Encyclopedia of
MONGOLIA AND THE MONGOL EMPIRE

Christopher P. Atwood

Indiana University, Bloomington

Facts On File, Inc.

For Jeffrey and Claire

Encyclopedia of Mongolia and the Mongol Empire

Copyright © 2004 by Christopher P. Atwood

Facts On File, Inc.
132 West 31st Street
New York NY 10001

Library of Congress Cataloging-in-Publication Data

Atwood, Christopher Pratt, 1964–
Encyclopedia of Mongolia and the Mongol empire / Christopher P. Atwood.
p. cm.
Includes bibliographical references and index.
ISBN 0-8160-4671-9
1. Mongolia—Encyclopedias. I. Title.
DS798.4.A88 2004
951.7'3'003—dc222003061696

Facts On File books are available at special discounts when purchased in bulk quantities for businesses, associations, institutions, or sales promotions. Please call our Special Sales Department in New York at (212) 967-8800 or (800) 322-8755.

You can find Facts On File on the World Wide Web at http://www.factsonfile.com

Text design by Joan M. Toro
Cover design by Cathy Rincon
Maps by Dale Williams

Printed in the United States of America

VB Hermitage 10 9 8 7 6 5 4 3 2 1

This book is printed on acid-free paper.

14734849

CONTENTS

LIST OF ILLUSTRATIONS AND MAPS

Photographs & Illustrations

Maps

INTRODUCTION

For many centuries the Mongols have been both familiar and unknown in the Western world. The great empire builder Chinggis (Genghis) Khan has passed into folklore somewhere between Attila the Hun and Conan the Barbarian, yet the Mongols themselves remain shadowy figures in the wastes between the more familiar Middle East and China. A number of fine works have appeared in recent years on the Mongol Empire, while the breakup of the Soviet bloc has sparked a harvest of books on contemporary Mongolia, yet in all these writings the two Mongols—the conquerors of the Middle Ages and the democratic reformers of today—remain separate, stranded on opposite sides of 600 years of intervening history and culture.

The aim of this encyclopedia is to cover both the history and culture of the Mongolian peoples and of the Mongol Empire in the 13th and 14th centuries. While many see Mongol history simply as an outward explosion of a vast empire that left little legacy, the story of Mongol history and culture is also one of a people and heritage that developed from prehistory to the present on the same windswept plateau. In this encyclopedia the article on history surveys Mongolian history and the various interpretations of it.

Many envoys and travelers left descriptions of the customs and ways of life of the nomadic Mongols, so different from the sedentary peoples of Europe, the Middle East, and China. From the 18th century, outside observers again began to describe the culture of these Mongolian peoples, thus forming a vast ethnographic literature now being expanded at a great rate by Mongol scholars themselves. This information on the continuities and changes in ordinary Mongolian life is introduced in articles on agriculture, hunting and fishing, clothing and dress, food and drink, yurts, and, of course, animal husbandry and nomadism. Articles on religion, shamanism, literature, oral poetry and tales, epics, medicine, and education survey the spiritual culture of the Mongols.

The background of Mongolian history is treated in articles on the Mongolian plateau, on climate, fauna, and flora, and on the fossil record and prehistory. The nomadic empires that successively dominated Mongolia— the Xiongnu, or Huns; the Türks; the Uighurs; and the Kitans—and their archaeological remains are given separate articles. Throughout their history, these peoples' relations with China have proved crucial; the peculiar features of these relations are described in the article on the tribute system.

The Mongol Empire is summarized in the article of that name, in which reference is made to further articles on the great khans, the major battles, and the institutions of the empire. At its height, the Mongol Empire touched the destiny of almost all Eurasia, and readers will find articles on all the major peoples and dynasties conquered by the Mongols as well as those who successfully resisted the Mongol invasions. Contrary to the stereotypes, the Mongols were very much interested in the cultures of the peoples around them. Articles on the empire's religious policy and on the four main religions of the empire—Buddhism, Christianity, Taoism, and Islam—and on history writing under the empire— Christian, East Asian, Islamic, and Mongolian—provide an entryway for exploring the Mongols' cultural interaction with the conquered peoples.

In the third generation after its founding, the Mongol Empire broke up into four rival empires, or khanates, each ruling a different part of Eurasia and headed by a different branch of the Mongol imperial family: the Il-Khanate in the Middle East, the Chaghatay Khanate in Central Asia, the Golden Horde on the Russian steppes, and the Yuan dynasty in East Asia. Separate articles survey each of these khanates and provide cross-references to articles on significant persons, cultural achievements, and historical events. The three western dynasties shared a common fate over the course of the 14th century, breaking up amid dynastic rivalries that threw up previously unimportant branches of the imperial family or new Mongol dynasties unrelated to the great family of Chinggis Khan. Articles on the Blue Horde, the Mangghud, the Jalayir, Moghulistan, Timur, and the Qara'unas describe these Islamized Mongol epigones.

The Mongols of today are descendants, however, of those who remained in East Asia during the Mongols' Yuan dynasty. After 1368 those Mongols who had remained nomads in the heartland were joined by those expelled from China. Over the following centuries these Mongols created a unique culture of Buddhist nomads, receiving influences from Tibet, China, and the hunting peoples of Siberia and Manchuria and synthesizing them with their own pastoral nomadic traditions. For the Mongols of today, the culture of the empire period is only the beginning of their national history, one that continues in succeeding dynasties and confederations: the Northern Yuan, the Oirats, Zünghars, the Khalkha, and others. Articles on the Eight White Yurts, the 17th-century chronicles, Buddhist fine arts, the Second Conversion to Buddhism, and the great lineages of the "living Buddhas" give an orientation to the cultural and religious developments of this era.

By the 17th century, people of Mongolian origin had expanded again, forming the Upper Mongols in Tibet, the Daurs in Manchuria, the Buriats in Siberia, the Xinjiang Mongols in Turkestan, and the Kalmyks along the Volga in Europe. The encyclopedia devotes separate articles to each of these far-flung branches of the Mongol peoples as well as to the Khalkha and Inner Mongolian peoples that dominate the Mongol heartland. Other articles describe remnant populations stranded from Afghanistan to Manchuria by the receding tide of the 13th- and 14th-century world empire. While such groups, including the Mogholis, Dongxiang, and Tu (Monguor), are not part of the Mongolian community today, they do speak languages related to Mongolian, and their history sheds light on the fate of the Mongol Empire. Entries on the Kazakhs, Tuvans, and Ewenkis describe non-Mongol peoples who have long been in contact with the Mongols and form minority populations on the Mongolian plateau.

By 1771 almost all the Mongolian peoples had fallen under the rule of the Manchus, who also ruled China as its last Qing dynasty. Only the Buriats in Siberia and the Kalmyks in the southern Russian steppes came under Russian rule. Articles are devoted to the institutions that the Qing Empire used in ruling Mongolia, such as the fieflike banners, the leagues, and the *ambans*, or viceroys, who supervised them; other entries refer to social classes under the Qing dynasty and to the slow advance of Chinese colonization, trade and moneylending, and the influence of Chinese fiction.

In the 20th century the Mongol peoples in both the Qing and czarist empires faced much more rapid colonization. Only the Khalkha, occupying "Outer Mongolia," that is, the center of the Mongolian plateau, were able to form an independent nation, first declared in 1911 as a theocracy and now called the State of Mongolia. The communist regimes in Russia and China organized various autonomous units for the Mongol peoples within their borders, ones which still exist. Readers seeking information on the overall geography, economy, political system, ethnic and social makeup, and administrative histories of independent Mongolia or these autonomous units should turn first to articles under their contemporary names: Mongolia, State of; Inner Mongolia Autonomous Region; Buriat Republic; Kalmyk Republic; Bayangol Mongol Autonomous Prefectures; Haixi Mongol and Tibetan Autonomous Prefecture; and so on. The entry "Mongolia, State of" provides cross-references to the major personalities, events, periods, and institutions in the life of independent Mongolia from 1911 on. The major provinces and cities of Mongolia and Inner Mongolia are all given separate articles. The more important persons and events in Inner Mongolian and Buriat history are also given separate entries. Russia (or, in its communist avatar, the Soviet Union), China, and Japan have all exercised powerful influences on Mongolia, and articles treat each of these countries' relations with modern Mongolia.

The encyclopedia articles are organized alphabetically. Titles of articles that begin in numerals are alphabetized by the first letter in the title. Cross-references to other articles are given in SMALL CAPITAL LETTERS. Suggestions for further reading are given at the end of articles for which important works exist. These are limited to the English-language literature, although preference has been given to items with extensive and multilingual bibliographies. Ready reference to the major events in Mongolian history is provided by the chronology. Since Mongolia, China, and Russia all use the metric system, measurements and figures are provided first in metric units. The equivalents in the British/American system are only approximate and in most cases are derived from the original metric measurements.

Given the wide variety of languages in which sources on Mongolian history have been written, it is understandable that there is considerable variation in spellings. During the 20th century sources written in the Mongolian language itself have become more important as the Mongols have begun to write their own history. In this encyclopedia Mongolian spellings have been generally used. Despite the impression sometimes given, neither diacriticals (apart from the umlaut) nor unfamiliar signs are necessary to render Mongolian names satisfactorily in English. Nevertheless, the Mongolian language itself has undergone much change, and rigid adherence to either the medieval or the modern forms necessarily results in a great number of unfamiliar forms. On the other hand, the normally reasonable precept to use the most familiar spelling is impossible to follow consistently, since most names and terms exist in English in several spellings, no one of which has achieved clear predominance. Thus, the encyclopedia follows what is hoped is a reasonable compromise of transcribing Mongolian consistently but in ways adapted to the broad changes of pronunciation in the differing eras of Mongolian history. In reverse order, from the present to the Middle Ages, the principles are as follows:

1. For geographical terms in Mongolia and for names of persons active after 1940, forms are based on the Cyrillic script, which was designed in 1941 and introduced as the official script in 1950. There is today considerable variation in the transcription of these terms, but based on pronunciation and historical considerations, I have used *kh* instead of *h*, *z* rather than *dz*, *y* rather than *ï*, and *w* rather than *v*.

2. For the period from around 1635 to 1940, the spellings are based on the Uighur-Mongolian script spellings with the modern pronunciation of its letters. Thus, *kh* is used for *k/q* and *g* for *g/γ*. Following the modern pronunciation in Khalkha Mongols, *ch* or *ts* is written for the scholarly *č*, and *j* or *z* is written *ǰ*. *Sh* is used instead of *š* and before i. For the "broken i" and the intervocalic *g/γ*, which disappear in spoken pronunciation, the modern pronunciation is followed. Thus, *Shara Nuur* would be written for *sir-a naγur*. These rules are also generally followed for names and terms in Inner Mongolia, where the Uighur-Mongolian script is still used.

3. For the period from the fall of the Mongol Empire in 1368 to the rise of the Qing dynasty around 1635, the encyclopedia follows the Uighur-Mongolian script, as its pronunciation is seen in the transcriptions in the Chinese sources that form much of our knowledge of the period. This is similar to that in the period of 1635–1940, except that *kh* and *gh* are used before *a, o,* and *u* but *k* and *g* before *e, i, ö,* and *ü*. *G* is used at the end of a syllable. *Ch* is used for *č* and *j* for *ǰ*.

4. For the period of the Mongol Empire, the spellings are based on the Uighur-Mongolian script as pronounced in the Mongolian language of the time. This pronunciation is particularly clearly represented in the invaluable Persian sources. Compared with the preceding periods, *q* (not *kh*) and *gh* are used before *a, o,* or *u,* and *q* is used after those vowels. (Around other vowels, *k* and *g* are used.) The apostrophe is used to mark the silent *gh/g* in words such as *ba'urchi,* "steward," or "*Hüle'ü*"; the *i* is never "broken"; and the *-y-* is written out in diphthongs like *sayin* or *Quyildar*.

Words used in Mongolian dialects or languages outside independent Mongolia are generally given in the form most appropriate according to the pronunciation. Buriat words and terms follow the Buriat Cyrillic script, while Kalmyk-Oirat words and terms follow either the modern Kalmyk Cyrillic script or the older clear script. The rendering of sounds in Kalmyk-Oirat is roughly as no. 3 above. Z is pronounced in Kalmyk-Oirat and Buriat like English z in *zoo.* Buriat *zh* is like the *z* in English *azure.* Kalymk-Oirat *ä* is like the *a* in American English *at.*

It should be noted that the spelling of the great conqueror commonly known as Genghis Khan is given here throughout as Chinggis Khan, a usage that is historically correct and strongly preferred by the Mongolians themselves and increasingly by Western writers on Mongolian history. The old spelling "Genghis" was occasioned in the 18th century by a misreading of the Persian sources. Pronounced in English with a completely unwarranted hard *g* at the beginning, this spelling has now become quite misleading. As a noun, *Mongolians* refers to citizens of independent Mongolia ("Outer Mongolia"), regardless of ethnicity, while *Mongols* refers to ethnic Mongols, regardless of citizenship.

Chinese names and terms are given in the Pinyin system. It should be noted that in this system, *x* is pronounced like English *sh*, *q* like English *ch*, *zh* like English *j*, *c* like English *ts*, and *z* like English *dz*. Thus Qing is pronounced roughly like "ching," Xu like "shoe," Zhou like "Joe," Chucai like "choot's eye," and Ze like "dzuh."

Mongolian words are spelled roughly as they sound. Stress is generally on the first syllable. Long vowels, which are written doubled, may be treated by the non-Mongolian speaker simply as strong stress. The pronunciation of consonants is roughly as in English, with the following exceptions: 1) the medieval consonant *q* is like a *k*, only farther back in the throat; 2) *gh* (and even the modern *g* before the vowels *a, o,* and *u*) is much deeper than an English *g* and close to the uvular *r* in the French pronunciation of "au revoir"; 3) *kh* is like the *ch* in the German pronunciation of "Bach"; 4) *z* is like the *dz* in English "adze"; 5) *g* is always hard, regardless of the following vowel.

The vowels have changed greatly, and the modern pronunciations of several vowels are rather different from anything found in any European language. The following notes provide an approximate pronunciation: 1) *a* is like *a* in English "father"; 2) *o* is like the *o* in English "top"; 3) *u* sounds superficially like the *o* in English "toll" but is actually articulated farther back and lower down; 4) *ö* is pronounced something like the *eu* in French "feu"; 5) *ü* is pronounced like the English *oo* in "pool"; 6) short (single) *e* and *i* both approximate the *i* in English "kit"; 7) long (double) *ee* is like the *a* in English "dale"; 8) long (double) *ii* is like the *ea* in English "team." In modern Mongolian, *ai* is pronounced like the *a* in American English "ban," while *oi* is pronounced like the Mongolian *ö* but with a glide into a slight *i* sound.

I present this encyclopedia to the reading public with great trepidation, aware that I have attempted to cover a vast topic with only limited powers. My only justification is that such a single-volume reference work on Mongolia, the Mongol peoples, and the Mongol Empire has long been a desideratum. It is my hope that the presentation to a wide public of the substantial achievements of specialists in Mongolia all over the world outweighs whatever errors of fact and interpretation that undoubtedly remain and for which I must take full responsibility. In authoring a work of this nature, I have benefited from the expertise of numerous scholars who have helped with facts and data: A. Hurelbaatar, Christopher Kaplonski, György Kara, Erjen Khamaganova, Peter Marsh, John R. Krueger, Ellen McGill, Elena Remilev Schlueter, Elena Songster, Natalia Simukova, and Nikolay Tserenpilov. Susie Drost has, through her indefatigable work as office manager and treasurer of the Mongolia Society, assisted in the production of this book more than she knows through facilitating conferences, book trade, and other forms of intellectual exchange between the Mongol lands and the United States. Apart from those with whom I have consulted personally, I have also followed the research of the widest array of scholars, many of whom have been acknowledged in the suggestions for further reading. I find it distressing not to be able to record my debt to so many who write in non-English languages and who have given guidance and assistance, either personally or through their books, particularly the scholars in Mongolia and Inner Mongolia on whose work I have in many cases relied heavily. My mother, Nancy Atwood, helped me by reading several articles and offering editorial suggestions. Finally, as always, I thank my wife, Okcha, for her support and assistance in all phases of this project, and my children, Jeffrey and Claire, who acquired from many dinner-table conversations a gratifying fondness for Mongolia's grasslands and horses and a slightly excessive scorn for those who start the word *Genghis* with a hard *g*. To them this book is dedicated.

Abadai *See* ABATAI KHAN.

Abatai Khan (Abadai, Abudai) (1554–1588) *Outer Mongolian Prince who began the Khalkha conversion to Buddhism and built the temple Erdeni Zuu*

Abatai, the son of the northern KHALKHA Mongol prince Noonukhu Üizeng (b. 1534), was born with his index fingers smeared in blood, an omen of war such as that of his ancestor CHINGGIS KHAN. From 1567 to 1580 he warred on the OIRATS to the west, receiving the title of Sain Khan for his victories. In the mid-1580s he crowned his war with a victory over the Oirats' Khoshud tribe at Köbkör Keriye, making his son Shubu-udai khan of the Oirats.

In 1581 Abatai heard from merchants about the Inner Mongolian ruler ALTAN KHAN's conversion to Buddhism and invited the lama Shiregetü Güüshi Chorjiwa (fl. 1578–1618) from Altan's Inner Mongolian city Guihua (modern HÖHHOT), who taught Abatai the rules of fasting and the vow of right conduct. In 1585 Abatai took stones from the ruins of QARA-QORUM to begin building the monastery ERDENI ZUU. In 1586 he visited Guihua, where the Third Dalai Lama (1543–88) was staying. Presenting rich gifts, Abatai received the Tantric Hevajra initiation and images and relics, which he installed in Erdeni Zuu. After his death his remains were interred at Erdeni Zuu.

Although Abatai's son Shubuudai was soon after killed by the Oirats and his power eclipsed, his descendants include the later Tüshiyetü khans and the great lama-politician, the First Jibzundamba Khutugtu. Abatai's huge YURT, which could hold up to 300 persons, was later consecrated by the First Jibzundamba in Khüriye (modern ULAANBAATAR). Ceremonies were held there to celebrate Mongolian independence in 1912, and the yurt was used for the secret party oath by the revolutionaries in 1919 (*see* 1921 REVOLUTION). The tent was destroyed in 1938 and the site replaced by a Young Pioneers camp.

See also JIBZUNDAMBA KHUTUGTU.

'Abbasid Caliphate As a symbol of Islamic unity and rule, the caliphate in Baghdad challenged the Mongol Empire's claim to universal rule until its destruction in 1258.

The Arab family of 'Abbas had founded the second Arab-Islamic dynasty in 750. Seated in Baghdad and bearing the title of caliph (*khalifa*), or "successor" of the Prophet, the 'Abbasid caliphs were eventually reduced to purely symbolic influence, confirming sultans in their titles and symbolizing mainstream Sunni Islamic legitimacy. Shi'ite Muslims, however, rejected the whole institution of the caliphate.

After centuries of purely symbolic influence, Caliph an-Nasir li-dini'llah (r. 1180–1225) rebuilt the 'Abbasids as a significant local power. Ruling the area roughly of modern Iraq, an-Nasir built up an army of Turkish military slaves and Kurdish mercenaries (*see* KURDISTAN). While often engaged in conflict with the Islamic powers, the caliphate continued to dispose of immense religious prestige among Sunni Muslims. The sense of invulnerability about the house of 'Abbas rose in autumn 1217, when the Khorazm-shah, an-Nasir's most formidable enemy, was foiled in an attack by unusual snows and retreated only to be destroyed by CHINGGIS KHAN (Genghis, 1206–27) two years later (*see* KHORAZM).

In 1230 three *tümen*s of Mongol soldiers (nominally 30,000 men) under CHORMAQAN arrived in Azerbaijan with the mission to destroy the last Khorazm-shah Jalal-ud-Din Mengüberdi and extend Mongol rule. In 1231 Jalal-ud-Din was killed, and the Mongols raided the northern borders of the caliph's sphere. From 1236 Mongol raids on Irbil and the caliphate, even down to the walls of Baghdad, became an almost annual occurrence, although the armies of the caliphate defeated Mongol detachments in 1238 and 1245.

Despite these successes the caliph's ministers hoped to come to terms with the Mongols, and by 1241 they were sending a rich annual tribute to the Mongols. Envoys from Baghdad attended both the coronation of GÜYÜG KHAN in 1246 and that of MÖNGKE KHAN in 1251. Güyüg Khan insisted that the caliph fully submit and attend the Mongol court in person and probably planned the conquest of Baghdad. However, the Khan died in 1248, and succession struggles blocked further action. When Möngke Khan ascended the throne, he sent his brother HÜLE'Ü to Iran, demanding that the caliph come to meet Hüle'ü personally and send troops to assist the Mongols in reducing the strongholds of the radical Shi'ite sect, the ISMA'ILIS. If the caliph refused, then Hüle'ü was to siege and destroy Baghdad. The caliphate rejected the Mongol demands, and in March 1257, having conquered the main Isma'ili fortresses, Hüle'ü set out for Baghdad.

Baghdad's situation was difficult. From 1242 devastating floods and sectarian riots among adherents of various Islamic schools had devastated the city, culminating in the great flood and anti-Shi'ite riots of 1256. The caliph, al-Musta'sim b'illah (r. 1242–58), was a weakling who refused to spend money to maintain the army built by his predecessors, not so much from greed as from an inability to conceive that the line of 'Abbas could possibly fall. The caliph's Shi'ite vizier, or prime minister, Mu'ayyid-ad-Din Ibn 'Alqami, vainly advocated submitting to the Mongols. For this, the caliph's Dawatdar (inkpot-holder), or secretary, Mujahid-ad-Din Aybeg, accused Ibn 'Alqami of being secretly in the pay of the Mongols. At the same time, the war party had completely unrealistic expectations of how long Baghdad could resist.

In November 1257, Hüle'ü's troops advanced on a front extending from Luristan to al-Dujayl. The left wing and center converged on Baghdad, while the right wing crossed the Tigris and attacked Baghdad from the west. Despite the Dawatdar's momentary victory west of the Tigris, the Mongols began the assault on Baghdad's flood-weakened walls on January 29, 1258. Despairing, the caliph came out under safe conduct on February 10 and the city was given over to pillage for a week. Hüle'ü hesitated over what to do with the caliph, but fear of the caliphate's prestige pushed him to put him and the entire male 'Abbasid family to death on February 20. The Shi'ite populations of Hilla and Najaf welcomed the Mongols,

who accorded them relative autonomy, but the Sunnis of Wasit resisted and were massacred. The conquests of Basra, Khuzistan, and Irbil rounded out the subjugation of the caliphate. A surviving 'Abbasid later escaped to MAMLUK EGYPT, and a shadow of the caliphate was continued there.

The Baghdad area formed the Mongol Il-Khans' winter pasture and a major revenue source, although the city's commercial importance declined relative to the Il-Khan capital, Tabriz.

See also BAGHDAD, SIEGE OF; IL-KHANATE; ISLAM IN THE MONGOL EMPIRE.

Further reading: John Andrew Boyle, "The Death of the Last 'Abbasid Caliph: A Contemporary Muslim Account," *Journal of Semitic Studies* 6 (1961): 145–161.

Abudai *See* ABATAI KHAN.

Academy of Sciences The Mongolian Academy of Sciences expanded from a committee of eight scribes and folklorists in 1921 to become Mongolia's center for scholarly research and publication in all fields.

Established by the government on November 9, 1921, the Books Institute (Nom-un khüriyeleng; Russian Mongol'skii uchenyi komitet, "Mongolian Academic Committee," or Uchkom for short), later renamed the Philology Institute (Sudur bichig-ün khüriyeleng), was a committee of eight men headed by the chairman Jamiyan (O. Jamyan, 1864–1930) and secretary Batuwachir (Ch. Bat-Ochir). The Buriat TSYBEN ZHAMTSARANO was the organization's dynamo. The institute had a budget of 3,000 silver dollars and met in Jamiyan's yurt until the institute purchased a log cabin in 1922.

The institute began with a language and literature cabinet in 1921, adding a history and geography cabinet and a library in 1924 and a national archives in 1927. The language and literature cabinet located, purchased, and preserved the rare block prints and manuscripts found all over the Mongolian countryside, building up a library of 6,000 books in Mongolian and foreign languages by 1925. The institute translated and reprinted Mongolian, Buddhist, and European classics, from the wise sayings of CHINGGIS KHAN, to Indian folktales, to the *Communist Manifesto*. The institute also sent students to Leningrad and Paris to study.

After the leftist turn of 1929, the reprinting of Buddhist classics and the dispatch of students to the "bourgeois" nations were discontinued. Translations, cooperation with Soviet scientific and geographical expeditions, and publications continued. It was renamed the Institute of Sciences (Shinjlekh ukhaany khüreelen) in December 1930; new departments were added: the arable agriculture cabinet and the Revolutionary Museum in 1931, the animal husbandry cabinet in 1943, and the Sükhebaatur

Museum and Marxism-Leninism cabinet in 1946. After World War II the Institute of Sciences improved its facilities while preserving its mostly philological and historical orientation.

In 1957 the renamed Institute of Sciences and Higher Education began to move into natural science, beginning with an observatory at Khürel Togoo and reorganizing itself into four subinstitutes: animal husbandry, social sciences, natural sciences, and medical sciences. In February 1960, however, opponents of this move returned the institute back to its purely social-scientific mission, yet when the academic impresario-turned-historian BAZARYN SHIRENDEW became chairman of the institute in July 1960, he reversed this decision. In May 1961 the institute was reborn as the Academy of Sciences (Shinjlekh ukhaany akademi), modeled on the Soviet Academy of Sciences as an all-around research organization. Meanwhile, in September 1959 the First International Congress of Mongolists finally reopened limited contact with non–Soviet-bloc countries in the field of Mongolian studies.

The academy expanded under Shirendew for 20 years, yet Mongolia's maximum leader YUMJAAGIIN TSEDENBAL disagreed with Shirendew's aim of developing the natural sciences in Mongolia. His preferred model was the Science and Technological Information Center, set up in 1972 as a database for disseminating in Mongolia research done in other Soviet-bloc countries. The party dismissed Shirendew in 1981 and publicly ridiculed the physicist B. Chadraa in 1982 for daring to attempt the production of advanced electronic components in Mongolia.

Democratization from 1989 opened up full scientific cooperation with all interested countries in all spheres. It also cast into question the traditional Franco-Russian model of an academy completely separate from teaching and raised the issue of new connections with the market economy. A thorough reorganization followed under Chadraa, the new chairman. In addition to 17 institutes and centers (10 in natural sciences, seven in humanities and social sciences), the academy now contains Ulaanbaatar University (founded 1992) and controls nine corporations involved in research and development in animal products, construction, energy, and other fields.

See also CHINGGIS KHAN CONTROVERSY; DAMDINSÜREN, TSENDIIN; MONGOLIAN PEOPLE'S REVOLUTIONARY PARTY; REVOLUTIONARY PERIOD; RINCHEN, BYAMBYN; TÖMÖR-TOGOO, DARAMYN.

A-chu   *See* AJU.

Aga Buriat Autonomous Area (Aginskiy, Agin)   Cut off from the Buriat Republic in 1937, Aga is ironically the most Buriat of Russia's Buriat autonomous units.

GEOGRAPHY AND ECONOMY

The Aga Buriat Autonomous Area occupies 19,500 square kilometers (7,530 square miles) along the ONON RIVER's northern bank. Administratively it is subject to Siberia's Chita Region. In 1989 the area's population was 77,188, of which 42,362 (54.9 percent) were Buriat. The terrain is low steppe (elevation 500–700 meters, or 1,650–2,300 feet, above sea level) in the south and east and forested uplands (elevation 800–1,000 meters; 2,600–3,300 feet) in the north and west. The Alkhanai peak, at 1,662 meters (5,453 feet) above sea level, is the highest point.

Aga's economy is based on stock breeding, farming, and industry (food processing, lumber, and nonferrous metals). In 1989 the population was 31.6 percent urban. The Orlovskii Ore-Dressing Plant producing tantalum concentrate was opened in 1960. A tentative recovery from the serious post-Soviet depression began in 1997–99. The Trans-Siberian Railway runs north of Aga, while the Chinese Eastern Railway cuts through Aga's eastern section. The capital, Aginskoye, is a small town of 9,286 (1989) originally formed around the Aga datsang (Buddhist monastery).

Traditional Buriat husbandry focused on large stock; figures for 1924 show 231,035 head, of which 50 percent were sheep and goats, 36 percent cattle, and the remainder horses with a few camels. Soviet plans promoted sheep breeding to feed the wool industry, and by 1968 the herd totaled 866,200 head, of which almost 93 percent were sheep and goats and only 6 percent cattle. As pastures degraded, animals were trucked over the border to be grazed in Mongolia during the summer, a practice that Mongolia halted in 1990. The unsustainable Soviet herd had diminished in 1998 to about 302,000 head, of which 23 percent were cattle and 73 percent sheep and goats. Sown acreage, insignificant before the Russian Revolution, rose to 180,000 hectares (444,780 acres) in 1968. Again, pasture degradation with the general post-Soviet depression forced retrenchment, as sown acreage declined to 118,500 (292,814 acres) in 1990 and 34,700 (85,744 acres) in 1998. Meanwhile, pigs, still only 1,900 head in 1968, have become a key subsistence stock, reaching 27,300 in 1998.

HISTORY

The Aga steppe was part of the MONGOL TRIBE'S ONON RIVER–KHERLEN RIVER homeland in the 12th and 13th centuries. By the 16th century Transbaikalia was mostly settled by Khamnigan "Horse" EWENKIS and around the Aga area by Mongol clans under KHALKHA Mongolian rule. Khori BURIATS fleeing from east of the Ergüne settled briefly on the Aga–Onon steppe. After submission to the Russians in 1647, the Khori Buriats returned to Aga, subjecting the local Khamnigans to tribute. Nine of the Khori's 11 clans settled in Aga; the main ones are the Galzuud, Sagaan, Sharaid, and Khalbin. By 1727 the Aga Buriats were confirmed as subjects of the czar. Subsequently,

Russian Cossack stations were set up south of Aga to block the frontier with Mongolia. Originally administered as part of the Khori tribe, in 1837 the Aga Buriats received a separate "steppe duma," or autonomous administrative organ, and a head taisha (*akhalagsha taisha*) of the Galzuud clan.

The Aga Buriats converted to Buddhism early in the 19th century. Within barely 30 years from 1801, nine *datsangs* (monasteries) were built along the Onon and Aga rivers. Aga (founded 1816) and Tsugol (founded 1801) *datsangs* together had 1,400 lamas. Buddhist culture strongly influenced the laity. Of the 38,784 Aga Buriats in 1908, 14 percent were literate, half in Mongolian, more than two-fifths in Tibetan, but fewer than 10 percent in Russian. This rate of literacy exceeded not only the Buriat but the general Siberian average. The noted Aga intellectuals Gomobozhab Tsybikov (1873–1930), Bazar Baradiin (1878–1937), and TSYBEN ZHAMTSARANO were all prominent in the Buddhist reformist movement. On the eve of the Russian Revolution, Aga's ethnic Russian population was still negligible, and the Buriats still nomadized in YURTS.

During the Russian Revolution, many Aga Buriats had their land seized by Russian peasants; some Buriats fled to Mongolia and HULUN BUIR. By 1926 the region's Buriat population dropped to only 31,700 (88 percent) out of a total of 36,000. (See BURIATS OF MONGOLIA AND INNER MONGOLIA.) From 1921 Aga was included as a noncontiguous AIMAG (province) of 27,400 square kilometers (10,580 square miles), first in the Buriat-Mongolian Autonomous Region and then in the Buriat-Mongolian Autonomous Soviet Socialist Republic (BMASSR). Due to strong resistance, collectivization was not generally implemented in Aga until 1933–35. In 1934 all monasteries were closed, and soldiers billeted in Aga *datsang*. Finally, on September 26, 1937, Aga was transferred in shrunken form to Chita Region as a national area (*okrug*), the lowest level of national autonomy in the Soviet system. (In 1977 Russia's "national areas" were renamed "autonomous areas," although without any practical difference.)

Massive migration reduced the Buriat percentage in the area to only 47.6 percent of 49,100 in 1959. Despite Russification, by 1989 Aga still had the highest percentage of Buriats claiming to speak their national language: 98 percent as compared with 90 percent in Ust'-Orda and 89 percent in the BURIAT REPUBLIC. In 1946 Aga monastery was reopened on a small scale.

During the Buriat cultural revival of the late 1980s and early 1990s, Tsugol *datsang* was revived in 1988, and Aga *datsang* established new schools of Tibetan medicine and astrology. A new environmental consciousness culminated in the creation of the Alkhanai National Park in 1999. Although Buriat officials have controlled the area's new democratic politics since 1990 and Aga was made an equal member of the Russian Federation in 1993, the area is in serious financial difficulties. Since 1997 the governor has been Bayr B. Zhamsuev (b. 1959). In search of influence, Aga elected in September 1997 a Moscow singer with underworld ties, Iosif Davidovich Kobzon, as its representative to Russia's State Duma (legislature). Kobzon caused great controversy with his lobbying for a restoration of Buriatia's pre-1937 boundaries, yet the area's autonomy remains threatened by Moscow's plans for administrative consolidation.

See also BURIATS; CLIMATE; DESERTIFICATION AND PASTURE DEGRADATION; ENVIRONMENTAL PROTECTION; FAUNA; FLAGS; FLORA; MONGOLIAN PLATEAU.

Agin *See* AGA BURIAT AUTONOMOUS AREA.

Aginskiy *See* AGA BURIAT AUTONOMOUS AREA.

agriculture *See* ANIMAL HUSBANDRY AND NOMADISM; FARMING.

Ahmad Fanakati (d. 1282) *Qubilai Khan's notorious financial officer, who strengthened and expanded the imperial monopolies*
A native of Fanakat in the Ferghana valley, Ahmad served CHABUI, QUBILAI KHAN's future empress, before her marriage and later served as provisioner for Qubilai's household in North China. In 1262 Qubilai Khan appointed Ahmad fiscal commissioner in chief (1262) and prefect of his Inner Mongolian capital, Kaiping (SHANGDU). Ahmad increased revenues in the various metal, mineral, and salt monopolies, raising, for example, the salt tax quota for Taiyuan in 1264 from 150 *ding* (YASTUQ) of silver to 250, and in 1271 to 1,000 *ding*. While himself of the privileged SEMUREN (western immigrant) class, he pushed Qubilai to curtail the tax exemptions given to *semuren* ORTOQ merchants, clergy, soldiers, and craftsmen.

In September 1264 Qubilai promoted Ahmad to be one of four managers (*pingzhang*) in the secretariat, the central government organ. Ahmad's relations with the secretariat's officials, mostly Mongols and Chinese sympathetic to CONFUCIANISM, were hostile. In 1270 Qubilai approved the creation of a department of state affairs, headed by Ahmad, which would be independent of the secretariat. When this arrangement proved inefficient, Ahmad was brought back into the secretariat, again as manager, but this time with his own collaborators in key positions. He also began promoting his family, making his son Husain route commander for DAIDU, the southern capital (modern Beijing). Ahmad unsuccessfully opposed the Chinese institution of the censorate, repeatedly requesting that it be prohibited from "uselessly conducting inspections" and "arbitrarily summoning clerks at the granaries and storehouses."

Impressed by Ahmad's knowledge and debating skills, Qubilai called him the most talented of his Turkestani advisers and claimed he could "clarify the way of Heaven, investigate the principles of Earth, and exert himself in Man's affairs." Ahmad's nominal superior, however, Grand Councillor Hantum, a Mongol aristocrat of the JALAYIR clan, despised him and his coterie as mere "businessmen" who "caught the profits of the whole world in their nets." Qubilai's heir apparent, JINGIM, also hated Ahmad and once even assaulted him at a court audience. In 1275, as the Yuan armies occupied South China, Ahmad convinced Qubilai to convert Song paper money to the Yuan bills at the confiscatory rate of 50 to 1 and to extend the monopolies immediately to the conquered territories, to be administered by special fiscal commissions appointed by Ahmad himself.

Chinese sources accuse Ahmad of oppressive taxes, multiplication of offices, judicial murder, nepotism, peculation, and accumulating concubines from the wives, sisters, and daughters of officials seeking to curry favor. He won over powerful opponents or pushed them to the sidelines, and a few obscure opponents he executed on trumped-up charges. Despite claims that Ahmad's corruption immediately caused government spending to soar, emissions of paper currency began to skyrocket only in 1274 due to both increasing silver supplies and campaigns against the Song. The key to Ahmad's favor with Qubilai was the administrative acumen he showed in supplying the revenues needed for the conquest of South China. As a hated outsider, he naturally preferred to work through new offices staffed by his friends and allies. Although Muslim opinion later viewed him as a victim of Chinese envy, Ahmad was in no sense a leader of any Muslim clique; in fact, most of his top cronies were Han Chinese.

In 1282 Wang Zhu (1254–82) and Gao Heshang (Monk Gao) formed a plot to kill Ahmad for reasons that remain obscure. With Qubilai and Jingim departed for Shangdu, on the night of April 26 the conspirators sent messages to the palace staff announcing that Jingim was returning for a secret Tantric Buddhist initiation and that the officials should greet him. Pretending to be Jingim's entourage, Wang and Gao gained access to the palace and killed Ahmad, Zhang Hui, and several other of his cronies. In the end other officials rallied the guards and captured the conspirators, who were executed shortly thereafter.

Only after Ahmad's death did his accusers finally turn Qubilai against him. The emperor abolished hundreds of offices created by Ahmad, executed his sons, confiscated his property, and dismissed those who had presented women in their families to Ahmad and his sons as concubines.

Further reading: H. Francke, "Ahmad," in *In the Service of the Khan: Eminent Personalities of the Early Mongol-Yuan Period (1200–1300)*, ed. Igor de Rachewiltz et al. (Wiesbaden: Otto Harrassowitz, 1993), 539–557.

aimag (*ayimaq, ayimagh, aimak*) Originally meaning "class" or "type," the word *aimag* was used by the 18th century for the four traditional divisions of Khalkha and then for the provinces of Mongolia and the subregional units of Inner Mongolia.

The term *aimag* (*ayimaq* in Middle Mongolian) basically means class or division. It was occasionally used in Middle Mongolian for traditional tribal-political units but more commonly for provinces of China or Tibet. In the 17th century the word came to be used for the divisions of the larger Buddhist monasteries, each formed of monks from a similar district.

In the 17th century, *aimag* occasionally appeared next to the administrative term OTOG. Combined with *ulus* (realm, people under one ruler), it designated a particular political unit (traditionally called a "tribe," although not consanguineous). In this sense the word was used for the people of Khalkha, who after 1725 were divided into four *aimag*s: Setsen Khan (or Tsetsen Khan), Tüshiyetü Khan, Sain Noyan, and Zasagtu Khan.

The word *bu* or *buluo*, "tribe," widely used in QING DYNASTY (1636–1912) administrative literature, was translated into Mongolian as *aimag*. *Aimag*, now seen as "tribe," became the designation for the Mongols' traditional ethnographic-political units: the Chakhar, the Dörböd, the Üjümüchin, and so on, yet the main Qing administrative system was built on BANNERS (appanages, or *khoshuu*) and LEAGUES (*chuulgan*), which rarely coincided with these "tribes," or *aimag*s. Only among the Khalkha were the four traditional *aimag*s coterminous with the four leagues.

After the 1911 RESTORATION of Mongolian independence, the designation of "league" was abolished as a Manchu imposition and only the name *aimag* retained. (Sain Noyan was renamed Sain Noyan Khan to give it equality with the others.) In 1924–25 the traditional names of the *aimag*s were changed, and the *aimag* designation was extended to the Great Shabi (hitherto ecclesiastical serfs) and the western Khowd frontier. Finally, in 1931 Mongolia replaced the traditional *aimag*s with 13 *aimag*s, or provinces, roughly equal in size. Expanded in number to 18 by 1940 and 21 in 1994, they form the current local administrative framework. The traditional ethnographic divisions of the Mongols are now termed *yastan*, or subethnic groups (literally "bones").

In Buriatia, the term *aimag* was used from 1921 to 1965 for the traditional Buriat ethnic-geographic units in place of Russian administrative terms. In Inner Mongolia after 1947, the traditional leagues (Mongolian, *chuulgan*; Chinese, *meng*) were renamed *aimag* in Mongolian but left as *meng* (league) in Chinese. Since then, the leagues/*aimag*s have undergone frequent administrative changes. From 1983 on many were turned into vast municipalities, leaving only the least developed regions as leagues/*aimag*s.

See also APPANAGE SYSTEM.

aimak   See AIMAG.

'Ain Jalut, Battle of ('Ayn-Jalut)

At the Battle of 'Ain Jalut on September 3, 1260, the Mamluks of Egypt delivered a sharp check to the Mongol advance in the Middle East. Dissension among the Mongol khans prevented them from avenging the defeat.

As HÜLE'Ü (r. 1256–65) brought Aleppo and Damascus under Mongol rule, he sent envoys demanding the surrender of Egypt. Sultan Qutuz (r. 1259–60) of MAMLUK EGYPT had already welcomed a plethora of Muslim forces fleeing the Mongol advance, including his great successor, Baybars Bunduqdari ("the arbalester," r. 1260–77). On Baybars's counsel, Qutuz sawed the Mongol envoys in half and advanced into Palestine on July 26 with Baybars as vanguard.

Hüle'ü had meantime received the news of the death of MÖNGKE KHAN and returned to Ahlât in Armenia on June 6, 1260. KED-BUQA of the Naiman tribe remained in Syria with a single *tümen* (10,000) of Mongols, 500 Armenians, and Syrian auxiliaries. When the Mongol vanguard at Gaza was driven back into northern Palestine, Ked-Buqa advanced to 'Ain Jalut ("Goliath's Spring," near modern Bet She'an in Israel).

When the Mamluks approached on September 3, the Mongols charged the Mamluks' left wing twice, nearly putting them to flight. Qutuz rallied the lines until the weight of his greater numbers showed, and the smaller Mongol force was surrounded on three sides. (Half of the Syrians had quickly deserted.) Ked-Buqa refused to retreat and was captured and beheaded, while other Mongol units were surrounded and destroyed. After the battle the Mamluks swept north into Syria, killing the Mongol overseers (DARUGHACHI) and capturing Ked-Buqa's base camp and family.

See also MILITARY OF THE MONGOL EMPIRE.

airag   See KOUMISS.

Aju (Azhu, A-chu) (1234–1287) *Qubilai Khan's toughest field commander in the conquest of South China*

Aju, grandson of the famous SÜBE'ETEI BA'ATUR of the Uriyangkhan clan, first went off to war with his father, Uriyangqadai (1199–1271), in 1253 against Dali (modern YUNNAN), VIETNAM, and the SONG DYNASTY. In 1254 Aju led the storming of Yachi (modern Kunming). When Uriyangqadai fell ill, Aju took over his field command until they rendezvoused with QUBILAI KHAN's armies in 1259. Aju had experience in inland naval warfare, and in 1263 Qubilai Khan appointed him chief commander in Henan, facing the largely waterborne Song armies. From 1268 to 1273 Aju with Liu Zheng (1213–75) successfully besieged Xiangyang (modern Xiangfan). In 1274 Aju proposed to Qubilai a final campaign of annihilation against the Song. Qubilai made BAYAN CHINGSANG the supreme commander and Aju his main field commander. By using portages and lakes, Aju avoided the heavy Song fortifications on the Han River, and on January 11, 1275, he led his vanguard in person on a daring amphibious assault across the Yangtze. Aju also commanded the navies at the great Mongol victory of Dingjia Isle (March 19). For the rest of the campaign Aju contained the Song forces on the lower Yangtze, while Bayan led the advance on the capital. After burning the Song fleet with crack fire-arrow archers at the battle of Jiaoshan Mountain (July 26), Aju besieged Yangzhou until its surrender on August 23, 1276.

Despite high honors from Qubilai and Bayan, Aju was taciturn and unpopular among his colleagues. After participating in campaigns against rebels in Mongolia in 1286, he died on his way to the front at Turpan.

See also XIANGYANG, SIEGE OF.

Alan Gho'a *Legendary ancestress of the Mongols' ruling Borjigid lineage*

In the genealogy of Chinggis Khan, Alan Gho'a is the pivotal figure, whose impregnation by a heavenly light created the BORJIGID lineage destined to rule. Alan Gho'a (Alan the Fair) was the daughter of Qorilartai Mergen of the Tumad tribe and married Dobun Mergen (Dobun the Sharp-Shooter) of the Borjigid lineage. After Alan Gho'a bore two sons to Dobun Mergen, he died, leaving Alan Gho'a widowed. She then bore three other sons, which her two older sons took to be children of a slave boy in the camp. Alan Gho'a told her sons, however, that a bright yellow man entered the YURT (or *ger*) through the smoke hole and rubbed her belly, then went out in the form of a dog and up the beams of the sun or moon. She then explained that the three sons were the sons of Heaven and destined to be sovereign khans over the commoners. In the SECRET HISTORY OF THE MONGOLS she emphasized the brothers' need for unity by quoting the widespread fable of separate arrows being easy to break, but those bound together being unbreakable. The youngest of the heavenly born sons, Bodonchar, became the ancestor of the Borjigid in the strict sense, including CHINGGIS KHAN, while the others were ancestors of less distinguished lineages.

Alaqai Beki (fl. 1211–1230) *Third daughter of Chinggis Khan, regent of the Önggüd tribe, and commander and official in North China*

When the ruler of the ÖNGGÜD tribe of Inner Mongolia, Ala-Qush Digid-Quri, assisted CHINGGIS KHAN's invasion of the Jin in 1211, Chinggis bestowed his daughter Alaqai Beki (Princess Alaqai) on Ala-Qush's son Bai Sibu (Buyan-Shiban) to cement the alliance. Other leaders of the Önggüd objected and killed both Ala-Qush Digid-Quri and Bai Sibu. Alaqai Beki then seized her stepsons Boyaoha and Zhenguo and fled by night to her father with his army at Datong. Dissuaded from massacring the

Önggüd, Chinggis Khan had Alaqai Beki marry Zhenguo, and she ruled the Önggüd as regent for several decades. She and her famous staff of women played an important role in both military campaigns and civil administration. Zhenguo died early, and Alaqai thereupon married Boyaoha. Her son by Zhenguo, Negüdei, died in Ögedei KHAN'S reign while campaigning against the Song, and the line of Önggüd princes continued through Boyaoha's sons by a concubine. The seal of Alaqai Beki's representative in her appanage of North China has recently been discovered in Inner Mongolia.

Alashan (Alxa) The only area in Inner Mongolia predominantly covered by dunes, far-western Alashan is inhabited by Oirat Mongols who were stationed there in the 17th and 18th centuries. (Generally written "Alashan" in Mongolian, the name is often pronounced Alshaa or Alagshaa.)

Traditionally, Alashan and Ejene (or Ejene Gol) were two independent banners not assigned to any of Inner Mongolia's six leagues. Since 1979 Alashan Left and Right (Alxa Zuoqi and Youqi) Banners and the Ejene (Ejin) Banner have formed a single Alashan league within Inner Mongolia. The league covers 270,244 square kilometers (104,342 square miles) with a population of 165,570, of which 41,974 (25.3 percent) are Mongol. Virtually all Mongols in these banners speak Mongolian. Although the Alashan Mongols are by origin OIRATS, their dialect lost much of its Oirat features through KHALKHA and Inner Mongolian influence (*see* MONGOLIAN LANGUAGE and KALMYK-OIRAT LANGUAGE AND SCRIPT).

Situated at about 800 to 1,400 meters (2,600–4,600 feet) above sea level, average annual precipitation in Alashan league varies from 120 millimeters (4.72 inches) in the east to only 37 millimeters (1.46 inches) in the west. The Badain Jiran and Tenggeri Deserts are the largest areas of dunes. Characteristic vegetation includes sagebrushes (*Artemisia sphaerocephala* and *A. ordosica*) and *Calligonum,* with patches of xerophytic trees and bushes such as saxaul. Rivers in Ejene Banner are flanked by scattered poplar (*Populus diversifolia*) forests. Usable pasture totals 127,000 square kilometers (49,000 square miles) and supports 1,425,000 head of livestock, of which 1,235,000 are sheep and goats. The league's 145,000 camels make up a third of China's total CAMEL herd (1990 figures). Irrigation has brought 10,000 hectares (24,710 acres) into cultivation. Extraction of minerals, principally coal and salt, is also an important part of the local economy.

In the 11th to 13th centuries, the XIA DYNASTY ruled Alashan, leaving behind the Xia imperial tombs in the Helan Mountains and the beautifully preserved desert fortress of Khara-Khota (Heishui). In 1686 the KHOSHUD noble Khoroli of the Oirats defected with his people to the QING DYNASTY and was enfeoffed as grand duke (r. 1697–1707) of Alashan banner. Later, in 1698, a Torghud

Kalmyk nobleman, Arabjur, went on pilgrimage to the Dalai Lama with his family and 500 subjects. Unable to return home, Arabjur in 1704 agreed to become a Qing subject and was stationed as a grand duke (r. 1704–29) with his people at Serteng (modern Aksay) in western Gansu. Under his son Danjüng (r. 1729–40) the TORGHUDS were moved to Ejene.

In 1928 China's Nationalist government assigned Alashan and Ejene to the newly created Ningxia province. As the last area in Inner Mongolia outside Communist control, it was the scene of PRINCE DEMCHUG-DONGRUB's final autonomy movement of 1949. In 1956 the two banners were transferred to Inner Mongolia, and in 1961 Alashan was split into Right and Left Banners. During the anti-Mongol policies of the Chinese Cultural Revolution, from 1969–79, the three banners were temporarily split off again from Inner Mongolia.

See also BAYANNUUR LEAGUE; CLIMATE; INNER MONGOLIA AUTONOMOUS REGION; INNER MONGOLIANS; MONGOLIAN LANGUAGE; WUHAI.

Further reading: Mary Ellen Alonso, ed., *China's Inner Asian Frontier: Photographs of the Wulsin Expedition to Northeast China in 1923* (Cambridge, Mass.: The Museum, 1979); Nasan Bayar, "History and Its Televising: Events and Narratives of the Hoshuud Mongols in Modern China," *Inner Asia* 4 (2002): 241–276.

Ali-Haiya *See* ARIQ-QAYA.

Altaic language family The Altaic language family includes the Mongolic, Turkic, and Manchu-Tungusic families. Many relate Korean and Japanese to the Altaic family as well. Debate continues over whether the Altaic language family is a real language family of branches developed from a common ancestor or a *sprachbund* (areal family) of independent languages that have converged over time through intimate contact. A genetic link to the Uralic family, including Hungarian, Finnish, and Estonian, is now generally rejected, although Hungarian does have many Turkic and Mongolic loan words.

THE ALTAIC LANGUAGES

By far the most commonly spoken Altaic language subfamily is the Turkic family, which includes the national languages Turkish (the largest Altaic language with 70 million speakers), Uzbek, Kazakh, Azerbaijani, Turkmen, and Kirghiz, as well as Uighur, spoken in China's Xinjiang Autonomous Region, and Tatar, Bashkir (Bashkort), Tuvan, Altay, Yakut (Sakha), and other languages spoken in Russia. The total number of Turkic speakers approaches 150 million. The Turkic languages are divided into two groups, one called Common Turkic and including all the above-mentioned languages, and the other including only Chuvash and the (now extinct) Old Bulghar languages of the Volga region in Russia. (The first rulers of Bulgaria also spoke this type of

Turkish language, although they were later assimilated by their Slavic subjects. *See* BULGHARS). The earliest Turkish inscriptions in an archaic form of Common Turkic date to the second half of the seventh century. (*See* RUNIC SCRIPT AND INSCRIPTIONS.)

The next most widely spoken family is Mongolic. In this family only the MONGOLIAN LANGUAGE, with perhaps 5 million speakers, is a major language; it is the national language of Mongolia and a regional language in China's Inner Mongolian Autonomous Region. All the other extant Mongolic languages, found in Russia, China, and Afghanistan, clearly derive from the well-attested 13th-century Middle Mongolian, although one, Daur, preserves traces of the highly divergent Kitan, a now-extinct language attested in inscriptions from the 11th century.

In the Manchu-Tungusic family only Shibe in Xinjiang (about 33,000 speakers in 1990) and the Solon Ewenki dialect in Inner Mongolia (about 25,000 speakers) are not endangered. Manchu, the language of the Manchu conquerors of China who founded the QING DYNASTY (1636–1912), is now extinct. Inscriptions in the Jurchen language date to the 12th century, when the Jurchen people founded the JIN DYNASTY.

ALTAIC FEATURES

The Altaic languages (along with Korean and Japanese) share a common syntax characterized by a usually subject-object-verb (SOV) word order and adjunct-head (modifier-modified) order. Absent external influences, Altaic languages form relative clauses not with relative pronouns but by verbal noun phrases (thus, not "I saw the meat that you ate," but "I the your-eaten meat saw"). The verb "to have" is absent, with possession generally being marked by case endings and the verb "to be" (thus, not "They have a question," but "To them a question is"). Altaic languages are typically agglutinative, marking grammatical relations by clearly demarcated morphemes, and use only suffixes, not prefixes. As is expected for agglutinative languages, natural gender is weak or absent. The role of conjunctions tends to be replaced by a large number of special verb endings or converbs.

Despite these common features, linguistic typology shows that many of them form a linked complex of features all deriving from the SOV word order. Since SOV is the most common order among languages, more or less "Altaic"-type syntax is quite common, being found, for example, in the Dravidian languages of southern India and even Quechua in Peru.

Altaic phonology also has certain distinctive features. Syllables are simple, with no initial consonants clusters and usually no final consonant clusters. Absent foreign influences, initial "r" is not allowed. Most distinctive is vowel harmony, in which all a word's vowels must come from a particular class, depending on the root's initial vowel. Thus, all case-endings have multiple forms. In modern Mongolian, for example, *gar*, "hand," takes the ablative ("from") in -*aas*, while *ger*, "home, yurt," takes the ablative in -*ees*. Vowel harmony is also found in the Uralic and, with quite different principles, in the Chukotko-Kamchatkan languages.

Linguists have also reconstructed a fairly large Altaic common vocabulary, along with many morphemes (noun and verb suffixes), yet while Mongolian shares much vocabulary and many morphemes with Manchu-Tungusic to its east and with Turkic to its west, Turkic and Manchu-Tungusic have very little common vocabulary. Moreover, much basic vocabulary, such as numbers, has no common elements. Many linguists thus argue that the common vocabulary is due to borrowing rather than genetic affinity.

Advocates of borrowing posit three distinct strata of Turkic loanwords in Mongolia, one borrowed from a Turkic language of the Bulghar-Chuvashic subfamily before the second century C.E., a second from a Qipchaq-type Turkish language (such as ancestral to modern Tatar or Kazakh) from the sixth to 10th centuries, and finally Buddhist and academic vocabulary from written Uighur Turkish in the 13th-14th centuries. (*See* BULGHARS; QIPCHAQS; UIGHURS.) Heavy Mongolic influence on the Manchu-Tungusic languages began no later than the Kitan Empire's rise in the 10th century and continued through the Manchu adoption of the UIGHUR-MONGOLIAN SCRIPT in the 17th century.

ALTAIC CULTURE

Regardless of whether they are descended from a common ancestor or converged through long association, the medieval Altaic peoples shared many cultural traits. Organized into strong patrilineal and exogamous clans, their peoples all had male or female shamans who beat drums and went on spirit journeys to cure illness and singers who chanted poetry in alliterative (not rhyming) verses. Herding livestock and farming in varying proportions, they all shared a fascination with the HORSE, which was sacrificed at the death of their leaders. Since the Middle Ages, migrations, lifestyle changes, and adoption of world religions have attenuated much of this common culture.

See also EWENKIS; KAZAKHS; MONGOLIC LANGUAGE FAMILY; ROURAN; TUVANS; UIGHURS; XIANBI; XIONGNU; YOGUR LANGUAGES AND PEOPLES.

Further reading: Sir Gerard Clauson, *Turkish and Mongolian Studies* (London: Royal Asiatic Society of Great Britain and Ireland, 1962); Bernard Comrie, *Languages of the Soviet Union* (Cambridge: Cambridge University Press, 1981): 39–91; Juha Janhunen, *Manchuria: An Ethnic History* (Helsinki: Finno-Ugrian Society, 1996); Roy Andrew Miller, *Japanese and the Other Altaic Language* (Chicago: University of Chicago Press, 1971); Nicholas Poppe, *Introduction to Altaic Linguistics* (Wiesbaden: Otto Harrassowitz, 1965).

Altai Range Forming the traditional western border of Mongolia, the Altai Range and associated ranges extend more than 1,600 kilometers (1,000 miles) from northwest to southeast. The name is of Turkish origin and means "golden."

To the north in Russia's Altai Republic, the Altai system is about 350 kilometers (220 miles) wide, tapering to the southeast to about 150 kilometers (90 miles). In the central Mongolian Altai, the ridges have an average altitude of 3,000–3,500 meters (9,800–11,500 feet) above sea level. High peaks include Belukha (4,506 meters; 14,783 feet), on the Russia-Kazakhstan frontier; Khüiten (4,374 meters; 14,350 feet), at the meeting of Mongolia, China, Russia, and Kazakhstan; and Mönkh-Khairkhan (4,231 meters; 13,881 feet), south of KHOWD CITY. All these peaks and many others are glaciated. In the arid Gobi-Altai Range, the peaks diminish toward the southeast from around 3,500 to 1,700 meters (11,500–5,600 feet) above sea level.

The Mongolian Altai presents relatively gentle slopes to the northeast toward the GREAT LAKES BASIN and steep slopes to the southwest toward Xinjiang's Zünghar (Junggar) Basin. The transverse Siilkhem/Sayluygem Range along the Russia-Mongolia frontier divides the Ob' drainage from the Great Lakes Basin inland basin. The Mongolian Altai divides the Irtysh drainage and the Zünghar inland basin to the west from the Great Lakes Basin to the east.

See also ANIMAL HUSBANDRY AND NOMADISM; BAYANKHONGOR PROVINCE; BAYAN-ÖLGII PROVINCE; CLIMATE; FAUNA; FLORA; GOBI-ALTAI PROVINCE; KHOWD PROVINCE; MONGOLIAN PLATEAU; SOUTH GOBI PROVINCE; UWS PROVINCE.

Altai Uriyangkhai (Uriankhai, Urianhai, Uryangkhai) The term *Uriyangkhai* in modern Mongolia denotes a vaguely defined *yastan* (subethnic group) in western Mongolia. The Altai Uriyangkhai form a coherent group within this artificial subethnic group.

In the 13th century RASHID-UD-DIN described the "Forest" Uriyangkhai as an extremely isolated Siberian forest people living in birchbark tents and hunting with skis (*see* SIBERIA AND THE MONGOL EMPIRE). Despite the similarity in name to the famous Uriyangkhan clan of the MONGOL TRIBE, Rashid-ud-Din clearly states that the two had no ongoing connection. The language of the "Forest" Uriyangkhai is unclear.

By the early 17th century, *Uriyangkhai* was a general Mongolian term for all the dispersed bands to the northwest, whether Samoyed, Turkish, or Mongolian in origin. The Uriyangkhai in this sense were subjugated first by KHOTOGHOID Khalkha and then by the ZÜNGHARS. With the disintegration of the Zünghars, the QING DYNASTY in 1757 organized the far northwestern frontier into a series of Uriyangkhai BANNERS: the Khöwsgöl Nuur Uriyangkhai, Tannu (Oyun), Kemchik, Salchak, and Tozhu (Toja) Uriyangkhai (all TUVANS), and the Altan-Nuur Uriyangkhai (Altayans). In the Altai Range, seven Altai Uriyangkhai banners were organized into two wings attached directly to Qing AMBANS (assistant military governors) of KHOWD CITY. Their territory included modern BAYAN-ÖLGII PROVINCE and eastern KHOWD PROVINCE as well as Xinjiang's Altay district north of the Ulungur River. Their principal duties were to guard the 12 Altai passes, man the postroads to Tarbagatai, and pay an annual tribute of 800 sables. Most were Oirat Mongolian speakers with Oirat, Buriat, or Mongolian CLAN NAMES, but some were Tuvan speakers.

In the aftermath of the great rebellion in Xinjiang (1864–77), KAZAKHS migrated into Altai Uriyangkhai territory, leading to repeated lawsuits between the expanding Kazakhs and the impoverished Uriyangkhais from 1822 on. In 1906 the Qing dynasty transferred western Mongolia's Altai Uriyangkhai, New Torghud, and Khoshud banners from Khowd's jurisdiction to the new Altai district, with its capital at Chenghua (modern Altay in Xinjiang). In 1913 the Altai district was divided between newly independent Mongolia and the Chinese province of Xinjiang, leaving some Altai Uriyangkhais in far northern Xinjiang. The Altai Uriyangkhais on the Mongolian side of the border were administratively attached to the DÖRBÖDS. In 1940, however, Kazakh and Uriyangkhai areas were separated to form the Bayan-Ölgii province. The Kazakhs dominated the new province, and both emigration and a growth rate slower than the national average have reduced the Altai Uriyangkhai percentage there by 2.5 times from 1940 to 1989.

Mongolia's Uriyangkhai people numbered 15,800 in 1956 (1.9 percent of Mongolia's population) and 21,300 in 1989 (only 1.0 percent of the population), inhabiting Bayan-Ölgii, Khowd, and KHÖWSGÖL PROVINCES. (In those census figures, the Altai Uriyangkhai were not separated from the Tuvans or the Khöwsgöl Uriyangkhai, also of Tuvan ancestry.) The Uriyangkhai Mongols in Xinjiang number more than 5,000 (1999).

The Uriyangkhai are one of Mongolia's most poorly educated ethnic groups, with only 13.1 percent holding white-collar positions, compared with the national average of 21.4 percent (1989 figures). Most Altai Uriyangkhais currently emphasize their Mongolian origins, disclaiming connection with the Tuvans.

Altan Khan (1508–1582) *Successful warrior khan who made peace with China and initiated the Mongols' Second Conversion to Buddhism*
Altan (Golden) and his twin sister, Mönggön (Silver), were born on January 20, 1508, to Barsu-Bolod Sain-Alag (d. 1519), the *jinong* (Chinggisid viceroy) of the Three Western Tümens (modern southwestern Inner Mongolia). Altan spent his first years in hiding when the ORDOS

people rose in rebellion against his grandfather, BATU-MÖNGKE DAYAN KHAN (1480?–1517?). Protected by locals, the boy was safely delivered to his grandfather's court.

On his father's death, Altan, as a second son, inherited the TÜMED *tümen* living around modern HÖHHOT in Inner Mongolia. From 1524 he began regular campaigns against Kökenuur, Ming China, and the northwestern Uriyangkhan. In 1538, under Bodi Alag Khan (1519?–47) of the Yuan, he participated in the all-Mongol attack on the Uriyangkhan. In 1550 Altan conducted a massive raid on China's MING DYNASTY, circling the walls of Beijing, although he never seriously intended to besiege it. As Altan's prestige grew, the Yuan Khan Daraisun (1548–57) was forced to grant Altan and his brother Baiskhal of the KHARACHIN the title of KHAN. Daraisun Khan himself moved east of the GREATER KHINGGAN RANGE.

By 1551 Buddhist White Lotus sectarians from China were hailing Altan as their deliverer from oppressive Ming rule. They and other Chinese refugees came to Altan Khan's realm to settle, serving as guides for Mongol raiding parties and smuggling goods over the frontier. By 1563 there were 12 large and 32 small sectarian settlements, or *baishing* (buildings), with a total of 16,000 inhabitants. Altan Khan encouraged agriculture, although his Tümed Mongol subjects remained mostly pastoral. There were perhaps 50,000 Chinese under Altan's rule. The largest settlement was renamed Guihua (modern HÖHHOT) in 1571.

After 1558 Altan Khan campaigned against the OIRATS, and the two sides established QUDA (marriage ally) relations, with the Oirat chiefs recognizing Altan as khan and he granting them the traditional title of TAISHI. He also established relations with the Chaghatayid rulers of MOGHULISTAN in Turpan and Hami on the basis of their common Chinggisid ancestry.

Altan Khan had two senior wives, but nothing is known of them. By 1568 Altan had married his own daughter's teenage daughter, Noyanchu Jünggen (Sanniangzi, 1551–1612). Since Noyanchu Jünggen had originally been promised to another, Altan sent her betrothed another granddaughter instead, one originally promised to his foster son Daiching-Ejei. Disgusted, Daiching-Ejei defected in 1570 to the Ming. The Ming official Wang Chonggu used Daiching-Ejei as bait to make peace successfully between China and Altan Khan. Speaking for all the Three Western Tümens (Tümed, ORDOS, and Yüngshiyebü/Kharachin), Altan Khan received the title prince of Shunyi and annual "gifts" from the Chinese court, and the Ming opened border horse fairs. In return the Mongols ceased their raids and joined the TRIBUTE SYSTEM. Defectors from both sides were sent back; Daiching-Ejei again became a favorite, and the White Lotus sectarians were executed by the Ming. Noyanchu Jünggen controlled much of the tribute-gift and horse-fair revenues, causing violent rivalry with Altan's eldest son, Sengge-Düüreng (d. 1586).

From 1571 Altan Khan and Noyanchu Jünggen received Buddhist catechetical instruction from a Tibetan monk, Ashing Lama, trained at the sacred Wutai Mountain in northern China. With the new influence from Tibetan lamas, Altan Khan built a new temple, Maidari Juu. In 1575 he and Noyanchu Jünggen, with the Three Western Tümens, invited the Tibetan cleric bSod-nams rGya-mtsho (1543–1588) to instruct them personally. At their meeting at Chabchiyal Temple in Kökenuur (near modern Gonghe) in summer 1578, bSod-nams rGya-mtsho hailed Altan Khan as a Buddhist universal monarch and incarnation of QUBILAI KHAN, while Altan Khan granted the title Dalai Lama to bSod-nams rGya-mtsho. Another Tibetan INCARNATE LAMA, Manjushri Khutugtu, accompanied Altan Khan back to Kökekhota. In 1580 Altan Khan became sick with gout and planned to apply the old traditional remedy of having his feet washed within the chest of a slave. Manjushri Khutugtu strongly objected and healed the khan, thus inspiring the nobility to rededicate themselves to Buddhism. Shamanizing and the keeping of the native *ongghon*s, or spirit dolls, was banned. Altan Khan died on January 13, 1582. Noyanchu Jünggen kept the seal of the prince of Shunyi, which gave rights to the tribute-gift payments. The Tümed nobility demanded that the Ming court pass the seal to Sengge-Düüreng, and in November Sengge-Düüreng married his stepmother and became prince of Shunyi in April 1583.

Although often seen as attempting to reunify the Mongols, Altan Khan's true ambition was to build his Tümed into an independent power center. As Barsu Bolod's second son, he could be neither great khan of the Yuan nor even *jinong* (viceroy) of the Three Western Tümens. Instead, through military campaigns, peace with China, and Buddhist conversion, he received new high titles thrice over and became the acknowledged, if unofficial, leader of the Western Mongols. His peace with China and his patronage of the Dalai Lama, far from being a submission, made him in his own eyes the unifier of China, Tibet, and Mongolia under his own sway. This influence was, however, purely personal, and his sons and grandson were simply Tümed rulers without larger ambitions.

See also ALTAN KHAN, CODE OF; NORTHERN YUAN DYNASTY; SECOND CONVERSION.

Further reading: Carl Johan Elverskog, *Jewel Translucent Sutra: Altan Khan and the Mongols in the Sixteenth Century* (Leiden: E. J. Brill, 2003).

Altan Khan, Code of The Code of ALTAN KHAN (1508–82) is the earliest extant body of Mongolian law. Despite its religious preface extolling the TWO CUSTOMS, through which "the laws of religion are like knotted silk-ribbons" and the "laws of the emperor are like a golden yoke," the code makes no provision for the prohibition of blood sacrifices or other native religious practices or the imposition of Buddhist norms.

The code covers ordinary legal cases: homicide in various forms, injuries, theft, breaking of marriage engagements and marital assaults, cases involving infectious diseases and contact with dead bodies, game laws, rewards for rescue of livestock and persons, assault of government envoys, and return of fugitives. The sections on theft, which details military supplies in particular, and on envoys, which specifies both punishments for resisting envoys and also the number of horses, officials, and servants an envoy may take, show the attention paid to enforcing government prerogatives. Most offenses receive livestock fines grouped in Nines and Fives, with serious offenses also meriting a flogging. Most cases are addressed to free men, but when mentioned, servants, particularly Chinese, are treated as of lower value. The only capital crime is theft by a servant. The provisions of the law are similar to those found in 17th-century codes such as the MONGOL-OIRAT CODE (Mongghol-Oirad Tsaaji) of 1640.

Further reading: Sh. Bira, "A Sixteenth-Century Mongol Code." In *Studies in the Mongolian History, Culture, and Historiography* (Tokyo: Institute for Languages and Cultures of Asia and Africa, 1994), 277–309.

Altan tobchi (Golden Summary) *Altan tobchi* denotes two Mongolian chronicles both composed in the mid-17th century. The more important was composed by the "state preceptor" (*güüshi*, a Buddhist title) Lubsang-Danzin (Tibetan, Blo-bzang bsTan-'dzin). Nothing is known of his life, although he may have been a Buddhist translator from ÜJÜMÜCHIN banner. His history was compiled shortly after 1651.

In producing what was probably the first of the 17th-century chronicles, he used six types of written materials: 1) traditional, undated Mongolian accounts of CHINGGIS KHAN, the fall of the YUAN DYNASTY, and the Mongol-Oirat conflicts; 2) various *biligs* (wise sayings) and testaments attributed to Chinggis Khan; 3) the SECRET HISTORY OF THE MONGOLS; 4) various Tibetan historical works, which as a lama he could read; 5) dated king lists of the Mongolian great khans and Chinese Ming emperors; and 6) genealogies of the Mongolian nobility. Putting these materials together, Lubsang-Danzin put completeness above coherence, including, for example, most of the *Secret History* side by side with contradictory Mongolian traditions. Sometimes he noticed the contradiction, as when he put "it is said" before the *Secret History*'s statement that Chinggis was born with a clot of blood in his hand; the traditional account, which Lubsang-Danzin preferred, was that he was born with a precious jade seal in his hand. In harmonizing discrete episodes of the 15th-century Mongol-Oirat conflict with one another and with the king lists (themselves frequently in error on the dates, although not on the order and names of the khans), Lubsang-Danzin often became completely confused, breaking up episodes

that belong together, assigning events to wrong khans, and so on. Despite these defects, Lubsang-Danzin's *Altan tobchi* preserves very valuable material, including the *Secret History* text, otherwise lost *biligs*, and KHORCHIN traditions on the benefits the Khorchin *ongs* (princes) had shown the Chinggisid khans. Roughly contemporary with Lubsang-Danzin's *Altan tobchi* is an anonymous abridged *Altan tobchi*, which eliminated most of the *Secret History* and the Tibetan materials and all the *biligs* and genealogies.

Further reading: C. R. Bawden, trans., *Mongol Chronicle Altan Tobci* (Wiesbaden: Otto Harrassowitz, 1955); Hidehiro Okada, "Chinggis Khan's Instructions to His Kin in Blo-bzang-bstan-'dzin's *Altan Tobci*," in *Meng-ku wen hua kuo chi hsueh shu yen tao hui lun wen chi*, ed. Chün-i Chang (Taipei: Mongolian and Tibetan Affairs Committee, 1993), 228–236; Hans-Peter Vietze, "Blo-bzan bsTan-'jin Güüsi's Rhymes," in *Proceedings of the 35th Permanent International Altaistics Conference*, ed. Chieh-hsien Ch'en (Taipei: Center for Chinese Studies Materials, 1993), 469–476.

Altyn Khans   *See* KHOTOGHOID.

Alxa   *See* ALASHAN.

Amar, Agdanbuugiin   *See* AMUR.

Amar, Anandyn   *See* AMUR.

Amarsanaa   *See* AMURSANAA.

amban The Manchu word *amban*, or "high official" (Mongolian *said*), was used unofficially for the imperial residents supervising Inner Asia (including Mongolia) under the QING DYNASTY (1636–1912).

Direct Qing administration in Outer Mongolia began with the *jiangjun* (Chinese for "general in chief") of ULIASTAI, created in 1733. Another *jiangjun* was appointed to KHOWD CITY in 1734. In the narrow sense, Mongolian *amban* or *said* refers, however, to the office of *dachen* (imperial resident), first instituted in Kökenuur for the UPPER MONGOLS (1725) and in Lhasa for Tibet (1728). In 1754 the general in Khowd was redesignated as, in Manchu, the *hebei amban* (Mongolian *khoobiyin said*; Chinese *canzan dachen*), and shortly after two *ambans* were appointed to administer Khüriye (*see* ULAANBAATAR) and its monasteries. The senior of the two positions, established in 1758, was entitled in Mongolian *khereg-i shidkhegchi said* (minister handling affairs; Manchu, *baita ichihiyara amban*; Chinese, *banshi dachen*), while the junior position, established in 1761, was entitled the *hebei amban/khoobi-yin said*, as at Khowd. Since the senior position was restricted to Khalkha Mongolian princes and the junior to officials from the Qing's EIGHT

BANNERS system, the two positions were known as the "Mongol *amban*" and the "Manchu *amban,*" respectively. Despite their theoretical subordination, the Manchu *amban*s actually had greater influence.

In 1758 the *jiangjun* of Uliastai, then a Khalkha prince, Tsenggünjab (d. 1771), received civil authority over Outer Mongolia (including Tuva) in addition to his supreme military authority. Under the *jiangjun* at Uliastai were two *amban*s, or imperial residents (Manchu *hebei amban;* Mongolian *khoobi-yin said*), again an Eight-Banners official and a Khalkha prince. In 1786, however, Outer Mongolia's eastern provinces, Setsen Khan and Tüshiyetü, were put under the *amban*s in Khüriye.

In the 18th century the Uliastai *jiangjun* and the Khowd *amban* were generally Khalkha Mongol princes, often serving a decade or more in office. After 1796 *jiangjun*s and *amban*s were all, except for those positions reserved to Khalkhas, officials from the Eight Banners. The *amban*s, two-thirds of whom were ethnically Manchu and one-third Mongol, were career officials specializing in military-police functions or border affairs and rarely held office in Mongolia more than three years.

Outside Outer Mongolia the autonomous Mongol BANNERS (appanages) were, as military auxiliaries for the dynasty, all placed under the supervision of Eight-Banners garrisons. These garrisons were headed by commanders variously titled in Chinese *jiangjun* (general in chief; Manchu *amba janggin*), *dutong* (military lieutenant-governor; Manchu *gûsa-be kadalara amban*), or *fudutong*s (deputy military lieutenant-governors; Manchu *meiren-i janggin*). The *jiangjun* of Ili (Yining) supervised the Mongols of Xinjiang; those of Ningxia (Yinchuan) and Suiyuan (modern HÖHHOT) supervised southwest Inner Mongolia; and those of Mukden (Shenyang), Jilin, and Qiqihar supervised eastern Inner Mongolia and the Butha Daurs. The *dutong*s in Zhangjiakou and Chengde supervised the central and southeastern Inner Mongols, and the *fudutong* of HULUN BUIR supervised the BARGA, Solons, and Daurs of Hulun Buir. *Dutong*s and *fudutong*s were often loosely referred to as *amban*s.

The 1911 RESTORATION of Outer Mongolia's independence abolished the *amban* system there. Republican China retained the *dutong*s of Suiyuan, Zhangjiakou, and Chengde as governors of Inner Mongolia's regions.

See also DAUR LANGUAGE AND PEOPLE; EWENKIS.

Further reading: Veronika Veit, "The Qalqa Mongolian Military Governors of Uliyasutai in the 18th Century," in *Proceedings of International Conference on China Border Area Studies,* ed. Lin En-shean (Taipei: National Chengchi University, 1984), 629–646.

Amur (Agdanbuugiin Amar, Anandyn Amar) (1886–1941) *A career official who served twice as prime minister*

Amur was the son of a poor TAIJI or petty nobleman, Agdanbuu, of Daiching Zasag banner (Bugat *Sum,* Bul-gan). Amur's original name was Gonggor. As a child he was tutored in Mongolian before studying in the school attached to the banner temple for three or four years and becoming a banner clerk. He clerked for his banner's PRINCE KHANGDADORJI in the AIMAG/league office, the banner office, and in the office dealing with gold-mining leases (*see* MINING). He married the daughter of Danjin Gabju (doctor of Buddhist philosophy), the lama who had cast his horoscope at birth. From 1913 he worked in Mongolia's foreign ministry, receiving the title of *beise* (grand duke). With the REVOCATION OF AUTONOMY, he returned to his home banner. He changed his name to Amur after suffering a serious illness.

In 1923 he returned to Khüriye (modern ULAAN-BAATAR) and joined the party. He served as foreign minister (October 1923–November 1924), party presidium member (August 1924 on), economy minister (December 1924–26), deputy prime minister and concurrent head of the planning commission, and after Tserindorji's death, prime minister (February 1928–March 1930). In these positions Amur showed an unsentimental understanding of Mongolia's precarious international position. Reliably pro-Russian in a geopolitical sense, he had no interest in Soviet ideology and strongly opposed all pan-Mongolist adventures. In 1937 a Soviet security operative described him as "a quiet, secretive person, a true Oriental; he is well respected by the people, especially the clergy."

Ironically, Amur's competence and well-known conservative patriotism made him, indispensable to Moscow's Communist International (Comintern) during the early LEFTIST PERIOD (1929 on). At the Eighth Party Congress (March–April 1930), however, the Comintern felt confident enough to demote him to head the Institute of Sciences. With the New Turn Policies in June 1932, he was made chairman of the Little State Khural (i.e., titular head of state) and from October 1934 was again a party presidium member. In 1934 he published the first volume of *Monggol-un tobchi teüke* (A Short History of Mongolia), which was the first connected account of the Mongolian world empire written by a Mongolian that took into account European research.

Promoted to replace GENDÜN as prime minister on March 22, 1936, Amur was again a token. Real power lay with the interior minister Choibalsang and his hatchetman Lubsangsharab (D. Luwsansharaw, 1900–40), as Joseph Stalin's Great Purge swept the country. In 1936, Amur and Dogsum (D. Dogsom, 1884–1941) attempted to release the victims still imprisoned in the bogus LHÜMBE CASE. In 1937 he pleaded with the state prosecutor to be skeptical of Choibalsang's manufactured conspiracies. Finally, on March 7, 1939, Lubsangsharab arrested Amur in a presidium meeting. In July he was deported to the Soviet Union. Interrogated with torture, he confessed to various imaginary crimes and was executed on February 10, 1941.

See also CHOIBALSANG, MARSHAL; REVOLUTIONARY PERIOD; THEOCRATIC PERIOD.

Amursana *See* AMURSANAA.

Amursanaa (Amursana, Amarsanaa) (1722?–1757) *Khoid leader who first rebelled against the Zünghars and then attempted to revive the Zünghar principality*
Amursanaa's mother, Botolog, was the daughter of TSEWANG-RABTAN KHUNG-TAIJI (1694–1727), or prince of the ZÜNGHARS. Tsewang-Rabtan had first married her to Galdan-Danzin, son of Lhazang Khan (1698–1717) of the UPPER MONGOLS in Tibet. After executing her first husband, Tsewang-Rabtan gave her in marriage to Üizeng-Khoshuuchi of the Khoid. While Amursanaa was thus legally accounted Üizeng-Khoshuuchi's son, rumor had it that he was actually the posthumous son of Galdan-Danzin and thus the grandson of a ruler on both sides of his family.

After the death of Galdan-Tseren, the ruler of the Zünghars, in 1745 the deceased ruler's eldest son by a lowborn wife, Lamdarja, seized the throne in 1749. He met the widespread opposition with violent repression. Amursanaa, together with Dawaachi of the ruling lineage, fled to the Kazakh sultan Abilay, whose daughter Amursanaa married. In 1752 with Kazakh help, Amursanaa and Dawaachi overthrew Lamdarja. Dawaachi belonged to the sovereign lineage and became *khung-taiji* ("prince," the ruling Zünghar title), but Amursanaa was unsatisfied. In summer 1754 he and his half brother Banjuur (Botolog and Galdan-Danzin's first son) surrendered to the QING DYNASTY's Qianlong emperor (1736–96) with 4,000 men. In spring 1755 the Qing general Bandi and Amursanaa marched on Zünghaxia. Resistance disintegrated, and Dawaachi was captured near Kashgar and deported to China. Qianlong now decreed that each of the OIRATS' four tribes would receive a khan: Banjuur would be khan of the Khoshuds and Amursanaa khan of the Khoid.

Again dissatisfied with his reward, Amursanaa and Banjuur conspired with Mongol noblemen in Bandi's army (*see* CHINGGÜNJAB'S REBELLION). Bandi got wind of the plots, executed Banjuur, and dispatched Amursanaa to Beijing. Due to the laxity of his escort, Amursanaa and 300 men escaped and returned to Ili, where he captured the local Qing garrison commander. In November Qianlong remobilized his army, and Amursanaa proclaimed himself khan of all the Zünghars (February 17, 1756) before rallying his men and killing Bandi and his garrison. Sultan Abilay supported Amursanaa, but the Sultan's KAZAKHS plundered their Zünghar allies mercilessly. Although a vast Qing expedition defeated Sultan Abilay's Kazakhs twice in July–August 1756, and forced Sultan Abilay to abandon his son-in-law, the Qing armies did not stay in the field and withdrew to Barköl. Amursanaa returned to the Ili valley in late 1756, where he again destroyed the Qing garrisons. Faced with another massive Qing expedition under Zhaohui, Amursanaa fought on with a dwindling force until he fled with 4,000 followers (largely women and children) to Semipalatinsk (modern Semey) on July 28. Forwarded by the Russian authorities to Tobolsk, he died of smallpox on September 21. His followers were eventually merged with the Volga KALMYKS.

Further reading: Fang Chao-ying, "Amursana," in Arthur W. Hummel, *Eminent Chinese of the Ch'ing Period* (Washington, D.C.: U.S. Government Printing Office, 1943), 9–11; Junko Miyawaki, "The Khoyid Chief Amursanaa in the Fall of the Dzungars: The Importance of the Family Trees Discovered in Kazan," in *Historical and Linguistic Interaction between Inner-Asia and Europe*, ed. Árpád Berta and Edina Horváth (Szeged, Hungary: University of Szeged, 1997), 195–205.

anda The *anda* relationship was a blood brotherhood formed by unrelated men. As such it formed an important complement to the patrilineal kin-based Mongol society.

In the Mongol clan society before the rise of CHINGGIS KHAN (Genghis, 1206–27), patrilineal kinship formed the chief language of alliance and hostility. In general, those who were kin were allies; those who were not were enemies. The relationship of *anda*, or blood brotherhood (modern Mongolian *and*), introduced a vital flexibility into this system. Found in many Turco-Mongol nomadic societies, the ritual of blood brotherhood involved drinking from a cup into which blood from both parties had been poured. The "brothers" would then exchange gifts and usually spend some time living in the same YURT, or *ger*. Blood brotherhood formed an important way of cementing political alliances. Thus, a chief of the MONGOL TRIBE, YISÜGEI BA'ATUR, made an alliance of *anda* with Toghril Khan (later named ONG KHAN) of the KEREYID tribe. Toghril's assistance later proved essential to the rise of Yisügei's son Chinggis Khan. Chinggis, as a child and a teenager, made himself blood brother of JAMUGHA, a Mongol from the Jajirad clan. In the end, however, the *anda* tie could not prevent war between Chinggis and both Ong Khan and Jamugha. After the rise of the MONGOL EMPIRE, the significance of the *anda* tie declined somewhat, although together with QUDA, or the marriage ally concept, it continued to link khans to their favored commanders (NOYAN). In the 20th century the idea of blood brotherhood has undergone a revival in nationalist movements.

Aniga (Anige, A-ni-ko) (1244–1278) *Nepalese-Newari artist who under Mongol patronage defined a long-lasting Inner Asian imperial style of Buddhist art*
Aniga early showed an aptitude for Buddhist art, memorizing the scriptures on the canonical proportions of icons after hearing them only once. In 1260 QUBILAI

KHAN's state preceptor, 'PHAGS-PA LAMA (1235–80), applied to Nepal for artists to complete a gold stupa in Amdo (Qinghai). Aniga, only 16 at the time, volunteered to lead the 80 artists and was appointed by the astonished 'Phags-pa as their supervisor.

Upon completing the stupa in 1261, Aniga was presented at court to Qubilai Khan, who commissioned him to improve a defective bronze diagram of acupuncture and moxibustion points presented by SONG DYNASTY envoys. After Aniga successfully completed the project in 1265, he was commissioned to produce a variety of Buddhas and stupas in SHANGDU and DAIDU, steel Dharma-wheels used as imperial standards, and portraits for the imperial temple in brocade appliqué. In 1273 he was appointed overseer of artisans; his sons Asanga and Ashura inherited his position. Extant works produced under Aniga's supervision include the White Pagoda in Beijing and an icon of the fierce deity Mahakala. Aniga's Nepalese style continued to have a strong influence on Tibetan art produced for the Yuan and Ming dynasties (1368–1644) as well as on the Mongolian master of sculpture Zanabazar (1635–1732).

See also BUDDHISM IN THE MONGOL EMPIRE; BUDDHIST FINE ARTS; JIBZUNDAMBA KHUTUGTU, FIRST; TIBET AND THE MONGOL EMPIRE.

A-ni-ko *See* ANIGA.

animal husbandry and nomadism Animal husbandry has long been and still is the principal economic pursuit of the Mongols. Today about 35 percent of Mongolia's families are nomadic herders, and about 45 percent of the working population make a living in the animal husbandry sector.

LIVESTOCK

Mongolian pastoralism is based on what is called the "five snouts of livestock" (*tawan khoshuu mal*): HORSES, CATTLE, CAMELS, SHEEP, and GOATS, in order according to their traditional prestige. All of these livestock are milked. In the Middle Ages sheep and goats, and on ceremonial occasions horses, were slaughtered for food, but today among most Mongols sheep, goats, and cattle are the main meat animals. Horses are, of course, used for riding, while cattle and camels are used as beasts of burden. Hides of all five animals are used. Horsehair is used for certain speciality purposes, but sheep's wool and camel's hair are the main fibers.

The five animals differ according to their pasturing properties. Sheep and goats are best kept together in herds of about 1,000, controlled throughout the day by a herder (who can be a child or adult, and of either sex), usually on foot. Big dogs help keep wolves away but are not used for herding. Herders often pool their herds to reach this optimal size and minimize their labor. During breeding season, sheep and goat herds are also sometimes split by age or sex. They spend the night near the camp or at a fixed winter corral and are led out each day. Cattle also spend the night near the camp but can go out to pasture and come back to the camp in the evening by themselves. While one or two riding horses are always kept near the camp, large horse herds spend the night three kilometers (two miles) or more from the camp under the guard of a stallion. The horses are supervised by mounted male herders, day and night, during foaling, and the herd is brought to camp for special events: switching the riding horses, gelding, milking mares, and so on. Sheep flocks and especially horse herds require heavy labor, while cattle are much less labor intensive.

The quality of pasture for animals on the MONGOLIAN PLATEAU varies with rainfall and evaporation, generally being better in the north and east and poorer in the south and west. In recent decades the *khangai* (mountain forest-steppe) areas support more than 75 sheep stocking units per 100 hectares, the steppe support about 50 to 75, the desert-steppe about 25 to 50, and the *gobi* (habitable desert) fewer than 25 (*see* FLORA; in sheep stocking units, sheep are counted as 1, goats as 0.9, cattle as 5, horses as 6, and camels as 7). Within any given region sheep, goats, cattle, and horses all use roughly similar pasture, although cattle and horses generally need more lush pasture, while goats do fine on the poorer pasture of the desert-steppe and *gobi*. Sheep are found everywhere, although they are relatively less common in the *gobi* habitat. Yaks (considered by the Mongols to be cattle) prefer to graze in high elevations over 2,750 meters (9,000 feet), while camels prefer dry *gobi*-type or soda-impregnated pasture.

To survive, every herding family needs at least one riding horse and access to at least 20 or so sheep, whether by owning them or herding them for others (*see* COLLECTIVIZATION AND COLLECTIVE HERDING; DECOLLECTIVIZATION; SOCIAL CLASSES IN THE QING PERIOD). Cattle or a second riding horse is not usually considered necessary until a herder has 50 or so sheep. Only when the sheep herd reaches 200 or so is a third horse considered necessary. More successful herders sometimes keep a horse herd with milking mares.

The Mongols do not traditionally practice selective breeding. The vast majority of males of all species are castrated before reaching sexual maturity. The yields of meat, milk, wool, and so on of all Mongolian breeds are thus far below those of European purebred types, yet the Mongolian breeds are all adapted for feeding on open range, sometimes on extremely scanty pasture and in very cold weather in the winter, and with low water needs. Improved breeds usually need far more water and shelter than do Mongolian livestock.

Mongolian livestock also supply the Mongols with fuel. The most common type of fuel is *argal*, or dried cattle dung, similar to the "buffalo chips" used by pioneers on the American plains. This is collected by using a wooden fork to flip the dung into a basket slung over the shoulders, although the 14th-century Arab traveler Ibn Battuta was shocked to see even high-ranking Mongols pick up and put in the chest of their robes especially fine bits of *argal* for later use. Sheep and goat dung (*khorgol*), naturally found in small pellets, is generally collected in crushed form from the animals' winter corrals. Horse dung (*khumuul*) is bad fuel and is not used if other dung is available.

NOMADISM

Mongolian pastoral nomadism must not be confused with the large-scale migrations that nomadic peoples sometimes undertook to escape enemies, seize fine new pastures, or deal with climatic pressures. Instead of such one-time movements, pastoral nomadism is the cyclical use of differing pastures through the year. The primary driving force is the insufficiency of the pastures in a single campsite to provide enough fodder for the animals through the year. Other factors that influence the type of migration are seasonality of the grass (in Mongolia grass grows from May to September), availability of water (well water is often needed in the birthing seasons, while in the winter, snow will serve), protection from winter winds, north-south and high-altitude–low-altitude temperature differences, terrain (animals are weak in the spring and cannot handle steep slopes), and protection from biting insects in the summer (windy areas have fewer mosquitos).

The combination of these factors has created four basic nomadization regimes in modern Mongolia: 1) in western and southwestern Mongolia around the high and dry ALTAI RANGE, herders make their summer camps in the mountains and winter in the lowlands; 2) in the steppe zone in eastern and central Mongolia, herders summer in the north and winter in the south; 3) in relatively lush north-central Mongolia around the lower KHANGAI RANGE and KHENTII RANGE, herders summer in the valleys and winter in the mountains; and 4) in the eastern Gobi and desert steppe, herders summer in exposed areas and winter in hollows. During the 13th century the khans and princes in the Khangai Range followed the first pattern, not the third, a difference that may be due to climatic, vegetational, or density changes.

Traditional animal husbandry made use of hay mowing along rivers, springs, and marshy low-lying ground. In the 19th century wet meadows were divided up by the banner (local administration) authorities and auctioned in the summer for a tax to be paid by the mowers.

While herds are owned by separate families, single families of Mongol herders rarely nomadize alone by choice. Instead, families camp together to form *khot ails*, or "camp families." The *khot ail* system allows the pooling of animals, especially sheep, to achieve the optimum number of about 1,000. Before collectivization it also allowed labor-poor but animal-rich families to put their animals out under close supervision to labor-rich but ani-

Collecting *argal* (dried dung) for fuel. Shiliin Gol, Inner Mongolia, 1987 *(Courtesy of Christopher Atwood)*

mal-poor families (*see* SOCIAL CLASSES IN THE QING PERIOD). Even during collectivization, however, it satisfied social needs. Among the OIRATS of western Mongolia, *khot ails* were generally formed at least partly along the lines of patrilineal kinship with a father and his married sons. Among the KHALKHA, for whom the clan organization had disintegrated, *khot ails* were often formed by unrelated friends or along the lines of matrilineal kinship (*see* MATRILINEAL CLANS). Within the *khot ail* the YURTS are generally lined up in an east–west line, with the senior household to the west (or right in the Mongols' southward orientation). With decollectivization, traditional forms of labor-sharing in the *khot-ail* are reviving.

Nomadism depends on the mobile yurt, or felt tent (Mongolian *ger*), the forms of which have varied over the centuries. Today nomads in the MONGOLIAN PLATEAU generally move about four or five times a year, although some move up to 12 times. Poor families, whose herds are usually just sheep with a riding horse, tend to be less mobile since they have to borrow or rent the necessary pack animals (cattle or camels). Also, the denser the population of people and animals, the shorter and fewer the nomadic movements. Nomads both in premodern and modern times have built sedentary structures (corrals, wells, etc.), which then become permanent pivot points in the yearly nomadic cycle. Mongolian traditional codes recognized a right of usufruct for those improving the pasture in this manner.

PASTORALISM IN PREMODERN MONGOLIA

Pastoralism in Inner Asia dates back to the Neolithic era, beginning about 4000 B.C.E. Fully nomadic pastoralism did not appear until the saddling of the horse and mobile dwelling carts after 800 B.C.E. gave sufficient mobility. Such innovations appeared first among the Cimmerians and Scythians in Eastern Europe and then in Mongolia among the XIONGNU of the third century B.C.E. (*see* ANIMAL STYLE; PETROGLYPHS; PREHISTORY).

Among the imperial nomads military needs made horses far more common than they are today. In 1188 the KITANS in eastern Inner Mongolia were herding a flock that was 32 percent horses, 59 percent sheep and goats, and 9 percent oxen. While quantitative data are absent, the universal impression of observers that the Mongols of the 13th-century MONGOL EMPIRE relied heavily on KOUMISS (fermented mare's milk, or *airag*) in the summer and mutton in the winter indicates a similar composition.

Sheep and horses were also the main marketable commodities for nomads. During eras when the nomads faced unified Chinese dynasties, horse markets were often opened at the borders, where horses for the Chinese armies could be exchanged on a massive scale for household goods. In the Mongol Empire Uighur, Turkestani, and Chinese traders and peddlers entered the Mongolian plateau to buy sheep and sheepskins. Camels were also of interest as beasts of burden and for their hair, but by contrast Mongolian cattle had no comparative advantage over the abundant oxen of China and other sedentary societies and hence were useless for trade.

Up to the 18th century the Mongols nomadized in much larger groups than did those observed by travelers and ethnographers in recent centuries. During times of war or tension the Mongols nomadized in *küriyen,* or yurts arranged in a circle for defense, with the leader's yurt or palace-tent (*ORDO*) in the middle. A similar arrangement was used in the 17th and 18th centuries by the great monastery Nom-un Yekhe Khüriye of the great lamas, the Jibzundamba Khutugtus, which became the nucleus of Mongolia's capital, ULAANBAATAR. During the period of the empire, when the khans had no fear of surprise attack, they arranged their main palace tents, or *ordo*s, in an east–west line, with the senior wife's *ordo* in the west and with servant yurts trailing behind their mistress's *ordo* in a line. This tremendous concentration of people was not matched by a similar concentration of herds. Instead, the herds were kept dispersed at far-off locations under the care of attached herders, with daily supplies of koumiss and sheep for slaughter being delivered to the main camp.

MODERN PASTORALISM

By the early 19th century Mongolia had been at peace for almost half a century; the massive *küriyen* of the past had either become sedentary towns or broken up; and commercial ties with China created a strong demand for sheep (*see* CHINESE TRADE AND MONEYLENDING). Under these conditions the composition of the Mongolian livestock herd became roughly similar to that of today. In representative figures for animal numbers in eastern Khalkha from 1764 to 1841, horses show a decline from 15 percent of all livestock in 1800 to 13 percent in 1841, while sheep and goats are 68–76 percent, cattle about 8–17 percent, and camels about 2 percent. Figures for all Khalkha in 1918 show just less than 12 percent of livestock as horses, 74 percent as sheep and goats, 11 percent as cattle, and a little more than 2 percent as camels. As indebtedness transferred increasing numbers of animals into the hands of Chinese merchants and their export increased livestock numbers steadily declined. For example, the recorded livestock totals for the eastern Setsen Khan province dropped from 1,817,508 in 1828 to 1,224,690 in 1841 and 1,037,501 in 1907.

During the 20th century animal husbandry was influenced by the demands of both markets and the command economy. At first during the 1920s, the decrease in the prestige of the nobility, who were the principal horse herders, the repudiation of the Chinese debt, and the strong foreign market for sheep's wool resulted in a rapid expansion of both livestock as a whole and sheep as a percentage. In 1929 Mongolia's 21.95 million head was more than 82 percent sheep and goats with 7 percent horses, 8.5 percent cattle, and 2 percent camels. In Inner Mongolia's BARGA, where commercialization remained high, a sample in 1945 showed a similar composition: 82 percent sheep and goats, 11 percent cattle, and 6 percent horses. (Camels were a negligible 0.02 percent.)

The closing of Mongolia's border with countries outside the Soviet bloc, the relaxation of pressure on rich herders after the failed attempt at collectivization in 1930–32, and the military needs of WORLD WAR II boosted somewhat the numbers of horses and other large stock compared with sheep and goats. By 1960 the total number of livestock had stabilized at about 22–24 million, of which horses were 11 percent, sheep 52 percent, goats 25 percent, cattle 8 percent, and camels 4 percent.

From the 1930s in Russian Buriatia and Kalmykia and in Japanese-occupied Inner Mongolia and from the 1950s in Mongolia and in China's Inner Mongolia, ambitious modernizers have attempted to revolutionize the productivity of animal husbandry by reducing winter die-off. Late winter and early spring are the bottleneck period for livestock, and the usual strategy to increase pastoral productivity is to use hay, fodder crops, and shelters to reduce this die-off and thus allow much higher growth in livestock numbers. Moreover, by introducing vastly more productive, improved breeds of sheep and cattle, productivity per head can be improved, but only at the price of supplying the many wells, shelters, hay, and fodder these more delicate breeds require. This intensive management reduces mobility and increases the intensity of grazing on selected spots, a change accelerated by politically motivated sedentarization in Russia and in some parts of Inner Mongolia. Fodder cropping also increases the damage to topsoil, leading to erosion. This model of intensive rangeland management in Russian and Chinese steppe lands produced vast increases in animal numbers at the price of pervasive pasture degradation and growing desertification. While independent Mongolia aimed to follow this model under collectivization, investment in the pastoral sector was never sufficient to allow it much success. Livestock and offtake numbers increased, but with only incremental changes in pastoral nomadic techniques. Pastures were thus left mostly intact.

Under the collectivized herding regime of 1959–93, the Mongol herders remained nomadic, but the previous organization by generalist households linked in *khot ail* was changed. Instead, herders specialized in one stock, and *khot ail*s served purely social needs. During this period sheep and cattle were the preferred animals, supplying wool for the textile industry and milk and beef for the city folk. With DECOLLECTIVIZATION in 1992–95 and the reopening of relations with China, another boom in pastoral cash-cropping like that of the 1920s occurred, this time in CASHMERE goats. At the same time, the fodder farming, well maintenance, and other infrastructural investments essential to Mongolia's attempted intensive grazing strategy disintegrated. A collapse in cashmere's world price in 1996 and a massive ZUD, or winter die-off, in the year 2000 have put the future of this cashmere boom in question.

See also COLLECTIVIZATION AND COLLECTIVE HERDING; DESERTIFICATION AND PASTURE DEGRADATION; FARMING; HUNTING AND FISHING; SOCIAL CLASSES IN THE MONGOL EMPIRE.

Further reading: Christopher P. Atwood, "The Mutual-Aid Co-operatives and the Animal Products Trade in Mongolia, 1913–1928," *Inner Asia* 5 (2003): 65–91; Jerker Erdstöm, "The Reform of Livestock Marketing in Post-Communist Mongolia: Problems for a Food Secure and Equitable Market Development," *Nomadic Peoples* 33 (1993): 137–153; Caroline Humphrey and David Sneath, *End of Nomadism? Society, State, and the Environment in Inner Asia* (Durham, N.C.: Duke University Press, 1999); Tomasz Potkanski and Slavoj Szynkiewicz, *The Social Context of Liberalisation of the Mongolian Pastoral Economy* (Brighton, U.K. and Ulaanbaatar: Institute of Developments Studies at the University of Sussex and the Research Institute of Animal Husbandry, 1993); Dennis P. Sheehy, "Grazing and Management Strategies as Factors Influencing Ecological Stability of Mongolian Grasslands," *Nomadic Peoples* 33 (1993): 17–30; John Masson Smith, "Mongol Nomadism and Middle Eastern Geography: Qishlaqs and Tümens," in *The Mongol Empire and Its Legacy,* ed. Reuven Amitai-Preiss and David O. Morgan (Leiden: E. J. Brill, 1999), 39–56; Sevyan Vainshtein, *Nomads of South Siberia,* trans. Michael Colenso (Cambridge: Cambridge University Press, 1980).

animal style This term, introduced by the Russian archaeologist Michael Rostovtzeff (1870–1952) to describe Scythian art in the Ukraine and southern Russia, has been applied to similar art in the period of the early nomads (ninth century B.C.E. to second century C.E.) from the Ukraine to Inner Mongolia. While the style does not exclude the human figure and is by no means uniform, the term does highlight a common artistic heritage in the steppe of the first millennium B.C.E.

The animal style's most characteristic motifs are the recumbent elk with antlers laid along the back, the coiled or crouching feline, and the raptor beak, either alone or attached to an eagle or a griffon. The bodies are typically formed of planes, with sharply differentiated anatomical units, and with one animal or body part frequently transforming into another. ELK STONES and PETROGLYPHS of the Altai and Mongolia contain clear precursors of the recumbent elk motif. Representations of raptors and crouching felines appeared in the east in roughly the eighth century B.C.E. and quickly moved west. From the fifth century the theme of animal combat swept the steppe. The grave art of the Scythian *kurgans* (Ukraine, fifth–fourth centuries B.C.E.), Ysyk (southeast Kazakhstan, fifth–fourth centuries B.C.E.), Pazyryk (Russian Altai, fourth century B.C.E.), and the Siberian hoard of Peter the Great exemplify the "classic" animal style in many media: openwork bronze belt plaques, hammered gold quiver covers, wood, felt hangings, saddle cloths, and even tattoos.

The shared bronze cauldrons for boiling funerary meals, poletops capped by totemic animals, and figures of a mounted man approaching a seated goddess indicate common religious practices and beliefs, yet the wide variety of burial customs, languages, and races affiliated with the animal style shows it was based not on common ethnicity but on a charismatic style associated with pastoral nomadism and shared beliefs of the hereafter. The early XIONGNU graves of NOYON UUL (Mongolia, first century B.C.E.–first century C.E.) contain fine examples of the style, yet its popularity slowly declined throughout the steppe from 200 B.C.E. on.

See also PREHISTORY.

Further reading: Emma Bunker, ed., *Ancient Bronzes of the Eastern Eurasian Steppes from the Arthur W. Sackler Collections* (New York: Arthur M. Sackler Foundation, 1997).

anthem With the 1911 RESTORATION of Mongolian independence, the new theocratic government adopted a new national flag, seal, and anthem. In 1914, as a military band was being formed under Russian guidance, a national anthem was composed by the Russian composer A. V. Kadlets, based on a KHORCHIN Mongol folk tune. The lyrics, entitled "Ambling Mules Worth a Hundred Taels," were a coronation poem in the traditional Buddhist *shabdan* genre (*see* DANSHUG), expressing devotion to the theocratic Bogda Khan (Holy Emperor; *see* JIBZUNDAMBA KHUTUGTU, EIGHTH). After the 1921 REVOLUTION the poet BUYANNEMEKHÜ composed another song, "Mongolian Internationale," whose lyrics, also sung to a Mongolian folk tune, praised the Communist International as the leader of the world's poor and oppressed people against capitalists and reactionaries. After the Bogda Khan's death in 1924, this became the de facto national anthem of Mongolia. In 1950 a new anthem was composed, with lyrics by the scholar and author TSENDIIN DAMDINSÜREN, music by the composer B. Damdinsüren (no relation), and an arrangement by L. Mördorj (1919–97). In 1961 Ts. Gaitaw and Ch. Chimed were commissioned to remove the names of Stalin and MARSHAL CHOIBALSANG from the second stanza, while leaving in Lenin and GENERAL SÜKHEBAATUR. After democratization in 1990, the whole stanza about the leaders was dropped from the official version, which is otherwise unchanged from Damdinsüren's text.

Further reading: G. Kara, "A Forgotten Anthem," *Mongolian Studies* 14 (1991): 145–154.

appanage system   The Mongol Empire was from the beginning a family venture under which the imperial family and its meritorious servants shared a collective rule over all their subjects, Mongol and non-Mongol alike. Members of the family thus deserved a "share" (*qubi*) in all the benefits of empire. The appanages of the Mongol nobility in sedentary areas were notorious for misrule, yet their presence established a web of empirewide exchanges that both held the empire together and facilitated intercultural exchange.

CHINGGIS KHAN (Genghis, 1206–27) gave almost a fourth of the Mongol population as shares to his immediate family: his mother, Ö'elün, his four brothers, and his three eldest sons, JOCHI, CHA'ADAI, and ÖGEDEI KHAN. Along with people, he gave them grazing grounds. The lands of his mother and brothers stretched from eastern Mongolia to Manchuria, while his sons' pastures were in the west: Jochi's along the Irtysh, Ögedei's on the Emil and Qobaq (Emin and Hobok) Rivers, and Cha'adai's around Almaligh (near Yining or Gulja). TOLUI, as the youngest son and the *odchigin* (guardian of the hearth), inherited the remaining people in the center. Ögedei occupied the center when he became khan, however, and Tolui's later appanage, inherited by his own *odchigin* Ariq-Böke, was along the ALTAI RANGE.

Shares of booty were distributed much more widely. Empresses, princesses, and meritorious servitors all received full shares. This booty included prisoners of war, especially craftsmen, who were sometimes kept as "house-boys" (*ger-ün kö'üd*) at the beneficiary's ORDO (palace-tent and its camp) and sometimes resettled elsewhere but in any case remained the property of the recipient.

Chinggis Khan distributed Han (ethnic Chinese) districts in Manchuria to his brothers, and in 1236 Ögedei Khan (1229–41) distributed "shares," or appanages, in North China, KHORAZM, and Transoxiana on a large scale to princes, empresses, princesses, imperial sons-in-law, and distinguished generals. In 1256, with the pacification of Iran, MÖNGKE KHAN (1251–59) divided up appanages there as well. Thus, Cha'adai and his descendants, for example, held not only their nomadic grounds around Almaligh, but also Kat and Khiva towns in Khorazm, Taiyuan prefecture in Shanxi, and certain cities and towns in Iran. As a result the empire was interlaced with a network of interlocking appanages that kept every prince directly interested in every region.

YELÜ CHUCAI, speaking for the Chinese officials and generals, protested to Ögedei that this distribution could lead to a disintegration of the state. Ögedei thus decreed that the appanage holders could appoint overseers (DARUGHACHI) and judges (JARGHUCHI) in the appanages, but the court would appoint other officials and collect taxes. While every two regular households paid one catty of silk in tax to the central government, in the appanages every five households paid one catty, the lighter burden compensating for what they paid to the appanage holders. Appanage households thus became known in Chinese as "five-households-silk households" (*wuhusi hu*). Despite Ögedei's regulations, appanage holders continued to demand excessive revenues, driving the inhabitants into flight. In one appanage, originally counted as 10,000 households, the population had fallen by 1251 to 500 to 700. QUBILAI KHAN (1260–94) enforced Ögedei's regulations but otherwise respected appanage rights. From 1311 to 1318 Grand Councillor TEMÜDER sought to increase revenues by restricting both the number and autonomy of the appanages, but fierce opposition defeated his measures.

During the civil strife in the MONGOL EMPIRE from 1260 to 1305, hostility among the territorial khanates strained the network of appanages. The CHAGHATAY KHANATE in Central Asia had few resources, and its first independent khan, Alghu (1260–65/6), confiscated the appanages and personnel of Berke (1256–66), khan of the Jochid GOLDEN HORDE, in Transoxiana. In 1266–67 Alghu's successor, Baraq (1266–71), sent his vizier to the Middle Eastern IL-KHANATE, ostensibly to inspect his appanages there but in reality to spy on Abagha Khan (1265–82). Despite incidents like these, appanage revenues crossed the Mongol lands until the middle of the 14th century. As allies, the Il-Khans in Iran and the YUAN DYNASTY in China sent administrators to and received revenues from appanages in each other's territories as regularly as communications allowed, ceasing only with the breakup of the Il-Khanate in 1335. The Yuan emperors actually expanded Jochid appanages in China and from 1339 sent revenues annually to ÖZBEG KHAN (1313–41) and his sons until rebellion in both realms disrupted communication.

After the fall of the Mongol Empire, appanage systems continued to divide the Mongols into districts ruled by hereditary noblemen. The units in such systems were called *tümen* and OTOG under the NORTHERN YUAN DYNASTY (1368–1634), *ulus* or *anggi* under the OIRATS and ZÜNGHARS, and BANNERS (*khoshuu*) under the QING DYNASTY (1636–1912). While the systems varied, they all combined the idea of patrimonial rule and the union of pasture and people.

See also AIMAG; ANIMAL HUSBANDRY AND NOMADISM; CENSUS IN THE MONGOL EMPIRE; FAMILY; HISTORY; PROVINCES IN THE MONGOL EMPIRE; SIX TÜMENS.

Further reading: Thomas T. Allsen, "Sharing Out the Empire: Apportioned Lands under the Mongols," in *Nomads in the Sedentary World,* ed. Anatoly M. Khuzanov and André Wink (Richmond, Surrey: Curzon Press, 2001): 172–190; Peter Jackson, "From Ulus to Khanate: The Making of the Mongol States, c. 1220–c. 1290," in *The Mongol Empire and Its Legacy,* ed. Reuven Amitai-Preiss and David O. Morgan (Leiden: E. J. Brill, 1999), 12–38.

Ara Khangai   *See* NORTH KHANGAI PROVINCE.

archaeology   Despite its nomadic tradition, Mongolia contains important and visible remains of ancient cultures. Archaeological monuments in Mongolia may be divided into seven types: 1) Stone Age sites; 2) petroglyphs; 3) ELK STONES; 4) "STONE MEN"; 5) graves; 6) ancient settlements and walls; and 7) inscriptions. (Monuments of an eighth type, temples and stupas, were in use constantly up to the 20th century and will not be considered here.) Except for the first, all of these categories contain visible monuments that have been recognized as remains of the past by the local people. While "stone men" suffered from iconoclasm probably in the Buddhist conversion, they and other rock monuments have more frequently been reverenced as sacred objects. Many travelers recorded legends about city ruins.

The scholarly study of Mongolian archaeological remains began in 1889–90 with the investigation of Mongolia's seventh-to-ninth-century Runic inscriptions by the Russian explorers and scholars N. M. Iadrintsev (1842–94), D. A. Klements (1848–1914), and V. V. Radlov (W. Radloff, 1837–1918). In the 1920s true excavations began with the 1922–28 Central Asian expedition of the American Roy Chapman Andrews (1884–1960) and the 1923–26 Mongolian-Tibetan Expedition under P. K. Kozlov (1863–1935). Kozlov's finds at NOYON UUL and Andrews's Neolithic excavations at Bayanzag (Bulgan, South Gobi), incidental to his more famous dinosaur finds, showed the possibilities of Mongolian archaeology. In 1933–34 D. Bukenich made small digs at the city ruins of Khar Balgas (medieval ORDU-BALIGH) and the temples of TSOGTU TAIJI. All finds were removed from Mongolia, and none of these expeditions trained local Mongolian archaeologists.

Soviet scholars began systematic research on Mongolian sites in the postwar period. In 1948–49 S. V. Kiselev (1905–62) led a team investigating the cities of Mongolia and Tuva, including QARA-QORUM and Ordu-Baligh. In 1949 A. P. Okladnikov (1908–81) led the Mongolian-Soviet Joint Historical and Ethnographic Research Expedition, which investigated, among other things, Stone Age sites and XIONGNU barrows. Although the material excavated was again removed to the Soviet Union, the expedition did train Mongolia's first archaeologists. When further Soviet expeditions to Mongolia were canceled in 1950, Kh. Perlee (1911–82), a graduate of the Kiselev expedition, excavated Züün Kherem and other Kitan cities and the empire-period AWARGA site in 1952–55, while Ts. Dorjsüren conducted excavations at Noyon Uul in 1954–55. In 1961 Soviet archaeological expeditions to Mongolia began again, but now with Mongolian archaeologists as colleagues.

Postwar archaeology focused on developing a basic classification of Mongolian historical eras. The interpretive schema was that of Friedrich Engels's *Origin of the Family, Private Property, and the State* (1884; published in Mongolian in 1928), which made putative social developments such as the transition from matriarchy to patriarchy almost automatic consequences of technical discoveries: pottery, pastoralism, and so on. At the same time the Mongolian government's ambitious plans of urbanization and agricultural self-sufficiency promoted interest in documenting native cities and farming.

Publications resulting from these early researches included studies of Qara-Qorum (Kiselev, 1966), the KITANS and Mongolian urbanism (Perlee, 1959, 1961), Northern Xiongnu (Dorjsüren, 1961), and the TÜRK EMPIRES (Ser-Odjaw, 1970). In the 1970s and 1980s a new generation of Mongolian archaeologists synthesized existing data on the Neolithic (D. Dorj, 1971), the Bronze Age (D. Nawaan, 1975), the Chandmani Iron Age culture (D. Tseweendorj, 1978, 1980), and petroglyphs (D. Dorj and E. A. Novgorodova, 1975). Discoveries in the 1980s opened up the field of the Mongolian Paleolithic as first summarized by Okladnikov in 1986.

After 1986 political changes created new possibilities for Mongolian archaeology. With the normalization of Sino-Russo-Mongolian relations, new chances arose to overcome the nationalist tendency to compartmentalize South Siberian, Mongolian, and Inner Mongolian data. The dethroning of Marxism opened the possibility to question the traditional interpretations based on Engels's evolutionary schema. International cooperation has widened greatly. The 1989 Mongolian-Hungarian-Soviet expedition was followed by various projects involving American, German, Japanese, South Korean, and Turkish archaeologists. Although some expeditions, using new technology and research methodologies, have made important discoveries, others have pursued sensationalist research agendas, as exemplified by the "searches for CHINGGIS KHAN's tomb," funded first by the Japanese newspaper *Yomiuri Shimbun* (1990–93) and then by the American futures trader Maury Kravitz (2001–02).

See also DINOSAURS; FOREIGN RELATIONS; FUNERARY CUSTOMS; PREHISTORY; RUNIC SCRIPT AND INSCRIPTIONS.

Archangaj   *See* NORTH KHANGAI PROVINCE.

archery   Originally the basis of the Mongols' military power and later almost driven to extinction by the advent of firearms, archery has been revived in Mongolia as a purely recreational sport.

Mongolian archery in the Middle Ages had great military significance. The earliest surviving piece of Mongolian writing is a stone inscription set up in 1226, which records a 335-fathom (about 575 yards) bow shot made by CHINGGIS KHAN's nephew Yisüngge. The Franciscan friar JOHN OF PLANO CARPINI observed that Mongols began shooting from their second year and that from child to adult they were all excellent marksmen. Mongolian men spent most of their time making their own arrows, which had a number of different heads made with bone or iron.

Mongol soldier with a bow and arrow, bow case and quiver, and flintlock, around 1870 *(From N. V. Prschewalski,* Reisen in der Mongolei, im Gebiet der Tanguten und der Wüsten Nordtibets *[1877])*

Under the QING DYNASTY (1636–1912) training in archery was required of all bannermen. The military compound bow used was only about 1 1/4 meters (four feet) long, although ones more than two meters (six feet) long were also used for hunting. Bows were composed of a goat horn or deer antler core covered by wood (larch, elm, or bamboo) and wrapped in animal tendons. The bow's powerful tension made it spring back when unstrung, and Mongolian EPICS frequently cite the difficult task of stringing a powerful bow as the distinguishing test of the hero. The bowstrings were made of silk threads or leather wrapped in tendons, the arrows of pine, birch, or willow fletched with feathers of a lammergeier, eagle, or falcon, and fitted with heads of deer antler, bone, or iron. Well-constructed compound bows and arrows were highly prized and fetched high prices. Hunters used this powerful war bow for large game, but small game was also taken with a simpler bow made of strips of fir or larch cut from the stems and wrapped with tendon. The bowstring was a length of hide, preferably horsehide.

Mongolian traditional bow technique involved putting the arrow on the right, or outer, side of the bow. The arrow was held with the thumb and forefinger and the bowstring drawn with the thumb, which was protected by heavy leather or a polished stone ring. The string was released by rolling it off the ring. Under the Qing the ability to handle a pull weight of about 37 kilograms (80 pounds) was considered the minimum for a grown man, and one of about 60 kilograms (133 pounds) was necessary for men who wished to participate in the imperial hunt. Training encompassed not only shooting from a standing position but also shooting while galloping on horseback, when the reins were taken up in the left hand or mouth while the right hand pulled back the bow. The targets for these military competitions were made of sheepskin stretched over wooden frames or wooden balls placed on poles about 1.7 meters (5.5 feet) high. Since the Mongols found it disturbing for target shooters to target a person or animal, even in their imagination, the target was sometimes called a *mangas*, or monster.

In the NAADAM "games" that accompanied religious rituals, archery was practiced with large, blunt ivory heads. The most common target was a pyramid or line of *sur*, made of leather straps rolled into a cylinder and filled with oak bark or leather, which was to be knocked over. At the beginning of the competition, the umpires (*uukhaichin*, or "*uukhai* sayers") gave a cry of *uukhai*, accompanied by a circular motion of their arms with the hands pointed up to the sky to summon good fortune. The same cry accompanied each striking of the target and the final tallying of the score. The victorious archer received the title *mergen* (sharpshooter, but also wise man).

By the late 19th century, however, firearms were clearly more useful in hunting and warfare, and the archery competitions became desultory. Among the lamas of Khüriye (modern ULAANBAATAR), who were forbidden by the letter of the *vinaya* (monastic discipline) from even being in the presence of weapons of war, shooting astragali (*shagai*) became a widespread sport. In it lamas shot lined-up astragali (*shagai*) at a distance of 3 meters (9 feet) with horn or ivory bullets flicked by the middle finger from a wooden plank.

In 1922 the army Naadam in Mongolia (later the National Holiday Nadaam) and in 1924 the Sur-Kharbaan (Archery) games in the BURIAT REPUBLIC became annual events, beginning the revival of archery as a sport. In the National Holiday Naadam rules, each man fires 40 arrows at a distance of 75 meters (246 feet). In the 1960s women began to compete in the event, shooting 20 arrows at a distance of 60 meters (197 feet). This innovation had been adopted first among the BURIATS and in the 1950s in Inner Mongolia. While traditional bows are still used in Mongolia with the traditional fingering, Buriat and Inner Mongolian archers use European-style professional model bows and have adopted the Western shooting style.

See also HUNTING AND FISHING; MILITARY OF THE MONGOL EMPIRE.

architecture *See* AWARGA; CHOIJUNG LAMA TEMPLE; DAIDU; ERDENI ZUU; HÖHHOT; IL-KHANATE; ORDU-BALIGH; PALACES OF THE BOGDA KHAN; QARA-QORUM; SARAY AND NEW SARAY; SHANGDU; THEOCRATIC PERIOD; TIMUR; ULAAN-BAATAR; YURT.

Arghun Aqa (d. 1275) *Reformer of the administration of Iran under Güyüg, Möngke, and the early Il-Khans*
Originally of the Oirat tribe, Arghun's father sold him to Qada'an for a side of beef during a famine. Qada'an gave Arghun as a page to his son Ilügei, then serving as a night guard in the KESHIG (imperial guard) of ÖGEDEI KHAN. Arghun knew the UIGHUR-MONGOLIAN SCRIPT, and when disputes arose over the governorship of Iran, Arghun was appointed one of the judges.

After Ögedei died in 1241 Empress TÖREGENE executed Governor KÖRGÜZ and appointed Arghun in his place as part of her wholesale rearrangement of the offices. Arghun continued Körgüz's policies in Khorasan (eastern Iran) and in 1243–44 extended civilian administration to Tabriz, formerly under Chormaqan's army, while his assistant Sharaf-ud-Din collected extortionate taxes there. In the years after Sharaf-ud-Din died (c. 1245), Arghun developed intimate ties with the Khorasanian elite and converted to Islam. When GÜYÜG was elected khan in 1246, he reversed his mother Töregene's policies, but Arghun stayed in favor by gifts and his proven efficiency.

After Güyüg died Arghun went to the court in 1249, and, again by adroitly cultivating SORQAQTANI BEKI, he kept his position when her son, MÖNGKE KHAN, was elected in 1251. Arghun's reports to the new khan formed the basis for Möngke's reforms, commuting the irregular in-kind *qubchiri* (contributions) to a regular silver tax, payable on a scale from 1 to 10 dinars.

Losing his supreme governorship to Saif-ud-Din Bitigchi (d. 1262) and then Shams-ud-Din Juvaini (d. 1284) under Möngke's brother HÜLE'Ü (r. 1256–65), Arghun worked in the Caucasus, raising the maximum *qubchiri* to 500 dinars and extorting money from local Christian lords. After 1262 he returned to Khorasan. Arghun fought under Abagha Khan (1265–81) in the battle of Qara-Su (1270) against the invading Chaghatay khan, Baraq. By this time he was known as Arghun Aqa (Elder Brother Arghun), a sign of his seniority and respect. His son NAWROZ inherited his position in Khorasan.

See also PROVINCES IN THE MONGOL EMPIRE.

Arhangai *See* NORTH KHANGAI PROVINCE.

Arik Buka *See* ARIQ-BÖKE.

Ariq Bögä *See* ARIQ-BÖKE.

Ariq-Böke (Ariq-Bögä, Arik Buka) (d. 1266) *The younger brother and rival of Qubilai Khan*
Ariq-Böke was the youngest son of CHINGGIS KHAN'S son TOLUI and of his main wife, SORQAQTANI BEKI, born a decade or more after his brothers QUBILAI KHAN and HÜLE'Ü. Sorqaqtani Beki was a Christian, and in 1254 WILLIAM OF RUBRUCK observed Ariq-Böke making the sign of the cross and claiming, "We know that the Messiah [Jesus] is God." Sometime after 1248 Ariq-Böke's older brother, Qubilai, recommended to Sorqaqtani Beki a Confucian tutor for Ariq-Böke, yet, unlike Qubilai, Ariq-Böke formed no close bond with Chinese scholars. Ariq-Böke's oldest brother, MÖNGKE KHAN, was elected great khan in 1251. With the death of Sorqaqtani Beki the next year, Ariq-Böke inherited his mother's ORDO (palace-tent), which nomadized from the ALTAI RANGE in the summer to the banks of the Ürüngü River in the winter.

When Möngke Khan died on a campaign in Sichuan in August 1259, Ariq-Böke was in Mongolia. Möngke's chief scribe, Bulghai, and his governor in North China, 'Alam-Dar hoped to forestall the coronation of their enemy, Qubilai. With the support of Möngke's son Asudai and his general Qundughai, they delivered Möngke's great seal to Ariq-Böke, who used it to issue documents mobilizing soldiers in Mongolia and North China. After Qubilai proclaimed himself khan in April 1260, Ariq-Böke did the same in a general assembly, or QURILTAI, near QARA-QORUM city. The CHAGHATAY KHANATE and the GOLDEN HORDE supported him over Qubilai. 'Alam-Dar was dispatched to Gansu as DARUGHACHI (overseer) with the commander Qundughai.

Qubilai's main weapon against his brother was blocking the shipment of Chinese grain to Mongolia. In response, Ariq-Böke and his court made their base in the

South Siberian agricultural colony of Kem-Kemchik (Tuva) and the Yenisey Kyrgyz lands (modern Khakassia; *see* SIBERIA AND THE MONGOL EMPIRE). In August Qubilai occupied Mongolia, seizing Ariq-Böke's four *ordo*s and detaching an army to the Gansu corridor. On October 27, 1260, 'Alam-Dar and Qundughai were defeated and killed at Guzang. Ariq-Böke sent messengers surrendering, and Qubilai returned to his capital. The next summer Ariq-Böke routed Qubilai's commanders in Mongolia. During a second invasion Qubilai defeated Ariq-Böke at Shimu'ultu Na'ur (Mosquito Lake) on November 27, 1261, but Ariq-Böke's rearguard, under Asudai, bloodied Qubilai's overconfident troops shortly afterward. Battles, cold, and the continuing blockade had, however, decimated Ariq-Böke's forces, reducing him at one point to drafting the clergy of Qara-Qorum into his army.

In summer 1260 Qubilai had sent two Chaghatayid princes in his entourage west to challenge Ariq-Böke's control there, but Ariq-Böke's envoys intercepted and killed them. Ariq-Böke then sent his own Chaghatayid prince Alghu, who raised an army of 150,000, while messengers sent by Ariq-Böke began collecting requisitions throughout the Chaghatay lands. Alghu, jealous of the lost wealth, killed Ariq-Böke's messengers and threw his support to Qubilai.

As Qubilai was now occupied with rebellion in North China, Ariq-Böke's entourage moved west, where Asudai crushed Alghu's army and captured his *ordo*s. Alghu fled to the Tarim Basin, and Ariq-Böke camped outside Almaligh (near modern Yining). By winter 1263–64 vengeful purges of Alghu's army had cost Ariq-Böke valuable support. In Iran Hüle'ü ordered his son Jumqur to leave Ariq-Böke's army, while one of Möngke's sons, Ürüng-Tash, deserted to Qubilai with Möngke's seal. Meanwhile, Alghu prepared to attack Ariq-Böke. In increasing difficulties, Ariq-Böke and Asudai surrendered to the court of Qubilai on August 21, 1264, where Qubilai received his younger brother with tears.

Qubilai appointed a board of Chinggisid princes and commanders (NOYAN) to try Ariq-Böke's case. Bulghai and nine other of Ariq-Böke's *noyan*s were executed, but Ariq-Böke, Asudai, and the other princes were pardoned as descendants of Chinggis Khan. Ariq-Böke died in autumn 1266.

Ariq-Böke's young sons had remained in his *ordo* in the Altai when he surrendered. In 1269 Qubilai summoned them to court, and they entered the emperor's service. In 1277–78 Yomuqur and Mingliq-Temür (erroneously written Melik-Temür) joined a rebellion led by Möngke Khan's son Shiregi, eventually fleeing to QAIDU (1236–1301). Yomuqur returned in 1296 and was pardoned, but in 1300 Mingliq-Temür was still with Qaidu. After the fall of the Mongols' YUAN DYNASTY in China, Yisüder, a descendant of Ariq-Böke, allied with the OIRATS and murdered the Qubilaid khan in 1388. Other Ariq-Bökids, including Dalbag (1412–14) and probably

Oiradai (1415?–25?), became puppet khans with Oirat support.

Ariq-Qaya (Ali-Haiya) (1227–1287) *Uighur peasant's son who under Qubilai Khan became one of the conquerors of South China*
Born a peasant, Ariq-Qaya studied the UIGHUR-MONGOLIAN script for a month and went to Mongolia to seek his fortune, joining the prince Qubilai's entourage. After Qubilai was elected great khan in 1260, Ariq-Qaya rose through the ranks of the secretariat. From 1268 he assisted AJU and Liu Zheng (1213–75) in their siege of Xiangyang (modern Xiangfan). Ariq-Qaya's request in 1272 to the court to put into action two Iraqi artillery technicians marked a turning point in the siege. The fall of Xiangyang led to an all-out invasion of the SONG DYNASTY in South China. The supreme commander BAYAN CHINGSANG dispatched Ariq-Qaya with 40,000 men to advance up the Chang (Yangtze). The Song general Gao Shijie's 1,000-boat flotilla and Yuezhou (modern Yueyang) city surrendered with little fight on April 18, 1275, and Jiangling (modern Shashi) surrendered on May 2. Tanzhou (modern Changsha) and Jingjiang (modern Guilin), however, were defended by desperate Song loyalists and fell only after costly sieges and mass suicides (January 1276 and April 1277). Ariq-Qaya fought in Guangxi and Hainan Island, blockading seaborne Song loyalists and pacifying tribal chiefs until 1281. QUBILAI KHAN made Ariq-Qaya senior grand councillor of the Huguang Branch Secretariat (modern Hunan, Guangxi, and parts of Hubei and Guangdong), but the area's notorious lawlessness, tribal disaffection, and oppressive taxation continued.

armed forces of Mongolia Despite the many constant features of Mongolia's geopolitical position, the size and mission of the modern Mongolian military has undergone major changes, depending primarily on relations between Russia/the Soviet Union and China and/or Japan.

See also MILITARY OF THE MONGOL EMPIRE. *On later Mongolian armies, see* NORTHERN YUAN DYNASTY; OIRATS; TUMU INCIDENT; ZÜNGHARS.

STRATEGY AND MISSION

Mongolia's strategic situation up to 1990 was governed by three constants: 1) Mongolia's primary strategy was alliance with Russia/the Soviet Union against China (or Japan from 1931 to 1945); 2) Mongolia's population is very small and has no defense industry whatsoever; 3) The Mongolian government has been civilian in nature and has, except for the LEFTIST PERIOD in 1929–32, commanded enough popular support, or at least acquiescence, to dispense with extensive internal garrisons.

Given these realities, the Mongolian army has suffered from a difficult institutional dilemma: In times of security paramilitary border guards seem to be all that is required, but in times of tension self-defense seems wholly impossible. There is thus a cycle of virtual demilitarization alternating with military buildups concurrent with Soviet occupation. Given Russian/Soviet material and psychological dominance over its southern rivals and superior supply facilities, Soviet and Mongolian troops have always garrisoned the frontier, while Chinese/Japanese troops have as a rule been kept far back for defense in depth.

With the breakup of the Soviet Union in 1991, Mongolia has become in theory and in fact neutral between China and Russia, maintaining normal relations with both. The Mongolian military is now supplementing its overwhelmingly Soviet/Russian equipment and traditions with defense ties with China and the United States. Budget troubles have added to the armed forces' difficulty in defining their mission.

THEOCRATIC PERIOD

The military inherited from the QING DYNASTY was essentially a militia system, trained and armed to fight 18th-century wars. The new independent government mobilized militiamen first during the expulsion of the Qing AMBANS from Khüriye (modern ULAANBAATAR, November–December 1911), next during the siege of KHOWD CITY (May–August 1912), and finally during the Inner Mongolian campaign (1913). The government also recruited a number of bandit or volunteer forces, particularly among Inner Mongolian refugees and exiles. In 1914 the theocratic government had approximately 10,000 men under arms. Soldiers mobilized in these three waves served permanently. Pay and supply still came from their original LEAGUES and BANNERS and was very inadequate, leading to sickness, mutinies, and high desertion rates.

Originally armed with Russian Berdans (single-shot rifles) and even more obsolete weapons, in February 1913 the Mongols received 10,000 Russian Mosin magazine rifles, 32 artillery pieces, and 65 machine guns. From early 1912 Russia maintained a mission in Khüriye to train soldiers in cavalry, infantry, machine-gun, and artillery skills. Around 3,200 soldiers completed some training.

REVOLUTIONARY PERIOD

Against the occupation of Khüriye first by about 8,000 Chinese soldiers and then by BARON ROMAN FEDOROVICH VON UNGERN-STERNBERG's 11,400 soldiers of mixed origin, the 1921 revolutionaries, armed and trained by Soviet Russia, originally planned to fight a partisan or guerrilla war. In June 1921, however, the Russian Red Army intervened in force, sending 13,100 troops into Khüriye under K. A. Neiman.

The partisan forces that made up the "People's" or "Democratic Army" (*Arad-un jirumtu tserig/Ardyn juramt tsereg*) numbered around 700 before the revolutionary victory. After seizing Khüriye in July 1921, the partisans

planned to establish a regular European-style army, unlike the traditional soldiers of the theocratic period or the ragged partisans of the revolution. With Soviet Red Army troops holding Khüriye until 1925, the Russians felt no urgency to supply a local Mongolian military, and growth was slow. Cavalry was the principal branch, with an artillery and a machine-gun regiment and a communications company. The supreme command was exercised by a commander in chief, supervised for the government by the army minister and for the Mongolian People's Revolutionary Party by a military council with its chairman. In 1921 GENERAL SÜKHEBAATUR held all three position, but in 1922 he lost the army ministry and chairmanship of the military council. Up to 1932 the chiefs of staff were always Soviet advisers.

In 1924–25 the Mongolian People's Red (or Revolutionary) Army was thoroughly reorganized. In late 1925 the government finally discharged the 1921 soldiers and moved to a conscription system with a two-year tour of duty. This turned the military into a mechanism for educating the young male population. Of those serving in 1925, 19 percent were fully literate, 38 percent were semiliterate, and 42 percent were learning the alphabet. By 1927 the army numbered 8,300, of which 46 percent were members of the People's Revolutionary Party or Youth League. Separate border troops were organized under the Office of Internal Security, and armored cars, transport planes, and biplane bombers were received from the Soviet Union.

In 1932 the importance of the People's Revolutionary Army increased dramatically. The Japanese conquest of Manchuria (1931–33) and the massive insurrection against the leftist policies in 1932 made military expenditures jump from 5.4 million (1931) to 12 million tögrögs (1932). By 1936 military expenditures had doubled again, to 24 million tögrögs, and were eating up half the budget, a situation that would last through WORLD WAR II. Modernization of the army was rapid, especially in motorized transport and armored cars, and involved a rise in the number of Soviet trainers from 14 in 1924 to 110 in 1936. Even so, from 1930 to 1937 the Soviet-educated commander in chief MARSHAL DEMID dominated the army as no one had since the time of Sükhebaatur, building up a Mongolian officer corps, keeping the number of Soviet advisers within bounds, and appointing the first Mongolian chief of staff.

WORLD WAR II AND AFTER

Border incidents with Japanese troops along the undemarcated frontier began in January 1935 and increased in 1936. In March 1936 MARSHAL CHOIBALSANG became de facto leader, and in June 1936 Soviet armored and aircraft units entered Mongolia again. In August 1937 Marshal Demid died in mysterious circumstances, and the Soviet Seventeenth Army entered Mongolia, bringing the total of Soviet troops up to 30,000 men stationed almost entirely in the east. Within the Mongolian military, the GREAT PURGE of 1937–39 devastated the officer corps. In all, 187 high-ranking commanders were executed, and the medical corps and air squadrons were rendered almost completely ineffectual. By 1939 the number of Soviet instructors had shot up to 681.

In 1936 tours of duty were extended to three years, and no officers were retired or demobilized during World War II. From February 1942 "People's Self-Defense Volunteer Cavalry Detachments" were organized. The Mongolian military increased from 18,000 in 1939 to 43,000 in 1945, in addition to 10,500 border troops, its largest recorded size. The Mongolian army received BT-7 and T-34 tanks, and 76-, 106-, and 122-mm guns and howitzers, but was still primarily a cavalry force. After the August 8 Soviet declaration of war, which Mongolia joined, Japan surrendered on September 2, 1945, and by December 1945 the Mongolian army had demobilized almost to its projected 18,000-man peacetime level.

With the SINO-SOVIET ALLIANCE of 1950, the Mongolian military seemed almost redundant. The last cavalry units were retired in 1954, and the army's World War II–era tanks, artillery, and airplanes were all decommissioned in 1956. Combat soldiers dropped from 90.3 percent of all personnel in 1945 to only 24.5 percent in 1955. That same year command and service personnel reached 28.3 percent, and construction troops reached 39.0 percent; the army ministry was combined with the security ministry, marking the Mongolian military's low point. Soviet troops remained in Mongolia to 1956, but only as construction workers working on the Trans-Siberian Railway.

SINO-SOVIET TENSIONS

With the beginning of the SINO-SOVIET SPLIT, in 1959 a defense ministry was restored. By 1964 the core of the renamed Armed Forces of Mongolia was a special motor rifle brigade with a motor rifle regiment, one special artillery division, and a special tank battalion. Independent antiaircraft, radio engineering, and tank repair units were also re-created. Communications, chemical, engineering-sapper, and special intelligence units were added in 1965. From 1961 to 1965 463 Mongolians trained in Soviet military institutions, and in 1964 the Soviet Union agreed to donate 700,000 rubles of military equipment annually, including MiG 17 jet fighters. Mongolian troop numbers remained around 17,500, although now combat troops predominated.

From 1966 Soviet troops again entered Mongolia. In 1978 the Soviet defense minister, D.A. Ustinov, asked the Mongolian leader YUMJAAGIIN TSEDENBAL to double Mongolia's military, which reached 33,000 army troops, 3,500 air force personnel, and 15,000 police and border troops. Equipment included 650 main battle tanks, 650 artillery, 200 air defense guns, 300 SAM-7 surface-to-air missiles, and 17 MiG 21 fighter jets. Defense spending regularly exceeded 10 percent of the budget from 1975 on, hitting almost 15 percent in 1980. Meanwhile, Soviet troops and air force personnel reached 75,000 (120,000 in some reports) deployed in KHOWD, SOUTH GOBI, EAST GOBI, and EASTERN PROVINCE as well as around ULAANBAATAR.

CONTEMPORARY

The resolution of Sino-Soviet tensions and the withdrawal of Soviet troops from 1987 to 1990 led to a return to the situation of the 1950s, in which the military faced no clear threat. Defense spending declined to 6–7 percent of the budget after 1990. In 1997 the armed forces totalled fewer than 20,000, distributed as follows: army 8,500; air force, 500; construction troops, 1,500; border guards, 5,000; internal troops, 1,400. While national security is still a major concern for Mongolia, it is now as likely to be seen in economic, demographic, and cultural terms as in military terms. In close cooperation with the U.S. military, however, Mongolia's armed forces have developed a new task of peace-keeping. In September 2003, Mongolia contributed 180 soldiers to carry on reconstruction with the U.S.-led force in Iraq.

Armenia   *See* GEORGIA; LESSER ARMENIA.

artisans in the Mongol Empire   The Mongol emperors paid special attention to artisans, exempting them as a rule from the massacres of the conquest and from all axes in return for lifelong service. The MONGOL EMPIRE was unique in its appreciation of craftsmanship from a wide variety of civilizations, perhaps due to its own lack of a distinctive luxury craft tradition.

Artisans entered Mongol service both as booty of war and by periodic requisitions. Both sorts were divided among the Mongolian aristocracy, and their conditions of life varied widely. As slaves they were known by the Mongolian title *ger-ün kö'üd,* or "houseboys." Many such artisans lived in separate households, handing over their finished products to their masters and receiving necessities, including cash, in return. Others, however, lived by the palace-tents (ORDO) of their masters, sharing the nomadic life and being counted as Mongols. Such slaves often suffered severely from hunger and cold. All craftsmen held the status of *darqan* and thus were immune to the *qubchiri,* or occasional requisitions levied incessantly by passing imperial envoys.

The Mongols held in service an extraordinary variety of captives, who became part of the intimate workings of the princely households. In 1252–53 WILLIAM OF RUBRUCK found Saxon miners from Transylvania, Hungarians, Russians, Germans, and even a Parisian goldsmith serving the Mongol lords. Foreign artisans soon mastered the making of the Mongol tents, or yurts, and a captive woman from Lorraine prospered by crafting YURTS. In 1253 MÖNGKE KHAN deported 500 households, probably from China, to repair and maintain the imperial *ordos.* The palaces in the Mongol capital of QARA-QORUM, built by ÖGEDEI KHAN (1229–41), were constructed by separate North Chinese and Muslim colonies of craftsmen.

The Mongols showed particular interest in weapons makers, Middle Eastern weavers of silk and gold brocade (Arabic *nasij,* Persian *nakh,* Mongol *nashishi,* called baldachin or "cloth of Tartary" in Europe), Chinese ceramics, architecture, and Buddhist statuary. The Mongols established many colonies of weavers and artisans in North China, often centered around deported Middle Eastern craftsmen. CHINQAI, the Uighur minister in Mongol service, administered a North Chinese artisan colony in Hongzhou (modern Yangyuan), to which were later added 300 households of Muslim *nasij* weavers and 300 weavers of serge and wool from the Jin capital of Kaifeng. Hasan, an early Muslim adherent of CHINGGIS KHAN (Genghis, 1206–27), administered a Muslim craftsmen colony at Simmalum, near modern Zhangjiakou, that practiced military and civil crafts. The Kitan Xiao Baiju administered a colony at Tanzhou (modern Miyun) that produced arrows, long bows, and crossbows and kept the imperial mews. Even craftsmen who were not deported, such as the arms makers in Tabriz and Bukhara, were placed in factories under the rule of a DARUGHACHI, or overseer, where they received instructions in how to make Mongol-style weapons.

Under the Mongol YUAN DYNASTY (1271–1368) in China, the administration of artisans was rationalized and expanded but underwent no fundamental change. In his first year of rule QUBILAI KHAN (1260–94) conscripted an additional 1,100 households as apprentice artisans and moved part of the Hongzhou colony closer to the capitals of SHANGDU and DAIDU (modern Beijing). In 1264 and 1272 additional conscriptions of apprentices drew in displaced households, freed slaves, mendicant Buddhist monks, Taoist priests, and other unaffiliated persons. At the same time, new offices were set up to supervise the colonies now found all over North China. These offices were headed by *darughachis* who were by law either Mongols or SEMUREN (various sorts, or non-Chinese) and generally attached to the palaces or *ordo*s of the imperial family. Due to manpower shortages in 1260–64, a number of craftsmen were also conscripted as soldiers, contrary to their customary immunity.

In the IL-KHANATE in Iran HÜLE'Ü (1256–65) added to existing Chinese colonies at Merv (Mary) and Tabriz a Chinese artisan colony at Khvoy around his Buddhist temple. Government weapons factories, such as at Tabriz, produced about 2,000 suits of armor a year. Purchases of raw materials and payment to the artisans were often disorganized, however, and GHAZAN KHAN (1295–1304) eventually decided to purchase most weapons on the open market, keeping only a small number of weapons makers to produce less commonly used items. This reform marked a movement away from requisitioning services and toward purchasing them, which eventually replaced the traditional Mongol policy on craftsmen in the Il-Khanate.

CLAN NAMES found among the 16th-century Mongols, such as *Urad,* "craftsmen," and *Ke'üd* "boys," mark the descendants of deported artisans among the nomads. Among the 18th-century ZÜNGHARS such new craft camp districts (OTOG) were still being organized, probably from captured Turkestani artisans.

See also CENSUS IN THE MONGOL EMPIRE; CLOTHING AND DRESS; MASSACRES AND THE MONGOL CONQUEST.

Further reading: Thomas T. Allsen, *Commodity and Exchange in the Mongol Empire: A Cultural History of Islamic Textiles* (Cambridge: Cambridge University Press, 1997).

assassins   *See* ISMA'ILIS.

astrology   Astrology was an area of great interest for the khans in the Mongol Empire and today is still widely practiced. Most astrologers today are lamas, trained and employed in the monasteries. Manuals of astrology and divination form a large part, sometimes the majority, of all comprehensive collections of Mongolian manuscripts from the 19th and early 20th centuries. Astrology forms one method of seeking guidance and averting ills; others practiced among the Mongols include the observation of omens and the seeking of auspices, especially through SCAPULIMANCY.

ASTROLOGY IN THE MONGOL EMPIRE

The Mongols, like the Turkish steppe empires before them, certainly had a native calendrical system, probably kept by the shamans, and drew astrological predictions from them. A Qongqotan stargazer (presumably the famous shaman TEB TENGGERI) was said to be active in 1209, and certainly by the 1250s the shamans were predicting eclipses, casting horoscopes, and declaring auspicious and inauspicious days. The new or full moons were considered auspicious for beginnings.

As they built their empire, the Mongols exempted astrologers, like artisans, physicians, and clergymen, from killing during war and from paying taxes in peace. Successful astrologers and diviners often became trusted advisers, such as the Kitan scholar YELÜ CHUCAI with CHINGGIS KHAN, Nasir-ud-Din Tusi (1201–74) with HÜLE'Ü, AND LIU BINGZHONG with QUBILAI KHAN. The IL-KHANATE, the Mongol YUAN DYNASTY in China, and the non-Chinggisid JALAYIR and Timurid successor dynasties (*see* TIMUR) all funded the construction of observatories and the compilation of celestial almanacs and star charts. The Mongol conquest resulted in the exchange of observational methods and data between China and the Middle East, while Qubilai's chief Buddhist chaplain, 'Phags-pa Lama (1235–80) used Chinese observations in composing a revised Tibetan calendar.

The *baqshis,* or Buddhist clergy, whether from Tibet, KASHMIR, Uighuristan, or China, soon became the most numerous astrologers among the Mongols. In Buddhism astrology and divination are seen as the science of the bodhisattva Manjushri, which, while dealing with merely conventional reality, is useful for living beings within that sphere. Uighur astrological works were translated into Mongolian in this period and became the basis for Mongolian astrological terminology.

BUDDHIST ASTROLOGY

In recent centuries Mongolian astrological manuals have included Chinese, Uighur, and Tibetan elements, all of which draw in varying degrees on Indian astrology. Within the Tibetan Buddhist tradition the Kalachakra (Wheel of Time) Tantra includes a separate calendar for astrological calculations. Tibetan methods of calculation were taught in the monasteries. The Buddhist Uighur astrological tradition was transmitted among the Mongols during the empire period, while Chinese methods were popularized by official almanacs with auspices for each day, issued in Chinese, Manchu, and Mongolian by the QING DYNASTY (1636–1912) court.

Mongolian astrology thus uses several calendars (although all of the East Asian lunar–solar type, with the new year around January–March) and a vast array of astronomical categories: the sun, moon, and planets; the Indian 28 nakshatras, or lunar mansions, and the Chinese 12-ANIMAL CYCLE, both of which are used to number months, days, and hours; the 12 Chinese "lords of the day;" the five elements (wood, fire, earth, metal, water); and the Chinese Eight Trigrams. Astrological calculations not only determined the time when an activity should take place, but also frequently its cardinal direction and sometimes the color of clothes worn or of the horse ridden. Given the presence of several different systems and vast numbers of ramifications in each one, any given event could always yield many different, often contradictory, indications, the resolution of which was the job of the astrologer. Ordinary people, however, often followed on their own much simpler "folk" versions of these complex nets of prognostications.

Modern astrologers, or zurkhaich (Uighur-Mongolian, jirukhaichi), have mostly been lamas trained in monasteries, although there were and are occasional lay astrologers as well. Virtually no ritual in the monastery can be held without first determining the proper time astrologically. Among the laity a visit to a zurkhaich was (and to a large degree still is) an inevitable part of preparing a wedding (both to determine the compatibility of the bride and groom and to determine the time and mode of the bride's arrival) and a funeral. Astrological predictions are also sought for new children (about their general fortune, dangerous times or directions, personalities, and so on), and for major birthdays (particularly every ninth and 12th year). The more scrupulous avoided unlucky days for going on a trip, making and first wearing new clothes, and many other activities. In old Mongolia astrologers were often consulted about where to look for a lost horse or other animal. If the astrological indications for a given event were unfavorable, the usual remedy was to have certain indicated scriptures read.

In the 20th century Communist regimes among the Mongols in Russia, Mongolia, and China first criticized astrology as charlatanism, then persecuted it, but finally tolerated it as a remnant of superstition fit only for the most backward elements of society. Nevertheless, astrologers were always trained in the few remaining monasteries and surreptitiously consulted in Mongolia even by high officials. Today among Russia's BURIATS and KALMYKS and in Mongolia proper, astrological considerations are observed at all levels of society. In ULAANBAATAR the astrological consultation booth to the west of GANDAN-TEGCHINLING MONASTERY is very busy, and the astrological tables prepared by L. Terbish are bestsellers.

See also CALENDARS AND DATING SYSTEMS.

Further reading: Thomas T. Allsen, *Culture and Conquest in Mongol Eurasia* (Cambridge: Cambridge University Press, 2001).

A'uruq *See* AWARGA.

Autonomous Period *See* THEOCRATIC PERIOD.

Awarga (A'uruq, Aurug)　Located in Delgerkhaan Sum, Khentii province, the Awarga ruins have been identified with the *a'uruq,* or "base camp," of CHINGGIS KHAN mentioned in the *SECRET HISTORY OF THE MONGOLS.* (The current name Awarga, "huge," may be a distortion of the Middle Mongolian *a'uruq.*)

The site, on a hill overlooking the Awarga River, occupies 4.5 square kilometers (1.7 square miles) and included an artisans' quarter in the east with three streets and many small dwellings, a series of 13 walled platforms ranged east to west, each with traces of three or four buildings, a palace covering 180 square meters (1,938 square feet), and a double-walled temple covering 81 square meters (872 square feet) just to the north of the settlement center. The palace was built with hexagonal polished columns, of which 40 bases have been uncovered. Remains uncovered in the area include a forge for casting iron with associated slag and cast-iron pieces, plowshares, grains, numerous pottery, iron, bone goods, and Chinese bronze coins, particularly of the JIN DYNASTY (1115–1234).

Although Chinggis Khan's palace-tents (ORDO) certainly remained nomadic, Awarga may mark one of the points, probably the winter camp, of the nomadic route, and the 13 raised platforms may be where the *ordos* were placed. The temple, built later in Chinese style, may be that erected by QUBILAI KHAN's grandson Gammala (d. 1302) near the site of Chinggis Khan's shrine.

See also ARCHAEOLOGY.

ayimaq   *See* AIMAG.

Ayuka   *See* AYUUKI KHAN.

Ayuki   *See* AYUUKI KHAN.

Ayuuki Khan (Ayouki, Ayuki, Ayuka) (b. 1641, r. 1669–1724) *Powerful Torghud khan who raised the Kalmyks to the height of their influence and prestige*
Ayuuki Khan was the son of the Kalmyk ruler Puntsog (r. 1661–69) but spent his childhood with his mother's kin among the ZÜNGHARS of eastern Turkestan, returning to his Torghud tribe on the Volga in 1654. After forcing newly arrived Khoshud people into submission and unifying the KALMYKS, Ayuuki swore allegiance in 1673 to the Russian czar, yet from 1680 on he repeatedly turned to the CRIMEA and Ottoman Turkey when disappointed with Russian treatment. In 1690 he received a seal as KHAN from the regent of the Fifth Dalai Lama, and by 1708 the czar recognized him as khan and began supplying him with cannons and firearms. In 1697–98, Ayuuki married his daughter to the Zünghar ruler TSEWANG-RAB-TAN KHUNG-TAIJI (r. 1694–27) and received Tsewang-Rabtan's cousin Darma-Bala in return. In 1699, angered by Ayuuki's lack of respect for them, his older sons revolted. One fled to the Zünghars with 15,000 households, but the eldest, Chagdarjab, was reconciled with his father by Russian ambassadors in 1701. Ayuuki made Chagdarjab his heir apparent in 1714, but with the heir's death in 1722 a bitter succession struggle broke out. The rebellion of Dasang, Chagdarjab's eldest son, was defeated in November 1723, but the succession remained uncertain at Ayuuki's death on February 19, 1724.

Further reading: Junko Miyawaki, "Background of the Volga-Kalmyk Khanship: The Case of Ayouki Khan of the Torguts," in *Altaic Religious Beliefs and Practices*, ed. Géza Bethlenfalvy et al. (Budapest: Research Group for Altaic Studies, 1992), 239–244; Johann Christian Schnitscher, *An Account of the Kalmyk Land under Ayuki Khan*, trans. John R. Krueger (Bloomington, Ind.: Mongolia Society, 1996).

Azhu   *See* AJU.

B

baba   *See* "STONE MEN."

Badmadorji (Badamdorj) (d. 1920) *This lama official was both the confidante of the nationalist Jibzundamba Khutugtu and a notoriously pro-Chinese intriguer.*

Badmadorji's origin is unknown, but his elder sister kept an inn. From at least 1900 to 1911 Badmadorji was one of the chief lama officials in the estate of the high lama, the Eighth Jibzundamba Khutugtu (1870–1924, called the Bogda [Holy One] by the Mongols), first as *da lama* and then as ERDENI SHANGDZODBA. He also taught the Bogda the Mongolian script.

Despite being dismissed and detained by QING DYNASTY officials, once for corruption and once for following the Bogda's orders to protect lamas who had led an anti-Chinese riot, he opposed secession from China. In September 1911 he revealed to the AMBAN Sandô the Bogda's entire conspiracy to seek Russian aid. Even so, after the 1911 RESTORATION of independence, Badmadorji became "minister to assist religion and state," a new cabinet-level office of the Shangdzodba.

In October 1915 he became minister of the interior. For bribes, Badmadorji and his underlings sold the right to join the GREAT SHABI and allowed the falsification of census figures. Neglected by Chen Yi's "soft" approach to the REVOCATION OF AUTONOMY that respected traditional Mongolian rights, Badmadorji in revenge became an eager tool of Xu Shuzheng's "hard" approach that promoted Chinese assimilation of the Mongols. In May 1920, realizing his unpopularity, he retired to the countryside, where he died suddenly.

See also JIBZUNDAMBA KHUTUGTU, EIGHTH; THEOCRATIC PERIOD.

Baghdad, siege of   The siege of Baghdad, while lasting only from January 29 to February 10, 1258, destroyed what had once been the world center of Islamic culture and political authority.

From 1257 the Mongol prince HÜLE'Ü (1256–65), founder of the Mongols' Middle Eastern IL-KHANATE, had demanded that the caliph submit. When the 'Abbasid caliph in Baghdad, al-Musta'sim b'illah (r. 1242–58), rejected submission, Hüle'ü led the Mongol army's center through KURDISTAN to the Tigris River at Ctesiphon and ordered the right wing to cross the river on a pontoon bridge near Ad-Dujayl. The right wing proceeded to about 25 miles from Baghdad. The caliph's *dawatdar* (inkpot holder), or secretary, Mujahid-ad-Din Aybeg, leading an infantry levy from the suburb of Karkh, defeated the Mongols, but that night as the caliph's soldiers celebrated, the Mongol commander BAIJU cut the dykes and flooded the enemy's camp. The next day (January 18) the Mongols attacked, and the *dawatdar* barely got back alive to Baghdad. The right wing then occupied the suburbs west of the Tigris, while the left wing covered Baghdad's southern walls, and Hüle'ü camped opposite the wall's Ajami tower on January 22. The Mongol army, said to have been 200,000 strong, prepared missiles and siege towers. The Tigris was bridged above and below the city, and patrols watched the banks for escape attempts.

When the assault began on January 29, the caliph tried to mollify Hüle'ü by sending out his Shi'ite vizier, Mu'ayyid-ad-Din Ibn 'Alqami, and Mar Makika, the catholicos of the Church of the East (Nestorians), both considered sympathetic to the Mongols. Hüle'ü sent them back and demanded that the *dawatdar* and other advocates of resistance be sent out. Meanwhile, the catapults breached Ajami tower on Friday, February 1, but stiff resistance drove back the Mongols. By Sunday, however, the Mongols held the walls. The *dawatdar* tried to escape down the Tigris, but Mongol patrols sank three boats and forced him back. From that time the caliph despaired and sent envoys to arrange surrender. Hüle'ü promised the caliph's son favorable treatment, and on Sunday, February 10, the caliph and his sons came out with a party of 3,000 dignitaries.

On February 13 the Mongol army entered the city with a warrant to kill everyone while the treasures were gathered in mountainous heaps outside the Mongol command's *kirü'ese*, or hitching post. Only the Christians under the catholicos's protection were spared. After one week Hüle'ü declared an amnesty for the survivors and left the putrid air of Baghdad. On February 20 the caliph with his entire family and court were executed. That same day the vizier Ibn 'Alqami and other reliable officials were restored to their posts under the eye of a Khorazmian DARUGHACHI (overseer), Ali Ba'atur. The walls and moats were leveled, and 3,000 Mongol soldiers were deputed to dispose of the dead bodies and clear the marketplaces.

See also 'ABBASID CALIPHATE; MASSACRES AND THE MONGOL CONQUEST; MILITARY OF THE MONGOL EMPIRE.

Baiju (fl. 1243–1260) *Mongol commander who conquered Seljük Turkey*

A relative of JEBE of the Besüd clan and a quiver bearer in the imperial guard (KESHIG), Baiju commanded 1,000 troops in the army sent with CHORMAQAN to conquer western Iran. In 1243 Empress TÖREGENE appointed Baiju to succeed Chormaqan, now an invalid. That summer Baiju invaded the sultanate of Rum in TURKEY. At Köse Daği (June 26, 1243) Baiju's army totally defeated Sultan Ghiyas-ad-Din Kay-Khusrau, and the Mongols took Erzincan, Kayseri, and Sivas. By releasing David, the illegitimate son of the Georgian royal family, from prison in Kayseri, he also obtained an effective tool of Mongol policy there. Meanwhile, King Het'um I (1226–69) of LESSER ARMENIA and Sultan Badr-ad-Din Lu'lu' (1233–59) of Mosul surrendered voluntarily. The caliph of Baghdad, however, defeated Mongol raids in 1238 and 1245. Baiju prided himself on the conquest of Rum, but GÜYÜG Khan (1246–48) found Baghdad's resistance irritating and blamed it on Baiju. Güyüg appointed new rulers in Rum and GEORGIA and in 1247 demoted Baiju, appointing his own partisan Eljigidei in his place. When MÖNGKE KHAN (1251–59) ascended the throne, he had Eljigidei executed and ordered Baiju again into Rum, where the sultan 'Izz-ad-Din was still resisting Mongol control. After Baiju defeated 'Izz-ad-Din at Aksaray (October 1256), Möngke ordered Baiju to put his troops at the service of his brother HÜLE'Ü. Baiju mobilized an army of 80,000 and participated ably in Hüle'ü's campaign against Baghdad and Aleppo. RASHID-UD-DIN FAZL-ULLAH reports, however, that Hüle'ü later executed Baiju and put Chormaqan's son, Shiremün, in his place.

See also 'ABBASID CALIPHATE; BAGHDAD, SIEGE OF; KÖSE DAĞI, BATTLE OF.

Baikal, Lake (Baykal) Lake Baikal, the world's oldest and deepest lake, lies in southern Siberia between Russia's BURIAT REPUBLIC and Irkutsk province. Its drainage basin of 557,000 square kilometers (215,060 square miles) covers most of the Buriat Republic and north-central Mongolia, including LAKE KHÖWSGÖL. Lake Baikal extends 636 kilometers (395 miles) southwest to northeast and is 79 kilometers (49 miles) wide at its maximum; total surface area is 31,500 square kilometers (12,162 square miles). The lake bottom is everywhere more than 800 meters (2,625 feet) deep and is 1,637 meters (5,371 feet) deep in the center. Baikal's 23,000 cubic kilometers (5,520 cubic miles) of water hold one-fifth of the world's unfrozen freshwater reserves. Tectonic processes formed the rift valley of Lake Baikal more than 25 million years ago, and it contains more endemic species than any other lake. The *nerpa,* or Baikal seal, is the world's only freshwater pinniped.

Lake Baikal is closely rimmed by mountain ridges, particularly on its western shore. All major affluents—the SELENGE RIVER, the Barguzin River, and Upper Angara River—enter the lake from the eastern side, while the only effluent, the Angara, flows northwest from the lake's southern end.

The waters of Lake Baikal are exceptionally clear and are fully oxygenated to the bottom by currents. The vast volume of water delays and moderates seasonal climate changes throughout the lake basin; neighboring air temperatures range from an average of 11°C (52°F) in August to –19°C (–2°F) in February. The lake's surface water does not exceed 12°C (54°F) even in the summer, except near the shore. Ice around 0.7–1.15 meters (2.3–3.75 feet) thick covers Baikal from January to May.

The *tenggis,* or ocean, crossed by the Mongols' mythical ancestors in the *SECRET HISTORY OF THE MONGOLS* is generally identified with Lake Baikal, and BARGA, Khori, and Buriat Mongols have inhabited the lake shores since at least the 12th century (*see* BURIATS). The lake's largest island, Ol'khon (Buriat Oikhon) occupies about 730 square kilometers (282 square miles) and has around 1,500 inhabitants. The Ekhired branch of the western Buriats settled the island in the 17th century, and it has been a stronghold of SHAMANISM ever since. The island is held to be the source and location of powerful shaman spirits, particularly at Shaman's Rock, which juts into Lake Baikal. The Ol'khon district, including adjacent mainland areas, has 8,711 inhabitants, of whom 4,237 (49 percent) are Buriat (1989 figures).

Despite a pulp and paper mill in Baykal'sk, the lake's water is still clean by international standards. In April 1987 Moscow established a coastal protection zone around Baikal, banning logging and planning less environmentally damaging development. In 1996 Baikal was made Russia's only UNESCO World Heritage site and in May 1999 this was reinforced by a special federal law. The paper and pulp mill remains in operation, however. Recently environmental concerns have led to development plans for Lake Baikal that envision phasing out commercial fisheries and developing tourism based on amateur sport fishing.

See also HUNTING AND FISHING.

Bait   *See* BAYAD.

Bajan-Ölgij   *See* BAYAN-ÖLGII PROVINCE.

balish   *See* YASTUQ.

Baljuna Covenant   At Baljuna Lake in summer 1203, CHINGGIS KHAN swore an oath that if he became ruler, he would reward those who had suffered with him in his rise to power. The Baljuna covenanters formed a group of hereditary servants of the dynasty.

After Chinggis was defeated by ONG KHAN of the KEREYID khanate at the battle of Qalaqaljid Sands (spring 1203), he fled east to the area of modern Hulun Buir. Many of the MONGOL TRIBE had deserted Chinggis, and his following fell to only 2,600. That summer Chinggis moved to Lake Baljuna in northeast Mongolia. There he was joined both by Mongol tribes, such as the QONGGI-RAD, and also by outsiders: Muslims such as Hasan, a trader resident in Mongolia, and JABAR KHOJA, a descendant of Muhammad, UIGHURS such as the scribe CHINQAI, and KITANS such as Yelü Ahai, a renegade envoy from the JIN DYNASTY court in North China (*see* YELÜ AHAI AND TUHUA). Short of food, Chinggis and 19 companions were reduced to eating a wild ass, and drinking the muddy water of the shallow lake. Chinggis then swore an oath to share his future goods with those who had shared his present poverty. These men received the title of "Baljuna men" (*Baljunatu*). The oath takers were mostly not Mongols, and it marked their incorporation into Chinggis's inner circle. Sources suspicious of these non-Mongol interlopers, such as the SECRET HISTORY OF THE MONGOLS, thus ignore the Baljuna Covenant.

Further reading: Francis Woodman Cleaves, "The Historicity of the Baljuna Covenant," *Harvard Journal of Asiatic Studies* 18 (1955): 357–421.

banners   The system of autonomous banners was the basic sociopolitical unit of the Mongols under the QING DYNASTY (1636–1912). The autonomous Mongolian banners must be clearly distinguished from the EIGHT BAN-NERS system that formed the Qing dynasty's garrison soldiers. Although the Eight Banners system also included Mongolian banners, those Mongols lived in garrisons in China and Manchuria under a different legal and administrative system.

ORIGINS

The autonomous banners were first organized in Inner Mongolia in 1634 by the Manchu emperor Hong Taiji (r. 1627–43), after the defeat of the last independent Mongol emperor LIGDAN KHAN (1604–34). Commissioners traveled Inner Mongolia to 1) fix the territory of each Mongolian ruler, or ZASAG (Inner Mongolian *jasag*); 2) assign each *zasag* his subjects; and 3) divide the population into *sumus* (modern Mongolian SUM, arrow), each to supply 50 soldiers. These demands in themselves did not change traditional Mongolian social structure. Mongol commoners had long been subject to TAIJI (BORJIGID, or Chinggisid nobles) and had occupied designated pastures. No attempt was made to break up traditional clan affiliations among the commoners. What was new was that these new appanages, called "banners" (*khoshuu*), were defined and controlled by non-Mongols.

STRUCTURE

By 1670 the banner system in Inner Mongolia had achieved its final form with 49 banners. The banner consisted of a certain body of people on a territory, defined in triennial censuses and detailed maps. Copies of both were forwarded to the LIFAN YUAN (Court of Dependencies), the organization responsible for supervising the Mongol banners. The Lifan Yuan issued to the *zasag* his seal, which granted the right to rule.

In Inner Mongolia each banner office had five officials: two administrators (*tusalagchi*), one adjutant (*zakhirugchi*; Inner Mongolian, *jakhirugchi*), and two deputy adjutants (*meiren*). The administrator was required to be a *taiji* (nobleman), and the senior *tusalagchi* held the seal as regent if the *zasag* was underage. The adjutant and deputy adjutants were by custom commoners.

The banner population was divided into *sums*, each of which had 150 households and supplied 50 on-duty fighting men. The *sumus* were further divided into 50s, 20s, and 10s. In larger banners every six *sumus* were organized into a "regiment" (*khariya*; Manchu, *jalan*), headed by a "colonel," or *zalan-u zanggi* (Inner Mongolian, *jalan-u janggi*).

The banner office kept extensive records, all in Mongolian, which was the administrative language of all autonomous banners. All literate commoners were required to put in two-month terms as banner clerks. Runners (*boshokho* or *khöögchi*) functioned as bailiffs, transmitting banner orders, collecting requisitions, and arresting criminals.

Banner operations were set up to operate without extensive taxation. Only the *zasag* received a large salary.

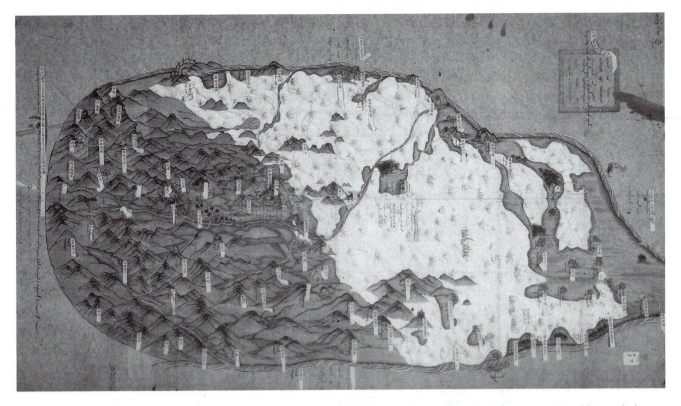

Map of Ongni'ud Left Banner, Inner Mongolia. Such illustrated maps of each banner were regularly produced and forwarded to the Lifan Yuan, which kept them on file. *(Courtesy Staatsbibliothek zu Berlin—Preussischer Kulturbesitz, Orientalabteilung)*

Qing regulations capped taxes at two sheep per 40, six woks full of grain per two head of horned cattle, and a horse, an ox, and cart per 10 households. Since the officials and runners were unpaid, overcollection and embezzlement were routine.

THE KHALKHA AND OIRAT BANNERS

In 1691 the newly submitted Khalkhas were organized into 34 banners, which the Qing authorities multiplied to 86 by 1759. Since the Khalkha population was considerably smaller than Inner Mongolia's, the multiplication of banners meant that each banner had on average two *sumus*, while the Inner Mongolian banners had on average 28. As a result, the official hierarchy in Khalkha was simplified, with only one administrator, an adjutant, and a regimental colonel.

The Khalkha and Inner Mongolian banners differed in the relation between the *taiji*'s personal subjects and the banner commoners. In each Mongolian banner the numerous noble *taiji* class (usually Borjigid) was originally assigned a body of commoners to provide domestic and pastoral services. In Khalkha the commoners were separated into "*sumu* commoners," or *albatu* (taxpayers), who performed only public services, and *khamjilga,* who performed only private duties for their *taiji* lords. In Inner Mongolia all banner commoners were assigned to the *taiji*s, with a smaller number reserved as *khamjilga*,

exclusively serving their *taiji*. Thus, most commoners performed both public service for the banner and the Qing empire and personal service for their lords.

The Oirat banners of Xinjiang, Kökenuur, and western Mongolia were similar to the Khalkha banners in size. In western Mongolia the *taiji* role was played by *zaisang*s, who had no *khamjilga*s.

DIFFERING BANNER TYPES

In several areas banners straddled the divide between the Eight Banners and the autonomous banners. Among the Höhhot TÜMED after 1636 and the CHAKHAR after 1675 the Qing abolished the *zasags* (*jasags*) and the *taiji* class. The areas were organized into banners in the Eight Banners system with (among the Chakhar) auxiliary "pastures" (*sürüg*) providing pastoral products for the emperor's table. Banner heads were appointed officials, although an oligarchy of a few non-Borjigid families dominated their ranks. Borjigid clansmen still existed but had no special status. Mongolian and Manchu languages were used together. The New and Old Bargas in HULUN BUIR and the Daurs in Butha were treated as "New Manchus" and settled under a similar Eight Banners system, with Manchu as the dominant administrative language. All of these banners, however, were subject to the LIFAN YUAN's Mongol law code, the *LIFAN YUAN ZELI.*

In western Mongolia after the collapse of the ZÜNG- HARS in 1755, new autonomous banners for the DÖRBÖDS and TORGHUDS were created, but alongside them were several banners without *zasags*: ZAKHACHIN, ÖÖLÖD, MING- GHAD, and ALTAI URIÁNGKHAI. These banners' chiefs were appointed by the AMBAN (imperial resident) of Khowd. The remaining Zünghars in Xinjiang were also organized into Öölöd banners, which lacked the autonomy of *zasag* banners.

THE BANNERS AS COMMUNITIES

Each of the Mongolian autonomous banners formed a more-or-less closed community. Rituals organized and financed by the banner included the "seal assembly" of the lunar new year in which the banner seal was worshiped and the coming budget discussed by the top officials, OBOO (cairn) worship, summer KOUMISS (fermented mare's milk) festivals, and NAADAM (games). Each banner also supported a common banner monastery. Banner membership was hereditary and virtually impossible to change. Banner members could nomadize freely anywhere within the banner, open land for hay mowing or farming, or exploit natural resources (salt lakes, timber, etc.) with at most nominal fees. Outsiders, however, whether Mongol or Chinese, paid substantial fees for such rights. For all but a few high-ranking noblemen, career mobility outside the banner was impossible.

In Inner Mongolia the banners were usually explicitly associated with a particular subethnic identity within the Mongols (Khorchin, Baarin, Üjümüchin, etc.). Among the Khalkha, however, all but two of the 86 banners belonged to the Khalkha subethnic group. For this reason banner identity was considerably stronger in Inner Mongolia than among the Khalkha. At the same time, the members of all the autonomous Mongol banners were a recognized and distinct ethnolegal caste within the Qing Empire. In this sense membership in the autonomous Mongol banners was one of the major foundations of the modern sense of Mongolian nationhood.

MODERN CHANGES

In the late 19th century the banner system began to show significant strains. The irresponsibility of the *zasags*, who had no incentive to frugality, and embezzlement by the unpaid officials led most banners into a permanent fiscal crisis. The usual response of renting out banner natural resources was itself pervaded by corruption. In Inner Mongolia this led to heavy Chinese colonization that turned the banner residents into rentiers living off meager annuities. In remoter banners auslander Mongols displaced by colonization became a large percentage of the residents, yet without rights or duties beyond paying a special tax. In Outer Mongolia many banners became virtual wards of Chinese moneylending firms.

Outer Mongolia's post-1911 independent theocratic government did not alter the banner system. The post-1921 revolutionary regime eliminated the *zasag* system and the *taijis*' privileges in 1922–24, and in 1931 a comprehensive administrative reform eliminated the banner (*khoshuu*) as a unit, replacing it with completely new AIMAGs (provinces) and *sumus* (districts). In Inner Mongolia under the Republic of China (1911–49), the banner (*khoshuu*) remained the unit for Mongol administration even where Chinese counties (*xian*) shared the land. The *zasag* (*jasag*) system finally collapsed in 1945, but the banner remained the basis for local administrative units despite colonization and administrative amalgamation. Among the OIRATS of Xinjiang and Qinghai (Kökenuur), the banner system was completely replaced by Chinese-style counties after 1949.

See also APPANAGE SYSTEM; *DUGUILANGS*; EDUCATION, TRADITIONAL; THEOCRATIC PERIOD.

Further reading: Henry Serruys, "Five Documents Regarding Salt Production in Ordos," *Bulletin of the School of Oriental and African Studies* 40 (1977): 338–353; ———, "A Question of Land and Landmarks between the Banners Otog and Üüsin (Ordos)," *Zentralasiatische Studien* 13 (1979): 213–23; ———, "A Socio-Political Document from Ordos: The *Dürim* of Otog from 1923," *Monumenta Serica* 30 (1972–73): 526–621.

Banzarov, Dorzhi Banzarovich (1822–1855) *The first person of Mongol ancestry to obtain a doctorate from a European university*

Born into the family of a Buriat Cossack petty officer in Lower Ichetui (near modern Petropavlovka), Dorzhi Banzarov was of the Tabunanguud clan of Selenge Buriats. After completing primary school at age nine, Dorzhi attended the Russo-Mongolian Military Academy. In 1835, recognizing his brilliance, the Buriat chief or *taisha* (*see* TAISHI) N. Wampilov arranged for him to be exempted from the Cossacks' regular 25-year tour of duty to attend the gymnasium (classical high school) in Kazan' on the Volga, where Dorzhi mastered the main languages of Inner Asia and Europe. Graduating with high honors, he went on to study at the University of Kazan'. His dissertation on *The Black Faith, or Shamanism among the Mongols* (1846), drew scholarly attention to SHAMANISM as the pre-Buddhist religion of the Mongols. His methodology of trying to identify remnants of shamanism within contemporary Buddhist practice was immensely influential. In 1850 he returned to Buriatia on the staff of East Siberia's governor-general, N. N. Murav'ev. Although he published articles on *paizas*, the "Stone of Chinggis Khan" of 1226, and other monuments of ancient Mongolian philology, the difficulties of pursuing scholarship in Siberia often depressed him. His premature death in 1855 was greeted with dismay by Russia's scholarly world.

See also BURIATS; NEW SCHOOLS MOVEMENTS.

Further reading: Dorji Banzarov, trans. Jan Nattier and John R. Krueger, "The Black Faith, or Shamanism among the Mongols," *Mongolian Studies* 7 (1982): 53–91.

Bao'an language and people (Bonan, Pao-an)

The Bao'an are a small (12,212 in 1990) nationality in China's Gansu province who speak a Mongolic language. Muslim in religion, they live in close contact with the Mongolic-speaking Dongxiang, the Turkic-speaking Salar, and the Hui (Chinese-speaking Muslims) in Jishishan county.

ORIGINS

The name Bao'an (pronounced Baonang in their own language) comes from the Bao'an fort built just north of the modern Tongren county seat in the early MING DYNASTY (1368–1644) and settled by military farmers of various origins. By the mid-Qing dynasty (1636–1912) the Bao'an fort itself and the outlying Xiazhuang and Gashari (or Gasiri) hamlets were settled by Muslim speakers of a Mongolic language, living among the Chinese, Hui, Tibetans, and Mongolic-speaking Buddhist Tu.

With no further information available about the origin of these Mongolian-speaking Bao'an Muslims, some see them basically as Tu who converted from Buddhism to Islam during the time of Ma Laichi (fl. 1698–1747), a miracle-working Sufi master who is known to have converted a nearby Tibetan community and probably the small Tuomao group of UPPER MONGOLS. Bao'ans themselves in the 1980s, however, argued that their nationality originates among SEMUREN, the Turkestani immigrant class in the MONGOL EMPIRE who later came to speak a Mongolic tongue.

LANGUAGE

The Bao'an language belongs to the Gansu-Qinghai subfamily of the Mongolic family. Bao'an resembles Tu in the use of many initial consonant clusters formed by dropping first-syllable vowels (njige, "donkey," from Middle Mongolian eljige; mba-, "to swim," from Middle Mongolian umba-; ftə~fu̥tə, "long," from Middle Mongolian dialect form *hutu), the presence of word-initial r- (re, "come," from Middle Mongolian ire-), the relatively loose constraints on final consonants, and the presence of many Tibetan loanwords. These features reflect mostly the Tibetan sound and lexical environment and apparently developed largely independently.

In fact, a number of elements connect Bao'an more closely to Dongxiang, which, due to massive Chinese influence, superficially seems quite different. Words like "two" (Bao'an guar, Dongxiang gua versus Tu goor), "big" (Bao'an fguo, Dongxiang fugiə versus Tu shge), "bladder" (Bao'an doləkh, Dongxiang dawala versus Tu dabsag), the plural marker -la, and the instrumental case guala show forms shared with Dongxiang and different from Tu. One Bao'an innovation is the change of word-final -n to -ng.

It was estimated in the mid-1980s that Bao'an speakers totaled about 9,000, the same number as the nationality, although the majority of Bao'ans in Dahejia and other major Bao'an villages in Jishishan by then used Chinese.

Paradoxically, 2,000–3,000 people registered as Tu in Tongren county speak Bao'an, albeit with small lexical differences. These are probably remnants of the original Bao'an population who were forcibly converted (or reconverted) to Buddhism.

HISTORY AND SOCIETY

In 1862 long-standing quarrels over water rights and increasing communal tensions led a body of Tibetans and Tu, mobilized by Rong-bo (Longwu) Monastery, to attack the Muslim Bao'an villagers, demanding that they become Buddhists. When Tibetans and Tu sacked the fort, the surviving Muslims, assisted by a friendly Tibetan tribe, fled to Xunhua, briefly settling among the Salars, a Turkic Muslim people. Not welcomed by the Salars, the Bao'an were mobilized by Ma Zhan'ao, a leader of the great Hui rebellion of 1862, and settled after Ma's surrender to the Qing dynasty at Dahejia village in Jishishan. Bao'an Muslims from Gashari and Xiazhuang later settled in neighboring villages.

The Ma family under the military commander Ma Zhan'ao and his son Ma Anliang owned two-thirds of the land in Dahejia, and the akhunds (Chinese ahong, an Islamic religious leader) of the 42-local monasteries were appointed by the Ma family. In 1896 Ma Anliang executed about 30 Bao'ans for joining an 1895–96 sectarian rebellion among the Salars.

In the early 20th century Bao'an merchants became active in the Tibetan trade. Those with larger capital were called "Tibetan guests" and conducted a trade in luxury goods as far away as India. The "Songpan guests" had less capital and conducted local trade in Songpan and other areas along the eastern border of the Tibetan plateau, bartering consumer goods for wool. The Bao'an also have a strong artisan tradition, exemplified by the knives of Gaozhaojia village.

After 1930 conflicts became frequent between the Bao'an farmers and the wealthy "Eight Families" over water rights and usury. Taxes and conscription under the Hui warlord Ma Bufang also became onerous.

Most of the Bao'ans honor the Yatou or Gaozhaojia menhuans (lodges of hereditary Sufi, or Islamic mystic masters). The Yatou menhuan was founded by Ma Wenquan (1840–82) of the Qadiriya Sufi lineage, and the Gaozhaojia menhuan, founded by Ma Yiheiya, split off from that in 1926. Both lineages have maintained their continuity despite persecutions in the Maoist period. With the revival of religion after the Cultural Revolution, the Yatou menhuan had about 5,000 followers, and the Gaozhaojia menhuan had about 3,000.

DISTRIBUTION AND CURRENT CONDITIONS

In 1952 the new People's Republic of China fixed the Bao'an as a separate nationality. According to the 1982 census there were 9,027 Bao'an people in China, of whom only 170 lived in the old home of Tongren county. Ethnic affiliation was apparently determined on the basis of religion rather than language, so that the 2,000–3,000 Buddhist Bao'an speakers of Tongren were made Tu rather than Bao'an. Of the registered Bao'an, 93 percent lived in Jishishan county (1982 population 169,483), concentrated in a few villages. Jishishan was made a Bao'an, Dongxiang, and Salar Autonomous County in September 1981. Jishishan is one of China's poorest counties, and in 1982 more than 93 percent of the Bao'an were employed primarily in agriculture. About 77 percent of those over six were illiterate, and fewer than 15 percent of school-age children attended primary school.

See also ALTAIC LANGUAGE FAMILY; DONGXIANG LANGUAGE AND PEOPLE; ISLAM IN THE MONGOL EMPIRE; MONGOLIC LANGUAGE FAMILY; TU LANGUAGE AND PEOPLE; YOGUR LANGUAGES AND PEOPLES.

Further reading: Henry Schwarz, *Minorities of Northern China: A Survey* (Bellingham: Western Washington University Press, 1984), 137–143.

Baotou (Pao-tou)   Inner Mongolia's largest city and main industrial center, Baotou accounts for one-third of the region's total industrial output.

Baotou municipality covers 9,991 square kilometers (3,858 square miles) and has a population of 1,779,314 people, of whom only 35,098 are Mongol (1990 figures). Administratively, this municipality is divided into Baotou proper, a suburban district, two mining districts, TÜMED Right Banner (Tumd Youqi), and Guyang county. The three widely separated urban districts comprising Baotou proper—Kundulun, Qingshan, and Donghe—cover 205 square kilometers (79 square miles) and together have a population of 950,000 (1990 figures), of which Mongols are only 20,000. The Shiguai mining district supplies Baotou's coal, while the noncontiguous Bayan Oboo district to the north supplies iron, niobium, and rare-earth ores. Bayan Oboo has the world's leading reserve of rare-earths oxides, totaling 103 million metric tons (113 million short tons).

Baotou's current territory was originally the grazing ground of the Tümed and Urad Mongols (*see* ULAANCHAB). The suburban area still includes the Agarautai *sumu* (SUM, or pastoral district) of Urad Mongols, whose 751 inhabitants in 1982 were 66 percent Mongol. Badgar Juu (Wudang Zhao), a Tibetan-style monastery which housed 1,200 lamas at its height, lies in the Shiguai district. CHINESE COLONIZATION established Baotou town (today's Donghe district) in 1806, and the Shiguai coal mines were opened in the 1860s. Railroads reached Baotou in 1923. In 1925 Chinese geologists discovered the ores of Bayan Oboo. In 1952 the new Chinese government, with Soviet assistance, began planning a massive steel metropolis. Baotou's industrial output reached 3.77 billion *yuan* in 1990 and is roughly one-third metals and one-third machine tools.

See also INNER MONGOLIA AUTONOMOUS REGION.

Barag   *See* BARGA.

Barga (Barghu, Barag, Bargut)   The Barga Mongols are Mongols who speak a Buriat-type dialect that came under the rule of the QING DYNASTY (1636–1912) and were resettled in Inner Mongolia. They were frequently active in pan-Mongolist movements; the failure of these movements has led small groups of Barga Mongols to emigrate to Mongolia.

Inner Mongolia's Old Barga (Chen Barag) banner and two New Barga (Xin Barag) banners together have a total area of 66,376 square kilometers (25,628 square miles). The combined 1990 population was 125,200, of whom 73,600 were Mongol, mostly Barga with some auslanders. Of these, 72 percent live in the New Barga banners. Most of the 20,700 Mongols of nearby Hailar and Manzhouli cities are also Barga. Barga in Mongolia numbered 2,100 in 1989. Inner Mongolia's Barga banners have a total of 1,318,000 head of livestock, of which 1,017,000 are sheep and goats (all figures from 1990). While the Barga are sometimes called BURIATS, this is incorrect. Their dialect is similar to the Buriats, but historically they have never borne that name, and history has made their culture distinct from the Buriats of Russia, even those of the same clan and lineage.

ORIGINS

The name *Barga* has been linked to the Bayirqu, who appeared in the early seventh to ninth centuries as one of the components of the predominantly Turkish Uighur confederation living in the Selenge valley. While plausible, such a connection is unproved.

In the 12th–13th centuries the Barga appear as a tribe or clan inhabiting the Barghujin Hollow (modern Barguzin in Buriatia) and were linked to the MONGOL TRIBE by marriage ties. (CHINGGIS KHAN's legendary ancestress ALAN GHO'A was of Barga ancestry.) In the MONGOL EMPIRE Ambaghai of the Barga (fl. 1211–56) commanded a *tümen* (10,000) of catapult operators. The Barga share the same 11 clans into which the Khori Buriats were traditionally divided, and Barga dialect is a type of Buriat Mongolian.

SETTLEMENT IN HULUN BUIR

While incorporated into the Mongol Empire, the Barga were never directly ruled by the descendants of Chinggis Khan. Early in the Northern Yuan (1368–1634) the Barga joined the OIRATS' coalition against the Northern Yuan emperors, and some were scattered widely among the Mongols and Oirats. The main body of the Barga-Khori tribe moved east to the area between the Ergüne (Argun') River and the GREATER KHINGGAN RANGE, where they became subject to the Solon (Daurs and Solon Ewenki) confederation. Around 1594 a large body of Barga-Khoris fled back east to the Onon-Uda-Nercha area, where they faced harassment from the Horse EWENKIS (Khamnigans) and demands for tribute from the KHALKHA Mongols.

While some sought Russian protection and become ancestors of the Khori Buriats, others remained tributary to the Khalkhas' Setsen Khan. Meanwhile, when China's QING DYNASTY counterattacked against the Cossacks in the Ergüne and Shilka Rivers in 1685–89, those Barga remaining east of the Ergüne were deported with the Solons to Manchuria.

The Qing authorities dispersed some of these Barga among the CHAKHAR banners but in 1732 moved a body of 275 Barga soldiers in Manchuria with their households west over the Greater Khinggan Range to the HULUN BUIR steppe as part of a 3,000-man-strong "Solon" (again Daur and Ewenki) banner force. These Barga, called the Old Bargas, or Chibchins (a somewhat derogatory term), were enrolled as Bordered White and Plain Blue banners within the Solon Left-Flank banners. As part of the EIGHT BANNERS system, each Old Barga banner was organized into three "arrows" (Manchu *niru,* Mongolian *sumu; see* SUM).

In 1734 the Barga who had been left in Khalkha's Setsen Khan province complained to the Qing authorities of mistreatment from the Khalkha aristocracy. The Qing authorities thus selected 2,400 Barga men in Khalkha and stationed them and the families, too, in Hulun Buir, east of the Solon-Old Barga banners. These New Barga Mongols formed eight banners in two wings, again each with three "arrows."

CULTURE AND LIFESTYLE

The traditional lifestyle of both Barga peoples was based on fully nomadic pastoralism. As part of the Eight Banners system, both Old and New Barga used Manchu as their administrative language, and some Manchu loanwords, such as *khala,* "clan," entered their language. Administration, while theoretically meritocratic, was based on an oligarchy of leading clans holding banner offices hereditarily. In Old Barga the top banner officials were almost all Daurs from Hulun Buir's capital, Hailar, but in New Barga they were Barga.

The Old and New Bargas differed substantially in folkways, with the New Barga showing greater Khalkha influence. The two dialects differ slightly from each other but preserve distinctive Buriat features, although today influence from the standard Inner Mongolian taught in schools and from recent KHORCHIN immigrants is strong. The Old Barga lived among Ewenkis and Daurs, neither of whom had accepted Buddhism, and they, too, preserved their pre-Buddhist native religion. The New Barga, however, were Buddhists, building many local monasteries. The annual fair at New Barga's Ganjuur Temple brought traders from Khalkha, Manchuria, and even Beijing.

Qing loyalism strongly colored the active New Barga literary culture, which was carried on almost entirely in the Manchu language, although Classical Mongolian was also taught. Küberi (1831–90) wrote Manchu-language histories of both the Mongols and his own New Barga people as well as advice for the young. This tradition of Manchu-language didactic and historical writing continued into the 20th century.

Under the Japanese occupation of 1932–45, Mongolian became the Barga's official language. After 1952, when the new Chinese Communist government designated the Daurs as a separate, non-Mongolian, nationality, the Old Barga were freed from Daur tutelage. Since then Barga culture has been more closely integrated into that of Inner Mongolia.

Despite heavy Chinese immigration into Hulun Buir, the Barga banners' Chinese population is found mostly in small administrative centers or in mining districts. The rural population is mostly Mongols who completely dominate rural police and administration. Most rural Barga are today seminomadic, often living in houses for part of the year. Traditional religious and clan life have also revived since 1979.

BARGA OF MONGOLIA

Mongolia's Barga population originated as political refugees. After the failed pan-Mongolist insurrection of summer 1928 (*see* MERSE), hundreds of New Barga refugees fled to Mongolia and were resettled in Eastern province's Gurwanzagal Sum, which is now about two-thirds Barga. In autumn 1945 a New Barga militia official, Ya. Shaariibuu (b. 1909), led 1,103 people from Barga to emigrate to Mongolia. His people were resettled in Eastern province's Khölön Buir Sum, which is now overwhelmingly Barga. In 1989, Mongolia's Barga numbered about 2,100.

See also DAMDINSÜRÜNG, GRAND DUKE; INNER MONGOLIA AUTONOMOUS REGION; INNER MONGOLIANS.

Bargu *See* BARGA.

Bargut *See* BARGA.

bariach *Bariach,* or bone setters, practice a distinct form of traditional healing among the Mongols, separate from either shamanist treatment or Tibeto-Mongolian medicine, although some *bariach* are also simultaneously shamans or lama-physicians. They are found in Mongolia, Inner Mongolia, Buriatia, and among other peoples of Siberia. The name is spelled *bariyachi* in the UIGHUR-MONGOLIAN SCRIPT and *baryaashan* in Buriat.

Bariach practice by means of massages, using, as they say, no equipment but their 10 fingers. By this method they treat broken bones, sprained and dislocated joints, and pulled muscles as well as various intestinal conditions seen as caused by cold wind penetrating the stomach. The most common problem they treat today is mild concussion (or "brain shaking"), a condition to which is attributed a wide variety of illnesses, particularly in children, throughout the former Soviet bloc. While some *bariach* do have medical training, they are mostly non-professional healers.

While *bariach* do not treat illnesses caused by spirits, their healing power is linked to a force believed to flow through the fingers, variously identified with a *bariach* ancestor, the WHITE OLD MAN, or Manal (the Buddhist medicine Buddha Manla or Bhaishajyaguru), or even Allah (by a Kazakh *bariach*) or "bioelectricity" (by a non-religious *bariach*). *Bariach* can be either male or female, and, like shamans, they usually begin to practice due to an accident or inexplicable malady, which is interpreted as a demand by the *bariach* ancestors to begin practicing. In an initiation ceremony, called *chandruu*, the afflicted person "takes the lineage" and becomes a *bariach*.

The practice of bone setting is attested to among famous Mongolian and Manchu physicians in Beijing in the 18th century. The Manchu bone setter Aishin Gioro Isangga of the Qianlong period (1735–96) trained his pupils by heaping tangled reeds and having his students massage them into order. During the early Communist era some were persecuted as charlatans, but by the 1960s and 1970s arrests were rare and brief. From 1985 on famous *bariach* in ULAANBAATAR and the countryside rapidly developed a public clientele, although medical opinion in Mongolia remains divided on the value of their services.

See also MEDICINE, TRADITIONAL.

Further reading: Daniel J. Hruschka, "*Baria* Healers among the Buriats in Eastern Mongolia," *Mongolian Studies* 21 (1998): 21–41.

basqaq   *See* DARUGHACHI.

Batmönkh   *See* DAYAN KHAN, BATU-MÖNGKE.

Batmönkh, Jambyn (Batmönh) (1926–1997) *Last Communist leader of Mongolia*
Born on March 10, 1926, in Bayan Mandal Uula banner (modern Khyargas Sum, UWS), Batmönkh belonged to the first generation to come of age after the GREAT PURGE. After attending Mongolian State University, from 1951 Batmönkh lectured at Mongolian State University and then at the Higher Party School. After studying at the Soviet Communist Party's Academy of Social Sciences in Moscow (1958–61), he headed the Institute of Economics and then Mongolian State University.

In 1973 he entered the MONGOLIAN PEOPLE'S REVOLUTIONARY PARTY's Central Committee as chairman of its science and educational department. In June 1974, when the Mongolian ruler YUMJAAGIIN TSEDENBAL chose to resign his post as premier (head of the government) and become head of state (previously a figurehead position), Batmönkh was chosen to be the new premier as an unthreatening newcomer outside the ruling circle. Both Tsedenbal and Batmönkh were of the Dörböd tribe.

In August 1984 the Soviet leadership engineered Tsedenbal's dismissal, and Batmönkh replaced him as the party's general secretary and head of state. After 1986 Batmönkh mechanically imitated the Soviet leader Mikhail Gorbachëv's "openness" and "restructuring" campaigns until December 1989, when antigovernment demonstrations broke out in Mongolia. Lacking Soviet support for a crackdown, the party leadership collapsed, and Batmönkh resigned all positions in March 1990. He has played no public role in the new democratic Mongolia.

See also MONGOLIAN PEOPLE'S REPUBLIC; SOVIET UNION AND MONGOLIA.

Batu (Baty) (d. 1255) *Chinggis Khan's grandson, founder of the Golden Horde and kingmaker in the 1251 election*
Batu was the second son of JOCHI, CHINGGIS KHAN's eldest son. His mother, Öki, of the QONGGIRAD, was the daughter of Chinggis's brother-in-law Alchi Noyan. Despite having an elder brother, Hordu (Hordu), Batu succeeded his father by Chinggis's order and helped enthrone his uncle ÖGEDEI KHAN as great khan at the election QURILTAI (assembly) in 1229.

In 1235 Ögedei proposed to complete the conquest of the western steppe originally entrusted to Batu's father. In spring 1236 Batu and princes from all the Chinggisid lines set out for the conquest of the QIPCHAQS, Russians, and neighboring peoples. According to the will of Chinggis, Jochi's sons inherited all the lands won in this massive campaign, from the Volga to Hungary, thus making Batu the greatest Mongol lord next to the great khan himself. Yet Batu had to live down both his irresolution at the battle of Muhi (April 11, 1241) and an embarrassing incident at Kozel'sk (spring 1238), where he struggled for two months against a town his cousins Qadan (son of Ögedei) and Büri (grandson of CHA'ADAI) stormed in three days. Büri complained of the unfairness of Batu receiving such a vast and fertile steppe, and, along with Ögedei Khan's son GÜYÜG and the non-Chinggisid commander (NOYAN) Harghasun, ridiculed Batu as an "old woman with a beard."

The death of Ögedei (December 11, 1241) brought a close to Batu's brief military career. Withdrawing from Hungary, he made his camps along the banks of the Volga. By this time he was afflicted, like many Mongol princes, with gout and announced his inability to attend any immediate *quriltai*, thus delaying the succession for several years. Eventually, Güyüg was elected great khan on August 24, 1246, with Batu's older brother, Hordu, representing the Jochid lineage.

After Ögedei's death Batu became a kind of viceroy over all the western parts of the empire, controlling routine affairs among the Russian princes, nominating Jochid retainers as governors of Iran, and receiving in audience grandees from the Caucasus. At no point, however, did he openly challenge the authority of the great khan. Suspicions between Batu and Güyüg increased, however, when Güyüg replaced the officials in Iran and the Caucasus with his own men, including Eljigidei, the father of Harghasun Noyan. When Güyüg began moving westward, ostensibly to campaign in the Middle East, SORQAQTANI BEKI, widow of Chinggis Khan's youngest son, Tolui, secretly warned Batu that he was actually Güyüg's intended target. Only Güyüg's sudden death in April 1248 averted a possible civil war.

During the succeeding regency Batu called a special *quriltai* in his own territory, attended mostly only by minor representatives of the great families. When Batu proposed elevating Möngke, Tolui's eldest son and one of the few high-ranking princes present, as KHAN, he began a revolution that pitched the Jochid and Toluid families against his old Chaghatayid and Ögedeid rivals. Möngke had also served in the western campaign of 1235–41 but had not joined in the ridicule of Batu. Deputing his brother Berke to represent the Jochids, Batu secured Möngke's election at the general *quriltai* in Mongolia (July 1251). When Möngke purged the opponents of the new election, Batu demanded and received custody of Büri and Eljigidei, who were both executed.

During MÖNGKE KHAN's reign Batu's prestige as king-maker and the great khan's viceroy in the west reached its height. Even so, Batu allowed Möngke's census takers to operate freely in his realm and scrupulously forwarded foreign representatives, such as WILLIAM OF RUBRUCK, to Möngke. Batu dispatched a large Jochid delegation to participate in HÜLE'Ü's expedition to the Middle East, little suspecting that it would result in eliminating the Jochid predominance there. He received the posthumous title Sayin Khan (The Good, i.e., Late, Khan). Möngke appointed first Batu's son Sartaq (r. 1255–56) and then Sartaq's son Ula'achi (Ulaghchi, 1256–57) as Batu's successors, but both soon died, perhaps by poison, leaving the throne to Batu's brother Berke.

See also GOLDEN HORDE; KIEV, SIEGE OF; MUHI, BATTLE OF; RUSSIA AND THE MONGOL EMPIRE; SARAY AND NEW SARAY.

Further reading: W. Barthold, trans. John Andrew Boyle, "Batu," in *Encyclopaedia of Islam*, 2d ed., Vol. 1 (Leiden: E. J. Brill, 1960–), 1,105–1,106.

Baty *See* BATU.

Bayad (Bait) The ethnonym Bayad (rich ones, from *bayan*, rich) appears early in Inner Asian history among various Mongolian and Turkish peoples in related forms. In the *SECRET HISTORY OF THE MONGOLS*, the clan name Baya'ud appears among the Mongols, while the ethnonym Bayid appears in Central Siberia. Only the latter appears to be connected to the modern Bayad people of western Mongolia (*see* SIBERIA AND THE MONGOL EMPIRE).

The Bayad appear to be Siberian peoples subjugated by the DÖRBÖD tribe of the OIRATS. In 1753 they followed the Dörböd prince Tseren-Möngke (d. 1757) into submis-

sion to the QING DYNASTY. Like all the Oirat tribes, the Bayads were (and are) not a consanguineal unit but a political-ethnographic one, formed of at least 40 different *yasu*, or patrilineages, of the most diverse origins. Of the 14 BANNERS ruled by the Dörböds' Choros lineage princes, 10 were mostly Bayad in composition, giving rise to the phrase "the Ten Bayad."

Today the Bayad are found in six *sums* of UWS PROVINCE between Lakes Uws and Khyargas and the Tes River. They numbered 11,600 in 1929, 15,900 in 1956, and 39,200 in 1989.

Bayan (1281?–1340) *The last powerful Yuan dynasty minister to oppose Confucianism and cooperation with the Chinese*
A MERKID Mongol, Bayan served Prince Haishan in Mongolia from 1299 on, winning the title *ba'atur* (hero) for exploits against Chabar's troops (*see* QAIDU KHAN). With Haishan's enthronement in 1307, Bayan served in the department of state affairs and as overseer (DARUGHACHI) of the Ossetian (Asud) Right Guards. Under Haishan's successors Bayan held a variety of provincial posts.

In September 1328, as manager (*pingzhang*) in Henan, Bayan backed EL-TEMÜR's coup d'état that brought Haishan's son Tuq-Temür (r. 1328, 1329–32) to the throne; Bayan headed Tuq-Temür's KESHIG (imperial guard). After the successive deaths of Tuq-Temür and El-Temür, Bayan helped Budashiri, Tuq-Temür's QONGGIRAD widow, enthrone the late emperor's nephew Toghan-Temür (r. 1333–70). Bayan became supreme grand councillor (*da chengxiang*) and tutor for El-Tegüs, Tuq-Temür's son and the heir apparent.

From November 1335 Bayan tried to revive the old ethnic hierarchy, abolishing the Confucian examination system and reemphasizing restrictions against Chinese holding certain offices, bearing arms, or learning Mongol or SEMUREN (West and Central Asian) languages. At the same time he encouraged agriculture and reduced the oppressively high salt monopoly fees. All Confucians, Mongol and *semuren* as well as Chinese, opposed his anti-Confucian policies and blamed popular unrest on his discouragement of Confucian learning. Bayan's persecution of distinguished Mongol and *semu* opponents added to the opposition. Several incidents led Bayan to fear assassination from disgruntled Chinese, while wild rumors spread that he intended to execute all Chinese of the surnames Zhang, Wang, Liu, Li, and Zhao. While Bayan was outside the capital hunting, his nephew TOQTO'A (1314–56) on March 14, 1340, convinced the emperor to exile him. Bayan died a month later.

Bayan Chingsang (1236–1295) *The conqueror of South China under Qubilai Khan*
Bayan's Nichügün Baarin clan, one of CHINGGIS KHAN's old *NÖKÖR* families, had followed the Mongol army west to

Iran. In 1264 HÜLE'Ü, the Mongol ruler there, sent Bayan as his envoy to the court of QUBILAI KHAN in China. Bayan's appearance immediately impressed the emperor, who detained Bayan for his own service. Within a year Qubilai had married him to his empress CHABUI's niece and briefly appointed him junior grand councillor (*chengxiang* or *chingsang*).

In 1274, with the Song weakening, Qubilai reappointed him junior grand councillor and assigned him an army of 100,000 to conquer South China. Bayan Chingsang, with his hard-fighting junior colleague AJU, personally led the advance down the Han River. Using portage through lakes and canals to avoid the Song fortresses of Yingzhou (modern Zhongxiang) and Ezhou-Hanyang (modern Wuhan), Bayan and Aju's combined land–sea force, numbering 10,000 ships, defeated the 10,000 ships of the Song general Xia Gui at Yangluobao Fort (January 12, 1275) and the 130,000 men and 2,500 boats of the Song's supreme commander, Jia Sidao, at Dingjia Isle (March 19). By April the Yuan armies held Jiankang (modern Nanjing), and Qubilai, fearful of soldier deaths from the southern heat, called off all operations and summoned his generals to an imperial audience in SHANGDU in August 1275. Less worried about Song resistance than about minimizing destruction in the rich lower Chang (Yangtze), Qubilai diverted the aggressive Aju to besiege Yangzhou while Bayan moved on the Song capital at Lin'an (modern Hangzhou). Bayan was promoted to senior grand councillor, with Aju as his junior colleague.

The final assault on the Song began in late November, as Bayan Chingsang's army launched a three-pronged advance south from Zhenjiang. Stiffened by loyalist scholars and volunteers such as Wen Tianxiang (Wen T'ien-hsiang, 1236–83), the Song armies took their last stand in Changzhou city, which the Mongols first stormed and then massacred on December 6 after a two-day siege. Bayan's armies met no resistance as they camped before the Song capital on February 5, 1276, and he escorted the Song empresses north and was received in the victory celebrations at Shangdu on June 14, 1276.

During and after the conquest of the Song, Bayan Chingsang (Grand Councillor Bayan) achieved legendary status. Chinese songs and folklore spoke of him as "Hundred Eyes" (*bai yan* in Chinese), and his red banner could incite panic in Song troops by its sudden appearance. Even so, Qubilai's chief mandate to Bayan was to kill no more than necessary, and Changzhou was the only city where he ordered wholesale massacre. In 1311 a temple was dedicated to him in Lin'an by imperial decree.

During his stay in the south, the development of water transport, both inland and overseas, had impressed him, and in 1282 he advocated both the construction of canals in the north and the overseas transportation of southern grain to the capital. These proposals bore fruit, however, only after he had been dispatched to the Mongolian frontier.

In 1277–78 Bayan had been briefly sent to Mongolia to deal with a sudden crisis caused by the rebellion of several frontier princes. Afterward the situation steadily deteriorated under pressure from Qubilai's rival QAIDU (1236–1301) and the growing disloyalty of the frontier Mongols, aristocrats and commoners alike. Returning to Mongolia in 1285, Bayan faced serious supply problems, and he set his troops to supplementing their diet with steppe roots and their clothing with marmot skins. In 1287 he advised Qubilai to use Chinese troops against NAYAN'S REBELLION. Bayan's defensive strategy against Qaidu caused enemies at court to denounce him as sympathetic to the enemy. In 1292 Qubilai ordered him replaced by Öz-Temür (1242–95).

Bayan remained in Datong (modern Datong) in semidisgrace until January 1294, when Qubilai fell ill. Bayan was summoned to the emperor's side at DAIDU (modern Beijing), and when Qubilai died in February 1294 Bayan served as regent in the capital until May, when Qubilai's grandson Temür was elected great khan. Bayan died on January 11, 1295, covered with honors.

Further reading: Francis Woodman Cleaves, "The Biography of Bayan of the Bārin in the *Yüan shih*," *Harvard Journal of Asiatic Studies* 19 (1956): 185–303; C. C. Hsiao, "Bayan," in *In the Service of the Khan: Eminent Personalities of the Early Mongol-Yuan Period (1200–1300)*, ed. Igor de Rachewiltz et al. (Wiesbaden: Otto Harrassowitz, 1993), 584–607.

Bayan Khongor *See* BAYANKHONGOR PROVINCE.

Bayan Ülegei *See* BAYAN-ÖLGII PROVINCE.

Bayanchongor *See* BAYANKHONGOR PROVINCE.

Bayangol Mongol Autonomous Prefecture (Bayingolin, Bayinguoleng) The Mongol autonomous prefecture (subprovincial unit) of Bayangol lies in central Xinjiang, the Uighur autonomous region of China. The Mongol inhabitants are OIRATS or western Mongols, related to Russia's KALMYKS.

On July 14, 1954, four counties in the north of the traditional Karashahr district were made the Bayangol Mongol Autonomous Prefecture with its capital at Yanqi (the new name for Karashahr city). At that time Mongols were about 35 percent of the prefecture's population. This original or northern Bayangol territory stretches from the alpine pastures of Bayanbulag (Zultus), set 2,500 meters (8,200 feet) above sea level amid the snow-capped Tianshan Mountains, east long the Kaidu River to Bosten Lake, 1,048 meters (3,438 feet) above sea level. Hejing county occupies the uplands in the west, while Khoshud (Hoxud), Bohu (Bagrash), and Yanqi counties surround Bosten Lake. These four counties together occupy 55,600 square kilometers (21,470 square miles) and in 1999 had

403,618 inhabitants, who were 10 percent Mongol, 56 percent Chinese, 22 percent Uighur, and 11 percent Hui (Chinese-speaking Muslim). The Mongols of Bayangol were settled from Kalmykia in 1771: TORGHUDS in Hejing, and KHOSHUDS in the other three counties. Mongols totaled about 36,700 in 1982 and 40,623 in 1999; seven out of 10 are Torghud.

In 1960, as part of the administrative gerrymandering in minority regions during Mao Zedong's Great Leap Forward, Bayangol's capital was moved to Korla city, and the vast Korla district added to Bayangol's territory, thus re-creating the pre-1954 Karashahr district. The newly added Korla district, covering almost 425,000 square kilometers (164,100 square miles) of the arid Tarim Basin, was originally almost purely Uighur in ethnic composition; in 1999 its 608,641 people were 56 percent Chinese, 42 percent Uighur, and 2 percent Hui. The 3,918 Mongols in Korla in 1999 are white-collar employees and their families, who moved there after 1954 to work in the prefectural administration and cultural organs.

In northern Bayangol 54,019 hectares (133,481 acres) were cultivated in 1999, and total livestock (including pigs) was about 1,460,000 head, of which 949,800 were in Hejing county. About half of the Bayanbulag alpine pasture suffers from overgrazing. China's railroad system reached Korla in 1979.

See also FLIGHT OF THE KALMYKS; XINJIANG MONGOLS.

Bayanhongor *See* BAYANKHONGOR PROVINCE.

Bayankhongor province (Bayanhongor, Bayanchongor, Bayan Khongor) Created in 1942 out of South Khangai and Altai provinces, Bayankhongor lies in southwestern Mongolia. Its territory includes parts of KHALKHA Mongolia's prerevolutionary Zasagtu Khan and Sain Noyan provinces and ranges from the southern slopes of the KHANGAI RANGE, the easternmost spur of the ALTAI RANGE, and into the GOBI DESERT. The province has a short frontier with western Inner Mongolia in China. It has an area of 116,000 square kilometers (44,776 square miles) and is relatively dry. The population has grown from 42,100 in 1956 to 85,300 in 2000. The province is one of Mongolia's most purely pastoral, with the largest total herd (2,3375,700 head in 2000) and the most goats, raised particularly for CASHMERE (1,190,000 head). As a mostly *gobi*-type region, the number of camels is also relatively large (37,100 head). There is no significant agriculture. The center of the province is Bayankhongor town, with 22,100 people (2000).

Bayannuur league (Bayannur, Bayannao'r) Bayannuur league today includes the sparsely inhabited Urad BANNERS in Inner Mongolia's GOBI DESERT and the densely farmed Hetao region along the Huang (Yellow) River. The league covers 64,400 square kilometers (24,865 square miles) and has 1,562,560 inhabitants, of whom 65,592, or 4 percent were Mongols (1990). The capital is Linhe.

Bayannuur league was originally the name given in 1956 to what is now ALASHAN league. In 1958 the three Urad banners, previously part of ULAANCHAB league, and the Hetao district, previously a non-Mongol district within the INNER MONGOLIA AUTONOMOUS REGION, were added to it. In 1969 the Alashan banners were stripped from Inner Mongolia, and the Bayannuur league was left in its present form.

See also INNER MONGOLIANS; ORDOS.

Bayan-Ölgii province (Bayan-Ölgiy, Bajan-Ölgij, Bayan Ülegei) Mongolia's only majority non-Mongol province, Bayan-Ölgii was carved out of KHOWD and UWS provinces in 1940 in the far west of Mongolia to be a province for the Turkic-speaking KAZAKHS and the Mongolian-speaking ALTAI URIYANGKHAI. It has a long frontier with Xinjiang in China and the Altay Republic in Russia. The area was part of the Khowd frontier until 1906, when it became part of the Altai district. It was occupied by the Mongols in the 1911 RESTORATION of independence. Frequent border disputes with China and the continued moving back and forth of the Kazakh population over the frontier disturbed conditions until the final border demarcation in 1964. The province, covering 45,700 square kilometers (17,645 square miles), occupies the ALTAI RANGE and contains Mongolia's highest peak, Khüiten Uul (4,374 meters, 14,350 feet high). The population was 38,300 in 1956 and 94,600 in 2000, making it one of Mongolia's most densely inhabited rural provinces. The total herd of livestock is 1,310,400 head and has a typical dry-region composition, with relatively fewer horses and horned cattle and relatively more goats and sheep. The provincial capital of Ölgii has 28,100 inhabitants (2000 figures). Although the 1992 constitution recognizes only Mongolian as the official language, education and many social activities take place in Kazakh. The Kazakh percentage of the population steadily increased from 1940. In 1989 it reached 91.3 percent of the total population of 89,862, while the Altai Uriyangkhais were 5.7 percent, TUVANS 0.8 percent, and DÖRBÖD 1.5 percent. From 1992 to 2001 an estimated net 15,000 Kazakhs emigrated to newly independent Kazakhstan. The province's percentage of Kazakhs declined to 80 percent, while Altai Uriyangkhais increased to 17 percent. Unemployment, which was at Mongolia's worst in 1992 at 18.9 percent, has declined to 4.3 percent in 2000, slightly below the national average.

Further reading: Louisa Waugh, *Hearing Birds Fly: A Nomadic Year in Mongolia* (London: Little, Brown, 2003).

Bayan-Ölgiy *See* BAYAN-ÖLGII PROVINCE.

Bayingolin *See* BAYANGOL MONGOL AUTONOMOUS PREFECTURE.

bKa'-'gyur and bsTan-'gyur (Kanjur or Kangyur and Tanjur or Tengyur)   The translation of the Tibetan Buddhist canon, formed by bKa'-'gyur (translated scriptures) and the bsTan-'gyur (translated canonical treatises), was a major achievement of Mongolian Buddhism.

In Indian Buddhism, scriptures, or the "word of the Buddha" (*buddhavacana*), were classified into "three baskets" (Sanskrit, *Tripitaka*): sutras (Mongolian, *sudur*), or discourses on liberation; *vinaya* (Mongolian, *winai*), or the code of discipline; and *abhidharma* (Mongolian, *iledte nom*, or *abidarma*) or systematic expositions of doctrine. The Chinese Buddhist canon preserved this threefold structure.

The Tibetans did not organize their extensive translations of the scriptures and Indian Buddhist scholarship until the reign of the Mongol Yuan emperor Ayurbarwada (titled Buyantu, 1311–20). With the support of Ayurbarwada's Tibetan chaplain 'Jam-dbyangs Bagshi, sNar-thang Monastery (near modern Xigazê) produced the first edition of the canon. The first and subsequent Tibetan editors combined all the "word of the Buddha" into the bKa'-'gyur (translated word; Mongolian, *Ganjuur*), divided into *vinaya*, sutra, and tantra (Mongolian, *ündüsü* or *dandra/dandris*). The treatises (*shastra*; Mongolian, *shastir*) and commentaries of Indian Buddhist writers such as Nagarjuna, Shantideva, and Ashvaghosha were organized into the bsTan-'gyur (translated treatises; Mongolian, *Danjuur*). The bKa'-'gyur contains 108 volumes and the bsTan-'gyur 225; together they include roughly 4,567 separate works. The first printing of the bKa'-'gyur was in Beijing in 1410 under the Chinese MING DYNASTY (1368–1644).

After a decline in Mongolian Buddhism in the 15th and 16th centuries, the newly converted ALTAN KHAN (1508–82) patronized Ayushi Güüshi (fl. 1578–1609), Shiregetü Güüshi Chorjiwa (fl. 1578–1618), and other translators in his capital Guihua (modern HÖHHOT). In 1587 Ayushi Güüshi created a complete set of new *galig* (transcription) letters to enable the UIGHUR-MONGOLIAN SCRIPT to render all the different letters of Sanskrit and Tibetan. This was important to ensure the proper pronunciation of the *dharanis* (Mongolian, *tarni*), or spells, that sealed initiations and meditative visualizations. A complete bKa'-'gyur translation was said to have been finished in 1607 under Altan's grandson, Namudai Sechen Khan (Chürüke, 1586–1607), but no copies have survived. Some treatises from the bsTan-'gyur were also translated.

LIGDAN KHAN (1604–34), as part of his program of reviving the YUAN DYNASTY, commissioned Gungga-Odser to produce a complete bKa'-'gyur translation in 1628–29. Gungga-Odser's team mostly appropriated the work of the Höhhot translators, often excising the previous translators' names and introducing their own. Their final product was a special manuscript edition in gold letters on a blue ground and five plainer manuscript copies.

Only a very small number of individual chapters from this edition have survived.

In 1717–20 the Qing dynasty's Kangxi emperor (1662–1722) sponsored the block printing of the complete Mongolian bKa'-'gyur in Beijing, based on Ligdan Khan's manuscript edition. A Tu (Monguor) INCARNATE LAMA from western Gansu, the Tuguan Khutugtu, Agwang-Choiji-Jamsu (Tibetan, Ngag-dbang Chos-kyi rGya-mtsho, 1680–1735), headed an editorial committee composed of mostly Inner Mongolian lamas resident in Beijing.

In 1742–49 the Qianlong emperor (1736–96) sponsored the translation of the bsTan-'gyur. The chief of the editorial committee, the Second JANGJIYA KHUTUGTU Rolbidorji (1716–86), had a very low opinion of the existing translations. As a prolegomena to his work, he and his large team, including Inner Mongolian translators such as DUKE GOMBOJAB and Tibetan specialists in particular fields such as sculpture, medicine, and linguistics, first created a terminological dictionary, the *Merged garkhu-yin oron* (Font of Scholars; Tibetan, *Dag-yig mkhas-pa'i 'byung-gnas*). Copies of the printed Mongolian bsTan-'gyur are today very rare.

Despite the translations, the vast majority of monasteries performed services in Tibetan, and the coveted bKa'-'gyur remained much easier to obtain in the Tibetan language than in Mongolian. When the Eighth Jibzundamba Khutugtu sponsored a new printing of the bKa'-'gyur in Khüriye (*see* ULAANBAATAR) in 1908–10, it was in Tibetan, not Mongolian. In any case, only a few monks went beyond the often highly able Tibetan-language handbooks and commentaries, and copies of the full canon were not the basis of practical instruction. Even so, the importance of the bKa'-'gyur is seen even in Mongolian EPICS, in which the hero's bride often brings a copy of the canon in her dowry.

See also LITERATURE; SECOND CONVERSION; TIBET AND THE MONGOL EMPIRE; TIBETAN CULTURE IN MONGOLIA; TU LANGUAGE AND PEOPLE.

Further reading: Walther Heissig, *A Lost Civilization: The Mongols Rediscovered*, trans. D. J. S. Thomson (London: Thames and Hudson, 1966); Karénina Kollmar-Paulenz, "A Note on the Mongolian Translator Ayusi Güsi," in *Tractata Tibetica et Mongolica*, eds. Karénina Kollmar-Paulenz and Christian Peter (Wiesbaden: Otto Harrassowitz, 2002), 177–187.

Black Death   The Mongol Empire may have played a pivotal role in spreading the bubonic plague, which convulsed its realms and ushered in the Eurasiawide catastrophe of the mid-14th century.

By 1304 the various successor states of the divided MONGOL EMPIRE had reached a new period of stability. Traditional Mongol policy subsidized long-distance commerce by plowing regressive taxation into capital for tax-exempt merchant partners (ORTOQ), who operated with government guarantees of their profit and safety. Indian Ocean sea trade and Inner Asian caravans linked China, Central Asia, India, the Middle East, and Europe. The increase of international trade created the conditions for transfer of diseases.

The European Black Death began in the Genoese port city of Caffa (Feodosiya) in the CRIMEA, whence Italian traders carried goods from the Mongol GOLDEN HORDE all over the Mediterranean. The Crimean port cities paid tribute but were often in conflict with the inland Mongol rulers. In 1346 plague broke out among Golden Horde soldiers besieging Caffa, who catapulted the bodies of the dead into the city. Italian trading ships then carried the plague all over the Mediterranean, hitting Alexandria, Aleppo, and Marseilles in 1347 and Cairo, Paris, and London by 1348.

Although the plague spreads to human populations from fleas that infest black rats, the plague bacillus, *Pasteurella pestis,* is fatal to humans and rats and hence needs a separate long-term reservoir. In nature it exists as an endemic disease in burrowing rodent populations. In the 20th century, for example, after spreading by ship from Hong Kong to port cities of North and South America, it became nativized among Andean and Rocky Mountain ground squirrels and marmots. Since plague outbreaks occasionally reached the Mediterranean but never became a constant threat before the great outbreak of 1347, the plague bacillus, now endemic among marmots in the neighboring Black Sea steppe zone, probably became nativized there only in the 14th century. From then on the burrowing rodents of the Black Sea and Caspian steppes served as reservoirs for constant outbreaks in western Eurasia until trade and lifestyle changes occurred in the 17th century.

The 14th-century Black Death first appeared in Mongol-ruled China. From 1313 a series of epidemics struck Henan province; they culminated in 1331 with an epidemic that supposedly killed nine-tenths of the population. Epidemics broke out in coastal provinces in 1345–46. Finally, in 1351 massive epidemics began to strike throughout China yearly up to 1362, causing catastrophic population decline. William McNeill has thus speculated that the plague was originally native to burrowing rodents of the Himalayan foothills. The Mongols, by joining YUNNAN on the southeastern skirts of the Himalayas to China proper and hunting marmots there, inadvertently transmitted the plague to Henan and the Chinese heartland by 1331, if not before. From there Mongol activity introduced it into the marmot colonies of Inner Asia, whence it began to spread west. European and Muslim writers virtually all recorded the plague as beginning in China and then crossing the steppe to the Crimea. Excavations of a Christian cemetery near Ysyk-Köl Lake (Kyrgyzstan) suggest a devastating outbreak of plague in 1338–39. Muslim writers noted the progress of the plague from KHORAZM in 1345 to the center of the Golden Horde in 1346 and south to Mongol soldiers in Azerbaijan in 1346–47. Mongol military operations then spread it to Mosul and Baghdad in 1349. Early outbreaks in Sindh had probably followed caravan routes south from Khorazm; evidence of an Indian Ocean transmission route is slim.

In recent centuries, while poorer Mongols continue to enjoy marmots as food and sell their pelts, hunters have followed rigorous customary rules against hunting sick or weak individuals. The Tu (Monguor) nationality in the Qinghai province of China even prohibit the eating of marmot, saying it is to them what pork is to Muslims. A scholar-lama of the Tu, Sumpa mKhan-po Ishi-Baljur (1704–87), observed that bubonic plague spread from marmots (see MEDICINE, TRADITIONAL). The influx of Chinese hunters, unfamiliar with the danger of sick marmots, sparked plague epidemics in Manchuria in 1911 and 1921, and the hardships after the fall of the Japanese Empire in 1945 led to another outbreak of bubonic plague, which devastated Inner Mongolia.

See also CHAGHATAY KHANATE; INDIA AND THE MONGOLS; TU LANGUAGE AND PEOPLE; WESTERN EUROPE AND THE MONGOLS; YUAN DYNASTY.

Further reading: Michael W. Dols, *Black Death in the Middle East* (Princeton, N.J.: Princeton University Press, 1977); William H. McNeill, *Plagues and Peoples* (New York: Anchor Book/Doubleday, 1998).

Blue Horde (White Horde, Princes of the Left Hand)

This autonomous area within the Golden Horde, in central and eastern Kazakhstan, eventually nurtured forces that would overthrow the Golden Horde's rulers and create a host of successor states.

The patrimony of CHINGGIS KHAN's eldest son, JOCHI was known to the Russians as the GOLDEN HORDE. This territory was itself soon divided into two wings, right and left, under the supreme rule of the family of BATU, Jochi's second son. Four of Jochi's sons, including Hordu (the eldest) and Toqa-Temür, were the "princes of the left hand," the east, while the rest formed the right, or western, half under the Batids. The "left hand" is called the "Blue Horde" in Russian sources, but the "White Horde" in Timurid sources. While Western scholarly tradition has favored the second, the use of "Blue Horde" by Ötemish Hajji (fl. 1555), a Khorazmian scholar intimately familiar with the Horde's oral traditions, indicates the Russian usage is correct.

Although displaced as Jochi's successor by order of Chinggis Khan, Jochi's eldest son, Hordu (fl. 1225–52), headed the "princes of the left hand" and received a *tümen,* nominally 10,000, as his half-share of Jochi's army. Hordu's main camp was at Alakol Lake, and his territory contained no significant cities, although a number of small farming villages in its territory have been excavated. The fur trade in Siberia was an important part of its economy (see SIBERIA AND THE MONGOL EMPIRE). The cities along the Syr Dar'ya, held first by Shiban of the "right hand" and later by the Chaghatayids, came under Blue Horde rule after 1320. At first the Jochid "left hand" was not sharply separate from the rest of the empire. Hordu participated in the western campaign of 1236–42, his son Qurumshi nomadized along the Dnieper at least to 1256, and in 1252 Hordu assigned his son Quli to represent the Golden Horde during HÜLE'Ü's expedition against Baghdad.

In the Mongol civil wars after 1260, Hordu's successors followed the policy set by the rulers of the Golden Horde as a whole, supporting first ARIQ-BÖKE and then QAIDU against QUBILAI KHAN. From 1284, however, Hordu's immensely fat grandson, Qonichi (fl. 1277–96), turned away from Qaidu to establish friendly relations with the Yuan and the IL-KHANATE, receiving luxury gifts and grain from the Yuan as reward. Qaidu then sponsored a rival, Köbeleg (or possibly Küilüg), against Hordu's son Bayan (fl. 1299–1304), leading to civil war.

In Bayan's time the leading non-Chinggisid commanders (NOYAN) were all of Mongol clans: Keniges, QONGGI-RAD (later Turkish Qunghrat), Jajirad, and Besüd. RASHID-UD-DIN also mentions 4,000 Jalayir clansmen commanded by OIRATs. Hordu's family were QUDA (marriage allies) of Qonggirad as well as of the Jajirad, KEREYID, NAIMAN, MERKID, TATARS, Arghun (probably a branch of the Önggüd in KHORAZM), and Qipchaqs, while another Jochid married a woman of the Töles (a Siberian people). From Qonichi's time, at least, the Blue Horde had its own KESHIG or royal guard. Hungarians, Circassians, and probably Russians served as discrete units in Bayan's armies.

Under Bayan's successors Sasi-Buqa (r. 1313–20/21) and Irzan (r. 1320/21–44/45), the Blue Horde's center moved south to the Syr Dar'ya. Previously, the descendants of Shiban, easternmost of the "right hand" princes, held the Syr Dar'ya valley, but now they apparently joined the "left hand." Irzan was also the first Muslim ruler of the Blue Horde, sponsoring urban madrasahs (schools), mosques, and Sufi (mystic) lodges. Nevertheless, the Horduid lineage did not survive the BLACK DEATH that traversed the Golden Horde from 1338 to 1346. By 1362 Urus Khan (d. 1377), of the line of Toqa-Temür, was ruling the Blue Horde from Sighnaq (near modern Chiili).

The western half of the Golden Horde was hit even harder by the plague, however, and Blue Horde lineages (including the Shibanids) streamed west to seek their fortune. In 1360 a Shibanid, Khizr (Khydyr) Khan, overthrew Khan Nawroz (1360) and occupied the Golden Horde's capital of New Saray. Meanwhile, Bulat-Temür and his son Arab-Shah, also Blue Horde princes, occupied Kazan. In 1373 Urus Khan overthrew Khizr Khan's family. Urus Khan and his sons were overthrown in 1377 by another Toqa-Temürid, TOQTAMISH (fl. 1375–1405), and his commander in chief (beglerbegi), Edigü (d. 1420), of the Manghit (Mongolian, MANGGHUD) clan, both protegés

of the Central Asian conqueror TIMUR (Tamerlane). Toqtamish went on to occupy Saray in 1378 and defeat Emir Mamaq (Mamay) of the Qiyat (Kiyad) in 1380, the last powerful defender of the "right hand" leadership.

Despite Toqtamish's later overthrow by Timur (1395), the Blue Horde Chinggisids continued to dominate the Qipchaq steppe, yet the tribal composition had changed considerably from the time of Bayan. Toqtamish's four chief clans were the Shirin, Baarin, Arghun, and Qipchaq. The Shirin and Qipchaqs were local Turkish clans, but the Baarin were descendants of the Mongol myriarchs (commanders of 10,000) on the Irtysh (see SIBERIA AND THE MONGOL EMPIRE). These clans under Toqa-Temürid dynasties formed the tribal core of both the Crimean (1449–1783) and the Kazan (1445–1552) khanates.

East of the Volga Shibanid princes dominated the old Blue Horde and western Siberia, forming khanates in the course of the 15th and 16th centuries: the khanate of Tyumen' that emerged under Ibrahim Ibaq (fl. 1473–1500) and the Uzbeks (or Özbegs) that coalesced around Abu'l-Khayr (b. 1412, r. 1428–68) and occupied Mawarannahr (Transoxiana) in 1512. Meanwhile, Urus Khan's family fled east to escape Abu'l-Khayr's rule, becoming KAZAKHS (from qazaq, freebooter) on the border of MOGHULISTAN; they returned to dominate the steppe under Qasim Khan (d. 1523). Non-Chinggisid rulers also played a major role: the Manghits (or Nogays) on the Ural River, the Qonghrats (Qonggirads) in Khorazm, and the Taybughids (probably of KEREYID ancestry) around Sibir' (modern Tobolsk). These ethnopolitical confederations formed part of the origin of the modern Uzbek, Kazakh, Tatar, Bashkir (Bashkort), Karakalpak, and Nogay nationalities.

Further reading: Th. T. Allsen, "The Princes of the Left Hand: An Introduction to the History of the *Ulus* of Orda in the Thirteenth and Early Fourteenth Centuries," *Archivum Euraiae Medii Aevi* 5 (1985 [1989]): 5–40; Allen Frank, *The Siberian Chronicles and the Taybughid Biys of Sibir* (Bloomington, Ind.: Research Institute for Inner Asian Studies, 1994).

Bodô (Dogsomyn Bodoo) (1885–1922) *A leader of the 1921 Revolution who resigned as prime minister under criticism and was later shot as a counterrevolutionary*
Bodô was born in the Maimaching (Chinatown) of Khüriye (modern ULAANBAATAR), as a member of the GREAT SHABI or ecclesiastical serfs. He became a clerk in the office of the ERDENI SHANGDZODBA, or the administration of the Bogda's (Holy One, the Jibzundamba Khutugtu) estate. Educated as a lama, he knew Mongolian, Tibetan, Manchu, and Chinese. In 1913 he left to become a teacher of Mongolian in the Russian-Mongolian Translators' School and helped TSYBEN ZHAMTSARANOVICH ZHAMTSARANO publish his progressive journal. Bodô wrote both Buddhist *surgal shilüg* (teaching verses) and

Chinese-style fiction (*see* DIDACTIC POETRY and CHINESE FICTION).

With the REVOCATION OF AUTONOMY in autumn 1919, Bodô's yurt in the Consulate Terrace area became the center of a secret anti-Chinese *nam* (faction or party), including Chagdurjab (D. Chagdarjaw, 1880–1922), a wealthy lama friend with a wide social network, MARSHAL CHOIBALSANG, a Russian-trained interpreter, and occasionally local Russian Bolshevik sympathizers. The group eventually merged with another anti-Chinese *nam*, the East Khüriye group, to form the People's Party of Outer Mongolia. On July 27, 1920, Bodô and Chagdurjab were sent to Russia to appeal for assistance. Joined by other party organizers, Bodô with Danzin of the East Khüriye group took the lead in negotiations with the Soviet authorities in Irkutsk. By this time Bodô had already emerged in clashes with Danzin as the most radical of the leaders, while Danzin criticized him as vain and intellectually arrogant.

In September Bodô returned to Mongolia with Dogsum (D. Dogsom, 1884–1941) of the East Khüriye group. Chinese arrests made revolutionary activity impossible, and he escaped east, where he was impressed into BARON ROMAN FEDOROVICH VON UNGERN-STERNBERG's White Russian army, which had invaded Mongolia. In mid-March 1921 he escaped the Whites and returned to the Mongolian border town of Altanbulag, which had become the base for the Soviet-allied People's Party. On April 16 he replaced the unpopular Chagdurjab as prime minister of the provisional government and on July 8 delivered with his comrades the terms of the new government to the Bogda.

Bodô became prime minister and concurrent foreign minister of the new constitutional monarchy and deputy party chairman under Danzin. From September 29, while Danzin and GENERAL SÜKHEBAATUR were away in Russia negotiating a friendship treaty, Soviet advisers described Bodô as the most reliable and forward looking of the revolutionaries. On his own authority he brought Chagdurjab back into the government as his deputy and organized a People's Mutual-Aid Cooperative on October 16, a plan that Chagdurjab had briefly attempted in 1918. Danzin had preferred to leave constitutional arrangements unsettled, but Bodô had the Bogda approve a nine-article "sworn treaty" on November 1. Later, his frequent contact with the Bogda's court, the clemency shown to the alleged lama-conspirators led by Shagja Lama, and his publication of a controversial note by Danzin treating the constitutional monarchy as a temporary expedient made him look pro-clerical.

As a result, when Danzin returned on December 22, he had more than enough ammunition for his insistence that Bodô was "fickle and weak." Ill and depressed, Bodô twice tried to resign; the second time, on January 7, 1922, his resignation was gratefully accepted by Danzin, Sükhebaatur, and ELBEK-DORZHI RINCHINO. He refused an appointment as ambassador to Moscow saying he would "not abandon his country or religion" and returned to private life, living with his wife in the countryside near Ulaanbaatar. That spring the youth league, headed by Bodô's pupil Choibalsang, began cutting off "feudal" ornaments on Mongolian clothing: large cuffs, women's jewelry, and high shoulders. The resulting storm of controversy was blamed on Bodô. In August he was arrested by the Office of Internal Security and investigated by a Soviet adviser, Sorokin. Bodô's first statement maintained his innocence, but in a later statement, after torture, he confessed to plotting to overthrow the government. Upon approval by the government (including his old enemies Danzin and Sükhebaatur) Bodô and 14 others, including Chagdurjab, were executed without trial on August 31.

See also JIBZUNDAMBA KHUTUGTU, EIGHTH; 1921 REVOLUTION; REVOLUTIONARY PERIOD; THEOCRATIC PERIOD.

Bodoo, Dogsomyn *See* BODÔ.

Bogda Khan Period *See* THEOCRATIC PERIOD.

Bolad Chingsang (d. 1313) *Ambassador from the Yuan to the Il-Khanate and cultural broker*
Bolad's father, of the Dörben clan, served as imperial *ba'urchi* (steward) and guards commander for CHINGGIS KHAN. In the 1240s Prince Qubilai (1215–94) arranged tutoring for Bolad from the Chinese scholar Zhang Dehui (1197–1274), and Bolad became fluent in Chinese. After Qubilai's election as khan in 1260, Bolad served as *ba'urchi,* designer of court ritual, censor, and chief of the agricultural administration. Bolad also served as judge in the sensitive cases of ARIQ-BÖKE (1264) and the murder of AHMAD (1282). From 1283–85 Bolad went as Qubilai's envoy to the Mongol Il-Khan Arghun (1284–91) in the Middle East. His return was blocked by QAIDU's insurgency, and he remained in the Il-Khanate. Bolad received command in Arghun's KESHIG (royal guard) and a royal concubine as a new wife. Subsequently, he served as consultant on institutions and usages in China and at Qubilai's court, including on paper money (*chao*) and on Mongol customs, history, and genealogy. In 1302 GHAZAN KHAN made him commander of a new guards unit of redeemed Mongol slave boys. Under Öljeitü (1304–16), Bolad achieved great influence as *chingsang* (*chengxiang,* grand councillor) and *aqa* (elder). Working closely with RASHID-UD-DIN, Bolad Chingsang was a major purveyor of Chinese culture in Iran.

See also QUBILAI KHAN.

Further reading: Thomas T. Allsen, *Culture and Conquest in Mongol Eurasia* (Cambridge: Cambridge University Press, 2001).

Bolor erikhe (*Bolor Erike; Bolor Erkh*) The *Bolor erikhe* (Crystal Rosary), written in 1774–75, was the first

Mongolian chronicle to use the Chinese-language sources on the Mongol YUAN DYNASTY. Its author, Rashipungsug, was a third-rank TAIJI and administrator (*tusalagchi*) of Baarin Right Banner (modern Bairin Youqi) in JUU UDA league. His only other known work is a history of a local temple.

After discussing the nature and origin of the Mongols, Rashipungsug traces the Mongol khans from their legendary ancestors among the Indian and Tibetan kings, through CHINGGIS KHAN, to Ligdan Khan's death in 1634. A fourth chapter gives the genealogy of the descendants of BATU-MÖNGKE DAYAN KHAN and the fifth chapter that of the other Mongolian *zasags* (banner rulers).

While drawing heavily on previous Mongolian chronicles, for the period from 1206 to 1368 Rashipungsug incorporated extensive selections from 1) the *YUAN SHI*'s basic annals, 2) the *Zizhi tongjian gangmu* (*xu bian*), and 3) the *Gangjian huizuan*, all MING DYNASTY (1368–1644) works available in Mongolian or Manchu translation. Rashipungsug discussed contradictions in his sources, criticized Chinese prejudices against the Mongols and Confucian prejudices against Buddhism, and defended apparent blemishes in the record of the Mongolian rulers. While by no means a critical historian, he illustrated the new intellectual horizons opened by contact with Chinese culture and furnished the background for the later Inner Mongolian author, Injannashi's, rejection of blind filiopietism.

Bonan   *See* BAO'AN LANGUAGE AND PEOPLE.

Bo'orchu (Borghochin)   *Chinggis Khan's earliest and most trusted* nökör, *or companion, and one of four heads of his* keshig, *or imperial guard*

Bo'orchu was the only son of Naqu the Rich, a herdsman of the Arulad lineage, one of the free Dürlükin (non-noble) lineages of the MONGOL TRIBE. Once, when Temüjin (later CHINGGIS KHAN) was tracking horse thieves who had stolen his eight geldings, he passed Bo'orchu milking his father's mares. Bo'orchu, then 13 years old, immediately joined Temüjin in the chase, and they recovered the horses. Bo'orchu returned home, but with his father's blessing soon joined Temüjin's camp as his first NÖKÖR, or companion. From then on Bo'orchu shared all the conqueror's hardships. Accounts of Chinggis's rise all contain vivid stories of the sufferings Bo'orchu loyally endured although the details differ. Bo'orchu, with Boroghul, MUQALI, and Chila'un of the Suldus, formed the khan's "four steeds." After Chinggis Khan's coronation in 1206, Bo'orchu received command of the entire right wing of the army. Bo'orchu, like the other "four steeds," also shared titular command of the KESHIG, or imperial guard, governing it for three days out of 12. Bo'orchu received 17,300 households in North China's Guangping (near Handan) as appanage. Bo'orchu's

Arulad clansmen served the khans in high positions both in the YUAN DYNASTY in China and in the CHAGHATAY KHANATE in Turkestan.

boqta   Virtually all travelers in the MONGOL EMPIRE remarked on the *boqta*, the headdress worn by married Mongol women. Portraits of Mongol rulers from both Iran and China in the 13th and 14th centuries show this striking piece of clothing. The *boqta* (modern Mongolian *bogt*) had a round base that fit on top of the head, a tall column, and a square top. On the square top was fitted a tuft formed of willow branches or rods covered by green felt. The framework of the *boqta* was light wood, covered with green or red silk. The column and the tuft at the top were decorated according to the wearer's rank and wealth: peacock feathers, mallard or kingfisher down, or precious stones. The *boqta* stood just over a meter or about 3.5 feet high. The *boqta* was worn over a hood into which the wearer would put up her hair in a chignon and was tied on below the chin. Wearing the *boqta* was so closely associated with the status of a married lady that *boqtala-* (modern *bogtlo-*), "to put on the *boqta*," became a synonym for marriage. The *boqta* may be the model for other high headdresses found in Europe and the Middle East during the late Middle Ages, such as the Flemish *hennin*. The *boqta* disappeared sometime before the late 16th century. Fashion designers in Mongolia have recently included *boqta*-style hats in their designs.

See also CLOTHING AND DRESS; FAMILY; JEWELRY.

Borghochin   *See* BO'ORCHU.

Borjigid (Borjigin)   The clan of CHINGGIS KHAN, named the Borjigid or, in a narrower sense, the Kiyad, formed the ruling class among the Mongols, Kazakhs, and other peoples of Inner Asia. (Borjigin and Kiyan are singular forms, while Borjigid and Kiyad are the plural. Kiyan/Kiyad is spelled in Turkish and Middle Mongolian as Qiyan/Qiyat.) Recent genetic research has confirmed that as many as 16 million men from Manchuria to Afghanistan may have Borjigid-Kiyad ancestry.

IN THE MONGOL TRIBE

The clan names Borjigid and Kiyad, which appear to be synonymous, were both applied to the leading lineage within the 12th-century MONGOL TRIBE. Sometimes they were used as a general term for all branches of the dominant *Niru'un* ("backbone") patrilineage of the Mongol tribe, while at other times they were applied only to the narrower branch that produced the khans. The *Niru'un* moiety contained about 20 major sublineages, all claiming common ancestry, although controversies were rife over the legitimacy of this or that sublineage's inclusion.

As in the Türk ancestor myths, supernatural wolf descent justified Borjigid supremacy. The patrilineage began with Blueish Wolf (Börte Chino'a) and his consort Fallow Doe (Gho'ai Maral), and the supernatural animal motif was repeated when ALAN GHO'A, the Fair, the widowed wife of Blueish Wolf's 11th-generation descendant, Dobun Mergen, was impregnated by a ray of light, which metamorphosed into a "yellow dog" (dog here is probably a euphemism for wolf). Alan the Fair's youngest son became the ancestor of the later Borjigid.

IN THE MONGOL EMPIRE

The rise of Chinggis Khan narrowed the scope of the Borjigid-Kiyad clans sharply. Virtually all of his uncles and first cousins had died, and from then on only the descendants of YISÜGEI BA'ATUR (i.e., Chinggis and his brothers) formed the real Borjigid. This separation was emphasized by the intermarriage of Chinggis's descendants with the Barulas, Baarin, MANGGHUD, and other branches of the original Borjigid. (As patrilineages were exogamous, the fact of intermarriage made clans *qari,* or foreign.) In the western khanates the Yürkin (Jürkin) and perhaps other lineages near to Chinggis's lineage used the clan name Kiyad or Qiyat but did not share in the privileges of the Chinggisids.

Within the empire the descendants of Chinggis's four brothers (Qasar, Qachi'un, Temüge Odchigin, and his half-brother, Belgütei) lived in the east along both sides of the GREATER KHINGGAN RANGE, while his sons JOCHI, CHA'ADAI, and ÖGEDEI KHAN had their appanages west of the ALTAI RANGE. The reigning khan and/or descendants of Chinggis's youngest son, TOLUI, held the middle. Family politics later led to the dispersal of the Ögedeid line and the creation of new Toluid centers in North China and in the Middle East.

In 1335, with the disintegration of the IL-KHANATE, the first of numerous non–Borjigid-Kiyad dynasties appeared. Established by QUDA (marriage partners) of the Kiyad rulers, these dynasties included the Suldus (*see* CHUBAN) and JALAYIR dynasties in the Middle East, the Barulas dynasties in Central Asia and India (*see* TIMUR), the Mangghud and QONGGIRAD dynasties in the GOLDEN HORDE and Central Asia, and the OIRATS in western Mongolia. Yet the Chinggisid Kiyad continued to rule in the CRIMEA, Kazan', Kazakhstan, and MOGHULISTAN until the Russian and Chinese conquest. The Qiyat clan name is still found among the KAZAKHS, Uzbeks, and Karakalpaks.

After the expulsion of the Toluid dynasty from China in 1368, the emperors in Mongolia faced repeated challenges from rival Borjigid descendants as well as from the non-Borjigid Oirat. Meanwhile, descendants of Chinggis Khan's brothers, Qasar and Belgütei, surrendered to the Ming in the 1380s and became tributary princes of the THREE GUARDS. (Descendants of Temüge Odchigin nomadized with the Belgüteids.) By 1470 virtually all these lines were severely weakened, and Mongolia was in almost total chaos.

BORJIGID RULE IN MONGOLIA

Under BATU-MÖNGKE DAYAN KHAN (1480?–1517?) a broad Borjigid revival reestablished Borjigid supremacy among the Mongols proper and even influenced the western Oirats. Among the Khalkha and in western Inner Mongolia, the descendants of Dayan Khan proliferated to become a new ruling class. The eastern Khorchins were under the Qasarids, and the Ongni'ud and Abagha Mongols under the Belgüteids and Odchiginids (*see* JUU UDA; SHILIIN GOL). Meanwhile, a fragment of the Qasarids deported by the Oirats became the KHOSHUDS, the only component tribe in the Oirat confederacy to claim Borjigid ancestry.

The QING DYNASTY (1636–1912) formalized the class distinction between the Borjigid ruling class (whether Chinggisid or of the fraternal lineages), called TAIJI, and their subjects. Genealogies of the Borjigid of each banner were updated triennially. *Taijis* had the right to certain services from their subjects and were distinguished from them by distinguishing marks, such as rank buttons, while only their wives could wear a sleeveless outercoat, or *uuji.* The Borjigid generally numbered about 10 percent to 20 percent of the male lay population, although in some BANNERS or districts they reached as much as 42 percent.

As an exogamous patrilineage, the Borjigid generally married either commoners or the *taiji* from southeastern Inner Mongolia's KHARACHIN and Monggoljin banners (*see* FUXIN MONGOL AUTONOMOUS COUNTY), who were not Borjigid. By the 18th century, however, Chinggisid Borjigid were also taking wives from the KHORCHIN *taiji* and other fraternal lineages, despite disapproval from rigorists such as Rashipungsug (fl. 1775; *see* BOLOR ERIKHE).

In every banner the *taiji* traditionally gathered for clan sacrifices carried on in various manners, depending on the influence of Buddhism, CONFUCIANISM, or the Mongol native religion. These sacrifices were dedicated not only to Chinggis or his brothers but also to more recent ancestors of the Borjigid nobility, such as KHUTUGTAI SECHEN KHUNG-TAIJI in Üüshin banner and ABATAI KHAN in Khalkha. The largest of these clan sacrifices occurred at the EIGHT WHITE YURTS in Ordos. Some were open to all Mongols, but others were open only to the *taiji.*

IN THE MODERN ERA

The linking of Borjigid descent to the privileges of aristocracy made them a target of attack for 20th-century revolutionary governments. In Mongolia CLAN NAMES were replaced by PATRONYMICS in an effort to break down class distinctions. The democratization of the cult of Chinggis Khan also diluted the previous close link of Borjigid status with Chinggis Khan. Even so, when the Mongolian government decided to revive clan names in 1998, many if not most of the Mongols preferred the name Borjigid. In Inner Mongolia the Borjigid or Kiyad name became the basis for many Chinese surnames. In eastern Inner Mongolia *taiji*s took the surname Bao (from Borjigid), and in ORDOS Qi (from Kiyad).

See also APPANAGE SYSTEM; KINSHIP SYSTEM.

Further reading: Tatiana Zergal et al., "The Genetic Legacy of the Mongols," *American Journal of Human Genetics* 72 (2003): 717–721.

Borotala Mongol Autonomous Prefecture (Bortala)

Borotala is a Mongol autonomous prefecture, or subprovincial unit, situated within Xinjiang, China's autonomous region for the Uighur nationality. Covering more than 27,000 square kilometers (10,425 square miles), the prefecture centers on the valley of the Borotala River draining into Ebi Nuur Lake, which lies 189 meters (620 feet) above sea level. The Borotala valley is flanked by the Kökechin Mountains to the south and the Alatau Mountains to the northwest, whose peaks soar to more than 4,000 meters (13,100 feet). Sayram Lake, 2,073 meters (6,801 feet) above sea level, is a major tourist attraction. The prefecture is divided into two counties, Wenquan and Jinghe, and a municipality, Borotala (Chinese, Bole). Since 1990 railways linking Kazakhstan and Xinjiang have passed through Jinghe.

Despite being a Mongol autonomous unit, the prefecture's 26,448 Mongols are only 6.6 percent of its 403,733 people (1999 figures) and are outnumbered by Chinese (66 percent), Uighurs (13 percent), and KAZAKHS (10 percent). In 1982 the 21,500 Mongols were 7.4 percent of the population.

The original core of Borotala's Mongol population was more than 1,800 CHAKHAR soldiers assigned to garrison the area in 1757–67 after its conquest by China's QING DYNASTY. The area's remaining ZÜNGHARS were attached to the Chakhar banners (*see* EIGHT BANNERS). The area of Jinghe county in the east was settled in 1771 by Torghud Oirats fleeing from the Volga (*see* FLIGHT OF THE KALMYKS). With the Chinese Communist entry into Xinjiang, Borotala was made an autonomous prefecture on July 1, 1954, at which time Mongols were 25 percent of the population. Total livestock (including pigs) number 146,000 head (1999). Since 1950 the Chinese People's Liberation Army has operated military farms throughout the lowlands, and farmland has increased 8.9 times, to 63,800 hectares, or 157,650 acres (1999). Ebi Nuur Lake is drying out, and dust storms have made 70 percent of Jinghe county's steppe unusable.

See also FLIGHT OF THE KALMYKS; TORGHUDS; XINJIANG MONGOLS.

Bortala *See* BOROTALA MONGOL AUTONOMOUS PREFECTURE.

Börte Üjin (1161?–1237?) *The principal wife of Chinggis Khan and the mother of his four famous sons*

Börte Üjin (Lady Börte) was the daughter of Dei Sechen of the QONGGIRAD lineage and his wife Chotan. When she was 10, YISÜGEI BA'ATUR (Hero Yisügei), a leading Mongol chief, stopped by Dei Sechen's camp with his nine-year-old son Temüjin (later CHINGGIS KHAN). Yisügei Ba'atur agreed to Dei Sechen's proposal to betroth the two children and left his son with Dei Sechen. On Yisügei Ba'atur's murder a servant of Yisügei fetched back Temüjin to his mother's camp.

As Temüjin and Börte entered adolescence, Temüjin went to marry Börte. Dei Sechen worried that the young orphan could not protect his wife, but Börte's younger brother Alchi convinced his father to agree. Börte thus joined Temüjin's family, bringing a sable coat as dowry. Temüjin gave the sable coat as a present to the powerful KEREYID khan Toghril (later ONG KHAN), and when Temüjin's teenage bride was kidnaped by MERKID tribesmen, Toghril Khan helped him rescue Börte from her captors. Soon after her rescue, Börte bore her first son, JOCHI, who was widely suspected of not being Temüjin's.

Temüjin and Börte had no further children for a few years, and he encouraged her to adopt the orphan SHIGI QUTUQU. Eventually she bore Temüjin three more sons, CHA'ADAI, ÖGEDEI (b. 1185), and TOLUI (b. 1192), and five daughters. During Temüjin's rise to power as Chinggis Khan, he placed great store by Börte Üjin's words. She first advised him to break with JAMUGHA and around 1210 convinced him that the shaman Teb Tenggeri posed a mortal threat to the new dynasty. She survived her husband, keeping his ORDO (palace-tent) into the 1230s.

See also ÖGEDEI KHAN.

Buddhism *See* BUDDHISM, CAMPAIGN AGAINST; BUDDHISM IN THE MONGOL EMPIRE; BUDDHIST FINE ARTS; CHAGHAN TEÜKE; CHOSGI-ODSIR; DANZIN-RABJAI; DIDACTIC POETRY; DORZHIEV AGWANG; INCARNATE LAMAS; JANGJIYA KHUTUGTU; JIBZUNDAMBA KHUTUGTU; LAMAS AND MONASTICISM; LITERATURE; 'PHAGS-PA LAMA; RELIGION; SECOND CONVERSION; TIBETAN CULTURE IN MONGOLIA; "TWO CUSTOMS."

Buddhism, campaign against

The campaign in revolutionary Mongolia against Buddhism both as an institution and as a belief system ended with virtually complete victory in 1940.

EARLY CONFLICTS

Although the movement leading to the 1921 REVOLUTION began as a defense of faith and nation against the Chinese, the Mongolian People's Party's appeal to Soviet Russia in 1920 raised the specter of atheism. During the 1921 battles the revolutionaries, in fact and in song, raised the red flag of the People's Party with the yellow flag of Buddhism, yet Buddhism had so long been associated with Mongolia's existing social order that calls for serious social reforms excited strong clerical opposition.

Until 1924 the theocratic lama-emperor Bogda Khan was retained as a constitutional monarch, but with his death in May, the 1924 CONSTITUTION enjoined a strict separation of church and state, the abolition of the *shabi-nar* (personal subjects of monasteries or INCARNATE LAMAS), and the abolition of any secular jurisdiction of religious figures. Estimates in 1924 showed about 113,000 lamas, yet this figure must include many who lived essentially as laymen. After the government insisted on treating these "part-time lamas" as laymen, probably some increased their commitment to retain their monastic status, while other accepted de facto laicization. In 1925 lamas resident in monasteries were estimated at 87,300 persons, or about 25 percent of the male population, a major increase over past numbers, and the *jisa* (modern Mongolian, *jas*), or monastic herds, at 21 percent of all livestock. In 1925–26 the government ordered that no child could be ordained before age 18, that only those with two brothers could become ordained, and that the *jisa/jas* be taxed.

Implementation of these measures caused isolated disturbances at monasteries from winter 1924–25 on. Apocalyptic chain letters warned believers against associating with the polluted party and the youth league members. Disaffected believers looked to proposed reincarnations of the JIBZUNDAMBA KHUTUGTU, or the Sixth (or Ninth) Panchen Lama (Chos-kyi Nyi-ma, 1883–1939), who had left Tibet and was traveling in North China and Inner Mongolia. As the party touched more lives through the draft, new schools, the mutual-aid cooperatives, and new party and league cells, the countryside polarized into religious and anticlerical camps. Even so, in 1929 only 5,773 children were being trained in public schools, while 18,995 children aged eight to 17 were being educated in the monasteries.

THE LEFTIST PERIOD

The leftist period, from 1929 to 1932, saw the first comprehensive attack on the Buddhist clergy. Writers and popular propagandists denounced the corruption of the clergy and the Panchen Lama as the tool of Japanese and/or Chinese imperialism. After 1930 crude attacks and desecration of sacred objects organized by Youth League members escalated.

By late 1929 114 incarnations and high lamas had had their property confiscated. By 1930 649,526 head of the monastic *jisa/jas* herds had been transferred to poor and middle-class herders and 1,224,565 head to the newly organized collectives. The total *jisa/jas* dropped from 3,598,329 head in 1927 (17 percent of all livestock) to 3,034,568 head in 1930 (about 13 percent), and 392,322 head in 1933 (2 percent). Heavy taxes were levied on lamas of military age in lieu of service. Any form of education within the monasteries was prohibited, as was any new religious construction.

Executions and show trials intimidated the high lamas. The Khalkha Zaya Pandita was arrested in 1929 and executed in February 1930. From March 1930 38

persons, mostly clerics, were tried in the Eregdendagwa case. The Yegüzer Khutugtu Galsangdashi (1870–1930) was executed with the lay TAIJI Eregdendagwa and his confederates on September 30, and the Diluwa Khutugtu Jamsrangjab (1883–1964) fled the country. Another large group was tried in November 1931.

In spring 1930 uncoordinated resistance broke out against the party's *tsonjin shashin,* or "religion of weapons," as the lamas called it, in Dörböd territory (UWS PROVINCE) and at Bandida Gegeen Monastery (Rashaant Sum, Khöwsgöl). A far bloodier rebellion began at Bandida Gegeen Monastery on April 12, 1932. The lamas organized an insurrectionary government while hoping for the aid of the Panchen Lama and the soldiers of Shambala, the hidden Buddhist realm whose soldiers will destroy the enemies of Buddhism at the end of the age. By July the new rebel government had 13 bands with more than 3,000 men, who sacked 35 *sum* government offices in NORTH KHANGAI PROVINCE, KHÖWSGÖL PROVINCE, SOUTH KHANGAI PROVINCE, and ZAWKHAN PROVINCE.

THE LEGAL CAMPAIGN

The scale of this rebellion, which was not finally stamped out until October 1932, shocked the government into removing the most offensive features of the new regime. The existing tax system remained, however, and the old economic position of the monasteries was not restored. The *jisa/jas* numbers steadily declined to 108,644 head in 1936 and 84,605 the next year. The military tax, set on a sliding scale, had averaged 14.5 tögrögs per lama up to 1934 but after that jumped every year to an average 116.1 per person in 1938. A special tax on lamas with high scholarly or administrative ranks was instituted in April 1936, with top rates of 75 percent of income. By 1938 the monasteries were supplying one-quarter of total government revenues. Representatives reporting to the party and security organs were appointed to each monastery in 1934, and the lamas lost the ability to discipline their own ranks. Even so, the number of lamas increased after 1932 and remained steady at around 75,000 to 1937. The lamas were maintained by the staunch generosity of the people; the government estimated that believers donated 2.7 million tögrögs worth of livestock in 1936 and 1937.

THE FINAL CAMPAIGN

From 1934 the Soviet ruler Joseph Stalin had been insisting on the elimination of the lamas in Mongolia. When Prime Minister GENDÜN proved unwilling to do so, he was replaced in March 1936, and real power was given to the interior minister MARSHAL CHOIBALSANG. Given its continued strength, the elimination of Buddhism could not be achieved solely by taxation. In 1936 100 lamas were executed in SOUTH GOBI PROVINCE. In 1937 35 border monasteries were closed, with more than 2,000 lamas executed for resistance. The number of military-age lamas declined from 40,953 in 1937 to 23,254 in 1938 and 13,613 in 1939. Marshal Choibalsang noted that by November 1939 he had formally arrested 17,335 lamas and "made an end of" 20,356. About 50,000 lamas returned to lay life, some after time in prison. Late in 1939 the great monasteries of ULAANBAATAR were closed, and by 1940 lamas numbered fewer than 500. The final liquidation netted 5,916 kilograms (13,042 pounds) of silver religious articles, 336,734 head of livestock, and 5,470 buildings. The silver was melted down and the buildings mostly cannibalized for wood and bricks.

See also GANDAN-TEGCHINLING MONASTERY.

Further reading: Owen Lattimore and Fukiko Isono, *The Diluv Khutagt: Memoirs and Autobiography of a Mongol Buddhist Reincarnation in Religion and Revolution* (Wiesbaden: Otto Harrassowitz, 1982); Larry William Moses, *Political Role of Mongol Buddhism* (Bloomington: Indiana University Press, 1977).

Buddhism in the Mongol Empire

Probably the first foreign religion to be given official status by the Mongols, Buddhism eventually became the main religion of the Mongol Yuan dynasty in the East.

The earliest Inner Asian empire to accept Buddhism was the western branch of the first Türk Empire (552–659), under which Buddhism became the court religion. The succeeding Uighurs turned to Manicheism, but by 982 the Uighur oasis kingdom in Turpan (Turfan) and Besh-baligh (near modern Qitai) was Buddhist, mixing the native Nikaya (Hinayana) tradition with strong Chinese Mahayana influences (*see* UIGHUR EMPIRE and UIGHURS). Chinese Buddhism also exerted a profound influence on the KITANS, who founded the Liao dynasty (907–1125) in Inner Mongolia and the Tangut XIA DYNASTY (1038–1227) in Northwest China. The Liao emperors sponsored the first critical edition of the Buddhist scriptures in Chinese in 1063.

During the 12th century Tibetan Buddhism eclipsed Chinese Buddhism among the Tangut. The later Xia emperors invited monks from central Tibet to serve as state preceptors (*guoshi*) and bestow on them Tantric initiations, while the Tibetan monks recognized the Xia rulers as incarnations of a bodhisattva. Among the northern nomads the Xia emperor became known as the Burqan Khan, or "Buddha Khan." Under the JIN DYNASTY (1115–1234), which replaced the Liao and conquered North China, Dhyana (Zen) Buddhism flourished. The QARA-KHITAI Empire (1131–1213), formed by Kitan refugees in predominantly Muslim Turkistan, also patronized Buddhism, as did their eastern Uighur vassals.

The Mongols' early contacts with Buddhism were all with the Dhyana (Zen) school. In 1215 YELÜ CHUCAI, a Kitan scholar and lay disciple of the Dhyana master Wansong Xingxiu (1166–1246), entered CHINGGIS KHAN's service. In 1219 SHII TIANZE, a Chinese general in Mongol service, enrolled as a lay disciple of the Dhyana master Zhongguan (d. 1220) and his disciple Haiyun (1202–57), introducing them to MUQALI, the Mongols' viceroy in North China. On Muqali's recommendation Chinggis Khan granted both clerics the status of DARQAN, or tax exempt, and allowed them to gather monks under their protection. That same year Yelü Chucai's opposition defeated a plan to conscript Buddhist monks for the army.

Chinggis Khan's later contacts with the Taoist (Daoist) MASTER CHANGCHUN gave the latter the opportunity to take over Buddhist monasteries, sparking a long-standing conflict between Buddhists and Taoists. Under ÖGEDEI KHAN Yelü Chucai and Haiyun defended Buddhist interests and promoted Mongol appreciation of Chinese culture generally. Buddhist monasteries were also established in the new Mongolian capital of QARA-QORUM. In 1247 GÜYÜG Khan (1246–48) appointed Haiyun chief of all the Buddhist monks of the empire, and this was confirmed in the first year of his successor, MÖNGKE KHAN (1251–59). From 1255 to 1258 Möngke and his brother Qubilai, his regent in North China, repeatedly demanded that the Taoists cease their denigration of Buddhism.

Under Möngke Khan, however, Tibetan and Kashmiri Buddhism began to replace Chinese Buddhism in imperial favor. Under Ögedei Khan the Kashmiri brothers Otochi and Namo attended the Mongol court, where Otochi served as a physician. In 1253 Möngke made Namo chief of all the Buddhist monks of the empire. In 1240 KÖTEN, Ögedei's second son, dwelling in the old Tangut territory, had dispatched an expedition to central Tibet to renew the Tangut link with the monasteries there. In 1247 the hierarch of the Sa-skya-pa order and head of the aristocratic 'Khon family, Kun-dga' rGyal-mtshan (1182–1251), known as Sa-skya Pandita (Scholar of the Sakya), met Köten and won the sickly prince's favor by healing him. In 1251–52 Möngke Khan ordered the initial conquest of Tibet. As part of the conquest Möngke also extended the tax exemption of all Buddhist clergy to Tibet and granted its monasteries as appanages to various Mongolian princes. The Tibetan Karma Bakhshi (1206–83), famed for his miraculous accomplishments, also received Möngke's patronage. In 1253 Sa-skya Pandita's nephew 'Phags-pa (1235–80) was summoned from the late Köten's camp to that of Qubilai, Möngke's brother. That same year 'Phags-pa conferred on Qubilai the initiation of the Tantric protector deity, Hevajra. Such Tantric initiations became regular among Qubilai's descendants, accounting for the many Sanskrit names in the imperial family.

The new Tibetan and Kashmiri Buddhists at the Mongol court assisted the Chinese Buddhists in their dispute with the Taoists. In the 1258 debate with the Taoists in the presence of Qubilai, 'Phags-pa and Namo joined forces with Fuyu (1203–75), abbot of Qara-Qorum's Shaolin Monastery and a discipline of Wansong Xingxiu, and LIU BINGZHONG (1216–74), a disciple of Haiyun's, to humiliate their Taoist interlocutors. As a result 237 Taoist monasteries were returned to Buddhist control. The

Tibetan Buddhist familiarity with the Indian textual tradition and training in debating techniques impressed Qubilai and helped 'Phags-pa win the debate.

When Qubilai became khan (1260–94) Liu Bingzhong remained a trusted councillor, but Dhyana Buddhism declined in importance. Qubilai appointed 'PHAGS-PA LAMA his state preceptor on the Xia or Tangut model, giving him power over all the empire's Buddhist monks, Chinese and Tibetan. In 1270, after 'Phags-pa created the SQUARE SCRIPT on the basis of the Tibetan alphabet as a common writing system for the empire, Qubilai promoted him to imperial preceptor (*dishi*). The displays of levitation and other magical accomplishments at court by the *baqshis* (Buddhist teachers) astounded visitors such as MARCO POLO.

For the rest of the Mongol YUAN DYNASTY in China to 1368, Tibetans were the most influential Buddhist clergy. In 1264 Qubilai created the Supreme Control Commission (Zongzhiyuan) under the state preceptor to administer affairs of both Chinese and Tibetan monks. During 'Phags-pa's frequent absences in Tibet, power devolved onto a coterie of Buddhist bureaucrats, including the Tibetan SANGHA. In 1288 Sangha, who had in the meantime risen to high office, had the office renamed the Commission for Buddhist and Tibetan Affairs (Xuanzhengyuan), while displacing 'Phags-pa's 'Khon family in favor of less-highborn Sa-skya-pa monks. In 1315 the position of imperial preceptor moved back to the 'Khon family, where it stayed until the end of the Yuan.

In DAIDU (modern Beijing) Qubilai built the White Pagoda Temple (Baitasi), which became a center for Buddhist translations from Tibetan into both the Mongolian and Uighur languages. (The temple's pagoda is still extant.) 'Phags-pa Lama authored the *Shes-bya Rab-gsal* (1278), a detailed outline of Buddhist dogmatics dedicated to Qubilai's son and heir apparent, JINGIM. In this work 'Phags-pa first linked the Mongol khans to the historical succession of Buddhist monarchs. In the famous multilingual Juyongguan inscription of 1345 Qubilai and his successors were hailed as long-prophesied bodhisattva khans.

Under Mongol patronage the Indo-Tibetan Buddhist textual tradition strongly influenced the long-standing Chinese and Uighur Buddhist scholarship as well as the infant Mongolian tradition. When the Chinese Buddhist canon was reprinted in 1285–87, all items were collated with Tibetan translations and the Sanskrit titles added from Tibetan sources where the Chinese lacked them. Tibetan Tantric Buddhism continued to be patronized by the succeeding MING DYNASTY (1368–1644), becoming a part of Buddhism in China proper to the present. At the same time familiarity with the standardized Chinese canon probably inspired 'Jam-dbyangs Bagshi, a cleric at the Mongol court, to sponsor the creation of the first Tibetan canon, or bKa'-'gyur, at sNar-thang monastery (near modern Xigazê) around 1320.

Contact with Tibetans at court also brought about literacy in Tibetan among the Uighurs. Karunadasas, one of the first Uighur interpreters in 'Phags-pa's entourage, translated in 1302 the Indo-Tibetan devotional lyrics for the bodhisattva Manjushri. During the early and mid-14th century, Uighurs in Kumul (Hami), Gansu, and Beijing translated many Tibetan works. Uighur and Mongolian translators, such as Sonom-Gara and CHOSGI-ODSIR

The White Pagoda in Beijing, designed by Aniga. It is the only remaining monument of the Yuan dynasty in its former capital. *(Photo courtesy of Lynn Struve)*

(fl. 1307–21) with his disciple Shirab-Singgi in Beijing, rendered many Tibetan Buddhist works into Mongolian, including sutras, devotional works, the biography of the Buddha, and guides to lay Buddhist life. The translators also composed original hymns in alliterative verses. The only Buddhist work known to be translated into Mongolian from Chinese was the *Sutra of the Big Dipper,* translated by Alintemür in 1328.

Buddhist monks shared in the privileges of the favored classes under Mongolian rule: tax exemptions for them and their dependents and the right to use the JAM (postroad). After the Mongol conquest of South China, from 1277 to 1291 Yang Rin-chen-skyabs (Yang Lianzhenjia) actively reconverted Taoist temples and the defunct SONG DYNASTY's palaces into Buddhist monasteries, even desecrating Song tombs. In 1297 Emperor Temür (1294–1307) decreed that those who struck or insulted monks would have their hands or tongues cut off, while Emperor Shidebala (1320–23) sponsored memorial halls for 'Phags-pa throughout the empire. The frequent arrogance of Tibetan monks and the expense of Buddhist rituals at court caused deep but muted dissatisfaction among Chinese Confucian officials.

With the Mongol reunification of China, Chinese Buddhist monks were organized into Dhyana (Meditation or Zen), Doctrine (principally the Garland or Huayan school), and Discipline schools. (The popular but plebeian Pure Land tradition was ignored.) Other sects of Buddhist origin strong in the south, such as the White Cloud and the Dhuta sect, were granted tax exemptions as separate religions, not as part of Buddhism. Dhyana monks were favored over other Chinese Buddhists; after palace lectures Qubilai concluded that their approach was complementary to that of the Tibetan lamas. Debates with Taoism continued until 1281, when Qubilai ordered Taoist scriptures burned, a measure that the Dhyana monks enthusiastically endorsed. In 1288 Dhyana Buddhists, with the assistance of Yang Rin-chen-skyabs, also won a court debate against the Garland school.

Despite the Mongol Empire's division in 1260, Buddhist *baqshis* (teachers) continued to travel the length of the empire. The Il-Khans in Iran held the 'Phag-mo-gru-pa order in central Tibet as their appanage, and HÜLE'Ü (r. 1256–65), Abagha Khan (1265–82), and Arghun Khan (1284–91) lavishly patronized a variety of Indian, Kashmiri, Chinese and Tibetan monks. Muslim sources claim the khans mainly sought immortality from the monks and that an Indian *baqshi*'s elixir of cinnabar killed Arghun. In 1295 GHAZAN KHAN, recently converted from Buddhism to Islam, approved the total destruction of Buddhism in Iran, destroying all Buddhist temples, even those containing a portrait of his father, Arghun, and forcing the *baqshis* to chose Islam or death. Ghazan Khan later allowed surviving Buddhists to either emigrate or to remain at court as long as they did not openly practice

their religion. The history of Buddhism is less well known in the CHAGHATAY KHANATE, but the very name of the khanate's first strong Muslim khan, Tarmashirin (1331–34), indicates he was raised a Buddhist. Numerous fragments of Buddhist literature found at Turpan in the mid-14th century show the continuing popularity of Buddhist literature among Mongols and Uighurs in the khanate's eastern half. In the GOLDEN HORDE, especially under Toqto'a Khan (1291–1312), Islam receded in face of the "Uighur" religion and their *baqshis*, which were promoted by Toqto'a's great NOYAN Saljidai of the QONGGIRAD and his wife, Kelmish-Aqa, QUBILAI KHAN's niece. In 1288 the dissident prince NOQAI of the Golden Horde sealed his alliance with Arghun by presenting a *sharil* (relic) of the Buddha. Following Islamization under ÖZBEG KHAN (1313–41), the term *baqsi* (from *baqshi*) came to mean "shaman" and/or "bard" among the KAZAKHS and other descendants of the Horde.

The MONGOL EMPIRE marked a major epoch in the history of Buddhism. The conversion of the Mongols and the establishment of Tibetan Buddhism in China and Mongolia created the beginnings of the Inner Asian Buddhist commonwealth that would last to the 20th century.

See also ASTROLOGY; BKA'-'GYUR AND BSTAN-'GYUR; EAST ASIAN SOURCES ON THE MONGOL EMPIRE; KASHMIR; RELIGIOUS POLICY IN THE MONGOL EMPIRE; TIBET AND THE MONGOL EMPIRE; *TREASURY OF APHORISTIC JEWELS.*

Further reading: Yüan-hua Jan, "Chinese Buddhism in Ta-tu: The New Situation and New Problems," in *Yüan Thought: Chinese Thought and Religion under the Mongols,* ed. Hok-lam Chan and Wm. Theodore de Bary (New York: Columbia University Press, 1982), 375–417.

Buddhist fine arts Only recently recognized by international art historians, Mongolia formed one of the great centers of Buddhist painting, sculpture, and temple banners.

PURPOSE

The primary purpose of Buddhist art is to aid contemplation by yogis. Tantric meditation in particular is based on the visualization of the deities and gurus. This visualization can be either for progress in the spiritual path, for devotion, or to consecrate some object. Images also serve as objects of worship in a conventional sense by those unable to practice meditation. All images also instruct, and certain genres, such as the depictions of the wheel of samsara, serve primarily this purpose.

FORMS

The deities of Mahayana Buddhism are divided into peaceful (*amurlingghui*) and wrathful (*dogshin*) classes. Buddhas and great bodhisattvas, such as Manjushri and Avalokitshvara, have blue hair with a topknot and wear only a religious toga. Historical gurus lack these and usu-

The Wheel of Samsara, showing the six births, clockwise from top: gods, titans (firing arrows at the gods), animals, hell-beings, hungry ghosts, and humans. Note the yurts, felt making, hunting, lamas, and other scenes of Mongolian life in the human panel. *Thangka* (mineral paints on cotton), kept in the Buriat Historical Museum. *(From* Buddiiskaia zhivopis Buriatii *[1995])*

ally (but not always) wear monastic robes and a hat. Buddhas and gurus of this miserable world wear a robe made from scraps and have no ornamentation. Those from perfected worlds have rich ornaments and fine robes. The wrathful deities have three glaring eyes, snarling tusks, wild orange-red hair, and a halo of flames. They include the tall *yidams*, or protectors of the various Tantric cycles, and the squat Bodhisattva Vajrapani and the Dharmapalas, or protectors of the Buddhist dharma.

All figures are specified by precise mathematical proportions. On paintings these are drawn out beforehand in geometrical forms. Within each class specific deities are marked by attributes (book, rosary, begging bowl, bell, scepter, etc.) and by hand gestures (*mudra*). The central figure is commonly surrounded by minor figures, illustrating other deities of the family. In INCARNATE LAMA images, the previous incarnations are often represented.

Forms of Buddhist art not centered on a deity figure include the stupas, or reliquary, from several centimeters to several meters high, which consists of a pedestal, a vessel holding the sacred remains, and a spire. Mandalas depict a perfected world around the deity of a Tantric initiation in schematic form. Another type of painting or temple banner represents offerings of various types to aid a yogi in visualizing things to be offered to the deity. Finally, illustrations of the 12 deeds of the Buddha Shakyamuni or of the six births in the wheel of samsara (cyclic existence) are intended primarily for teaching and often are painted on the outside of temple walls.

MATERIALS

Most of these types of art could be made in several media. Sculpture was used for the chief offering site of every temple that could afford it. The most valuable were gilt bronze and (more rarely) silver. At the other end of the market were amulets of papier-maché or terra-cotta stamped from metal molds. Painted wood was also used, particularly for complex three-dimensional representations of paradises or divine realms. The large demand for Buddha figures created an industry in Buddha images both at Dolonnuur and (from the 1880s to 1914) in Warsaw. In use the main sculptures are clothed, hatted, and garlanded. Evanescent media used for particular rituals included colored sand for mandalas and painted dough figures (*baling*) for exorcisms.

Considerably less expensive than sculpture were *thangka* paintings. These are painted on a cotton scroll with mineral paints in a size of animal fat. Some paints were also made with crushed scale insects. All these features involving killing disturbed the more scrupulous lamas, as did the artists' frequent use of spit to moisten the paint. (Some paintings, however, were valued precisely because they contained the spit of great painters, such as "BUSYBODY" SHARAB.) Gold leaf could also be used for fiery halos. Finally, temple banners, or appliqués (*zeegt naamal*), were modeled on *thangkas* but had the

advantage of being sturdier when stored in rolled-up form. These were made by sewing pieces of colored cloth onto a cotton background. In the richer examples, pearls and other precious stones were sewn on.

EXECUTION AND STYLES

The first distinctive style of Buddhist art associated with Mongolian patronage was that of Aniga (1244–78), who 'PHAGS-PA LAMA had invited from Kathmandu in Nepal. Aniga's school established a Sino-Tibetan style, which continued for centuries.

Zanabazar (1635–1723, *see* JIBZUNDAMBA KHUTUGTU, FIRST) began native Mongolian sculpture with works of genius unsurpassed later. His school's images, of gilt bronze or copper cast in two pieces, continued his Nepalese-influenced style through the 18th century. Works of his school outside Mongolia have been identified particularly by the drum-shaped bases and the distinctive gilded double *vajra* (powerbolt) on the bottom of the base. By the 19th century, however, Dolonnuur (modern Duolun) became the main center for both routine and superior Buddhist images. Sculptures of the Dolonnuur school were made of hammered copper or bronze sheets and assembled in many pieces. Billowing scarves, distinctive flat crowns and earrings attached separately, and profuse inlays of precious and semiprecious stones distinguish masterpieces of this style from those of the Zanabazar school.

The only surviving paintings of the SECOND CONVERSION are the wall paintings of Maidari Juu (near BAOTOU) and ERDENI ZUU, both dating from the late 16th century. The background of the former already shows the influence of Chinese landscape painting, with its attendant cool palate of greens and blues that forms so much of the overall look of Qing-era Tibetan and Mongolian *thangka*s. Extant Mongolian *thangka*s date mostly from the 19th and early 20th centuries, although surviving examples from the time, if not the hand, of Zanabazar are similar stylistically.

A distinctive feature of Mongolian guru portraits, particularly of the Jibzundamba Khutugtus, is the interest in individual portraiture. Zanabazar's self-portraits showed an early interest in this, and the Fourth Jibzundamba Khutugtu (Lubsang-Tubdan-Wangchug, 1775–1813) had portraits of his predecessors made from their mummified remains. Early in the 20th century painters such as "Busybody" Sharab used the new medium of ink to draw the flesh of the Khutugtus while drawing the clothing and attributes in the traditional manner in mineral paints.

By 1900 about 40 master artists were working in Khüriye (modern ULAANBAATAR). The antireligious campaigns of the mid-20th century almost ended the tradition of Buddhist art among the Mongols. In Inner Mongolia Buddhist temples had already become so dependent on Chinese artisans working on commission that no distinctly Mongolian Buddhist art survived the Cultural Revolution (1966–76). In Mongolia *thangka* painting survived on a small scale, to be revived after 1990 with the advent of religious freedom. The expensive and labor-intensive sculptural and temple banner traditions were less hardy and have not been revived beyond purely functional needs.

See also BUDDHISM IN THE MONGOL EMPIRE; CHOIJUNG LAMA TEMPLE; MONGOL *ZURAG;* PALACES OF THE BOGDA KHAN; THEOCRATIC PERIOD.

Further reading: Patricia Berger and Theresa Tse Bartholomew, *Mongolia: The Legacy of Chinggis Khan* (San Francisco: Asian Art Museum of San Francisco, 1995); N. Tsultem, *Development of the Mongolian National Style Painting "Mongol Zurag" in Brief* (Ulaanbaatar: State Publishing House, 1986); ———, *Mongolian Architecture* (Ulaanbaatar: State Publishing House, 1988); ———, *Mongolian Sculpture* (Ulaanbaatar: State Publishing House, 1989).

Buin Nemkhu *See* BUYANNEMEKHÜ.

Bulgan province Created in 1937 from Khöwsgöl, Gazartarialan (modern Selenge), Central, and North Khangai provinces, Bulgan lies in north-central Mongolia with a frontier on Buriatia in Russia. Its territory was mostly part of KHALKHA Mongolia's prerevolutionary Tüshiyetü Khan province, with small parts of Sain Noyan province. Teshig Sum, on the northern border, is primarily Buriat, however. The new ERDENET CITY was removed from Bulgan's jurisdiction in 1976. The province's 48,700 square kilometers (18,803 square miles) cover the northern foothills of the KHANGAI RANGE and the valleys of the SELENGE RIVER and the ORKHON RIVER. It is a relatively wet province. The population has risen from 30,900 in 1956 to 62,600 in 2000. Bulgan is one of Mongolia's leading arable agricultural provinces, accounting in 2000 for about 19 percent of the country's wheat harvest. The province's 1,522,800 head of livestock in 2000 included the third-largest number of cattle (225,800 head). The capital, Bulgan town, was originally Wang-un Khüriye, a combined monastery town and residence of the prince of Daiching Zasag banner. Its population in 2000 was 16,200.

See also AMUR; BURIATS IN MONGOLIA AND INNER MONGOLIA; DAMBA, DASHIIN; KHANGDADORJI, PRINCE; MAGSURJAB; TSOGTU TAIJI.

Bulgaria *See* BYZANTIUM AND BULGARIA.

Bulghars (Greater Bulgaria) The Mongols conquered the Bulghars, a northern people on the Volga, who engaged in the fur trade, during the great western expedition of 1236.

The Bulghars first appeared north of the Black Sea in 481 as a nomadic people speaking a Turkic language of the Oghur subfamily, close to modern Chuvash. (*See* ALTAIC LANGUAGE FAMILY.) Around 670 the Khazar khanate dispersed the Bulghars, most of whom moved west to subjugate the Balkan Slavs and form the nucleus of modern Bulgaria. Another group, however, moved north to the confluence of the Volga and the Kama Rivers. By 921–22 these northern Bulghars controlled the trade of fur and slaves to the Middle East and KHORAZM. Khorazmian merchants converted the Bulghars to Islam. The capital city was known as Bulghar. The Bulghar warred constantly with the advancing Russians, but by 1150 they controlled the lower Volga city of Saqsin.

In 1224 the Bulghars ambushed the Mongol army of SÜBE'ETEI BA'ATUR and JEBE as it passed Saqsin. In 1229 under ÖGEDEI KHAN (1229–41), Kökedei and Sönidei attacked Bulghar outposts on the Yayiq (Ural) River, besieged Saqsin, and camped in the Bulghar heartland in 1232. The Bulghar cities and the local Qipchaq and Bashkir (Bashkort) nomads resisted successfully, and in 1235 Ögedei mobilized a much larger army under his nephew BATU (d. 1255). In 1236 Sübe'etei took the city of Bulghar, butchering the entire population. Saqsin city and the Bashkirs (Bashkort) were subdued in the same year.

Despite the conquest, the city of Bulghar reached its apogee of development in the 13th and 14th centuries. The GOLDEN HORDE under Batu and his successors allowed emirs of the old Bulghar families to continue ruling while paying the same fur tax. The Golden Horde encouraged caravan trade and began again to coin money. In the time of ÖZBEG KHAN (1313–41) the Mongols adopted Islam and soon became Turkicized in language, forming a new people called the TATARS. The revived Russians sacked Bulghar again in 1399, and the crisis of the late 14th century that shattered the Golden Horde also broke up Bulghar's prosperity. In 1446 the Chinggisid prince Ulugh Muhammad and a large body of Tatars occupied Kazan' (a new and nearby rival of old Bulghar city), founding the independent Kazan khanate. Ivan IV, czar of Russia, conquered Kazan' in 1552. The contemporary Tatars of Tatarstan are descendants of the fused Bulghar and Tatar peoples; the neighboring, mostly non-Muslim, Chuvash preserve a rustic form of the medieval Bulghar language.

See also OSSETES; QIPCHAQS; RUSSIA AND THE MONGOL EMPIRE.

Further reading: Th. T. Allsen, "Prelude to the Western Campaigns: Mongol Military Operations in the Volga-Ural Region, 1217–1237," *Archivum Eurasiae Medii Aevi* 3 (1983): 5–24.

Buqa (Bögä, Boka) (d. 1289) *Supreme Mongol commander and vizier under Arghun Khan, ruler of the Mongols of the Middle East*
Born of a minor branch of the JALAYIR clan, Buqa and his brother Aruq were raised in the personal entourage of the Il-Khan Abagha (1265–82) in the Middle East.

Appointed as to *tamghachi* (keeper of the commercial tax), Buqa unsuccessfully supported Abagha's son Arghun as khan after Abagha's death. Qutui Khatun, mother of the victorious candidate, Ahmad (r. 1282–84), protected Buqa from retaliation, however. When Ahmad arrested Arghun in 1284, Buqa freed Arghun on the night of July 4, seized the camp, and led the army against Ahmad.

Once victorious, Arghun (r. 1284–91) appointed Buqa simultaneously commander in chief (*beglerbegi*) and vizier, holding the supreme red seal (*al tamgha*). QUBILAI KHAN in China awarded Buqa the title of *chingsang* (*chengxiang*, grand councillor). Buqa's brother Aruq received the lucrative governorships of Baghdad and Diyarbakır.

Buqa's ruling clique included junior Jalayirids like himself, ambitious Persian rivals of Shams-ud-Din Juvaini, the Assyrian Christian governors in Mosul and Irbil, and the Georgian king Dmitri (1273–89; *see* GEORGIA). Eventually Buqa's tight control alienated Mongol commanders such as TA'ACHAR. Arghun dismissed Aruq after the Jewish clerk SA'D-UD-DAWLA promised to double revenues and then gave the crown territories (*injü*) to Ta'achar and command of the center (*ghol*) to Qunchuqbal of the QONGGIRAD, thus vitiating Buqa's financial and military power. Buqa feigned illness while plotting to overthrow Arghun. The plan betrayed, Arghun executed Buqa (January 16, 1289), Aruq (February 22), their families and supporters. The torture and demotion of Buqa's Assyrian confederates sparked anti-Christian rioting in Mosul.

Buriad *See* BURIATS.

Buriat language and scripts

Buriat language and scripts   Buriat is the language of the Buriat Mongols of southern Siberia and northeastern Mongolia and Inner Mongolia. According to the 1989–90 census figures, there were about 463,000 BURIATS worldwide and up to 93,000 of the allied Bargas.

In the 13th and 14th centuries BARGA and Buriat tribes inhabited the present-day Barguzin valley and the lands west of LAKE BAIKAL. The Barga were in close contact with the Mongols and form the ancestors of the modern Barga and of the Khori Buriats. The Buriats of that period appear to be the ancestors of today's Ekhired-Bulagad group. The location of the Khongoodor tribe, ancestors of the Tünkhen and Alair Buriats, is not clear.

DIALECTS AND SOCIOLINGUISTICS

Buriat language in its pure form is quite different from Mongolian and very difficult for a speaker of Modern Mongolian to understand, yet the Kyakhta Treaty of 1727 that fixed the boundary of the Russian and Manchu Qing Empires (including Mongolia and Inner Mongolia) included KHALKHA Mongols of the Tsongol, Sartuul, and other OTOGs (camp districts) on the Russian side of the boundary. To this day the dialect of these "Selenge Buriats" is close to Khalkha Mongolian and quite far from standard Buriat. The Khori Buriats, by contrast, share CLAN NAMES with Barga Mongols who were resettled on the Manchu Qing side of the frontier. Barga Mongols numbered perhaps 70,000 to 90,000 in 1990. New and Old Barga dialects differ somewhat from each other and rather more from Khori Buriat. In addition, 2,100 Bargas live in Mongolia. After 1920 thousands of Buriats fled Bolshevik control to Mongolia and Inner Mongolia. Their descendants in Mongolia numbered 35,444 in 1989 and have been estimated at about 6,500 in Inner Mongolia.

In Russia Buriat has been divided into five dialects. The most widely spoken is Khori, found along the Uda valley from around Onokhoi northeast to Romanovka on the upper Vitim. It is also spoken in Aga and among the Buriats of Inner Mongolia and northeast Mongolia. The Ekhired-Bulagad (Russian Ekhirit-Bulagat) group is spoken in Ust'-Orda east of the Angara and the Ol'khon, Barguzin, and Selenge delta districts around Lake Baikal. The Alair-Tünkhen (Russian, Alar-Tunka) dialect group includes Tünkhen dialect in southwest Buriatia and Alair of western Ust'-Orda. Extinct today is the very archaic Nizhneudinsk dialect far to the west. Finally, the Khamnigan dialect is found among Buriatized EWENKIS (a Manchu-Tungusic people) subject to the Aga Buriats and has been carried with them also into Mongolia and China. Some linguists consider Khamnigan dialect to be a separate archaic Mongolian language.

The Buriat language is nowhere used in secondary or higher education and is, compared with Mongolian in Mongolia or even Inner Mongolia, in an advanced stage of loss. With rapid urbanization since 1970, almost half the republic's Buriats now live in cities or towns. Official figures show the percentage of Russia's Buriats claiming Buriat as their native language dropping from 98.1 percent in 1926 to 86.3 percent in 1989, but surveys taken in 1988–90 indicate only 39 percent of Buriats in the republic have actually mastered the spoken language and only 19 percent the written language. While 62 percent speak Buriat with their parents, only 31 percent (and only 11 percent in the cities) speak it with their children; only 19 percent use the language at work. Taught only in primary schools and in subordination to Russian even there, the Buriat language, whether spoken, printed, or broadcast, is not a significant vehicle of public discourse. While the Buriats of Mongolia and Inner Mongolia still largely speak Buriat, education and books are in standard Mongolian.

DISTINCTIVE FEATURES

The most distinctive feature of the Buriat dialects is the transformation of all affricates into fricatives or spirants. Sharing with the Khalkha and Kalmyk-Oirat the splitting of Middle Mongolian *j* and *ch* into *j* or *ch* before *i* and *dz* or *ts* before all other vowels, Buriat has gone further, transforming *j* and *ch* into *zh* and *sh*, and *dz* and *ts* into *z* and *s*. Thus *sharga*, "sled" (from Middle Mongolian *chirgha*), becomes a homonym with the horse color *sharga*, "light bay" (Middle Mongolian *shirgha*). Perhaps to avoid this sort of convergence, Buriat changes Middle Mongolian *s* to *h* before a vowel. Thus, Middle Mongolian *chagha'an sara*, "white moon, Lunar New Year" (Mongolian *tsagaan sar*), becomes *sagaan hara*.

Buriat shares with the East Mongolian dialect of Inner Mongolia the Manchurian areal feature of replacing *e* by ə (conventionally written *e*). Short *ö* disappears, replaced by *ü* in the initial syllable and *e* afterward, so that Khalkha *tölöölögch* becomes in Buriat *tülöölegshe*.

Buriat and Khalkha share the merger of final *-n* and *-ng* into *-ng* (conventionally written *-n*). Like Kalmyk-Oirat, however, Buriat retains the unstable *-n* in the nominative (thus, Buriat *oshon*, spark versus Mongolian *och*) and has formed personal conjugations from postposed pronouns (for example, *yabadagbi*, "I go," from *yabadag*, "go(es)" + *bi*, "I," or *yerebesh*, "you came," from *yerebe* "came" + *shi*, "you"). While a few idiosyncratic sound changes resemble Kalmyk-Oirat, Buriat morphology is quite distinct from either Kalmyk-Oirat or Mongolian with its accusative in *-iiye* rather than *-iig*, ablative in *-ha* (from reconstructed *-sa*) rather than *-aas*, and genitive after consonants in *-ai*, rather than *-iin*. Buriat also contains unique forms (e.g., *niutag*, homeland, compared to Mongolian *nutag*, Kalmyk *nutg*; *orïyool*, "peak," compared to Mongolian *orgil*, Kalmyk *örgl*), and unique vocabulary, such as *zon*, "people," and *basagan*, "girl."

Buriats have been in close contact with Russians longer than any other Mongolic people and in addition to usual recent political and technical vocabulary, have a number of old, assimilated loanwords such as *büülkhe* or *khileemen*, "bread" (from *búlkha* or *khleb*), *khartaabkha*, "potato" (from *kartófel'*), and *khapuusta*, "cabbage" (from *kapústa*).

SCRIPTS

The UIGHUR-MONGOLIAN SCRIPT was introduced among Russia's Buriats in the 18th century from Mongolia. By the 19th century there was a significant body of Buddhist religious texts, genealogies, chronicles, law codes, and primary school textbooks. In 1895 the first bilingual Russian-Buriat Mongolian newspaper was published. The vocabulary, morphology, and orthography of Buriat Uighur-Mongolian works clearly reflect the distinctive features of the Buriat dialects. Czarist regulations, however, blocked the Uighur-Mongolian script from spreading to the Buriats west of Lake Baikal. There Christian Buriats Iakov V. Boldonov (1808–49) and N. S. Boldonov (1835–99) designed a Cyrillic script for Buriat and printed pamphlets, liturgies, and catechetical works from 1840, producing a modest degree of Cyrillic literacy.

During the 1905 Revolution the new Buriat intelligentsia demanded an end to the educational separation of the western Buriats. The learned lama AGWANG DORZHIEV (1853–1937) introduced a modified Uighur-Mongolian script called the Vagindra script after its creator's pen name, intended for use among the western Buriats. The script was popularized by Buriat intellectuals from 1905 to 1910 but never achieved success. The Latin script introduced by the Buriat intellectual Bazar Baradiin (1878–1937) in 1910 likewise did not succeed, although his device, borrowed from Finnish, of writing long vowels with double letters was later adopted into Buriat and Mongolian Cyrillic scripts.

After the Russian Revolution of 1917 overthrew the czarist religious and educational policies, the new Soviet regime strongly promoted Buriat literacy in the Uighur-Mongolian script, especially after the 1923 administrative unification of the eastern and western Buriats. Yet some western Buriats still preferred Cyrillicization. Suddenly, in 1930 Latinization became the general policy for Soviet nationalities. After discussions Bazar Baradiin produced a new Latin script in January 1931 based on the literary language, which he hoped would be used by all Mongols, not just Buriats. When it was decided that summer to choose a living dialect, not a literary language, as the new script's standard, Tsongol was chosen, one close to Khalkha Mongolian.

In 1936, with the growth of Russian nationalism under Joseph Stalin, the Khori dialect, one very different from Khalkha, was chosen as the standard dialect. Finally, in 1938 it was decided to switch the Buriats from the Latin script to a new Cyrillic script based on the Khori dialect. A new design, relatively close in structure to the former Latin script but quite different from the previously introduced Kalmyk Cyrillic scripts, was created in 1939. The only new letters used for Cyrillic Buriat were ö, ü, and the distinctive Buriat *h*. In imitation of Bazar Baradiin's Latin script, long vowels were marked by doubling rather than a diacritical. Rather than using the "half i" (й) for the consonant *y*, *e* was always written as ə, and the Cyrillic palatalized vowels were used to mark the consonant *y-*: я (*ya*), е (*ye*), ё (*yo*), and ю (*yu* or *yü*). Finally, the Cyrillic ы (*y*, or back *i*) was introduced for the long *ii* in certain case endings. All of these devices were later also adopted in designing Mongolia's Cyrillic script (*see* CYRILLIC-SCRIPT MONGOLIAN). The Buriat Cyrillic script has been used until the present both in the BURIAT REPUBLIC and in the Ust'-Orda and Aga autonomous areas, which were separated from it in 1937.

See also KALMYK-OIRAT LANGUAGE AND SCRIPT; MONGOLIAN LANGUAGE.

Further reading: James E. Bosson, *Buriat Reader* (Bloomington: Indiana University, 1962); Yeshen-Khorlo Dugarova-Montgomery and Robert Montgomery, "The Buriat Alphabet of Agvan Dorzhiev," in *Mongolia in the Twentieth Century: Landlocked Cosmopolitan*, ed. Stephen Kotkin and Bruce A. Elleman (Armonk, N.Y.: M.E.

Sharpe 1999), 79–97; Juha Janhunen, *Material on Manchurian Khamnigan Mongol* (Helsinki: Castrenianum Complex of the University of Helsinki and the Finno-Ugrian Society, 1990).

Buriat Republic The Buriat Republic is the main homeland of the South Siberian Buriat Mongols. Founded in 1923 as an Autonomous Soviet Socialist Republic (ASSR) within the Soviet Union, the republic adopted a new constitution as a constituent republic within the Russian Federation in 1992. The ASSR originally included the Aga, Ust'-Orda, and Ol'khon districts, but they were stripped from the republic's territory in 1937. (*See* AGA BURIAT AUTONOMOUS AREA and UST'-ORDA BURIAT AUTONOMOUS AREA.) In 1989 the republic's population was 1,038,252, of which 249,525, or 24 percent, were Buriat. The capital is ULAN-UDE. (*For the history and culture of the Buriats as an ethnic group, see* BURIATS.)

GEOGRAPHY AND DEMOGRAPHY

Buriatia occupies 351,300 square kilometers (135,638 square miles) along the southern and eastern side of LAKE BAIKAL, linking the MONGOLIAN PLATEAU to the East Siberian uplands. It is mostly over 800 meters (2,600 feet) above sea level. The highest peak is Munku-Sardyk in the Sayan Mountains at 3,491 meters (11,453 feet), and the lowest spot is the shores of Lake Baikal at 456 meters (1,496 feet) above sea level. Siberian taiga forest covers 67 percent and high mountain tundra or barren rock 16.0 percent of the territory, but the lowlands contain patches of steppe and forest steppe.

Ranges divide Buriatia into six major valleys or basins: 1) the middle Selenge and its tributaries; 2) the Khori area around the Uda (Buriat, Üde), Kholoy (Buriat, Khooloi), and Khudan valleys and the Yeravna (Buriat, Yaruuna) lakes; 3) the Barguzin (Buriat, Bargazhan) valley; 4) the Irkut valley; 5) the Upper Angara-Muya valley; and 6) the Baikal basin. In the northeast and southwest are the sparsely inhabited Vitim plateau and Sayan Mountains uplands.

Buriatia's population is concentrated in the steppes of the middle Selenge, Khori, Barguzin, and Irkut valleys and around the Selenge delta by Lake Baikal. The Selenge valley and its tributaries from the Mongolian border to Ulan-Ude are Buriatia's economic hub, whether in industry, grain farming, or the raising of sheep for wool and cattle for meat and milk. The Khori area and the Barguzin valley are more purely rural, with sheep and cattle breeding and some grain farming. In the Irkut valley cattle breeding predominates, while along the southern shores of Lake Baikal pig and cattle breeding dominate. Average rural population densities range from 5.5 persons per square kilometer (14.2 per square mile) in the middle Selenge valley to 1.5–2.3 per square kilometer (3.9–6 per square mile) in the other steppe valleys and as low as one person per 5 square kilometers (0.5 per square mile) elsewhere.

Russians moved into Buriatia in several distinct waves. The "old-timers," whether Cossacks or peasants, settled in the valleys around the Cossack forts in the 17th and 18th centuries. Many came without women and married Siberian natives. Cossack units remained on the frontier until the Russian Revolution. Old Believers, exiled for protesting liturgical innovations in the Russian Orthodox church, were, by contrast, settled with their families around Mukhorshibir', Bichura, Tarbagatai, and Zaigraevo from 1756 to 1780. Political dissidents, beginning with the Decembrists of 1825, often added to the area's cultural development. In 1890–1905 emancipated peasants streamed west to settle on former Buriat land newly opened by the czarist authorities. Finally, in the Soviet industrialization and during World War II, whole industrial populations were resettled as a bloc in Ulan-Ude and elsewhere.

Since 1939, when Buriats formed 21.3 percent of the republic's population of 545,800, Russian immigration has matched the higher Buriat birthrate, doubling the population while maintaining the ethnic balance. Buriats form relatively high percentages of the population in the Barguzin valley (41 percent), the Khori valley (48 percent), the western side of the Selenge valley (32 percent), and the southwestern districts (61 percent). In the Akha (Russian, Oka) district in the far southwest, Buriats (including the Soyots) total 91 percent. Even where Buriats are a small minority, however, in the rural areas they generally live in villages separate from Russians. While traditionally purely rural, by 1989 44.5 percent of the Buriat lived in urban areas, forming 17.3 percent of the urban population. Ewenki reindeer herders and hunter-fishers dwell in the northern Barguzin and Upper Angara valley and the Vitim plateau, while Turkish-speaking Soyots (allied to the TUVANS and DUKHA) live in the Sayan Mountains.

From 1926 to 1989 the absolute number of persons living in the countryside changed relatively little, from 338,500 to 397,800, although as a percentage of the total population rural dwellers dropped from 87 percent to 37 percent. The countryside weathered the post-Soviet economic-demographic crisis better than did the cities, and by 1996 its population had risen absolutely and relatively to 425,400 or 40 percent.

Until 1975 Ulan-Ude, the capital, was Buriatia's only major urban center. Subsequently, Gusinoozërsk (1989 population 29,790) in the Selenge valley grew around a massive new coal-fired thermal-electric energy plant, and Severobaikal'sk (28,336) developed on the Baikal-Amur Railway in northern Buriatia. Both declined in population in the 1990s.

AUTONOMOUS SYSTEM

From 1923 to 1992 the Buriat ASSR was a Soviet-style republic within the Russian Soviet Federated Socialist Republic, which in turn was one of 15 "union republics"

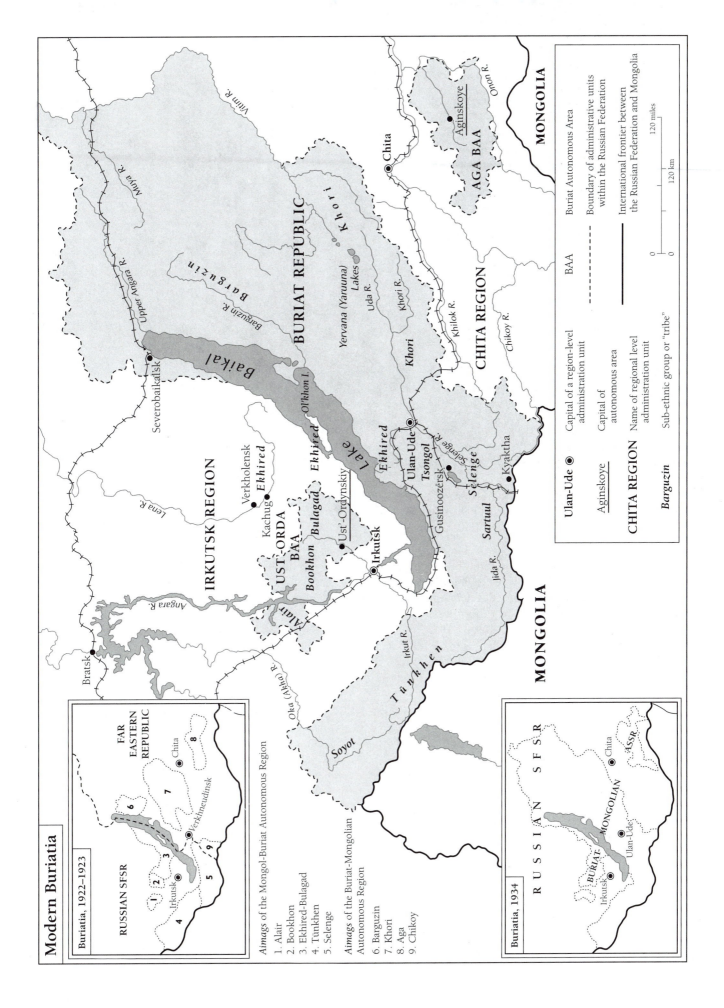

Modern Buriatia

Buriatia, 1922–1923

RUSSIAN SFSR

FAR EASTERN REPUBLIC

Chita

Irkutsk

Verkhneudinsk

1. Alair
2. Bookhon
3. Ekhired-Bulagad
4. Tünkhen
5. Selenge

Aimags of the Mongol-Buriat Autonomous Region

6. Barguzin
7. Khori
8. Aga
9. Chikoy

Aimags of the Buriat-Mongolian Autonomous Region

Buriatia, 1934

R U S S I A N   S F S R

Chita

BURIAT-MONGOLIAN ASSR

Irkutsk

Ulan-Ude

MONGOLIA

Bratsk

Angara R.

IRKUTSK REGION

Verkholensk *Ekhired*

Kachug

Lena R.

Severobaikalsk

Muya R.

Upper Angara R.

Vitim R.

Barguzin R.

Barguzin

BURIAT REPUBLIC

Khori

Yervana (Yaruuna) Lakes

Uda R.

Khori R.

Khilok R.

CHITA REGION

Chikoy R.

Ol'khon I.

Ekhired

Lake *Baikal*

Ekhired

Ekhired

Ulan-Ude

Tsongol

Selenge

Selenge R.

Gusinoozërsk

Sartuul

Kyakhta

Jida R.

Chita

Aginskoye

AGA BAA

Onon R.

MONGOLIA

UST'-ORDA BAA

Bulagad

Bookhon

Ekhired

Ust'-Ordynskiy

Irkutsk

Aldır

Oka (Akha) R.

Irkut R.

Tünkhen

Soyot

Legend

BAA — Buriat Autonomous Area

- - - Boundary of administrative units within the Russian Federation

——— International frontier between the Russian Federation and Mongolia

Ulan-Ude ◉ — Capital of a region-level administration unit

Aginskoye ● — Capital of autonomous area

CHITA REGION — Name of regional level administration unit

Barguzin — Sub-ethnic group or "tribe"

0   120 miles
0   120 km

The town of Kyren (Buriat, Khüren) in the valley of the Irkut (Buriat, Erkhüü) River. This town is the center of the Tunka (Buriat, Tünkhen) district and the Tunka National Park. *(Courtesy Katherine Metzo)*

within the Soviet Union. While lacking the formal "right to secede" enjoyed by the "union republics," the Buriat ASSR did have its own rarely used flag and seal. The governmental form was specified in three successive local constitutions, adopted in 1923, 1937, and 1978, and was essentially identical to that in other region-level Soviet governments, although until 1965 rural districts and settlements were given Buriat names such as AIMAGs and somons.

The Communist Party of the Soviet Union, as the sole permitted political party before 1990, had committees parallel to each level of government, controlling both the elections and the voting behaviors of the soviets (i.e., local and ASSR legislatures). The party-state strictly controlled all legal media and cultural organizations and allowed no criticism of Moscow's policies. The socialist economic system, which put major industrial enterprises directly under economic ministries in Moscow and governed all economic activity according to All-Union Five Year Plans, further diminished any real Buriat autonomy.

In 1939 the Buriat writing system was switched from the UIGHUR-MONGOLIAN SCRIPT to a new Cyrillic script, which was somewhat modified later for use in Mongolia (*see* BURIAT LANGUAGE AND SCRIPTS). Education in this new standard Buriat language was, however, restricted to

grade school. Written materials were few and almost exclusively propagandistic, folkloric, literary, or pedagogical in character. In 1970 Buriat language instruction in schools was abolished.

The Soviet system enacted preferential policies for nationalities in their own areas. These preferences, combined with ambitious ethnic Russians' tendency to emigrate, resulted in a striking overrepresentation of Buriats both in government organs and in the intelligentsia.

During the disintegration of the Soviet system, Buriatia declared itself sovereign in 1990. After renaming itself the Buriat Republic in 1992, a new constitution with a new flag and seal based on the Mongolian SOYOMBO SYMBOL was adopted on February 22, 1994. A new language law passed in 1992 made Russian and Buriat equal official languages. The new constitution provides for a 65-member standing legislature, the People's (or National) Khural (Assembly), a directly elected president, and a government responsible to the president. Supreme Court justices are appointed by the president and confirmed by the People's Khural. On June 30, 1994, Leonid V. Potapov (b. 1935), a Russian engineer and party cadre raised in Kurumkan, won a direct election to a four-year term as president of Buriatia. While Russians have captured the visible top positions, Buriats are still heavily overrepresented in official ranks. As elsewhere in Russia, no new stable party structure has appeared. Potapov won reelection in 1998 and 2002 and has expressed support for Moscow's plans for administrative consolidation.

Faced with overwhelming economic and financial problems, Potapov signed a power-sharing agreement with Russia's federal government on August 29, 1995. Buriatia is represented as an autonomous unit in Russia's upper house, the Federation Council. Federal-regional disputes continue, however, both over constitutional matters and over federally owned enterprises.

ECONOMY

The current Buriat economy is primarily urban. In 1991, at the beginning of the post-Soviet economic crisis, the sectoral composition of the gross regional product was as follows: industry, 37.0 percent; services, 32.7 percent; agriculture, 16.2 percent; and construction, 13.8 percent. In 1993 23.4 percent of employed persons were in industry and only 14.9 percent in agriculture (including herding). A further 9.2 percent were employed in trade, 15.2 percent in culture, and 2.9 percent in management. These employment trends were all relatively close to those elsewhere in Russia.

Only 9.0 percent of Buriatia's land is usable for arable agriculture, hay mowing, or pasture. Pastures total about 16,700 square kilometers (6,450 square miles), with another 3,500 square kilometers (1,350 square miles) used for hay mowing. With collectivization in 1929–32, the agricultural sector (including herding) was forced into kolkhozes, or collective farms, and sovkhozes, or state-owned farms worked by wage labor, often transient. In 1970 kolkhozes numbered 71, and sovkhozes numbered 58. In 1979 collective farmers were only 8.8 percent of the population.

Soviet agricultural policy stressed farming over herding and commercial products over subsistence, along with mechanization and economies of scale. From 1940 to 1969 the total sown area in Buriatia (excluding acreage dedicated to fodder) increased from 384,000 hectares (948,860 acres) to 524,000 (1,294,800 acres). Summer wheat and oats largely replaced the traditional Siberian crop of winter rye, and agriculture was heavily mechanized. In 1970 2,800 grain harvesting combines were in operation. Pigs about doubled, from 79,000 (1941) to 153,000 (1969). Animal husbandry accounted for more than two-thirds of the total agricultural product in the 1970s, due in large part to the commercialization of herding. In 1941 Buriatia's herders herded 407,000 cattle and 637,000 sheep and goats, but by 1970 emphasis on wool production expanded sheep and (relatively rare) goat numbers to 1,706,000, while cattle reached only 440,000. Animal husbandry supplied 53,000 metric tons (58,422 short tons) of meat (including pork and poultry), 5,600 metric tons (6,173 short tons) of wool, and 103,900 metric tons (114,530 short tons) of milk in 1969. In border areas many sheep were actually fattened in Mongolia. As pasture degraded, more animals had to be fed on fodder, acreage of which grew from 34,000 hectares (84,010 acres) in 1940 to 291,000 (719,060 acres) in 1970.

In 1940 industry in Buriatia was based primarily on electric power production (81.9 million kilowatt-hours), coal (39.1 thousand metric tons; 43.1 thousand short tons), lumber, glass, (2 million square meters; 21.5 million square feet), and food industries. In the 1950s woolen textiles were added and in the 1960s machine tools, instruments, and so on. By 1969 coal production reached almost 1.3 million metric tons (1.4 million short tons) and electricity 871 million kilowatt-hours. Other products mined included tungsten and molybdenum near Zakamensk and gold near Bagdarin and Irakinda. In the 1970s the new thermal-electric plant at Gusinoozërsk was built with an installed capacity of 1.25 gigawatts. From 1974 to 1989 the Soviet government poured money and energy into the Baikal-Amur Railway (BAM) project of building a northern parallel to the Trans-Siberian Railway. As part of Soviet policy, regional interdependence was emphasized, and Buriatia exported two-thirds of its industrial products and imported 89 percent of its consumer goods.

By the late 1980s pasture degradation and newly assertive Mongolia's prohibition on cross-border grazing forced a sharp decrease in sheep numbers. By 1995 Buriatia herded about 380,000 cattle, 475,000 sheep and goats, and 65,000 horses. Meanwhile, sown acreage (excluding fodder) shrank to 376,000 hectares (929,100 acres) as farmers found the cost of operating machinery soaring while grain prices stagnated. Still, grain farming is generally more profitable than livestock.

This profound rural depression, combined with the strong traditions of collectivism and the absence of any marketing, financial, or technical infrastructure, made the rural "privatization" campaign ordered by Moscow in 1992 a fiasco. While the kolkhozes are mostly bankrupt, they are still preferred to private farms. Families subsist by keeping hay- or fodder-fed cattle and raising vegetables and pigs. Thus, fodder acreage (348,600 hectares, or 861,390 acres, in 1994) and pig numbers (160,000 in 1995) have remained steady. From 1991 to 1996 the consumption of potatoes rose by 29 percent, while that of meat declined 61 percent.

Meanwhile, the urban economy faced equal or greater challenges. Not only did the economy contract sharply in absolute terms, there was, as elsewhere in the former Soviet bloc, a sea change in its sectoral composition. By 1998 services dominated the economy, accounting for 50.8 percent of the gross regional product, while industry and construction declined to 24.8 percent and 6.45 percent, respectively. Farming and herding produced 17.3 percent of the region's goods and services. Electricity from Gusinoozërsk remained an important product, exported to both Chita and Mongolia. In 1995 industrial output was 36.5 percent in fuel and energy, 17.3 percent in machine tools and metalworking, 16.8 percent food processing, 7.5 percent in lumber and woodworking, and 6.1 percent in construction materials.

In 1995 Buriatia's average income was 21 percent lower than that of Russia as a whole, while its living costs were 17 percent higher. The overall infant mortality rate in 1993 was 20 per 1,000 births. More than two-thirds of the population live below the poverty line, and while the government aims to attract foreign investment, the business climate is estimated as one of Russia's worst.

ADMINISTRATIVE HISTORY

With the Red Army's reconquest of eastern Siberia in January–March 1920, western Buriatia fell to the Russian Soviet Federated Socialist Republic (RSFSR), while eastern Buriatia came under the Far Eastern Republic, a Communist-controlled buffer state between Russia and Japan. In the Far Eastern Republic the new constitution of April 1921 created a Buriat-Mongolian Autonomous Region of four *aimags*, and on January 9, 1922, a Mongol-Buriat Autonomous Region with five *aimags* was created in the RSFSR. Both of these autonomous regions united several discontinuous chunks of territory within the modern Buriat Republic, Aga, Ust'-Orda, and Ol'khon. The RSFSR Buriat region had 185,192 people, of whom 129,000 were Buriats, and the 108,800 people in the Far Eastern Republic were likewise mostly Buriat.

In October 1922 Japan withdrew from Siberia, and the RSFSR absorbed the Far Eastern Republic. The two autonomous regions were merged to form the Buriat-Mongolian ASSR on May 30, 1923. In order to form a contiguous territory, intervening Russian territories were annexed. As a result, while the new republic included 90 percent of Russia's Buriats, its population of 491,000 was only 43.8 percent Buriat (1926 figures). In 1927 the ASSR was slightly further enlarged by annexing the Kabansk district, and certain districts north of the Baikal were added subsequently, bringing the total area to 424,100 square kilometers (163,746 square miles).

On September 26, 1937, in the middle of Joseph Stalin's GREAT PURGE, the Central Executive Committee of Moscow's Supreme Soviet partitioned the Buriat-Mongolian ASSR, giving Aga *aimag* to the Chita region and the Alair, Bookhon (Russian, Bokhan), and Ekhired-Bulagad *aimags* to Irkutsk. This partition, undertaken in a panic over a possible Japanese invasion, cut the percentage of Buriats in the ASSR to 23.1 percent. Later, on July 7, 1958, Moscow's Supreme Soviet again changed the republic's name from "Buriat-Mongolian" to simply "Buriat," confirming the death of pan-Mongolist dreams.

In 1990 the Buriat legislature, supported by scholars and activists, protested the illegality of the 1937 and 1958 decisions, which were never approved by the ASSR's legislature, yet Ust'-Orda and Aga's economic dependence on their current parent regions makes any expansion of Buri-atia most unlikely. Indeed, projected plans of Russian administrative consolidation have raised the possibility of merging the Buriat Republic with Irkutsk and Chita into one large Baikal district.

See also CLIMATE; DESERTIFICATION AND PASTURE DEGRADATION; ENVIRONMENTAL PROTECTION; FAUNA; FLAGS; FLORA; MONGOLIAN PLATEAU.

Further reading: Caroline Humphrey, "Buriats," in *The Nationalities Question in the Soviet Union*, ed. Graham Smith (London: Longman, 1990), 290–303; Caroline Humphrey, *Marx Went Away, but Karl Stayed Behind* (Ann Arbor: University of Michigan Press, 1998); G. V. Manzanova, "Problems of Employment and Unemployment in Buryatia," in *Culture and Environment in Inner Asia*, vol. 2, *Society and Culture*, ed. Caroline Humphrey and David Sneath (Cambridge: White Horse Press, 1996), 49–60; Larisa R. Pavlinskaya, "Reindeer Herding in the Eastern Sayan," *Cultural Survival Quarterly* 27.1 (spring 2003): 44–47.

Buriats (Buryats, Buriyad, Buriad) The Buriats are the northernmost branch of the Mongolian peoples. Inhabiting southern Siberia on both sides of LAKE BAIKAL, they were brought under Russian control in the 17th century. Early in the 20th century the Buriat Mongols seemed poised to become leaders of the entire Mongolian world, with a generation of brilliant scholars, publicists, and thinkers who combined profound attachment to their Mongolian heritage with mastery of modern thought. Yet the increasingly repressive and closed Soviet regime under which the Buriats lived aborted this possibility. Only in the 1980s did the Buriats awaken after a period of long-standing Russification.

DEMOGRAPHY, LIFESTYLE, AND ETHNIC IDENTITY

The Buriats of the Soviet Union numbered 421,000 in 1989. Since 1937 they have been principally distributed among the Buriat Republic (59 percent of all Buriats) and two nearby but noncontiguous districts, Aga (10 percent) and the Ust'-Orda (12 percent), all in the Soviet Union's Russian Republic. Only in Aga, however, are the Buriats a majority.

Traditionally, the Buriats were heavily rural, and this is still true in Aga and Ust'-Orda, where 81 percent and 84 percent, respectively, of the Buriats live in country villages (defined as settlements of fewer than 15,000 people). Rural Buriats today are all sedentarized and live in Russian-style houses, although those herding on far pastures may use traditional yurts for temporary camps. In the republic, however, only 55 percent live in the countryside. Urbanization and an orientation toward success in Russian society have largely broken the transmission of Buriat language, so that only 62 percent of adult Buriats today speak Buriat with their parents and only 31 percent speak it with their children. This percentage falls to only 11 percent in the cities. Buriats, like INNER MONGOLIANS in China, are grossly overrepresented in educational, cultural, and civil administrative positions but underrepresented as technical specialists and industrial workers. Of the Buriat Republic's secondary and higher education staff, 74 percent are Buriat.

The question of Buriat identity is complex. Traditionally, Buriats have been distinguished from the Mongols proper by their dialect, strong clans, lack of a Chinggisid aristocracy, and greater attachment to SHAMANISM. However, by this definition the Buriats of Russia's Selenge valley would have to be considered Mongols, while the BARGA of Inner Mongolia would be considered Buriats. In practice, by 1900 *Buriat* had come to mean all the czar's more-or-less Mongolian subjects in Siberia. The Buriats' indubitable Mongolian connections led the Transbaikal Buriats in the early 20th century to adopt a dual "Buriat-Mongolian" identity. At first encouraged by the Soviet authorities, this dual identity was officially "canceled" by Moscow in 1958. The nation-building process under the Soviet period has powerfully shaped modern Buriat identity; Buriats frequently look down on Mongols as backward. While the Mongolian connection is being revived, the Buriats function socially and politically today as a nationality, or people, within Russia, distinct from the Mongols despite their acknowledged Mongolian origin and affinity.

"Tribal," or subethnic, stereotypes and conflicts among the Buriats are still strong. While western, or Ust'-Orda, Buriats are considered to be effective politicians who look out for one another, the Khori are often seen as mutually jealous despite their leadership in cultural, technical, and scientific fields. The Selenge Buriats, who had no prerevolutionary tradition of political leadership, are stereotyped as poor, passive, and very religious.

The official Buriat population until recently included the Soyots in the Akha (Russian, Oka) region in the far west and the Khamnigan EWENKIS in and around Aga. The Soyots are a branch of reindeer-herding TUVANS. In Soviet times they were officially merged with the Buriats, and their reindeer herding was slated for extinction. By 1999, however, more than half of the 4,000 "Buriats" of Akha had declared themselves as Soyots again. A similar movement has expanded the numbers of Khamnigan Ewenkis, who had been assimilated by the more powerful Buriat clans in the 19th and 20th centuries.

EARLY HISTORY TO 1628

Scholars have connected both the Bayirqu and the Quriqan (Chinese "Guligan"), who appear in the early seventh to ninth centuries, to the ancestry of the Buriats. The name *Bayirqu* is linked to the BARGA (Middle Mongolian, Barghu), a component of the Buriats east of Lake Baikal, while the Quriqan are mentioned in western Baikalia. The Angara and Upper Lena valleys and Lake Baikal's western shore were major areas of settlement of

the TÜRK EMPIRES (552–742). Remains of settlements and old Turkish Runic inscriptions have been found in Ust'-Orda territory and the upper Lena (*see* RUNIC SCRIPT AND INSCRIPTIONS), but not in Transbaikalia.

During the rise of CHINGGIS KHAN in the 12th to 13th centuries, the Buriats proper lived along the Angara River and its tributaries. Meanwhile the Barga appeared both west of Lake Baikal and in northern Buriatia's Barguzin valley, described as the MONGOL EMPIRE's coldest, northernmost land. Linked also to the Barga were the Khori-Tumad along the Arig River in eastern KHÖWSGÖL PROVINCE and the Angara. All of these peoples (and their Turkic neighbors to the west) were skillful skiers with many shamans living deep in forests and hunting the abundant squirrels and sables. Neither the Selenge valley in today's southern Buriatia or the Aga steppe had at this time any connection with the Buriats; these were the lands of the MERKID tribe and the MONGOL TRIBE proper.

The Barga had long intermarried with the Mongols and appear to have joined their cause early. In 1207 Chinggis Khan's son JOCHI subjugated the "forest peoples," including the Buriats, west of Lake Baikal and made them pay a tribute of furs (*see* SIBERIA AND THE MONGOL EMPIRE). Commanders of note in the Mongol army came only from the Barga of Barguzin Hollow; the other tribes did not participate in the imperial venture.

During the first half of the Northern Yuan (1368–1635), the Buriats and Bargas joined the Oirat alliance against the great khans. Some of the forest peoples moved south: The Tumad, Barga, and Bulaghachin clans later appear in Mongolia proper and Inner Mongolia. When Russian Cossacks in the Yenisey valley first heard of the Buriats in 1609, they were still west of Lake Baikal paying fur tribute to the KHALKHA Mongols while themselves collecting fur tribute from the Ket and Samoyed peoples on the Kan and the EWENKIS (Tungus) on the lower Angara. Buriat lands then extended west as far as Nizhneudinsk and north as far as Verkholensk and Bratsk. They were arranged in an intermarrying confederation of two allied groups, the Bulagad (sables) in the Angara and Oka as far as Nizhneudinsk and the Ekhired (twins) in the Lena region. Scattered Mongol or Oirat clans lived among these Buriats. Although intermarrying, the Ekhired and Bulagad saw themselves as distantly related by a common descent from the Bull Lord (Bukha Noyon) descended from heaven.

Meanwhile 11-clan alliance of the Khori-Barga had migrated out of the Barguzin valley eastward to the lands between the GREATER KHINGGAN RANGE and the Ergüne (Argun') River. Around 1594, to escape subjection by the Daurs (*see* DAUR LANGUAGE AND PEOPLE), most of them migrated back to the Aga and Nerchinsk steppes. After 1607 most of the Khori Buriats migrated farther west to Ol'khon (Buriat, Oikhon) Island and the Selenge delta to escape harassment by the "Horse" Ewenkis (Khamnigans) and Khalkha Mongols. (Those who remained east of the Ergüne and in the Transbaikal steppe became ancestors of Inner Mongolia's Old and New Bargas, respectively). While the Khori did not call themselves Buriats and claimed descent not from the Bull Lord but from a swan maiden, they did speak a Buriat-type dialect (*see* BURIAT LANGUAGE AND SCRIPTS). Finally, in Mongolia's modern Khöwsgöl province lived the Khongoodor tribe also speaking a Buriat dialect.

RUSSIAN CONQUEST AND BURIAT MIGRATIONS, 1628–1727

From 1628 the Cossacks advanced along Siberia's rivers into Buriat lands using muskets to extort *yasak* (from Mongolian *jasaq*), or tribute, in furs from the Siberian natives. The advance was decentralized, with fortress commanders (*voevoda*) competing to explore new lands, build new fortresses, and put the natives to tribute. As under the Mongol Empire, the new conquerors also traded in slaves, mostly women and children captured in raids or sold by the impoverished natives (*see* SIBERIA AND THE MONGOL EMPIRE). Following the conquest, Russian peasants moved into the often depopulated river valleys.

The primary Cossack advance into Buriatia came up the Angara, through southern Lake Baikal, up the Selenge to Verkhneudinsk (modern ULAN-UDE), and thence by land across Transbaikalia to Nerchinsk. There their advance met the independent advance from Yakutsk into the Amur basin. A secondary advance came up the Lena from Yakutsk, by portage to northern Lake Baikal, and thence up the Upper Angara and Barguzin Rivers to Baunt Lake. By 1647 fortresses had been founded on both the southern and the northern reaches of Lake Baikal, and by 1676 Cossack forts controlled the territory roughly up to the present Russo-Mongolian frontier.

Bands of Ewenkis roamed the uplands and forests around the Buriats, who primarily inhabited the patches of steppe in the valleys. These Ewenkis were the main hunters of valued sables, and the Russian demand for fur tribute from the Buriats exacerbated hostilities between the Buriats and Ewenkis. The Selenge valley, as before, was inhabited by Mongol clans, such as the Khatagin, Tsongol, Sartuul, and Tabunanguud, under the rule of the Khalkha khans. The Transbaikal steppe around the ONON RIVER, Shilka River, and Ergüne River was inhabited mostly by Bargas and "Horse" Ewenkis, who had adopted the Mongolian pastoral way of life and paid tribute to the Khalkha khans.

Resistance to the Cossack advance came from both the local Buriats and from the Khalkha khans. Until about 1645 western Buriat resistance was relatively local, but in 1644–46 the Ekhired and Bulagad tribes cooperated to field at one point 2,000 men. They were defeated despite sieging Verkholensk, but rebellions continued until 1695–96. By 1652 the Khalkha khans were also protesting the Russian incursions into Transbaikalia, and from 1666 on Khalkha raiding parties reached as far as Bratsk, Il'imsk, Yeravninsk, and Nerchinsk, while the khans besieged the forts on the Selenge. At the same time, however, the Khoris along the Uda River in 1647 surrendered as a block to the Russians to escape paying tribute to the Khalkhas. Smaller Mongol clan fragments also defected north to the protection of Cossack forts. The invasion of Khalkha by GALDAN BOSHOGTU KHAN in 1688 stopped Khalkha resistance to the Cossack advance and sent more Mongol refugees fleeing into Russian control. In 1703 the Khori chiefs confirmed their submission to the czar in return for an imperial patent guaranteeing a cessation of Cossack abuses.

The Buriat reaction to these invasions created the contemporary ethnic geography as groups moved mostly east, leaving only a small body of Buriats (numbering 1,598 in 1897) isolated near Nizhneudinsk. The core of the Bulagad settled in today's central and western Ust'-Orda, while the Ekhired remained on the upper Lena. The Khori had vacated Ol'khon and the Selenge delta, settling along the Uda River before using their alliance with the Russians to attack their old rivals, the Horse Ewenkis, and seize the Aga steppe. Ekhireds and Bulagads occupied the vacant Ol'khon Island and in 1704 crossed the Baikal to occupy the Selenge delta. Meanwhile, the Khongoodor in the late 17th century moved from Khöwsgöl north to escape Mongol rule, occupying today's southwestern Buriatia (Tünkhen) and western Ust'-Orda (Alair). In 1740 a group of Ekhireds from Verkholensk crossed the frozen Baikal and subjugated the Ewenkis there, settling in Barguzin valley. The Selenge Mongols, cut off by the new border from their Khalkha kinsmen and mixed with displaced Buriats and Khori, gradually accepted the Russian designation as Buriat, forming the final component of the Buriat people.

SOCIETY AND ADMINISTRATION, 1727–1898

In 1708 Siberia was made a civilian province (*guberniia*), with eastern Siberia to be supervised from Irkutsk. The rise of Verkhneudinsk east of the Baikal created a division of the Baikal lands and hence the Buriats into 1) Cisbaikalia, directly under Irkutsk, and 2) Transbaikalia, under Verkhneudinsk. This division persisted through numerous administrative reorganizations. Russian demographic and administrative pressure was stronger in Cisbaikalia than in Transbaikalia, a fact that accentuated preexisting cultural differences. However, it must be remembered that this division does not correspond exactly to Buriat cultural or ethnographic distinctions. The Transbaikal Buriats of the Selenge delta, for example, remain closer to their Ekhired-Bulagad cousins than to the Khori or Selenge Buriats.

The Buriats' native political structure differed sharply from that of the Mongols' in its complete absence of the Chinggisid BORJIGID ruling lineage and the legitimizing charter of Chinggis Khan's conquest and rule. This was true even of the Selenge Buriats, among whom only subject clans and no Borjigid were found. Instead, Buriat tribes or confederations were formed of large numbers of exogamous clans, whose senior leaders jostled for influence while claiming some remote fraternal origin.

Buriat society varied greatly by tribal origin and by economic origin. The agropastoral Buriats of Ekhired, Bulagad (including the Barguzin), and Khongoodor origin lived in tight groups of 20 to 200 closely related persons nomadizing between winter and summer pastures. Each group, called an *ulus* by Russian administrators, held pasture in common and periodically redistributed the fertilized hay fields vital to their cattle-based husbandry. These Buriats lived in round wooden yurts or Russian-style cabins rather than Mongol felt yurts. Fishing played a large role for the Verkholensk Ekhired and especially the Ol'khon Island Buriats, and the Ekhireds still engaged in large-scale battue hunting. The Khori and Selenge Buriats, however, were far more nomadic, living mostly or, in Aga, entirely in felt yurts. As with the Mongols, the Khori nomadized frequently in small camps of one to three yurts, raising much larger numbers of diverse livestock: sheep, goats, horses, cattle, and a few camels.

While remaining basically nomadic, in the late 19th century wealthier Buriats began adopting Russian patterns of progressive ranching, using horse-drawn haymaking machines and milk separators, developing livestock breeds such as the Buriat horse, and building wooden yurts at their winter campsites. In home life the Buriat women adopted sewing machines. Nomad Buriats replaced the open fire and trivet, which filled the yurt with eye-watering and health-endangering smoke, with portable stoves and metal stovepipes.

Russian administration was applied through the native political leadership they found among the Buriats. Among the western Buriats, on average 30 *uluses*, or more than 2,000 persons, in a single valley formed a single tribal community. Those of Ekhired and Bulagad origin generally contained segments of many different clans bound by long-standing marriage alliance (QUDA) relations, but those of Khongoodor origin were often formed by branches of a single clan. On the Khori and Aga steppes the 11 Khori clans, numbering from several

Two Transbaikal Buriat *taisha*s with their wives and three daughters, 1890. *(Courtesy Staatliche Museen zu Berlin, Ethnologisches Museum)*

hundred to several thousand, formed the natural units between the household and the tribe as a whole.

All these units had their chiefs, who were generally hereditary, being designated on the basis of clan seniority. Those of the smaller *uluses* had general titles such as *darga* (head, boss) or *zasuul* (administrator), but those of larger units bore ranks similar to that which had existed under the NORTHERN YUAN DYNASTY and the OIRATS: *shülengge, zaisang,* and *taisha* (from Mongolian TAISHI), in ascending order of dignity. The Khori *taishas* borrowed rank buttons and other marks of status from Mongolia. The *taisha* of the Galzuud clan was recognized as the head *taisha* (*akha-lagsha taisha*) and titular head of the Khori people.

In 1822 the Russian reformer Michael Speransky rationalized the system of Siberian native administration. The *ulus* was defined as the "clan administration" and grouped according to valleys or other existing units as "native administrations." Finally, those "native administrations" among the Buriats that had a history of tribal unity were grouped into 12 "steppe dumas." These were composed of clan chiefs elected by their peers. All native officials were unpaid and had similar tasks: apportioning taxes, keeping track of their subjects, serving as intermediaries between Russian local officials and their subjects, and administering justice according to the "Steppe Code," which Speransky developed on the basis of existing Buriat codes. The titles *zaisang* and *taisha* were apportioned to "clan administrators" depending on their size, while "native administration" or steppe duma heads were titled head *taisha*. Taxes included the fur *yasak,* which since 1727 could be paid in cash and by the late 18th century was often paid primarily in grain. Speransky's attempts to limit taxation failed, however.

Entirely apart from the native Buriat administration were Buriat Cossack units. These were organized in the 1760s from Selenge Buriat frontier guards recruited in 1727. In 1851 these Buriat Cossacks were yoked with Russian units in the Transbaikal Cossack army. They were organized into seven stations (*stanitsa*), all in the Selenge valley, and in the 1897 census numbered with their families 26,782 persons, or 14.9 percent of the Transbaikal Buriats. Like the Buzava Cossacks among the KALMYKS, the Buriat Cossacks became strongly Russianized in their lifestyle and organization and had a number of bilingual Russian-Mongolian schools. From Cossack ranks came DORZHI BANZAROVICH BANZAROV (1822–55), the first Buriat Ph.D., Sanzhimitab Budazhapovich Tsybyktarov (1877–1921), the first Buriat M.D., and Tsyrempil Ranzhurov (1884–1919), the first Buriat Bolshevik. Unlike the Buzavas, however, who remained staunchly Buddhist, the Buriat Cossacks frequently converted to Russian Orthodoxy.

RELIGION AND CULTURE, 1727–1898

During the 18th and 19th centuries the Transbaikal Buriats progressively converted to Buddhism. Originally part of the Khalkha, the Tsongol and Sartuul had been familiar with Buddhism decades before the Cossack conquest of the Selenge valley. Yurt *dugangs* (assembly halls) already existed in 1700, and sedentary *datsangs* (monasteries) were soon built in Sartuul and Tsongol territories. In 1728 the authorities prohibited the further entrance of Mongolian lamas among the Buriats but authorized the ordination of two tax-exempt lamas per clan. In 1741 a decree by the Russian empress Elizabeth authorized the creation of 11 *datsangs* in Transbaikalia with 150 lamas each. In 1764 this official Buddhist structure was completed with the selection of the *shireetü lama* (throne lama) Damba-Darzhaa Zayaev (d. 1777) of Tsongol Monastery as the Pandita Khambo-Lama (Learned Abbot Guru) with authority over all Buriat Buddhists. Buddhism soon spread to the Khori, where monastery construction began in 1758. Monasteries began on the Aga steppe in 1801, among the Alair and Tünkhen Khongoodors in 1814–17, and in Barguzin in 1818. Buddhism remained primarily a Selenge-Khori-Aga phenomenon, however, and was never officially authorized in Cisbaikalia.

The attitude of the Russian authorities to Christian missionary activity in Siberia was at first ambivalent, as becoming a Russian Orthodox believer earned exemption from *yasak*. As *yasak* became less important as revenue, Orthodox missionary activity became an important part of Russification. Moreover, while Russian churchmen did not find shamanism threatening, the spread of Buddhism in Cisbaikalia alarmed them, prompting a renewed missionary activity by the Russian Orthodox Church, establishing mission stations and appointing priests, especially in Tünkhen, Alair, and neighboring Bulagad areas. While the Speransky legislation guaranteed freedom of religion, bribery and coercion were pervasive, whether in ordinary mass conversions or in high-profile successes, such as the 1857 conversion of the Tünkhen *taisha* Khamakov and his son Damba.

At the time of the Russian conquest, the Selenge Buriats and possibly the Khori had some experience with the UIGHUR-MONGOLIAN SCRIPT, but the other Buriats were illiterate. Education among the Transbaikal Buriats was dominated by the Tibetan-language education in the monasteries and Mongolian-language clerical education sponsored by the chiefs (*see* EDUCATION, TRADITIONAL). In 1800 the Barguzin Buriats invited teachers from Khori to begin instruction in the Uighur-Mongolian script. Schools for Buriats conducted in Russian spread in both Cis- and Transbaikalia during the 19th century but by the late 19th century had a combined enrollment of only 600. In Cisbaikalia education was almost entirely in Russian; a new Cyrillic-script Buriat designed for Christian materials was little used, and the Uighur-Mongolian script not at all. Despite the relatively shallow reach of Russian-language education, a number of Buriats after Dorzhi Banzarov received some kind of Russian higher education

Pallas Samlung. II Theil. Platte XII.

Buddhist temple at Gusinoozersk (Goose Lake) around 1770 (*From Peter Simon Pallas,* Sammlungen historischer Nachrichten über die mongolischen Völkerschaften *[1976]*)

and conducted important academic research on Buriat folklore, religion, and Mongolian literature.

By the late 19th century copies of most of the major genres of Tibetan and Mongolian Buddhist literature circulated both in manuscript and from the late 19th century in block print form from Tsugol, Aga, and other monasteries. New works included translations of Buddhist classics, histories of Chinggis Khan, and records of pilgrimages to Tibet. Particular to the Khoris were Buriat-language legal documents based on Speransky's steppe code and long genealogical records.

Tugultur Toboev (Toba-yin Tegülder), Aga's head *taisha* from 1853 to 1878, wrote a pioneering chronicle of Khori and Aga history in 1863. Tegülder's work inspired two subsequent Khori-Aga chronicles as well as Selenge chronicles. Wandan Yumsunov's *Khori-yin arban nigen etsige-yin zon-u ug izagur-un tuuji* (Tale of the lineage of the people of the eleven fathers of the Khori, 1875) is the richest in material, describing in four chapters the origins of the Khori, Buddhism, shamanism, and administration. The Barguzin *taisha* Tsydeb-Jab Sakharov (b. 1839) published a history of the Barguzin in Russian in 1869, later writing another briefer history in Buriat-Mongolian

(1887). Most of the chronicles use a common Buriat-Mongolian language written in the Uighur-Mongolian script but with a strong influence of Buriat dialect. While the Khori and Selenge chronicles link their history to Chinggis Khan and Tibetan Buddhism and are strongly critical of shamanism, they also show a sense of common Buriat identity and strong loyalty to the czar.

By 1897 Russia's first census quantified the striking differences between the Cisbaikal and Transbaikal Buriats. The 108,937 Cisbaikal Buriats were now 90.9 percent primarily farmers and only 5.9 percent herders. (Those who were mixed farmers and herders were counted as farmers.) Religiously, they were 47.6 percent shamanist, 41.8 percent Russian Orthodox, and only 10.6 percent Buddhist. By contrast, 77.2 percent of the 179,726 Transbaikal Buriats were livestock herders and 20.1 percent practiced farming. Religiously, 91.9 percent were Buddhist, 6.7 percent, mostly Cossack, were Orthodox, and only 1.5 percent were shamanist. Literacy among men in Cisbaikalia was 9.2 percent and in Transbaikalia 16.4 percent (that of women was much lower—0.8 percent and 0.6 percent, respectively). The nature of literacy was also different: 93 percent Russian in Cisbaikalia, and only 16 percent Russian in Transbaikalia (the balance in both cases was Tibetan and/or Mongolian). One thing that both groups shared was their almost purely rural character.

CRISIS, REVIVAL, AND REVOLUTION, 1898–1923

From 1890 the Russian government began to implement aggressive Russification among the Buriats, as it did with other nationalities. Communally held land was stripped from the Buriats of both Cis- and Transbaikal and assigned to Russian peasants. The building of the Trans-Siberian Railway in 1898–1900 increased the flood of Russian settlers. In 1901 Speransky's steppe dumas and steppe code were finally abolished and replaced by direct administration of Buriats as individuals in districts (volost') of 300 to 3,000 persons. In World War I 12,000 Buriats were conscripted for labor battalions.

An expanding network of Buriat lamas, scholars, and publicists protested Moscow's new policies. Education was expanding this new intelligentsia as secular schools under the Russian Ministry of Education grew from only six in 1890 to 36 in 1911. (See NEW SCHOOLS MOVEMENTS.) With the shaking of czarist rule in the 1905 Revolution, suppressed religions revived: shamanism in the east and Buddhism in the west. Cisbaikal Russian Orthodoxy suffered massive defections. The established leadership of taishas hoped to have the Speransky system revived; their spokesman in the Russian Duma of 1907 was the Aga schoolteacher and assistant to the taisha, Bato-Dalai Ochirov (d. 1914). He and the Bulagad Buriat Mikhail Nikolaevich Bogdanov (1878–1920), educated in St. Petersburg, Berlin, and Zürich, also pursued detailed research on the rural economy and advocated organizing rural cooperatives. Other leaders, however, allied with the socialists by demanding the prohibition of land privatization, elected leadership, progressive taxation, and women's equality. Despite these conflicts with czarist policy, Transbaikal Buriats such as AGWANG DORZHIEV and TSYBEN ZHAMTSARANOVICH ZHAMTSARANO (1881–1942) vigorously promoted Russia's interests in Tibet and Mongolia.

Buriats reacted quickly to the Czar's abdication on March 15, 1917 (March 2 in the old calendar). On May 3–8 (April 20–25) the Buriat National Committee (Russian abbreviation, Burnatskom), led by Tsyben Zhamtsarano, Elbek-Dorzhi Rinchino (1888–1938), and the chairman M. N. Bogdanov, was organized at Chita. The congress renamed the Buriat administrative hierarchy with terms taken from Mongolia: somon (old ulus), khoshuun (old volost'), and AIMAG (roughly the steppe dumas), and advocated autonomy with elective administrations, common land ownership, a reformed Buriat code, and universal Buriat-language education in the Uighur-Mongolian script, capped by a Buriat National Duma as an autonomous legislature. The Burnatskom's insistence that secular education precede Buddhist training caused conflict with conservative lamas.

The chaos and poverty of revolutionary Russia prevented the realization of the Burnatskom's aims, especially in spreading the Uighur-Mongolian script to the western Buriats. Increased land seizures by Russian peasants led in August to the formation of Buriat militias. Still, in the November 1917 election the Burnatskom (now headed by Tsyben Zhamtsarano) received 26,155 (14.7 percent) votes in Transbaikalia and 15,464 (7.2 percent) in Irkutsk, making it the region's second party.

Siberia's Russian settlers overwhelmingly supported the peasant-based Social Revolutionary Party, which won more than 56 percent of the combined Irkutsk-Transbaikal vote in November 1917. Its Siberian oblastniki (regionalist) wing was allied to the Burnatskom. By contrast, the Bolsheviks' core supporters were workers and soldiers from the front, both of whom were rare in Siberia. The Third Buriat All-National Congress in December 1917 denounced the Bolshevik seizure of power, but that winter the Bolsheviks seized power in the Baikal area, aided by Cossacks returning from the front.

Under Bolshevik rule the Burnatskom elected the socialist Rinchino as its chairman but was attacked in May 1918 as anti-Soviet. Even so, the local Bolsheviks had to accept provisionally the somon-khoshuun-aimag system despite their opposition on principle to autonomy. Under the slogan "socialization of land," they egged on Russian peasants to seize Buriat and Cossack territories, a movement that reached a crescendo of violence in 1918. As rumors spread of an apocalyptic conflict between Buriats and Russians and a mass Buriat "return" to Mongolia, Khori and Aga Buriats began migrating in April 1919 to northeastern Mongolia and HULUN BUIR, while Selenge Buriats migrated to north-central Mongolia. (See BURIATS OF MONGOLIA AND INNER MONGOLIA.)

Meanwhile, a charismatic lama of Khori's Kizhinga monastery, Samtan Tsydenov (1850–1922), proclaimed himself "king of the dharma" and "subduer of the Three Worlds" who would destroy the enemies of Buddhism at the end of the era and built an independent regime in Khudan valley. His unorthodox ideas and dangerous insubordination to the czar had long alienated the regular clergy, while the Burnatskom opposed his seemingly backward character.

With the overthrow of Bolshevik rule by Czechoslovak prisoners of war and White Guards, the half-Russian Buriat Cossack Grigorii M. Semënov in November brought together a faction of Burnatskom supporters led by Elbek-Dorzhi Rinchino into what was called the long-awaited Buriat National Duma in November 1918. Relocated to Chita, this Duma grew into a pan-Mongolist DAURIIA STATION MOVEMENT involving Hulun Buir and Inner Mongolian delegates, but it foundered by autumn 1919. Most Buriat nationalists kept their distance and Semënov had M. N. Bogdanov shot and Samtan Tsydenov imprisoned; the latter's mysterious escape only increased his fame. By this time local partisan movements sprang up against White rule and the Red Army advance put the Bolsheviks again in charge of Buriatia by March 1920. To avoid complications with Japan, a puppet Far Eastern Republic was maintained in Transbaikalia from April 1920 to November 1922.

Through Russian peasant attacks, emigration, and civil war, Russia's Buriat-speaking population dropped from 1897 to 1926 by more than 50,000, from 289,100 to 236,800. At first under the new regime, the *taisha*s and other wealthy Buriats were tolerated, although they were disenfranchised. Incomplete figures show the number of lamas declining from 11,276 in 1916 to 7,566 in 1927, although the number of monasteries actually increased to 47. Tsydenov was again briefly imprisoned by the Bolsheviks, and after his death his movement was harassed into virtual extinction by 1924.

While the Irkutsk party organization remained hostile to autonomy, V. I Lenin and Joseph Stalin (then heading the People's Commissariat of Nationalities) insisted that Buriat autonomy was necessary for foreign political reasons. Soviet leaders hoped Buriat autonomy would serve as a showcase for Communist minority policy among the Mongols, Tibetans, and other Buddhist peoples of the Far East. With this aim the Far Eastern Republic's new constitution already guaranteed Buriat autonomy, and a Buriat-Mongol Autonomous Region (*oblast'*) of four noncontiguous *aimag*s, Aga, Khori, Barguzin, and Chikoy (around KYAKHTA CITY) was created in April 1920. Leadership was in the hands of a mix of nonparty Buriats and Russian Bolsheviks. On January 9, 1922, a Mongol-Buriat (*sic*) Autonomous Region was created in the Cisbaikal territories of the Russian Soviet Federated Socialist Republic (RSFSR), again with five mostly noncontiguous *aimag*s: Alair, Bookhon (Russian, Bokhan), Ekhired-Bulagad, Tünkhen, and (western) Selenge. Here leadership was in the hands of a small number of rapidly recruited Buriat Bolsheviks.

BURIATS IN THE BURIAT-MONGOLIAN REPUBLIC, 1923–1937

When the Far Eastern Republic was absorbed into the RSFSR (subsequently itself merged into the Soviet Union), Moscow again insisted in 1923 that the discontinuous *aimag*s be merged into the Autonomous Soviet Socialist Republic with urban centers and a mostly contiguous territory. As a result, the new Buriat-Mongol Autonomous Soviet Socialist Republic (BMASSR) included 90 percent of Russia's Buriats, but its population was only 43.8 percent Buriat. The capital of the new republic was the small city of Verkhneudinsk, which with the neighboring stretch of the Trans-Siberian Railway had been previously excluded from Buriat autonomy. Only 0.6 percent of the Buriats were urban, and in the Buriat regional Communist Party apparatus only 153 of the 1,326 members and candidate were Buriats, most from the western *aimag*s.

A core of relatively assimilated Alair and Bulagad Communists was used to control the less reliable but more influential Transbaikal Buriat intelligentsia. The republic's initial leadership troika included the party secretary Mariia M. Sakh'ianova (1896–1981, Balagan), premier MIKHEI NIKOLAEVICH ERBANOV (1889–1938, Alair), and head of state Matvei I. Amagaev (1897–1944, Balagan); all had joined the party in 1917. The old Burnatskom intellectuals led cultural and educational activities. Other pan-Mongolist movement alumni, particularly Elbek-Dorzhi Rinchino, were assigned to Mongolia. Buriat agents served the Soviet Union as far as Inner Mongolia.

M. N. Erbanov diligently implemented the centrally approved policy of *korenizatsiia* (nativization), increasing the percentage of Buriat party members, cadres, and workers and the public use of the Buriat language. Language policy milestones included the creation of a Buriat newspaper (in the Uighur-Mongolian script) in 1921, the Buriat Academic Committee (Buriatskii uchenyi komitet, or Buruchkom) in 1922, a Buriat pedagogical vocational high school in 1924, and Buriat-language radio broadcasts in 1931, two years after the first Russian broadcasts from Verkhneudinsk. Despite the Russian cadres' criticism of nativization, by 1939 Buriat city dwellers had risen to more than 20,741, or 9 percent, of Buriats as preferential policies enticed Buriats out of the countryside.

From 1908 western Buriat students in Irkutsk had begun producing theater pieces, and the movement grew into a virtual craze of playwriting after 1917. In 1918 the Burnatskom intellectual and reform Buddhist Bazar Baradiin (1878–1937) of Aga set up a Buriat printing press in Chita, where he printed first a comedy of manners based on the Aga nobility and then historical tragedies. The dean of Soviet Buriatia's socialist realist literature, the Khori schoolteacher Khotsa Namsaraiev (1889–1959), began his writing career with the play *Kharankhii* (Darkness, 1919) before going on to write prolifically in every genre. The other major genre of early Soviet literature was poetry. Pëtr Nikiforovich Dambinov of Bookhon *aimag* published his first poem, "Sesegte Tala" (Flowery steppe, 1922), under the pen name Solbone Tuya (or Solbonoi Tuyaa, "Rays of the Morning Star"). He later became the first secretary of the Buriat Writers' Union.

After 1928 popular opposition to the increasingly radical and violent policies initiated by Soviet ruler Joseph Stalin stoked Moscow's fears of pro-Japanese pan-Mongolism. In May 1929 pan-Mongolism was attacked, and the old Burnatskom intellectuals were gradually exiled to Moscow or Leningrad. The Buruchkom and many literary journals were closed down, and "nativization" of the cadres wound down after 1932. The introduction in 1931 of a Latinized Buriat script destroyed existing native-language literacy just as the political impetus for developing non-Russian literacy was weakening. To strengthen the impact of political theater, a studio was organized in 1928 and an art technicum in 1930, which eventually grew into the Kh. Namsaraiev Buriat Dramatic Theater in 1950.

On a mass level the impact of these policies was dwarfed by that of forced collectivization and sedentarization begun in 1929. Widespread revolt broke out, particularly among the Buriats in Tüngkhen and the Russian Old Believers in the eastern Selenge valley. As in 1919, the Buriat rebels were inspired by apocalyptic preaching and the idea of a return to Mongolia. The Buriats resisted fiercely the demand to surrender their livestock to the collectives, slaughtering their animals before surrendering them. The number of Buriatia's livestock fell 62.5 percent from 1929 to 1932. By 1934 75.8 percent of the republic's agricultural-pastoral households had been collectivized, and in 1937 the number reached 91.6 percent. Even then, the number of livestock was only 51 percent of the 1929 figure.

Meanwhile, Buriat Buddhism came under frontal attack. In May 1928 the *datsang*s were labelled "the republic's biggest reactionary force." By 1933 lamas were reduced to 2,758 in 29 *datsang*s, almost all along the Mongolian frontier. The campaign climaxed in 1935. Of the remaining 1,219 lamas, 617 were repressed, 150 to 180 fled to Mongolia or Inner Mongolia, 120 to 130 became herders, and 280 to 320 became workers in the cities. Lama physicians at the Atsagat medical *datsang* numbered 440 in 1925 but only 53 in 1937. In the next year the remains of organized Buddhism were crushed. All these cultural campaigns were mostly implemented at the grass roots by a new generation of convinced Buriat believers in the Soviet system.

M. N. Erbanov, now the Buriat party committee's first secretary, presided over this cultural devastation until his own time came in 1937 during Stalin's Great Purge. The fabricated "Case of the A[gwang] Dorzhiev Organization," built on bogus testimony extracted by torture that implicated 1,303 Buddhist clerics, eventually metastasized into a new "Japanese-Buriat Counterrevolutionary Center" case that eventually implicated 723 members of the republican leadership and Buriat intelligentsia: Erbanov himself, second secretary A. A. Markizov, premier D. D. Dorzhiev, head of state I. D. Dampilon, the Writers' Union secretary Solbone Tuya, and so on. As elsewhere in the Soviet bloc, countless smaller cases annihilated a whole generation of party and social leaders. On September 26, 1937, the same month as the show trial that sentenced Erbanov and 53 other supposed confederates to death, Buriatia was dismembered, and the Aga and Alar, Bookhon, and Ekhired-Bulagad *aimag*s were separated as the Aga and Ust'-Orda "national areas."

The 1939 census revealed that as a result of the campaign against Buddhism, the Great Purge, and collectivization, the ethnic Buriat population had declined even further, from 238,100 to 224,719. Literacy had risen from 28.5 percent in 1926 to 67.6 percent in 1939, but another body of intellectuals like that destroyed in the Great Purge would not appear again.

WARTIME AND POSTWAR BURIATS, 1937–1984

During World War II Buriats served mostly in Irkutsk and Transbaikal divisions and were heavily decorated. The several Heroes of the Soviet Union among the Buriats included the major general Il'ya Vasil'evich Baldynov and colonel Vladimir Buzinaevich Borsoev; after the war three other Buriats achieved the rank of general. During the Soviet Union's brief war on Japan in Manchuria and Inner Mongolia, Buriats served both as combat soldiers and, like S. D. Dylykov, as translators and political officers. Perhaps as a reward for this loyalty, a Buriat first party secretary, A. U. Khakhalov, and premier, D. Ts. Tsyrempilon, were again chosen for the ASSR in 1951.

During World War II and its aftermath, Moscow tolerated religious activity, and the war deaths reinvigorated the cults of the dead; many Buriats held large *tailgan*s (sacrifices) to the spirits of war before being shipped out to the front. In 1946 the Ivolga and Aga *datsang*s were reopened as Buddhist centers, with two dozen married lamas; the *khambo-lama*, or abbot of Ivolga *datsang*, chaired the Central Spiritual Administration of Buddhists and became titular head of Soviet Buddhism. The GESER epic was also encouraged in the war years as a way of developing martial patriotism. In 1948–49, however, the epic was attacked as exemplifying feudal reaction and implicitly resistance to Russian rule. This attack ceased only in 1953, after Stalin's death. In the early 1960s Moscow began a new campaign against superstitions and religious beliefs that for the first time targeted shamanism more than Buddhism. Still, the sincere and militant atheism of the revolutionary activists became rare in postwar generations.

The 1937 purges and dismemberment of Buriatia marked the abandonment of Moscow's aim to use it as a model for Mongolia and Inner Mongolia. In the postwar period Moscow slowly eliminated the remaining traces of the earlier policy. In 1958 the ASSR was renamed simply the Buriat ASSR, dropping the word *Mongol*. In 1965 the Buriat local administrative terms of *aimag* and *somon* were abolished. Meanwhile, the dominant theory of the Russian archaeologist A. P. Okladnikov maintained that the Buriats were actually Mongolized Turks, thus minimizing links to the Mongols (*see* ARCHAEOLOGY). The elevation of Aga and Ust'-Orda "national areas" to the level of "autonomous areas" in 1977 was applied to all Russia's "national areas" and had no special Buriat significance.

During the postwar period the Buriats showed moderately high population growth, increasing 39.5 percent from 1959 to 1979, a rate close to that of Yakuts and Kalmyks. This increase was almost twice that of the Russians but much lower than that of the Soviet Muslim peoples. Urbanization in the ASSR increased during World War II, when many industries were relocated to Ulan-Ude along with their Russian workers. The percentage of ASSR Buriats living in urban areas (towns of more than 15,000) increased from 16.6 percent in 1959 to 35.9 percent in 1979, while the Buriat percentage of the republic's urban population rose from 8.1 percent to 14.5 percent.

As with the Mongols of Inner Mongolia, preferential policies in employment and education acting on a relatively low population base exerted a strong "pull" toward white-collar cultural and administrative positions. By 1970 the Buriats had a higher percentage of "specialists" (156.5 of 1,000) than did any other Soviet nationality except the Jews. Under ANDREI URUPKHEEVICH MODOGOIEV, an Ust'-Orda Buriat who ruled Buriatia from 1960 to 1984, this pull also drew educated Aga and Ust'-Orda Buriats to migrate to the Buriat ASSR. From 1970 to 1979 the Buriat population grew by only 8.3 percent in Aga and actually declined 6.0 percent in Ust'-Orda, even while growing 15.8 percent in the ASSR. In 1989 Buriats formed 50 percent of the regional party apparatus, 45 percent of the city and local party cadres, and 60 percent of the responsible ASSR officials. In the countryside the rural intelligentsia was heavily Buriat, and public recognition went mostly to Buriat-dominated collective farms.

Russification of the Buriat elite caused the official Soviet-style Buriat-language culture to languish. While output of Buriat belles lettres, particularly poetry and theater, continued, it was unsupported by Buriat-language nonfiction or by education above the high school level. Increasing urbanization and familiarity with Russian further diminished the appeal of the heavily rural-oriented Soviet Buriat culture. In 1970 Buriat-language education was eliminated, and although many Buriat poets such as Dondok A. Ulzytuev (1936–72) and Bayir S. Dugarov (b. 1947) saw themselves as voices of Buriat national continuity, their audience was limited. Buriat language ability, particularly at advanced levels, declined swiftly.

Despite the decline in the Buriat language, much traditional religious and spiritual culture was maintained. By the 1960s the most important calendrical rituals were sagaalgan, the lunar new year, or WHITE MONTH of the Mongols, and the summer sur-kharbaan, or ARCHERY festival, similar to the Mongolian NAADAM. The former was associated with Buddhism and frowned upon, while the latter was coopted by the state. Tailgans and worship at OBOO (cairns for Buddhist or shamanist worship) were frequent and well attended in many collective farms although also still officially frowned upon. Shamans still existed, although even devoted clients considered them to have but a shadow of their ancestors' spiritual power. Detailed genealogical knowledge remained widespread, and clan exogamy was practiced, although many rituals were conducted by the collective farm community, not clans. Ivolga and Aga datsangs were maintained by discrete popular devotion throughout the late Soviet era, but the lamas were strictly forbidden to conduct Buddhist activities outside the datsang. Unofficial Buddhism was strictly forbidden. Bidiyadara D. Dandaron (1914–74), a Khori Buriat chosen by Samtan Tsydenov as his future incarnation, was jailed three times (1937, 1948, and 1972), the last time for attempting to revive Buddhist rituals outside the monastery with Buriat and non-Buriat participants. Even so, once again foreign policy needs— now the desire to highlight the Soviet Union's greater benevolence compared with Maoist China—pushed Moscow to allow the Fourteenth Dalai Lama several visits to Ivolga from 1979 on.

NATIONAL REVIVAL AFTER 1984

The wave of liberalization in the Soviet Union after 1985 came only slowly to Buriatia. In 1984 the new Soviet leadership retired the long-ruling Buriat apparatchik Modogoiev and replaced him as party secretary with A. M. Beliakov, a Russian. At the same time Buriat-language education was revived in the primary schools, and in 1989 the sagaalgan was openly celebrated.

In 1990–91 the existing ASSR leadership was forced to respond to the breakup of the Soviet Union and the new multiparty situation. As in other autonomous units, a declaration of sovereignty, a new flag, a declaration of equal official status for the local language (i.e., Buriat) and Russian, and finally in 1992 a new constitution followed. Nevertheless, just as in other regions of Russia, Buriatia soon found financial needs overwhelming desires for greater autonomy. While the elections of 1994 brought the Buriat Republic a Russian president, overall the Buriats remained in a strong position governmentally. In the legislature 40 percent was Buriat (compared with 50 percent in 1989), as were 70 percent of the republic's ministers. Even so, Moscow's plans for administrative consolidation threaten to merge the Buriat Republic with one or more neighboring Russian provinces.

With the new freedom of expression, historical and cultural questions are being frankly discussed. Renewed contacts with the Buriats of China, who seem to have preserved their traditions so well, have only accentuated the Russification of the Buriats in their homeland. In this situation the question for the Buriats was expressed in the title of the noted historian Shirap B. Chimitdorzhiev's book: Kto my Buriaty? (Who are we Buriats?).

Many Buriats have looked for the answer to this question in religion, specifically Buddhism and shamanism. A Buddhist revival began in 1988, and by 2000 25 monasteries and religious organizations existed on Buriat soil. The role of Buddhism was recognized by the republican government with the 1991 celebration of the 250th anniversary of the empress Elizabeth's recognition of Buriat Buddhism. Shamans, too, have organized on an official level, forming the Association of Shamans of Buriatia in 1993, which sponsored large-scale tailgans, or clan sacrifices, at Ol'khon Island in 1993 and 1996. However, as in the early 20th century, new connections with Tibetans and non-Buriat Buddhists have created controversial organizations and sparked criticism of clerical marriage and alcohol consumption tolerated by the Traditional Buddhist Sangha (Monastic Community) of Russia, the successor of the Soviet-era organization of Buddhists.

The lasting division between Buddhism and shamanism and the new divisions in Buddhism have made the epic hero Geser the most consensual symbol of Buriat identity. In 1990 the Buriat republic's legislature declared 1990 the 1,000-year anniversary of Geser. From 1991 to 1992 a series of Geser readings, coinciding with summer *sur-kharbaan* festivals and the movement of the official Geser banner, was staged successively at the birthplaces of famous Geser singers in Ust'-Orda, Khori, and Aga. Both Ust'-Orda and the new Tunka National Park have adopted the tourist slogan "Land of Geser."

A more sensitive question is that of Buriat unity and the link to Mongolia. The Buriat legislature officially charged on August 27, 1990, that Moscow's dismemberment of the republic in 1937 was illegal since it had never been approved by the ASSR itself, yet the practical obstacles to restoring the pre-1937 boundaries have proved insuperable. Thus, both the relatively mainstream All-Buriat Association for Cultural Development (founded February 1991) and the more political Congress of the Buriat People (July 1996) have sought nonadministrative ways to strengthen Buriat unity. While often denounced by Russians both in Buriatia and elsewhere, pan-Mongolism has not had any practical success. The word *Mongol* in the republic and the autonomous areas' names has not been revived, and pan-Mongolian parties have as yet obtained no share in power. Many of their more talented alumni have, however, been coopted as individuals into the government. The vogue of Chinggis Khan seems to be quite superficial compared to the profound veneration in Mongolia and Inner Mongolia. Even so, the continuing economic and social crises have again stimulated apocalyptic rumors that after some great catastrophe, Russians will take over the land and the Buriats will return to Mongolia.

See also AGA BURIAT AUTONOMOUS AREA; CLOTHING AND DRESS; DANCE; EPICS; HUNTING AND FISHING; JEWELRY; RELIGION; UST'-ORDA BURIAT AUTONOMOUS AREA; WEDDINGS; YURT.

Further reading: James Forsyth, *A History of the Peoples of Siberia: Russia's North Asian Colony, 1581–1990* (Cambridge: Cambridge University Press, 1992); Roberte Hamayon, "Emblem of Minority, Substitute for Sovereignty: The Case of Buryatia," *Diogenes* 49.2 (2002): 16–25; Caroline Humphrey, "Buryats," in *The Nationalities Question in the Soviet Union*, ed. Graham Smith (London: Longman, 1990): 290–303; Caroline Humphrey, *Marx Went Away, but Karl Stayed Behind* (Ann Arbor: University of Michigan Press, 1998); Caroline Humphrey, "The Uses of Genealogy: A Historical Study of the Nomadic and Sedentarized Buryat," in *Pastoral Production and Society* (Cambridge: Cambridge University Press, 1979): 235–260; Helen Sharon Hundley, "Speransky and the Buriats: Administrative Reform in Nineteenth Century Russia" (Ph.D. diss., University of Illinois at Urbana-Champaign, 1984); Rinchen, *Four Mongolian Historical Records* (New Delhi: International Academy of Indian Culture, 1959); Robert A. Rupen, *Mongols of the Twentieth Century,* 2 vols. (Bloomington: Indiana University Press, 1964); Elena Stroganova, "Millenarian Representations of the Contemporary Buriats," *Inner Asia* 1 (1999): 111–120; Natalya L. Zhukovskaya, "Religion and Ethnicity in Eastern Russia, Republic of Buriatia: A Panorama of the 1990s," *Central Asian Survey* 14 (1995): 25–42.

Buriats of Mongolia and Inner Mongolia Established by BURIATS fleeing Russian peasant attacks in 1919, the Buriat communities in Mongolia and in China's Inner Mongolia have often been leaders in modern reforms in their communities.

In Mongolia Buriats number 35,400, or 1.7 percent of the population (1989 figures). In China the Buriats remain socially distinct, although they are officially registered as Mongols. Due to this fact, no official figures on their population exist, although their numbers were estimated in 1990 at more than 6,000.

With the establishment of the Russia-Qing frontier in 1727, the Buriats of Russia and the KHALKHA Mongols under Manchu Qing rule were separated by wide border zones manned by frontier guards. As Russia established its sphere of influence in Mongolia in the early 20th century, Buriats began using pasture in HULUN BUIR and along the northern border of Mongolia. With the 1911 RESTORATION of Mongolian independence, educated Buriats also served as translators, interpreters, and schoolteachers, working for both the Russian consulate and the Mongolian government.

During the Russian Revolution attacks and land seizures by Russian peasants intensified against the Buriats. In April 1919 Aga and Khori Buriats, along with many Khamnigan (Buriat-influenced EWENKIS), in desperation fled over the border to today's EASTERN PROVINCE and KHENTII PROVINCE in Mongolia and to Hulun Buir in Inner Mongolia, while Tünkhen and Tsongol Buriats fled to areas in today's SELENGE PROVINCE, BULGAN PROVINCE, and KHÖWSGÖL PROVINCE. Buriats fighting for the White Russian cause likewise took refuge in Hulun Buir. The Buriats and the native Bargas and Khalkhas frequently clashed over pastures and incidents of armed robbery and horse theft.

After the 1921 REVOLUTION many Buriat intellectuals again returned to Mongolia's capital as prominent political figures, while the rural Buriat refugees petitioned to receive refuge in Mongolia. Since many were anti-Communist, this was a sensitive issue for Mongolia's new

Soviet-aligned government. On February 5, 1922, the Buriats in the capital convened and established a Buriat Assembly, which served as the new People's Government's liaison with the rural Buriats in Mongolia until 1925. From 1922 to 1923 the government established six special Buriat banners in Setsen Khan and Tüshiyetü Khan provinces. Finally, at Mongolia's First Great Khural in November 1924, the Buriats of Mongolia, numbering 4,361 households and 16,093 persons, were collectively naturalized as Mongolian citizens. In 1931, with the provincial reorganization, the Buriat banners were replaced by ordinary *sums*.

In Hulun Buir the autonomous banner authorities agreed on December 3, 1921, to allow the Aga Buriat and Khamnigan herder refugees to stay permanently. They based their decision in part on sympathy with the refugees' sufferings at the hands of the Reds and in part on Hulun Buir's historical connection with the Aga and Khori Buriats and the Khamnigans (*see* EWENKIS). The next year a new banner was formed on the Shinekhen (Xinhen) River in Solon Ewenki territory (modern Ewenki Autonomous Banner) with about 160 households and 700 people. While Buriat emigration to Mongolia ceased after 1921, anticommunist Buriats continued to move into Hulun Buir, bringing the Shinekhen population in 1931 up to about 800 households and 3,000 people.

In both Mongolia and Hulun Buir the Buriats introduced new handicrafts, farming techniques, hay-mowing machines, improved horse and cattle breeds, sewing machines, and enclosed portable stoves with stovepipes instead of the old open fires. Mostly nomadic, in Mongolia's wooded KHENTII RANGE they built supplementary log cabins and in Hulun Buir mud-brick houses. The Buriats built many Buddhist temples throughout their new banners.

With the beginning of Mongolia's leftist period in 1929, Buriat intellectuals with "White" (i.e., anticommunist) pasts were dismissed from government positions. The Japanese occupation of Manchuria increased the Soviet advisers' sense of threat from pan-Mongolist Buriat espionage. In July 1933 the LHÜMBE CASE became the first manufactured spy case to affect the Buriats, sending 251 to execution or lengthy prison sentences. The GREAT PURGE of 1937–39 had a far more terrible impact. By one count Buriats in Dornod and Khentii provinces accounted for 5,368 of the 25,785 persons known to have been unjustly shot or imprisoned, as special execution squads in trucks (*khorpoodlog*) roamed the Buriat countryside.

These grim years left a legacy of suppressed bitterness among Mongolia's Buriats, expressed by both the dissident poet RENTSENII CHOINOM and the orphaned spirits that possessed Buriat shamans. Still, the Buriats remained occupationally successful. In 1989 27.7 percent of the Buriats were white-collar workers, the highest of any subethnic group in Mongolia. Mongolia's prime minister from 1991 to 1992, D. Byambasüren, was a Buriat.

While the Shinekhen Buriats prospered during that time in Hulun Buir, they remained wary of possible Soviet invasion. By 1945 more than half the Buriats had migrated south from Hulun Buir and were living in SHILIIN GOL and Jirim leagues. The Soviet invasion in August 1945 swept scores of Inner Mongolia's Buriat lamas and many more laymen into Soviet labor camps, although the major leaders evaded capture. During the ensuing Chinese civil war the Shiliin Gol Buriats waged a guerrilla war against the Chinese Communists. Defeated, many Buriats were executed, while others fled west as far as Kökenuur. By 1956 the surviving Buriats had all been resettled back at Shinekhen, where in October 1957 they were made citizens of China. In 1990 the three Buriat SUM (districts) had about 5,950 Buriats out of 7,981 residents; another 1,000 were Khamnigan Ewenkis.

With liberalization in China after 1980 and in Mongolia after 1990, the distinctive Buriat culture of wellkept genealogies, strict clan exogamy, lamas, BARIACH (Buriat, *baryaashan,* bone setters), and shamans has been openly revived. Mongolian and Shinekhen Buriats both preserve their Buriat tongue, wear distinctive Buriat clothing on festive occasions, and frown on intermarriage with local Mongols, whether Khalkha, or BARGA. Only in Mongolia, however, can the memories of persecution be openly recalled. Buriats of Russia have become interested in both groups, but especially the Shinekhen Buriats, as preservers of traditional Buriat culture.

See also AGA BURIAT AUTONOMOUS AREA; BURIAT LANGUAGE AND SCRIPTS.

Further reading: A. Hurelbaatar, "An Introduction to the History and Religion of the Buryat Mongols of Shinehen in China," *Inner Asia* 2 (2000): 73–116; Ippei Shimamura, "The Roots Seeking Movement among the Aga-Buryats: New Lights on Their Shamanism, History of Suffering, and Diaspora," in *A People Divided: Buryat Mongols in Russia, Mongolia and China,* ed. Konagaya Yuki (Cologne: International Society for the Study of the Culture and Economy of the Orclos Mongols, 2002).

Buriyad *See* BURIATS.

Burma (Myanmar) Mongol campaigns in Burma (modern Myanmar) shattered the Pagan kingdom but did not lead to permanent conquest.

In the 11th century the rulers in Pagan adopted Theravada Buddhism, the scholastic sect of Buddhism based in Sri Lanka. At the same time they subdued the more civilized realm of the Mon, a people speaking a language related to Khmer on the coast. Called Mian by the Chinese, Burma had abundant gold, which attracted traders from Bengal in the east to YUNNAN in the west.

In 1271 and 1273, the Mongol administration in Yunnan sent monks as envoys to Pagan's king Narathihipate (Narasihapati, r. 1256–87) but the Pagan kingdom in reply began harassing the Gold-Tooths (ancestors of the modern Dai and then Mongol subjects) along the Yunnan-Burma border, launching a full-scale attack in March 1277, with a large army including elephants. The 700-man Mongol garrison under Qutuq rallied Achang and Gold-Tooth tribesmen along the Yunnanese border and defeated the Burmese at Nandian (near Tengchong). In November the Mongol official Nasir-ad-Din (d. 1292; see SAYYID AJALL) raided Burma with an army of 3,840 Mongols, Cuan (Yi), and Mosuo, reaching the Irawaddy at Jiangtou (probably modern Katha). In December 1283 10,000 soldiers from Sichuan and Miao tribal auxiliaries, all under the Mongol prince Sang'udar, advanced by raft and by land to Jiangtou and Biao-Dian (probably modern Mabein), garrisoning them before taking Tagaung. Peace negotiations proved inconclusive.

In November 1286 QUBILAI KHAN's grandson Esen-Temür, the prince of Yunnan, set out from Yunnan with 6,000 troops and 1,000 Gold-Tooth auxiliaries. While King Narathihapate's son Thihathu (Sihasura) seized the throne and murdered his father at Shrikshetra (modern Prome), the Yuan army garrisoned Tagaung and Mong-Nai-Dian (near modern Molo). Esen-Temür advanced that spring to Pagan, but disease decimated the Mongols, and they withdrew. The Pagan kingdom fell into anarchy.

In 1297 Thihathu's brother Tribhuvanaditya submitted to the Yuan court, but in 1299 his younger brother Athinkaya murdered him. Another expedition was dispatched to suppress Athinkaya, but already involved with the Babai-Xifu of northern Thailand, the Yunnan authorities recommended accepting Athinkaya's preferred submission. Central and southern Burma soon came under Thai rulers who paid nominal tribute to the Yuan, and only the north remained under Mongol control.

Buryats *See* BURIATS.

buuz Meat dumplings, generally called *buuz,* are the most typical holiday fare among the Mongols, always served during the WHITE MONTH and for welcome guests. Adopted during the Qing dynasty (1636–1912), *buuz* (from Chinese *baozi*) are meat dumplings wrapped in thin skins of leavened flour and cooked in a steamer. The meat filling, or *shanz* (from Chinese *xianzi,* today *xianr*), is made of ground mutton or beef mixed with onions, cabbage, salt, and today black pepper. In wrapping the skins, cooks leave a small hole at the top with a whirl pattern around it to allow steam to escape. *Buuz, bānshi* (small meat dumplings in soup), and such foods are generally eaten during the winter months; vast amounts are made and frozen to be eaten during the course of the White Month (lunar new year). During the summer they are served only when special guests come. Dumplings are particularly popular in Mongolia's capital, ULAANBAATAR, where *buuz,* potato salad, slices of sausage with onion, and shots of vodka form the standard food for guests.

See also FOOD AND DRINK.

Buyannemekhü (Sonombaljiriin Buyannemekh, Buin Nemkhu) (1902–1937) *Mongolia's first revolutionary poet and playwright*

Buyannemekhü was born in Tüshiyetü Zasag banner (in modern Delgerkhangai Sum, Middle Gobi) but was early taken to Khüriye (modern ULAANBAATAR). At age 10 he was adopted by the Inner Mongolian anti-Chinese rebel Togtakhu Taiji (1863–1922) and tutored in Mongolian, Manchu, and some Chinese. Buyannemekhü also listened to the minstrels who entertained Togtakhu. At age 16 Buyannemekhü was enrolled in Mongolia's new public primary school and studied Mongolian, Russian, and Chinese. Buyannemekhü greatly appreciated CHINESE FICTION and Beijing opera.

Fleeing Chinese rule, Buyannemekhü joined the Mongolian People's Party at Troitskosavsk (in modern KYAKHTA) on February 27, 1921. His "Mongolian Internationale" became for many years the de facto national ANTHEM. After working as a publicist in Irkutsk, he returned to Khüriye in late 1921 and became a leader in the MONGOLIAN REVOLUTIONARY YOUTH LEAGUE. Buyannemekhü and his comrades wrote and performed *shii jüjig* (Beijing opera style plays) in Mongolian with revolutionary or historical themes: *Oirakhi tsag-un tobchi* (A survey of modern times, written 1922, revised 1924), covering Mongolian history from 1911 to 1921, and *Bagatur khöbegün Temüjin* (The heroic boy Temüjin, written March 3, 1928), describing the boyhood of Temüjin (CHINGGIS KHAN).

Naive and excitable in his politics, Buyannemekhü was briefly imprisoned during the Third Congress (August 1924). Terrified by the congress's execution of opponents, Buyannemekhü fled to Inner Mongolia, where he worked with the Daur revolutionary MERSE for more than a year. After reconciling with the new Mongolian regime, he did propaganda work in Buriatia until August 1928.

In January 1929 he helped form the Writers' Circle with TSENDIIN DAMDINSÜREN, BYAMBYN RINCHEN, and other writers. The group's first collective anthology, *Uran üges-ün chuglagan* (A gathering of artistic words), contained several of his songs, poems, and essays.

Buyannemekhü's first wife, Dulmajab, divorced him while he was in Inner Mongolia. His alcoholism and her jealousy made his second marriage with a Tatar woman, Zhena, miserable. In 1930 he was expelled from the party for his controversial past and irregular personal life. In March–September 1932 he was imprisoned for his involvement with Merse and other INNER MONGOLIANS.

During the succeeding NEW TURN POLICY, however, Buyannemekhü became a leading journalist and playwright. Buyannemekhü's most famous play, *Kharangkhui Zasag* (A dark regime, 1934), pictured all the characters of Qing-era Mongolian society and the way they conspired to destroy the lowborn couple Tsetseg and Chuluunbaatar. His reminiscence about his 1922 meeting with Lenin, published in 1935, was widely reprinted. In 1936 he received the Star of Labor. With the GREAT PURGE, however, Buyannemekhü was arrested on September 11, 1937, and executed on October 27. In 1963, with de-Stalinization, he was posthumously exonerated and his collected works reprinted in Cyrillic.

See also LITERATURE; MONGOLIAN PEOPLE'S PARTY, THIRD CONGRESS OF; REVOLUTIONARY PERIOD.

Byzantium and Bulgaria Mongol contacts with Byzantium and Bulgaria resulted from Mongol advances into the Black Sea steppe and the Caucasus. As the Mongol prince Batu's armies retreated from Hungary, they crossed the Danube and forced Bulgaria to pay tribute (1242–43). After the Mongols dispatched an embassy to Byzantium in 1254, Michael VIII Palaeologus (1259–82) allied with Il-Khan HÜLE'Ü (1256–65), to Mongol ruler of the Middle East, partly from fear and partly to gain an ally against Turkmen raids.

In 1262, however, MAMLUK EGYPT sought a three-power alliance against Hüle'ü among Egypt, Byzantium, and Berke (1257–66), Mongol khan of the GOLDEN HORDE. Michael at first temporized until NOQAI, the Golden Horde's commander, invaded in 1264 with 20,000 troops and Bulgarian allies, forcing Michael to join the alliance. In 1265, however, Michael married a natural daughter to Hüle'ü's son Abagha (1265–82), who agreed to be baptized. Thereafter, Michael managed to remain friendly to both warring Mongol parties and Egypt as well.

Bulgaria and Byzantium remained, however, generally hostile to each other, and in 1272 Michael concluded an alliance against Bulgaria with Noqai, then nomadizing west of the Dnieper, sealing it with another natural daughter. From then until his death Noqai served as a reliable ally for Byzantium in its rivalry with Bulgaria. Even after the new Bulgarian czar George I Terter (1280–92) sent his son Teodor Svetoslav as hostage and his daughter as wife for Noqai's son Jöge (Bulgarian, Chaka), Noqai continued to raid Bulgaria.

In autumn 1299, however, the new khan of the Golden Horde, Toqto'a (1291–1312), overthrew Noqai. Noqai's son Jöge/Chaka fled with Teodor Svetoslav to Bulgaria, where Teodor had Chaka crowned czar. Within a year, however, Toqto'a invaded Bulgaria, and Teodor overthrew his former protegé, becoming czar himself (1300–21). From then on the Golden Horde was firmly allied to Bulgaria. Wary of this development, Byzantium, too, cultivated relations with both the Golden Horde and the Il-Khans. In the palace a special school was set up to train girls of noble or lowly family as the emperor's adoptive daughters, who played a role in diplomacy. Toqto'a, his successor ÖZBEG KHAN (1313–41), the Il-Khan Öljeitü (1281–1316), and many lesser princes all received such fictive daughters, Özbeg apparently twice.

Despite this marriage diplomacy, from 1320 Özbeg repeatedly raided Thrace, partly in service of Bulgaria's wars against both Byzantium and the rising power of Serbia but just as much in pursuit of loot. Usually the Mongol detachments were small, 2,000 to 3,000, but in 1324 12 *tümen*s (nominally 120,000 men) pillaged Thrace for 40 days; on the last raid in 1337 they pillaged for 15 days and supposedly took 300,000 captives. Özbeg's successors did not continue his aggressive policy, and contacts with Byzantium and Bulgaria lapsed.

Further reading: Bruce G. Lippard, "The Mongols and Byzantium, 1243–1341" (Ph.D. diss., Indiana University, 1983).

C

calendars and dating systems Since the 13th century at least, the Mongols have used the traditional East Asian lunar-solar calendar, with the WHITE MONTH, or lunar new year, around January or February. While this has been replaced in the 20th century by the solar Gregorian calendar, the lunar-solar calendar is still used for traditional festivals and astrological calculations.

CALENDARS

The complexity and variations of the world's calendrical systems stem from the discrepancy between the length of the year (approximately 365 1/4 days) and that of 12 lunar phase cycles that formed the early basis for the months (approximately 354 1/2 days). While European calendars opt to ignore the Moon and Islamic calendars to ignore the Sun, East Asian calendars, including the Mongolian, use both. The full moon must always fall on the 15th of the month, yet the new year should fall around late January, when the Sun is in the constellation Aquarius. To achieve this balancing act, traditional East Asian calendars insert an extra intercalary lunar month approximately every three years. Differences between various East Asian calendars stem from different calculations for inserting the intercalary moon and for calculating the beginning of the (then invisible) new moon.

At the time of the TÜRK EMPIRES, the Turks used a lunar-solar calendar that followed the moon but with a new year timed to the rising of the Pleiades. This autumnal new year was reflected in the Turk and Uighur designations of the month according to the TWELVE-ANIMAL CYCLE, even though by 1200 the Uighur astrologers used the full Chinese calendar. Meanwhile, the 12th-century Mongols had their own indigenous names for the lunar months and calendar of festivals, probably kept by shamans. After the Mongol khans conquered North China, their Kitan adviser YELÜ CHUCAI (1190–1244) promulgated in their name a Chinese-style calendar, corrected by comparison with Middle Eastern astronomical observations. From the beginning the Mongol khans celebrated the new year in late January or early February and continued to do so even after the conversion of the western khanates to Islam, which had its own calendar.

In the 17th century Tibetan lunar-solar calendars and the Chinese lunar-solar calendar used by the Manchu QING DYNASTY (1636–1912) were introduced into Mongolia for astrological and administrative purposes. The Khalkha of Mongolia proper, however, used an independent lunar-solar calendar designed by the scholar-lama Sumpa mkhan-po Ishi-Baljur (1704–87), somewhat different from both the Chinese and Tibetan calendars. After the 1921 revolution, this Mongolian calendar was used for official purposes alongside the "European" (i.e., solar, or Gregorian) calendar until 1924, when only the Gregorian calendar was used (*see* REVOLUTIONARY PERIOD). Traditional festivals are still calculated according to the Mongolian calendar. In Inner Mongolia, as part of China, only the Gregorian calendar has been used for official purposes since 1912, but the Chinese lunar-solar calendar is still used to date both Mongol and Chinese traditional festivals. Thus, the White Month (*tsagaan sar*) is sometimes celebrated on different days in Mongolia and Inner Mongolia.

THE WEEK

Since the time of the MONGOL EMPIRE, if not long before, the Mongols have reckoned time in seven-day weeks. At least since the 16th century the days of the week were named after either the Sanskrit or Tibetan names of the

Sun, Moon, and five visible planets. In the 20th century numerical names replaced them in both Mongolia proper and Inner Mongolia, although not in exactly the same way. Thus, Tuesday (Mars's day) may be referred to either as *anggarig* (Sanskrit), *migmar* (Tibetan), *khoyordokh ödör* (day second, in modern Mongolia), or *garig-un khoyar* (second planet, modern Inner Mongolia). Since 1989 the Tibetan names have again become more widely used in Mongolia. Mongolia and Inner Mongolia have a five-and-a-half day workweek, working a half day on Saturday.

DATING SYSTEMS

The Mongolian dating systems include the twelve-animal cycle, the imperial reign years, and the Christian, or common, era. The choice of such systems has always been closely associated with sovereignty and power.

The twelve-animal cycle was adopted from China by the Türk and Uighur Empires in the sixth to ninth centuries. Its use was continued by the Mongols in the 13th and 14th centuries. From 1260, however, QUBILAI KHAN introduced the simultaneous use of Chinese *nianhao*, or reign years. These auspicious-sounding titles were proclaimed on the coronation of a new emperor or to commemorate dramatic events. For example, in 1260 Qubilai Khan proclaimed Year One of Central Unification (*Zhongtong*) to mark his coronation. In 1264, when his rival ARIQ-BÖKE surrendered, he proclaimed Year One of Returning to the Fundament (*Zhiyuan*). Such Chinese reign years were proclaimed by the Mongol great khans even after the Mongol dynasty was expelled from China in 1368. They went out of use some time between 1450 and 1500, leaving the twelve-animal cycle the only dating system.

With the revival of Mongolian historiography around 1600, the twelve-animal cycle, which often led to confusion, needed to be refined. The ancient Chinese system of concurrent 10- and 12-year cycles producing a 60-year cycle was thus adopted, first in various Uighur or Tibetan forms. Around the same time the Mongols submitted to the Manchu Qing dynasty (1636–1912) and adopted the Manchu reign years, which were proclaimed not just in Chinese but also in Manchu and Mongolian versions. Thus, 1821 was Year One of Daoguang (Brilliant Way, Chinese) or Törö-Gereltü (Brilliant State, Mongolian).

With the restoration of Mongolian independence, the new Mongolian theocratic government proclaimed 1911 Year One of Olan-a Ergügdegsen (Cyrillic, Olnoo Örgögdsön), "Elevated by the Many." This title was a translation of the name of the first monarch at the dawn of time, according to the Buddhist scriptures. This reign year continued in use after the 1921 Revolution. In 1924, with the proclamation of a republic, it was replaced by the "year of Mongolia," yet this year was still numbered from 1911, so that 1925 was "year 15 of Mongolia" (*see* REVOLUTIONARY PERIOD).

In Inner Mongolia the Mongols were forced to use the "Year of the (Chinese) Republic" from 1912 on. Most preferred, however, to use the twelve-animal cycle dates instead. In 1936 the nationalist Inner Mongolian government of Prince Demchugdongrub declared year 731 of "Holy Chinggis," dating from his coronation in 1206. This system continued until the fall of his government in 1945.

The Christian dating system from the birth of Christ first appears in Mongolian-language documents among the BURIATS in czarist Russia. From 1921 these dates were added on official documents in Mongolia proper as the "European year." This system did not actually replace the "Year of Mongolia," however, until the adoption of CYRILLIC-SCRIPT MONGOLIAN in 1945–50. In 1949 the People's Republic of China adopted the Christian, or common, era.

See also ASTROLOGY; FIVE-YEAR PLANS; FOOD AND DRINK; KOUMISS; *NAADAM; QURILTAI.*

camels The Bactrian, or two-humped, camel of Mongolia is used as a draft animal, for its fine hair, for milk, and for its hides and meat. In the year 2000 camels in Mongolia numbered 322,900, or only 1.1 percent of total stock. The two-humped camel, or *Camelus bactrianus*, is better adapted to cold but less hardy in extremely dry and hot conditions than is the one-humped camel, or dromedary (*C. dromedarius*) of Arabia and the Sahara Desert. The two-humped camel is primarily an animal of the GOBI DESERT. The endangered wild two-humped camel (*khawtgai*) is found in southwestern Mongolia.

The Alashan breed, a typical breed of the Mongolian camel, weighs on average 608 kilograms (1,340 pounds) for the bull and 454 kilograms (1,001 pounds) for the cow. It produces 4 to 5 kilograms (9–11 pounds) of hair a season and can carry loads of 150–250 kilograms (330–550 pounds) for 30–40 kilometers (19–25 miles) daily, while geldings can pull up to 428 kilograms (944 pounds). Mongols ride camels with a soft felt saddle with attached stirrups placed between the humps; it is controlled with a halter and reins and a separate rope attached to a wooden stake through the camel's nose. Loads are placed between felt or wool pads along the animal's sides and are held in place by two wooden poles tied in front and back and underneath the camel's belly.

Wild and domestic camels are commonly found on Mongolian and southern Siberian PETROGLYPHS from the Upper Paleolithic to the Bronze and early Iron Ages (1500–500 B.C.E.). Literary evidence and petroglyphs show that camels regularly drew the Inner Asian YURT carts. When the collapsible yurt replaced the yurt cart, the camel remained the main beast of burden for nomadic movements.

In 1924 275,000 camels formed only 2 percent of independent Mongolia's total herd. In 1953 the number of Mongolia's camels reached 888,000, or 3.9 percent. With the camel's role as transport slowly yielding to motorized transportation, the number steadily declined from then on to 537,500 (2.1 percent) in 1990, and sales of camel hair likewise declined from a high of 3,900 metric tons (4,299 short tons) in 1955 to 2,300 metric tons (2,535 short tons) in 1990. After 1990 the fuel crisis put camels once more in demand for local transport, but herders have turned to more marketable commodities, throwing camel numbers into a steady decline. SOUTH GOBI PROVINCE has always been by far the leading camel-herding province, with EAST GOBI PROVINCE, MIDDLE GOBI PROVINCE, GOBI-ALTAI PROVINCE, BAYANKHONGOR PROVINCE, and KHOWD PROVINCE containing most of the rest. Traditionally about 21 to 23 percent, South Gobi's percentage of Mongolia's camel herd reached 29 percent in 2000.

While camels were traditionally raised in Kalmykia and in the Aga steppe, they were eliminated by Soviet economic planners. In Inner Mongolia the total number of camels in 1947 was 110,000. The number peaked at 344,000 in 1978 before declining as commercialization advanced to 247,000 in the middle of 1990. In 1990 (year end), the total number was 222,900, of which 149,700 lived in ALASHAN league. By 2003, droughts and commercialization further reduced Alashan's camel herd to only 68,000.

"Campaigns of Genghis Khan" See SHENGWU QINZHENG LU.

Čaqar See CHAKHAR.

Caracathay See QARA-KHITAI.

cashmere

Cashmere refers to the soft undercoat of cashmere goats and the fabric made from weaving such fibers. Since the 1970s the Mongolian plateau has been producing the great majority of the world's cashmere. Mongolia and China's Inner Mongolia have become the main rivals in the world production of cashmere. Cashmere goats flourish particularly in dry areas of the GOBI DESERT, covering Mongolia's BAYANKHONGOR PROVINCE, GOBI-ALTAI PROVINCE, and SOUTH GOBI PROVINCE and Inner Mongolia's ALASHAN, BAYANNUUR, and ORDOS leagues.

Responding to insistent Soviet demands before and during WORLD WAR II, Mongolia's cashmere production shot up from 100 metric tons (110 short tons) in 1940 to 800 metric tons (882 short tons) in 1945. Later, in the collectivized economy, cashmere production increased from an average of 1,193 metric tons (1,315 short tons) in 1960–65 to 1,327 (1,463 short tons) in 1986–90. Concerted efforts improved the average cashmere yield per goat from 200 grams (7.1 ounces) in 1960 to 295 grams (10.4 ounces) in 1990.

Japanese war reparations paid in 1972 created the state-owned Gobi Cashmere Factory in ULAANBAATAR to knit cashmere as well as camel hair goods. As cashmere goods production rose from 38,900 pieces (1980) to

275,700 (1990), the percentage of cashmere exported in raw form fell to barely 25 percent.

In China the Inner Mongolian Yekhe Juu (also spelled Ih Ju) League Cashmere Factory was founded in 1972 in Dongsheng City (Ordos) with the ability to process 200 metric tons (220 short tons) of cashmere annually. As in Mongolia before the creation of Gobi Cashmere, poor production technology meant most of the raw cashmere was exported. In 1979 the Japanese firm Mitsui invested 3 billion yen (13 billion *yuan*) in the Dongsheng plant, with further investment in 1987. By 1990 the factory was the world's largest cashmere factory. Inner Mongolia's total production in 1989 reached 1,976 metric tons (2,178 short tons) of cashmere, 637.47 metric tons (702.69 short tons) of hairless cashmere, and 137.25 metric tons (151.29 short tons) of knitted goods. Of this, 130 metric tons (143 short tons) of hairless cashmere and 268,000 cashmere sweaters were exported annually.

In the 1990s, with the opening and PRIVATIZATION of the Mongolian economy, cashmere production in Mongolia proper rose from 1,500 metric tons (1,653 short tons) in 1990 to 3,300 (3,638 short tons) in 1999. Even so, Mongolian factories did not modernize their equipment, and Mongolia's fiber width showed a worrying increase while the capacity of Inner Mongolia's factories expanded past 4,500 metric tons (4,960 short tons). After Mongolia's export controls were eliminated, 45–60 percent of Mongolia's total cashmere production has been exported in raw form to Inner Mongolia. Since 1996, however, the glut on the world market has caused prices to plummet. The Gobi Cashmere Joint-Stock Company, still Mongolia's largest single buyer of cashmere and maker of cashmere goods, has lobbied in vain for reinstatement of export controls on raw cashmere. Despite being one of the state sector's most profitable enterprises, in 2001 the Gobi Company was scheduled to be privatized.

See also COLLECTIVIZATION AND COLLECTIVE HERDING; DECOLLECTIVIZATION; ECONOMY, MODERN.

cattle

Mongolian cattle in ancient times were used for milk and as draft animals but were rarely, if ever, eaten. Today beef and dairy cattle are both major parts of Mongolian animal husbandry. Most cattle are ordinary domestic cattle (*Bos taurus*), but yaks (*Bos grunniens*) and yak–cattle crossbreeds are kept in Mongolia's mountainous west. In 2000 Mongolia had 3,097,600 head of cattle.

The traditional breed of Mongolian bulls are about 1.2 meters (3.9 feet) high at the shoulder and 1.37 meters (4.49 feet) long and weigh about 300–400 kilograms (660–880 pounds). Cows are about 1.1 meters (3.6 feet) high and 1.27 meters (4.17 feet) long and weigh about 250–350 kilograms (550–770 pounds). The dressing percentage is about 53 percent, and milk production on good pastures is about 500–700 kilograms (1,100–1,540 pounds) annually, with 5.3 percent butterfat content. In fact, real annual milk production per cow in Mongolia averages around 290–350 kilograms (640–770 pounds). While meat and milk production are thus far below those of purebred cattle, Mongolian cattle are adapted to live on open range with little water and through very cold winters. They are also very disease resistant. The quality of meat and milk is high.

Mongolian yaks inhabit primarily the KHANGAI RANGE and ALTAI RANGE. They are particularly common in certain *sum*s (districts) of KHOWD PROVINCE, GOBI-ALTAI PROVINCE, and BAYANKHONGOR PROVINCE and are also found in the mountainous areas of NORTH KHANGAI PROVINCE, SOUTH KHANGAI PROVINCE, ZAWKHAN PROVINCE, KHÖWSGÖL PROVINCE, BAYAN-ÖLGII PROVINCE, and UWS PROVINCE. In Tibet yaks do not breed or work well in altitudes below 3,000 meters (9,800 feet), but Mongolian yaks are bred in altitudes as low as 2,500 meters (8,200 feet). Like Tibetans, the Mongolians produce common cattle-yak crossbreeds, called *khainag*, which can be found as low as 1,600 meters (5,250 feet).

In the early steppe empires cattle appear to have been rather rare on the Mongolian plateau. In the eastern Inner Mongolian pastures under the JIN DYNASTY in 1188,

only 9 percent of the animals were cattle. Thirteenth-century travelers reported that the cattle were used mostly as draft animals, to pull carts and the mobile YURTS of the period. They were milked but eaten only rarely. The 1640 MONGOL-OIRAT CODE prescribed fines of CAMELS, HORSES, SHEEP, and GOATS, but none of cattle.

Cattle became more common in the 19th century. In 1924 cattle in Mongolia proper totaled 1,512,100 head, or 11 percent of all livestock. The absolute numbers in 1940 reached 2,722,800 head (10.3 percent). At this time the herders were selling more beef than mutton to the state procurement agencies, although this illustrates only the eating habits of the small urban class. The numbers declined absolutely and relatively in the 1950s but gradually increased again in the succeeding decades to 2,848,700 head (11 percent). The increase was primarily in dairy cows, as average annual production of milk rose from 219,600 metric tons (242,067 short tons) in 1961–65 to 306,100 metric tons (337,417 short tons) in 1986–90, while annual beef production rose only from 62,300 metric tons (68,674 short tons) to 66,200 metric tons (72,973 short tons) from 1960 to 1990.

With the market transition of 1990 the production of both beef and milk increased sharply, as the number of cattle reached 3,824,700 in 1999 (11.4 percent of total

Khainag (yak-cattle crossbreeds) grazing near the shore of Lake Khöwsgöl, 1992 *(Courtesy of Christopher Atwood)*

livestock). In that year beef production reached 104,600 metric tons (115,302 short tons) and milk 467,000 metric tons (514,779 short tons). In the following year a massive ZUD (winter die-off) hit the cattle-breeding provinces especially hard. Most of Mongolia's cattle are in the wetter northern provinces, especially North Khangai province, Khöwsgöl province, KHENTII PROVINCE, South Khangai province, and CENTRAL PROVINCE.

In Inner Mongolia the number of cattle rose from 1,764,000 head in 1947 to 4,932,000 in 1965. After declining during the Cultural Revolution, the number again expanded from 3,585,000 in 1978 to 4,398,000 in 1990 (all June figures). Of the 3,853,000 left after the 1990 fall slaughter, almost 80 percent lived in central SHILIIN GOL and the three eastern districts of TONGLIAO, KHINGGAN, and CHIFENG (see KHORCHIN and JUU UDA), with 819,000 (21 percent) in Tongliao Municipality (formerly Jirim) alone.

A number of cattle breeds have been developed by improving Mongolian cattle or crossbreeding them with other breeds. Dual-use breeds include the improved Kalmyk cattle, the crossbred Three Rivers cattle produced in HULUN BUIR by White Russian ranchers, and the crossbred Steppe Red cattle of central Inner Mongolia developed from 1953 on. The Selenge, developed in Mongolia, is a beef breed.

See also ANIMAL HUSBANDRY AND NOMADISM; DAIRY PRODUCTS; FOOD AND DRINK.

census in the Mongol Empire The census first appeared among the Mongols in 1206 when CHINGGIS KHAN numbered his people as part of his DECIMAL ORGANIZATION. In the *SECRET HISTORY OF THE MONGOLS*, Chinggis Khan ordered SHIGI QUTUQU, the first *JARGHUCHI* (judge) of the MONGOL EMPIRE, to record in a "blue register" (*köke debter*) all the households under their proper decimal units. The register was to be a permanent record of the assignment of the people to their units. This first census was remarkably complete; when Chinggis Khan put his companion (NÖKÖR) Degei over the "hidden households," they made only 1,000 out of the 95,000 counted. Since all Mongols served the government in the same way, this census did not divide them into categories, although the merits of the decimal unit commanders were recorded and updated in the registers. Chinggis repeated the census around 1225.

The conquest of the sedentary regions required new census practices. In Chinggis Khan's time subjects in a newly conquered city were sorted and classified, but there was no written register of the subject population. ÖGEDEI KHAN (1229–41) ordered the first census of sedentary peoples under Mongol control in 1233 in North China. This first census of the subject peoples led to a debate between YELÜ CHUCAI and Mahmud Yalavach (*see* MAHMUD YALAVACH AND MAS'UD BEG) over the definition of a household. In China, where the extended family was the ideal, married sons living with their father were one household, but in Turkestani and Mongol practice every adult man was head of a separate household for tax purposes. Yelü Chucai prevented the application of this standard to China, at least temporarily.

In 1235 Shigi Qutuqu was sent as judge to North China, and the census was repeated with much greater thoroughness. Local censuses also took place in the 1240s in Russia and TURKEY. GÜYÜG Khan (1246–48) ordered an empirewide census, but his death aborted the enterprise. Thus, it was MÖNGKE KHAN (1251–59) who in 1252 first counted the empire's entire population. The extent of the empire made the census very time consuming; while that of North China was completed in 1252, Novgorod in the far northwest was not counted until winter 1258–59.

The new census was far more complicated than the old census, counting not just the number of households but also the number of men aged 15 to 60 and the number of fields, livestock, vineyards, and orchards. Since some subject people paid taxes while others served in the military, there were separate registers of military and civilian households. Another registry listed those in the personal appanages of the Mongol nobility. Within the civilian register craftsmen were also listed separately, while in the military registers auxiliary and regular households were distinguished. Clergy of the approved religions were separated and not counted. The census took place in winter, during the slack season, and evaders faced beatings and even execution. In Novgorod, Armenia, and other tributary districts the census and the regressive taxation it facilitated sparked popular riots and resistance. The large census teams combined both Mongol clerks from the court of the khans and experienced local staff, at least where it was available, as in China and Iran. When the new "blue register" was completed, probably in both the local administrative language and in Uighur or Mongolian, one copy was returned to Qara Qorum and one copy kept for the local administration.

As taxation, corvée, and military levies depended on census records, government power depended on a regular census, yet in all the Mongol successor states the census eventually lapsed. In the Mongol YUAN DYNASTY of China the records were revised yearly from 1262 to 1275. After that year the conquest of South China and a general slackening of administration broke off the yearly census. The vastly enlarged realm was counted in 1291–93 and again in 1330, but efforts to increase tax revenues by accurately investigating land holdings failed in the face of widespread opposition. The census of military households likewise lapsed after 1289. In the IL-KHANATE in Iran the census continued in HÜLE'Ü's reign (1256–65) but then lapsed until the time of GHAZAN KHAN (1295–1304), who ordered a new census. In the GOLDEN HORDE a second census was carried out in 1274–75. The lapse of the census marked the transformation of Mongol rule from a charismatic regime based on expansion into a traditional regime based on support of a stable upper class.

See also APPANAGE SYSTEM; ARTISANS IN THE MONGOL EMPIRE; MASSACRES AND THE MONGOL CONQUEST; MILITARY OF THE MONGOL EMPIRE; RUSSIA AND THE MONGOL EMPIRE.

Further reading: Thomas T. Allsen, *Mongol Imperialism: The Policies of the Grand Qan Möngke in China, Russia, and the Islamic Lands, 1251–1259* (Berkeley: University of California Press, 1987).

Central Europe and the Mongols   Despite devastating invasions in 1241–42 and later, Hungary and Poland remained outside the Mongol Empire. Hungary and Poland first learned of the Mongols through their eastern neighbors. The Hungarians, themselves of steppe origin, had dispatched Friar Julian to convert their relatives in "Greater Hungary" (the modern, now Turkicized, Bashkirs or Bashkort). Julian returned in 1237 warning King Bela IV (r. 1235–70) about the advancing Mongols. In the same year the chief KÖTEN (Kotian, Kötöny) of the QIPCHAQS (Comans) also sought refuge in Hungary with 40,000 cavalrymen. King Bela welcomed the Qipchaqs as bulwarks both against the Mongols and the nobility. Meanwhile, both Poland and Hungary had long been involved in southeastern Russia (modern western Ukraine), and when the Mongols destroyed Kiev in December 1240 and sacked Halych (Galich) and Volodymyr (Vladimir), Prince Daniel of Halych (d. 1264), his brother Vasil'ko of Volodymyr (d. 1269), and Michael of Chernihiv (Chernigov, d. 1246) all took refuge in Poland.

When the Mongols demanded that Bela IV deport Köten, he refused, and the Mongols thus invaded in five columns, commanded by SÜBE'ETEI BA'ATUR in the vanguard, along a vast front from Poland to Wallachia. Hordu (CHINGGIS KHAN'S senior grandson) commanded the attack in Poland, at that time divided among nine princes of the Piast dynasty. The Mongols drove through Poland, sacking its major cities before defeating a combined Polish–German army at Liegnitz (Legnica) on April 9, 1241. Hordu's army then crossed Moravia to rejoin the others in Hungary. The other four columns crossed the Carpathian Mountains through separate passes and linked up in northeast Hungary. The Mongols found the Hungarian army under Bela formidable, even though the Qipchaqs had revolted after jealous barons murdered Köten. Hordu's brother BATU and his generals Boroldai and Sübe'etei crushed the Hungarians on April 11 at Muhi (just south of Miskolc), and Bela escaped first to Austria and then to Croatia. As Pope Gregory IX (r. 1227–41) and the Holy Roman Emperor Frederick II (r. 1220–50) issued conflicting calls for a crusade, the Mongol army summered in Hungary and then under

Prince Qadan (son of ÖGEDEI KHAN) crossed the frozen Danube in December 1241. Qadan chased Bela to Ragusa, until news of Ögedei Khan's death on December 11, 1241, prompted the Mongols to return through Bulgaria to the Qipchaq steppe in spring 1242. Mongol princes carried thousands of Hungarians and Transylvanian Saxons captive to their appanages as slaves.

Despite famine, after the invasion King Bela poured resources into castle building. He also resettled refugee Qipchaqs and OSSETES back in Hungary, marrying his son to a Qipchaq princess, and sought Russian allies. The Poles, too, sought to use Russian princes against the Mongols, first supporting Michael of Chernihiv, then Daniel of Halych. Daniel later turned for assistance to the pagan Lithuanians and expelled the Mongol garrisons from his territory in 1256. When the Lithuanians betrayed the alliance and invaded Halych, Batu's brother Berke (r. 1257–66) dispatched Boroldai to reassert Mongol authority. Daniel fled to Poland, but his brother Vasil'ko and his sons joined Boroldai in 1259 to ravage Lithuania and Poland, massacring Sandomierz. Another Russian–Mongol raid on Poland, instigated by Daniel's son Lev, followed in 1280.

By 1280 Noqai, leader of a junior Mongol line, had established a virtually independent realm from the Dnieper to the Danube, ruling Ossetes, Vlachs (Romanians), and Russians of Halych and Volodymyr. King Ladislaus IV (r. 1272–90), Bela IV's grandson, whose mother was Qipchaq, had fought with the nobility and the church and had adopted the Qipchaq lifestyle. In winter 1285–86 Noqai and the future khan, Töle-Bugha (r. 1287–91), invaded Hungary. Noqai plundered Transylvania, while snow bogged down Töle-Bugha in the Carpathians. The Poles exploited the absence of the Russian princes with the Mongols and raided Russian land, so the next year Noqai and Töle-Bugha raided Poland in reprisal.

As Hungary and Poland assimilated their eastern elements, the Mongols lost interest in conquest. In 1290 Qipchaq malcontents murdered Ladislaus, ending the Qipchaq interlude in Hungarian history. Poland annexed Halych in 1349, and while it would later suffer from raids by the TATARS, descendants of the GOLDEN HORDE, conquest was never again a threat.

See also BYZANTIUM AND THE BALKANS; CHRISTIAN SOURCES ON THE MONGOL EMPIRE; KIEV, SIEGE OF; LIEGNITZ, BATTLE OF; RUSSIA AND THE MONGOL EMPIRE; WESTERN EUROPE AND THE MONGOLS.

Further reading: Nora Berend, *At the Gate of Christendom: Jews, Muslims, and "Pagans" in Medieval Hungary, c. 1000–c. 1300* (Cambridge: Cambridge University Press, 2001); James Chambers, *The Devil's Horsemen: The Mongol Invasion of Europe* (London: Cassel, 1988).

Central province (Töv)   Created in the 1931 reorganization of Mongolia, Central province surrounds the capital ULAANBAATAR in east-central Mongolia. In the early 1950s Selenge was combined with Central province, but the two were separated again in 1959. The borders of Ulaanbaatar, a separate province-level unit, with Central province were readjusted in 1994. Its territory was entirely included in KHALKHA Mongolia's prerevolutionary Tüshiyetü Khan province.

Covering 74,000 square kilometers (28,572 square miles), Central province includes the well-watered and wooded KHENTII RANGE in the northeast and steppe in the west and south. It is crossed by the TUUL RIVER. Its population of 82,000 in 1956 dropped to 63,600 in 1969 due to the separation of Selenge but reached 98,000 in 2000. The province's livestock, numbering 2,022,100 head, contains high numbers of HORSES (249,500 head) and SHEEP (1,101,200); cattle, including milking cows supplying Ulaanbaatar, number 184,200. Central province is also an important arable agriculture center, producing 11 percent of Mongolia's grain, 21 percent of its potatoes, and 15 percent of its vegetables. Since 2003, a rich gold mine at Bornuur is being operated by a Canadian company. Zuunmod, with 16,200 people, is the province's administrative center.

See also NATSUGDORJI.

17th-century chronicles The Mongolian chronicle tradition, founded in the 17th century, expressed and transmitted the traditional Mongolian sense of history into the 20th century.

COMMON STRUCTURE AND THEMES

The basic structure of Mongolian chronicles is illustrated in the earliest mature examples of the tradition: the ALTAN TOBCHI, or "Golden summary" (c. 1655), compiled by Lubsang-Danzin, and the ERDENI-YIN TOBCHI, or "Precious summary" (1662), by SAGHANG SECHEN. Later chronicles fall into two schools, an "eastern school" based on the *Altan tobchi*, followed by the *Asaragchi neretü-yin teüke* (History of Asaragchi, composed in KHALKHA in 1667), and 18th-century writers such as DUKE GOMBOJAB, Rashipungsug (*see* BOLOR ERIKHE), and Lomi; and a "western school" represented by the *Erdeni-yin tobchi*, the *Shira tughuji* (Yellow, i.e., Imperial, tale) and later ORDOS chronicles.

The chronicles begin with the primeval king of India, Mahasammata, and his successors. Branches of this lineage move first to Tibet and then to Mongolia, becoming the ancestors of CHINGGIS KHAN as recorded in the 13th-century SECRET HISTORY OF THE MONGOLS. This text is quoted extensively at least through the childhood of Chinggis but is followed by apocryphal material focusing on Chinggis Khan's divine mandate, his rivalry with his brothers Qasar and Belgütei, and his people's desire for his rule. The spatial horizon of the legendary material is limited to the MONGOLIAN PLATEAU, northwest China's Tangut XIA DYNASTY, Inner Mongolia's ÖNGGUD (Enggüd) tribe, and Korea.

After the death of Chinggis Khan the common material in the *Altan tobchi* and the *Erdeni-yin tobchi* includes a list of khans up to Toghan-Temür (1333–70) and some material, drawn from Tibetan sources, on their Buddhist chaplains. A story cycle follows, recounting the fall of the Yuan, Toghan-Temür's escape, his lament over lost DAIDU (*see* "LAMENT OF TOGHAN-TEMÜR"), and how his queen gave birth to the Ming's Yongle emperor (1402–24), who was thus truly Mongolian.

With the reign of Elbeg Khan (1392?–99?) the Mongolian chronicles begin a cycle of Mongol-Oirat conflicts. Most of the names can be identified with figures who appear in MING DYNASTY frontier reports but with frequent divergences of narrative caused by numerous inaccuracies in both types of materials and by their radically differing interests: tribal and genealogical politics for the Mongols and frontier raids for the Ming writers. The chronicle episodes, all told from a Mongolian and anti-Oirat standpoint, emphasize the priority of loyalty to blood, the Chinggis cult and sovereignty, rivalries with princes descended from Chinggis Khan's brothers Qasar and Belgütei, and the need for Mongol unity.

Lubsang-Danzin's *Altan tobchi* includes a genealogical appendix identifying the origins of the Mongol noble lines that survived the Manchu conquest. The *Erdeni-yin tobchi* interlards even richer genealogical material on the Ordos and TÜMED nobles in the text. In later chronicles the genealogical material expanded tremendously.

Throughout, the chronicles typically date not events, but only the births, coronations, and deaths of khans, often with their ages at coronation and/or death. Certain divergences among the lists and episodes and clear interpolations show that these were based on king lists, whether of the Mongol great khans or Ming emperors, which circulated separately.

SOURCES AND COMPILATION

The shared contents of the 17th-century chronicles fall into three categories: 1) narrative episodes unique to the chronicles with a strong Chinggisid emphasis; 2) material taken from other written sources, such as the *Secret History,* collections of *biligs* (wise sayings) of Chinggis Khan, and Tibetan historical handbooks; and 3) king lists that gave the dates of the khans' births, coronations, and deaths in the 12-ANIMAL CYCLE, probably with their length of reigns and ages at coronation and death. The chroniclers worked by integrating these three classes of materials with varying degrees of skill and then adding further materials, both scholastic and legendary.

The original common chronicle material concerned only the life of Chinggis Khan (1162–1227), Toghan-Temür's loss of Daidu (1368), and the Mongol-Oirat conflict (1392–1517). While the Chinggis Khan material appears to be a single tradition, episodes in the Mongol-Oirat conflict in the *Altan tobchi* and *Erdeni-yin tobchi* show both extensive sharing and significant divergences.

Thus, a common body of material on the 1392–1517 period, already in written form, must have been reworked and expanded independently by the compilers. As the latest common episodes relate to BATU-MÖNGKE DAYAN KHAN (1480?–1517?), the common chronicle material on the Mongol-Oirat wars must have been first written down shortly after then. In addition to supplying independent "updates" of post–Dayan Khanid material, the two early chronicles each incorporated historical episodes not found in the other. That in the *Altan tobchi* is primarily CHAKHAR and KHORCHIN related, while that in the *Erdeniyin tobchi* is Ordos related.

The incorporation of written materials into these legend cycles is illustrated by the use of *Secret History* materials in the account of Chinggis Khan. The original 16th-century stage of the chronicle tradition is documented by the recently published *Chinggis khaghan-u altan tobchi* (Golden summary of Chinggis Khan), which contains the chronicle legends of Chinggis Khan without any *Secret History* materials. When the text of the *Secret History* reappeared, apparently some time before 1650, Lubsang-Danzin incorporated the bulk of it into his *Altan tobchi* alongside the apocryphal *Chinggis khaghan-u altan tobchi* material. Given the contradictions that resulted, however, this was not a popular solution. An abridged *Altan tobchi* used only an abbreviated version of the *Secret History* up to Chinggis Khan's marriage to BÖRTE ÜJIN, a solution also followed by Saghang Sechen. The *Asaragchi neretü-yin teüke* also included the tale of Börte's kidnapping by the MERKID.

Both Lubsang-Danzin and Saghang Sechen incorporated Tibetan material on the formation of the world, Tibetan lamas at the Mongolian court, and so on. The *Asaragchi neretü-yin teüke* added a preface from the Fifth Dalai Lama's (1617–82) didactic work *Festival of Youth*. The abbreviated *Altan tobchi*, however, cut most of the Tibetan materials.

Interpolated king lists in the *Altan tobchi* is date to 1655 and 1624, and the earliest king lists used by any of the chroniclers must, given their documented inaccuracies and regional divergences, have been composed after the death of Daraisun Khan (1548–57).

HISTORICAL VALUE

Given the nature of the 17th-century chronicles, their historical value is uneven. Material taken from Tibetan or *Secret History* sources is obviously of no independent value, although the use made of it is of intellectual-historical interest. The king lists are useful when corroborated by Ming reports. The episodic material, both common and regional, is, however, of great importance. The material from the period from ESEN (d. 1454) to Dayan Khan can be confirmed extensively from the Chinese sources and supplies the crucial tribal-political motives and structures ignored by the Chinese frontier observers. From Elbeg to Esen (1392–1454) the material is less reliable but still important. Finally, that on Chinggis Khan and Toghan-Temür, while worthless as a historical source, is of great value in explaining the political and tribal issues related to the Dayan Khanid period.

See also EIGHT WHITE YURTS; LITERATURE.

Further reading: Hidehiro Okada, "Mongol Chronicles and Chinggisid Genealogies," *Journal of Asian and African Studies* 27 (1984): 147–154; C. Žamcarano, *Mongol Chronicles of the Seventeenth Century,* trans. Rudolf Loewenthal (Wiesbaden: Otto Harrassowitz, 1955).

Cha'adai (Chaghatai, Chaghaday) (d. 1242) *Second of Chinggis Khan's sons and founder of the Chaghatay khanate* Cha'adai was the second son of CHINGGIS KHAN's main wife BÖRTE and his first son of indubitable paternity. He campaigned with his brothers JOCHI and Ögedei against Inner Mongolia (1211) and Hebei and Shanxi (1213) and with Ögedei against Otrar (winter 1219–20) and Urganch (April 1221). With his personal retainer, Zhang Rong (Chang Jung, 1158–1230), Cha'adai supervised the road and bridge building for the KHORAZM campaign. Chinggis Khan bestowed Almaligh (near modern Huocheng) as Cha'adai's summer pasture, and his winter pastures ranged from Samarqand to Besh-Baligh (near modern Qitai). Chinggis also assigned him 4,000 or 8,000 men (the sources differ). Cha'adai had two main wives, Yisülün and Tögen, both of the QONGGIRAD clan, and eight sons, but his favorite son, Mö'etüken, was killed at the siege of Bamiyan (1221).

His campaigns in North China and Central Asia won him the city of Taiyuan and his two stewards: Vajir, a Uighur from North China and a master of the Chinggisid *biligs* (wise sayings), and Qutb-ud-Din Habash 'Amid from Otrar. Chinggis Khan praised Cha'adai's devotion to the Mongol JASAQ (law) and *yosun* (custom) but considered him obstinate and narrow-minded. He appointed first BO'ORCHU of the Arulad and then Köke Chos of the Baarin to train him, yet still Cha'adai openly insulted Jochi as being a bastard.

Cha'adai supported ÖGEDEI KHAN's enthronement in 1229, and as the oldest surviving Chinggisid, he secured the empire's stability in the crucial first post-Chinggisid generation by his strict deference to the khan. He vainly remonstrated against Ögedei's excessive drinking. He strictly prohibited Islamic ablutions and slaughtering in his territory, and his anti-Islamic image influenced his descendants for several generations. Cha'adai became the obvious kingmaker after Ögedei's death in 1241 but soon died himself. Yisülün accused Vajir of poisoning him and put him to death, setting Habash 'Amid as steward in his stead. The decision of GÜYÜG Khan (1246–48) to set aside Cha'adai's designated successor, Qara-Hüle'ü (d. 1252–53), and make his alcoholic son Yisü-Möngke his heir disordered the khanate's succession for decades.

See also CHAGHATAY KHANATE.

Chabchiyal *See* JUYONGGUAN PASS, BATTLE OF.

Chabi *See* CHABUI.

Chabui (Chabi) (d. 1281) *The empress of Qubilai Khan and his partner in the administration of the empire*
Chabui was the daughter of Alchi Noyan of the QONGGI-RAD. Since 1237 the Qonggirad had been promised that in every generation one of their daughters would be empress and one of their sons would receive a princess. Chabui was QUBILAI KHAN's second wife, probably marrying him around 1240. Chabui bore Qubilai, then a prince with little political clout, four sons: Dorji, JINGIM, the future heir apparent (1243–85), Manggala (d. 1280), and Nomuqan (d. 1301). She soon eclipsed Qubilai's first wife, and although Qubilai during her life married five other wives and had many concubines, Chabui never faced any real rival in her husband's esteem. Chabui was famous for her frugality. Before Qubilai's coronation she gave her sons both Buddhist initiations and Confucian educations, and as empress she supported Confucian officials. Thus, she once criticized LIU BINGZHONG for not opposing a plan of Qubilai's KESHIG nobility to make the

Empress Chabui (d. 1281), wife of Qubilai Khan, wearing a *boqta*. Anonymous court painter *(Courtesy of the National Palace Museum, Taipei)*

suburbs of the capital a grazing ground. During the victory celebrations over the Song in 1276, she warned Qubilai, "Your handmaiden has heard that from ancient times there has never been a kingdom that lasted for a thousand years. To not let our descendants reach that point [that the Song did] will be happiness." Chabui also tried to improve conditions for the captured Song empress, Madame Quan. After Chabui's death in 1281, Qubilai married her niece Nambui, to whom he bequeathed Chabui's ORDO.

Chaghan teüke **(The White History)**   In the late 16th century KHUTUGTAI SECHEN KHUNG-TAIJI circulated a work whose full name was *Arban buyantu nom-un chaghan teükei* (White history of the dharma with ten virtues), which he found in Songzhou (near modern CHIFENG) and attributed to QUBILAI KHAN (1260–94). The text describes the "TWO CUSTOMS" of (Buddhist) religion (*shashin*) and state (*törö*), which had supposedly been observed in all countries and especially in Tibet and which Qubilai had reestablished. The realization of this ideal lies in assigning proper titles to monks and officials, who are to perform tasks grouped in numbered categories (three great deeds, four great principles, six great examples, etc.) and to receive prescribed rewards or punishments for meditative and governmental accomplishments or moral demerits. The realm is defined by the scheme of "five colors and four foreigners," a mandalalike arrangement of the Koreans, Chinese, Turkestanis, and Tibetans around the "blue" Mongols, and a calender of Buddhist and pastoral festivals. Despite Khutugtai Sechen's claim, the text shows no connection in language or themes to real Yuan-era documents. Significantly, the government titles closely resemble those in use at the EIGHT WHITE YURTS, the shrine of CHINGGIS KHAN, and one manuscript closes with a list of donors to the shrine. The history is likely a late 16th-century utopia, retrojected to Qubilai's time, envisioning Buddhist reunification of Mongolia around the Eight White Yurts.

Chaghatai *See* CHA'ADAI.

Chaghatay Khanate   The Chaghatay Khanate had the most turbulent history of any of the MONGOL EMPIRE's successor states, with frequent changes of dynasty, territory, and political orientation. The name *Chaghatay* is the Turkish form of the founder's Mongolian name, CHA'ADAI, and is the realm's common name in the Islamic histories that form our main source on the dynasty.

FORMATION OF THE DYNASTY

The roots of the Chaghatay Khanate as a separate state lay in CHINGGIS KHAN's allotment to Cha'adai (d. 1242), his second son of four (Rasid-ud-Din) or eight (the *Secret History*) 1,000s of subjects and the summer pastures around Almaligh (near modern Huocheng) and Quyas (east of the Ysyk Köl). Chinggis Khan did not, however, give Cha'adai any special rights or control over the Mawarannahr (Transoxiana) region of Samarqand and Bukhara, although Cha'adai's winter camp was in that area.

Chinggis Khan's third son and successor, ÖGEDEI KHAN (1229–41), appointed Mahmud Yalavach governor of the region from the Amu Dar'ya to Uighuristan (see MAHMUD YALAVACH AND MAS'UD BEG). At the same time, as a reward for his elder brother's support, Ögedei granted him for the first time areas of Mawarannahr as his personal property (INJE or emchü). Then and later there was considerable friction between the great khans' governors and the ulugh ev (Turkish, great house), or Cha'adai's ORDO (palace-tent). The Chaghatayids also held appanages in Taiyuan in North China and in Kat and Khiva in KHORAZM and had representatives among the TAMMACHI (garrison) soldiers in Iran and Afghanistan.

The early death of Mö'etüken, Cha'adai's second son, in the siege of Bamiyan (1221) caused controversy over the succession. Cha'adai desired Mö'etüken's son Qara-Hüle'ü to succeed him after his death. When Ögedei's son GÜYÜG became khan (1246–48), however, he appointed his friend, Yisü-Möngke, Cha'adai's fifth son, head of Cha'adai's ulus. By this time the Chaghatayids had become closely allied with the Ögedeids against the other branches of the Chinggisid family. Thus, of the Chaghatayid family only Qara-Hüle'ü and Mochi-Jebe, a concubine's son slighted in the inheritance, attended the controversial general assembly or QURILTAI of 1251 that overthrew the Ögedeid family and elected Möngke of the Toluid branch as khan. MÖNGKE KHAN gave the headship of the Chaghatay ulus to Qara-Hüle'ü. Again, unfortunately for Chaghatayid dynastic continuity, Qara-Hüle'ü's death was untimely (late 1251). His Oirat wife Orghina, a daughter of Chinggis Khan's daughter Checheyiken, carried out the execution of Yisü-Möngke and ruled with Möngke's sanction as regent for her young son, Mubarak-Shah.

After Möngke's death the 1260–64 civil war between Möngke's brothers QUBILAI KHAN and ARIQ-BÖKE again upset Chaghatayid dynastic continuity. Orghina fled to Ariq-Böke's court in Mongolia, while Ariq-Böke and Qubilai tried to set their own candidates on the throne. Ariq-Böke won the first round, getting his man, Alghu, to the Chaghatay realm first and killing Qubilai's candidate, Abishqa, in Gansu. Meanwhile, the Muslim clergy in Bukhara, backed by Jochid retainers in Bukhara, actively sought the intervention of the Muslim Mongol khan Berke (1257–66) of the GOLDEN HORDE. Alghu (1260–65/6) made his court in the Kashgar area, with 15 tümens (nominally 150,000), and sent another prince, Negübei, to Mawarannahr with 5,000 men and a staff. While gathering as much taxes as possible, Alghu's agents crushed the challenge from the Jochid partisans before attacking north into Khorazm and Otrar, part of the Jochid territory, and south into the Qara'una garrisons in Afghanistan. His aim was to turn the small, interlocking set of Cha'adai's appanages into a large compact territorial realm. In this sense Alghu's was the first attempt to make the Chaghatayids a real khanate. As alliance with Ariq-Böke in impoverished Mongolia was more costly and constricting than that with Qubilai in North China, Alghu betrayed Ariq-Böke around 1262 and allied with Qubilai.

With Ariq-Böke's fall Qubilai made the Chaghatayid realm virtually a satellite of his own. Qubilai's agent Qonggiradai revised the census in 1264. After Alghu's death without an heir in 1265–66, Orghina and Cha'adai's old retainer Qutb-ud-Din Habash 'Amid finally put her son Mubarak-Shah on the throne, but Qubilai dispatched another grandson of Mö'etüken, Baraq, to seize power. Once in control of the khanate, Baraq Khan (1266–71) continued Alghu's policy of expanding north, fighting the Ögedeid QAIDU KHAN and the Jochids. He also turned on Qubilai, raiding the Tarim Basin. Defeated by the Jochid Golden Horde, Baraq in 1269 reversed his policy and joined an alliance of Qaidu and the Golden Horde, to whom he had to leave one-third of Mawarannahr. The price of his adherence was his allies' support for his southward invasion of Khorasan (northeast Iran–northwest Afghanistan). The armies of the Mongol IL-KHANATE in Iran defeated Baraq at Qara-Su near Herat (July 22, 1270), and with Baraq's untimely death the next year, Qaidu secured almost complete control over the Chaghatay Khanate. Thus the second attempt to built a strong Chaghatay Khanate again failed. Not until 1282, with Qaidu's selection of Baraq's son Du'a, was something like a stable dynasty created, and not until Qaidu's death in 1301 did the Chaghatay khans really control their own realm.

GEOGRAPHY AND FOREIGN RELATIONS

Histories frequently treat the Chaghatayid Khanate as a unified realm under the descendants of Cha'adai, stretching from China proper to the Amu Dar'ya and centered on Samarqand and Bukhara. In fact, this situation existed for only a few decades. Although the khanate achieved dominant influence over the turbulent QARA'UNAS in Afghanistan as early as the 1260s they did not secure control over the Tarim Basin until 1290. The Mawarannahr area was actually only rarely the realm's power center, and by 1335 the Khanate had begun to split into the Qara'unas in Afghanistan and the Dughlats in eastern Xinjiang.

Qubilai's early grants to Alghu and Baraq describe the Chaghatay realm as stretching from the Altai to the Amu Dar'ya. It thus included Zungharia (Junggar Basin) and the Ili Valley in northern Xinjiang, modern Kyrgyzstan, and the Mawarannahr (Transoxiana) area of Samarqand and Bukhara, together with the neighboring steppes of

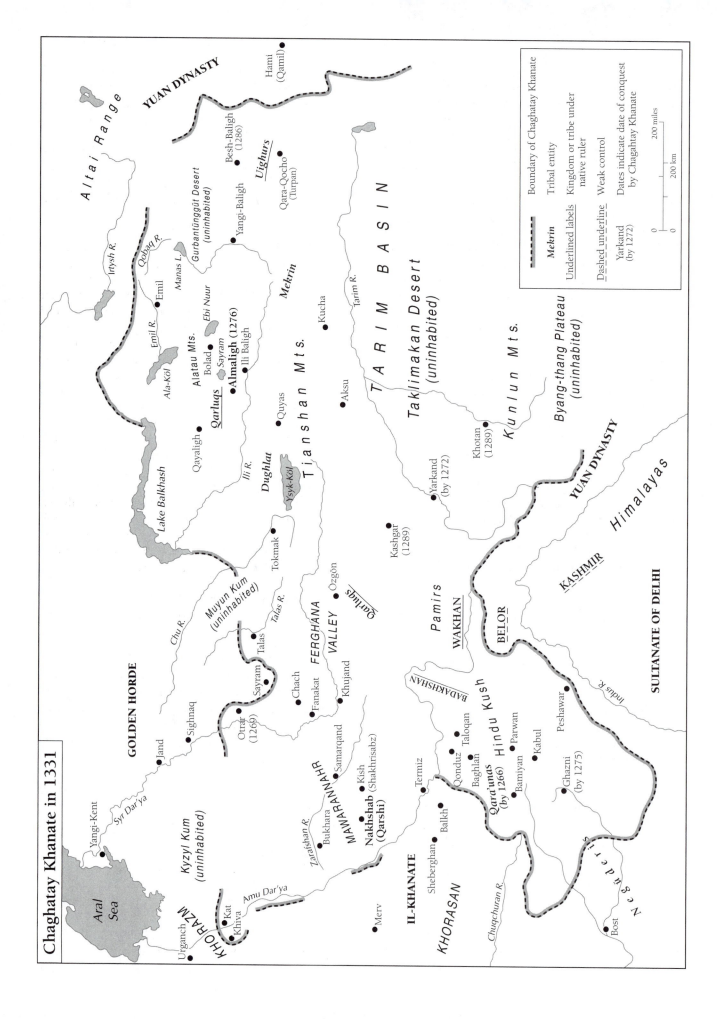

Chaghatay Khanate in 1331

YUAN DYNASTY

Altai Range

Hami (Qamil)

Besh-Baligh (1286)

Uighurs

Gurbantünggüt Desert (uninhabited)

Yangi-Baligh

Qara-Qocho (Turpan)

Irtysh R.

Qobaq R.

Manas L.

Emil R.

Emil

Ala-Köl

Ebi Nuur

Alatau Mts.

Bolad · Sayram

Almaligh (1276)

Ili Baligh

Mekrin

Kucha

T A R I M   B A S I N

Tarim R.

Taklimakan Desert (uninhabited)

Kunlun Mts.

Byang-thang Plateau (uninhabited)

YUAN DYNASTY

Qayaligh

Qarluqs

Quyas

Aksu

Himalayas

Lake Balkhash

Ili R.

Dughlat

Ysyk-Köl

T i a n s h a n   M t s.

Khotan (1289)

Yarkand (by 1272)

KASHMIR

Tokmak

Kashgar (1289)

Muyun Kum (uninhabited)

Chu R.

Özgön

Qarluqs

Pamirs

WAKHAN

BELOR

SULTANATE OF DELHI

Talas R.

GOLDEN HORDE

Talas

Sayram

FERGHANA VALLEY

Chach

Fanakat

Khujand

BADAKHSHAN

Indus R.

Sighnaq

Otrār (1269)

Termiz

Qonduz

Taloqan

Baghlan

Hindu Kush

Parwan

Peshawar

Jand

Syr Dar'ya

Bukhara

Samarqand

MAWARANNAHR

Kish (Shakhrisabz)

Nakhshab (Qarshi)

Qaraunas (by 1266)

Bamiyan

Kabul

Ghazni (by 1275)

Yangi-Kent

Kyzyl Kum (uninhabited)

Zarafshan R.

Sheberghan

Balkh

KHORASAN

IL-KHANATE

Chughuran R.

N e g ü d e r i s

Bost

Aral Sea

Urganch

Kat

Khiva

KHORAZM

Amu Dar'ya

Merv

Legend

Boundary of Chaghatay Khanate

Mekrin   Tribal entity

Kingdom or tribe under native ruler

Underlined labels

Weak control

Dashed underline

Yarkand (by 1272)   Dates indicate date of conquest by Chaghatay Khanate

200 miles

200 km

southeastern Kazakhstan. As Baraq complained in 1269, it was a "miserable little *ulus* (realm)," compared to the YUAN DYNASTY, the IL-KHANATE, or the Golden Horde, and until 1300 the Chaghatay khans' foreign policy was expansionist. Since its neighbors were all Mongol khanates, the Chaghatayids became the prime instigators of intra-Mongol divisions. After 1300, however, expansion was primarily south against India and Khorasan, and the Chaghatay khans became conciliatory toward the Yuan.

In the early alliances and conflicts with Qubilai, Kashgar, Ysyk-Köl, and Almaligh changed hands several times. The Yuan lost Almaligh to the Chaghatayids for good in 1276 and the Tarim Basin a decade later. Uighuristan (Turpan and Hami) came under loose Chaghatayid control sometime between 1295 and the general Mongol peace of 1304. While Möngke and Qubilai Khans had assigned all the land south and west of the Amu Dar'ya to the Il-Khan HÜLE'Ü (1217–65), Chaghatayid influence soon spread to Afghanistan, and the family of Cha'adai's eighth son, Baiju, held Ghazni from around 1275. The absorption of the Qara'unas gave the Chaghatayids a frontier on India, which they raided from 1292 on. It also facilitated Chaghatay pressure on Khorasan, which increased after 1291.

Chaghatayid relations with the Golden Horde fluctuated. In the decade after Möngke Khan's death, the Jochids and Chaghatayids were hostile, yet the Golden Horde shared the Chaghatayid's hostility to the Il-Khanate. After 1269 this common hostility won out, and the Golden Horde allied with Qaidu and the Chaghatayids. However, when the latter became powerful in the 1280s, the Golden Horde khans dropped out of the coalition. Subsequently, the two were sporadically allied against the Il-Khans. After the disintegration of the Chaghatay Khanate, Janibeg (1342–57) briefly reasserted Jochid dominance over the Chaghatayids.

TRIBAL STRUCTURE

The original Chaghatayid army was the 4,000 or 8,000 men granted Cha'adai by Chinggis Khan and apparently composed of four non-Chinggisid clans: the Barulas, Arulad, JALAYIR, and Suldus. IBN BATTUTA, who visited the court of Sultan Tarmashirin (1331–34), recorded how the court of the Chaghatay khans was composed of the KESHIG, or imperial guard, divided into day and night guards, and the four commanders: the sultan's deputy, the vizier, the chamberlain, and the keeper of the *al-tamgha* (red seal). In the time of TIMUR (1336?–1405) at least, these chief positions were hereditary in four clans then residing in Mawarannahr (Jalayir, Barulas, Qa'uchin) or northeast Khorasan (Arulad). The Qa'uchin (old ones), the name for hereditary army units recruited in Mawarannahr, apparently replaced the Suldus.

East of Ferghana the Dughlat (Dogholad), a Mongol clan, eventually rose to prominence in the Almaligh-Ysyk Köl-Aksu area. Exactly when the Dughlat first entered this area is unclear. To the south the Qara'unas, of extremely diverse clan origins, occupied Afghanistan in two broad swaths from Qonduz-Baghlan to Ghazni and from Qandahar to Sistan. After 1300 the Cha'adai realm thus had three competing power centers: the Dughlad in the east, Mawarannahr and Ferghana in the center, and the Qara'unas in the south. Rulers generally nomadized in the east or center, appointing viceroys with their own guards *tümen* (10,000) for the other two areas. In several cases these *tümen*s became permanent nomadic groupings.

ADMINISTRATION

Lack of native Chaghatayid historical traditions has left internal Chaghatay administration quite obscure, but bureaucratic administration seems to have been undeveloped compared with that in the Il-Khanate in the Middle East or the Yuan Dynasty in the East. The Mongol census and organization of the local population into decimal units, divided into military and civilian households, continued through the 14th century. Likewise, the early Mongol division of the subject population into appanages survived Alghu's infringements and continued into the early 14th century. Cha'adai and his immediate successors had bad relations with Mahmud Yalavach, KÖRGÜZ, and other governors implementing civilian rule. The regent Orghina, however, followed the advice of Mas'ud Beg and Cha'adai's old adviser Qutb-ud-Din Habash 'Amid to limit and regularize taxation (*see* MAHMUD YALAVACH AND MAS'UD BEG). Although Alghu and Baraq continued to employ Mas'ud Beg, both plundered Bukhara when the treasury required it. Mas'ud Beg was finally able to significantly limit such extortionate exactions only after Qaidu's rise in 1282. Even so, civil wars devastated Mawarannahr for seven years after 1275–76 and again after Qaidu's death in 1301.

The most concrete evidence of Chaghatayid fiscal administration is in its coinage. Local issues of coins began in the Syr Dar'ya cities around 1270–72 and in Bukhara and Samarqand from 1281 on. Issues peaked around 1286–87 but then declined, ceasing by 1294–95. Not until about 1319 did large-scale coinage resume under the khan Kebeg. The initial decline in issues after 1286–87 seems to be connected to a general Eurasian silver shortage, but the prolongation of this hiatus past 1300 indicates a fiscal crisis peculiar to the Chaghatay Khanate.

MILITARY

The Cha'adai military, despite its success in expansion in both the Tarim Basin and Khorasan, is little known. The Armenian knight Hetum estimated the total available military reserves, Mongol and local, available to the combined Chaghatayid-Ögedeid realm under Qaidu's son Chabar as 40 *tümen*s, fewer than all but the Il-Khanid realm. (A *tümen* nominally numbered 10,000.) Their troops were considered very skillful and hardy but relatively poorly equipped despite the khans' frequent demands on armories in their appanages in Bukhara and Samarqand. Baraq's invasion of Khorasan in 1270 is said to have involved 90,000 men, while Kebeg's invasion of 1313–14 involved four or five *tümens*. During the unsuccessful siege of Kusui (Afghanistan, 1295) the Chaghatay armies employed 12 catapults, 100 naphtha throwers, and a tower higher than the city walls, yet the Chaghatay armies scored few, if any, successes in siege warfare.

POLITICAL HISTORY

Building on earlier attempts by Alghu and Baraq, Baraq's son Du'a built the mature Chaghatay Khanate. After being raised by Qaidu as the Chaghatay khan, Du'a campaigned aggressively against Qubilai Khan's Yuan dynasty in 1285–89, forcing Yuan garrisons out of the Tarim Basin and making Uighuristan the frontier zone. In the south Du'a installed his eldest son, Qutlugh-Khoja (d. 1298–99), over the Qara'unas. From 1292 Qutlugh-Khoja began regular raids on India and southern Iran. From 1291 on Chaghatayid princes exploited the revolt of NAWROZ to invade Khorasan; in 1295 Du'a personally occupied Mazandaran, southeast of the Caspian Sea, for eight months. In a 1298 attack on the Yuan frontier, he captured Körgüz, a son-in-law of Qubilai. From 1300 on, however, Du'a proposed peace with the Mongol realms to revive trade and warred against India to fill the treasury. After Qaidu's death in the next year, Du'a enthroned Qaidu's weak son, Chabar, while opening peace talks with the Yuan dynasty. In autumn 1304 all five lines of the Mongol Empire—Du'a of the Chaghatayids, Qaidu's son Chabar, the Yuan, the Il-Khanate, and the Golden Horde—made peace. Meanwhile, Du'a strengthened his dynastic position. Several years of turbulence followed Du'a's demotion of the Ögedeids, after which several princes and their people resettled in Khorasan under the Il-Khanate. Du'a acquired the title Du'a Sechen (Du'a the Wise), and although never a Muslim, by the 16th century he was being honored in an Islamic shrine in Yarkand.

Du'a's son and successor, Könchek (1307–08), however, became a virtual satellite of the Yuan. The Chaghatay princes received lavish gifts from the Yuan emperor Haishan while allowing Haishan's envoy in autumn 1308 to collect a third of Samarqand's, Talas's, and other cities' revenues from their traditional appanages. Könchek's death in spring 1308 reopened the dormant conflict among rival Chaghatayid lines. Many held that only Du'a's sons were eligible, yet with Esen-Buqa among the Qara'unas and Du'a's other sons too young, Nalighu (erroneously written Taliqu, r. 1308–09), from a fraternal line of the sons of Mö'etüken, seized the throne. Nalighu, a Muslim and son of a Kerman princess, tried to destroy Du'a's descendants, but a conspiracy of emirs and princes under Du'a's son Kebeg murdered him.

After suppressing a sudden rebellion by Ögedei's descendants and driving Chapar into exile in the Yuan, Kebeg enthroned his elder brother Esen-Buqa, newly arrived from Afghanistan, as khan (1309–18?). Esen-Buqa nomadized between the Ysyk-Köl and Talas, while Kebeg became viceroy in Ferghana and Mawarannahr. Da'ud-Khoja, son of Qutlugh-Khoja, replaced Esen-Buqa as viceroy in Afghanistan.

Despite the conciliatory attitude of Du'a's sons, the Yuan and the Il-Khans eventually attacked them. First, in 1312 the Il-Khans exploited opposition to Da'ud-Khoja to win over the Qara'unas in Ghazni. Second, the Yuan in 1314 invaded under the Qipchaq general Chong'ur. To secure his rear, Esen-Buqa dispatched Kebeg to invade Khorasan in winter 1313–14. A shortage of provisions forced Kebeg to withdraw, while Chong'ur's forces reached as far as Chimkent (modern Shymkent) in 1315. The disaster was completed when Prince Töre-Temür deserted to the Yuan in 1315 and Prince Yasa'ur (1289–1320) defected to the Il-Khanate in 1316, after plundering Samarqand, Kish (modern Shakhrisabz), and Nakhshab (modern Qarshi), and dragooning their inhabitants to Khorasan.

Kebeg (1318?–27), however, reversed this decline. Yasa'ur's revolt against the Il-Khanate in summer 1318 drove the Il-Khan to make peace with Kebeg (June–July 1320), who also reestablished Chaghatay dominance over the Qara'unas of Afghanistan, appointing first Da'ud-Khoja and then his brother Tarmashirin as viceroy. Kebeg enjoyed peaceful relations with the great khans from 1322 on, and despite Chong'ur's reestablishment of nominal Yuan control there, a 1326 document shows Kebeg exercising authority in Uighuristan. While Esen-Buqa had adopted the Qara'una policy of government by plunder, Kebeg controlled his soldiers, winning the title of "the Just." Building a palace at Nakhshab, he transferred the dynasty's political center to Mawarannahr. Kebeg also renewed the large-scale raids against India. Booty from these raids and a revival of transit trade supplied the silver for renewed coinage. Kebeg's brother Eljigidei (1327–30) had even more expansive ambitions, supporting Qoshila as a candidate for the Yuan throne, while Tarmashirin, still viceroy of the Qara'unas and based in Termiz, invaded India again (1328–29).

MONGOL LIFE, RELIGION, AND COURT CULTURE

The Chaghatayid Mongols retained the Mongolian language and nomadism throughout their history as a unified khanate. MOGHULISTAN in the east and the Qara'unas in the south preserved spoken Mongolian well into the 16th century. In Mawarannahr, however, the record is less clear. Ibn Battuta records both Kebeg and Tarmashirin as speaking Turkish at court, but that hardly excludes their knowing Mongolian. The Mongol conquest also revived the use of the Uighur script for writing Turkish.

As in other Mongol realms, interaction with the sedentary world sparked increasing social differentiation among the Mongols. In Mawarannahr Mongol military commanders, while not farmers themselves, acquired interest in agriculture and craftsmanship as lords of landed estates, mills, and weaving workshops. At the same time, impoverished Mongols sold themselves or their families into slavery. An Islamic *waqf* (pious endowment) document of 1326 from Bukhara records the purchase of Mongol, Chinese, and Hindu slaves who were converted and manumitted as tenants.

In his territory around Almaligh and Quyas, Cha'adai built only pools to attract waterfowl, storehouses along his nomadic routes, and a small town or village. His successors, too, were not great builders. The official Mas'ud Beg built a grand *madrasa* (school) in Bukhara, which was sacked by an invading Il-Khan army in 1273, and Kebeg built a palace at Nakhshab. The relatively modest remaining Chaghatay cultural monuments, such as the tomb of Buyan-Quli Khan (1348–58), have been completely overshadowed by the cultural efflorescence under the succeeding Timurid dynasty.

Cha'adai's legacy of loyalty to the Chinggisid JASAQ (law) retarded the spread of Islam among his descendants. Until Tarmashirin (1331–34) only marginal princes converted to Islam, and none ruled successfully as a Muslim. The first well-known Muslim khan, Tarmashirin, was overthrown in part because of his overly close identification with Islamic law as opposed to the *jasaq*, yet by his time perhaps 50–70 percent of the Barulas clansmen had Arabic names, generally a sign of Islamization. Despite the many powerful Sufi (Islamic mystic) lodges in Mawarannahr, historical records show relatively little evidence of their influence on the Chaghatay Mongols. While several Muslim khans remonstrated against harassing the peasantry, one famous Muslim prince, Yasa'ur, was a notorious practitioner of the nomadic tradition of plunder.

Du'a and his sons actively patronized Buddhism. In 1285–90 Du'a supported the 'Bri-gung (modern Zhigung) Monastery in Tibet, sending an otherwise unknown Prince Rinchen against Qubilai in Tibet. Yuan records also show Eljigidei (1327–30) sharing in the Yuan dynasty's patronage of Buddhist temples. Even Tughlugh-Temür Khan (1347–62), known in Islamic sources as the one who converted the eastern Chaghatay realm to Islam, invited the Tibetan Buddhist INCARNATE LAMA Rol-pa'i rDo-rje (1340–83) of the Karma-pa to his realm.

A Mongolian-language document trove from Turpan, dating from 1326 to 1369, offers glimpses of Mongol culture in eastern Turkestan. Numerous copies of both translations and original Mongol poetry by CHOSGI-ODSIR and other Yuan monks and fragments in SQUARE SCRIPT illustrate the tremendous influence of the Yuan Buddhist culture on Uighuristan. A decree of exemption given to a Buddhist temple likewise demonstrates continuing royal patronage, yet a translation of the Alexander (Mongolian, Sulqarnai) romance and an Arabic-style divination text show Western influence was not lacking. Given Uighuristan's frontier status and continued autonomy, however, it is unclear how typical these documents are even of eastern Chaghatay culture.

FALL OF THE DYNASTY

After the brief reign of Töre-Temür (1330–31), Tarmashirin became the last of Du'a's many sons to rule as Chaghatay khan. Tarmashirin accelerated Kebeg's policies, ignoring the Almaligh area, establishing a reputation among his Tajik subjects as a just ruler, and encouraging agriculture. Perhaps to avoid opposition from his emirs, he did not summon annual *quriltais*, as was the Mongol custom. He also ruled as a Muslim, favoring Muslim emirs and imposing *shari'a*, or Islamic law. By this time, many of the Mongol soldiers and emirs were already Muslim, including Tarmashirin's viceroy for the Qara'unas, Burundai, but the neglect of the *quriltais* and the Almaligh heartland caused a revolt among his nephews in 1334. The several short-lived Dü'aid khans who followed were based in Almaligh and rejected Islam; Changshi (1335–38) supposedly erected Buddhist idols in every mosque. In reaction, an Ögedeid prince, 'Ali Sultan, seized power and for a few months persecuted non-Muslim religions.

The following exceedingly obscure decade saw the final incorporation of Khorasan into the Chaghatayid sphere after the disintegration of the Il-Khanate in 1335, devastating outbreaks of the BLACK DEATH beginning in the east in 1338–39, conflicts with the ambitious local dynasty in Herat, and the effective disintegration of the khanate. The traveler Ibn Battuta tells of a descendant of Yasa'ur turned Sufi *faqir* (mendicant), Khalil, who on the instigation of Herat rose up and defeated the non-Muslim khans in Almaligh, but this is echoed only vaguely in other sources. The election of Qazan Khan (1343?–46/7), a non-Dü'aid Chaghatay prince, demonstrated the breakdown of dynastic consensus. Finally, the Chaghatay realm disintegrated when the Qara'una emir Qazaghan overthrew Qazan and set up an Ögedeid puppet khan. Emir Dolaji of the Dughlat clan in the east thereupon set up his own puppet khan in 1347, creating the foundation for an independent Moghulistan in the east. The later rise of Timur (1336?–1405) from the Barulas clan in Mawarannahr created a third contender for the mantle of the now-divided Chaghatay realm.

THE IMPACT OF THE MONGOLS ON CENTRAL ASIA

Mongol rule affected Central Asia deeply. The initial conquest of the Tarim Basin and the cities north of the Tianshan Mountains was bloodless and that of Mawarannahr considerably less devastating than the conquest of Khorasan. Nevertheless, the persistence of the unreformed

Mongol traditions of administration, the endemic dynastic instability, and the blockage of trade caused by hostilities with the neighboring khanates all militated against urban recovery. When Ibn Battuta visited Mawarannahr in 1333, he found the cities there in a half-ruined state compared with flourishing Tabriz and Khorazm. Perhaps for this reason, the Chaghatay territory did not, with the exception of the appended Arabic notes in Jamal Qarshi's Persian lexicon, produce any significant historical writings before 1350. Even so, Timur and his successors, who built a new empire centered in Mawarannahr and brought the area prosperity and cultural renaissance, continued to think of themselves as Chaghatays, a name Western scholars later gave to the Turkish language of poetry and history from the 14th to the 19th centuries.

See also APPANAGE SYSTEM; ARTISANS IN THE MONGOL EMPIRE; BUDDHISM IN THE MONGOL EMPIRE; CENSUS IN THE MONGOL EMPIRE; CHRISTIANITY IN THE MONGOL EMPIRE; INDIA AND THE MONGOL EMPIRE; ISLAM IN THE MONGOL EMPIRE; ISLAMIC SOURCES ON THE MONGOL EMPIRE; MONEY IN THE MONGOL EMPIRE; PROVINCES IN THE MONGOL EMPIRE; RELIGIOUS POLICY IN THE MONGOL EMPIRE.

Further reading: W. Barthold, "Čaghatay Khanate," trans. John Andrew Boyle, in *Encyclopaedia of Islam*, 2d ed., vol. 2 (Leiden: E. J. Brill, 1960): 3–4; Michal Biran, *Qaidu and the Rise of the Independent Mongol State in Central Asia* (Richmond, Surrey: Curzon Press, 1997); Peter Jackson, "Chaghatayid Dynasty," in *Encyclopedia Iranica*, vol. 5, 343–347; Kazuhide Kato, "Kebek and Yasawr: The Establishment of the Caghatai-Khanate," *Memoirs of the Toyo Bunko* 49 (1991): 97–118; Beatrice Forbes Manz, *Rise and Rule of Tamerlane* (Cambridge: Cambridge University Press, 1989).

Chahar   *See* CHAKHAR.

Chakhar (Chahar, Tsakhar, Caqar, Qahar) The appanage of the last independent Mongol emperors in the 16th and 17th centuries, the Chakhar Mongols were tightly controlled by China's Qing dynasty (1636–1912). To the KHALKHA Mongols and BURIATS, *Chakhar* was long a synonym for Inner Mongolians. Today the Chakhar dialect is the basis for standard Inner Mongolian (*see* MONGOLIAN LANGUAGE).

GEOGRAPHY

Traditionally divided into left- and right-flank BANNERS, Chakhar today is divided between SHILIIN GOL and ULAANCHAB leagues in China's Inner Mongolia Autonomous Region. The three major Chakhar left-flank banners, Plain Blue (Zhenglan), Plain and Bordered White (Zhengxiangbai), and Bordered Yellow (Xianghuang), cover 21,000 square kilometers (8,100 square miles) in southern Shiliin Gol and have a total population of 174,700, of which 65,700, or 38 percent, are Mongols. Livestock

numbering 1,855,600, including 1,550,300 sheep and goats, graze the steppe there (1990 figures). Although the 5,400 Chakhars in the southernmost Taipusi banner are only 2 percent of the banner's total population, they are concentrated in a single steppe district completely surrounded by ethnic Chinese-inhabited farmland. Virtually all Mongols in these banners speak Mongolian.

The three contemporary Chakhar right-flank (Qahar Youyi) banners now in Ulaanchab were heavily colonized by Chinese farmers after 1903. At present covering fewer than 11,000 square kilometers (4,250 square miles), their total population is 683,100, of which only 19,300 (3 percent) are Mongol. Few, if any, Mongol children here speak Mongolian fluently.

HISTORY

The Chakhars first appear in the second half of the 15th century as one of the Mongols' SIX TÜMENS. At that time the current Chakhar territory was inhabited by the Yüngshiyebü *tümen* (partly ancestors of today's KHARACHIN Mongols), while the Chakhars themselves inhabited modern northern Shiliin Gol. After the reign of BATUMÖNGKE DAYAN KHAN (1480?–1517?), the Chakhar *tümen* became the personal appanage of the Chinggisid great khans of the NORTHERN YUAN DYNASTY. Under Daraisun Küdeng Khan (1548–57) the Chakhar moved east over the GREATER KHINGGAN RANGE into the Shara Mören (Xar Moron) valley.

In 1627 the princes of Chakhar's Sönid, ÜJÜMÜCHIN, Naiman, and Aohan OTOGs (camp districts) revolted against the centralization of Ligdan Khan (1604–34). After being attacked by the rising Manchus in 1632, Ligdan Khan took the remaining Chakhars and fled west to ORDOS and then Kökenuur (Qinghai). After his death his sons surrendered to the Manchus' new QING DYNASTY (1636–1912), and the remaining Chakhars were resettled as autonomous banners in south-central Inner Mongolia. The rebellious *otogs* were resettled separately in Shiliin Gol and JUU UDA leagues.

In 1675 Ligdan's grandsons Burni and Lubsang revolted against the Qing along with the prince of Naiman banner. After Burni and Lubsang's defeat the Chakhars' Chinggisid nobility was stripped of its prerogatives, and the Chakhar banners were integrated into the directly controlled EIGHT BANNERS system. In addition to the Eight Banners, each named by the color of its banner (Plain Yellow, Bordered Yellow, Plain White, etc.), the Qing court also established four "pastures" (*sürüg*), which supplied meat, mounts, and DAIRY PRODUCTS for imperial use. The 12 Chakhar banners and pastures, together with the DARIGANGA pastures, were all put under the *dutong*, or Manchu official, stationed in Zhangjiakou (Kalgan).

In the 18th and 19th centuries unofficial CHINESE COLONIZATION nibbled away steadily at the Chakhars' southern boundaries. In 1903, with the sinicizing NEW

POLICIES, the Qing court forced the Chakhar right-flank banners to accept massive new colonization, which was further accelerated by railway construction from 1907 on. In 1928 the Republic of China divided Inner Mongolia into provinces, with Chakhar's right-flank banners assigned to Suiyuan and the left-flank banners and pastures assigned to Chahar. Under the Japanese occupation (1937–45) Chakhar officials played an important role in PRINCE DEMCHUGDONGRUB's autonomous Mongolian regime. After 1945 China's civil war between the Communists and the Nationalists wracked the Chakhar's left-flank banners, until they were incorporated into the Communist-established Inner Mongolian Autonomous Government in 1947. The Communists occupied Suiyuan province in 1949, which in 1954 was transferred with the Chakhar right-flank banners into the INNER MONGOLIA AUTONOMOUS REGION. In 1958 the Chakhar left-flank banners, previously a separate league, were transferred to Shiliin Gol league, while the right-flank banners were transferred from the Pingdiquan district to ULAANCHAB league.

See also INNER MONGOLIANS; JEWELRY; MONGOLIAN LANGUAGE; NEW SCHOOLS MOVEMENTS; SAINCHOGTU, NA.; WEDDINGS.

Further reading: David Aberle, *Chahar and Dagor Mongol Bureaucratic Administration* (New Haven, Conn.: HRAF Press, 1953); Henry Serruys, "The Čaqar Population during the Qing," *Journal of Asian History* 12 (1978): 58–79; Henry Serruys, "A Study of Chinese Penetration into Čaqar Territory in the Eighteenth Century," *Monumenta Serica* 35 (1981–1983): 485–544; Herbert Harold Vreeland III, *Mongol Community and Kinship Structure* (New Haven, Conn.: HRAF Press, 1957).

Cham *See* TSAM.

Champa *See* SOUTH SEAS.

Chang Jou *See* ZHANG ROU.

Chang-chia *See* JANGJIYA KHUTUGTU.

Changchun, Master (Qiu Chuji, Ch'iu Ch'u-chi) (1148–1227) *Taoist master of the Complete Realization sect who instructed Chinggis Khan in religious principles*
Qiu Chuji was born in Qixia county in the Shandong peninsula, then as now a stronghold of Taoism (Daoism). At age 18 he entered the Taoist retreat at Kunlun Mountain in Ninghai (modern Mouping) and became a disciple of Wang Zhe (Master Chongyang, 1112–70), founder of the Complete Realization (Quanzhen, Ch'üan-chen) sect of Taoism. The Complete Realization school focused on the achievement of immortality by transforming the internal organs, with a tight control of bodily functions.

This procedure, called "internal alchemy," depended on the preservation of semen, which entailed complete celibacy. The asceticism and eccentricity of its devotees generated great controversy. Before Master Chongyang died in 1170 he appointed Qiu Chuji, titled Master Changchun, his successor. Traveling North China, Changchun's fame grew, and the JIN DYNASTY emperor summoned him to an audience in 1188. With the emperor's death, however, Changchun's opponents had him confined to his hometown of Qixia, yet continued support from the imperial family soon allowed him freer movement within Shandong.

When the Mongols invaded North China, peninsular Shandong did not suffer from direct Mongol invasions. In 1213 widespread insurrections against Jin rule broke out, and many of the insurgents went over to the SONG DYNASTY in South China. Both the Jin dynasty, which moved its capital south in 1214 to Henan, and the Song unsuccessfully sought Changchun's support.

CHINGGIS KHAN's personal physician, Liu Zhonglu (Liu Wen), told the khan that Changchun was a *tenggeri möngke kü'ün,* "heavenly immortal man," aged 300 years, and possessing pills of immortality. More skeptical advisers, such as YELÜ CHUCAI, hoped that Changchun might be able to moderate the conqueror's harsh measures. In 1219, as he was traveling west to destroy KHORAZM, Chinggis Khan summoned Changchun to an audience. Liu Zhonglu and JABAR KHOJA delivered the message to Shandong, and Changchun quickly accepted the summons. Changchun traveled through Mongolia and Turkestan, making numerous observations of the natural and human environment, including a measurement of a lunar eclipse. He arrived at Chinggis Khan's camp in Parwan, Afghanistan, on May 17, 1222.

At the first interview Changchun told Chinggis Khan that he had been misinformed and that he had no pills of immortality. Renewed warfare in Afghanistan interrupted the instruction until October. To achieve long life Changchun recommended periodic abstention from sexual intercourse. He also advised Chinggis Khan to remit taxes in North China for three years. When a massive snowfall struck the imperial camp, he interpreted this as heaven's anger at the Mongols' lack of filial piety. Later he used a hunting accident to reprove the Mongol custom of hunting as violating heaven's love for life. Chinggis Khan approved these discourses and issued a PAIZA (tablet of authority) and decree exempting Changchun's monasteries from taxation, followed by another decree appointing him chief of all monks in China. The two parted in spring 1223, and Master Changchun arrived at Zhongdu (modern Beijing) a year later, spending the rest of his life there. With the powers granted him by Chinggis Khan, he converted many Buddhist monasteries to those of his Complete Realization sect, destroying their Buddhist images. Recruiting war refugees and ransoming captives, he also enrolled 20,000 to 30,000 men in his temples. This aggressive expansion infuriated the Buddhist Yelü Chu-cai, who had come to see Changchun as a corrupt fraud.

Changchun died on August 22, 1227. The record of Changchun's western journey written by Li Zhichang (Li Chih-ch'ang; translated by Arthur Waley as *Travels of an Alchemist*) is a valuable source on Chinggis Khan and Mongol rule in North China and Central Asia.

See also RELIGIOUS POLICY IN THE MONGOL EMPIRE; TAOISM IN THE MONGOL EMPIRE.

Further reading: Li Chih-ch'ang, *Travels of an Alchemist,* trans. Arthur Waley (1931; rpt., New York: AMS Press, 1979).

Chen-chin *See* JINGIM.

chess Mongolian chess has the same basic pieces and moves as international chess but lacks a few of the modern rules developed to speed up the opening. Mongolian chess sets label their pieces as follows: lord (*noyon*) for the king, tiger (*bars*) for the queen, camels (*temee*) for bishops, horses (*mori*) for knights, carts (*khangai* or *terge*) for rooks, and boys (*khüü*) for pawns. In Mongolian chess only the boy/pawn in front of the lord/king or tiger/queen can move two spaces in its first move; other pawns can move only one space on their first move. Castling is also not allowed. Once a boy/pawn gets to the end of the board, he is turned into a tiger/queen but diagonally can move only one space at a time. Other forms of chess with different boards were also played by children. In eastern Inner Mongolia Chinese chess is played. In Russia's KALMYK REPUBLIC the current president, Kirsan N. Ilümzhinov (b. 1962), an amateur chess master, is now head of the international chess association, Fédération Internationale des Échecs (FIDE). Chess is now a required topic in all Kalmyk schools.

Chifeng municipality (Ulanhad) Chifeng is a small city in southeastern Inner Mongolia with a metropolitan population of 235,000 (1990), of which 26,400 are Mongol. The name means "red peak," or in Mongolian, Ulaankhad (Ulanhad). Since 1983 Chifeng municipality has also administered the seven Mongol BANNERS and three Chinese counties of former JUU UDA league. The expanded Chifeng municipality has an area of 84,000 square kilometers (32,400 square miles) and a population of 4,105,758. Mongols number 677,012, or 16 percent.

Chifeng city was originally established as a Chinese county in Ongni'ud Right Banner territory in 1778. From 1914 it was part of Rehe, and in 1935 Chifeng was reached by railways. In 1955 Rehe province was broken up, and Chifeng county, along with the neighboring KHARACHIN banner, was assigned to Inner Mongolia as part of Juu Uda.

See also INNER MONGOLIA AUTONOMOUS REGION.

Chin dynasty *See* JIN DYNASTY.

China and Mongolia Farming people of China and pastoral nomads of Mongolia have been in contact for almost 3,000 years. After China's unification in the third century B.C.E., the Chinese dynasties tried to channel relations with the northern nomads through the TRIBUTE SYSTEM. At times peoples of nomadic origin conquered all or part of China, culminating in the Mongol conquest of the 13th century. Finally, in the 17th century the Mongolian and Chinese peoples fell under the Manchu QING DYNASTY (1636–1912), which melded Chinese and Inner Asian institutions. Only in the 20th century has China been forced to recognize Mongolia as an equal sovereign nation in a multistate system.

EARLY INTERACTIONS

From the third century B.C.E. to the 18th century, the northern nomads were the chief foreign policy preoccupation of China's dynasties. The nomads themselves both coveted the goods of China, which their own economies could not supply, and feared the ability of Chinese diplomacy to instigate civil wars and divisions.

Peoples of Mongolic origins several times conquered all or part of China. In the fourth to sixth centuries C.E., XIANBI dynasties ruled North China. In the 10th century the KITANS from Inner Mongolia conquered the area around modern Beijing. Finally, the Mongols under CHINGGIS KHAN (1206–26) began the conquest of all China, which was completed under his grandson QUBILAI KHAN (1260–94). At the time of the Mongol conquest, China was already divided into three dynasties: the JIN DYNASTY in the north and Manchuria, the XIA DYNASTY in the northwest, and the SONG DYNASTY in the south. Of these, only the Song was founded by ethnic Chinese. During these conquest dynasties, the nomadic peoples and the Han (ethnic Chinese) came to live in close proximity. "Barbarian" and Han officials served side by side in the court, while the dominant non-Chinese military caste settled in landed estates and camps in the Chinese countryside and formed garrisons in the main cities.

The Mongol YUAN DYNASTY (1206/1271–1368) was the first nonethnic Chinese dynasty to conquer all of China. Many Chinese generals and local strongmen surrendered and served the Mongols faithfully, while others conducted a bitter guerrilla resistance in the hills of North China. Thousands of Song loyalists killed themselves rather than surrender to the Mongols. The Mongols created a formal class system that divided the Chinese into northern and southern and put both below the Mongols and Central and West Asian immigrants. Ambitious Chinese officials responded by adopting Mongol names and mores in order to pass as Mongols. While often portrayed simply as a nationalist Chinese uprising, the insurrections from 1351 on that finally overthrew Mongol rule in China likewise came from a complex mix of millenarian Buddhist movements, piracy, economic catastrophe associated with the BLACK DEATH, and ethnic resentment that rallied to the cause of restoring the Song. To the end of the Yuan dynasty, ethnic Chinese were willing to fight and die for it, and the Yuan produced its share of loyalists who refused any association with the succeeding MING DYNASTY. (*On Chinese-Mongol interaction in the Yuan, see* BUDDHISM IN THE MONGOL EMPIRE; CHANGCHUN; DAIDU; DAOISM IN THE MONGOL EMPIRE; EAST ASIAN SOURCES ON THE MONGOL EMPIRE; LI TAN'S REBELLION; LIU BINGZHONG; MASSACRES AND THE MONGOL CONQUEST; MUQALI; PROVINCES IN THE MONGOL EMPIRE; *SEMUREN;* SHII TIANZE; SOCIAL CLASSES IN THE MONGOL EMPIRE; YAN SHI; ZHANG ROU.)

The succeeding Ming Dynasty (1368–1644) has often been portrayed as a purely Chinese regime, yet the founder, Zhu Yuanzhang, actively recruited Mongols into his armies and praised many aspects of the Yuan regime. Relations with the Mongols of Mongolia were again regulated by the tribute system. A vocal group of Chinese literati denounced the Mongols as incurably barbaric, but their voice was rarely heeded by the decision makers. Only in the wake of the TUMU INCIDENT (1449) did the nationalist elements temporarily dominate the court.

THE QING DYNASTY

Under the QING DYNASTY (1636–1912) both China and Mongolia were taken over by the Manchu ruling family that set its capital in Beijing. While seen as a Chinese dynasty by foreign powers, the Mongols saw the Qing as the dynasty of a fellow Inner Asian people. Mongol relations with ethnic Chinese settlers and merchants were generally not friendly but were sometimes mutually advantageous. In the 19th century, however, Chinese domination of the Mongolian economy increased. Scattered attacks on settlers and even occasional rebellions broke out in Inner Mongolia from the 1870s. In 1901 the Qing introduced the NEW POLICIES, which aimed at the comprehensive sinicization of China's Inner Asian frontier. This led to violent opposition from the highest to the lowest levels and eventually to the 1911 RESTORATION of Mongolian independence. (*On ethnic Chinese and Mongols in the Qing Dynasty, see* BOLOR ERIKHE; CHINESE COLONIZATION; CHINESE FICTION; CHINESE TRADE AND MONEYLENDING; EIGHT BANNERS; FOOD AND DRINK; INJANNASHI; *LIFAN YUAN ZELI;* NEW POLICIES.)

THE MONGOLIAN QUESTION, 1911–1949

In autumn 1911 the Mongolian independence movement and the Chinese republican revolution against Qing rule broke out simultaneously. The Chinese 1911 Revolution was in part a Han (ethnic Chinese) uprising against the Manchu rulers, yet the new republican authorities were determined to hold on to China's Inner Asian dominions. The new Republic of China created a flag with five stripes, each standing for one of the five races of China: Han, Manchu, Mongol, Tibetan, and Muslim. Despite the new government's weakness, the Chinese public and politicians were alike committed to maintaining whatever claim possible on all the former Qing territories.

From 1912 to 1915 the Republic of China's new president, Yuan Shikai (1859–1916), attempted to retain as much control as possible over Inner and Outer Mongolia. With Outer Mongolia his task was complicated by Chinese public opinion, which demanded aggressive action against Russian support for Mongolian secession, action that militarily was completely unrealistic. This public opposition prevented Russo-Chinese negotiations from coming to any conclusion until Yuan Shikai had suppressed the domestic opposition parties. On November 5, 1913, he agreed to respect Outer Mongolia's internal autonomy and meet in a trilateral conference with Russia and Outer Mongolia. In return, Russia recognized a legitimate Chinese claim on Outer Mongolia and pressured the Mongolian government into calling off the invasion of Inner Mongolia (*see* SINO-MONGOLIAN WAR). The subsequent KYAKHTA TRILATERAL TREATY of June 1915 confirmed China's full control of Inner Mongolia, and defined China's power in Outer Mongolia as suzerainty, and allowed China to station a high commissioner in Mongolia. (*On the Chinese administration in Inner Mongolia from 1911 to the present, see* INNER MONGOLIA AUTONOMOUS REGION and INNER MONGOLIANS.)

The outbreak of World War I and then the Russian Revolution weakened Russia's strong position, and in 1919 the Mongolian rulers, frightened of the chaos in Russia, agreed to a REVOCATION OF AUTONOMY, albeit with guarantees against ethnic Chinese colonization. However, the general "Little" Xu Shuzheng of the pro-Japanese Anfu clique aimed to colonize Mongolia as a power base and, once stationed in Mongolia, implemented an openly sinicizing regime. The Mongolians in response turned to either White Russian or Soviet support. These two warring forces together drove the Chinese out of Mongolia by March 1921. The Red Army then installed a new People's Government in Khüriye (Ulaanbaatar).

With the Soviet-supported 1921 REVOLUTION China lost all the suzerain rights over Outer Mongolia it had been granted in the 1915 Kyakhta Trilateral Treaty. While the warlords Zhang Zuolin (1875–1928) and Feng Yuxiang (1882–1942) were successively entrusted with the task of recovering Mongolia militarily, Chinese diplomats aimed to use Chinese recognition of the Soviet Union to win concessions in Mongolia. In May 1924 they seemed to have succeeded, with the Soviet Union explicitly recognizing Chinese sovereignty (i.e., full control) over Mongolia in return for China's recognition, yet China as before was unable to conquer Mongolia, and the called-for general conference was never held.

From 1921 on Soviet agents also cultivated friendly forces in China: the Chinese Communist Party, the Nationalist Party, and Feng Yuxiang. For all of these forces, at least de facto recognition of the new MONGOLIAN PEOPLE'S REPUBLIC (MPR's) legitimacy was the price of Soviet financial and military support. The more respectable Chinese politicians tried to avoid publicizing this concession, and even most Communists hoped for some kind of postrevolutionary federal unification with Mongolia. While reuniting China in 1927–28, the new Nationalist Party government under Chiang Kai-shek (1888–1975) turned against the Soviet Union and again denounced Soviet Russia's "red imperialism" in Mongolia. The Communists, now subject to ferocious repression, confirmed their total alienation from legal Chinese society by vociferously supporting Mongolian and other minority self-determination. Although the Japanese invasions of China from 1931 on brought about a Sino-Soviet rapprochement in the mid-1930s, the Nationalist government's categorical rejection of any Mongolian independence did not change.

By May 1945 the Nationalist Party was evolving a more liberal position under American influence and recognized "high-level autonomy" for Mongolia and Tibet. As the Soviet Union became a world power during WORLD WAR II, Joseph Stalin got the United States and Great Britain at Yalta to formally concede Mongolian independence from China before forcing Chiang Kai-shek in August 1945 to likewise concede full Mongolian independence (see PLEBISCITE ON INDEPENDENCE). Protests in the Chinese legislature were easily overriden, showing the purely abstract and ideological nature of Chinese claims to Outer Mongolia. Although China formally recognized Mongolian independence in February 1946, the two countries did not settle the outstanding border issues or exchange ambassadors.

Since 1944 the MPR had cultivated the KAZAKHS and Mongols in the northern part of China's Xinjiang province, where Mongolia had traditional territorial claims. In late May 1947, as China's authorities tried to strengthen their claims on the area and recruit Kazakhs, Mongolians and Chinese clashed over the ill-defined border at Baytik Shan (Baitag Bogd). In June Mongolian troops drove the Chinese and Kazakhs south, while in June–July 1948 Mongolia again attacked pro-Chinese Kazakhs camping in Mongolian territory. These clashes revived the Chinese Nationalist government's strong hostility to Mongolia.

SINO-MONGOLIAN FOREIGN RELATIONS

In October 1949, as the Chinese Communist armies swept away the Nationalist regime, the People's Republic of China (PRC) under Mao Zedong recognized Mongolia. For the next 10 years Mongolia, China, and the Soviet Union were formally allies (see SINO-SOVIET ALLIANCE). During World War II Mao Zedong had expressed his confidence that Mongolia would naturally join China after the Communist victory. In 1949 and again after Stalin's death in 1954 and in 1956, both Mao and Premier Zhou Enlai asked the Soviet Union to "return" Outer Mongolia to China to be united with Inner Magnolia in an autonomous region. The appointment as China's first ambassador to Mongolia of the Inner Mongolian revolutionary Jiyaatai (1901–68), rather than a career diplomat, exemplified the new Chinese leadership's initial view of Mongolia as not truly a foreign country.

When these reunification bids were flatly rejected, Beijing turned to wooing Mongolia as an independent country. From 1958 the SINO-SOVIET SPLIT made the wooing more urgent. State visits and negotiations in the late 1950s and early 1960s resolved the long-disputed border issue, but by 1962 China's hopes of winning Mongolia over to an anti-Soviet position were dashed. From then on relations deteriorated rapidly. In 1964 the two sides were publicly denouncing each other, and in 1967 Chinese Red Guards attacked Mongolian diplomatic personnel in Beijing. Relations continued in deep freeze until the late 1980s. Meanwhile, Chinese policy in Inner Mongolia has been crucially influenced by its perceived rivalry with the MPR. During periods of liberalization Inner Mongolia's economic growth has been used to demonstrate the folly of Mongolian independence, while during periods of repression police measures have been used to crush real and imagined subversion from Mongolia (see "NEW INNER MONGOLIAN PEOPLE'S REVOLUTIONARY PARTY" CASE).

While the Nationalist government in refuge on Taiwan had canceled its recognition of Mongolian independence in 1952, the People's Republic of China's (PRC's) position remained more complicated. Formally, the PRC has continued to recognized Mongolia and exchange ambassadors. Ideologically, the PRC equally insisted that all of Mongolia was historically an inalienable part of China, that the 1911 Restoration was a Russian conspiracy with "feudal upper-stratum elements," and that the Mongolian people have always opposed all "splittist" attempts. Nevertheless, because Lenin and Stalin had blessed Mongolian independence, Maoist writers, when mentioning the 1921 Revolution, had to treat it favorably. Only Soviet ties with Mongolia after Stalin's death in 1952 could be criticized as manifesting continuity with czarist policies and becoming "social imperialism" in the 1960s.

After 1989 Sino-Mongolian relations again became multifaceted and important. The decline in Soviet power facilitated the normalization of relations, while the transition from socialist to market economies in both countries has transformed economic relations. Politically, China and Mongolia have returned to normal relations, with high-level visits since 1989 leading to the April 29, 1994, treaty on friendly relations. While criticism of post-1952 Mongolian foreign policy is now muted, the previous paradoxes of historical delegitimation and pragmatic recognition still define the PRC's official position on Mongolian independence. Even so, China's increasing nationalism and ties with overseas Chinese have revived in unofficial circles the idea of Mongolian independence as illegitimate, a viewpoint expressed in the 1993 book *Wai Menggu duli neimu* (The inside story of Outer Mongolian independence). After a protest from the Mongolian government, the book was banned in China.

For its part the Mongolian government has scrupulously distanced itself from any support of Inner Mongolian independence while maintaining that it does have an interest in purely cultural ties with Mongols abroad. Even so, Mongolia's periodic visits from the Dalai Lama, seen in China as a Tibetan splittist, and its tolerance as a democracy of the occasional protests of China's Inner Mongolia policy are irritants. In the immediate aftermath of Mongolia's 1990 democratic revolution, Chinese authorities smashed nationalist study circles in Inner Mongolia for circulating Mongolian democratic works. Ironically, however, the long-term result of renewed contact between the Mongols of Inner Mongolia and Mongolia proper has been mutual estrangement, as the two sides realize how decades of separation have made them different from each other. Nevertheless, Mongolia still has a network of Inner Mongolian dissidents and their supporters serving as middlemen between Inner Mongolia and the West.

Economically, China (including Hong Kong and Macao) has become Mongolia's dominant trading partner, receiving 58.9 percent of Mongolia's exports and supplying 20.5 percent of its imports (2000 figures). China has replaced the former Soviet Union as the buyer of Mongolia's copper and molybdenum concentrates and other important mineral exports. Moreover, in 2000 Chinese firms were partners in one-third of Mongolia's 1,252 joint ventures and supplied more than 25 percent of Mongolia's total foreign investment, a fact that has generated considerable anxiety in Mongolia. Human interchange has also increased, with Chinese businessmen and Inner Mongolian students, artists, and translators making extended stays in Mongolia and Mongolian peddlers, tourists, students, and businessmen visiting China.

CHINESE IN MONGOLIA

Mongolian independence in 1911 made the Chinese community in Mongolia an expatriate one, made up mostly of male traders and craftsmen concentrated in Khüriye/ULAANBAATAR, KYAKHTA CITY, and SELENGE PROVINCE. The Chinese faced considerable hostility from the Mongols. The 1911 government tried to keep Mongols and Chinese segregated, but the use of Mongolian names and the taking of Mongolian wives accelerated after 1921.

In those years Chinese and Russians were the bulk of Mongolia's tiny working class, and the Mongolian trade unions maintained a separate Chinese section with its own Chinese club and entertainment program. In 1924 Chinese members of the Mongolian Trade Unions

(including many white-collar workers) totaled 2,161 or more than half. Subsequently, however, the numbers of Chinese workers in Mongolia's principal enterprises declined to 16.6 percent in 1932 and 5.2 percent in 1938. Large numbers of Chinese were targeted in the GREAT PURGE in 1937–40 and the 1948 Port Arthur Case. In 1956 the Chinese still numbered 16,200, or 1.9 percent of the population but were undergoing rapid assimilation. The president of Mongolia from 1992 to 1997, Punsalmaagiin Ochirbat, had a Chinese grandfather, a fact on which his political opponents attempted to capitalize.

A lasting legacy of the Sino-Mongolian alliance of the 1950s was a new population of Chinese guest workers who settled in Ulaanbaatar near the traditional Chinatown (Maimaching). Peaking at more than 13,000 in 1961, the population was numbered at 6,000 in 1981. At first working in construction, the remaining Chinese, numbering several thousand, were mostly displaced by Russian and Mongolian workers in the 1960s. After 1981 the Mongolian government began exiling many to western Mongolia as antisocial elements and security risks. After the thaw in the late 1980s these Chinese returned to Ulaanbaatar, where most make a living raising vegetables, pigs, chickens, and other goods for the market. They remain mostly citizens of China.

See also FOREIGN RELATIONS; KYAKHTA; MONGOLIA, STATE OF; MONGOLIAN PEOPLE'S REPUBLIC; REVOLUTIONARY PERIOD; SELENGE PROVINCE; THEOCRATIC PERIOD.

Chinese colonization   Since the Han dynasty (202 B.C.E.–220 C.E.) Inner Mongolia has been a border area sometimes settled by ethnic Chinese and sometimes by nomadic peoples. Under the Mongol Empire the Mongols themselves brought in displaced Chinese to farm as far north as Tuva, but these colonies disappeared after 1368. After the TUMU INCIDENT in 1449 the Mongols advanced far south, establishing the frontier of settlement around the line of the current Great Wall. The rebellions and wars of the early QING DYNASTY (1636–1912) devastated the Chinese population and relieved any incipient land pressure. As the Chinese population grew from 100–150 million in 1650 to 410 million in 1850, farmers began to spill over into Inner Mongolia, Manchuria, the Tibetan plateau, and China's own mountain slopes and coastal sandbars.

Scattered evidence shows Chinese immigration moving north into Inner Mongolia by the early 18th century and accelerating slowly through the 18th and 19th centuries. The general Qing policy, announced in 1748, was to prohibit colonization without its prior approval. At first exceptions were made provided the settlers returned south of the wall every winter, but by the 19th century such regulations were no longer enforced. In southern Rehe district, including Josotu and southern JUU UDA leagues (land on both sides of the modern Inner Mongolia-Liaoning border), the Qing government permitted farming Mongols, who had already divided up their banner land (a very exceptional procedure), individually to hire Chinese tenants. This policy was also later followed among the HÖHHOT TÜMED. By 1800 the officially recognized Chinese settler population within modern Inner Mongolian frontiers was more than 425,000 (not including those in traditional Mongol lands now included in neighboring provinces).

Until 1901 this process of colonization had no government sanction. Some settlements were begun by miners, who had a particularly lawless reputation. While a few families of Chinese might simply show up in a likely looking spot and start farming, lasting colonization was usually arranged by land developers (*dishang*), who brokered settlements with the local banner authorities, dug canals, recruited tenants, and organized self-defense, often through secret society organizations. The land development industry often grew out of trading stations, when Chinese merchants induced indebted banners and noblemen to settle the debts with a grant of land. Official recognition of the fait accompli and the establishment of subprefectural (*ting*) and then county (*xian*) administrations usually lagged decades behind the first settlement.

Mongolian attitudes toward colonization varied greatly depending on its nature and scale. Chinese land practice allowed for "bottom-soil" rights, which gave the owner a fixed rent from a plot of land without any right to remove the renter or control use. Since banner land was usually held in common, bottom-soil rents were divided among the banner members. In 1736 the ORDOS Mongols approved colonization along the Great Wall and hoped to extend it to increase their bottom-soil rents. Renting of land or other resources was a common way to handle new expenses. By 1905 the government of Prince Güngsangnorbu (1871–1931) of KHARACHIN Right Banner (modern Harqin Qi) in Rehe was using the leasing of mines and other resources to finance new schools without increasing banner taxes. Transfer of land to pay debts, however, left no bottom-soil rights and was hence unpopular, particularly as the debts were often the private ones of the banner ZASAG (ruler). Widespread corruption in the process of pricing, surveying, and assigning the land made the process all the more objectionable. In any case, colonization deals were not registered with the Qing authorities and so bound both the Mongolian BANNERS (appanages) and the Chinese developers in an underground economy.

After the 1870s the frequent lawlessness of the settlers and the dawning realization that colonization was not a one-time event but an accelerating process provoked increasing numbers of antisettler attacks by Mongols. In the Hetao, for example, the first Mongol attacks on settlers came in 1882, which were in turn resisted by the settlers led by a dynamic canal builder, land developer, and vigilante leader, Wang Tongchun (1851–1925).

In southeastern Inner Mongolia Mongolian banner governments in the 19th century began to collect bottom-soil rents by force from increasingly assertive Chinese tenants and tried to restrict Chinese use of banner resources (forests, remaining pastures, etc.). This conflict exploded during the 1891 Jindandao ("Golden Pill Way") rebellion of Chinese sectarian peasants, who killed or drove north scores of thousands of Mongols.

In 1901 with the NEW POLICIES, the Qing government suddenly embarked on a full-scale program of colonization to assimilate and strengthen the frontier. New colonization commissioners, such as the notorious Yigu (d. 1926) in Suiyuan (southwest Inner Mongolia), assigned vast tracts of virgin steppe to colonization. The Qing exercised their right of eminent domain and appropriated for their own treasury bottom-soil rights, not only in unopened areas but in already colonized lands governed by unofficial agreements. In Ordos the people organized DUGUILANG, or vigilante "circles," to resist, while in Jirim league (eastern Inner Mongolia) Mongol insurrectionists armed with Russian and Japanese rifles, such as Togtakhu Taiji (1863–1922), killed government surveyors and soldiers and looted Chinese shops (*see* FRONT GORLOS MONGOL AUTONOMOUS COUNTY). Rebellions broke out again in 1912–13 in coordination with Khalkha Mongolia's declaration of independence and invasion of Inner Mongolia. Many more colonization projects were created on paper than were actually implemented, but even so by 1912 the number of Chinese in Inner Mongolia's current frontier was about 1,550,000, substantially outnumbering the Mongols.

After 1912 the provincial warlords of the Republic of China continued government colonization programs in Inner Mongolia as railroad construction integrated the colonized areas into the national market. Now the establishment of counties preceded the actual settlement. Farming Mongols in eastern Inner Mongolia were frequently evicted to make way for Chinese tenants imported by land developers. The last great revolt, led by Gada Meiren (1893–1931), broke out in KHORCHIN Left-Flank Middle banner (Horqin Zuoyi Zhongqi) in 1929 against another massive colonization project. The rebellion was crushed in 1931 and the Mongol farmers evicted, but the actual colonization was forestalled by the Japanese occupation of Inner Mongolia (1931/1937–45). In 1937 the Chinese population of Inner Mongolia was already more than 3,700,000.

The Chinese Communist programs of land reform applied from 1947 to 1952 canceled bottom-soil rights and hurt Mongol interests in areas such as Rehe, where they rented land to Chinese immigrants. At the same time the new Inner Mongolian Autonomous Region government was cautious about pushing the agricultural frontier any further. Instead, Chinese were transferred into Inner Mongolia to run mines and railroads and deliver administration and services, building nonagricultural towns on the steppe. From 1958 agricultural immigration resumed, and in 1960 alone about 1 million refugees fleeing the countrywide famine of the Great Leap Forward streamed into Inner Mongolia, plowing up previously untouched steppe. Yields soon declined due to the destruction of the topsoil, and in the next two years 590,000 refugees returned to their homes. Large new strips of Chinese settlement remained, however. From 1984 the Inner Mongolian government has tried to shift many marginal Chinese farming communities threatened by severe desertification to herding.

See also BAOTOU; CHAKHAR; CHIFENG MUNICIPALITY; CHINA AND MONGOLIA; CHINQAI; DESERTIFICATION AND PASTURE DEGRADATION; ENVIRONMENTAL PROTECTION; FARMING; INNER MONGOLIA AUTONOMOUS REGION; INNER MONGOLIANS; QARA-QORUM; SIBERIA AND THE MONGOL EMPIRE; TONGLIAO MUNICIPALITY; WUHAI.

Further reading: C. R. Bawden, "A Document concerning Chinese Farmers in Outer Mongolia in the Eighteenth Century," *Acta Orientalia* 36 (1982): 47–55; Paul Hyer, "The Chin-tan-tao Movement: A Chinese Revolt in Mongolia (1891)," in *Altaica: Proceedings of the 19th Annual Meeting of the Permanent International Altaistics Conference,* ed. Juha Janhunen (Helsinki: Finno-Ugrian Society, 1977), 105–112; G. Navaangnamjil, "A Brief Biography of the Determined Hero Togtokh," in *Mongolian Heroes of the Twentieth Century,* trans. Urgunge Onon (New York: AMS Press, 1976), 43–76; Henry Serruys, "Two Complaints from Wang Banner, Ordos, regarding Banner Administration and Chinese Colonization (1905)," *Monumenta Serica* 34 (1979–80): 471–511.

Chinese fiction   Chinese novels and short stories in written translations and retold by minstrels formed a popular and important part of Mongolian literature, as they did for other countries of east and southeast Asia. Until the 19th century the *Journey to the West* (*Xi you ji,* first Chinese edition 1592), a magical Buddhist-Taoist version of the Tang monk Xuanzang's journey to India, was the most widely circulated Chinese novel among the Mongols. Translated and annotated in 1721 by Arana (d. 1724), a high Mongol official in the EIGHT BANNERS system, it was printed in CHAKHAR in 1791 and circulated as far as Buriatia and Xinjiang. It was read as a Buddhist text, although both the original text and Arana's commentary were far from orthodox. Similarly, an obscure Chinese versified novel about the ancient Chinese queen Zhong Wuyuan was widely copied and read as an incarnation tale of the powerful Buddhist protectress-deity Lhamo. The *Three Kingdoms* (*Sanguo yanyi,* printed 1522) circulated in Mongolia in an imperially sponsored Manchu print edition but was first translated into Mongolian in the first half of the 19th century. Again, its surface message of loyalty and heroism guaranteed it a wide circulation, although a deeper reading sometimes led to profound cynicism.

In the mid-19th century the Mongols of southeast Inner Mongolia were also swept up in the fashion for the tragically thwarted love of young lord Jia Baoyu for his cousin Lin Daiyu told in *Dream of the Red Chamber* (*Hong lou meng,* printed 1792). In 1847 "Khasbuu" (probably a pseudonym) made an annotated and abridged translation of the work. These works and the later Mongolian "continuations" written by INJANNASHI (1837–92) were intended for like-minded readers who saw their own experiences in the trials of the sensitive young lovers.

From 1800 to 1925 manuscript translations, sometimes illustrated, of at least 80 different Chinese novels were made in Inner Mongolia and Khalkha. Popular genres included historical dramas, supernatural combats, detective tales of Judge Bao and Judge Shi, romances, adventures, and erotic melodramas. Chinese novels before the mid-20th century circulated in a bewildering variety of sequels, prequels, and abridged, "improved," or annotated texts, and the Mongolian translators frequently worked from now-obscure versions. The EIGHTH JIBZUNDAMBA KHUTUGTU (1870–1924) was an eager reader, yet purely secular works were never printed until 1925, when the KHARACHIN printer Temgetü (1887–1939) printed *Three Kingdoms* in Beijing. Since then Mongolian translations of the most critically respected traditional Chinese novels have been regularly in print in Inner Mongolia.

Chinese novels also circulated in performing traditions. Beijing opera troupes were some of the most popular entertainers and drew their material largely from historical fiction. The *Journey to the West* was performed as drama in several monasteries in Khalkha. Mongolian minstrels (*khuurchi*) in eastern Inner Mongolia, eastern Khalkha, and Khüriye (*see* ULAANBAATAR) performed episodes of Chinese novels, particularly of the adventure and historical genres. Delivered in mixed prose and rhyme, these "booklet stories" (*bengsen üliger*) mixed motifs from Mongolian EPICS and songs and Indian tales with a pseudohistorical Chinese background. Musical accompaniment and mime enlivened the narrative.

The influence of Chinese authors on Inner Mongolian writers such as Injannashi has long been known, but Chinese fiction also had an important impact on fiction and drama writers of early 20th-century Mongolia proper. Mongolia's first revolutionary prime minister, BODÖ (1885–1922), penned a romance based on the Chinese story of lost love "The Pearl-Sewn Shirt," and the founders of modern Mongolian literature, especially BUYANNEMEKHÜ (1902–37), appreciated Chinese literature in both written and performed forms.

See also FOLK POETRY AND TALES; LITERATURE; THEOCRATIC PERIOD.

Further reading: Christopher P. Atwood, "The Marvellous Lama in Mongolia: The Phenomenology of a Cultural Borrowing," *Acta Orientalia* 46 (1992–93): 3–30; ———. "'Worshiping Grace': The Language of Loyalty in

Qing Mongolia," *Late Imperial China* 21 (2000): 86–139; C. R. Bawden, "The First Systematic Translation of Hung Lou Meng: Qasbuu's Commented Mongolian Version," *Zentralasiatische Studien* 15 (1981): 241–305; Claudine Salmon, *Literary Migrations: Traditional Chinese Fiction in Asia (17th–20th Centuries)* (Beijing: International Culture Publishing Corp., 1987).

Chinese trade and moneylending

Before the submission of the Mongols to the QING DYNASTY (1636–1912), trade with China was carried on through the TRIBUTE SYSTEM and regulated horse markets at the frontier towns. This trade was seen as a political concession to the Mongols and, to avoid Mongolian raids, was generally conducted on favorable terms.

From early in the Qing dynasty Inner Mongolian dukes and princes began attending audiences in Beijing every three years, and shops in Beijing began to cater to the Mongolian trade. Shop agents also began to accompany the princes back to their territories. With the surrender of Khalkha in 1691 and the Zünghar wars, Chinese merchants served the Qing armies in Mongolia as supply agents. They also began to trade with Russian merchants at Khüriye (*see* ULAANBAATAR) and KYAKHTA CITY, a trade regularized in the Russia-Qing treaty of 1727.

Chinese merchants in Mongolia were at first tightly regulated. In 1722 the Qing authorities decreed that every Chinese merchant going to Mongol lands had to obtain a permit from Guihua (modern HÖHHOT), Zhangjiakou (Kalgan), or Dolonnuur (modern Duolun) specifying the merchant's name, destination, type of goods, and expected length of the journey. A quota of permits was set by the LIFAN YUAN, the agency in charge of the Mongols. Permits were issued for only one year, and traders could reside only in a certain number of trading towns. Around 1720 zarguchis (judges; *see* JARGHUCHI) were stationed in Khüriye and later in Kyakhta (modern Altanbulag), ULIASTAI, and KHOWD CITY. Expanding trade and the limitations of the permit system made Guihua, Zhangjiakou, and Dolonnuur major commercial centers. The number of firms trading in Mongolia located in Zhangjiakou rose from about 10 in 1662 to more than 230 in 1820. Shanxi firms dominated the Mongolian trade, but those from Beijing, Huangxian in Shandong, and Leting in Hebei were also active. Chinese firms separated financiers, who generally remained in China, from the managers, who were shareholders and received both a salary and bonuses in the form of additional shares. Shop assistants were paid at first in room and board and only later by salary. A few able assistants rose to become shareholding managers.

By the Qing's final campaign against the ZÜNGHARS in 1753–57, official Khalkha debts had risen to 155,739 taels of silver. CHINGGÜNJAB'S REBELLION led to widespread looting of Chinese shops. Qianlong (1736–96) ordered

Storefront of a Chinese firm in Khüriye (modern Ulaanbaatar). Note the sign board in Chinese, Tibetan (top), Mongolian (left), and Manchu (right). *(From Tsedendambyn Batbayar. Modern Mongolia: A Concise History [1996])*

68,000 taels of the war debt paid out of the imperial treasury, while the merchants were pressured to forgo the remaining 85,700. From 1776 to 1781 Qianlong pushed the local authorities to liquidate all official and much of the Mongols' private debts and strictly enforce the restrictions on Chinese merchants. In 1797, however, the new emperor, Jiaqing (1796–1820), removed the restrictions on trading in the countryside. The new ability to trade in the countryside became a tremendous advantage to Chinese merchants. In the trading towns competition was stiff, and Mongols could drive good bargains, but in the countryside there was usually no competition.

The Chinese merchants purchased livestock, wool, hides, furs, and deer antlers in Mongolia. The largest item sold was TEA, followed by cotton drill. Other items included tobacco, flour, grain, liquor, wine, opium, pipes, scissors, needles, thread, guns, bullets, traps, Buddhas, ritual implements, glass, beads, and luxuries. Chinese artisans in Guihua and elsewhere were soon making boots, jewelry, steels and flints, bowls, and other goods in the Mongolian style, devastating local Mongolian manufactures except among the DÖRBÖD and other far western Mongols. Trade was conducted at first in barter, with goods reckoned either in bricks of tea or sheep, but in the second half of the 19th century a silver economy was established.

Chinese shops sold goods on credit and loaned silver. Qing regulations limited interest to 3 percent a month uncompounded, or 36 percent a year, and prohibited interest from exceeding the principal, yet the great demand, both private and public, for capital broke through all regulations. Unscrupulous merchants in Mongolia, as in China itself, worked unwary borrowers into a state of inextricable debt, which finally gave the firm complete ownership of the debtor's herd. Chinese merchants also competed fiercely for the right to become official "partners" (*tüngshi*, from Chinese *tongshi*), supplying interest-bearing loans for the cash-poor BANNERS (appanages) and LEAGUES. Even monasteries, which were the largest institutions in Mongolia, were often reduced to rolling over debts repeatedly. Private debts of banner princes were supposed to be paid by their private subjects (*khamjilga*) but were often imposed on the banner population at large. In Inner Mongolia indebted princes often sold their banner lands to the merchants, who would then organize colonization and settlement of the land by Chinese tenants (*see* CHINESE COLONIZATION). In the mid-19th century 15 or so firms were capitalized at 100,000 taels or more, and the great Dashengkui firm, *tüngshi* to banners all over Mongolia, was capitalized at 20,000,000 taels.

From about 1865 Chinese trade and offtake of animals greatly increased. In 1884 official debt of Khalkha's three eastern AIMAGS and the GREAT SHABI (the Jibzundamba Khutugtu's estate) reached 1.8 million *taels*. In 1900–10 an estimated 800,000 sheep and 100,000 live horses were driven from Outer Mongolia to China annually, while in 1909 1.6 million boxes of tea went to Mongolia through Zhangjiakou. One growing factor was China's involvement in the world hide and wool trade. In 1879 the export of camel wool from Tianjin reached 10,000 *piculs* (1 *picul* = 133.33 lbs.), while in 1885 the export of sheep wool reached more than 200,000 *piculs*, (although roughly half of the sheep wool came from the Tibetan plateau). By World War I the United States had become the final destination for most of the wool exported from Mongolia, whether through Vladivostok or Tianjin.

In the first decade of the 20th century, as the Qing switched its policy to assimilation, looting of Chinese shops and the burning of debt records became frequent. The 1911 RESTORATION of Mongolian independence devastated Chinese trade. Although the new theocratic government tried to prevent violence against merchants, shops and records of debts were destroyed in 1912 in Khowd and elsewhere. At the same time the Mongolian government encouraged direct ties with American, British, and German merchants. The upheaval of the Russian Revolution (1917–21) spilled over into Mongolia and northeast Inner Mongolia, and when trade revived after 1923 Chinese firms were almost completely dependent on British and American capital. The 1928 leftist turn in Mongolia finally expelled Chinese firms, and the 1931–37 Japanese conquest reduced their role in Inner Mongolia to minor retail trade.

See also ANIMAL HUSBANDRY AND NOMADISM; MONEY, MODERN; SOCIAL CLASSES IN THE QING PERIOD; THEOCRATIC PERIOD.

Further reading: M. Sanjdorj, *Manchu Chinese Colonial Rule in Northern Mongolia*, trans. Urgunge Onon (New York: St. Martin's Press, 1980); Henry Serruys, "A Mongol Banner Pays Its Debt," *Monumenta Serica* 36 (1984–85): 511–544.

Ch'ing   *See* QING DYNASTY.

Chingay   *See* CHINQAI.

Chinggisids   *See* BORJIGID.

Chinggis Khan (Genghis, Jenghiz, Chingiz) (1162?–1227) *Founder of the Mongol Empire and national hero of the Mongol people*
Like that of most great conquerors, the legacy of Chinggis Khan has been very controversial. In his day many non-Mongols called him an accursed bandit and killer destined for hell, while others described him as a man of tremendous gifts and charisma who had received his mission of rule from God. The Mongols themselves traditionally called him the "Holy Lord," and his cult became a cornerstone of Mongol civic and religious traditions.

CHILDHOOD AND YOUTH

Chinggis was the son of YISÜGEI BA'ATUR and so a member of the Mongols' ruling BORJIGID lineage. His birthplace of Deli'ün Boldaq on the Onon River is placed sometimes in Dadal Sum in Mongolia's Khentii province and sometimes on the southern border of Aga Buriat Autonomous Area, in Russia. Yisügei himself was a grandson and nephew of two of the first Mongol khans. When his first son by his principal wife, Ö'ELÜN, was born, Yisügei was returning to his camp from battle against the hostile Tatar tribe with a captive named Temüjin (blacksmith). Yisügei thus named his son, the future Chinggis, Temüjin. The fact that he was born with a blood clot in his hand was later taken as an augury of his violent rise to universal rule. When Temüjin was only nine years old, his father was poisoned while at the camp of some TATARS.

The *SECRET HISTORY OF THE MONGOLS*, the earliest monument of Mongolian literature, presents the following period as one of almost total isolation and deprivation for Yisügei's two widows and their sons. The Persian historian RASHID-UD-DIN and the *SHENGWU QINZHENG LU* (a Mongolian chronicle preserved only in Chinese translation), however, imply that Yisügei's brothers stood by their sister-in-law. The sources do agree, however, that most of Yisügei's subject tribesmen deserted him and that dominance over the Mongols passed to the rival TAYICHI'UD clan. As a child Temüjin spent some time with Dei Sechen of the QONGGIRAD and his daughter BÖRTE; before his death Yisügei and Dei Sechen had betrothed the children to each other. He also formed a blood brotherhood (ANDA) with JAMUGHA, who later grew up to be his rival.

As he entered adolescence Temüjin's life became dangerous. Ö'elün's older sons, Temüjin and Qasar, came into conflict with Begter and Belgütei, the sons of Yisügei's other wife. Eventually Temüjin and Qasar murdered Begter but spared Belgütei. Temüjin faced repeated threats from the hostile clans and tribes, horse thieves, and other dangers of the steppe. The rival Tayichi'ud clan at one point imprisoned him, perhaps for his murder of Begter, but he escaped. Probably shortly after this episode Temüjin went to claim his betrothed bride, Börte, bringing her to his camp. The MERKID tribe had long desired vengeance for Ö'elün, who had been stolen by Yisügei from one of their tribesmen. Now, hearing that Temüjin had a new wife, the Merkid raided his camp, kidnapping Börte and Yisügei's other wife, while Ö'elün and the brothers fled. With the aid of Toghril Khan of the KEREYID and his blood brother Jamugha, Temüjin and his brothers succeeded in rescuing Börte. Soon after, Börte gave birth to a son, whom Chinggis named JOCHI, or "guest." The name reflected Temüjin's doubts about his son's paternity, doubts that later caused family conflict.

Börte later gave birth to three other sons and five daughters. Chinggis had four other major wives, but of these four most were childless, and only one son, Kölgen, by his second wife, Qulan, survived to adulthood.

TEMÜJIN'S RISE TO POWER

The counterattack against the Merkid, perhaps around 1180, marked Temüjin's entrance onto the larger Mongolian stage. Toghril Khan, ruler of the Kereyid Khanate occupying central Mongolia, had been Yisügei's blood brother, and now he took Temüjin under his wing. Soon after, he and Jamugha had a falling out, after which Temüjin's uncles, together with a significant part of the MONGOL TRIBE, declared Temüjin khan of the Mongols.

The details of Temüjin's subsequent rise to chief of the Mongol tribe are told in the *Secret History of the Mongols,* the *Shengwu Qinzheng Lu,* and in Rashid-ud-Din's *COMPENDIUM OF CHRONICLES.* While often sharing episodes, they also diverge on many points, particularly chronology, and it is difficult, if not impossible, to reconstruct a synoptic narrative of his political vicissitudes before 1201. The only incident that can be firmly dated is his 1196 participation in an attack on the Tatar tribe, his hereditary enemies. This attack had been planned by the JIN DYNASTY in North China, and for his participation the

dynasty gave Temüjin the Chinese title of Zhaotao, or "Pacification Commissioner," and Toghril the title of ONG KHAN, or "Prince Khan."

By 1201 Temüjin had fought his way to dominance among the Mongol clans. The Tayichi'ud and other remaining opponents within the Mongols, with the support of the Tatars, the NAIMAN, the Merkid, and other tribes, elected Jamugha khan in an attempt finally to block Temüjin's rise. Temüjin's subsequent defeat of Jamugha and his virtual annihilation of the Tayichi'ud made him the recognized leader of the Mongol tribe, yet many disaffected Mongols preferred to submit directly to Ong Khan rather than acknowledge Temüjin's rule. Together with Ong Khan, Temüjin warred against the Tatars, the Naiman, and the Merkid. In 1202 Temüjin and his Mongols crushed the Tatars, whose adult population he massacred and whose children he distributed to his people as slaves.

Temüjin's powerful position in the court of his ally Ong Khan eventually raised the fears of Ong Khan's son that the Mongol planned to usurp rule over the Kereyid Khanate as well. Temüjin tried to cement their alliance by requesting Ong Khan's daughter as a bride for his son Jochi and by giving his own daughter to one of Ong Khan's sons. Ong Khan pretended to agree but instead planned a sudden attack on Temüjin and his troops. Fortunately, Temüjin was warned by two herdsmen, Badai and Kishiliq, who heard the news from their lord and warned him of the danger. Even so, the Kereyid and a large part of the Mongol tribe under his command decisively defeated Temüjin at the battle of QALAQALJID SANDS (spring 1203). Regrouping in the east, only 2,600 of Temüjin's once scores of thousands of men were left. At the muddy waters of Baljuna Lake he promised that should he regain his position, he would always honor those faithful few who had shared the water with him and their descendants (see BALJUNA COVENANT).

Before the year was out, however, Temüjin had gathered new adherents among the Mongols, tricked Ong Khan and the Kereyid with a fake message of surrender from his brother Qasar, and crushed the Kereyid forces at the battle of Jeje'er Heights (autumn 1203). Ong Khan was killed in his flight, and the Kereyid as a whole surrendered to Temüjin. Now the victories followed in rapid succession. In 1204 he defeated the Naiman tribe inhabiting the ALTAI RANGE at the battle of Keltegei Cliffs, and then he crushed the Merkid troops at Qaradal Huja'ur. Meanwhile, the ruler of the ÖNGGÜD, along the frontier between Mongolia and China, had joined Temüjin and received his daughter in marriage. With these victories Temüjin united the nomadic peoples of the Mongolian plateau for the first time in centuries.

THE 1206 *QURILTAI* AND CHINGGIS'S NEW INSTITUTIONS

In 1206 Temüjin held a great assembly (*quriltai*) on the ONON RIVER, where he was acclaimed as Chinggis Khan, ruler of the "Great Mongol Empire." The term *Chinggis* has often been interpreted as being meaning *Tenggis,* or "Ocean," thus referring to Chinggis's pretension of universal rule, yet Igor de Rachewiltz's identification of *Chinggis* with a Turkish word meaning "hard" or "severe" seems more probable. The name was pronounced "Chingiz" in the Turkish and Persian languages, and a misreading of the Persian manuscripts by pioneering French scholars in the 18th century produced the European "Genghis" or "Jenghiz."

The 1206 assembly also founded the core institutions of the new MONGOL EMPIRE. Both the Naiman and the Kereyid had a more centralized monarchy than did the tribal Mongols, and Chinggis borrowed extensively from them. He moved his headquarters to Ong Khan's Shira Ordo, or "Yellow Palace Tent," and created a large imperial guard (KESHIG) divided into day guards and night guards on the model of the Kereyid guard. Chinggis ordered the Naiman's chief Uighur scribe, TATAR-TONG'A, to instruct his sons and the adopted foundling SHIGI QUTUQU in the mystery of writing, thus inaugurating the UIGHUR-MONGOLIAN SCRIPT, which has remained in use up to the present. He also divided all the Mongols into 10s, 100s, 1,000s, and 10,000s, each with its own commander. Chinggis Khan personally appointed all the commanders of rank of *chiliarch* (commander of 1,000) and above. This DECIMAL ORGANIZATION, part of a long tradition in Inner Asia, created a hierarchy of nested cells through which he could easily mobilize forces of a desired size and transmit orders.

Perhaps the most important measures for Chinggis were the rewards decreed for those who had been faithful to him in his rise to power. Virtually all his uncles and cousins and most of the major clan heads had turned against him during his rise, so Chinggis found his supporters among individual companions (NÖKÖR) often hailing from clans of very low rank in the traditional Mongol order. Chinggis's mother, Ö'elün, had raised foundlings, discovered in the camps of defeated Tayichi'ud, the Yürkin, and the Tatar, to be adoptive brothers for her son, and Chinggis Khan gave many of them, such as Shigi Qutuqu, high position. The list of these positions in the *Secret History of the Mongols* divides them into several categories, such as the "four steeds" and the "four dogs." Chinggis expected both unwavering loyalty and effective service from his "dogs" and "steeds," and he received it from them virtually to a man. As a result their clans, such as MUQALI's JALAYIR, Boroghul's Üüshin, and Chila'uns Suldus, among the "steeds," and Qubilai's Barulas, among the "dogs," became powerful aristocratic families for the next few centuries, holding vast appanages and major political power in North China, Turkestan, Persia, and the Inner Asian steppe.

While hardly any of Chinggis's uncles and cousins even survived the brutal politics of his rise, his brothers, sons, daughters, and sons-in-law all became powerful

Chinggis Khan (1206–1227). Anonymous court painter
(*Courtesy of the National Palace Museum, Taipei*)

members of the new ruling class. Chinggis's relations with his brothers were not free of tension. Qasar, his full brother, had often wavered in his support. Chinggis had excluded his half-brother Belgütei from his intimate counsels for his indiscretions, and his youngest brother, Temüge Odchigin, he considered too lazy for any serious posts. Even so, he assigned subjects and territory to all of them. To his sons he assigned subject peoples and advisers as well as chances to show themselves in battle. In accordance with the Mongolian tradition of QUDA, or marriage alliance, the families of his sons' wives and of his sons-in-law (*kürgen*) also shared in his good fortune.

CHINGGIS KHAN'S RELIGIOUS MANDATE

Before Chinggis Khan's birth the Borjigid aristocracy among the Mongols had justified its rule through predestination by "Eternal Heaven" (*see* TENGGERI) and legends of its divine origin from its ancestress ALAN GHO'A. Chinggis Khan himself came to see heavenly predestination in his extraordinary rise to power. A key role in this religious aspect of his early rise was played by TEB TENGGERI, a shaman and the son of "Father" Münglig, to whom Chinggis had granted his widowed mother, Ö'elün, in marriage. Teb Tenggeri's visions and austerities earned great influence among the Mongols, and he proclaimed that Temüjin was heaven's chosen lord of the world. It was Teb Tenggeri who chose the title "Chinggis" for Temüjin. After Chinggis's coronation the power of Teb Tenggeri and his brothers grew, and around 1210 they challenged Chinggis's new dynasty, attacking his brothers. Had Teb Tenggeri prevailed, rule over the new Mongolian empire might well have turned into a nonhereditary, charismatic succession of prophets, much like the early caliphate in Islamic history. Protests by Chinggis's family, particularly his mother, Ö'elün, and his wife, Börte, however, convinced him to defend the dynastic nature of the state, and he allowed his brother Temüge Odchigin to fight back against Teb Tenggeri and kill him.

After Teb Tenggeri's death Chinggis Khan would personally commune with "Eternal Heaven," seeking his approval before major campaigns, such as that against the Jin empire in China and against KHORAZM in the West. Chinggis Khan thus replaced Teb Tenggeri as the empire's voice of heaven's will. The *Secret History of the Mongols* detailed the repeated signs that heaven had destined him for rule, from the blood clot he held in his hand at his birth to the oxen that butted Jamugha's tent and bellowed, "Heaven and Earth have taken counsel: Let Temüjin be Lord of the Nation." Contemporary stories from people in contact with the Mongols emphasized that Chinggis Khan was not just a conqueror but a Moseslike lawgiver and prophet for the new nation.

In future years, after conquering the sedentary powers, Chinggis Khan would fashion a distinctive religious policy that saw all religions as praying to one god, or heaven. Heaven's will was made known primarily by success in this life, and Chinggis expected religious figures to recognize that his extraordinary career was the direct result of heaven's favor and not a chance event. Despite his conflict with Teb Tenggeri, Chinggis Khan sought out holy men of various religions, and those who impressed him by their irreproachable conduct and wisdom would receive tax privileges and immunities for them and their followers. After meeting in 1222–23 with a Chinese Taoist priest, Master CHANGCHUN, who urged him to show respect for life, Chinggis Khan tried to give up hunting, encourage filial piety, and show more humanity on his campaigns, but such resolves had no lasting effect.

THE FOREIGN CONQUESTS

After his coronation in 1206 Chinggis Khan strengthened his new Mongol state and prepared for a final confrontation with the Jin dynasty by concluding marriage alliances with the Siberian tribes to the north, with the UIGHURS and QARLUQS, both Turkish-speaking peoples in the oases of Turkestan, and with the Tanguts' XIA DYNASTY in northwest China (*see* SIBERIA AND THE MONGOL EMPIRE). These alliances having been secured by diplomacy or force, Chinggis Khan led the Mongols into a full-scale invasion of the Jin dynasty in 1211. Before Chinggis the Mongols had suffered heavily from the Jin dynasty's punitive expeditions and its policy of encouraging tribal

conflicts on the Mongolian plateau, and Chinggis Khan conducted the campaign against the Jin with appalling ruthlessness. Repeatedly defeated but refusing to submit, the Jin rulers fled south of the Huang (Yellow) River in 1214, abandoning their capital at Zhongdu (modern Beijing; *see* ZHONGDU, SIEGES OF). Chinggis Khan's original plan of making the Jin tributary turned into a policy of occupying and administering North China according to Mongol norms.

While Muqali, Chinggis Khan's viceroy in northern China, began a systematic destruction of remaining resistance in North China, Chinggis turned to the west. In 1204 remnants of the Naiman and Merkid had fled west of the Altai into the QARA-KHITAI empire in Turkestan. The resulting turmoil and the disintegration of the Qara-Khitai due to religious strife opened the way for the Mongols to occupy all of eastern Turkestan. In 1218–19, Chinggis dispatched his general SÜBE'ETEI BA'ATUR and his eldest son, Jochi, to pursue the refugees and conquer the Qara-Khitai, bringing the Mongols' frontier up to the border of the new Muslim Turkish dynasty of Khorazm, then ruling Central Asia, Iran, and Afghanistan. Tension between these two powerful states erupted into war when Sultan Muhammad executed Mongol merchants and envoys in 1218–19. The result was another campaign of vengeance on the part of Chinggis Khan, one that brought Central Asia, eastern Iran, and Afghanistan under Mongol rule. In eastern Iran and Afghanistan, in particular, the Mongols faced dogged resistance and responded with repeated horrific massacres.

It was in these years that a rift arose between Chinggis Khan's eldest son, Jochi, and his two younger brothers, CHA'ADAI and Ögedei. Bitter at being passed over for Ögedei as Chinggis's designated heir, Jochi nomadized with his camp and subjects to the western steppe of Kazakhstan and refused to see his father again until his untimely death around 1225.

Returning to Mongolia, Chinggis planned for his final campaign against the Xia, who had refused to supply troops for his western campaign. Chinggis took this refusal as a personal insult, and the campaign against the Xia was marked by general massacres as well as incidents of unpredictable clemency. At some point in the campaign he fell ill, perhaps after a fall from a horse. By summer 1227, with the Xia campaign effectively over and warned by astrological signs of his impending death, Chinggis attempted to delay the inevitable with a proclamation against killing and looting. On August 25, after giving his generals a final plan for the destruction of the Jin, he died, probably at age 66. His body was buried at a site he had chosen before his death, called Kilengu, somewhere in the KHENTII RANGE. Xu Ting in 1235–36 described the site as surrounded by the KHERLEN RIVER and the mountains. His palace tents, perhaps located at AWARGA, became the site for his cult that began in his son ÖGEDEI KHAN's reign. (*See* EIGHT WHITE YURTS.)

CHINGGIS'S PERSONALITY AND LEGACY TO THE MONGOL EMPIRE

Despite the obscurity of the sources on the chronology of his early rise, Chinggis Khan's personality emerges clearly in the historical record. The death of his father and the consequent turmoil left a deep impression on him, reinforced by his mother, Ö'elün's, repeated exhortation to remember the wrong done to him by the rival Tayichi'ud clan. In reaction, Chinggis grew up with an ideal of a unified and harmonious society, with clear lines of authority and obedience, that he would eventually realize in his imperial institutions. Family loyalty was his touchstone of worth, and disorder was anathema.

Intensely loyal to his companions, Chinggis also took deep pleasure in the thorough destruction of his enemies, thus realizing the ideals of the Mongol tribal moral code, which emphasized the idea of *achi qari'ulqu*, or returning good for good and evil for evil. Ironically for such a famous conqueror, we know little of Chinggis's tactical battle skills; indeed, the major sources, taken at face value, suggest that his skill was not so much as a battle commander but as a ruler who discovered and used talent. Part of this skill was his openness to criticism and correction from those within his trusted circle. In the court of Chinggis Khan one finds relatively little of the constant intrigues endemic to despotic government. Perhaps due to his upbringing, Chinggis also had no difficulty in receiving advice from the strong women around him, particularly his mother, Ö'elün, and his first principal wife, Börte. When Börte was raped and gave birth to Jochi, he never rejected her or her son, a magnanimity unusual in his age.

All these personal characteristics would find clear reflection in the empire Chinggis built. The Mongols impressed all who encountered them with their loyalty and forbearance with one another and their implacable hatred toward those who defied them. Deeply aristocratic in its ethos, the MONGOL EMPIRE depended on the esprit de corps shown by the Mongols as a whole and more narrowly by the descendants of Chinggis Khan and his companions.

See also CHINGGIS KHAN CONTROVERSY; EIGHT WHITE YURTS; HISTORY OF THE WORLD CONQUEROR.

Further reading: Igor de Rachewiltz, "The Title Činggis qan/qaghan Re-examined," in *Gedanke und Wirkung,* ed. Walther Heissig and Klaus Sagaster (Wiesbaden: Otto Harrossowitz, 1989), 281–298; Paul Ratchnevsky, *Genghis Khan: His Life and Legacy,* trans. Thomas Nivison Haining (Oxford: Basil Blackwell, 1991); B. Ya. Vladimirtsov, *The Life of Chingis-Khan,* trans. Prince D. S. Mirsky (London: Routledge and Sons, 1930).

Chinggis Khan controversy

From 1949 the assessment of Chinggis Khan's historical role became a sensitive issue between Mongolia and the Soviet Union and between the Soviet Union and Maoist China.

In the early 20th century the Mongols' traditionally religious image of CHINGGIS KHAN as a sacred ancestor and culture founder was replaced by one of Chinggis as a military conqueror and world historical hero straddling Europe and Asia. This new vision also drew the attention of foreign powers to the possibility of using the image of Chinggis Khan to garner Mongolian support. During their occupation of Inner Mongolia from 1931 to 1945, Japanese officials supported Inner Mongolian efforts to honor Chinggis Khan, such as the construction of an 822-square-meter temple to Chinggis Khan at Wang-un Süme (Ulanhot). Meanwhile, China's Nationalist government removed the traditional cult objects of Chinggis Khan in ORDOS to Gansu to prevent them from falling into the hands of the Japanese. Even the Chinese Communist leader, Mao Zedong, in a 1935 manifesto addressed to the INNER MONGOLIANS, exhorted them to follow the spirit of Chinggis Khan in resisting Japan.

In Mongolia proper (Outer Mongolia) Chinggis Khan's stature grew after the 1921 Revolution with the secularization and Europeanization of Mongolian historical consciousness (he was, of course, the only Mongol most Europeans knew). AMUR's 1934 history of the MONGOL EMPIRE and TSENDIIN DAMDINSÜREN's 1947 modern Mongolian version of the long-lost *SECRET HISTORY OF THE MONGOLS* accelerated the secularization of the image of Chinggis Khan. In 1940 Joseph Stalin casually agreed when Mongolia's ruler, MARSHAL CHOIBALSANG (r. 1936–52) asked about including the standard of Chinggis on Mongolia's new seal, but the Mongols thought better of it.

With the conclusion of WORLD WAR II and the apogee of Great Russian nationalism, Soviet Communist authorities began attacking the heroic figures, real or legendary, of non-Russian peoples, such as the Mongolian epic hero GESER. In line with this trend, in 1949 the MONGOLIAN PEOPLE'S REVOLUTIONARY PARTY's Politburo attacked Chinggis Khan and his "campaigns of plunder," demanding that their feudal and reactionary side be emphasized. While attacks on epic heroes ceased after Stalin's death, this anti-Chinggis line strongly influenced the first edition of the *History of the Mongolian People's Republic* (1954), produced by a team of Soviet and Mongolian scholars.

Meanwhile, in China the Communist government continued the 1930s strategy of winning Mongolian support by honoring Chinggis Khan. On April 23, 1954, the chairman of the INNER MONGOLIA AUTONOMOUS REGION, ULANFU, presided over sacrifices to celebrate the return of Chinggis Khan's cult objects to Ejen-Khoroo, and in 1956 the relics were housed in a 1,500-square-meter mausoleum built with state funds. Even the Japanese-sponsored Temple of Chinggis Khan in Ulaankhota (Ulanhot) was restored and honored.

With the 800th anniversary of Chinggis Khan's birth approaching in 1962, members of Mongolia's party leadership proposed to rethink the 1949 resolutions and allow historians in the Mongolian ACADEMY OF SCIENCES to discuss the issue. Although the top leader, YUMJAAGIIN TSEDENBAL, expressed reservations, commemorative stamps were issued, and a front-page editorial in the party daily, Ünen (Truth), on May 31, 1962, offered a mostly favorable appraisal, as did an academic conference. An 11 meter (36 foot) high stone monument with a carved portrait of Chinggis Khan was erected near the khan's presumed birthplace of Gurwan Nuur in Dadal Sum, Khentii province. Informed of the conference, Soviet historians had been strongly critical, while Chinese scholars were either critical or praised Chinggis as a unifying figure in *Chinese* history. When in spring 1962 the Inner Mongolians held their own celebrations, this focus, with an implicit reference to bringing Mongolia back within China, was the theme. The Soviet embassy soon attacked the Mongolian academics, claiming they had belittled Russia's contribution to Mongolian independence and had criticized Soviet historians by name. On September 10, 1962, at a special Politburo meeting, Tsedenbal saddled the regime's chief theoretician, DARAMYN TÖMÖR-OCHIR, with responsibility for the debacle, and he was dismissed.

After Sino-Soviet relations deteriorated into violent polemics in 1963–64, Soviet spokesmen denounced some favorable articles on Chinggis Khan published in China from 1961 to 1964. In this way Chinggis Khan became a minor issue in the SINO-SOVIET SPLIT. In fact, the Chinese Communists had little interest in Chinggis Khan. During the Cultural Revolution from 1966 to 1976 many Inner Mongolians were persecuted for supposedly venerating Chinggis Khan above Chairman Mao, and both the Ejen Khoroo mausoleum and the Ulaankhota temple were gutted; restoration was completed at the sites only in 1984 and 1987, respectively. In 1975, however, the Mongolian ruler Tsedenbal again accused the Chinese of "making a fetish" of Chinggis Khan to justify their expansionist aims, thus strangely linking contempt for Chinggis Khan with defense of Mongolian independence. In the late 1980s ideological pressure against the Mongolians' veneration of Chinggis Khan was removed. In 1992 Lenin Avenue in ULAANBAATAR was renamed Chinggis Khan Avenue.

See also CHINA AND MONGOLIA; EIGHT WHITE YURTS; JAPAN AND THE MODERN MONGOLS; SOVIET UNION AND MONGOLIA.

Further reading: J. Boldbaatar, "The Eight-Hundredth Anniversary of Chinggis Khan: The Revival and Suppression of Mongolian National Consciousness," in *Mongolia in the Twentieth Century: Landlocked Cosmopolitan*, ed. Stephen Kotkin and Bruce A. Elleman (Armonk, N.Y.: M. E. Sharpe, 1999), 237–246; Paul Hyer, "The Chinggis Khan Shrine in Eastern Inner Mongolia," in *The Chinggis Khan Symposium in Memory of Gombojab Hangin* (Ulaanbaatar: Mongol Sudlal Hevlel, 2001), 113–138.

Chinggünjab's Rebellion (Chingünjav) This ill-coordinated and unsuccessful rebellion of 1756–57 marked the depth of Khalkha Mongol frustration with QING DYNASTY (1636–12) controls and weariness with the Zünghar wars. After many years of war between the Qing Dynasty and the OIRATS mostly fought on Khalkha soil, 1753–55 were particularly difficult years. In 1753, when the DÖRBÖD tribe of the Oirats surrendered, livestock and pasture were purchased from the Khalkha Mongols at state-dictated prices to aid them, and in 1754–55 a difficult winter caused great hardship. Meanwhile, by 1755 the Oirat chief AMURSANAA (1722?–57), serving with an army of Khalkhas, Inner Mongols, Oirats, and Chinese in the pacification of the Züngharia, became dissatisfied with his rewards and plotted rebellion against the Qing with Sebdenbaljur of the Inner Mongolian KHORCHIN, Tsebdenjab, high-ranking prince of Khalkha's Sain Noyan AIMAG, and Chinggünjab (1710–57). Tsebdenjab revealed the disaffection to the expedition's overall commander, Bandi, who separated the conspirators, sending Chinggünjab to pacify the "Uriyangkhai" (Altayan Turks) on the Katun' (Upper Ob') River and recalling Amursanaa to Beijing. Amursanaa's escorting officer, a high-ranking Khalkha prince, Erinchindorji, allowed him to escape with 300 Oirat soldiers, and Amursanaa launched his rebellion that autumn. In spring 1756 the emperor Qianlong (1736–96) executed Erinchindorji, despite his being a son of a Manchu princess and half-brother of the Mongolia's supreme lama, the SECOND JIBZUNDAMBA KHUTUGTU. Discontent over this execution became rife.

Unaware of these events, Chinggünjab was unable to join Amursanaa's rebellion. As the senior prince of the KHOTOGHOID Khalkha, Chinggünjab was originally high in rank among the Zasagtu Khan princes. Repeated breaches of discipline had lost him his position until it was restored in 1754. In summer 1756 he was ordered with 800 men to pursue Amursanaa. Instead, he wrote a letter denouncing the emperor's cruelty and burdensome requisitions before moving into the Khöwsgöl area on the Shishigt River and sending letters claiming the Jibzundamba Khutugtu supported his opposition. The effect of Chinggünjab's missives were immediate. By September 14 the border guards and postroads had virtually all been abandoned. Bands sometimes numbering in the hundreds looted Chinese shops, occupied Mongolian KYAKHTA (modern Altanbulag), and rioted in Khüriye (*see* ULAANBAATAR), yet Chinggünjab failed either to arrest the main loyalist princes or to recruit an army.

Initial enthusiasm did not translate into organization or staying power. Prompted by the Qing court, the second Jibzundamba Khutugtu disavowed the rebellion in letters and assemblies. The Qing brought up Inner Mongolians to man the postroads and border guards before calling up soldiers from the Khalkha *aimag*s. In Setsen Khan famine blocked the call-up, and in Tüshiyetü Khan the khan Yampildorji was either unable or unwilling to implement the order. The Zasagtu Khan and Sain Noyan *aimags*, however, eventually called up their troops, and most of the Khalkha *jasags* (ruling nobility) reported for duty. Tsenggünjab (d. 1771), brother of the repentant conspirator Tsebdenjab, set out in November to capture the rebel leader. Chinggünjab retreated toward the Russian frontier while desperately trying to contact either Amursanaa or the Jibzundamba Khutugtu as his supporters fell away. Chinggünjab was captured in mid-January 1757 and executed on March 11 in Beijing. In the succeeding repressions probably hundreds of rebels and rioters were executed and their families enslaved to loyalist nobles. A succeeding smallpox epidemic of winter 1757–58 added to the Khalkhas' suffering.

Further reading: C. R. Bawden, "The Mongol Rebellion of 1756–1757," *Journal of Asian History* 2 (1968): 1–31; ———, "Some Documents concerning the Rebellion of 1756 in Outer Mongolia," *Bulletin of the Institute of China Border Area Studies* 1 (1970): 1–23.

Chingünjav *See* CHINGGÜNJAB'S REBELLION.

Chinkai *See* CHINQAI.

Chinqai (Chinkai, Chingay, Zhenhai) (1169–1252)
Early adherent of Chinggis Khan and chief scribe under Ögedei Khan and Güyüg Khan

Ethnically a Turk of Uighur origin, Chinqai had a Chinese name (True Ocean, pronounced today Zhenhai), and his religion was Christian. A wealthy caravaneer, he was familiar with both the Mongolian plateau and with North China. He joined CHINGGIS KHAN early, participating in his campaign against the TATARS (1202) and in the BALJUNA COVENANT of 1203. He won merit in subsequent campaigns against the XIA DYNASTY and the JIN DYNASTY in North China. Chinggis Khan ordered him to settle 10,000 Chinese prisoners of war on a state farm in Mongolia named Chinqai City. Under ÖGEDEI KHAN (r. 1229–41) Chinqai served as one of the three chief scribes along with YELÜ CHUCAI in North China and Mahmud Yalavach in Turkestan (*see* MAHMUD YALAVACH AND MAS'UD BEG). Closest to the khan, Chinqai countersigned all documents issued by the other two. After Ögedei's death his widow, TÖREGENE, pursued her grudges against the regular officials, and Chinqai fled to the court of her son, Prince KÖTEN, in Northwest China. When Töregene's son GÜYÜG became khan (1246–48), he restored Chinqai and made him more powerful than ever. After Güyüg's death Chinqai supported Güyüg's widow OGHUL-QAIMISH as regent and opposed the election of Möngke as khan. When MÖNGKE KHAN proved victorious, Chinqai was executed in November–December 1252. Recent archaeological surveys have tentatively identified ruins in Sharga Sum (Gobi-Altai province) as the medieval Chinqai City.

Further reading: P. D. Buell, "Činqai," in *In the Service of the Khan: Eminent Personalities of the Early Mongol-Yuan Period (1200–1300)*, ed. Igor de Rachewiltz et al. (Wiesbaden: Otto Harrossowitz, 1993), 95–111.

Ch'iu Ch'u-chi *See* CHANGCHUN, MASTER.

Choibalsang, Marshal (Khorloogiin Choibalsan, Choybalsan) (1895–1952) *One of the "first seven" revolutionaries of 1921 chosen by Stalin as Mongolia's supreme dictator in 1936*

Choibalsang remains one of the most controversial figures in Mongolian history. Set up as ruler of Mongolia by Stalin's decree, he later showed unexpected nationalist tendencies. While Mongolia began to achieve its often-thwarted goal of internationally recognized independence under his rule, Choibalsang came to power through the murder of tens of thousands of his fellow citizens and the virtual annihilation of Mongolian Buddhism.

CHILDHOOD

Choibalsang was the youngest of four children of the woman Korlô (Khorloo, d. 1915), a *shabi* (lay disciple, or subject) of an INCARNATE LAMA living in the territory of Achitu Zasag banner, near Sang Beise-yin Khüriye Monastery (modern Choibalsang city, EASTERN PROVINCE). Korlô was a poor, devout, and hard-working woman whose foul temper always broke up her relations with men. Her liaison with Choibalsang's father, a Daur from Inner Mongolia named Jamsu, ended before his birth, and Korlô had the boy, originally named Dugar, raised first by an old woman in the neighborhood and then by her eldest daughter. Choibalsang claimed not to know who his father was, but Korlô's liaison with the Daur was well known locally. It is possible this fact influenced his attitude toward Inner Mongolia, which combined pan-Mongolism with contempt for Inner Mongolian expatriates.

At age 12 he began living at a temple, where he was given the monastic name Choibalsang. At age 16 he ran away with another novice to the capital Khüriye (modern ULAANBAATAR). Although the authorities picked up his trail to Khüriye, a Buriat teacher, Nikolai T. Danchinov (1886–1916), arranged his enrollment in the Russian-Mongolian Translators' School, which prevented his deportation back to the monastery. After a year of studying, he was enrolled in a gymnasium in Irkutsk until 1917. Choibalsang learned serviceable conversational Russian but did not read or write it well and never became familiar with Russian or European high culture.

IN THE 1921 REVOLUTION

From 1917 Choibalsang worked as a translator at the Khüriye telegraph office and lived in the house of BODÔ, his former teacher at the Translators' School. With the Chinese REVOCATION OF AUTONOMY in 1919–20, Choibalsang was drawn into Bodô's anti-Chinese group, interpreting for him at occasional meetings with local Russian radicals. In late June 1920, after Bodô's group merged with another to form the Outer Mongolian People's Party, Choibalsang accompanied a party leader, DANZIN, to Soviet Russia to ask for aid to overthrow the Chinese.

Eventually seven members (the famous "first seven"), including Choibalsang's mentor, Bodô, gathered in Irkutsk. From August Choibalsang stayed in Irkutsk with the seven's only military man, SÜKHEBAATUR, and in November he accompanied Sükhebaatur back to Troitskosavsk (in modern KYAKHTA) to recruit soldiers along the border. Although Sükhebaatur and Bodô did not get along, Sükhebaatur became Choibalsang's second mentor. In the ensuing military operations Choibalsang executed several important assignments well and on May 20, 1921, became deputy to the newly appointed General Sükhebaatur. He was assigned to fight the White Russians in western Mongolia.

OFFICIAL IN THE NEW REGIME

Once the People's Party was established in Khüriye as the new government, Choibalsang continued as Sükhebaatur's deputy. During Sükhebaatur and Danzin's absence in Russia (September 29 to December 22, 1921), however, Choibalsang came under the prime minister Bodô's influence again, supporting several of his controversial leftist moves. Remaining loyal to his first mentor, Choibalsang lost his full party membership and deputy commandership as a result of Bodô's resignation and eventual execution. Nevertheless, protected by his second mentor, Sükhebaatur, Choibalsang avoided execution and by the end of 1922 was again holding responsible military positions. After Sükhebaatur's premature death, Choibalsang went for military training in Moscow in August 1923. On his return in summer 1924, he supported the execution of Danzin, Sükhebaatur's successor as commander in chief, at the People's Party's Third Congress. As a reward, Choibalsang became party presidium member and the next commander in chief.

In 1921 Choibalsang married Borotologai, a devout Buddhist and seamstress in the household of the Bogda (Holy One, Mongolia's theocratic ruler until 1924). In the 1920s Choibalsang, despite being an avid hunter and target shooter, was one of the few leaders openly to keep a Buddhist altar in his house. Around 1929 Choibalsang's affair with the actress Diwa (Dewee) poisoned his home life to the point that he donated his yurt-courtyard to the party and lived in his office. One colleague saw him weeping at the grave of Sükhebaatur about his loneliness. Still, Choibalsang and Borotologai did not divorce.

Russian observers and agents at the time analyzed Choibalsang as a "rightist" (i.e., supporter of the party chief DAMBADORJI), but weak, unstable, and more pro-

Russian. During the LEFTIST PERIOD (1929–32) Choibalsang was "kicked upstairs" to become chairman of the Little Khural (i.e., titular head of state). Despite his work as chairman of the commission on confiscating the property of feudals, he never became part of the leftists' inner circle. In 1930 he was made foreign minister and then demoted to head of Mongolia's museum before becoming minister of agriculture.

THE PURGES

In 1933 Choibalsang's name came up in the LHÜMBE CASE, just as it had in the Bodô case, yet Choibalsang avoided implication this time through high-level Soviet intervention. In December 1934 he was at Stalin's advice promoted to deputy prime minister under Gendün. The next year Stalin personally presented 20 GAZ automobiles to Choibalsang as a sign of his favor.

In 1935 Borotologai requested a divorce, fearing that a plain Buddhist wife such as she would impede his rise. Choibalsang married a modern woman, B. Gündegmaa. Choibalsang had no children by either of his wives. In 1937 he adopted a boy, named Nergüi, of one of his Interior Ministry subordinates. Rumors claim that Nergüi was in fact Choibalsang's illegitimate son. Later Gündegmaa adopted a girl, Suwd.

In February 1936, again on Soviet direction, Choibalsang became head of the Interior Ministry, the new security organ, and received the title of marshal. From that time on the Interior Ministry began the final liquidation of the monasteries. In August 1937, with the mysterious death of the commander in chief, MARSHAL DEMID, whose fame Choibalsang always resented, and the arrival of the Soviet security chief M. P. Frinovskii, the preparations for the complete purge of the party leadership were complete.

From September 1937 to the end of 1939, Choibalsang effected an almost complete annihilation of the existing Mongolian elite. By official records, certainly incomplete, Choibalsang through his special purge commission personally approved the execution of 20,099 "counterrevolutionaries" and the imprisonment of 5,739 more. His own notes speak of 56,938 arrests and 20,356 lamas liquidated (how much overlap there is between these and the commission victims is unclear). Throughout the purge process Choibalsang followed the lead of his Soviet trainers. At times Choibalsang seemed to have been helpless to save his friends, and the second half of 1938 he spent in Russia consulting with Stalin and recovering from stress. Even so, Choibalsang certainly guided the purges, making sure that Borotologai and her Tibetan lover survived, for example. In March 1939 a new team of Soviet intelligence operatives arrived headed by Ivan A. Ivanov (1906–48), the new "political representative" (ambassador), who became Choibalsang's ever-present shadow.

The arrest of the last two remaining members of the "first seven" in 1939 and the extermination of the old elite cleared the way for a new mythological history in which Sükhebaatur and Choibalsang created the People's Party and led the revolution. In 1941 the town of Bayantümen (former Sang Beise-yin Khüriye) and EASTERN PROVINCE were both renamed Choibalsang. Mongolia's first major factory, the Industrial Combine in Ulaanbaatar, was also renamed after him.

THE MARSHAL

After 1940 Choibalsang was the unquestioned lord of the new government. In winter 1939–40 he promoted 3,000 new cadres to high positions, creating virtually a whole new ruling elite overnight. Holding until his death, or nearly so, the rank of marshal and positions of premier, foreign minister, army minister, and commander in chief, in 1940 he gave up the position of interior minister to his protegé, B. Shagdarjaw, and made the newly minted economist YUMJAAGIIN TSEDENBAL (1916–91) the party's general secretary. Only G. Bumtsend, a kindly old partisan from 1921 and a political nonentity who had been chosen as titular head of state, and Sükhebaatur's widow, S. Yanjmaa, now a party Politburo member, dared treat "the marshal" familiarly. While usually friendly and down to earth, the marshal's occasional outbursts of rage terrified his entourage.

After the final cases in 1940 to clean up witnesses, terror was no longer a mass phenomenon. Torture was still standard procedure in political cases, however, and was formally approved in a secret Politburo decision in 1943. Incidents such as the 1948 "Port Arthur Case," a supposed plot to kill Choibalsang that led to 80 arrests and 42 executions among Mongolia's Chinese residents, seemed minor only in relation to the wholesale slaughters of 1937–40.

Choibalsang always felt his lack of education and after 1940 arranged regular private tutoring from Soviet advisers and Soviet-educated Mongolians on topics of history and economics. From 1934 his key policy decisions were always approved in his regular meetings with Stalin in Moscow. Even on minor matters Choibalsang never felt comfortable about any decision until he knew that Soviet advisers had approved it. His reliance on Soviet advice led to the 1941–46 switch from the traditional UIGHUR-MONGOLIAN SCRIPT to CYRILLIC-SCRIPT MONGOLIAN.

Despite this dependence, however, Choibalsang did not loose all national feeling. In 1945, with Mongolian participation in WORLD WAR II, Choibalsang let loose a brief wave of pan-Mongolist nationalism through the press, calling for unification of Inner Mongolia with the MONGOLIAN PEOPLE'S REPUBLIC. The Sino-Soviet treaty of August 1945 blocked this unification and temporarily embittered his relations with Stalin. In 1950, when his young protegés proposed that Mongolia follow the example of Tuva and join the Soviet Union, Choibalsang gave them a severe dressing-down.

In winter 1951 Choibalsang went to Moscow for medical treatment, where he died of kidney cancer on January 28, 1952. A national day of mourning was decreed for January 29, the first day of the WHITE MONTH (lunar new year), beginning the new leadership's campaign against that traditional holiday.

LEGACY

The Choibalsang cult remained intact until Soviet ruler Nikita Khrushchev's 1956 speech on de-Stalinization. Criticism of the Choibalsang cult was carried further in 1963, when Choibalsang province and the Industrial Combine were renamed. Despite these criticisms, the fundamental distortions of 1921 revolutionary history lasted until democratization in 1990. Even so, while his victims have now been exonerated, Choibalsang still has many defenders in Mongolia, who honor him for his nationalism and blame the purges and the destruction of the monasteries on either Soviet pressure and/or the needs of the time. Choibalsang city is still named after him, and his statue remains in front of Mongolia's National University.

See also BUDDHISM, CAMPAIGN AGAINST; GREAT PURGE; MONGOLIAN PEOPLE'S PARTY, THIRD CONGRESS OF; 1921 REVOLUTION; REVOLUTIONARY PERIOD; THEOCRATIC PERIOD.

Choijung Lama Temple (Choijin) This temple housed the official oracle of the Eighth Bogda (Holy One), or Jibzundamba Khutugtu (1870–1924). In 1883–84 the Eighth Bogda's tutor, Yonzin Khambo (Yonzon Khamba), diagnosed the fainting spells of the Bogda's younger brother, Lubsangkhaidub (1872–1918), as being possession by Choijung-Setab (Tibetan, Chos-skyungs bSe-khrab), an oracle deity. In 1884 the deity was formally invited from Tibet, and Lubsangkhaidub was eventually able to channel three forms: Naichung (gNas-'chung), Dizimur (rTse-ma-ra), and Dorji-Shugdan (rDo-rje Shugs-ldan). The temple was built in 1899–1901 by local Chinese contractors, while the main images were made by Mongolian sculptors. It received imperial recognition in 1906. The "Speaker Lama," Lubsangpeljai, who interpreted Lubsangkhaidub's sounds, managed the temple. From 1916 a distinctive TSAM dance was performed there. In 1938 the temple was closed down, and in 1941 it became a museum.

See also JIBZUNDAMBA KHUTUGTU, EIGHTH; THEOCRATIC PERIOD.

Choinom, Rentsenii (1936–1979) *A poet jailed for lamenting the humiliation of the Mongol heritage in the smug conformity of the socialist regime*
Born in 1936 into a Buriat herding family in Khentii province's Darkhan Sum, Choinom attended school for four years until his father's death in 1950 forced him to withdraw. In 1953, however, he took a job as copyist,

typesetter, and printer. Painfully shy as a child, he was very interested in drawing and technology. In 1955 he was imprisoned for nine months for stealing 1,000 tögrögs from his workplace. In 1956 he contracted tuberculosis and after treatment in 1957 began working as an artist. Until January 1967 he alternated stints as an artist with treatment for bone tuberculosis and periods of writing poems.

Having begun writing poems by 1954, in 1961 he wrote his epic (*nairaglal*) *Altai*, inspired by the Kazakh national author Abay Kunanbayev. He also published a verse novel, *Khün* (Man), in 1964. Subsequently, he was able to publish only a few scattered poems. He married his first wife, Lhagwajaw, in 1962; they had one child and divorced after two years. In 1965 he married a second wife, Nina, and had two children, but his in-laws forced a divorce because of his alcoholism in 1967. With the divorce, the inability to publish his poems and his recurring bone tuberculosis, he began drinking heavily. Meanwhile, his unpublished notebooks included melancholy paeans to alcohol and to himself as a poet, bittersweet love lyrics to Nina, praises of the glories of the Mongol past destroyed by a philistine government, poetic accusations, and sarcastic barbs about the party-state: "Since they butchered in the thirties / Brilliant minds as reactionaries / Cattle numbers just shoot higher / Yes, our party's wisdom does not tire." Investigated for rumored antisocial poetry, he was imprisoned in a labor colony from 1969 to 1973, yet he continued writing and returning to the theme of the great past and tortured present of the Mongols as well as the BURIATS, as expressed in his 1973 long poem *Buriat*.

After his release he was kept under strict surveillance until his death in late May 1979 at the house of an artist friend, Demberel. In 1989 Choinom's works were first publicly praised, and the reprinting of his surviving poems began.

See also LITERATURE; MONGOLIAN PEOPLE'S REPUBLIC.

Choir city (Choyr, Čojr) During the Soviet buildup after 1966, Choir, along the TRANS-MONGOLIAN RAILWAY, became the largest Soviet airbase in Mongolia. With the withdrawal of Soviet troops from Mongolia in 1989–91, the Mongolian government hoped to use its facilities, including 259 buildings and Mongolia's longest airstrip, as an economic attraction. The area was made a directly administered city in 1991 and a free trade zone in 1992. In 1994 the city and its surrounding Sümber Sum were separated from EAST GOBI PROVINCE and made Gobi-Sümber province. To date, however, significant development has not materialized. Unemployment reached 8.3 percent in 1995, and emigration reduced the province's population from 13,000 in 1995 to 12,200 in 2000, of whom 9,000 lived in Choir city. Its territory of 5,540 square kilometers (2,140 square miles) is steppe in terrain and relatively dry in climate (196.5 millimeters, or 7.74 inches, of precipitation annually).

Chormaghun   *See* CHORMAQAN.

Chormaqan (Chormaghun) (fl. 1221–1241) *Mongol commander and conqueror of western Iran, Armenia, and Georgia*
Under CHINGGIS KHAN Chormaqan of the Sönid clan served as quiver bearer in the KESHIG (imperial guard). In 1229 the newly elected ÖGEDEI KHAN sent him to conquer the Middle East west of the Amu Dar'ya River and to suppress Jalal-ud-Din Mengüberdi, the fugitive sultan of KHORAZM. Ögedei gave him three *tümen*s (10,000s) of TAMMACHI (garrison) troops, partly Mongol and partly Central Asian. Chormaqan was to settle permanently in the area and appoint all the overseers (DARUGHACHI) in his territory. Chormaqan passed rapidly through Khorasan (northeast Iran), racing to capture Jalal-ud-Din by surprise. In August 1231 his troops raided Jalal-ud-Din's camp, in Kurdistan and the sultan fled to the hills, where a local Kurd killed him. Meanwhile, Fars and Kerman in southern Iran submitted voluntarily. From 1232 on Chormaqan wintered in the Mughan steppe on the Azerbaijan-Iran border and sent out annual expeditions against the remaining citadels in Azerbaijan, KURDISTAN, Armenia, and GEORGIA. The Armenian and Georgian nobility eventually agreed to pay an annual tribute, supply the army's needs, and accompany Chormaqan's army on campaign. Chormaqan led the sack of Amid (Diyarbakır) in 1241, but soon after he became deaf; his wife, Elteni, then shared command with his successor, BAIJU. Armenians generally saw Chormaqan and his Christian wife, Elteni, as protectors from the crueler elements of the Mongol army.

Chosgi-Odsir (Chos-kyi 'Od-ser, Choiji-Odser) (fl. 1307–1321) *Translator and poet who first rendered many classic Buddhist texts into Mongolian*
Chosgi-Odsir, called a "Western monk" in the YUAN SHI (History of the Yuan, 1370), was probably of Uighur origin. Trained in the Sa-skya school of Tibetan Buddhism, he thoroughly mastered both the Tibetan and the Mongolian languages.

By command of Emperor Haishan (1307–11), Chosgi-Odsir translated Shantideva's guide to the Mahayana path, the *Bodhicaryavatara*, and wrote an original Mongolian commentary. In 1312 Haishan's brother and successor Emperor Ayurbarwada (1311–20) had the translation and commentary printed in 1,000 copies at Baitasi (Monastery of the White Pagoda) in DAIDU (modern Beijing).

The court rewarded Chosgi-Odsir with 10,000 *ding* (*yastuq*) in paper currency in 1313 and in 1321 assigned him an honor guard in his monastery at the capital.

Chosgi-Odsir also assisted Asanga (son of ANIGA) in designing Buddhist iconography. Even so, when Chosgi-Odsir appealed for clemency for a disgraced official, Ayurbarwada silenced him by interjecting, "Monks should chant the scriptures—why should they participate in government business?"

Chosgi-Odsir's other extant works include the Tibetan *Twelve Deeds of the Buddha*, digested from Ashvaghosha's classic biography and later translated into Mongolian by his disciple Shirab Singgi, and a versified Mongolian hymn to the four-armed Mahakali, protectress deity of the Sa-skya order. None is, however, complete. The translation of the mantra collection entitled *Pancaraksha* ("Five Amulets"), traditionally ascribed to Chosgi-Odsir, was actually the work of his disciple Shirab-Singgi. While the Mongolian grammar *Jirükhen-ü tolta* (Aorta of the heart) is traditionally ascribed to Chosgi-Odsir, no Middle Mongolian text of it is extant, and the known "commentaries" all date from the 17th century or later.

See also BUDDHISM IN THE MONGOL EMPIRE; EDUCATION, TRADITIONAL; LITERATURE.

Chovd   *See* KHOWD CITY.

Chövsgöl   *See* KHÖWSGÖL PROVINCE.

Choybalsan, Horloogiin   *See* CHOIBALSANG, MARSHAL.

Choyr   *See* CHOIR CITY.

Christianity in the Mongol Empire   Despite its early influence in Mongolia, Christianity never achieved a leading position in the MONGOL EMPIRE and virtually disappeared in Inner Asia with the empire's fall. The territory of the Mongol Empire contained the lands of several Christian churches: the Georgian, Ossetian (Alan), and Russian branches of the Eastern Orthodox Church, the Armenian Apostolic Church, and the Assyrian Church of the East, called the "Nestorians" by outsiders. The latter church, seated in Baghdad and using the Syriac language in its liturgy, had early made converts in Central Asia, forming Christian communities among the largely Buddhist UIGHURS of Turfan.

In 1007 a khan of the KEREYID tribe in central Mongolia received baptism with 200,000 of his subjects. The Assyrian metropolitan of Merv (Mary), Abdisho, granted special dispensations for these new nomadic Christians: Lenten diet could include milk, and the Eucharist was offered with no bread and KOUMISS for wine. By 1200 Christianity of the Assyrian Church of the East dominated the ÖNGGÜD of Inner Mongolia and influenced the Kereyid and NAIMAN. An undated Syriac inscription in western Mongolia testifies to a Christian presence in Naiman territory. After CHINGGIS KHAN (Genghis,

1206–27) conquered these peoples, his family intermarried extensively with the royal families of the Kereyid and Önggüd. Conquest later brought them in contact with the Armenian, Georgian, Russian, and Ossetian Christian churches. The Mongols included Christians, whom they called *erke'ün* (plural *erke'üd*), as one of the four favored religions—also Buddhism, Taoism, and Islam—of the empire, whose clergy received tax exemptions and a measure of patronage in return for their prayers.

The Church of the East, accustomed to Mongol ways, saw the empire as a great blessing. Other Christians, however, were disgusted by Mongol food and marriage customs and viewed the conquest as punishment for their sins. Armenian writers identified the Mongols as the "Nation of the Archers," whose coming foretold the approaching end of the world. The Russian church declared that fermented mare's milk was unclean, so that any priest who lived with the Mongols was disqualified from holding the Eucharist. Even as Armenians and Georgians hoped for Mongol assistance against Muslim rulers, nobles and people alike resented court intrigues, tax collectors, and undisciplined soldiery, while the clergy impotently opposed political marriages with the alien conquerors.

Many third-generation Mongol princes raised by Christian mothers and tutors, such as Sartaq in CRIMEA, HÜLE'Ü (1216–65) in Iran, and GÜYÜG as great khan (1246–48), showed favor to the Church of the East, employing its adherents as scribes, physicians, and astrologers and keeping Christian priests at their ORDOs, or palace-tents. At court Assyrian Christian clergy often linked up with Buddhist monks to oppose Muslim influence. Christian writers sincerely praised Mongol Christian women such as Eltani (Chormaqan's wife, fl. c. 1240) and Hüle'ü's wife, TOGHUS KHATUN (d. 1265), yet Mongol men at this point typically refused baptism.

In the Mongol YUAN DYNASTY in China, the Buddhist QUBILAI KHAN (1260–94) treated Christianity favorably. The Önggüd and Uighurs formed the main body of Christian people, together with thousands of deported OSSETES and Russians and occasional Assyrian, Armenian, and European merchants. Christians formed part of the SEMUREN, or "various sorts," the second class in the Yuan structure, below the Mongols but above the native Chinese. The Church of the East appointed new metropolitans for DAIDU (modern Beijing), Tangut (northwest China), and Uighuristan. Assyrian immigrants such as 'Isa (Aixie, fl. 1248–1312) served Qubilai with astronomical and medical skills, while the Yuan government supervised the Christian church through the "Commission for the Promotion of Religion" (*Chong-fusi*), headed by 'Isa and later by his son Ilya (d. 1330). In the Chinese-Mongol Confucian reaction to the reign of Yisün-Temür (titled Taidingdi, 1323–28), under which *semuren* had dominated, Ilya was executed for sedition and witchcraft.

In the Chaghatayid Khanate of Central Asia, the Church of the East created new metropolitanates in Samarqand, Kashghar, and Almaligh. Excavations at a Christian cemetery in Ysyk-Köl (Kyrgyzstan), dating from 1249 to 1345, demonstrate a sizable community near the capital of the Chaghatayid realm. Tarmashirin Khan's (1331–34) conversion to Islam led to a Mongol reaction favoring Christianity under his immediate successors. This in turn led in 1338 to a bout of persecution of the church.

The Russian church began to recover from the conquest by 1249–50, when the new metropolitan Cyril arrived from investiture in Byzantium. Taking up residence not in ruined Kiev, but in Vladimir (near Moscow), he strongly supported cooperation with the Mongols of the GOLDEN HORDE and resistance to the Catholic advance. The declaration of the Russian church's complete tax exemption by Mengü-Temür Khan (1267–80) began a great increase in church wealth. Metropolitan Peter's (d. 1342) close association with Moscow and the mid-14th-century monastic revival sparked by St. Sergius (d. 1392) shaped the classic Russian Orthodox church. In the GOLDEN HORDE steppe, Cyril had created a bishopric of Saray. After the Golden Horde's conversion to Islam under ÖZBEG KHAN (1313–41), however, Christian influence among the QIPCHAQS, OSSETES, and other steppe peoples rapidly declined, producing by 1400 a clear division between Christian forest and Muslim steppe.

After Hüle'ü's conquest of Baghdad, the Assyrian church received the former palace of the caliph as a church and built new monasteries in the capital, Maragheh (see BAGHDAD, SIEGE OF). Despite periodic Muslim riots up to 1295, Assyrian and Uighur Christians generally held the governorship in Assyria (northeast Iraq), while others served as privileged ORTOQ merchants and ambassadors to the European powers. Mongol patrons in the Middle Eastern IL-KHANATE frequently allied with local Christians during communal tensions, and in 1281 the Church of the East elected an Önggüd catholicos (patriarch), MAR YAHBH-ALLAHA (1244–1317), for his familiarity with Mongol language and customs. Although several queens and princes of the blood, including Abagha Khan (1265–81), were baptized, as adults the princes frequently preferred Buddhism or Islam. After putting GHAZAN KHAN (1295–1304) on the throne, the Muslim Mongol NAWROZ instigated massive pogroms against non-Islamic faiths, costing the Church of the East vast sums of money and many lives and churches in Iran and Assyria. With the fall in Nawroz in 1297, however, Ghazan Khan strongly repudiated anti-Christian persecution and showed favor to Mar Yahbh-Allaha. Sultan Öljeitü (1304–17), once baptized by Mar Yahbh-Allaha but now a Muslim, protected church properties but ceased royal patronage. Öljeitü's Kereyid father-in-law, Irinjin, however, interceded for Christian interests, staving off attempts by Islamic jurists to impose

the poll tax and degrading badges until 1318. Irinjin's execution in 1319 by Abu-Sa'id (1317–35) deprived Christianity of its last patron.

During the late 13th century eastern trade between China and the Mediterranean and Black Sea ports abetted a network of Catholic missions in Soltaniyeh, Saray, Almaligh, and Daidu (modern Beijing). Except in China, where they served the Ossetian and Armenian population, missionaries focused on the Mongol elite, although without lasting success.

Despite the Christian sympathies of the early Il-Khans and Chaghatayids, the Mongol conquests in the Middle East and Turkestan expanded pastoralism at the expense of agriculture, which furthered the displacement of sedentary Assyrian, Armenian, and Greek Christians by nomadic Muslims, such as the Turks and Kurds. The crisis of the mid-14th century destroyed both the old network of the Church of the East and the new Roman Catholic network. Persecution under Ulugh-Beg (1393–1447) finally destroyed Christianity in Samarqand (see TIMUR). A small population of *erke'üd* (Christians) survived among the Mongols of ORDOS, Inner Mongolia, and they even preserved their tax exemption to 1920 but retained few traces of Christian beliefs.

See also BUQA; BYZANTIUM AND BULGARIA; CHRISTIAN SOURCES ON THE MONGOL EMPIRE; GEORGIA; KED-BUQA; KURDISTAN; LESSER ARMENIA; RELIGIOUS POLICY IN THE MONGOL EMPIRE; RUSSIA AND THE MONGOL EMPIRE; SARAY AND NEW SARAY.

Further reading: Erica C. D. Hunter, "The Conversion of the Kerait to Christianity in A.D. 1007," *Zentralasiatische Studien* 22 (1989/1991): 142–163; Samuel Hugh Moffet, *A History of Christianity in Asia*, vol. 1, *Beginnings to 1500* (San Francisco: HarperCollins, 1992), 399–517.

Christian sources on the Mongol Empire While never possessing the insider access of Mongolian, Chinese, and Islamic sources, Christian chroniclers of Russia and the Middle East and travelers from Latin Christendom add an important alternative perspective.

At the time of the Mongol conquest, Russia and Armenia had a flourishing historical tradition. In addition to their terse references to particular incidents, the Russian chronicles contain discrete "tales" (*povest'*) on the Mongol conquest, such as that on the Kalka River battle (1223; *see* KALKA RIVER, BATTLE OF), Mongol sack of Ryazan' (1237), and the oppressive DARUGHACHI (*basqaq*) Ahmad (1284). Certain tales circulated separately, such as the 14th-century *Tale of the Destruction of Ryazan'*. The 1380 defeat of the Mongols by Dmitrii Donskoi of Moscow created a famous epic, Sofony of Ryazan's *Zadonshchina* (*see* KULIKOVO POLE, BATTLE OF). The sense of opened horizons found in many Islamic histories and in Chinese and European travel accounts, however, is completely absent from the Russian chronicles. The Russian chronicles treat the Mongol conquest as a series of isolated episodes of oppression, assimilating them to biblical or apocalyptic categories or previous nomadic raids.

Armenian sources, while also using familiar biblical, apocalyptic, and historical categories, show far more interest in the MONGOL EMPIRE itself. The second half of the *History of the Armenians* (1266–67) by the monk Kirakos of Gandzak (c. 1205–71/2) is a vivid and well-informed account of Mongol conquest and rule. Captured and briefly held prisoner by the Mongols as a scribe, Kirakos was familiar with the Mongolian language and leaders. Shorter and less personal is the *History of the Nation of the Archers* (1271) by Grigor of Akants'. Both authors also give considerable information on the Mongols in GEORGIA. The rulers of LESSER ARMENIA, Constable Smbat and King Het'um I (1230–69), left records of their dealings with the Mongols. The *Les Flor des estoires de la terre d'Orient* (1307) of the knight-turned-monk Hayton (Het'um), dictated in French at Poitiers, gave Europe one of the most accurate accounts of the geography and history of the Middle East, together with an account drawn from personal knowledge of the campaigns of the Il-Khans against MAMLUK EGYPT. The only significant Georgian source, *The Georgian Chronicle*, while important for the later reigns of the Mongol Il-Khan dynasty (1256–1335), lacks the broader vision of the Armenian histories.

Among monuments of Syriac literature, the *Yish'iata demar Yahbaladha vderaban Sauma* (History of the MAR YAHBH-ALLAHA and of Rabban Sauma, translated as *Monks of Kublai Khan*, c. 1318) is a hagiography of the ÖNGGÜD Christian clerics Mar Yahbh-Allaha and Rabban Sauma. Originally in Persian but extant only in Syriac translation, this work illustrates the Church of the East's ties with the Il-Khans. In his *Chronography* (*Makhtebhanuth zabhne*), Gregory Abu'l-Faraj Bar Hebraeus (1225–86), maphrian (primate) of the East for the Syrian Orthodox (Jacobite) Church, used oral and written sources (he praises 'ALA'UD-DIN ATA-MALIK JUVAINI highly, for example) for his history of the Mongols. Unencumbered by official position, Bar Hebraeus was free to focus his informed good sense on communal riots, tribal turbulence, and other phenomena that official chroniclers such as RASHID-UD-DIN tried to bury. His church history section is also a main source on the early conversion of the KEREYID to Christianity. A continuator brought his political history forward to 1297.

Apart from the famous accounts of the papal envoy JOHN OF PLANO CARPINI, the missionary WILLIAM OF RUBRUCK, and the merchant MARCO POLO, a number of other Latin Christian sources exist. Simon of St. Quentin recorded the 1247 embassy to BAIJU. Latin works from Poland and Hungary included the travelogue of Friar Julian, who visited the Bashkirs (Bashkort) just as the Mongols were invading, and the narrative poem *Carmen miserabile* on the destruction of Hungary. Friars involved in Roman Catholic missions of 1294 in the Mongol successor states also left letters and reports: John of Monte Corvino (1246–1328), Odoric of Pordenone (1286–1331), and John of Marignolli (fl. 1338–57). The merchant handbook *La Pratica della Mercatura* (1340) of the Florentine Francesco Balducci Pegolotti describes trade in the Mongol world on the eve of its collapse in the wake of the BLACK DEATH.

See also CENTRAL EUROPE AND THE MONGOLS; CHRISTIANITY IN THE MONGOL EMPIRE; RUSSIA AND THE MONGOL EMPIRE; WESTERN EUROPE AND THE MONGOLS.

Further reading: Robert Bedrosian, *Kirakos Gandzaketsi'is History of the Armenians* (New York: Sources of the Armenian Tradition, 1986); Robert F. Blake and Richard N. Frye, "History of the Nation of the Archers (the Mongols)," *Harvard Journal of Asiatic Studies* 12 (1949): 269–399; E. A. Wallis Budge, trans., *Chronography of Gregory Abu'l Faraj 1225–1286* (1932; rpt., Amsterdam: APA, 1976); E. A. Wallis Budge, *The Monks of Kublai Khan, Emperor of China* (1928; rpt., New York: Ams Press, 1973); Charles J. Halperin, *Tatar Yoke* (Columbus, Ohio: Slavica, 1985); Hetoum, *A Lytell Cronycle: Richard Pynson's Translation (c. 1520) of La Fleur des histories de la terre d'orient (c. 1307)* (Toronto: University of Toronto Press, 1988); Robert Michell and Nevill Forbes, trans., *Chronicle of Novgorod, 1016–1471* (London: Offices of the Society 1914); George A. Perfecky, trans., *The Galician-Volynian Chronicle* (Munich: Wilhelm Fink, 1973); Robert W. Thomson, "The Historical Compilation of Vardan Arewelc'i," *Dumbarton Oaks Papers* 43 (1989): 125–226.

Chuban (Chopan, Chupan, Jupan) (d. 1327) *Chief commander under the last Il-Khan reigns*
Descendant of Chila'un of the Suldus, one of CHINGGIS KHAN's "four steeds," Chuban first supported Geikhatu as khan (1291–95) and in August 1295 deserted Baidu Khan for GHAZAN KHAN (1295–1304). Chuban was an able commander, winning credit at the otherwise disastrous Syrian (1303) and Gilan (1307) campaigns. Ghazan's brother, Sultan Öljeitü (1304–16), made him commander in chief (*beglerbegi*) and granted him his daughter, Dowlandi (d. 1314). Chuban rejected, however, Öljeitü's Shi'ite faith. Under Öljeitü's son, Abu-Sa'id (1317–35), Chuban married Öljeitü's other daughter, Sati Beg. In 1318 Chuban's client Taj-ud-Din 'Alishah successfully plotted RASHID-UD-DIN's execution and become vizier himself, while Chuban ferociously suppressed a 1319 rebellion against his regency.

Chuban was a dedicated Sunni Muslim and followed up this victory with attacks on churches, brothels, and wineries. He was also friendly to the Il-Khans' traditional opponents in MAMLUK EGYPT, and after arranging peace in 1323 he funded a school and tomb for himself in Egyptian-controlled Medina. He also received high titles from the YUAN DYNASTY for his promotion of intra-Mongol harmony.

Eventually, the arrogance of Chuban's sons Temür-tash and Dimashq-Khoja alienated the khan. Abu-Sa'id's thwarted desire for Chuban's daughter Baghdad Khatun, wife of the JALAYIR emir "Big" Hasan (Hasan Buzurg), also poisoned their relationship. In August 1327, while Chuban was campaigning in Khorasan, Abu-Sa'id executed Dimashq-Khoja. Chuban marched in a rage against Abu-Sa'id but was deserted by his emirs. He fled to Herat, whose governor killed him in December 1327. Temürtash fled to Egypt, where he was executed in 1328.

Abu-Sa'id married Baghdad Khatun, who protected Chuban's surviving relatives and possibly poisoned the khan. In the chaos after Abu-Sa'id's death, Temürtash's son, "Little" Hasan (Hasan Küchek) raised the Suldus banner, defeated "Big" Hasan's Jalayirs in 1338, and established a Suldus regime that controlled Azerbaijan to 1357.

Further reading: Charles Melville, "Wolf or Shepherd? Amir Chupan's Attitude to Government," in *Court of the Il-Khans, 1290–1340*, ed. Julian Raby and Teresa Fitzherbert (Oxford: Oxford University Press, 1996), 79–93; ———, "Abu Sa'id and the Revolt of the Amirs in 1319," in *Iran face à la domination mongole*, ed. Denise Aigle (Tehran: 1997), 89–120.

Chung-tu   *See* ZHONGDU, SIEGES OF.

Chü-yung-kuan Pass   *See* JUYONGGUAN PASS, BATTLE OF.

clan names   Patrilineal clan names remained important among the Mongols from their earliest recorded history in the 12th century through the 18th century. After that time clan names began to decline among those Mongols ruled by the BORJIGID (Chinggisid) aristocracy. New clanlike formations took their names from a particular ancestor or a guardian deity. The Borjigid clan identity was attacked in the revolutionary period as a bulwark of feudalism, but in recent decades interest in clan names has revived.

Mongol lineage or clan names were not historically fixed. From their earliest known history the Mongol and Oirat (West Mongol) tribes and their component clans (including up to several thousand people in one territory under common rule) were composed of lineage branches and individual families drawn from many ancestries ("bones"). Among them was usually one dominant lineage that gave its name to the clan or tribe as a whole. Thus, clan names actually in use could be of one's clan, of the lineage fragment, or "bone," within that clan, or of one's whole tribe, depending on one's social context. Moreover, new families drafted by rulers to perform special functions usually acquired a clan name and identity from that function.

From the 13th to the 17th century many clan names of differing origin appear in history: 1) the original 35 or so clans of the MONGOL TRIBE: the JALAYIR, MANGGHUD,

QONGGIRAD, and so on; 2) the tribes on the Mongolian plateau or southern Siberia, which were conquered by the Mongols: MERKID/Merged, KEREYID, NAIMAN, and so on; while all these tribes were originally divided into clans, these subdivisions fell into disuse after their incorporation into the Mongol realm; 3) fragments of conquered peoples assimilated into the Mongols: Sartuul (Turkestani Muslims), Tangut (*see* XIA DYNASTY), Asud (OSSETES), and so on; 4) clans formed by groups performing functions at court: KHARACHIN ("black" KOUMISS distillers of Qipchaq origin), Urad (craftsmen), Khali'uchin (otter hunters), and so on. Ruling all of these was the Borjigid clan, composed of the descendants of Chinggis Khan and his brothers.

A similar clan name need not mean common origin. Many clan names—*dörben/dörbed/dörböd*, "the four," *bayad/baya'ud*, "the rich ones," *ikires/ekhired* "twins," *bulaghachin/bulagad*, "sable hunters"—appear to have arisen more than once independently as clan names in Inner Asia. In other cases common names have been used for groups that are geographically and socially distinct.

Ethnographic research from the 18th century on has vastly increased the number and type of Mongol clan names known, particularly among the OIRATS (West Mongols) and the northern forest Mongols, such as the DARKHAD and BURIATS. Some are names of Siberian peoples, often originally Turkic speaking, who became incorporated into the Oirats or northwestern Mongols. From the 18th century genealogical knowledge declined sharply among the Khalkha and Inner Mongolians. Only the TAIJI (nobility) emphasized genealogical knowledge. In some areas, however, new commoner clans, named after their apical ancestor and sometimes matrilineal, formed on the ruins of forgotten clan identities (*see* MATRILINEAL CLANS). Some clans took their names from the colors of the horses they dedicated to the clan protector deity, such as Sharanuud, "yellows," Kharanuud, "blacks," and Khuanuud, "bays" (*see* RELIGION).

When surnames were introduced among the Buriats and KALMYKS of Russia in the 19th century, PATRONYMICS (names based on one's father's name), not clan names, were used. The same was also true in 20th-century Mongolia, where the rule of the Borjigid clan was attacked in the REVOLUTIONARY PERIOD. In Inner Mongolia no official patronymic or clan name system has been introduced, but the BARGA and the Daurs still frequently use their clan names. In 1997 the Mongolian government decided to introduce clan names again to reduce the number of people with identical names but this has been stymied by the general ignorance in the populace about their actual clan identity.

See also KINSHIP SYSTEM; NAMES, PERSONAL.

clear script   The clear script (originally *todorkhoi üzüg; tod üzg* in modern Kalmyk; *tod üseg* in modern Mongolian) was created in winter 1648–49 by ZAYA PANDITA NAMKHAI-JAMTSU among the OIRATS. Based on a modification and refinement of the UIGHUR-MONGOLIAN SCRIPT, it was long the main script of the Oirats and is still used in Xinjiang.

By the 17th century with the spread of literacy a number of devices had arisen to resolve the ambiguities of the old, unreformed Uighur-Mongolian script. Single dots were used to mark "n" from the vowels "a" and "e," double dots were used to distinguish "gh" and "kh" from each other, a pointed versus rounded distinction in the form of the "ch" distinguished ch and j, and so on. Zaya Pandita made use of these devices as well as many others of his own invention.

The Mongols did not pursue a thought-out reform of the Uighur-Mongolian script or eliminate all its ambiguities, but the Manchus and Oirats did. Manchu script reformers in 1623–33 preserved the cursive character and "look" of the Uighur-Mongolian but made extensive use of added dots and circles. Zaya Pandita adopted a more radical approach, changing letter forms to virtually eliminate the differing initial, medial, and final forms of the letters. He also modernized the orthography. He invented a mark below the vowel to indicate long vowels, eliminating the Uighur-Mongolian silent "g"/"gh." Suffixes were sometimes written in classical forms and sometimes in forms closer to those of the spoken language.

As it happened, Zaya Pandita frequently adopted opposite distinctions for his clear script from those that became current in the reformed Uighur-Mongolian script. Thus, while in the reformed Uighur-Mongolian script "j" was indicated by a rounded form and "ch" by an angular form, in the clear script it is the opposite. Similarly, the double dot marks the "gh" in Uighur-Mongolian but the "kh" in the clear script.

The clear script was first used for Buddhist translations, of which Zaya Pandita and his disciples had completed 214 by 1690. The first original work written in the script was the *Sarayin gerel* (Light of the Moon), a biography of Zaya Pandita by his disciple Ratnabhadra written around 1690. The script became the official script of the Zünghar and Kalmyk Oirats and was used for the full range of writings: official documents, legal texts, personal letters, histories, hagiographies, prayers and devotional texts to Buddhist and native deities, and EPICS. The fall of the Zünghars and their annihilation by the Qing caused many manuscripts to be destroyed, yet under the Qing the script continued to be used for official and private purposes by the Torghud and Khoshud refugees from the Volga who resettled in Xinjiang. The QING DYNASTY'S LIFAN YUAN (Court of Dependencies) accordingly maintained a school in the clear script to train central government officials to handle this alphabet. The Oirats in western Mongolia (modern KHOWD PROVINCE and UWS PROVINCE) at first used only the clear script. In 1768 the Qing dynasty established a clerical school in KHOWD CITY that enrolled 20 new students each year (three DÖRBÖDS, four ALTAI URIYANGKHAIS, and two each from the TORGHUD, ÖÖLÖD, ZAKHACHIN, and MINGGHAD banners). The school taught Manchu and Uighur-Mongolian, and under its influence the clear script began to recede in official use, although it was still used for histories, epics, and nonofficial writings.

In Kalmykia the clear script was replaced in 1925 with a newly designed Cyrillic script. It is, however, still studied by scholars and KALMYKS interested in their literary heritage. With Mongolia's independence in 1912 the clear script was discouraged as a sign of Oirat separatism. Scholarly interest in and small-scale reprinting of clear script manuscripts revived in the 1960s. In China the clear script remained in official use among the Oirat Mongols of Xinjiang through the 20th century. Further diacriticals were introduced, distinguishing "ts" from "ch" and "z" from "j"; this distinction in Mongolian words is based on the succeeding vowel and hence not strictly necessary. With the explosion in minority-language publishing after 1979, the script was used for newspapers, the academic journal *Khaan tenggeri,* school textbooks, and humanistic works. The small number of Xinjiang Oirads (fewer than 150,000), however, meant a growing influence of Inner Mongolian books and culture. This led in 1981 to a decision to replace the clear script gradually from 1982 to 1990 with the Uighur-Mongolian script used in Inner Mongolia. Publications in the clear script continued, however, at least into the 1990s.

See also KALMYK-OIRAT LANGUAGE AND SCRIPTS; XINJIANG MONGOLS.

Further reading: György Kara, "The 'Clear Script,'" in *The World's Writing System,* ed. Peter Daniels and William Bright (New York: Oxford University Press, 1996), 548–550; Attila Rakos, *Written Oirat* (Munich: Lincom Europa, 2002).

climate Deep in Asia, the climate of Mongolia is dry and extremely continental, with ranges of 40°C (72°F) and more between summer and winter average temperatures. The climate throughout the MONGOLIAN PLATEAU (including Mongolia and neighboring areas of Transbaikalia and Inner Mongolia) is generally governed by the Asiatic high pressure region centered on the LAKE UWS region. This extreme high pressure system is responsible for the sparse cloud cover, giving Mongolia 200 to 500 more hours of sunshine annually than other areas at the same latitude. It also creates a steady prevailing wind from the north and west over most of the plateau, which in the spring causes vast duststorms that deposit fine loess soil in North China. Mongolia is not directly reached by the monsoon rains, but weather patterns concentrate 65–75 percent of precipitation in the three summer months, while only 8–10 percent falls in the cold season. Thus, the lowlands generally lack permanent snow cover, particularly in the south. Since the first frosts come in the first week of September, crops and vegetation must begin growing without the benefit of extensive runoff or spring rains.

The line of average annual temperature below freezing passes through the middle of Mongolia's eastern plain and steppe zone, between the GOBI DESERT and the northern ranges. Except around LAKE BAIKAL, whose waters delay the onset of the seasons, the Mongolian plateau is warmest in July and coldest in January. In the lowlands average January temperatures range from –12°C (10°F) in ALASHAN to –26°C (–15°F) in Barguzin in northern Buriatia (with an average nighttime low of –33°C, or –27°F), while average July temperatures range from 26°C (79°F) in Alashan to 14°C (57°F) in Barguzin. In ULAANBAATAR average temperatures in January range between a daytime high of –19°C (–2°F) and a nighttime low of –32°C (–26°F). In July daytime highs average 22°C (72°F), while nights average 11°C (52°F).

The overall amount of precipitation generally increases toward the east but is heavily dependent on altitude. In most of the ranges precipitation is about 300–500 millimeters (12–20 inches), and the core of the Sayan and KHENTII RANGES receive more than 500 millimeters (20 inches) of average annual precipitation. Lake Baikal moistens the neighboring ranges, giving the Khamar-Daban, Ulan-Burgasy, and Barguzin Ranges areas with more than 1,000 millimeters (39 inches) of average annual precipitation. In the steppe near the ranges, on the eastern plain, and in the valleys of Transbaikalia, precipitation is around 200–300 millimeters (8–12 inches). In the Gobi Desert and the GREAT LAKES BASIN precipitation is generally less than 150 millimeters (6 inches), and it drops below 50 millimeters (2 inches) in much of Alashan.

Climate change in Mongolia can be directly measured only since about 1940, but tree-ring research is extending this record back many centuries. Trends are similar to those elsewhere in the northern hemisphere, showing a few extremely cold years around 1600–05 brought on by the Huanyaputina eruption in the Andes and another milder cooling period in 1625–75 followed by a steady warming trend to around 1780. This was followed by a period of prolonged cooling from then to about 1870, followed by a rapid climb in temperature since then. From 1940 to 1995 average winter temperature has risen from around –21°C (–6°F) to above –18°C (0°F), while average summer temperatures cooled from about 16.5°C (61.7°F) to about 15.8°C (60.4°F). (The figures on local temperatures given in the first part of the article are from the 1980s.) Precipitation shows much less clear trends, although it has recently been increasing, particularly in summer.

See also HÖHHOT; KALMYK REPUBLIC; ULAN-UDE; UST'-ORDA BURIAT AUTONOMOUS AREA.

Further reading: Academy of Sciences, MPR, *Information Mongolia* (Oxford: Pergamon Press, 1990), 22–26; G. C. Jacoby, R. D. D'Arrigo, N. Pederson, B. M. Buckley. Ch. Dugarjav, and R. Mijiddorj, "Temperature and Precipitation in Mongolia Based on Dendroclimatic Investigations," *IAWA Journal* 20 (3): 339–350.

clothing and dress　Until the 20th century Mongolian clothing for both men and women was based on a long caftan, or *deel* (Buriat, *degel;* Kalmyk, *lawshg*), fastened under the right shoulder and bound by men with a belt or cloth sash. (Since married women did not wear a sash [*büs*], adult women came to be called *büsgüi,* meaning "beltless.") Fastenings were made of knots or metal buttons hooked into loops. Often an overcaftan or waistcoat was worn over the *deel.* Underneath the *deel* Mongols always wore trousers. From the 16th century dress became more elaborate and distinctive, until the revolutionary movements of the 20th century again promoted a simple style.

The Mongols did not weave, and so native materials were restricted to furs, leather, and felt. Mongolian women did, however, skillfully sew clothes from imported fabrics, particularly cotton, silk, and especially silk brocade. During the empire period they sewed with threads of wound tendons, but later with cotton and silk thread. Linings in the winter were of silk stuffing for the

Deel (or caftan) from a Yuan-era tomb excavated on the Onon River in the Chita region, southern Siberia. Silk lined with skins *(From Dowdoin Bayar,* Altan urgiin yazguurtny negen bulshiig sudalsan ni *[2000])*

very rich or cotton stuffing, fine raw wool, or sheep- and goatskins for the ordinary Mongols. Trimmings were of sable, ermine, squirrel, fox, and other furs.

Traditionally, the Mongols did not wash their clothes or bodies, as it was feared that polluting the water would anger the dragons that control the water cycle and bring thunderstorms. Except for holidays, clothes were not changed until they fell apart. The smell attached to these constantly worn unwashed clothes was seen as a precious memento of the wearer. Thus, a gift of clothes actually worn by a khan and carrying his smell was a high honor.

CLOTHING IN THE MONGOL EMPIRE

In the empire the caftan most often had a collar slanting from the neck to the underarm, like a bathrobe. Some men's caftans, as seen in a portrait of ÖGEDEI KHAN, had a square collar. The skirt of the caftan was usually sewn on separately with ruffles. Frequently, the caftan was tied with both a thin leather belt passing below the belly and a broad sash covering the belly.

Upon marriage women no longer wore their sashes and wore a very full caftan with a slanting collar, sometimes with a short-sleeved jacket opening down the front. While most women wore caftans overlapping on their right, they sometimes wore caftans overlapping on their left. Women's caftans often were decorated with a thick border of brocade along the overlapping collar. Great ladies wore caftans with very full sleeves and a train held by servants.

Materials varied greatly according to the status of the wearer. The most favored materials in the summer were Middle Eastern silk and gold brocades called *nashish* (from Arabic *nasij*) and *nakh*. Middle Eastern brocade weavers were deported to China in settlements to supply the needs of the Mongol court in the east. Valuable furs, especially sable and ermine, were worn in winter. One prince, NOQAI (d. 1299), even proudly wore dog skins as a sign of his adherence to old Mongol ways. In winter the underlayers were made of skin with the fur inmost, while with the outer layer the fur faced out, at least on the upper part.

During the great assemblies (QURILTAI) the khans bestowed on their courtiers clothing of set colors. Such court clothes were called *jisün*, "color," from the designation of a special color for each day. During the WHITE MONTH all present wore white silk, while in the great summer *quriltais* all those attending wore a different color each day. Unauthorized use of these *jisün* robes was strictly punished.

SIXTEENTH TO TWENTIETH CENTURIES

By the late 16th century the Mongol nobility wore over the caftan a long sleeveless or short-sleeved overcaftan buttoned down the center of the chest and open below the waist. A detachable tippet (*zaam*) of brocade or fur attached to the caftan was worn around the neck. Only

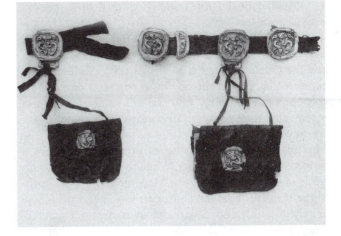

Leather belts and pouches decorated with silver plaques from a Yuan-era tomb in the Chita region *(From Dowdoin Bayar, Altan urgiin vazguurtny negen bulshiig sudalsan ni [2000])*

sashes, never leather belts, were now worn by men and unmarried girls. The sleeves for men and women were narrow and ended in distinctive horse-hoof cuffs. This style was also used among the rising Manchus and with a little modification became the basis for QING DYNASTY (1636–1912) court dress, worn by the Mongolian nobility at audiences with the Qing emperor. The court *deel*, or caftan, was embroidered with dragons and clouds and at the lower border with the world mountain, Sümber (Mt. Meru in Sanskrit), surrounded by waves and diagonal lines in colors symbolizing the five directions. The court overcaftan (Mongolian, *uuj*) was long-sleeved for lords and sleeveless for ladies. It was plainer in appearance but also embroidered with dragons. The form and number of dragons were governed by sumptuary laws. Lords wore large rosaries as necklaces.

Like the Chinese, Mongols saw fastening caftans on the right as a sign of civilization. When the KHALKHA were debating in 1689 whether to rely on the Russians or the Manchu Qing dynasty, the FIRST JIBZUNDAMBA KHUTUGTU noted that since the czar was not Buddhist and "moreover the edge of his garment is wrongly turned, it is not acceptable," while the "garment of the emperor of the Manchus is like the garment of a god."

In later Qing-era regional dress among the Mongols, the distinctions of status, sex, and region became striking. Outside court men no longer wore the sleeved overcaftan over the *deel*, only a sleeveless waistcoat (Mongolian, *khantaaz*; Buriat, *khantuuza*) overlapping and buttoning to their right. Women also frequently wore the waistcoat, or *khantaaz*, over the *deel*, either alone or under an *uuj*. Among women the sleeveless *uuj* was restricted to the wives of the TAIJI (nobility). The increasingly elaborate brocade used to border women's *deel*, *uuj*, and *khantaaz* accentuated the differences of the sexes.

Regional distinctions among Mongol dress became very clear in this period. The KALMYKS and the OIRATS of western Mongolia, such as the Dörböd, Bayad, and Uriyangkhai, shared a distinctive broad-shouldered *uuj*, and the Oirats of western Mongolia retained the flat tippet, or collar, on the shoulders. Among most of the Mongols proper (Khalkha and INNER MONGOLIANS) and BURIATS, the tippet changed into a distinctive standing collar sewn to the *deel*. Among the ÜJÜMÜCHIN and Kheshigten of Inner Mongolia and among the Kalmyks, it formed a folded-down collar. While the caftan was usually made of one piece among the Mongols and Oirats, in the Buriat women's *degel* the upper part was always made separately from the pleated skirt and lower sleeves. Facings of colored cloth or brocade highlighted the seams between the upper part and the skirt and between the lower and upper sleeves. The overlap of Buriat men's caftans was bordered by colored bands. Buriat women's *degels* had puffy shoulders, an innovation adopted in greatly exaggerated form in Khalkha. The Buriats were also the only Mongolian peoples still to use leather belts. Among the KHORCHIN, Daurs, and other eastern Inner Mongolians, women's caftans were modeled on Manchu styles, with wide sleeves and no horse-hoof cuffs. These robes were decorated with less brocade and more flower embroidery.

Accessories were hung either from the sash (men) or from long cords attached to loops sewed onto the armpits of the *uuj* (women). Men's accessories included a knife, sometimes with chopsticks, a flint and striker, and a cloth pouch holding a snuff bottle. Women's accessories, usually hung from a metal wheel, butterfly, or similar object, included pouches for aromatic herbs, nail cleaners, tweezers, toothpicks, and earpicks. Women also sometimes attached colored scarves to the armpits of the *uuj*. Pockets were not necessary, as the caftan's loose fit and the tight sash created ample area in the chest.

FOOTWEAR

Traditional boots among the Mongols were similar to those elsewhere in East Asia, with no heel and no distinction of right and left. Whether made of leather, cotton, or silk, the boots were sewn out of multilayered flat soles and separate uppers and legs, each divided into right and left sides. The preferred color scheme was dark legs and uppers, with light soles and light leather strips along the seams. Boots were worn over cotton or felt stockings depending on the weather.

While boots in the empire period were sometimes pointed or slightly upturned, the distinctive Mongolian riding boots with their highly upturned "pig-snout" front first appear in the 16th century, although they may have existed earlier. Painted leather appliqués enlivened these boots both for men and women. Court-dress boots were made of cloth, not leather, and did not have the upturned front. Buriat boots also did not have the upturned front. In eastern Inner Mongolia women wore Chinese-style embroidered cloth shoes. By the 19th century Chinese craftsmen in HÖHHOT and elsewhere made most of the Mongolian boots following local preferences.

HAIRSTYLES AND HEADGEAR

In Inner Asia men's hair was partly shaven and partly braided. In the empire period Mongol men shaved most of the top of the head, leaving only a small forelock. The hair was grown long and tied in braids, often hooked up behind the ears. The Manchu Qing dynasty imposed on Mongol men their own style of shaving the front half of the head and putting the hair in a single braid down the back.

The most common men's winter hat in the empire was a skin "falcon" hat with the brim short and upturned in front and covering the neck in back. Similar to this was a kind of helmet with a brim projecting all around, a knob on the top, and a hanging flap of leather protecting the neck. The summer hat was conical and made of wood with tassels hanging down from the pointed top.

By the 16th century the men's winter hat was perfectly circular, with the brim raised in the back as well. Tassels were often attached to the center of the crown, and a strip of cloth was always hung from the top down the wearer's back. In the Qing dynasty the winter hat with the upturned circular brim and the bamboo conical hat became the official court winter and summer hats. As such, they were surmounted by buttons of various semiprecious stones according to the wearer's rank. Instead of a cloth strip peacock feathers were attached to the top of the court hat.

Informal variants of the winter hat with the upturned brim were made with differing widths of the brim and height and steepness of the crown. Another type of hat, today called the *jangjin malgai*, or "general's hat," from General Sükhebaatar, has a bell-shaped crown and a brim in four folded-up flaps. The Khori Buriats wore a pointed hat sewn from two roughly diamond-shaped pieces with the bottom point functioning as earflaps to be tied under the chin or behind the head.

In the empire period married women wore the distinctive high BOQTA hat, described with admiration by travelers from every county. The hair was kept in a bun under the *boqta*. By the end of the 16th century the *boqta* was no longer worn, and the hair was now kept in two braids down the front of the chest. Women wore hats similar in style to those of men. From the 17th century JEWELRY worn on the head became very expensive and complicated. Among the western Buriats and Kalmyks, however, braids were worn under a cylindrical skullcap (*khalwng*, in Kalmyk). Among Kalmyk women skullcaps were lavishly decorated with gold thread embroidery and brocade and capped with tufts of silk thread.

MODERN CHANGES

By 1900 Mongolian clothing and jewelry, particularly in Khalkha, had become very elaborate. The high-brimmed hat, the great horns of artificial hair, the high, padded shoulders, the horse-hoof cuffs, and the upturned boots of married women constituted the "five prides" of Khalkha. With the 1921 REVOLUTION youths began to criticize these and the old Qing court dress as linked to feudal customs. In 1922 members of the Revolutionary Youth League began stopping women in the streets and cutting off their high shoulders, cuffs, and jewelry and confiscating men's hats with rank buttons and peacock feathers. The campaign soon caused widespread disaffection and was repudiated by the government.

Nevertheless, by 1924 the traditional dress attacked by the youth had, in fact, almost completely disappeared. The caftan was retained, but with no cuffs, *uuj*, or *khantaaz*, and no brocade. Instead cavalry boots, cigarettes (rather than a pipe), a fedora or peaked cap for men, and bobbed hair for women were adopted. Women also began to wear the sash after marriage. From around 1929 to 1940 Soviet-style military uniform or suits and ties gradually replaced this modernized Mongolian costume among Mongolia's leaders. In Inner Mongolia similar changes occurred from the 1930s to the 1950s (*see* REVOLUTIONARY PERIOD).

Today the modern-form *deel* is worn in Mongolia proper by both sexes in the countryside, particularly in the winter, and for ethnic and ceremonial occasions in the cities. Newscasters, for example, wear the *deel* around the White Month and NAADAM celebrations. A long-sleeved jacket, or *khürem*, with traditional styling is popular with young men. In Inner Mongolia *deel*s are worn daily only in the HULUN BUIR and SHILIIN GOL steppe. In Mongolia the "general's hat" with a cloth knot on the peak is commonly worn, but in Inner Mongolia men wear European-style headgear and rural women wrap their heads in turbans.

Further reading: Thomas T. Allsen, *Commodity and Exchange in the Mongol Empire: A Cultural History of Islamic Textiles* (Cambridge: Cambridge University Press, 1997); Henny Harald Hansen, *Mongol Costumes* (London: Thames and Hudson, 1993).

Čojr *See* CHOIR CITY.

collectivization and collective herding Collectivization of the nomadic herders was completed in Mongolia in 1958–59. While the process involved collective ownership of most of the livestock, there was no attempt to sedentarize the nomads.

EARLY EXPERIMENTS IN COLLECTIVIZATION

The Mongolian government first attempted collectivization during the LEFTIST PERIOD of 1929–32. The movement provoked a massive slaughter of livestock and insurrection. After the fiasco of collectivization in 1931–32, the Mongolian government remained hesitant of further collectivization experiments for years. Leninist doctrine insisted strongly, however, on the ultimate necessity of collectivizing the "peasantry" both for economic growth and for the Communist regime's safety.

In 1934 People's Producers Associations (*Ardyn üildwerchinii negdel*; the term "association," or *negdel*, was used instead of either "cooperative," *khorshoo*, or "collective," *khamtral*) began to be formed on a strictly voluntary basis. At first such associations merely pooled labor, but with the publication of model bylaws in 1942 they were transformed into cooperatives in which members voluntarily chose what implements and livestock they wished to pool, income from which was partly added to the association's fixed capital and part distributed as wages.

COLLECTIVIZATION

As late as 1953 the *negdel*s, along with the state-owned hay-mowing stations and state farms, held only 3.3 percent of Mongolia's livestock. The authorities began actively promoting collectivization in that year. Collectivization proceeded from the northern *khangai* (wooded mountain steppe) to the central *kheer* (steppe) and the southern gobi (habitable desert); in 1954 collectivized livestock in the three zones reached 8.4 percent, 4.6 percent, and 3.1 percent, respectively, of the total. In 1955 a congress of model workers from the *negdel*s, renamed "Agricultural (or Rural) Associations" (*Khödöö aj akhui negdel*), issued new model guidelines. Members should give at least 75 working days per year to the *negdel*, and their private livestock should not exceed 100 head in the khangai and kheer and 150 in the gobi. Members of the whole family, including children up to 16, had to join with the head of the family (previously only family heads joined, and dependents often worked full time on private herds).

By 1957 34.3 percent of all rural households with 40.2 percent of the total herd had joined collectives. In 1958–59 the government finally dared to order holdouts to join, and by April 1959 97.7 percent of all rural households belonged to the *negdel*s. With procurement prices deliberately raised, the number of livestock continued its rise from 23.1 million in 1955 to 23.8 million in 1959. In reality, however, the high limits on private livestock meant that 48 percent of all livestock were still privately owned, albeit by *negdel* members. That year the party Central Committee ordered that this number be cut in half: 50 in the khangai and 75 in the gobi. Thus, in 1960 *negdel* members composed about 96 percent of the agricultural and animal husbandry workers (the balance belonged to state farms and mowing stations), while 74 percent of Mongolia's livestock belonged to the *negdel*s and only 22 percent to *negdel* members privately.

THE *NEGDEL*S

Amalgamation made the *negdel*s, numbering 289 in 1965, conterminous with the *sum*, or district, the subprovincial unit of rural administration, the two often being referred to together as the *sum-negdel*. The membership of the *negdel* was the same as that of the *sum,* except for excluding children under 16 and transient specialists (physicians, veterinarians, school teachers, etc.). Every *sum-negdel* had a settlement that served as an administrative, commercial, and cultural center. The *sum, negdel,* and settlement all had different names, so that the same unit could be referred to as, for example, Khairkhandulaan *sum,* or New Victory *negdel,* or even Marzat settlement.

Administration of the *sum-negdel* was similarly trifurcated: The *sum* members elected a local legislature (assembly of people's deputies), which chose a chairman to head the local government; *negdel* members elected a governing board, which chose a *negdel* chairman, who was responsible for fulfilling the five-year plan; and finally the local party committee elected the party secretary. In fact, the membership of the assembly, the governing board, and the party committee usually overlapped to form a leading oligarchy that administered the *sum-negdel* as a whole. Leadership, while strongly paternalistic, was usually not distant from herders. At the same time, the FIVE-YEAR PLANS and party apparatus exercised tight control from outside the *sum-negdel.*

The average *negdel* contained about 500 households and was divided into four brigades. At the *sum-negdel* center most *negdels* had one auxiliary brigade handling carpentry, small-scale manufacture, and so on, while a small number of *negdels* had farming brigades. (Most farming took place at the state farms, however.) The regular herding brigades were divided into *suuri* (literally settlements, but more accurately nomadic camps), of two to five households. Unlike in the past, each camp specialized in taking care of only one animal, assigned by *negdel* officials in consultation with the households involved.

Negdel members received a basic wage in addition to the proceeds of the sale of assigned animals to the state procurement agencies, with bonuses and penalties for meeting or not meeting production quotas. These wages were paid in cash, while herders used their allowed private herds for subsistence needs. In practice, however, neither the bonus nor the penalties were very large, and income was largely guaranteed. Likewise, the state rarely punished *negdels* severely for consistently failing to meet state-set production targets. Thus, neither *negdels* nor individual *negdel* herders had strong material incentives to produce. *Negdel* herders received pensions on retirement at age 55 (women) or 60 (men).

The *negdel* organization effectively delivered consumer goods and medical and educational services through the stores, boarding schools, and clinics in the *sum-negdel* center. *Negdel*-owned trucks also assisted members in nomadization. More directly related to production was the organization of veterinary services and the mobilization of labor to build and maintain wells and corrals and to mow hay.

Especially in the first five years, the *negdel* authorities used brigade assignments to break up clans and lineages. Vigilance by *negdel* officials and limitations on private livestock also curtailed tradition feasts (*nair*) and sacrifices, such as cairn (OBOO) worship. Along with compulsory education delivered in boarding schools at the *sum* center, these changes were part of the "cultural revolution" desired by the government. Later, however, zeal for cultural transformation flagged. Legally, the *negdels,* like the old BANNERS (appanages), were a closed community that members could not enter or leave without permission. Approved migration to the province towns and cities was common, however.

THE PERFORMANCE OF COLLECTIVE HERDING

The *negdel* system did not create the productivity breakthrough advertised by its planners. Total productivity per head of livestock showed no great increase, whether in sheep's wool, cow's milk, or the slaughter weight of beef cattle, sheep, or goats. Only in CASHMERE did a steady increase in livestock productivity appear, rising from 200 grams (7.1 ounces) per goat in 1960 to 295 grams in 1990. While the overall herd size fluctuated from 22.5 to 24.8 million head, the herd composition was altered to reflect government purchasing priorities, so that the average value of output per head of livestock grew from 52 tögrögs in 1960 to 73 in 1985. Since urbanization reduced the number of working *negdel* members from 234,100 to 142,100 in the same period, labor productivity in Mongolia's livestock sector rose from 5,260 tögrögs per herder in 1960 to 10,901 in 1985. This increase in productivity resulted partly through increased investment in wells, corrals, and other installations. Reflecting this investment, survival rates of lambs and kids increased from 65 percent and 53 percent in 1960 to 77 percent and 69 percent in 1980. (That of large livestock remained stagnant.)

Collectivized herding's mixed record led to major reforms in the late 1980s, which, with democratization, turned into wholesale DECOLLECTIVIZATION in the 1990s.

See also ANIMAL HUSBANDRY AND NOMADISM; ECONOMY, MODERN; MONGOLIAN PEOPLE'S REPUBLIC.

Further reading: Danuta Markowska, "Urbanization of the Steppes," in *Poland at the 8th International Congress of Anthopological and Ethnological Sciences* (Wroclaw: Zaklad Narodowy im. Ossilinskich, 1968), 171–192; Zofia Szyfelbejn-Sokolewicz, "On the Applicability of the Concept 'Local Community' to the Study of Culture Change in Present Day Mongolia," in *Poland at the 8th International Congress of Anthopological and Ethnological Sciences* (Wroclaw: Zaklad Narodowy im. Ossilinskich, 1968), 211–223; Slawoj Szynkiewicz, "The Role of the Herdsmen's Co-operatives in Modernizing the Country Life in Mongolia," in *Poland at the 8th International Congress of Anthopological and Ethnological Sciences* (Wroclaw: Zaklad Narodowy im. Ossilinskich, 1968), 195–210.

Comans *See* QIPCHAQS.

Compendium of Chronicles (Jami' al-tawarikh)
RASHID-UD-DIN FAZL-ULLAH's *Compendium of Chronicles* is both an invaluable encyclopedic account of the Mongol Empire and an unprecedented attempt at multicivilization history. GHAZAN KHAN (1295–1304), Mongol ruler in Iran, was worried that the now-Islamic Mongols might loose sight of their ancestral traditions and commissioned Rashid-ud-Din to produced a comprehensive history of the people. His successor Sultan Öljeitü (1304–17) further asked him to add accounts of all the known peoples of the world, particularly the earlier Hebrew, Persian, and Islamic dynasties, as well as those of India, China, and Europe. The resulting *Compendium of Chronicles* was compiled under Rashid-ud-Din's direction by a team including many foreign consultants, particularly the Mongol BOLAD CHINGSANG. The style throughout is plain and impersonal.

The history of the Mongols is the *Compendium's* most valuable part. Rashid-ud-Din incorporated large parts of 'ALA'UD-DIN ATA-MALIK JUVAINI's *HISTORY OF THE WORLD CONQUEROR*, editing out his elaborate style and predestinarian theory of history. For contemporary Islamic history he used Ibn al-Athir's *al-Kamil fi'l Ta'rikh*. For the history of CHINGGIS KHAN and his predecessors, he used the Mongolian chronicle now preserved in the first chapter of the *YUAN SHI* (History of the Yuan) and in Chinese translation as the *SHENGWU QINZHENG LU* (Campaign undertaken by the lawgiving warrior). The Mongolian *Altan debter*, to which he refers occasionally, may well be the *SECRET HISTORY OF THE MONGOLS*, but if so, he was shown only isolated portions of it.

Other sections on the Mongols were new. The description of the Mongol tribes and clans, the annotated list of Chinggis Khan's captains, the Persian translations of Chinggis's *biligs* (wise sayings), and accounts of the khans' wives and children, all produced by extensive interviews with Bolad Chingsang and other Mongol informants, are indispensable sources on Mongol social history. His history of QUBILAI KHAN, evidently derived from Bolad Chingsang, excellently complements Chinese histories. Even when incorporating existing source material, he carefully corrected and added material from his Mongol consultants or from now-lost Mongolian written sources.

In his history of the Middle Eastern Il-Khans, however, Rashid aims to conceal as much as reveal. Despite the wealth of data, he reveals few intimate details, and, as is typical in Islamic histories, he systematically excises the substantial role of Christianity and Judaism at court. The final section on Ghazan Khan's reforms is, however, a unique firsthand description of administration and finance in a medieval Islamic state.

In his tomb complex of Rab'-i Rashidi, Rashid arranged for one illustrated copy each in the Persian original and Arabic translation to be made annually. Four of these copies have survived as well as a number of later manuscripts. Rashid-ud-Din's work became the primary source on the Mongol conquest in the Islamic world and from the 18th century in Europe as well, and it remains a strong influence on the historical view of the Mongols even today.

See also ISLAMIC SOURCES ON THE MONGOL EMPIRE.

Further reading: Thomas T. Allsen, *Culture and Conquest in Mongol Eurasia* (Cambridge: Cambridge University Press, 2001); Rashid al-Din, *Successors of Genghis Khan*, trans. John Andrew Boyle (New York: Columbia University Press, 1971); Rashiduddin Fazlullah, *Jami'u't-Tawarikh: Compendium of Chronicles, A History of the Mongols*, 3 vols., trans. W. M. Thackston (Cambridge, Mass.: Harvard University Press, 1999).

Confucianism Although the Mongols have traditionally resonated with Confucianism's patriarchal and filiopietist social values and orientation toward service to the state, Confucianism's teachings have usually been assimilated more through reading histories than through abstract metaphysical texts.

EARLY INTERACTIONS

While North China's XIANBI dynasties in the fifth–sixth centuries had translated Confucian classics into their own Mongolic language, the KITANS, another Mongolic people who founded the Liao dynasty (907–1125), showed little interest in Confucian works. Although CHINGGIS KHAN (Genghis, 1206–27) was fascinated by Buddhist and Taoist holy men, he too showed no interest in Confucianism, although his entourage included Confucian-trained officials such as YELÜ CHUCAI. Under Chinggis Khan's successor, ÖGEDEI KHAN (1229–41), however, Yelü Chucai and Inner Mongolian ÖNGGÜD men began instructing the emperor in Confucianism. From 1233 on trained Confucian scholars received the same privileges given Buddhist and Taoist clergy (*see* RELIGIOUS POLICY IN THE MONGOL EMPIRE), a descendant of Confucius was enfeoffed as duke, and a Confucian temple was built in the imperial capital of QARA-QORUM. From 1240 Yelü Chucai's influence declined, and Ögedei's immediate successors showed no interest in Confucianism, allowing the provisions protecting scholars to lapse.

QUBILAI AND HIS SUCCESSORS

In the 1240s, the prince Qubilai, under the influence of the Buddhist monk Haiyun (1202–57) and the master diviner LIU BINGZHONG (1216–74), began interviewing Confucian scholars. Zhao Bi (1220–76), a Shanxi scholar in Qubilai's entourage, translated into Mongolian the commentary by Zhen Dexiu (1178–1235) on the Confucian classic *Great Learning*, while Yao Shu (1203–80) lectured Qubilai's son JINGIM on the *Classic of Filial Piety*. The records of their conversations kept by Zhang Dehui

(1197–1274) show Qubilai coming to grips with the almost purely ethical character of Confucianism yet worried by the conventional wisdom that excessive Confucianism had ruined the earlier JIN DYNASTY.

From 1252 Qubilai began applying these lessons as brother of the khan and viceroy in China. With Qubilai's election as khan in 1260, Confucian scholars for a brief period began to dominate the councils of the ruler. While QUBILAI KHAN eventually rejected their advice as too dogmatic, Confucians remained a presence in the government, supported by Qubilai's Confucian-trained son Jingim and many Mongolian aristocrats. These Confucian Mongols tended to focus on Confucianism's historical and dynasty-building experiences rather than on the ritual or metaphysical side of the teaching.

Under the civilian registration policies Confucian scholars were defined as those who were either descended from a degree holder under the previous Chinese dynasties or had demonstrated Confucian knowledge in an examination. Government quotas kept the number of Confucian households at well under 1 percent of the population, hardly a fifth of the Buddhist or Taoist clergy. Most of these Confucians were schoolteachers, receiving positions in the local administration only at advanced ages.

Qubilai's early Confucian advisers were not members of any organized school. The northern Dongping school, which emphasized literary composition, was discredited when its key adherent at court, Wang Wentong, was executed for involvement in LI TAN'S REBELLION. Xu Heng (1209–81), a northern Confucian at Qubilai's court, was the first to disseminate in North China the teachings of the metaphysical and rigorist school of Zhu Xi (1130–1200) that had dominated the SONG DYNASTY (960–1279) in South China. While at first Confucians of the fallen Song refused to serve the Yuan, by 1310 a new generation of South Chinese scholars had begun serving in government positions as well as teaching and tutoring in the dynastic schools. When the emperor Ayurbarwada (titled Renzong, 1311–20) finally established the examination system in 1315, Zhu Xi's interpretations of the *Four Books* were established as standard. In 1324 the "Classics Mat," or program of Confucian lectures for the emperor by senior scholar officials, was also instituted. Despite these victories for the Zhu Xi school, leading Yuan Confucians even in South China, such as Wu Cheng (1249–1333) and Yu Ji (1272–1348), reflected the Mongol focus on law and administration and avoidance of narrow sectarianism.

From Qubilai's reign on Confucianism dominated the formal education of well-born Mongol boys. In 1269 state-sponsored Mongolian schools were established in the provinces, and in 1271 a Mongolian School for the Sons of the State was established in the capital, all staffed by accredited Mongol teachers instructing children in the MONGOLIAN LANGUAGE in the SQUARE SCRIPT. The school textbooks were all translated from Chinese: the *Difan* (Plan for an emperor) by the Tang emperor Taizong (597–649), the institutional compendium *Zhenguan zhengyao* of Wu Jing (640–749), the massive history *Zizhi tongjian* (Comprehensive mirror in aid of government) of Sima Guang (1019–86), and Zhao Bi's translation of the commentary on the *Great Learning*. The court printed Mongolian translations of the *Zizhi tongjian* in 1282 and the elementary *Classic of Filial Piety* in 1307. Only in 1329 was a Directorate of Literature established for the comprehensive translation of Chinese classics into Mongolian.

MONGOL CONFUCIANISM IN THE QING DYNASTY

After the expulsion of the Mongols from China in 1368, Confucian influence disappeared. Only the *Classic of Filial Piety* was still transmitted; all other translations were lost. With the Mongols' submission to the QING DYNASTY (1636–1912) they once again came in contact with Confucianism, yet since the Mongols in the autonomous BANNERS (appanages) were not allowed to participate in the dynasty's Confucian examination system or even invite teachers to give instruction in Chinese, such contact was indirect.

Certain Chinese books that were translated into Mongolian for other reasons contained some Confucian content, particularly the 1644 court-sponsored printings of an abridged Mongolian translation of the Chinese YUAN SHI (History of the Yuan), or standard Yuan dynasty history. Manchu versions of the *Four Books* were also printed, and many learned Mongols could read Manchu (far more than could read Chinese). Other printed didactic texts frequently used as textbooks taught elementary Confucian concepts such as the *Shengyu Guangxun* (Holy instruction), written by the Kangxi emperor in 1670 and revised by his son the Yongzheng emperor in 1724, and the translated Chinese primer *Three-Character Classic* (*Sanzijing*). Historians of Buddhism such as DUKE GOMBOJAB (fl. 1692–1749) and the lama Jamba-Dorji of Urad (fl. 1849) in describing Chinese Buddhism incidentally touched on other Chinese schools, including Confucianism. Finally, by the 19th century the increasing number of Chinese settlers in Inner Mongolian banners made Chinese literacy more common. In the early 19th century a Höhhot TÜMED author, Galsang (fl. 1838), translated all of the *Four Books*, which were printed in bilingual Chinese-Mongolian editions.

In 1775 the eastern Inner Mongolian author Rashipungsug became the first Mongolian historian to confront the Confucian view of the Mongols in his BOLOR ERIKHE. While very much sympathetic with Confucianism's social values, he was offended by the criticisms of Buddhism offered by Confucian scholars in the course of the histories he read. While Rashipungsug remained firmly committed to the priority of Buddhism, INJANNASHI

(1837–92) engaged Confucian thought at a much deeper level. Quoting Qubilai's early conversations with Zhang Dehui, Injannashi then offered his own Confucian-influenced views reconciling cultural relativism with common human morals, yet his subtle ideas were not followed up.

By 1900 certain aspects and catchphrases of Confucian teachings were widely circulated among the Mongols but without the larger context of systematic doctrine. In Inner Mongolia citations from the Chinese classics increased in the years immediately after 1912, when the Manchu Qing dynasty fell and the Mongols were directly incorporated into the Republic of China. In Mongolia some conservative scholars responded to the 1921 Revolution by emphasizing the family- and state-oriented secular values of Confucianism. Thus, *Mandukhu naran-u tuyaga* (Rays of the rising sun), published in 1923 by Batuwachir (Ch. Bat-Ochir, b. 1874), expressed Confucian ideas on family and personal cultivation. In both areas, however, Soviet-influenced revolutionary movements advocating revolutionary changes in society and the family and vehemently denouncing feudal and Oriental traditions, soon swept away these nascent Confucian trends.

See also LIAN XIXIAN; RELIGIOUS POLICY IN THE MONGOL EMPIRE; REVOLUTIONARY PERIOD; SAYYID AJALL.

Further reading: John W. Dardess, *Confucianism and Autocracy: Professional Elites in the Founding of the Ming Dynasty* (Berkeley: University of California Press, 1983); Igor de Rachewiltz, "The Preclassical Mongol Version of the *Hsiao-Ching*," *Zentralasiatische Studien* 16 (1982): 7–109.

1924 Constitution

The 1924 Constitution confirmed the elimination of the constitutional monarchy under the JIBZUNDAMBA KHUTUGTU and made Mongolia a people's republic. With the death of the Bogda Khan (Holy Emperor, *see* JIBZUNDAMBA KHUTUGTU, EIGHTH) in May 1924, the Mongolian revolutionary leadership proclaimed Mongolia a republic. On October 24, 1924, the government created a commission to draft a new constitution. The commission's draft was supplied by the Russian legal adviser P. V. Vseviatskii and translated into Mongolian by ELBEK-DORZHI RINCHINO. The First Great Khural (November 8–28, 1924) adopted it essentially without change.

The new constitution was of the Soviet form, putting all sovereign power nominally in the hands of an indirectly elected supreme legislature or Great State Khural, which elected a standing legislature or Little State Khural and a government (i.e., cabinet). In reality, the Presidium of the MONGOLIAN PEOPLE'S REVOLUTIONARY PARTY (nowhere mentioned in the constitution) was the real decision-making body. Although the constitution guaranteed various rights, they were restricted to the "real people" (*jingkhini arad tümen*), and the constitution's preface defined the republic's aim as the destruction of internal and external reactionaries. All natural resources and for-

eign trade were reserved to state monopoly. The constitution confirmed the abolition of the previous legal estates and the privatization of religious belief. It also disenfranchised the aristocracy, full-time monks, and all "greedy exploiters" and persons living on interest payments. The more radical class struggle and socialist provisions were not actually implemented until the LEFTIST PERIOD beginning in 1929.

See also REVOLUTIONARY PERIOD.

1940 Constitution

The 1940 Constitution, passed at the eighth Great Khural (June–July 1940), held after the annihilation of the Buddhist clergy and the GREAT PURGE, confirmed the destruction of the prerevolutionary social order.

The government organs created in the 1940 Constitution resembled those of the 1924 CONSTITUTION, but the standing legislative body, the Little State Khural, was renamed the Great Khural's Presidium; its chairman remained titular head of state. The government, or cabinet, elected by the supreme legislature or Great State Khural, was renamed the Council of Ministers and the prime minister renamed the chairman of the Council of Ministers. The Great State Khural's deputies' terms were extended to three years.

The preface of the constitution defined the MONGOLIAN PEOPLE'S REPUBLIC as a state composed of three nonantagonistic strata: herders, workers, and intellectuals, now pursuing "noncapitalist development" toward the future building of socialism. The constitution followed the expropriation of the aristocracy, destruction of the Buddhist church, and limitation of private ownership of capital to the animal husbandry sector. "Exploiting classes" such as those who lived on rents or interest, high lamas, titled nobility, oppressive taiji (petty nobility) counterrevolutionaries, and influential *kulaks* (rich farmers or herders) were all disenfranchised. Freedom of religion was now paired, as in Soviet constitutions, with "freedom of antireligious propaganda."

In 1949 the indirect election of the Great State Khural deputies by open ballot was amended to direct election by secret ballot, and the political disabilities of the earlier "exploiting classes" were removed. As before, however, only one candidate, that nominated by the MONGOLIAN PEOPLE'S REVOLUTIONARY PARTY, stood for each position. The Cyrillic version of the constitution published in 1949 also made numerous changes in language from the original UIGHUR-MONGOLIAN SCRIPT version.

1960 Constitution

Approved on July 6, 1960, at the close of the successful collectivization campaign, the 1960 Constitution celebrated the MONGOLIAN PEOPLE'S REPUBLIC's coming of age as a fully socialist country.

The 1960 Constitution's preamble was the first to tie explicitly Mongolia's freedom and development to the

October Revolution, V. I. Lenin's teaching, and Soviet assistance. It was also the first to identify explicitly the MONGOLIAN PEOPLE'S REVOLUTIONARY PARTY as the ruling party.

The 1960 Constitution defined the state's class basis as the workers, the collectivized *arat*s (Mongolian, *arad/ard*, people, commoners, here used to match Russian peasants), both herders and farmers, and the intellectuals. The text repeatedly emphasized that all property in Mongolia, whether owned by the state or the rural cooperatives, was socialist and that all resources were to be dedicated to socialist construction and development, culminating in a communist society.

The 1960 Constitution retained the government structure created in 1940 as amended in 1949, although the supreme legislature or Great State Khural was renamed the Great People's Khural. At first the Khural grew with the population, but in 1981 its size was fixed at 370. With greater prosperity, the section on civil rights was expanded to include, for example, the right to free health care and a steadily shortening work week with improving services. At the same time, the list of civil duties was lengthened by requiring various good behaviors, including "proletarian internationalism" (i.e., a pro-Soviet, pro-Russian attitude).

In May 1990, during the 1990 DEMOCRATIC REVOLUTION, the 1960 Constitution was amended to allow multiparty elections until a new constitution could be drawn up. A 430-seat Great People's Khural was elected by a first-past-the-post system, while a new Little State Khural with 50 seats became the standing legislature, elected by proportional representation.

1992 Constitution   The Mongolian 1992 Constitution was intended to consolidate the social and political system created by the 1990 DEMOCRATIC REVOLUTION. It was the first Mongolian constitution to guarantee effectively a pluralistic society that respects human rights and decides political leadership through competitive elections. The constitution defines Mongolia's current state structure.

The 1992 Constitution was adopted on January 13, 1992, by the Great People's Khural (Assembly), which had been elected in May 1990 after the advent of multiparty elections. Drawn up after comparison with a wide variety of world constitutions, the initial draft, presented at the end of October 1991, was subject to 76 days of discussion in the Great People's Khural. In these debates the initial draft's proposed official name for the country was changed from the Republic of Mongolia (*Bügd Nairamdakh Mongol Uls*) to State of Mongolia (*Mongol Uls*), the old 1945 flag basically preserved (*see* FLAGS), a new seal adopted, and possible land PRIVATIZATION carefully circumscribed.

The 1992 Constitution is divided into a preamble and six chapters. The first chapter, on the State of Mongolia's sovereignty, defines Mongolia as a unitary state, allowing the stationing of foreign troops only by parliamentary approval and restricting private land ownership to improved urban and farm land, while reserving subsoil resources, forests, and pasture to state ownership. Ownership of land by foreign nationals is prohibited. Religion and state are enjoined to support each other without either encroaching on the other's sphere.

The second chapter defines the rights and freedoms of Mongolian citizens. Given the history of gross abuse by previous Mongolian governments, these carefully spell out rights to property, to join political parties and peacefully protest, to enjoy freedom from unlawful searches, detention, or any form of torture, and to a fair trial based on a presumption of innocence. Capital punishment is limited to the most serious crimes. Guarantees of free education, health care, and other vaguer rights, such as to a balanced ecology, to favorable work conditions, and to engage in creative work, are also offered. Citizens are required to respect the constitution and others' rights, as well as, when required, to pay taxes and do military service. (There is no provision for conscientious objection.)

The third chapter defines the structure of the state: 1) The Great State Khural (*Ulsyn Ikh Khural*), or parliament; 2) the president; 3) the government (i.e., cabinet) with its prime minister; and 4) the judiciary. The Great State Khural is composed of 76 members elected for four-year terms. The president is directly elected to, at most, two four-year terms and has a veto power that can be overridden only by two-thirds of the parliament. He or she must be born in Mongolia. The government and prime minister are nominated by the president for confirmation by the Great State Khural. The selection of judges, including those of the Supreme Court, is entrusted to a general council of courts, with confirmation by the parliament and appointment by the president, and is limited to those with a formal legal education and legal experience.

The fourth chapter defines a three-tier system of local administration. Below the national level are: 1) provinces (AIMAGS) and the capital city, ULAANBAATAR; then 2) rural *SUMS* and urban districts (*düüreg*); and 3) rural *bag* (teams) and urban *khoroo* (wards). Local governments are indirectly elected; a general meeting (in the lowest level) or part-time *khural*, or assembly (in the upper levels), elects a standing presidium and nominates a governor. The governor then must be approved by the next higher level.

The fifth chapter creates a nine-member Constitutional Tsets, or court. The parliament, president, and Supreme Court each appoint three members who serve for six years. This body exercises the predominant power on issues of constitutionality. The sixth chapter allows constitutional amendments either by a three-fourth majority of the parliament or by a national referendum called for by two-thirds of the legislature.

The first amendment to the 1992 Constitution concerned the relation of the government and prime minister to the president and Great State Khural. Originally, the constitution forbade members of parliament to serve in the government. In 1998 members of the parliament in both main parties passed a constitutional amendment to change this provision and to create a more clearly parliamentary system. President N. Bagabandi's veto was overridden, but the Constitutional Court invalidated the amendment due to procedural irregularities. President Bagabandi also refused to accept the government nominated by the majority parliamentary party, as the candidates were under investigation for corruption. After further controversy, in May 2001 a new parliament passed, and the Constitutional Court accepted, the constitution's first amendment clearly establishing the principle of a government responsible to parliament and composed of parliament members.

See also MONGOLIA, STATE OF.

Court of Colonial Affairs   *See* LIFAN YUAN.

Crimea

Under the Mongols Crimea continued to export northern commodities—grain, fish, salt, beeswax, honey, skins and furs, and slaves—to Byzantium, Italy, and Egypt. In the 13th century the main ports for Black Sea commerce were Sudak (Italian, Soldaia) and Caffa (Russian, Feodosiya). Inland from both was the administrative center of Qirim (modern Staryy Krym). Goths, Greeks, Armenians, Jews, and Anatolian Turks settled the coastal ports and villages, while Qipchaq nomads dwelled in the northern plains. During the Latin occupation of Constantinople (1204–60) the Venetians established a factory at Sudak, where MARCO POLO's family kept a house.

In spring 1223 a detachment of Mongols sacked Sudak as part of a massive raiding expedition through the Qipchaq lands. As the Mongols conquered the Black Sea steppe from 1236, famine-struck Qipchaq refugees crowded into Crimea. The Mongol conquest of Crimea in 1238 depopulated the Crimean steppe and glutted the port markets with Qipchaq slaves. Sudak now became MAMLUK EGYPT's key supplier of mamluks (military slaves).

After the Mongol conquest the port cities paid customs duties to the GOLDEN HORDE khans on the Volga, but the revenues were divided among the whole empire's Chinggisid princes, in accordance with the APPANAGE SYSTEM. Crimea's salt lakes also generated major revenue for the Horde. In 1260 the Byzantines recovered Constantinople and gave to the Genoans vast trade concessions in the Black Sea. In 1267 the khan Mengü-Temür (1266–80) granted the Genoese the administration of Caffa, while Venice held a factory at Azaq (Italian, Tana, modern Azov), center of the fish trade. By 1340 Crimea was the Mediterranean's major supplier of Far Eastern wares.

In the 1290s conflicts between the khan Toqto'a (1291–1312) and the senior prince NOQAI (d. 1299) spilled over into Crimea. In the 14th century Christian-Muslim tensions increased with the immigration of Anatolian Turks. These tensions periodically provoked conflict with the Mongol rulers, who sacked Caffa in 1308 and Sudak in 1322 and besieged Caffa unsuccessfully in 1343 and 1345–46. In 1332 Ibn Battuta found Caffa flourishing under Genoese control, but Sudak was partly in ruins and under Turkish control. Qirim and Azaq were heavily Muslim and ruled by governors from the Horde.

During the 1345–46 siege plague spread from the Horde's army to the Crimean cities, claiming 85,000 lives. In the succeeding troubles Far East trade dried up, and defeated khans and emirs restocked their treasuries by looting Caffa. The same chaos, however, allowed the Genoese to unify the port cities and renegotiate their status (1380).

In 1426–27 a line of Chinggisid khans established themselves in Crimea, and in 1449 the Chinggisid Hajji Giray declared himself khan of an independent Crimea. In 1475 the Ottoman Turks conquered Caffa and the port cities. The Crimean khanate occupied the Crimean inland and the neighboring steppe as an Ottoman protectorate until the Russian conquest in 1783.

See also BYZANTIUM AND BULGARIA.

Crusaders   *See* LESSER ARMENIA; MAMLUK EGYPT; WESTERN EUROPE AND THE MONGOLS.

Cyrillic-script Mongolian

The Cyrillic (Russian) script was adapted for writing the Mongolian language in a lengthy process from 1941 to 1951, and it is still Mongolia's official script.

INTRODUCTION OF THE SCRIPT

Russia's Buriat Christians and folklorists first experimented with transcribing MONGOLIAN LANGUAGE texts into Cyrillic. In 1925 the KALMYKS (Oirat Mongols) in European Russia adopted a Cyrillic script to write their language. In 1939 the Buriat Mongols in Siberia moved from the Latin script they had adopted in 1931 to a new Cyrillic script. On March 25, 1941, the MONGOLIAN PEOPLE'S REPUBLIC rejected Latinization and, to increase familiarity with Soviet writings and culture, decided to replace the traditional UIGHUR-MONGOLIAN SCRIPT with the Cyrillic script instead. The Mongolian scholar TSENDIIN DAMDINSÜREN designed the new script in less than a week. The Khalkha dialect of Mongolian, spoken by 70 percent or more of the population of the Mongolian People's Republic, was naturally chosen as the basis for the Cyrillic script orthography.

After desultory educational efforts the Mongolian government tried to switch to the new script in July 1945, but passive resistance was widespread. In July 1946 a serious push was begun to transfer to the new script, and by October 1947 42.2 percent of adults were literate in the Cyrillic. From July 1, 1950, government business was officially conducted in the new script. Even so, important political works were published in the Uigher-Mongolian Mongolian script as late as 1951. From 1955 to 1958 the Inner Mongolian government in the People's Republic of China planned to introduce the Cyrillic script in place of the Uighur-Mongolian script, but this idea was canceled for political reasons (*see* KHAFUNGGA).

DESIGN OF THE SCRIPT

In commissioning Damdinsüren to design the script, YUM-JAAGIIN TSEDENBAL ordered that the Russian script not be "cut up," that is, that all its letters must be used. At the same time, non-Russian letters were to be kept to an absolute minimum. Damdinsüren fulfilled this mandate largely by imitating the existing Buriat Cyrillic script. Russian "ж" (zh) and "з" (z) were used for the Mongolian "j" and "z," even though the Mongolian pronunciation was different (like *j*am and a*dz*e, not like a*z*ure and *z*oo). The use of Cyrillic "н" (n) for both Uighur-Mongolian "-n" and "-ng" complicated the noun declension system. Palatalized Russian vowels (е, ё, я and ю) represented the consonant "y," even though this created ambiguities between, for example, "ye" and "yö."

Vowels were more complicated. Damdinsüren adopted the Cyrillic Buriat "ө" and "γ" for the Mongolian front rounded vowels (conventionally transcribed ö and ü). At first long vowels were distinguished by an added apostrophe and then by a macron (e.g., ō). In May 1945, however, it was decided to follow Buriat by representing long vowels with double vowels, thus avoiding diacritics. The Russian soft sign (ь) and hard sign (ъ) and the "61 i" (ы) had no obvious use in Mongolian, but Damdinsüren used the soft sign to represent a reduced etymological "i" that palatalized the preceding vowel and the "61 i" in case endings.

In all new Mongolian languages (Mongolian proper, Buriat, and Kalmyk-Oirat) short noninitial vowels are more or less reduced, losing their distinctive character but mostly still being pronounced as a "schwa." While the Kalmyk Cyrillic script drops them all and the Buriat Cyrillic script retains them all, Damdinsüren adopted a middle course together with complex rules of dropping and retention of short vowels in noun and verb inflection. These rules, which include switching between the soft sign (ь) and the "i" (и), give considerable trouble to Mongolian children.

CONTEMPORARY USE

Although the older generation in Mongolia continued to use the Uighur-Mongolian script privately, the Cyrillic script soon became completely dominant. In 1986, with the beginning of liberalization, the Uighur-Mongolian script was introduced as a compulsory subject in seventh and eighth grades (equivalent to American ninth and tenth grades). In 1991, with full-scale democratization, the Mongolian legislature ordered the Uighur-Mongolian script restored as Mongolia's official script by 1994. For a few years primary school pupils were taught solely in the Uighur-Mongolian script. In a democratic environment the inadequate materials and poor teacher training in the Uighur-Mongolian script could not overcome passive resistance from the population, and in 1996 the Cyrillic script was reconfirmed as the official script, with the Uighur-Mongolian script to be taught as a required secondary school subject. While Latinization has influential adherents, Cyrillic will remain Mongolia's primary script for the foreseeable future.

See also BURIAT LANGUAGE AND SCRIPT; KALMYK-OIRAT LANGUAGE AND SCRIPT.

Further reading: Stephane Grivelet, "An Attempt to Change the Official Script of Mongolia," *Turkic Languages* 2 (1998): 233–246; ———, "Latinization Attempt in Mongolia," in *Historical and Linguistic Interaction between Inner-Asia and Europe,* ed. Árpád Berta and Edina Horváth (Szeged, Hungary: University of Szeged, 1997), 115–120.

D

Dadu *See* DAIDU.

Dagor *See* DAUR LANGUAGE AND PEOPLE.

Dagur *See* DAUR LANGUAGE AND PEOPLE.

Da Hinggan Ling *See* GREATER KHINGGAN RANGE.

Dahur *See* DAUR LANGUAGE AND PEOPLE.

Daidu (**Dadu, Ta-tu, Khanbaligh**) Moving his capital to Daidu (modern Beijing) marked the importance of North China in QUBILAI KHAN's realm, yet he also preserved much of his Mongol background in his palace there.

The site of present-day Beijing, traditionally named Yanjing, was a secondary capital of the Liao dynasty (907–1125) founded by the Inner Mongolian KITANS. In 1153 the Jurchens' JIN DYNASTY renamed the city Zhongdu, or "Central Capital." In 1215 the city was besieged and sacked by the Mongols (*see* ZHONGDU, SIEGES OF). Afterward, under the name Yanjing, it served as the seat of Mongol administration in North China.

When Qubilai Khan (1260–94) was first elected khan, he placed the secretariat, his main organ of administration, at Yanjing. Cut off from his ancestors' palace-tents (ORDOS) by war, he built an ancestral temple there with earth and grass from the steppe. Finally, in 1266 Qubilai ordered a new capital to be built northeast of old Yanjing centered on today's Forbidden City. *Feng-shui* expert and adviser LIU BINGZHONG based the city's overall placement on the Chinese classic *Zhou Li* (Rites of the Zhou dynasty), and the Turkestani architect Igder

designed the buildings. Qubilai held his first formal audience in the new palace in February 1274. Renamed Daidu (Great Capital, modern Chinese pronunciation Dadu) in 1272, the city was called by its many foreign residents Khan-Baligh, "City of the Khan."

The new city's 15 meter (50-foot-high) whitewashed walls extended five kilometers (three miles) east to west and somewhat less than seven kilometers (five miles) north to south. Respectable residents from the old city were housed in extended-family compounds in plots of around 3 hectares or more than an acre each. The six broad alleys and strict grid organization gave the city an impressively spacious look. Suburbs stretched for miles outside the new city's 12 gates, while old Yanjing became almost desolate. Following Mongol custom, burials and any bloodshed were strictly forbidden inside the city. A curfew testified to the Mongols' continuing fears of rebellion.

Following a model begun at QARA-QORUM, Qubilai's palaces, including Daming Hall for formal audiences and Yanchun Pavilion for confidential meetings and Buddhist rituals, occupied elevated platforms inside the palace grounds. The outer-palace grounds, walled with watchtowers and arsenals, were a stocked game park, crisscrossed by elevated walkways and graced by the lake Taiye Chi (modern Bei- and Nanhai).

The Yuan-era population has been estimated at 600,000 persons, and they served as a magnet for all forms of commerce. Even so, feeding the court establishment was a major task. In 1292 Guo Shoujing dredged the Tonghui Canal, bringing water into the very walls of the city. After the fall of the city to the MING DYNASTY in 1368, the site was retained and renamed Beijing (Northern Capital). The only extant monument of the Mongol city is Baita or "White Pagoda" north of Bei-hai Lake.

See also "LAMENT OF TOGHAN-TEMÜR."

Further reading: Nancy R. S. Steinhardt, "The Plan of Khubilai Khan's Imperial City," *Artibus Asiae* 44 (1983): 137–158.

dairy products Historical and ethnographic accounts show that Mongolian dairy products have generally been processed in identical ways from the 13th century to today, although the terminology differs somewhat from region to region. Mongols milk all five of the animals but they tend to put the milk to different uses. Thus, mare's milk is generally fermented into KOUMISS, sheep and goat's milk is mostly used in TEA or cheeses, while cow's milk is used for all three purposes.

Zöökhii, or cream, is one of the simplest dairy products to make, being produced by letting the milk curdle in a warm place for six to eight hours and skimming the cream off the top. This cream is strained and churned to form "white oil" (*tsagaan tos*), which is then gently

"Yellow milk" being fermented to make *khuruud* (a hard cheese). Shiliin Gol, Inner Mongolia, 1987 *(Courtesy of Christopher Atwood)*

melted to separate the "yellow oil" (*shar tos*), or clarified butter. The residue from the separation of "white oil" is *tsötsgii*, a delicious cream eaten in recent times mixed with cane sugar and fried millet.

Once the cream is skimmed off, the rest of the milk may be poured into a kettle over a gentle flame until it separates into curds and "yellow milk" (*sharasü*). The yellow milk is boiled and then mixed with culture and allowed to ferment, forming *chagaa*. The *chagaa* is then placed in sacks and the liquid squeezed out with a weight, forming a semisolid *aarts*. Dried in the sun, *aarts* becomes *khuruud*, a kind of rockhard cheese. This cultured cheese can be preserved indefinitely and was part of the regular rations of soldiers on campaigns. It is reconstituted for eating by placing it in hot water. In the Middle Ages this was done by putting it in a skin and beating it, while in modern times it is often placed in tea. Today the *aarts* is frequently mixed with sugar and squeezed through a meat grinder to form wormlike pieces of sweet *aaruul*, a popular holiday and gift product. Another form of *khuruud* is made today without culture by pressing unfermented curds into molds to make pieces of hard, round, dry curds used to decorate hospitality plates.

In the fall *öröm* rather than *zöökhii* is made. *Öröm* is a kind of coagulated foamy cream. By gently heating (to about 80°C, or 176°F) and ladling the milk, a foam is produced, which when the fire is weakened coagulates. By carefully adding new milk around the edges and reheating three to four times, a thick layer of *öröm* is formed, which after cooling overnight can be removed.

Cheeses (*biyaslag*) are made by adding fermented milk to foaming milk, heated over a gentle flame. The curdled milk is then strained through cloth, wrapped, and placed under a stone to remove the liquid. This procedure can also be followed with the milk left over from *öröm*. Culture is also added directly to milk (fresh or leftover from making *öröm*) to make yogurt (*tarag*).

Fermented, slightly alcoholic liquors are made from mare's, cow's, and camel's milk. That from mare's milk is the famous koumiss (from Turkish *qumiz*, Mongolian, *airag* or *chigee*), the drink of choice for Inner Asian men. This is produced by vigorously churning cultured milk. Koumiss has a natural tendency to separate into turbid white dregs and a potent clear liquid. While today only plain koumiss is usually drunk, in the empire period the clear liquid, called "black koumiss" (*qara qumiz*) in Turkish (all clear liquids are "black" to the Mongols), was the rulers' preferred drink. Today, instead, distilled milk liquors are made with home-distilling equipment set up over a kettle of boiling fermented milk. The resulting liquor, called *shimiin arkhi* in Mongolia or *saali-yin arikhi* in Inner Mongolia, is 10–12 percent alcohol. Double-fermented milk liquor, or *arz*, reaches 30 percent alcohol.

See also FOOD AND DRINK.

Kalmyk women and children in a yurt, brewing distilled milk liquor (*From Peter Simon Pallas*, Sammlungen historischer Nachrichten über die mongolischen Völkerschaften *[1976]*)

Dalai Lama, fourth (Yon-tan rGya-mtsho) (1589–1617)
The only Dalai Lama of non-Tibetan origin
In 1588 the Third Dalai Lama, bSod-nams rGya-mtsho (1543–88) died while in Inner Mongolia. In February 1589 a boy born to Sümer Taiji, grandson of ALTAN KHAN (1508–82) and a lady variously known at Bigchog Beiji or Baigha-Jula, showed remarkable religious attainments from birth. In 1592 the boy's uncle Tümed khan Chürüke and his queen, Noyanchu Jünggen, visited his father's camp at Chaghan Nuur (Qagan Nur), and the boy was enthroned as the Dalai Lama at Guihua (modern HÖHHOT). The Tibetans, believing the Mongols to have "little wisdom and much pride," ignored the boy until 1601, when the chief monasteries of the Dalai Lama's dGe-lugs-pa (Yellow Hat) order sent a delegation to test him. Once the boy passed the test, the Tibetans insisted that he be brought to Lhasa. On November 3, 1603, he was ordained at Lhasa with the name Yon-tan rGya-mtsho. Within a year tensions flared with the rival Karma-pa lamas, who saw the new Dalai Lama's Mongo-

lian escorts as illiterate barbarians and dGe-lugs-pa bigots. The Tibetan king, based in gZhis-ka-rtse (Xigazê), also saw the escorts as a threat and had them expelled in 1605. As the dGe-lugs-pa were strong in the dBus district around Lhasa, while the Karma-pa and the Tibetan king were based in the gTsang district, regional tensions flared. Only the affection between the young Dalai Lama and his tutor, Blo-bzang Chos-kyi rGyal-mtshan (1567–1662), the first Panchen Lama, who presided over bKra-shis Lhun-po Monastery in gZhis-ka-rtse, moderated the tensions. In 1617 the Dalai Lama died; his heart and other organs were brought back to Tümed as relics.

Damba *See* DAMBADORJI.

Damba, Dashiin (1908–1989) *Mongolian party leader who was ousted for attempting to implement de-Stalinization more aggressively than the maximum leader, Tsedendal, wished*

Born on March 29, 1908, in Daiching Zasag banner (Teshig *Sum,* Bulgan), Damba joined the MONGOLIAN REVOLUTIONARY YOUTH LEAGUE in 1924 and participated in the expropriation of the nobility's property in 1929–30. After studying in the party school in ULAANBAATAR, he became a commissar in the armed forces (*see* ARMED FORCES OF MONGOLIA) from 1932 to 1938.

After serving as provincial party secretary, he was elected to the party presidium in July 1939 while participating in the arrest of the 1921 revolutionary and deputy interior minister Losal (D. Losol, 1890–1940). With the arrest and torture of the new party secretary Basanjab (B. Baasanjaw, 1906–41), Damba was implicated as well, but Mongolia's leader, MARSHAL CHOIBALSANG, had the charges dropped. Damba remained in the Politburo but was not part of Choibalsang's inner circle.

After Choibalsang's death Damba took the position of the party's first secretary, while YUMJAAGIIN TSEDENBAL became premier. The Soviet-educated Tsedenbal despised Damba as a "backward" man who shirked work to visit the countryside, was not a reader, and did not write his own speeches. In 1956, with de-Stalinization in the Soviet Union, a special commission headed by BAZARYN SHIRENDEW was formed to reevaluate purge victims in the Stalin-Choibalsang years. Damba supported giving the commission access to top-secret Interior Ministry files, but Tsedenbal was opposed. In 1957, when Tsedenbal wished to arrest Shirendew and another rival as "imperialist spies," Damba persuaded him to delay and then drop the charges. In November 1958 Tsedenbal dismissed Damba. After his dismissal he headed a machine tractor station and eventually became deputy director of the Institute of Agriculture.

See also MONGOLIAN PEOPLE'S REPUBLIC.

Dambadorj, Tseren-Ochiryn   *See* DAMBADORJI.

Dambadorji (Tseren-Ochiryn Dambadorj, Damba Dorji, Damba) (1899–1934) *Mongolia's leader in 1925–1928 who resisted complete dependence on the Soviet Union*

Dambadorji's father, Tsering Wachir, was head of the telegraph bureau of Mongolia's theocratic government. His son Dambadorji was born in Maimaching, the Chinatown of Khüriye (modern ULAANBAATAR). His father enrolled him in 1913 in the translator's school attached to the Russian consulate and then in the gymnasium (high school) in Troitskosavsk (in modern KYAKHTA). After graduating he worked in the telegraph bureau. In winter 1920–21 he joined the Mongolian revolutionaries in Troitskosavsk, later participating in the October 1921 siege at Tolbo Nuur (Tolbo Sum, Bayan-Ölgii). From December 1921 to January 1923 he was chairman of the Mongolian People's Party. After being replaced as chairman by the more conservative "Japanese" Danzin (1875–1934), he traveled to Germany and other Euro-

pean countries, wrote articles, and translated several works of Friedrich Engels.

At the People's Party's Third Congress (August 1924) he allied with the Buriat revolutionary ELBEK-DORZHI RINCHINO to overthrow GENERAL DANZIN and regain his old position. After Rinchino's recall to Russia in July 1925, Dambadorji as party chairman and his allies ran Mongolia. Under Dambadorji's rule state control of the economy and Soviet presence slowly increased, yet he strictly disciplined radicals who demanded the replacement of experienced old officials. With Moscow's encouragement Dambadorji supported both the Chinese warlord Feng Yuxiang and Inner Mongolian revolutionaries. His short-lived first marriage in 1925 to a Chinese actress, Wang Shuqin, diminished his popularity. In 1927 he married a Mongolian woman, Batsükh.

His attempts to open diplomatic relations with Japan and his opposition to the Communist International's radicalization of the allied Inner Mongolian party incurred Moscow's hostility. After more than a year of pressure, Dambadorji's regime was overthrown at the People's Revolutionary Party's Seventh Congress (September–December 1928). Dambadorji was exiled to Moscow for study with Batsükh and their son, Abmad. After 1932 he worked in Mongolia's embassy in Moscow before dying of disease in 1934.

See also MONGOLIAN PEOPLE'S PARTY, THIRD CONGRESS OF; MONGOLIAN PEOPLE'S REVOLUTIONARY PARTY, SEVENTH CONGRESS OF; REVOLUTIONARY PERIOD; THEOCRATIC PERIOD.

Dambijantsan (Ja Lama) (d. 1922) *Mysterious adventurer said to have had magic powers who helped drive the Chinese out of Khowd and became the border warden in western Mongolia*

Dambinjantsan is generally said to have been a Kalmyk. A Dambijantsan (known as Ja Lama, from "Jantsan") traveled western Mongolia and Tibet in 1889–90, 1892, and from 1900 to perhaps 1904 as a lama from the west, prophesying the fall of the Qing and the rise of the Mongols and calling himself a reincarnation of AMURSANAA (1722?–57).

In 1910 a Dambijantsan reappeared in western Mongolia, although those who knew both doubted if it was the same person. In 1912 he persuaded the Dörböd rulers to support the 1911 RESTORATION and joined GRAND DUKE DAMDINSÜRÜNG, MAGSURJAB, and the JALKHANZA KHUTUGTU in the siege of KHOWD CITY. Dambijantsan's annihilation of Chinese reinforcements coming from Chenghua (modern Altay) and his capture of their carbines marked a turning point in the siege and also began the legend of his invulnerability to bullets.

After the Mongolian victory he took the title Dogshin Noyan Khutugtu Nom-un Khan (Fierce Lordly Incarnation, Dharma King) and was appointed commissioner of the Western Marches by Mongolia's theocratic government. He built a new monastery near LAKE UWS, forcing the lamas to dig an artificial pond, collecting 2,000 subjects, or *shabi* (lay disciples), and mooting various Russifying reforms. Despite stories of his gun magic, clairvoyance, and prophetic gifts, his requisitions and extreme cruelty soiled his and the theocratic government's reputation, and sparked a *DUGUILANG*-style movement of Dörböd lamas against their prince and the Mongolian government, one that had to be suppressed by force. In 1914 the western Mongolian people appealed directly to the Russian government, and Dambijantsan, a Russian citizen, was arrested and deported.

After penal exile in Tomsk and Yakutsk, he returned to Astrakhan and in 1918 reappeared in Khalkha's Zasagtu Khan AIMAG. Again winning over some of the princes, he set up a stockade at Gongpoquan, north of Mazong (Maajin) Shan in the northwest Gansu borderlands (modern SUBEI MONGOL AUTONOMOUS COUNTY). He remained neutral in the conflict between the White Russians and the Soviet-supported revolutionaries in 1921–22 but was assassinated by agents sent from the revolutionary Office of Internal Security in early December 1922. Until the moment of his death even his assassins worried about his reputation for invulnerability.

See also THEOCRATIC PERIOD.

Further reading: John Gaunt, "Mongolia's Renegade Monk: The Career of Dambijantsan," *Journal of the Anglo-Mongolia Society* 10 (1987): 27–41.

Damdinsüren, Jamsrangiin *See* DAMDINSÜRÜNG, GRAND DUKE.

Damdinsüren, Tsendiin (1908–1986) *Mongolian author and scholar who became a leader in the preservation and study of Mongolia's prerevolutionary literary heritage*

Born in Üizeng Zasag banner (modern Matad Sum, Eastern), the second son of the banner clerk Tsengde, who served briefly as banner deputy adjutant (1921–22) before retiring due to illness, Damdinsüren was first tutored at home. In 1923 he became a banner clerk in his banner and in 1925 volunteered as a scribe for a company of soldiers stationed at Tamsag. While in the army, he began collecting books. From 1927 to 1929 he served as editor of *Ünen* newspaper and first became acquainted with Marxism in an evening study group with the Buriat "Wooden Leg" Gombozhab and the Russian adviser Koniaev. In the succeeding LEFTIST PERIOD (1929–32) he briefly served on Mongolia's trade union council before being sent to organize herding collectives in GOBI-ALTAI PROVINCE.

From 1933 he studied at the Oriental Institute in Leningrad (St. Petersburg). In 1936 he married a Russian-Jewish woman, L. V. Zevina, who was studying Mongolian there. They had four children: Lev, Konstantin,

Mikhail, and Anna (Dulmaa). After his return in 1938 he was arrested in the GREAT PURGE on November 4 and tortured—a blow with a red-hot iron lost him several teeth—but was not executed. After his release on January 27, 1940, MARSHAL CHOIBALSANG employed him to design Mongolia's Cyrillic script. From 1942 to 1946 he was again *Ünen* newspaper's editor in chief. From 1946 to 1950 he studied for his master's degree in Moscow, writing his thesis on the GESER epic. Subsequently, he worked at the Mongolian State University and the ACADEMY OF SCIENCES and published 56 scholarly papers and monographs.

Damdinsüren began his writing career as a poet and a short story writer. His first story, "The Rejected Girl" ("Gologdson khüükhen"), written for the leftist Writer's Circle in January 1929, followed a poor family through its troubles into the revolutionary years. Altered by pressure from his colleagues, the original, less ideological version was to Damdinsüren's later regret lost. In Leningrad Damdinsüren wrote his famous poem "My Silver-Haired Mother" ("Buural ijii mini," 1934) in a strongly rhythmic folkloric style, speaking of his homesickness as well as his determination to study. In 1950 he composed the lyrics to the Mongolian national ANTHEM.

After 1940, however, Damdinsüren put his major effort into scholarship, paraphrasing the *SECRET HISTORY OF THE MONGOLS* in modern Mongolian (1947) and publishing the extraordinary pioneering anthology *Monggol uran zokhiyal-un degeji zagun bilig oroshibai* (One hundred best works of Mongolian literature, 1955), which presented prerevolutionary works, almost all of which had existed only in manuscript, in a modern format with notes and commentary. Works covering virtually every field of prerevolutionary Mongolian literature followed.

In 1963 the party Politburo attacked Damdinsüren for recklessly reprinting Buddhist and shamanist texts and for encouraging his students to do the same. In 1970 his 1967–69 Russian-Mongolian dictionary was recalled, and Damdinsüren was fined 5,600 tögrögs for its "chauvinistic" chronological appendix. Foreign, particularly Russian, appreciation of his work prevented further persecution.

See also CYRILLIC-SCRIPT MONGOLIAN LITERATURE; MONGOLIAN PEOPLE'S REPUBLIC; SOVIET UNION AND MONGOLIA.

Damdinsürüng, Grand Duke (Jamsrangiin Damdinsüren) (1874–1920) *A Barga Mongol and one of the chief generals of the Mongolian theocratic government*

Born the only surviving son of a *SUM* captain in Plain White banner of New BARGA left flank (modern Xin Barag Zuoqi), Damdinsürüng became a clerk before enrolling as a militiaman at age 18. In 1908, while staying in Beijing to receive his lieutenant's commission, he met the Khalkha PRINCE KHANGDADORJI (1870–1915). After bannermen in

HULUN BUIR (including Barga) overthrew the local Chinese authorities in January 1912, Hulun Buir joined Khalkha Mongolia's new theocratic government, and Damdinsürüng was made duke (later grand duke) and deputy foreign minister. Damdinsürüng and MAGSURJAB commanded the successful Mongolian siege of KHOWD CITY (August 1912), and in 1913 he became supreme commander in the southeast during the SINO-MONGOLIAN WAR. As deputy foreign minister Damdinsürüng helped draft the Mongolian-Tibetan treaty of March 1913. After 1915 Hulun Buir was made a "Special Region" in China, but some New Barga bannermen and CHAKHAR soldiers were resettled in Mongolia as Damdinsürüng's subjects. Damdinsürüng, like many INNER MONGOLIANS, found the arrogance and mismanagement of the Khalkha nobility and lamas frustrating and proposed numerous reforms. After the disappointment of the 1915 KYAKHTA TRILATERAL TREATY and the REVOCATION OF AUTONOMY in 1919, he drank heavily. The Chinese authorities in Mongolia arrested him on September 10, 1920, and he died in prison.

See also THEOCRATIC PERIOD.

Further reading: Sh. Natsagdorj, "Damdinsüren the Forefront Hero," in *Mongolian Heroes of the Twentieth Century*, trans. Urgunge Onon (New York: AMS Press, 1976), 77–104.

dance Due to clerical opposition, dance virtually disappeared from central Mongolia. Folk dances have remained only in the peripheral areas of the Mongol world. In the 20th century new folk dance traditions were created.

A story of an early QURILTAI of 12th-century Mongols tells of them dancing around a lone tree and stamping their feet so strongly they pounded a ditch as deep as their knees. European travelers also observed a kind of drinking dance in which the dancer teased and encouraged a partner to drink. In the ancestral temple built by QUBILAI KHAN (r. 1260–94), dances were performed, but of what style is unknown.

In modern times essentially no dances are known among the central Khalkha Mongols, except for the Garuda dance of the wrestlers and the TSAM dance of the monasteries. A circle dance, or *yookhor*, was popular among the western BURIATS. In it the dancers make a circle, hold hands, and slowly circle while singing. Games are also associated with dances. Among the eastern Buriats dance is performed only during weddings, due to Buddhist opposition.

The OIRATS of western Mongolia, Xinjiang, and Kalmykia perform a dance called *bii* or *biyelgee*. This dance, performed inside the yurt, involves only the arms, hands, head, and shoulders and mimes either daily activities or worship rituals. While often etymologized by Mongols as related to *biye*, "body," and thus expanded to the form *biyelgee*, the word, in fact, originates from Kazakh *bi*, "dance" thus indicating its foreign origin.

Among the KALMYKS on the Volga the *bii* dances were strongly influenced by Cossack forms.

In ORDOS dances involving only the upper body are also performed. One involves holding a pair of chopsticks and clicking them on each other and parts of the body, while another involves balancing liquor cups on the head.

Eastern Inner Mongolian dances include the Andai of southeastern Inner Mongolia, which was performed by villagers on a specially prepared ground when a shaman identified a young woman as suffering from lovesickness or post-partum depression. The dance, which was avoided by the respectable strata or society, was performed by dancers, villagers, and eventually the patient herself and involved waving handkerchiefs and stamping.

With the development of professional folk performance ensembles in the Mongol regions of Russia, Mongolia, and China, the idea that the Mongols *ought* to have a flourishing dance tradition took hold. Emblematic movements from the various dances described above were taken and added to the ensemble jumps and twirls of Russian Cossack dance to manufacture a synthetic folk dance style.

Further reading: Carole Pegg, *Mongolian Music, Dance, and Oral Narrative* (Seattle: University of Washington Press, 2001).

danshug (modern, *danshig*) In Mongolia the *danshug* (from Tibetan *brtan-zhugs*, firm abiding) ritual of asking an INCARNATE LAMA to abide longer in this world became a vital part of the offering site–almsgiver (or priest–patron) relationship established between the KHALKHA nobility and the JIBZUNDAMBA KHUTUGTU (*see* "TWO CUSTOMS"). Begun in Tibet by the First Panchen Lama (1567–1662), this type of ritual was first performed in Mongolia for the FIRST JIBZUNDAMBA KHUTUGTU in 1657 at ERDENI ZUU, when it was accompanied by the Maitreya procession. From 1696 on the Khalkha nobility of all four AIMAGs and the GREAT SHABI presented the *danshug* annually or more often. These offerings began with a poem in the Tibetan *shabdan* (from *zhabs-brtan*, firm feet) genre requesting the lama to remain in this world for the sake of sentient beings and the presentation of a silver mandala, then followed with a gilt statue of Ayushi (Amitayus), Buddha of eternal life, and the scripture Tsendoo, written in five jewels. Accompanying the offerings were "The Danshug Games of the Seven Banners [of Khalkha]," *Doloon khoshuun-u danshug naadum*. During the reign of the Fifth Jibzundamba (1815–42), the Qing government restricted this all-Khalkha *danshug* to once in three years, but the GREAT SHABI continued annual offerings. After 1912 annual *danshugs* were held in the last month of summer, becoming the basis of today's NAADAM festival.

See also THEOCRATIC PERIOD.

Danzan, Soliin   *See* DANZIN, GENERAL.

Danzanravjaa   *See* DANZIN-RABJAI.

Danzin, General (Soliin Danzan) (1885–1924) *One of the leaders of the 1921 Revolution, he served as national leader until his execution during the party's Third Congress* Danzin was born to an unwed mother, Soli, in Süjügtü Zasag banner (modern Khotont Sum, North Khangai). When Soli married, Danzin stayed behind with his paternal grandfather. Placed in a banner monastery, he soon ran away and became a hired herder. Eventually, he became notorious in the local BANNERS as an incorrigible horse thief. In the early 1910s he fled south to the Gobi before ending up in Khüriye (modern ULAANBAATAR) around 1915. There he found employment in the Finance Ministry supervising leases and MINING concessions. He worked as liaison to the Russian Witte expedition and to the Russian financial adviser S. A. Kozin, although he never learned much Russian.

When the REVOCATION OF AUTONOMY was still impending, Danzin joined with Dindub and Dogsum (D.

Dogsom, 1884–1941) to form a *nam* ("faction," later "party") called the "Officials' Faction," or the East Khüriye Group, to fight Chinese control. After merging with another anti-Chinese faction, the "Consulate Terrace Group" headed by BODÔ, and forming the "People's Party of Outer Mongolia," Danzin set out for Soviet Russia with an interpreter, Choibalsang, on June 28–29.

From the beginning Danzin insisted that the Mongolian party needed to be representing the Bogda, as the established ruler of Mongolia, to have any credibility with the Russians. This insistence brought him into repeated conflict with Bodô. The uneducated Danzin, whom Russian advisers assessed as "not a man of great range," considered the intellectual Bodô to be pretentious and vain. Once in Russia the two could not work together, and they split up, Danzin going to Moscow to negotiate assistance while Bodô returned to Mongolia.

In mid-February 1921 Danzin returned to the border, where GENERAL SÜKHEBAATUR and others had been building a partisan army. Danzin dominated the March 1–3, 1921, assembly at which the People's Party program was adopted, and he was elected the party chairman. In mid-spring Bodô returned, and Danzin went to Khüriye to do

Elbek-Dorzhi Rinchino (third from right) and General Danzin (in fedora at left) picnicking with their families and friends, summer 1924 *(From* XX Zuun Mongolchuud, *2000)*

undercover work among Mongols in the White Russian army that had occupied Khüriye. On the way back he injured himself when his pistol went off during cleaning.

With the successful intervention of the Red Army in Mongolia, Danzin became finance minister and Bodô prime minister in the new government. From September 29 to December 22 Danzin, with General Sükhebaatur and Deputy Foreign Minister TSERINDORJI, went to Moscow to negotiate the November 5 friendship treaty. During their absence Bodô made a series of erratic decisions. Now Danzin, Sükhebaatur, and the Buriat revolutionary ELBEK-DORZHI RINCHINO all desired Bodô's resignation, which occurred in January 1922. To calm public opinion, Danzin went personally to western Mongolia to invite the JALKHANZA KHUTUGTU DAMDINBAZAR, a well-respected high lama, to serve as prime minister. In June Danzin criticized the Youth League as overly radical and insisted Mongolia would have to develop step by step. In August Danzin with the other ministers approved the execution without trial of 15 well-known dissenters, including Bodô.

After Sükhebaatur's death in February 1923, Danzin took his position as commander in chief, although his prime interest remained finances. After the chaos and depression of the 1919–22 years Mongolia's international trade through China began to pick up again in 1923. Hoping to revive Mongolia's economy and finances, Danzin encouraged Chinese firms to return to Mongolia. This friendliness to Chinese firms alienated his former ally Elbek-Dorzhi Rinchino, and Danzin's political supporters began to criticize openly the Buriat advisers as clever pied pipers of the naive young Mongols. Criticism of Danzin's administration increased at the People's Party's Third Congress in August 1924, when Danzin suddenly withdrew in a huff to the city garrison. He may have been planning a coup d'état against Rinchino, but he did not have the soldiers' support and was himself arrested and executed without a trial on August 30.

See also MONGOLIAN PEOPLE'S PARTY, THIRD CONGRESS OF; MONGOLIAN PEOPLE'S REVOLUTIONARY PARTY; 1921 REVOLUTION; REVOLUTIONARY PERIOD; THEOCRATIC PERIOD.

Danzin-Rabjai (Danzanravjaa, D. Ravjaa) (1803–1856)
A wild incarnate lama, Danzin-Rabjai was Mongolia's greatest traditional poet and playwright and the focus of innumerable legends.
Born in Mergen Wang banner (modern East Gobi province), Danzin-Rabjai's parents were so poor his mother had to beg for soup from a camel herder for the customary meat meal after childbirth. Local legends speak of him being raised by his father, Dulduitu, but the poems and early biographies speak of Dulduitu as his mother and say nothing of his father, who apparently disappeared early from his family's life.

In 1809 Danzin-Rabjai took vows as a *bandi* (novice) and the next year at age eight (seven in the Western

count) first revealed his poetic talent. Sitting by the door of a YURT on a rainy day, his area, while covered by the worst felt, did not drip, while the area of honor did. When kidded about this by the master, he spoke his poem "Indra" (*Khormusta tngri*), saying that just as seating does not matter in the rain, so age does not at the moment of death.

Shortly afterward Danzin-Rabjai was enthroned as the fifth incarnation of the Gobi-yin Noyan Khutugtu (Lordly Incarnation of the Gobi) lineage, affiliated with the bKa'-brgyud-pa order of Tibetan Buddhism. Since the previous incarnation, Jamiyang-Oidub-Jamtsu, had stabbed a lama, the Qing authorities had canceled the lineage in 1794, and the enthronement was somewhat secret. In 1817 he first studied the Tibetan verses of the A-mdo Tibetan lama sKal-ldan rGya-mtsho (1607–77) of Rong-bo (Longwu) monastery and then studied philosophical debate at Badgar Juu (north of BAOTOU). A cryptic autobiographical poem seems to refer to his first sexual experience at age 17 and his mother's death in spring the next year. Later he wrote of his grief that "the kindness of a mother is greater than the Buddha's."

TRAVELING INCARNATION

From 1822 his life alternated between building hermitages in his Mergen Wang banner and wanderings in Inner Mongolia and Khalkha. He became a particular disciple of the Third JANGJIYA KHUTUGTU (1787–1846). From 1825 consorts accompanied him on his journeys, and his frequent drinking spells and bouts of rage earned him the epithet *dogshin* (terrible). In 1839, hearing of an illness of the Fifth Jibzundamba Khutugtu (1815–42), he rushed to Khüriye (modern ULAANBAATAR) and performed services for healing. The next year, however, he was refused entrance to the city as a wild and drunken "Red Hat" (bKa'-brgyud-pa) lama. In 1841 even his teacher, the Jangjiya Khutugtu, ordered him to stay in his banner, which he did. In 1852, after performing a cursing ritual against Chinese rebels at the invitation of the Manchu AMBAN and the Khalkha khans, the *dogshin* lama became welcome again in prominent Khalkha circles, although not in Khüriye. In 1856 he felt ill but hoped to revisit Maidari Juu near Höhhot. He died on the way in Dörben Kheükhed (Siziwang) banner.

SONGS AND POEMS

Danzin-Rabjai's songs combine a language and PROSODY close to folk songs with a profound multilayered understanding of the Buddhist concept of emptiness. Danzin-Rabjai had many women in his life, and while a large number of his lyrics are still sung as love songs, a deeper level of meaning is always available. His most famous song, *Ülemji-yin chinar* (Extraordinary qualities), extolled the ravishing of the poet's senses by the sight, sound, smell, taste, and touch of his beloved. Legend said he composed this song for his great love, the singing girl

Dadishuari, in gratitude for her cure of his near-fatal illness. At the same time, its imagery follows the Buddhist "five qualities of enjoyment" frequently offered to gurus in meditation. Danzin-Rabjai's devotional lyrics to deities and gurus are sometimes filled with the sentiments of a lover and at other times with profound filial longing.

The theme of what was said to be Danzin-Rabjai's first poem, *Khormusta Tngri,* was death and impermanence. His two conversation songs, now sung as folk songs, *Galuu khün khoyor* (The goose and the man) and *Öwgön shuwuu* (The old man and the bird) use bird migrations to illustrate the transitory nature of affections and the power of past lives.

Danzin-Rabjai, like many Tantric and Dhyana (Zen) practitioners, ridiculed institutionalized religion, saying to Dadishuari on his deathbed that a good horse that can go a long distance is better than boring scriptures, yet he also authored a number of didactic poems. His famous *Ichige, ichige* (For shame, for shame) is a marginally rewritten version of some verses by the THIRD MERGEN GEGEEN (1717–66), but *Tsagasun shibagu* (The kite) is a fresh rephrasing of traditional didactic sentiments. In another song he playfully tweaks the common didactic trope about the preciousness of human birth, saying that realizing your own self-deception is better than a human birth.

THE OPERA *MOON CUCKOO*

Danzin-Rabjai had directed TSAM performances from 1827. In 1831, inspired by a visit to ALASHAN (Alxa), where Tibetan-style opera was performed, he built a theater in his Khamar Hermitage and wrote the opera *Saran Khökhögen-ü Namtar* (Tale of the moon cuckoo). In 1833 his first performances began. Danzin-Rabjai not only wrote the libretto but also composed the tunes, designed the costumes, and trained and directed the troupe. The story, an adaptation of a Tibetan work of the same name, revolves around a noble prince and his evil companion who have mastered the technique of transferring their souls into other bodies. When the two enter cuckoos' bodies, the evil companion stealthily returns to the prince's body, destroys his own, and becomes ruler, while the prince begins to teach Buddhism to the birds. The imposture is eventually noticed by the prince's faithful wife, and the evil companion is driven out, but the cuckoo cannot return. The opera alternated lively action and didactic passages, with a number of pieces sung in Tibetan. The actors, instead of wearing masks as in *tsam* drama, used makeup in the style of the Chinese operas. The performances were popular and made Danzin-Rabjai's monasteries quite a bit of money.

HIS LEGACY

Danzin-Rabjai also had talents as a physician and a painter whose works ranged from images of his incarnation lineage, to ink portraits of CHINGGIS KHAN, to erotica.

Danzin-Rabjai (1803–56), the fierce Lordly Incarnation of the Gobi and perhaps Mongolia's greatest poet *(From D. Tsagaan and Z. Altangerel,* Ikh Gowiin Dogshin Noyon Khutugtu *[n.d.])*

Copies of his writings, paintings, and effects were kept by his *takhilchi* (curator), Balchinchoijai, and his descendants. The opera was performed in his banner until the 1920s, and legends flourished about the incarnation. During the anti-Buddhist campaigns of 1937–40, the then-*takhilchi*, Tüdew, hid as much as he could in caves. The 1962 publication of his poems in Cyrillic by D. Tsagaan was a milestone in academic study of Danzin-Rabjai. In 1990, with the end of communism, Tüdew's grandson Altangerel exhumed Danzin-Rabjai's effects and founded a museum dedicated to Danzin-Rabjai in the city of Sainshand.

See also LITERATURE.

Further reading: Marta Kiriploska, "Icige, Icige (A Poem of Danjin Rabjai)," *Central Asiatic Journal* 45 (2001): 254–265; ———, "Who Was Dulduitu? (A Note on Rabjai)," *Zentralasiatische Studien* 29 (1999): 97–108; Michael Kohn, "A Lonely Battle in Mongolia to Save Buddhist Relics." *New York Times,* 12 August 2002, p. 4; Nicholas Poppe, "Noyan Khutugtu Rabjai and Mongol

Folklore," in *Studia Sino-Mongolica,* ed. Wolfgang Bauer (Wiesbaden: Otto Harrassowitz, 1979), 191–196; D. Tsagaan and Z. Altangerel, *Ih Gobiin Dogshin Noyon Hutuqtu* (Ulaanbaatar: UULS Studio, n.d.).

Daoism   *See* TAOISM IN THE MONGOL EMPIRE.

Darhan   *See* DARKHAN CITY.

Darhat   *See* DARKHAD.

Dariganga   Living along Mongolia's southwestern frontier, the Dariganga *yastan* (subethnic group) numbers 28,600 (1989) and has a dialect and lifestyle quite similar to the KHALKHA Mongols. In 1697, after driving the invading ZÜNGHARS out of Khalkha, the Manchu Qing emperor Kangxi established a special imperial stud in the Dariganga area, manned by Khalkhas from Setsen Khan province and SHILIIN GOL Mongols from Abaga (Abag) and Sönid BANNERS (appanages). The Dariganga herds were eventually expanded into two camel herds, two horse herds, and a sheep herd, annually supplying 800 stallions, 300 bull camels, and first 4,000 and then, after 1831, 7,270 rams. Dariganga was under the Inner Mongolian CHAKHAR banners and had no hereditary nobility (*see* EIGHT BANNERS).

In March 1912, after the 1911 RESTORATION of Mongolian independence, the Dariganga officials petitioned to join Mongolia. The new Republic of China sent the Chakhar official Jodbajab to recover the territory, but his troops were dispersed. He was arrested on August 28 and returned to China after the KYAKHTA TRILATERAL TREATY in 1915. The requisitions due the Qing emperor were transferred to the new theocratic emperor. Many Dariangas escaped them, however, by joining the GREAT SHABI, or the emperor's personal estate.

Dariganga continued under Outer Mongolian administration after the 1915 KYAKHTA TRILATERAL TREATY. After the White Russian seizure of Khüriye in February 1921, however, China again dispatched Jodbajab to recover Dariganga. That August, however, a task force of Soviet Kalmyk troops, assisted by Mongolian partisans, drove Jodbajab again out of Dariganga. The new revolutionary regime in 1924 reorganized Dariganga as a banner with an elective government. In 1931 Dariganga was attached to EASTERN PROVINCE but in 1941 was transferred to SÜKHEBAATUR PROVINCE. Treated simply as Khalkha in the 1930s, the Dariganga were recognized as a separate subethnic group from the 1956 census on.

See also DASHBALBAR, OCHIRBATYN; THEOCRATIC PERIOD.

Darkhad (Darkhat, Darhad)   The Darkhad of Mongolia are a Mongolian-speaking *yastan* (subethnic group) numbering 14,300 (1989) and living in far northern Khöwsgöl province. Originally they were *shabi* (lay disci-

ples) of Mongolia's great lama lineage, the Jibzundamba Khutugtu. The Darkhad name means "Exempt Ones" (cf. Middle Mongolian DARQAN). They received the name when the KHALKHA Mongolian nobleman Deleg and his lady, Dejid Akhai, donated themselves and their subjects to the FIRST JIBZUNDAMBA KHUTUGTU (1635–1723). From then on they formed part of the GREAT SHABI, the personal estate of the Jibzundamba Khutugtu, and as such were exempt from state requisitions. The Darkhad were divided into three OTOGs (camp districts), each ruled by a *daruga* (chief) and inspected every three years by *zaisang*s (officials) dispatched by the ERDENI SHANGDZODBA office administering the Khutugtu's estate. In 1861 the Darkhad numbered 7,015 persons, but by 1915 had decreased to 5,130. The Darkhad principally occupied the Darkhad basin around the upper Shishigt River west of LAKE KHÖWSGÖL; they were pastoral nomads living in YURTS (*ger*), although a few used Tuvan-style birchbark tepees. The Darkhad *otog*s were almost entirely illiterate. Darkhad Monastery (at the seat of today's Rinchinlhümbe Sum) had more than 1,000 lamas, yet then and now the Darkhad were also active patrons of shamans and did not taboo fish, as did other Mongolian Buddhists.

Under the QING DYNASTY the Darkhad territory was included in Tannu Uriyangkhai province and separated from the Khalkha Mongols by frontier pickets. Around the Darkhad were organized several Khöwsgöl Uriyangkhai BANNERS inhabited by TUVANS.

The origin of the Darkhad appears to be mixed Mongolian and Tuvan. The most common CLAN NAMES are Mongolian and Buriat ones. The Khuular clan, however, are Turkish-origin Tuvans. The Darkhad dialect today is quite close to Khalkha but contains forms that indicate it was originally a Kalmyk-Oirat type dialect later subject to very strong Khalkha influence (*see* KALMYK-OIRAT LANGUAGE AND SCRIPT; MONGOLIAN LANGUAGE).

After the 1911 Restoration the Khöwsgöl area, unlike the rest of Tannu Uriyangkhai, remained part of Mongolia. In 1925 the Darkhad and their neighboring Khöwsgöl Uriyangkhais were put under the new Delger Yekhe Uula province, which in 1931 was merged with neighboring Khalkha areas to form the new KHÖWSGÖL PROVINCE. By that time the Darkhad population had rebounded to 6,893. In 1989 the Darkhad were the most rural of Mongolia's ethnic groups, with 61.5 percent collective herders, 10.1 percent white-collar employees, and 28.4 percent workers or state farm employees, compared to the national averages of 27.8 percent, 21.4 percent, and 50.6 percent, respectively.

darkhan   *See* DARQAN.

Darkhan city (Darhan, Darchan)   Created in 1961 as an industrial center, Darkhan city became a center of Mongolia's construction materials industry.

The site of Darkhan was chosen in Selenge province to take advantage of the presence of limestone, sand, clay, marble, marl, and other construction raw materials. The nearby Sharyn Gol brown coal (lignite) field, with reserves of 696 million metric tons (767 million short tons), supplied power, while the site's location on the TRANS-MONGOLIAN RAILWAY facilitated transportation and communication. Construction began on October 17, 1961, and in 1962 Darkhan was put under direct central government administration. The resident population reached 23,300 by 1969 and 65,800 in 2000. More than 90 percent of the population is under 35 years of age (1990 figure), and 86 percent live in apartment blocks (2000 figure). Soviet and East European (especially Czechoslovak) aid played a major role in constructing the city.

Major components of the Darkhan industrial complex include the Sharyn Gol strip mine (opened in 1964), a thermal power plant with a capacity of 50,000 kilowatt-hours (renovated with German assistance in 1993), a building materials combine, a cement factory, and a prefabricated house-building combine. By 1985 Darkhan itself (not including Sharyn Gol) produced 9.7 percent of Mongolia's total industrial output; of that, 36.4 percent was building materials, 22.7 percent food processing (meatpacking, poultry, flour), and 15.8 percent fuel.

Mongolia's manufacturing did not fare well in the economic liberalization of the 1990s, particularly outside ULAANBAATAR. The Russo-Mongolian joint-stock company Mongolrostsvetmet (formerly Mongolsovtsvetmet) built a new minimetallurgical plant in 1993–94 in Darkhan with Japanese technology, but the city's share of Mongolia's total industrial sales dropped from 5.2 percent in 1995 to 3.3 percent in 2000 as unemployment reached 7.8 percent.

In 1994 the area of Darkhan was renamed Darkhan-Uul province and expanded from an original 200 square kilometers (77 square miles) to a current 3,280 square kilometers (1,266 square miles). Darkhan-Uul's population was 83,300 in 2000. The newly expanded province grows a significant grain and potato crop and in 2000 accounted for more than 18 percent of Mongolia's total vegetable harvest.

Darkhan-Uul province See DARKHAN CITY.

Darkhat See DARKHAD.

darqan (darkhan, tarqan) In the Turco-Mongolian tradition, exemption from imposts was one of the most important privileges accorded to classes and persons. Those accorded these exemptions bore the title *tarqan* (Turkish) or *darqan* (Mongolian, modern *darkhan*). This term first appears under the Türk empire (552–745) as one of the titles of the great leaders of the empire. It followed the Turks west into the Islamic world, where Mahmud al-Kashghari defined it in the 11th century as "a pagan word meaning emir (i.e., commander)."

In the MONGOL EMPIRE the title *darqan* was also a title of honor, but with a somewhat different connotation. In the famous SECRET HISTORY OF THE MONGOLS the range of possible rights and exemptions associated with the word *darqan* or its derivatives include: the right to nomadize freely over wide territory, the right to hold women captured in war without forwarding them to the khan, immunity to prosecution for up to nine transgressions, the right to serve as quiver bearers for the khan, and the right to drink the *ötög*, a special ceremonial liquor (probably a milk liquor) offered at the great assemblies (QURILTAI). All these rights were hereditary, being granted "unto the seed of the seed." Rewards of subjects and goods inevitably accompanied them, too.

While many in the Mongol elite received these exemptions, the actual title of *darqan* was mostly reserved for those outside the ruling inner circle. *Darqan* was a purely honorary title; the bearer was not expected to fill any office. The "classic" *darqan*s, whose descendants were known not by name but simply as "Darqan," were Badai and Kishiliq of the Oronar clan, herdsmen who had warned CHINGGIS KHAN (Genghis, 1206–27) of an attack by ONG KHAN. Similarly, MÖNGKE KHAN (1251–59) granted the title to a camel herder who warned him of a coup attempt; HÜLE'Ü (1256–65) in Iran to a Georgian wrestler; Abagha Khan (1265–82) to a Hindu who had led the camp of his mother and stepmother through hostile territory; and GHAZAN KHAN (1295–1304) to a Persian who alone in a village had supplied him with horses after a defeat. Sometimes, however, the *darqan* or his descendants could become important officials. Thus Kishiliq's descendant HARGHASUN DARQAN became grand councillor in the Mongol YUAN DYNASTY.

Tax exemption was also granted to other people in the empire who did not have such exalted status. Criminals exempted from punishment in return for frontline service were called *darqan*. All craftsmen were enrolled on the census and placed under direct state control. In return they too were exempted from taxes. This exemption made them *darqan*; one meaning of *darkhan* in modern Mongolian is simply "craftsman." Those persons dedicated to the service of the palace-tents (ORDO) of the deceased Chinggis were also freed from imposts and hence also received the name of *darkhad* (plural of *darkhan*). Such Darkhad people still exist at the EIGHT WHITE YURTS of Chinggis Khan in Ordos in Inner Mongolia. Under the QING DYNASTY (1636–1912) local Mongol rulers continued to grant *darqan* status to those rendering special services; regulations dealing with the financial problems this could cause were being issued as late as 1923 in Inner Mongolia.

See also CENSUS IN THE MONGOL EMPIRE; MOGHULISTAN; *NÖKÖR*; RELIGIOUS POLICY IN THE MONGOL EMPIRE.

darughachi (*basqaq, shahna*) The *darughachi* was an overseer used by the Mongols to supervise local officials in subject kingdoms. The term in Mongolian is sometimes used in the form of *darugha* (modern *darga*), which indicates a chief or boss of any sort.

The institution of *darughachi* seems to have originated with the QARA-KHITAI, or Western Liao Empire, in Turkestan. The Qara-Khitai emperor and his small core of ruling Kitan people appointed overseers to reside at the court of the many tributary rulers to ensure that they obeyed Qara-Khitai policy. In Persian these overseers were called *shahna* and in Turkish *basqaq*. During the MONGOL EMPIRE the Persian and Turkish terms were used as interchangeable equivalents for the Mongolian word *darughachi*. These officials always worked alongside existing local authorities.

Despite this clear connection in terminology, no *shahna*s in the Mongol Empire are known before 1214, even though several sedentary kingdoms had become tributary to the Mongols by then. In these early years CHINGGIS KHAN preferred to use marriage ties to attach sedentary rulers to himself and did not require tributary states to accept *darughachi*s. *Darughachi*s were first appointed after 1214 when Chinggis resolved to exterminate North China's JIN DYNASTY (1115–1234), which had broken its tribute agreement. More *shahna*s, or *darughachi*s, were appointed in Mawarannahr (Transoxiana) during Chinggis Khan's campaign of vengeance against the sultanate of KHORAZM. From the reign of Chinggis's successor, ÖGEDEI KHAN (1229–41), on, however, states voluntarily submitting to tribute were also required to accept a *darughachi*. Such *darughachi*s were sometimes accompanied by troops and paid special attention to ensuring the collection of Mongol-imposed taxes.

The term *darughachi* did not refer to a specific function but simply meant an official representing the Mongol rulers to a particular non-Mongol population. Thus, the early *darughachi*s oversaw units ranging from a single prominent family, a ward in a city, or a town, to a regional capital. The last were called "great *darughachi*s." *Darughachi*s were also assigned to non-Mongol artillerymen and Iranian craftsmen. The length of tenure of *darughachi*s was indefinite, and sons frequently inherited the position from their fathers. More important than function in defining the distinct role of the *darughachi* was ethnicity. Virtually all early *darughachi*s were allied people who had surrendered early to the new empire: ÖNGGÜD, UIGHURS, KITANS, QARA-KHITAI, NAIMAN, or Muslim traders in the Mongolian plateau. Combining implicit loyalty with knowledge of sedentary society, such political middlemen were invaluable.

All of the successor states of the Mongol Empire retained the institution of *darughachi*. In the Mongol YUAN DYNASTY (1271–1368) in China, QUBILAI KHAN and his successors transformed the *darughachi* into a type of local official. In each district the magistrate, his assistant, and a clerk would discuss all business with a *darughachi* who controlled the seal that made any document valid. *Darughachi*s were supposed to serve for only 30 months and be Mongols or SEMUREN (various sorts), while the officials were ethnic Chinese. Sons of *darughachi*s received preferential promotion but did not directly inherit offices. In fact, however, tenure was often much longer, and the rules on ethnicity were frequently subverted.

In the IL-KHANATE (1256–1335) in Iran the *shahna* or *basqaq* (the Mongol term *darughachi* only gradually became common) served alongside the Persian governor and (in great cities like Baghdad) an auditor general and Mongol commander. The *shahna* participated in all legal cases involving Mongols and in smaller cities commanded the garrison and exercised police functions. As in the Yuan system, *shahna*s and governors were supposed to exercise surveillance over each other, but the two often colluded in corruption. There is no data on specific tenure in office, but rotation was normal. Most *shahna*s were Mongols with Persian staffs, and the few Muslim *darughachi*s were old servants of the Mongols.

In the GOLDEN HORDE (1257–1480) in Eastern Europe, overseers governed the sedentary areas of the empire, such as the Crimean trading cities and the Russian principalities. Up to the 1320s they were called *basqaq*s (Russian *baskak*). The *basqaq* of Vladimir, the most powerful Russian principality, was called the Great Basqaq. In the early 14th century, however, the Russian princes of Moscow and elsewhere won greater autonomy, and the *basqaq* institution declined, being replaced by ad hoc messengers or envoys (*posoly*, from Mongolian *elchi*). The 15th-century term *doroga* (or *daruga*) as used in the Golden Horde designated the head of a secretariat dealing with a particular area or appanage (such as Moscow). How it developed from the *darughachi* is unclear.

See also ARTISANS IN THE MONGOL EMPIRE; BAYAN; KASHMIR; KÖRGÜZ; MAHMUD YALAVACH AND MAS'UD BEG; *ORTOQ*; SA'D-UD-DAWLA; PROVINCES IN THE MONGOL EMPIRE; RUSSIA AND THE MONGOL EMPIRE; SAYYID AJALL; SHIMO MING'AN AND XIANDEBU; *TAMMACHI*; YELÜ AHAI AND TUHUA.

Further reading: Elizabeth Endicott-West, *Mongolian Rule in China: Local Administration in the Yuan Dynasty* (Cambridge, Mass.: Harvard University Press, 1989).

Dashbalbar, Ochirbatyn (1957–1999) *One of Mongolia's great modern poets and from 1996 an ultranationalist politician speaking for those alienated by Mongolia's democratic transition*
Dashbalbar was born in Dariganga Sum (Sükhebaatur province). After eight years in the local school, he attended a professional high school in Omsk in agricultural science. He abandoned that field for literary studies

at Moscow's Gorky Literature Institute, becoming a professional writer while making a living writing for his provincial newspaper and later as a translator.

Dashbalbar's vision of poetry was formed by Mongolian and foreign poets such as DANZIN-RABJAI, NATSUG-DORJI, B. Yawuukhulan, Alexander Blok, Sergei Esenin, Walt Whitman, and Rabindranath Tagore. In his earliest published poetry collection, *Oddyn ayalguu* (Melody of the stars), Dashbalbar proclaimed: "Like two icebergs in the Atlantic grinding each other to powder/I would write poems," His early poetry bore witness to his lust for experience heightened to the utmost, while at the same time testifying to his love for his DARIGANGA homeland and especially his deceased father. Dashbalbar always had a high appreciation of the poet's vocation, and his poem "Nökhdöd" (To the comrades, 1986), revealed his aim to "Toss away the petty private thoughts/Like powdered dust shaken from my shoulder" and seek the truth. His 1990 prose–poetry collection *Burkhny melmii* (Eyes of the Buddha) testified to the rest he found in the Buddha's teaching of impermanence.

From 1991 Dashbalbar ran the literary journal *Zokhist ayalguu* (Harmonious melody) of the newly formed nationalist Mongolian National Free Writers' Union and the Mongolian Buddhist Center. Dashbalbar's commitment to the truth of Buddhism and his long-standing dedication to filial piety and the Mongolian land propelled him to denounce land PRIVATIZATION, feminism, Christian evangelism, and the new Democratic movement in general as being foreign-directed conspiracies to destroy Mongolia. Elected to the new democratic legislature in 1990, he was a vocal opponent of liberalization in the debates over the 1992 constitution. In 1996 he again won election to the Great State Khural (the parliament) from SÜKHEBAATUR PROVINCE, representing the Mongolian Traditional United Party and then in 1999 the Mongolian Party for Tradition and Justice. He died of a liver complaint on October 16, 1999, leaving three children from his previously divorced wife.

See also LITERATURE; MONGOLIA, STATE OF.

Daur language and people (Dagur, Dagor, Dahur, Dawor)

The Daurs, numbering 121,357 in 1990, are a Mongolic-speaking people mostly inhabiting northeast Inner Mongolia and Manchuria. Although the Daur language is distinctly different from Mongolian and heavily influenced by Manchu, in the 20th century the Daurs adopted a Mongol identity. In the early 1950s, however, the Chinese government designated them a separate nationality distinct from the Mongols. In Mongolian and Manchu the name is written Dagur or Dahur, respectively, but is pronounced "Daur" by the Daurs themselves.

ORIGINS

The name *Daur* goes back to the medieval KITANS, speakers of a very distinct language of the Mongolic

family who called their 10th- to 12th-century empire the "Daur Gurun," or Daur Empire. The Daur language today retains a few Kitan features, such as the peculiar word *kasoo* for "iron" (versus Mongolian *temür,* a borrowing from Turkic), yet the Daur language is mostly a development of Middle Mongolian, the language of the Mongol Empire (*see* MONGOLIAN LANGUAGE). Moreover, the Daur clan name Boskochaina may be the same as the QONGGIRAD tribe's Bosqur lineage, from whom came CHINGGIS KHAN's wife BÖRTE ÜJIN. The Daurs thus appear to be a population of provincial Kitans who were heavily "Mongolized" during Mongolian rule in Manchuria (*see* MANCHURIA AND THE MONGOL EMPIRE).

The Daurs emerged into history in 1616, when the nascent Manchu Empire found "Solon" tribesmen distributed along the northern bank of the Amur River from the Shilka to the Bureya and north along the Zeya. These Solons were divided into *khala*s (clans), a Manchu-Tungusic word, and composed of predominantly agricultural Daurs in symbiosis with bands of hunting and farming EWENKIS, a Manchu-Tungusic people. Daurs and Ewenkis intermarried yet maintained their distinctive languages. The BARGA, then occupying northern HULUN BUIR, were also tributary to these "Solons," and place names show that Daur territory at times stretched north to the Aldan River and west to the upper Shilka and Ergüne valleys.

LANGUAGE

Daur language is, along with Mogholi, the most archaic of the extant Mongolic languages. It has preserved the initial h- (e.g., *heleg,* "liver," from Middle Mongolian *helige,* cf. Modern Mongolian *eleg*), virtually all the diphthongs (e.g., *aol,* "mountain," from Middle Mongolian *a'ula,* cf. Modern Mongolian *uul*), and the q- as a stop (e.g., *kuaangart,* "bell," from Middle Mongolian *qongqa,* cf. Modern Mongolian *khonkh*).

At the same time it shows a number of progressive features related to its Manchurian environment and probable Kitan ancestry. The transformation of medial -b- to -w- is rather complete (e.g., *taawu,* "five," from Middle Mongolian *tabun*), and it shares with the Buriat and East Mongolian dialects the transformation of /e/ to /ə/ and the disappearance of ö (e.g., *uku-,* "to give," from Middle Mongolia *ög-*). Daur also shows a number of idiosyncrasies, such as the transformation of final -l to -r, the lengthening of short vowels, and the creation -ua- diphthongs from u or o (eg., *duand,* "middle," from Middle Mongolian *dumda*).

There are at present three principal dialects of Daur: Butha, Qiqihar, and Hailar (spoken in the Hulun Buir steppes). The number of Daur speakers in the 1980s was estimated at 90,000 of 94,014 Daurs (1982 census). Most Daurs today are multilingual, knowing Chinese, Mongolian, and often Ewenki as well as Daur (*see* ALTAIC LANGUAGE FAMILY; MONGOLIC LANGUAGE FAMILY).

THE DAURS AS MANCHU BANNERMEN

By 1643 Manchu raids had subdued the Daur-Ewenki tribes. The next year Cossacks arriving from Yakutsk began pillaging Solon villages. While some paid tribute to the Cossacks, others moved south to escape them. By 1667 both voluntary flight and the Qing generals' scorched-earth policy had driven all the Solons south of the Amur to the well-watered and forested valley of the Nonni (Nen) River.

The Qing set up small garrisons of Daurs and Ewenkis at Aihui (modern Heihe) on the Amur River and Mergen (modern Nenjiang) on the upper Nonni, and a larger force at Qiqihar in Heilongjiang province. In 1731 the Daurs and Ewenkis still on the lower Nonni River were formally incorporated within the Manchu EIGHT BANNERS system as the Butha (Hunting) Eight Banners.

In 1732 26 Daur and Ewenki *niru* (arrows, each nominally 300 households) were transferred to Hulun Buir steppe, west of the GREATER KHINGGAN RANGE. The Daurs did not adapt well to the new environment, and most returned to Butha, leaving three Daur *nirus* in and around Hailar city as mixed farmers and ranchers. Despite their small numbers, they monopolized most of the high positions in the Hulun Buir banner administration. In 1763 Daurs were sent to help garrison Xinjiang, being stationed in modern Tacheng (Qöqek).

The modern distribution of the Daurs still reflects these Qing military assignments. In 1982 36.5 percent of the 94,014 Daurs lived in the Butha area, 8.2 percent on the upper Nonni around Nenjiang (both areas now divided between Inner Mongolia and Heilongjiang), 22.2 percent in the Hulun Buir steppe west of the Greater Khinggan Range, 17.6 percent in Qiqihar and its suburbs, 2.7 percent on the Amur around Heihe, and 4.6 percent in Xinjiang. (The remaining 8 percent lived outside traditional Daur areas.)

TRADITIONAL ECONOMY, RELIGION, AND CULTURE

The Butha Daurs mainly planted millet along with buckwheat, barley, and kitchen gardens. They kept mostly horses, cattle, and pigs, milking only the cows. After the influx of Chinese settlers, hunting of elk for medicinal products and logging supplemented their income. Daurs lived in Chinese-style houses with *kangs* (heated sleeping platforms). The ideal was the compound household of married brothers living together under the supervision of a family patriarch, and family life was governed by strict hierarchies of age and sex. The lifestyle of the Hailar Daurs was similar, except that sedentary ranching of sheep, horse, and cattle replaced grain farming as the main pursuit.

Unlike most Mongolic peoples, the Daurs rejected Buddhism. Clan elders, sometimes assisted by *baksh* (learned men), carried on the twice-yearly worship of heaven and mountain spirits at clan cairns (OBOO),

accompanied by games of WRESTLING, ARCHERY, HORSE RACING, and field hockey (see NAADAM). Families lit bonfires on new year's day to worship heaven (see WHITE MONTH). Shamans (*yadgan*), whether male or female, used clan spirits for healing physical and psychic diseases but were, like women, kept away from the main clan rituals. Special women's rituals from which men were excluded included worship at women's *oboos*, river worship, and certain *lurgel* dances.

After joining the Eight Banners the Daurs and Ewenkis used Manchu for writing. Daurs read Manchu-language primers, collections of Qing memorials, and Manchu translations of Chinese historical romances. By the 19th century Daurs began writing in their own language using the Manchu script. Changshing (Arabdan, 1809–85?), born in Nantun village outside Hailar, wrote poems and travelogues. Mamegchi, a Butha Daur official, wrote a poetic travelogue of a journey to Hulun Buir, criticizing Buddhist superstition, while the songs of Qin Tongpu (1865?–1940?) described events in ordinary life and offered warnings against lust, greed, and anger.

MODERN HISTORY

Chinese immigration into Manchuria, the progressive sinicization of the Manchus, and the late Qing NEW POLICIES promoting the assimilation of frontier regions such as Hulun Buir all pushed the Daurs, particularly in Hailar, to adopt a Mongol as opposed to a Manchu identity. The building of the Russian-operated Chinese Eastern Railway and the growth of Japanese influence in Manchuria also opened new horizons, as students studied in Tokyo, Moscow, and Leningrad. Daurs joined in the 1912 anti-Chinese insurrection in Hulun Buir and became officials in independent Mongolia's theocratic government. After the restoration of Chinese control in 1920, Hailar Daur intellectuals such as MERSE (Guo Daofu, 1894–1934?) and Fumingtai (Buyangerel, 1898–1938) worked with Inner Mongolian politicians to bring Mongolia's 1921 REVOLUTION to Hulun Buir and Inner Mongolia. Fumingtai's uncle Duke Tsengde (1875–1932) became the first person in Mongolia to restore the original text of the SECRET HISTORY OF THE MONGOLS from the Chinese transcription.

Under the Japanese occupation of 1932–45, Hulun Buir and Butha were each made autonomous Mongolian provinces. Daurs, who were now considered Mongols, played the leading role in both provinces as Mongolian replaced Manchu and Chinese as the official language. In the civil war between the Chinese Communists and the Kuomintang that followed the end of WORLD WAR II in 1945, the Communists won Daur support by continuing the Japanese autonomy program. As elsewhere, however, the land reform and rural class struggle campaigns of 1946–48 created lasting bitterness within Daur communities.

In 1952 in Heilongjiang and in 1954 in Xinjiang, Daur nationality townships were set up, marking them as a separate nationality. In Inner Mongolia the question of separating the Daurs from the Mongols was more controversial, since it would deprive the Daurs of their leadership role among the Hulun Buir Mongols. Chinese ethnographers preferred a separate designation, however, and in September 1956 a Daur nationality township was created in Inner Mongolia. While the Inner Mongolian chairman ULANFU advocated setting up a Daur autonomous banner, many Daur officials demanded a larger autonomous prefecture covering all the territory from Hailar to Qiqihar, even though the Daurs would be only a small percentage of such a prefecture's population. In May 1957 Ulanfu publicly criticized this proposal, and in August 1958 the Chinese government created a Morin Dawa Daur Autonomous County in the Butha heartland, now in northeastern Inner Mongolia. Eventually, a total of seven small Daur nationality townships were established in Qiqihar, Hulun Buir, Xinjiang, and elsewhere.

In the 1910s and 1920s Qin Tongpu experimented with a Cyrillic script and Merse with a new Latin script. In 1957–58 a Daur committee designed a Cyrillic script based on the Qiqihar Daur dialect, but this was canceled in 1958 due to the growing SINO-SOVIET SPLIT. In 1983 Daur scholars introduced a new Latin script based on Morin Dawa's Butha dialect and the Chinese *pinyin* Latinization scheme. Daurs mostly still use Chinese or Mongolian for writing, however.

Further reading: David Aberle, *Chahar and Dagor Mongol Bureaucratic Administration* (New Haven, Conn.: HRAF Press, 1953); Caroline Humphrey, *Shamans and Elders: Experience, Knowledge, and Power among the Daur Mongols* (Oxford: Oxford University Press, 1996); G. Kara, *Daurica in Cyrillic Script* (Budapest: MTA Altajisztikai Kutatócsoport, 1995); Samuel E. Martin, *Dagur Mongolian Grammar, Texts, and Lexicon* (Bloomington: Indiana University, 1960); Herbert Harold Vreeland III, *Mongol Community and Kinship Structure* (New Haven, Conn.: HRAF Press, 1957).

Dauriia Station Movement The pan-Mongolist movement of Dauriia Station in 1919 briefly brought together the Cossack forces of the half-Buriat Mongol commander Grigorii Semënov, Inner Mongolian bandits still unreconciled to the Chinese 1911 revolution, earnest Buriat and Daur nationalists, and Japanese advisers. It ended in failure, but it bequeathed a term and a legacy to later Soviet demonology.

After the Bolshevik seizure of power in Russia, Japan's army-dominated Terauchi cabinet nurtured anti-Communist volunteer detachments under Ataman (Cossack commander) Grigorii M. Semënov (1890–1945). Tokyo supported Semënov not only against Bolsheviks but also against more pro-American White (anti-Communist)

Russian forces in Siberia. From August 1918 Semënov controlled the railway lines east of Lake Baikal through HULUN BUIR into Manchuria.

Among the troops joining Semënov's forces were about 800 men under Duke Fushengge (Chinese, Fuxing'a) from Baarin (Bairin) banner. Fushengge was the former chief of staff for Babujab (1870–1916), an Inner Mongolian bandit from Monggoljin (Fuxin) banner who had fought successively for Japan, for independent Mongolia, and for the Chinese monarchist party. By summer 1918 Semënov was toying with the idea of a pan-Mongolian state and on Fushengge's advice brought in the Neichi (Neisse) Gegeen, an INCARNATE LAMA of Guisui (modern HÖHHOT), as a prestigious figurehead. The Japanese role in instigating this pan-Mongolist plan, while often assumed, is unclear.

In November 1918 Semënov convened a Buriat National Duma in Verkhneudinsk (modern ULAN-UDE). The Buriats, through their landsmen in Khüriye (modern ULAANBAATAR), tried to contact the theocratic government of Outer Mongolia but got no firm answer. On January 12–14, 1919, Semënov with his chief Japanese adviser, Kuroki Tikanori, convened delegates from the Buriats, Hulun Buir, and Inner Mongolia at Dauriia Station, a Russian railway just over the border from Hulun Buir and China. From February 25 to March 6, 1919, the Dauriia delegates joined the Buriat National Duma in Chita under the chairmanship of Neichi Gegeen and inaugurated a new pan-Mongolian government with Neichi Gegeen as head of state, the Buriat Dashi Sampilon (d. 1937) as finance minister, the Hulun Buir Daur Lingsheng (1889–1936, a.k.a. Fuxiang) as war minister, and ELBEK-DORZHI RINCHINO as adviser. Semënov was granted the title of prince. The new government sent a three-man delegation to the Paris Peace Conference via Tokyo in late April.

By this time, however, Japan's military-dominated Terauchi cabinet had been replaced by the civilian Hara Kei cabinet. Hoping to withdraw from the Siberian adventure, the new cabinet refused to allow the delegation to go to Paris and demanded that Japanese officers cease assisting the pan-Mongolist venture. Meanwhile, the Outer Mongolian government, while feigning sympathy, began seeking Chinese help against the movement.

Stymied in their hopes for recognition, the Buriat nationalists deserted. By July Fushengge began entertaining emissaries from China's monarchist party. Before he could act Semënov, the Neichi Gegeen, and other Inner Mongolian troops attacked and killed Fushengge in September. The movement broke up, and in December Neichi Gegeen with 400 Mongols was transferred to Verkhneudinsk. In January 1920 this force was to be thrown against the advancing Bolshevik armies, but Neichi Gegeen led a mutiny against the Russian officers and fled to Mongolia, occupied since September 1919 by Chinese troops. The Chinese at the KYAKHTA border town murdered Neichi Gegeen and his top confederates at a banquet before sending the ordinary fighters on to reinforce the Chinese garrison in Khüriye.

While the Dauriia Station Movement was a complete failure, it established the image of pan-Mongolism and Lamaist theocracy as tools of Japanese imperialism that Soviet policy makers repeatedly invoked from 1925 on. In this way it paved the way for the GREAT PURGE and the annihilation of Buddhism (*see* BUDDHISM, CAMPAIGN AGAINST).

See also REVOCATION OF AUTONOMY; THEOCRATIC PERIOD.

Further reading: Uradyn E. Bulag and Caroline Humphrey, "Some Diverse Representations of the Pan-Mongolian Movement in Dauria," *Inner Asia: Occasional Papers of the Mongolia and Inner Asia Studies Unit* 1.1 (1996): 1–23.

Dawor *See* DAUR LANGUAGE AND PEOPLE.

Dayan Khan, Batu-Möngke (Batmönkh, Dayun Khan) (b. 1475?, r. 1480?–1517?) *Khan who united the Mongols under Chinggisid supremacy in the northern Yuan dynasty (1368–1634)*

About 1480 a kidnapped boy said to be seven years old was presented to MANDUKHAI, SECHEN KHATUN, regent and empress of the late khan Manduul (1473?–79), with the claim that he was the son of Manduul's former Chinggisid *jinong* (viceroy), Bolkhu (fl. 1470–79). The khan and the *jinong* had previously come to blows, and Bayan-Möngke had fled and been murdered. Manduul's TAISHI (regent), Ismayil, had then taken in Bolkhu's wife Shiker. The kidnapper's story, recounted in the Mongolian chronicles, was that, afraid for his life, Shiker had given her only child, Batu-Möngke, to a commoner family to nurse and that the kidnappers had seized the boy from them to bring him back to court. The truth of this tale is impossible to assess.

Mandukhai, then 33, married the boy and had him crowned the Great Khan of the Great Yuan at the Eshi Khatun (First Lady) shrine (that of SORQAQTANI BEKI) kept by the CHAKHAR. Batu-Möngke's reign title, Dayan Khan, was derived either from *dayan,* "all, whole," or from *Dayun,* "Great Yuan" (from *dai ön*). She then led the Mongol armies in 1483 against Ismayil Taishi, who fled in defeat to Hami, where he was killed (c. 1486). Shiker was brought back, unwillingly, to the Mongols and given the title *taikhu* (empress dowager). Around that time, Mandukhai also broke the power of the OIRATS.

From 1480 raids on China had been virtually constant, and under Dayan Khan they reached a new level of organization. Dayan Khan sent "tribute" missions to China from 1488 to 1498, but as a mature ruler he had no interest in joining the Ming's TRIBUTE SYSTEM. Dayan Khan allied with Tölöögen and his son Khooshai, chief of the Monggoljin clan in ORDOS. In 1500 he and Man-

dukhai moved into Ordos to the EIGHT WHITE YURTS, or shrine of Chinggis Khan, and launched a massive raid on Ningxia. Barely escaping an unexpectedly vigorous Chinese counterattack the next year, however, Dayan Khan relocated to the KHERLEN RIVER, yet large-scale raids all along the frontier continued through 1507.

While Dayan Khan kept the support of the Monggoljin in Ordos, Iburai Taishi, probably a Uighur, and Mandulai ("the Ordos elder") soon dominated the area. In 1508 a delegation of western Inner Mongolia's three *tümens* (Ordos, TÜMED, and Yüngshiyebü), discontented with Iburai's power, invited Dayan Khan to rule them. Dayan Khan dispatched to them his second and third sons, Ulus-Baikhu (often given as Ulus-Bolod) and Barsu-Bolod Sain-Alag (d. 1521). As Ulus-Baikhu was being enthroned as *jinong,* he was killed in a riot over a horse. Barsu-Bolod escaped, and Dayan Khan led his Three Eastern Tümens (Chakhar, KHALKHA, and Uriyangkhan) with the KHORCHIN and Abagha to attack the Three Western Tümens. Although first defeated at Türgen Stream (probably in present-day Tümed territory), in 1510 Dayan Khan's army crushed the Three Western Tümens at Dalan-Terigün (modern Yin Shan Mountains). Mandulai was killed, and Iburai fled to Kökenuur, where he remained active to 1533. Rejecting advice to enslave the Three Western Tümens, Dayan Khan had Barsu-Bolod enthroned as *jinong* in 1513. All his soldiers at Dalan-Terigün he made DARQAN (exempt from imposts).

From 1513 raids on China recommenced. Dayan Khan built forts in the Xuanfu (modern Xuanhua) and Datong areas and stationed 15,000 cavalry on Ming territory. Invasions in 1514 and 1517 involved up to 70,000 cavalry.

Although beginning as a puppet Chinggisid like many others, Dayan Khan became one of Mongolia's most important rulers. He and Mandukhai eliminated Oirat power and abolished the TAISHI system, making him the first Chinggisid khan in a century actually to rule. His victory at Dalan-Terigün reunified the Mongols and solidified their corporate identity as a Chinggisid people, distinct from the Oirats. Finally, his decision not to enslave the Three Western Tümens but to divide the Six Tümens as fiefs for his sons created a decentralized system of BORJIGID clan rule that secured domestic peace and outward expansion for a century.

See also NORTHERN YUAN DYNASTY.

Further reading: Hidehiro Okada, "Dayan Khan in the Battle of Dalan Terigün," in *Gedanke und Wirkung: Festschrift zum 90. Geburtstag von Nikolaus Poppe,* ed. Walther Heissig and Klaus Sagaster (Wiesbaden: Otto Harrassowitz, 1989), 262–270; Hidehiro Okada, "Life of Dayan Qaghan," *Acta Asiatica: Bulletin of the Institute of Eastern Culture* 11 (1966); 46–55; Wada Sei, "A Study of Dayan Khan," *Memoirs of the Research Department of the Toyo Bunko* 19 (1960); 1–42.

decimal organization The decimal organization, in which households were grouped in 10s, 100s, and 1,000s, was a traditional Inner Asian method of social and military organization. From the first XIONGNU (Hun) Empire founded in 209 B.C.E., nomadic states grouped their peoples in 10s. The well-documented decimal organization of North China's JIN DYNASTY (1115–1234), founded by the Jurchen people of Manchuria, was based on a 300-household "clan" (*mouke*). A hundred households in each "clan" supplied regular soldiers, and 200 supplied auxiliary soldiers. Ten "clans" made up a "thousand" (*meng'an*). In Mongolia, perhaps under Jin influence, the KEREYID Khanate also divided its people into 1,000s. CHINGGIS KHAN in turn first divided his people into 100s and 1,000s in 1204, a year after conquering the Kereyid.

After his coronation in 1206 Chinggis Khan repartitioned all his Mongol subjects into a decimal organization. The smallest group was a unit of 10 households (*harban*). Ten 10s made 100 (*ja'un*), and ten 100s made 1,000 (*mingghan*). Each unit had its own head, or chief (*darugha*). Chiliarchs, or heads of a thousand, were appointed directly by Chinggis Khan and later participated in the election of his successors at the great QURIL-TAI assemblies, but centurions, or heads of 100s, and decurions, or heads of 10, were appointed by their superiors and had no political role. Chiefs at each level received an appropriate PAIZA, or badge of rank. Normally, the chiliarchs passed their offices to one of their sons, although the emperor retained complete freedom to dismiss or replace them. Centurions and decurions were not supposed to be hereditary.

Some 1,000s, but not all, were organized into 10,000 (*tümen*). The *SECRET HISTORY OF THE MONGOLS* states that in 1206 Chinggis Khan had 95 thousands and appointed three commanders of *tümen*: BO'ORCHU on the right wing, MUQALI on the left, and Naya'a of the Baarin in the center. (The myriarchy of Naya'a is unconfirmed elsewhere, however.) Peng Daya, a Chinese envoy, mentions eight myriarchs among the Mongols under ÖGEDEI KHAN (1229–41). RASHID-UD-DIN FAZL-ULLAH numbers Chinggis Khan's people as 129 thousands and mentions *tümen*s but does not list them. In any case, many 1,000s were assigned to members of the imperial family and did not come under any *tümen*. Later, as the number of troops expanded and sedentary soldiers were levied, the number of myriarchs exploded both among the Mongol commanders and among the sedentary peoples.

During peacetime the chiefs of 1,000s were lords of the households under them. They governed the use of the pasture lands and received from their subjects tribute of DAIRY PRODUCTS (particularly KOUMISS) and meat animals. For campaigns or garrison duty the emperor or prince estimated the number of soldiers needed and asked for a certain ratio of the army's total strength, for example, two of 10. In that case each decurion, or chief of 10, would select two adult men and forward them to the rendezvous point. Knowing the total number of 1,000s under his command, the ruler could mobilize troops of any number desired without the need for elaborate recordkeeping. Natural increase and decrease of households and resources would eventually wreck havoc on such a system, and Ögedei Khan required units that fell below the minimum of households be replenished by those from a different wing and that every owner of 100 sheep contribute one for the poor of his unit.

Outside observers of the Mongol conquest all found this system a fascinating aspect of Chinggis Khan's law-giving activity. Modern observers have often seen in this system an attempt to shatter traditional tribal allegiances and replace them with a rational system of total conscription. Such a view seems inaccurate, however. As noted above, chiliarchs were hereditary and in peacetime had the same privileges as the clan chiefs of old. Many 1,000s, in fact, were explicitly formed out of single clans or traditional clan segments, and exact numbers were not strictly required. Records of the Mongol YUAN DYNASTY show that units were classified as being 30 percent, 50 percent, and 70 percent of nominal strength. Thus, the decimal organization did not break up natural units of pastoral life; instead, it was adjusted to fit them. The point of the decimal organization lay in allowing troop mobilization without records and enforcing a relatively equal military burden among the tribes, clans, and camps.

As the Mongols developed a more sophisticated system of conscription and taxation, the sedentary people were also numbered and divided into 10s, 100s, 1,000s, and 10,000s. Here again, though, there was no attempt to enforce rigid exactness of numbers. In Tibet, for example, the 11 *tümen*s ranged in size from 5,850 to 500 households! The resulting system was quite similar to that of the Jin dynasty. In the Mongol Yuan dynasty in China, at least, only a minority of subject households were put in the military registers, and even among those, one or two auxiliary households would assist a single regular household in providing one soldier liable for active duty. The sedentary decimal units joined the Mongol units as a military caste, subject to their own officers in peace and war. Again natural demographic change made it inevitable that in a few generations some units would have too few adult men and others too many. Constant reregistration was thus necessary to maintain an effective use of manpower. Up to about 1290 this occurred but afterward lapsed. The registration of sedentary *tümen*s in the IL-KHANATE of Iran and the GOLDEN HORDE in Eastern Europe seems to be similar, although less is known of it.

The traditional decimal organization with the division into two wings was retained even into the 16th century in the Crimean khanate, a splinter state of the East European Golden Horde. Among the Mongols of the NORTHERN YUAN DYNASTY (1368–1634) in Mongolia itself, only the term *tümen* survived, and in a way that had no numerical meaning at all. The SIX TÜMENS into which the Mongols were divided in the 16th century were each composed of 10 or so OTOGs (camp districts), which were themselves named after clans. There is, however, no mention whatsoever of a census.

The Manchu QING DYNASTY (1636–1912) imposed on the Mongols their banner militia system, which retained traces of the Inner Asian decimal tradition. This banner system provided for a triennial census as well, although the real strength of the units diverged from the paper strength. This final form of the Inner Asia decimal organization was abolished only in the 20th century.

See also BANNERS; CENSUS IN THE MONGOL EMPIRE; SUM.

decollectivization

decollectivization The breakup of the collectives in Mongolia, while not initiated or even desired by the herders, proceeded swiftly and relatively efficiently.

INITIAL EXPERIMENTS

By 1989 Mongolian herders had been herding collectively for 30 years, specializing in one form of animal and receiving salaries and pensions, with small bonuses for exceeding production quotas. Most had become comfortable with a system that, although it offered little incentive for high productivity, supplied many free services, both social and herding related, and virtually eliminated risk. Moreover, allowances of private animals amounted to about 20 percent of collectives' total herd. From 1986 to 1989, during the era of Soviet-inspired perestroika (restructuring), the Mongolian government changed the basic payment system to offer greater incentives and allowed the herders a variety of contract and lease arrangements to increase productivity. In leases the herder leased the animals, paying a fee and charges for use of once-free herding-related services: hay, corrals, veterinary services, and transportation. In return the herders received payment for meeting production targets of products and young and could keep excess offspring. (Shortfalls were made up by the herders' private herds.) By 1990 private animals reached 32 percent of all livestock.

DECOLLECTIVIZATION POLICY

In September 1990 the new democratically elected government, headed by Prime Minister D. Byambasüren (b. 1942), embarked on a reform plan emphasizing PRIVATIZATION. In January 1991, while approving price changes that worsened the terms of trade for herders and boosted meat targets, the government put all herders on the lease system for a period of five years. Meanwhile, some proposed immediate and full decollectivization as China had done in Inner Mongolia in 1983, while the *negdel* leadership, supported at least passively by most herders, sought to maintain the *negdel* structure but improve the terms of trade and perhaps allow a free market in animal goods.

After announcing the overall privatization plan in May, the government fine-tuned its application to the collectives. In late 1991 every Mongolian received vouchers redeemable for state and collective property, 30 percent in pink vouchers for "small privatization" and 70 percent in blue vouchers for "large privatization." While privatization legislation set guidelines for how to use the vouchers, *negdel*s were allowed, in practice, to make their own decisions. Most *negdel*s conducted only "small privatization" in late 1991, dividing up 30 percent of the animals and winter-spring shelters and other dispersed infrastructure. Animals were divided to members by family size, with extra shares for length of service in the *negdel* weighted by various formulas. Nonherding rural residents were expected to receive shares of fixed assets only, but some *negdel*s gave them animals as well. The other 70 percent of the collective stock was held by a shareholding company run by the old *negdel* leaders, which funded salaries and pensions from anticipated profits, supplied services (for fees), and organized marketing. Herders exchanged their blue vouchers for shares in this shareholding company and continued the leasing operation they had been following since 1991 with the company's animals. After five years or so the herders were expected to be ready for full privatization, and the government, over the objection of the *negdel* leaders, guaranteed that herders who so wished could leave the company, not with their blue vouchers but with their share of livestock.

RESULTS OF DECOLLECTIVIZATION

In fact, however, privatization proceeded much more rapidly than planned. In the general economic crisis the shareholding companies, despite being run by the same people who had run the *negdel*s, proved generally unable to meet their traditional obligations. The company itself was blamed for these problems, and most were dissolved by their shareholders after a year. The total number of livestock in private hands reached 54.9 percent in 1991, 70.4 percent in 1992, and 89.6 percent in 1993. By 1995 the companies had essentially disappeared except for a few former state farms specializing in one pastoral cash crop. In place of the old companies many herders set up voluntary cooperatives (*khorshoo*) to handle marketing and bulk purchasing of consumer goods.

The new private livestock economy differed in several ways from the old *negdel*s. Herders went back to the precollectivization pattern of herding a mix of stock and cooperating in *khot ails*, or camps. The initial distribution of livestock was based almost entirely on family size and age, and livestock ownership has not, as many expected, become concentrated in a small class of entrepreneurial herders. The number of herding households with more than 200 head of stock rose from 12.3 percent in 1995 to 14.5 percent in 2000, yet the number of households with fewer than 30 head simultaneously decreased from 33 percent to 26.7 percent. With the removal of the *negdel* administration and many town and city residents moving back to the countryside, there was considerable confusion and conflict over usufruct rights to favored camping spots. (The pastures are held in common by all *SUM*, or district, residents.) Where herders had been moved from traditional family routes under the *negdels*, they now moved back to strengthen their old family claims.

Decollectivization in Mongolia took place simultaneously with a serious bout of inflation and a breakdown in urban-rural trade. As a result herders held on to animals rather than marketing them. The number of livestock slaughtered for consumption dropped sharply from 1992 to 1995, while the total number soared from 25.2 million head in 1993 to 33.5 in 1999. By 1998 the currency had stabilized, and a new private network that had replaced the old state companies and marketing levels first reached and then in 1999 exceeded 1990–92 levels.

Private livestock herding has proved, however, weak in infrastructure. Hay mowing, fodder crops, and wells have not been maintained. Traditional herding skills were replaced under the *negdels* by professional livestock management, which has now disappeared. Survival rates of young animals decreased from 94.4 percent in 1990 to 90.5 percent in 1999. The tendency of new and less skilled herders to hug settlements or natural water sources has increased pasture degradation. The vulnerability of these large herds was highlighted by the *ZUD* (winter disasters) of 1999–2000 and 2000–01, which reduced the livestock to 26.1 million head by late 2001 and cut survival rates of young animals in 2000 to 83.5 percent. International aid and government relief prevented a humanitarian catastrophe, but the future success of private herding appears to depend on both a revival of traditional herding skills and mobility and infrastructural investment by local *sum* (district) governments.

See also ANIMAL HUSBANDRY AND NOMADISM; COLLECTIVIZATION AND COLLECTIVE HERDING; MONGOLIA, STATE OF.

Further reading: Melvyn C. Goldstein and Cynthia M. Beall, *Changing World of Mongolia's Nomads* (Berkeley: University of California Press, 1994).

deer stones *See* ELK STONES.

Demchungdongrub, Prince (De Wang, Prince Teh) (1902–1962) *Conservative prince of the high steppe who became the leader of the Inner Mongolian autonomous movement under the Japanese*
Born in Sönid Right Banner (modern Sonid Youqi), Demchugdongrub was a prince in SHILIIN GOL, the most traditional and conservative Inner Mongolian league. His father died just before his birth, and in 1919 Prince De (a respectful abbreviation of Demchugdongrub) attained his majority and was enthroned as prince.

Despite China's 1911 revolution, the young prince was a QING DYNASTY (1636–1912) loyalist, keeping his queue, or braided ponytail, and opposing the Chinese-educated nationalist Mongols. After the victory of the Chinese Nationalist Party in 1928, he opposed the administrative reforms of the KHARACHIN Mongol politician Wu Heling (Ünenbayan b. 1896).

By 1933 the Japanese had occupied Manchuria, including eastern Inner Mongolia. From October 1933 Prince De, based at Batukhaalga (Bailingmiao), led a movement of China's remaining Inner Mongolian BANNERS to demand autonomy from China's Nationalist government. In 1934 China's ruler, Chiang Kai-shek, agreed to form a Mongol Political Council, but Japanese infiltration of the strategic CHAKHAR area and subversion from local Chinese warlords opposed to any autonomy paralyzed the council.

With autonomy thwarted, Prince De used Japanese assistance to create first a Mongol army and then a military government in February 1936. Using units only nominally under Prince De's control, Japanese advisers then provoked the army into a losing battle with Fu Zuoyi in September–November 1936, which greatly damaged the prince's prestige. The Japanese invasion of North China of August 1937, however, drove Fu Zuoyi west and delivered most of central and western Inner Mongolia to Prince De's government. By this time he favored the educated "Young Mongol" nationalists.

In October 1937 Prince De set up an autonomous government in HÖHHOT, yet by September 1939 the chief Japanese adviser, Kanai Shoji, forced his nationalist government into a merger with two Chinese collaborationist regimes to form the Mongol Border (*Mengjiang*) government, with its capital in Zhangjiakou (Kalgan). Only with the transfer of Kanai Shoji did Prince De gain back more than nominal authority in the government, renamed the Mongol Autonomous State, in August 1941. Wearied by constant political struggles, Prince De redirected his attention to educational, publishing, and economic reforms among the Mongols.

During the Soviet-Mongolian invasion of Japanese-occupied Inner Mongolia in August 1945, De Wang fled to Beijing. His four children in Sönid Right Banner near the frontier surrendered to the Soviet-Mongolian forces and were taken to Mongolia and enrolled in schools. While the Chinese Nationalists did not treat him as a collaborator, De Wang remained semiretired. In January 1949, however, he attempted again to secure Mongol autonomy in far western ALASHAN, one of the few regions not under the advancing Chinese Communists. In the end he fled the Communist advance and crossed over the border to independent Mongolia in December but was arrested and extradited to China on September 18, 1950. At the same time his children in Mongolia were arrested or sentenced to internal exile.

Sentenced by the new Chinese government as a counterrevolutionary, Demchugdongrub did hard labor in the Fushun coal mines until his release on April 9, 1963. He died on May 23, 1966, on the eve of the Cultural Revolution.

Reviled by Chinese, Russian, and Mongolian Communists, Prince De is still respected by most INNER MONGOLIANS. Very stubborn by nature and conscious of his privileges as a prince, he transmuted this will and class feeling into an insistence on the Mongols' right to be treated as equals by neighboring powers.

See also JAPAN AND THE MODERN MONGOLS.

Further reading: Sechin Jagchid, *The Last Mongol Prince: The Life and Times of Demchugdongrub, 1902–1966* (Bellingham: Western Washington University Press, 1999).

Demid, Gelegdorjiin   *See* DEMID, MARSHAL.

Demid, Marshal (Gelegdorjiin Demid) (1900–1937)
Mongolia's commander in chief during the early buildup against Japan

Demid was born in Setsen Zasag banner (modern Ikhtamir Sum, North Khangai), and in addition to herding livestock he followed his father as a carpenter and caravaneer. In 1921 he volunteered for the People's Party's partisan army and in 1922 joined the second class of Mongolia's fledgling military academy. After serving as a course instructor in cavalry and as a company captain for three years, in 1926 he entered the Red Army military school in Tver'. In 1929 he became director and commissar of Mongolia's military academy. In March 1930, during the Eighth Party Congress at the height of the LEFTIST PERIOD, he was appointed Mongolia's commander in chief. With the NEW TURN POLICY in June 1932, Commander in Chief Demid became one of Mongolia's top leaders. In 1936 he was made marshal. Demid's program for the military emphasized technological modernization. From 1930 to 1936 the number of armored cars increased 20 times, trucks 17 times, airplanes 4 times, machine guns 12 times, and artillery 6 times. While opposed to excessive reliance of Soviet advisers, Demid opposed Prime Minister Gendün's subordination of the party to the government and by late 1935 advocated inviting Soviet troops into Mongolia. He survived Gendün's downfall but on August 22, 1937, died of food poisoning while on a train to Moscow. Soon after his death he was denounced as a Japanese spy.

See also ARMED FORCES OF MONGOLIA; REVOLUTIONARY PERIOD.

1990 Democratic Revolution
The 1990 democratic revolution bloodlessly overthrew 70 years of one-party rule and ideological conformity and created a new political system based on pluralism, respect for human rights, and competitive multiparty elections. PRIVATIZATION, DECOLLECTIVIZATION, and market economy followed. Culturally, a new period of national assertiveness, religious renaissance, and pop culture began.

ORIGINS OF THE MOVEMENT

The 1990 revolution, like the 1921 REVOLUTION, was overwhelmingly an affair of young city dwellers. The movement leaders were virtually all born between 1954 and 1964. While a number had rural backgrounds, most had some training in other Soviet-bloc countries and worked in white-collar nonmanagerial positions: journalists, lecturers, teachers, and researchers in fields such as economics, philosophy, biology, and physics. While the movement coincided with a religious revival, the leaders were strongly secular.

Another crucial part of the revolution was older reformers who stayed within the Mongolian People's Revolutionary Party (MPRP). By arguing against repressive measures and taking over the leadership of the ruling party when the old guard resigned, they were essential to the peaceful success of the revolution. These reformist leaders, such as P. Ochirbat (b. 1942), the Buriat D. Byambasüren (b. 1942), and the Kazakh union chief Q. Zardykhan (b. 1940), were generally Moscow educated. All eventually broke with the MPRP, but only after the establishment of the multiparty system.

The democratic movement had no living connection with the pre-1940 resistance and unlike democratic movements elsewhere in the Soviet bloc had no support from an emigre population. The movement leaders were animated by anger at the compulsory obeisance to Soviet Russian models and sorrow and shame at the regime's betrayal of Mongolia's past. They were frustrated with Mongolia's backwardness and felt stifled by conformist and careerist thinking. Most saw the 1921 revolutionaries as basically good men whose cause had been slowly twisted by dogmatic Soviet advisers. Rising living standards and the pervasive regime propaganda about Mongolia's glorious achievements ironically created a revolution of rising expectations, which was amplified by East Asian economic successes and the reforms in China.

The seeds of the democratic revolution were planted by the Soviet ruler Mikhail Gorbachev's policies of glasnost' (openness, Mongolian, *il tod*) and perestroika (restructuring, Mongolian, *öörchlön shinechlelt*) from 1985 on. In Mongolia openness allowed increased criticism of the legacy of YUMJAAGIIN TSEDENBAL, Mongolia's ruler from 1952 to 1984. Politicians, academics, and ordinary citizens who had been exiled or disgraced in that period were exonerated. Meanwhile, in Eastern Europe, Mongolian students saw firsthand the movements against Soviet control that culminated in the electoral victory of Poland's opposition union Solidarity, the fall of the Berlin Wall on November 9, 1989, and the execution of Romania's Communist ruler Nicolae Ceaucescu on December 25.

In 1988–89 several semilegal or underground student and youth organizations pushed the bounds of acceptable "openness." The biophysicist B. Batbayar (b. 1954) began circulating his *Büü mart! Martwal sönönö* (Don't forget! If you forget you perish) under the pseudonym "Baabar." The work criticized Russian expansionism in Mongolia, meditated on the contrast of utopian promises and bloody reality in the French and Russian revolutions, and reevaluated Mongolian history, highlighting the Tsedenbal era's cronyism, ecological disasters, Russification, and moral crisis. With the news of Eastern European events, a group of students at the Mongolian National University began discussing a new National Progress Party. Finally, on December 2–3, 1989, at a Conference of Young Creative Artists certain members of the above groups, encountering a tentative approval of the MPRP leaders attending, founded the Mongolian Democratic Association (MDA) with the ostensible aim of furthering perestroika. The leader was SANJAASÜRENGIIN ZORIG.

DEMONSTRATIONS

The new association leaders were worried about a crackdown and rushed to develop support. On December 10, International Human Rights Day, a date they hoped would give the government pause before cracking down, they held an outdoor meeting that gathered 300 people, demanding a constitutional amendment ending the MPRP's one-party rule (required under the 1960 CONSTITUTION), respect for human rights, a new election for the Great People's Khural, a free press, abolition of special privileges for government leaders, market socialism, and an investigation of the past errors and crimes of the Mongolian leaders and the MPRP. To avoid a violent reaction, the movement leaders continued to affirm socialism (albeit in its "market" form), doffing their hats at one point in memorial to Lenin and strictly prohibiting personal ridicule of serving leaders. The demonstrators sang as their anthem "Song of the Bell" (*Khonkhny duu*), whose lyrics by S. Tsogtsaikhan of the folk-rock band Soyol Erdene (Culture Jewel) spoke of an awakening of the Mongolian people.

In responding to the demonstrations the Mongolian leadership was paralyzed by Moscow's indecisive attitude and demands from figures in the party itself, such as Deputy Premier Byambasüren, for much swifter reform. From December to February demonstrations increased in size and frequency, despite symbolic concessions from the government, such as the removal of the Stalin statue in front of the State Library on February 22, 1990. On Sunday, March 4, 100,000 persons gathered in front of Victory Cinema before marching to Sükhebaatur Square in front of the government palace to demand that a special congress of the MPRP be called to dismiss the current leadership, separate the party and government, and elect a new multiparty Provisional People's Assembly.

By this time the movement had crystallized into three groups, all led by academics. The MDA had reached 30,000 members by January 21 and held its first congress on February 18, demanding the replacement of the whole party and government leadership and a cessation of exploitative MINING contracts with the Soviet Union. Meanwhile, the Democratic Socialist Association, formed around "Baabar" (B. Batbayar) on January 22, and the New Progressive Association (NPA) was organized on February 16. On February 24 the Mongolian Student Association (MSA) convened the three associations, which issued a common communiqué and began cooperating. These three associations with the MSA itself became for two months the four "democratic forces." In March the three associations formed parties: the Mongolian Democratic Party, the Social Democratic Party, and the National Progress Party, respectively. The parties soon each had their own newspapers, although paper shortages kept publication irregular. The differences among the organizations were mostly of tone and social circle, with the rather more academic and moderate Democratic Socialists contrasting with the more populist and aggressive Democratic Association.

HUNGER STRIKES

On March 7, after the MPRP Politburo member Ts. Namsrai rejected the demand for resignation and a new leadership, 10 Democratic Association members began a hunger strike in Sükhebaatar Square. Over the next two days prodemocracy demonstrations spread to the provinces, while loyalist organizations, too, began to organize to "defend our party" (i.e., the MPRP) and to oppose the democratic movement. The top MPRP leadership, however, had no stomach for the mass repression that would be necessary to crush the democratic movement now, particularly as support for such a move could be expected only from China, not Russia. Shrewdly gambling that the MPRP still had the support of the majority, the party's first secretary, JAMBYN BATMÖNKH, and his colleagues sacrificed their careers to refashion the MPRP as a democratic party.

In roundtable discussions the two sides came to a face-saving compromise. While not agreeing to an immediate resignation of either the Politburo or the Great People's Khural, the question of a totally new leadership would be presented to upcoming party and state congresses, and the hunger strike was called off. Batmönkh publicly announced the compromise in a radio and television address on the evening of March 9. On March 12–14 at the plenary meeting of the MPRP Central Committee, the entire MPRP Politburo resigned, the Tsedenbal legacy was denounced, and multiparty democracy accepted. On March 21–23 the Great People's Khural replaced the old legislative and government leaders. A draft law legalizing multiple parties was introduced on April 1.

Despite these agreements the democratic coalition, formalized on April 15, still demanded a Provisional People's Assembly and an immediate separation of party and government. While the government vainly requested an end to demonstrations, demonstrators and Government Palace guards at Sükhebaatur Square almost came to blows on April 26, until Zorig calmed the crowd. Cartoons ridiculing the new leaders appeared, while on April 28 the government passed a law authorizing force to disperse unlawful demonstrations. A day later the KHÖWS-GÖL PROVINCE government arrested Democratic Party organizers, and a new hunger strike began in Möron (Khöwsgöl's capital). On May 4 this new crisis, too, was resolved, as the speaker of the Great People's Khural voided the Khöwsgöl arrests while defending the limits on demonstrations as consistent with human rights. Instead of a Provisional Assembly, a Little State Khural would be directly elected by proportional representation.

THE CAMPAIGN

On May 10 the long-awaited Great People's Khural met and amended the 1960 Constitution to prepare for multiparty elections to its next session and to the Little State Khural. Parties registered, and on May 15 a 75-day campaign season began, with the election commission chaired by Mongolia's cosmonaut J. Gürragchaa. The challenge for the democratic parties in facing the MPRP's institutional advantages was made clear by the official membership data presented at party registration: Democratic Party, 7,200; Social Democrats, 2,900; National Progress Party, 1,800; MPRP, 94,000. Smaller parties representing single-issue agendas, such as ecology or those in the private economy, also existed. Public organizations such as the Women's Association and the MONGOLIAN REVOLUTIONARY YOUTH LEAGUE also registered as parties. Despite a pledge to swear off direct state subsidy, the MPRP's continuing vast financial resources gave it a colossal advantage. Financial assistance to the new parties was so meager that the National Progress Party donated its share to charity in protest.

In the pressure of the campaign, the Democratic Forces coalition broke down. On June 27 the Democratic Party decided unilaterally to boycott the campaign and was publicly denounced by both the Social Democrats and the National Progress Party. The MDA leader and hunger striker G. Boshigt (b. 1942) was expelled for opposing this policy, and he bitterly denounced his former comrades as "Stalinists." By pushing back the date of the election, summoning local officials to ULAANBAATAR to order them to cease obstructing opposition party activities, and inviting foreign observers, P. Ochirbat brought the Democrats back into the election, although the coalition remained ruptured.

On July 22–26 the election and the runoff were held. The MPRP won 51.74 percent of the vote, while the Democrats received 24.33 percent, the National Progress Party 5.95 percent, and the Social Democrats 5.52 percent. In the new Great People's Khural, elected in a first-past-the-post system, this resulted in 357 seats for the MPRP, 16 for the Democrats, five for the National Progress Party, and four for the Social Democrats. (There were 36 nonparty deputies and nine from the youth league.) In the proportional representation Little State Khural the MPRP took 31 seats, the Democrats 13, the National Progress Party three, and the Social Democrats three.

Despite its clear victory, the MPRP was not interested in retaining sole power. By 1990 the economy was already in trouble as gross domestic product sank from 10,546.8 million tögrögs in 1989 to 10,281.4 million in 1990 (in 1986 prices), while inflation, formerly unknown, reached 52.7 percent by 1991. The first conference of the Mongolian Unemployed Persons Association on August 9 underlined the importance of the gathering economic crisis. The crisis was linked to that of the whole Soviet bloc, but the Soviet Union, on the verge of disintegration itself, had neither the ability nor interest to assist Mongolia. In this context the MPRP delegates realized that securing aid from Western countries was essential and that some painful adjustments were in store. For both purposes it would be helpful to have the democratic forces associated with the government, rather than outside. Thus, while P. Ochirbat was elected president unopposed and D. Byambasüren prime minister, the vice presidency was reserved for one of the new parties. The victory of the Social Democrat R. Gonchigdorj (b. 1954) over the Democrat Zorig for the vice presidency further embittered Social Democrat–Democrat relations. D. Ganbold (b. 1957), economist and leader of the National Progress Party, and D. Dorligjaw (b. 1959) of the Democratic Party were brought in as deputy prime ministers.

THE NEW REGIME

The formation of the new multiparty government and legislature marked the stabilization of the 1990 Democratic Revolution. The 1992 CONSTITUTION institutionalized multiparty democracy, but the prime practical task was to manage Mongolia's ongoing economic crisis. By summer 1992, in a backlash against the hardships of the transition and scandals associated with what the MPRP portrayed as feckless young Democrat officials, the Mongolian electorate gave the MPRP 72 of 76 seats in the new legislature. The new MPRP deputies were largely provincial officials quite out of tune with the reformist wing of the MPRP. One of the officials who had resigned in March 1990, P. Jasrai (b. 1933), now returned as prime minister. In 1994 demonstrations in Sükhebaatur Square were banned. Even so, the 1990 revolution was irreversible, and the MPRP worked through democratic means until in 1996 it was voted out of office by a reformed Democratic Coalition. Religious, press, and associational freedoms won in 1990 remained intact.

Vital parts of these freedoms were the new associations that emerged from February 1990 to represent previously ignored social groups and points of view: the Believers' Association, the Free Labor Party (representing those in the private economy), the Green Party, the Association of Unemployed, and the Human Rights Association. Previously party-controlled institutions such as the Mongolian Trade Unions and the Mongolian Revolutionary Youth League, both of which had given facilities and assistance to the fledgling democratic movement, elected new independent leaders in March 1990. While these new or reformed organizations did not succeed as actors in the electoral process, they did place a strong stamp on the values and interests of the new democratic society.

See also MONGOLIA, STATE OF.

Further reading: Tom Ginsburg, "Nationalism, Elites, and Mongolia's Rapid Transformation," in *Mongolia in the Twentieth Century: Landlocked Cosmopolitan*, ed. Stephen Kotkin and Bruce A. Elleman (Armonk, N.Y.: M. E. Sharpe, 1999), 247–276; György Kara, "Baabar's 'Don't Forget!' Analysis of a Mongolian Social Democrat's Treatise, 1990," *Acta Orientalia* 46 (1992–93): 283–287.

Demotte *Shahnama* The earliest surviving masterpiece of Persian painting, the Demotte *Shahnama* was produced at the Mongol court late in the IL-KHANATE. First composed by Firdausi (d. 1020) of Tus in 1010, the great epic *Shahnama*, or *Book of Kings*, gives a legendary account of the historical dynasties of Iran. Ironically, the epic achieved great popularity with Iran's foreign rulers, including the Turkish Seljük dynasty, the Mongol Il-Khans, and the Turco-Mongol Timurids. In 1334–35, it underwent a major revision by Hamdullah Mustaufi Qazvini (b. 1281–82). The only known copy of the illustrated Demotte *Shahnam* survived more-or-less intact until shortly before World War I, when the French art dealer Georges Demotte cut out the illustrations for separate sale and discarded the rest. As reconstructed by art historians, the original manuscript contained about 280 folios with perhaps 120 illustrations, of which 58 survive. The illustrations focus on themes of royal legitimacy, death, and mourning, the fantastic, and the intrigues of women. While art historians agree that the illustrations allude to episodes from Mongol history along with their ostensible subjects from the *Shahnama*, there is no consensus on the exact episodes represented. The manuscript as a whole, clearly prepared for a learned court audience, indicates the high appreciation of Iranian culture and its fusion with Chinggisid legitimacy at the court of Abu-Sa'id Ba'atur Khan (1317–35) or his immediate successors.

Further reading: Oleg Grabar and Sheila Blair, *Epic Images and Contemporary History: The Illustrations of the Great Mongol Shahnama* (Chicago: University of Chicago Press, 1980); Abolala Soudavar, "The Saga of Abu-Sa'id Bahador Khan: The Abu Sa'idname," in *Court of the Il-*

Alexander killing the Habash monster, from the Demotte *Shahnama*. This scene may also be seen as an allusion to Chinggis Khan's soldiers meeting the jiaoduan beast (presumably a rhinoceros) near the Indus River. Yelü Chucai used this occurrence to convince Chinggis Khan to abandon his aim to return to Mongolia via India and Tibet. *(Opaque watercolor, gold, and ink on paper. 59.05 × 39.69 centimeters. Denman Waldo Ross Collection. Photograph© 2003 Museum of Fine Arts, Boston; 30.105)*

Khans, 1290–1340, ed. Julian Raby and Teresa Fitzherbert (Oxford: Oxford University Press, 1996), 95–218.

Derbet *See* DÖRBÖDS.

desertification and pasture degradation In the 20th century desertification has become a serious problem in Kalmykia and Inner Mongolia. In Buriatia desertification has not yet begun, although pasture degradation is severe. In independent Mongolia, while much of the pasture is mildly or moderately degraded, desertification is not yet a pressing issue.

Desertification in Inner Mongolia was early on recognized as a serious problem. By 1988 the total pasture had shrunk to 78.8 million hectares (195 million acres) from about 88 million hectares (217 million acres) in the 1960s. Of this the usable pasture was only 63.5 million hectares (157 million acres). By 1995 the situation was accelerating, with 15 percent of Inner Mongolia's land area desertified into bare gravel, salt flats, or dunes, and another 45 percent was estimated to be in the process of desertification. Droughts in 1999 and 2000 and a locust plague in 2002 covering Inner Mongolia from ULAANCHAB to KHINGGAN leagues exacerbated the crisis. In Mongol areas of Xinjiang and Russia's Buriatia and Kalmykia virtually all pastures are degraded, and in Kalmykia up to 80 percent of the territory is affected by desertification, with about half severely or very severely affected.

Pasture experts generally identify four main causes of desertification and pasture degradation: 1) plowing up of vulnerable pasture and use of heavy agricultural machinery, which lead to topsoil blowing off in the spring winds; 2) general overstocking of livestock, which increases the pressure on the forage and changes the vegetation from nutritious grass-legume assemblage to a less nutritious or even harmful sedge-forb assemblage; 3) a change in animal composition from large animals to sheep and goats, such as karakul sheep and CASHMERE goats, whose hooves are sharper and foraging more destructive; and 4) lowered mobility, which results in rapid degradation of overused pasture. (Since nonuse does not restore pasture as rapidly as overuse degrades it, the lower use of remote pasture does not compensate for the degradation of accessible pasture.)

This decrease in mobility is itself the result of several factors including: 1) the simple increase in rural human and livestock densities in Mongolia and especially Inner Mongolia; 2) forced sedentarization for political reasons in Buriatia and Kalmykia and parts of Inner Mongolia; 3) a shift to less hardy animals crossbred with high-yield European breeds, which need more well water and stall feeding; and 4) the tendency of poorer and less skilled herders to "hover" around small towns and fixed installations for ease, cultural benefits, and to minimize transportation costs when nomadizing or selling animal products.

While the problem has long been recognized, proposed solutions have usually predicated maintaining or even increasing the tendency to sedentary cash-based ranching and so have been either ineffective or even harmful. In Russia since 1990 the general economic crisis and the shift to subsistence livestock have at least temporarily reduced agricultural acreage and cut back overstocking of sheep. In China the government in 1984 took the important step of prohibiting further agricultural colonization but a year later ordered rangeland privatized and fenced while encouraging hay mowing and fodder crops. Intended to encourage responsible care of the pastures, these policies have sharply reduced mobility and actually increased degradation. Since 1999, as dust storms filled with Inner Mongolian topsoil have covered Beijing and even at times crossed the Pacific Ocean, the Chinese central government has intervened, ordering vast areas fenced off and planning to move as many as 650,000 "ecological emigrants," mostly Mongols, off the steppe to cities and stable farming areas.

See also ENVIRONMENTAL PROTECTION; FLORA.

Further reading: Chen Shan, "Inner Asian Grassland Degradation and Plant Transformation," in *Culture and Environment in Inner Asia,* vol. 1, *The Pastoral Economy and the Environment,* ed. Caroline Humphrey and David Sneath (Cambridge: White Horse Press, 1996), 111–123; E. Erdenijab, "An Economic Assessment of Pasture Degradation," in *Culture and Environment in Inner Asia,* vol. 1, *The Pastoral Economy and the Environment,* ed. Caroline Humphrey and David Sneath (Cambridge: White Horse Press, 1996), 189–197; Hong Jiang, "Culture, Ecology, and Nature's Changing Balance: Sandification on Mu Us Sandy Land, Inner Mongolia, China," in *Global Desertification: Do Humans Cause Deserts?* ed. J. F. Reynolds and D. M. Stafford Smith (Berlin: Dahlem University Press, 2002).

De Wang   *See* DEMCHUGDONGRUB, PRINCE.

didactic poetry   Traditional Mongolian literature contained several genres of didactic poetry, all very popular. Folk poetic genres including the "THREES OF THE WORLD"; proverbs of course have substantial didactic content, as do many songs. Sanskrit and Tibetan didactic verses translated by the 17th century included Nagarjuna's *A Drop of Nourishment for the People* (*Arad-i tejiyekhüi dusul*), and Sa-skya Pandita's TREASURY OF APHORISTIC JEWELS. These were both collections of aphoristic quatrains that made frequent reference to Indian fables, explained in commentaries. The *Oyun tülkhigür* (Turquoise key, often mistranslated as Key of wisdom), despite its attribution to CHINGGIS KHAN, is a collection of probably 17th-century Mongolian proverbs specifically inspired by these models. The verses are of irregular length and not consistently alliterated.

The literary form is much more refined in the genre of *surgal shilüg* (teaching verses, modern *surgaal shüleg*). The well-known *surgal* (teaching) of Ishidandzanwangjil (or Dandzanwangjil, 1854–1907), an INCARNATE LAMA and physician in ORDOS, exemplifies the classic form. Each verse, or stanza (*shilüg*, from Sanskrit *shloka*), contains four head-rhyming lines (*shad*, from Tibetan). Each line contains six trochees and a concluding dactyl, with a cesura after the first four trochees. Sinners excoriated include oppressive banner rulers, ungrateful children who devote themselves to romance, indulgent parents, uxorious husbands, ignorant lamas, those who kill animals for sacrifices, children who stint funerary expenses for deceased parents, opium smokers, drunkards, and so on. Arguments used to enforce good behavior include the pains of hell, repaying the grace of the Qing emperor, and, most insistently, the precious opportunity of human birth, which should be used to collect merit.

The composition among the Mongols of *surgal shilügs* in Tibetan began with the first Tibetan-language writers in Mongolia, such as the First Zaya Pandita of Khalkha Lubsang-Perenlai (1642–1715). The THIRD MERGEN GEGEEN LUBSANG-DAMBI-JALSAN (1717–66) is the first known author of extensive *surgal shilügs* in the MONGOLIAN LANGUAGE. His poems show several patterns of strict isosyllabic PROSODY. Some *surgals* were written in the seven-foot lines later used by Ishidandzanwangjil, while others were cast in seven-foot couplets. The concluding section of an untitled *surgal* used eight-feet lines, each describing a fault of a particular people and concluding with the exclamation *ichigüritei* (shameful!). DANZIN-RAB-JAI later copied this device for his poem *Ichige, ichige,* and it also (directly or indirectly) inspired the Kalmyk poet Boowan Badma (1880–1917).

Since it was directed to a simple audience, didactic poetry eschewed the involved style of the Sanskrit and Tibetan courtly poetry (*kavya* or *snyan-ngag*). Poetic skill was expressed through images or juxtapositions that strikingly illustrated the evil and foolishness of behavior that contravened the expectations of religion and state.

The aim of an original and appealing vehicle for an old message was exemplified in the genre of *üge,* or speeches. Featuring words put in the mouth of animals or inanimate things, they formed a particularly piquant way of expressing moral lessons. In the famous "Conversation between a Sheep, a Goat, and an Ox," for example, the abbot Agwang-Khaidub (or Agwang-Lubsang-Khaidub, 1779–1838) pictures these three animals trussed up in a monastery courtyard. The sheep and ox are sure it cannot be because they are to be slaughtered, since the monks recite so often the Buddha's prohibitions on killing. They are, of course, destined for slaughter, and the author criticizes the lamas' surrender to habit and convention in doing what they know is wrong.

Traditional didactic poetry flourished into the 20th century. In Kalmykia aphorisms and *surgal shilügs* both revived as exemplified by Boowan Badma's *Chiknä khujr* (Ornament of the ear, 1916). Loroisambuu (1884–1939) in Ordos observed in his *surgal* that even with a steamship one cannot escape the sea of samsara. Soon, however, social changes replaced the traditional didactic poem with new Soviet and Chinese models.

See also FOLK POETRY AND TALES; LITERATURE; MUSIC; SANGDAG, KHUULICHI.

Further reading: C. R. Bawden, "Conversation between a Sheep, a Goat and an Ox," *New Orient* 5 (1986): 9–11; Henry Serruys, "Two Didactic Poems from Ordos," *Zentralasiatische Studien* 6 (1973): 425–483; N. S. Yakhontova, "The *Oyun Tülkigür* or 'Key to Wisdom': Text and Translation Based on the MSS in the Institute for Oriental Studies at St. Petersburg," *Mongolian Studies* 23 (2000): 69–137.

dinosaurs Mongolian dinosaur exploration began with the 1922–25 Central Asiatic Expedition of Roy Chapman Andrews (1884–1960) sponsored by the American Museum of Natural History (AMNH), which was originally looking for mammal and human fossils. Finds of the dinosaur *Protoceratops* with well-preserved eggs at the Flaming Cliffs of Shabarakh Usu (currently called Bayan-zag, in Bulgan Sum, South Gobi) changed the direction of research. Soviet paleontologists surveyed Mongolia from 1925 on, but large-scale work began only with the 1946–49 Mongolian Paleontological Expedition headed by I. A. Efremov, which shipped 120 metric tons (132 short tons) of bones from Mongolia, chiefly found at Nemegt and Altan Uul sites (Gurwantes Sum, South Gobi). Paleontological work in Mongolia ceased for a decade but began again with the Polish-Mongolian Paleontological Expedition (1963–71) and the Joint Soviet (later Russian)-Mongolian Paleontological Expedition (1969 on). These later expeditions trained Mongolian paleontologists and shared specimens with the Mongolian Academy of Sciences. Since 1990 the AMNH has again sponsored exhibitions.

Mongolia's dinosaur fossils virtually all date from the Cretaceous period (currently dated to 138–63 million years ago). Cretaceous deposits in Mongolia span the entire period except for the final stages, and are divided into Early and Late. A distinctive feature of the Mongolian dinosaur fauna is their inland distribution, contrasting with the littoral distribution of most other Cretaceous dinosaur sites. The two pterosaur genera known from Mongolia, for example, appear to have eaten either insects or freshwater fish, in contrast to the usually marine types known elsewhere.

Mongolia's Late Cretaceous presents probably the world's richest assemblage of large and small theropods (meat-eating and "ostrich" dinosaurs), with seven major lineages and perhaps 25 species documented. Particularly fine specimens include the complete *Velociraptor* skeleton found at Tögrög (Bulgan Sum, South Gobi), the approximately 20 skeletons of *Oviraptor* uncovered at Ukhaa Tolgod (Gurwantes Sum, South Gobi), several skeletons of *Gallimimus* of varied ages from Nemegt, and several complete skeletons of the massive tyrannosaurid *Tarbosaurus* from Nemegt.

Among herbivorous dinosaurs sauropods have been found in all levels of the Mongolian Cretaceous, including two skulls similar to *Diplodocus,* but none of the skeletons is complete. The bipedal ornithopods are well represented in Mongolia, with iguanadontians in the Lower Cretaceous and hadrosaurs ("duck-billed" dinosaurs) in the Upper Cretaceous. Finds of both types are quite similar to European and North American examples. With the exception of the hadrosaur *Saurolophus,* of which 15 skeletons were found at Altan Uul, most of the finds are incomplete. The ankylosaurs (armored dinosaurs usually regarded as vegetarian, although anteating has also been suggested) appear in Mongolia in the late Lower Cretaceous and last through the final Cretaceous deposits. At present, however, pachycephalosaurs ("dome-headed" dinosaurs) are known in Mongolia only from Late Cretaceous sediments. The ceratopsians, an order restricted to eastern Asia and western North America, are represented in Mongolia by two very well-documented genera, *Psittacosaurus* of the Lower Cretaceous and *Protoceratops* of the middle Late Cretaceous, both of which are quite small and archaic in appearance. More than 80 skulls of *Protoceratops* from Mongolia illustrate every stage of growth from egg to adulthood. A few other ceratopsian genera are known by fragmentary remains, but the massive horned ceratopsians such as *Triceratops* have so far not been found in Asia.

Due to the well-drained soils with high pH that formed the two countries' red beds, Mongolia and China have the world's most extensive remains of dinosaur eggs, sometimes with beautifully preserved embryonic skeletons inside. The vast majority of Mongolian eggs are Late Cretaceous. About 13 "oogenera" (genera defined by egg types) have been described for Mongolia. Embryos link one oogenus in the dinosaurid-spherulitic category with therizinosaurs (a herbivorous theropod family), while context links others with sauropods and various hadrosaurs. The therizinosaur and sauropod eggs were incubated underground in moist soil. The dinosauroid-prismatic type includes Roy Chapman Andrews's original eggs associated with *Protoceratops*. Finally, embryos of both *Oviraptor* (a beaked theropod) and of true birds have been found in ornithoid-type eggs, which were laid in dry conditions with parental care.

See also ARCHAEOLOGY; FOSSIL RECORD; SOUTH GOBI PROVINCE.

Further reading: Michael J. Benton, ed., *The Age of Dinosaurs in Russia and Mongolia* (Cambridge: Cambridge University Press, 2000).

Dolonnuur Assembly

At this assembly in Dolonnuur from May 30 to June 3, 1691, the KHALKHA nobility officially submitted to the QING DYNASTY. For 15 years the Khalkha's two main rulers, the western or Zasagtu Khan and eastern or Tüshiyetü Khan, had been engaged in disputes. In autumn, 1687, the Oirat GALDAN BOSHOGTU KHAN intervened on the side of the young Zasagtu Khan Shara. The Khalkha Tüshiyetü Khan Chakhundorji (r. 1655–99) then killed Shara and Galdan's brother. In reply Galdan invaded Khalkha in spring 1688, driving the Tüshiyetü Khan, his brother the great INCARNATE LAMA known as the FIRST JIBZUNDAMBA KHUTUGTU, and vast numbers of other Khalkha nobles and commoners into flight to the Inner Mongolian border. There, after appeals by Chakhundorji and the Jibzundamba Khutugtu, the Qing emperor Kangxi (1662–1722) allowed the Khalkhas to enter Inner Mongolia and receive relief grain.

While Manchu armies invaded Mongolia and defeated Galdan, a great assembly was held at the Inner Mongolian religious and trade center Dolonnuur (mod-ern Duolun) to welcome the Khalkhas' submission and announce the reconciliation of Chakhundorji and the Zasagtu Khan in the person of the late Shara's brother Tsewangjab. On May 30 the emperor personally received the homage of and gave rewards to the Jibzundamba Khutugtu, the Tüshiyetü Khan, the Setsen Khan, Tsewangjab, and 549 other Khalkha representatives seated on the right and a comparable number of Inner Mongolian and EIGHT BANNERS nobility seated on the left. The assembly closed on June 3, and the emperor returned to Beijing with the Jibzundamba Khutugtu. In 1701 Tsewangjab officially succeeded as the new Zasagtu Khan.

Dongxiang language and people (Santa, Tunghsiang)

Although virtually nothing definite is known of their early history, the Dongxiang, at 373,872 (1990), are the most numerous of the nationalities who speak a "peripheral" Mongolic language. As Muslims in China's Gansu province, the Dongxiang have always been intimately linked to China's Hui (Chinese-speaking Muslim) people.

ORIGINS

The name Dongxiang (Eastern Village) was originally a toponym east of Linxia. No contemporary records mark the formation of the Dongxiang nationality. The two chief pieces of evidence are 1) the group's Mongolic language, which indicates connections with the MONGOL EMPIRE and more recently with the Mongolic-speaking Buddhist Tu and Muslim Bao'an people nearby, and 2) their self-designation as "Santa," derived from "Sartaq," Mongolian for "Turkestani" and/or "Muslim." Dongxiang scholars see themselves as a people formed by deported Turkestanis, both soldiers and artisans, under Mongol officers who were settled in northwest China (*see* SEMUREN). The continuing prestige of immigrant sayyids (descendants of Muhammad's son-in-law 'Ali) and sheikhs (Sufi or Islamic mystic masters) among the Dongxiang illustrates the importance of connections to the outside Islamic world. Another theory sees the Dongxiang as an offshoot of the Tu people who converted to Islam under Hui influence. The name "Santa" would then have been adopted in its sense of "Muslim."

LANGUAGE

Dongxiang language belongs to the Qinghai-Gansu subfamily of the Mongolic languages. A number of phonetic, morphological, and semantic innovations are shared with Tu and Bao'an: the common use of Turkish *tash*, "stone," for Mongolian *chuluu*, a tendency to aspirate unaspirated initial stops when followed by an aspirate stop (for example, Middle Mongolian *batu*, "firm," becomes *putu* in Dongxiang or *padə* in Tu), anomalous unrounding of the ö (for example, Middle Mongolian *dörben* becomes *jiəron* in Dongxiang and *deeren* in Tu), and the development of the verb "to place" from Middle Mongolian *talbi-* to *tai-*

(Dongxiang) or *taii-* (Tu), and so on. While they all tend to eliminate diphthongs (Middle Mongolian *a'ula,* "mountain," becomes *ula* in Dongxiang and *ulaa* in Tu), these languages do retain the Middle Mongolian initial h- (for example, *hula'an,* "red," becomes Dongxiang *khulan* and Tu *fulaan,* and *hüker,* "cattle," becomes Dongxiang *fugiə* and Tu *fugor*).

Dongxiang differs substantially from Tu, however, in ways that reflect its pervasively Chinese environment. Semantically, Dongxiang shows a large number of Chinese loanwords, including basic vocabulary such as *gao* (Chinese *hao,* "good"), *naidzu* (Chinese *nai,* "milk"), *khai* (Chinese *xie,* "shoes"), the numbers above 20, as well as all of its modern political, administrative, and technological terminology. Religious terms are Arabic and Persian. Phonologically, while Dongxiang does show the tendency of Tu to drop first-syllable vowels, it, like Chinese, has no initial consonant clusters. Phonemic vowel length and vowel harmony have both disappeared. The syllable-final consonants have been simplified to -n; where the originally Mongolian word has some other consonant, it is either changed (Middle Mongolian *sartaq,* "Turkestani, Muslim" to Dongxiang *santa*) or dropped (*ghar* to *qa*). The Chinese copula verb *shi,* "to be," is used in sentences as a kind of topic marker after the subject.

Virtually all Dongxiang people speak the Dongxiang language. The three dialects, Suonanba, Wangjiaji, and Sijiaji, pose no problem of intercommunication. Inner Mongolian linguists devised a written language for Dongxiang in the early 1980s, but it is not in general use; writing is done in Chinese.

HISTORY

Since the Dongxiang were, like the Hui, generally regular subjects of the Chinese county administration and mostly lacked autonomous institutions, they did not have the political visibility of the Tu and the Yogur. One *tusi,* or hereditary "aboriginal official," did operate in Dongxiang, living in Baihe village and administered several dispersed hamlets with his surname, He. This lone *tusi's* authority was curtailed around 1725 and abolished early in the 20th century.

Dongxiangs participated in the revolt of the proscribed Jahriya sublineage of Naqshbandi Sufis (Islamic mystics) in 1781, and as a result several villages were destroyed and Dongxiang Islamic activity was subjected to imperial regulation. Ma Wuzhen of the Dongxiang was one of the local leaders during the great Hui revolt of 1862 before surrendering in 1872 and being enrolled in the Qing army. Dongxiang men also participated in the rebellion of the Mufti *menhuan* (Sufi lodge) in 1895–96.

Under the Chinese Republic, with the suppression of Ma Zhongying's 1928 rebellion, the Dongxiang territory was divided in 1930 among four counties. The Hui warlord Ma Bufang relied heavily on Islamic recruits, and conscription was very onerous. The Dongxiang army deserter Mutefeile (Ma Muge) led a widespread antitax rebellion in 1943.

Although all are Muslim, the Dongxiang are divided into many sects. In 1954 77,616, or 67 percent, were affiliated with one of nine *menhuan,* or Sufi lodges (the "Old Teaching"), and 532 mosques existed in Dongxiang territory. The Dongxiang Ma Wanfu (1853–1934), after making the pilgrimage to Mecca, came under the influence of Wahhabism, and on his return to Gansu he founded a Chinese branch of the anti-Sufi Ikhwan (Muslim Brotherhood, or "New Teaching") movement. Although he excoriated Chinese accretions to Islam, his movement did not become politically hostile to the Chinese Republic.

In the People's Republic of China the Dongxiang districts were reunited as a Dongxiang autonomous area in September 1950 (defined as an autonomous county in 1955). The native ethnonym Santa, which in practice meant simply "Muslim," was rejected and the previously purely geographic term Dongxiang adopted for the nationality. In 1981 nearby Jishishan county, with more than 8,000 Dongxiang, was made a Bao'an, Dongxiang, and Salar nationality autonomous county.

In 1982 more than 145,000 of the total 279,397 Dongxiangs lived in the Dongxiang Autonomous County in Gansu's Linxia Hui Autonomous Prefecture, where they formed more than 77 percent of the county's total population of 187,310. Despite this high percentage, only about 60 percent of the higher county officials and 59 percent of the party members were Dongxiang. Almost 97 percent of the Dongxiang are engaged in agriculture. Dongxiang county is one of China's poorest, and with fewer than 10 percent of school-age children in primary schools and illiteracy among those six and over reaching almost 90 percent, the Dongxiang were China's least educated nationality.

See also ALTAIC LANGUAGE FAMILY; BAO'AN LANGUAGE AND PEOPLE; ISLAM IN THE MONGOL EMPIRE; MONGOLIC LANGUAGE FAMILY; TU LANGUAGE AND PEOPLE; YOGUR LANGUAGES AND PEOPLES.

Further reading: Henry Schwarz, *Minorities of Northern China: A Survey* (Bellingham: Western Washington University Press, 1984); ———, "A Script for the Dongxiang," *Zentralasiatische Studien* 16 (1982): 153–164.

Doquz *See* TOGHUS KHATUN.

Dörbed (of western Mongolia) *See* DÖRBÖDS.

Dörbed Mongol Autonomous County (Dorbod, Durbote, Durbet) Located in northeast China's Heilongjiang province, Dörbed county had about 235,675 people in 1990, of whom 42,775 (18.15 percent) were

Mongols. In 1982 the Mongol population numbered 32,429, almost 16 percent of the population. The county has 44 villages that are all or mostly Mongol. Dörbed lies on the eastern bank of the Nonni (Nen) River, south of Qiqihar in marshy, low-lying ground. In 1987 the total number of livestock in Dörbed (excluding pigs) was 147,414 head, of which 29.5 percent were oxen, 14.5 percent milk cows, 19 percent horses, and 37 percent sheep and goats. In 1988 707,000 hectares (1,747,000 acres) were cultivated for a total yield of 100,200 metric tons (110,450 short tons) of grains and soya. Average income that year in the Mongol villages was 260 *yuan*. Surveys of the county's mainly Mongolian villages found that 78 percent of the Mongols there could speak Mongolian.

The Dörbed were an important clan among the Mongols in the 12th–13th centuries. Submitting to the QING DYNASTY in 1624, the Dörbed clan was organized into a banner in Jirim league ruled by descendants of CHINGGIS KHAN's brother Qasar. In 1900 the Russian-managed Chinese Eastern Railway was extended through Dörbed territory, and after 1913 massive state-sponsored colonization established three Chinese counties there as the Mongols were sedentarized.

The Japanese excluded Dörbed banner from Manchukuo's Mongol autonomous provinces of Khinggan established in 1932. After 1945 the Chinese Communists established a new banner government, and in October 1956 it was converted to an autonomous county.

See also INNER MONGOLIANS; KHORCHIN.

Dörbet *See* DÖRBÖDS.

Dörböds (Dörwöd, Dörbed, Dörbet, Derbet) The Dörböds are a tribe of Oirat Mongols. (Oirat tribes were not consanguineal units but political-ethnic units.) A Dörben clan existed within the MONGOL TRIBE in the 12th–13th centuries, but the Dörböds appear as an Oirat tribe only in the latter half of the 16th century. What their relation, if any, is to the Dörben clan of the 12th–13th centuries is unclear. (Dörben and Dörböd both mean "the four" and may have originated independently. The word is written Dörböd in the CLEAR SCRIPT, Dörwd in Cyrillic-script Kalmyk, and Dörwöd in CYRILLIC-SCRIPT MONGOLIAN.)

The Dörböd and Zünghar tribes were ruled by collateral branches of the Choros "bone," or lineage. In 1616 Russian diplomats identified the Dörböds' Baatur Dalai Taishi as the most powerful Oirat prince. In 1677 Dalai Taishi's son Solom-Tseren (d. 1684?) joined the KALMYKS on the Volga with 4,000 households, occupying the westernmost pastures. In 1699 a body of Dörböds joined the Don Cossacks, eventually becoming the Buzava Kalmyks. Trapped west of the Volga, the Dörböds could not join the 1771 FLIGHT OF THE KALMYKS east and hence dominated the remaining Kalmyks. By 1806 these Volga Dör-

böds had split into the "Lesser" Dörböds (actually larger in number) under the Tundutov princes (descendants of Dalai Taishi's third son, Toin), and the "Greater" Dörböds under the Khapchukov princes (descendants of Dalai Taishi's fourth son, Ombo Daiching Khoshuuchi). The Lesser Dörböds live in northern Kalmykia, while the Greater Dörböds live around Lake Manych-Gudilo.

Meanwhile, the Dörböds in the Oirat homeland remained a major tribe of the ZÜNGHARS. In 1753, as the Zünghar principality disintegrated, the "three Tserens"—Tseren, Tseren Ubashi (both descendants of Ombo Daiching Khoshuuchi), and Tseren-Möngke (descendant of Dalai Taishi's younger brother)—surrendered to the QING DYNASTY (1636–1912). First given pastures along the Baidrag River (northern BAYANKHONGOR PROVINCE), the Dörböds were resettled in 1759 in modern UWS PROVINCE. The Dörböds were formed into 16 BANNERS of the Sain Zayaatu Left and Right LEAGUES. The Dörböd nobility's approximately 15,000 subjects included many BAYADS and a small number of captured Turkestanis, or KHOTONGS.

Until the 1880s Dörböd society and economy differed significantly from that of the Khalkhas to their west. Governmental duties were lighter, monasteries were fewer, and Chinese merchants rarer. While basically pastoral and nomadic, as many as one-fourth of the Dörböd households also practiced some irrigation agriculture, as did monasteries, and local handicrafts were also preserved to a greater degree than in Khalkha. From the 1880s, however, Dörböd socioeconomic trends converged with those of the Khalkhas. After Mongolian independence in 1911, separatist feeling remained strong among the Dörböds into the 1930s. The Kalmyk adventurer DAMBIJANTSAN was at first welcomed in 1911 as a kinsman, and the Dörböd monasteries of Tegüs-Buyantu and Ulaangom were centers of anticommunist disturbances in 1930. Even Dörböd officials in the revolutionary government, such as Badarakhu (Ö. Badrakh, 1895–1941), proposed secession from Khalkha and direct annexation to the Soviet Union. Many Dörböds achieved high office, however, under YUMJAAGIIN TSEDENBAL and JAMBYN BATMÖNKH, Mongolia's rulers from 1952 to 1990, who were both Dörböd. The Dörböds in Mongolia, numbering 25,700 in 1956 and 55,200 in 1989, are the largest western Mongolian *yastan*, or subethnic group.

See also KALMYK REPUBLIC.

Further reading: Arash Bormanshinov, "The Buzava (Don Kalmyk) Princes Revisited," *Mongolian Studies* 16 (1993); 59–63; ———, "Prolegomena to a History of the Kalmyk *Noyans* (Princes). I. The *Buzâva* (Don Kalmyk) Princes," *Mongolian Studies* 14 (1991); 41–80; Uradyn Erden Bulag, "Dark Quadrangle in Central Asia: Empires, Ethnogenesis, Scholars, and Nation-States," *Central Asian Survey* 13 (1994): 459–478.

Dorjeev, Agvan *See* DORZHIEV, AGWANG.

Dorjieff *See* DORZHIEV, AGWANG.

Dorjiev, Agvan *See* DORZHIEV, AGWANG.

Dornod *See* EASTERN PROVINCE.

Dornogov' *See* EAST GOBI PROVINCE.

Dörwöd *See* DÖRBÖDS.

Dorzhiev, Agwang (**Agvan Dorjiev, Dorjeev, Dorjieff**) (1853–1938) *Buriat lama who advised the Thirteenth Dalai Lama and promoted Buddhist learning in Russia*

Agwang Dorzhiev's ancestors were Ekhired Buriats of Verkholensk who in 1811 migrated east to the lands of the Khori Buriats' Galzuud clan. His father, Dorzhi Iroltuev, and mother, Dolgar, lived in the *ulus* (district) of Kharashibir' on the Uda (Buriat, Üde) River (35 kilometers, or 22 miles, northeast of Onokhoi).

His parents were devout Buddhists, and Agwang received lay initiations as a boy and made a pilgrimage to Khüriye (modern ULAANBAATAR). By reading hagiographies and the *SUTRA OF THE WISE AND FOOLISH*, Dorzhiev was inspired to leave his new wife and become a monk. In 1873–74 he and his teacher, Baldan-Choimpel, followed a party of Khalkha nobles going to Lhasa to escort the infant EIGHTH JIBZUNDAMBA KHUTUGTU back to Mongolia. His teacher had also secretly agreed with the Russian Geographical Society to bring back information on Tibet.

After returning to Khüriye and being ordained as a *gelüng* (full-fledged monk), Dorzhiev visited his family before making a pilgrimage to China's sacred Wutai Mount. From there he reached Lhasa in 1878, where he joined the Mongol monks in Lhasa in the sGo-mang *datsang* (college) of 'Bras-spung Monastery. After 10 years of study of *tsanid* (higher Buddhist studies) curriculum, he received the most prestigious Lharamba degree and was given advanced initiations along with the young Thirteenth Dalai Lama (1876–1933), to whom he remained ever devoted. While editing a new bKa'-'gyur edition, Dorzhiev widely praised the czar's tolerance of Buddhism and advocated a pro-Russian policy for Tibet. This advocacy revealed his Buriat origin (Russian subjects were not then allowed in Tibet) and made him political enemies, but in 1897–98 he was sent by the Dalai Lama to Russia via India and Beijing to propose Russian protection of Tibet.

From then on Dorzhiev shuttled several times between Russia and Lhasa with letters for the Dalai Lama and the czar and lavish gifts of gold butter lamps, gilding, food, cloth, and temple hangings for the Tibetan monasteries. The British began to see him as the evil genius behind the Dalai Lama's anti-British policy. After vainly warning the Tibetans of the futility of resisting Britain's 1904 incursion into Tibet, Dorzhiev followed the Dalai Lama in flight to Mongolia. Sent from there to appeal to the czar, Dorzhiev found that Russia's involvement in the Russo-Japanese War precluded any assistance. Dorzhiev's last visit to the Dalai Lama in autumn 1912 came as Tibet and Mongolia were securing their independence with the fall of China's last dynasty. After parting from the Dalai Lama for the last time, he passed through Mongolia and in January 1913 negotiated a formal Tibeto-Mongolian alliance.

From 1898 Dorzhiev also began touring both Buriat and Kalmyk monasteries, advocating reform of the religious life of Buddhist monks in Russia. He instituted *tsanid* studies in four Khori monasteries in 1898 and in Kalmykia after 1900 and gave mass lay initiations to the KALMYKS. In Kalmykia, isolated from other Buddhist centers since the 18th century, Dorzhiev's activities were especially important and controversial. The chief Kalmyk lama protested as unsettling innovations the new-style *tsanid* schools and Dorzhiev's preaching against snuff and liquor, but the aristocrat Tseren David Tundutov supported him.

In Buriatia controversy arose with Russian Orthodox missionaries, who protested Dorzhiev's plans for a Buddhist temple among his native Ekhired shamanists west of LAKE BAIKAL. To this controversy was added in 1910 Dorzhiev's proposed *datsang*, or Buddhist college, in St. Petersburg. Despite Orthodox opposition, a committee of scholars, explorers, artists, and Kalmyk princes lobbied for the czar's approval, and with 50,000 gold rubles donated by the Dalai Lama at their last parting in 1912 and 30,000 rubles gathered by Dorzhiev himself from Buriat and other donors, the St. Petersburg *datsang* was built between 1913 and 1915, the first Buddhist temple in a European city.

Dorzhiev's also tried to reform the script of the Buriat Mongols. In 1905 he created a printing house, Naran, in St. Petersburg and a press in the Atsagat medical *datsang* near his hometown. In fall 1905 Dorzhiev designed a new script to unify the Buriat language. Called the Vagindra script from Dorzhiev's Sanskrit pen name, the script was a semiphonetic improvement of the UIGHUR-MONGOLIAN SCRIPT based on Buriat dialects. Although he was assisted in this endeavor by secular intellectuals, the Vagindra script made no headway against official Russian opposition, and by 1921 Dorzhiev himself had abandoned it.

The outbreak of the Russian Revolution in March 1917 (February in the Old Style) was a welcome development for Dorzhiev. Dorzhiev maintained good relations with socialist intellectuals such as ELBEK-DORZHI RINCHINO and hailed the proclamation of freedom of religion, which allowed Buddhism to expand freely to the western Buriats. The later Communist persecution of the "Jesus long-hairs" (Russian Orthodox priests) he saw as just retribution for their persecution of Buddhism. Even so, during the Civil War the St. Petersburg *datsang* was closed down until 1924, and Dorzhiev was arrested while touring Kalmyk monasteries. Released through the intervention of Russian scholars, he continued his work in Kalmykia, seeking to rebuild the devastated *tsanid* schools.

With the end of the civil war and the revival of Russia's Oriental policy, Dorzhiev was invited to the September 1920 conference of the Toilers of the East at Baku and addressed the Communist Party Politburo with Rinchino a month later. In letters accompanying offerings to the Thirteenth Dalai Lama, Dorzhiev argued that the Communists, with their policy of helping weak nations, might still prove friendlier to Tibet than was Britain or China.

Dorzhiev advocated the elimination of lamas' private property on both Buddhist and Communist grounds and participated actively in the First All-Union Buddhist Congress in January 1927 in Leningrad, which supported this policy. At the same time, he argued publicly that, unlike Christianity, Buddhism supported the Soviet regime. He also defended the reputation of Buddhist medicine.

In 1931, with increasing antireligious persecution, Dorzhiev was confined to Leningrad. On May 30, 1935, the lamas of the Leningrad *datsang* were arrested. Dorzhiev was deported in January 1937 to the Atsagat medical *datsang,* where he was arrested on November 13 on the fabricated charge of being a leader of a Japanese spy ring doing "wrecking work" in the collectives and preparing an armed insurrection. He died of heart failure in prison on January 29, 1938.

See also BURIAT LANGUAGE AND SCRIPT; BURIATS; MEDICINE, TRADITIONAL; THEOCRATIC PERIOD; TIBETAN CULTURE IN MONGOLIA.

Further reading: Alexandre Andreyev, "An Unknown Russian Memoir by Aagvan Dorjiev," *Inner Asia* 3 (2001); 27–39; Thubten J. Norbu and Dan Martin, *Dorjiev: Memoirs of a Tibetan Diplomat* (Tokyo: Hoka Bunka Kenkyu, 1991); John Snelling, *Buddhism in Russia: The Story of Agvan Dorzhiev, Lhasa's Emissary to the Tsar* (Shaftesbury, Dorset: Element, 1993).

D. Ravjaa *See* DANZIN-RABJAI.

dughuyilang *See* DUGUILANG.

duguilang (*dughuyilang*) Duguilangs were a special form of popular protest in ORDOS (southwest Inner Mongolia), which after 1900 evolved into relatively permanent vigilante organizations. The name *duguilang,* or "circle," referred to the members' manner of both assembling and signing their letters. By sitting and putting their names in a circle, they prevented the identification of a ringleader who could be punished. This custom persisted

long after *duguilang*s had become armed organizations with open leaders.

The earliest known *duguilang* occurred in 1828 in Ordos. *Duguilang*s were formed to send petitions to league authorities against banner rulers, to intimidate unpopular or abusive banner officials, to enforce community norms, and to defend the banner territory against encroachment, whether by other BANNERS, Chinese colonization, or foreign missionaries. Since the laws of the QING DYNASTY (1636–1912) did not allow subjects directly to sue their own banner ruler (*see* ZASAG), the *duguilang*s had to use the threat of violence or riot to force the league authorities to relent. Where the *duguilang*s were better entrenched, they engaged in direct action, mobbing their targets and then frightening or torturing them into good behavior. The first known example of this type of vigilante action was around 1884, also in Ordos. Repression from the authorities could likewise be severe. Strong banner rulers often meted out their own tortures, while the Qing law punished insubordination with exile to a Chinese province for the ringleaders, with enslavement of their family, and 100 lashes and cattle fines for the rest.

Membership in the *duguilang*s included commoners, TAIJI (petty nobility), and often banner office clerks and militia leaders. The Ordos *duguilang*s from the beginning saw one of their tasks as protecting Buddhism and the cult of CHINGGIS KHAN (*see* EIGHT WHITE YURTS). A *duguilang* league in 1913 in Üüshin was sealed with a *khanggal,* or Buddhist offering of bull's blood to the *dogshin* (fierce) protector deities. After 1911 the role of lamas in these movements increased.

Quite similar struggles against misrule have been documented from elsewhere in Mongolia as far back as the 18th century, although without the name *duguilang* or its trademark round-robin signatures. From the late 19th century, *duguilang* organizations spread to Khalkha. Famous *duguilang*s included that led by Ayushi (1858–1939) of Darkhan Zasag banner (modern Tsetseg Sum, Khowd) and that formed against the impious and drunken prince of Khurts Zasag banner (modern Erdenetsagaan Sum, Sükhebaatur) in 1919. The lamas of the western Mongolia Dörböds in 1913 also used vigilante action, surrounding the banner ruler's palace-tent and forcing him to hear their accusation. They called this "setting up a screen" (*khashig bosgokhu*). The Dörböd lamas' Tegüsbuyantu rebellion against the leftist antireligious policy of 1930 began as a similar movement.

The growth of Ordos *duguilang*s from occasional activities to permanent organizations was ironically begun by the authorities themselves. In 1900 Ordos rulers responded to Boxer emissaries, then favored by the Qing court, by encouraging *duguilang*s to attack Catholic missionaries. When the Qing dynasty turned to forced colonization (in part to pay Boxer reparations), the powerful *duguilang* movement moved into opposition (*see* CHINESE COLONIZATION; NEW POLICIES).

Üüshin had 12 and neighboring Otog eight permanent *duguilangs*, effectively dividing the banners into semi-independent districts.

After the 1912 fall of the Qing, the Üüshin *duguilangs* actually seized control in Üüshin in 1913, putting government in the hands of a *gong hui* (public assembly), a kind of representative assembly of the *duguilangs*. By 1920, however, the Ordos rulers and the Chinese authorities had crushed the *duguilangs*, disarmed the people, and prohibited assembly. Only in Otog, where the ruler was an ineffectual opium addict, did the eight separate *duguilangs* remain a force, able to challenge local strongmen but not to rule.

In 1924 Ordos *duguilang* leaders exiled in Beijing petitioned the revolutionary government in Mongolia for assistance. In 1926 Soviet-supported Inner Mongolian revolutionaries armed the *duguilang* leaders Öljeijirgal (Shine Lama, 1866–1929) and the INCARNATE LAMA Jamyangsharab (1887–1946), who ruled Üüshin and Otog banners, respectively, as military strongmen until their deaths. The last recorded *duguilang* in Ordos drove the Chinese Nationalist office out of Khanggin (Hanggin) banner in 1950.

Further reading: Christopher P. Atwood, *Young Mongols and Vigilantes in Inner Mongolia's Interregnum Decades, 1911–1931* (Leiden E. J. Brill, 2002); C. R. Bawden, "A Joint Petition of Grievances Submitted to the Ministry of Justice of Autonomous Mongolia in 1919," *Bulletin of the School of Oriental and African Studies* 30 (1967): 548–563; Sh. Natsagdorj, "Arad Ayush the Commoner," in *Mongolian Heroes of the Twentieth Century*, trans. Urgunge Onon (New York: AMS Press, 1976), 1–42; Henry Serruys, "Documents from Ordos on the 'Revolutionary Circles.' Parts I and II," *Journal of the American Oriental Society* 97 (1977); 482–507 and 98 (1978); 1–19.

Dukha (Tsaatan) The Dukha are Mongolia's only reindeer herders, known to the Mongolians as Tsaatan, or "reindeer people." The Dukha, who speak the Tuvan language, numbered about 80 households in the 1990s and lived in the northwest of Mongolia's far-northern KHÖWS-GÖL PROVINCE. The 36 households that actually herd reindeer are divided about equally into North (*Züün*) and South (*Baruun*) Taiga bands. The Uighur-Uriyangkhai in northeastern Khöwsgöl also call themselves Dukha (*see* TUVANS).

The North Taiga band was organized under the QING DYNASTY from 1755 to 1912 as part of the Tozhu (Toja) Uriyangkhai banner. With Mongolian independence, the Tozhu banner became part of Tuva, soon annexed by Russia, leaving only this band on the Mongolian side of the frontier. The South Taiga group fled over the frontier from Tuva to avoid collectivization and conscription in the 1930s–40s. At first the Mongolian government treated both groups as illegal aliens, repeatedly deporting them back to Tuva. In 1956 the government finally gave them Mongolian citizenship, settling them at a fishery station at Tsagaan (Dood) Nuur Lake on the Shishigt River. A market remained for furs and deer antlers, however, and in 1985 the government organized a fur-trapping and reindeer-herding state farm in Tsagaan-Nuur Sum (district) to employ some Dukha. In 1995, with economic liberalization, the reindeer herds were privatized. Inbreeding among the reindeer, poaching by outsider hunters, and cancellation of the government wolf-control program have damaged the Dukhas' living.

Further reading: Batulag Solnoi, Purev Tsogtsaikhan, and Daniel Plumley, "Following the White Stag: The Dukha and Their Struggle for Survival," *Cultural Survival Quarterly* 27.1 (spring 2003); 56–58; Alan Wheeler, "The Dukha: Mongolia's Reindeer Herders," *Mongolia Survey*, no. 6 (1999): 58–66.

Dundgov' *See* MIDDLE GOBI PROVINCE.

Dzabkhan *See* ZAWKHAN PROVINCE.

Dzakhachin *See* ZAKHACHIN.

Dzavhan *See* ZAWKHAN PROVINCE.

Dzungar *See* ZÜNGHARS.

E

East Asian sources on the Mongol Empire While usually impersonal in tone, Chinese, Korean, Vietnamese, and Tibetan sources cover the MONGOL EMPIRE from beginning to end and supply vast amounts of information. Chinese writings on the conquest begin in 1221 with the *Meng-Da beilu* (A complete record of the Mong-TATARS) of Zhao Gong, an envoy of the Song, which is the first written account in any language of the Mongol conquest and the only one written during the reign of CHINGGIS KHAN himself. Later the Song envoys Peng Daya and Xu Ting combined their accounts to produce the important *Heida shilue* (A sketch of the Black Tatars, 1237). In Zhao Gong's time the Song considered using the Mongols as allies against the Jin, but by Peng and Xu's time, the Song saw the Mongols as their new northern rival, and attitudes hardened. Few records on the Mongols from writers serving the Jurchen JIN DYNASTY in North China have survived. The *Runan yishi* (The lost cause at Runan, translated as *Fall of the Jurchen Chin*) of Wang E (1190–1273) described the Jin dynasty's last stand in 1234. In 1260 QUBILAI KHAN ordered the collections of Jin records to prepare the defunct dynasty's history, but disagreement over how to handle the issue of legitimacy long delayed publication. A commission under the Mongol grand councillor TOQTO'A (1314–56) finally published the *Jin shi* (History of the Jin) and the *Song shi* (History of the Song) in 1344 and 1345. Both sources contain valuable information, although the Mongol editors eliminated much sensitive information from the *Jin shi* in particular.

Taoist writings on the Mongols began with Chinggis Khan inviting the Taoist adept MASTER CHANGCHUN to his mobile court in Afghanistan. The journey of the Taoist Changchun to Chinggis Khan's court in Afghanistan sup-plied the occasion for the earliest writings by Chinese scholars in the employ of the Mongols. In 1228 Changchun's disciple, Li Zhichang (1193–1256), and Chinggis's Confucian secretary, YELÜ CHUCAI, wrote opposing accounts, entitled *Xi yu ji* (Notes on a journey to the West, translated as *Travels of an Alchemist*) and *Xi yu lu* (Record of a journey to the West), respectively. Li Zhichang's work is usually published with a number of Mongol decrees written for the Taoist patriarch. Qubilai's interviews with Chinese Confucians in the 1240s produced several accounts, of which the *Lingbei jixing* (Travels north of the range, 1248) by Zhang Dehui (1194–1274) is extant. Wang Yun (1227–1304) in the *Zhongtang shiji* (Records of the secretariat's office) described QUBILAI KHAN's early conferences with his Confucian ministers.

Su Tianjue (1294–1352) collected prose writings of Chinese scholars under the Mongol YUAN DYNASTY, such as memorials, prefaces, and obituaries, in his *Guochao wenlei* (Anthology of the dynasty) and used the biographical material to compile the *Guochao mingchen shilue* (Sketches of the dynasty's eminent ministers, 1328). The latter work, which assembled biographies of North Chinese, Mongols, and a few SEMUREN (Central and West Asians) dating from the time of Chinggis Khan to the accession of Ayuribarwada (titled Renzong/Jen-tsung, 1311–20), was the first Chinese summation of Mongol rule. Su portrayed the Yuan as a true Confucian dynasty that unified the previously divided world. He focused on Chinese Confucians but also praised the Mongol noblemen who assisted them in fighting against corrupt officials. *Geng/shen waishi* (The unofficial history of 1380), written by Quan Heng in the succeeding MING DYNASTY, chronicled the Yuan from 1328 to its fall in 1368 in jaded but objective terms. The *Zhuo geng lu,* a wide-ranging compendium of anecdotes and miscellaneous information by Tao Zongyi (fl. 1360–68), and the imperial cookbook, *Yinshan zhengyao* (1330), by the Uighur Hu Sihui (Qusqi), reflect different facets of Yuan society.

The Yuan dynasty sponsored little public history writing in Chinese. (*On the court chronicle, or Veritable Records, see* MONGOLIAN SOURCES ON THE MONGOL EMPIRE.) One of the few extant official historical works is the *Ping Song lu* (Record of subjugating the Song) by Liu Mingzhong (1243–1318). Official publications on law and administrative policy include two extant collections of administrative decrees, the *Yuan dianzhang* (compiled 1320–22) and the *Tongzhi tiaoge* (1321), which are extremely valuable despite being written in an often impenetrably literal translation from Mongolian into Chinese. The dynasty also sponsored a complete digest of Yuan administrative history in more readable Chinese. This *Jingshi dadian* (Compendium on administering the world, 1330) has mostly been lost, although its chapter prefaces and its chapters on Mongol horse administration and the Korean and Burmese conquests have survived.

After the fall of the Mongol Yuan dynasty in 1368, the new Ming dynasty rapidly compiled the YUAN SHI (History of the Yuan, 1370) using sources such as the *Jingshi dadian* and the *Guochao mingchen shilue* as well as a host of others, mostly now nonextant. Because the sources are not usually identified, it is thus a digest of many of the Chinese accounts of Mongolian history.

In Korea the *Koryŏ sa,* or standard history of the Koryŏ dynasty (918–1392), compiled in Chinese in 1451 under the succeeding Chosŏn or Yi (1392–1910) dynasty according to the same annals-treatises-biographies format as the *Yuan shi,* contains unusually detailed accounts of the Mongol invasions and occupation. Other Korean sources include the annalistic *Tongguk t'onggam* (Comprehensive mirror of the eastern kingdom, 1484) by Sŏ Kŏjong, and *Ikchae-chip,* the complete works of the poet and scholar Yi Chehyŏn (1287–1367). The earliest extant history of Vietnam, Ngô Sĩ Liên's *Đai Viêt Su' Ký Toàn Thu'* (Comprehensive volume of the historical records of Vietnam, 1479) makes use of earlier annals to describe the Mongol invasion. The *An Nam Chí Lu'o'c* (*Annan zhilue,* Sketch of Annam), compiled in Chinese by Lê Tác (Li Ze), a Vietnamese defector to the Yuan who settled in China in the 1280s, covers the Yuan invasions of Vietnam from the Yuan perspective.

The most important Chinese Buddhist source on the Mongols is the *Fozu lidai tongzai* (Complete records of the Buddhist patriarchs through history), by Shi Nianchang (b. 1282), which covered Buddhist activities in China chronologically up to 1331. Chinese Buddhist monks also played a key role in transmitting information about China to other cultures. RASHID-UD-DIN FAZLULLAH's history of China was derived from a compilation like Nianchang's, transmitted by two Chinese Buddhist monks in Iran. In 1285 another Chinese monk translated Chinese historical records into Tibetan. Kun-dga' rDo-rje (1309–64) incorporated these translations into his pioneering general history of Tibet and Tibetan Buddhism, the *Hu-lan deb-ther* (composed 1346–63). The invaluable 1434 genealogical encyclopedia *rGya-Bod yig-tshang* (Sino-Tibetan records), by Shribhutibhadra (Tibetan dPal-'byor bZang-po), quoted wholesale from Yuan law codes and documents about Tibet, giving the most detailed surviving picture of myriarchy (*khri-skor,* Mongol *tümen*) organization in sedentary regions. Other monuments of the new Tibetan historiography under the Mongols include the *Si tu'i bka'-chems,* or testament of Byang-chub rGyal-mtshan (1302–64), and the memoirs of the INCARNATE LAMA Rang-byung rDo-rje (1284–1339) at the Mongol court, incorporated into the 1775 history of his Karma-pa lineage, *Karma Kam tshang brgyud-pad.*

See also BUDDHISM IN THE MONGOL EMPIRE; CONFUCIANISM; FOOD AND DRINK; MEDICINE, TRADITIONAL; TAOISM IN THE MONGOL EMPIRE; TIBET AND THE MONGOL EMPIRE.

Further reading: Dan Martin; *Tibetan Histories: A Bibliography of Tibetan Language Historical Works* (London: Serindia, 1997); Lao Yan-shuan, "The Chung-t'ang shih-chi of Wang Yün: An Annotated Translation with an Introduction," Ph.D. diss., Harvard University, 1962; Š. Bira, "Some Remarks on the *Hu-lan Deb-ther* of Kundga' rdo-rje," *Acta Orientalia* 17.1 (1964): 69–79; Hoklam Chan, *China and the Mongols: History and Legend under the Yuan and Ming* (Hidershot, Hampshire: Ashgate, 1997); Hok-lam Chan, *The Fall of the Jurchen Chin: Wang E's Memoir on Ts'ai-chou under the Mongol Siege (1233–1234)* (Stuttgart: Franz Steiner, 1993); Peter H. Lee and Wm. Theodore de Bary, ed. *Sources of Korean Tradition,* vol. 1, *From Early Times through the Sixteenth Century* (New York: Columbia University Press, 1997).

Eastern Mongols *See* INNER MONGOLIANS; KHALKHA.

Eastern province (Dornod) One of the original provinces created in the 1931 administrative reorganization, Eastern province occupies Mongolia's far eastern frontier with the Hulun Buir region of Inner Mongolia in China. It also abuts central Inner Mongolia and Russia's Chita district. It was renamed Choibalsang province (after Mongolia's then ruler MARSHAL CHOIBALSANG) in 1941 but was changed back to Eastern (Dornod) province in 1963. Composed entirely of KHALKHA Mongolia's prerevolutionary Setsen Khan province, the province has received as immigrants Buriat Mongols from Russia, BARGA Mongols from HULUN BUIR, and ÜJÜMÜCHIN Mongols from central Inner Mongolia. The province's 123,600 square kilometers (47,720 square miles) are occupied mostly by Mongolia's low-lying eastern steppe. Khökh Nuur Lake, at 554 meters (1,818 feet) above sea level, is Mongolia's lowest spot. Its population of 35,100 in 1956 increased to 74,200 in 2000.

Eastern's total livestock herd is 826,600 head. Dornod's capital, Choibalsang, had a population of 41,700 in 2000, making Eastern one of Mongolia's most urbanized provinces. The city was originally Sang Beise-yin Khüriye, a monastery town and seat of the grand duke of Achitu Zasag banner. It was renamed Bayantümen in 1923 and Choibalsang in 1941. Linked to the Soviet Union by a railway constructed for military purposes in 1938–39, Choibalsang was developed as a food-processing and light industrial city, powered by the nearby Aduunchuluun coal mine, and accounting for 2.7 percent of Mongolia's whole industrial output in 1985. It also had a major Soviet military presence. The 1990 transition to an open economy struck Eastern province particularly hard. Light industries and arable agriculture have almost collapsed, and unlike elsewhere, animal husbandry has not picked up the slack. By 2000 unemployment had grown to 12.6 percent, the highest in Mongolia.

See also BURIATS OF MONGOLIA AND INNER MONGOLIA; DAMDINSÜREN, TSENDIIN; MINING; SOVIET UNION AND MONGOLIA; YADAMSÜREN, ÜRJINGIIN.

East Gobi province (East Govi, Dornogov') One of the original provinces created in the 1931 administrative reorganization, East Gobi lies in southwestern Mongolia with a long frontier with Inner Mongolia in China. The urban province Gobi-Sümber (*see* CHOIR CITY) was carved out of its territory in 1994. Its territory lies mostly in KHALKHA Mongolia's prerevolutionary Tüshiyetü Khan province with some taken from Setsen Khan province. The province's 109,500 square kilometers (42,280 square miles) are mostly pure *gobi* (habitable desert), with a dry and hot climate. Its population has increased from 23,400 in 1956 to 51,100 in 2000, but still slightly fewer than one person inhabits every two square kilometers (1.3 per square mile). The TRANS-MONGOLIAN RAILWAY, completed in late 1955, made East Gobi's mineral resources accessible; these include the oil wells at Züünbayan and the fluorspar mines at Khar-Airag. The railway border town of Zamyn-Üüd serves both visitors from China and transit passengers. The 1,036,600 head of livestock (2000 figures) have a typical *gobi* composition, with relatively many camels (29,800 head), sheep (453,900 head), and goats (344,600 head). The capital, Sainshand, had 25,200 people in 2000, and posted Mongolia's hottest recorded temperature of 40.8°C (105.4°F). American atlases frequently misidentify Sainshand as Buyant-Uhaa. The museum of the province's famed author DANZIN-RABJAI (1803–56) is the city's principal cultural attraction.

See also GOBI DESERT; MATRILINEAL CLANS; MINING; SANGDAG, KHUULICHI.

economy, modern In 1940 Mongolia had a private herding-based economy, with a small state-owned indus-trial sector serving domestic needs. After 1970 Soviet assistance created a hothouse of industrialization that transformed Mongolia's lifestyle and foreign trade profile. Moving from a Soviet-bloc economy to a globalized economy after 1990, small-scale provincial industries were devastated, leaving the decollectivized herds and the vast Soviet-era mining enterprises as the main economic pillars. Through all these transformations, however, the Mongolian economy has been plagued by persistent trade imbalance and dependence on foreign aid.

ANIMAL HUSBANDRY

The elimination of the nobility and the monasteries, together with the failure of the first attempt at collectivization in 1930–32, left medium-scale private pastoral herders as the majority of the rural producers. From 1941, to boost exports to the Soviet Union, a system of compulsory sale at state-set low prices was implemented. This system produced major increases in output of all animal commodities except for those such as sheep wool and beef cattle, which were already heavily commercialized. Growth in production of most animal products slowed in the mid-1950s, when, following an analysis of the government's agriculture expert, N. Jagwaral, the government accepted that only collectivization could create growing output without the rise of social stratification.

Completed by 1960, collectivization did not live up to its promise. In general, by moving the herders away from subsistence production, collectivization somewhat increased the average income generated per animal. Modest increases in total output despite a diminishing rural population showed that while collectivization was not making a great contribution to the national economy, it was allowing resources and labor to be diverted to other fields without causing serious shortages. The most important change in animal husbandry was an investment in strategies to avoid winter-spring die-off: wells, corrals (*khashaa*), and fodder.

CREATING NEW ECONOMIC BRANCHES

The leaders of Mongolia in the 1950s were firmly committed to creating a diversified economy. The addition of wheat sheathes and a cogwheel to the national seal in 1960 expressed the regime's aspirations, one that were realized in the 1970s and 1980s.

With Soviet grain supplies cut off during WORLD WAR II, Mongolia created a crash program to expand grain FARMING and flour milling. After the war, however, the program lapsed. In March 1959, with the Soviet Union embarking on its Virgin Lands program, the party announced the goal of making Mongolia self-sufficient in grain. Vast amounts of equipment, including 5,400 tractors, were imported from the Soviet Union to create a mechanized agricultural sector. Most arable agriculture took place on state farms. Mongolia achieved self-sufficiency in grain by 1970.

The earliest industries in Mongolia were coal and gold MINING. In spring 1934 the opening of the Industrial Combine in ULAANBAATAR, which united a 1,000-kilowatt coal-fired power plant with factories for woolen clothing, felt, tanned hides, sheepskins, and shoes, began the Mongolian light industrial sector. This development of light industry continued during World War II and afterward. In 1949 Soviet-Mongolian joint-stock companies began mining and drilling for uranium, fluorspar, and oil in eastern Mongolia and the Gobi, although the results were disappointing.

Purely military needs required Mongolia's first railway between Borzya and Choibalsang, built in 1938–39. The long-planned line from ULAN-UDE to Ulaanbaatar was finally completed in 1949, and the SINO-SOVIET ALLIANCE mandated a further extension to China in 1956. Air transport began in 1947 and connected all provinces with the capital by the mid-1950s. Mongolia's road system remained rudimentary, however, as the relative ease of driving over the open steppe made paving less urgent.

A domestic construction and building materials industry had begun by 1930, with brick, whiting, and woodworking mills. A peculiarity of the construction industry was, however, the prevalence of non-Mongolian labor. Japanese prisoners of war (1945–47), Soviet soldiers in penal units for surrendering to Germany and other offenses (1947–56), Chinese guest workers (1956–63), and Soviet construction workers (1960–69) built most of what a visitor now sees in central Ulaanbaatar.

A new city, DARKHAN, apparently first planned with Chinese labor and a steel mill in mind, was redirected in 1961 into a Soviet–Eastern European–Mongolian project built around factories producing construction materials, as well as metalworking and repair shops and clothing and food-processing industries. After 1972 Japanese reparations built the Gobi CASHMERE factory in Ulaanbaatar, a significant advance into international-quality cashmere and camel hair knitted goods.

In the 1970s and 1980s Mongolia entered full scale into mining, opening the ERDENET CITY copper-molybdenum ore-dressing plant, one of the 10 largest in the world. In EASTERN PROVINCE, SÜKHEBAATAR PROVINCE, and EAST GOBI PROVINCE fluorspar, tungsten, uranium, and aluminum mines were vastly expanded. Based on these investments Mongolia now supplies 15 percent of the world's fluorspar. To fuel these energy-hungry plants and to warm Mongolia's apartment dwellers through the winter, massive investments in electricity, thermal power production, and coal production created a coal–thermal power–nonferrous mines triangle that proved to be the most robust portion of Mongolia's new economy.

As a result of these developments, the composition of Mongolia's output changed radically. The share of industry (including mining, manufacturing, and utilities) in the gross national product rose from 12.7 percent in 1940 to 48.9 percent in 1990, while animal husbandry's and agriculture's share fell from 64 percent to 15.7 percent.

THE PLANNED ECONOMY

From 1948 to 1990 the Mongolian economy was developed according to FIVE-YEAR PLANS on the Soviet model. Specifying quantity and prices of both the inputs and outputs of all economic enterprises, the planning process was oriented primarily to produce higher output figures for desired commodities rather than toward the most efficient satisfaction of needs. As such, it was quite well suited to the Mongolian leaders' desire to produce a diversified range of products as a good in itself.

At the same time the Mongolian leaders at many points sacrificed efficiency and profitability to social harmony. Consumer prices were essentially fixed despite constant increases in production costs, particularly after the 1970s. Enterprises were never closed, even when chronically unprofitable. These policies were sustainable only due to the continuous supply of Soviet aid.

At the same time the creation of new branches of production was at all points dependent on Soviet aid and hence on Soviet priorities. Estimates of Soviet aid to Mongolia in the 1980s range from 11 percent to 33 percent of Mongolia's total gross national product. Mongolia was assigned a role within Soviet-bloc planning primarily as a producer of raw materials. The development of massive capital-intensive enterprises when Mongolia had no indigenous heavy industry increased both Mongolia's dependence and its balance of payment problem. From 1960 to 1990 Mongolia regularly ran trade deficits of 25–30 percent, with the difference being made up by Soviet loans. Even within arable agriculture, the appearance of self-sufficiency was illusory, as the heavily mechanized agriculture depended on continuing supplies of equipment, spare parts, fuel, and even seeds from the Soviet Union. Given Mongolia's geopolitical importance to the Soviet Union in the SINO-SOVIET SPLIT, however, constant deficits were not a problem.

While industrialization did steadily increase labor productivity, the high prices of necessary imported inputs were reflected in the steadily worsening situation in specific consumption of materials. The amount of tögrögs in material expense required for one tögrög of national product rose from 0.7 in 1960 to 1.3 in 1986. Capital productivity declined as well: 1 tögrög of fixed installation produced 0.77 tögrögs of national income in 1960 but only 0.24 tögrögs in 1990.

THE MARKET ECONOMY

By 1986 Mongolian economists were well aware of the efficiency problems, while the East European nations (and to a lesser degree the Soviet Union) were expressing dissatisfaction with the seemingly bottomless pit of Mongolian aid. Such complaints were swallowed up in the collapse of the Soviet Union as a whole, which led in

1991 to the cessation of all aid, cancellation of all ongoing projects, and complete chaos in the international trade on which Mongolia depended. With democratization Western nations and multilateral lending institutions suddenly became a new source of aid, currently averaging US $320 million annually. Stimulated both by Western advice and by Mongolia's own desire to emulate the success of other Asian nations, Mongolia embarked on a rapid program of PRIVATIZATION and free trade. The results have so far been mixed, with many of the problems attributable to an incompetent and corrupt banking sector.

The immediate difficulties of the transition were severe. The gross domestic product (GDP) fell from a high of 10,546.8 million tögrögs in 1989 to 8,193.6 million tögrögs in 1993 (in 1986 prices). Inflation, unknown in consumer goods for decades, reached 325.5 percent in 1992. At the same time pervasive shortages led to rationing for the first time since WORLD WAR II. By 1994, however, inflation had fallen to a manageable 66.3 percent, free consumer prices had resolved the shortages, and rationing was lifted. Since 1995 the GDP has risen from 550,253.7 million tögrögs to 632,640.7 million tögrögs in 2000 (1995 prices), an increase powered by recuperation in the trade and repair, mining, and transport-communications sectors. By 2000 inflation had fallen to 8.1 percent, and the tögrög's value against the U.S. dollar had stabilized.

The opening of the 1990s fundamentally shook up the Mongolian economy. (It also changed statistical practices, which makes comparison sometimes difficult.) Manufacturing has been almost wiped out, going from around 70 percent of total industrial output in 1990 to 27 percent in 2000. Grain and fodder farming have likewise virtually collapsed, with sown acreage dropping from 790,000 hectares (1,952,090 acres) in 1990 to 210,000 (518,910 acres) in 2000. Truck farming for urban populations has, however, increased steadily.

Mining has weathered the transition well and now produces more than 50 percent of Mongolia's total industrial output and supplies 40–50 percent of total exports. The other two legs of the 1980s heavy-industrial triangle, power and coal, have also remained important, although coal output has declined. The mining and power industries, which remain mostly state owned, have benefited from both foreign aid and foreign investment. Direct foreign investment in gold, petroleum, and copper extraction promises continued growth in the mining sector.

Decollectivized animal husbandry at first showed very powerful growth, as the number of livestock shot up from 23 million in 1988 to 33.5 million in 1999, while the agricultural share of GDP rose from 19.2 percent in 1990 to 37 percent in 1999. The breakdown in state-owned trading organs kept herders from being able to market their surpluses until private trading companies picked up the slack in the late 1990s. Concerns about overstocking were underlined by two successive ZUD (winter disasters in spring 2000 and 2001), which cut livestock to 26.1 million in 2001 and threatened the livelihood of scores of thousands of herding families. The decline in fodder production and wells that the collectives formerly encouraged have exacerbated vulnerability. Private construction of simple roofless khashaas (corrals) has not compensated for this weakening pastoral infrastructure.

In the second half of the 1990s the wholesale and retail trade sector, now almost wholly privatized, accounted for almost half of Mongolia's economic growth and became second to agriculture in total production. The mixed public–private transportation and communications sector has likewise made a strong recovery. The construction industry, notoriously inefficient before 1990, was devastated by the transition, and privatized construction has only slowly picked up the slack.

Mongolia's foreign trade profile has dramatically changed. In the 1920s Russia received Mongolia's exports, but Mongolian consumers preferred Chinese goods. Now, with Mongolian consumers showing strong preferences for European goods, the opposite prevails: China buys 59 percent of Mongolia's exports and supplies only 21 percent of its imports, while Russia supplies 34 percent of Mongolia's imports but purchases only 10 percent of its exports. A new trend is exports to the United States (20 percent in 2000); clothing manufacturers elsewhere in Asia take advantage of America's lack of import quotas on Mongolian clothes to ship clothing components to Mongolia, where assembly is finished for export to the United States.

Early on in the transition, the collapse in the tögrög's purchasing power slashed imports, leading in 1993 to Mongolia's first trade surplus since World War II. In 1996, however, low prices for copper and cashmere devastated Mongolia's exports, particularly to the European Union, South Korea, and Japan. Wildfires that year also damaged the economy, as did the summer droughts and ZUD of 1999–2000 and 2000–01. Since then Mongolia has again funded large trade deficits by continuous loans from foreign patrons.

From 1996 to 2001, unfavorable price trends and zud conditions kept Mongolia's overall growth rate a modest 2–3 percent. By 2003, however, growth had increased to an annual 5 percent. Future plans for Mongolia include a refinery to complement its renewed oil production financed by international aid and a zinc mine funded by Chinese capital. Several large companies, including the national airline, MIAT, and Gobi Cashmere Company, are slated for privatization. In 2000 the Mongolian government announced its intention to seek investment for a "Millennium Road" project to build a paved east–west trunk road across Mongolia.

See also ANIMAL HUSBANDRY AND NOMADISM; COLLECTIVIZATION AND COLLECTIVE HERDING; DECOLLECTIVIZATION.

Further reading: Tumuriin Namjim, *The Economy of Mongolia: From Traditional Times to the Present*, ed. William Rozycki (Bloomington, Ind.: Mongolia Society, 2000); National Statistical Office of Mongolia, *Mongolian Statistical Yearbook 2000* (Ulaanbaatar: National Statistical Office, 2001); Frederick Nixson et al., *The Mongolian Economy: A Manual of Applied Economics for a Country in Transition* (Cheltenham, England: Edward Elgar, 2000); State Statistical Office of the MPR, *National Economy of the MPR for 70 Years* (Ulaanbaatar: State Statistical Office, 1991).

education, traditional Traditional methods of education in Mongolia emphasized the senses and memory. Formal education began in Mongolia during the empire period. Buddhist monastic education became widespread after 1578, and education of scribes was promoted by the administration in the QING DYNASTY (1636–1912) BANNERS (appanages).

(*On the early pioneers of a modern-style education, see* NEW SCHOOLS MOVEMENTS. *On modern education among the Mongols of Russia, see* BURIATS *and* KALMYKS. *On that among the Mongols in China, see* INNER MONGOLIANS. *On modern education in Mongolia, see* MONGOLIA, STATE OF; MONGOLIAN PEOPLE'S REPUBLIC; REVOLUTIONARY PERIOD; THEOCRATIC PERIOD.)

TRADITIONAL CHILD RAISING

In the MONGOL EMPIRE children began to ride as early as two or three years of age. A pillow was generally placed on the saddle when children rode. As soon as a boy could ride a little, he was given a small bow and trained to shoot little birds and other animals. Girls rode as well as boys and sometimes learned to shoot, also. In recent centuries horse riding begins later, at around five to six years of age. Early horse riding is not only practical but is held to develop courage. By age 13 or 14, children are expected to be able to bridle, saddle, hobble, and ride even difficult horses, and soon after they begin to be able to herd semi-wild horse herds on the steppe.

In unschooled pastoral families, intellectual training began at age two or three with the names of seasons, directions, and familiar objects, moving on to tongue twisters and memorization games. From age 10 girls began to sew, while boys began to work at carpentry and repair YURTS, saddles, and other things. Respect was inculcated by having children serve their elders food and liquor reverently, and children were trained through public shaming to play harmoniously with others. Specifically pastoral skills taught included knowing the proper names for the different colors of livestock, for which an extensive and exact vocabulary exists in Mongolian. At the same time children's senses were trained to see and count things far off, to track wild animals, and to observe weather signs. The names of mountains and other geographical features marking one's own banner territory were also memorized.

EDUCATION IN THE EMPIRE PERIOD

Under the MONGOL EMPIRE the khans generally appointed non-Mongol scribes and religious figures—Taoist, Christian, Buddhist—as tutors for their children. Formal education among the Mongols began around 1204 with CHINGGIS KHAN appointing the Uighur scribe Tatar-Tong'a as tutor for his sons, to teach them the newly adopted UIGHUR-MONGOLIAN SCRIPT. Under ÖGEDEI KHAN the Christian scribe Qadaq and the Taoist priest Li Zhichang tutored imperial princes. QUBILAI KHAN appointed the Confucian scholars Yao Shu (1203–80) and Xu Heng (1209–81) as tutors for his son JINGIM, and Abagha Khan appointed the Uighur Maichu *baqshi* (teacher) and a Chinese Buddhist monk as tutors for his grandson GHAZAN KHAN.

From 1269 Qubilai Khan also established a system of local schools in the provinces intended to educate young Mongols in the new SQUARE SCRIPT. The Mongolian school system was capped by a Mongolian School for Sons of the State in the capital. In 1315 this educational network was linked to an examination system, which became an important path of upward mobility for Mongols. In all these schools and exams, the curriculum was dominated by a rather eclectic mix of CONFUCIANISM and Chinese historical and administrative works. While BUDDHISM was the court religion, the relative rarity of Buddhist names indicates that a monastic education was not common among the Mongols.

TRADITIONAL BUDDHIST AND SCRIBAL EDUCATION

Nothing is known of formal education between the fall of the Mongol YUAN DYNASTY in China in 1368 and the SECOND CONVERSION to BUDDHISM begun in 1575.

The building up of a native monastic class began in 1578, when the newly converted ALTAN KHAN (1508–82) and his aristocracy dedicated 108 children to be trained as monks. More such officially inspired dedications occurred as Buddhism spread, although often the aristocrats preferred to hire substitutes. By the 19th century the monasteries were by far the largest institution of formal education. The basic curriculum emphasized reading and memorizing the Tibetan texts chanted during the regular services in the Buddhist temples. Only after completing this program would monks be allowed to learn the MONGOLIAN LANGUAGE. Most monks entered the monasteries at eight to 10 years of age and left at around age 17, mostly with a knowledge of the Tibetan letters (*see* LAMAS AND MONASTICISM; TIBETAN LANGUAGE AND SCRIPT). Of those lamas who stayed in the monasteries a small minority became fluent in written Tibetan and in Mongolian. Lamas were responsible for much, if not most, of the Mongolia- and Tibetan-language literature and history writing produced among the Mongols.

The banners, or local administrations, of Mongolia under the QING DYNASTY (1636–1912) trained clerks for banner (local appanage) administration. Many BANNERS maintained a small school that enrolled 15 to 25 boys. They learned how to write Mongolian in the Uighur-Mongolian script as well as Manchu, written with a similar script. Penmanship was emphasized over comprehension. Boys graduated by age 13 and from then until their 60th year performed a three-month rotation as a scribe every year. Because of this duty the banner schools were not popular, although some clerks parlayed their skills into a career as a banner official. The Manchu AMBANS maintained similar schools in Khüriye, ULIASTAI, and KHOWD CITY, where Chinese was also taught. In addition to this official scribal schooling, most officials regularly tutored a few boys and occasionally girls in their home, including their own children. Of these, at least one in 10 had to be instructed in official penmanship and registered for the scribal rotation. The others were taught to read, not write, so as to avoid this duty. Among the Volga KALMYKS a decree in the 1740s fined the father of any boy still illiterate by age 15.

Initial instruction for the lamas was based on simple poems in Tibetan describing the letters. Scribal instruction was based mostly on DIDACTIC POETRY, such as the *Oyun tülkhigür* (Turquoise key), or translated Chinese primers, such as the *Three-Character Classic* (*Sanzijing*). Unsatisfied by these options, the ORDOS poet Kheshigbatu (1849–1917) composed his own alliterated primer based on the kind of instruction given to pastoral children. Mongolian lamas also composed a number of grammatical textbooks structured as "commentaries" on the no longer extant *Jirükhen-Tolta* (Artery of the heart) attributed to CHOSGI-ODSIR (fl. 1307–21). The earliest and most widespread of these was by the ÜJÜMÜCHIN INCARNATE LAMA Danzin-Dagba (fl. 1723–36); new traditional grammars were being produced as late as the 1920s. For scribal use the Qing court commissioned an official dictionary (*Khorin nigetü tailburi toli*, Dictionary in twenty-one headings, completed in 1717) with pronunciation guides in the Manchu script.

Statistics on traditional literacy are hard to find and harder to interpret. About 45 percent of the male population in Khalkha and about 17–20 percent in neighboring Inner Mongolian areas passed through the monasteries, yet few of these people could be considered genuinely literate. Those officially registered as scribes were about 0.3–0.7 percent, but they were perhaps as little as a tenth of those tutored in reading and writing in banner and home schools. A detailed survey of the Aga steppe in southern Siberia in 1908 may be representative of Mongolian areas. Of the 39,000 persons, about 6 percent were literate best in Tibetan, 7 percent best in Mongolian, and 1 percent best in Russian. (In Mongolia proper, Manchu and Chinese replaced Russian). Female literacy was less than 1 percent. In Aga's two major monasteries about half the lamas were considered literate in Tibetan.

Further reading: Y. Rinchen, "Books and Traditions (From the History of Mongol Culture)," in *Anacleta Mongolica*, ed. John G. Hangin and Urgunge Onon (Bloomington, Ind.: Mongolia Society, 1972), 63–76.

Eg River (Egiin Gol, Egiyn Gol) Flowing from LAKE KHÖWSGÖL into the SELENGE RIVER, the Eg River is 475 kilometers (295 miles) long and drains an area of 42,400 square kilometers (16,370 square miles). Since 1991 the Mongolian government has sought to build a hydroelectric power plant on the Eg River 6 2/3 kilometers (four miles) above its confluence with the Selenge but had not been able to finance the project as of 2000. The prospect of flooding the river valley hastened archaeological investigations since 1991, and tombs dating from the Bronze Age to the MONGOL EMPIRE have been excavated and above-ground Buddhist sites identified.

Egiyn Gol *See* EG RIVER.

Eight Banners The Eight Banners were the military foundation of the QING DYNASTY (1636–1912). Although organized at first for the Qing dynasty's ruling Manchu people, the Eight Banners had Mongolian and Chinese-martial units as well. The Eight Banners system must not be confused with the autonomous banner system (*see* BANNERS) that governed the vast majority of Mongols who remained in Inner and Outer Mongolia.

ORIGINS

The formation of the Eight Banners went hand in hand with the rise of the MANCHU EMPIRE. By 1601 the Qing dynasty's founder, Nurhachi (b. 1558, r. 1616–26) had created the first "arrows" (Manchu, *niru*; Mongolian; *sumu; see* SUM), which each enrolled 300 soldiers with their families as permanent military units. By 1615 Nurhachi had begun combining these "arrows" into divisions (Manchu, *gûsa*; Mongolian, *khoshuu*). The divisions were distinguished by their banners: plain yellow, white, red, or blue, or bordered yellow, white, red, or blue (the border was red or, in the case of the red banner, white). The Chinese name *qi* (banner) used for these divisions has given the traditional English name for these units.

THE EIGHT BANNERS MONGOLS

Mongolian units also joined the rising new dynasty. In 1621 two South Khalkha (later renamed JUU UDA league) *taiji* (noblemen) surrendered to Nurhachi with 600 households. Nurhachi formed them into two "arrows." The number of Mongolians surrendering or donated to the throne by submissive Mongol lords increased, and in 1635 Nurhachi's successor, Emperor Hong Taiji (1627–44), divided the now approximately 10,000 Mongols into 80 "arrows," or *sumus*, organized into eight separate Mongol banners. By 1657 the banner soldiery was approximately 32 percent Manchu, 17 percent Mongol, and 51 percent Chinese-martial.

Only those Mongols who had physically moved toward the Manchu homeland in modern eastern Liaoning province were enrolled in the Eight Banners. Hong Taiji organized the great majority of his Mongol subjects who had remained in Inner Mongolia into quite different autonomous banners ruled by hereditary *jasags* (Khalkha, ZASAG) of the noble, or *taiji*, caste. While the Eight Banners Mongols included a wide variety of clans, including the Chinggisid BORJIGID clan, Chinggisid privileges were not recognized in the Eight Banner system, and few officials were Borjigid. Arrow and banner offices were all theoretically open to merit, although in reality virtually every Mongolian *sumu* captain passed his office to his son.

Some Mongols in the steppe were, however, incorporated into the Eight Banners: the Höhhot TÜMED (1636), CHAKHAR (1675), and the BARGA Mongols, Solons (*Ewenkis*), and Daurs of HULUN BUIR (1732–34). While enjoying many privileges of Eight Banners membership, legally they were subjected to the Lifan Yuan's criminal code. These bannermen were never stationed within China proper and so remained socially distinct from the other Mongol Eight Banners people.

MONGOL SOCIETY IN THE EIGHT BANNERS

With the Manchu conquest of China in 1644, approximately half the Eight Banners soldiers were moved to Beijing, while 30 percent were stationed in garrisons in the strategic parts of the empire. Each garrison contained a selection of all the ethnic units and banners within the system. Thus, Mongol Eight Banners troops, numbering 43,636 in 1720, were distributed throughout the empire as salaried soldiery. Within the banner hierarchy Mongols shared numerous privileges with the Manchus that were denied the Chinese-martial bannermen.

All Eight Banners officials were required to know Manchu; those in the Mongol Eight Banners had to know Mongolian in addition. Knowledge of Chinese was also widespread. During the 18th century Mongol bannermen participated fully with Mongols from the autonomous banners in Beijing's active Mongolian and Tibetan-Buddhist culture. Arana (d. 1724), of the Chakhar Umi clan, completed the first Mongolian translation with commentary of a Chinese novel, *Journey to the West*, in 1721. The *Menggu shixi pu* (Mongolian genealogy), written in Chinese and Manchu in 1735 by Lomi (b. c. 1670) of the Kharachin Borjigid, fused the Mongolian tradition of the 17th-CENTURY CHRONICLES with intense Qing loyalism. Mongol bannermen were dedicated in their patronage of Tibetan-rite Buddhist temples, yet already by the 1730s there were reports that Mongol Eight Banners soldiers no longer spoke Mongolian well. From the 1740s to the end of the dynasty, a number of distinguished Chinese-language poets from the Mongol banners appeared, including Fashshan (Chinese, Fa Shishan, 1753–1813) and Sandô (Chinese, Sanduo, b. 1875). In 1865 the Mongol bannerman Chongqi (father-in-law of the Tongzhi emperor, 1862–75) won first place in the palace examinations.

The decline in Mongolian-language skills coincided with an increasing use of Mongol bannermen in the Qing dynasty's Inner Asian administration. After 1750 Mongol Eight Banners officials served frequently as AMBANS (imperial residents) and *jiangjuns* (generals in chief) in Tibet, Kökenuur (Qinghai), Xinjiang, and Inner and Outer Mongolia. Despite their ancestry, these Mongol Eight Banners soldiers were usually seen as "Manchus" by the local Mongols. After 1901 prominent Mongol Eight Banners officials, such as Xiliang (1853–1917) and Sandô, loyally implemented the Qing's hated NEW POLICIES in Tibet and Mongolia.

In the 1911 revolution that overthrew the Qing, garrison bannermen and their families in China suffered massive pogroms followed by widespread discrimination under the Republic of China (1911–49). Many bannermen denied their ancestry, particularly outside Beijing. Discrimination eased under the People's Republic (1949 on). Since 1982 many Chinese-speaking pure- or mixed-blood descendants of Eight Banners Mongols in China proper have revived their designation as Mongols.

Further reading: Roger DesForges, *Hsi-liang and the Chinese National Revolution* (New Haven, Conn.: Yale University Press, 1973); Mark Elliot, *The Manchu Way: The Eight Banners and Ethnic Identity in Late Imperial China* (Stanford, Calif.: Stanford University Press, 2001).

Eight White Yurts (mausoleum of Genghis Khan)

The Eight White Yurts, or Palaces (*Naiman chaghan ger/ordon*), in ORDOS, Inner Mongolia, was the largest and most widely honored of the many cult places of CHINGGIS KHAN and his family in Mongolia. While other cult objects were dispersed throughout northeast Ordos, the most important were kept at Ejen Khoroo (Ejin Horo), or "the Court of the Lord [Chinggis]." The complex of sacrificial objects is also called the ONGGHON (grave or sacred thing) of Chinggis Khan. Since 1956 the cultic objects have been centralized in a mausoleum of Genghis Khan built at Ejen Khoroo by the Chinese government.

THE OBJECTS

Since the 18th century at least, the Eight White Palaces (*Naiman chaghan ordon*) have been traditionally enumerated as the three yurts of Chinggis Khan's wives (BÖRTE ÜJIN, Qulan, and the fictional Gürbeljin Ghoa) and five other sacred objects (Chinggis's white horse dedicated to the god Indra, his milk pail, his arrows and quivers, his reins and saddles, and his treasury containing old writings and sacrificial articles). All but the treasury, which stayed close to Börte's YURT, nomadized in different spots over northeastern Ordos and the neighboring Höhhot Tümed banners, congregating together at a special place only for the great spring offering.

The yurts were not the collapsible yurts used by the Mongols in recent centuries but archaic *chomchog* yurts, squarish in plan with a bell-shaped top, which were moved only on carts. The Golden Palace (Altan ordon), or *chomchog*-yurt, was a double yurt, with one placed in front as a kind of antechamber communicating by a door with the one behind as the holy of holies. In front of this double yurt in the open was kept a black standard or four-tailed standard, which was believed to be Chinggis Khan's war standard. Also kept nearby was a two-wheeled "yellow *khasag*-cart," pulled by white camels.

Inside the inner chamber of the Golden Palace was a box or casket containing, it was believed, the remains of Chinggis Khan and his principal wife, Börte (also written Börtegeljin). The casket measured 1.20 meters long, 0.77 meters wide, and .995 meters high (3.94 by 2.53 by 3.26 feet). In and around the casket were also kept other cult objects and manuscripts. A similar casket with remains existed in Empresses Qulan and Gürbeljin Ghoa's *chomchog*-yurt.

Other objects of worship associated with Chinggis Khan's family in Ordos included the *chomchog*-yurt of TOLUI, Chinggis Khan's youngest son, and his wife SORQAQTANI BEKI, known as Eshi Khatun (First Lady). In it was an *ongghon*-portrait of Tolui and his flint and belt buckle. This shrine was kept at the border of Ordos's

Otog and Khanggin (Hanggin) banners with its own Darkhad population. Its chief officiant, or *iröölchi*, (*see* YÖRÖÖL AND MAGTAAL) carried on the highly secret *garli* offering at the Eight White Palaces.

OFFICIANTS

The custodians of the sacred objects and officiants at the sacrifices were known as the "500 Yellow Darkhad," who were tax exempt, or *darkhan* (Middle Mongolian DAR-QAN), hence their name. Since they were to be in eternal mourning for Chinggis Khan, they were forbidden to put on mourning for other authorities. The Darkhad were of diverse clan origins and were scattered among the banners of Ordos along with the sacred objects of which they had custody. (These Darkhad have no relation to the DARKHAD of northern Mongolia.) Ruling the non-Chinggisid Darkhad was a Chinggisid prince bearing the title *jinong*, who was the tituler ruler of all Ordos.

The Darkhad were divided into two groups of *yamutad* (literally, government officials): the Right *yamutad* of civil officials guarding Chinggis's court, and the Left *yamutad* of military officials guarding his standard. Those of the Right were said to be supervised by BO'ORCHU and his descendants and those on the Left by MUQALI and his descendants. The two wings of the Darkhad had titles that at the upper levels (TAISHI, *taibuu*, *jaisang*, *chingsang*, etc.) roughly paralleled court titles in use from about 1300 to 1500.

CEREMONIES

Since the 16th century the worship at the shrine consisted of four seasonal offerings: 1) the "Sacrifice of the White Herd of Spring" on the 21st of the last moon of spring, when Chinggis's 99 white mares were first milked and aspersions (*satsal*) of mare's milk made; 2) the "Sacrifice of the Lake of Summer" on the 16th of the middle moon of summer, as the white mares foaled; 3) the "Sacrifice of the Muzzles of Autumn" on the 12th of the last moon of autumn, when the milking season ceased; and 4) the "Offering of the Placing of the Hides" on the third of the first moon of winter, when the *tasama*, or goathide, wrapping Chinggis's casket was anointed. In addition to these offerings, there were minor monthly offerings.

All these offerings consisted of sacrificial offerings of nine sheep and one mare and aspersions of nine measures of milk liquor (*sarkhud*). In most offerings the meat and liquor were shared out to all the audience, who eagerly sought it as evidence of the grace of Lord Chinggis. Certain others, though, were limited to the 60 Darkhad officiants, or the TAIJI (descendants of Chinggis Khan). The spring sacrifice was by far the largest, and the only one in which all the "Eight White Palaces" were gathered. During this sacrifice, the casket of Chinggis's remains was put on the yellow *khasag*-cart and driven to the "palace" of the quiver. The night before occurred the secret *garli*-offering, in which nine sheep bones were burned both

The coffin of Chinggis Khan and Börte being moved from the Palace of the Quiver (background) into a tent on the "yellow-*khasag* cart" (foreground) after the spring sacrifice in 1935 (*Courtesy the Owen Lattimore estate*)

outside and inside the Golden Palace to the family *ong-ghon* (sacred thing) of Chinggis Khan. The next day the *jinong* officiated over a public offering.

Apart from these calendrical rituals there was an anointing ritual held whenever the felt of the *chomchog* yurts was replaced. In it a sable skin and five-colored cloth strips were anointed and hung from the Golden Palace's ridgepole. Other calendrical offerings were dedicated to the black four-footed standard and the quiver and arrows. Darkhad lamas also performed Buddhist ceremonies during the major sacrifices.

Associated with the sacrificial offerings were prayers offered by the *khonjin*, or speaker, giving glory to Chinggis Khan and his companions and seeking his blessing. A unique form of prayer was made of repetitive syllables uttered by the *chargichi*, or player of a sacred wooden clapper (*chargi*), during the offerings of milk liquor. Called by the Mongols the "language of the gods" (TENG-GERI), these strings of repetitive syllables are clearly fossilized examples of glossolalia, or "speaking in tongues," characteristic of ecstatic worship throughout the world and first spoken in a trance state perhaps induced by the rhythmic clapper. At present, however, the cult includes no spontaneous or ecstatic elements.

THE CHINGGIS KHAN CULT IN THE MONGOL EMPIRE

The offerings of the Eight White Palaces as they existed in the descriptions of ethnographers and the memories of old Darkhad men are a combination of elements dating from the time of the empire and innovations from about 1450–1510. The idea of eight halls and four seasonal sacrifices with aspersions of mare's milk, the *garli* sacrifice of burning bones, the title *jinong*, and the physical form and terminology of many of the objects all go back to the time of the MONGOL EMPIRE. At the same time, the names and legends of Chinggis's family and companions associated with the cult and the cult portraits and texts are all 16th-century in origin. Most important, the link with the territory of Ordos and the belief that Chinggis Khan's remains are actually kept there certainly postdate 1450, when the Mongols first occupied the area.

There is no serious doubt that after his death in 1227 in northwest China, Chinggis Khan was transported to the KHENTII RANGE. The area around the grave, called the "great *qoruq*" or forbidden ground at Kilengu, was guarded thereafter by men of the Uriyangkhan clan. At the coronation QURILTAI of his successor, ÖGEDEI KHAN, in 1229, three days of offerings were made and 40 maidens of good family sacrificed to him.

The center for the Chinggis Khan cult was the four palace-tents (ORDO) of his principal wives and the *ong-ghon* (felt, silk, or bronze anthropomorphic dolls inhabited by his family spirits) kept in carts near them. Chinggis Khan had four *ordo*s, each controlled by a principal wife: Börte Üjin (QONGGIRAD clan), Qulan (MERKID),

Yisüi, and Yisügen (both TATARS and sisters). Both Ögedei and Möngke Khans are known to have attended Chinggis Khan's *ordo*s, and the latter is said to have "sacrificed to its standard and drums."

Chinggis Khan's descendants also established their own cult sites. His grandson BATU on the Volga kept a cult figure (*ongghon*) of Chinggis Khan in a cart in front of his palace-tent. The offerings at this shrine consisted of aspersions of the first fruits of milk, sacrifices of animals, particularly sheep and horses, in which the bones would be burned and the meat placed in the shrine and consecrated before being eaten, and the dedication of animals to the *ongghon*, which would then be allowed to roam freely and never be ridden.

In 1260 QUBILAI KHAN, another of Chinggis Khan's grandsons, installed ancestral spirits in his civil capital, DAIDU. Although the rituals became more Chinese in style after an ancestral temple was built in 1280, seasonal milk aspersions and prayers in Mongolian continued to be offered to Chinggis by shamans. By 1266 eight "halls" (probably yurts kept in the palace temple) were arranged west to east for worshipping Chinggis, his father, YISÜGEI, and his sons and successors up to MÖNGKE KHAN.

In 1292 Qubilai appointed his grandson Gammala (1263–1302) prince of Jin to supervise the great *qoruq* at Kilengü and Chinggis Khan's *ordo*s. Khans continued to be buried at Kilengu, and there were now nine *ordo*s rather than just four. RASHID-UD-DIN mentions constant incense offerings to the *ongghon* there; presumably aspersions and sacrifices were conducted as well. The title of prince of Jin (Jinwang, or in medieval Chinese, Jinong), inherited by Gammala's son and grandson, became the title for the supervisor of Chinggis's *ordo*s. The remains of Gammala's cult center have been excavated at AWARGA.

CREATION OF THE EIGHT WHITE YURTS

After the Mongol khans fled their capital, Daidu, in China and returned to the steppe in 1368, nothing is known of the cult of Chinggis Khan for almost a century, except that it must have continued in some form. After the 1449 TUMU INCIDENT the Mongols swarmed into the Ordos area of Inner Mongolia south of the Huang (Yellow) River. Evidently, as they poured in, they brought with them some of the yurts and sacred objects of the cult of Chinggis Khan. Reconstituted in the new territory, the cult was intertwined with apocryphal stories now linked to local geography and the known fact of Chinggis's death nearby. Qulan was turned into a Korean empress, and the fictitious Gürbeljin Ghoa of the XIA DYNASTY replaced the historic Yisüi and Yisügen. These apocryphal legends were later incorporated into the 17TH-CENTURY CHRONICLES of Mongolian history. New cultic regulations were attributed to Qubilai Khan, the supposed author of the *CHAGHAN TEÜKE* (White history), a late 16th-century apocryphal religiopolitical utopia.

By 1452 the title of *jinong* (the old prince of Jin) began to appear again as a leader of the western branch of the Mongols proper. From 1508 on the Eight White Yurts (*Naiman chaghan ger*) were one of the two centers of the Mongols' NORTHERN YUAN DYNASTY. There the *jinong* made daily incense offerings to Lord Chinggis, and the great khans were crowned. The Eight White Yurts were still mobile and on occasion accompanied the khans on campaign. ALTAN KHAN (1508–82) at least twice dedicated conquered Mongol enemies to the service of the shrine, and this is probably the origin of many, if not all, of the Darkhad, although legend attributed their selection from the Mongols to Qubilai Khan. During this period the four great sacrifices, the arrows and quiver, the sacred sable skin, the *chomchog* yurts, the Darkhad titles, and the idea of Chinggis being buried in Ordos are all mentioned. Also mentioned, however, was the palace-tent of Chinggis's mother, Ö'ELÜN ÜJIN, a shrine that apparently no longer exists.

Ordos had the most revered but by no means the only Chinggisid cult objects. An ancient shrine of Chinggis Khan's brother Qasar existed in ULAANCHAB's Muuminggan banner with 16th-century texts and cult portraits. Another cult place, where glossolalia-style prayers were also read, was kept in Khalkha Mongolia until 1937. The tent of Tolui and Eshi Khatun (Sorqaqtani Beki) was worshipped among the CHAKHAR; this may be, in fact, the same one later found in Ordos. The last Mongol khan, Legdan, fled west from Chakhar to Ordos to escape the rising Manchus in 1632 and may have brought the Eshi Khatun shrine with him. Ligdan dedicated a saddle to the Eight White Yurts but in 1634 fled farther west to Kökenuur, taking the Eight White Yurts with him.

THE CHINGGIS KHAN CULT IN THE QING

Although the cult objects (possibly with Ligdan's Eshi Khatun shrine added) were returned to Ordos after Ligdan's death, the fall of the Mongol dynasty and the submission of the Mongols to the Qing cast the shrine into eclipse. There is no evidence of the cult of Chinggis Khan in Ordos until 1720, when the Manchu emperor Kangxi recognized the cult. Manchu imperial attention increased under Emperor Qianlong (1735–96), under whom all the current features of the Eight White Palaces can be seen. The title of *jinong* remained hereditary among the Ordos nobility until 1764, when it was attached by imperial order to whichever Chinggisid prince was the captain general of the Yekhe Juu league, the administrative name for Ordos (*see* LEAGUE).

While the memories of Chinggis Khan were strongest in Ordos, the cult continued to flourish in the 18th and 19th centuries throughout Mongolia. Many banners claimed to have been the site of Chinggis's life and burial, kept standards and other cult objects, and conducted sacrifices and prayers in the "language of the gods." Indeed, every banner among the Mongols in being ruled by a Chinggisid nobleman, having its own banner standard, and conducting the same seasonal mare's milk sprinkling and marriage rituals sanctified by his example was, in a sense, an incarnation of Chinggis's realm.

Chinggis Khan also appeared within the Buddhist pantheon in Mongolia and even Tibet. From the 17th century Tibetan lamas had identified Chinggis Khan as an incarnation of the fierce bodhisattva Vajrapani, just as the Manchu emperor in China was an incarnation of the bodhisattva of wisdom, Manjushri. In Kökenuur the Tibetans included him in worship as a local deity of the Ordos Mongols. The INCARNATE LAMA, the Third Mergen Gegeen (1717–66), composed prayers for the worship of Lord Chinggis and his black and white standards as part of his nativization of Buddhist worship.

In 1873 Hui (Chinese Muslim) rebels raided Ordos and set fire to the shrine of Chinggis Khan. Many books in the treasury palace-tent were lost, but a timely rain is said to have rescued the cult objects in the Golden Palace tent from destruction. In 1915 Chinese bandits again looted the shrine, although taking only gold and silver and leaving the other cult articles.

THE SHRINE IN CHINESE POLITICS

In 1916 the government of the new Republic of China built a brick Chinggis Khan Temple, but the Darkhad refused to cooperate, claiming that the structure was of ill omen and that Chinggis Khan's will forbade residence in dirt walls. In 1927 the Darkhad tore the new temple down.

In May 1939 China's Nationalist government, worried about the use Japan might make of the remains, ordered the most holy objects—the caskets of Chinggis, and Börte and of Qulan and the black four-footed standard—transported to a Taoist temple in Yuzhong county, Gansu. The worship was maintained by teams of Darkhad rotating from Ordos. In 1949 the cult objects were moved farther west to sKu-'bum (Ta'ersi) Monastery in Qinghai (Kökenuur) in a futile effort to escape the Chinese Communist advance.

At first the new Chinese Communist government of Suiyuan province, which had jurisdiction over Ordos, was happy to have the cult objects gone and held the spring sacrifices as a purely secular NAADAM, with athletic contests and musical performances. By contrast, the ethnic Mongol Communist Ulanfu and the eastern Inner Mongolian cadres in the Inner Mongolian Autonomous Region saw the shrine as a monument to Inner Mongolian national feeling. Championing it also strengthened the autonomous region's claim to speak for the Mongols of Suiyuan. Late in 1953 the Inner Mongolian government petitioned to have the cult objects moved back from sKu-'bum to Ordos. In 1954 Beijing agreed to move the cult objects back, fund a new mausoleum, and annex Suiyuan to Inner Mongolia. Ulanfu's attendance at the April 1954 celebration of the return of the caskets and standard was thus a personal triumph.

The new 1,500-square-meter mausoleum destroyed many of the earlier traditions. In 1956 the spring sacrifice was moved permanently to May 15, and made the only main one. The legal privileges of the Darkhad were abolished, although those living near the shrine continued to officiate. The west wing housed the black four-footed standard, which had never before been allowed under a roof, as well as saddles, the sword, and other standards and cult objects from all over Ordos. The east wing held a new *chomchog*-yurt for Tolui and Eshi Khatun (Sorqaqtani Beki). In the rear chamber the caskets for Chinggis and his three empresses were crowded into a single *chomchog*-yurt. These were flanked by new *chomchog*-yurts for Chinggis's brothers Qasar and Belgütei, added to appeal to those non-Ordos Mongols who traced their ancestry to them. The front hall housed a large statue of Chinggis Khan.

During the Cultural Revolution the Darkhad were driven out, and all the tents and cult objects desecrated or destroyed. In 1979 Beijing again issued funds to restore the mausoleum, seek out the Darkhad, and have imitations of the old tents and cult objects made. While the mausoleum's many Mongol visitors still treat the sanctuary with honor, the sense of fear and power that used to make the Darkhad speak only in a whisper about things such as the *garli* sacrifice is certainly gone.

See also CHINGGIS KHAN CONTROVERSY; FUNERARY CUSTOMS; *JEWEL TRANSLUCENT SUTRA*.

Further reading: Peter Alford Andrews, *Felt Tents and Pavilions: The Nomadic Tradition and Its Interaction with Princely Tentage* (London: Melisende, 1999), 1: 351–386; Elizabetta Chiodo, "'The Book of the Offerings to the Holy Cinggis Qaghan': A Mongolian Ritual Text," *Zentralasiatische Studien* 22 (1989–91): 190–220 and 23 (1992): 84–144; N. Hurcha, "Attempts to Buddhicize the Cult of Chinggis Khan," *Inner Asia* 1 (1999): 45–58; Henry Serruys, "A Mongol Prayer to the Spirit of Činggis-qan's Flag," in *Mongolian Studies,* ed. Louis Ligeti (Amsterdam: Gruner, 1970): 527–535; ———, "A Prayer to Cinggis-qan," *Études Mongoles . . . et Sibériennes* 16 (1985): 17–36.

Eleuth *See* ÖÖLÖD.

Elista (Kalmyk, Elstä) The capital of Russia's KALMYK REPUBLIC, Elista is a relatively small town situated in western Kalmykia. Covering 21 square kilometers (8 square miles), the city proper had a population of 89,682 in 1989, of which 49.7 percent were Kalmyk. It has grown rapidly in the post-Soviet transition, and its population reached 105,765 in 2002. The name *Elista* is from Kalmyk *elstä,* "sandy."

During the early Soviet period construction materials, woodworking, and wool, meat, and milk plants were developed in Elista. In 1969 the city was connected by railroad to Stavropol'; highways were subsequently built to Volgograd and Astrakhan. After 1975 oil production became the major industry, currently accounting for 70.5 percent of the city's industrial output. A thermal energy plant is being planned. Elista is Kalmykia's center of administration, culture, and education, including the Kalmyk State University (founded 1970). In 2002 Elista accounted for 31 percent of Kalmykia's population, more than 70 percent of its retail trade and catering, and 45 percent of its industrial production. Elista has become a showpiece for the plans of the Kalmyk president Kirsan N. Ilümzhinov (b. 1962), who is also head of the world Fédération Internationale des Échecs (FIDE) CHESS association. In 1998 Elista hosted the World Chess Olympiad at a newly built "City Chess" complex.

Founded in 1865, Elista remained only a minor settlement until 1928, when it was made capital of Kalmykia. By 1939 the city's population had reached 17,000. After occupation by the German army from August 12, 1942, to January 1, 1943, Joseph Stalin exiled the KALMYKS from the territory and put Elista, renamed Stepnoi, under Stavropol' Territory. In 1957, with the exoneration and return of the Kalmyks, the name Elista was revived, and it again became capital of Kalmykia.

elk stones (deer stones, stag stones) Elk stones are the most characteristic funerary monument of the Mongolian Bronze and early Iron Ages (12th–5th centuries B.C.E.), occurring in the KHANGAI RANGE, KHENTII RANGE, and ALTAI RANGE of Mongolia, as well as in Transbaikalia and Tuva. None are found in the GOBI DESERT or Inner Mongolia. Made of granite or sometimes marble, they generally range from 1.5 to 2.5 meters (4.9 to 8.2 feet) tall, although examples as small as 0.8 meters (2.6 feet) or as tall as 3.55 meters (11.65 feet) have been found. The elk stone of Tsokhiotyn Am (Shine-Ider, Khöwsgöl) shows an early example that is both cruder and less stylized than the "classic" elk stone. The classic elk stone has several stylized upward-facing elks (British red deer, *Cervus elaphus*) stacked on top of one another, each with long antlers with curved tines laid along the back, legs reduced to nubs, large, round eyes, and grossly elongated lips. At the top of the stone, separated by a belt, is a solar disk, sometimes accompanied by a smaller disk (sun and moon?). Various articles—bows and arrows, daggers, axes, mirrors, shields—may be between the deer or hanging from another belt at the bottom. Classic elk stone figures are also found on PETROGLYPHS. Elk stones are virtually always found in or near slab tombs, rectangular grave enclosures made of large stones set on edge.

See also PREHISTORY.

Further reading: Esther Jacobson, *The Deer Goddess of Ancient Siberia: A Study in the Ecology of Belief* (Leiden: E. J. Brill, 1993).

El-Temür (d. 1333) *Qipchaq officer who engineered the 1328 coup d'état that restored the children of Haishan to the throne*

A grandson of TUTUGH, El-Temür headed the KESHIG (imperial guard) and Palace Provisions Commission for Emperor Haishan (1307–11) of the Mongols' Yuan dynasty in China. Losing favor after Haishan's death, he was an official in the Military Affairs Bureau in DAIDU when the emperor Yisün-Temür (1323–28) died at SHANGDU. On September 8 El-Temür arrested Yisün-Temür's top officials in Daidu and summoned Haishan's sons Qoshila and Tuq-Temür to the capital. Escorted by the Henan governor BAYAN (1281?–1340), Tuq-Temür arrived from South China and was enthroned in Daidu. El-Temür's and Bayan's support from the rich central and southern provinces forced Yisün-Temür's partisans in Shangdu to surrender on November 23. When Haishan's elder son, Qoshila, arrived from the CHAGHATAY KHANATE to Mongolia, he was elected khan on February 27, 1329. Fearing Chaghatayid influence on the Yuan dynasty, El-Temür assassinated Qoshila on August 30 and reenthroned Tuq-Temür. Under Tuq-Temür (1328–32) El-Temür held the court's highest offices, controlled the Qipchaq guards, and displaced the QONGGIRAD as the imperial QUDA (in-law family). Not personally of Confucian sympathies, he exploited the Confucians' resentment of Yisün-Temür's largely Muslim faction and patronized scholarship. After Tuq-Temür's death in 1332, El-Temür disagreed with Bayan and the empress dowager Budashiri over the succession. Following El-Temür's illness and death in 1333, his old co-conspirator Bayan executed his children in 1335.

environmental protection The Mongolian tradition of religiously based prohibitions on damaging sacred areas developed in the late 20th century into an ecologically based system of natural parks and strictly protected areas.

In the Mongolian world empire damaging living things around the imperial cemeteries and battue hunting during the calving season were prohibited. During the hunting season in fall, however, the Mongol khans organized immense hunts that must have denuded whole areas of animals. Later, after the conversion to Buddhism, hunting, logging, and farming were prohibited around monasteries. Bogd Uul, a mountain south of Mongolia's largest monastery in the present capital, ULAANBAATAR, thus became from the 18th century a protected area. In Inner Mongolia the protected strip around monasteries, called the *jaarig*, was often the only area of unplowed steppe preserved from CHINESE COLONIZATION, forming small islands of pastoral nomadic Mongolian population surrounded by Chinese farms. Buddhist didactic poets and preachers inveighed fiercely against hunting.

Under the Mongolian People's Republic (1924–92) the modernizing government encouraged population and livestock growth, predator-control programs to expand herds, fencing for railways, and farming. Hunting was avidly pursued by leaders such as MARSHAL CHOIBALSANG. Logging was begun on Bogd Uul after 1929. Herds of Mongolian gazelles were cut down from millions in 1950 to perhaps 300,000 in 1965–70. In the late 1960s the Przewalskii's horse disappeared from its last refuge in the southwestern Gobi, a victim of hunting early in the century and later of competition from domestic livestock.

In 1972 the Mongolian government began planning for environmental protection, to which regular funding was assigned from 1976 on. In 1975 two areas in the Trans-Altai GOBI DESERT, spanning southern BAYANKHONGOR PROVINCE, GOBI-ALTAI PROVINCE, and KHOWD PROVINCE, were set aside as nature reserves. In 1978 43.8 square kilometers (16.9 square miles) of Bogd Uul were again granted legal protection. By 1990 10 other small nature reserves were created. In 1992 the nature reserve system was reorganized into four levels of descending strictness: 1) strictly protected areas (translating Russian *zapovednik*), for pristine areas of world ecological importance; 2) natural parks, for wilderness areas of historical, cultural, or environmental importance; 3) natural reserves, dedicated to preserving particular valuable areas, whether ecosystems, rare species, fossil beds, or geological formations; and 4) natural and historical monuments, protecting natural and manmade monuments of touristic, historic, and cultural importance. At present about 8 percent of Mongolia's territory is covered by the nature reserve system, which is administered by the Ministry for Nature and the Environment.

The Great Gobi Strictly Protected Area, with 5,300 square kilometers (2,050 square miles), remains by far the largest nature reserve in Mongolia. This area of the Trans-Altai Gobi Desert preserved the habitats of the last remnants of the wild two-humped camel (*Camelus bactrianus ferus*), the Gobi bear (*Ursus arctos pruinosus*), and largest remaining herds of the wild ass, or chigetai (*Equus hemionus hemionus*). Other large strictly protected areas include the Khan Khentii Strictly Protected Area (1,200 square kilometers; 460 square miles), with its associated Gorkhi-Terelj Natural Park (286.4 square kilometers; 110.6 square miles), established in the area of the legendary Burqan Qaldun mountain in the KHENTII RANGE; the LAKE UWS Strictly Protected Area (771 square kilometers, or 298 square miles, in four discontinuous areas) in the northwest, with a large nesting waterfowl population; the Nömrög Strictly Protected Area in the far-eastern GREATER KHINGGAN RANGE (311.2 square kilometers; 120.2 square miles); and the Eastern Mongolia Strictly Protected Area (570 square kilometers; 220 square miles), which protects herds of Mongolian gazelles along the frontier with China. The Gurwansaikhan Natural Park, covering 2,000 square kilometers (770 square miles), protects populations of argali sheep, ibex, snow leopard, and the huge lammergeier vulture as well as saxaul forests and dinosaur fossil sites. LAKE KHÖWSGÖL Natural Park, with an area of 838 square kilometers (324 square miles), was established to protect the second largest body of freshwater in Central Asia.

In Mongol areas of Russia and China, environmental damage has been much more severe, particularly in the steppes. Farming and overstocking have caused widespread pasture degradation and desertification, and industrialization has degraded air and water quality. In 1969 in the Soviet Union's BURIAT REPUBLIC, a Baikal Reserve (165.7 square kilometers; 64 square miles) was set up on the lake's southern shores, joined by the Jerga Reserve in 1974 (42.2 square kilometers; 16.3 square miles). In 1986–87 the Soviet government created the Barguzin Strictly Protected Area (111.1 square kilometers; 42.9 square miles) and the Transbaikal National Park (256 square kilometers; 98.8 square miles) on LAKE BAIKAL's northeastern shore and the Ol'khon National Park (418 square kilometers; 161.4 square miles) on its western shore, while putting the entire Baikal region under special environmental supervision. In 1991 the Tunka National Park (1,183.7 square kilometers; 457 square miles) was established along the upper Irkut valley. All of these areas cover taiga and mountain-taiga areas. In 1999 the Alkhanai National Park (138.2 square kilometers; 53.4 square miles) was created in a mountain-steppe area of the AGA BURIAT AUTONOMOUS AREA with several Buddhist religious sites. The saiga antelope of the KALMYK REPUBLIC is protected in the Black Lands (Chernye Zemli) Strictly Protected Area (1,219 square kilometers; 470.7 square miles) established in 1990. Russian national parks, unlike strictly protected areas (*zapovedniks*), allow human use, and, in fact, the Tunka National Park covers the entire Tunka (Buriat, Tünkhen) district with more than 26,000 people (61 percent of whom are Buriat).

In 1988 the Chinese government extended its system of nature preserves (*ziran baohuqu*) to Inner Mongolia with the Daqinggou Preserve in KHORCHIN Left-Flank Rear banner (Horqin Zuoyi Houqi, 81.8 square kilometers; 31.6 square miles), protecting valuable broadleaf forests. Other preserves that protect forests include the Helan Shan Preserve in ALASHAN Left Banner (Alxa Zuoqi, 667.1 square kilometers; 257.6 square miles) set up in 1992 to protect the Qinghai spruce, the pine *Pinus tabulaeformis*, and wild animals, and the Hanma Preserve (1,073.5 square kilometers; 414.5 square miles) in northern Genhe city, protecting since 1996 remaining patches of primeval boreal forest in the Greater Khinggan Range. Wetland preserves in Mongol areas include the Dalai Nuur Preserve (1,194.1 square kilometers; 461 square miles) in Kheshigten (Hexigten) banner that protects native and migratory waterfowl; the Khorchin Preserve (1,269.9 square kilometers; 490.3 square miles) in Khorchin Right-Flank Middle banner (Horqin Youyi Zhongqi) that protects wetland waterfowl and bush and

thin steppe-forest terrain; and Bayanbulag Preserve (1,000 square kilometers; 386.1 square miles) set up in 1988 to protect swans, other waterfowl, and swamps in Hejing county of Xinjiang's BAYANGOL MONGOL AUTONOMOUS PREFECTURE. The SHILIIN GOL Steppe Preserve, covering 10,786 square kilometers (4,164.5 square miles) south of Shiliin Khot (Xilinhot) city, protects marshy meadows, classic steppe, and sparse desert forests, while the Western ORDOS Preserve (5,558.5 square kilometers; 2,146.2 square miles) in Otog banner and WUHAI city protects endangered desert relic flora, including the deciduous shrub *Tetraena mongolica* (Zygophyllaceae) and the rockrose (*Helianthemum ordosicum*; Oistaceae). These two and the Dalai Nuur Preserve were set up in December 1997.

Since the breakup of the Soviet bloc and the easing of political tensions, international cooperation in environmental protection has advanced. In 1994 Russia, Mongolia, and China coordinated nature protection in the Aga steppe–northeast Mongolia–HULUN BUIR triangle to protect the Daurian steppe ecology and many rare birds, such as the white-naped crane (*Grus vipio*). The program includes the Dalai Lake Nature Preserve in Inner Mongolia, covering 7,400 square kilometers (2,860 square miles) of lake, wetlands, and steppe (set up in 1992); the Mongolian Daurian Strictly Protected Area (1,030 square kilometers; 397.7 square miles) in two discontinuous patches near Torei Lake and the Ulz River; and the Daurskii Strictly Protected Area in Russia's Chita Region.

Despite these extensive systems of nature preserves, loss of habitat and declines in endangered species continue, even within the protected areas. Many of the preserves still exist more on paper than in reality, and few are large enough on their own to offer protection against widespread desertification, particularly in Kalmykia and Inner Mongolia. Gold mining, now freed from state monopoly, has damage riverine ecosystems in Mongolia. Meanwhile, declines in the 1990s in legal effectiveness in China, Russia, and Mongolia and the booming market in prosperous Asian-Pacific nations for blood antlers, bear gall, and other wild products have made poaching harder to combat. Despite the creation of the Black Lands Strictly Protected Area, for example, Kalmykia's saiga antelope populations have plummeted since 1998, to fewer than 18,000. In many parks coordinating natural protection with native pastoral land use is also an unresolved issue.

See also ANIMAL HUSBANDRY AND NOMADISM; DESERTIFICATION AND PASTURE DEGRADATION; FAUNA; FLORA; HUNTING AND FISHING.

Further reading: Caroline Humphrey, Marina Mongush, and B. Telengid, "Attitudes to Nature in Mongolia and Tuva: A Preliminary Report," *Nomadic Peoples* 33 (1993): 51–62; C. Finch, *Mongolia's Wild Heritage* (Boulder, Colo.: Mongolia Ministry for Nature and Environment and UNDP, 1999); Tsui Yenhu, "A Comparative

Study of the Attitudes of the Peoples of Pastoral Areas of Inner Asia towards Their Environments," in *Culture and Environment in Inner Asia,* vol. 2, *Society and Culture,* ed. Caroline Humphrey and David Sneath (Cambridge: White Horse Press, 1996): 1–24.

epics The epics of the Mongolian peoples, sung in alliterative verse, resemble not so much the historically based European epics (*Iliad, Song of Roland,* etc.) as fairy tales told on a vast and heroic scale. Mongolian epics take place in a timeless fantasy world in which the hero (*baatar*) confronts the monster (*mangas*). The epic hero, while not usually of divine ancestry, has the ability to transform himself into an animal or some other form. Sometimes the hero is alone, but sometimes he travels with his brother or companions. Most epics are built on one of two narrative structures: 1) the hero's search (with the hero transformed into a snot-nosed urchin) for a beautiful wife whom he wins by victory in an athletic contest; or 2) his search for his beautiful wife stolen by a multiheaded monster who must be killed by first killing his extracorporeal souls. While the hero or his consort often recites Buddhist scriptures, lamas who appear are always transformed monsters, while shamans are the monster's assistants. (Lamas and shamans generally never appear in the same epic.) The hero always has a wonderful and wise steed who gives him the best advice, which the hero either follows, thus achieving success and concluding the episode, or ignores, thus losing his life. If dead or spell enslaved the hero must be revived by some miraculous tool brought by his horse, wife, or sister. Endless feasting concludes each episode.

The most distinctive feature of Mongolian epic style is hyperbole. The hero's body is made of bronze, his ribs have fused into solid bone, his consorts' cheeks flash rays, his arrows pierce mountains, his saddle cannot be lifted by 70 men, his journeys cross continents, and so on. Characters are flat, and the difference between positive and negative characters is always sharp. Epics are sung in alliterative verses that tend toward parallel couplets.

Since at least the 17th century, epics have been written down by Mongolian singers. While epic singers usually learn to perform from another singer, often a close relative, singers also learn new episodes from written versions. The GESER epic, for example, appears to have been first introduced into Mongolia from Tibet entirely through writing but was soon nativized as a fertile oral epic tradition.

Epic performances were usually sung within a narrow register; Oirat Mongolian epic singers sang in a special voice called *khäälkh* (Khalkha, *khailakh*). Singers accompanied themselves on a lute or fiddle depending on their region. Epic songs are believed to have a powerful effect on the environment and thus must be performed and heard carefully and reverently. Performing the epic at the wrong time (e.g., in daytime or summer), making mis-

takes in the performance, breaking it off unfinished, or sleepiness in the audience can cause storms or other disasters, while performing it well can heal diseases, give sight to the blind, or bring success in endeavors, particularly the hunt. In recent years, however, such restrictions on epic performances have disintegrated. Women epic singers, previously prohibited, have also begun to appear.

The material and spiritual culture (tobacco, spyglasses, Buddhist terms, etc.) and occasional historical figures (Russians, Dalai Lama, etc.) mentioned all indicate that Mongolian epics in their current form date from the late 17th century at the earliest. The close similarity in themes between the Tibetan Geser epic and other Mongolian epics indicates considerable mutual influence. Mongolian epics can be divided into four regional types: Buriat, Kalmyk-Oirat, Khalkha, and eastern Inner Mongolian. Epic singers of the BURIATS were the most accomplished, traditionally knowing on average 20 epics of 2,000 to 15,000 lines. Buriat epics, of which the "Abai Geser" and "Alamzhi Mergen" are the best known, reflect their primarily forest hunting culture. By contrast, heroes of the Khalkha Mongol and Oirat epics are wealthy nomad lords living in a YURT with endless numbers of horses and livestock. The long JANGGHAR epic of the KALMYKS and OIRATS is the closest in the Mongolian tradition to a realistic historical epic. Khalkha epics, of which "Khan Kharankhui" (Dark Khan) was the most famous, were generally shorter than the Jangghar or Buriat epics and were sung unaccompanied; by the beginning of the 20th century the Khalkha epic singer's art was often breaking down into prose tales. In eastern Inner Mongolia minstrels sang epic tales but purely for entertainment. Based on literary predecessors, including Indian and Chinese tales and novels, these minstrel tales had far more complicated and diverse plots than did other epics.

See also FOLK POETRY AND TALES; HUNTING AND FISHING.

Further reading: C. R. Bawden, trans., *Eight North Mongolian Epic Poems* (Wiesbaden: Otto Harrassowitz, 1982); ———, "Mongol (The Contemporary Tradition)," in *Traditions of Heroic and Epic Poetry,* vol. 1, *The Traditions* (London: Modern Humanities Research Association, 1980): 268–299; W. Heissig, "New Mongolian Minstrel Poems," *Orientalia Romana* 4 (1972): 1–70; Nicholas Poppe, *The Heroic Epic of the Khalkha,* trans. John R. Krueger, D. Montgomery, and M. Walter (Bloomington, Ind.: Mongolia Society, 1979). Boris Ya. Vladimirtsov, "The Oirat Mongolian Heroic Epic," trans. John R. Krueger, *Mongolian Studies* 8 (1983–84): 5–58.

Erbanov, Mikhei Nikolaevich (Yerbanov) (1889–1938)
One of the chief founders of the Bolshevik Party in Buriatia
Born on March 10 to the Buriat peasant Nikolai-Sukhe (1861–1927) and his wife, Mariia Viktorovna, in Great

Bakhtai *ulus,* or village (in modern Alair District of UST'-ORDA BURIAT AUTONOMOUS AREA), Mikhei learned his letters from a Russian villager before attending school in Balagansk from 1903 and a commercial course in Tomsk from 1908. He later worked in Tomsk, Barnaul, and Irkutsk. Associating with a social democratic group in Barnaul in 1913, he joined the Bolsheviks in Irkutsk in December 1917. Erbanov worked with the partisans in late 1919 and participated in the execution of Siberia's White commanders Kolchak and Pepeliaev.

As one of the few Buriat Bolsheviks, Erbanov became from late 1919 the Irkutsk Communist Party organization's "man in Buriatia," heading both the party committee's Buriat section and nonparty Buriat organizations. From January 1922 Erbanov chaired the government of the new western Buriat autonomous region, and when the eastern and western Buriat regions were merged to form the Buriat-Mongolian republic in 1923, Erbanov chaired its Council of People's Commissars.

Erbanov strongly defended the "nativization" policy that gave preference to Buriat cadres and promoted the Buriat-Mongolian language. In 1928 he was elected first secretary of the Buriat Regional Party Committee and member of the Communist Party's Central Committee in Moscow. In 1937, however, he was arrested in Joseph Stalin's GREAT PURGE and shot in 1938.

See also BURIAT REPUBLIC; BURIATS.

Erdenet city

Erdenet city was built around the colossal Erdenet copper and molybdenum ore-dressing plant, the largest mine of its kind in Asia, built from 1974 to 1983 with Soviet aid. The developing city was separated from BULGAN PROVINCE in 1975 and made a centrally administered city. By 1979 Erdenet's population had already reached 31,900.

By 1985 Erdenet city accounted for 17.9 percent of Mongolia's total industrial output; the ore-dressing plant accounted for 70.7 percent of the city's industrial output, with the remainder generated by a carpet factory, a woodworking plant, and other small industries. Erdenet was developed by the Soviet-Mongolian joint-stock company Erdenet Ore-Dressing Dressing Plant, with the Soviet Union holding 51 percent of the stock and appointing the director and the Mongolian government holding 49 percent and appointing the vice director. Soviet and Mongolian workers were integrated on the shop floor to facilitate training of the latter. In 1990 about 15 percent of Erdenet's residents were non-Mongolian, mostly Russians.

After economic liberalization Erdenet's mine became more important than ever for Mongolia. In 1994 Erdenet city's territory was expanded from 60 square kilometers (23 square miles) to 840 (324 square miles) and renamed Orkhon province. Orkhon's total population reached 76,000 in 2000, of which 68,300 lived in the urban area.

The province's share of Mongolia's total sales of industrial product, generated overwhelmingly by the mine, leaped to 42 percent in 1995 before recovery of other industrial sectors in Mongolia reduced it to 32 percent in 2000. The Mongolian government now owns a 51-percent share in the renamed Erdenet Concern, which has a Mongolian director. The mine currently has about 6,240 employees, of whom about 600 are foreign specialists from Russia, Kazakhstan, and elsewhere. Foreign investment is playing a major role in renovating the plant's technology. Erdenet's manufacturing industries, however, have suffered, and unemployment has remained at more than 5 percent, somewhat above Mongolia's average and well above that of ULAANBAATAR.

See also ECONOMY, MODERN; MINING; SOVIET UNION AND MONGOLIA.

Further reading: Simon Strickland-Scott, "Urban and Rural Life in Post-Communist Mongolia," *Mongolian Studies* 24 (2001): 7–39.

Erdene Zuu   *See* ERDENI ZUU.

Erdeni Shangdzodba   *See* SHANGDZODBA, ERDENI.

Erdeni tunumal   *See* JEWEL TRANSLUCENT SUTRA.

Erdeni Zuu (Erdene Zuu)

This temple, founded in 1585, is the most ancient and venerated monastery of the KHALKHA Mongols. ABATAI KHAN first built the temple in 1585 on a spot identified (correctly) by the Mongols as ÖGEDEI KHAN's QARA-QORUM. A monk from the city Guihua (modern HÖHHOT) in Inner Mongolia performed the first consecration, and after Abatai Khan returned from his meeting with the Third Dalai Lama in 1586, three main temples (*zuu*) were built to house the Buddha images and relics he had received. In the early history of the temple Sa-skya-pa lamas played the major role. Only after the return of the supreme Khalkha cleric the FIRST JIBZUNDAMBA KHUTUGTU from meeting with the Fifth Dalai Lama in 1658 was the monastery made a dGe-lugs-pa (Yellow Hat) establishment. Little building was done in the 17th century, but from 1701 on construction of new temples and restoration of the old were virtually constant. In 1796, to mark the accession of the Qing's Jiaqing emperor (1796–1820), the Khalkha lay and religious leaders undertook a particularly large-scale renovation that established the monastery's final layout. From 1803 to 1813 the monastery's outer wall, 400 meters (1,310 feet) square, was constructed with 108 stupas, each financed by donations from Khalkhas of all walks of life. Also in 1803 four great gates were funded by the fourth Jibzundamba Khutugtu on the occasion of his trip to Tibet. At its height the monastery had 62 temples or assembly halls and thousands of monks, although not all were resident. During the late 19th century the monastery declined with the financial means of its patrons. The antireligious campaigns of 1937–39 left only 18 salvageable temples and assembly halls, and the site was made a museum in 1944. Since 1990 Buddhist services are once again being conducted at the site.

See also JIBZUNDAMBA KHUTUGTU, SECOND.

Erdeni-yin tobchi (Precious summary) The most widely read of the traditional Mongolian chronicles, the *Erdeni-yin tobchi*, Precious summary, written in 1662, covers Mongolian history up to the Manchu conquest.

The *Erdeni-yin tobchi*, written by the ORDOS nobleman SAGHANG SECHEN, was the second of the 17TH-CENTURY CHRONICLES. Disposing of materials similar to those used in Lubsang-Danzin's ALTAN TOBCHI (c. 1655), Saghang Sechen created a much more unified work, recasting the 12-animal dates in the more precise 60-year system, moving genealogical material into the body of the work, and reordering the confused narratives of the Mongol-Oirat conflict (1392–1517). To avoid contradictions with his traditional Mongolian material on CHINGGIS KHAN, he used *Secret History* material sparingly while broadening the scope of his history with a lengthy discussion of the formation of the world and a brief digression on Chinese history before the Mongols. His concluding chapter on the new Manchu khans was the first Mongol summary of the topic. In addition to the Mongolian chronicle tradition, Saghang Sechen used Tibetan and at least one Chinese history and made use of riddles and other folkloric materials.

The most valuable part of Saghang Sechen's work is his extensive coverage of events in his homeland of Ordos up to the revolt against Mongolia's last Chinggisid emperor LIGDAN KHAN and the Manchu conquest of 1628–35. He particularly honored the work of his great-grandfather KHUTUGTAI SECHEN KHUNG-TAIJI, who initiated the conversion of the Ordos Mongols to Buddhism. Despite his praise of the Manchus' unification of the realms through finely graded titles, his discrete silence on the 1632–36 Manchu conquest, which he witnessed personally, indicated his regret over the loss of Mongolian independence.

Saghang Sechen's work was the most popular Mongolian chronicle. In 1766 the Khalkha nobleman Tsenggünjab (d. 1771) presented a copy to the Manchu emperor Qianlong, who had it translated and published in a trilingual Mongolian-Manchu-Chinese edition. In 1829 I. J. Schmidt produced a German translation, the first Mongolian work translated into a European language.

Further reading: John R. Krueger, trans. *The Bejewelled Summary of the Origin of Khans (Qad-un Ündüsün-ü Erdeni-yin tobči). A History of the Eastern Mongols to 1662* (Bloomington, Ind.: Mongolia Society, 1964); John R. Krueger, *Poetical Passages of the Erdeni-yin tobči* (The Hague: Mouton, 1961); Tetsuo Morikawa, "The Manuscripts and Manuscript Families of the *Erdeni-yin tobči*," *Memoirs of the Toyo Bunko* 59 (2001): 49–86.

Erduosi   *See* ORDOS.

Esen (r. 1438/1453–1454) *Powerful Oirat Mongolian commander who captured the Chinese emperor*
Esen was son of the Oirat TAISHI (grand preceptor, i.e., regent), Toghoon Taishi (d. 1438), of the Choros clan (possibly of Uighur origin; *see* OIRATS). His early campaigns were against the Chaghatayid khans of MOGHULISTAN in modern Xinjiang. Esen three times defeated and twice captured the Moghuli ruler, Ways Khan (1417–32). In both cases Esen treated Ways Khan with the honor due a khan of CHINGGIS KHAN's blood. The second time, however, he forced Ways Khan to grant him his sister in marriage. After his father died Esen inherited his position as *taishi* for the reigning Chinggisid khan Togtoo-Bukha (titled Taisung, 1433–52). In 1443–45 he subjugated the Chaghatayid principality of Hami and the three MING DYNASTY guards (*wei*), including the Chigil Mongolian Guard, in eastern Gansu. In 1446–47 he also attacked the Ming's THREE GUARDS (ethnically Mongols) in eastern Inner Mongolia and received the submission of the Jurchen in Manchuria.

Since 1439 Esen Taishi and his khan, Togtoo-Bukha, had been sending vast "tribute" missions to China, often numbering more than 1,000 men. (The TRIBUTE SYSTEM actually functioned as a kind of state-subsidized monopoly trade.) Esen encouraged hundreds of Hami- and Samarqand-based Muslim merchants to accompany his mission. In response to this inflation of numbers, in winter 1448–49 the Chinese government gave only one-fifth of the agreed-upon "gifts." Esen's request for a Chinese princess was also rejected.

Incensed by this slight, Esen planned a multifront attack on the Ming, with Togtoo-Bukha attacking Liaodong, Alag Chingsang (grand councillor) attacking Xuanfu (modern Xuanhua), Esen attacking Datong, and another column attacking Ganzhou (modern Zhangye). Esen's invasion was unexpectedly crowned with the capture of the Ming's Zhengtong emperor (1436–49, reenthroned as Tianshun, 1457–64) on September 1, 1449 (*see* TUMU INCIDENT). Esen offered the emperor his sister in marriage, but the emperor refused a marriage alliance. The response of the Chinese officialdom, who elevated the Zhengtong emperor's brother to the throne, stymied Esen, and he sent the emperor back in 1450. Despite the Tumu crisis, tribute missions continued until Esen's death. In 1450–51 Esen and Togtoo-Bukha again invaded the Three Guards, devastating the area around the Nonni-Sungari confluence.

Esen's religious beliefs are unclear. Esen's grandfather Mahmud (d. 1418), bore a Muslim name, and as the price of his marriage with Ways Khan's sister Makhtum Khanim, Esen converted to Islam. Makhtum Khanim's two sons by Esen, Ibrahim and Ilyas, were Muslims, yet Esen's other sons were not. From at least 1446 to 1452 Esen had a Buddhist monk as state preceptor (*Guoshi*), for whom he requested Buddhist articles. In 1446 he also requested medicines and books on *yin-yang* and divination from the Ming.

By 1451 Esen and the khan Togtoo-Bukha had a falling out. From 1449 Togtoo-Bukha had opposed Esen's policy of confrontation with the Ming. When the two quarreled over the designation of the heir of the throne, Togtoo-Bukha supported the Three Guards, who had suffered from Esen's cruelty, and led the Mongols against the Oirats in 1452. Togtoo-Bukha fled in defeat when his own brother Agbarji Jinong (viceroy) deserted to the Oirat side. Although promised by Esen the title of khan, Agbarji was murdered instead, and in 1453 Esen himself took the title of Great Khan of the Great Yuan. Esen gave his son the title of *taishi*, an action that led his commander Alag Chingsang, who had expected to receive the title himself, into rebellion. Esen Khan fled and was killed by the son of a man he had earlier executed.

Esen saw his conquests as restoring the Yuan heritage, but his vision did not extend beyond Mongolia. Viewing the local Mongolian Chinggisids, the Chaghatay khans, and the Ming emperor all as possessors of a comparable charisma, his aim was not conquest but the creation of a relationship in which he partook of that charisma, through marriage and titles, while holding real power and receiving commercial benefits. The Ming's frustrating resistance to this program apparently encouraged his failed attempt to seize the throne and that charisma for himself. The 17th- and 18th-century Zünghar rulers considered themselves to be descendants of Esen Taishi.

Evenk   *See* EWENKIS.

Ewenkis (Evenk, Owenk'e; Tungus)   Originally reindeer herders speaking a Manchu-Tungusic language, many Ewenki (as they call themselves) were subjugated by the Buriat, BARGA, and Daur clans and so came under heavy Mongolian influence. Traditionally the Ewenkis are called Tungus in Russia; the division and naming of official Ewenki nationalities was conducted inconsistently in modern Russia and China. The Ewenkis of Russia (29,900 in 1989) are actually ethnographically closer to China's Orochen (6,965 in 1990) than to most of China's 26,315 (1990) Ewenkis.

ORIGINS

The Ewenki have been traced to the SHIWEI, who inhabited the GREATER KHINGGAN RANGE-Amur River area in the fifth to ninth centuries, but such a connection is merely conjectural. Ewenki language forms the northern branch of the Manchu-Tungusic language group and is closely related to Even (Lamut) and Negidal in Siberia and more distantly related to Jurchen and Manchu in Manchuria. Ewenki dialects can be divided into three broad groups: 1) Siberian Ewenki, spoken by Russia's Ewenkis in the Lena and Yenisey valleys, as well as (confusingly) by China's Orochen; 2) Solon Ewenki, spoken by most of the Ewenkis in China; and 3) Khamnigan, originally spoken by the Ewenkis of Russia's Transbaikal steppe. (The term *Khamnigan* is simply the general Buriat-Mongolian term for all Ewenkis, but it may be used more narrowly for the Ewenkis of Transbaikalia.) Russian linguists usually treat Solon Ewenki as a separate language.

By 1600 the Ewenkis of the Lena and Yenisey valleys were successful reindeer herders. These Reindeer Ewenki wore distinctive deerskin leggings, open collarless jackets, and aprons and lived in birchbark tepees. By contrast, the Solons and Khamnigan had picked up horse breeding and the Mongolian *deel,* or robe, from the Mongols. The Solons nomadized along the Amur River and its northern tributaries in birchbark tepees, fishing, and hunting boar, elk, and reindeer for food and tigers, sables, and lynx for furs. They also planted millet, barley, oats, and buckwheat. Their only livestock was horses. Their tribes were closely linked with the Daurs, a more agricultural Mongolic-speaking people. To the west the Khamnigan were another body of horse-breeding Ewenkis in the Transbaikal area. They were tributary to the KHALKHA Mongolian princes. Also in the Amur valley was a body of Siberian Ewenki-speaking people called Orochen by the Manchus. Some were "Pedestrian" (i.e., no horses or reindeer) and others "Horse" Orochen.

MANCHU AND RUSSIAN CONQUEST

Manchu attacks from 1636–37 and Russian Cossack attacks from 1643–47 affected both the Solons and the Khamnigans. Like the Daurs, the Solons were first subjugated by the Manchus then raided by the Cossacks and finally deported by the Manchus into the lower Nonni (Nen) River valley. In 1731 they were reorganized as members of the Butha (Hunting) Eight Banners along with their Daur partners. Their lifestyle remained a combination of hunting (both individual and in battue), farming, and fishing, and they paid a regular tribute of furs.

The Manchus dispatched the Solon Ewenkis together with the Daurs widely over Inner Asia as garrison soldiers. Groups were stationed in the upper Nonni, in the HULUN BUIR steppe in 1732, and in Xinjiang after 1755. Those in Hulun Buir formed six of the Solon Eight Banners (the other two were filled by Barga Mongols). The Hulun Buir Solons became completely pastoral people, living in Mongolian YURTS and herding animals like the Mongols. In 1982 roughly 38 percent of the approximately 17,420 Solons lived in the Butha homeland, 12 percent in the upper Nonni, 42 percent in the Hulun Buir steppe, and about 5 percent in Xinjiang. Solon Ewenkis used Manchu and sometimes Mongolian for writing, and 18th-century Solon generals such as Oboshi and Hailancha commanded Qing forces as far as Nepal and Xinjiang. While preserving their native religion, the Solon Ewenkis adopted the Mongolian and Daur custom of OBOO (cairn) worship.

The Orochen were also moved south by the Manchus and the "Horse Orochen," enrolled in the banners as auxiliaries to the Butha and Solon banners. The "Pedestrian Orochen" remained outside the banner system. Both were primarily hunters.

The Transbaikal Khamnigan around Nerchinsk and the Aga steppe faced both Cossack demands for tribute and Khori BURIATS trying to occupy their pastures. Most of the Khamnigan preferred Cossack rule, and some enrolled in Cossack regiments in the Selenge valley. The Aga steppe was mostly taken over by the Khori, however. Those Khamnigan who fled to the Manchus at this time were merged into the Solons. The Khamnigan chief Gantimur (later Prince Peter Gantimurov) caused a long-lasting diplomatic contretemps by fleeing first to the Manchus and then defecting back to the Russians in 1667. In 1740 Ekhired Buriats migrated east and conquered the Siberian Ewenkis of Barguzin valley northeast of LAKE BAIKAL. Under the Speransky system of 1822, the Aga Khamnigans, horse-keeping hunters until the late 19th century, were supervised by clan officials organized into the Urul'ga "Steppe Duma" and paid an annual three-ruble poll tax. The Siberian Ewenkis of Barguzin and elsewhere were put under a simpler native authority.

MODERN CHANGES

After 1880 Russia's Khamnigan gradually moved to seminomadic herding of cattle, sheep, camels, and horses. While some of the wealthy dwelt in Russian-style houses, most lived in Buriat-style yurts and used tepees covered with birchbark or felt on hunting expeditions. Of the 24,000 "Tungus" of Transbaikal (mostly Khamnigan with some Siberian Ewenkis) in 1897, almost 5,000 spoke Buriat as their first language. After 1918 many of the Khamnigan, along with some of their Buriat neighbors, fled over the border into Mongolia and Hulun Buir, forming the present Khamnigan communities there. Virtually all the remaining Khamnigan in the Aga steppe were registered as Buriats until the 1990s.

From 1900 the Russian-built Chinese Eastern Railway crossed Solon Ewenki territory in Hulun Buir. Under the Japanese occupation of 1932–45, Butha and Hulun Buir were declared autonomous Khinggan East and North provinces, respectively. The Ewenkis and Orochens were all treated as Mongols, and Mongolian was made the administrative language.

In Russia and China the Communist governments established autonomous units for the Ewenki and Orochen peoples, although their wide dispersion made territorial autonomy in any real sense virtually inapplicable. Russia merged the Orochen and some Khamnigans into the Ewenki nationality, while China combined Solon, Khamnigan, and a small body of Siberian Ewenkis into their Ewenkis, but left the Orochen as a separate nationality. Russia's vast far-northern Ewenki Autonomous Area with its capital in Tura is only 14 percent Ewenki in population and contains only 12 percent of Russia's scattered Ewenkis. More than 12 percent of Russia's Ewenkis (4,300 people in 1989) inhabit northern Buriatia, Chita, and Irkutsk. All but a small number around Aga are Siberian Ewenkis. A band of these Siberian Ewenkis entered Inner Mongolia in the 19th century, forming along the Jiliu River China's only population of reindeer herders (numbering 323 in 1990).

The decision of the new Chinese Communist government to make the Daurs a separate nationality separated the Solons from their long-standing Daur partners. In Hulun Buir part of Solon banner territory was separated out as the Ewenki Autonomous banner in 1958. At the time Ewenkis were 24.6 percent of the banner's 10,535 people, Mongols were 36.2 percent, and Daurs 22.3 percent. With Chinese immigration into the Dayan and Yimin coal-mining districts, the banner's population by 1990 had ballooned to 129,000 inhabitants, of which more than 60 percent were Chinese. Ewenkis totaled 8,700 (including about 300 Khamnigan), Mongols 21,600 (including about 5,950 Buriats), and the Daurs more than 14,000. These minorities still dominate the steppe, but the steppe today account for only 14 percent of the banner's population. The banner in 1990 had 240,000 livestock, of which 135,000 were sheep and goats. Mongolian is the socially dominant language outside the towns, but multilingualism and intermarriage of Ewenkis with Mongols and Daurs are common.

The Orochen Autonomous banner in Hulun Buir, established in 1952, has a population of 293,800, of which only 1,900 are Orochen and another 2,800 are Solon Ewenkis. The banner is in modern China's major forestry area.

The Khamnigan of Mongolia, numbering about 300 families, are scattered among the Buriats. They speak only the Khamnigan dialect of Buriat Mongolian and are officially considered Buriats. Those in Hulun Buir, who still speak Khamnigan, totaled 1,600 in 1988. Those left in Russia live in and around AGA BURIAT AUTONOMOUS AREA and speak Khamnigan-dialect Buriat and Russian. In the 1990s, the Khamnigans of Buriatia began to revive an ethnic consciousness as people separate from the Buriats.

See also DAUR LANGUAGE AND PEOPLE; HUNTING AND FISHING.

Further reading: M. G. Levin and L. P. Potapov, *The Peoples of Siberia*, trans. ed. Stephen Dunn (Chicago: University of Chicago Press, 1964), 620–654; Henry Schwarz, *Minorities of Northern China: A Survey* (Bellingham: Western Washington University Press, 1984), 171–188; Juha Janhunen, *Material on Manchurian Khamnigan Evenki* (Helsinki: Finno-Ugrian Society, 1991).

F

falconry The tradition of falconry in Inner Asia, one of the great sports of the khans, has now disappeared in Mongolia except among the KAZAKHS of BAYAN-ÖLGII PROVINCE, who hunt with golden eagles. During the MONGOL EMPIRE the Mongol nobles hawked with goshawks, gerfalcons, peregrine falcons, and saker falcons. In the MONGOL TRIBE falconry was associated with the Kiyad/BORJIGID ruling moiety, whose symbol was the white gerfalcon, and under the empire it was allowed only for the ruling family and captains. The required tribute of white gerfalcons from Siberia and the Manchurian coast were very onerous, and the keepers of the imperial mews often bullied and extorted goods from the common people.

At the court of QUBILAI KHAN (1260–94) the emperor went hawking during the winter and spring months. In the winter he hawked with eagles, taking foxes, small deer, and even wolves. In the early spring he hawked with falcons and hawks taking game birds and cranes. The birds were always cast with the right hand, not the left, as in Europe. The imperial hawks and falcons had little tablets of silver attached to their feet with the name of the keeper.

The Mongols today do not hawk. The Kazakhs of Bayan-Ölgii hawk with golden eagles, killing foxes, rabbits, and occasionally wolves. The eagles are caught when young and kept until they are 10, when they are released again to breed. While kept they live together with the falconer's family and so become unusually tame. Kazakhs cast eagles with the right hand.

family Under the MONGOL EMPIRE elite Mongol families were based on polygamy and strong paternal authority. Marriage was stiffened by the substantial payments that had to be made. By the 19th century polygamy had become rare, and cohabitation often began without any formal marriage or wedding at all. In the 20th century new law codes have reestablished the family on a legal basis similar to that in other modern societies.

MARRIAGE

The Mongol family in empire times was formed through arranged marriage. The groom's family paid a high bridewealth in livestock, which purchased rights over the bride's fertility (all children were now of the groom's clan) and gave her the right to wear the BOQTA, or married woman's headdress. The bride received from her family an *INJE,* a dowry or premortem inheritance, consisting of livestock or, for Chinggisids, human subjects. There were also gifts (*shidkül*) of clothing or household ornaments presented by the bride's family to the groom's mother. Such high payments could be avoided through a direct exchange of daughters between two families, or through the groom working for the father-in-law before his marriage. (CHINGGIS KHAN did this for his wife BÖRTE ÜJIN.)

Since marriage linked clans in a continuing connection, the tie was preferably not broken, even after death. Thus, widow remarriage was very rare except in the form of levirate marriage, in which a deceased man's wives would be taken by either his surviving youngest son or, if lacking a son, a younger brother. Historical examples show the first marriage was arranged for high-born children in their mid- or late teens. In polygamous families each wife had her own YURT; they camped in a line west to east, with the senior wife on the west.

FAMILY LIFE

In the household most of the work was done by women: loading yurts and carts and driving them, herding and milking all livestock except horses, processing DAIRY PRODUCTS, making felt, cooking, and sewing. Men herded and milked livestock, especially horses, which they alone milked, and made bows and arrows, horse gear, carts, and yurts. Their main task was hunting and making war.

The family tone was strongly patriarchal. White hair and long beards were a sign of dignity in old men, and youth were expected not to speak to elders unless spoken to. Fathers had authority over sons, elder brothers over younger brothers, husbands over wives, and mothers-in-law over daughters-in-law. At the same time, fathers and older brothers were expected to avoid strictly any familiarity with their sons' or younger brothers' wives. ÖGEDEI KHAN decreed that women who were jealous of their husbands' other wives or wore excessive finery should be publicly humiliated and bridewealth gathered for the husband to marry another wife. While small children were treated indulgently, older sons were expected to show rigorous obedience to their fathers. These strongly hierarchical relations often prevented father–son intimacy, and many khans were closer to their grandsons than to their sons.

Marital relations were complicated, although 13th-century travelers saw Mongolian women as remarkable in their docility, diligence, and lack of jealousy. Since each wife had her own yurt, the husband had to chose every day with which wife to eat and sleep. Among the Chinggisids a surprising number followed the example of Chinggis himself and were deeply attached to one main wife. Often the first marriage, arranged by the parents, was loveless and sterile, and stepmothers inherited from a father were often treated more as respected companions and advisers than as romantic partners. Sexual liaisons of princes with maidservants were common and in the event of a child being born were often regularized by a marriage ceremony. While many outside observers stated that the Mongols made no difference between children of wives and concubines, the khans often favored sons by their main wife over all others, leaving sons of maidservants feeling alienated, particularly if the father had not formally married the mother.

INHERITANCE

The laws of inheritance of livestock among Mongol herders have remained roughly constant even to the present. Among the nobility the "flock" distributed included human subjects as well. Upon marriage a son received a share of the family stock as a premortem inheritance and lived either in a separate yurt in the camp or formed a new camp. The favorite son, usually the youngest, lived with his father until death and inherited the remaining stock on his father's death. This youngest child was called the *odchigin* (Turkish for hearth chief) or today *otgon* (from *od-qan*, hearth khan). The youngest child inherited the most, although other shares were most of the time equal. (In the empire period the elder may have received

a larger share.) Daughters also received shares through their *inje* (dowry) of stock. Land was held in common by the clan and so not inherited. (*See* APPANAGE SYSTEM.)

CHANGES IN THE NINETEENTH CENTURY

The provisions in the MONGOL-OIRAT CODE of 1640 and the *KHALKHA JIRUM* (Khalkha regulations) of 1709 outline practices of marriage similar to those in force under the Mongol Empire. Fathers and mothers-in-law were allowed physically to discipline their adult sons and daughters-in-law within reason; daughters could be married from age 14 and were expected to be married by 20; and bridewealth was legally required for a legitimate marriage. The caps set in the 1640 code for bridewealth were extremely high, and a dowry of clothes, horse harnesses, and other household goods was also required. While the theoretical death penalty for adultery, running off with a married woman, and elopement said to have been enacted by Chinggis Khan lapsed after 1600, the more realistic heavy livestock fines remained. Divorce is not mentioned in the codes, but marital discord was generally settled between the two families, with the civil authorities intervening only if the families could not come to agreement. Divorce was relatively rare.

By 1900, however, the impression of observers was that the earlier marriage and family system was breaking down in Khalkha and the high steppe of Inner Mongolia, although little hard statistical evidence is available. Formal marriage with the payment of bridewealth became rare among the poor and remained common only among the TAIJI (nobility). One factor was the increasing number of boys taking religious vows in monasteries (*see* LAMAS AND MONASTICISM). A man who had taken vows could not formally marry. Thus, while most of the 45 percent of Khalkha men in 1918 who were lamas were actually living with wives and children, they did not pay bridewealth and were not formally married.

The decline in formal marriage coincided with a rise in female-headed households, probably due to the sex imbalance arising from widespread monasticism as well as from the economic decline after 1825. Despite the presumed imbalance of men and women, polygamy seems to have become statistically insignificant. In areas of the Gobi traditional marriage disappeared among commoners, and even long-term male-female cohabitation became rare (*see* MATRILINEAL CLANS). In Ordos all women conducted some form of wedding ceremony, but the numerous unwed mothers would marry the *khii mori* (prayer flag), and the children would be accounted children of heaven.

In CHAKHAR, eastern Inner Mongolia, and among the Daurs, however, where the influence of CONFUCIANISM was strong, strictures against extramarital sex grew stricter. Among these sedentary ranchers and mixed agropastoral farmers, the new family lived in a single compound with the groom's parents and with the extended family under strict rules of decorum and authority divided by age and sex. At the same time, bridewealth disappeared, being replaced by an indirect dowry (i.e., gifts given by the groom's family to the bride's, but returned with the bride at marriage).

MODERN FAMILY LIFE

Already in the 1910s the Khalkha Mongols noticed a new trend in family life toward greater equality between husbands and wives, while from around 1920 frequent elopements without bridewealth gradually broke down the custom of arranged marriages even in respectable families. After the 1921 REVOLUTION the MONGOLIAN REVOLUTIONARY YOUTH LEAGUE attacked wife beaters and elders who tyrannized their children. Similar campaigns occurred among the KALMYKS and BURIATS in Russia after 1920 and among the INNER MONGOLIANS in China after 1945.

In all Mongol areas marriage was put on a similar legal basis in the 20th century based on monogamy, the consent of the bride and groom, age limits (18 in Mongolia and 20 in China since 1978), prohibition of bridewealth or dowry, equal rights of divorce, general male–female equality, and so on. The ideal of companionate marriage, romantic love, and the beauty and duty of motherhood were all promoted, while the old society was castigated in part for its immorality as evidenced by widespread sexually transmitted diseases. Civil registration of vital events (birth, death, marriage, divorce, and adoption) was established in Mongolia in 1951. In the urban areas registering these events was crucial for obtaining housing and other benefits from the state sector.

Women had always worked in animal husbandry, and labor shortages and socialist ideas of women's social roles kept the number of urban homemakers few. Since WORLD WAR II women's literacy and workforce participation in independent Mongolia have become virtually equal to those of men. While the total fertility rate reached 8 children in 1963, it declined to 4.5 in 1990 and 2.2 in 2000. Marriage generally occurs at an early age (20 for women and 24 for men). Courtship generally includes sexual relations, and pregnancy frequently sparks the decision to marry. Divorce is easily obtainable but relatively uncommon; in 2000, marriages amounted to 9 per 1,000 persons over 18 annually, while divorces were 0.6 per 1,000. While female-headed households numbered 56,491, or 10.2 percent, in 2000, the number of children growing up in single-parent households was only 45,262, or fewer than 5 percent.

See also KINSHIP SYSTEM; WEDDINGS.

Further reading: Pao Kuo-yi [Ünensechen], "Family and Kinship Structure of the Khorchin Mongols," *Central Asiatic Journal* 9 (1964): 277–311; Pao Kuo-yi "Child Birth and Child Training in a Khorchin Mongol Village," *Monumenta Serica* 25 (1966): 406–439; Sara Randall, "Issues in the Demography of Mongolian Nomadic Pastoralism," *Nomadic Peoples* 33 (1993): 209–229; Herbert Harold Vreeland III, *Mongol Community and Kinship Structure* (New Haven, Conn.: HRAF Press, 1957); Mei Zhang, "Effect of Privatisation Policies on Rural Women's Labour and Property Rights in Inner Mongolia and Xinjiang," in *Culture and Environment in Inner Asia*, vol. 2; *Society and Culture*, ed. Caroline Humphrey and David Sneath (Cambridge: White Horse Press, 1996), 61–96.

farming Although Mongolia is always associated with animal husbandry and pastoral nomadism, farming has also played a perennial, albeit subsidiary, role. Since 1959 the Mongolian government has developed a highly extensive and mechanized agriculture. This article primarily describes agriculture in Mongolia proper. (*For agricultural colonization by the Chinese in Inner Mongolia, see* CHINESE COLONIZATION. *On agriculture in Inner Mongolia after 1911, see* INNER MONGOLIAN AUTONOMOUS REGION.)

While observers from widely varying periods generally treat farming among the Mongols as an innovation, Mongolian farming shows substantial continuity. One reflection of this is the consistent vocabulary used for grain farming, including not only the names of the grains but also of the implements, such as plows and sickles. By contrast, names for vegetables and fruits vary in almost all dialects and are generally borrowed.

TRADITIONAL FARMING

Chinese travelers in both the 13th and the late 16th centuries noted that Mongols grew millet, and cultivation methods have been documented by ethnographers from the 19th and early 20th centuries. Nomadic farmers cultivated land near the spring and autumn pastures so that they could be conveniently visited in sowing and harvest time. Mongolian farming was generally dependent on surface water and took place near rivers and springs in Tuva, western Mongolia (particularly around KHOWD CITY), in the SELENGE RIVER valley and its tributaries, the ORKHON RIVER and TUUL RIVER, and in southern Inner Mongolia, particularly among the Höhhot Tümed, eastern KHORCHIN, KHARACHIN, Daurs (*see* DAUR LANGUAGE AND PEOPLE) and neighboring Mongols. In some spots farming was done around springs or river banks where winter flooding irrigated the land. In northwestern Mongolia irrigation systems existed with channels and even simple aqueducts made of hollow logs (*onggocha/ongots*). Many of these irrigation systems were ancient, dating back to the military farms created under the Mongol Empire (*see* CHINQAI; QARA-QORUM; SIBERIA AND THE MONGOL EMPIRE).

Much Mongolian farming was carried on by ordinary banner members who had a traditional right to cultivate any unoccupied land in the banner. Disputes over land were rare and were settled by investigating whose family or clan had cultivated the land first. Near the border of

China land tenure became more complex, with several levels of ownership. Both monasteries and the QING DYNASTY authorities at various times and places sponsored farming on their lands to supply monks' and soldiers' grain needs (see ZAKHACHIN).

During sowing the Mongols broadcast the seeds by hand from a hat. A simple wooden plow pulled by an ox formed furrows and partially turned the soil. Fields were fenced with willow branches or even stacked sheep dung, and scarecrows of stuffed hawks were set up. Having sown the seeds, the Mongols usually moved away and would not return until harvest time. Sometimes poor families (who had few pack animals and had trouble moving anyway) remained in the area to watch the fields in return for part of the harvest. Harvesting was done with a sickle or knife. The simplest way of threshing was to clear an open space with a post in the center and simply drive several oxen or horses over the grain for two or three days. More developed farmers used a large circular stone over which a roller was pulled by an ox. Millet and barley were the main crops, and the yield per hectare for millet was around 25 kilograms (22 pounds per acre). Wheat could yield 90–120 kilograms per hectare (80–107 pounds per acre) but without some tending it was liable to produce no crop at all and so was rarely planted.

Grain was stored either in a tent or in pits in the ground. Flour was made by mortar and pestle from earliest times. Steamed breads or boiled noodles, however, appear to have become common only after the 17th century; before then flour was usually mixed with milk or soup.

FARMING IN MONGOLIA, 1911–1959

During the late 19th century Chinese farming in the Selenge valley expanded, reaching perhaps 60,000–70,000 hectares (148,300–173,000 acres). With the 1911 RESTORATION of Mongolian independence, many of the Chinese farmers fled. While the theocratic government encouraged agriculture both in the Selenge valley and in the former military fields around Khowd, buying improved Russian farm implements and distributing them to the local administrations, it was unable to reach the earlier levels of cultivation. The revolutionary government after 1921 continued the same policy, and by 1925 cultivation reached more than 75,000 hectares (185,300 acres), much of which was still cultivated by Chinese or Russian farmers. By 1938, however, political turmoil had again forced an exodus of ethnic Chinese farmers, and privately cultivated fields had declined to 16,000 hectares (39,500 acres). During WORLD WAR II a shortage of grain from Russia prompted a temporary boom in both farming and milling based on indigenous technology.

VIRGIN LANDS FARMING

In 1959 Mongolia initiated a "Virgin Lands" campaign, imitating Soviet ruler Nikita Khrushchev's program, with the aim of becoming self-sufficient in grain. The crops and technology were completely borrowed from the Soviet Russian system and relied on mechanization and fertilizers. Most arable agricultural enterprises were organized as "state farms" (sangiin aj akhui), in which the laborers were paid employees of the state and the farm directors directly appointed by the central government. The main crops were wheat, barley, oats, potatoes, and fodder crops, particularly corn. While at least a few farms were set up in virtually every province, SELENGE PROVINCE was the main arable agriculture center.

By 1960 265,500 hectares (656,050 acres) were under cultivation, and the 1960 harvest reached 256,500 metric tons (282,750 short tons) of grain, 6,800 metric tons (7,500 short tons) of vegetables, 18,500 metric tons (20,400 short tons) of potatoes, and 34,400 metric tons (37,900 short tons) of fodder. From that point cultivation expanded until in 1985 1,240,000 hectares (3,064,040 acres) were cultivated, with 64 percent under plow and 36 percent fallow. In that year each hectare sown with wheat yielded an average 1,430 kilograms (1,275 pounds per acre), while the potato yield averaged 11,010 kilograms (9,825 pounds per acre). The production of fodder, which in 1985 amounted to 18 percent of the total acreage, made animal husbandry increasingly dependent on farming.

Despite the success in making Mongolia self-sufficient in grain, this new agriculture was heavily dependent on imported inputs. As Soviet-bloc countries began to demand higher prices for these goods after 1985, both the scale and the productivity of agriculture dropped. From 1991 the decline became precipitous as trade suddenly shifted to hard currency. On a market basis the economics of mechanized agriculture have become dubious. By 2000 the wheat harvest had virtually collapsed, to 138,700 metric tons (152,891 short tons) from 1990's 596,200 metric tons (657,198 short tons), while the potato harvest was only 58,900 metric tons (64,926 short tons) compared with 131,100 (144,513 short tons) in 1990. One of the few profitable markets for grain and potatoes is the distilled liquor industry. This decline was the result of sharp decreases in both acreage and yields per acre. Fodder production has virtually ceased. Only vegetable farming has increased, fueled by small private plots on the outskirts of cities. The future direction of Mongolian agriculture is uncertain.

See also ANIMAL HUSBANDRY AND NOMADISM; HUNTING AND FISHING.

Further reading: Walther Heissig, "Mongol Farming," *Contemporary Manchuria* 3, no. 4 (1939): 79–96; Sevyan Vainshtein, *Nomads of South Siberia*, trans. Michael Colenso (Cambridge: Cambridge University Press, 1980).

fauna   Mongolian fauna is mostly similar to that of the forest, steppe, and desert belts that sweep east to west across Eurasia. There are, however, a few distinctive relict species. The fauna of the MONGOLIAN PLATEAU (including neighboring areas of Transbaikalia and Inner Mongolia) belongs to the Palearctic (Old World) subzone of the Holarctic (pan-Boreal) province and includes such ubiquitous Holarctic fauna as the wolf, peregrine falcon, golden eagle, crow, shrew (*Sorex*), vole (*Clethrionomys, Microtus*), and hare (*Lepus*). Distinctive East Asian fauna include the musk deer (*Moschus moschiferus*) of the wooded ranges, the raccoon dog (*Nyctereutes procyonoides*) of eastern Mongolia, and the Siberian tiger that up to the 20th century inhabited the forests of the GREATER KHINGGAN RANGE in northeastern Inner Mongolia. Mongolia shares with eastern Siberia and North America the tundra vole (*Microtus oeconomus*), arctic ground squirrel (*Citellus undulatus*), and pika (*Ochotona*), while its only poisonous snake, the shield-snouted viper (*Agkistrodon halys*), is a relative of the American cottonmouth.

Within Mongolia proper, identified species include 136 mammals, 436 birds, 22 reptiles, eight amphibians, and 75 fish. About 20,000 invertebrates have been identified.

FOREST AND MOUNTAIN WILDLIFE

The forest fauna is essentially that typical of Europe and Siberia, such as the elk or red deer (*Cervus elaphus*), roe deer (*Capreolus capreolus*), moose, wild boar, red fox, wolverine, lynx, brown bear, and smaller rodent and insectivore fauna. Likewise, forest bird life in Mongolian, Buriat, and Khinggan forests includes the loon, great spotted woodpecker (*dendrocopus major*), goshawk, stone capercaillie, hazel hen, three-toed woodpecker (*Picoides tridactylus*), and surd cuckoo (*Cuculus saturatus*). The black kite (*Milvus migrans*; Mongolian, *elee*) is the most common forest raptor. Fur-bearing animals such as the sable (*Martes zibellina*), ermine or stoat (*Mustela erminea*), solongo (*Mustela sibirica* and *M. altaica*), otter, and beaver have become rare, while the muskrat has been locally introduced. In Mongolia proper, estimates in 1965–70 of forest ungulate populations included 140,000 elk, 100,000 roe deer, 80,000 musk deer, 40,000 wild boar, and 15,000 moose.

The reindeer (*Rangifer tarandus*), both wild and domestic, is found in isolated patches of taiga forests and alpine tundras of KHÖWSGÖL PROVINCE and Buriatia. The great argali sheep (*Ovis ammon*), first described by MARCO POLO, and the ibex or wild goat (*Capra sibirica*), are the largest wild animals of the ALTAI RANGE, KHANGAI RANGE, and GOBI-ALTAI range and were estimated in 1965–70 at 50,000 and 100,000, respectively. Their main predator, aside from hunters, is the endangered snow leopard (*Uncia uncia*), with an estimated population of 500–1,700. Alpine birdlife includes the endemic Altai snowcock (*Tetraogallus altaica*), rock pigeon (*Columba rupestris*), and ptarmigan.

STEPPE AND DESERT WILDLIFE

In the past the steppe and desert fauna of Mongolia was dominated by a few large ungulates in vast flocks, but hunting and competition from domestic livestock have devastated them. The Mongolian, or white, gazelle, *Procapra* (or *Gazella*) *gutturosa*, of the eastern steppe was estimated at 300,000 in Mongolia in 1965–70, while the black-tailed gazelle (*Gazella subgutturosa*) of the GOBI DESERT numbered about 60,000.

Apart from gazelles, rodents are now the only wild steppe or desert fauna commonly seen: marmots (*Marmota*), ground squirrels (*Citellus*), and pikas (*Ochotona*) are common in the steppe, while several species of jerboas (some endangered), hamsters, and gerbils dwell in the Gobi. Predators include the widespread but very wary wolf, corsac fox (*Vulpes corsac*), steppe cat (*Felis manul*), polecat (*Mustela eversmanni*), and marbled polecat (*Vormela peregusna*). Characteristic steppe or desert bird life includes the skylark, magpie, great bustard (*Otis tardus*), wheatears (*Oenanthe*), tawny eagle (*Aquila rapax*), upland buzzard (*Buteo hemilasius*), and steppe falcon (*Falco naumanni*). The saxaul sparrow (*Passer ammodendri*) frequents the saxaul thickets of the Gobi. Mongolia's largest bird is the lammergeier (*Gypaetus barbatus*; Mongolian, *yol*), a vast vulture of the mountains and deserts with a wing span of 2.4–3 meters (8–10 feet). Lizards in the steppe and desert include the agamids *Phrynocephalus versicolor* and several species of *Eremias*.

Rare or endangered Gobi animals include the Mongolian saiga antelope (*Saiga tatarica mongolica*), wild ass (*Equus hemionus hemionus*, called "chigetai" from Mongolian *chikhtei*, long-eared one, although the real Mongolian name is *khulan*), wild two-humped camel (*Camelus bactrianus ferus*), and Przewalskii's horse (*Equus caballus przewalskii*). The wild camel's population is estimated at only 300 and is declining. The Przewalskii's horse died out in the Gobi in the late 1960s but has recently been reintroduced into both the Great Gobi Protected Area and the Khustain Reserve near ULAANBAATAR in forest-steppe terrain. Mongolia now has more than 60 wild horses. Rare Gobi predators include the red dhole (*Cuon alpinus*) and the Gobi bear (*Ursus arctos pruinosus*), estimated at about 30 in 1985.

WATER FAUNA

The lakes and rivers of the Mongolian plateau include a large number of waterfowl, both native and migratory. Cormorants, great egrets (*Egretta alba*), ducks (mallard, mandarin, and shelduck), geese, common terns, herring gulls, coots, and marsh harriers (*Circus aeruginosus*) are common forms; swans, Dalmatian pelicans (*Pelicanus crispus*), white-naped cranes (*Grus vipia*), ospreys (*Pandion haliaetus*), and fish eagles (*Haliaetus*) are less common. The Mongolian plateau's rivers and lakes belong to the Pacific (ONON RIVER, KHERLEN RIVER), Arctic (ORKHON

RIVER, TUUL RIVER, EG RIVER, SELENGE RIVER, LAKE BAIKAL, Barguzin), and inland (GREAT LAKES BASIN, Valley of the Lakes) basins. Larger fish in the Pacific and Arctic watersheds include Baikal and Amur sturgeons (*Acipenser baeri* and *A.schrencki*), troutlike lenoks (*Brachymistax lenok*), salmonlike taimens (*Hucho taimen*), and pikes (*Ezox*). The omul (*Coregonus autumnalis*), a type of whitefish, is Lake Baikal's main food fish.

Waters of the Mongolian plateau contain a number of fauna of evolutionary-biological interest. Lake Baikal, the world's deepest lake, has 2,630 identified species, of which two-thirds are unique to the lake, including the nerpa, or Baikal seal, the world's only freshwater pinniped. The Altai Mountain dace (*Oreoleuciscus potanini*), isolated in the Great Lakes Basin, has diversified into a number of divergent types inhabiting different ecological niches.

See also ENVIRONMENTAL PROTECTION; FOSSIL RECORD; HUNTING AND FISHING; KALMYK REPUBLIC.

Further reading: Academy of Sciences, MPR, *Information Mongolia* (Oxford: Pergamon Press, 1990), 44–48.

fine arts   *See* ANIGA; BUDDHISM IN THE MONGOL EMPIRE; BUDDHIST FINE ARTS; CHOIJUNG LAMA TEMPLE; DEMOTTE *SHAHNAMA*; IL-KHANATE; JIBZUNDAMBA KHUTUGTU, FIRST; MONGOL *ZURAG*; PALACES OF THE BOGDA KHAN; SHARAB, "BUSYBODY"; THEOCRATIC PERIOD; YADAMSÜREN, ÜRJINGIIN.

fire cult   The Mongolian fire cult is an example of the widespread and ancient Eurasian worship of the family fire as a symbol of family continuity. The family hearth, or *golomt,* is the symbol of the continuity of the family, so that destroying the fire is equivalent to destroying the family, and vice versa. The wedding ceremony thus includes both the groom contributing to the worship of the bride's fire and the bride worshipping her new family's fire. New family hearths are founded by an ember from an old fire.

Traditionally, the sanctity of the household fire has been guarded by many prohibitions. One must not pour water on the fire, cut it with a knife, or walk over it. The fire has the power to purify things that are from outside the family or are polluted. Envoys to the Türk khans of the seventh century and the Mongol great khans of the 13th century were passed between two fires to purify them, a custom that continues today for the mourners at funerals. Clothing or hats that have been stepped on and stray or borrowed objects brought to the YURT are also purified before use by waving them over the fire.

Traditionally, rituals of the fire were conducted on daily, monthly, seasonal, and yearly bases. Daily care consisted of feeding it a small amount of grain (traditionally fried millet) mixed with sugar and butter and reciting the mantra *om a hung* three times. Monthly or seasonal worship was carried on only by some households, but all families were expected to worship the household fire during the last lunar month in preparation for the WHITE MONTH (lunar new year). This date was traditionally on the 23rd, 24th, or 29th of the 12th lunar moon, depending on the region and social status of the people. Among the KALMYKS, where the new year was switched to autumn, the fire sacrifice (*ghal täklghn*) was celebrated on the 22nd of the ninth lunar month.

In rural areas today, the annual fire worship begins when the stars become fully visible. The family members all gather in new clothes before the fire, before which a table has been placed on a clean white felt. Sometimes preceded by an incense offering, a sheep's chest wrapped with woolen yarn and decorated with strips of silk and wrapped in the fat of the animal's intestines is waved three times in a clockwise direction with the invocational cry *khurui* repeated three times. Once this is placed in the fire, liquor, butter, jujube fruits, scraps of silk, and grains are also added. As the fire burns high, the family bows down, a fire prayer is read, and then the family members make their own individual offerings or light incense sticks. A brief prostration is also made on new year's day itself.

The fire prayers occur in several distinct forms, although all known fire prayer texts, without exception, align the cult with the Buddhist tradition. The most common type invokes the fire as the child of Indra (Khormusta), the Buddha, or the seed-syllable *ram*, but also of steel and flint, heaven (Tenggeri), Mother Etüken (the earth goddess), and CHINGGIS KHAN and his queen BÖRTE ÜJIN, all implicitly identified with the household's master and mistress. Blessings sought include sons, daughters, and daughters-in-law, a peaceful state, and a flourishing property. Similar in meter, alliteration, and formulas to Mongolian EPICS, these prayer texts appear to date from the 16th or 17th century. The THIRD MERGEN GEGEEN (1717–66) authored a version in Tibetan-style alliterative quatrains, added a more structured ritual, and emphasized the role of Buddhist deities. Finally, a third type of text prescribes complex ritual actions and tantric-style visualizations to be carried out by the officiant, clearly to be a lama.

These differences in the ritual texts parallel differences in the name of the deity and who conducts the ceremony. The deity of the fire is usually simply "Fire-Ruler" (Turkish, *odkhan*, or Mongolian, *galaikhan*) or "Mother Fire-Ruler," but sometimes Miraja Khan, the "Hermit God" (Mergen Gegeen), or "the seven sisters, khans of fire" (tantric texts). In different areas and in different households the mistress of the household, the master, a respected lay ritualist, or a lama carried out the annual ritual.

The fire cult is unquestionably an ancient part of Mongol religious life but one that was easily incorporated into Buddhism. Unlike the cult of the *ONGGHON*, it was never opposed by Buddhist missionaries; indeed, the fire cult is part of the oldest traditions of Indian Buddhism.

This religious confluence accounts for the fire cult's apparent increase in importance and complexity after the Buddhist conversion.

See also FOLK POETRY AND TALES; LITERATURE.

Further reading: Christopher P. Atwood, "Buddhism and Popular Ritual in Mongolian Religion: A Reexamination of the Fire Cult," *History of Religions* 36 (1996): 112–139.

five-year plans The system of five-year plans, first adopted in the Soviet Union in 1929, was applied in Mongolia in 1948–90 as a crucial part of a noncapitalist economy. Mongolia originally formulated a wishful five-year plan in 1931, but it was canceled by the NEW TURN POLICY in 1932. In 1941 a Board of Planning, Accounting, and Control (later renamed the State Planning Commission) began sketchy annual plans. The first five-year plan in 1948–52 again sought ambitious goals: doubling the output of Mongolia's fledgling industry and increasing livestock from 21 million in 1947 to a projected 31 million in 1952. In fact, output in key industrial goods, such as coal and shoes, actually declined, while livestock numbers did not pass 23 million. Despite the disappointment, Mongolia's economy was governed from then on by five-year plans (with one three-year plan in 1958–60) until the eighth and last in 1986–90. Collectivization, completed in 1959, theoretically brought the entire economy under state control.

From 1966 Mongolia's five-year plans were integrated with the politicoeconomic planning calendar in the whole Soviet bloc, with plans being drawn up simultaneously and in consultation in all Soviet-allied countries. Each plan was drawn up by the Ministry of Finance and the State Planning Commission. This plan, and the detailed plans dependent on it, were structured around using specified inputs (labor, materials, investment, etc.) to meet specified output indexes. Prices for all goods transferred between enterprises and nations were set by the plan. Based on the nationwide plan, ministries drew up detailed plans for branches of the economy, provincial and town government drew up plans for their regions, and finally enterprises drew up subordinate plans for themselves. Enterprises were publicly praised or blamed for meeting or not meeting their quotas. The five-year plans proved effective at directing resources to specified branches, thus helping Mongolia build up numerous industries from scratch, but only at the cost of systematic inefficiency.

With democratization and PRIVATIZATION the five-year plan system was abolished. Today planning has been replaced by economic management using prices, now freed from state control, as the main indicator and money supply and tax policy as the major tools.

See also COLLECTIVIZATION AND COLLECTIVE HERDING; ECONOMY, MODERN; MONGOLIAN PEOPLE'S REPUBLIC; MONGOLIAN PEOPLE'S REVOLUTIONARY PARTY.

flags In Mongolia proper (KHALKHA or Outer Mongolia) the SOYOMBO SYMBOL has been a constant on the flag and an object of great veneration. In Mongolian regions of China and Russia, the symbolism has been more varied. The new flag of the 1911 RESTORATION of Mongolian independence expressed the nation's theocratic ideals. About three times wider than long, the flag had three pointed tails at the upper, center, and lower fly. A thick border along the hoist, top, and bottom edges enclosed a field. In the center of the field was a multicolored Soyombo symbol of Zanabazar (*see* JIBZUNDAMBA KHUTUGTU, FIRST) placed on a lotus and surrounded by an aureole of flames, a placement used for fierce protector deities. On both sides of the Soyombo were written Buddhist seed syllables in Zanabazar's SOYOMBO SCRIPT, while on the field was printed 39 lines of Tibetan prayers, as on a *khii mori* (wind horse, or prayer flag). Different versions were sewn in different colors, often with brocade cloth, although the Tibetan-rite Buddhist colors of red and yellow predominated.

In the 1921 REVOLUTION the partisans raised red and yellow flags bearing the Soyombo, taking advantage of the Buddhists' and Soviets' shared affinity for red and yellow (or gold). The 1924 CONSTITUTION specified that the national flag of the MONGOLIAN PEOPLE'S REPUBLIC be red with a (golden) Soyombo on a lotus in the middle. Usually, the flag was more-or-less square. The 1940 CONSTITUTION lengthened the flag to a 1:2 ratio and replaced the Soyombo with the new Soviet-style state seal, but this flag was not long used. Just before Mongolia joined WORLD WAR II in 1945, a new design again incorporating the Soyombo was adopted. The flag, again twice as long as wide, was divided into three vertical stripes, the center blue and the fly and hoist red. On the red stripe on the hoist was a golden Soyombo without the lotus but surmounted by a five-pointed golden star. Confirmed by constitutional amendment on February 23, 1949, the same basic design has been used ever since. The new democratic 1992 CONSTITUTION removed the Communist star but otherwise left the flag unchanged.

During the Republic of China (1912–49) Inner Mongolian autonomous movements proposed a variety of party and state flags. In 1936 the Mongolian military government under PRINCE DEMCHUGDONGRUB adopted a new flag with a blue field and a canton with three vertical stripes of red, yellow, and white. In 1942, however, the Japanese forced the INNER MONGOLIANS to accept another flag formed of horizontal stripes with red, for Japan, in the center. In 1946 a pan-Mongolist, pro-Soviet East Mongolian autonomous government in Wang-un Süme (modern Ulanhot) flew a flag of three horizontal stripes with the central blue and red flanking. In the center of the blue stripe was a crossed hoe and *uurga* (Mongolian lasso pole) signaling eastern Inner Mongolia's agropastoral economy. The Chinese Communists added a five-pointed star above the hoe and *uurga* before abolishing the flag altogether in 1949.

War flag of the theocratic state, 1911–19 *(Courtesy Christopher Atwood)*

Before 1991, as autonomous Soviet socialist republics within the Soviet Union's Russian Soviet Federated Socialist Republic (RSFSR), the BURIAT REPUBLIC and KALMYK REPUBLIC occasionally flew a version of the RSFSR flags with the republics' names or initials added on. After the breakup of the Soviet Union, both the Buriat and Kalmyk Republics designed new flags. Kalmykia's first flag, adopted in October 1992, was replaced in July 1993 by one with more clearly Buddhist symbolism: a yellow field with a blue circle in the center and a white nine-petaled lotus in the blue circle. Buriatia in October 1992 adopted a blue, white, and yellow horizontal tricolor, adding at the upper hoist in yellow the Buddhist symbol of the crescent moon, sun, and flame found on the Soyombo and Buddhist stupas. The AGA BURIAT AUTONOMOUS REGION and UST'-ORDA BURIAT AUTONOMOUS REGION have also adopted new flags. That of Aga mixes the crescent moon, sun, and flame with the Russian tricolor, but the Ust'-Orda flag has no special Mongolian symbolism.

Flight of the Kalmyks   In 1771 the bulk of the Kalmyks on the Volga fled increasing Russian control to try to reconquer Züngharia. Ravaged by hunger and Kazakh attacks, on their arrival in Züngharia they had no choice but to surrender to the QING DYNASTY. Their descendants are now the bulk of the current Xinjiang Mongols.

After the death of AYUUKI KHAN (r. 1669–1724) Russian encouragement of Christian conversions, interference in Kalmyk politics, and increasing colonization periodically stimulated the idea of returning to Züngharia (Junggar basin). Soon after her coronation Empress Catherine II (1762–96) decreed that the Kalmyk ruler's *zarghu* (court or council) no longer be a privy council of the khan's Torghud retainers but a genuine legislative body with members elected by the nobility (*noyod; see* NOYAN) from the KALMYKS' three tribes (TORGHUDS, KHOSHUDS, and DÖRBÖDS) and the monasteries. This decision and the empress's program of colonization on the Volga led Ubashi (b. 1745, r. 1762–71, d. 1774) to decide to flee. The leading advocates of flight were Tsebeg-Dorji (d. 1778), whose bid for rule over the Kalmyks the Russian authorities had rejected, and Tseren, who had fled from the Qing dynasty's conquest of Züngharia and been resettled among the Kalmyks with 10,000 households. Tseren believed that Züngharia had been left empty by the Qing and that the Kalmyks could easily seize the area.

In autumn 1770 Ubashi's court crossed the Volga, ostensibly to guard against Kazakh raids. After waiting in vain for the Volga to freeze and allow the others over, Ubashi revealed the decision to the people on January 4 (old style), plundered the Russian merchants and soldiers in the camps, and the next day set out with 30,909 households and 169,000 persons. Left stranded west of the Volga were 11,198 households. The forts on the Ural River were in rebellion and let the Kalmyks pass, but the governor of Orenburg vainly attempted to pursue them. He also notified the KAZAKHS, however, who harassed and plundered the Kalmyks as they moved across Kazakhstan. The Kyrgyz also looted their camps savagely near Lake Balkhash. In early August the Kalmyks reached the Ili Valley. Having lost all but a third of their cattle and been reduced to 70,000 people, the Kalmyks could not fight, and they surrendered to the Qing. Overriding advisers suspicious of the former anti-Qing refugee Tseren, the emperor Qianlong (1736–96) issued livestock, TEA, rice, sheepskins, cloth, cotton, YURTS, and silver in great amounts in relief. Qianlong saw Ubashi's imperial audience in October at his summer palace as the culmination and vindication of his Mongolian policy. In 1774 Qianlong resettled the refugees into 17 BANNERS (appanages). Ubashi, Tsebeg-Dorji, and other "Old" Torghud and Khoshud princes of the Kalmyks received pastures in central and northern Xinjiang (*see* XINJIANG MONGOLS). Tseren and his "New" Torghuds were resettled in the Khowd frontier (modern Bulgan Sum, Khowd).

flora   Mongolia's vegetation ranges from the taiga forests of Siberia to the gravelly sands of the GOBI DESERT. The vegetation of the MONGOLIAN PLATEAU (including Mongolia and neighboring areas of Transbaikalia and

Inner Mongolia) can be divided into three "pure" zones: the mountain taiga forest (Mongolian *taiga*), the steppe (Mongolian *kheer*), and the Gobi Desert (from Mongolian *gobi*). The mountain forest steppe (*khangai*) and the desert steppe are intermediate forms. On the high peaks of the ALTAI RANGE, the KHANGAI RANGE, the Sayan, and the higher ranges along the Baikal there are also alpine and subalpine tundra.

Mountain taiga forest covers KHÖWSGÖL PROVINCE, the Sayan and KHENTII RANGES, and the lower ranges along the Baikal. The main species are the larch (*Larix sibirica* in the west and *L. dahurica* in the east) and the Siberian pine or cedar (*Pinus sibirica*), with areas of birch (*Betula*), spruce (*Picea obovata*), and fir (*Abies sibirica*). The forests usually have a thick undergrowth of shrubs, herbs, berries, and wildflowers, such as *Rhododendron dahurica*, bilberry (*Vaccinium vitis*), and wild marsh azalea (*Ledum palustre*). Larch (*L. dahurica*) forests with areas of low-lying meadow and swamp cover northeast Buriatia.

The steppe belt is wide in eastern Mongolia and in HULUN BUIR, SHILIIN GOL, and Aga areas but gradually narrows westward. Discontinuous areas of steppe are found in Buriatia along the Selenge and its tributaries, on the upper Uda (Buriat, Üde), and around the Yeravna (Buriat, Yaruuna) Lakes and in the Barguzin (Buriat, Bargazhan) valley. Important grasses include *khyalgana*, or feather grasse (*Stipa baicalensis* in the wetter east and *S. krylovii* in the drier west), June grass (*Koeleria*), rye grass (*Leymus chinensis*), fescue (*Festuca*), wheat grass (*Agropyron cristata*), and *Cleistogenes squarrosa*. Sedges (*Carex*), legumes, and shrubs such as sagebrushes (*Artemisia*) and pea shrubs (*Caragana*) form an important component of the flora. The east forms the Daurian-Mongolian floral zone, with more species characteristic of Manchuria. In *solonchaks*, or low-lying salt marshes, splendid feather grass (*Achnatherium splendens*, Mongolian *ders*), couch grass (*Aneurolepidium*; Mongolian, *khiag*), and wheat grass (*Agropyron cristata*) grow. Willows and poplars line major watercourses.

The forest steppe covers the lower Khangai and Khentii and the valleys of the Barguzin and the Selenge and its tributaries in Buriatia. Here forests of larch (*Larix sibirica*) in the Khangai and of cedar (Siberian pine, *Pinus sibirica*), pine (*Pinus sylvestris*), and birch in Buriatia and the Khentii occupy the northern slopes, while steppe

Khangai (forest-steppe) landscape. Bulgan province, 1992 *(Courtesy Christopher Atwood)*

vegetation covers the southern slopes. The grass is like that of the steppe, but with bluegrass (*Poa attenuata*) being common. This area supports the highest density of livestock.

The desert steppe stretches between the Gobi and the steppe. (In China *gobi* is used for this desert steppe zone, not for drier shrub desert.) The Valley of the Lakes and the GREAT LAKES BASIN are basically desert steppe, as are the lower slopes of the Altai. There, feather grasses (*Stipa* sp.), taana onion (*Allium polyrrhizum*), sagebrushes, and *Ajania* (a flowering shrub of the Asteraceae family) are the most characteristic vegetation.

The classic Gobi Desert of south-central and southwestern Mongolia, ULAANCHAB, and northern ALASHAN has a very thin vegetation cover of shrubs and semishrubs such as ephedra (*Ephedra przewalskii*) and members of the goosefoot family (Chenopodiaceae): saxaul (*Haloxylon ammodendron*), tumbleweed (*Salsola passerina*), and others. The trans-Altai Gobi of KHOWD PROVINCE forms the edge of the Zünghar zone, with species characteristic of northern Xinjiang.

PASTURES, FORESTRY, AND GATHERING

Mongolian wild vegetation is used for fodder, lumber, and culinary-medicinal purposes. As fodder it is the basis of Mongolia's most important economic pursuit both historically and today, animal husbandry. Mongolian pastures contain about 5,000 species of plants, of which 600 are forage species and 200 particularly nutritious for livestock. Standing crop ranges from 3,500–4,000 kilograms per hectare (3,120–3,570 pounds per acre) in the forest-steppe to 375–1,500 (335–1,340 pounds per acre) in the desert steppe. Overgrazing first shortens the stems and then begins to cause an increase in poisonous or otherwise harmful grass. Pasture degradation is significant in Mongolia and very serious in Buriatia and Inner Mongolia. Cultivation or extremely heavy grazing in marginal lands can lead to full-scale desertification, a problem particularly serious in Kalmykia and southwestern Inner Mongolia.

With transportation a key bottleneck, the main forestry centers in Mongolia and Buriatia are along the lower SELENGE RIVER and its main tributaries, the Yöröö and the Uda, and the Baikal, with smaller centers in eastern Khentii and western Khangai. In Inner Mongolia the northern GREATER KHINGGAN RANGE is China's main area of forestry and has been heavily developed with railroads, roads, and a vast influx of Chinese workers.

Many herbs, mushrooms, and berries are collected for both culinary and medicinal purposes. The sea buckthorn (*Hippophaë rhamnoides*), bilberry (*Vaccinium vitis*), blueberry (*Vaccinium uliginosum*), currant (*Ribes altissimum* and *R. nigrum*), and bird cherry (*Padus asiatica*) are found throughout the Khangai and Khentii. Pine nuts (*Pinus sibirica*) are also widely eaten. Edible mushrooms are collected in the Khentii.

Perhaps the most important root plant gathered, particularly in forest areas, was the lily bulb (*Lilium tenuifolium* and *L. martagon*), the Mongolian name for which, *tömös*, later became the term for potato. Other important roots used as flavorings included *Phallerocarpus gracilis* (Mongolian *yamaakhai*), silverweed (*Potentilla anserina*, Mongolian, *gichgene*), and snakeweed (*Polygonum vivparum*, Mongolian, *mekheer*) in the forest steppe and beach grasses *Psammochloa villosa* and *Leymus racemosus* (Mongolian, *suli*) and the goosefoot *Agrophyllum pungens* (Mongolian, *tsulikhir*) in the gobi zone.

Medicinal plants included the flowers *Lophanthus chinensis* (Mongolian, *sadagnagwa*), *Oxytropis pseudoglandulosa* (Mongolian, *ortuuz*), and *Rhodiola rosea* (Mongolian, *altangagnuur*), while the "camel's tail" pea shrub (*Caragana jubata*) is boiled for medicinal teas. Leaves of the juniper (Mongolian, *arts*) are the main incense in Mongolian traditional religious ceremonies, only partially replaced by artificial joss sticks.

See also ALASHAN; ANIMAL HUSBANDRY AND NOMADISM; DESERTIFICATION AND PASTURE DEGRADATION; ENVIRONMENTAL PROTECTION; FOSSIL RECORD; KALMYK REPUBLIC; KHORCHIN; ORDOS.

Further reading: Peter D. Gunin, et al. *Vegetation Dynamics of Mongolia* (Dordrecht: Kluwer Academic Publishers, 1999); B. Gomboev et al., "The Present Conditions and Use of Pasture in the Barguzin Valley," in *Culture and Environment in Inner Asia*, vol. 1, *The Pastoral Economy and the Environment*, ed. Caroline Humphrey and David Sneath (Cambridge: Cambridge University Press, 1996), 124–140; Sodnomdarjaa Jigjidsüren and Douglas A. Johnson, *Mongol orny malyn tejeelin urgamal/Forage Plants in Mongolia* (Ulaanbaatar: Research Institute for Animal Husbandry, 2003); S. Tserendash and B. Erdenebaatar, "Performance and Management of Natural Pasture in Mongolia," *Nomadic Peoples* 33 (1993): 9–16.

folk art   *See* CLOTHING AND DRESS; HORSE-HEAD FIDDLE; HORSES; JEWELRY; MUSIC; SHARAB, "BUSYBODY"; YURT.

folk poetry and tales   Mongolian literature has always been closely connected to folk poetry and orally transmitted tales. This connection goes both ways: Not only do writers take up folk poetic themes and genres, but also written literature frequently exercises a profound influence on folk poetry. Many pieces of Mongolian poetry first collected as "folksongs" have later been identified as works first written by Mongolian poets or liturgists, particularly the THIRD MERGEN GEGEEN and DANZIN-RABJAI. Finally, many originally orally transmitted works were written down not just by ethnographers but by the Mongols themselves and subsequently circulated as literature.

While Mongolian EPICS and folk poetry are often given impossibly ancient dates (going back to 1000), a precise dating of orally transmitted works is obviously impossible. By the late 18th century, certainly, one can say that folk literature had essentially the cast considered traditional today. Judging from the common Chinggisid themes, much of the wedding poetry and FIRE CULT prayers seem to have originated in the milieu surrounding the Chinggisid restoration during and following the reign of BATU MÖNGKE DAYAN KHAN (1480?–1517?). Hunting prayers and shamanist invocations are likely to have a roughly similar age.

Blessing (yörööl) and praise (magtaal) poetry were some of the most important genres of Mongolian folk poetry, connected to religion, games (naadam), and virtually every part of everyday life (see YÖRÖÖL AND MAGTAAL). Political addresses (jorig) were similar. Handbooks for speaking appropriate words of blessing or praise at every occasion circulated, particularly in ORDOS. In the 19th and 20th centuries Geligbalsang (1846–1943) of KHALKHA and Gamala of ÜJÜMÜCHIN (1871–1932) became famous for their beautiful praises and blessings.

Mongolian proverbs and riddles frequently appear in literature but were rarely collected by the Mongols themselves until modern times. A distinctive genre of Mongolian gnomic poetry is the "THREES OF THE WORLD."

Mongolian epics in their present form date from the late 17th century at the earliest and in some cases certainly later. The GESER epic, first printed in Mongolian in 1716, later became nativized as a Mongolian epic. The JANGGHAR epic appears to have taken its final form among the KALMYKS in the early and mid-18th century. While the Jangghar is less commonly found in written versions, both the Geser epic and the Khalkha epic Khan Kharankhui exist in a number of manuscripts, both in the UIGHUR-MONGOLIAN SCRIPT and in the CLEAR SCRIPT.

In eastern Inner Mongolia, HULUN BUIR, eastern Khalkha, and old Khüriye (modern ULAANBAATAR), a distinctive style of khuurchi (fiddlers') tales, grew up. While the epics were connected to hunting magic, fiddlers' tales were purely for dramatic entertainment. They drew their material mostly from written sources: the Geser epic, CHINESE FICTION such as the novels *The Water Margin* and *Three Kingdoms*, and Indian story cycles such as the *Thirty-Two Wooden Men*. They were thus also sometimes called *bengsen-ü üliger,* or "chapbook tales." Pajai (1902–62) of Jarud banner was perhaps the most famous of these fiddlers.

Mongolian folktales include the widespread animal fables, explanations of natural phenomena, and so on. Some can be linked to similar themes in East Asian literature, while others share motifs with Indian or Tibetan tales. Stories about ethnic origins and historical figures have been widely gathered today, and such material has found its way into many old Mongolian, Buriat, and Kalmyk-Oirat chronicles. In Khalkha and Inner Mongolia many epics are now told as prose stories.

See also EIGHT WHITE YURTS; FIRE CULT; LITERATURE; MUSIC; PROSODY; WEDDINGS.

Further reading: Damdinsurengiin Altangerel, ed., *How Did the Great Bear Originate? Folk Tales from Mongolia* (Ulaanbaatar: State Publishing House 1988); ———, *The Legend of Cuckoo Namjil: Folk Tales from Mongolia* (Ulaanbaatar: State Publishing House, n.d.); John Gombojab Hangin, ed., *Mongolian Folklore: A Representative Collection from the Oral Literary Tradition* (Bloomington, Ind.: Mongolia Society, 1998); Nassenbayar et al., trans., *Mongolian Oral Narratives: Gods, Tricksters, Heroes, and Horses* (Bloomington, Ind.: Mongolia Society, 1995); Nicholaus Poppe, *Tsongol Folklore: Translation of the Language and Collective Farm Poetry of the Buriat Mongols of the Selenga Region* (Wiesbaden: Otto Harrassowitz, 1978); Henry Serruys, "A Genre of Oral Literature in Mongolia: The Addresses," *Monumenta Serica* 31 (1977): 555–613; Archer Taylor, *An Annotated Collection of Mongolian Riddles* (Philadelphia: American Philosophical Society, 1954).

food and drink Mongolian food has changed in many ways since the MONGOL EMPIRE, but mutton and traditional dairy products remain at the heart of it. Food in Mongolia is traditionally divided into "white foods" (tsagaan idee), or DAIRY PRODUCTS, and "red foods" (ulaan idee), or meat. White foods are the staple of the summer and red foods of the winter. This division, however, takes account only of the most honored foods and leaves out several important categories of food: various forms of grain, which even for a pure nomad supply much of the caloric intake, game, wild vegetables and herbs, wild fruits and berries, and salts for seasoning.

Mongolian animals are slaughtered in a distinctive style. The animal is thrown on its back, and its legs are held or, with powerful animals like the horse, tied. The butcher cuts a hole below the breast bone and suddenly reaches in and rips open the aorta, causing a catastrophic internal hemorrhage. This slaughtering is aimed at keeping all the blood in the body, exactly the opposite aim of Jewish and Muslim slaughtering. The blood is scooped out after the organs are removed and used for sausages. Attempts to impose this slaughtering style in Muslim lands caused conflict in the empire period. The Mongols were also notorious in the empire and later for eating animals that had died naturally or had been killed by wild animals.

DAILY FOOD IN THE MONGOL EMPIRE

Travelers to Mongolia in the 13th century observed that the Mongols lived primarily on KOUMISS, or fermented mare's milk, during the summer and on mutton during the winter. Observers also noticed the importance of wild meat in the Mongolian diet. Animals hunted included rabbit, deer, wild boar, ibex, gazelle, and the kulan, or wild ass. Muslim and Christian observers were particularly disgusted by the Mongols' liking for wild rodents, such as hamsters, ground squirrels, and especially marmots. Large fish was also taken in the winter by ice fishing.

For important occasions meat was prepared by roasting on a spit with salt as the only seasoning. For daily meals bones and meat were boiled together with seeds, grains, and wild onions and grasses to make a thick soup (*shöl*). While the Mongols rarely slaughtered animals during the summer, they were always careful to preserve the flesh of animals that died naturally (again to the disgust of Christian and Muslim observers). This they did by cutting the meat into strips and drying them in the sun and wind. This process, still common today, produces *borts* (jerky), which can be kept for several seasons. The intestines of horses would be made into sausages and eaten fresh. During the winter sheep were the only domestic animal frequently slaughtered. Horses were slaughtered only on ritual occasions, when a great feast was made.

Millet was also eaten boiled in gruel at least twice a day in winter. The millet was sometimes grown on the MONGOLIAN PLATEAU, sometimes received in tribute by noble-born Mongols, and sometimes bought by well-off commoners by selling sheep and skins to Uighur and Chinese peddlers.

Descriptions of mealtime etiquette exist only for roasted meat eaten among men of consequence. The meat was cut up into small pieces, and the order of eating was determined by the host. Pieces were served to the guests skewered on prongs. Those in charge of cutting and presenting the food were the *ba'urchis* (stewards), belonging to the *keshig*, or imperial guards, and had a high position. It is likely that, as is reported of the Turks, different clans were assigned different parts of meat according to their prestige and that part of the *ba'urchi*'s role was to know these hierarchies. Food was eaten with the fingers, and hands were wiped on clothes or grass.

During the early empire the most common imported foodstuff was liquor, both Chinese rice wine and Turkestani grape wine. CHINGGIS KHAN first saw grape wine when it was presented to him in 1204 in tribute by a Mongol tribe envoy and disapproved, as the liquor was dangerously strong. Certainly drunkenness was frequent at Mongol gatherings. Singing and a kind of teasing dance accompanied the drinking of liquor, which proceeded according to a complex ritual of offering and counteroffering.

At the court of the Mongol rulers in China, as seen in the *Yinshan zhengyao* (1330), a cookbook by the Uighur Hu Sihui (Qusqi), Turkestani and Middle Eastern influence on Mongolian food was very strong. Noodles became a major part of the diet, and Mongolian soups were enlivened with spices such as cardamom and Middle Eastern ingredients such as chickpeas and fenugreek seeds. The khans enjoyed genuine Turkish or Middle Eastern dishes such as sherbet, the pastries *börek* and *güllach* (an early version of baklava), and the bread *yufka*.

LATER TRADITIONAL MONGOLIAN FOOD

After the breakup of the Mongol Empire, much Mongolian food remained the same. A Chinese frontier official in 1594 described the continued dominance of mutton and the near-absence of beef, the preparation of thick meat stews, and the brewing of fermented milk liquors. Fried millet, flour, and noodles were prepared and mixed with meat stews or with milk. Both meat and flour stew (*bantang*) and noodles with meat chunks (*goimon*) are still common everyday dishes. The KALMYKS on the Volga bought rye flour from Russian farmers and made a rye porridge (*budan*).

Several changes were already in progress, however. Hunting was declining as a source of meat. TEA entered Mongolia together with the conversion to Buddhism from 1578 on; tea was already an absolutely indispensable part of Tibetan Buddhist monastic life and soon spread to the laity as well. Mongolian tea was made with milk, salt, and butter. Millet and meat were frequently added to it to make it a kind of thick soup. Wooden and, for the rich, silver bowls were used for tea, and spoons also came into use.

During the QING DYNASTY (1636–1912) these changes amplified. The large group hunts became rare, and game became only a small part of the diet. Fishing was abandoned under Buddhist influence. Cane sugar and rice imported from China became more common; a special dish for the days leading up to the WHITE MONTH (lunar new year) was millet or rice suspended in melted butter and served with sugar on top. *Bortsog*, or breads fried in animal fat, also became an important part of the meal. Among the UPPER MONGOLS of Kökenuur and those in western Mongolia, *zambaa* (from Tibetan *rtsam-pa*), or parched barley flour, usually moistened with tea and dairy products and rolled into balls, began to be eaten.

Serving styles also changed. Rather than pieces served with a skewer, festive meals were dominated by a metal plate piled with food, which was presented to visitors to take what they wanted. A hospitality plate, still kept regularly by every rural family and many urban ones, consisted of layers of *bortsog*, molded dried curd (*süün khuruud*), Chinese moon cakes (*yeewen*, from Chinese *yuebing*), *öröm*, candies, sugar cubes, and so on. Whole boiled mutton for ceremonial occasions, or *shüüs*, was arranged on a plate with the four legs sticking out, the fatty tail covering the rear and the boiled head on top, often with a piece of *süün khurud* crowning the head. The more respectable Mongols adopted a combination of chopsticks and a knife, both carried in a wooden sheath and hung on the sash. Eating with the fingers and knife was still common, however.

The Mongols during this time adopted a variety of Chinese-style dumplings and steamed buns. These included *mantuu* (from Chinese *mantou*), a fluffy steamed and leavened bun, *bänshi* (from Chinese *bianshi*, simple food), or dumplings of meat stuffing wrapped in a thin skin and boiled in soup, *khuushuur* (from *huxianr,* today *xianrbing*), a flattened patty stuffed with meat, vegetables, and salt and fried on a griddle, and especially BUUZ (from *baozi*). Another form of food adopted from China was round griddle cakes made with leavened dough and fried (*bin,* from Chinese *bing,* pancake) or roasted (*gambir,* from Chinese *ganbing,* dry pancake).

Roasted meat became almost unknown except in certain districts such as Alashan. Apart from boiling in a wok, another cooking method is to use hot stones to cook an animal in its own skin. This method is used for both marmots (*tarwagany boodog*) and sheep and goats (*khorkhog*). In the latter case water is also added to make a broth.

MODERN CHANGES

In the 20th century European and Chinese cuisine has exercised a powerful influence on Mongolian food. In both areas cheap distilled liquors with alcohol contents ranging from 45 percent (Mongolian vodka) to 60 percent (Chinese *baijiu*) have become the main liquor, far outstripping native milk liquors.

In Mongolia since the 1930s the state-owned hotels and restaurants have served a completely European fare. Chopsticks are no longer used, having been replaced by a varying combination of European utensils and the traditional knife and hands. Fried millet also disappeared from independent Mongolia's traditional cooking in the 1930s with the breakoff of economic relations with China. Beef has become a major part of the Mongolian diet, although still less consumed than mutton and goat's meat. Bread, once unknown, is now served with every meal among urban Mongolians, yet the Mongolian palate remains in many ways quite traditional, tending to a combination of fatty (dairy and animal) and salty or sweet and strongly averse to hot spices. Even today 88 percent of the Mongolians' consumed fat is of animal or dairy origin, the highest percentage in the world, yet cholesterol levels remain relatively low. Vegetables include cabbage, onions, potatoes, carrots, and radishes. The main seasoning is black pepper, although Chinese spices are again being used since 1990. Fruits include apples, watermelons, and imported oranges and tangerines. Urban families buy wild *chatsargana,* or sea buckthorn (*Hippophaë rhamnoides*), and pine nuts (*Pinus sibirica*) in season; *chatsargana* is made into juice.

Milk tea, noodle soups, flour stew (*bantan*), fat-fried breads (*bortsog*), griddle cakes (*bin, gambir*), and fried noodles are standard fare in both urban and rural areas. Urban families still try to secure a full *shüüs* for the White Month, while sausage and onion slices, potato salad, and heaps of *buuz,* washed down with vodka, are served for guests and special occasions. Rural families still produce the full range of milk products; of these *aaruul* (a kind of wormlike sweetened hard cheese) and *shimiin arkhi* (fermented milk liquor) are also sold in packaged format, while *zöökhii* (cream), *tsötsgii* (sour cream), yogurt (*tarag*), and fermented mare's milk (koumiss) are mostly sold unpackaged and seasonally. Unhomogenized milk and European-style butter, called *maasal* from Russian *maslo,* is also regularly available commercially. Pork and fish remain relatively unfamiliar foods.

In Inner Mongolia restaurants and hotels generally serve Chinese fare, and most Mongols are now familiar with highly spiced food. Noodles, buns, and dumplings are made in ways very close to the Chinese, but milk tea, fried millet, traditional dairy products received from relatives in the countryside and the higher percentage of meat differentiate the urban Mongol diet from that of their ethnic Chinese neighbors. In eastern Inner Mongolia pork is now common, and melted pork fat sometimes replaces butter in traditional dishes.

See also ANIMAL HUSBANDRY AND NOMADISM; FARMING; HUNTING AND FISHING.

Further reading: Thomas T. Allsen, *Culture and Conquest in Mongol Eurasia* (Cambridge: Cambridge University Press, 2001); Paul D. Buell, "The Mongol Empire and Turkicization: The Evidence of Food and Foodways," in *The Mongol Empire and Its Legacy,* ed. Reuven Amitai-Preiss and David O. Morgan (Leiden: E. J. Brill, 1999), 200–223; Paul D. Buell, Eugene N. Anderson, trans., *A Soup for the Qan: Chinese Dietary Medicine of the Mongol Era as Seen in Hu Szu-hui's Yin-shan cheng-yao* (London: Kegan Paul International, 2000).

foreign relations From 1911 to 1989 Mongolian foreign policy relied on the northern power (Russia/Soviet Union) to secure independence from the southern power (China, and from 1931 to 1945, Japan). From 1989, with the breakup of the Soviet bloc, Mongolia has pursued a new foreign policy based on evenhanded relations with Russia and China while promoting relations with both "third neighbors" and multilateral institutions to promote its independence and security.

RUSSIAN PATRONAGE AND ATTEMPTS AT RECOGNITION, 1911–1928

While the 1911 RESTORATION of Mongolian independence relied on Russian patronage, the new theocratic government persistently sought recognition from outside powers. On October 29, 1912, Mongolia's foreign ministry announced to all foreign powers its independence and asked to open relations. At this time the international treaties governing China's status allowed for spheres of influence, such as Russia's in Mongolia, but precluded any change in China's formal frontiers. Hence, all the addressed powers ignored the proposal. Late in 1913 the foreign minister, PRINCE KHANGDADORJI, met with a Japanese officer, "Kodama Toshimasa" (real name Odate Kamikichi), in an effort to open relations, but the Russians got wind of the affair and it came to nothing. Only the Tibetan government, in a similar situation to Mongolia's, recognized the new government in a February 4, 1913, treaty signed in Khüriye (modern ULAANBAATAR).

In 1915 the KYAKHTA TRILATERAL TREATY officially defined Outer Mongolia as an area under Chinese suzerainty, limiting its relations to Russia and China. In 1919, in the face of Chinese pressure (*see* REVOCATION OF AUTONOMY), the theocratic emperor secretly appealed to the U.S. and Japanese embassies in Beijing. This appeal and the growing American share in the wool trade led to the opening of a U.S. consulate in Zhangjiakou (Kalgan).

After a chaotic period of Chinese and White Russian occupation, the 1921 REVOLUTION put Mongolia back in the situation of 1911: recognized by Russia, seen as a breakaway province by China, and ignored by the rest of the world. On September 14, 1921, the prime minister, BODÔ, issued another announcement of Mongolia's independence and readiness to open relations with all nations. The new American consul in Zhangjiakou, Samuel Sokobin, visited Mongolia five times from August 1921, but his own anti-Soviet feelings and the Mongols' suspicion soon led to a complete break.

The Soviet government, unlike the czarist, made no attempt to bring Mongolia and China to the same negotiating table, preferring to deal with each separately. From 1925, however, the DAMBADORJI regime in Mongolia actively sought at least informal relations with foreign countries. By this time 124 non-Soviet, non-Chinese citizens lived in Ulaanbaatar, and American, British, and German firms were important players in the Mongolian wool trade. From 1926 to 1929 the Mongolian government sent 39 students to Germany and four to France. Dambadorji twice attempted to invite Japanese diplomats to Mongolia, but each time pressure from Moscow blocked the invitation

EXCLUSIVE SOVIET RELIANCE, 1928–1952

These attempts at an independent foreign policy led Moscow to engineer Dambadorji's dismissal in 1928. The leftists who controlled the new government voluntarily renounced any relations with the non-Soviet world, whether in diplomacy, trade, culture, or human relations, and restricted their ties to the Soviet Union and Mongolia's fellow Soviet satellite, the Tuvan People's Republic. Mongolia's few veteran diplomats were exterminated in the 1937–40 GREAT PURGE. Talks with the Japanese-controlled Manchurian government in 1935 and 1939–40 eventually resolved some frontier issues but without leading to recognition.

The final days of WORLD WAR II marked a tentative rebirth of Mongolia's foreign relations. The U.S. vice president, Henry Wallace, briefly visited Mongolia in May 1944 as part of his tour of the Soviet Union and the Far East. The Soviet Union's declaration of war on Japan led to both the Sino-Soviet treaty of August 14, 1945, and Mongolia's participation in the war. The first led to the

Republic of China's recognizing Mongolia's independence on January 6, 1946 (*see* PLEBISCITE ON INDEPENDENCE), while the second led to Mongolia's unsuccessful first application for membership in the UNITED NATIONS (UN). In 1948–50 Mongolia exchanged recognition first with Albania and North Korea, then the new People's Republic of China (PRC), and finally the Soviet Union's six East European satellites.

Despite these seemingly impressive advances, Mongolia's ruler, MARSHAL CHOIBALSANG (r. 1936–52), treated recognition as purely symbolic, showing no interest in exchanging ambassadors (although the PRC on its own initiative sent an ambassador to Mongolia in 1950) or engaging in any further contacts with the countries that recognized it. The rare opportunities of contact with the non-Soviet world were squandered by defensiveness and suspicions.

MONGOLIA AND THE SOVIET BLOC, 1952–1986

Choibalsang's death and the accession of a new generation gradually led for the first time to real multi–nation foreign relations, at least within the Soviet bloc. The first step was the new prime minister YUMJAAGIIN TSEDENBAL's visit to Beijing, the first of any Mongolian leader to a non-Soviet country, in October 1952, which led to the appointment of Mongolia's ambassador to Beijing, again the first not accredited to Moscow. In 1955–56 Mongolia began exchanging ambassadors with the other Soviet-bloc nations. In 1955 India became the first noncommunist country to recognize Mongolia and post diplomats to Ulaanbaatar. (In the 1970s India's Soviet alliance and common hostility to the PRC became a basis for fruitful political and cultural relations with Mongolia.) In 1961 Mongolia was finally admitted to the United Nations, and a mission was set up in New York.

Mongolia's admission to the Council of Mutual Economic Assistance (Comecon) in 1962 opened up all-around relations with Eastern Europe. Prodded by the Soviet Union, the East European nations, especially Czechoslovakia and East Germany, financed numerous aid projects in Mongolia. Mongolian students also studied in Eastern Europe, whose more open economy and culture opened new horizons for them. Despite these investments, the share of Mongolian trade held by the non-Soviet Comecon countries (i.e., Eastern Europe plus Vietnam and Cuba) actually declined from 19.8 percent in 1970 to 13.2 percent in 1985. By 1986 the East European countries were expressing donor fatigue.

Mongolia steadily expanded the number of countries with which it had relations, but such relations outside the Soviet bloc and India generally had little substance. From 1952 Chiang Kai-shek's Chinese Nationalists on Taiwan revoked their recognition of Mongolian independence, and put pressure on those countries that recognized it, most notably the United States and Japan, to continue denying recognition to Mongolia. Mongolia's admission to the UN led to the establishment of diplomatic relations with Britain (1963) and France (1964), but the U.S. State Department's hope to establish relations was blocked by lobbyists for the Nationalist government on Taiwan. Japan and Mongolia opened relations just before the U.S. 1972 opening to the PRC, but by this time Mongolia, prompted by the Soviet Union, refused any relations with the United States.

NEW MONGOLIAN FOREIGN POLICY, 1986 TO THE PRESENT

Mikhail Gorbachev's more open Soviet policy allowed the establishment of U.S.-Mongolian diplomatic relations in 1987 and the normalization of Sino-Mongolian relations in 1989. As the Soviet bloc disintegrated in 1989–91, Mongolia found itself for the first time truly neutral and unaligned. China and Russia in 2000 still accounted for 37 percent and 23 percent of Mongolia's foreign trade, respectively, yet other countries—Japan, the United States, the European Union, and South Korea—have become important as what Mongolia calls "third neighbors." While good relations with Russia and China remain a vital priority, Mongolia has attempted to increase its freedom of action by cultivating relations with these "third neighbors," both bilaterally and multilaterally. Despite the occasionally acrimonious electoral debates, particularly over relations with China, this consensus runs through Mongolia's elite in all parties.

Foreign aid has replaced Soviet aid in the Mongolian economy. Mongolia joined the International Monetary Fund (IMF) and the Asian Development Bank (ADB) in 1990, the World Bank in 1991, and became a charter member of the World Trade Organization in January 1997. International aid, of which Japan is the largest national source and the ADB the largest multilateral source, exceeds US $300 million annually, in 1999 reaching US $92 per capita, one of the highest levels in the world. With this aid has come both fresh debt, added to the existing debt burden owed Russia, and a major role of multilateral aid organizations, such as the IMF, in determining Mongolian economic policy. Aiming to solidify its relationship with the United States, Mongolia strongly supported the U.S. position in the first Gulf War of 1991, and sent 180 troops to join the U.S.-led occupation of Iraq in 2003.

See also ARCHAEOLOGY; CHINA AND MONGOLIA; ECONOMY, MODERN; JAPAN AND THE MODERN MONGOLS; MONGOLIAN PEOPLE'S REPUBLIC; MONGOLIA, STATE OF; REVOLUTIONARY PERIOD; RUSSIA AND MONGOLIA; SOVIET UNION AND MONGOLIA; THEOCRATIC PERIOD.

Further reading: Alicia J. Campi, "Early U.S.-Mongolian Diplomatic Contacts," *Mongolia Survey*, no. 6 (1999): 47–57; J. Tumurchuluun, "Mongolia's Foreign Policy Revisited: Relations with Russia and the PRC into the 1990s," in *Mongolia in the Twentieth Century: Landlocked Cosmopolitan*, ed. Stephen Kotkin and Bruce A. Elleman (Armonk, N.Y.: M. E. Sharpe, 1999), 277–289; Serge M. Wolff, "Mongol Delegations in Western Europe, 1925–1929, Parts I and II," *Journal of the Royal Central Asiatic Society* 32 (1945): 289–298 and 33 (1946): 75–92.

fossil record The present landmass of Eurasia can be divided into a number of terranes, which during the Paleozoic era, currently dated from 570 to 240 million years ago (mya), were minicontinents occupying separate tectonic plates in the ocean north of Gondwanaland, then on the south pole. These terranes came together (with the rest of the continents) to form the massive single continent Pangea in the Triassic period (240–205 mya). Most of Mongolia appears to have been part of the Amuria plate, formed from smaller units in the Ordovician (500–435 mya), but the Khangai-Khentii areas occupied the margins of the Siberian plate. The Amuria plate moved northward from the southern tropics in the Cambrian (570?–500 mya) to relatively high northern latitudes by the Triassic.

PALEOZOIC

Rocks from the Paleozoic show a typical sequence of marine fossils. Just before the Cambrian stromatolites (colonies of cyanobacteria, or "blue-green algae") and oncolites (nodules of sand- or clay-covered cyanobacteria or algae) are common. In the Cambrian hard-bodied forms appear, first plankton, mollusks, hyoliths (mollusk-like fossils of uncertain classification), and brachiopods, and then trilobites and archeocyaths (reef-building spongelike animals). In the middle Ordovician bryozoans, bivalve mollusks, and early coelenterates appear, and in the Silurian (435–410 mya) jawless fish. Devonian deposits (410–360 mya) show distinct zones of coastal, outer, and deep waters with brachiopods, tabulate corals, and radiolarians (protozoan plankton with siliceous skeletons) dominating the respective zones. In the Carboniferous period (360–290 mya), fusilinids (an extinct type of foraminifera), bryozoans, corals, and sea lilies (crinoids) formed vast reefs. Mongolia's first known land fossils, those of the giant club moss *Lepidodendron*, appeared in this period. Late in this period and in the succeeding Permian (290–240 mya), as the Amurian plate moved into higher latitudes, cooling climates were reflected in both land plants and sea animals.

MESOZOIC

By the Triassic the Amurian, North China, Kazakhstan, and Siberian plates had all come together, making Mongolia an inland landmass. Conifers and horsetails dominate the land fossil record, now deposited in rivers and lakes, which shows clear differentiation between the cooler north and warmer south. In the Jurassic (205–138 mya) first the cooler, then the warmer flora dominates. Insect fossils have also been found—cockroaches, beetles, dragonflies, and orthopterans—as well as fragmentary vertebrate remains. It was in the late Jurassic–early Cretaceous that tectonic developments created in Mongolia the contrast of the low south-southeast and the mountainous north-northwest. From the late Cretaceous fossil-bearing deposits become restricted to the relatively low-lying Gobi.

The famous dinosaur fossils of Mongolia all date from the Cretaceous period (138–63 mya), when Mongolia experienced a warm climate with large lakes. Early Cretaceous flora was mostly conifers: cheirolepids (extinct conifers with juniperlike leaves) and early pines, later succeeded by *Araucaria* (relatives of the monkey-puzzle tree and Norfolk Island pine) and gingkos. In the early Cretaceous the most common dinosaur form was the herbivore *Psittacosaurus,* progenitor of the horned DINOSAURS. Other fossils include herbivorous iguanadons, ankylosaurs, sauropods, and various carnivorous theropods. Bird feather impressions, lizards, early mammals, including placentals, and a wide variety of insects round out the faunal remains.

In the later Cretaceous vast lakes provided habitat for distinctive freshwater mollusks. The land fauna was now dominated by flowering plants and modern conifers. Dinosaurs, including *Protoceratops,* hadrosaurs (so-called duck-billed dinosaurs), ankylosaurs, theropods such as *Tarbosaurus,* a close relative of *Tyrannosaurus,* and smaller "ostrich dinosaurs," established a classic late Mesozoic fauna, also including turtles, crocodiles, fish, lizards, and mammals. The richness and high quality of preservation of Mongolia's Cretaceous vertebrata make it one of the world's leading areas for research on dinosaurs, early mammals, and other fauna.

CENOZOIC

Mongolia's terrain rose in the transition from the Cretaceous to the Paleogene (63–24 mya), accentuating the Gobi-Khangai split as the Gobi lakes retreated. Forests of *Taxodium* (related to the bald cypress) and the broadleafed *Trochodendroides* dominated the lower Paleogene flora (Paleocene, 63–55 mya), while the fauna contains archaic mammals typical of Asia: insectivores, anagales (an extinct, mostly herbivorous order unique to Asia), various creodonts (archaic meat eaters), condylarths (archaic ungulates), notoungulates (an extinct ungulate order later restricted to South America), pantodonts, dinocerates (uintatheres), and the probably egg-laying extinct mammalian order Multituberculata.

In the middle Paleogene (Eocene, 55–38 mya) early examples of the modern ungulate orders appear: artiodactyls, including ancestral ruminants (tragulids) and piglike animals, and perrisodactyls, including early horses, tapirs, and brontotheres. After a warming period in the earlier Eocene, when myrtles, laurels, maples, and oak fossils were deposited in the Gobi, the collision of India with Asia first raised the Himalayas and began a cooling and drying trend. Late Eocene flora included more grasses and in better-watered areas elms, beeches, aspens, and poplars. Rich fossil beds at Ergel Zoo (Erdene Sum, East Gobi) and Khoyor Zaan (Khöwsgöl Sum, East Gobi) show new rhinoceratoid families: hyracodontids ("running rhinoceroses"), hippopotamus-like amynodontids, and horse-sized indricotheres. Burrowing rodents (cylindrodontids) and field mice (cricetids) appear. A two-toed flightless crane, *Ergilornis,* and giant tortoises shared the habitat. In the late Paleogene (Oligocene, 38–24 mya) Mongolia acquired true savannah conditions, and the fauna became more diverse, with colossal indricotheres, rodents, lagomorphs (rabbits and pikas), and piglike and ruminant artiodactyls flourishing. The small ancestral rhinoceros *Epiaceratherium* (*Alloceratops*) was a characteristic element.

The Neogene period (24 mya to present) saw the gradual elevation of the ALTAI RANGE and KHANGAI RANGE, the formation of the GREAT LAKES BASIN between them, and the initial formation of the current GOBI DESERT. Three-toed horses successively immigrating from North America, *Anchitherium* and *Hipparion,* supplied the most common remains. The *Anchitherium* fauna of the lower Neogene (early Miocene 24–5 mya) included an African immigrant, the early shovel-tusked elephant *Gomphotherium,* a small deerlike ruminant (*Lagomeryx*) immigrated from Europe, and true deer (*Dicroceras, Stephanocemas*) native to Asia. The *Hipparion* fauna of the middle Neogene (late Miocene) included hornless rhinoceroses (*Chilotherium*), okapilike early giraffids (*Palaeotragus* and *Samotherium*), field mice (cricetids), and mice (murids). The Pliocene (5–1.8 mya) fauna continued with *Hipparion,* gazelles, steppe rhinoceroses, ostriches, flightless storks, *Amphipelargus,* and pheasants. With the uplift of the northern mountains and the formation of deep valleys, sedimentation and fossils (including a fragmentary ape find) were for the first time since the lower Cretaceous deposited in northern Mongolia.

The distribution of the mostly modern Pleistocene (1.8 mya to 10,000 years ago) fauna was heavily influenced by the oscillations between glacial and interglacial periods. Mongolian Pleistocene deposits are quite poor in fossils. Famous Ice Age megafauna—mammoths, wooly rhinoceroses, bisons—persisted until the very end of the epoch and were pictured in cave art at sites such as Khoid Tsenkher.

See also CLIMATE; FAUNA; FLORA; GOBI DESERT; MONGOLIAN PLATEAU; PREHISTORY.

Further reading: Academy of Sciences, MPR, *Information Mongolia* (Oxford: Pergamon Press, 1990), 12–17.

Front Gorlos Mongol Autonomous County (Qian Gorlos, Guorluosi) Front Gorlos Mongol Autonomous County, in northeast China's Jilin province, had a population of 544,302 in 1982, of which 30,762 (5.7 percent were Mongol. The banner occupies 7,219 square kilometers (2,787 square miles) near the confluence of the Sungari (Songhua) and Nonni (Nen) Rivers in the Manchurian plain and is 120–260 meters (390–850 feet) above sea level. Approximately 32.4 percent of the territory is occupied by pastures. The 366,300 head of livestock in 1982 included about 148,700 pigs and 121,900 sheep. Corn is about 60 percent of the total grain and bean harvest of more than 250,000 metric tons (275,578 short tons).

In the 12th–13th centuries, the Gorlos (Middle Mongolian, Ghorulas) was a clan of the MONGOL TRIBE. Submitting to the QING DYNASTY in 1625, the eastern Gorlos clan was organized into two BANNERS (appanages), Gorlos Front and Gorlos Rear banners, in Jirim league, each ruled by descendants of CHINGGIS KHAN's brother Qasar. Chinese settled Front Gorlos from the 18th century, and the Mongols slowly became farmers. Massive CHINESE COLONIZATION from 1902 sparked an uprising led by Togtakhu Taiji. In 1910 the banner's collective land system was officially dissolved.

The Japanese excluded Front and Rear Gorlos banners from Manchukuo's Mongol autonomous provinces of Khinggan established in 1932. After 1945 the Chinese Communists coopted Front Gorlos's active Mongol nationalist movement, and in September 1955 it was made a Mongol autonomous county. Rear Gorlos banner was converted into Zhaoyuan county in 1956. In 1956 16,700, or 8.1 percent, of Front Gorlos's inhabitants were ethnic Mongol. Despite their small percentage of the population, 24.5 percent of upper- and mid-level cadres were Mongol in 1982.

See also INNER MONGOLIANS; KHORCHIN.

Further reading: G. Navaangnamjil, "A Brief Biography of the Determined Hero Togtokh," in *Mongolian Heroes of the Twentieth Century,* trans. Urgunge Onon (New York: AMS Press, 1976), 43–76.

Fuhsin   *See* FUXIN MONGOL AUTONOMOUS COUNTY.

funerary customs   Traditional funerary customs on the Mongolian plateau have included at different times and in different social groups burial, cremation, and many forms of "sky burial," or exposure of the body.

The earliest inhabitants of Mongolia left many graves and grave monuments (*see* ELK STONES; PREHISTORY; NOYON UUL; XIANBI; XIONGNU). Despite these numerous finds, survey ARCHAEOLOGY indicates that the number of actual graves is far fewer than one would expect given Mongolia's population, offering indirect evidence for exposure of the dead. Medieval Chinese accounts indicate that both the SHIWEI in the GREATER KHINGGAN RANGE, sometimes considered ancestors of the Mongols, and the Mongolic-speaking KITANS of eastern Inner Mongolia exposed their dead in trees, but only until the flesh

decomposed, at which point the bones were burned. Even after building a powerful Chinese dynasty, Kitans used the form of the YURT for funeral urns or coffins in a curious piece of nomad nostalgia.

DEATH AND BURIAL IN THE MONGOL EMPIRE

In the MONGOL EMPIRE travelers' accounts make no mention of exposure, only burial. The Mongols feared the contagion of death and avoided the sick. Seriously ill persons put up a spear with a black felt strip outside their yurts, which only shamans and close relatives would pass. Once the person died, the relatives of the deceased and his or her possessions became unclean and had to pass between two fires, while shamanesses sprinkled them with water and prayed (*see* FIRE CULT). Viewing property of the dead as unclean, the Mongol khans abolished estate taxes in all the lands they conquered.

The Mongols were generally buried on open ground. Sources describe commoners as being buried inside a yurt with some meat and KOUMISS (fermented mare's milk), and beside the yurt a mare with a foal and a bridled and saddled gelding. One or more horses were sacrificed; the meat was eaten and the head and hide hung on a pole by the grave site. The bones, within which resided the life of the animal and which symbolized patrilineal ancestry, were burned for the dead. While the sources agree that men- and maidservants were buried with the khans, they are not consistent in their details. The corpses of the khans were kept in caskets, which were moved around the palace-tents (ORDO) for lengthy mourning before burial. Burial caskets have been confirmed by archaeology. Again, the sources differ on whether riches were buried with them, although clothing, armor, horse equipment, and other daily goods certainly were.

Burial took place on clan territory. People often selected their own burial spots before their death, and if a man died abroad on campaign, every effort was made to bring his body back to the chosen spot. Burial was often at the base of mountains and/or marked by a lone tree or copse; the branches of such trees were thereafter sacred. The Mongols carefully replaced the grass to avoid otherwise marking the gravesite, although the Turks erected "STONE MEN" and sometimes cairns (*see* OBOO).

There was an imperial cemetery for the Chinggisid nobility in the KHENTII RANGE, called Kilengu in the Chinese sources, where most of the great khans were buried. This forested area was qoruq, or forbidden, to enter or to pluck so much as a branch. The other khanates established their own "great qoruqs" in their lands: that of the IL-KHANATE at Kuh-e-Shahu, northwest of Kermanshah, and that of the GOLDEN HORDE in the steppe between the Ural and Volga Rivers. No qoruq has as yet been excavated.

After a death the deceased's name was avoided and no cult offered for three years. Only then, when the flesh and bones had disintegrated and the soul become an ancestral spirit, were sacrifices regularly offered to

Casket of a Mongol burial from the 13th–14th centuries *(From Dowdoin Bayar,* Altan urgiin yazguurtny negen bulshiig sudalsan ni *[2000].)*

the ONGGHON, or crude spirit figures made for the deceased's spirit. In these rituals some sacrificial meat and bones soaked with milk liquors (*sarqud;* modern *sarkhad*) were placed in holes in the ground and burned, while the descendants ate the rest of the meat and liquor. Animals were also dedicated to the dead, after which they were not used for common purposes. After the death of a Chinggisid prince his palace-tents (*ordo*) were always maintained under the care of their mistresses. As might be expected, the funerary cult of CHINGGIS KHAN was especially important (*see* EIGHT WHITE YURTS).

Religious changes brought about changes in funerary practices. By the 1270s Mongol nobles frequently visited relics and tombs of Buddhist, Islamic, and Christian saints and had Christian or Buddhist services performed for the dead. In the Il-Khanate, GHAZAN KHAN (1295–1304) and his brother Sultan Öljeitü (1304–16), after converting to Islam, built for themselves large Islamic-style mausoleums with attached on-site charitable foundations. Buyan-Quli Khan (1348–58) of the Chaghatayids built a similar mausoleum, but the *qoruq* custom was maintained among the Muslim Golden Horde khans until at least the 15th century. In the Mongol YUAN DYNASTY in the east, the Tibetan 'Phags-pa Lama began holding Buddhist services in the ancestral temple in the capital of DAIDU in 1270, but the burial ground in Kilengu was still used.

Despite the emphasis on burial in the sources, it is most unlikely that even the ritual described for commoners could be carried out except by the well-off. The form of burial for the ordinary Mongol thus seems unrecorded.

THE BUDDHIST ERA

The Mongolian funerary customs described here, including human sacrifice, were still observed virtually unchanged in the mid-16th century. After the SECOND CONVERSION to Buddhism, from 1575 on, Mongolian funerary customs underwent relatively rapid change, although many underlying ideas remained the same. While exposure appears in the sources as a Buddhist innovation borrowed from Tibet, it may have long been practiced among ordinary people.

In Buddhist funerals death was still viewed as extremely polluting, and the dying person was attended only by a lama. The lama recited to the dying in Mongolian the so-called *Tibetan Book of the Dead,* which gave instruction on how to avoid rebirth. Once the person died, astrologers were consulted to choose an appropriate *buyanchi* (merit maker) to prepare the corpse in the correct lion's position (assumed by the Buddha at Nirvana), wrap it in a shroud, and choose the proper time of day and direction for bringing out the corpse and the proper burial site. Lamas performed services in a neighboring YURT while the deceased's yurt was censed from the outside by circumambulating lamas. These ceremonies averaged about three days but were shorter or longer depending on astrology and the survivors' willingness or ability to pay. From the earliest years of conversion, human sacrifice was banned, and at first the customary grave gifts (clothes, armor, horses, etc.) were explicitly assigned to the lamas instead.

Burials for ordinary people were basically by exposure, although with small variations, depending on astrological calculations (drenched in water, placed on a wooden plank, etc.). Around the body the lamas erected poles with *dartsag,* or colored strips, hanging from them. Sometimes a wind-powered prayer wheel was also erected. Upon completion of the ceremony, the mourners and the lama left the body, which was quickly consumed by dogs or wild animals. The funeral party had to return home without looking back and, if on horseback, riding furiously. The mourners and the deceased's possessions were purified by waving them over a fire and/or by a special service of the lama in the deceased's yurt.

The nobility and rich had long services of up to 49 days performed for them. Noblemen were often buried in a *bunkhan,* or small brick pyramid, sitting in an upright position, praying. They and noted lamas were also sometimes cremated. After cremation the ashes would be gathered, mixed with clay, and formed into a Buddhist statue or relic to be kept in a stupa. In any case, noblemen were always returned to their native BANNERS (appanages). The Jibzundamba Khutugtu and other high lamas were embalmed and their bodies kept in monasteries.

MODERN FUNERARY CUSTOMS

Exposure continued to be the primary method of disposal of the dead in Mongolia into the 1950s. Early in the 1920s a cemetery was opened outside ULAANBAATAR at Altan-Ölgii, where GENERAL SÜKHEBAATUR and other distinguished revolutionary figures were buried. In 1955 the Mongolian government prohibited exposure as a "disgusting remnant of the past" that perpetuated Buddhist influence and class distinctions. At the same time ordinary Mongols were limited to four cemeteries in the capital, and access to Altan-Ölgii was restricted to high officials, labor heroes, and other worthy personages. (Russians, Chinese, and KAZAKHS all have separate cemeteries.) In limitation of the Russian embalming of Lenin, the government attempted to preserve the corpse of maximum leader MARSHAL CHOIBALSANG after his death, but the embalming failed. Even so, he and the exhumed remains of General Sükhebaatur were housed in a *bunkhan,* or tomb, north of Sükhebaatur Square.

Despite the pressure against religious beliefs in the Communist period, the vast majority of burials then and now involve lamas and traditional astrological calcula-

tions on how, where, and at what hour the body should be removed and buried. The *buyanchi*'s role in preparing the corpse has been reduced to a symbolic touch but is still important, and fire purification is still practiced on the return home, before the funeral feast. Despite these traditional features, innovations disliked by the elders are common: coffins, covering the corpse's face with a KHADAG (scarf), funeral cortèges, and graveside eulogies with the corpse's face uncovered. In remoter areas of the countryside, exposure continues, with the corpse in the lion position, wrapped in a felt, and a fire lit nearby. Even there, however, the custom of covering the face with a *khadag* has entered the customary ritual.

During the 1950s and 1960s gravesites in Ulaanbaatar imitated Russian forms, with a slab, headstone, and iron railings. Since the 1970s, however, the tendency has been toward more natural-looking rocks, the use of traditional symbols, and the UIGHUR-MONGOLIAN SCRIPT or SOYOMBO SCRIPT for the inscription. The new practice of placing a small metal yurt on the gravesite curiously recalls the Kitan yurt-shaped coffins and urns. In 1990 exposure was once again legalized, but inhumation continues to be the regular urban practice. Grave marking is now generally a single stone with name, dates, signature, and signs of the deceased's life, whether Buddhist, professional, or the cross of the newly spreading Christian religion.

Further reading: Caroline Humphrey, "Rituals of Death in Mongolia: Their Implications for Understanding the Mutual Constitution of Persons and Objects and Certain Concepts of Property," *Inner Asia* 1 (1999): 59–86; John R. Krueger, "The *Altan Saba* (The Golden Vessel): A Mongolian Lamaist Burial Manual," *Monumenta Serica* 24 (1965): 207–272.

Fuxin Mongol Autonomous County (Fuhsin, Monggoljin)   Located in northeast China's Liaoning province, the Fuxin Mongol Autonomous County had a population of 683,672 in 1984, of which 130,303 (19 percent) were Mongol. The autonomous county occupies 6,264 square kilometers (2,419 square miles) of hilly terrain; of its farming villages, 128 are purely Mongol. Fuxin city, a major coal mining center, is entirely surrounded by the autonomous county but not included in its jurisdiction. In the early 1980s about 90 percent of the population was engaged in agriculture, growing sorghum, millet, and soybeans.

Around 1600 Fuxin's Mongol community was formed from native Uriyangkhan Mongols of the Ming dynasty's THREE GUARDS and Monggoljin Mongols migrating from the TÜMED *tümen* around HÖHHOT. Submitting to the QING DYNASTY in 1629, they were reorganized as Tümed Left Banner of Josotu league under a ruler descended from CHINGGIS KHAN's companion (NÖKÖR), Jelme of the Uriyangkhan. It was popularly called Monggoljin banner.

In 1891 Chinese sectarian and anti-Mongol rebels of the Jindandao sect ravaged Monggoljin banner for 10 days, killing up to 10,000 and forcing many more to flee. Mongolian Fuxin City was founded by Chinese settlers as a coal town in Monggoljin territory in 1902.

The Japanese excluded Monggoljin banner from Manchukuo's Mongol autonomous provinces of Khinggan established in 1932. By that time impoverished Monggoljin emigrants, maintaining a distinctive Mongolian-speaking farming culture, were wandering eastern Inner Mongolia as farmworkers, bandits, Mongol doctors, and lamas. Even today most of the lamas in Beijing's Yonghegong Temple are Monggoljin Mongols. The Chinese Communists began operating in the country after 1945. In 1953 various Mongol nationality villages were designated, and on October 18, 1957, Fuxin county was transformed into a Mongol autonomous county. In 1984 Mongols made up about 28 percent of all administrative officials.

See also INNER MONGOLIANS; KHARACHIN.

G

Galdan Boshogtu Khan (b. 1644, r. 1678–1697)
Zünghar ruler who challenged the Manchus for domination of Mongolia
Galdan was born the son of Erdeni Baatur Khung-Taiji (d. 1653), of the Choros clan, a descendant of ESEN Taishi (r. 1438–54). His mother, Amin-Dara, was the daughter of TÖRÖ-BAIKHÛ GÜÜSHI KHAN of the Khoshud.

Galdan, the second son of Baatur and Amin-Dara, was early recognized as the emanation body of the Tibetan INCARNATE LAMA dBen-sa sPrul-sku, who had been active in Mongolia. In 1656 Galdan went to central Tibet and became a disciple of the First Panchen Lama (1567–1662) and then the Fifth Dalai Lama (1617–82). In 1666 he returned home where his brother Sengge was ruling the Zünghar tribe. In 1670 two of Sengge's older half-brothers, dissatisfied with their inheritance, assassinated Sengge. Galdan renounced his vows to avenge his brother's death and married Anu-Dara, Sengge's previous wife and the granddaughter of Ochirtu Tsetsen Khan, the highest authority among the OIRATS. With his victory the Dalai Lama designated Galdan Khung-Taiji (Viceroy to the Khan). In 1676, however, Galdan imprisoned Ochirtu Tsetsen Khan, and in winter 1678 the Dalai Lama bestowed on Galdan the title Boshogtu Khan (Khan with the Mandate).

Galdan saw himself as the enforcer of the Dalai Lama's supreme prestige among all the Mongols and Oirats. In turn the Fifth Dalai Lama and then the Dalai Lama's regent (*sde-srid* or *sde-ba*), Sangs-rgyas rGya-mtsho (r. 1679–1703), supported him to the end of his career. Both the QING DYNASTY's Kangxi emperor (1662–1722) and the Khalkha's Tüshiyetü Khan Chakhundorji (r. 1655–99), however, publicly censured Galdan's overthrow of Ochirtu Tsetsen Khan. Moreover,

Galdan perceived the rising status of the FIRST JIBZUN-DAMBA KHUTUGTU Zanabazar (1635–1723), Chakhun-dorji's brother, as a threat to the Dalai Lama's supremacy among the Mongols and Oirats. Since Galdan believed he himself, in his previous life as the dBen-sa sPrul-sku, had actually administered monastic vows to the Jibzun-damba in 1639, such insubordination seemed particularly insulting.

Galdan brought East Turkestan under Zünghar rule for the first time, bringing the oasis cities of Turpan and Hami under tribute in 1679 and installing the exiled Khoja Afaq, head of the White Mountain branch of the Naqshbandi Sufi (Islamic mystic) order, over the Tarim Basin in 1680. Like his predecessors, he maintained close relations with Bukharan merchants, through which the Bukharans got safe access to the Chinese and Siberian markets, yet Galdan regularly raided the KAZAKHS and the Ferghana valley. Unlike Sengge, Galdan maintained cordial relations with Russia.

In 1686 at Khüren-Belcheer, a meeting was called to resolve a festering conflict between the two Khalkha rulers, the Tüshiyetü and Zasagtu khans. At this meeting the Jibzundamba Khutugtu and the Dalai Lama's representative occupied seats of equal height, which Galdan protested as an infringement of the Dalai Lama's prerogatives. When Chakhundorji exploited the new Zasagtu Khan's youth to delay the agreed-on resolution, the young Zasagtu Khan Shara (r. 1686–88) appealed to Galdan. At that point Chakhundorji invaded the Zasagtu Khan and killed Shara and Galdan's brother Dorjijab. Galdan invaded Khalkha with 30,000 men, defeating the Tüshiyetü Khan's son Galdandorji at Tömör (early July 1688) and then the Tüshiyetü Khan himself at Olgoi Nuur (August 28–29, 1688). Seeing the Jibzundamba's insubordination as the root of the conflict, Galdan plundered and burned Khalkha's temples and images, generating deep hostility.

For the next year Galdan camped in Khalkha territory and hoped to keep the Qing Empire, now hosting scores of thousands of refugee Khalkhas, neutral. His position deteriorated, however, as Sengge's son TSEWANG-RABTAN KHUNG-TAIJI, revolted in spring–summer 1689 and the Qing secured Russian neutrality by the Treaty of Nerchinsk (August 29, 1689). In July 1690 Galdan moved into Inner Mongolia, ostensibly to negotiate with the Qing, while the Qing hoped his approach would bring him in range of their armies. On September 3 Qing armies decisively defeated Galdan at Ulaan-Budung in Kheshigten (Hexigten) banner. Meanwhile, Tsewang-Rabtan made himself master of Züngha^M.

Galdan's only ally remained the Tibetan regent Sangs-rgyas rGya-mtsho whose intervention dissuaded the Qing and Tsewang-Rabtan from following up on their advantage. Only in late spring 1696 did the Qing armies finally march into Khalkha. On June 12 General Fiyanggü crushed Galdan's 10,000 remaining men at Zuunmod. Qing artillery fire killed Anu-Dara, and Zünghar prisoners revealed the Dalai Lama's long-concealed death, shattering the Tibetan regent's authority. Galdan escaped, but his men dwindled to 400 or 500 in March 1697. By the time the Kangxi emperor personally marched out to finish him off, Galdan had already died of disease near the ALTAI RANGE on April 5, 1697. Cheated of a personal victory, Kangxi falsified the records to make Galdan's death a suicide on May 4.

Further reading: Fang Chao-ying, "Galdan." In *Eminent Chinese of the Ch'ing Period,* ed. by Arthur W. Hummel (Washington, D.C.: U.S. Government Printing Office, 1943), 265–268; John R. Krueger, "Three Oirat-Mongolian Diplomatic Documents of 1691," *Central Asiatic Journal* 12 (1969): 286–295; Hidehiro Okada, "Galdan's Death: When and How," *Memoirs of the Research Department of the Toyo Bunko* 37 (1979): 91–97.

Galdan-Tseren (Galdantsering) (r. 1727–1745) *Zünghar ruler who made peace with the Qing Empire*
With the death of his father, TSEWANG-RABTAN KHUNG-TAIJI (1663–1727), prince of the Zünghars, Galdan-Tseren executed his Torghud (Kalmyk) stepmother for poisoning him and exiled her son Luuzang-Shonu. Domestically, Galdan-Tseren lavishly patronized Buddhism. He also reorganized the ZÜNGHARS into 24 directly ruled *OTOG*s (camp-districts) and 21 aristocratic appanages, or *anggis*.

In 1730 the QING DYNASTY mobilized 60,000 men and built the advance fortress of KHOWD CITY. Galdan-Tseren sent two armies into Khalkha, one in autumn and winter 1731, with 20,000 men, and another in August 1732, with 30,000 men, but both were defeated. The Qing and

the Zünghars made peace in 1739. The Zünghars sacrificed Tuva and the GREAT LAKES BASIN but received the right to send commercial delegations to Beijing every four years and to Chinese border towns every three years. The Zünghars could also trade freely with Tibet and maintain representatives there. After the treaty Galdan-Tseren attacked first the KAZAKHS from 1740 to 1743 and then prepared to assault the Russian forts that had deprived the Zünghars of their traditional Siberian tribute, but he died before the campaign could be completed.

Gandan-Tegchinling Monastery (Gandantegchinlen)
Originally the *tsanid* (higher Buddhist studies) college for the monks of Khüriye (modern ULAANBAATAR), Gandan-Tegchinling, or Gandan, was from 1944 to 1989 Mongolia's only functioning monastery.

The monks of a *tsanid* college are full-time scholars specialized according to the branch of the scriptures (including tantra, astrology, and medicine) that they study. A *tsanid datsang* (college) was established by the SECOND JIBZUNDAMBA KHUTUGTU in 1755, but without separate facilities. In 1809 a new *tsanid* campus was built on a small hill to the west of Khüriye. In 1836, having ordered the entire clergy of Khüriye to move west, away from encroaching Chinese shops, the Fifth Jibzundamba Khutugtu (1815–42) built his palace, named Gandan-Tegchinling (Mongolian, Tegüs-Bayaskhulangtu, Complete Rejoicing), just south of the *tsanid* college in 1838. Gandan-Tegchinling also became the *tsanid* college's permanent name. In 1855, however, the Jibzundamba Khutugtus with their monks moved back to their original palace near the current city center.

Behind Gandan palace were four *dugangs* (assembly halls), with two larger ones built in the marquee style of the main Khüriye *tsogchin* (great assembly hall). The temple complexes were surrounded on all sides except for directly south by the yurt-courtyards of the *tsanid* scholars. From 1911 to 1913 a striking Tibetan-style temple housing a 24-meter (80-foot)-high gilt-copper image of the Buddhist deity Migjid Janraisig (Eye-Opening Avalokiteshvara) was built north of the assembly halls (*see* THEOCRATIC PERIOD).

During the anti-Buddhist persecutions the temples of Gandan and Khüriye were finally closed late in 1939, and the surviving buildings of Gandan were used to house the administration of Central province. In 1940 the Migjid Janraisig Temple area was placed under Soviet military command and made a firing range. The image was dismantled and melted down (*see* BUDDHISM, CAMPAIGN AGAINST).

In 1944, on Joseph Stalin's recommendation, Mongolia's ruler, MARSHAL CHOIBALSANG, reopened Gandan as Mongolia's only working monastery. The original DUGANGS having been razed, the palace's main hall became the new *tsogchin dugang* (great assembly hall). The temple housed many of Mongolia's remaining Bud-

The Migjid Janraisig (Eye-Opening Avalokiteshvara) Temple, stupa, and sacred pole at Gandan-Tegchinling Monastery *(Courtesy Christopher Atwood)*

dhist treasures, including a self-portrait and a Vajradhara by Zanabazar (1635–1723), and a 50,000-volume library. The total number of lamas was 100, and Gandan's abbot (*khamba lama*) became the officially approved spokesman for Mongolian Buddhism. In 1947 Mongolian scholars aided by a few Soviet advisers intervened to save the Migjid Janraisig Temple from demolition, and in 1961 it was made a national cultural monument. Despite city construction, the quarters around Gandan have remained occupied by the yurt-courtyards of the lamas and their families. (One deliberately provocative act was the establishment of a hunting museum directly south of the grounds.)

With the advent of religious freedom in 1990, Gandan expanded to 200 monks and underwent a full-scale renovation. In 1997, with government and private funds, a new full-scale Migjid Janraisig statue, modeled on the old, was dedicated.

See also LAMAS AND MONASTICISM; PALACES OF THE BOGDA KHAN.

Genden, Peljidiin *See* GENDÜN.

Gendün (Peljidiin Genden) (1895–1937) *At first a leading leftist, he became prime minister during the conservative New Turn policy and was shot during Stalin's purges.*

Gendün was born in July 1895 in Üizeng Zasag banner (Taragt Sum, South Khangai). His unwed mother's great uncle, the respected "Old Tsorji" (vicar) Namjiljab (1835–c. 1935) of Arbai Kheere-yin Khüriye Monastery (modern Arwaikheer), raised the boy, and the banner administrator tutored Gendün in Mongolian and a little Tibetan. From age 15 he began earning a living as a caravaneer, hired herder, and substitute for postroad duty. In 1920–21 Gendün was mobilized into the banner militia to fight off Chinese troops.

Despite escapades as a rustler, from July 1922 to March 1924 Gendün took part in Üizeng banner's new Youth League cell, its first elective government, and its new party branch. In November 1924 he became a delegate to the First Great Khural (assembly) in Ulaanbaatar. Impressed by such glib talk from a country delegate, Prime Minister TSERINDORJI and deputy party chairman Jaddamba (N. Jadamba, 1900–41) arranged Gendün's election as chairman of the Little State Khural, Mongolia's titular head of state. Gendün immediately moved in with the late GENERAL SÜKHEBAATUR's old tutor, Jamyan (O. Jamyan, 1864–1930), who taught him history and literature, while the elder statesman TSYBEN ZHAMATSARANOVICH ZHAMTSARANO taught him Russian. In 1926 he married Donjid, daughter of a hometown WRESTLING champion; a year later they had a daughter, G. Tserendulam. An auto accident in early 1928 left him permanently lame.

Within a few years Gendün and Badarakhu (Ö. Badrakh, 1895–1941) began leading the *khödöö* (rural) opposition against the city-bred party leaders, demanding the party follow its leftist rhetoric about relying on the poor and middle-class rural masses. In September 1927 Gendün was dropped from the party presidium and the Little Khural, keeping only his honorary positions as head of the Mongolian trade unions and chairman of the board of the state bank.

At the party's Seventh Congress (autumn 1928) Moscow's Communist International (Comintern) mobilized the *khödöö* faction to overthrow the party chief DAMBADORJI, and Gendün was appointed one of three new party secretaries. When, in December 1929, the Comintern demanded the party go beyond confiscating the property of the aristocracy and high lamas and move into collectivization, annihilation of the feudal classes, and direct attacks on religion, Gendün, unlike his fellow party secretaries Badarakhu and Shijiye (J. Shijee, 1901–41), began to have cold feet. He was also strongly opposed to Badarakhu's Dörböd separatism.

Gendün's muted skepticism about the leftist policies served him well when Stalin canceled them in May–June 1932. Badarakhu and Shijiye were exiled to Moscow, while Gendün became prime minister. As prime minister Gendün became the strongest advocate for the New Turn policies. He declared that the party was simply the government's "Red Corner" (propaganda center) and that petty persecution of the lamas was bad for the government. He kept defense spending moderate and adopted the slogan "Get rich!" (*bayajigtun*) for the herders. From his first summit meeting with Stalin on November 15, 1934, however, Stalin pushed him to be tougher on the lamas.

Gendün was a disciple of the lama Puntsugtsering in his home banner, and in 1924 he exclaimed that the Buddha and Lenin were the world's greatest geniuses. As prime minister he resumed his yearly pilgrimages to his teacher, a gesture important in restoring the population's confidence, yet he was also a boorish man whose antics worsened when he was drunk. Stories such as that of Gendün breaking Stalin's pipe, while often told in Mongolia as heroic acts of defiance, were, in fact, episodes of drunken buffoonery that only exposed him to ridicule.

After tension-filled meetings with Stalin in December 1935 to January 1936, Gendün finally agreed to invite Soviet troops to Mongolia. Roundly criticized for impeding Soviet-Mongolian friendship at the next party plenum, Gendün was relieved of all his duties on March 20, 1936, and exiled with his family to Crimea. On July 17, 1937, as part of Stalin's GREAT PURGE, he was arrested at Sochi and shot as a Japanese spy on November 26.

See also LEFTIST PERIOD; MONGOLIAN PEOPLE'S REVOLUTIONARY PARTY, SEVENTH CONGRESS OF; REVOLUTIONARY PERIOD.

Genghis Khan   *See* CHINGGIS KHAN.

Georgia (Iberia)

The Mongols forced the Georgian kingdom to pay tribute and eventually divided it in two, yet Georgian cavalry fought for the Mongols in all their battles in the Middle East.

On the eve of the Mongol conquest, the Georgian kingdom had reached the apex of its medieval power. Under Queen Tamara (1184–1211/2) and her son Giorgi Lasha (1212–23), the Georgians conquered the surrounding Turkish emirates and raided beyond Tabriz. The core of the Georgian army was the *aznaur*s, or knights, of the landed Georgian nobility. As it expanded the Georgian kingdom came under increasing Armenian influence. Queen Tamara's dynasty, the Bagratid, was of Armenian origin, as was the Zakarian (Mkharghrdzeli) family of Iwané, her chief commander. The land reconquered by the Zakarian family (roughly modern Armenia and western Azerbaijan) formed an autonomous realm within the Georgian kingdom.

From 1220 to 1228 first the Mongol generals JEBE and SÜBE'ETEI BA'ATUR and then the Qipchaq tribesmen and Jalal-ud-Din Mengüberdi, both fleeing from the Mongols, repeatedly crushed Georgian armies under Iwané and sacked Tiflis, Gandzak (Ganja, Gäncä), and Nakhichevan (Naxçıvan). In 1232 the Mongols returned to the Caucasus under CHORMAQAN. After subduing Azerbaijan and Greater Armenia, Chormaqan took Tiflis in 1236, while Queen Rusudani (Giorgi Lasha's sister) fled to K'ut'aisi. The Georgio-Armenian nobility, led by Iwané's son Awag and cousin Vahram (Waram) of Gagi (south of Shamkhor), submitted and agreed to supply the Mongol army's needs. Most onerous for the nobility were demands for *tangsuq*s, or delicacies: gold cloth, falcons, hunting dogs, and fine horses. The Mongols set overseers (DARUGHACHI) in the cities and systematically destroyed Georgian fortifications. Under Chormaqan's successor, BAIJU, Armenian and Georgian forces participated in the sack of Erzerum (1242) and the battle of Köse Dağı (1243) against the Turkish sultanate of Rum (*see* TURKEY). Chormaqan and his wife Elteni's patronage of the Christian church won clerical support, but the Georgio-Armenian nobility, despite their submission and intermarriage with the chief Mongol families, still deeply resented Mongol rule.

Awag negotiated the submission of Queen Rusudani in 1243, and shortly before her death her son David attended the court of BATU (d. 1255), founder of the Mongol GOLDEN HORDE on the Volga, and of Great Khan GÜYÜG (1246–48) in Mongolia. After the defeat of Rum, Baiju also dispatched Vahram to free David, Giorgi Lasha's illegitimate son, from Turkish imprisonment. He, too, was sent on to Batu and Güyüg. Güyüg was presented with two Davids: David Narin ("the Slim," son of the queen, 1258–93), and David Ulugh ("the Big," son of Giorgi Lasha, 1247–69). The khan made David Ulugh the senior king, and Baiju and Vahram set him on the throne in Tiflis.

Under MÖNGKE KHAN (1251–59) ARGHUN AQA of the Oirat, as governor of Iran, and Najm-ud-Din, as Batu's representative in the Caucasus, took a census and imposed the Mongols' DECIMAL ORGANIZATION on the Georgians, dividing them into six *tümens* (each nominally 10,000). The *qubchiri* (commuted silver tax) was fixed by decimal unit, and evasion was harshly punished. Meanwhile, the financial needs of Möngke's brother HÜLE'Ü (1256–65), founder of the Mongols' Middle Eastern IL-KHANATE, pushed the *qubchiri* to extreme levels. Uncertain of Hüle'ü's attitude and denounced by the Persian tax farmer Khoja 'Aziz for withholding back taxes, both Davids sooner or later fled to K'ut'aisi. Only in November 1262, with the execution of Khoja 'Aziz, did David Ulugh return to Tiflis. As David Narin remained in K'ut'aisi, the kingdom was now divided.

The appanage of Batu had long included Iran and the Caucasus, and in 1251 Möngke Khan assigned Georgia to Batu's brother Berke (1257–66). Berke did not nomadize in Georgia, but several Golden Horde princes accompanying Hüle'ü campaigns settled in the steppes of Azerbaijan and harassed the inhabitants, particularly the monasteries. The Georgians and Armenians thus welcomed Hüle'ü's suppression of their armies in 1262. Berke's subsequent invasion and sack of Tiflis in 1266 only confirmed the Georgian preference for the IL-KHANATE over Berke's Golden Horde.

After 1262 David Narin in K'ut'aisi paid nominal homage to the Il-Khans, while David Ulugh in Tiflis was reduced to a minor governor. The sons and younger brothers of the nobles were taken into the KESHIG (imperial guard) partly as hostages and partly as hard-fighting *ba'aturs* (heroes) who participated in every major campaign of the Il-Khans. Like other Christian officials of the Il-Khanate, David Ulugh's son Dmitri (1273–89) became a partisan of BUQA, vizier of Arghun Khan (1284–91), and was executed in Buqa's fall in 1289. GHAZAN KHAN's conversion to Islam (1295–1304) initially resulted in much destruction of churches, but he later repudiated this policy; even Christian monks lauded him for his reform of rampant abuses in Mongol administration.

The execution of King Dmitri in 1289 and the death of his uncle David Narin in 1293 opened a period of disintegration in the Georgian kingdom. The Mongols and the powerful Jaqeli family in Samtzkhé (around Artvin)

put forward several Bagratid candidates both in K'ut'aisi and in Tiflis. One Tiflis candidate, David VI (1292–1310), retreated to the Caucasus Mountains and sent envoys both to the Il-Khans and to Toqto'a Khan (1291–1312) of the Golden Horde; another, Wakhtang III (1301–10), loyally led the Georgian cavalry in Il-Khan's Öljeitü's (1304–17) Gilan campaign. In 1316 the commander, CHUBAN, of the Suldus restored Giorgi V (1316–46) to the throne in Tiflis. This king, with the support of his maternal relatives in the Jaqeli family, reestablished the authority of the throne. In 1330 he reunited the divided kingdom, and when the Il-Khanate broke apart in 1335, he made Georgia again a major power in the Caucasus.

See also CHRISTIAN SOURCES ON THE MONGOL EMPIRE; CHRISTIANITY IN THE MONGOL EMPIRE; KÖSE DAĞI, BATTLE OF; LESSER ARMENIA.

Further reading: Robert Bedrosian, "Armenia during the Seljuk and Mongol Periods," in *The Armenian People from Ancient to Modern Times,* ed. Richard G. Hovannisian (New York: St. Martin's Press, 1977), 241–272; ———, *Kirakos Gandzakets'i's History of the Armenians* (New York: Sources of the Armenian Tradition, 1986); Robert P. Blake and Richard N. Frye, "History of the Nation of the Archers (the Mongols)," *Harvard Journal of Asiatic Studies* 12 (1949): 269–399.

Geser   The Geser epic (in Tibetan Ge-sar), originally of Tibetan origin, became widespread among the Mongolian peoples. Particularly among the Buriat Mongols, it has become a repository of native religious ideas and identity.

The Geser epic is episodic in structure and in some of its many versions can contain hundreds of episodes. The main episodes of most Tibetan and Mongolian Geser versions tell of a god who is born to be a hero to suppress disorders arising throughout the world. At first he is Joru (Tibetan, Byi-ru), a snotty-nosed boy although possessing hidden supernatural powers. Geser comes into his own as a hero by defeating his wicked uncle Chotong (Tibetan, Khro-thung) in a horse race and winning Rogmo the Fair (Tibetan, 'Brug-mo) as his wife. An evil monster (Emperor of the Dragons in Tibetan, a 12-headed northern monster in Mongolian) steals another of Geser's wives (Me-bza' 'Bum-skyid in Tibetan, translated as Tümen-Jirgalang in Mongolian). Geser fights to regain her and succeeds, but she drugs him into forgetting to return home. While he is away, three kings (either of Hor/Mongols in the Tibetan versions or of Sharaigol/Yogurs in the Mongolian versions) steal Rogmo, and Geser has to be recalled to fight them. Geser also makes a peaceful trip to China and with his cleverness and magical powers wins the emperor's daughter. Finally, Geser descends to fight the lord of hell and free his mother from torment there. Geser fights his battles with a mixture of supernatural might, transformations, magic weapons, and much low cunning. He is also assisted by companions and his elder brother, who remains in heaven.

The earliest traces of the Geser epic are attested to in the songs of the Tibetan yogi and poet Mi-la-ras-pa (Milarepa, 1040–1123), which mention "Geser of Phrom," which has been explained as "Caesar of Rome." Today Geser is called in Tibetan versions "Geser of Gling," a principality in eastern Tibet (near modern Dêgê), and the Tibetan Geser shows a basically eastern Tibetan geography. The traditional rulers of Gling considered themselves descendants of Geser's half-brother. In any case, the current form of the Geser episodes is primarily governed by widespread folkloric motifs, religious beliefs and practices, and the demands of an exciting narrative, rather than any historical background.

The Tibetan Geser tales are sung by bards who are believed to be possessed by the spirit of Geser. A typical performance of the epic, undertaken over several days, includes short prose narratives linking 50 to 100 songs, each with about 100 lines on average. New episodes are interpreted as newly recovered memories of a previous life in which the bard was a companion of Geser. While written versions exist, they are definitely secondary to the oral versions. Among the Mongols, however, the prose written versions formed the basis for the versions sung by minstrels, such as Pajai (1902–62) of the Jarud. Yet the Geser narrative was also taken up by true epic poets among the Oirat and Buriat Mongols (see below).

Fragments of Mongolian Geser texts survive from at least the early 17th century. The "classic" Mongolian Geser, similar but not identical to any Tibetan original, was block printed in Beijing in 1716, with nine chapters mostly in prose with short versified passages. Other manuscripts with texts more or less parallel to the Beijing block print also contain up to six additional episodes. The written Ling Geser text, by contrast, is a direct Mongolian translation of a Tibetan Geser of Gling tale.

The Geser epic in both Tibet and at least at first in Mongolia was associated with Buddhist beliefs not of the dominant dGe-lugs-pa (Yellow Hat) order, but of the "Old Order" (rNying-ma-pa) of married Tibetan lamas. While born by a decree of Shakyamuni Buddha, Geser is an incarnation in the Mongolian version of the god Indra (Mongolian, Khormusta Tngri), and his role is not to teach enlightenment but to destroy the enemies of good, an important, although secondary, task. The Nomchi Khatun Geser text appends a story of how the Dalai Lama, contemplating the disorder of the world, has a vision of Geser, who gives him instructions on how to build merit and asks that he circulate these instructions throughout the world. Even so, the popularity of the Geser epic offended the stricter adherents of dGe-lugs-pa Buddhism; ordered by the emperor Qianlong to compose a prayer for Geser, a dGe-lugs-pahierarch sourly complained that most hold "an inhuman bully [i.e., Geser] as a savior better than the lama." Many of the stories in the Beijing block print have a distinctly anticlerical edge, such as that in which Geser is turned into a donkey by a monster disguised as an INCARNATE LAMA. Rescued by one of his wives, Geser tricks the monster into entering a flammable meditation chamber and burns him alive.

Buriat Mongol versions of the epic, called Abai Geser (Worthy Geser) or Abai Geser Khübüün (Worthy Boy Geser), chanted by epic singers, have abandoned the Buddhist environment entirely. All begin with a conflict in heaven between the 55 white gods in the west and the 44 red gods in the east. Geser, as one of the western gods, assists their struggle, but when the flesh of the defeated eastern chieftain is flung to earth, its stink causes all manner of evil; to subdue these evils Geser volunteers to be born on earth. Both the hunt and the ANDA QUDA (blood brother and marriage ally) relations figure prominently. While in most versions the names and episodes of the Tibetan and literary Mongolian Geser can be seen, however faintly, in that sung by Manshud Imegenov (1849–1908) in 1906 for the folklorist TSYBEN ZHAMAT-SARANOVICH ZHAMTSARANO, the original Tibetan elements have almost completely disappeared.

Consonant with his role as a minor god protecting Buddhism, Geser was the object of an active cult. The QING DYNASTY rulers identified Geser with Guan Yu, the hero of the Chinese historical romance *Three Kingdoms*, and under this form they patronized his cult as an exemplar of martial loyalty. Mongolian prayers to Geser show him as a typical mounted protector deity, defending herds, suppressing demons, and bringing success in war, hunting, and athletic contests.

Geser has been one of the chief topics of investigation by Buriat, Mongolian, and Inner Mongolian folklorists, such as Zhamtsarano and BYAMBYN RINCHEN. Among the BURIATS the Abai Geser epic was criticized in the late Stalin era, like all non-Russian martial heroes, for its supposedly feudal character. Since 1990 Geser has become a key plank in Buriat national identity. This politicization has popularized academically insupportable ideas, such as that Geser began among the Buriats around 1000 and that the Manshud Imegenov version represents the original, "pre-Buddhist" form.

See also FOLK POETRY AND TALES; TIBETAN CULTURE IN MONGOLIA; TSAM.

Further reading: Bayir Dugarov, "Geser Boyda-yin Sang: A Little-Known Buryat-Mongolian Sutra." In *Writing in the Altaic World*, ed. Juha Janhunen and Volker Rybatzki (Helsinki: Finnish Oriental Society, 1999), 49–61; Robin Kornman, "Geser of Ling." *Religions of Tibet in Practice*, ed. Donald S. Lopez, Jr. (Princeton, N.J.: Princeton University Press), 39–68.

Ghazan Khan (b. 1271, r. 1295–1304) *Mongol khan who converted the Middle Eastern Il-Khanate to Islam and undertook comprehensive reforms of Mongol administration*
Born on November 4, 1271, Ghazan was the son of Arghun, then crown prince and viceroy in Khorasan

(eastern Iran) for Abagha Khan (1271–82). From his fourth year Abagha Khan took over his grandson's education, placing him in the ORDO (palace-tent) of his childless senior wife, Bulughan Khatun (d. 1286) of the Baya'ud and having a Chinese Buddhist monk teach him Mongolian and Uighur scripts and Buddhism. After Abagha's death Bulughan Khatun and Arghun married while wintering in Baghdad in 1282–83; Bulughan's ordo moved to Khorasan with Ghazan. Arghun became khan in 1284 and left with Bulughan Khatun for Azerbaijan, leaving Ghazan in Khorasan as titular viceroy. Later, after Bulughan Khatun died, Arghun had her ordo with its treasuries sealed in trust for Ghazan.

As an adult Ghazan was both sickly and unusually slight and ugly. While he hunted like other Mongol princes, his favorite hobby was practicing handicrafts. Although the exclusively Islamic culture of Khorasan had permeated local Mongol life, Ghazan built a major Buddhist temple at Khabushan (modern Quchan). Despite these disadvantages, Ghazan built up in Khorasan a loyal entourage of Mongol commanders (NOYAN) such as Qutlughshah (d. 1307) of the Mang'ud, Nurin Aqa (Elder) of the Yürkin (d. 1303), and the Persian administrator Sa'd-ud-Din Savaji (d. 1312). In 1289 NAWROZ (d. 1297), scion of the chief Mongol family in Khorasan, rebelled. When Arghun Khan was murdered in 1291, renewed invasions by Nawroz, rebellion in Nishapur city, and famine in Khorasan kept Ghazan from pressing his claims in the capital and avenging his father. By 1292 the new khan, Ghazan's uncle Geikhatu, had taken over most of Arghun's wives and ordos. In autumn and winter 1294–25 Nishapur and Nawroz, both exhausted by war, negotiated their surrenders. When Geikhatu was overthrown in March 1295, Ghazan was finally free to pursue his claim to his father's wives, ordos, and throne.

In seizing the throne, Ghazan followed the guidance of the newly submitted Nawroz, making a rapid march to surprise the rival khan Baidu at Qongghor-Ölöng (near Soltaniyeh). A thunderstorm disrupted Ghazan's planned night attack, however, and on May 23, outnumbered by Baidu's columns, Ghazan withdrew on Baidu's promise to divide the kingdom and return to Ghazan all of Arghun's ordos. At this point Nawroz, himself a dedicated Muslim, convinced Ghazan that he ought to accept Islam. Ghazan and all his army formally converted in a joyous public ceremony near Rayy (June 17). After keeping the Ramadan fast, Ghazan advanced again in September. Nawroz's diplomacy bore fruit when TA'ACHAR, Baidu's disgruntled beglerbegi (commander in chief), deserted. Ghazan entered Tabriz victoriously on October 4 and recovered his old ordos and Abagha's wives. (One of these new wives, the younger Bulughan Khatun of the QONGGIRAD, later bore him his only two children, a son who died in infancy, and a daughter.) On October 19 he ordered the destruction of all churches, synagogues, and Buddhist temples. At first Ghazan Khan elevated recent adherents,

such as Nawroz and Sadr-ud-Din Zanjani (d. 1298), but later he carefully weeded out suspicious officials. By 1298 only his long-time Khorasanian entourage controlled the government: Qutlughshah as beglerbegi, Sa'd-ud-Din Savaji as vizier, with the assistance of RASHID-UD-DIN FAZL-ULLAH (1247–1318), and Nurin Aqa guarding Khorasan with Ghazan's half-brother Kharbanda (1281–1316).

By 1298 Ghazan's attachment to Islam had become deep and personal. He dreamed of angels and of Ali, feeling special kinship with Muhammad's family. While prohibiting the restoration of his father's ruined memorial Buddhist chapel, he honored his ancestors' pre-Buddhist worship of heaven as a kind of proto-Islamic monotheism. Ghazan also soon saw the political necessity of respecting the religion of the IL-KHANATE's Georgian and Lesser Armenian client kings. From spring 1296 he renewed the traditional privileges of the Christian churches and cracked down on anti-Christian pogroms, eventually becoming friendly with the Assyrian catholicos (patriarch) MAR YAHBH-ALLAHA.

Ghazan invaded Mamluk-held Syria three times, in 1299–1300, 1300–01, and 1303. Ghazan's decisive victory near Homs (December 22, 1299), in which he had showed great personal courage, had broken the string of Mamluk victories, yet he lacked sufficient troops to adequately garrison Syria. After the last campaign, in which Qutlughshah allowed the Mongol army to be defeated at Marj al-Suffar, south of Damascus (April 30, 1303), Ghazan ordered his beglerbegi beaten at court.

Rashid-ud-Din's COMPENDIUM OF CHRONICLES (Jami'al-tawarikh) gives an extensive record of Ghazan Khan's reforms. The continued political crisis, aggravated by the Eurasian silver shortage of the 1280s and 1290s, had emptied the Il-Khanate treasury. Ghazan Khan understood that being the openhanded khan of Turco-Mongol ideals paradoxically required strict attention to imperial finances. From around 1300 he planned a comprehensive reform of Mongol administration, aiming to replace the anarchy of PAIZA (badges) with a regulated system of taxation. He also unified weights, measures, and coinage. The abolition of the ORTOQ system followed Islamic precepts and buttressed the authority of the traditional Muslim administrative-landlord ruling class.

In his final illness he made his brother Kharbanda his heir. After Ghazan's death on May 17, 1304, Kharbanda (known as Sultan Öljeitü, 1304–16) retained Ghazan's personnel and policies with little change.

Further reading: Charles Melville, "Padshah-i Islam: The Conversion of Sultan Mahmud Ghazan Khan," *Pembroke Papers* 1 (1990): 159–177.

goats Goats have traditionally been the least valued of the Mongols' five kinds of livestock, used mostly for meat, milk, skins, and hair, but not as valued as other livestock. The international market for CASHMERE caused a boom in goat populations through the 1990s. In the year 2000 Mongolia had 10,269,800 goats. Mongolian goats are herded along with sheep and have traditionally been counted together with them. Goats and sheep are milked around the same time in May–June. Most male sheep and goats are castrated, and the testicles are, unlike those of large animals, eaten.

When goats were first distinguished from sheep in Mongolian censuses in 1929, they numbered 3,339,300, or 15 percent of Mongolia's total livestock. The number of goats reached 5,631,300, or 24 percent, in 1960. During the collectivization era the numbers were usually fewer than 5 million, or about 20 percent, despite the creation of a cashmere industry in Mongolia. In 1990 the number was 5,125,700, or 19.8 percent of total. With the opening of the Mongolian economy, the cashmere market boomed. The total number of goats swelled to 11,033,900, or almost 37 percent, in 1999. The ZUD of 2000 checked the rise in these numbers. Goats are particularly numerous in the drier western and southwestern provinces, such as GOBI-ALTAI PROVINCE, BAYANKHONGOR PROVINCE, SOUTH GOBI PROVINCE, and KHOWD PROVINCE.

In Inner Mongolia goats numbered 2,282,000 in 1947, or 28 percent of the total number of the traditional five kinds of livestock. This number rose to 13,709,000, or 34 percent, in 1965. For the next two decades the number of goats was generally fewer than 10 million. By 1990 it had risen to 12,209,000, or 27 percent, of livestock.

See also ANIMAL HUSBANDRY AND NOMADISM; DAIRY PRODUCTS; FOOD AND DRINK.

Gobi Desert *Gobi* (Cyrillic, *gowi*) in Mongolian refers to gravelly or sandy desert, drier than the grassy steppe and uninhabited by marmots but still with some vegetation and human habitation. (Totally uninhabited land is called *tsöl.*) The Gobi Desert occupies roughly the southern third of Mongolia proper, and while the term is not so commonly used in Chinese geographical classification, it also includes the land along China's northern border from Sönid Left Banner (Sonid Zuoqi) in Inner Mongolia to Barköl in Xinjiang. The Gobi Desert occupies about 775,000 square kilometers (300,000 square miles), or about 1 million square kilometers (390,000 square miles) if the mostly *tsöl*-deserts of ALASHAN are included.

The Gobi is a mostly level plain 700–1,600 meters (2,300–5,250 feet) above sea level and entirely enclosed

Gobi landscape, east of Sainshand, 1992 *(Courtesy Christopher Atwood)*

within the Central Asian inland drainage basin. Annual precipitation is generally less than 150 millimeters (6 inches), and average temperatures range from 25°C (77°F) in July to –15° to –20°C (5° to –4°F) in January. Strong winds in the spring and fall create powerful dust storms. The core of the Gobi along southern Mongolia and Urad and northern Alashan banners is gravelly with scattered thickets of deep-rooted xerophytic trees and bushes such as saxaul (*Haloxylon ammodendron*), *Reaumuria soongarica,* and *Ephedra przewalskii*. To the north and east there are zones first of Gobi feather grass (*Stipa glareosa*) and grey sagebrush (*Artemisia xerophytica*), and then of steppe needle grass (*Stipa krylovii*) and pasture sage (*Artemisia frigida;* Mongolian *agi*), and finally genuine steppe. The Gobi zone south of the ALTAI RANGE is called the Trans-Altai Gobi.

Gobi herding emphasizes meat and semi-finehaired sheep, goats, and two-hump camels. The desert's few towns are mostly small administrative and retail trade centers; Sainshand and Saikhan Tal along the TRANS-MONGOLIAN RAILWAY and the mining town of Bayan Oboo are the only ones with populations more than 20,000.

See also ANIMAL HUSBANDRY AND NOMADISM; BAYANKHONGOR PROVINCE; CLIMATE; EAST GOBI PROVINCE; ENVIRONMENTAL PROTECTION; FAUNA; FLORA; GOBI-ALTAI PROVINCE; KHOWD PROVINCE; MIDDLE GOBI PROVINCE; MINING; MONGOLIAN PLATEAU; SHILIIN GOL; SOUTH GOBI PROVINCE; ULAANCHAB.

Further reading: John Man, *Gobi: Tracking the Desert* (New Haven, Conn.: Yale University Press, 1997).

Gobi-Altai province (Govi-Altai, Gov'-Altaj)

Originally named Altai province, Gobi-Altai was one of the original provinces created in Mongolia's 1931 administrative reorganization. Lying in southwestern Mongolia, all of its territory was included in KHALKHA Mongolia's prerevolutionary Zasagtu Khan province. It has a long boundary with the desert areas of Gansu and Xinjiang in China. The province's area of 141,400 square kilometers (54,600 square miles) is, as its name suggests, mostly gobi (habitable desert) or true desert (*tsöl*) and is traversed from east to west by the eastern ALTAI RANGE's parallel ranges. The area north of the Altai is part of the GREAT LAKES BASIN between the KHANGAI RANGE and Altai range. That south of the Altai is part of Mongolia's driest and hottest southern zone. Here the area's Great Gobi Nature Preserves protect much of Mongolia's rarest wildlife: the argali sheep, the snow leopard, the wild camel, the Gobi bear, and the newly reintroduced Przewalskii's horse (*see* ENVIRONMENTAL PROTECTION). Gobi-Altai's population of 41,000 in 1956 had grown to 63,600 in 2000, but still slightly less than one person inhabits every two square kilometers (0.77 square miles). Gobi-Altai is one of Mongolia's major pastoral provinces, with 2,035,100 head of livestock. Cattle and horses are relatively few, but the province has some of Mongolia's largest herds of camels (31,800 head), sheep (847,600), and especially CASHMERE-producing goats (1,003,800). In the year 2000 18,000 people lived in the capital, Altai (previously named Yisünbulag).

See also SHARAB, "BUSYBODY."

Gobi-Sümber province   *See* CHOIR CITY.

Go-dan   *See* KÖTEN.

Golden Horde (Qipchaq Khanate, *Ulus* of Jochi)

The Golden Horde, founded by CHINGGIS KHAN's eldest son, Jochi, unified for the first time the lands around the Kazakh, Caspian, and Black Sea steppes. Successors to the Golden Horde ruled under Russian sovereignty into the 20th century. The name *Golden Horde* derives from the gold-hung palace-tent (*horda* or ORDO) at which ÖZBEG KHAN (1313–41) received visitors. When Russian chronicles mentioned "going to the Horde," *horde* was being used in its proper sense of a nomadic palace, not the later European sense of a mass of people. As the realm disintegrated, the chroniclers referred to other *ordo*s at the center of splinter regimes: the BLUE HORDE, the Volga Horde, the Great Horde, and so on. Implicitly, the palace-tent stood for the people gathered around their ruler. Not until the 16th century, however, did Russian chroniclers begin explicitly using *Golden Horde* to designate this Mongol successor state. Persian sources of the 13th and 14th centuries, undoubtedly reflecting Mongol usage, spoke either geographically of the *Dasht-i Qifchaq,* "Qipchaq Steppe" (*see* QIPCHAQS) or dynastically of the "*ulus* (realm) of JOCHI," Chinggis Khan's eldest son and ancestor of its khans.

FORMATION OF THE DYNASTY

The Golden Horde, originally the *ulus,* or people, of Jochi (d. 1225?), emerged as a separate entity earlier than any other of the successor states of the MONGOL EMPIRE. The family's early separatist tendency reflected Jochi's alienation from his father, Chinggis Khan (Genghis, 1206–27). Jochi's successor, BATU (d. 1255?), was an immense distance from Mongolia and suffered from gout and a reputation as a coward. As a result, he preferred to defend his autonomy rather than compete for rule in Mongolia.

Perhaps in compensation for passing him over as heir, Chinggis Khan's original grant to his eldest son Jochi was exceptionally generous. Starting from the Chu River and KHORAZM, by 1242 it extended west to the Danube and north to the Arctic. Under the appanage system Jochi and his descendants were also assigned shares in the sedentary cities: Pingyang (modern Linfen), Zhending, and Jinzhou (modern Jinxian) in North China, 5,000 households in Bukhara, and so on. (Other princes, though, also had shares in Jochid cities such as Khorazm and the CRIMEA.) Finally, under Chinggis Khan's son ÖGEDEI KHAN (1229–41), the Jochids exercised certain rights in the Middle East: the right to nominate the governors from their own retainers, the right to receive first tribute from the client kings, and the right to a fifth share of all war booty.

After Ögedei's death, however, the Jochids' rights in the Middle East were curtailed. The regent, TÖREGENE (1242–46), and her son GÜYÜG Khan (1246–48) appointed ARGHUN AQA and Eljigidei as governor and commander there, respectively. Eljigidei's son had earlier joined a group of young princes, including Güyüg himself, in publicly ridiculing Batu's battlefield ineptitude. Batu had his revenge when he skillfully arranged the coronation of MÖNGKE KHAN (1251–59), from the family of Chinggis's youngest son, Tolui. Batu's surviving tormentors were all executed, and Möngke explicitly assigned GEORGIA in the Caucasus to Batu's brother Berke. In his own Qipchaq steppe, Batu was almost completely autonomous, and Arghun Aqa personally visited Batu's *ordo* several times to consult with him.

At this point Möngke mobilized a vast campaign in the Middle East under his brother HÜLE'Ü (1217–65). For the first time a prince, not just a non-Chinggisid NOYAN, would be operating in the Jochid preserve west of the Amu Dar'ya. Möngke ordered princes from every branch to participate, and several Jochid princes—Quli, Balaqan, Dutar, and others—participated. Despite their participation, Hüle'ü soon held all real power south of the Caucasus, and did not send the accustomed portion of booty to Batu's successor Berke. Hüle'ü had Balaqan and/or Dutar and their attendant shamans (*bö'e*) executed for sorcery in February 1260. The suspicious death of Quli sent the Jochid princes' entourage into panic. Some fled to the Qipchaq steppe, some to Egypt, and some joined Negüder, a Jochid retainer in southern Afghanistan, who had been challenging Hüle'ü's authority in Herat (*see* QARA'UNAS).

During the first years of Hüle'ü's expedition, first Batu, then Batu's son Sartaq, and finally Sartaq's boy Ula'achi (Ulaghchi) had died within two years (1255–57). As a result, Batu's brother Berke succeeded him. While Sartaq and his son had been Christians, Berke was a Muslim, and his accession added a religious element to the developing Jochid-Hüle'üid feud. Christians believed Berke had poisoned Sartaq and Ula'achi, while Muslims hoped Berke would oppose war on Muslims. Now, although the late Jochid princes had all played their part in the destruction of the caliphate, Berke suddenly expressed his anger at Hüle'ü's sack of Baghdad. In autumn 1262 Berke invaded the IL-KHANATE. This inconclusive campaign marked the first battle between Mongol regional powers. Stymied by his failure, Berke sought a joint attack with Sultan Baybars (1260–77) of MAMLUK EGYPT, thus allying with a non-Mongol against a Mongol relative. When the Byzantine Empire detained Egyptian envoys, Berke sent an army through Bulgaria effecting the release of the envoys and forcing Byzantium's adherence to the new alliance. A second invasion in summer 1265 broke through Derbent but withdrew after Berke's death in Tiflis.

Berke's expansive interpretation of Jochid rights also generated hostility in the east. In 1259 the Muslim elite and the Jochid retainers in Bukhara attempted to declare Berke sovereign there, leading Alghu Khan (1260–65/6) of the Chaghatayid dynasty to smash the Jochids' Bukharan appanage before invading Jochid territory in Khorazam and Otrar. Alghu's successor, Baraq (1266–71), continued the northward pressure on the Jochids' eastern domains.

Faced with a two-front war, Berke's successor, a grandson of Batu, Mengü-Temür (Möngke-Temür, 1267–80) had to call a truce with the Il-Khans before sending an army of 50,000 under Jochi's son Berkecher to push Baraq south. Letters sent to Egypt demonstrate that Mengü-Temür had not abandoned hope of recovering Azerbaijan. In 1269, with Baraq suitably chastened, Mengü-Temür formed a grand alliance of the Jochids, Chaghatayids, and Ögedeids aimed at attacking the Toluid states, especially the Il-Khanate.

TRIBAL STRUCTURE

The core of the Golden Horde was the vast steppe stretching from the Irtysh in the east to the Danube in the west. Jochi and his wives proved sufficiently fertile to fill this vast steppe. Jochi's sons, 14 of whom are known by name, divided the steppe into longitudinal strips, nomadizing north to south along the main rivers, often with hundreds of kilometers between summer and winter camps. Despite Berke's temporary assignment to Georgia, no Jochid princes ever settled permanently south of the Caucasus, the Aral Sea, or the Syr Dar'ya.

The steppe was divided between the princes of the right (i.e., western) hand and the left (i.e., eastern) hand. Jochi was succeeded not by his oldest son, Hordu, but by his second son, Batu. Batu thus headed the right-hand princes, while Hordu headed the left-hand princes. Right-hand prince Shiban's appanage, from the Ural and Irgiz valleys through the desert north of the Aral Sea and along the Syr Dar'ya to the Sarysu-Chu confluence, marked the border of the two halves. All the Golden Horde's urban centers fell to the princes of the right hand.

While RASHID-UD-DIN FAZL-ULLAH's list of the four 1,000s assigned by Chinggis to Jochi—the Sanchi'ud, Keniges, Üüshin, and Je'üred clans—has often been taken as the total number of Mongols in the Golden Horde, this is clearly not so. The *SECRET HISTORY OF THE MONGOLS* says Jochi's *ulus* had eight 1,000s, and Vassaf states that on Jochi's death his army was divided between Batu and Hordu, with each receiving a *tümen* (nominally 10,000). Moreover, several other Mongol clans existed in the Golden Horde. Around 1300 troops and/or commanders

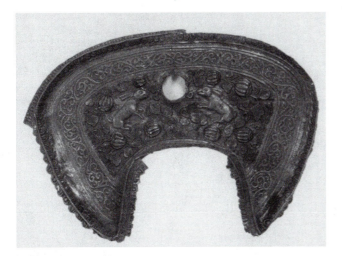

Saddle arch of gilt silver, from Ternenis village, near Melitopol'. The rabbit may refer to the rider's year of birth in the 12-animal cycle. Gold saddle arches with dragons (a sign of royalty) have been found in Yuan-era tombs of Inner Mongolia. (*Courtesy State Hermitage Museum, St. Petersburg*)

(*noyan*) of the Sanchi'ud, Üüshin, Je'üred, QONGGIRAD, and ÖNGGÜD clans and a *tümen* of the Qiyat (Kiyad) clan served the princes of the right hand, while *noyan*s of the Keniges, Qonggirad, Jajirad, Besüd, and Arghun (a branch of the Önggüd) clans and four *tümen*s of JALAYIR led by OIRAT *noyan*s served the princes of the left hand. Little is known about the clans' regional distribution, although the Qonggirads and the Önggüd nomadized around Khorazm in modern Karakalpakstan.

The Franciscan friar WILLIAM OF RUBRUCK's account suggests a substantial depopulation of the native Qipchaqs, particularly in the west, while the glut of Qipchaq slaves in the Black Sea ports shows that much of the surviving population was enslaved, losing any previous clan structure. From 1400 a so-called Qipchaq clan appeared in the Blue Horde and its successors indicating that previous subtribal affiliations had been forgotten. The disappearance of preconquest leading CLAN NAMES, such as Ölberi and Terteroba, shows the "detribalization" inflicted on the subjugated Qipchaqs.

ETHNIC GEOGRAPHY

Around the Golden Horde's steppe core were several sedentary civilizations. To the southeast was Khorazm and its capital, Urganch, a Turkic-speaking Muslim land based on irrigation agriculture with a long tradition of scholarship and trade between the Volga and Central Asia. The smaller cities along the Syr Dar'ya were similar in culture. In the southwest the port cities of CRIMEA, inhabited by Goths, Greeks, Armenians, Anatolian Turks, and (after 1204) Italians, thrived on the export of grain, fish, honey, and slaves and the import of silver and luxuries for the khans. At the Volga-Kama confluence the BUL-GHARS had built an Islamic urban civilization on the export of grain, honey, furs, slaves, and transit trade between Khorazm and the Baltic. Competing with Bulghar for control over the fur trade and the Volga were the Russians (including at this time the Ukrainians and Belarussians) with a rich yet insular Christian civilization. Russia's largest city, Novgorod, was important for the Golden Horde as its only outlet to the Baltic Sea trade.

The Golden Horde also contained a number of tribal peoples in the Caucasus and the Volga watershed. Centered in the Caucasus foothills, but also found in pockets throughout the steppe from the Volga to the Prut, were the OSSETES (Alans), while the Circassians (Cherkes) occupied the Kuban Basin and neighboring Caucasus foothills. Both Eastern Orthodox in religion, neither was ever fully subdued by the Mongols. In the middle Volga, squeezed between the Bulghars, the Russians, and the Qipchaq steppe, were the Mordvins (including the Moksha), speaking a language related to Finnish and Estonian, and the Burtas, a Turkicized body of Ossetes. East of the Urals were the Bashkirs (Bashkort), who through the 13th century retained both the language of, and sense of kinship with, the Hungarians. Northeast of them were Samoyeds. The Mongols put all of these northern peoples, including the Russians and Bulghars, to the fur tribute.

On the steppe itself the khans established several towns. By 1255 Batu had founded the new settlements of Saray (Selitrënnoye, north of Astrakhan) and Ügek (Uvek, south of Saratov) at the southern and northern limits of his migrations. In the 14th century new cities flourished under sultans ÖZBEG KHAN (1313–41) and Janibeg (1342–57) on the Volga (Astrakhan, Beliamen, and the new capital, New Saray), the Kuma (Majar), the Ural (Saraychik), and the Dniester (Aq-Kerman, modern Bilhorod-Dnistrovs'kyy). The khans remained nomadic, however; Özbeg wintered near Saray and summered either at Bish-Dagh (Pyatigorsk) near Majar or in the southern Urals.

FOREIGN RELATIONS

A constant of Golden Horde foreign policy was hostility to the Il-Khans. While some rulers did not actively pursue their claims beyond the Caucasus, none, except possibly Toqto'a (1291–1312), ever considered abandoning them. Ultimately, Sultan Özbeg's sons and grandson pursued this claim to ultimate success by occupying Tabriz, in modern Iran, in 1357–59, although they could not hold on to their conquest. To outflank the Il-Khans, the Golden Horde maintained the Egyptian alliance begun by Berke and Baybars. Although the alliance never produced the hoped-for military benefits, it did play a substantial role in the cultural and religious life of the Horde. Geography dictated that this alliance needed the Byzantine Empire as a third partner, and keeping Byzantium in line

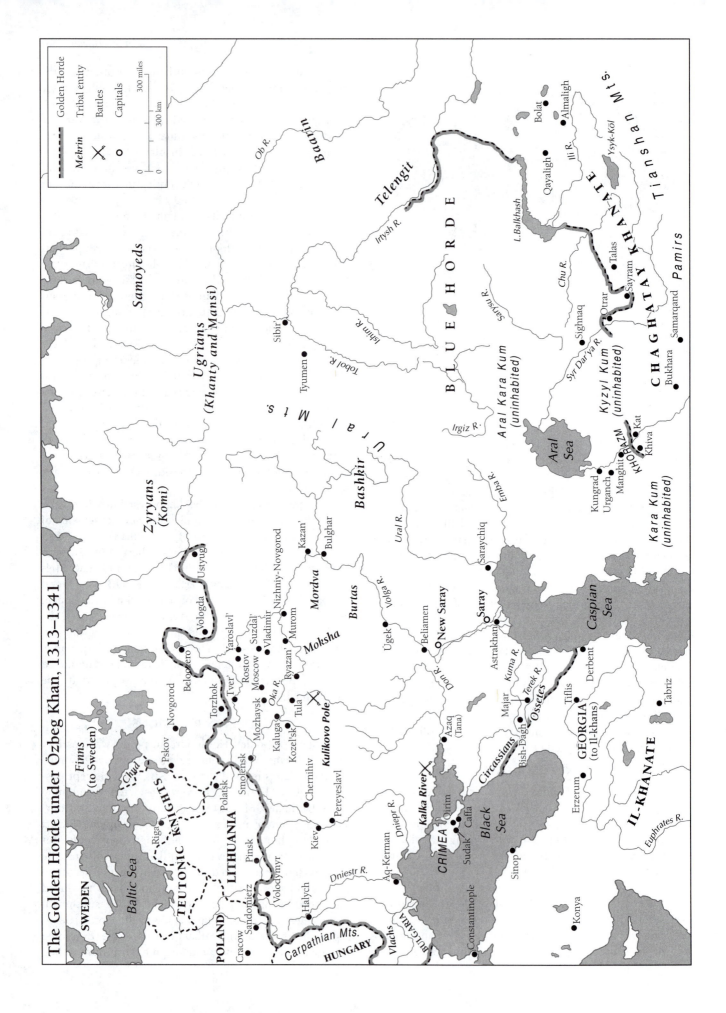

The Golden Horde under Özbeg Khan, 1313–1341

Golden Horde
Tribal entity
Battles
Capitals

Mekrin
X
o

300 miles
300 km

SWEDEN

Baltic Sea

Finns
(to Sweden)

Chud

Riga

TEUTONIC KNIGHTS

Pskov

Polatsk

Smolensk

Pinsk

LITHUANIA

POLAND

Cracow

Sandomierz

Volodymyr

Halych

Carpathian Mts.

HUNGARY

Vlachs

BULGARIA

Dniestr R.

Aq-Kerman

Dniepr R.

Kiev

Pereyeslavl

Chernihiv

Kozel'sk

Kaluga

Tula

Kulikovo Pole

Oka R.

Ryazan'

Mozhaysk

Moscow

Rostov

Tver'

Torzhok

Novgorod

Beloozero

Vologda

Ustyug

Zyryans
(Komi)

Yaroslavl'

Suzdal'

Vladimir

Murom

Nizhniy-Novgorod

Kazan'

Bulghar

Mordva

Moksha

Burtas

Bashkir

Ural Mts.

Ural R.

Ügek

Beliamen

Don R.

New Saray

Saray

Astrakhan

Volga R.

Saraychiq

Emba R.

Kara Kum
(uninhabited)

Caspian Sea

Majar

Kuma R.

Terek R.

Ossetes

Bish-Bagh

Derbent

Circassians

GEORGIA
(to Il-khans)

Tiflis

Erzerum

Euphrates R.

IL-KHANATE

Tabriz

Konya

Sinop

Black Sea

Constantinople

CRIMEA

Qirim

Caffa

Sudak

Kalka River

Azaq
(Tana)

Kalka River

Samoyeds

Ugrians
(Khanty and Mansi)

Sibir

Tyumen

Tobol R.

Ishim R.

Ob R.

Baarin

Telengit

Irtysh R.

BLUE HORDE

Sarysu R.

L.Balkhash

Qayaligh

Bolat

Almaligh

Ili R.

Ysyk-Köl Mts.

Tianshan Mts.

CHAGHATAY KHANATE

Talas

Sayram

Chu R.

Otrar

Sighnaq

Syr Dar'ya R.

Bukhara

Samarqand

Pamirs

Kyzyl Kum
(uninhabited)

Aral Kara Kum
(uninhabited)

Irgiz R.

Aral Sea

KHORAZM

Kat

Khiva

Manghit

Urganch

Kungrad

necessitated land access to Constantinople, which in turn necessitated control over Bulgaria. From Berke to Özbeg these requirements were more or less maintained.

Eastward, the Golden Horde's primary interest lay in thwarting the Chaghatayids' ambitions toward Khorazm and the Syr Dar'ya cities. From 1269 to 1284 the khans pursued this aim by encouraging QAIDU and the Chaghatayids' ambitions to the south and east. From 1284, however, the Golden Horde became wary of Qaidu's expansion and opened friendly relations with the YUAN DYNASTY.

Central Europe impinged on the Golden Horde primarily as a source of instability among the Russian principalities. Local Jochid princes and noyans met Lithuanian and Polish raids on southwestern Russian towns (modern western Ukraine) with counterraids, which were, however, often as damaging to the local Russians through whom the Mongol soldiers passed as to the Poles or Lithuanians.

ADMINISTRATION

Little is known of the Golden Horde's formal court organization. The rulers bore the title qan, "khan," not qa'an, "great khan," but were otherwise fully sovereign (see KHAN). JOHN OF PLANO CARPINI stated that Batu had "door-keepers and all officials just like their Emperor." By Qonichi's time (fl. 1277–96) the left hand, too, had a separate KESHIG, or royal guard. The Horde's great noyans stemmed from the realm's original Mongol clans, were QUDA (marriage ally) to the sovereign, and commanded a keshig unit, a 1,000, or tümen. In both Hordu and Batu's family the Qonggirad were the most important quda partners.

Özbeg Khan adopted the Yuan and Il-Khanate system of having the keshig's four three-day shift commanders (termed ulus emirs) countersign the khan's orders. These shift commands all belonged to old Mongol clans. The senior of the four was beglerbegi, "commander in chief" and "deputy to the khan," while another ulus emir was vizier. Except for the influential position of tutor to the crown prince held mostly by immigrant Islamic clergymen, there was no avenue of advancement open to lowborn or non-Mongol men.

Evidence on local administration is fragmentary. In the indirectly ruled Russian lands three censuses were carried out in 1245–46, 1256–59, and 1273–74, and the entire population was registered in the Mongols' DECIMAL ORGANIZATION. Church estates were exempt from all taxation and JAM (postroad) stations and princely appanages were also separated out. In the 13th century basqaqs (overseers; see DARUGHACHI) supervised administration, and Muslim tax farmers collected taxes, but under Toqto'a and his successors the Russian princes took over the functions of both institutions in their own lands. Administrative trends in Bulghar were probably similar. In the cities of Crimea, the Black Sea, the Volga, and Khorazm, however, the Horde ruled directly. Mongol and Khorazmian noyans served as darughas, in effect governors, overseeing a staff of secretaries, customs agents, "weighers" (customs assessors), and bazarde-tarkhans, or market inspectors.

ECONOMY

Caravan trade was the foundation of the Golden Horde's state finances. MUHAMMAD ABU 'ABDULLAH IBN BATTUTA in 1332 remarked on the immensely profitable trade of horses from the Black Sea steppe via Khorazm to India. Furs, falcons, and slaves traveled the same route. Transit trade from China and India also passed through Khorazm to Saray and thence to Crimea. Trade from the Middle East and Central Asia to Russia and the Baltic Sea passed along the Volga, while Persian authors describe caravans passing south through Derbent into Azerbaijan during years of peace. The Horde's Mediterranean exports, notably slaves, furs, and falcons, moved out through Crimea and Azaq (Azov). This trade was taxed through the Tamagha (Russian, tamga), or commercial tolls, collected in all major cities.

The principal import was metals, particularly silver. In the 1240s and 1250s the steppe and Russian economies were not monetized, using cloth bolts and squirrel pelts as currency. Bulghar, however, had mints that struck coins under the name of Möngke and (under Berke) ARIQ-BÖKE. Mengü-Temür and his successors issued currency in their own names, and minting expanded to Khorazm, Saray, and Qirim (Staryy Krym) in Crimea. The main silver currency, however, was not coinage but sommo (Italian; Ibn Battuta's sawma), an ingot weighing 206 grams, or 7.3 ounces (see YASTUQ).

Russian tribute helped finance this monetarization. The tribute to the Horde was collected at first in furs, sparking an intensified exploitation of the northern fur market. When necessary ortaqchis (tax-exempt traders operating with government capital; see ORTOQ), who traded in furs and often doubled as tax farmers, undoubtedly supplied on ruinous interest the furs necessary to pay the taxes. By the middle of the 14th century, however, the tax was fully monetized, and the Russian princes inserted themselves as middlemen between the ortaqchis and the taxpayers. Wills of the Russian princes show even small hamlets being required to pay on a regular basis 650 to 900 grams (23 to 32 ounces) of silver. Since silver mines did not open in Russia until the 17th century, this silver must have been imported from either Europe or Central Asia. Russia thus became the Horde's leading silver source, a fact noted by Ibn Battuta and MARCO POLO, although they erroneously attributed the influx of sommo to silver mines.

MILITARY

The Golden Horde army was the largest of the three western khanates but neither as battle worthy nor as well equipped as those of the CHAGHATAY KHANATE and the Il-Khanate. During the 1357 invasion of Azerbaijan, the conventional wisdom said the Horde's vast army was "horsemen without weapons." The bulk of the army must have been Mongol clans and their native Turkish subjects. Still, Rashid-ud-Din speaks of Russians, Hungarians, and Circassians being brought into both right- and left-hand armies, and they do figure occasionally in battle accounts. In 1277 the Russian prince of Rostov won distinction in the siege of an Ossetian fortress.

POLITICAL HISTORY

In 1269 the Golden Horde khan Mengü-Temür had fashioned a grand alliance of the Golden Horde, Qaidu, and the Chaghatay Khanate. By this alliance the perpetually aggressive Chaghatayids were directed south against the Il-Khans and east against QUBILAI KHAN's Yuan dynasty. Unfortunately, Baraq's 1270 invasion of Iran failed. In the east, however, there was unexpected success. In 1277 dissident princes rebelling against Qubilai Khan captured Qubilai's son Nomuqan (d. 1301) and handed him over to Qaidu, who sent him on to Mengü-Temür. The Golden Horde had never had much quarrel with Qubilai Khan, and Mengü-Temür's mother-in-law, Kelmish Aqa, was actually Qubilai's niece. She ensured that Nomuqan was treated well and tried to have him returned.

After becoming khan Mengü-Temür's brother Töde-Mengü (Töde-Möngke, 1280–87) converted to Islam and began neglecting state affairs for Sufi gatherings. As a result, collateral Jochid princes Qonichi of the left hand and NOQAI (d. 1299) west of the Dnieper became effectively co-khans. In 1283–84 the three sent Nomuqan back as a gesture of peace to Qubilai Khan, yet in the Russian lands Töde-Mengü and Noqai could not agree on whom to appoint grand prince, sparking a decade-long conflict. In 1287 four of his nephews overthrew Töde-Mengü, calling him insane. The four nephews nominated their eldest, Töle-Bugha (1287–91), khan and ruled collectively, yet dissension increased. When Töle-Bugha reopened war against the Il-Khanate in 1288 and 1290, Noqai, by contrast, sent peace envoys to the Il-Khan. In 1291 one of the nephews, Toqto'a, Mengü-Temür's fifth son, fell out with his brothers and fled to Noqai, who helped him seize the throne.

Noqai himself remained in his territory, and Toqto'a Khan's (1291–1312) chief adviser became Salji'udai (d. 1301–02) of the Qonggirad, who was not only Toqto'a's father-in-law but his grandmother Kelmish's husband as well. A personal quarrel embittered Noqai's relations with Salji'udai, and by 1296 Noqai was seeking alliance with the Il-Khans against Toqto'a. Finally, in 1299 Toqto'a defeated Noqai, reunifying the princes of the right hand. Meanwhile, Qaidu tried to restore his declining influence in the Horde by sponsoring his own candidate in a civil war against Qonichi's successor, Bayan (fl. 1299–1304). Toqto'a abandoned Noqai's aggressive policy in the Balkans, and after Qaidu's death in 1301 he strongly supported the Mongol states' general peace of 1304, sending two *tümens* to buttress the Yuan frontier. Around 1310 Toqto'a reunified the Horde's coinage, closing down mints outside Saray.

Despite Toqto'a's successes, his policies were largely reversed after this death. During the interregnum after his death in 1312 his nephew Özbeg marched from Khorazm and seized the throne. After his election Özbeg Islamized his titulature, taking the throne as Sultan Muhammad Özbeg and proscribing Buddhism among the Mongol elite. He thus reversed the spread of Yuan culture that had flourished under Toqto'a. The policy of Islamization was not applied, however, to non-Mongols. Özbeg also reversed Toqto'a's peaceful foreign policy, menacing the young Il-Khan, Sultan Abu-Sa'id (1317–35), in 1318–19, 1324–25, and in 1335, but without success. Despite Egypt's 1323 peace treaty with the Il-Khans, Özbeg also revived Noqai's Balkan ambitions. In Özbeg's time the left-hand princes recovered control of the Syr Dar'ya valley while also adopting Islam. Yuan envoys seem to have backed a rival candidate after Toqto'a's death, but in 1326 Özbeg reopened friendly relations with the Yuan. From 1339 on Özbeg and his successors received annually 24,000 *ding* in Yuan paper currency from their Chinese appanages.

MONGOL LIFE, RELIGION, AND COURT CULTURE

The Egyptian geographer al-'Umari (1301–49) wrote that "when the TATARS [i.e., Mongols] took possession of [the Qipchaq Steppe] . . . they mixed with [the Qipchaqs] and entered into kinship with them, and the land won the upper hand over their natural and racial qualities and all of them became just like the Qipchaqs." At the highest social levels, however, the direct exchange *quda* marriage system limited the number of marriages with non-Mongol clans. Of the 25 marriages in the Jochid royal family recorded by Rashid-ud-Din, only two involved local Turkish people (a Qipchaq and a Siberian Töles). All the rest were with clans that arrived in the Mongol conquest. The Horde's letters to Egypt were written entirely in Mongolian throughout their relationship. Mongolian poetry written on birchbark and SQUARE SCRIPT fragments, unfortunately undated but probably from Toqto'a's reign, testify to the continued use of Mongolian. By the 1380s, however, if not before, the khans' decrees were being written in Turkish.

Nomadism remained dominant in the Horde up to its disintegration in the 15th century, and clan affiliations lasted far longer. In Khorazm, for example, the Qonggirad and MANGGHUD (Manghit) clans retained distinct identities into the 20th century. To the extent that sedentarization occurred, it was more urban than rural. The discovery of YURTS in the courtyards of houses in New Saray shows the continuing attachment to nomadism among the Horde's urban elite.

Unlike in the Il-Khan or Chaghatay realms, Islam in the Golden Horde proceeded not "up" from the conquered population, but "in" from abroad and then "down" from the Mongol elite. Berke's original conversion was due to the Bukharan sheikh (Sufi master) Saif-ud-Din Bakharzi, and his alliance with Egypt added another element to the Horde's Islamic culture. Like Berke, Özbeg was converted by a Bukharan sheikh, Ibn 'Abd-ul-Hamid, and the cosmopolitan character of the Horde's Islam continued. In traveling the Horde, Ibn Battuta met clerics and Sufis of most diverse origins: three Bukharans (including Ibn 'Abd-ul-Hamid), two Iraqis, and one each of Egyptian, Khorazmian, Lezgian (from Dagestan), Ossetian, and Greek origin. The Central Asian Hanafi school of legal interpretation, which allowed the consumption of both mead and KOUMISS, predominated, but the Middle Eastern Shafi'ites had official standing, too.

Engraved silver stemcup with a lid from the Golden Horde. The lid consisted of two perforated disks between which herbs could be placed to spice the wine. Similar stemcups have been found in Yuan-era tombs in Inner Mongolia and they were probably used at *quriltais* (grand assemblies). *(Courtesy State Hermitage Museum, St. Petersburg)*

After Berke's conversion, which happened in his early youth, Jochi, or perhaps Batu, assigned the Muslims in the Jochid army to his entourage, thus giving his appanage a strong Islamic identity. During his reign Berke claimed to have converted several of his brothers and most of his emirs, yet Islam did not continue as the state religion. A later spread of Buddhism reflected the influence of Kelmish Khatun and Salji'udai and the Yuan dynasty's prestige, a prestige seen also in the numerous Chinese artistic and architectural motifs in Saray.

When Özbeg came to power he killed emirs and Buddhist clerics who resisted Islamization, not necessarily to convert all the Mongols but to proscribe any non-Muslim communal identity for them. Ibn Battuta noted in 1332 that only "some" of the ethnic Mongols actually practiced Islam, yet to be a Mongol of the Golden Horde was, from then on, to be in some sense a Muslim. Janibeg ordered his army into the turban and woolen cloak of the Sufi mystic. By contrast, Ibn Battuta in 1332 noted that the Qipchaqs were still predominantly Christian, and Franciscan friars carried on, despite occasional violence, an active apostolate among them.

Due to its insularity, the Russian Orthodox culture had little influence on the khans. The closest Russo-Mongol social interaction occurred with the favored princely family of Rostov and vicinity. Gleb of Beloozero (d. 1278) received a Mongol bride at Great Khan Möngke's court and subsequently spent years at Mengü-Temür's court. Fedor of Mozhaysk and Yaroslavl' (d. 1299), spent years at Töde-Mengü's court, handing the khan his goblet and receiving a Mongol princess in marriage on the other. A Jochid prince, called by the Russians "Czarevich Peter of the Horde," was baptized in 1259 and settled in Rostov with Gleb's brother Boris (d. 1277), marrying into another family of Mongol converts already settled there. Despite these links there is little evidence of any lasting cultural interchange between Rostov and Saray.

DISINTEGRATION OF THE GOLDEN HORDE AND ITS SUCCESSOR KHANATES

With the disintegration of the Il-Khanate in 1335 and of the Chaghatayid realm in 1339, the Golden Horde prospered as *ortoq* merchants and trade fled to the Qipchaq steppe. Coinage, linked to commerce and the silver supply, grew slowly after the general peace of 1304 and reached unprecedented levels under Özbeg's son Janibeg (1342–57). Demanding submission from the emirs in strife-torn Azerbaijan, Janibeg boasted that "today three *uluses* are under my command."

The Golden Horde succumbed, however, to the continentwide catastrophe of the BLACK DEATH. Reaching the Horde's eastern borders from China in 1338–39, the plague ravaged Khorazm in 1345 and Saray in 1346 before being transferred to Caffa and the entire Mediterranean by soldiers waging Janibeg's self-destructive grudge war against Italian interests. Economic hardship was exacerbated by political instability as Özbeg's sons established an ominous pattern of intrafamilial murder. Janibeg had murdered his brother Tïnïbeg (1341–32) to seize the throne. By some accounts, Berdibeg (1357–59) murdered his father, Janibeg; in any case Berdibeg was killed by his brother, who in turn was killed by the third brother, Nawroz (1360).

In 1360 various princes of the left hand, now known as the BLUE HORDE, sensed opportunity and seized power, first in Saray and then in Bulghar. Thus began what the Russian chronicles called "the Great Troubles." From 1362 Emir Mamaq (Mamay, d. 1381) of the Qiyat clan ruled through puppet khans and tried to fight off the usurpers from his base by the Sea of Azov. From 1378, however, whole clans of the Blue Horde, mostly Turkish in origin, moved west under the Jochid prince TOQTAMISH (fl. 1375–1405). The struggle between Toqtamish and Mamaq was thus a struggle of the Horde's two sections, right and left. Mamaq was defeated in 1381, and the right-hand clans virtually disappeared, perhaps due to their greater urbanization, which rendered them more vulnerable to the Black Death.

Districts isolated from the great struggles tried to preserve their independence. The Genoans in Crimea forced Mamay to recognize their autonomy. The family of Özbeg's Qonggirad (Qonghrat) commander, Naghatay, assisted by the descendants of the sheikh Ibn 'Abd-ul-Hamid, made Khorazm independent. In Russia Dmitrii of Moscow ("Donskoi," 1359–89) began the path that led to the pyrrhic victory of Kulikovo Pole (1380). Despite a proliferation of local mints, urban markets declined precipitously in the 1370s, and urban life did not recover from TIMUR's (Tamerlane) 1395 sack of New Saray, Azaq, and other cities.

With Toqtamish's overthrow in 1395, a new clan, the Manghit (see MANGGHUD), under the non-Chinggisid commander in chief Edigü (d. 1420), emerged between the Volga and the Emba. Edigü maintained something of the Horde's unity until 1411, but by 1425 independent regimes were ensconced throughout the Golden Horde's territory. Khanates of Blue Horde origin formally proclaimed themselves in Crimea (1449), Kazan' (or Bulghar al-Jedid "New Bulghar," 1445), and Kasimov (1453). The Crimean khanate finally dispersed the "Great Horde" (Ulugh Orda), composed of the right-hand Sanchi'ud (Turkish Sijuvut) clan, in 1503.

THE IMPACT OF THE MONGOLS ON THE INNER ASIAN STEPPE

The Golden Horde played a formative role in the state formation and ethnogenesis of all the Turkic peoples of the Inner Asian steppe. The Crimean and Volga Tatars, while actually in dynastic and clan affiliation of Blue Horde origin, inherited what was left of the Golden Horde cities. Their very name, from the Russian term for the Mongols, marks them as, in Russian eyes, the descen-

dants of the feared and reviled "lawless Tatars." Debates among both peoples continue on whether they are the inheritors of the Golden Horde, as opposed to the classical civilizations of Crimea or early medieval Bulghar. In any case, the Golden Horde played an indisputable role in Islamizing Crimea and in forming the modern Volga Tatar language.

The Kazakh, Uzbek, Karakalpak, Nogay, and Bashkir (Bashkurt) all share a background in the early 15th-century Manghit and Blue Horde confederations, a background reflected in common CLAN NAMES and a common folklore. Until 1919, for example, the leaders of the liberal nationalist Alash-Orda Party in Kazakhstan proudly traced their descent either to Chinggis or to the Arghun clan of the Blue Horde. The Islamization of the steppe and the Turkicization of the Bashkirs were powerfully promoted by the prior Islamization and Turkicization of the Golden Horde's Mongol elite. While the centralization and urbanization of the Golden Horde was a comparatively short-lived episode in premodern steppe history, it left a legacy of literacy, money economy, and larger political ambitions that did not wholly disappear in the crisis of the 14th and 15th centuries.

See also APPANAGE SYSTEM; ARTISANS IN THE MONGOL EMPIRE; BUDDHISM IN THE MONGOL EMPIRE; BYZANTIUM AND BULGARIA; CENSUS IN THE MONGOL EMPIRE; CENTRAL EUROPE AND THE MONGOL EMPIRE; CHRISTIAN SOURCES ON THE MONGOL EMPIRE; CHRISTIANITY IN THE MONGOL EMPIRE; INDIA AND THE MONGOL EMPIRE; ISLAM IN THE MONGOL EMPIRE; ISLAMIC SOURCES ON THE MONGOL EMPIRE; MONEY IN THE MONGOL EMPIRE; RELIGIOUS POLICY IN THE MONGOL EMPIRE; RUSSIA AND THE MONGOL EMPIRE; SARAY AND NEW SARAY; WESTERN EUROPE AND THE MONGOL EMPIRE.

Further reading: B. Spuler, "Batu'ids," in *Encyclopaedia of Islam*, 2d ed., vol. 1 (Leiden: E. J. Brill, 1960 on), 1106–1108; Devin DeWeese, *Islamization and the Golden Horde: Baba Tükles and the Conversion to Islam in Historical and Epic Tradition* (University Park: Pennsylvania State University Press, 1994); Charles J. Halperin, *Russia and the Golden Horde: The Mongol Impact on Medieval Russian History* (Bloomington: Indiana University Press, 1985); Peter Jackson, "The Dissolution of the Mongol Empire," *Central Asiatic Journal* 22 (1978): 186–243; George Vernadsky, *Mongols and Russia* (New Haven, Conn.: Yale University Press, 1953).

Gombojab, Duke (mGon-po-skyabs) (fl. 1692–1749)
One of Mongolia's pioneers in Tibetan and Chinese studies
Duke Gombojab was the son of Udari (d. 1692), the administrator (*tusalaghci taiji*) of ÜJÜMÜCHIN West banner and younger brother of its prince, Sudani (r. 1658–90). Both Sudani and Udari having been posthumously implicated in plotting with GALDAN BOSHOGTU KHAN, Gombojab succeeded to his father's ducal title in 1692 only by

special imperial dispensation. Moving to Beijing, Gombojab mastered the Mongolian, Manchu, Tibetan, and Chinese languages and sometime after 1723 became headmaster of the Lifan Yuan's "Tangut" (i.e., Tibetan) school. He was later granted a princess of the imperial family in marriage.

His Tibetan textbook was the foundation of future Tibetan-Mongolian dictionaries. His only Mongolian-language book was *Gangga-yin uruskhal* (Flow of the Ganges, 1725), a brief genealogical handbook of the Mongolian BANNERS. Much more original was his *rGya-nag chos-'byung* (1735) (How the dharma arose in China), a Tibetan-language history of China and its Buddhism from Chinese sources. Block-printed in Lhasa in 1746, this work was Tibetan and Mongolian scholars' basic source on China until the 20th century. Inspired by the story of the pilgrimage to India by the Chinese monk-translator Xuanzang (596–664), Gombojab also translated Xuanzang's record of Turkestan and India into Tibetan. From 1742 to 1749 he helped lead the imperially sponsored Mongolian translation of the bsTan-'gyur (scriptural commentaries) and the terminological dictionary *Merged garkhu-yin oron* (Font of scholars) that formed its prolegomena. He then joined the team translating into Tibetan all Chinese Buddhist scriptures not available in that language. His date of death is unknown.

See also MEDICINE, TRADITIONAL.

Görgüz   *See* KÖRGÜZ.

Gov'-Altaj   *See* GOBI-ALTAI PROVINCE.

Govi-Altai   *See* GOBI-ALTAI PROVINCE.

Greater Bulgaria   *See* BULGHARS.

Greater Khinggan Range (Da Hinggan Ling, Khingan Range, Ta Hsing-an Ling)   The traditional eastern boundary of Mongolia, the Greater Khinggan Range runs northeast to southwest through eastern Inner Mongolia. Independent Mongolia touches the Khinggan foothills only in the far east. (The Lesser Khingan Range lies farther east in Manchuria.) The Greater Khinggan Range is about 1,400 kilometers (870 miles) long and 200–450 kilometers (125–280 miles) wide. The ridges have an average altitude of around 1,000–1,600 meters (3,300–5,200 feet) above sea level; the highest peak is the Khonggo Peak (Honggaoliang or Huanggangliang, 2,029 meters, or 6,657 feet) near the range's southern end. The eastern slopes are relatively steep, while those in the west slope gently toward the MONGOLIAN PLATEAU. Nowhere do slopes exceed 500 meters (1,640 feet) in height, and the range's ridges are rounded and indistinct, with flattened summits. The range separates the Manchurian drainage basins of the Shara Mören (Xar Moron) and the Nonni (Nen) Rivers to the east from the Mongolian basins of the Ergüne (Argun') River and the Central Asian inland basin to the west.

In the far north and west, forests of larch (*Larix sibirica*) and white birch form China's leading timber area. Along the eastern slopes north of the Tuur (Tao'er) River are forests of oak (*Quercus mongolica*). South of the Tuur (Tao'er) River Manchurian steppe vegetation with *Filifolium sibiricum* prevails.

Great Lakes Basin   The Great Lakes Basin is an inland basin in western Mongolia bounded by the ALTAI RANGE to the west, the KHANGAI RANGE to the east, and the Tannu Ola (Tagna Uul) Range to the north. It contains several of Mongolia's largest lakes, including the mostly salt UWS (3,350 square kilometers; 1,293 square miles in area) and Khyargas (1,407 square kilometers; 543 square miles) Lakes, and the mostly fresh Khar Us (1,852 square kilometers; 715 square miles) and Khar (575 square kilometers; 222 square miles) Lakes. The basin itself is about 600 kilometers (370 miles) long and 200–250 kilometers (125–155 miles) wide at an elevation ranging from about 1,500 meters (4,900 feet) above sea level in the south to 759 meters (2,490 feet) above sea level at LAKE UWS in the north. Several ridges and lone mountains divide the basin into subbasins. Precipitation is less than 100 millimeters (4 inches) annually and very unpredictable. The basin contains Mongolia's largest sand dune fields. To the south, the basin communicates with the Valley of the Lakes, which extends for 550–600 kilometers (340–370 miles) between the Khangai and Gobi-Altai Ranges.

See also ANIMAL HUSBANDRY AND NOMADISM; CLIMATE; ENVIRONMENTAL PROTECTION; FLORA; GOBI-ALTAI PROVINCE; KHOWD PROVINCE; MONGOLIAN PLATEAU; UWS PROVINCE; ZAWKHAN PROVINCE.

Great Purge   From 1937 to 1939 Joseph Stalin's purges in the Soviet Union spilled over into Mongolia, destroying almost the entire revolutionary generation in Mongolia and leaving Stalin's man, MARSHAL CHOIBALSANG, as the satellite country's unquestioned dictator. From 1925 on Communist publicists and Moscow officials became increasingly free in linking pan-Mongolism, Lamaism, and Japanese espionage as a single charge used against political enemies not only in Mongolia but also among the BURIATS of southern Siberia (*see* DAURIIA STATION MOVEMENT; RINCHINO, ELBEK-DORZHI). The Great Purge proper began as frequent clashes with Japanese troops on the eastern border stoked this long-standing anxiety into a full-fledged hysteria. It also brought the Soviet Red Army into Mongolia in August 1937, ensuring that any resistance could be crushed. Not surprisingly, the Great Purge was carried on simultaneously with the destruction of the lamas and the remaining aristocrats (*see* BUDDHISM, CAMPAIGN AGAINST).

Another piece of the Great Purge was Marshal Choibalsang's grudge against his colleagues and rivals. Of the 11 members of the party presidium elected in 1934, two died before the purges began (MARSHAL DEMID and Eldebwachir) and were posthumously denounced, while all the others except for Choibalsang were executed as spies and traitors between 1937 and 1940.

However, the purge's fundamental cause was the extension to Mongolia of Stalinism. Following the methods used in Russia, thousands upon thousands of Mongols in all walks of life, many of whom had dedicated their lives to the regime, were tortured into signing grotesque tales of espionage and wrecking before being executed.

CHOIBALSANG'S RISE

After the LHÜMBE CASE (1933) of supposed Japanese espionage, with which he was at first connected, Choibalsang was exiled to Moscow. Escaping involvement by assisting in the interrogation of other suspects, in 1934 he was appointed Mongolia's deputy prime minister by Stalin's order. In February 1936 Choibalsang was appointed head of the new Interior Ministry. One-fourth of the ministry's staff, including Choibalsang's personal adviser Chopiak, were Soviet trainers. That May the procedures for arresting high government officials were loosened, although through 1936 and early 1937 the focus remained on lamas, culminating in the show trial of 23 lamas on October 4–7, 1937.

PURGES BEGIN

From July 17, 1937, arrests of "pan-Mongolists" and "Japanese spies" by the Soviet security organs began in Russia with the former prime minister GENDÜN, Buriats who had once worked in Mongolia, and with Russian embassy staff and advisers in ULAANBAATAR. In August Soviet troops in Mongolia were brought up to 30,000 men, and the Stalin's deputy security chief, M. P. Frinovskii, arrived in Ulaanbaatar. By pushing Chopiak and Choibalsang, he came up with an initial list of 115 officials to arrest in Mongolia. From September 10 mass arrests began in Ulaanbaatar in the "Gendün-Demid Case." Virtually all those arrested succumbed to torture and implicated others. On October 18–20 the first 14 cases were disposed of in a show trial at the Central Theater; all were sentenced to execution. From October 2, 1937, to April 22, 1939, a "Special Commission" headed by Choibalsang, party secretary Lubsangsharab (D. Luwsansharaw, 1900–40), and justice minister Tserindorji (G. Tserendorj) discussed 25,785 cases and ordered 20,099 executions; the remainder all received lengthy prison sentences. Choibalsang's work on this commission was guided throughout by Chopiak's replacement, Golubchik. The destruction of the monasteries continued apace, as did attacks on Mongolia's KAZAKHS and Buriat Mongols, largely emigrés from the Soviet Union (see BURIATS OF MONGOLIA AND INNER MONGOLIA). Mongolia's Inner

Mongolian expatriates, with their ties to their Japanese-occupied homeland, were virtually exterminated, and the Chinese workers were decimated. A similar purge was also going on in Buriatia at the same time.

FINAL STAGES

From August 1938 to January 1939 Marshal Choibalsang left Mongolia for medical recuperation in the Soviet Union. While there, Stalin's crony Kliment Voroshilov instructed Choibalsang to have Lubsangsharab arrest Prime Minister AMUR and then himself arrest Lubsangsharab and other officials who had been directing the purges. The arrest of Amur took place on March 7. On April 20 newly arrived Soviet instructors explained at a national conference of Interior Ministry personnel that the purges had gone too far, pinning the blame on previously selected Mongolian and Soviet operatives. In July–August the remaining key witnesses of the purges, Lubsangsharab, certain Interior Minister leaders, and their Soviet advisers, together with the last 1921 revolutionaries Losal (D. Losol, 1890–1940) and Dogsum (D. Dogsom, 1884–1941), were arrested, deported to the Soviet Union, and executed. In 1940 Justice Minister Tserindorji and a number of recently promoted top officials were arrested so as to open the way for even younger, Soviet-educated, and presumably totally loyal officials. Repression would continue, but the Great Purge was over.

RESULTS

The Great Purge destroyed the previous governing elite and opened the way for a new generation of Soviet-educated, and often Russian-married, officials, such as YUM-JAAGIIN TSEDENBAL. Special persecution against Inner Mongolians and Buriats nativized the ranks of Mongolia's white-collar intelligentsia, while that against the Chinese nativized the working class.

See also REVOLUTIONARY PERIOD.

Further reading: Baabar [Bat-Erdene Batbayar], trans. D. Sühjargalmaa, S. Bürenbayar, H. Hulan, and N. Tuya et al, ed. C. Kaplonski, *Twentieth Century Mongolia* (Cambridge: White Horse Press, 1999); D. Dashpurev and S. K. Soni. *Reign of Terror in Mongolia, 1920–1990* (New Delhi: South Asia Publishers, 1992); Shagdariin Sandag and Harry H. Kendall, *Poisoned Arrows: The Stalin-Choibalsang Mongolian Massacres, 1921–1941* (Boulder, Colo.: Westview Press, 2000).

Great Shabi (Shav') The Great Shabi of the Jibzundamba Khutugtu constituted the personal subjects of the great INCARNATE LAMA who supported his monastic establishment. The Great Shabi began with the donation of 108 persons by the nobility to the FIRST JIBZUNDAMBA KHUTUGTU (1635–1723) at his enthronement in 1639. The donated persons, whether lamas or laymen, were all considered disciples (*shabi;* modern, *shawi*) of the "Holy

One" (Bogda). Shabi "disciples" was the general term for monastic serfs; the estate of the JIBZUNDAMBA KHUTUGTU, being by far the largest in Khalkha, was called the "Great Shabi" (*Yekhe Shabi*; modern *Ikh shawi*).

The Great Shabi rapidly expanded, particularly in the 18th century. Donations to the Bogda from 1719 to 1811 totaled 17,000 persons. The Great Shabi reached 69,698 persons in 1764 and achieved its maximum size of 111,466 by 1825. The great majority of these donations came from Khalkha's Tüshiyetü Khan province, with some from Setsen Khan province and SHILIIN GOL league in Inner Mongolia. Only small numbers came from western Khalkha. While most *shabi* were in eastern Khalkha, only the DARKHAD of modern Khöwsgöl province, all *shabi*, had their own exclusive territory.

Shabi duties included annual payments directly to the Office of the ERDENI SHANGDZODBA (treasury of the Bogda), called the "offering tea," in-kind payments, and labor services to monasteries as well as occasional expenses connected with special services, invitation of a new Bogda from Tibet, and so on. Like the serfs (*khamjilga*) of secular lords, the Great Shabi, too, had to pay any private debts of the Bogda. The Great Shabi was divided into OTOGS (camp districts), originally 12 but numbering 114 by 1830. The *otog*s, each headed by a lay *zaisang*, were themselves divided into 50s, or *bag*s (teams) and 10s. Until the fall of the Qing, the Great Shabi used the old law code, KHALKHA JIRUM, alongside the Qing codes.

The status of *shabi* was an attractive one. Lay *shabi* could nomadize anywhere within the four Khalkha AIMAGS and were free of the onerous postroad, guard, and militia duty of the taxpayers (*albatu*). In 1837 the Qing administration prescribed that able-bodied *albatu* could no longer be donated, only *khamjilga*, slaves, bastard sons, children, or the aged. These measures and the general decline in Mongolian population reduced the Great Shabi to 55,479 in 1909.

Under the Bogda's independent theocratic government after 1911, however, the Great Shabi's ranks again swelled, reaching 89,392 by 1921. Petitions to enter the *shabi* were now rarely rejected. Wealthy persons eagerly entered the Great Shabi to gain tax exemption.

After the 1921 REVOLUTION the Great Shabi offices were made elective in 1923. With the first provincial (*aimag*) election of 1925 the Great Shabi was renamed Delger Yekhe Uula province, with its territory confined to the DARKHAD lands and neighboring Khöwsgöl Uriyangkhai banners. All connection to the monastic estates was abolished.

See also KHÖWSGÖL PROVINCE; REVOLUTIONARY PERIOD; THEOCRATIC PERIOD; TUVANS.

Great Wall of China   *See* MING DYNASTY.

Green Palace   *See* PALACES OF THE BOGDA KHAN.

Guihua   *See* HÖHHOT.

Guisui   *See* HÖHHOT.

Guo Daofu   *See* MERSE.

Güüshi Khan, Törö-Baikhu (Gushri) (b. 1582, r. 1642–1655) *Oirat Mongolian ruler who established the supremacy of the "Yellow Hat" order and the Dalai Lamas in Tibet*

Güüshi Khan was born Törö-Baikhu, the third son of Akhai Khatun, who had married two cousins, both chiefs of the Oirats' Khoshud tribe, in succession: Yadai Chingsang and Khanai Noyan Khongghor. Her five sons by different fathers were collectively known as the "Five Tigers." Törö-Baikhu was the son of Khanai Noyan Khongghor. At age 12 he had already won renown in battle against the Turkestanis. In 1630 he succeeded his elder brother Baibaghas as chief of the Khoshud with the title Güüshi Taishi. In 1634 an appeal came to the OIRATS in Z üngharia from the Fifth Dalai Lama, Ngag-dbang Blo-bzang rGya-mtsho (1617–82), and the dGe-lugs-pa ("Yellow Hat") monasteries for help against Karma-pa ("Red Hat") and Bon-po (the non-Buddhist religion of Tibet) partisans such as TSOGTU TAIJI. In response Güüshi Taishi invaded Kökenuur (northeast Tibet) in winter 1636 with 10,000 men. On new year's day (January 26, 1637) his men crushed Tsogtu Taiji at Ulaan-Khoshuu. From 1639 Güüshi proceeded methodically to destroy the Dalai Lama's enemies: the Bon-po king of Be-ri (near Garzê) in winter 1640–41, the king of gTsang at gZhis-ka-rtse (modern Xigazê) in 1642, and finally rKong-po (near modern Gongbo'gyamda). On April 13, 1642, the Dalai Lama proclaimed Güüshi king (Mongolian, khan) of Tibet. Güüshi Khan died in January 1655, and his son Dayan succeeded him.

See also UPPER MONGOLS.

Güyüg Khan (Guyuk) (b. 1206, r. 1246–1248) *Chinggis Khan's grandson and a strict and intelligent emperor, Güyüg Khan was unable to achieve much due to his ill health and divisions in the Mongolian ruling family.*

GÜYÜG'S EARLY LIFE AND CORONATION

The MONGOL EMPIRE's first khan in the third generation from its founder, CHINGGIS KHAN, Güyüg Khan was also the first khan to face significant disaffection among his relatives. Güyüg was the eldest son of ÖGEDEI KHAN and his principal wife TÖREGENE. Little is known of his early life. His wife was OGHUL-QAIMISH, a woman of MERKID origin. In 1233 his father, Ögedei, assigned him and his maternal cousin Alchidai the task of destroying the Eastern Xia regime, which a rebellious Jin official had created in Manchuria in 1215. The Eastern Xia regime was not strong, and the two dispatched it in a few months. In 1235 Ögedei assigned two of his sons, Güyüg and Qadan, to join the great western expedition against the QIPCHAQS and their allies, the Russians, the BULGHARS, and the OSSETES (Alans). Güyüg participated in the siege of the Russian city of Ryazan' in 1237 and in the lengthy siege of the Ossetian capital at Magas in 1239–40.

While this battle experience gave Güyüg the kind of stature necessary for a future khan, the campaign also began the feud with BATU (d. 1255) that would blight Güyüg's reign. Batu, the son of CHINGGIS KHAN's eldest son JOCHI, had not had great success in his sieges. When Batu presumed on his seniority to receive an extra portion during a feast, the SECRET HISTORY OF THE MONGOLS tells how first Güyüg's nephew Büri, then Güyüg, and finally one of Güyüg's men, Harghasun Noyan, ridiculed Batu as an effeminate weakling. Batu appealed to Ögedei to restrain his sons; when Güyüg returned for an audience, Ögedei harshly criticized him and then sent him and Harghasun back to Batu for judgment. Büri he dispatched to his father, CHA'ADAI. Other sources show that the dispute was real, yet also that Güyüg did not return to Mongolia during Ögedei's life. Ögedei recalled both him and Möngke, son of Tolui, sometime around December 1240 to January 1241.

When Ögedei died in December 1241, Güyüg had apparently still not returned to the court. Güyüg's mother, Töregene, took over as regent and began to persecute Ögedei's officials. Ögedei had expressed his wish that his favorite grandson, Shiremün, be his successor, but given Shiremün's age and inexperience this bequest got no support. Töregene wished to elect Güyüg khan, and the only other serious contender was Güyüg's sickly younger brother, KÖTEN, in the Tangut area. Given this lack of real opposition, it is hard to understand why the QURILTAI (assembly) was delayed until 1246. The most likely reason is that Töregene hoped to fix the direction of imperial policy in a congenial direction before calling the quriltai, while Güyüg for his part delayed his coronation until he secured independent support among the princes and so would not be merely his mother's puppet. When Güyüg was formally elected khan on August 24, 1246, several officials that Töregene had tried to dismiss, such as CHINQAI, Mahmud Yalavach, and Mas'ud Beg, were back in office, and Töregene soon departed west to her own ORDO (palace-tent) in the Emil valley.

GÜYÜG'S REIGN

Once the coronation was concluded, Güyüg demonstrated that he would follow his father's policies, not his mother's. Over his mother's vehement objections, he had one of her intimates arrested and executed for bewitching Köten, and 'Abd-ur-Rahman, Töregene's choice for governor of North China, was also executed. Of the provincial officials appointed under Töregene, only the Oirat official ARGHUN AQA remained. Güyüg handled other challenges

to his power carefully. Temüge Odchigin, Chinggis Khan's youngest and sole remaining brother, had tried to seize the throne during Töregene's regency; Güyüg had this delicate case investigated by Hordu (of the Jochid line) and Möngke, and they had Odchigin executed. The Ögedeids and Cha'adaids always had a close connection, but CHA'ADAI's family was now headed by a child. To secure his base, Güyüg replaced this child with Yisü-Möngke, a close friend.

In the Secret History of the Mongols Ögedei scolds his son as a self-confident, even arrogant, disciplinarian who ruled his troops with fear. Sources during his reign describe him as strict and very intelligent but rather morose and sickly. Heavy drinking did not improve his health. Claiming it would improve his condition, he left QARA-QORUM to move the court to his father's appanage on the Emil and Qobaq (Emin and Hobok) Rivers. The plan increased his personal security at the cost of political isolation. Like his father, Güyüg strove to make a name for himself and win favor by heroic generosity, emptying the treasury with his gifts. He also proposed to complete Ögedei's campaigns by warring against the SONG DYNASTY in South China and reducing the 'ABBASID CALIPHATE in Iraq and the fortresses of the "Assassins," or ISMA'ILIS, in Iran to obedience.

Religiously, Güyüg departed from his father's policy. Unlike earlier Mongol rulers, Güyüg allowed Christian prayers to be offered openly in his ordo. Ögedei had carefully balanced three bureaucratic cultures: the largely Christian eastern Turk network, the Islamic group around Mahmud Yalavach (see MAHMUD YALAVACH AND MAS'UD BEG), and the North Chinese. While he restored Mahumd Yalavach and his associates to positions in the provinces and treated ZHANG ROU and other Chinese commanders favorably, Güyüg's key advisers were all in the first group: his secretaries, the Uighur Christian Chinqai and the Uighur Buddhist, Bala, and his tutor and judge (JARGHUCHI), the NAIMAN Christian Qadaq. His physicians were also Christian. Muslim writers considered him pro-Christian and hostile to Islam, yet in his letter to the pope, Güyüg firmly rejected the papal claim to speak for God, and he asserted the Mongol Empire's divine mandate of world rule.

While the empire seemed to accept Güyüg as khan, Batu, head of the Jochid line, had not attended the quriltai due to gout. His absence allowed suspicions to fester. Under Ögedei the Jochid house had nominated or at least approved all the military and civil officials west of the Amu Dar'ya. Töregene had broken this tradition by appointing Arghun Aqa. Güyüg ruptured it further by appointing Eljigidei, a former officer in Ögedei's KESHIG (imperial guard) and the father of Batu's old irritant Harghasun Noyan. Eljigidei would command the troops of CHORMAQAN in western Iran and Armenia. As Güyüg began to move west to join Eljigidei, rumors circulated in the ruling family that he was actually aiming against Batu. While en route in April 1248, his health deteriorated, and he died at Qum-Senggir. Güyüg's empress, Oghul-Qaimish, assisted by Chinqai, Bala, and Qadaq at her *ordo* and Eljigidei in the west, took power as regent.

See also BUDDHISM IN THE MONGOL EMPIRE; CENSUS IN THE MONGOL EMPIRE; CENTRAL EUROPE AND THE MONGOLS; CHRISTIANITY IN THE MONGOL EMPIRE; INDIA AND THE MONGOLS; ISLAM IN THE MONGOL EMPIRE; JOHN OF PLANO CARPINI; KOREA AND THE MONGOL EMPIRE; MANCHURIA AND THE MONGOL EMPIRE; PROVINCES IN THE MONGOL EMPIRE; RELIGIOUS POLICY IN THE MONGOL EMPIRE; TAOISM IN THE MONGOL EMPIRE; WESTERN EUROPE AND THE MONGOLS.

H

haan   *See* KHAN.

Hafeng'a   *See* KHAFUNGGA.

Ha-feng-a   *See* KHAFUNGGA.

Hai-hsi   *See* HAIXI MONGOL AND TIBETAN AUTONOMOUS PREFECTURE.

Haixi Mongol and Tibetan Autonomous Prefecture (Hai-hsi)   Located in the northwest of China's Qinghai province, Haixi covers 328,970 square kilometers (127,016 square miles) on the northern edge of the Tibetan plateau. In its center lies the Great Tsaidam (Qaidam) Basin, about 2,600–3,000 meters (8,500–9,800 feet) above sea level and rimmed by mountains rising to over 5,500 meters (18,050 feet). Haixi also administers the noncontiguous Tanggula district, a virtually uninhabited district on the borders of the Tibet Autonomous Region. The Tsaidam is somewhat warmer and drier than other lands in Tibet. Haixi's capital is Delingha township.

In 1982 Haixi's population was 272,178, of which 18,682, or 7 percent, were Mongol, 9 percent Tibetan, and 78 percent Chinese. The Mongols inhabit the eastern counties of Ulaan (Ulan) and Dulaan (Dulan) and the Utu-Mören district of Golmuud (Golmud). Tibetans live in Tianjun, Dulaan, and Tanggula districts. In 1982 2,283,000 head of livestock grazed Haixi, including 1,568,000 sheep, 424,000 goats, 223,000 cattle, 38,900 horses, and 25,000 camels. Among the Mongols 93 percent were nomadic herders.

The UPPER MONGOLS of Haixi were traditionally organized into eight appanages, or BANNERS, all of the KHOSHUD tribe. From 1929 Hui (Chinese-speaking Muslim) and Han (ethnic Chinese) farmers from eastern Qinghai began cultivating land, bringing 7,300 hectares (18,040 acres) under plow by 1949. From 1935 KAZAKHS from Xinjiang settled in Haixi, frequently plundering the Mongols. After the entry of the Chinese People's Liberation Army, Dulaan county was declared a Mongol autonomous county in 1952, and Kazakh and Tibetan autonomous counties were proclaimed the next year. In 1954 the autonomous counties were subsumed into the Haixi Mongol, Tibetan, and Kazakh Autonomous prefecture. In 1984, after the small Kazakh population was returned to Xinjiang, the prefecture was redesignated only a Mongol and Tibetan autonomous unit.

Since 1956 oil, gold, potassium and other salts, borax, asbestos, lead, and zinc have all been extracted from the Tsaidam. Paved road construction in the Tsaidam began in 1947, and the Qinghai-Tibet Railway reached Golmuud in 1981. The previously virtually uninhabited Tsaidam has been divided into the townships of Mangnai, Lenghu, Dachaidan (Da Qaidam), and Golmuud city, all almost entirely inhabited by immigrant Han Chinese. By 1982 cultivated acreage, mostly in western Dulaan county, had expanded to 475,000 hectares (1,173,700 acres), but desertification has became a major problem.

In the 1990s illegal private gold miners, organized by Hui syndicates, operated widely in southeast Haixi. In 1999 controversy canceled international funding for a plan to dam the Xiangride River and resettle in Dulaan county 58,000 Hui and Chinese farmers from eastern Qinghai.

See also DESERTIFICATION AND PASTURE DEGRADATION; SUBEI MONGOL AUTONOMOUS COUNTY.

Halh *See* KHALKHA.

Hangai *See* KHANGAI RANGE.

Harchin *See* KHARACHIN.

Harghasun Darqan (1257–1308/9) *Mongol aristocrat who delivered the throne to Haishan and Ayurbarwada in the disputed succession of 1307*

Harghasun's ancestor, Kishiliq of the Oronar, had warned CHINGGIS KHAN of ONG KHAN's treacherous attack and received the perpetual title of DARQAN (exempt). Entering QUBILAI KHAN's court as a KESHIG centurion in 1272, Harghasun was appointed to the Court of the Imperial Clan, the empire's supreme judicial organ, in 1285, where he cut back executions by as much as three-fourths. From 1291 to 1298 he served as manager (*pingzhang*) of Huguang province, stretching from Wuhan to Vietnam, suppressing widespread banditry. Under Emperor Temür (1294–1307) he rose to be right grand councillor in the secretariat. Friendly to Confucian scholars, he opened the first Confucian temple in DAIDU (modern Beijing). During Temür's final illness Harghasun nursed him personally while commanding the *keshig*. After his death one faction hoped to enthrone Ananda, the Muslim prince of Anxi, but Harghasun sent messengers evading their blockade and summoning to Daidu the brothers Haishan from Mongolia and Ayurbarwada (with their mother Targi) from Shanxi, meanwhile holding off demands to appoint Ananda's supporter, Empress Bulughan of the Baya'ud, as regent. When Ayurbarwada and Targi reached the Daidu suburbs, Harghasun executed the opposition leaders and Prince Ananda. After Haishan's (1307–11) election as khan, however, Harghasun fell from favor and was appointed to the new QARA-QORUM branch secretariat, where he resettled refugees and revived military farms.

Harqin *See* KHARACHIN.

Harqin Zuoyi Monggol Zizhixian *See* KHARACHIN.

Hazaras Descendants in part of the Mongol Qara'unas, the Hazaras form a large and distinctive ethnic minority in Afghanistan.

ORIGINS

The modern Hazaras stem from the merger of the ruling Mongol class of QARA'UNAS with their mountain Tajik subjects. The Hazaras are first found under that name (Persian for 1,000, from the Mongol military's DECIMAL ORGANIZATION) in the histories of Babur (1483–1530) and Abu'l Fazl ibn Mubarak (1551–1602), who describe them as important nomads (*aimaq,* or modern Mongolian

AIMAG "tribe") dominating Afghanistan from Meydan to Balkh and from Ghazni to Qandahar. Although they had been ruling over Tajik mountaineers and mixing with Turkish nomads since 1230 or so, some of them still spoke Mongolian. Abu'l Fazl mentions that those of Meydan and Behsud (from the Mongolian clan name Besüd) were already in the process of settling. Allying in the 17th century with Iran's Safavid dynasty (1499–1736), Hazara emirs converted to Twelver (Imami) Shi'ism, isolating them religiously from their neighbors.

DISTRIBUTION AND TRADITIONAL LIFE

By the 19th century the main body of Hazaras, dwelling in the Hazarajat (Bamiyan and Oruzgan provinces and vicinity), were purely sedentary farmers speaking Persian. An emotional Shi'ite religiosity was widespread. While the former nomadic rulers had settled and adopted the culture of their subjects, the Hazara *mir*s (from emir, commander) formed powerful endogamous "bones," or lineages, that controlled most of the land and resided in *qal'a,* or mud-brick fortresses. The Hazaragi dialect of Persian still contains a number of Mongol-origin words not found in any other language of Afghanistan, principally for secondary body parts, animal and plant names, and geographical features. The physical appearance of the Hazarajat Hazaras is distinctly Mongol, although more Middle Eastern faces are not unknown. The term *hazara* also designates a number of smaller, lesser-known groups. Of these the Sheikh-'Ali Hazaras, dwelling from Bamiyan to Pol-e Khomri, are seminomadic, dwelling in the summer in YURTS. Although predominantly Sunni with an Isma'ili minority, they identify with the Hazaras. The Hazaras numbered 1,403,000, or 9 percent, of Afghanistan's population in 1989; recent exiles in Pakistan have been estimated at 17,000 to 70,000 persons.

MODERN HISTORY

As the Afghan (Pashtun) rulers in Kabul solidified their rule over modern Afghanistan, Hazara rebellions broke out in 1888–90, 1892, and 1893. The Afghan ruler Abdur-Rahman (1880–1901) responded with harsh repression, labeling the Shi'ite Hazaras infidels and importing Pashtun settlers into Hazarajat. Thousands of Hazaras emigrated to Iran and British India. In the 20th century Hazara migrants formed mostly proletarian communities in all major cities of Afghanistan, especially the capital, Kabul. After the Communist coup d'état of April 1978, Hazara insurgents under the Shura-e Ittifaq (Solidarity Council) freed all Hazarajat except Bamiyan from Communist control, maintaining an implicit agreement of mutual noninterference with the Soviet occupation forces. Iranian-educated clerics replaced the *mir*s as leaders. From 1982 civil war raged between Iranian-financed and native factions, resolved in 1987 by the formation of an Iranian-supported umbrella organization, Hizb-e Wahdat-e Islami (Islamic Unity Party). The Hizb-e Wahdat joined the victorious Mujahideen coalition government that overthrew the Communist government in 1991, but the coalition warlords' massacre of hundred of Hazaras in the Afshar ward of Kabul (February 11, 1993) shocked the Hazaras and revived conflicts over political alliances. In 1998 the Pashtun-based Sunni Taleban militia occupied Bamiyan, declaring the Hazaras to be infidels and perpetrating massacres at Yäkauläng, Robatak Pass, and elsewhere. Hezb-e Wahdat forces reoccupied Hazarajat in November 2001 as part of the Northern Alliance offensive that overthrew the Taleban regime.

See also ISLAM IN THE MONGOL EMPIRE; MOGHOLI LANGUAGE AND PEOPLE.

Further reading: Sayed Askar Mousavi, *Hazaras of Afghanistan: An Historical, Cultural, Economic and Political Study* (New York: St. Martin's Press, 1997); H. F. Schurmann, *Mongols of Afghanistan: An Ethnography of the Moghols and Related Peoples of Afghanistan* (The Hague: Mouton, 1962).

Henan Mongol Autonomous County (Ho-nan)

Located in the southeast of China's Qinghai (Kökenuur) province, Henan Mongol Autonomous County has an area of 7,000 square kilometers (2,700 square miles). Henan lies on the eastern edge of the Tibetan plateau at an altitude mostly over 3,500 meters (11,500 feet) and shares the plateau's strong sunlight, cool summers, and extremely unpredictable weather.

The total population in 1982 was 21,237, of which 18,236 persons were herders and 3,001 town dwellers. Mongols numbered 18,076, or 85 percent, in 1982. While the Mongols now speak Tibetan, many Tibetans have recently changed their designation to Mongols. About 93 percent of the territory is usable pasture, and in 1939 livestock were estimated at 223,500 head. By 1974 the increase of livestock had leveled off at around 760,000 head. Of these, 249,700 in 1984 were bovines: 80 percent yaks and 19 percent yak–common cattle hybrids. The county also had 17,500 head of eastern Tibet's fine Hequ horses.

The UPPER MONGOLS of Henan were traditionally divided into four BANNERS (appanages), three of the KHOSHUD tribe and one TORGHUD. The "Henan Princes" of the Khoshud's Front First banner were Qinghai's senior Mongol rulers and the chief lay patrons of the great Bla-brang Monastery (modern Xiahe). After 1912 the Henan princes maintained their region's autonomy against the Hui (Chinese-speaking Muslim) warlords of Gansu and Qinghai. In 1942 the ruling princess, Dashi-Tsering (c. 1918–66), married the son of the local Tibetan warlord, who was a brother of the Bla-brang INCARNATE LAMA. In 1952 she allowed the Chinese Communists to begin organizing in Henan and to suppress mostly Hui anticommunist guerrillas. In October 1954 Henan was made a directly administered autonomous county, with Dashi-tsering as chairwoman. Grassroots control was secured

only after crushing a serious Mongol insurrection against collectivization in 1958. During the Cultural Revolution of 1966–76 Red Guards hounded Dashitsering to death as a feudalist.

Further reading: Yangdon Dhondup and Hildegard Diemberger, "Tashi Tsering: The Last Mongol Queen of 'Sogpo' (Henan)," *Inner Asia* 4 (2002): 197–224.

Hentiy *See* KHENTII PROVINCE.

Herlen *See* KHERLEN RIVER.

Hiagt *See* KYAKHTA CITY.

history Mongolian history may be analyzed in terms of dynasties, religious growth, cycles of unity and disintegration, and changing social formations.

DYNASTIES

The dynastic method of periodization is useful as a general framework for placing historical events. While periodization based on social or intellectual trends (feudal society, Renaissance, and so on) are often controversial, dating by dynasties has the benefit of being relatively clear cut. The history of the MONGOLIAN PLATEAU begins with a succession of peoples from the third century B.C.E. to the ninth century C.E., each with its own ruling family. These include the XIONGNU (or Huns), the XIANBI, the ROURAN (or Avars), the TÜRK EMPIRES, and the UIGHUR EMPIRE. All these successive dynasties are best known from Chinese records, although Greek and later Arabic histories and inscriptions from the Türk and Uighur Empires valuably supplement our knowledge.

The period from 840 on was a time of disunity. The Mongolian-speaking TATARS became the main tribe on the Mongolian plateau, assimilating the Turkish-speaking tribes. The Tatars came in part under the Liao dynasty (907–1125), founded by the Inner Mongolian KITANS. After the fall of the Liao, tribes fought for control until CHINGGIS KHAN (Genghis, 1206–27) of the MONGOL TRIBE burst into world history and founded the MONGOL EMPIRE. This empire broke up in 1260 into four successor states: the YUAN DYNASTY in China, Mongolia, and the east, the CHAGHATAY KHANATE in Turkestan, the GOLDEN HORDE in Eastern Europe and Kazakhstan, and the IL-KHANATE in the Middle East.

Modern European historians first formed detailed accounts of these events from the Jesuits at the 18th-century Chinese court. Following Chinese annals European histories adopted the idea that the Mongols' own Yuan dynasty did not really begin until the final conquest of all China in 1279 and ended with their expulsion from China in 1368, to be succeeded by the Ming who ruled to 1644. Problematic even for China, this "short" Yuan dynasty scheme makes no sense for Mongolia.

After the empire's breakup the Mongols ruled China as the Yuan dynasty until 1368. Despite their expulsion from China, the Mongol emperors in Mongolia continued to rule in the name of the Yuan from 1368 to 1634; this is the NORTHERN YUAN DYNASTY.

In 1636 the Inner Mongolians surrendered to the Manchu QING DYNASTY, which in 1644 also conquered China's MING DYNASTY (1368–1644). The KHALKHA (Outer Mongolians) surrendered to the Qing in 1691, and the Qing Empire reached its height in 1755 with the destruction of its last enemies, the ZÜNGHARS (a branch of the OIRATS, or West Mongols). The Qing dynasty ruled Mongolia until the rebellions of 1911–12 forced the emperor to abdicate, and Mongolia regained its independence in the 1911 RESTORATION.

From 1911 to 1921 the great INCARNATE LAMA, the Jibzundamba Khutugtu, was the unquestioned supreme authority in Mongolia proper, or Outer Mongolia, although the country's international status was subject to several sharp changes. This period can thus be called the THEOCRATIC PERIOD in Mongolian history.

After the 1921 REVOLUTION Mongolia was under a Soviet-supported People's Government with the Jibzundamba Khutugtu as the head of state. Only in 1924, with the death of the Jibzundamba Khutugtu, was a people's republic proclaimed. This MONGOLIAN PEOPLE'S REPUBLIC lasted from 1924 to 1992, yet the real break with the past came not in 1924 but through the destruction of organized religion and the purges of 1937–39. From 1921 to 1940 can be considered the REVOLUTIONARY PERIOD, when Mongolia's government was transformed from a Soviet-supported and vaguely left-wing junta to a genuinely Communist dictatorship of one man. This dictatorship lasted until the 1990 DEMOCRATIC REVOLUTION, which resulted in a new 1992 CONSTITUTION renaming the country the STATE OF MONGOLIA and guaranteeing a democratic system.

RELIGIONS AND IDEOLOGIES

Another way to look at the long span of Mongolian history is through the successively dominant religions or ideologies. The impact of world religions on the nomads of the Mongolian plateau began with the Türk Empires' acquaintance with Buddhism, the Uighur Empire's adoption of Manicheism, and the adoption of Christianity in the 11th century by the KEREYID and ÖNGGÜD tribes. Under the Mongol Empire many religions competed to win over the great khan, although SHAMANISM remained the leading religion at court (see RELIGIOUS POLICY IN THE MONGOL EMPIRE). After 1260 Tibetan-rite Buddhism became the court religion of the Yuan dynasty. During the Northern Yuan dynasty Buddhism's role declined, until in 1578 ALTAN KHAN met the Third Dalai Lama, beginning what Mongolian historians called the SECOND CONVERSION of the Mongols to Buddhism.

From about 1635 to 1921 Tibetan-rite Buddhism of the "Yellow Hat" (dGe-lugs-pa) order was the unques-tioned official religion of the Mongols. This dominance influenced every aspect of Mongolian culture, including literature, social life, family structure, language, folk poetry, food, and even practices of shamans and others who rejected Buddhism (see TIBETAN CULTURE IN MONGOLIA). This was the Buddhist era in Mongolian history.

From 1921 to 1940 the established Buddhist church and the new revolutionary government competed for dominance. At first many government figures hoped to preserve some place for religion in the new society, but after 1928 radical new leaders acceded to Soviet pressure and began a campaign that would eventually destroy the established church (see BUDDHISM, CAMPAIGN AGAINST). From 1940 to 1990 Mongolia was a monolithically Communist society, dominated by Soviet Russian culture and ideology. From the late 1980s Mongolia began to open up to non-Soviet influences, and with the fall of the Communist government have come a Buddhist revival, new religions, European, American, and Asian-Pacific pop cultures, and new nationalism, thus creating a mixed pluralistic culture.

CYCLES AND SOCIAL EVOLUTION

In the 1920s and 1930s a number of scholars began to propose macrohistorical models of social change in Mongolia. Such models can be divided into two types: cyclical and social evolutionary.

The cyclical model treated nomadism as a distinctive type of human society, one in which class divisions, state formation, and attendant social change are dependent not on internal but external factors. In this view nomadic states were primarily methods of extorting goods from the wealthier sedentary civilizations, particularly China, whether through exploiting the TRIBUTE SYSTEM or through conquest. Thus, premodern Mongolian history was essentially a series of cycles in which the steppe or the sown alternated dominance. Mongolia's modern history from the Qing era on was thus seen as a radical break with the past induced by new technology and new social changes. Major works in this school include Owen Lattimore's *Inner Asian Frontiers of China* (1940), Sechin Jagchid's *Peace, War, and Trade along the Great Wall* (Chinese edition 1972, English edition 1989), and Thomas Barfield's *Perilous Frontier* (1989).

By contrast, the Russian Mongolist Boris Ya. Valdimirtsov, in a work published posthumously in 1934, analyzed Mongolian society as a type of "nomadic feudalism." To him nomadism did not define a peculiar type of society but was instead compatible with a feudalism analogous to that of Europe. Feudalism, he believed, already existed under the Mongol Empire and continued past the fall of the Qing dynasty. While Vladimirtsov's views have been ascribed to Soviet Marxist influences, they actually flow out of his prerevolutionary work and the general trends of Russian Mongolian studies. While European, American, and pre-1949 Chinese writers usually worked from Chinese sources on the early steppe empires before the Qing, Russia's pioneering Mongolists, including Vladimirtsov, all began with deep immersion in the contemporary society and culture of Mongols, BURIATS, and KALMYKS, whose aristocratic social structure the cyclical school tended to dismiss as a late product of foreign domination.

After World War II Vladimirtsov's view of premodern Mongolian society as basically feudal became the consensus in the Soviet Union, Mongolia, China, and Japan. This view was expressed in Tayama Shigeru's comprehensive 1954 study of Mongolian society under the Northern Yuan and Qing. In editions of the *History of the Mongolian People's Republic* from 1955 on (English translation 1973), Soviet and Mongolian editors placed this concept in a comprehensive Marxist-Leninist analysis of Mongolian social evolution. Thus, Mongolia's primitive communal society began to break down under the Xiongnu in the third century B.C.E., forming the first early feudal state, the Rouran Empire, in the fifth century C.E. Under the Mongol Empire feudal relations deepened, while aggressive wars of conquest damaged productive forces. The result was first the "feudal disintegration" of the 15th–16th centuries and then increasing exploitation under the Manchu yoke. The national liberation movement struggled in vain with the clerical and lay feudalists and foreign imperialists until the 1921 Revolution and Soviet assistance put Mongolia on the road of noncapitalist development to socialism, which was achieved with collectivization of the countryside in 1960.

In China a new version of this Marxist-Leninist social evolutionary viewpoint developed by the late 1970s. This school emphasizes the discontinuity between the earlier steppe empires and the developing Mongol tribe. The Mongols proper were in a primitive communal society until class differentiation from 1050 to 1200 produced an early slave state under Chinggis Khan. The conquest of foreign feudal regimes, especially China, accelerated the advance toward feudalism, which under QUBILAI KHAN (1260–94) replaced the slave society. While this view rightly emphasize the rapid social change both among the preimperial Mongols and after the conquest and the significance of slavery and war captives in early Mongol society, any analogy with Greco-Roman slavery noted by Marx and Engels seems very forced.

The breakdown of the post–World War II ideological barriers opens the possibility for rethinking both social evolutionary and cyclical schemes for understanding Mongolian history. A more flexible and realistic understanding of the interaction between exogenous and endogenous forces also seems needed. Cultural anthropological approaches, such as Roberte Hamayon's ambitious 1990 analysis of shamanist Mongolian culture in terms of society divided into moieties engaged in marriage exchange, offer fresh new views.

See also ANIMAL HUSBANDRY AND NOMADISM; APPANAGE SYSTEM; KINSHIP SYSTEM; SOCIAL CLASSES IN THE MONGOL EMPIRE; SOCIAL CLASSES IN THE QING PERIOD.

Further reading: Thomas J. Barfield, *Perilous Frontier: Nomadic Empires and China* (Cambridge, Mass.: Basil Blackwell, 1989); Bat-Ochir Bold, *Mongolian Nomadic Society: A Reconstruction of the 'Medieval' History of Mongolia* (Richmond, Surrey: Curzon Press, 2001); Roberte Hamayon, *La Chasse à l'ame: Equisse d'une théorie du chamanisme siberien* (Nanterre: Société d'éthnologie, 1990); *History of the Mongolian People's Republic* (Moscow: Progress Publishers, 1973); Sechin Jagchid and Paul Hyer, *Mongolia's Culture and Society* (Boulder, Colo.: Westview Press, 1979); Owen Lattimore, *Inner Asian Frontiers of China* (1940; rpt., Oxford: Oxford University Press, 1988); B. Vladimirtsov, *Le Régime social des Mongols: Le féodalisme nomade,* trans. Michel Carsow (Paris: A. Maisonneuve, 1948).

History of the World Conqueror (Ta'rikh-i jahan gusha) The *History of the World Conqueror,* written in Persian, is invaluable not only for its detailed picture of the Mongol conquests and administration but also for its view of the role of nomads in Islamic history. The Persian landholder and bureaucrat 'ALA'UD-DIN ATA-MALIK JUVAINI began his *Ta'rikh-i jahan gusha,* or *History of the World Conqueror,* during his first visit to the Mongol capital of QARA-QORUM in 1252–53 as a young scribe in the entourage of his father and the Mongol governor ARGHUN AQA. The narrative reaches up to the destruction of the Isma'ili fortresses in 1256, although isolated pieces of information date from as late as 1259. Juvaini certainly planned to write more; spaces are left blank in one autograph manuscript, and several promised chapters were never written. He may have broken off his writing due to the press of business attendant on the governorship of Baghdad that he received in 1259, but more likely he found writing about living khans to involve too much sacrifice of honesty to make the task worthwhile.

The *History of the World Conqueror* is a classic example of the ornate style of Persian composition, full of extended similes, puns, and poetry, both original and quoted. Structurally it consists of three parts tracing 1) the rise of CHINGGIS KHAN and his successors ÖGEDEI KHAN and GÜYÜG KHAN from poverty and obscurity to world dominion; 2) the fall of the KHORAZM shahs, and with them Iran as a whole, from wealth and glory to humiliation and destruction; and 3) the rise of MÖNGKE KHAN and the Toluid branch of the Chinggisid family to the khanship, displacing the descendants of Ögedei. He also digresses on the history of the UIGHURS and the ISMA'ILIS. As this summary makes clear, the ultimate theme of the work is the instability of human affairs. Juvaini believed deeply in the divine predestination of all events, including those that were the most catastrophic for Islam, such as the Mongol invasion. While he pointed out certain advantages that Mongol rule was bringing to orthodox Islam, such as the resettlement of Muslims in

Mongolia and China and the destruction of the Isma'ili "Heretics," his belief in God's ultimate inscrutability freed him from the need to palliate the disaster, and he described in harrowing detail both the massacres of the conquest and the rampant maladministration of Mongol rule. Only the third part, on the rise of the serving emperor Möngke, sometimes degenerates into the flattery of the court historian.

Juvaini's history was widely read in the Persian world. His successor as historian of the Mongols, RASHID-UD-DIN FAZL-ULLAH, incorporated in both Persian and Arabic large parts of the *History of the World Conqueror* into his encyclopedic *Jami'al-tawarikh*, or COMPENDIUM OF CHRONICLES, with editing to match his own plain style and differing point of view. In this form Juvaini's historical accomplishment reached an even wider readership.

See also ISLAMIC SOURCES ON THE MONGOL EMPIRE.

Further reading: 'Ala'ud-Din Ata-Malik Juvaini, *The History of the World Conqueror,* 2 vols., trans. John Andrew Boyle (Cambridge, Mass.: Harvard University Press, 1958).

Hoboksar *See* KHOBOGSAIR MONGOL AUTONOMOUS COUNTY.

Hö'elün *See* Ö'ELÜN ÜJIN.

Höhhot (Huhhot, Kökeqota, Khökhkhot, Huhehaote; Guisui) First built by Altan Khan in the 16th century, Höhhot had become a provincial Chinese frontier town before being chosen in 1954 as the capital of China's Inner Mongolian Autonomous Region. The name, from Mongolian Khökhe-Khota, means "Blue Town." Höhhot is situated on the Tümed plain in central Inner Mongolia at slightly over 1,000 meters (3,280 feet) above sea level. The level and well-watered plain abuts the Huang (Yellow) River and is separated from the MONGOLIAN PLATEAU to the north by the Daqing Shan Mountains. Average temperatures range from 21.8°C (71.2°F) in July to –13.5°C (7.7°F) in January. The average annual precipitation is 426.1 millimeters (16.8 inches).

POPULATION AND ECONOMY

Administratively, Höhhot municipality includes three urban districts, the suburban district, Tümed Left Banner (Tumd Zuoqi), and Tohtoh county. Covering 6,100 square kilometers (2,355 square miles), the municipality has 1,441,641 people of whom 132,659 are Mongols. Höhhot's three urban districts—New Town (Chinese, Xincheng), Yuquan (commonly called Old Town), and Huimin (Hui People)—occupy 58 square kilometers (22 square miles) and had a population of 625,900 in 1990. These include 72,900 Mongols (12 percent), 28,000 Hui (Chinese-speaking Muslims), and more than 17,000

Manchus. The Han (ethnic Chinese) are everywhere dominant, demographically, culturally, and linguistically. The suburban district occupies 2,000 square kilometers (770 square miles) and has 322,000 people, of whom Mongols form 25,000 and other nonethnic Chinese minorities 3,800.

Höhhot is Inner Mongolia's center of administration, communications, publishing and media, education, and health care. Of the region's higher education institutions, 80 percent are in Höhhot. It is also Inner Mongolia's second largest industrial center after the steel city of BAOTOU, producing 15 percent of Inner Mongolia's total industrial output. Machine tools, textiles, and food processing are the main industrial sectors.

Höhhot's Mongol population is composed of local Chinese-speaking TÜMED Mongols and auslanders who arrived after 1954 to staff the autonomous region's central administrative offices and Mongolian-language cultural organs. Since the children of the auslanders growing up in Höhhot's Chinese-speaking urban environment generally cannot communicate effectively in Mongolian, new Mongolian-language teachers, broadcasters, editors, and so on are continually being brought into Höhhot from Inner Mongolia's rural areas.

HISTORY

Höhhot began as one of several small towns built on the Tümed plain under the Mongol ruler ALTAN KHAN (1508–82) from 1557 on. Altan Khan's Tümeds had long been at least semiagricultural, and the khan attracted religious, economic, and political refugees from China and patronized Buddhism.

In 1575 the Chinese MING DYNASTY bestowed on one of Altan Khan's towns the title Guihua, "Return to Culture." Guihua was called Höhhot in Mongolian. In Guihua Altan Khan and his successors constructed many temples: Yeke Juu (Great Monastery, Chinese, Dazhao, 1579), Shireetü Juu (1602), and Five-Pagoda Monastery (Chinese, Wutasi, 1727). A small fortress was built in the north of the built-up area. The fortress and temples were the nucleus of Höhhot's "Old Town," or Yuquan district. Hui merchants gathered north of the gate of Guihua's fortress, building a mosque in 1693 and forming the nucleus of the modern Hui Peoples' district. In the 18th and 19th centuries, Guihua was a hub of caravan trade with Outer Mongolia.

In 1735–39 the QING DYNASTY built a large garrison town, Suiyuan (Rule the Distant), about 3 kilometers (2 miles) northeast of Guihua. The town's *jiangjun*, or general in chief (*see* AMBAN) supervised southwestern Inner Mongolia with a garrison of EIGHT BANNERS bannermen. Suiyuan boasted a regular grid of wide streets, unlike Guihua's warren of winding lanes, but Guihua remained the commercial center.

In 1913 the government of the new Republic of China unified Guihua and Suiyuan as Guisui. Although

Five-Pagoda Monastery (Chinese, Wutasi) 1727, in Höhhot *(Courtesy of Christopher Atwood)*

the Mongolian caravan trade declined, Guisui became the seat of Suiyuan, a special region, and then (from 1928) a province covering modern southwest Inner Mongolia. In 1921–22 railroads, electricity, and telephones all came to Höhhot. In 1937, with Japanese occupation, Guisui was renamed Höhhot (Chinese, Houhecheng) and became briefly the center of PRINCE DEMCHUGDONGRUB'S autonomous Inner Mongolian government. With Japan's surrender Inner Mongolia's Höhhot again became Suiyuan's Guisui, continuing as such through the 1949 surrender to the Communists. In 1954, however, Suiyuan was annexed to the Inner Mongolian Autonomous Region, and on April 25 Guisui was renamed Höhhot (Chinese, Huhehaote) and made capital of the INNER MONGOLIA AUTONOMOUS REGION. Only since then have the "Old," "New," and Hui towns merged into one conurbation.

See also BKA'-'GYUR AND BSTAN-GYUR; CHINESE TRADE AND MONEYLENDING; INNER MONGOLIANS; SECOND CONVERSION; *SUTRA OF THE WISE AND FOOLISH.*

Further reading: Piper Rae Gaubatz, *Beyond the Great Wall: Urban Form and Transformation on the Chinese Frontiers* (Stanford, Calif.: Stanford University Press,

1996); William R. Jankowiak, *Sex, Death, and Hierarchy in a Chinese City: An Anthropological Account* (New York: Columbia University Press, 1993).

Ho-nan   *See* HENAN MONGOL AUTONOMOUS COUNTY.

höömii   *See* THROAT SINGING.

Horchin   *See* KHORCHIN.

Horqin   *See* KHORCHIN.

horse-head fiddle (*morin khuur, morin huur*)   The horse-head fiddle is the emblematic musical instrument of traditional Mongolian music.

The horse-head fiddle, or *morin khuur,* is one of several Mongolian fretless spike fiddles. The horse-head fiddle, as its name suggests, has a horse head carved on the scroll. It has two strings and lateral tuning pegs called "ears." The body is a trapezoidal box with the thicker end downward. A movable wooden bridge or string loop is used to modify the pitch. Traditionally, the body was covered with the hide of suckling camel, sheep, or goat or sometimes snakeskin. The strings are made of horsehair from a gelding, preferably a champion racer. The average modern fiddle is a little over 1 meter or about 3.5 feet long. The horse-head form is traditional among the KHALKHA and INNER MONGOLIANS, but not among the OIRATS.

Mongolian two-string fiddles are traditionally played with the musician seated on the ground and the instrument between the legs. The fiddle's base is placed in the ground, and the sound box is rested against the left thigh face outward. The strings are not pressed against the neck, but rather pushed lightly, by a knuckle or nail, from the side, above, or below. In bowing, the tension on the bow hairs is governed by the bow hand's pinkie finger.

The horse-head fiddle was traditionally used to accompany long songs (*urtyn duu*). In YURTS it was kept in the honored *khoimor* (rear) section on the western (male) side, with a KHADAG scarf tied to the bridge. Menstrual taboos prevented it being placed between a woman's legs, barring them from playing it. Legends of the origin of the first horse-head fiddle speak of a man,

The Old Fiddler, by Ü. Yadamsüren, 1958. Mongol *zurag* style (gouache on cotton). 78 × 65 centimeters *(From* Orchin Üyeiin Mongolyn Dürslekh Urlag *[1971])*

sometimes of celestial origin, who traveled to his fairy love on a magical winged horse. When his jealous ordinary wife clipped the horse's wings, the horse died; the first horse-head fiddle was made as the horse's memorial.

The horse-head fiddle's status as the emblem of Mongolian tradition was marked in the painting *Old Fiddler* (1958) by ÜRJINGIIN YADAMSÜREN, one of the path-breaking works in the neotraditional MONGOL *ZURAG* style. In visits from 1966 to 1968, the award-winning Russian violin maker Denis Vladimirovich Iarovoi trained Mongolian fiddle makers in new ways to make the horse-head fiddle more effective as a concert hall instrument. Iarovoi and his Mongolian pupils established the new standard in the fiddle's construction, in which the sound box was made entirely of wood, with two *f*-shaped sound holes, and the bow was flat, not arched. The tuning and fingering were also changed to accord with Western instruments. The social role of the instrument also changed. Women began to play the fiddle, and the Ikh Chuulga folk orchestra was created with horse-head fiddles, ranging in size up to that of the countrabass, as one of the main instruments. A parallel process of modernization, influenced by Chinese performance ideas, took place in Inner Mongolia.

See also MUSIC.

Further reading: Peter K. Marsh, *The Horse-Head Fiddle and the Reimagination of Tradition in Mongolia* (New York: Routledge Press, 2004).

horse racing Horse racing is one of Mongolia's "three manly games," although ironically it is today most often performed by young boys and girls. Mongolian horse racing was one of the important games (NAADAM) connected with summer religious ceremonies, such as the libation of mare's milk, the OBOO sacrifice, and the DANSHUG ceremonies offered to INCARNATE LAMAS. In both Mongolian EPICS and in the Tibetan versions of the GESER epic the hero wins the hand of his bride by winning at a horse race. This seems to indicate that at the time of the crystallization of the epic tradition, around the late 17th–early 18th centuries, young men were the only riders. Today adults race only in special races to test amblers (*joroo mori*), which attract considerably less interest than the fast children's races.

In many ways Mongolian horse racing is more a test of the horse than of the rider and is an expression of the deep love and admiration that country-bred Mongols have for beautiful and strong horses. In fact, even if the jockey falls off, the horse is still considered as having completed the race if it crosses the finish line. In the National Holiday Naadam, the national championship in Mongolia, horses are divided into age categories, with only those six years and older racing the full 30 kilometers (19 miles). The youngest horses are only two years old and have a five-kilometer (3.1-mile) course. In provincial *naadams* in western Mongolia, younger horses

Regular (left) and felt racing saddle (right) hung up near the door of a yurt. Shiliin Gol, Inner Mongolia, 1987 *(Courtesy Christopher Atwood)*

OMBO, a red star (common in the days of communism), a blue star (common today), or the "endless knot" (a Buddhist symbol).

About 1,300 to 1,600 horses compete in Mongolia's National Holiday Naadam. The various age classes each begin the race with an elder leading the children in several clockwise circumambulations of the starting ground. The children sing a special song called the *giingoo* and slowly build up speed until the signal is given, and they sweep off at a gallop. Elders also accompany the race to make sure no one is injured and no horses are lost. When the horses finally pass the finish line, the judge chants a long *magtaal* (praise) of the winning horse (*see* YÖRÖÖL AND MAGTAAL) and presents the jockey with a handful of crumbly cheese before anointing the leading horse's head and flanks with KOUMISS, or fermented mare's milk. Taking a sip of koumiss himself, he passes it to the winning jockey, who sips it and passes it to the horse's owner, who also sips. This is then repeated with the second horse and so on. Different praises and titles are given to the leading horses in differing numbers, five in Mongolia today, nine in traditional ORDOS, and so on. The very last horse, called the *bayan khodood* (rich belly), is also given a *magtaal* and an anointing. Prizes are given to the owners of the lead horses, who generally share them with the jockey.

are sometimes banned on the grounds that premature racing can ruin their promise. Mongols usually ride only geldings, and mares are not allowed in the race. Dark colored horses are preferred.

The horse trainer, or *uyaach,* begins training and conditioning the horse a month or two before the race, paying special attention to its weight. The proper child is also selected. Before racing, the tails and manes of the horses are tied, both to make it easier for the horses to run and to excite the horses for the race. The harness and saddle are also given ornamental studs.

Today the jockeys are children from six to 10 years old, whose light weight permits the horses to go farther and faster in the grueling cross-country race. Instead of the wooden Mongolian saddle, jockeys traditionally ride on light felt pads without stirrups to ease the horse's running. Today, however, the children in Mongolia's national *naadam* ride with regular saddles and stirrups. Jockeys wear a special colored shirt and a cap with a conical front. Emblematic symbols on the cap include the SOY-

horses   The horse was not only the basis of Mongolia's ancient military prowess, virtually the sole means of human transport, and the source of nourishing KOUMISS (fermented mare's milk), it was also the wise councillor in Mongolian EPICS; its hair supplied the standards that symbolized the majesty of the state; and its picture is a frequent adornment of Mongols' homes. Mongolia has 2,660,700 horses, the seventh largest horse herd in the world and is the only country where horses outnumber people.

Traditional Mongolian regional breeds average from 130–131 centimeters (12.8–12.9 hands) high for stallions and 125–129 centimeters (12.3–12.7 hands) for mares and weigh from around 316–370 kilograms (697–816 pounds) for stallions and 296–350 kilograms (653–772 pounds) for mares. The head is large, the croup is sloping, and the belly of a range-fed horse is large. Despite these (to the European eye) unattractive proportions, Mongolian horses are famous for their ability to run hard and long on very scanty fodder and are generally good natured. While shoeing has been known from the Middle Ages, it is done only on either very valuable horses or those used on paved ground. Mongolian mares are milked six to eight times a day and with good pasture can produce about 7.5 liters (7.9 quarts) of milk daily. The hair of horse manes is used to make brushes, brooms, ropes, and the girths for Mongolian YURTS.

Before Buddhism horses were the most honored sacrificial animal. The horse sacrifice and meal was a key part of Inner Asian funerary practice from the Bronze Age (1500–800 B.C.E.) through the great nomadic empires. Horse sacrifices to the ancestors continued during the summer among the shamanist western BURIATS of Ust'-Orda and Ol'khon. Elsewhere missionaries of the SECOND CONVERSION to Buddhism in the 16th–17th centuries successfully aroused disgust with this killing and had the horse sacrifice banned. Since then, for most Mongols eating horsemeat has became somewhat disreputable. (The cult of CHINGGIS KHAN at the EIGHT WHITE YURTS was an exception.) The ancient practice continued of dedicating horses and other livestock to heaven (*TENGGERI*), the clan, or local spirits by having *seter* (Tibetan, *se-ter*), or colored cloth strips, tied to them. Such animals could not be ridden or sold.

The Mongolian saddle is formed of a wooden framework mounted on a leather flap and is placed over a felt saddle pad. The seat is high, with only a small space between the high pommel and cantle, and has an attached padded cushion. Leather strips hanging from the saddle in pairs are used to tie game or other items. Stir-rups were anciently made of wood or bone but are today made of steel and have a round base. The stirrup leather is relatively short and usually not adjustable to the rider's height. Saddle girths are usually made of a braided rope of wool or camel's hair twisted with horse or cattle molt. Leather girths are sometimes used but are considered to be hard on the horse for long journeys. The Mongols use a snaffle bit. Mongolian whips have a long wooden body, a thong for holding, and a strap of 25–30 centimeters (10–12 inches) at the end for whipping. Spurs are not used. For capturing horses the Mongols use primarily an *uurga*, formed of a two-piece wooden pole 6–7 meters (20–23 feet) long and a 1.5–2 meters (5–6.6 feet) long leather strip tied in a loop on the end. Sometimes a simple lasso is used.

Mongols generally ride geldings, and riding a mare is considered unmanly. The gelded testicles of large animals are not eaten but either offered to the fire (*see* FIRE CULT) or hung on the horse's mane or tail; in any case they must be kept from birds and dogs. After gelding the horse is fed on milk and cheeses for three to seven days. Countryside

Mongolian horse with saddle. A white padding has been placed over the saddle. Ordos, Inner Mongolia, 1987 *(Courtesy Christopher Atwood)*

Mongols keep at least one horse always available at their camp for riding, while the other horses roam on the steppe in a semiwild state. Since riding horses cannot graze well, they must be rotated every week or so. When horses need to be switched, gelded, or milked, the horse herd is brought to the camp or other convenient spot. Horse herding is considered men's work.

HISTORY

After first domesticating the horse around 4000 B.C.E. in Ukraine as a draft animal, the people of the Inner Asian steppe began riding around 800 B.C.E. The overwhelming importance of the horse as a weapon of war is illustrated by the fact that in 1188 C.E. 32 percent of the animals on the eastern Inner Mongolian pastures were horses. Since horses were so numerous, it is not surprising that koumiss, or fermented mare's milk, is by far the most commonly mentioned dairy product in the Mongol diet of the 13th century. (*On the training and armor of Mongolian war mounts, see* MILITARY OF THE MONGOL EMPIRE.)

The long peace in the 19th century allowed the percentage of horses to decline. Figures for the eastern Khalkha show the percentage of horses at about 15 percent in 1800 and 13 percent in 1825–41. By 1918 the percentage of horses among Mongolia's livestock had dropped to 11.9 percent. Nobles still kept vast numbers of horses: In 1841 the 20 *zasags* (ruling noblemen) of Setsen Khan province each had on average almost 700 horses, which formed 22.8 percent of their combined total herds. By contrast the average commoner (*arad*) family had only 3.4 horses, which formed only 11.0 percent of their combined herds.

After the 1921 REVOLUTION the percentage of horses dropped as low as 7.1 percent in 1929 before rising again to more than 10 percent. Absolute numbers temporarily peaked at 2,502,700 head in 1960, with horses forming 10.9 percent of all livestock before beginning a slow decline. From 1990 to 1999 the number of horses increased along with those of Mongolia's total herd, jumping from 2,262,000 (8.7 percent) in 1990 to 3,163,500 (9.4 percent) in 1999. Horse numbers were seriously damaged by the 2000 and 2001 ZUD (winter disaster). Mare's milk production in 1992 was 8 million liters (2.1 million gallons), or 6.9 percent of Mongolia's total milk production. While horses are found all over Mongolia, the KHANGAI RANGE is the center of horse breeding. NORTH KHANGAI PROVINCE and SOUTH KHANGAI PROVINCE, CENTRAL PROVINCE, KHENTII PROVINCE, and KHÖWSGÖL PROVINCE have high numbers of horses. In Inner Mongolia the number of horses rose from 487,000 in 1947 to 1,963,000 in 1980, but since then has declined to 1,692,000 (1990, midyear figures) or 1,567,500 (year-end figure).

Traditional Mongolian horses are found in several local breeds, such as the Tes River, Galshar, small Darkhad, and Üjümüchin horses. The Buriat horse, crossbred with Russian, is slightly larger than the Mongolian horse and yields more milk. Improved breeds, with heights of 140–150 centimeters (13.8–14.8 hands), in China include the Three Rivers horse, created by White Russian refugees in HULUN BUIR, and the Khorchin horse.

See also ANIMAL HUSBANDRY AND NOMADISM; DAIRY PRODUCTS; FOOD AND DRINK; HORSE RACING.

Hoshut   *See* KHOSHUDS.

Hoton   *See* KHOTONG.

Hovd   *See* KHOWD CITY.

Hövsgöl   *See* KHÖWSGÖL PROVINCE.

hP'ags-pa Lama   *See* 'PHAGS-PA LAMA.

Hsien-pi   *See* XIANBI.

Hsi-Hsia   *See* XIA DYNASTY.

Hsiung-nu   *See* XIONGNU.

Huan'erzui, Battle of   At the Battle of Huan'erzui (Badger's Mouth) in February 1212, the Mongols under CHINGGIS KHAN delivered a legendary defeat to the field armies of the Jin dynasty in North China.

Although the Mongols had advanced as far as the capital of North China's JIN DYNASTY in 1211, they withdrew to the Jin frontier in Inner Mongolia that winter. In February 1212 the Mongols took the border prefecture of Huanzhou (near modern Zhenglan Qi) and besieged Fuzhou. The Jin emperor dispatched the bandit-suppression commissioner, Heshilie Jiujin, to lead the crack cavalry of the ruling Jurchen people and KITANS, assisted by Han (ethnic Chinese) infantry under two civil officials, Duji Qianjianu and Hu Sha. The force totaled several hundred thousand.

Leaving Hu Sha with infantry at Huihebao Fort (modern Huai'an), Heshilie Jiujin and Duji Qianjianu advanced past Yehuling (Fox Range) into Inner Mongolia. While certain Kitan commanders advocated a surprise attack, Heshilie Jiujin preferred to advance his troops in a body and sent an envoy to Chinggis Khan denouncing his invasion. The Mongols besieging Fuzhou (in Inner Mongolia) had been eating breakfast but formed up quickly after hearing of the Jin advance. Although the Mongols were vastly outnumbered, MUQALI, Chinggis Khan's trusted *NÖKÖR* (companion), led a cavalry charge, discomfiting the Jin ranks. The main Mongol force then moved up to shatter the Jin troops. Pursuing the fugitives more than 48 kilometers (30 miles) they met Hu Sha's rear guard at Huihebao Fort, crushing it. The flower of Jin soldiery was destroyed in this battle, which became legendary among the Mongols. The victory was attributed to the fighting qualities of the Mongol cavalry, Heshilie Jiujin's excessive caution and reliance on numbers, and the disaffection of many Kitan commanders, who resented Jurchen control.

See also MILITARY OF THE MONGOL EMPIRE.

Huhehaote   *See* HÖHHOT.

Huhhot   *See* HÖHHOT.

Hulagu   *See* HÜLE'Ü.

Hülegü   *See* HÜLE'Ü.

Hüle'ü (Hülegü, Hulagu) (1217–1265) *Conqueror of Baghdad and founder of the Mongol Il-Khan dynasty in the Middle East*
Hüle'ü was the third son of TOLUI (1191?–1232) and his Kereyid main wife, SORQAQTANI BEKI (d. 1252). Hüle'ü's first wife, Güyüg (or Köpek) Khatun of the OIRATS, was Hüle'ü's second cousin on her mother's side. She bore him a son, Jumqur (1234–64), and a daughter before dying early. She was replaced as wife by the QONGGIRAD Qutui Khatun and by Güyüg's half-sister Öljei, yet two-thirds of Hüle'ü's 21 known children and all his favored sons were born of concubines.

CONQUESTS AND DEFEATS IN THE MIDDLE EAST

Immediately after his eldest brother, MÖNGKE KHAN's, election as khan in 1251, Hüle'ü was appointed to administer North China. In summer 1252, however, Möngke gave North China to Hüle'ü's elder brother QUBILAI KHAN and assigned to Hüle'ü the conquest of the caliph of Baghdad (*see* 'ABBASID CALIPHATE). In preparation Möngke ordered two of every 10 men in the Mongol military to accompany Hüle'ü, along with imperial princes of the Jochid and Chaghatayid lines and commanders (NOYAN) of his in-law (QUDA) clan, the Oirats.

Around this time Hüle'ü also married his KEREYID stepmother, TOGHUS KHATUN. Although they had no children, he greatly respected her judgment, and she accompanied him on campaigns along with Öljei Khatun and several concubines. He also took his sons Abagha (1234–82) and Yoshmut (d. 1271) but left Jumqur behind along with Qutui Khatun.

Arriving in Khorasan in winter 1255–56, Hüle'ü victoriously besieged the Isma'ili fortress of Alamut (November 20, 1256), the 'Abbasid caliph in Baghdad (February 10, 1258), Aleppo (January 1260), and many lesser cities, butchering the vanquished (*see* BAGHDAD, SIEGE OF). Since several had come out with guarantees of safety, Hüle'ü acquired a reputation for perfidy. Mean-

while, Öljei Khatun's brother Buqa-Temür sacked Wasit (February–March 1258), and Hüle'ü's son Yoshmut and his commander Elege of the JALAYIR captured rebellious Mayyafariqin (near modern Silvan, fell in spring 1260) and Mardin. Only Homs, Hamath, and Damascus (February 1260) were not destroyed.

After the fall of Aleppo, Hüle'ü received news of Möngke Khan's August 1259 death in China and withdrew to Armenia, leaving his vanguard commander, KED-BUQA, in the Levant with 10,000 or so soldiers. Sensing opportunity, the sultan of MAMLUK EGYPT, Qutuz, advanced on the reckless Ked-Buqa, killing him at the Battle of 'Ain Jalut (September 1260) and quickly recovering from the Mongols all the lost land up to the Euphrates. Qutuz's successor, Sultan Baybars, defeated a second Mongol expedition into Syria in December. In 1261 the Mamluks instigated rebellions in Mosul and Jazirah (Cizre), suppression of which occupied the Mongols until summer 1262.

THE NEW KHANATE

Hüle'ü, although infuriated by these challenges, was unable to respond due to the hostility of the Jochid ruler, Berke (1257–66). Previously, Iran and the Caucasus had belonged to the Jochid branch, but Möngke and Hüle'ü covertly planned to turn the area into a separate *ulus* (realm) of the Toluid branch. From around 1258 Hüle'ü proclaimed his status as *Il-Khan* (subordinate khan), using his allegiance to Great Khan Möngke to carve out for himself a new realm. The suspicious deaths of a number of Jochid princes and Hüle'ü's destruction of the caliph and many Muslim cities added to the anger of Berke, a Muslim convert.

After Möngke's death his brothers Qubilai and ARIQ-BÖKE went to war. Hüle'ü's son Jumqur, left behind in Almaligh, joined Ariq-Böke's army, but Berke supported Ariq-Böke, and by 1262 Hüle'ü threw his support to Qubilai. Hüle'ü ordered his son to leave Ariq-Böke's army and join him in the Middle East. Jumghur and Qutui Khatun set out, but Jumqur died on the way, and Qutui Khatun reached Iran only after Hüle'ü's death.

In summer 1262 Berke sent his nephew NOQAI south against Hüle'ü. Both sides mobilized vast resources, but the seesawing conflict ended with a humiliating defeat for Hüle'ü's advancing army on the Terek (January 13, 1263). Meanwhile, Qubilai Khan, having defeated Ariq-Böke, confirmed Hüle'ü as the Mongol ruler from the Amu Dar'ya to Egypt. Hüle'ü's dynasty for decades remained hostile to Egypt to the southwest and to the Jochids' GOLDEN HORDE to the north and allied with Qubilai as great khan in the east.

TERRITORIES AND ADMINISTRATION

To feed his nomadic appanage, Hüle'ü took over the rich steppes of Azerbaijan, relocating the *TAMMACHI* (garrison) army of Baiju to Seljük TURKEY. In 1262 Hüle'ü gave

Khorasan and Mazandaran to his heir apparent, Abagha, and northern Azerbaijan (Arran) up to the Caucasus to Yoshmut. He himself nomadized in southern Azerbaijan and Armenia, building a palace at Ala Dağ. The Kurdish area of the upper Tigris was also assigned to his newly arrived Mongol entourage (*see* KURDISTAN).

While Hüle'ü received the full submission of the client kingdoms of southern Iran, virtually all the previously tributary Muslim rulers in the west rebelled against his rule. Only the Turkmen Seljukid and Artuqid dynasties in Anatolia and Mardin survived as major client kingdoms. Hüle'ü's early reign also saw trouble with the Mongols' Christian subjects. From winter 1258–59, Hüle'ü's agent in GEORGIA, ARGHUN AQA, pressed Hüle'ü's heavy tax demands and arrested many Georgio-Armenian nobles, driving the Georgian kings into flight. Only in November 1262, when Hüle'ü had his vizier, Saif-ud-Din Bitigchi, and several of his underlings executed, did he and his new vizier, Shams-ud-Din Juvaini, try to implement a more sustainable administration (*see* JUVAINI, 'ALA'UD-DIN ATA-MALIK AND SHAMS-UD-DIN MUHAMMAD).

RELIGIOUS INTERESTS

Hüle'ü's mother, Sorqaqtani Beki, had been a Christian of the Assyrian Church of the East, and although raised by a non-Christian nurse, the memory of his mother gave Hüle'ü a sentimental attachment to her Christian faith. Toghus Khatun was openly Christian, keeping a chapel at her ORDO (palace-tent) and interceding for Christians. When permitted by his interests, Hüle'ü showed special favor to Armenian and Georgian nobles and clergy. In the siege of Baghdad Christians were spared, and the palace of the caliph was given to the Assyrian catholicos (patriarch) as a church. Christian writers admired Hüle'ü as a scourge of their Muslim oppressors.

Nevertheless, Hüle'ü's personal beliefs revolved around astrology, Buddhism, and alchemy. During the attack on Baghdad the commander and astrologer Husam-ud-Din predicted catastrophe for anyone who harmed the caliph. Hüle'ü was nervous until the Isma'ili scholar Nasir-ud-Din Tusi presented historical counterexamples. Afterward, when the conquest was accomplished, he had a magnificent observatory built at Maragheh for Nasir-ud-Din and executed Husam-ud-Din. Chinese artisans constructed a Buddhist temple at Khvoy, where Hüle'ü frequently performed Buddhist prostrations. Hüle'ü patronized alchemists claiming to have the elixir of life, and the Assyrian bishop Henan Isho (d. 1268) in rebellious Jazirah (Cizre) rescued his city and became its governor by promising to reveal the art of transmuting base metals into gold.

Hüle'ü's fell ill in February 1265 after several days of banqueting and hunting, and he died early on February 8 as a comet appeared in the sky. He was buried in a *qoruq* (forbidden spot) with treasure and maidens at Kuh-e-Shahu (northwest of Kermanshah). Toghus Khatun died soon after, and Abagha (r. 1265–82) succeeded his father as Il-Khan that summer.

See also 'AIN JALUT, BATTLE OF; IL-KHANATE; TIBET AND THE MONGOL EMPIRE.

Hulun Buir (Khölön Buir) The Inner Mongolian Autonomous Region's most multiethnic region, Hulun Buir has always had a distinct identity from the rest of Inner Mongolia.

MODERN POPULATION AND ECONOMY

Traditionally, Hulun Buir included the region west of the Khingan watershed extending to the borders of KHALKHA Mongolia and Russia. This area, now including the Barga, Ewenki, and Ergüne (Ergun) BANNERS and Yakeshi, Hailar, and Manzhouli cities, covers more than 161,000 square kilometers (62,160 square miles). This area's population of 1,264,100 in 1990 included 146,400 Mongols, or 12 percent of the total. Daurs were another 2 percent, and EWENKIS (Solons) 0.08 percent. The Mongols here belong to four quite different groups: 1) the BARGA, settled in the area in 1732–34; 2) the ÖÖLÖD, who were settled in the area in 1732; 3) the Buriats, newly immigrated from Russia in 1922 (*see* BURIATS OF MONGOLIA AND INNER MONGOLIA); and 4) recent Inner Mongolian immigrants, mostly KHORCHIN.

Economically and demographically, old Hulun Buir may be divided into two areas, the steppe zone, including the Barga and Ewenki banners, and the forest zone, including Yakeshi and the two Ergüne banners. The steppe zone, where most of the area's Mongols live, has 1,670,000 head of livestock, of which 1,215,000 are sheep and goats. Coal mining is also important. The forest zone, sparsely inhabited by Öölöd Mongols, Daurs, and Ewenkis in 1949, has been intensively developed since then as China's largest forestry region. The region's capital, Hailar, has a population of 205,700 (1990 figures).

In 1949 the eastern slopes of the GREATER KHINGAN RANGE and the Nonni (Nen) valley were also attached to Hulun Buir. Within these larger boundaries Hulun Buir covers 250,000 square kilometers (96,500 square miles) and has a population of 2,551,763, including 185,400 Mongols (7 percent), 65,318 Daurs (2.5 percent), 22,808 Ewenkis, and 2,744 Orochens. The economy of Hulun Buir east of the Khingan watershed is based on farming in the lowlands and forestry in the uplands.

SETTLEMENT

From the mid-17th century Hulun Buir was temporarily vacant due to the wars and deportations accompanying the rise of China's last QING DYNASTY (1636–1912). In 1732 the Qing resettled the Hulun Buir steppe with "Solons" (Ewenkis and Daurs), Old Barga and Öölöd Mongols, and Orochens to fortify the newly defined border with Russia. Two years later another large contingent of New Barga Mongols were settled there as well. All these ethnically diverse peoples were enrolled in the EIGHT BANNERS militia forces and used Manchu for official purposes.

Under the Qing, Hulun Buir was administered by the *fudutong* (deputy military lieutenant governor; Manchu, *meiren-i janggin*) resident in Hailar, who was always a bannerman from Manchuria or Beijing. While generally called "Bargas" by Russians and Khalkhas, Hulun Buir's soldiery was multiethnic, including on the official roster 864 New Bargas, 185 Old Bargas, about 1,295 "Solons" (mostly Ewenkis but with about 200 Daurs), 117 Orochen, and 136 Öölöds.

MODERN HISTORY

In 1900 Russia built the Chinese Eastern Railway across Northern Manchuria, bringing Hulun Buir into the Russian sphere of influence. In 1908 the Qing's NEW POLICIES curtailed Hulun Buir's autonomy and promoted colonization. These moves bred violent opposition, and on January 15, 1912, the Hulun Buir bannermen occupied Hailar, declaring their merger with newly independent Mongolia. New Barga officials such as GRAND DUKE DAMDINSÜRÜNG (1874–1920) won high position in Mongolia. In 1915, however, Russian pressure forced Hulun Buir to became an autonomous "special region" under joint Russo-Chinese supervision.

In 1920, with the chaos of Russia's civil war, the officials in Hailar negotiated a return to China under semiautonomy. In 1922 Buriat anticommunist refugees were organized into their own banner on the Shinekhen River. During the 1920s Hulun Buir became a major center of the wool trade, dominated by American and British companies. Meanwhile, young Daurs and Barga Mongols pursued education in Japan, Russia, Mongolia, and even the United States and formed pan-Mongolist parties. In July–September 1928 the Daurs MERSE (Guo Daofu, 1894–1934?) and Fumingtai (Buyangerel, 1898–1938) led an unsuccessful pan-Mongolist insurrection in New Barga territory.

In 1932, after Japanese occupation, Hulun Buir was made the autonomous Khinggan North province. All Hulun Buir's bannermen were now officially considered Mongols, and Mongolian replaced Manchu as the official language. The Soviet Union's August 1945 invasion raised pan-Mongolist hopes despite widespread destruction and plunder, yet diplomatic considerations again blocked unification with Mongolia. The Soviet authorities reappointed the old officials to a new Hulun Buir Autonomous government.

Pan-Mongolist revolutionary parties operated in Soviet-dominated Hulun Buir until October 1947, when Chinese Communist pressure brought Hulun Buir into its Inner Mongolian Autonomous government as a LEAGUE. In 1949 Hulun Buir league was made a constituent part of the Inner Mongolian Autonomous Region after being merged with the Daur and Ewenki-inhabited Nonni valley east of the Greater Khinggan Range. In 1954 the addition of the northern Khorchin areas further diluted Hulun Buir's distinct identity. The steppe herds were collectivized in June–September 1958. During the Cultural Revolution (1966–76) former rich herders were attacked, and Mongols and Daurs with knowledge of Russian or connections over the Mongolian frontier were savagely persecuted in the "NEW INNER MONGOLIAN PEOPLE'S REVOLUTIONARY PARTY" CASE. In 1969, at the height of the SINO-SOVIET SPLIT, Hulun Buir was detached from Inner Mongolia and attached to Heilongjiang province.

In 1979 the Cultural Revolution policies were denounced, and Hulun Buir was returned to Inner Mongolia. (The Khorchin area was no longer included, leaving Hulun Buir league with the steppe and Nonni valley areas.) In 1983–85 first herds and then range land were privatized. In January 1988 Beijing made Hulun Buir an experimental area for economic reform, resulting in increased trade, investment, and tourism with Russia. In 2002 Hulun Buir league was renamed Hulun Buir municipality.

See also DAUR LANGUAGE AND PEOPLE; INNER MONGOLIA AUTONOMOUS REGION; INNER MONGOLIANS; THEOCRATIC PERIOD.

Further reading: A. Hurelbaatar, "The Transformation of the Inner Mongolian Pastoral Economy: The Case of Hulun Buir League," in *Culture and Environment in Inner Asia*, vol. 2, *Society and Culture*, ed. Caroline Humphrey and David Sneath (Cambridge, Mass.: White Horse Press, 1996), 160–175; Burton Pasternak and Janet W. Salaff, *Cowboys and Cultivators: The Chinese in Inner Mongolia* (Boulder, Colo.: Westview Press, 1993).

Hungary *See* CENTRAL EUROPE AND THE MONGOLS.

Huns *See* XIONGNU.

hunting and fishing Hunting and fishing were important activities for the ancient Mongols, which, however, by the 18th century had fallen into disrepute among the strongly Buddhist-influenced Mongols of Khalkha and Inner Mongolia. Hunting among the Mongols had two main forms: the battue hunt carried on by a large number of people and the small-scale hunt involving one or a few hunters. In the 13th century game formed a substantial part of the Mongols' meat supply. At QUBILAI KHAN's court the great khan's table was supplied from October to March with meat sent by court hunters and by game sent as tribute from nearby commanders, while skins were sent from those farther away. Battue hunting was strictly seasonal and forbidden during the birthing season or the summer, but small-scale hunting was carried on throughout the year, limited only by natural conditions.

The fur trade was a long-standing part of North Asian political institutions. From ancient times the Siberian and Manchurian peoples have both sold and surrendered in tribute furs to their nomadic neighbors (*see* GOLDEN HORDE; RUSSIA AND THE MONGOL EMPIRE; SHIWEI; SIBERIA AND THE MONGOL EMPIRE). The nomads then either used these furs themselves or traded them to the sedentary peoples to the south. Some Mongolian peoples, such as the BURIATS of southern Siberia and the ALTAI URIYANGKHAI of northwestern Mongolia, themselves paid a fur tribute, whether to Khalkha Mongols of the steppe or to the Russian or Manchu Qing Empires. Squirrels and sables were always the principal animals in this fur trade, but ermine, marten, bear, lynx, otter, fox, and wolf were also hunted for their furs and given in tribute. Furs were also used by forest and steppe peoples alike for money or moneylike uses such as bridewealth. Hunting was (and is) undertaken not only for food or furs but also to control predators, especially the wolf.

BATTUE HUNTS

Accounts of battues from the 13th century, the late 16th century, and from the western Buriats, Tuva, the Gobi Khalkha, and ORDOS in the 18th–19th centuries are all similar. Men were mobilized to serve as beaters in a vast circle. Making noise, they gradually pulled the circle tighter. Eventually the animals would be coralled and shot with their arrows. Under the great khans, the Tümed rulers of the 16th century, or the *jinong* (viceroy) of Ordos, thousands participated, and the lines extended over scores of kilometers, while among the TUVANS or Buriats 20 to 100 or so might participate and the circles were up to a few kilometers wide. Each man carried only a limited number of arrows (30 among the Buriats), which they recovered and reused during the hunt. Allowing an animal to escape the circle was a grave fault, but a few animals were always released at the end to avoid tempting fate.

Such battues were often conducted against traps, such as ropes of horsehair attached to stakes, as described in 13th-century Mongolia. Modern ethnographers describe the use of nets of goats' hair tied to sagebrush in the desert for catching rabbits or foxes, pens or pits in the steppe for saiga antelopes or gazelles, and barricades of felled logs in mountain passes for deer, elk, and moose.

During these great collective hunts the Mongol rulers also used beasts and birds of prey to kill the game: leopards, lynxes, tigers (against wild boar, bears, wild asses or kulans, elk, and roebuck), goshawks, gerfalcons, peregrine and saker falcons, eagles, and mastiffs (*see* FALCONRY). Falconry has disappeared among the Mongols, but the Ordos Mongols still hunt with greyhounds (*taiga*).

SMALL-SCALE HUNTS

Small-scale hunting techniques, practiced by individuals or small parties before the use of firearms, varied with the animal. Smoke was used to block marmots or badgers from leaving their holes while other hunters burrowed into their holes. Elongated loops of horsehair triggered by hand or on long sticks were used to catch birds and small animals. The northern forest peoples, or "Uriyangkhai," of the 13th century and the Tuvans today hunt on skis and exhaust the prey with a long chase. Bears were sometimes hunted by blocking the mouth of their dens, provoking them to try to come out, and firing at them. Crossbows with triggers set up in animal paths were the main method used against moose, elk, deer, bear, and fur-bearing mammals; the 17th–18th-century Mongolian legal codes contained provisions for compensating persons injured by such traps. Roe deer and musk deer were lured with squeakers. Whistling arrows were used to disorient or flush out prey.

In hunting, a mount was helpful but not necessary. Some Tuvans and the EWENKIS in the Siberian mountain taiga used reindeer to reach their hunting grounds and to carry bag. Among the western Buriats and the Khamnigan Ewenkis of the Onon-Shilka valleys and the Solon Ewenkis of the Amur basin, horses were adopted before other livestock as mounts for hunting.

HUNTING CULTURE

In recent centuries forest hunters have conceived of game as the gift of the "Lord of the Forest," known variously as Bayan-Khangai, "Rich Land" (Buriats) or Bayin-Achaa "Rich Father" (Daurs) or as "King of Beasts," Manakhan or Mani-Khan among the Khalkha. Bayan Mani, "Rich-Mani," in Ordos seems to merge Manakhan with the Lord of the Forest. Prayers to the deity were required with the burning of aromatic herbs, while vaunting or boasting was prohibited. As a gift, all meat had to be shared equally by the participants, whether in battues or in small-group hunting, although the man who actually brought down the animal usually received the hide or other nonmeat parts. Certain body parts were preserved and replaced in the forest so as to preserve the game animals' spirit. Before the hunt direct reference to either the hunt itself or to the prospective game animal was avoided by using circumlocutions.

Hunting was the quintessential manly activity, often seen as taking in marriage the seductive daughter or sister of the Lord of the Forest, who thus became the hunter's marriage ally. Fidelity in intention to this intended bride meant that sexual relations were forbidden before the hunt. Women were not allowed to step over hunting equipment lest they pollute it with their menstrual blood. Shamans, whose sex-role identity was ambiguous, were also frequently excluded from hunting.

With the conversion to Buddhism hunting was attacked as a violent and evil activity. Neichi Toin (1557–1653), a Buddhist missionary, was shocked into becoming a monk by witnessing the death throes of a pregnant wild ass. By the 19th century government-organized battue hunts in the central Mongolian lands were no longer held. Even so, small-scale hunting continued to engage as many as half of poorer herding households, although avid young hunters often did penance later in life for their killing. In the 20th century, however, the new revolutionary governments encouraged hunting precisely because of its manly, antireligious, and lower-class character and imbued it with a new ideology of warring on nature.

FIREARMS AND TRAPS

Firearms appeared in Siberia and Mongolia in the 17th century in the form of flintlock rifles. Flintlocks were the only firearms used in most areas until the turn of the 20th century. While local gunsmiths were rare, many hunters in remote districts could cast their own shot in stone molds and mix gunpowder from saltpeter, charcoal, and sheep's dung. The flintlock on a stand not only increased the effectiveness of existing forms of hunting, it allowed new methods of hunting, such as waiting by marmot holes and shooting them as they emerged.

Breech-loading rifles appeared in the late 19th century among the Buriats, but not until around 1900 among the Mongols and related peoples of the Manchu Qing Empire. After that political events rapidly increased the number and potency of firearms. The Ewenkis and Daurs of Manchuria, for example, began to acquire the single-shot Berdan rifle in 1900–01, the Russian Mosin magazine rifle around 1911, and the Japanese Arisaka and Chinese-made Mauser 7.9 mm magazine rifles in the early 1930s. Metal traps from Russia also began to appear after 1850.

This new technology drove into extinction the battue hunt and most of the traditional hunting styles in the early 20th century. While marmots remain a great delicacy, furs are the only economically significant product of hunting today. A marmot-skin craze in 1920s Germany made marmot skins temporarily a major export. From 1960 to 1990 annual state purchases of marmot skins declined from more than 1 million to fewer than 700,000 while those of squirrel pelts declined from 140,000 to around 8,000 to 20,000. Purchases of wolf skins remained steady at 3,000 to 5,000 annually. Mongolia has also earned foreign currency by selling licenses to foreigners at high prices to take coveted game, such as argali sheep, ibex, and snow leopards. Since 1990 Mongolian deer herds have been harmed by poachers seeking blood antlers for sale in China, while herders have complained that the discontinuation of the government-run predator-control program (due to budgetary, not environmental reasons) has allowed wolves to run rampant.

FISHING

While never as important as hunting, fishing was seen as a similar activity. The most common form of fishing in the Mongol Empire was ice fishing in lakes and rivers. Only large fish were taken. Like hunting, fishing was seen as a gift, in this case from water deities, and was hedged about by many of the same traditional prohibitions. Fishers used bow and arrows, hooks, their bare hands, horsehair loops as snares, gaffs, spears, and baskets. Ice fishing was conducted along the shore where the ice was thin.

After the SECOND CONVERSION to Buddhism in the 17th century, however, fishing declined even more than hunting as an activity. (The reason for the Buddhist prohibition on fish eating is sometimes said to be the similarity of the unblinking gaze to that of the Buddha and sometimes the fear of eating loved ones reincarnated as fish.)

By the 19th century fish resources in Mongolia were mostly unexploited. Elsewhere, however, the devoutly Buddhist KALMYKS had worked in Russian fisheries on the Caspian Sea since the 18th century, although they did not eat their catch. Shamanist Buriats on Ol'khon Island in LAKE BAIKAL continued to fish, as did the Ekhireds in Verkholensk and the Selenge Delta.

See also ARCHERY; ENVIRONMENTAL PROTECTION; MILITARY OF THE MONGOL EMPIRE.

Further reading: C. R. Bawden, "Mongol Notes, II: Some 'Shamanist' Hunting Rituals from Mongolia," *Central Asiatic Journal* 12 (1968–69): 101–143; Sevyan Vainshtein, *Nomads of South Siberia,* trans. Michael Colenso (Cambridge: Cambridge University Press, 1980).

I

iascot   *See* YASTUQ.

Iberia   *See* GEORGIA.

Ibn Battuta, Muhammad Abu ʻAbdallah
(1304–1368/69) *Moroccan traveler who described all four successor states of the Mongol Empire*
Muhammad Abu-ʻAbdallah Ibn Battuta was born in Tangier into a family of CADIS, or Islamic judges. In 1325 he journeyed through MAMLUK EGYPT and Syria before going south to Mecca. From there he crossed Arabia into the Mongol IL-KHANATE in 1326. By this time he had apparently conceived his love of traveling for its own sake. Rulers at first welcomed him as an Arab jurist trained at Mecca but then came to honor him even more for his traveler's tales. After traveling to Tabriz in the entourage of the last Il-Khan, Abu-Saʻid (1317–35), he returned to Mecca in 1327. From there he traveled the monsoon waters of East Africa and the Persian Gulf before reaching Mecca a third time in 1330. By this time he planned to go to India but could not find a guide, and instead he went north to Turkish Anatolia (*see* TURKEY). From Sinope he crossed the Black Sea to the GOLDEN HORDE and the *ordo* (palace-tent) of ÖZBEG KHAN (1313–41). After visiting Constantinople in the entourage of Özbeg's Byzantine queen (1332), he finally set out for India via KHORAZM and the CHAGHATAY KHANATE, where he stayed with the khan Tarmashirin (1331–34). India, which he reached in September 1333, was a land of fabulous wealth, and Sultan Muhammad b. Tughluq lavishly rewarded him as *cadi* (Islamic judge) of Delhi. Dispatched as an envoy to the Mongol YUAN DYNASTY in China in 1342, he reached there, if at all, only after lin-

gering in ports from the Maldives to Sumatra. On his return to Morocco he witnessed the BLACK DEATH in Syria in 1348. Visits to Andalusia and the Mandingo kingdom in West Africa rounded out his itinerary. Upon his return the sultan of Morocco ordered him to dictate his account to Abu ʻAbdallah Ibn Juzayy, who penned it in elegant Arabic.

While avoiding fantastic elements, Ibn Battuta sometimes inserted bogus accounts of places he never visited. His visit to Mongol China may well be one, as the uprising of "Firuz," which supposedly broke out while he was in China, clearly reflects Qoshila's bid for the Yuan throne in 1328–29, more than 10 years before his visit. Even more obviously fictitious is his transposition of Qutulun Chaghaʻan, the legendary warlike daughter of the Central Asian Mongol QAIDU, to an island in the South China Sea. Even so, Ibn Battuta's indubitably genuine travels in the Islamized western Mongol successor states are one of the main sources on the Golden Horde and the Chaghatay khanate.

See also ISLAMIC SOURCES ON THE MONGOL EMPIRE; SARAY AND NEW SARAY.

Further reading: H. A. R. Gibb and C. F. Beckingham, trans., *Travels of Ibn Battuta, A.D. 1325–1354*, 5 vols. (London: Hakluyt Society and Cambridge University Press, 1956–2000).

Ih Ju   *See* ORDOS.

I-la Chʻu-tsʻai   *See* YELÜ CHUCAI.

Il-Khanate (1256–1335/56)   Created as a result of MÖNGKE KHAN's 1252 decision to send his brother HÜLEʻÜ

(1217–65) to the Middle East, the resulting Il-Khanate dynasty suffered from hostility on three fronts and severe social conflicts.

FORMATION OF THE DYNASTY

Until 1252 the Mongols' great khan, the Jochid GOLDEN HORDE, and the other princely lines shared rule over the area from Afghanistan to Turkey. The great khan appointed governors and confirmed client kings, but always with the prior approval of the Jochid ruler on the Volga. No member of the imperial family resided in this area, but many had appanages in the area and appointed representatives to guard their interests. Two TAMMACHI, or permanent garrison armies, occupied the area, one based in Afghanistan and the other based in Azerbaijan and Armenia. Neither was commanded by a member of the imperial family. In 1252 Möngke appointed his brother Hüle'ü to campaign personally in the Middle East, thus upsetting this balance. RASHID-UD-DIN FAZL-ULLAH claims that Möngke secretly intended from the beginning that Hüle'ü would stay permanently in the Middle East despite public plans for Hüle'ü to return at the end of his mission.

As soon as he crossed the Amu Dar'ya, Hüle'ü took the Azerbaijan area for himself, ordering Baiju Noyan, commander of the *tammachi* troops there, to relocate to Anatolia. After his conquest of Baghdad in February 1258, Hüle'ü began calling himself *Il-Khan,* or "obedient khan," implying a status as a deputy or viceroy of the great khan Möngke, despite the public statement that Hüle'ü would return to Mongolia. Thus, when Möngke Khan died in August 1259, Hüle'ü's status was unclear. By 1260 criminal accusations leveled against Jochid princes in Hüle'ü's service strained relations with the Golden Horde rulers, and in 1262 a complete purge of the Jochid princes and Hüle'ü's support for QUBILAI KHAN in his conflict with ARIQ-BÖKE brought open war with the Golden Horde. Nevertheless the special contempt shown toward the Il-Khans by the rulers of the Golden Horde and CHAGHATAY KHANATE demonstrated the khanate's latecomer status.

GEOGRAPHY

Although the Il-Khans successively designated Maragheh, Ujan, Tabriz, and Soltaniyeh as their capitals and built pavilions, palaces, and temples, particularly at their summer camps, they remained truly nomadic to the end of the dynasty, traveling in well-organized caravans with the realm's officials, treasury, and archives. The khans' nomadic routes covered central Iraq, northwest Iran, Azerbaijan, and Armenia.

The Il-Khans divided their realm into a center (*ghool*) and two wings. The center, including Iraq, the Caucasus, and western and southern Iran, was under direct Mongol administration, except for the client regimes of the Georgian king, the Artuqid sultan in Mardin, and the two chiefdoms of Luristan. The Shi'ite shrine city of Kufa was also autonomous. The Gilan area by the Caspian Sea remained independent until subjugated by Sultan Öljeitü (1304–16) as a tributary state in 1307. Iraq and Diyarbakır together supplied about 35 percent of the Il-Khanate's revenue.

The dynasties in Fars and Kerman (in southern Iran) had surrendered to ÖGEDEI KHAN (1229–41), but by 1305 only the minor Kurdish Shabankara dynasty in Fars remained as an even nominally autonomous client kingdom. The conquest had not devastated Fars, and that province supplied 20 percent of the Il-Khanate's revenue. Even so, the royal family rarely if ever toured there. Bahrain and Hormuz, as traditional dependencies of Fars and Kerman, paid tribute to the Il-Khans and served as the gateway to the Indian Ocean.

The right wing included Anatolian TURKEY (under the client Sultanate of Rum until 1307–08) and the kingdom of LESSER ARMENIA in Cilicia, although the smaller Turkmen elements in the Taurus Mountains and western Anatolia remained unruly. Anatolia was the richest single province, supplying almost a quarter of the Il-Khanate's revenues. Several *tümens* (10,000s) of Mongol troops nomadized in the central and eastern portion of Turkey, commanded either by a prince of the blood or a powerful commander (NOYAN).

Khorasan was an autonomous realm held by the crown prince with his own KESHIG (royal guard) of a Qara'una *tümen,* and it did not pay its taxes to the central treasury. The crown prince migrated among pastures from Herat to Gorgan and Semnan. Herat's local Kart dynasty was a significant force, and until 1289 the viceroy also shared power with family of the Mongol commander ARGHUN AQA. While according to Möngke's original grant Hüle'ü's sway extended to India, the Qonduz-Baghlan QARA'UNAS and the Sistan Negüderis preferred of Central Asia's Chaghatayid Mongols.

FOREIGN RELATIONS

The dynasty's traditional foreign policy revolved around three rivals, MAMLUK EGYPT, the Golden Horde, and the Chaghatay Khanate, and one ally, the YUAN DYNASTY. From the 1260 Battle of 'Ain Jalut, the Mamluks defeated the Il-Khanate's periodic forays into Syria and in return raided the Il-Khan frontier zone from Lesser Armenia to Mosul. Not until 1323 was peace made. With the Golden Horde, war began with Berke's invasion of Azerbaijan in 1262 and continued intermittently until the Il-Khanate victory in 1290. Since neither realm controlled Abkhazia or the Caucasus mountains, the pass of Derbent provided the only means of access. On the northeastern border Abagha Khan (1265–82) defeated the Chaghatay Khanate's invasion of 1270, but the Khorasan viceroys could not stop the frequent raids over the Amu Dar'ya and by the Chaghatays' Qara'una allies in Afghanistan. The general peace of 1304 only temporarily checked these attacks.

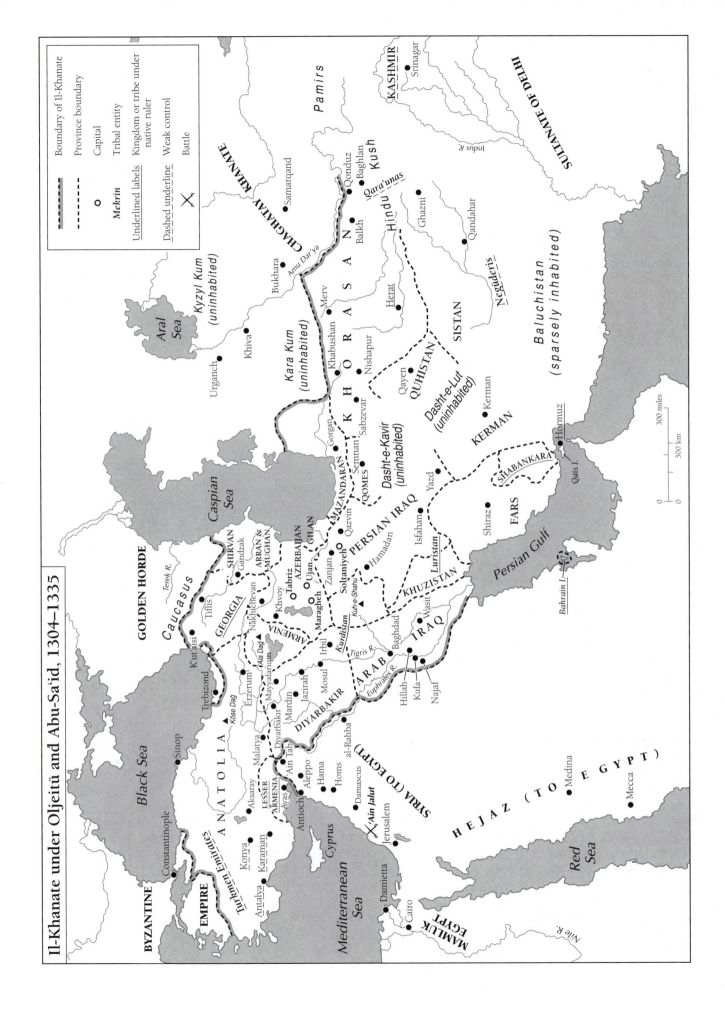

Il-Khanate under Oljeitü and Abu-Sa'id, 1304–1335

Boundary of Il-Khanate
Province boundary
○ *Mehrin* Capital
▲ Tribal entity

Underlined labels Kingdom or tribe under native ruler
Dashed underline Weak control
✕ Battle

BYZANTINE
EMPIRE

GOLDEN HORDE

CHAGHATAY KHANATE

KASHMIR
Srinagar

SULTANATE OF DELHI

Indus R.

Pamirs

Aral
Sea

Kyzyl Kum
(uninhabited)

Samarqand

Bukhara

Hindu Kush
Qonduz
Baghlan

Qara'unas

Ghazni
Qandahar

Khiva

Urganch

Kara Kum
(uninhabited)

Amu Dar'ya

Merv

Khabushan

Balkh

Negüderis

Baluchistan
(sparsely inhabited)

KHORASAN

Herat

SISTAN

Caspian
Sea

Gorgan
Nishapur
Sabzevar

QUHISTAN

Qayen

Dasht-e-Lut
(uninhabited)

Dasht-e-Kavir
(uninhabited)

Kerman

Hormuz
Qais I.

SHIRVAN

Terek R.

Caucasus

Gandzak

ARRAN &
MUGHAN

Semnan
QOMES

MAZANDARAN
Qazvin
GILAN

KERMAN

Yazd

FARS

SHABANKARA

Tiflis

Kutaisi

GEORGIA

Nakhichevan

AZERBAIJAN
Tabriz
Ujan

Soltaniyeh
Zanjan

PERSIAN IRAQ

Isfahan

Shiraz

Persian Gulf

Bahrain I.

Trebizond

Sinop

Black Sea

Erzurum
Köse Dağ

Khvoy
Maragheh
'Ala Dağ
ARMENIA
Mayyafiriqin

Irbil

Kurdistan

Hamadan

Luristan

KHUZISTAN

Wasit

Constantinople

ANATOLIA

Aksaray

Turkmen Emirates

Konya
Karaman

Antalya

LESSER
ARMENIA

Malatya

Diyarbakir
Mardin
Jazirah
Mosul

DIYARBAKIR

al-Rahba

Tigris R.

ARAB

Baghdad

Hillah
Kufa
Najaf

IRAQ

Euphrates R.

Ayas
'Ain Tab
Aleppo
Hama
Homs

Antioch

Cyprus

Mediterranean
Sea

Damascus

✕ 'Ain Jalut

Jerusalem

SYRIA (TO EGYPT)

HEJAZ (TO EGYPT)

Medina

Mecca

Damietta

MAMLUK
EGYPT

Cairo

Nile R.

Red
Sea

300 miles

300 km

The Mongol Yuan dynasty in the east retained suzerainty over the "obedient khans" (*Il-Khan*) to the end of its regime. Up to the realm of Geikhatu (1291–95) the Il-Khans proclaimed this suzerainty on their coinage. GHAZAN KHAN (1295–1304), however, publicly downplayed this relationship in favor of Islamic formulas of sovereignty. Nevertheless, active tributary relations between the Yuan and Il-Khans continued, and Il-Khan high officials still coveted Chinese titles such as *chingsang* (modern *chengxiang*, grand councillor) and *gong* (duke).

ADMINISTRATION AND FISCAL POLICY

The administration of the Il-Khans centered on the khan elected at a QURILTAI (assembly). Like previous Turkish dynasties in Iran, the Mongol dynasty did not have a fixed succession rule. Stable succession thus depended on consensus among the great commanders (NOYAN).

As in the Yuan dynasty, a threefold ethnic class distinction of the conquest elite, the subject class, and an intermediate mixed class permeated government. The division of the first two classes, often summarized as "Mongols and Muslims," was as much cultural, social, and political as strictly religious. *Mongol* meant the nomadic military class and *Muslim* the native sedentary Iranian and Iraqi population. The intermediate class was specialists and royal clients who were either foreign (Turkestanis), non-Muslim (Assyrians, Armenians, Jews), or both (UIGHURS, Chinese). Ghazan Khan's reign eliminated the intermediate class's previous power.

The core of the Mongol class was the khan's household, consisting of his own *keshig*, or imperial guard, and intimate servitors and the palace-tents (ORDO) of his wives with their affiliated estates. These estates, or *injü* (INJE), constituted the khan and his family's private demesne, in contrast to the *dalai*, or state lands. The *keshig* was divided into four three-day shifts, and from 1291 on the four shift chiefs, three of whom were drawn from the Mongol great *noyan*s, countersigned all decrees of the khan with their black seals. Among the chief *noyan*s, the families of Elege of the JALAYIR and Su'unchaq of the Suldus were the most prestigious. The OIRATS of Diyarbakır, frequent QUDA (marriage allies) of the khans, remained a discrete tribal body. Outside the court was the Mongol army, organized by the traditional DECIMAL ORGANIZATION and clan affiliations.

Opposite these Mongol *noyan*s was the financial administration, staffed by Persian Sunni Muslim clerks and headed by one or two viziers (always two after 1295), the senior of whom handled the supreme red seal, or *al tamgha*. Nevertheless the Mongol and Persian orders were not hermetically sealed. The great *noyan*s had their own appanages administered by Persian clients, provincial commanders and governors frequently colluded, and the senior vizier himself served in the *keshig* as the head of the khan's personal three-day shift.

By 1305 a number of autonomous client kingdoms had been turned into provinces, and Ghazan Khan's reforms of 1300 created for the first time a single coinage and standard of weights and measures. By the dynasty's end the Il-Khan regime had eight directly administered provinces of the center, in addition to the semi-independent viceroyalties of Khorasan and Anatolia. In addition to the universal *qubchiri*, or poll tax, the eight central provinces paid "divan dues" based on traditional agricultural taxes, while the center's 20 main cities paid separate *tamgha*, or commercial tolls. Major cities and the provinces received a (usually) Persian *malik* (governor) who handled finance and administration, a Mongol emir, or *noyan*, who commanded the troops, and a DARUGHACHI (Persian, *shahna*) of the Mongol or intermediate class. Assignment of important provinces (particularly GEORGIA, Diyarbakır, and Iraq) as camping grounds for princes offered a further layer of supervision.

The Il-Khanate practiced the traditional *muqata'at*, or tax-farming system. The treasury drew up contracts specifying the total amount of taxes paid and the deductions the tax farmer could take for expenses. *Malik*s of major provinces were usually concurrent tax farmers, subcontracting the taxes in districts and villages. Theoretically, the tax farmer could not collect more than the contracted amount, but supervision was lax and overcollection rife. The eager attention the Il-Khans usually paid to reports from *ayqaq*s (informers) about untapped or embezzled revenues put constant upward pressure on taxes and made the tenure of governors and viziers exceedingly uncertain—all but one of the viziers under the Il-Khans were executed with torture on charges of embezzlement, treason, or both.

Hüle'ü stored the booty of his conquests of 1256–58 in a tower by Lake Urmia, but by Sultan Ahmad's reign (1282–84) the tower had partially collapsed, and the remaining treasure was shared out as coronation gifts. From then on the treasury was carried in the khan's *ordo* in chests. Except under diligent khans such as Ghazan Khan, treasury procedures were lax and embezzlement routine. Unbudgeted drafts on outlying provinces hindered financial planning, and random seizures by messengers (*elchi*) damaged the economy. These problems peaked in the 1290s. Ghazan Khan's reforms did curb the abuses, particularly of the messenger system, but did not eliminate the constant pressure for more revenue.

MILITARY

The immigrant Mongols, composed of the *tammachi* (garrison) armies dispatched in the 1230s to Afghanistan and to the Armenia-Azerbaijan area, as well as Hüle'ü's new army, constituted the Il-Khan's military core. Nevertheless once counted and incorporated into the decimal organization, designated military households in the settled population also supplied infantry and cavalry that served under Mongol commanders in garrisons or the field. The theoretical reserve of the Il-Khan's army added up to 30 *tümen*s (each nominally 10,000), although *tümen*s averaged perhaps only 40 percent of paper strength. In reality the largest battlefield force ever mobilized was about 70,000 men. Thus, the Il-Khans had enough troops only to confront one of their three major enemies—Egypt, the Golden Horde, or the Chaghatayids—at a time. The court equipped and provisioned at most one out of five army units, leaving remoter units, Mongol or native, to feed and equip themselves. Even so, the Il-Khanid army was better armed than the larger Chaghatayid and Golden Horde forces. In addition to the Mongol units, Georgian cavalry participated in virtually every battle, and the client kingdoms of Lesser Armenia and Seljük Turkey in the west and Kerman and Fars in the east also supplied troops for major campaigns.

POLITICAL HISTORY

On Hüle'ü's death in 1265 the princes and *noyan*s unanimously elected his eldest son, Abagha (1234–82), khan. Abagha immediately faced an invasion from Berke, khan (1257–66) of the Golden Horde, which ended with Berke's fortuitous death in Tiflis. In 1270 Abagha defeated an invasion by the Chaghatay khan Baraq at Qara-Su near Herat (July 22), and his brother Yisüder went on to sack Bukhara in retaliation (January 1273). In 1277 Sultan Baybars of Egypt invaded Turkey, defeating the Mongol troops there at Elbistan. Stung by this defeat, Abagha executed the local regent, Mu'in-ad-Din Pervâne, for collusion, assigned Turkey to one younger brother, Qongqortai (d. 1284), and sent another, Möngke-Temür (1256–82), with a large army to invade Syria. Poor leadership led, however, to an even more humiliating defeat near Homs (October 29, 1281). Late in his relatively long reign, feeling increasing financial pressure, Abagha began to resent Hüle'ü's old *noyan*s and viziers. He promoted his foster son and *tamghachi*, BUQA, as commander in chief (*beglerbegi*) and countenanced Majd-ul-Mulk's accusations against the long-standing *sahib-divan* (or vizier) SHAMS-UD-DIN JUVAINI.

Abagha Khan's death led to the Il-Khanate's first contested election. While Abagha's entourage, commanding the Qara'una *tümen* Abagha had brought from Khorasan, preferred his son Arghun (1260–91), Hüle'ü's old-guard *noyan*s, such as Elege and Su'unchaq, and the princes delivered the election to Abagha's brother Tegüder (June 21, 1282), who promptly distributed the rest of the treasury to the Mongol aristocracy. A Muslim convert, Tegüder ruled as Sultan Ahmad (1282–84) but made no attempt to Islamize the realm. Ahmad's only policy initiative was an unsuccessful attempt to make peace with Egypt. Arghun, however, intrigued with Abagha's old Qara'una *tümen* while appealing to Qubilai Khan in the east, who believed that Islam and the Mongol JASAQ (law) were incompatible. In 1284 Ahmad, belatedly realizing the extent of Arghun's intrigues, executed Prince Qongqortai, imprisoned Abagha's *keshig* chiefs, and attacked Arghun in Khorasan. Although Arghun was captured, Buqa, whom Ahmad had unwisely trusted, freed him and overthrew Ahmad. Arghun's coronation (August 11, 1284) was confirmed by Qubilai in February 1286.

In Arghun's reign the khan for the first time showed outright hostility to Muslim officials as Buddhism reached its height of influence as the royal religion. Arghun defeated an invasion from the Golden Horde in 1290 but could not stop the increasingly destructive raids from Egypt or the rebellion of NAWROZ in Khorasan. Pushed by his empty treasury, Arghun allowed the viziers Buqa and then SA'D-UD-DAWLA to centralize expenditures tightly. Arghun's former partisans, led by TA'ACHAR (d. 1296) of the Baarin, fought this centralization, engineering the deaths of both viziers and finally murdering Arghun himself as he lay in a coma.

The conspirators originally planned to enthrone Baidu, who refused to appear at the *quriltai*, so instead they enthroned Geikhatu, Arghun's brother and viceroy in Anatolia. Under Geikhatu's reign (1291–95) social, financial, military, and political factors combined almost to destroy the Il-Khanate. Socially, Islamization among the Mongol rank-and-file had proceeded rapidly, isolating the court, which was still dominated by a pagan-Buddhist-Christian cousinage. First the conspirators and then Geikhatu had shared out the treasury to buy support, and a pan-Eurasian silver shortage from 1286 to 1297 made it impossible to rebuild the realm's finances. Nawroz's rebellion and famine continued to ravage Khorasan. The only bright spot was the peace with the Golden Horde.

Khan Geikhatu and his vizier Sadr-ud-Din Zanjani (d. 1298) tried to use short-term tricks to sustain the treasury, including a disastrous experiment with adopting the Yuan's paper money (*chao*). Geikhatu limited Ta'achar's power by relying on the old guard of Elege's sons Shigtür and Aq-Buqa, the khan's father-in-law, but Geikhatu's pederasty alienated most of the aristocracy. Eventually, Ta'achar and his clique overthrew Geikhatu and enthroned Baidu in his place.

By 1295 Ghazan (1271–1304), Arghun's son and viceroy in Khorasan, had made peace with Nawroz, and by October 1295 he overthrew Baidu. Ghazan Khan's reign refounded the khanate on a new basis. A recent convert to Islam, he Islamized the state, ordering all *noyan*s and Mongol soldiers to convert, destroying Buddhism, and thrusting Christianity into a secondary position. Careful management and the revival in the Eurasian silver supply rebuilt the treasury. Finally, he replaced the old elite wholesale with a loyal Khorasanian clique led by the commander in chief (*beglerbegi*) Qutlughshah (d. 1307) of the MANGGHUD, thus restoring the khan-*noyan* consensus necessary for stable government.

Reigning as Sultan Öljeitü, Ghazan Khan's brother Kharbanda (1281–1316) at first continued with his brother's personnel and policy. With the Syrian front quiet, Öljeitü and the aggressive Qutlughshah finally reduced Gilan, the last Iranian province free of Mongol rule, to tributary status, a pyrrhic victory that cost Qutlughshah his life (June 1307). Chaghatayid dissensions allowed Il-Khanid influence, coordinated with a Yuan advance, again to reach Sistan and Ghazni. The deaths of Qutlughshah and Sheikh Baraq Baba (1257/8–1307), Öljeitü's wild Sufi spiritual adviser, pushed Öljeitü, baptized a Christian, into a renewed spiritual quest that resulted in his adoption of Twelver Shi'ism as the state religion in winter 1308–09. Öljeitü's new commander in chief, CHUBAN (d. 1327) of the Suldus, refused to convert, and the Sunni urban centers rioted against Shi'ism. Under Chuban's influence Öljeitü's son Abu-Sa'id later returned the regime to Sunni orthodoxy.

Under Abu-Sa'id Ba'atur Khan (Mongolian, Busayid, b. 1305, r. 1317–35), the old Suldus and Jalayir families under Chuban and "Big" Hasan (Hasan Buzurg, d. 1356), respectively, reestablished their prestige. As regent during Abu-Sa'id's minority, Chuban faced two foreign challenges: a rebellion in 1318 of Chaghatayids and Qara'unas who had been resettled in Khorasan, and a desultory invasion by the Golden Horde's ÖZBEG KHAN in winter 1318–19. More threatening was the rebellion of Irenchin, the one-time emir of Anatolia, father-in-law to Öljeitü and Abu-Sa'id, successively, and patron of Christian churches. Demoted by Chuban, Irenchin and other Mongol emirs revolted and were bloodily crushed at the Battle of Zanjan-Rud (between Zanjan and Soltaniyeh, July 13, 1319). Chuban's victory strengthened his hold over Abu-Sa'id. Chuban first reconcile the Il-Khanate with the Chaghatay khan Kebeg (1318–26), who assisted "Big" Hasan in crushing the Chaghatayid rebels in Khorasan, and then signed a peace treaty with Egypt (1323). Despite these successes, Abu-Sa'id overthrew Chuban and his sons in 1327, giving chief command to "Big" Hasan.

MONGOL LIFE, SOCIAL CONFLICT, AND COURT CULTURE

The court of the Il-Khanate and its successor states remained trilingual until at least the middle of the 14th century, with documents written in Persian, Mongolian, and Uighur Turkish. All three languages influenced one another heavily, sharing vocabulary and idioms. The court also used the Islamic lunar calendar alongside the Chinese-based Mongol lunar-solar calendar and 12-ANIMAL CYCLE. The role of the WHITE MONTH (Mongolian new year), hunting, and liquor in cementing social relations continued in full force despite Islamization.

While in Mongolia Hüle'ü had frequent interviews with Chinese scholars and patronized the Tibetan Buddhist 'Bri-gung-pa and Phag-mo-gru-pa orders. Two sons, Yoshmut and Qongqortai, were born of Chinese concubines. This patronage of Chinese and Tibetan Buddhist culture continued in Iran. Thus, for example, both Ghazan Khan's nursemaid and his first tutor were Chi-

nese, and in 1292 he received as a wife Kökejin Khatun from the Yuan court. Even after Islamization Qubilai Khan's envoy BOLAD CHINGSANG reached the height of his influence under Öljeitü. Under Abu-Sa'id "tribute" missions reached their peak, and wealthy Persian Gulf merchant families carried on lucrative trade in China. Minorities also participated in this exchange. Thus, when an Assyrian Christian merchant returned from a trade mission to Qubilai, Abagha Khan appointed the envoy's son Mas'ud (d. 1289) as governor of Mosul and Irbil and Qubilai's Uighur Christian envoy Yashmut (d. 1284) darughachi.

The Il-Khans at first followed the Mongol religious policy of according equal patronage to the clergy of several favored religions. By Arghun's reign, if not earlier, Judaism replaced Taoism as one of the four exempt religions, along with Buddhism, Christianity, and Islam. This evenhandedness and Hüle'ü's conquests created deep disaffection among the Muslim populations, particularly in Iraq, Diyarbakır, and KURDISTAN, often expressed in communal rioting. From 1289 to 1295 this rioting became linked to Mongol political divisions and formed a vital force driving the Islamization of the dynasty. After 1297 Buddhism was proscribed, but Christian clergy retained their tax exemptions and limited subsidies. The full regime of discriminatory taxation and sumptuary regulations for lay Christians and Jews came in force only after 1319.

Until 1290 or so Assyrian Christian clergy and Buddhist baqshis (Uighur and Mongolian, "teacher") increased their influence among the Mongol elite in the central zone. The Assyrian church coexisted easily with Buddhism and unlike other churches performed funerary liturgies for Buddhist khans such as Hüle'ü and Arghun. At the same time Islamization among the rank-and-file Mongols appears to have made great strides in the 1280s. The ordinary illiterate Mongol trooper, often with captured local wives, lived in much closer contact with the Muslim majority than did the noyans and the royal family with its quda system of cross-cousin marriage exchange and education under Uighur or Chinese tutors. In the realm's center the numerous Mongol units competed for pasture with Turkmen and especially Kurdish pastoralists, but where their numbers were fewer they often merged with Turkmen tribes. In 1296 a whole tümen of Oirats in Diyarbakır deserted to Egypt over conflicts with the local Turkmen. In Khorasan the influence of Arghun Aqa, an early Muslim convert, probably accelerated Islamization, yet the Mongol military units of Khorasan maintained their Mongol identity, merging after the dynasty's fall with the Chaghatayid and Timurid-aligned Mongols in Afghanistan.

Mongol Islamic practice involved several different levels. The ecstatic séances conducted by Sufi dervishes attracted many converts, including Ahmad, Geikhatu's son Alafrang, and the young Öljeitü. Others, such as

Nawroz, embraced a militant Muslim-Mongol solidarity directed against the non-Muslim intermediate class. Ghazan Khan, in turning against Buddhist idolatry, linked Islam with the ancient monotheistic Mongol traditions, while Shi'ite-inclined Mongols identified the legitimacy of the 'Alid family in Islam with that of the Chinggisids in the empire. Chuban sought the strict application of Islamic law and international peace.

Religious change also affected Mongol customs. Following the native Mongol practice of absolute separation of the living and the dead, Hüle'ü and his immediate successors were buried in unmarked graves. Christian Mongols such as Irenchin, however, endowed masses for their parents, and Arghun endowed a Buddhist temple for his soul. After Islamization Ghazan and Öljeitü built Persian-style mausolea with attached charitable institutions, while Chuban built a similar tomb and school complex in Medina. Following Islamic traditions of tribal endogamy Sultans Ahmad and Öljeitü contracted marriages with Chinggisid princesses for themselves or their sons, although many Mongols continued to view such endogamy as monstrously incestuous.

Nothing of the Buddhist art sponsored by the earlier Il-Khans survived the persecution of 1295. Guided by Rashid-ud-Din and other Persian viziers, the later Il-Khans sponsored famous masterworks of Persian art: Ghazan Khan's and Sultan Öljeitü's renovation of the tomb of Bayazid at Bastam and Öljeitü's mausoleum complex at Soltaniyeh and his Hamadan and Mosul Qur'ans. As a child Abu-Sa'id received a thorough education in poetry and Persian and Uighur-script calligraphy; after completing a particularly fine piece of penmanship, his proud father Öljeitü sent it around the *ordo*s to be admired. The era's greatest artistic achievement was the Persian illustrated manuscript tradition, freed from previous Islamic strictures against visual representation and nourished by Chinese ink painting and landscape techniques and Christian iconography. Modeled on the Chinese Hanlin Academy, the new Persian library atelier (*kitabkhana*) institutionalized illustrated manuscript production. The era's masterpiece, the DEMOTTE *SHAHNAMA*, was probably created under Abu-Sa'id.

FALL OF THE DYNASTY

While Hüle'ü left 10 sons at his death, factional struggles up to 1295 had virtually wiped out the collateral lines. Ghazan had no surviving sons, his brother Öljeitü had only one, and Öljeitü's son Abu-Sa'id none. The virtual disappearance of the princely class removed a potent source of rebellion after 1295, yet it also increased the influence of the emirs (*noyan*s) and resulted in 1335 in the extinction of the royal family.

Abu-Sa'id's seizure for himself of "Big" Hasan's wife, Baghdad Khatun, who was Chuban's daughter, set in motion conflicts that would break out after Abu-Sa'id's death in 1335. Accused with Baghdad Khatun of attempt-

ing to assassinate the khan in 1332, Hasan was exiled to Anatolia. Non-Mongol emirs, particularly Sharaf-ud-Din Mahmud-Shah (d. 1336), who ruled the crown lands (*injü*), and the vizier Ghiyas-ud-Din Muhammad (d. 1336), son of the famous Rashid-ud-Din, acquired unprecedented military power, causing widespread dissatisfaction among the Mongol emirs.

Abu-Sa'id died suddenly in Karabakh (November 30, 1335) while confronting renewed Golden Horde attacks. Ghiyas-ud-Din immediately enthroned Arpa-Ke'ün (d. 1336), a descendant of Hüle'ü's brother Ariq-Böke. Rivals, each sponsoring implausible Chinggisids as titular rulers, successively occupied the royal seat of Azerbaijan: 'Ali-Padshah of the Oirats (1336–37), "Big" Hasan of the Jalayir (1337–38), and "Little" Hasan (Hasan Kuchek), grandson of Chuban (1338–43). Outside the old Il-Khanid center local dynasties soon threw off Mongol rule.

"Little" Hasan's Chubanid brothers held the Azerbaijan heartland until 1257, yet their rapacious policies led to general rejoicing when Janibeg, khan of the Golden Horde, overthrew the regime in 1357. "Big" Hasan having maintained Jalayirid rule in Baghdad, his son Sheikh Uwais (r. 1356–74) founded his own Jalayirid dynasty after Janibeg's death in 1357 and held Azerbaijan and Iraq until 1385. The chaos after 1335 diverted East-West trade to the Golden Horde and Mamluk Egypt. The Black Plague, first appearing among the Chubanid armies in 1346–47, completed the socioeconomic disaster.

THE IMPACT OF THE MONGOLS ON THE MIDDLE EAST

The Mongol invasion and rule of the Middle East played a major role in shaping some of the distinctive features of its late medieval Islamic civilization. Nomadic pastoralism expanded at the expense of sedentary agriculture due to the massacres and general devastation of the invasion, the immigration of the scores of thousands of Mongol nomads, and the system of taxation, which taxed agriculture to subsidize commerce. Hamdullah Mustaufi Qazvini (b. 1281/2) claimed tax revenues under the Mongols were one-fifth to one-tenth what they had been in previous dynasties. The particularly severe devastation in Khorasan turned that area, once the cultural center of Iran, into a backwater.

Mongol rule also changed the religious complexion of the Middle East. Despite early Mongol patronage, the expansion of nomadism and communal violence devastated the wholly sedentary Christian and Jewish communities. The clerical immunities the Mongols offered religious institutions also encouraged the growth of tax-exempt Sufi lodges. While their tenacious cultural identity limited their interest in urban *shari'a* (Islamic law)-based Islam, the Mongols actively patronized Sufi masters, adding further to their influence.

Cultural interchange, particularly with China, enriched Persian culture under the Il-Khans. By the dynasty's end the Mongol elite participated in and developed further the Persian high-culture tradition of calligraphy, poetry, illustrated manuscripts, and the national epic, *Shahnama*. Despite the chaos after the dynasty's fall, the Jalayirids continued this patronage, transmitting Il-Khanid cultural achievements to the Timurid dynasty.

See also APPANAGE SYSTEM; ARTISANS IN THE MONGOL EMPIRE; BUDDHISM IN THE MONGOL EMPIRE; BYZANTIUM AND BULGARIA; CENSUS IN THE MONGOL EMPIRE; CHRISTIAN SOURCES ON THE MONGOL EMPIRE; CHRISTIANITY IN THE MONGOL EMPIRE; INDIA AND THE MONGOL EMPIRE; ISLAM IN THE MONGOL EMPIRE; ISLAMIC SOURCES ON THE MONGOL EMPIRE; MONEY IN THE MONGOL EMPIRE; PAPER CURRENCY IN THE MONGOL EMPIRE; PROVINCES IN THE MONGOL EMPIRE; RELIGIOUS POLICY IN THE MONGOL EMPIRE; WESTERN EUROPE AND THE MONGOL EMPIRE.

Further reading: Thomas T. Allsen, *Culture and Conquest in Mongol Eurasia* (Cambridge: Cambridge University Press, 2001); John Andrew Boyle, ed., *Cambridge History of Iran*, vol. 5, *The Seljuk and Mongol Periods* (Cambridge: Cambridge University Press, 1968); Linda Comaroff and Stephan Carboni, *Legacy of Genghis Khan: Courtly Art and Culture in Western Asia, 1256–1353* (New York: Metropolitan Museum of Art, 2002); A. K. S. Lambton, "Mongol Fiscal Administration in Persia," *Studia Islamica* 64 (1986): 79–99 and 65 (1987): 97–123; Charles Melville, *The Fall of Amir Chupan and the Decline of the Il-Khanate, 1327–37: A Decade of Discord in Mongol Iran* (Bloomington, Ind.: Research Institute for Inner Asian Studies, 1999); Charles Melville, "The Itineraries of Sultan Öljeitü, 1304–1316," *Iran* 28 (1990): 55–70; ———, "The Ilkhan Öljeitü's Conquest of Gilan (1307): Rumour and Reality," in *The Mongol Empire and Its Legacy*, ed. Reuven Amitai-Preiss and David O. Morgan (Leiden: E. J. Brill, 1999), 73–125.

Il-qan *See* IL-KHANATE.

incarnate lama (living buddha)   In Buddhist belief an incarnate lama is an emanation body (*khubilgan;* Tibetan, *sprul-sku,* often written "tulku" in English) of a deity in a perfected realm who appeared for the benefit of sentient beings in this realm. The term "living Buddha" (*huofo*) is of Chinese origin and is disliked by Tibetan and Mongolian Buddhists. The ability to produce such emanation bodies is the height of "skill in means" (Mongolian, *arga;* Sanskrit, *upaya*), or the ability to use any effective method to save living beings. Generally such emanation bodies were linked to great bodhisattvas, such as Manjushri, Avalokiteshvara, and Tara rather than to Buddhas, such as Shakyamuni Buddha, the historical Buddha of our era. Nevertheless, the sanctity and power of such a lineage was far more dependent on the demonstrated supernatural charisma of its successive incarnations than on its identification with any particular bodhisattva.

Indeed, the exact identification of a lineage with a particular bodhisattva is often unclear and in any case of interest only to learned lamas and not ordinary believers. Since lay patrons benefit the faith as well, emanation bodies need not be lamas or monks. Thus, the Qing emperors in Beijing were identified as the emanation body, or incarnation, of Manjushri, while CHINGGIS KHAN was identified as the emanation body of the fierce bodhisattva Vajrapani.

The practice of finding incarnate lamas began in the Tibetan Karma-pa lineage in the 13th century. By the time of the SECOND CONVERSION to Buddhism (1578 on) in Mongolia, the practice was well entrenched in all monastic orders of Tibet, including the dominant dGe-lugs-pa. The greater incarnate lamas bore the title Khutugtu (also spelled Khutukhtu; modern Khutagt), while the less important ones had the title of Gegeen. Incarnate lamas were the most important figures in the Buddhist establishment, setting the tone both religiously and politically. The most powerful incarnate lama lineage in Mongolia was that of the Jibzundamba Khutugtu, held to be, like Chinggis Khan himself, an emanation of Vajrapani.

Incarnate lineages began more or less spontaneously after the death of any outstanding lama, promoted by a combination of homage to the departed lama's holiness and the tremendous increase in importance and revenue accruing to any monastery with an incarnate lama. Incarnate lamas were discovered among possible child candidates through divination, cryptic prophecies left by the previous emanation, dreams, portents, and the candidate's recognition of the previous emanation's personal effects.

The Qing emperor ordered all major incarnations, such as the Jibzundamba Khutugtu, to be found in Tibet, but minor ones were still found in Mongolia. The newly identified incarnate lama lived with his parents under the supervision of a senior monk until at age four or five the boy was invited to the monastery to spend the rest of his childhood among adult tutors. At age seven he began to learn to read, and after taking *getsül* vows at about age 16 he would begin to receive the worshipping public.

The main task of the incarnate lama was to receive devotions and give blessings. As adults most incarnate lamas took little interest in daily monastery administration, and their personal staff, headed by the *soibon* (Tibetan, *bso 'i-dpon*), and the temple staff handled all important business. The teenage years of an incarnate lama were often difficult times, when they began to challenge their tutors' rules and acquire passions for hunting, drinking, and/or sex. An incarnate lama's reputation for sanctity, however, did not necessarily depend on rigid adherence to monastic discipline. Many incarnate lamas of outwardly scandalous behavior still kept a reputation for miraculous healing powers and other signs of great holiness.

The Qing government recognized 57 incarnate lamas in Inner Mongolia and 19 in Outer Mongolia, but the actual number of incarnate lineages in Outer Mongolia was 35 to 44. Of the lineages, 13 had lay serfs or *shabinar* numerous enough to be given a seal and territory equivalent to a banner, while the Jibzundamba Khutugtu had a rank higher than any secular aristocrat in Khalkha. The *shabinar* of these incarnations were each under a *shangdzodba* and a *da lama*, whose selection had to be confirmed by the league administration or the Qing court (*see* GREAT SHABI).

From the beginning incarnate lamas had great political influence. Aside from the Jibzundamba Khutugtu, who was the supreme leader of Khalkha, many incarnate lamas played powerful roles in the 1911 RESTORATION, the new revolutionary government after 1921, and in Inner Mongolian nationalist movements from 1924 to 1945.

The institution of incarnate lamas did not exist among the Kalmyk or Buriat Mongols of Russia. In Mongolia proper it fell under suspicion as a potentially subversive force after the 1921 REVOLUTION and was banned in 1929. With the reappearance of religious freedom in Mongolia in 1990, all the incarnate lamas were long dead, and the institution has not been revived. In Inner Mongolia it continued unchallenged until 1945 and was not directly attacked by the Communist regime until 1958. When qualified religious freedom returned to China in 1979, many incarnate lamas, such as the line of the Ulaan Gegeen in HÖHHOT, still survived and have returned to a leadership role in Inner Mongolian Buddhist life.

See also DANSHUG; JANGJIYA KHUTUGTU; LAMAS AND MONASTICISM; REVOLUTIONARY PERIOD; SHANGDZODBA, ERDENI; SOCIAL CLASSES IN THE QING PERIOD.

Further reading: Paul Hyer and Sechin Jagchid, *A Mongolian Living Buddha: Biography of the Kanjurwa Khutughtu* (Albany: State University of New York Press, 1983); Owen Lattimore and Fukiko Isono, *The Diluv Khutagt: Memoirs and Autobiography of a Mongol Buddhist Reincarnation in Religion and Revolution* (Wiesbaden: Otto Harrassowitz, 1982); Aleksei M. Pozdneyev, *Religion and Ritual in Society: Lamaist Buddhism in Late 19th-Century Mongolia*, trans. Alo and Linda Raun (Bloomington, Ind.: Mongolia Society, 1978).

India and the Mongols Subject to incessant Mongol raids, India's climate and stiffening resistance from the sultans of Delhi blocked conquest for a century and a half.

At the time of the Mongol conquest the Islamic Delhi sultanate ruled northern India. Warring incessantly with the Hindu kings further south and east and always wary of the subjugated Hindu majority, the sultanate of Delhi was less a unified regime than a coalition of *malik*s (provincial military governors), of Qipchaq Turk, Ghurid (Afghan), and Khalaj Turk origin, each slaves of the sultan or his predecessors, each with his own personal army, and each ready at any point to seize the sultanate for himself.

When Jalal-ud-Din Mengüberdi of KHORAZM fled across the Indus River, CHINGGIS KHAN (Genghis,

1206–27) dispatched Dörbei the Fierce to pursue him. Dörbei did not locate Jalal-ud-Din but sacked Nandana and sieged Multan for 42 days in 1224 before retreating due to the summer heat. The heat and disease attendant upon summering in India long restricted Mongol invasions there to seasonal booty raids.

ÖGEDEI KHAN (1229–41) appointed Dayir Ba'atur commander of Ghazni and Mönggetü commander in Qonduz with two *tümen*s (10,000s) of TAMMACHI (permanent garrison) troops. In winter 1241 the Mongol force invaded the Indus valley and besieged Lahore. By this time many Indian merchants had acquired Mongol passes (PAIZA) for trade in Central Asia and hence influential townsmen advocated surrender. Dayir Ba'atur died storming the town, however, on December 30, 1241, and the Mongols butchered the town before withdrawing.

In 1253 MÖNGKE KHAN (1251–59) dispatched the Tatar tribesman Sali of the KESHIG (guards) to take command of the troops of both Dayir and Mönggetü (who had also died in the meantime) and to conquer Hindustan and KASHMIR. Simultaneously, several Indus valley *malik*s visited the Mongols and accepted allegiance, and in 1259–60 envoys passed between HÜLE'Ü (r. 1256–65), the founder of the Mongol IL-KHANATE in the Middle East, and Delhi. These intimations of submission soon evaporated, and Sali and his successors raided Hindustan regularly for the next few decades.

By the 1280s the Mongol khanates had become heavily involved in the trade to India. Indian exports included spices, precious stones, cottons, silks, and ivory, but the key import from Hormuz in Iran and from the GOLDEN HORDE was horses, with smaller markets in military slaves and falcons. Having ruined their own cities, the Chaghatay khans of Central Asia, descendants of CHA'ADAI, Chinggis's second son, depended on this transit trade. A general depression of trade in the 1290s thus hit the CHAGHATAY KHANATE realm hard. By 1270 the Mongols in Afghanistan formed a distinct body called QARA'UNAS, famed for their turbulence and said to be of mixed Mongol-Indian blood. Nominally subject to the Il-Khanate, the Chaghatayids of Central Asia soon acquired great influence among the Qara'unas, and from 1292 to 1306 the Chaghatay Khan Du'a (1282–1307) and his sons led several concerted efforts to conquer Delhi. Other Qara'unas responded to hardship by converting to Islam and settling in India as "New Muslim" auxiliaries of the sultan. After a two-month siege of Delhi in 1303, Sultan 'Ala-ud-Din Muhammad (1296–1315) reorganized his armies and won great victories in 1305 and 1306, meting out horrific punishments to the captured Mongols. After 1306 Chaghatayid and Qara'una attacks entirely ceased for more than a decade. Around 1310 'Ala-ud-Din killed envoys from the Il-Khan Öljeitü and massacred the entire 20,000–30,000 population of submitted "New Muslims."

Although Sultan Ghiyas-ud-Din Tughluq (1320–25) was in origin a poor Qara'una who took service with a merchant of Sind, clashes with the Mongols were again constant in his reign—he claimed to have fought them 29 times—but no longer threatened conquest. Under his son Muhammad (1325–50) Mongol raids reached as far as the Indian city of Meerut (Mirath) in 1328–29, and the booty from Indian raids, together with a trade resurgence, revived the Chaghatay economy. Thus, while the Chaghatayid pressure on India was constant, it was left to TIMUR and his descendants, the Mughals, to take Delhi and rule India.

See also SOUTH SEAS.

Further reading: Peter A. Jackson, *The Delhi Sultanate: A Military and Political History* (Cambridge: Cambridge University Press, 1992); André Wink, "India and the Turco-Mongol Frontier," in *Nomads in the Sedentary World,* ed. Anatoly M. Khazanov and André Wink (Richmond, Surrey: Curzon Press, 2001): 211–233.

Injannashi (Injannasi, Injanasi, Injinash) (1837–1892)
A complex and ironic author whose satires on blind superstition made him the icon of later Inner Mongolian nationalists
Injannashi was born on May 20, 1837, the youngest surviving son of the Chinggisid TAIJI (nobleman) Wangchinbala (Chinese name Bao Jingshan, 1795–1847) and his lady, Mayushaka (b. 1800), in Tümed Right Banner (modern Beipiao county, Liaoning province) in Josotu league. Wangchinbala's family, like the other Mongols of Josotu league, had long been settled as landlords of Chinese tenants.

Injannashi's family was highly literate in Mongolian, Manchu, and Chinese. Wangchinbala wrote poems in Mongolian while serving as banner *tusalagchi* (administrator), a position inherited by two of his sons, Gularansa (1820–51) and Süngwaidanjung (Chinese, Bao Songshan, 1834–98). These two also translated the Chinese novel *Shuihu zhuan* (Outlaws of the marsh) into Mongolian, and like their middle brother, Gungnechuke (1832–66), were poets.

Injannashi married twice—his first wife was the daughter of a KHARACHIN prince—and had two sons. A rebellion by his family's Chinese tenants in 1870 and the failure of their investment in a coal mine caused financial distress. He died in Jinzhou city in Liaoning on February 25, 1892.

Injannashi's artistic activities began with poetry and Chinese brush painting of landscapes and birds. His most famous work, the *Blue Chronicle of the Rise of the Great Yuan Dynasty* (Yekhe Yuwan ulus-un mandugsan törö-yin khökhe sudur), he claimed had been begun by his father and briefly worked on by his three brothers before he completed it himself in 1870–71. Internal evidence indicates, however, that the extant *Blue Chronicle* (Khökhe sudur) is entirely Injannashi's work. While Injannashi apparently planned to write a full history of the YUAN DYNASTY from the rise of Chinggis to 1368, the text breaks off in 1236. Following the precedent of Rashipungsug's *BOLOR ERIKHE,* with which Injannashi was familiar, he uncritically mixed Chinese histories, particularly the YUAN SHI, and traditional Mongolian chronicles (*see* 17TH-CENTURY CHRONICLES). Unlike Rashipungsug, however, Injannashi added verses and embellishments of his own creation. The result, while presented as a history, is similar to the Chinese historical novel *Romance of Three Kingdoms* (from which Injannashi also borrows episodes). Injannashi's freedom is even greater in a later incomplete manuscript of the work in the author's hand called the Tümed manuscript, with numerous entirely imagined episodes.

Injannashi's other novels *Nigen dabkhur asar* (One story pavilion) and *Ulagan-a ukilakhu tingkhim* (Pavilion of scarlet tears) were re-creations in Mongolian of the world of the Chinese novel *Dream of the Red Chamber* (or *Story of the Stone*) by Cao Xueqin (1724?–64). Injannashi borrowed heavily from two of the Chinese "continuations" inspired by the great novel of thwarted youthful love and karmic debts and evidently conceived of his work in the same lines. While much of the setting is autobiographical—the hero is the son of the "Marquis of the North," living in Zhongxinfu court, the very name of Wangchinbala's mansion—and embellishments are drawn from Mongolian life, the novels reflect primarily the *Red Chamber* craze that swept late Qing China.

Injannashi's fame in Inner Mongolia derived primarily, however, from the *Blue Chronicle*'s "Brief Introduction" (tobchitu tolta). In it Injannashi savagely satirizes the sensuality of the *taiji*s, the obscurantism of the clergy, the crudity of the Mongol nomads, and the pettiness of prejudiced Chinese scholars, earning praise from Inner Mongolian reformers and nationalists as a "democratic" writer. Injannashi crafted an original version of CONFUCIANISM, in which he saw the true *yirtinchü-yin yosu* (Chinese, *shidao*), or "way of the world," as avoiding both narrow-minded dogmatism and libertine skepticism. All the world's diversity was created through *arga bilig* (Chinese, *yin* and *yang*) and was, properly understood, good. This included both Buddhism and his own Mongolian people, who, despite their faults, deserved cultivation, a fact proved by the great phenomenon of CHINGGIS KHAN.

Originally circulated in manuscript, Injannashi's *Blue Chronicle* was printed in part in 1930 in Beijing and in full in 1940 in Kailu. His *Red Chamber* novels were published in 1938 and 1939. New editions were printed in HÖHHOT in 1957 and have been reprinted continuously ever since.

See also CHINESE FICTION; INNER MONGOLIANS; LITERATURE; "NEW SCHOOLS" MOVEMENTS.

Further reading: C. R. Bawden, "A Chinese Source for an Episode in Injanasi's Novel, *Nigen Dabqur Asar,*" in *Tractata Tibetica et Mongolica,* ed. Karénina Kollmar-Paulenz and Christian Peter (Wiesbaden: Otto Harrassowitz, 2002),

21–29; ———, "Injanasi's Romantic Novels as a Literary Tour-de-Force," in *Documenta Barbarorum*, ed. Klaus Sagaster and Michael Weiers (Wiesbaden: Otto Harrassowitz, 1983), 1–10; A. Craig Clunas, "The Prefaces to *Nigen Dabqur Asar* and Their Chinese Antecedents," *Zentralasiatische Studien* 15 (1981): 139–189; John Gombojab Hangin, *Köke Sudur (The Blue Chronicle): A Study of the First Mongolian Historical Novel by Injannasi* (Wiesbaden: Otto Harrassowitz, 1973).

inje (*injü*)   The term *inje* or dowry referred in the MONGOL EMPIRE to the human dowry of servants given with an aristocratic bride. Through the peculiarities of the Mongolian ORDO (palace tent) system the term sometimes came to designate the personal subjects of a khan.

The *inje,* which accompanied the bride to the groom's household at marriage, was both a daughter's share in her father's subjects and a support for her in her new family. (Due to exogamy, this was often far away from her natal home.) In the KEREYID Khanate of the 12th century, such dowries could reach up to 200 persons. The aristocracy of the Mongol Empire practiced polygamy, and each wife possessed her own *ordo,* among which the husband dwelt in rotation. The *ordo's* principal staff consisted partly of servants who had come with the wife as *inje* from her own people, and so in the khanates of Chaghatay in Turkestan and the Il-Khans in Iran the word *inje* (spelled *injü* or *enchü,* perhaps also influenced by *emchü,* personal property) came to refer to the khan's entire household, including inherited people, landed property, and subjects levied from his outer subjects as *keshigten* (imperial guards; *see* KESHIG).

In Mongolia, however, the term was used only in the original sense. Under the MONGOL-OIRAT CODE (*Mongghol-Oirad tsaaji*) of 1640, *inje* was restricted to livestock except among the greatest nobles, but the custom was retained on a much wider scale among the Qing (Ch'ing, 1636–1912) dynasty. In intermarriage with the dynasty's Manchu imperial family, sizable communities of Beijing bannermen and craftsmen were dispatched as *inje* with Manchu princesses to areas of Mongolia, where they long formed separate communities. Daughters of Mongolia's titled nobility received three to eight maidservants and two to five families as *inje,* depending on their rank. On the other end of the scale, the poorer TAIJI (descendants of CHINGGIS KHAN) usually sent only a single maidservant with their daughters. The revolutionary regime abolished the custom in 1923; in Inner Mongolia it continued until the Japanese occupation (1931–45).

See also FAMILY; QUDA; SOCIAL CLASSES IN THE QING PERIOD; WEDDINGS.

Further reading: Junko Miyawaki-Okada, "Women's Property in the History of Nomadic Societies," in *Altaic Affinities,* ed. David B. Honey and David C. Wright (Bloomington: Indiana University, 2001), 82–89.

Injinash   *See* INJANNASHI.

Inner Mongolia Autonomous Region   The Inner Mongolia Autonomous Region is China's third-largest provincial level unit, second only to Xinjiang and Tibet, and its main autonomous region for the Mongol nationality. Inner Mongolia covers 1,183,000 square kilometers (456,760 square miles) and has a population of 21,456,518, of which only 3,379,738 are Mongol (1990 figures). The region is heterogeneous in natural and ethnic geography. Much of it closely resembles neighboring Chinese provinces, but other areas are open steppe inhabited by Mongols in YURTS. While only about 16 percent of the population is Mongol, most Mongols live in areas in which they are, locally, the majority or a very large minority.

(On the social, cultural, and political history of Inner Mongolia's ethnic Mongols, *see* INNER MONGOLIANS.)

GEOGRAPHY AND DEMOGRAPHY

In physical geography Inner Mongolia forms a conglomeration of three different zones. The steppe and desert along the border with the State of Mongolia (Outer Mongolia) form part of the high MONGOLIAN PLATEAU. Eastern Inner Mongolia beyond the GREATER KHINGGAN RANGE is a more arid extension of the Manchurian plains, while Inner Mongolia south of the Yin Shan Mountains is part of the uplands flanking the North China plain. The Huang (Yellow) River valley cuts through these uplands and separates the deserts of the ORDOS plateau. In climate and vegetation, however, the region is more unified, being largely dry and continental with annual precipitation generally between 150 and 400 millimeters (6–16 inches). Most of the region is naturally steppe, with patches of dunes and sparse forests, but the southwestern third is desert and the northern Khinggan a vast boreal forest.

The human geography of Inner Mongolia was determined by the early pastoral settlement by Mongols and the advance of CHINESE COLONIZATION from the 18th to 20th centuries. Inner Mongolia can be divided into four large socioeconomic zones: pastoral, agropastoral, forestry, and agricultural.

The pastoral zone includes the areas along Mongolia's border (eastern HULUN BUIR, SHILIIN GOL, traditional ULAANCHAB, ALASHAN), northern JUU UDA east of the Khinggan, and the western part of the Ordos plateau, south of the Huang (Yellow) River. While containing more than 65 percent of Inner Mongolia's area, it has only 18 percent of its population. Mongols constitute an average 24 percent of the population in this zone, yet this low percentage is an average of 1) vast, sparsely settled pastoral areas proper, where Mongols are the majority, 2) small patches of high-density farming habitations that are virtually exclusively Han (ethnic Chinese) inhabited, and 3) cities and towns, where Mongols are a minority.

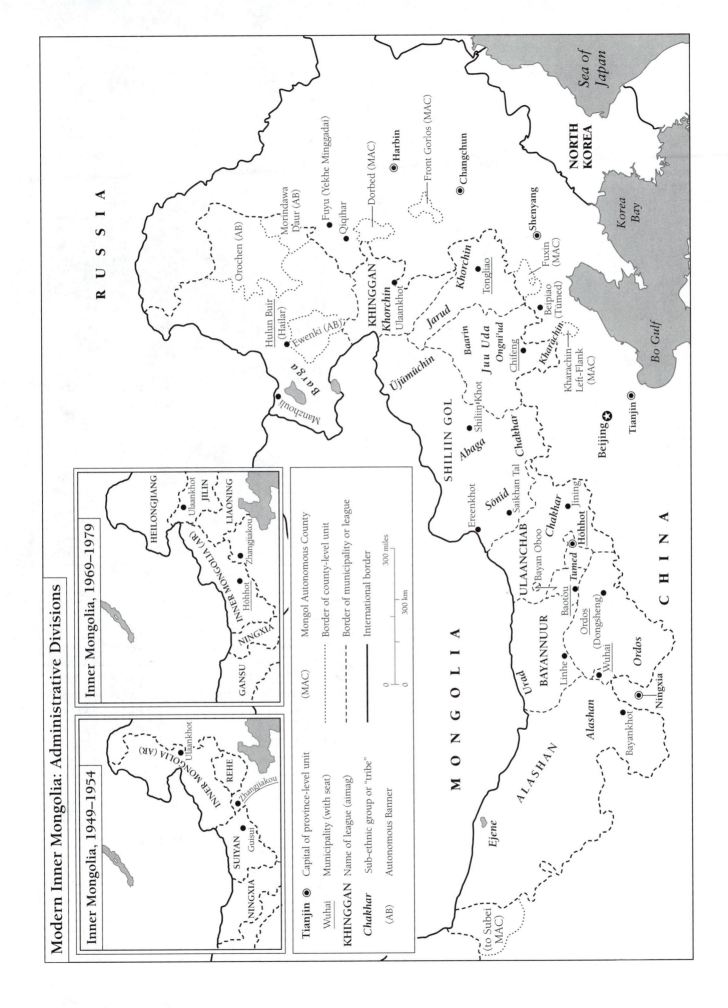

Modern Inner Mongolia: Administrative Divisions

Inner Mongolia, 1949–1954

NINGXIA
SUIYAN
  Guisui
INNER MONGOLIA (AR)
  Zhangjiakou
REHE
  Ulaankhot
NINGXIA

Inner Mongolia, 1969–1979

HEILONGJIANG
  Ulaankhot
JILIN
INNER MONGOLIA (AR)
  Zhangjiakou
  Höhhot
LIAONING
NINGXIA
GANSU

Tianjin ◉ Capital of province-level unit
Wuhai ◉ Municipality (with seat)
KHINGGAN Name of league (aimag)
Chakhar Sub-ethnic group or "tribe"
(AB) Autonomous Banner
(MAC) Mongol Autonomous County

········ Border of county-level unit
– – – – Border of municipality or league
——— International border

0   300 miles
0   300 km

RUSSIA

Manzhouli
Barga
Hulun Buir (Hailar)
Ewenki (AB)
Orochen (AB)
Morindawa Daur (AB)
Fuyu (Yekhe Minggadai)
Qiqihar
Dorbed (MAC)
Harbin ◉
Front Gorlos (MAC)
Changchun ◉

KHINGGAN
Khorchin
Ulaankhot
Khorchin
Jarud
Baarin
Juu Uda
Ongni'ud
Tongliao
Beipiao (Tumed)
Fuxin (MAC)
Shenyang ◉

NORTH KOREA

Sea of Japan

Üjümüchin
SHILIIN GOL
Abaga
Shiliin Khot
Chakhar
Ereenkhot
Sönid
Saikhan Tal
Chakhar
Jining
ULAANCHAB
Bayan Oboo
Tumed
Höhhot ◉
Baotou
Tumed
BAYANNUUR
Urad
Linhe
Ordos (Dongsheng)
Wuhai
Ordos
Ningxia ◉
Bayankhot
Alashan
ALASHAN
Ejene
(to Subei MAC)

Chifeng
Kharachin
Kharachin Left-Flank (MAC)

Beijing ✪
Tianjin ◉

Korea Bay
Bo Gulf

M O N G O L I A

C H I N A

A Khorchin farming village in Tongliao Municipality, around the White Month, 1988. The village is almost purely ethnic Mongol. *(Courtesy Christopher Atwood)*

In eastern Inner Mongolia KHORCHIN and neighboring districts are areas of agropastoral settlement, where the rural residents mix farming and stockbreeding. This zone is small both in area (7 percent) and in percentage of Inner Mongolia's population (11 percent) but contains almost 39 percent of Inner Mongolia's Mongols. It is the only zone where Mongols are the majority (54 percent).

The northeastern forestry zone in the Greater Khinggan Range contains 14 percent of Inner Mongolia's area and 9 percent of its population. Sparsely inhabited before 1950 by non-Mongol but culturally allied minorities—Daurs, EWENKIS, and Orochen—this area is now predominantly settled by Han. Mongols form only 3.5 percent of the population and other minorities an additional 8 percent.

The agricultural zone consists of areas along the Huang (Yellow) River and the borders with Inner Mongolia's neighboring provinces: Shanxi, Hebei, Liaoning, and Jilin. While accounting for only 13 percent of Inner Mongolia's area, the agricultural zone includes 61 percent of the autonomous region's population. Mongols are only 8 percent of this zone's population, but this 8 percent includes 31 percent of Inner Mongolia's Mongols. Some

dwell in small Mongol enclaves surrounded by Chinese settlements, while others, such as in KHARACHIN and TÜMED areas, dwell in mixed ethnic villages.

Urbanization is rapidly advancing in Inner Mongolia, with city dwellers jumping from 22 percent of the total population in 1978 to 36 percent in 1990. Inner Mongolian cities can be divided into four types: 1) administrative-commercial (e.g., HÖHHOT, Shiliin Khot); 2) industrial (e.g., BAOTOU); 3) mining (e.g., Bayan Oboo, WUHAI, Huolin Gol); and 4) railroad (e.g., Ereenkhot, Manzhouli). As a rule, only administrative towns in pastoral or agropastoral areas have a significant Mongol population.

Communications in China are based heavily on railways, which in Inner Mongolia tie Inner Mongolia's subregions more closely to the neighboring provinces than to each other. Early railroads that crossed Inner Mongolia include the Chinese Eastern Railway crossing Hulun Buir (1900) and the Beijing-Baotou railway (1923). Trunk lines constructed after 1949 include the TRANS-MONGOLIAN RAILWAY (1956), the Baotou-Lanzhou line (1958), and the Beijing-Tongliao line (1977). Mining and forestry centers are connected by branch lines. Only in 1994, with the completion of the Jining-Tongliao line, could one go by rail between eastern and western Inner Mongolia without passing through Beijing. Buses and trucks provide local transportation, and airlines have operated in eastern Inner Mongolia since 1931. In 1958 the system was overhauled, with Höhhot as the new hub.

AUTONOMOUS SYSTEM

Inner Mongolia is an autonomous region of China. As they have developed since 1949, China's minority autonomous areas are ranked in three levels: autonomous region, autonomous prefecture, and autonomous county, equal to a province, district, and county, respectively. All autonomous units are considered "inalienable parts of the People's Republic of China."

The actual degree of autonomy granted autonomous areas such as Inner Mongolia depends much more on general Chinese politics and the particular region's financial and cultural situation than on the formal "Nationality Regional Autonomy Law" adopted in 1984. China has long combined total centralization in theory with considerable local autonomy in practice, but such autonomy depends primarily on financial independence from the central government. Thus, despite the provisions of the law, autonomy for Inner Mongolia is rather limited, as its finances are dependent on large state-owned mining and metallurgical enterprises and central government subsidies.

Similarly, while China's minorities have rights of cultural expression that are, in practice, considerably beyond what are accorded minorities in most other Asian nations, these rights depend less on formal autonomous status than on the traditional and current cultural status of the nationality involved. The Mongols, with a long written tradition, a prerevolutionary secular education movement (see NEW SCHOOLS MOVEMENTS), and no currently active independence movement, share with the ethnic Koreans one of China's best developed minority-language educational systems. In 1990 about 60 percent of ethnic Mongol grade school students were learning in Mongolian and another 8 percent studying Mongolian as a second language. Mongolian-language higher education is also strongly developed, and minority students, especially those studying in the minority languages, receive extra points on the college entrance exam. However, the content of Mongolian-language education is, at the grade school level, entirely translated from nationwide textbooks and contains no special Inner Mongolian or ethnic Mongol content. Moreover, Mongolian-language education does not open access to the Chinese-dominated economy.

The primary practical consequence of regional autonomy is the preferential policies in education and employment for the area's titular nationality, including the guarantee that the head of the area's government will be of the titular nationality (i.e., in Inner Mongolia, a Mongol). Thus, the percentage of Mongols in Inner Mongolia's legislature, the People's Congress, has been fixed at 39–37 percent from 1954 to the present despite vast swings in the Mongol percentage of Inner Mongolia's population. The 35-person leadership of the Inner Mongolian People's Government elected in 1988 included 15 Mongols. The fact that the Mongols are simultaneously grossly overrepresented compared to their percentage of the population and still a minority in their own region's legislature and government has created in both Han and Mongol officials a strong sense of grievance, which they look to Beijing to address.

In local administration Inner Mongolia contains two parallel systems, one of leagues (Chinese, *meng*; Mongolian, AIMAG), BANNERS (*qi*; Mongolian, *khoshuu*), and *sumu* (SUM) for Mongol areas and one of municipalities (*shi*), counties (*xian*), and townships (*xiang*) for Han areas. While the two parallel administrative hierarchies are structured in the same way, only leagues, banners, and *sumus* are considered as Mongol autonomous units, which must be headed by Mongols. While many leagues and banners have Han majorities, the *sumus* are almost always majority Mongol, while the townships are Han. Local government in pastoral-zone *sumus* is totally dominated by Mongol cadres and carried on largely in Mongolian, with little participation from the recently immigrated Han minority. Since 1983 several leagues have been converted to municipalities.

Over the formal structures of government and autonomy is the reality of central Communist Party control and ideology. The most important plank of this ideology is Chinese nationalism, and the Inner Mongolian government exercises constant vigilance in denouncing and punishing even the most cautious expression of Mongol separatism. Described officially as a "people's democratic dictatorship," the Chinese system functions as an oligarchy with little public accountability. Since the 1980s corruption has become rampant. While many Mongols, particularly those who speak Mongolian and whose families were persecuted in the repeated campaigns of 1946–76, still nurse deep grievances against the regime, open dissent is rare.

ECONOMY

The basic composition of the modern Inner Mongolian economy was established by 1965. While in 1952 farming accounted for 60 percent of the total social product, herding for 15 percent, and industry (including mining) for only 10 percent, by 1965 the percentages had changed to 18 percent, 10 percent, and 45 percent, respectively. Despite rapid urbanization since 1965, farming still accounted for 17 percent and herding for 7 percent of the total social product in 1990, while industry's share has grown only to 49 percent. Inner Mongolia has shared in China's overall rapid growth since 1978, with total social product rising from 11 billion *yuan* to 53.5 billion in 1990 (in current prices).

Inner Mongolia has 86.67 million hectares (214.16 million acres) of steppe, of which 68 million hectares (168 million acres) are usable for livestock. Soviet confiscations at the end of WORLD WAR II resulted in great loss of livestock, but the number of traditional Mongol livestock (HORSES, CATTLE, CAMELS, SHEEP, and GOATS) rebounded after 1947 from 8.1 million head to 40.8 million head in 1965. By 1978 the number had declined to 34.4 million before increasing again to 45.9 million in 1990. In the same period (1947 to 1990) sheep and goats have increased from 70 percent to 86 percent of the total herd, and since 1985 the authorities have become concerned with overgrazing. While the number of herders in 1982 was only 547,000, or 6 percent of the employed population, the total value produced in animal husbandry since 1965 has averaged half or slightly less than that of arable agriculture.

Inner Mongolia's total plowed acreage peaked at around 5.6–5.7 million hectares (13.8–14.1 million acres) in 1957–65. Since then it has declined to about 5.0 million hectares (12.4 million acres), of which about one-quarter is irrigated. In 1982 farmers numbered 5,278,000, or 58 percent of the employed population. Since 1949 old-time staples—gaoliang sorghum, millet, and buckwheat in the east and naked oats in the west—have given way to wheat, corn (maize), potatoes, and oil crops. The number of pigs shot up from 1 million in 1949 to 6.1 million in 1979, before declining to 5–5.7 million in 1990. Many agropastoral Mongols now keep pigs, blurring the traditional saying in mixed-ethnicity areas that Mongols kept mastiffs and Han kept pigs.

Inner Mongolia's industrial product in 1990 was divided into 16 percent mining, 26 percent heavy industry, and 58 percent light industry. In the 18th century gold prospecting began in Ergüne (Ergun) and Ongni'ud banners, and in the 19th century coal mines in Wuhai and Baotou cities were opened. Today coal, oil, shale oil, ferrous metals, nonferrous metals, precious metals, and rare earths as well as a wide variety of minerals, salts, and stones used for metallurgical, chemical, and construction industries are all mined in Inner Mongolia. Inner Mongolia's deposit of rare earths form 95 percent of China's total, and proven coal reserves exceed 200 billion metric tons (220 billion short tons), second only to Shanxi in China. Total coal production reached 46.1 metric tons (50.8 short tons) in 1990 and 112.3 million metric tons (123.8 million short tons) in 2002; the promotion of coal as a household fuel has slowed deforestation, but is also responsible for smog in Inner Mongolian cities and acid rain. In 1990 production of iron ore reached 8,890,000 metric tons (9,799,545 short tons) and of gold reached 50 metric tons (55 short tons). Plans call for pumping 1 million metric tons (1.1 million short tons) of oil annually from Shiliin Gol.

Inner Mongolia's heavy industries are entirely based on processing the goods produced in the mining sector.

These include iron (2.81 million metric tons, or 3.1 million short tons, in 1990), steel (2.73 million metric tons, 3.01 million short tons), and 17 billion kilowatt-hours produced in Inner Mongolia's coal-fired electric generators. Major light industrial products include DAIRY PRODUCTS (22,000 metric tons, or 24,251 short tons, in 1990), wool thread (4,349 metric tons; 4,794 short tons), woolen textiles (10.4 million meters; 34.1 million feet), carpets (366,000), chemical fertilizers (134,794 metric tons, 148,585 short tons), cement (2.28 million metric tons, 2.51 million short tons), glass, and televisions (364,451 sets). International exports earning more than US $10 million annually include CASHMERE, frozen beef, carpets, soya, and rare earths.

Incomes in Inner Mongolia have risen rapidly in recent years. In 1990 average annual income was 1,050 yuan for the urban population, 906 yuan for the herders, and only 607 yuan for the farmers. Since 1980 that of herders has increased the fastest and that of urban areas the slowest. The infant mortality rate in 1981 was 24 per 1,000 live births, broken down into 20 per 1,000 in urban areas and 54 per 1,000 in rural areas. In the remote majority-Mongol herding banners, the infant mortality rate reached up to 91 per 1,000, while in the agropastoral banners of Khorchin it was around 36–59 per 1,000.

ADMINISTRATIVE HISTORY

The Inner Mongolian Autonomous Region had its origins in the Inner Mongolian Autonomous Government elected at the Inner Mongolian People's Congress in May 1947. While controlled by the Chinese Communists, one-third of the congress's delegates voted against ULANFU, the chief Mongol Communist, as leader and were subsequently eliminated. The autonomous government was, however, very different in structure and territory from the later autonomous region. The government consisted of Ulanfu as prime minister (Mongolian, yerüngkhei said, chairman, Chinese, zhuxi) and KHAFUNGGA as deputy prime minister, assisted by a 19-member government committee, several ministries, and an 11-member Small Khural (Mongolian for standing legislature) or advisory conference (Chinese, canhuiyi). Of the top 32 officials, 28 were ethnic Mongol. The government controlled the Inner Mongolian People's Self-Defense Army, flew its own flag, and printed its own money. At the time its territory consisted of Hulun Buir, Naun Muren (the Nonni River valley), Khinggan, Shiliin Gol, and CHAKHAR leagues. In 1948, as the Chinese Communists advanced, Jirim and Juu Uda were added. In these boundaries Inner Mongolia's population was about 35 percent Mongol. To the south and east were various extraregional banners of ambiguous status: Ongni'ud, Aohan, Kharachin, Fuxin, Gorlos, and Dörbed.

On December 12, 1949, the Inner Mongolian Autonomous Region was proclaimed, and the previous attributes of sovereignty were stripped away, while the constitutional structure of the region's government remained in limbo. Meanwhile, as the generals defending Suiyuan province (covering southwest Inner Mongolia) surrendered, Suiyuan was organized as a separate province. Suiyuan covered the traditional Ordos and Ulaanchab leagues, but its population was more than 90 percent Chinese. Ordos and Ulaanchab were organized within Suiyuan as autonomous prefectures.

In June 1954, after considerable controversy, Suiyuan was merged with Inner Mongolia, with the autonomous region's new capital in Suiyuan's former capital Guisui, now renamed HÖHHOT. While the unification of all Inner Mongolia was popular among Mongols, some explained the merger by Ulanfu's desire to bring his Höhhot Tümed homeland into Inner Mongolia. Inner Mongolia's ethnic Mongol percentage dropped to 13 percent. The autonomous region's First People's Congress, meeting in July 1954, was only 38 percent Mongol, and the government had only a bare Mongol majority. Similarly, the region's first Communist Party Congress elected a committee that was chaired by Ulanfu yet was two-thirds Han. In 1955 Rehe province was divided among Liaoning, Hebei, and Inner Mongolia. Although Inner Mongolia gained three banners, this newly annexed area, too, was overwhelmingly Chinese. Only the April 1956 annexation of Alashan brought in strongly Mongol areas.

In 1958 under the Great Leap Forward, internal administrative changes amalgamating Mongol and Han areas accompanied massive Han immigration. Before April 1958 Inner Mongolia consisted of eight leagues, two cities (Höhhot and Baotou), and two administrative districts, Pingdiquan and Heato, covering the most heavily Han areas of former Suiyuan. In 1958 Ulaanchab league was split and partly merged with Pingdiquan and partly with Hetao and Alashan. At the same time, Shiliin Gol, the only league with no farming townships, was merged with Chakhar. Meanwhile, from 1956 to 1961, administrative consolidation merged nine banners with neighboring counties. While in all but one case the resulting unit took the banner's name, the new units were all heavily Han. In 1962–64 some of these amalgamations were reversed.

In 1969–79, during the Cultural Revolution, Inner Mongolia was stripped of its eastern and far western areas. In the east Hulun Buir league was given to Heilongjiang, Khinggan and Jirim leagues to Jilin, and Juu Uda league to Liaoning provinces. In the west the Ningxia Hui Autonomous Region annexed Alashan Left Banner, and Gansu took Alashan Right and Ejene. While some of the league-banner terminology was maintained in the new provinces, banners in strategic areas were detached from the league system. Inner Mongolia was now only 7 percent Mongol and no longer included the eastern areas, which had been the cradle of the autonomous region. Despite this low percentage, when a new Inner Mongolian legislature was elected after the close of the Cultural Revolution in 1976, it was 36 percent Mongol. The chairman and 12 of the 15 vice chairmen of the Revolutionary Committee, or government, were Han.

In April 1979, with the new reform policies, Inner Mongolia's old frontiers were restored, while a Mongol replaced the Han chairman. In the forestry zone, however, the Jagdachi district, though theoretically returned to Inner Mongolia, was actually still administered by Heilongjiang province. The new 38 percent-Mongol parliament of 1983 selected a government headed by Ulanfu's son Buhe. Since then, Mongols have always chaired the government, but Mongols never regained their pre-Cultural Revolution political dominance.

See also BAYANNUUR LEAGUE; CHIFENG MUNICIPALITY; CLIMATE; ENVIRONMENTAL PROTECTION; FAUNA; FLAGS; FLORA; KHINGGAN LEAGUE; TONGLIAO MUNICIPALITY.

Further reading: *China's Inner Mongolia* (Höhhot: Inner Mongolia People's Publishing House, 1987); Peng Jianqun and Jia Laikuan, *Prosperous Inner Mongolia* (Beijing: China Today Press, 1992).

Inner Mongolians The Mongols of Inner Mongolia were separated from those of Mongolia proper in 1911–15 when they were forced to remain in the Republic of China after the 1911 RESTORATION of Mongolian independence. Since then the Inner Mongolians have alternated between periods of pan-Mongolian agitation and of pursuing educational reform and uplift under the auspices of sympathetic outside forces. Anxiety over the influx of Chinese and loss of ethnic identity have clouded the Inner Mongolians' view of the future.

The term *Inner Mongolia* (*Dotogadu Monggol*, or in Chinese *Nei Menggu*) stems from the distinction under the QING DYNASTY (1636–1912) between "inner" *zasags* (*jasags*, or rulers) of Inner Mongolia and the "outer" *zasags* of Outer Mongolia (today's State of Mongolia), Kökenuur, and Xinjiang. Under the Republic of China, when the region was divided into "special regions" and provinces, the unification of Inner Mongolia became a rallying cry, finally fulfilled in 1954. In 1947, under the influence of usage in the Mongolian People's Republic, "Inner (*Dotogadu*) Mongolia" was changed in Mongolian to "South (*Öbör*) Mongolia," although the Chinese *Nei Menggu*, or "Inner Mongolia," was retained. (*On the geography, economy, and institutions of Inner Mongolia, see* INNER MONGOLIA AUTONOMOUS REGION.)

In 1990 Mongols numbered 3,379,738, or 16 percent, of the Inner Mongolia Autonomous Region's total population. While the Mongols are a small part of the whole region's population, by 1990 three-fourths still lived in districts where they were locally the predominant population. Surveys indicate about 77 percent of the Inner Mongolians primarily use Mongolian, 10 percent use Mongolian with Chinese, and 13 percent have no functional Mongolian.

In 1982 75.2 percent of the Mongols in Inner Mongolia worked in herding or farming, compared with 68.3 percent of the region's Han (ethnic Chinese). While Mongols are traditionally seen as herders, in fact, just over half of the Inner Mongolian Mongols live in mixed agropastoral areas and almost 10 percent in purely agricultural areas. Within the urban economy Mongols are more likely than the Han to be employed in government, education, scientific, hygiene, and allied nonbusiness fields (12.5 percent versus 7.2 percent) but much less likely to be found in mining, manufacturing, construction, or commerce (12.3 percent versus 24.4 percent; all 1982 figures). In 1982 the Mongols had a slightly lower illiteracy rate than did the Han Chinese (24.5 percent of those over 12 as opposed to 26.2 percent).

Traditionally, Inner Mongolia also included several areas now in China's Manchurian provinces. These areas were excluded under the Japanese occupation in 1931–33, a decision ratified by the Chinese Communists. (See DÖRBED MONGOL AUTONOMOUS COUNTY; FRONT GORLOS AUTONOMOUS COUNTY; FUXIN MONGOL AUTONOMOUS COUNTY; KHARACHIN.)

"Tribal," or subethnic, identities and stereotypes are still strong among the Inner Mongolians. Inner Mongolians getting to know one another often first ask the other's native area. The eastern KHORCHIN, who speak a dialect heavily influenced by Chinese, are often resented for their success in climbing the political ladder. The ORDOS Mongols are seen as more religious, while those of ALASHAN are seen as the most backward. Those of northern SHILIIN GOL are seen as the most traditional, yet not very hardworking.

Before 1200 the nomadic peoples of Inner Mongolia were usually related to, but somewhat different from, those of Mongolia proper (see KITANS; ÖNGGÜD; XIANBI; XIONGNU). Under the Mongol YUAN DYNASTY (1206/71–1368) Inner Mongolia was occupied by the Turkish Önggüd, the Mongolian QONGGIRAD, and appanages under the descendants of CHINGGIS KHAN's brothers (see MANCHURIA AND THE MONGOL EMPIRE). Under the MING DYNASTY these appanages surrendered and were made the THREE GUARDS. In 1450, after the TUMU INCIDENT, Mongols flooded south from Mongolia proper and re-Mongolized Inner Mongolia. From then until 1636 Inner Mongolia was the political and cultural center of the Mongols (see NORTHERN YUAN DYNASTY). The Inner Mongolians surrendered to the Qing dynasty (1636–1912) in 1636 but until the 19th century remained culturally and historical close to the KHALKHA Mongols of Mongolian proper.

REFORMIST CURRENTS IN INNER MONGOLIA

During the 19th century an enlightenment movement began among the Mongols of eastern Inner Mongolia. Writers such as INJANNASHI (1837–92) and his family were inspired by CONFUCIANISM and Chinese literature to criticize the Mongols' crudity, religious obscurantism, and aristocratic idleness and immorality as well as Chinese ethnocentrism and anti-Mongol bigotry. After 1900 this intellectual current sparked a NEW SCHOOLS MOVEMENT in southeast Inner Mongolia led by the Kharachin prince Güngsangnorbu (Prince Güng, 1871–1931). Using revenues from leasing land and mines to Chinese farmers and merchants, he built schools, including Inner Mongolia's first girls' school, invited Japanese teachers, and sent students to Japan to study. Neighboring princes in JUU UDA and southern Khorchin and CHAKHAR and Daur officials also pursued similar reform programs.

Meanwhile, the Mongols in areas away from the advance of CHINESE COLONIZATION, such as Shiliin Gol, ULAANCHAB, Alashan, and northern Khorchin, remained strongly committed to traditional Mongolian values of Buddhist church and Chinggisid state. In Ordos, however, isolated between the Huang (Yellow) River and the Great Wall, resistance circles, or DUGUILANG, emerged first to petition against and gradually to fight against Chinese colonization and princely abuse of power. Culturally conservative and Buddhist, by 1901 the circles were openly opposing the nobility.

THE 1911 RESTORATION AND PAN-MONGOLISM

In November 1911 the restoration of Mongolian independence began in Khüriye (modern ULAANBAATAR), the center of Khalkha or Outer Mongolia. Although the Inner Mongolian expatriate Duke Haishan (1857–1917) had been one of the restoration's chief planners, the Inner Mongolian BANNERS (appanages) at first supported the Qing dynasty, which was simultaneously fighting the Chinese republican revolution in southern China. Only in isolated HULUN BUIR did the banners expel the Qing garrison and join independent Mongolia.

After the abdication of the last Qing emperor on February 12, 1912, the new president of the Republic of China, Yuan Shikai, sought to reassure the Inner Mongolian rulers that the republic would not infringe their princely prerogatives. At the same time he dispatched troops to hold Inner Mongolia's strong points and protested Russian support for the Khalkha Mongolian government. Faced with an ethnic Chinese republic most of the Inner Mongolian *jasags* (hereditary banner rulers; see ZASAG) now supported pan-Mongolism, but some, led by Prince Güng, opposed the theocratic nature of the new Khalkha Mongolian state and eventually supported Yuan Shikai's government. Although Outer Mongolia tried to drive the Chinese out of Inner Mongolia in 1912–13 (see SINO-MONGOLIAN WAR), Russian pressure forced the Mongolian government to abandon its pan-Mongolist policy.

THE CHINESE REPUBLIC AND INNER MONGOLIA, 1912–1931

In 1912 Inner Mongolia's population was estimated at 2.5 million, of which slightly more than 875,000 were Mongol. Administration in Inner Mongolia was based on ethnicity, with the Mongols subject to the traditional banners and their Chinggisid *jasag*s and the Chinese settlers subject to counties. In 1914, after the Mongolian troops withdrew, Yuan Shikai divided Inner Mongolia into three "special regions" governed by military lieutenant governors, or *dutong*s, in Chengde, Zhangjiakou (Kalgan), and Guisui (modern HÖHHOT) (*see* AMBAN). The Mongols of eastern Jirim league were divided among the Manchurian provinces. In 1920 fear of the spread of the Russian civil war pushed Hulun Buir to voluntarily rejoin China as a semiautonomous region.

After Yuan Shikai's death in 1917, his generals split into warlord factions. The *dutong*s joined these cliques and attempted to expand their wealth by promoting increased Chinese colonization, sparking *duguilang* resistance in Ordos and popular rebellions elsewhere. Violence became rife as the Mongols were disarmed, while Chinese bandits were hired as mercenaries in incessant wars.

Khalkha Mongolia's 1921 REVOLUTION breathed new hope into pan-Mongolist agitation. Mongol authors and politicians such as Bai Yunti (revolutionary alias Serengdonrub, 1894–1980) and MERSE (Guo Daofu, 1894–1934?), students in Prince Güng's Mongolian and Tibetan School in Beijing, and *duguilang* leaders all looked to the new regime in Outer Mongolia. Some politicians and students also supported either the Chinese Nationalists (or Guomindang) or the Chinese Communists, both of whom from 1924 espoused self-determination and autonomy for China's border nationalities. From 1925 the new Mongolian People's Republic and the Soviet Union trained scores of Inner Mongolian students nationalists, yet the Inner Mongolian People's Revolutionary Party (IMPRP), funded and armed by the Mongolian People's Republic and the Soviet Union, failed in its attempts from 1925 to 1928 to spark an Inner Mongolian revolution. During this period cultural nationalists such as Prince Güng's pupil the printer Temgetü (1887–1939) began laying the foundation for a new secular and progressive Mongol culture that looked to Chinggis Khan as a model of youthful determination.

When the Chinese Nationalists reunified China in May 1928, they quickly repudiated their autonomy program and continued to sponsor colonization. While Merse returned to education and writing, the Kharachin politician Wu Heling (Ünenbayan, b. 1896) lobbied for reforms in the autocratic *jasag* system that would preserve Mongolian autonomy. In Ordos *duguilang* leaders used Soviet-supplied rifles to maintain independent military regimes. The alienation and social disintegration in Inner Mongolia resulted in popular apathy toward the Japanese takeover of Manchuria and eastern Inner Mongolia.

JAPANESE RULE, 1931–1945

The Japanese occupied Khorchin and Hulun Buir in 1931–32. In 1933 they invaded Kharachin and Juu Uda areas. The occupation drew the attention of Chinese public opinion to disaffection in Inner Mongolia. The conservative Shiliin Gol PRINCE DEMCHUGDONGRUB (Prince De) used the Japanese threat to advance a Mongol autonomy movement from 1933 to 1935, but despite the agreement of the central government, northern China's local military governors were absolutely opposed to any limit on their authority over the Mongolian banners. Stymied by their opposition and encouraged by a wave of enthusiasm among Mongol nationalist intellectuals, Prince De accepted Japanese military aid in February 1936, yet the new Mongol force proved unable to handle China's warlord armies until Japan launched its own wholesale invasion of China in July 1937.

Japanese rule gave Inner Mongolia stability and much of the autonomy and reforms that nationalists had been looking for for decades. Colonization was immediately halted, and Mongolian and Japanese became the sole languages of education and administration. Government-funded education, cooperatives, and publishing aimed to improve the Mongols' economic, social, and cultural situation. In traditionally Mongol areas Mongol officials dominated the administrations, even where Mongols were now the minority. In Manchukuo, the new Japanese-controlled state under the last Qing emperor, Puyi, the remaining Mongol areas of eastern Inner Mongolia were organized into four autonomous Khinggan provinces. (Outlying Mongol banners in Manchuria were excluded from these provinces and from subsequent Inner Mongolia autonomous regions.) While nobles were given sinecures at the Manchukuo court, nationalist intellectuals rose to unprecedented influence. In central Inner Mongolia (Shiliin Gol, Chakhar, and half of Ulaanchab) Prince De headed an autonomous government under the Japanese-controlled administration of China.

By 1941 in Manchukuo, 23,742 students, of whom 17 percent were female, were studying in 201 Mongolian-language public primary schools, with another 1,475 in secondary schools and 550 in teachers' training schools. In Prince De's government 5,090 students (19 percent female) were studying in 74 public schools, 1,423 in 31 private schools, and 839 in four secondary schools. Culturally, the Japanese occupation saw the first printing of many prerevolutionary classics, such as the *BOLOR ERIKHE* and the *Khökhe sudur* of Injannashi, while the journals *Ulaan bars* (Red tiger) and *Shine Monggol* (New Mongolia) carried Inner Mongolia's first novella (in 1940), many poems, and essays by new authors.

Despite these reforms, Japanese rule was often oppressive. The Mongols resented the administrative manipulation that separated the four Khinggan provinces while forcing Prince De to work with North Chinese collaborationist regimes. Japanese advisers were usually high-handed and the Mongol officials often reduced to puppet status. Many of the nationalist intellectuals were

Soviet-educated former IMPRP members, who secretly looked to the Mongolian People's Republic for inspiration. In 1936 Lingsheng (1889–1936), the governor of Khinggan North province, was arrested by Japanese security police as a Soviet spy with more than 20 other distinguished officials; he and three others were executed. Only after 1941 did the Japanese try to win over the Mongols, unifying three of the Khinggan provinces and increasing the authority of Prince De and his Mongol officials. By this time, however, widespread shortages were causing serious discontent, and informed officials realized the Japanese Empire's days were numbered.

CHINESE CIVIL WAR

The Chinese Nationalists held on to southwestern Inner Mongolia during WORLD WAR II, and the Chinese Communists in Yan'an (Yenan) tried to infiltrate both Nationalist and Japanese-held Inner Mongolia. However, World War II in Inner Mongolia ended not with a Chinese advance but with a combined Soviet-Mongolian invasion. Despite massacres of lamas, confiscation of Inner Mongolia's livestock, and wanton destruction by Soviet troops, Inner Mongolian nationalists and people welcomed the possibility of pan-Mongolian unification brought by the invasion. Eventually, Sino-Soviet treaties blocked this possibility, but in the interval Mongol nationalist regimes headed by leftist intellectuals such as KHAFUNGGA (1908–70) took power in former Japanese-occupied Inner Mongolia, and revived the IMPRP in eastern Inner Mongolia.

The Chinese Communists quickly adapted to this new reality on the ground, coopting leaderless Mongol nationalists into a front organization under ULANFU (1906–88), a Höhhot TÜMED and long-time Communist.

Soldiers in an Inner Mongolian cavalry unit, under the Chinese Communist–aligned Inner Mongolian Autonomous Government, 1947 *(From* Öbör Monggol-un tegübüri jirug *[1947])*

Advocating federalism and national autonomy, Ulanfu used diplomacy, threats, and revolutionary appeals to push the nationalist regimes and their leftist leaders such as Khafungga into merging with his Communist front organization. Once the Chinese Nationalist assault of 1946–47 was beaten off, a new Inner Mongolian Autonomous Government claiming authority over the old Khinggan provinces, Shiliin Gol, and Chakhar was proclaimed on May 1, 1947, at Wang-un Süme (modern Ulanhot). Publicly, the new government seemed highly autonomous, with its own flag, currency, government (including an army ministry), and provisional parliament; Ulanfu held the position of prime minister.

The Chinese civil war was a time of deep suffering in Inner Mongolia. From 1937 to 1947 the estimated population dropped from 847,000 to 832,000 (age-set data confirm this drop occurred after 1942) and increased only to 835,000 by 1949. Soviet pillaging, outbreaks of the plague, and battlefield disruption devastated the population. From 1946 the Communists encouraged reprisals against Japanese-era "collaborators." These campaigns culminated in the violent land and herd reform campaign of eastern Inner Mongolia and Chakhar in 1947–48, in which "exploiters" (those who rented out land or livestock) were publicly humiliated, beaten, and often killed. Only Shiliin Gol and Hulun Buir areas along the Mongolian frontier were spared this struggle. In some areas as much as 25 percent of the population were labeled exploiters, and the targets responded by slaughtering their livestock, fleeing, or rebelling. In farming areas Chinese and auslander Mongol tenants benefited while the native Mongol bannermen lost. Even so, the Communists won the committed loyalty of most nationalist intellectuals and many ordinary Mongols, loyalty stiffened by the Chinese Nationalists' opposition to Mongol autonomy and revenge killings by anticommunist Mongols. Attempts by pro-Nationalist Mongols and Prince De to form an alternative Mongol center were swept away by the Communist advance, and all Inner Mongolia came under Communist control by 1949.

INNER MONGOLIA, 1949–1966: ECONOMIC DEVELOPMENT AND ETHNIC TENSIONS

In 1949 the Chinese Communists decisively recast Inner Mongolia's autonomy. The Inner Mongolian military and youth league were integrated with their Chinese counterparts, and propaganda campaigns began attacking the "upper stratum" nationalists who had founded the nationalist regimes of 1945–46. On October 10 the People's Republic of China (PRC) was proclaimed a unitary republic, and on December 3 the previous Inner Mongolian Autonomous Government was renamed the Inner Mongolia Autonomous Region, a mere local administrative organ of the PRC. The Inner Mongolian flag and federalist slogans disappeared. Ulanfu remained in charge of the government, party, and military.

The new regime continued to mop up resistance, although very little is known of the opposition. The new government accused anticommunist elements of killing 550 cadres and citizens from January to July 1950 and by 1952 had sentenced 9,324 people to death or imprisonment as counterrevolutionaries. From May 1955 to the end of 1957, another wave of convictions sentenced 1,788 persons as counterrevolutionaries.

In summer 1949 Inner Mongolia's capital was moved from Wang-un Süme, a center of East Mongolian nationalism, to Zhangjiakou in northern China. In 1954–56 Inner Mongolia was expanded to include the southwestern banners and areas in eastern Inner Mongolia that had not been included in the Khinggan provinces. As a result, the percentage of Mongols in the autonomous region, which had been about 35 percent in 1949–54, dropped to 12 percent. The new capital was put in Höhhot, near Ulanfu's homeland. By exacerbating the gap between the region's status as a Mongol region and its actual ethnic composition, this move sparked considerable ethnic tensions.

In contrast to the 1940s, the 1950s were boom years for both population and livestock. Wolf extermination, fodder cutting, new wells, and veterinary stations helped large stock (horses, cattle, and camels) increase from 3,043,000 head in 1949 to 6,646,000 in 1964 and sheep and goats from 5,755,000 head to 23,990,000 in the same period. With public health campaigns, disease eradication, and improved nutrition, the Mongol population increased from 835,000 in 1949 to 985,000 in 1953 and 1,384,355 in 1964. Land reform was extended to southwestern Inner Mongolia in 1952; the greater experience with pastoral areas and the regime's greater confidence kept the process less violent. In 1956–58 land and livestock were collectivized throughout Inner Mongolia, even in Shiliin Gol and Hulun Buir, leading to a 15 percent drop in livestock numbers but no mass slaughter. Except in the areas bordering Mongolia, the nomadic Mongols were sedentarized, although often with different summer and winter residences. Restrictions on private livestock under the communes were far stricter than in the collectives of the Mongolian People's Republic, and income was tied more tightly to work on communally owned herds.

From 1947 to 1958 Chinese immigration into Inner Mongolia revived, but in a changed pattern. Instead of opening virgin pasture, the government opened new administrative, mining, railway, and industrial towns on the steppe and intensified cultivation south of the existing frontier of settlement. The percentage of Mongols within Inner Mongolia's post-1956 frontiers dropped from 14.8 percent in 1947 to 11.2 percent in 1964. Completely new cities such as Shiliin Khot (Xilinhot), Bayan Oboo, and Saikhan Tal appeared, and existing cities such as BAOTOU were transformed.

In 1947–66 Inner Mongolian educational and publishing activities built on the previous achievements of the Japanese occupation, although there are no separate statistics on literacy rates for Mongols. Students in "ethnic" primary schools (mostly Mongol, but also including Daurs, ethnic Koreans, etc.) expanded from 22,500 in 1947 to 122,600 in 1956 and 233,500 in 1966. Inner Mongolia University was opened in 1957, with 60 lecturers and professors brought in from prominent Chinese universities. Mongolian radio and several publishing houses publishing in Mongolian as well as Chinese were also established. The new regime continued the Japanese-era reprinting of prerevolutionary writers such as Injannashi, adding duguilang poets to the canon and promoting new writers such as NA. SAINCHOGTU. Scholarship also expanded in cooperation with that in Mongolia and the Soviet Union. The Japanese legacy was maintained, however, in the use of Japanese as the main foreign language in Mongol-language schooling.

While the relative prosperity of the 1950s and the seemingly unassailable might of the new regime kept Inner Mongolian intellectuals and officials compliant, ethnic tensions remained. Han Chinese, particularly recent immigrants, resented the overrepresentation of Mongol cadres, particularly at the highest level, who generally had "bad class background" (intellectuals, wealthy peasants, etc.) and "complicated" pasts. In education preferential policies to assist Mongols were seen as not only unfair but perpetuating this "bad class background" elite into another generation. Mongols in their turn resented the powerful Chinese cultural influences in what was supposed to be China's Mongol autonomous region. East Mongols also resented the dominance of Ulanfu's Höhhot Tümeds.

In 1956, during the liberal "Hundred Flowers" campaign, the Inner Mongolian scholar Tübshin criticized the fact that young urban Mongols were not learning the MONGOLIAN LANGUAGE, and as a result in 1957 he was designated "Inner Mongolia's Biggest Rightist." In July 1955 the Cyrillic script used in the Soviet-aligned Mongolian People's Republic had been adopted, but in March 1958 its adoption was canceled as Sino-Soviet tensions increased.

Spurred by the Chinese ruler Mao Zedong's utopian and autarchic ideas, the Great Leap Forward from 1958 to 1962 enforced collectivization all over the steppe. Agricultural colonization was suddenly encouraged as administrative consolidation combined Mongolian banners and leagues with neighboring Chinese counties and districts. This planned immigration, together with refugees from the massive government-created famine that gripped China in 1959–60, resulted in the net immigration of 1,926,600 outsiders into Inner Mongolia in 1958–60.

The disasters of the Great Leap Forward were followed by a brief retreat. In 1961–62 a net 689,900 persons left Inner Mongolia, mostly refugees returning home due to the desertification of newly farmed steppes and improving conditions in China proper. Meanwhile, some of the administrative consolidations were reversed.

After the thaw of 1961–62, political tensions returned in 1964–66. The play Chasun dumdakhi checheg

(Flowers in the snow) by T. Damrin was attacked for not portraying the Inner Mongolian nationalists in 1945–47 negatively enough. At the same time, the "redraw class lines" campaign charged that Ulanfu's Tümed Mongols had been unfairly advantaged during land reform. Finally, an academic debate over whether to draw modern Inner Mongolian vocabulary from Chinese or Russian acquired sinister overtones in the light of Sino-Soviet polemics. Coinciding with these violent policy shifts and increased ethnic tensions was a serious rise both in political crimes and in armed robberies and murders. From the end of 1957 to 1966 the regime sentenced 18,230 persons as counterrevolutionaries, a yearly average of more than 2,000.

THE CULTURAL REVOLUTION, 1966–1976

Under the Cultural Revolution from 1966–76, Mao Zedong's reckless instigation of merciless civil strife turned these tensions into a ghastly mass persecution of Mongols. In May 1966 China's leaders attacked Ulanfu for "creating ethnic divisions" and trying to "set up an independent kingdom," and Red Guards (young Maoist vigilantes) tried to seize power. The region's military authorities opposed the Red Guards but were overthrown by "rebel" factions allied to Beijing by November 1967, while the Mongol Red Guards generally supported the "conservative" factions. As elsewhere in China, the opposing factions agreed only in savagely persecuting the old scapegoats—landlords, lamas, "rightist" intellectuals, former Japanese collaborators, and Guomindang officers—and vandalizing the prerevolutionary cultural heritage. Mongolian-language publications continued, although the content was now purely Maoist, and some Mongolian-language education in the countryside was maintained. However, Mongol-language schools in the cities and in some countryside areas were closed down as nests of ethnic solidarity and key links in Ulanfu's system of preferential policies.

From April 1968 the Han military man Teng Haiqing widened the Cultural Revolution's attack on the previous autonomy policy, an attack which turned into a virtually genocidal campaign against the Mongols as a political and social force. A vast underground conspiracy, the "New Inner Mongolian People's Revolutionary Party," was fabricated through interrogation and torture, eventually consuming almost the entire educated class among the Mongols. Official figures, widely considered as underestimates, put the death toll at 22,900 and those injured or crippled at 170,000. At the same time, the "redrawing class lines" campaign disenfranchised large numbers of Mongols (15 percent of Shiliin Gol's Mongols and in some areas up to 50 percent) as members of the "exploiting classes."

In May 1969 the scale of the "NEW INNER MONGOLIAN PEOPLE'S REVOLUTIONARY PARTY" ("New IMPRP") CASE was criticized, and in December Teng was dismissed and replaced by another Han military man, You Taizhong. In July 1969, as the SINO-SOVIET SPLIT reached warlike levels, Inner Mongolia was partitioned, with Hulun Buir and eastern Inner Mongolia being divided among Manchuria's provinces and Alashan being partitioned between Gansu and Ningxia. The rump Inner Mongolia contained hardly more than 15 percent of China's Mongols and was only 7 percent Mongol. In any case, the region was under direct military rule from Beijing until 1972.

The Cultural Revolution accentuated the emphasis on agriculture. Previously, Mongols, like Chinese city dwellers, received rations of grain food, but now such rations for rural Mongols were called "unjust grain," and Mongol districts were exhorted to grow their own. While Chinese immigration was encouraged, there was actually little free arable land left, and immigration rates for Inner Mongolia as a whole remained well below the 1950s rates. The one exception was the influx of "sent-down" Red Guards from China's cities, who left again after 1976.

CONTEMPORARY INNER MONGOLIAN POLITICS

The late Cultural Revolution was marked by numerous incidents of Mongol protest in both the cities and the countryside. In 1976, with the overthrow of the "Gang of Four," blamed for the excesses of the Cultural Revolution, Mongol demonstrations in Höhhot first openly contested the whole existence of the "New IMPRP." In 1979 China's new government acknowledged the "New IMPRP" case to have been a hoax from the beginning, restored Inner Mongolia's previous frontiers, abolished discrimination against "bad class backgrounds," and replaced You Taizhong with Kong Fei (1911–93), a Khorchin Mongol. East Mongol cadres continued to lobby for the punishment of Teng Haiqing, the return of the Jagdachi region in the GREATER KHINGGAN RANGE, which was left under Heilongjiang's administration, and the retention of Inner Mongolia's mineral wealth in Inner Mongolia.

On August 22, 1981, the Communist Party's new policy on Inner Mongolia was announced without addressing these points or the issue of Chinese migration. The next month students struck in Höhhot, demanding that Inner Mongolia's land, schools, administration, and party organs be of and for Mongols first and foremost. The demonstrations, covertly supported by Kong Fei and other East Mongol cadres, became a forum for airing the Mongol students' bitterness over the loss of their culture, the Communist Party's betrayal of their parents' generation's loyalty during the Cultural Revolution, and the continued Chinese domination of Inner Mongolia. In Alashan a fight between Han and Mongols students left six Mongols dead. After a futile appeal to Beijing by the students, the region's Han party secretary, Zhou Hui, in February 1982 quieted the demonstrations by promising nonretaliation for the demonstrators. Since 1982 economic and cultural liberalization and firm suppression of dissent have blocked ethnically based demonstrations.

After the demonstrations Ulanfu's son Buhe (Bökhe) became chairman of Inner Mongolia from 1982 to 1992. The numerous posts occupied by Ulanfu's Yun family became the subject of frequent jokes, yet the party secretaries continue to be Han outsiders. After Ulanfu's death in 1988 and Buhe's retirement in 1992, the Yun family gradually lost its position. By law, the chair of autonomous regions must be of the titular nationality, and in practice Höhhot Tümeds and eastern Inner Mongolians have alternated in the post. Since 2000 the region's chairwoman has been Oyunchimeg (Uyunqimg, b. 1942), a Liaoning Mongol.

The 1990 DEMOCRATIC REVOLUTION in independent Mongolia inspired many Mongol nationalists. Groups circulating Mongolian liberal and nationalist literature were smashed by police in 1991, and more arrests have followed periodically. Independent Mongolia's subsequent economic difficulties and cultural prejudices between Khalkha and Inner Mongolians have dampened enthusiasm for Mongolia as a model.

THE PASTORAL ECONOMY

In 1984 the obvious unsustainability of marginal farming and the burgeoning foreign and domestic market for meat, wool, and CASHMERE prompted a turn to promote herding. Further agricultural colonization was prohibited. In 1990 the average income of herders was 906 *yuan*, considerably more than the farmers' average 607 *yuan*, and Mongol herders have made China the world's chief producer of cashmere. Decollectivization of both farmlands and herds took place in 1983. Acting on the assumption that common pasture ownership would promote overuse, the Inner Mongolian authorities in 1985 took the unprecedented step of assigning pasture land to individual households to be fenced with barbed wire. This move and increasing population density are slowly sedentarizing the remaining nomads in Shiliin Gol and Hulun Buir.

However, given the expense of fencing and the ineffective legal remedies, only wealthy and politically well-connected herders can actually keep other herders' animals off their pasture. This policy thus accelerated the polarization of Inner Mongolian pasture into a few sheltered areas owned and intensively managed by official organizations or well-connected herders, and all other lands suffering rapid desertification. The culmination of this process is the Inner Mongolian government's current plans for "three-way restructuring": the most prosperous and management-oriented one-third of the herders will remain as pastoralists, while the marginal two-thirds will be relocated as farmers or town-based entrepreneurs. This has exacerbated border conflicts between various banners and districts, sometimes leading to violent altercations. This process was suddenly accelerated by disastrous droughts in 1999 and 2000 and a massive plague of locusts in 2002 that devastated herders, especially in Shiliin Gol. While herders responded with long-distance migrations (*otor*) to find new pasture, the Chinese government from 1999 to 2002 moved 30,000 "ecological migrants" off the steppe completely and plans to move 650,000 more by 2008.

CULTURAL POLICY

After 1979 the Inner Mongolian government vigorously promoted the revival of Mongolian language and culture, restoring Mongolian-language grade schools in both cities and countryside. Preferential policies assisted Mongol students in entering colleges and universities, where in 1989–90 87.5 percent of the ethnic Mongol teacher-training students and 35.6 percent of the ethnic Mongol graduate students were studying in Mongolian-language classes. Mongolian-language books, magazines, and journals were heavily subsidized. Inner Mongolian scholars have moved into the forefront of international Mongolian studies in the fields of folklore, linguistics, Kitan studies, and identifying and printing ancient manuscripts.

Nevertheless, Mongolian culture faces an uncertain economic future. Already in the 1980s some rural Mongols complained that Mongolian-language education was useless compared to knowing Chinese. From 1979 to 1989 the number of Mongol elementary school students in Mongolian medium schools dropped from 71.2 percent to 59.7 percent. Since then market reforms have exacerbated the education–employment mismatch, as students trained in Mongolian-language humanities find available jobs are overwhelmingly in the Chinese-dominated clerical, technical, and managerial areas. In 1993 certain officials proposed eliminating Mongolian-language education above the elementary school level to promote economic growth. While protests from East Mongol cadres defeated this proposal, the dilemma of Mongolian-language education in a Chinese-dominated society remains.

See also BARGA; CHINGGIS KHAN CONTROVERSY; CLOTHING AND DRESS; DAUR LANGUAGE AND PEOPLE; DANCE; DESERTIFICATION AND PASTURE DEGRADATION; EPICS; EWENKIS; FAMILY; FARMING; FOOD AND DRINK; HUNTING AND FISHING; JAPAN AND THE MODERN MONGOLS; JEWELRY; KOUMISS; LITERATURE; MUSIC; RELIGION; WHITE WEDDINGS MONTH.

Further reading: Asia Watch, *Crackdown in Inner Mongolia* (New York: Human Rights Watch, 1991); Christopher P. Atwood, *Young Mongols and Vigilantes in Inner Mongolia's Interregnum Decades, 1911–1931*, 2 vols. (Leiden: E. J. Brill, 2002); Uradyn E. Bulag, *The Mongols at China's Edge: History and the Politics of National Unity* (Lanham, Md.: Rowman and Littlefield, 2002); A. Hurelbaatar, "A Survey of the Mongols in Present-Day China: Perspectives on Demography and Culture Change," in *Mongolia in the Twentieth Century: Landlocked Cosmopolitan*, ed. Stephen Kotkin and Bruce A. Elleman (Armonk,

N.Y.: M. E. Sharpe, 1999): 191–222; Sechin Jagchid, *The Last Mongol Prince: The Life and Times of Demchugdonrob, 1902–1966* (Bellingham: Western Washington University, 1999); Owen Lattimore, *Mongol Journeys* (New York: Doubleday, Doran, 1941); Owen Lattimore, *Mongols of Manchuria* (1934; rpt., New York: Howard Fertig, 1969); Li Narangoa, "Educating Mongols and Making 'Citizens' of Manchukuo," *Inner Asia* 3 (2001): 101–126; David Sneath, *Changing Inner Mongolia: Pastoral Mongolian Society and the Chinese State* (Oxford: Oxford University Press, 2000); Bing Wang, "One School/Two Systems: An Ethnographic Case Study of a Mongol High School in China" (Ph.D. diss., University of Calgary, 1999); Dee Mack Williams, *Beyond Great Walls: Environment, Identity, and Development on the Chinese Grasslands of Inner Mongolia* (Stanford, Calif.: Stanford University Press, 2002).

Islam in the Mongol Empire   Although the Mongol conquest was widely perceived as a disaster for Islam, the conquest ultimately resulted in a substantial expansion of the Islamic world.

By the time of CHINGGIS KHAN (Genghis, 1206–27), Islam predominated among the QARLUQS, a Turk tribe in the Ili valley, and in the city states of the Tarim Basin up to the borders of Uighuristan (modern eastern Xinjiang). Muslim traders operated alongside Uighur merchants in North China, and the Arghuns, a Muslim minority, lived among the Christian ÖNGGÜD of Inner Mongolia. Involvement in the fur, falcon, and livestock trade of Siberia and Mongolia brought Muslim merchants such as Jabar (Ja'far) Khoja and Hasan in contact with Mongol nomad chiefs like Chinggis Khan. Chinggis won early support from the Qarluqs (1211), and after overthrowing the Buddhist QARA-KHITAI Empire in 1216–18, he proclaimed freedom of religion among the Tarim Basin cities. Already large numbers of Muslim caravan traders had become ORTOQ, or merchant partners, of the Mongols.

The Mongol campaign against KHORAZM, however, destroyed this early amity. In this campaign the Mongols proved unable to win virtually any local support and resorted to repeated wholesale massacres to root out stubborn resistance. Subsequently, Islamic states in Fars, Kerman, and KURDISTAN surrendered more or less peacefully, but the 1258 destruction of Baghdad and almost the entire 'Abbasid family again stoked the image of the Mongols as the most hideous enemies of the Islamic faith. Islamic historians such as Ibn al-Athir (1160–1233) in Mosul and Minhaj-ud-Din Juzjani (1193–ca.1265) in Delhi saw the Mongols as precursors of the end of the world; the setback to Islam seemed inexplicable otherwise. 'ALA'UD-DIN ATA-MALIK JUVAINI (1226–83), writing at the Mongol court, however, found much to commend in the Mongols and believed that their rule was actually extending the sway of Islam.

Under ÖGEDEI KHAN (1229–41) the Mongols' old merchant partners, Mahmud Yalavach and his son Mas'ud Beg, achieved high office (*see* MAHMUD YALAVACH AND MAS'UD BEG). Muslim perceptions of the khans fluctuated: Ögedei, his brother JOCHI (d. 1225), and his nephew MÖNGKE KHAN (1251–59) were seen favorably, while CHA'ADAI (d. 1242) and GÜYÜG khan (1246–48) were detested as anti-Muslim. Mongols such as Cha'adai attempted to implement Mongol beliefs proscribing bathing in summer and prohibiting the slaughter of meat in the Islamic fashion (*halal*). These practices ran directly contrary to Islamic rites and caused great friction. The brief 1238–39 uprising in Bukhara of Mahmud Tarabi, a faith healer and seer, demonstrated the continuing appeal of Islamically based resistance to Mongol rule.

The Shi'ite Muslim minorities received quite diverse treatment. The Sevener Shi'ites, or ISMA'ILIS, who maintained a theocratic state in the fortresses of the Elburz Mountains and Quhistan, incurred the wrath of the Mongols and were destroyed under Möngke Khan. The Twelver Shi'ites of southern Iraq, the Persian Gulf, and Iran's shrine cities of Qom and Meshed, however, had no political pretensions. After the destruction of Baghdad they announced their submission and gratitude for the destruction of what they considered an usurping and tyrannical caliphate. From then on the Shi'ite community at Najaf, site of the tomb of 'Ali, was an autonomous tax-exempt ecclesiastical polity.

With the division of the empire, the first khan to rule as a Muslim was Berke (r. 1257–66), Jochi's son, of the GOLDEN HORDE. Accounts of his conversion variously stress the milk of Berke's Muslim wet nurse or the persuasions of a Bukharan Sufi master or sheikh, Saif-ud-Din Bakharzi. Islam in the Golden Horde was closely connected to foreign policy and trade. Islam was not widespread in its territory, and Berke's conversion brought a close alliance with MAMLUK EGYPT against his cousin HÜLE'Ü. Under the non-Muslim Toqto'a Khan (1291–1312), Franciscan missionaries and Uighur *baqshis* (Buddhist teachers) eclipsed Islam. With his conversion again by a Bukharan Sufi, Ibn 'Abd-ul-Hamid (known as Sayyid Ata), and the purge of recalcitrant commanders, ÖZBEG KHAN (1313–41) made his court thoroughly Muslim and joined it to the international urban network of Muslim merchants and scholars, while Sufi *faqirs*, or miracle workers, brought Islam to the Golden Horde's various nomadic subjects.

While the early Il-Khans in the Middle East moved in a pervasively Islamic environment, they generally did not convert. The Sufi sheikh 'Abd-ur-Rahman won to Islam one of Hüle'ü's baptized sons, Tegüder, who in 1282–84 became the first Muslim Il-Khan under the name Sultan Ahmad. Ahmad neglected politics for dervish sessions of singing and dancing but continued royal patronage of other religions unchanged. Ahmad's attempt to make peace with Egypt ended with the imprisonment of Sheikh 'Abd-ur-Rahman, who he had sent as his trusted envoy.

By 1289 Islam was widespread among the ordinary Mongols in Iran and was resisted primarily by the royal family and certain high commanders. The khan Baidu (1295) had outwardly to act as a Muslim despite his strong Christian sympathies. In 1295 NAWROZ, a Muslim Mongol emir, induced GHAZAN KHAN (1295–1304), a main contender for the vacant throne, to convert to Islam. Ghazan Khan's victory was followed by Nawroz's edict to destroy all churches, synagogues, and Buddhist temples. In 1297, however, Nawroz fell from favor, and Ghazan Khan repudiated his persecution of Christianity, although he allowed the proscription of Buddhism to stand. Islamization did not, however, change the later Muslim Il-Khans' foreign policy.

Although the Central Asian CHAGHATAY KHANATE was demographically as Muslim or more so than the Il-Khanate, the anti-Islamic legacy of its founder Cha'adai retarded Islamization. Mubarak-shah (r. 1266), the first Muslim ruler, was deposed after less than a year of rule. Tarmashirin Khan (1331–34), while raised a Buddhist, was the first to rule as a Muslim. His excessive attention to the settled Transoxiana provoked a violent backlash from the less Muslim eastern area. The khanate split in half, and the eastern half, or MOGHULISTAN, did not convert to Islam until the Sufi sheikh Mawlana Arshad-ud-Din converted Tughlugh-Temür (r. 1360–62/3), who, with his 120,000 soldiers, accepted circumcision.

Mongol rule created a large Muslim community in China. Deported craftsmen from Central Asia and the Middle East had been settled there, and QUBILAI KHAN (1260–94) actively recruited Muslim physicians, musicians, astronomers, artillery operators, and ortoq merchants, setting up a Muslim Medical Office (1270) for the court, a Directorate of Muslim Astronomy (1271), and a Muslim School for the Sons of the State (1289), teaching Persian. Muslims were classified as SEMUREN, "various sorts," below the Mongols but above the native Chinese. Central Asian Muslim officials, such as AHMAD FANAKATI and 'UMAR SHAMS-UD-DIN SAYYID AJALL, achieved high position. In 1280, however, Qubilai became aware of Islamic (and Jewish) rejection of Mongol customs and he decreed death for those who performed Islamic-Jewish slaughtering or circumcision. In 1287 he revoked this decree, which was damaging commerce and revenues. The conversion to Islam of Qubilai's grandson Ananda (again supposedly through a Muslim wet nurse), who held an appanage in northwest China, opened the possibility of powerful patronage of Islam. In 1307, however, after HARGHASUN DARQAN thwarted Ananda's attempt to seize the throne, his family's appanage was abolished.

The peak of Muslim influence in Yuan China came under Yisün-Temür (titled Taidingdi, 1323–28), when the Muslims Dawla-Shah (d. 1328) as left grand councillor and 'Ubaidullah (d. 1328) as manager (pingzhang) dominated the administration. Dawlat-Shah had good relations with the Christians and granted both them and Muslims exemption from corvée. Ananda's son Örüg-Temür was reinstated in northwest China, and payments to mostly Muslim ortoq merchants selling pearls reached extraordinary levels. The conspirators who overthrew Yisün-Temür's son in 1328 executed both Dawla-Shah and 'Ubaidullah, abolished the position of cadi (Islamic judge) in the capital, DAIDU (modern Beijing), and after first putting all religions on an equal tax footing, later granted Buddhist and Taoist monasteries special exemption from the commercial tax. In 1332 Ananda's son Örüg-Temür was accused of treason and executed. Muslims never again achieved high office in the Yuan.

Islamization as a process is best recorded in the IL-KHANATE. Long before converting, non-Muslim Mongol rulers prayed at saints' tombs, patronized Sufi mystics, and attended Islamic festivals. The decisive stage of conversion involved undergoing circumcision and learning prayers, ablutions, and other daily rituals. After conversion came further changes: switching the Mongol hat for the turban, abandoning the Mongol burial practices for Islamic interment in a mausoleum, and contracting endogamous marriages. Many formally Muslim Mongol lords balked at these changes for years. At the same time, even profoundly Muslim khans such as Ghazan Khan retained a deep interest in the Mongols' pre-Islamic festivals and customs.

Turks and Central Asians had always adhered to the Hanafi school of Sunni Islam, which, by permitting consumption of horsemeat, KOUMISS, and mead, was more adapted to Inner Asian customs. In the Golden Horde, the Chaghatay Khanate, and the YUAN DYNASTY Muslim Mongols unanimously followed this lead. Many Mongols, such as Ghazan Khan, also felt a great devotion to the family of 'Ali, frequently visiting his tomb in Najaf. His brother Sultan Öljeitü (1304–16), influenced by the Mongol emir Taramtaz (himself the son of a Uighur baqshi), went further and converted to Twelver Shi'ism in 1309. Öljeitü saw a close parallel between Chinggisid privilege in the MONGOL EMPIRE and the Shi'ite claim of Islamic leadership (imamate) for 'Ali's family only. One extreme Turkish Sufi, Baba Baraq, supposedly claimed that Öljeitü was an incarnation of 'Ali, who was in turn an incarnation of God. Öljeitü's attempt to impose even moderate Shi'ism, however, brought widespread resistance, and his son Abu-Sa'id (1317–35) returned the Il-Khanate's Mongols to Sunni Islam.

The Mongol conquests ironically powered a dramatic expansion of Islam, implanting a sizable Muslim minority in China and stimulating the conversion of the Qipchaq steppe. The Mongol conquest also strengthened the role of Sufism in Islam. Sufi faqirs led the conversion, which in turn sparked the formation of more organized Sufi lodges with lineages going back to the various sheikhs credited with converting one or another Mongol ruler. The confrontation of the Mongol rulers by miraculous

Sufis formed legend cycles that gave the numerous ethnic groups stemming from the Golden Horde and the Chaghatayid Khanates—the Uzbeks, Nogays, and so on—a new communal identity as Muslim peoples.

See also 'ABBASID CALIPHATE; ARGHUN AQA; BAO'AN LANGUAGE AND PEOPLE; BLUE HORDE; BULGHARS; CHUBAN; CRIMEA; DONGXIANG LANGUAGE AND PEOPLE; HAZARAS; INDIA AND THE MONGOLS; ISLAMIC SOURCES ON THE MONGOL EMPIRE; KAZAKHS; MOGHOLI LANGUAGE AND PEOPLE; NOQAI; RELIGIOUS POLICY IN THE MONGOL EMPIRE; QARA'UNAS; SARAY AND NEW SARAY; TIMUR; TURKEY.

Further reading: Reuven Amitai, "The Conversion of Teguder Ilkhan to Islam," Jerusalem Studies in Arabic and Islam 25 (2001): 15–43; Devin DeWeese, Islamization and the Golden Horde: Baba Tükles and the Conversion to Islam in Historical and Epic Tradition (University Park: Pennsylvania State University Press, 1994); Kim Ho-dong, "Muslim Saints in the 14th to the 16th Centuries of Eastern Turkistan," International Journal of Central Asian Studies 1 (1996): 285–322; Charles Melville, "Padshah-i Islam: The Conversion of Sultan Mahmud Ghazan Khan," Pembroke Papers 1 (1990): 159–177; Judith Pfeiffer, "Conversion Versions: Sultan Öljeytü's Conversion to Shi'ism (709/1309) in Muslim Narrative Sources," Mongolian Studies 22 (1999): 35–67.

Islamic sources on the Mongol Empire

Islamic sources on the Mongol Empire The MONGOL EMPIRE sparked some of the greatest historical writing in the Islamic world, particularly in Persian, and these histories form one of the most important bodies of data and interpretation about the Mongol Empire. The earliest Arabic historian of the Mongol conquest was 'Izz-ad-Din 'Ali Ibn al-Athir (1160–1233) of Mosul, who fought for Salah-ad-Din (Saladin) against the Crusaders. In his al-Kamil fi'l Ta'rikh, which covered world history to the year 1231, Ibn al-Athir described the initial Mongol invasions, viewing them as an unprecedented, almost uncanny, catastrophe for Islam. Vivid depictions of Mongol atrocities enliven an otherwise rather dry narration. Shihab-ud-Din Muhammad an-Nasawi, the private secretary of the Mongols' die-hard foe, Jalal-ud-Din Mengüberdi, was familiar with the al-Kamil and supplemented it with a lively biography of his patron's struggle against the Mongols (1241/2). The extensive information on the IL-KHANATE and the GOLDEN HORDE in Arabic-language Mamluk writings is only now being analyzed. Al-'Umari's (1301–49) geography, al-Yunini's (1242/3–1326) general history, and the memoirs of Abu'l-Fida' (1273–1331) are three sources in this vast body that have received modern historians' attention. Also well known is the travelogue of the Moroccan jurist MUHAMMAD ABU 'ABDULLAH IBN BATTUTA (1304–68/9).

Persian histories of the Mongols begin with two major monuments, one favorable and one hostile. 'ALA'UD-DIN ATA-MALIK JUVAINI's (1226–83) HISTORY OF THE WORLD CONQUEROR (c. 1259) was the first non-Mongol attempt to pen a large-scale history of the Mongols and their conquest. Juvaini was in Mongol service and saw much to appreciate in their simplicity and vigor. Independently, Minhaj-ud-Din Juzjani (1193–c.1265), the chief cadi, or Islamic judge, in Delhi, added to his history of the Islamic dynasties, the Tabaqat-i Nasiri, a chapter on the "Irruption of the Infidels into Islam." As a writer at the court of the sultanate of Delhi, Juzjani saw the Mongol invasions as a forerunner of the apocalypse. As one might expect, the chapters on CHINGGIS KHAN's conquest of Afghanistan, which Juzjani witnessed in his youth, and on relations with the sultanate of Delhi are particularly useful.

With the conversion of the Mongol Il-Khans in Iran to Islam, Persian-language court historiography flourished. Vassaf wrote a continuation of Juvaini's history to 1328 that combined valuable historical information with an extremely ornate style. The Mongol period saw a renewed interest in the Persian national epic, the Shahnama of Firdausi, that was reflected in Hamdullah Mustaufi Qazvini's (b. 1281/2) versified world history, Zafar-nama (1335), one of the few sources on late-Il-Khan history. Qazvini's geographical text, Nuzhat al-qulub, also sheds light on Il-Khanid geography, finances, and administration. The crown of Il-Khanid history, however, was RASHID-UD-DIN FAZL-ULLAH's (1247–1318) COMPENDIUM OF CHRONICLES, covering the united Mongol Empire and its four successor states up to 1304. The authoritative stature of Rashid's work inspired many continuators. Abu'l-Qasim Kashani, who improbably claimed to have been the real author of the Compendium, composed a history of Sultan Öljeitü (1304–16), while Hafiz-i Abru (d. 1430), writing in Timurid Herat, covered the reign of Abu-Sa'id (1317–35). Rashid-ud-Din and Kashani both clearly used royal diaries kept on the Chinese model at the Il-Khanid court. Apart from histories focusing on the Mongols themselves, Persian local histories and hagiographies contain much valuable information.

Before 1400 neither the Golden Horde nor the CHAGHATAY KHANATE nurtured any significant historiographical traditions. In the Chaghatayid area, though, the succeeding Turco-Mongol Timurid dynasty (c. 1378–1512; see TIMUR) saw a revival of the Central Asian Persian historiography in authors such as Mu'in-ud-Din Natanzi and Ghiyas-ud-Din Kh^wandamir (1475–1535/6), all of whom also supply important information on the later phases of the divided Mongol Empire. Muhammad Haidar Dughlat (1499–1551) of MOGHULISTAN also worked in the same tradition. In the successor states of the Golden Horde a number of genealogical and local histories appeared from the 16th century, principally in Turkish. Ötermish Hajji's Tarikh-i Dust Sultan (also known as Chingiz name, c. 1555) is a rich repository of oral traditions in Jochid lands. Abu'l-Ghazi Bahadur Khan's (1603–68) Shejere-i

Türk, while of no great value on the earlier empire, was the earliest Islamic source on the Mongols to be translated into a European language. Sufi hagiographies and genealogies are also important sources in Central Asian and Golden Horde history.

See also INDIA AND THE MONGOLS; ISLAM IN THE MONGOL EMPIRE.

Further reading: Li Guo, *Early Mamluk Syrian Historiography: al-Yunini's Dhayl Mir'at al-zaman* (Leiden: E. J. Brill, 1998); Peter Holt, *Memoirs of a Syrian Prince: Abu'l-Fida', Sultan of Hamah (672–732/1273–1331)* (Wiesbaden: Otto Harrassowitz, 1983); Khʷandamir, *Habibu's-Siyar*, Vol. 3, *The Reign of the Mongol and the Turk*, trans. Wheeler M. Thackston (Cambridge, Mass.: Harvard University Press, 1994); Johannes Baptist von Loon, trans., *Tarikh-i Shaikh Uwais (History of Shaikh Uwais): An Important Source for the History of Adharbaijan in the Fourteenth Century* (The Hague: Excelsior, 1954); Minhaj-ud-Dîn Abû-'Umar-i-'Usman [Juzjani], *Tabakat-i-Nasirî*, 2 vols., trans. Major H. G. Raverty (1881; rpt., Calcutta: The Asiatic Society, 1995); Mustawfi Hamd-Allah, *The Geographical Part of* Nuzhat al-Qulub, trans. G. Le Strange (Leiden and Berlin: E. J. Brill and Luzac, 1919); W. M. Thackston, trans., *Mirza Haydar Dughlat's Tarikh-i-Rashidi: A History of the Khans of Moghulistan*, Vol. 2 (Cambridge, Mass.: Harvard University Press, 1996).

Isma'ilis (Assassins, Mulahidah) The Mongols smashed the Isma'ili state (1090–1271), famed for its fortresses and assassins, and persecuted the sect. Originating as a branch of Shi'ite Islam, the Isma'ilis separated from other Shi'ites over the precise succession of the imamate, or true leadership of Islam, among the descendants of 'Ali (Muhammad's son-in-law). When the Isma'ilis founded the Fatimid caliphate in Egypt (973–1171), the mainstream Sunni authorities ruthlessly persecuted their followers in Iran as subversives.

Hasan-i Sabbah (d. 1124), an indefatigable propagator of the teachings of the most radical Nizari subsect of the Isma'ilis, got control of the citadel of Alamut (1090), in the Elburz Mountains northeast of Qazvin, while his confederates finagled the keys of nearby Lanbasar (Lammasar, 1102) and Girdkuh (c. 1095) in the Quhistan district, around Qayen in eastern Iran. Facing the constant danger of extermination, Hasan-i Sabbah sent *fida'i* (fedayeen), or "self-sacrificers," also known as *hashishiyun* (assassins), or "hashish users," to murder his most dangerous enemies. While the Isma'ili leaders lived in an isolated fortresses, ordinary Isma'ilis adhered covertly to the faith in the surrounding districts, particularly in Quhistan and Syria. Hasan (1126/7–66), the keeper of Alamut, came to claim descent from the Fatimid caliphs in Egypt and announced an era of spiritual resurrection in which the rules of Islamic law, or *shari'a*, were annulled. Sunni Muslims and mainstream

Shi'ites treated these Nizari Isma'ilis as "heretics," or *mulahidah*, a term general even in contemporary European and Chinese accounts.

The first verifiable Isma'ili contact with the Mongols came as CHINGGIS KAHN's youngest son, TOLUI, campaigned in eastern Iran in 1221 and ravaged Isma'ili populations in Quhistan. Hasan's grandson Hasan Jalal-ud-Din (r. 1210–21) is said to have been the first ruler west of the Amu Dar'ya to submit to the Mongols. 'Ala'ud-Din (MARCO POLO's Alaodin, r. 1221–55) sent an envoy to ÖGEDEI KHAN's (1229–41) coronation, but this submission by no means met Mongol requirements. Meanwhile, 'Ala'ud-Din used fedayeen, or assassins, against Mongol commanders, killing Kül-Bolat, who had campaigned in Quhistan, and the commander Cha'adai Noyan (not to be confused with Chinggis Khan's son), who had campaigned in western Iran under CHORMAQAN.

In 1246 'Ala'ud-Din sent his governors in Quhistan as envoys to the Mongol QURILTAI (assembly), but GÜYÜG KHAN (r. 1246–48) ordered Eljigidei to command a great campaign against him. The khan's death and succession struggles aborted this proposal until the coronation of MÖNGKE KHAN (1251–59). Shams-ud-Din Qazvini, chief judge of the city of Qazvin, where hostility to the Isma'ilis was rampant, had denounced the menace of the "Heretics," and Möngke Khan saw the Mulahidah not only as rebels but as an evil cult deserving complete annihilation. Möngke Khan assigned the campaign to his brother HÜLE'Ü, and KED-BUQA of the NAIMAN tribe set out as a vanguard in 1252. From May 1253 to September 1254 Ked-Buqa sacked the citadels and massacred the towns of the Isma'ilis in Quhistan, but Girdkuh fortress still stood. Rumor said that 'Ala'ud-Din dispatched 400 assassins to kill Möngke, although no attacks are recorded.

Hüle'ü himself arrived in spring 1256 with a vast army, including 1,000 mangonel experts and naphtha throwers from North China, and began mopping up in Quhistan. 'Ala'ud-Din had been murdered by a slave in December 1255, and his young son Rukn-ud-Din Khur-Shah then at Maimun-Diz, hoped to come to some agreement with the Mongols. Hüle'ü reached the Elburz citadels in September 1256, and after an exchange of envoys and some minor operations, he put Maimun-Diz under siege on November 8. The advancing winter and fodder shortages worried some Mongol commanders, but Rukn-ud-Din came down on November 20. Hüle'ü treated him favorably, and Rukn-ud-Din secured Alamut's surrender on December 15.

In March 1257 Hüle'ü sent him on to Möngke Khan in Mongolia. The khan executed him and his whole party and pronounced an edict of extermination against all Mulahidah. He ordered Ötegü-Chino'a, then directing operations against Girdkuh, to collect and butcher those "heretics" who had already surrendered; 12,000 were killed. Lanbasar, ravaged by plague, surrendered late in 1257, and the survivors were massacred. Girdkuh held out an incredible 15 years, until December 1271.

The Mongols not only virtually exterminated Nizari Isma'ili believers but sought out and destroyed all copies of their books, of which only fragments survive. Hüle'ü preserved the life of several Isma'ili scholars, including the famous astronomer Nasir-ud-Din Tusi, for whom he built an observatory in Maragheh. "Assassin" communities remained in Syria, and Isma'ili fedayeen attempted to murder 'ALA'UD-DIN 'ATA-MALIK JUVAINI, the Sunni Persian governor of Baghdad for the Mongols, in 1271.

J

Jabar Khoja (Ja'far) (1110–1227) *Envoy of Chinggis Khan who assisted in the conquest of North China and became administrator of Zhongdu city*

Jabar Khoja's place of origin is unknown, but he was a Muslim and *sayyid* (descendant of Muhammad—Jabar was the Mongolian pronunciation of the Arabic name Ja'-far) and had traveled in North China. Meeting CHINGGIS KHAN while both were at the KEREYID court, he joined Chinggis Khan's standard, joined the BALJUNA COVENANT (1203), and served as envoy to North China's JIN DYNASTY. In 1213 Jin troops blocked the Mongols at Juyongguan Pass, and Jabar suggested an alternate route through thick forests. Thanks to his advice, the Mongols successfully bypassed Juyongguan and surrounded the defenders (*see* JUYONGGUAN PASS, BATTLES OF). In 1214 Jabar Khoja served as the Mongol negotiator in the talks that brought the Jin emperor to submit as a tributary to Chinggis Khan. When the Jin emperor rebelled and fled south, the Mongols besieged the former Jin capital of Zhongdu (*see* ZHONGDU, SIEGES OF). The city fell in May 1215, and Chinggis Khan gave Jabar a large part of the city as his appanage and made him its chief administrator with Shimo Ming'an (*see* SHIMO MING'AN AND XIANDEBU). Although a Muslim, Jabar Khoja shared Chinggis Khan's fascination with the Taoist adept MASTER CHANGCHUN and believed in his powers. Jabar Khoja is said to have lived to age 117.

Ja Lama *See* DAMBIJANTSAN.

Jalayir Once rivals of the Mongol tribe, many members of the Jalayir became powerful aristocrats in the MONGOL EMPIRE and its successor states.

The earliest appearance in history of the Jalayir (plural Jalayid) may be as the "Chaladi" found in Chinese records of 910 on eastern Inner Mongolia. In Mongolian oral history the Jalayir figure as enemies of CHINGGIS KHAN's ancestress Mother Monolun (or Nomulun). The Jalayir almost wiped out Monulun's BORJIGID clan, and the survivors fled north to the BARGA (Barghu) Mongols. Under her son Qaidu, the Borjigid conquered the Jalayir, making them "hereditary slaves," or *ötegü bo'ol*. This event might be dated around 1060. From then on the Jalayir was a subject clan, dispersed among the ruling chiefs of the MONGOL TRIBE.

Most if not all of the Jalayir came to be inherited by Chinggis Khan's father, YISÜGEI BA'ATUR, and the various Jalayir sublineages assisted Chinggis Khan's rise early on. His most famous Jalayir commander, MUQALI (1170–1223), subdued North China and received the title prince of state (*Guowang* or *Gui-ong*), acting as Chinggis's viceroy while the khan was campaigning against KHORAZM. Another Jalayir commander, Ilügei, served as tutor and adviser to Chinggis's son and heir, Ögedei (r. 1229–41); his son Danishmand was Ögedei's steward. The Jalayir MENGGESER NOYAN became chief judge, or *jarghuchi*, under MÖNGKE KHAN (1251–59).

In China Muqali's descendants inherited his title of prince of state. Muqali's great-grandson Nayan became close to QUBILAI KHAN (1260–94), and Nayan's son Shuti served Qubilai in the KESHIG (imperial guard) and in overseeing court ritual. Nayan and Shuti both shared Qubilai's interest in CONFUCIANISM, and the Jalayir aristocrats came to be mainstays of Confucian influence in the Mongol YUAN DYNASTY. Hantum (Antong), grand councillor under Qubilai, Baiju, grand councillor under Shidebala (titled Yingzong, 1320–23), and Dorji, grand councillor under Toghan-Temür (titled Shundi, 1333–70), were all descendants of Muqali, and all promoted Confucian scholars and doctrines.

The Jalayir were powerful in the other successor states as well. Chinggis Khan gave 1,000 men under Möge of the Jalayir to his son CHA'ADAI; Möge's descendants were one of the chief tribes both in the successor CHAGHATAY KHANATE in Turkestan and in the Central Asian dynasty founded by Temür (Tamerlane, r. 1370–1405).

The Jalayir Elege was a chief general of HÜLE'Ü (r. 1256–65), who founded the IL-KHANATE in Iran. BUQA (d. 1289), a Jalayir of a junior sublineage, served Hüle'ü's successors Abagha (r. 1265–82) and Argun (1284–91) as commander in chief (amir al-umara or beglerbegi) and vizier, holding the red seal. Elege's ninth son, Aq-Buqa (d. 1295), was Geikhatu Khan's (1291–95) father-in-law and chief commander, and Aq-Buqa's grandson, Hasan Buzurg ("Big Hasan"), served Abu Sa'id (r. 1317–35) as commander in chief. After the Il-Khanate broke up in 1338, Hasan Buzurg occupied Iraq, ruling in the name of various Chinggisid candidates until his death in 1356. Under his son, Sheikh Uways (1358–74) the Jalayirid dynasty flourished in Iraq and western Iran. Eventually, the dynasty fell to internal dissension and attacks from TIMUR and his successors. The Jalayirid dynasty, which lasted until 1432, patronized the arts, and the Il-Khans' illustrated manuscript tradition developed further under their rule.

No members of the Jalayir dynasty achieved fame in the GOLDEN HORDE, under Chinggis's son JOCHI. Even so, numerous Jalayir clans found today among its successor peoples—Uzbeks, Kazakhs, and Bashkirs (Bashkort)—attest to the presence of Jalayirs there as well. In Mongolia, too, after the expulsion of the Yuan from China, the Jalayir continued to be an important clan. In the 16th century the name Jalayir (as Jalair or Jalaid) was one of the 14 clans of the Khalkha in northern Mongolia. It is found at present as a clan name among the Khalkha of Mongolia as well as a banner and clan name in eastern and southeastern Inner Mongolia (see KHINGGAN LEAGUE).

Further reading: Igor de Rachewiltz, "Muqali, Böl, Tas, An-t'ung," in *In the Service of the Khan: Eminent Personalities of the Early Mongol-Yuan Period (1200–1300)*, ed. Igor de Rachewiltz et al. (Wiesbaden: Harrossowitz, 1993), 3–12; J. M. Smith, Jr., "Djalayir, Djalayirid," in *Encyclopaedia of Islam* (Leiden: E. J. Brill, 1960 on), 2d ed., vol. 2, 401–402.

Jalkhanza Khutugtu Damdinbazar (Jalkhanz Khutagt, Sonomyn Damdinbazar) (1874–1923) *Incarnate lama who served as prime minister under White Russian and revolutionary regimes*

Damdinbazar was born in Tsogtai Zasag banner (modern Tüdewtei Sum, Zawkhan) before being discovered as the Jalkhanza Khutugtu. At age 16 he visited Khüriye (modern ULAANBAATAR) and at age 20 joined the entourage of the Bogda (the Holy One, or the Jibzundamba Khutugtu). In 1902–05 he spent three years at the ÖÖLÖD and MINGGHAD temple in western Mongolia; he also performed pilgrimages to Tibet and India and became a famous meditation master. He participated in the 1911 enthronement of the Bogda as KHAN and was appointed in February 1912 the supreme authority in western Mongolia. His prestige helped recruit 1,300 soldiers among the western Mongols for the victorious siege of KHOWD CITY. After this he returned to his home monastery (in modern Tsagaan-Uul Sum, Khöwsgöl). During the REVOCATION OF AUTONOMY and after the Bogda used him to deliver secret appeals to the U.S. legation in Beijing. In February 1921 he was made prime minister under the White Russian BARON ROMAN FEDOROVICH VON UNGERN-STERNBERG, but he did not resist the Red Army's march into Khüriye. In February 1922 the revolutionaries, worried about disaffection among the lamas, recalled the Jalkhanza Khutugtu from retirement in his home monastery to serve as figurehead prime minister until his death.

See also JIBZUNDAMBA KHUTUGTU, EIGHTH; REVOLUTIONARY PERIOD; THEOCRATIC PERIOD.

jam (yam)
The *jam*, or courier and relay system, which linked together the MONGOL EMPIRE, had many prototypes in earlier empires but was an unusually potent institution under the Mongols.

ORIGIN OF THE *JAM*

While courier systems had been established as early as the Persian Empire, the immediate prototype for the Mongol courier system was that of the JIN DYNASTY (1115–1234) in North China. This dynasty, like its predecessors, maintained roads and relay stations, building bridges and ferries where necessary. Regular travelers at government expense, such as foreign envoys, were given room and board as well as fresh horses and pack animals, while messengers on the express post carried an official badge to receive rapid remounts. Food and stock were provided by the surrounding civilian population.

After conquering North China, CHINGGIS KHAN (Genghis, 1206–27) ordered civilians to supply envoys bearing tablets of requisition (PAIZA) whatever remounts and provisions they needed. Those riding on government business would simply exchange their own tired horses for any fresh horse they saw on the road, and any passing envoy became the honored guest of the local officials. The Mongols also built roads; Chinggis's son ÖGEDEI KHAN carved a military highway through the ALTAI RANGE.

ORGANIZATION OF THE *JAM*

Ögedei in his first year as khan (1229–41) organized a formal *jam* (modern *zam*, Uighur pronunciation *yam*), or road system. Relay stations with attached households were set up every 45 kilometers (25 miles). The staff tended the station's horse herd, supplied remounts to the envoys, and served specified rations to those on government business. Only those bearing an official *paiza*, or tablet, were to use the *jam*, but those carrying military intelligence or rarities for the emperor were allowed even without a *paiza*. Civilians near the stations paid a *qubchiri* tax to supply the goods, but the attached households, called *jamchi* or *ula'achi* (from *ula'a*, relay, Uighur, *ulagh*), were exempt from other taxes. Ferries, wells, and bridges were maintained, and even dogsled relays were used in remote areas of Manchuria and Siberia (*see* MANCHURIA AND THE MONGOL EMPIRE; SIBERIA AND THE MONGOL EMPIRE.) In settled zones the *jamchi*s were locals, while in the steppe they were mostly deported subject peoples. The *jam* inspectors, called *todqa'ul* in the west and *todghasun* in the east, were important officials. The two great lords in the west, CHA'ADAI in Turkestan and BATU by the Volga, controlled their *jam*s separately.

Abuses of the *jam* soon became notorious. The Mongol nobility as well as the court freely issued *paiza*s, often for personal business. The excess traffic meant that stations lacked horses, and envoys often came to blows over them. *Paiza* holders expected excellent service and beat the *jamchi*s when the food and drink was not up to par. Widespread banditry necessitated guards, and RASHID-UD-DIN FAZL-ULLAH noted that even minor persons would receive an escort of 200 horsemen, while major personages would have 500 to 1,000. MÖNGKE KHAN (1251–59) limited some of these abuses.

THE *JAM* IN THE SUCCESSOR STATES

The Mongol YUAN DYNASTY in China maintained Ögedei's system by dedicating vast resources and making reforms. QUBILAI KHAN (1260–74) in 1261 set up special "gerfalcon" posts exclusively for the highest officials. Even ordinary relays, though, had sumptuous hostels built. In 1269–71 the court limited the number of *paiza*s assigned to each office, set up a general administration of the *jam* under the ministry of war, and specified written records be kept of all horses issued. Around 1330 the Mongol Yuan dynasty maintained (according to incomplete figures) 1,400 stations, of which 913 were the conventional horse relays with 44,135 horses, 424 were water relays with 5,921 boats, and the rest sedan chair, ox cart, and foot relays. In Manchuria 15 dogsled relays disposed of 218 dogs.

Meanwhile, in Iran the *jam* system broke down under the weight of overuse. *Jamchi*s on well-traveled routes fled, and the system reverted to the random requisitions of Chinggis's time. GHAZAN KHAN (1295–1304) rebuilt the *jam* on a restricted scale, constructing a limited number of hostels for those traveling at government expense but prohibiting the requisitioning of goods. Envoys from the court received a per diem stipend, and those of the nobility traveled at their own expense. Only envoys bearing urgent military intelligence used the staffed postal relay service.

The *jam/yam* institution survived in the GOLDEN HORDE, financed by a *yam* tax, but little is known of its operation. The 1305 peace treaty between the Mongol successor states reopened the *jam* between them.

SEVENTEENTH CENTURY TO THE PRESENT

The QING DYNASTY (1636–1912) in Mongolia also maintained a postroad system that carried both urgent news and official goods. After establishing garrisons in Mongolia, the Qing set up a separate grain transport system, which operated along the regular postroad routes. The Qing postroad stations were called *örtege* (modern *örtöö*, Chinese, *taizhan*) and were divided into the official stations (*guanshe taizhan*) and the *sumu* stations (*sumu taizhan*). The former contained five main trunk roads (*jam* or *zam*) through Inner Mongolia, the main western road from Beijing to Xinjiang and the northern road from Zhangjiakou (Kalgan) to Khüriye (modern ULAAN-BAATAR), KYAKHTA CITY, and KHOWD CITY and on to Xinjiang. All of these were maintained by the central government in Beijing. The local *sumu* stations, however, were operated by the local banners (appanages) and *sumu*s (SUM). All the roads through Mongolia were manned as a public duty (*ulaga*, modern *ulaa*) by Mongols. By the 19th century, however, it was common for the more remote banner offices to hire substitutes nearer to the roads to fulfill their functions.

After 1911 this postroad system was inherited and maintained by the independent Mongolian governments (*see* REVOLUTIONARY PERIOD; THEOCRATIC PERIOD). Not until 1949 was the civilian duty of *ulaa* eliminated.

See also TEMÜDER.

Jamugha (Jamuqa, Jamukha) (c. 1160–1205) *Chinggis Khan's former blood brother and foremost rival within the Mongol tribe*
Jamugha belonged to the Jajirad (or Jadaran) clan, which considered itself a branch of the heavenly born BORJIGID lineage, but which rivals claimed was really of illegitimate birth. Jamugha was an orphaned only son, raised by women of his father's clan. In his childhood (around 1173) Jamugha first became ANDA (blood brother) with Temüjin (the later CHINGGIS KHAN), likewise orphaned by his father's murder. By around 1180 Jamugha had risen to significant influence among the Mongols. When Temüjin asked Toghril Khan of the KEREYID khanate for help against the MERKID tribe, who had kidnapped his bride, Jamugha joined him with a large force. Temüjin and Jamugha renewed their blood brotherhood, but the amity broke down, and the two blood brothers separated. When retainers of the two camps clashed over horse stealing, Jamugha and Temüjin assembled their followers and fought an inconclusive battle. The following years are obscure; at some point Jamugha surrendered to Toqto'a, chief of the Merkid tribe. In 1201 those Mongols opposed to Temüjin raised Jamugha as *gür-khan* (universal khan)

in alliance with the Merkid and other tribes. Temüjin and Toghril (now ONG KHAN) defeated Jamugha, who fled north. Eventually, Jamugha and his supporters went over to Ong Khan. When Temüjin conquered the Kereyid in 1203, Jamugha fled to the NAIMAN Khanate. After Temüjin defeated the Naiman, Jamugha was captured and executed. Mongol sources portray Jamugha as the opposite of Chinggis—glib, untrustworthy, and brutal toward his followers—and Chinggis's execution of his *anda* appears as a fratricidal sacrifice necessary to found the new order.

Jangar   *See* JANGGHAR.

Jangghar (Janggar, Jangar, Zhangar)
Jangghar is one of the great EPICS of the Mongolian peoples. It is the only epic of the KALMYKS on the Volga and one of the main epics among the Mongols of Xinjiang and western Mongolia. Only short versions are found among the KHALKHA. *Janggharchis*, or Jangghar singers, sing their tales in mostly alliterative verses organized into various episodes, varying from a few hundred to almost 2,000 lines. The recitation is always concluded with a "Praise of Holy Jangghar." In western Mongolia a "Jangghar *biyelgee*," or mime, is also performed. Texts have been recorded both in native Oirat and Mongolian manuscripts and, since the beginning of the 19th century, by folklorists. The best-known version is that recorded from the Lesser Dörböd bard Eelän Owla (Ilya Ovlaev) among the Kalmyks in 1908–10. Ultimately 26 episodes were recorded among the Kalmyks. Later publications from *janggharchis* among the Oirat Mongols of Xinjiang have expanded the number of episodes to more than 60, covering some 1,700 pages.

The hero Jangghar is the son of Üzüng Aldar Khan of the mythical Northern Land of Bumba. At age five his father is killed, and he is captured by the enemy Mighty Silver Shigshirge. This enemy's son, the boastful and drunken but good-hearted Red Swain, defends Jangghar. As a task the five-year-old Jangghar with his steed Aranzal is sent to steal the horses of Golden Chest. Hit by Golden Chest's arrow, Jangghar is cured by Red Swain, who brings Jangghar, Golden Chest, and Mighty Silver Shigshirge into alliance to rule the Northern Land of Bumba.

The subsequent episodes revolve around how Jangghar and his companions (Red Swain, The World's Handsome Mingyan, Fierce Black Thought, Heavy-Handed Claw, etc.) defeat the attacks of various monsters who steal horses, wives, and companions from Jangghar. Jangghar and his companions likewise steal horses, win brides, and turn their defeated enemies into companions. Their enemies include mythical monsters (White Camel, Blue-Headed Fly, etc.) and figures such as the Turkish khan and Fierce Black Kinas (from Russian *kniaz*, "prince") from the historical environment of the Kalmyks in the 17th–18th centuries. Frequent but only glancing references are made to the Buddhist cultural environment.

The time of origin of the Jangghar epic is not known, although its distribution, sketchy geography, and material culture (e.g., stained glass, bayonets) all suggest an origin among the late 17th-century Kalmyks. Jangghar's relatively realistic themes parallel the epics of the neighboring Turkic Muslim peoples, Nogay, Kazakh, and Kyrgyz, and some have related the hero's name to the Persian title *jihangir*, "world conqueror." In the early 20th century princes and monasteries among the Kalmyks, XINJIANG MONGOLS, and western Mongols (TORGHUDS, ZAKHACHIN, BAYADS, DÖRBÖD) patronized the *janggharchi* richly. Officially encouraged in the Soviet Union as a masterpiece of patriotic and nonclerical folk literature, on Joseph Stalin's recommendation 1940 was made the epic's 500th anniversary. The living tradition of Jangghar performance among the Kalmyks was, destroyed by their exile to Siberia in 1944, while that in Xinjiang was damaged by the Maoist Cultural Revolution (1966–76).

See also FOLK POETRY AND TALES.

Further reading: Arash Bormanshinov, "The Bardic Art of Eeljan Ovla." In *Fragen der Mongolischen Heldendichtung*, Vol. 2, ed. Walther Heissig (Wiesbaden: Harrassowitz, 1982): 155–167.

Jangjiya Khutugtu (Janggiya; Tibetan, lCang-skya, Changchya; Chinese, Zhangjia, Chang-chia)
The Jangjiya Khutugtus were a lineage of INCARNATE LAMAS who oversaw Mongolian Buddhism for the QING DYNASTY (1636–1912). The incarnate lama lineage originated among the Tu (Monguors) in western Gansu. The first Jangjiya Khutugtu, Agwang-Lubsang-Choidan (Tibetan, Ngag-dbang Blo-bzang Chos-ldan, 1642–1715), was a lama of dGon-lung (Chinese, Youning Si) Monastery in modern Huzhu county who had spent more than 20 years in Tibet (1661–83). In 1693 he was summoned to the court of the Kangxi emperor (1662–1722) as *Jasag da blama* (ruling head lama), nominally ruling all Mongolian monasteries, and in 1706 he was made *Da guoshi* (great state preceptor). Both titles were inherited by his successors. In 1697, while on a mission to Tibet, he encouraged the *TAIJI* (noblemen) of Kökenuur to surrender to the Qing. He supervised Huizong Temple (Mongolian, Khökhe Süme, Blue Temple) in Dolonnuur, built to commemorate the submission of the KHALKHA, and Songzhu Temple in Beijing, a major center for Mongolian and Tibetan block printing. Recognized in dGon-lung Monastery as the 14th of his lineage, the lineage's name, and sometimes the count of incarnations, was taken from his predecessor, a simple Tu lama of Zhangjia village.

In 1723 the next incarnation, Rolbidorji (Tibetan, Rol-pa'i rDo-rje, 1716–86, also called Ishi-Dambi-Rome/Ye-shes bsTan-pa'i sGron-me), was forced to flee as Qing troops ravaged the Tu monasteries, which had supported the Mongol prince Lubsang-Danzin's rebellion. In 1724 the new Yongzheng emperor (1723–35), who had been a disciple of his previous incarnation, rescued Rolbidorji from reprisals by summoning him to Beijing. Rolbidorji studied Manchu, Mongolian, and Chinese with the future Qianlong emperor (1736–96) in Beijing, and in 1745 Qianlong became Rolbidorji's pupil, receiving the Tantric Heruka initiation. Rolbidorji's tutors had experienced sharp conflicts with Yongzheng's brother, Prince Yunli (Kheng-ze, 1697–1738), who supported the rNying-ma-pa (Old Order), but their pupil became an articulate defender of dGe-lugs-pa (Yellow Hat) interpretations, both in debate and in his widely used textbook, *Presentation of Tenets* (*Grub-mtha'i rnam-bzhag*). Rolbidorji chaired the Mongolian translation of the bsTan-'gyur (canonical scripture commentaries), which was completed in 1749 with an accompanying terminological dictionary, *Merged garkhu-yin oron* (Font of scholars). Rolbidorji sponsored both Yonghegong, Beijing's first Tibetan Buddhist teaching temple, and a unique Manchu-language temple.

Ishi-Dambi-Jalsan (Tibetan, Ye-shes bsTan-ba'i rGyal-msthan, 1787–1846), from a Tibetan village near Xining, was confirmed by the Qianlong emperor as the third incarnation. He spent six years from 1800 studying in Tibet and was not officially enthroned until 1819. He sponsored the teaching of Mongolian in Beijing and was the guru of the famous Mongolian poet and incarnate lama DANZIN-RABJAI. The lineage's next two incarnations died at ages 26 and 10, respectively. The last incarnation, personally named Sangjaijab (Tibetan, Sangs-rgyas-skyabs, 1891–1958), was again a Tu. He received high honors under the Republic of China (1911–49) for his staunch opposition to both Mongolian independence and modern ideas, although his influence among the Mongols was slight. He fled to Taiwan in 1949.

See also TU LANGUAGE AND PEOPLE.

Further reading: E. Gene Smith, *Among Tibetan Texts: History and Literature of the Tibetan Plateau* (Boston: Wisdom Publications, 2001), 133–146.

Japan and the modern Mongols Invaded by Mongol soldiers in the 13th century, Japan came in contact with the Mongols again around 1900. After 40 years of the Manchu-Mongolian policy that put Japan in occupation of most of Inner Mongolia, Japan's catastrophic defeat in 1945 again cut off contact with the Mongols. Eventually Japan's old links to both Mongolia and Inner Mongolia were revived on a new footing, and after 1990 Japan became Mongolia's leading aid donor and the main destination of Inner Mongolian students. (*On the Mongol invasions of Japan, see* JAPAN AND THE MONGOL EMPIRE.)

EARLY CONTACTS

Japan's first modern contact with the Mongols came about as a result of the country's expanding influence in China. Mongolian aristocrats and lamas in Beijing were impressed by the discipline and demeanor of Japanese troops participating in the suppression of the Boxer movement in 1900. In 1903 Prince Güngsangnorbu (Prince Güng, 1871–1931) of KHARACHIN Right Banner visited Japan and was inspired by the country's modernization to invite Japanese teachers to staff a military academy and a girls' school in his banner. Neighboring princes of southeastern Inner Mongolia followed suit. During the Russo-Japanese War (1904–05) in Manchuria, the Japanese hired Mongolian and Chinese bandits as auxiliaries. With the conclusion of the war Prince Güng sent several of his best students to Japan for higher education; on returning to China they became leaders in Inner Mongolia's political and cultural life. Treaties between Russia and Japan from 1907 to 1910 defined Outer Mongolia and northern Manchuria as Russia's sphere and southern Manchuria as Japan's but left Inner Mongolia undefined.

From 1900 Japanese scholars, students, tourists, and Buddhist monks frequently visited Mongol lands, building up a vast fund of knowledge about the Mongols. The Japanese-owned South Manchurian Railway (Mantetsu) and the Kwantung (Guandong, Japanese, Kanto) Army that garrisoned the railway actively researched Mongolian conditions and attempted to expand Japan's influence there in ways sometimes unapproved by Tokyo.

STRATEGIC AND IDEOLOGICAL CONFLICTS, 1911–1931

During the 1911 RESTORATION of Mongolian independence from China and the overthrow of China's last QING DYNASTY, Kawashima Naniwa, a Japanese adviser in the Chinese government, encouraged Manchu and the eastern Inner Mongolian nobility to create a separate Manchuria under the Qing emperor. In December 1911 Kawashima arranged for loans and supplies of rifles for Prince Güng and other Inner Mongolian nobles in return for MINING concessions. That spring, however, the foreign ministry decided to recognize the Chinese Republic and in April recalled Kawashima to Japan. The arms shipments went forward, however, until mid-June 1912, when the new Chinese Republican authorities captured the weapons en route, resulting in several casualties on both sides. On July 8 Japanese and Russian negotiators defined southeast Inner Mongolia (Josotu, including Kharachin, JUU UDA, KHORCHIN, and Front Gorlos) as Japan's sphere. However, while maintaining informal contacts and subsidizing students, Tokyo did not imitate Russia's support for an autonomy movement within its sphere.

Compared to Inner Mongolia, Outer Mongolia's case was rather simple. When Outer Mongolia declared independence with Russian assistance in 1911, Japan's foreign ministry immediately recognized Russia's predominant influence there and refused Mongolia's several attempts to open relations. The ministry also disclaimed all connection with the unauthorized negotiations carried on in Mongolia in 1913 by Kodama Toshimasa, a Japanese naval reserve officer in the employ of Mantetsu.

During World War I (1914–18) and the Russian civil war (1918–20), Japanese commercial and politicomilitary influence on the mainland expanded rapidly, while that of Russia receded. The Japanese Mitsui firm established a representative in Outer Mongolia's capital, Khüriye, and in 1918 agents visited Outer Mongolia. In February 1918 the Japanese general staff sent arms and 49 trainers headed by Kuroki Tikanori to the headquarters of the half-Buriat Mongolian Cossack commander Grigorii M. Semënov (1890–1945), then planning to attack the new Soviet Russian regime. Semënov's pan-Mongolist plans eventually alienated both anticommunist Russians and the other world powers, and on May 16, 1919, the liberal administration of Japanese prime minister Hara Kei withdrew support from Semënov, forcing Kuroki and the other advisers to leave his camp in August. Despite this withdrawal, the Soviet leadership (and subsequent Communist historians) believed that Semënov's pan-Mongolist movement of 1919 and his subordinate BARON ROMAN FEDOROVICH VON UNGERN-STERNBERG's 1920–21 invasion of Mongolia were simply tactical variations in the advance of a unitary "Japanese imperialism" aiming not just at Mongolia but even the BURIATS of southern Siberia.

From the Soviet victory in the Russian Civil War and the Soviet-supported 1921 REVOLUTION in Outer Mongolia on, both sides sought influence throughout the region. The Japanese ideology of pan-Asianism and monarchic modernization and the Soviet ideology of anticolonialism and class revolution became intertwined with the two countries' national interests. Supported mostly by the monarchist nobility and bandit chiefs and the Tibetan Panchen Lama, then active in Inner Mongolia, Japan lost the support of young Mongols to Soviet-supported nationalist movements. Meanwhile, in the Soviet-oriented Mongolian People's Republic, Moscow stymied the DAMBADORJI regime's attempts from 1925 to 1928 to contact Japanese diplomats. Incidents such as the summer 1928 Soviet-inspired rebellion in HULUN BUIR caused violent press polemics, yet both sides avoided real clashes.

JAPANESE OCCUPATION IN INNER MONGOLIA

The Great Depression, China's increasingly hostile Nationalist regime, and enthusiasm in the Japanese press forced Tokyo to back the Kwantung Army's coup d'état of September 18, 1931, and occupy all of Manchuria, including eastern Inner Mongolia. The May 1933 campaign added Rehe (or Jehol, including Juu Uda, Kharachin, and Fuxin). While returning the last Qing emperor to the throne of "Manchukuo" and sending the former bandit Ganjuurjab to win over anti-Chinese militiamen, the Kwantung Army did not attract much more than passive support from young Mongol nationalists. The Japanese assumed the role of protect-ing the Mongols against CHINESE COLONIZATION and increased the power of local Mongol government. Nevertheless, instead of a unified Mongolian autonomous area, they set up four provinces, called Khinggan South, North, East, and West.

Once having occupied Manchuria, the Kwantung Army agents worked to infiltrate western Inner Mongolia. This time they paid special attention to the previously Soviet-affiliated nationalists. By August 1935 they had penetrated the Mongol nationalist circle in the autonomy movement of PRINCE DEMCHUGDONGRUB (Prince De). While Prince De at first hoped to secure greater autonomy from China, by 1936 he was working with the Kwantung Army to attack the northwest Chinese warlords. Not until the full-scale Japanese invasion of 1937, however, did Prince De and his Japanese backers gain control of most of western Inner Mongolia. By 1938 about 80 percent of the INNER MONGOLIANS were living under Japanese-controlled governments. Japanese scholarships and schools created a large number of Inner Mongolians fluent in Japanese by 1945.

While the Soviet Union allowed Japan to take over its interests in Manchuria for compensation, border clashes began along the Mongolian-Manchukuo boundary in January 1935. Since the border had never been demarcated, the Mongolian and Manchukuo governments held four sessions of talks from June 1935 to September 1937 to attempt to resolve border issues, yet Tokyo's and Moscow's growing suspicions of "their" Mongols helped prevent a peaceful resolution. In Khinggan North province (Hulun Buir) on Manchukuo's Soviet-Mongolian frontier, the Japanese executed the governmental chairman, Lingsheng (1889–1936), on April 24, 1936, as a Soviet spy and imprisoned many others, while the Soviet GREAT PURGE destroyed the Mongolian People's Republic's entire elite on charges of being "pan-Mongolist" spies for Japan. The conflict eventually resulted in the pitched BATTLE OF KHALKHYN GOL in May–September 1939, in which the Red Army won a decisive victory over Japanese forces. Quadrilateral Soviet-Mongolian-Japanese-Manchukuo negotiations from September 9–16, 1939, resulted in a recognition of the frontier claimed by the Soviet and Mongolian side. In May 1941 the Soviet Union and Japan signed a nonaggression pact.

Japanese rule in Inner Mongolia came to an end with the sudden Soviet-Mongolian invasion on the night of August 9–10, 1945. In Wang-un Süme (Ulanhot), the capital of the Khinggan provinces, the Mongols, led by KHAFUNGGA, rose up and killed their Japanese advisers. Elsewhere, the Japanese fled. While Mongolia declared war on Japan, it was not allowed representation in the peace conference or in the payment of reparations. Of the many thousands of Japanese prisoners of war captured by Soviet forces, 12,318 were sent to work in Mongolia in November–December 1945. Of these, 13 percent died before being sent back to the Soviet Union in October

1947 for ultimate repatriation to Japan. Many of the buildings they built, including the government palace in ULAANBAATAR, still exist.

FOREIGN RELATIONS, 1954 ON

In 1954 Japanese inquiries about prisoners of war in Mongolia opened the first channel of relations. Serious discussion about normalization of relations began with Mongolia's membership in the UNITED NATIONS in 1961. The main issue was reparations and the state of war. Mongolia demanded that Japan declare peace with Mongolia and pay reparations, while Japan felt that since Mongolia had been until 1946 de jure a part of China, no state of war existed and that any claim Mongolia had against Japan was canceled by Mongolia's callous and unlawful exploitation of Japanese prisoners of war. Only in February 1972 were these issues resolved, with Mongolia's legislature unilaterally abolishing its state of war with Japan and Japan paying reparations worth US $17 million by funding the Gobi CASHMERE Factory. The Soviet Union encouraged this denouement so as to strengthen Mongolia's economy by giving it access to the Japanese market but otherwise forced the Mongolians to keep Japan at arms length.

From 1987, with the growing liberalization in the Soviet bloc, Japanese-Mongolian relations flourished, accelerating after Mongolia's 1990 DEMOCRATIC REVOLUTION and the cessation of Soviet aid in 1991. Cultural ties between Japan and Mongolia have greatly expanded, whether in scholarship (see ARCHAEOLOGY), journalism, or religion. In August 1991 the Japanese prime minister, Toshiki Kaifu, became the first leader of a developed democracy to visit Mongolia, a visit repeated by Prime Minister Keizo Obuchi in 1999. From 1991 Japan has been consistently the largest aid donor to Mongolia. From 1993 to 1997 annual grant aid averaged US $52 million, technical cooperation $25.5 million, and loans almost $24 million. Mongolia began trading with Japan in the 1960s, but such trade by 1990 still amounted to only US $17.4 million, or 1 percent of Mongolia's total trade turnover. By the year 2000 it expanded to $81.4 million, or 7.5 percent. This percentage, however, remains below that of the United States or the European Union.

After 1945, Inner Mongolia came under Chinese Communist control, and all contact with Japan was cut off for over 30 years. Even so Japanese, rather than Russian or English, remained the major foreign language taught in Inner Mongolia's Mongolian-language schools, a status assisted by the similarities in Japanese and Mongolian grammar (see ALTAIC LANGUAGE FAMILY). With the opening of the People's Republic of China in 1979 many Inner Mongolian students again began to study in Japan. In 1999 the association of ethnic Mongol students from China studying in Japan had more than 330 members. The world's first test-tube goat was created in 1984 by Shuurgan (b. 1940), an Inner Mongolian scientist researching in Japan.

See also FOREIGN RELATIONS; MONGOLIA, STATE OF; MONGOLIAN PEOPLE'S REPUBLIC; REVOLUTIONARY PERIOD; SAINCHOGTU, NA.; THEOCRATIC PERIOD.

Further reading: Tsedendambyn Batbayar, "Mongolia and Japan in 1945–1995: A Half Century Reconsidered," in *Mongolia in the Twentieth Century: Landlocked Cosmopolitan,* ed. Stephen Kotkin and Bruce A. Elleman (Armonk, N.Y.: M. E. Sharpe, 1999), 191–222; Robert B. Valliant, "Inner Mongolia, 1912: The Failure of Independence," *Mongolian Studies* 4 (1977): 56–92.

Japan and the Mongol Empire   Qubilai's expeditions against Japan, finally wrecked by the famous *kamikaze* (divine wind), became great burdens on Mongol-ruled China and Korea. By the 13th century the military government in Kamakura (1185–1333), dominated by the Hojo family, had removed the emperor in Kyoto from actual administration. Japan had no formal relations with the mainland, but Japanese Buddhist pilgrims, merchants, and pirates all regularly crossed the East China Sea.

QUBILAI KHAN (1260–94) first learned of Japan in 1265 from a Korean interpreter. From 1266 to 1272 Qubilai's repeated dispatch of envoys was stymied first by Korean noncooperation and then by the Hojo family's refusal to allow the Japanese emperor to receive them. In July 1271 the Korean interpreter Cho Kaesǔng first proposed invasion. In November 1274 a fleet under Prince Hindu and the Korean Hong Tagu (1244–91), with 1,000 transport ships, 300 ba'atur (hero) light warships, and 300 smaller craft and 15,000 fighting men, set out from Korea against Japan. The flotilla seized a beachhead at Hakata (modern Fukuoka), defeating the Japanese defenders. Soon, however, a storm threatened the fleet, forcing it to reembark with heavy losses. The Hojo now extensively walled the Hakata waterfront and slew Qubilai's later envoys.

In 1280 Qubilai ordered the Song defector Fan Wenhu to lead what was said to be a 100,000-man fleet from Quanzhou (Amoy) against Japan. Korea was to ferry 40,000 North Chinese, under Aq-Taghai (1235–90) of the Suldus, on 900 ships and contribute 10,000 men. The northern fleet sailed on June 10, 1281, reaching Munakata. Fan Wenhu's fleet landed at Imari somewhat later. On August 15 and 16 a typhoon destroyed much of both fleets. Aq-Taghai and Fan Wenhu embarked for the mainland with the seaworthy ships, leaving the remaining troops to be crushed by the Japanese, who butchered the captured Mongol, Korean, and Han (North Chinese) men and enslaved the "Tang" (South Chinese). From 1283 to 1286 Qubilai amassed ships, grain, and sailors for another expedition, even recruiting tattooed criminals and former salt smugglers as marines. Qubilai finally canceled the expedition so as to facilitate his invasion of VIETNAM.

Shinto priests believed the storm that destroyed the Mongol fleet to be a "divine wind" (kamikaze). The *Moko shurai ekotoba* ("The Mongol Invasion Painted Scroll,"

c. 1293) is one of the masterpieces of Japanese painting and a valuable source on the invasion.

See also KOREA AND THE MONGOL EMPIRE.

Further reading: Thomas Conlan, *In Little Need of Divine Intervention: Takezaki Suenaga's Scrolls of the Mongol Invasions of Japan* (Ithaca, N.Y.: Cornell University Press, 2001).

Jargalant *See* KHOWD CITY.

jarghuchi (yarghuchi) The position of *jarghuchi*, or judge, was always linked to the census and taxes and tightly guarded by the khan's household. Conflicting traditions point to his adoptive son SHIGI QUTUQU or his brother Belgütei as being CHINGGIS KHAN's (Genghis, 1206–27) first *jarghuchi* (Uighur, *yarghuci,* modern Mongolian, *zargach*). Members of the KESHIG (imperial guard) assisted the *jarghuchi*s. Chinggis's sons and "companions" (NÖKÖR) all received their own *jarghuchi*s. Under ÖGEDEI KHAN (1229–41) CHINQAI, then chief scribe, tried important cases, but under the reigns of GÜYÜG (1246–48) and MÖNGKE KHAN (1251–59) the position of great judge (*yeke jarghuchi*) at court was separated from that of chief scribe.

In North China the supreme governor also began to bear the title "great judge" (Mongol, *yeke jarghuchi;* Chinese, *da duanshiguan*) from the appointment of Shigi Qutuqu in 1235. From then until 1259 the *yeke jarghuchi*s in Yanjing (modern Beijing) handled administrative and judicial matters. Judicial procedure routinely involved beatings to extract confessions. At this early stage there was no complete law code, and *jarghuchi* had enormous latitude, even in capital cases. The princes appointed their own *jarghuchi*s for their own appanages, who were even less accountable.

In the Mongol YUAN DYNASTY in China QUBILAI KHAN (1260–94) restricted the *jarghuchi*s to judicial affairs and organized them under the Court of the Imperial Clan, a high-ranking office always headed by a powerful nobleman and staffed by members of the *keshig*. Decisions from 1311 to 1328 eventually restricted the *jarghuchi*s' jurisdiction to cases involving Mongols, SEMUREN (various sorts), the *keshig* (imperial guard), and the postroads in the metropolitan area, while attempting to abolish the separate appanage *jarghuchi*s. In the IL-KHANATE the position of *yarghuchi*s (Uighur pronunciation of *jarghuchi*) was also reserved for Mongol nobles, but little is known of the institutional framework.

See also APPANAGE SYSTEM; CENSUS IN THE MONGOL EMPIRE; MAHMUD YALAVACH AND MAS'UD BEG; MENGGESER NOYAN.

jarliq (yarligh, yarlyk) The *jarliq*, or decree (Uighur, *yarligh,* modern Mongolian, *zarlig*), particularly the written patent conferring immunity from taxation on families or institutions, was one of the most important documents for subjects of the MONGOL EMPIRE. In 1204 the Uighur scribe Tatar-Tong'a entered the service of CHINGGIS KHAN (Genghis, 1206–27), and the court soon began issuing patents, or decrees, stamped with the emperor's vermilion seal (*al tamagha*). The term *jarliq* was most often used for written patents of immunity (DARQAN) granted religious institutions or those who had performed special service, and for warrants (accompanied by a tablet, or PAIZA) to use the postroads (JAM). Given the constant possibility under Mongol rule of irregular demands for provisions or room and board, such a *jarliq* (Uighur pronunciation, *yarligh*) was a vital protection to its possessor, as well as being a matter of honor and prestige. At the coronation of a khan, all old *jarliq*s with the vermilion seal were automatically renewed, so that conflicting and duplicate *jarliq*s circulated constantly.

QUBILAI KHAN began the practice of having the four great aristocrats in his KESHIG sign all *jarliq*s, a practice that spread to all other successor states. In the Mongol IL-KHANATE in Persia, GHAZAN KHAN (1295–1304) reformed the issuance of *jarliq*s, creating set forms and graded seals, ordering that all *jarliq*s be kept on file at court, and invalidating all *jarliq*s older than 30 years. In the GOLDEN HORDE the chancellery language switched to Turkish in the 14th century, and many Turkish *yarligh*s from the 15th century are preserved in the archives of Moscow and Istanbul.

Further reading: Francis Woodman Cleaves, "A Chancellery Practice of the Mongols," *Harvard Journal of Asiatic Studies* 14 (1951): 493–526.

jasaq (yasa, yasaq) The famous *jasaq* was the body of laws and practices decreed by CHINGGIS KHAN and his successors, which gradually came to form a sort of constitution of the MONGOL EMPIRE. As Chinggis Khan (Genghis, 1206–27) rose to power, he repeatedly declared judgments on various matters relating primarily to the administration of the army, court, and imperial prerogatives. These decisions and the punishments for the guilty, called *jasaq* (ordinance, modern *zasag,* Uighur pronunciation, *yasaq*), served as precedents for future cases, and with the adoption of writing such judgments were recorded permanently. At the coronation of Chinggis Khan's son ÖGEDEI KHAN (1229–41), the new khan proclaimed for the first time the "Great Jasaq" as an integral body of precedents, confirming the continuing validity of all the ordinances and commands of his father, while adding his own. While many of the *jasaq*s of Ögedei were in turn frequently cited, subsequent reigns provided much less in the way of new decisions.

By the time of MÖNGKE KHAN (1251–59), the *jasaq* had become a body of written precedents consulted at the great assemblies (QURILTAI) that elected new khans, mobilized campaigns, and dealt with administration. Collections of such precedents, called the *Great Book of Jasaq*s, were kept in the treasuries of the khan and the other great princes. Members of the Besüd clan always attended such readings of the *jasaq,* where they performed shamanic rituals. The *jasaq* shared its importance at the *quriltai*s with the codified *biligs,* or wise sayings of Chinggis and his descendants, which were also written down by scribes from day to day in versified form. Memorization and recital of these proverbs were important accomplishments of Chinggisid princes.

The *jasaq* must not be understood as a formal law code. Sources such as the *SECRET HISTORY OF THE MONGOLS* show how the promulgation of *jasaq*s was connected to specific events, without any effort at systematization. The repeated reference of Persian writers under the Mongols to the "*yasa/yasaq* [ordinances] and the *yosun* [customs]" show that the *jasaq* was only one part of a much larger body of unwritten customs, which were equally binding.

Despite this lack of codification, the *jasaq* came to exert a profoundly conservative influence on the Mongol Empire. Innovations, whether they were QUBILAI KHAN's (1260–94) partial adoption of Chinese administrative and legal precedents or the adoption of Islam in the IL-KHANATE of Iran or the CHAGHATAY KHANATE of Central Asia, gave opponents the slogan of defending the "ordinances and customs" of Chinggis Khan. However, the lack of systematization also made it easy for those bent on reform to advertise them as only a further elaboration of the ancient precedents.

The perception of the *jasaq* among the subject peoples was heavily influenced by their own ideas about law. Chinese writers minimized both Chinggis Khan's role in making Mongol institutions and the very term *jasaq* itself, emphasizing the role of Chinese advisers under Ögedei and especially Qubilai in developing formal institutions. Islamic writers saw the *jasaq* (Persian, *yasa*) as a Mongol equivalent of the wide-ranging *shari'a,* or code of Islamic law, some emphasizing their compatibility and others their antagonism. Armenian and Syriac Christian writers, by contrast, reduced the *jasaq* to a Mongol Ten Commandments made up of a small number of short, numbered, rules.

See also CHA'ADAI; QAIDU.

Further reading: Igor de Rachewiltz, "Some Reflections on Chinggis Qan's Jasagh," *East Asian History* 6 (1993): 91–104.

Java *See* SOUTH SEAS.

Javhlant *See* ULIASTAI.

Jebdzundamba *See* JIBZUNDAMBA KHUTUGTU.

Jebe (Yeme) *Commander of Chinggis Khan's vanguard of heavy cavalry*
Jebe belonged to the Besüd lineage, clients of the TAYICHI'UD branch of the BORJIGID. In 1201, when CHINGGIS KHAN crushed the Tayichi'ud, Jebe, fighting for his Tayichi'ud lords, shot one of Chinggis's favorite horses dead. After the battle Jebe boldly acknowledged his deed and promised to fight similarly for him. Chinggis admired his honesty and prowess and changed his name, originally Jirgho'adai, to Jebe, "weapon." Chinggis called Jebe, with Qubilai Noyan (not to be confused with the khan), Jelme, and SÜBE'ETEI BA'ATUR, his "four dogs," and from the 1204 Battle of Keltegei Cliffs on, used Jebe in the vanguard to command his heaviest cavalry. In the attack on North China in 1211, Jebe was the first to attack the JIN DYNASTY's frontier fortresses. Both at Juyongguan Pass (October 1211) and Dongjing city (January 5, 1213), Jebe lured the Jin defenders out by feigned retreat and then crushed them and seized the fortifications. In 1217–18 Chinggis Khan dispatched Jebe against Küchülüg, a fugitive NAIMAN prince who had taken over the QARA-KHITAI Empire in Turkestan. Jebe surprised Küchlüg at Kashgar and chased him into Badakhshan, where the locals captured him and handed him over. During the attack on KHORAZM Chinggis dispatched Jebe and Sübe'etei in May 1220 to capture the fugitive sultan 'Ala'ud-Din Muhammad. Racing through Iran, the Mongol force finally blockaded him on an island in the Caspian Sea. They then pursued his armies through western Iran, GEORGIA, and Azerbaijan, Jebe repeatedly using his trademark ambush. Passing north through Derbent, they defeated the OSSETES (Alans) and then the QIPCHAQS and Russians at the BATTLE OF KALKA RIVER (May 31, 1223), before riding home through the Kazakhstan steppe. Soon after this extraordinary display of military prowess Jebe died.

See also JUYONGGUAN PASS, BATTLES OF.

Jebtsundamba *See* JIBZUNDAMBA KHUTUGTU.

Jenghiz Khan *See* CHINGGIS KHAN.

Jetsun-Dampa *See* JIBZUNDAMBA KHUTUGTU.

jewelry From the 17th to 19th centuries jewelry in Mongolia began to develop in elaborate and distinctive forms for each AIMAG, or subethnic group. Such jewelry was rejected as feudal and old fashioned in the 20th century.

In the time of the MONGOL EMPIRE the khans and nobles avidly collected pearls and gemstones as *tangsuqs,* or precious things, encouraging ORTOQ merchants to present them by offering colossal sums for fine samples. The great khan Temür (1294–1307) once paid 140,000 *ding* of paper currency for a fine ruby weighing about 6 grams (two ounces). This he wore on his hat during the great assemblies of WHITE MONTH and the summer (*see QURILTAI*). Married women wore jewelry mostly on or hanging from their BOQTA (headdress). The forms of these pendants resemble later Mongolian jewelry.

Central Khalkha married woman's hat, with her hair pulled into "horns" and adorned with jewelry *(From* Mongolian Arts and Crafts *[1987])*

beads, like rosaries, wrapped around the head, and for married women a wooden pin built into the braids with a horizontal cross pin sticking out from which ornaments could be hung. Among the KHALKHA (including the MING-GHAD and the New BARGA), the hair swung out from behind the head into enormous "horns" held by silver hair clasps and fed into cylindrical silver braid cases. On top of the head was a silver skull cap. In central Inner Mongolia (CHAKHAR, SHILIIN GOL, ULAANCHAB, and ORDOS) the face was framed in cascades of beads of coral and semiprecious stones hanging from a decorated cloth bonnet or fillet on the head. The earrings were bowed plates, again so heavy they had to be hung from the top of the head. In Ordos the braids were still slung over the chest, but elsewhere in central Inner Mongolia they were often rolled up and encased in open coral nets, again with pendants. In eastern Inner Mongolia (KHORCHIN, JUU UDA, KHARACHIN, Daurs, etc.), however, an entirely different pattern of jewelry, based on the Manchu-style coiffure, was used, in which the hair was held in a bun with hairpins.

Like many distinctive pieces of Mongolian dress, such as the boots, jewelry was made by both Mongolian and Chinese craftsmen, although the latter always followed the local taste. The most common material in tra-

From the late 16th century onward, Mongolian jewelry developed a profusion of local forms. The starting point from which these designs evolved can be seen in both early temple painting and in the conservative styles current in 1900 among the DÖRBÖD, BAYAD, and ALTAI URIYANGKHAI of western Mongolia. This jewelry included earrings, sometimes linked underneath the chin, and a rosary or amulet as necklace, while the hair was gathered into two braids descending down the front of the chest and wrapped in black cloth. This braid case was sometimes ornamented with round silver plaques and ended in a pendant. Such jewelry (*zasal chimeg*) was prepared before a marriage by the groom's family and given to the bride's family. The bride then brought it to her new home as an indirect dowry. Other jewelry included amulets, breast ornaments, chatelaines, bracelets, and finger rings.

Among the other Mongolian *yastan,* or subethnic groups, jewelry became more complicated. The Khori BURIATS were distinguished by vast hoop earrings (slung from the head due to their weight), strings of large coral

Üjümüchin married woman's jewelry, typical of the central Inner Mongolian style *(From* Mongolian Arts and Crafts *[1987])*

ditional Mongolian jewelry was silver; gold was very rare. Silver was worked by embossing, chasing, engraving, filigreeing and enameling. Red coral was the favorite bead; agate, lapis lazuli, amber, and turquoise were also used. Inlays were held simply with wax and so were often lost.

Mongolian jewelry was highly polychrome, and virtually every flat surface was decorated. Most of the decoration is based on patterns of symbols, such as the dharma wheel, lotus, double fish, endless knot, "cash" symbol (a square inside a circle), interlocking circles and diamonds (symbolizing marriage), fan, vase, Chinese "double happiness" and *rui* characters, dragon, lion (often looking more like a dog), bat, and butterfly. Borders of key scrolls or vegetation were used profusely.

In the 1920s and 1930s the Mongolian headdress went out of living use due to revolutionary criticisms of its class character, its link to arranged marriages, and changing fashions. Rings and bracelets continue to follow the Mongolian jewelry tradition.

See also CLOTHING AND DRESS.

Further reading: Martha Boyer, *Mongol Jewelry* (London: Thames and Hudson, 1995).

Jewel Translucent Sutra (*Erdeni tunumal neretü sudur*)

This biography of ALTAN KHAN (1508–82) and his immediate successors, also known as *Altan Khaghan-u tughuji*, "The Biography of Altan Khan," is the major extant literary monument of the NORTHERN YUAN DYNASTY (1368–1634). The work, which survived in a single manuscript, was written in 1607 in quatrains of alliterative verse in an elegant style filled with Buddhist rhetorical tropes, although the author was evidently not a monk. The unknown author probably knew Chinese and is far more reliable on chronology than are later Mongolian chroniclers. The author used written sources, including a no longer extant account by Dayan Kiya, a powerful official at Altan and his successors' court.

The work describes how Altan Khan established the state through conquest, brought China into it through negotiations, and then how he became patron (alms-giver) to the Dalai Lama. It concludes with how Sengge-Düüreng (1582–86) continued his father's work and how the FOURTH DALAI LAMA was born under Altan's grandson Namudai Sechen (Chürüke, 1586–1607) and many Buddhist scriptures were translated from Tibetan into Mongolian.

The theme of the work is the harmony between the "TWO CUSTOMS" of Buddhist religion (*shashin*) and Chinggisid state (*törö*), the former incarnate in the Dalai Lama and the latter in the cult and lineage of CHINGGIS KHAN. It extolls the TÜMED *tümen* as the center of this restored legitimate rule.

See also EIGHT WHITE YURTS; LITERATURE.

Further reading: Carl Johan Elverskog, *Jewel Translucent Sutra: Altan Khan and the Mongols in the Sixteenth Century* (Leiden: E. J. Brill, 2003).

Jibzundamba Khutugtu (Jebdzundamba, rJe-btsun Dam-pa, Jebtsundamba, Jetsun-Dampa)

The INCARNATE LAMA lineage of Jibzundamba Khutugtus from 1639 to 1924 formed the center of KHALKHA religious beliefs, identity, and political life. The Jibzundamba Khutugtus were known among their Khalkha Mongols as the Bogda (Holy One) or Bogda Gegeen (Holy Brilliance or Holy Incarnate Lama). In Inner Mongolia, they were called the Aru Bogda, or "Northern Holy One."

RELIGIOUS STATUS OF THE JIBZUNDAMBA KHUTUGTUS

As finally canonized in the 18th century, the Jibzundamba (from Tibetan rJe-btsun Dam-pa, Reverend Noble One) Khutugtus of Mongolia formed only the conclusion of a long line of incarnate lamas in India and Tibet, stretching from the time of Shakyamuni Buddha to the 'Jo-nang-pa hierarch rJe-btsun (reverend) Taranatha (1575–1634). Despite this sequence, Jibzundambas are numbered from first Mongolian one.

The FIRST JIBZUNDAMBA KHUTUGTU (Zanabazar, 1635–1723) was the second son of the Khalkha khan Gömbö-Dorji. In 1639 he was enthroned as an incarnation and in 1647, even before visiting Tibet, was referred to in QING DYNASTY (1636–1912) court records as the Jibzundamba Khutugtu, clearly linking him to rJe-btsun Taranatha. The oldest Tibetan sources record the Jibzundamba simply as the emanation body of 'Jam-byangs (i.e., the bodhisattva Manjughosha or Manjushri).

When the Fifth Dalai Lama proscribed Taranatha's 'Jo-nang-pa lineage as heretical during the First Bogda's first visit to Tibet, the Jibzundamba Khutugtu was initiated into the dGe-lugs-pa (Yellow Hat) lineage. While Taranatha's prodigious scholarship preserved his place in the lineage, 'Jam dbyangs/Manjughosha was then reinterpreted as an old dGe-lugs-pa master 'Jam-dbyangs Chos-rje (1379–1449), giving the Jibzundamba Khutugtus a link to the dGe-lugs-pas lineage. The Jibzundamba Khutugtus were now seen as emanatron-bodies of the bodhisattva Vajrapani.

FIRST AND SECOND INCARNATIONS

The Jibzundamba Khutugtu was the foundation stone of Khalkha identity. The first two incarnations were found in the family of the Khalkha Tüshiyetü Khans. The First Jibzundamba Khutugtu, or Zanabazar, began the creation of Khüriye (modern ULAANBAATAR) in the KHENTII RANGE as the new Khalkha center. An accomplished artist, he sculpted many of the main *shitügen*s (objects of worship) of its temples. To him is also ascribed the design of the *tsogchin dugang*s (main assembly halls), the dress of the lamas, the exalted place of the *gebkhüi* (proctor) in the precedence, and the establishment of the *umdzad*, or cantors, of the Khüriye monasteries.

Politically, the First Jibzundamba aimed for reconciliation between the Khalkha princes and between Russia and China. Yet the Oirat ruler, GALDAN BOSHOGTU KHAN, saw in his growing importance a challenge to the authority of the Dalai Lama, which he took as his task to defend. When open war broke out between the Khalkhas and the OIRATS in 1688, the First Jibzundamba led the Khalkhas into allegiance to the Qing emperor Kangxi (1662–1722). The Bogda and the emperor established a strong bond, and the lama resided in China until 1702. From 1701 he began the reconstruction of Khalkha after the devastation of Galdan's invasions.

The Second Jibzundamba (1724–58), the great-grandson of the first's elder brother, continued to expand the monasteries of Khüriye. The Qing emperor Qianlong (1736–96) began to limit the autonomy of the Bogda, chastising him for traveling to ERDENI ZUU, for example, without authorization. The Bogda played an ambivalent role during the disturbances of CHINGGÜNJAB'S REBELLION (1756–57) but died soon after of smallpox. Religiously, his reign saw the inception of a college (*datsang*) of *tsanid* (Buddhist philosophy and scholarship); two *datsangs* of medicine followed shortly after his death in 1760.

THIRD AND FOURTH INCARNATIONS

With the death of the second Jibzundamba Khutugtu, the Qianlong emperor ignored the Khalkha candidates and decreed that the Third Jibzundamba be found in Tibet. The Khalkha nobility, in response, asked that in that case the Jibzundamba be moved to Dolonnuur and his estate, the GREAT SHABI, be dissolved. Both requests were rejected, and the Third Jibzundamba (Ishi-dambi-Nima, November 1, 1758–November 5, 1773) was identified in the family of the prince of Litang in eastern Tibet.

With the end of the short life of this Third Bogda, the Khalkha nobility again hoped for a Mongolian incarnation but were disappointed. The Fourth Jibzundamba Khutugtu (Lubsang-Tubdan-Wangchug, 1775–1813) was discovered in the family of the Seventh Dalai Lama's elder brother. Legendary for his "fierce aspect" (*dogshin düri*), he enforced clerical discipline with blows. He invited numerous images from Tibet and introduced the services and study of the Düinkhor (Kalachakra) Tantras into Mongolia. He also made many visits to China, during the last of which he caught a cold and died.

THE INSTITUTION

During the reigns of the Fourth through Seventh Jibzundambas, the institution reached its acme of wealth. The Bogda controlled a vast estate. In 1825 his personal herd reached 28,790 horses, 3,470 camels, 9,780 cattle, and 41,880 sheep and goats. His "disciples" (subjects) in the Great Shabi measured 27,779 lamas and 83,687 layfolk, distributed in 16,653 households and controlling 1,448,718 head of livestock. This entire estate was administered by the office of the ERDENI SHANGDZODBA, staffed by Khalkha lamas.

During this period the Bogda's principal function came to be simply to receive offerings and give blessings. Vast numbers of worshipers came from Khalkha, Inner Mongolia, Buriatia, and Tibet. The most ordinary form of worship, conducted once every two to five days, consisted of the Bogda in a litter placing a prayer wheel on the heads of worshipers. The Bogda also daily received silver mandalas from wealthier worshipers. Finally, annually and triennially, Mongolian nobles and lamas presented to the Khutugtu prayers and rich offerings at the ceremony of DANSHUG (firm abiding).

The discovery of the new Jibzundamba Khutugtu in Tibet involved the approval of the emperor in Beijing and the Dalai and Panchen Lamas. The final selection among the three final candidates was made by a drawing from a golden urn in Lhasa. The boy was then invited from Lhasa at about five years of age, the total expenses of which could reach 400,000 taels of silver. The Bogda also brought with him tutors and teachers of specialized topics as well as his relatives, who received titles and wealth. Upon his death the Jibzundamba Khutugtu was embalmed and his remains placed in a stupa. These stupas were housed in either Amur-Bayaskhulangtu Hermitage (Baruunbüren *Sum,* Selenge) or in Dambadarjaa Hermitage in Khüriye (Ulaanbaatar). The Fourth Jibzundamba had individualized images of the first and second incarnations made on the basis of these relics.

FIFTH INCARNATION TO 1900

From 1813 the Bogda's status with the Qing emperors steadily declined, as did the social origin of the families in which the Bogda was discovered: noblemen (First through Fourth), rich commoner (Fifth, born 1815), muleteer (Sixth, born 1842), and ordinary layman (Seventh, born 1850). (The Eighth was born in 1870, again in a high-ranking Tibetan family.) From 1835 the imperial treasury no longer subsidized the Bogda's trips to Lhasa. In 1837 donations of able-bodied taxpayers to the Bogda's Great Shabi were prohibited. The Beijing authorities restricted the great *danshug* ceremony to once every three years. The last imperial audience was granted, very unwillingly, in 1840. After 1865 the Khutugtu's estate went into a steady decline.

While the Fifth Jibzundamba had no distinctive character and the Sixth survived only 49 days in Mongolia, the Seventh and Eighth were famous, or notorious, for their self-willed lives. The Seventh Jibzundamba Khutugtu (1850–December 14, 1868) as a child was particularly attached to a court lama locksmith who showed him how to make Buddha figures. Around 1863, however, he came under the influence of the Setsen khan Ardashida, who reverenced the Bogda greatly after defeating the khan's shamanic powers. The khan and his two sons led the Bogda into ARCHERY, drinking, and smoking, and by 1868 the Bogda was living with Ardasida's daughter. The connection was broken and the Bogda died soon after. Around his 15th year the Eighth Jibzundamba (Agwanglubsang-Choijin-Nima-Danzin-Wangchug-Balsangbu, 1870–1924) also began to rebel and lived long enough to force the Khalkha and Qing authorities to accept his marriage to his consort, Dondugdulma (1874–1923).

IN THE TWENTIETH CENTURY

Despite his Tibetan origin, the Jibzundamba acquired a strong identification with Mongolia. From 1895 the Bogda began to take a political role. In December 1911, as the Qing dynasty was falling, the Eighth Jibzundamba declared Mongolia independent and was enthroned as the holy emperor (or Bogda khan) of religion and state.

In theocratic Mongolia, the Jibzundamba's establishment expanded tremendously in both wealth and prestige. Resentment of this expansion in clerical power was an important factor in pushing the secular nobility to approve the return to China in 1919. The Russian Whites under BARON ROMAN FEDOROVICH VON UNGERN-STERNBERG (1886–1921) briefly restored the theocratic government and the privileges of the Bogda Khan before being overthrown in turn by the revolutionary government installed with Soviet Russian troops in July 1921.

The new revolutionary government confirmed the Jibzundamba Khutugtu as the Bogda Khan, but as a "constitutional monarch." In fact, his powers were constantly whittled down. With the death of the Eighth Jibzundamba in 1924, 40,000 taels of silver were expended on his death, but in September 1925 the Bogda's property was confiscated for the state treasury. Meanwhile, all discussions of the continuation of his incarnation were postponed. The high lamas found a boy, this time in Mongolia, but in July 1925 the party authorities declined to accept him and instead proposed to consult with the Dalai Lama in Tibet. In September the party congress tactfully decided that the next Jibzundamba Khutugtu would be born in the hidden Buddhist kingdom of Shambala, and a mission was to be sent to the Dalai Lama to confirm this. Not until February 15, 1929, was the finding and enthroning of incarnate lamas categorically prohibited.

In Tibet, however, a child was discovered as the Ninth Jibzundamba (religious name, 'Jam-dpal rNam-grol Chos-kyi rGyal-mtshan; Mongolian, Jambal-Namdul-Choiji-Jaltsan, b. 1930), but he was not enthroned before the fall of the theocratic government in Tibet and his exile to India. With the establishment of religious freedom in Mongolia in 1990, the Fourteenth Dalai Lama (b. 1935) enthroned him as the Ninth Jibzundamba. In 1999 the Ninth Jibzundamba made his first visit to Mongolia.

See also THEOCRATIC PERIOD.

Further reading: C. R. Bawden, trans., *Jebtsundamba Khutukhtus of Urga* (Wiesbaden: Otto Harrassowitz, 1961); Alice Sárközi, *Political Prophecies in Mongolia in the 17–20th Centuries* (Wiesbaden: Otto Harrassowitz, 1992).

Jibzundamba Khutugtu, Eighth (1870–1924) *Last theocratic emperor of Mongolia, the Eighth Jibzundamba Khutugtu consistently supported Mongolian independence*
The Eighth Jibzundamba (religious name, Agwanglubsang-Choijin-Nima-Danzin-Wangchug-Balsangbu) was born on September 8, 1870, in Lhasa into the family of an official of the Dalai Lama's estate. He was brought back from Tibet in 1874 with his Tibetan parents. The Bogda (Holy One) lived in Khüriye (modern ULAANBAATAR) with his parents and a lama tutor until 1882, when, on his father's death, he was separated from his mother except for daily audiences. The Eighth Bogda was unusually intelligent and always fascinated with clocks, models, devices, and illustrated magazines from Russia. Beginning in the 1890s, he began to build a private zoo, which eventually even included an elephant.

From 1885 he began to rebel against his tutors; in 1887 his mother died. He began to drink, smoke, and travel the streets of Khüriye playing life-threatening practical jokes. He took regular trips to the rural Amur-Bayaskhulangtu Hermitage, where he felt freer than in Khüriye. Despite his wild behavior, most of the lamas and princes came to see in his behavior a deep religious significance, and the few skeptics muted their suspicions.

In his youth the Bogda had many lovers, male and female, and a married lady bore him an illegitimate daughter. In summer 1902 Dondugdulma (Dondogdulam, 1874–1923), a former maid and concubine of one of his noble-born companions, was enthroned as his consort. The two had no children, although after he became emperor of Mongolia the two adopted a boy, Lamyaa. At some point in his youth the Bogda contracted syphilis, and his eyesight began degenerating in 1911.

POLITICAL LIFE, 1895–1911

Already in his childhood the JIBZUNDAMBA KHUTUGTU lineage had reached the nadir of its prestige at the QING DYNASTY court in Beijing. As an incarnation of the FIRST JIBZUNDAMBA KHUTUGTU, who was a Chinggisid, the Eighth Jibzundamba believed himself to be a descendant of CHINGGIS KHAN and deeply resented the lack of respect shown to him and via him to Buddhism and Mongolia.

In 1891 the Bogda had a dream of meeting with an envoy of the god Indra, which he later recalled as an omen of achieving sovereign power. In 1900 (some sources say 1895) he secretly asked whether Russia would support Mongolian independence from the Qing, but the Russian authorities told him to be patient. In 1904 the Thirteenth Dalai Lama arrived in Khüriye after fleeing the British invasion of Lhasa and was housed in GANDAN-TEGCHINLING MONASTERY. A rivalry between the two great incarnations immediately developed, yet the

The Eighth Jibzundamba Khutugtu, painted by "Busybody" Sharab. Early 20th century. Mineral paints on cotton, 48 × 32 centimeters *(From N. Tsultem,* Development of the Mongolian National Style Painting "Mongol Zurag" in Brief *[Ulaanbaatar, 1986])*

clerical privileges. He remained a fearsome drinker, sometimes spending a full week in a stupor, and was strikingly indulgent with intimates such as BADMADORJI and the Darkhan Wang Pungtsugtsering, even if they betrayed his policies. Nevertheless he never became either an autocrat or a mere puppet.

Domestically, the Bogda's decrees most often treated religious and cultural topics. The cults of Mongolia's mountains and of Khalkha's first Buddhist khan, Abatai (1554–88), were revived and expanded. Statues of the female deity Baldan Lhamo with prayer texts were to be placed in every yurt in the land. Fowling and fishing were prohibited, as were drinking and gambling. Proper legal and Buddhist procedures were established for executions and intermarriage with Chinese was prohibited. While he turned previously appointive offices in HULUN BUIR, DARIGANGA, and western Mongolia into hereditary fiefdoms, he also created a parliament in 1914, albeit with limited powers. He donated 1,000 *taels* of silver to the fledgling Mutual-Aid Cooperatives, intended to displace Chinese merchants.

The Bogda also supported several construction projects, which were as distinguished artistically as they were damaging financially. The 24-meter (80-foot)-high statue of Migjid Janraisig ("Eye-Opening Avalokiteshvara," a Buddhist deity) cost 900,000 taels of silver, while the Andingmen Gate (Gate of Firm Peace, Mongolian, Amugulang Engkhe-yin Khagalga) cost 280,000 taels.

FOREIGN OCCUPATION AND REVOLUTION

By 1919 turmoil in Russia and the expansion of the Bogda's personal subjects (*see* GREAT SHABI) led an influential body of aristocrats to push for the REVOCATION OF AUTONOMY. Warned by dreams and his own long-standing beliefs, the Bogda opposed this from the beginning but did not crack down on the plans. The assimilationist policy of the Chinese general Xu Shuzheng (1880–1925) fully justified his fears.

In June 1920, however, Xu's warlord clique in Beijing was overthrown, and he fled. In July the Bogda, prophesying that Chinese rule would last only three years, authorized appeals to Soviet Russia and other countries. Several of his leading conspirators were arrested, but Mongolian People's Party commoners contacted Soviet Russia. On October 2 the Bogda secretly approved the offer of White Russian BARON ROMAN FEDOROVICH VON UNGERN-STERNBERG (1886–1921) to liberate Mongolia from the Chinese. The Chinese finally arrested the Bogda on October 26, holding him at their headquarters in Khüriye. The lamas performed exorcisms against the *gamings* (Chinese republicans), and on December 22 the Bogda was released, when China's "Mongolia hand," Chen Yi, tried a softer approach.

On February 1, as Baron von Ungern-Sternberg attacked Khüriye a second time, a 50-man commando force under the Tibetan Shagja Lama, Jamyangdanzin (d. 1922), invaded the Bogda's palace, killed his Chinese

Dalai Lama's presence showed the need to plan for future changes.

In 1909, as the Qing government began pushing the NEW POLICIES of colonization and modernization, the Bogda instructed his people in his *lüngden* (prophecy, or pastoral message) that they needed to consider new ways to maintain their old religion and way of life. From 1910 on he quarreled openly with the new Qing AMBAN, Sandô, and secretly discussed independence with his entourage. His plans for the 1911 RESTORATION of Mongolian independence were favored by Russian assistance and the times, and on December 29 the Bogda was proclaimed the holy emperor (Bogda Khan) and "Dual Ruler of Religion and State." Dondugdulma became the "Mother-Angel (*Ekhe Dagini*) and "mother of the nation."

AS THEOCRATIC RULER

Once the Mongolian government had declared independence, the Bogda Khan's influence was always on the side of full independence for Mongolia, the inclusion of Inner Mongolia in a pan-Mongolian state, and the expansion of guards, and escorted him and his consort through deep snows to Manjushri Hermitage, south of the city. On February 21 the Bogda was again enthroned as khan. By July, however, the baron's government disintegrated as the Red Army with the Mongolian People's Party revolutionaries marched into Khüriye. On July 11 the revolutionaries enthroned him as the constitutional monarch of the People's Government.

AS CONSTITUTIONAL MONARCH

In the oath of November 1, 1921, the Bogda Khan's supreme powers were restricted solely to religious affairs. In secular affairs his rights extended only to consultation with the prime minister. The Bogda and the new prime minister, BODÔ, agreed on the need to cultivate relations with other countries as an alternative to dependence on Russia. In December the Bogda's rescuer of February, the Shagja Lama, was arrested with 48 other lamas. They were released on the Bogda's appeal, but on August 31, 1922, Shagja, Bodô, and 13 others were executed. In May 1923 his personal physician, Lama Seriinün (Sereenen), was executed in another case.

Even in religious matters the government began rapidly abridging previous privileges, limiting and then abolishing his rights to public funds, the immunities of his personal subjects, or Great Shabi, and state-funded religious ceremonies. By February 1924 the party cell in the Shabi ministry proposed to register all the Bogda's property, but this he strenuously resisted, and the proposal was rejected.

In June 1923 the Bogda's consort, Dondugdulma, died, and a young wrestler's wife was chosen by the Bogda from a list prepared by princes in his entourage. During winter 1923–24 the Bogda became ill and was examined by Russian doctors, but he died on May 20. For a last time the religious ceremonies of his funeral were paid from state funds, while his seal as emperor was "temporarily" transferred to the interior ministry.

See also CHOIJUNG LAMA TEMPLE; PALACES OF THE BOGDA KHAN; THEOCRATIC PERIOD.

Further reading: C. R. Bawden, trans., *Tales of an Old Lama* (Tring, England: Institute of Buddhist Studies, 1997).

Jibzundamba Khutugtu, First (Zanabazar, Öndör Gegeen) (1635–1723) *Khalkha cleric, political leader, and artist*

The First Jibzundamba Khutugtu was born on November 4, 1635, the second son of the KHALKHA tüshiyetü khan Gömbö-Dorji. For his birth his father planned an early winter migration, camping his yurt near today's Yösön Züil (South Khangai), where tradition said ABATAI KHAN had had a vision of the Third Dalai Lama. The boy is said to have shown miraculous abilities, and the Khalkha prince Sholoi Makhasamadi Setsen Khan (1577–1652) named him Gegeen Keüken, "Brilliant Child." In 1638

the boy took the lowest *ubashi* vows and received the name Zanabazar (from Sanskrit *jñanavajra*). The next year the western Tibetan incarnate lama dBen-sa sPrul-sku administered further initiations, giving him the name Lubsang-Dambi-Jaltsan-Balsangbu at Shiregetü Tsagan Nuur (Bürd Sum, South Khangai). The Khalkha nobles presented the boy with 108 households, marking the beginning of the GREAT SHABI, or clerical estate of the JIBZUNDAMBA KHUTUGTU.

By this time the boy was recognized as an incarnation of Taranatha (1575–1634), a revered scholar of the Jo-nang-pa lineage of the Sa-skya-pa monastic order. In 1647 the Khutugtu (blessed one) paid symbolic homage to the Qing emperor in Beijing under the name Jibzundamba Khutugtu (from Tibetan rJe-btsun Dam-pa, Reverend Noble One). In 1649 Gömbö-Dorji escorted his son to Tibet. The hierarchs of the dGe-lugs-pa order, the Panchen and Dalai Lamas, were just then proscribing the Jo-nang-pa order for its heretical beliefs and seizing its monasteries for their own order. Even so, both received him, and the Panchen Lama administered the *getsül* (novice) vows and further initiations.

Print of the First Jibzundamba Khutugtu Zanabazar. Such prints were folded up and kept as amulets. *(From N. Tsultem, Eminent Sculptor Zanabazar [1982])*

Upon his return to Mongolia accompanied by Tibetan monks and artisans and scriptures from the former Jo-nang-pa monasteries, he began in 1654 a new establishment, Nom-un Yekhe Khüriye in KHENTII PROVINCE, which was finally completed in 1680, becoming the nucleus of Khüriye (modern ULAANBAATAR). He also introduced new rituals, such as the Maitreya procession he learned from the Panchen Lama's monastery of bKra-shis Lhun-po (modern Zhaxilhünbo, near Xigazê).

Zanabazar was known as the Öndör Gegeen, "Tall Majesty," due to his unusual height. Portraits made from his preserved body show a round-headed bald man with a kindly expression. Zanabazar, like many later Mongolian lamas, kept a consort. Supernatural and artistic powers, like those of Zanabazar himself, were ascribed to his "Girl Prince" (Kheükhen Noyan). After her death at age 18 (shortly after 1706), her ashes were included in the production of a scripture set.

POLITICAL ACTIVITIES

In 1686, at the behest of the Qing emperor Kangxi (1662–1722), the Jibzundamba Khutugtu joined representatives of the Dalai Lama and the emperor himself in an assembly to resolve the bitter feud between the eastern Tüshiyetü khan, now Zanabazar's elder brother Chakhundorji (r. 1655–99), and the western Zasagtu khan. Despite the seemingly successful conclusion to the conference in November 1686, the Oirat GALDAN BOSHOGTU KHAN, who was the incarnation of the dBen-sa sPrul-sku, who had initiated Zanabazar decades before, believed the Jibzundamba was being built up to reduce the influence of the Dalai Lama, with whom the OIRATS were closely allied. In 1687, after another outbreak of violence between the Tüshiyetü and Zasagtu khans, Galdan invaded Khalkha. Sought constantly by Galdan as his chief enemy, the Khutugtu fled with Chakhundorji's family and 300 disciples to Abaga (Abag) banner in Inner Mongolia, where in summer 1688 he appealed to the emperor Kangxi for assistance.

Later hagiographies claim that at Aru-Elestü in Inner Mongolia the Khalkha princes and khans assembled, and the Jibzundamba Khutugtu counseled that as the Qing were Buddhists and buttoned their clothes on their right they were acceptable, whereas the non-Buddhist Russians who buttoned their clothes on their left were not. In fact, such an assembly never occurred, but the story illustrates the reasoning that brought the Khalkha into the Qing orbit.

After the Qing armies defeated Galdan in 1689–90, a great assembly was held at Dolonnuur (modern Duolun) in May 1691, at which the Jibzundamba Khutugtu led the nobles in obeisance to the emperor (*see* DOLONNUUR ASSEMBLY). After the assembly Zanabazar followed the emperor back to Beijing, staying with him until 1701. Mongolian stories reflect a close sympathy between the emperor and the Mongolian cleric. Kangxi's grandmother,

Vajradhara, by the First Jibzundamba Khutugtu. Now kept in Gandan-Tegchinling Monastery (*From* Eminent Sculptor Zanabazar *[1982]*)

who was a KHORCHIN Mongol, had particularly deep faith in him.

In 1701, with Galdan dead and Khalkha resettled, Zanabazar returned to Khalkha's venerable ERDENI ZUU Monastery and supervised the repair of the tremendous damage done by Galdan. During the next 20 years he built many temples and reorganized the liturgy, dress, and music in Khalkha temples, following in most aspects the Panchen Lama's model. All the while, he diligently supported the Qing war effort, encouraging domestic peace among the princes, reporting on conditions to the emperor, and blessing the troops going off to war.

In 1722, hearing news of Kangxi's death, the aged lama traveled to Beijing, where shortly after the enthronement of his successor, the emperor Yongzheng (1723–35), the Jibzundamba died on February 18, 1723, poisoned, rumors said, by the new emperor. His embalmed body was returned to his monastery, and his reliquary was installed in 1728 at Amur-Bayaskhulangtu Hermitage, built with 10,000 taels of silver from the imperial treasury.

ARTISTIC AND CULTURAL ACTIVITIES

One of Zanabazar's greatest legacies to Mongolia was his sculpture. In 1655 he set up a forge at his retreat of Shibeetü-Uula, near Erdeni Zuu, and that year he sent his first mature images, now lost, to the Manchu court. His great masterpieces, including *Five Transcendent Buddhas* and the *Vajradhara,* now the main image of Ulaanbaatar's GANDAN-TEGCHINLING MONASTERY, were produced in 1683. His sculptures combine a faithful adherence to the standards of Indo-Tibetan iconography with extraordinarily lifelike human beauty. His masterworks of the female figure, *White Tara* and *Green Tara,* were said to be modeled on the "Girl Prince" in puberty and maturity, respectively. (The *Green Tara* was produced in 1706 for the restored temple of the deity.) The school of Zanabazar continued to produce masterpieces into the late 18th century.

Although Zanabazar is said to have been a master painter, no reliably attributed works survive. Zanabazar is also said to have designed numerous temples, the earliest being Baruun Khüriye (Shankh, South Khangai), begun in 1647. The innovative marquee-style roof of the *tsogchin dugang* (main assembly hall) at Nom-un Yekhe Khüriye became a canon for later Mongolian assembly halls.

Zanabazar was also skilled in literary arts, personally copying and block printing many scriptures. His *Byin-rlabs mTshog-stsol* (Mongolian, *Jinlab-Tsogdzol*), or blessing of peace, composed in Tibetan, became a widely memorized prayer for Khalkha Mongolian Buddhists. He also created a new script, the SOYOMBO SCRIPT, into which he translated a number of scriptures. The SOYOMBO SYMBOL, found at the inception of every text written in this script, became the symbol of the Khalkha as the people of the Jibzundamba and is now on the Mongolian national flag.

Further reading: N. Tsultem, *Eminent Mongolian Sculptor G. Zanabazar* (Ulaanbaatar: State Publishing House, 1982); J. Choinkhor, ed., *Undur Geghen Zanabazar* (Ulaanbaatar: Mongolian National Commission for UNESCO, 1995); Junko Miyawaki, "How Legends Developed about the First Jebtsundamba: In Reference to the Khalkha Mongol Submission to the Manchus in the Seventeenth Century," *Memoirs of the Toyo Bunko* 52 (1994): 45–67.

Jibzundamba Khutugtu, Second (1724–1758) *Last of the great incarnate lama lineage of the Jibzundamba Khutugtus to be born in Mongolia and ambivalent preserver of Qing rule in Mongolia*

The great lama First Jibzundamba had declared his great-grandnephew, the Darkhan Chin-Wang (prince of first rank) Dondubdorji, to be an incarnation of an Indian pandita. Dondubdorji reigned briefly as Tüshiyetü khan but was deposed in 1702 by the Kangxi emperor (1662–1722) for moral delinquency. In 1723 Kangxi's son, the Yongzheng emperor (1723–35), again raised Dondubdorji's rank for his achievements in battle against the ZÜNGHARS and bestowed on him a Manchu princess of the royal family. Hearing the First Jibzundamba's deathbed prophecy that the Darkhan Chin-Wang would father his successor with a woman born in the monkey or chicken year, the Darkhan Chin-Wang took another wife, Bayartu, from the KHOTOGHOID in northwest Mongolia, born in the monkey year (i.e., 1704).

Although a son was born nine months later on February 24, 1724, the KHALKHA nobility put forward several other candidates, of whom the child of the Setsen khan was the most probable. First the oracle in Lhasa and then the Yongzheng emperor decided that the son of the emperor's son-in-law was the incarnation. In 1728 Dondubdorji's son was given the initial *ubashi* (or *genen*) vows with the name Lubsang-Dambi-Döngmi and the next year was installed in Da Khüriye by the Khalkha princes as the second Jibzundamba Khutugtu. In 1730 he was immunized from smallpox in preparation for his journey to Beijing, but with the renewed Zünghar invasion of 1731 he was relocated to Dolonnuur (modern Duolun) in Inner Mongolia, where he stayed until 1735. After Yongzheng's death the boy traveled to Beijing, where the Qianlong emperor (r. 1736–96, d. 1799) treated him with great favor.

On his return to Khalkha the boy as an adolescent began to harass his entourage with murderous pranks, although the hagiographies say either that the victims were unharmed or that some karmic purpose was at work. Given a gold foil patent and golden seal from the LIFAN YUAN in 1738, the Khutugtu began a program of rebuilding and renovating the temples of both Khüriye (modern ULAANBAATAR) and ERDENI ZUU. From his youth the boy had studied *tsanid* (Tibetan, *mtshan-nyid,* academic study of Buddhist philosophy, discipline, and tantra), and in 1755 he founded and devised the statutes for the first *tsanid* school in Khalkha.

During the Second Jibzundamba's reign the Manchu court began to curtail his autonomy. In 1741 the Qianlong emperor ordered attendants placed by the side of the Khutugtu and suggested that the Khalkhas consider his removal to Dolonnuur, a proposal that they did not take up. An unauthorized visit by the Khutugtu to Erdeni Zuu in 1743 earned him a reprimand from the emperor. In 1756, while the Khutugtu and his distant cousin Yampildorji, the Tüshiyetü khan (r. 1745–58), were visiting Beijing, Qianlong ordered his half-brother Erinchindorji executed for allowing the rebel AMURSANAA to escape. That summer, as CHINGGÜNJAB'S REBELLION began, the Khutugtu and the Tüshiyetü khan secretly contacted the Russian commandant at Selenginsk.

The Second Jibzundamba Khutugtu. Note the scenes of his infancy among the Mongolian yurts. Mineral paints on cotton, 60 × 42 centimeters *(From N. Tsultem,* Development of the Mongolian National Style Painting "Mongol Zurag" in Brief *[Ulaanbaatar, 1986])*

Publicly, however, he maintained a loyal stance. On September 19 the Khutugtu transmitted with his endorsement an imperial decree against the rebels. In October the Khutugtu convened an assembly of the Khalkha nobles with the Second JANGJIYA KHUTUGTU of Beijing and the loyalist Khalkha general in chief of ULIASTAI to reiterate their loyalty to the Qing. While the nobility looked to him for leadership in any rebellion, the Khutugtu expressed his discontent with Qing rule only covertly. His request to spare Chinggünjab's life was ignored. That year a smallpox epidemic ravaged Khalkha, and he died on February 5, 1758, three days before the new year's assembly opened.

After his death the Qianlong emperor insisted on finding the next JIBZUNDAMBA KHUTUGTU in Tibet. One portrait of the Second Jibzundamba includes scenes of his childhood in a Mongol YURT, perhaps to distinguish him from the later Tibetans who occupied the throne.

Jin dynasty (Chin, Kin)

Jin dynasty (Chin, Kin) During the rise of the Mongols the Jin dynasty (1115–1234) ruled North China and became bitter enemies of the Mongols.

RISE AND RULE OF THE DYNASTY

The Jin dynasty arose in east Manchuria among the Jurchen people, who spoke a language in the Manchu-Tungusic family and were ancestors of the later Manchu people. By the 10th century the Jurchen had come under the power of the Liao dynasty, founded by the Kitan people of eastern Inner Mongolia. While the KITANS were seminomadic, the Jurchen were primarily farmers living in cabins and raising millet, wheat, flax, oxen, and pigs. Hunting, fishing, and ginseng collecting also played an important role in their economy. The Jurchen shared in the horse-based Inner Asian warrior tradition that used great collective hunts as training for war.

By the 10th century the Wanyan had become the leading Jurchen clan. Wanyan Aguda (1068–1123) challenged the Liao dynasty, defeating them with astonishing speed and proclaiming his own Jin, or "Golden," dynasty. (Due to this dynastic name, the Mongols called the Jin rulers "Altan Khan" or "Golden Khan"; this was the origin of MARCO POLO's "Golden King.") The SONG DYNASTY (960–1279), then ruling most of China, unwisely encouraged the Jurchen to destroy the Liao and then attacked the Jurchen themselves. The Jurchen thereupon defeated the Song, conquering all of North China. From then on until the Mongol conquest, the Jurchen Jin occupied North China, Manchuria, and Inner Mongolia, while the native Chinese Song dynasty held South China.

At its apogee around 1175, the Jin dynasty combined both traditional Chinese and Jurchen institutions. The capital was moved south to Zhongdu (Chung-tu, modern Beijing). A Chinese-style bureaucracy was set up with officials chosen by exams. While the Liao had patronized Buddhism, the Jin dynasty emphasized CONFUCIANISM. Nevertheless, Confucian scholars held little power, as the Jurchen generals and the prolific Wanyan clan monopolized high positions. The military was built around a militia of Jurchen households and their slaves organized into a DECIMAL ORGANIZATION of 100s and 1,000s. The Jin had created their own script to write the Jurchen language in 1119, which continued in use through the 14th century. Along the frontier the Jin recruited tribal auxiliaries, called Jiu (Mongolian Jüyin) and including Tangut, ÖNG-GÜD, and Kitan elements, to guard the frontier against nomadic incursions. This was somewhat risky, as many Kitans, in particular, nursed a deep grudge against the Jurchen as usurpers.

THE JIN AND THE MONGOLIAN TRIBES

While the Kitan Liao dynasty had occupied the Mongolian plateau, the Jurchens could not effectively pacify the area. The Jin collected tribute from the tribes and encouraged rivalries among them to keep them weak. Around the middle of the century, when the MONGOL TRIBE (in the narrow sense) unified under a charismatic khan, the Jin encouraged the Tatar tribe to whittle down the new khanate. The TATARS captured the Mongol khan Hambaghai and handed him over to the Jin frontier authorities, who nailed him to a wooden mule, and the Mongols swore vengeance against the "Golden Khan." Under the emperor Wanyan Yong (titled Shizong, r. 1261–90), Jin armies conducted regular punitive expeditions against the nomads, enslaving them or driving them north.

Under his successor, Wanyan Jing (titled Zhangzong, r. 1190–1209), Jin policy turned defensive. Ramparts were built in Inner Mongolia, and the Jiu border auxiliaries became restive. In 1196 the grand councillor, Wanyan Xiang, even allied with the Mongols and the KEREYID Khanate against their erstwhile Tatar allies. For their role in this expedition, the Mongol chieftain Temüjin was offered the title *zhaotaoshi*, or "bandit suppression commissioner," and the Kereyid khan Toghril received the title *ong*, "prince" (modern pronunciation *wang*). By 1202–04 both envoys and the Jiu border auxiliaries were defecting to Temüjin, yet the Mongols still paid tribute. When Temüjin was proclaimed emperor with the title CHINGGIS KHAN (r. 1206–27), the Jin were distracted by war with the Song. Wanyan Jing died in 1209, and his brother Wanyan Yongji (titled King of Weishao, r. 1209–13) usurped the throne. Wanyan Yongji had served on the frontier, and Chinggis despised him. From that year the Mongols discontinued tribute.

CONQUEST OF CHINA NORTH OF THE HUANG (YELLOW) RIVER

Chinggis Khan's ensuing campaign against the Jin can be divided into three stages. In the first stage, from spring 1211 to summer 1213, the Mongols had two aims: clearing away Jin fortifications down to the mountains bordering

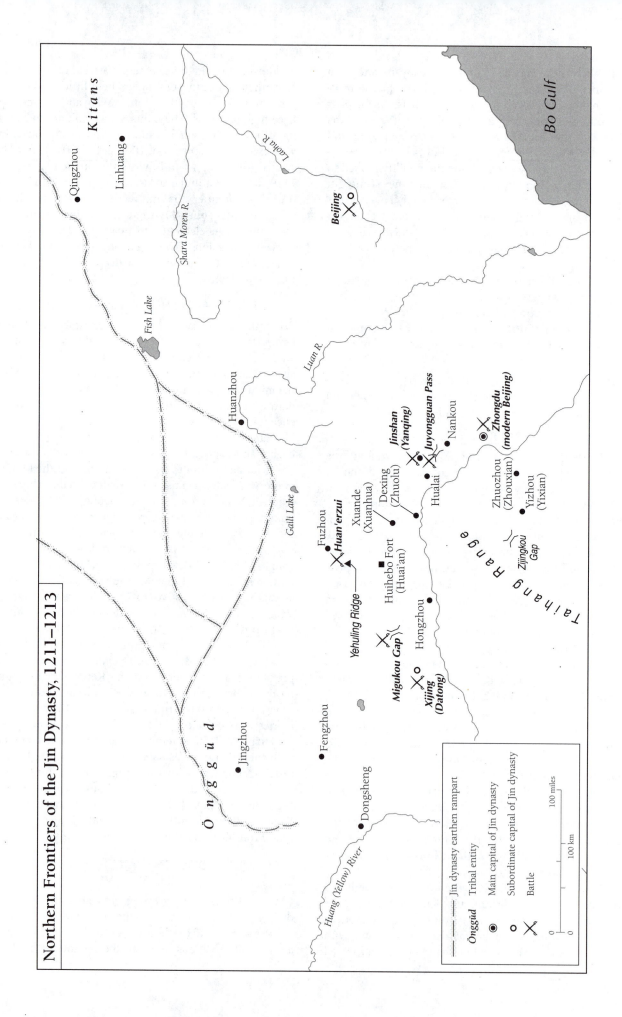

Northern Frontiers of the Jin Dynasty, 1211–1213

Bo Gulf

Kitans

Qingzhou

Linhuang

Laoha R.

Shara Moren R.

Beijing

Fish Lake

Luan R.

Huanzhou

Ö n g g ü d

Jingzhou

Fengzhou

Gaili Lake

Fuzhou
Huan'erzui

Yehuling Ridge

Migukou Gap

Hongzhou

Xijing (Datong)

Huihebo Fort (Huai'an)

Xuande (Xuanhua)

Dexing (Zhuolu)

Hualai

Jinshan (Yanqing)

Juyongguan Pass

Nankou

Zhongdu (modern Beijing)

Zhuozhou (Zhouxian)

Yizhou (Yixian)

Zijingkou Gap

T a i h a n g   R a n g e

Dongsheng

Huang (Yellow) River

Ônggüd Tribal entity

———— Jin dynasty earthen rampart

⊙ Main capital of Jin dynasty

○ Subordinate capital of Jin dynasty

✗ Battle

100 miles

100 km

the North China plain and seizing the passes through those mountains. Meanwhile, the Jin tried to defeat the Mongols in the field. In repeated battles, including Huan'erzui ("The Badger's Mouth," February 1212), and Jinshan (July to August 1213), the Mongols smashed Jin armies, each numbering, according to the sources, in the hundreds of thousands. They broke through Juyongguan Pass and Zijingkou Gap by November 1213.

In the second stage, from autumn 1213 through spring 1214, the Mongols roamed at will, pillaging the entire North China plain. The strategic aim was to force the Jin dynasty to surrender and become a tributary state. The Jin were now on the defensive, never venturing to meet the Mongols in the field. In summer 1213 the Jin general Heshilie Hushahu had murdered the emperor Wanyan Yongji and enthroned his nephew Wanyan Xun (title Xuanzong, r. 1213–24). This second stage ended when the Mongols besieged the capital, Zhongdu (modern Beijing), and the Jin temporarily agreed to become tributaries of the Mongols, presenting a Wanyan princess to the Mongols. Believing the war was over, Chinggis withdrew from the North China plain, although he still held the passes and the territory north of the ranges.

The third stage began when the new Jin ruler, Wanyan Xun, fled the capital to the southern city of Kaifeng, south of the Huang (Yellow) River, making it his redoubt against the Mongol invasions. Only then did Chinggis alter his strategic aim to one of actual Mongol conquest and rule of the North China plain. Beginning in December 1214 the Mongols first wiped out remaining Jin centers of control in southern Manchuria, then moved to the area of Zhongdu, starving it into surrender on May 31, 1215. They then systematically rooted out all resistance in Shanxi, Hebei, and lowland Shandong from 1217 to 1223. In these later campaigns, MUQUALI, Chinggis Khan's most trusted surviving NÖKÖR (companion), served as commander, while the khan fought in Central Asia. After 1217 regular Jin armies did not hold cities in the plains; the Mongols mostly fought local strongmen and deserters to the Jin or Song standards. From Muqali's death in 1223 to 1230, the Mongols could not challenge the Jin hold on Henan, central Shaanxi, and southeast Shandong.

The Mongols' destruction of what had been East Asia's most feared military machine is hard to explain, but the Jin leadership's incessant internal strife certainly played a part. This conflict peaked in summer 1213, when Heshilie Hushahu abandoned the defense of Xijing (modern Datong) and returned to Zhongdu to overthrow the emperor Wanyan Yongji and replace him with Wanyan Xun. Another weakness was disaffection among the Jin's ethnic auxiliary armies. When the Mongol attack began in 1211, the entire network of frontier tribes supposedly guarding the border was already on the Mongol side. Kitan army units and leaders repeatedly deserted the Jurchen cause. Finally, the experiences of the past had misled the Jin officials to expect that

northern nomads might raid but could never conquer walled cities.

THE JIN IN HENAN

The relocation of the Jin dynasty to Henan caused tremendous hardship yet also illustrated the regime's surprising strength: 420,000 military households migrated south, as did thousands of civil officials, straining local resources. While defections to the Mongols constantly drained Jin military strength, few civil officials went over to the Mongols, and even fewer deserted to the Song dynasty in South China. Not all defections to the Mongols were voluntary or permanent. The greatest general of the Jin's last stand, Wanyan Hada, had been forced by circumstances and rebellious troops to desert in 1213 but soon returned to the Jin standard. Indeed, by the 1220s the dynasty's remaining positions in Shaanxi and Shandong depended on the loyalty of warlords and volunteer forces ruling their cities and mountain fortresses as independent fiefdoms.

Guarded to the north by the Huang (Yellow) River and on the west by the Tongguan Pass, the remaining Jin heartland was hard to attack. When Chinggis Khan's son ÖGEDEI KHAN (1228–41) ascended the throne, he rebuffed Jin offers of peace talks. In 1230 he sent Doqulqu to attempt a frontal attack on Tongguan Pass, but Wanyan Hada first crushed Doquluqu's army and then defeated the famed general SÜBE'ETEI BA'ATUR. That autumn Ögedei and his brother Tolui campaigned personally, first subduing Fengxiang, the Jin's last major stronghold in Shaanxi. In spring 1232 Tolui led the Mongols through Song territory and invaded Henan from the south, while Ögedei pushed through the Tongguan Pass from the west. Tolui's troops killed Wanyan Hada on February 13, 1232. From then on the Jin's waning hopes rested on siege warfare. Sübe'etei invested the southern capital of Kaifeng from April 1232. Sensing correctly that Sübe'etei was planning a complete massacre, the inhabitants of the capital held out in desperate resistance. Finally, in February 1233 the emperor Wanyan Shouxu (titled Aizong, r. 1224–34) fled to Guide, and on March 5 the city surrendered. YELÜ CHU-CAI, once a Jin official and now Ögedei Khan's leading minister, intervened to spare the city from wholesale slaughter. Hunting down Wanyan Shouxu and besieging him in Caizhou, the Mongols, with the belated assistance of the Song, finished off the Jin in February 1234. The remaining Jin-held citadels in Shandong and Shaanxi surrendered at the same time.

LEGACY TO THE MONGOL EMPIRE

The relatively sophisticated Jin institutions had a delayed influence on the Mongols. While many institutions of Mongol rule in China, such as the decimal organization, a military system combining features of a tribal militia with a professional military caste, and the strong role for the imperial family, recall Jin practice, they were also the predictable results of the encounter of Inner Asian conquerors with Chinese traditions. Such civil administration as the Mongols had in North China under Chinggis Khan was mostly set up by former Jurchen officials, but chaotic conditions and Mongol indifference prevented any close imitation of the complex Jin bureaucracy. Under Ögedei Khan Yelü Chucai began to draw more successfully on Jin administrative precedents, despite considerable opposition from those who hated everything associated with the fallen regime. After the fall of Kaifeng, Yelü Chucai and sympathetic Chinese commanders in Mongol service protected and repatriated former Jin officials. They eventually came to gravitate around QUBILAI KHAN (1260–94), who interviewed and employed scores of them. Thus, the significance of Jin precedents for the later Mongol YUAN DYNASTY, while delayed and indirect, was profound.

See also HUAN'ERZUI, BATTLE OF; JUYONGGUAN PASS, BATTLES OF; KAIFENG, SIEGE OF; MANCHURIA AND THE MONGOL EMPIRE; MASSACRES IN THE MONGOL EMPIRE; ZHONGDU, SIEGES OF.

Further reading: Henry Desmond Martin, *Rise of Chingis Khan and His Conquest of North China* (Baltimore: Johns Hopkins Press, 1950; rpt., New York: Octagon Books, 1971); Hok-lam Chan, *Fall of the Jurchen Chin: Wang E's Memoir on Ts'ai-chou under the Mongol Siege (1233–1234)* (Stuttgart: Franz Steiner, 1993); Herbert Franke and Hok-lam Chan, *Studies on the Jurchens and the Chin Dynasty* (Aldershot, Hampshire: Ashgate, 1997).

Jingim (Zhenjin, Chen-Chin) (1243–1285) *The heir apparent of Qubilai Khan and patron of Chinese culture*
Born the second son of QUBILAI KHAN and his principal wife, CHABUI, Jingim was named "True Gold" ("Jingim" in 13th-century Chinese, "Zhenjin" in contemporary pronunciation) by the Chinese Dhyana (Zen) monk Haiyun. As a child Qubilai assigned Jingim Yao Shu (1203–80) as his senior Confucian tutor.

Qubilai's eldest son was sickly, and after being elected khan in 1260 he groomed Jingim to succeed him. In 1262 Jingim was made prince of Yan and concurrent director of the secretariat and commissioner of the bureau of military affairs. From 1264 he began attending meetings of the secretariat monthly. In 1273 he was formally designated heir apparent. While often joining the princes in sessions of reciting the Mongolian *bilig*s (wise sayings) and of ARCHERY, his private interests were in Chinese histories.

By the 1270s Jingim was publicly hostile of Qubilai's chief adviser, AHMAD FANAKATI, and he became the hope of the Confucian officials at court. Ahmad's death in 1282 brought Jingim into his own. In 1285 a South Chinese scholar unwisely composed a memorial asking that Qubilai abdicate in favor of Jingim. Despite Jingim's effort to hush it up, the text of the memorial leaked, and Qubilai became furious. In the midst of this crisis Jingim fell ill and died.

Jingim's widow, Bairam-Egechi (Kökejin), remained high in Qubilai's favor, however, and in 1291 Jingim's chief steward, Öljei, became the secretariat's senior grand councillor. Bairam-Egechi saw her third son, Temür, crowned in 1294. Jingim's eldest son, Gammala (1263–1302), who had a slight stammer, tried to contest the election, but at the QURILTAI Temür won in a competition to recite *bilig*s (wise sayings). After Temür died childless in 1307, the sons of Darmabala (1264–92), Jingim's second son, succeeded him. In 1323, after a coup d'état, Gammala's son Yisün-Temür was made emperor for five years before his death and a civil war returned the throne to Darmabala's descendants.

Jirim *See* KHORCHIN; TONGLIAO MUNICIPALITY.

Jochi (Jöchi, Jüchi, Tushi) (d. 1225?) *Ancestor of the khans of the Golden Horde and Chinggis Khan's eldest son; suspicions of illegitimacy alienated him from his father*
Jochi's mother, CHINGGIS KHAN's main wife, BÖRTE ÜJIN, gave birth to him after she had been raped by MERKID tribesmen. While Chinggis always treated him as legitimate, later taunts of illegitimacy, reflected in his very name, meaning "guest," dogged Jochi. His relations with CHA'ADAI, Chinggis's second son and the presumed heir should Jochi be disowned, were particularly bad.

By 1203 Chinggis Khan had arranged marriages for Jochi with both Börte's QONGGIRAD clan and with his KEREYID allies, suitable-in-laws (QUDA) for an heir apparent. Jochi held a command in the conquest of the northern Merkid tribe in 1204, and after the unification of Mongolia Chinggis dispatched Jochi in 1207 to Siberia, where he brought the forest peoples into submission (*see* SIBERIA AND THE MONGOL EMPIRE). Jochi campaigned with Cha'adai and Ögedei in southwest Inner Mongolia (November 1211) and in Hebei and Shanxi (autumn 1213). Jochi also accompanied SÜBE'ETEI BA'TUR's first campaign against the Qipchaqs (1218–19).

However, according to the *SECRET HISTORY OF THE MONGOLS*, Chinggis Khan passed over both Jochi and Cha'adai and chose Ögedei as his successor in 1219. Jochi's reputation solely as a hunter did not inspire confidence in his abilities as ruler. During the Central Asian campaign Jochi commanded the right flank, sacking the cities along the Syr Dar'ya (spring 1220) before joining his brothers Ögedei and Cha'adai at the destruction of Urganch (spring 1221).

Chinggis Khan assigned to Jochi KHORAZM and the steppes from the river Chu on west, intending them as a base for the conquest of the Qipchaqs. Instead, Jochi dallied in the hunt. Jochi presented his father with vast herds of wild asses in 1224, but by this time the two were seriously estranged. The gathering crisis ended when

Jochi died prematurely, leaving his *ulus* (people) to his second son, BATU. He received the posthumous title Ulus-Idi (Lord of the Realm).

See also BLUE HORDE; GOLDEN HORDE; ÖGEDEI KHAN.

John of Plano Carpini (1182–1252) *Papal envoy who wrote an important description of the Mongols' history, military, and customs*

Born at Plano Carpini (Italian Pianò Carpine, modern Magione) near Perugia, John became a Franciscan friar and served from 1221 as administrator of the order's mission in Germany. Interrupted by a brief stint in Spain, he served from 1228 as the provincial of Saxony, actively promoting the Franciscan order in North and Central Europe. The Council of Lyon (1245), chaired by Pope Innocent IV, responded to the Mongols' 1241–42 invasion of Central Europe by dispatching an envoy to deliver a papal bull to the invaders and to collect intelligence. Despite his obesity, John was chosen as envoy, probably because of his familiarity with Eastern Europe. In Poland Friar Benedict joined the embassy, probably interpreting for John's Slavic interlocutors. On his way John tried to promote an alliance between the Polish and Russian lords against the Mongols, which involved the Eastern Orthodox Russians accepting Catholicism. From Kiev the ambassadors entered Mongol jurisdiction on February 26, 1246, and crossed the steppe first to the realm of Prince Batu and then to Mongolia, where they arrived on July 22. After witnessing the great QURILTAI (assembly) that elected GÜYÜG KHAN and receiving Güyüg's flat rejection of the papal bull, the envoys returned to the West in November. Reaching Europe in June 1247, John delivered Güyüg's reply and his own report to Pope Innocent at Lyon. Pleased with his execution of the arduous mission, Pope Innocent appointed John in 1248 the archbishop of Antivari (modern Bar) in Dalmatia, where he stayed to his death.

John's Latin report, *Historia Mongolorum quos nos Tartaros apellamus* (History of the Mongols whom we call Tartars), is a major source on the MONGOL EMPIRE. The descriptions of the *quriltai* that elected Güyüg and the Mongol military are particularly valuable. The genealogy of the Chinggisid ruling family he provided is remarkably accurate for an outside observer, although superseded today. His historical section, however, mixes many reliable assertions with bizarre accounts of mythical creatures, which were derived from the Russian clerics with whom he associated throughout his journey. John's own view of the Mongols was intensely negative. While conceding many admirable features of their military organization, he believed that their victories were more the result of fraud than true valor. Despite advice from his Russian friends, he did not have enough gifts to participate in the lavish reciprocal gift giving that marked Mongol social interaction, and as a result he blamed his hosts for their lack of hospitality.

Once incorporated in Vincent de Beauvais's encyclopedic *Speculum Historiale* (Historical mirror), John's *History of the Mongols* was widely read during the Middle Ages. In 1832 a manuscript with a brief account written by his companion Benedict the Pole was also found in the Bibliothèque Nationale in Paris. In 1957, another manuscript, called the "Tartar Relation" (*Historia Tartarorum*) was discovered, which appears to be a copy of notes taken from a lecture John gave on his experiences in Asia. (Despite the controversy over the attached Vinland Map, the authenticity of the "Tartar Relation" is not in doubt.)

See also CENTRAL EUROPE AND THE MONGOLS; CHRISTIAN SOURCES ON THE MONGOL CONQUEST; KIEV, SIEGE OF; RUSSIA AND THE MONGOL EMPIRE; WESTERN EUROPE AND THE MONGOLS.

Further reading: Christopher Dawson, ed., *The Mongol Mission* (1955; rpt., New York: AMS Press, n.d.); R. A. Skelton, Thomas E. Marston, and George O. Painter, *The Vinland Map and the Tartar Relation* (New Haven, Conn.: Yale University Press, 1965).

Josotu See FUXIN MONGOL AUTONOMOUS COUNTY; INJANNASHI; KHARACHIN.

Jou-jan See ROURAN.

Juan-juan See ROURAN.

Jüchi See JOCHI.

Jungar See ZÜNGHARS.

Jungdu See ZHONGDU, SIEGES OF.

Ju Ud See JUU UDA.

Juu Uda (Zuu Ud, Ju Ud, Zhao Wuda) One of the traditional six leagues (*chigulgan*) of Inner Mongolia, the Juu Uda Mongols are partly farmers and partly herders, occupying the upper Shara Mören (Xar Moron) valley, east of the GREATER KHINGGAN RANGE.

Under China's last Qing dynasty Juu Uda contained 11 banners, or appanages, from eight "tribes" (AIMAG): Aohan, NAIMAN, Baarin (Bairin), Jarud, Aru Khorchin (Ar Horqin), Ongni'ud, Kheshigten (Hexigten), and KHALKHA (later merged with Khüriye/Hure). The neighboring "lay disciples," or subjects of Khüriye (Hure) Monastery, were an autonomous unit. Much of this territory has subsequently been lost to CHINESE COLONIZA-TION, and the remaining banners are now divided between CHIFENG MUNICIPALITY and TONGLIAO MUNICI-PALITY. The present banners of old Juu Uda cover more than 85,000 square kilometers (32,800 square miles) and have a population of about 2,798,000 (1990 figures). Of this, 707,000, or 25 percent, are Mongols; the highest percentage is in Khüriye banner (56 percent Mongol) and the lowest in Aohan (4 percent Mongol). Outside Aohan rural Mongols and Chinese live mostly in separate districts, and the great majority of Mongols speak Mongolian.

Economically, the Mongols of the old Juu Uda banners range from mostly pastoral to mostly farming. In Baarin Right Banner (Bairin Youqi) 58.1 percent of the total agricultural sales comes from herding, while in Khüriye it is only 3 percent. The total herd in the old Juu Uda banners was about 7.5 million (1990), in which the percentage of pigs ranges from negligible to about a quarter in Naiman and Khüriye.

HISTORY

The Shara Mören valley was the original home of the medieval KITANS. After the establishment of the 13th-century MONGOL EMPIRE, it became the territory of the QONGGIRAD clan. Under the Ming after 1449 it became the home of Taining (Ongni'ud) and Fuyu (Üjiyed), both Mongol guards for the Ming (see THREE GUARDS). By 1500 the Shara Mören valley's Mongols had been reorganized into the "five OTOGS (camp districts) of South Khalkha" (see SIX TÜMENS). These five otogs—the Qonggirad, Üjiyed, Baarin, Jarud, and Bayud clans—became the appanage of Alchu-Bolod, the fifth son of the Chinggisid BATU-MÖNGKE DAYAN KHAN (1480?–1517?). Meanwhile, the neighboring Ongni'ud were ruled by descendants of CHINGGIS KHAN's brother Temüge Odchigin. In the mid-16th century Daraisun Küdeng Khan (1548–57) moved his CHAKHAR people east to the Shara Mören valley, mixing them with the South Khalkha.

The fall of Ligdan Khan (1604–34) and the rise of the Manchu QING DYNASTY (1636–1912) again reshuffled the appanages, now called BANNERS. Descendants of Alchu-Bolod were recognized as rulers over Baarin and Jarud banners. The Naiman, Aohan, and Kheshigten banners were split off from the Chakhar and installed under their Chinggisid princes, the Naiman and Aohan under descendants of Dayan Khan's grandson and successor, Bodi Alag Khan (1519?–47), and the Kheshigten under descendants of Dayan Khan's sixth son, Wachirbolod. A body of KHORCHINS was settled in the Shara Mören valley under Manchu protection, becoming the Aru ("North") Khorchin. Finally, in 1665 a body of northern Khalkha Mongols, escaping strife in Zasagtu Khan province, surrendered to the Manchu Qing dynasty and were resettled in the same area. The Qing fixed the banners' new boundaries in 1636 and organized the Juu Uda league in 1674.

The Ongni'ud Right and Aohan banners began dividing up their fields and employing Chinese immigrants as tenants in the 18th century, following the KHARACHIN banner pattern. The anti-Mongol insurrection of the Jindandao ("Golden Pillway") sect of Chinese tenants in 1891 began in Aohan and devastated the Mongols of the southern Juu Uda, sending farming Mongols fleeing north. From 1908 state-sponsored Chinese colonization projects established a patchwork of almost purely Chinese counties among the Mongol banners of northern Juu Uda.

In 1933 the Japanese occupying forces designated the remaining Juu Uda banners (excluding Ongni'ud Right and Aohan) as Khinggan West province, putting the Chinese counties mostly under Mongol administration. After a brief period in 1945–46 under Mongol nationalist governments, the Chinese Communists took control of Juu Uda. They combined Kheshigten, Baarin, and Aru Khorchin as Inner Mongolia's Juu Uda league while assigning Jarud, Naiman, and Khüriye to Jirim league. Ongni'ud Left Banner was made a Mongol autonomous county in Rehe province. In 1954 Rehe was abolished and Aohan and Ongni'ud attached to Juu Uda league, along with several counties and Kharachin banner. In 1983 Juu Uda was renamed CHIFENG MUNICIPALITY.

See also BOLOR ERIKHE; FARMING; INNER MONGOLIA AUTONOMOUS REGION; INNER MONGOLIANS; MONGOLIAN LANGUAGE; NEW SCHOOLS MOVEMENTS.

Further reading: Rong Ma, "Migrant and Ethnic Integration in the Process of Socio-Economic Change in Inner Mongolia, China: A Village Study," *Nomadic Peoples* 33 (1993): 173–192; Dee Mack Williams, *Beyond Great Walls: Environment, Identity, and Development on the Chinese Grasslands of Inner Mongolia* (Stanford, Calif.: Stanford University Press, 2002).

Juvaini, 'Ala'ud-Din Ata-Malik (1226–1283) **and Shams-ud-Din Muhammad** (d. 1284) *Both high officials of the Mongols, 'Ala'ud-Din Ata-Malik was one of the great historians of the Mongols.*
The Juvaini family was one of the ancient landholding families of Khorasan (northeastern Iran), with ancestral estates in the Juvain district (modern Joghatay), northwest of Sabzevar. The Juvaini family had served the Seljuk (1037–1157) and Khorazmian (1138–1230/1) dynasties as *sahib-divan* (chiefs of the secretariat). In 1232–33, as the Mongols were mopping up resistance, Baha'ud-Din Muhammad (father of 'Ala'ud-Din and Shams-ud-Din) was brought before the local Mongol commander. Expecting death, he was instead appointed by the governor Chin-Temür to be *sahib-divan* for the administration in Khorasan. Baha'ud-Din served the Mongols as administrator until his death in Isfahan at age 60 (1253).

Against the advice of his father, who preferred a religious career for him, 'Ala'ud-Din entered the service of the Mongols as a scribe before his 20th year. With his father and ARGHUN AQA, the governor of Khorasan, he visited the Mongol capital of QARA QORUM in 1252–53. There, at the suggestion of his companions, he began his *Ta'rikh-i jahan gusha,* or *HISTORY OF THE WORLD CONQUEROR,* which he abandoned sometime around 1260 after recording Mongolian history up to 1256. From 1256 to 1259 'Ala'ud-Din Ata-Malik traveled in the entourage of the Mongol prince HÜLE'Ü (r. 1256–65). In 1259 Hüle'ü appointed him the governor of the caliph's former territories (southern Iraq and Khuzistan), a position he held until 1283. In Khorasan in 1256 and in Iraq he actively promoted irrigation and agriculture. As a Sunni Muslim, tensions with Shi'ite Muslims and Christians in Iraq marred his governorship, however, and led to the voluntary exile of the catholicos (Christian patriarch) from Baghdad in 1268.

In 1262, as Hüle'ü tried to improve his civil administration, he appointed Shams-ud-Din Muhammad vizier. Under Hüle'ü's son Abagha Khan (1265–82) Shams-ud-Din and 'Ala'ud-Din continued as vizier and governor of Baghdad, respectively. In 1280 Majd-ul-Mulk, a spurned client of the Juvainis, accused the family of massive embezzlement, royal pretensions, and treasonous communications with MAMLUK EGYPT, but the intercession of the queen, Öljei, saved Shams-ud-Din. In 1281 Abagha made Majd-ul-Mulk covizier with Shams-ud-Din. 'Ala'ud-Din was arrested, publicly tortured, and fined 3,000,000 gold dinars; he sold his sons to pay the ransom. Released, he was soon arrested again. When Abagha suddenly died, the new khan, Sultan Ahmad (1282–84), executed Majd-ul-Mulk and honored Shams-ud-Din. Abagha's son Arghun, however, believing that Shams-ud-Din had poisoned Abagha, accused 'Ala'ud-Din's men of embezzlement; 'Ala'ud-Din died of natural causes on March 5, 1283. Soon after Arghun's partisans overthrew Sultan Ahmad, and Shams-ud-Din was beaten to death and beheaded on October 16, 1284. Five years later Arghun executed his remaining sons.

Further reading: 'Ala-ad-Din 'Ata-Malik Juvaini, *History of the World Conqueror,* 2 vols., trans. John Andrew Boyle (Cambridge Mass.: Harvard University Press, 1958).

Juyongguan Inscriptions *See* MONGOLIAN SOURCES ON THE MONGOL EMPIRE.

Juyongguan Pass, battles of (Chü-yung-kuan; Chabchiyal) (October 1211 and autumn 1213) The Mongol victories against the heavily fortified Juyongguan Pass opened the way to Zhongdu, the Jin capital. Access to Beijing is blocked to the north and northwest by a chain of mountains, which successive Chinese dynasties have fortified in defense against the northern nomads. To protect their capital at Zhongdu (modern Beijing), the Jin garrisoned Juyongguan with the ruling Jurchens and hard-fighting Kitan auxiliaries.

During his first attack on the Jin in 1211, CHINGGIS KHAN defeated the Jin field army at Huihebao Fort (modern Huai'an), seized Dexing (modern Zhuolu), and ordered JEBE, commander of his heavy cavalry, to seize the pass. Jebe feigned an assault and then retreated north up the valley as far as Xuande (modern Xuanhua). When the defending general pursued, Jebe turned and scattered the Jin troops, opening the way to Zhongdu. The Mongols subsequently withdrew.

In 1213 the Mongols were ready to force the Jin to surrender, but the Jin by then were more familiar with Mongol tactics. In July–August 1213 Chinggis Khan took Xuande and Dexing again. Between Huailai and Jinshan (modern Yanqing) he crushed a vast army under the Jin marshal Shuhu Gaoqi, and the remnants fell back on their strong fortifications at Juyongguan. Following a proposal of JABAR KHOJA, Chinggis Khan had two QONGGIRAD commanders, Ketei and Bocha, guard the pass while Chinggis Khan and Jebe broke through the mountains at Zijingkou Pass, 75 miles to the southwest. Meanwhile, one of the Jin's Kitan commanders, Elu Bu'r, betrayed Juyongguan's northern mouth to the Mongols. Racing northeast along the plain, Jebe attacked Juyongguan's southern mouth, crushing the defenders and meeting Ketei and Bocha in the middle of the pass. From this time on the Mongols controlled access to Zhongdu and the North China plain.

See also MILITARY OF THE MONGOL EMPIRE; ZHONGDU, SIEGES OF.

K

kagan   *See* KHAN.

Kaifeng, siege of (K'ai-feng)   In this year-long siege, lasting from April 1232 to May 1233, Mongol armies finally broke the southern capital of the JIN DYNASTY, which once had ruled North China. Although the Jin emperor fled, he was run to ground soon after in the small town of Caizhou (modern Runan).

When the Mongols broke into Henan and killed the Jin dynasty's great commander Wanyan Hada in February 1232, the Jin lost hope of fielding armies against the Mongols. On April 5 the Mongols sent an envoy to the Jin capital of Kaifeng demanding complete surrender. The Jin emperor, Wanyan Shouxu (titled Aizong, r. 1224–34), sent out his brother, Wanyan Eke, as a hostage to the Mongols, but the Mongols, under the general SÜBE'ETEI BA'ATUR, suspected the Jin's good faith, and negotiations broke down.

Swollen by refugees and soldiers, the city's population reached 1,470,000 households, but at first morale among the defenders was excellent. The emperor personally visited the troops on the gates and threw open palace supplies for medicines and rewards, and political prisoners were released to join the struggle. At least 200,000 civilians were drafted into the army on pain of death, and the students in the Hanlin Academy pleaded to be allowed to join the artillery men on the walls. When the Mongols sent the Chinese envoy Tang Qing that summer to discuss surrender again, the defending generals killed him.

The Mongol assault used trebuchets, while the Jin catapulted cast-iron exploding shells and in close combat used metal tubes spitting flaming gunpowder (early European scholars mistranslated these weapons as cannons and rockets). The attackers responded by covering their trenches with cowhides as the defenders lowered larger explosive shells on iron chains. In August the besiegers drove off the last relief attempt. That summer it is claimed that plague killed 900,000 (not counting those too poor for burial), and by December the besieged were eating one another.

The emperor broke out with an army on February 5, and the Mongol final assault had to be delayed until the Jin army was scattered. The emperor, however, escaped to Guide. On March 5 Marshal Cui Li in Kaifeng rebelled, killing the defending Jin commanders and seizing the remaining imperial family and consorts to hold for negotiations. On May 27 Cui Li finally handed over more than 500 men of the Wanyan family to the Mongols, who butchered them all. The empresses were escorted to the Mongol court, and Sübe'etei entered the city.

Enraged by the heavy Mongol casualties, Sübe'etei asked ÖGEDEI KHAN for permission to slaughter everything alive, but after strenuous objections from his minister YELÜ CHUCAI, Sübe'etei was ordered to resettle the population north of the Huang (Yellow) River. Yelü Chucai and Chinese generals in Mongol service, such as ZHANG ROU and YAN SHI, protected the descendants of Confucius and Jin scholars and officials, but the highways were littered with the corpses of starving refugees.

K'ai-p'ing   *See* SHANGDU.

Kalaqin   *See* KHARACHIN.

Kalka River, Battle of   The Battle of Kalka River on May 31, 1223, was the disastrous first encounter of Russian armies with the Mongols. When the Mongol generals JEBE and SÜBE'ETEI BA'ATUR rode north through the Derbend Pass, they crushed the QIPCHAQS (Polovtsi) under Gyurgi (George), son of Könchek. The defeated Qipchaqs, led by Köten (Kotian), appealed to Köten's Russian son-in-law Mstislav the Daring (d. 1228) of Halych (Galich). The princes of southern Russia (modern Ukraine) met at Kiev, where they assented to the Qipchaq request.

Commanded by Mstislav the Old of Kiev (d. 1223) and Mstislav of Chernihiv (Chernigov, d. 1223), the Russians advanced down the west bank of the Dniepr to rendezvous with the Qipchaqs and other Russian contingents. Mongol envoys arrived to dissuade the Russians from hostilities, but they were killed. On Tuesday, May 23, 1223, the Russian vanguard crossed the Dniepr in boats and clashed with Mongol scouts, who fled leaving their livestock behind. Not realizing this was a ruse, the Russians and Qipchaqs seized the livestock and pursued the Mongols for eight days to the river Kalka (north of Mariupol'), where the Mongols were camped on the other side of the river.

Mstislav the Daring, without telling his commanders, ordered young Daniel of Halych (d. 1264) and the Russian-Qipchaq vanguard over the Kalka, and the Mongols again fell back in a feigned retreat. When the Mongols suddenly turned and showered the enemy with arrows, the vanguard broke and streamed back over the river, where the Qipchaqs, riding in headlong flight, disorganized the main force's unready lines. The other princes fled back to the Dniepr, but Mstislav the Old had set a stockade on a stony hill above the Kalka, where he and his two sons-in-law fought for three days, until they came out under a safe conduct offer from the Mongols. The three, however, were crushed to death under boards as the Mongols feasted on top of them.

In their pursuit to the Dniepr, the Mongols caught and killed Mstislav of Chernihiv and six other princes. Mstislav the Daring, however, crossed the Dniepr and cut loose the boats to end the pursuit. The Mongols sacked Novhorod-Sivers'kyy (Novgorod-Severskii) before riding back to Mongolia.

See also MILITARY OF THE MONGOL EMPIRE; RUSSIA AND THE MONGOL EMPIRE.

Further reading: George A. Perfecky, trans., *The Galician-Volynian Chronicle* (Munich: Wilhelm Fink, 1973).

Kalmucks *See* KALMYKS.

Kalmyk Republic The Kalmyk Republic, or Kalmykia, is the homeland of the KALMYKS, a branch of the OIRATS, or West Mongols living along the Caspian Sea, and a component republic of the Russian Federation. Europe's only Buddhist and Mongolian-speaking people, the Kalmyks were exiled as a people to Siberia from 1943 to 1957. The population of Kalmykia in 1989 was 322,579, of which Kalmyks formed 146,316, or 45 percent. This number included 84 percent of the Kalmyks of the old Soviet Union. Since 1991 the republic's population has declined and was estimated at 314,300 in 2001. In the Kalmyk language the republic's official name is *Khal'mag tangghch* (Kalmyk Nation).

GEOGRAPHY AND DEMOGRAPHY

The Kalmyk Republic covers 76,100 square kilometers (29,380 square miles) along the northwestern shore of the Caspian Sea. The territory is uniformly dry, low-lying steppe. Elevations range from 28 meters (92 feet) below sea level along the Caspian Sea to 222 meters (728 feet) above sea level in the Yergeni Highland on the republic's western border, which marks the watershed between the Black and Caspian Seas. In the south Kalmykia borders the Manych-Kuma depression. Kalmykia's long westward salient encloses the saline Lake Manych-Gudilo, which drains toward the Black Sea. Other bodies of water include only seasonal streams and shallow saline lakes.

Kalmykia's climate is warmer than that of the MONGOLIAN PLATEAU. Temperatures in January average from –7° to –12°C (19° to 10°F), while July averages range from 23° to 26°C (75° to 79°F). Precipitation varies with elevation, reaching 300–400 millimeters (12–16 inches) annually in the northwest and falling to 170–200 millimeters (7–8 inches) along the Caspian coast. It falls mostly in the summer, and winter snow cover is light or absent. Sunny days average 280 per year. Vegetation in Kalmykia is mostly of desert-steppe type, with species similar to those of Kazakhstan, although different from those of Mongolia. Sagebrushes (*Artemisia lercheana, A. pauciflora*), feather grasses (*Stipa ucrainica, S. lessingiana*), and fescue (*Festuca valesiaca*) grow in the wetter north and west, with groves of willow, aspen, and elm near surface water in the Yergeni Highlands. In the republic's dry "Black Lands" along the Caspian, sagebrush (*Artemisia pauciflora, A. astrachanica, A. arenaria*) and saltworts of the goosefoot family (*Atriplex cana, Anabasis salsa*) dominate, with stands of summer cypress or burning bush (*Kochia scoparia*) being useful as fodder. Animal life is typical of the western Eurasian steppe: ground squirrels, jerboas, mole rats, hamsters, Siberian polecats, corsac foxes, and wolves. In 1970 saiga antelope numbered 200,000 but are now fewer than 18,000. Birds include lark, wheatear, partridge, bustard, tawny eagle (*Aquila rapax*), and saker falcon (*Falco cherrug*).

Rural population densities range from around 1.4 persons per square kilometer (3.6 per square mile) in the center and southeast to more than 11 persons per square kilometer (28.5 per square mile) around Lake Manych-Gudilo. About 3.3 persons per square kilometer (8.6 per square mile) inhabit the Yergeni Highlands and the north, and about 4.7 per square kilometer (12.2 per square

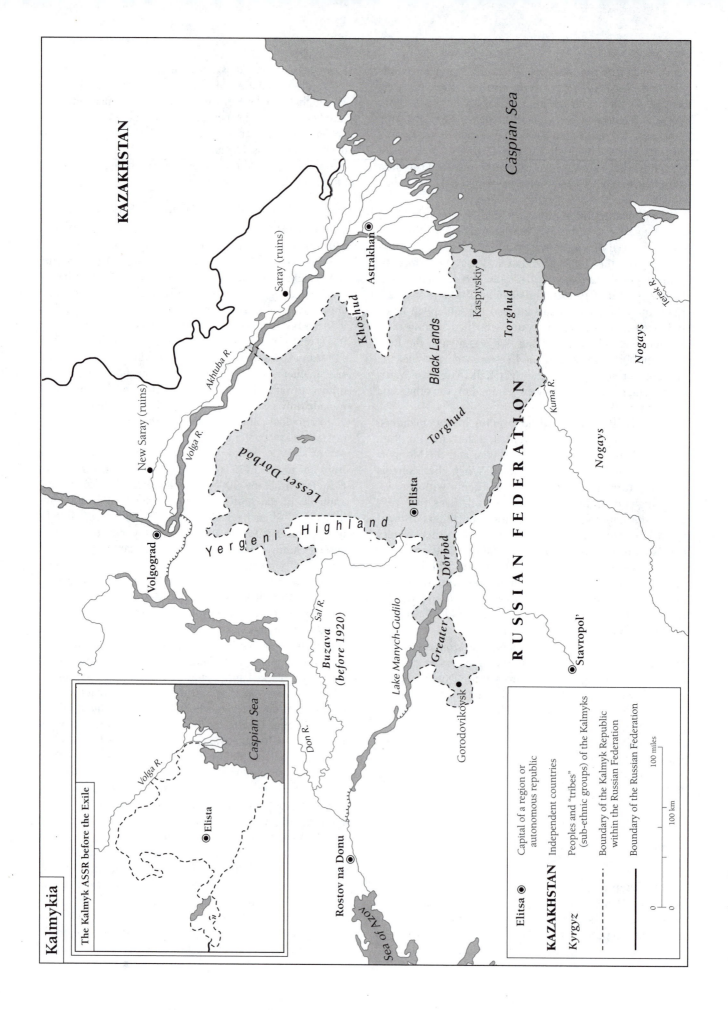

Kalmykia

The Kalmyk ASSR before the Exile

KAZAKHSTAN

Caspian Sea

Saray (ruins)

New Saray (ruins)

Astrakhan

Akhtuba R.

Volga R.

Khoshud

Kaspiyskiy

Torghud

Black Lands

Torghud

Nogays

Volgograd

Lesser Dörböd

Elista

Y e r g e n i   H i g h l a n d

Dörböd

RUSSIAN FEDERATION

Kuma R.

Nogays

Terek R.

Sal R.

Buzava
(before 1920)

Lake Manych-Gudilo

Greater

Gorodovikovsk

Stavropol'

Don R.

Volga R.

Elista

Caspian Sea

Rostov na Donu

Sea of Azov

Elitsa ◉ Capital of a region or
            autonomous republic

KAZAKHSTAN Independent countries

Kyrgyz Peoples and "tribes"
        (sub-ethnic groups) of the Kalmyks

– – – Boundary of the Kalmyk Republic
       within the Russian Federation

—— Boundary of the Russian Federation

100 miles

100 km

0

0

mile) inhabit the Caspian littoral. In 1989 the republic's only significant cities or towns included the capital, ELISTA (89,682 residents), Kaspiyskiy (15,770 residents), and Gorodovikovsk (12,016 residents); together with "urban-type communities" as small as 3,900 people, they accounted for 46 percent of the population. During the post-Soviet transition only Elista has grown relatively and absolutely, while the population of the minor towns has fallen even more rapidly that that of the countryside. By 2001 the urban percentage fell to an estimated 42 percent, while Elista's share of the population grew from 28 percent in 1989 to about 35 percent.

When it was first formed as an administrative region, Kalmykia was more than 75 percent Kalmyk in population. This had decreased to 48.6 percent in 1939, before the exile in 1943. The return of the Kalmyks after their exoneration in 1957 was rather slow, but by 1970 the republic was 41.1 percent Kalmyk. Since then the Kalmyks' higher birthrate has boosted their percentage of the population to 45.4 percent (1989). Traditionally, the Kalmyks were divided into Dörböd, Torghud, and Khoshud tribes, each with its own territory. Political events in the early 19th century split the DÖRBÖDS in two. Before the exile the Lesser Dörböd occupied the Yergeni Hills, the Greater Dörböds the area around Lake Manych-Gudilo, the KHOSHUDS the land along the lower Volga, and the TORGHUDS the central Black Lands territories as well as the Caspian coast and the Volga north of the Khoshuds.

Kalmykia's non-Kalmyk population is primarily Russian and other Slavic peoples (39.3 percent in 1989). Cossacks are an active presence in Kalmykia and include both Russians and descendants of the Buzava Kalmyk Cossacks, who were deported from their original territories on the Don after the end of the Russian civil war. Since the establishment of a Moravian colony at Sarepta in the 18th century, there has also been a small German population, 5,586 in 1989. About 26,600 various Muslim Caucasus peoples (Dargva, Chechens, Avars, Kumyks) also lived in Kalmykia in 1989; since then their numbers have been swelled by refugees from the Chechen war.

AUTONOMOUS SYSTEM

In 1920 Kalmykia was created as an autonomous unit. The territory was carved out of Astrakhan province west of the Volga and Stavropol' province around Lake Manych-Gudilo, home of the Greater Dörböds. In 1943, with the exile of the Kalmyks, the republic's territory was divided between Stavropol' and Astrakhan. With the return of the Kalmyks in 1957, the old territory was restored with the exception of two districts along the Volga River and a small piece of territory in Dagestan. The loss of these territories, which contain the historic Khoshud Khural (Buddhist temple), is still resented.

From 1920 to 1935 and in 1957–58 Kalmykia was an autonomous region (*oblast'*) within the Russian Soviet Federated Socialist Republic (RSFSR). From 1935 to the 1943 exile and from the 1958 return to 1992, Kalmykia was officially an Autonomous Soviet Socialist Republic (ASSR), again within the RSFSR. (The RSFSR was itself one of the 15 "union republics" forming the Soviet Union.) The difference between these two statuses was largely symbolic; as a republic the ASSR had a constitution, a (rarely used) flag and seal, and a government that imitated the form and titles of the government in Moscow. Kalmykia and the other ASSRs lacked the (entirely theoretical) "right to secede" possessed by the "union republics," evidence of their lesser importance, which rankled until the end of the Soviet Union.

Autonomy in Kalmykia, as everywhere in the Soviet Union, was strictly limited by Communist Party supervision, the FIVE-YEAR PLAN governing all economic activities, and the ideological control of all media. Soviet autonomy was thus not a matter of autonomous politico-economic decision making but of officially directed multiculturalism. The key planks in this regime involved preferential policies benefiting Kalmyk cadres (in both elective and appointive positions), special Kalmyk-language classes in grade schools, and official subsidies for Kalmyk publications, performing arts, and scholarship. While preferential policies rapidly produced a new Kalmyk Communist leadership in the 1920s, Kalmyk-language education remained limited. With the return from exile, "nationality classes" in Kalmyk language were briefly revived but in 1963 were canceled. From then on, although a newspaper, literary magazine, and a small number of books were published in Kalmyk, there was no formal Kalmyk-medium instruction.

With the breakup of the party-state and the disintegration of communism, Kalmykia, like many other autonomous areas, declared itself sovereign. The Kalmyk and Russian languages were given equal official status (October 1990), and in 1992 the Kalmyk ASSR was renamed the Kalmyk Republic with a new seal and flag. A new constitution created a directly elected president and vice president with seven-year terms, a 27-member unicameral legislature, the People's (or National) Khural (Assembly), with a four-year term, and a government with 15 ministries and a chairman. Official multicultural policies were revived, with the restoration of Kalmyk as a subject in 1991 and Kalmyk-language grade school education in 1993.

Since April 1993 the Kalmyk presidency has been held by the Kalmyk millionaire Kirsan N. Ilümzhinov (b. 1962), who has developed a pervasive personality cult. In 1998 he also assumed the position of chairman of the government. President Ilümzhinov has pursued an ambitious and eccentric economic and social policy while securing dissolving opposition parties and controlling the economy. The murder of Larissa Iudinova, the editor of the only opposition newspaper, has remained unsolved. Under Ilümzhinov Kalmyks occupy perhaps 90 percent of official positions, and criticism of his rule is often seen as criticism of Kalmyk autonomy. He won reelection for a seven-year term in October 1995, with 85 percent of the vote (there was no opponent). Due to his alliance with the Russian president Boris Yeltsin's network, federal subsidies amounted to 32 percent of the republic's budget in 1998. Since 1999, however, President Ilümzhinov has strongly resisted the recentralization policies of the new Russian president, Vladimir Putin, while growing internal opposition forced him into a runoff against another Kalmyk candidate in 2002, which Ilümzhinov ultimately won with 57 percent of the vote.

ECONOMY

The Kalmyk economy is based on livestock and mining, principally oil and natural gas. In the 1970s 64 percent of the 5.3 million hectares (13.1 million acres) of agricultural land was given over to pasture, 11 percent to hay mowing, 9 percent fodder crops, and only 8 percent to grain crops. Agriculture and herding were collectivized in the 1930s and in the late 1990s 62 percent of rural economic enterprises were agricultural cooperatives (essentially the old collective farms renamed), and 24 percent were state owned.

The traditional Kalmyk herd included GOATS and fat-tailed SHEEP (735,000 in 1916), cattle (259,000 in 1916), HORSES, and CAMELS. Soviet development emphasized the exploitation of fine-haired caracul (Astrakhan) sheep. By 1941 sheep and goat numbers rose to 1,046,200, while CATTLE numbers dropped to 212,900. Wool production was 3,700 metric tons (4,079 short tons) in 1940. By 1971, after the return of the Kalmyks, sheep and goat numbers reached 2,462,700 and cattle numbers 352,200; wool production that year was 13,600 metric tons (14,991 short tons). In 1991 the herd peaked at 3,150,600 head of sheep and goats and 357,900 head of cattle. The excessive numbers of sheep caused widespread desertification, amplified by the sharper hooves of the caracul sheep. The area covered by dunes expanded from 2–3 percent of the republic in 1959 to 33 percent in 1985, and fodder cropping was expanded to make up for pasture degradation.

Since 1991 these environmental problems and the general Soviet economic crisis slashed sheep and goat numbers to 830,000 and cattle numbers to 144,800 in 1998. Wool production in 1995 was little more than 3,000 metric tons (3,307 short tons). Horses numbered 13,000. In recent years, in response to environmental destruction, efforts have been made to reintroduce the traditional Kalmyk fat-tailed sheep as well as two-humped camels, which now number 370.

Grain farming, mostly of winter wheat, was developed in the west in the Yergeni Hills. The total harvest reached 416,000 metric tons (458,561 short tons) in 1971, almost double that of 1940. In 2000 the harvest had declined to 228,000 metric tons (251,327 short tons), before increasing to 432,000 metric tons (476,198

short tons) in 2002. Fisheries on the Caspian Sea are also an important industry, in which Kalmyks have participated since the 18th century.

Kalmyk industry is largely based on processing animal products: meat, butter, canned food including fish, knitted goods, and leather. A machine-tools plant was developed in Kaspiyskiy, and small construction industries were developed in the city centers. Since the 1990s wool-processing and leather plants have received some West European investment.

By 1971 the new petroleum industry extracted 352,000 metric tons (388,013 short tons) of petroleum and 549 million cubic meters (19,387.8 million cubic feet) of natural gas. Proven and probable reserves are currently estimated at 5.5 billion metric tons (6.1 billion short tons) of petroleum and 520 billion cubic meters (18,400 billion cubic feet) of natural gas, although major technical overhaul will be necessary to exploit most of this.

Kalmyk living standards remain among Russia's lowest, with income only 38 percent of Russia's average (the subsistence level is 10 percent lower than Russia's average). Unemployment is one of the highest in the nation (13.3 percent in 1996). Infant mortality, however, is 18 per 1,000 live births, lower than in Buriatia (20 per 1,000) or Mongolia (58 per 1,000). While the republic's population continues to fall due to emigration, it is actually one of only 10 Russian regions, mostly minority areas, where births outnumber deaths.

See also DESERTIFICATION AND PASTURE DEGRADATION.

Kalmyk-Oirat language and scripts Oirat, or Kalmyk, is spoken by people of Oirat Mongolian ancestry in Kalmykia (Russia), Xinjiang (China), and western Mongolia and Qinghai (China). This speech can be treated as either a relatively divergent dialect of Mongolian or a closely related language. (The term *Kalmyk* was used first by the Turks and Russians for all OIRATS. Today, however, it is generally used only for those Oirats in Kalmykia on the Volga.)

DISTRIBUTION AND SOCIOLINGUISTICS

Where uninfluenced by modern Mongolian (whether KHALKHA or Inner Mongolian), Oirat, or Kalmyk, is usually hard for a Mongolian speaker to understand. Only in Kalmykia, however, is Mongolian influence entirely absent, although it is relatively weak in Xinjiang. In western Mongolia and among the UPPER MONGOLS of Qinghai, Khalkha and standard Inner Mongolian, respectively, have heavily influenced the speech. Sociolinguistically, the speech of the KALMYKS must be considered a separate language from Mongolian, while those of western Mongolia and Qinghai are clearly only dialects. That of Xinjiang is in an intermediate stage.

Kalmyks in the KALMYK REPUBLIC number approximately 146,300 (1989 figures), while Oirats and Oirat-influenced Mongols in Xinjiang number approximately 138,000 (1990 figures), in Qinghai and Gansu approximately 79,600 (1990 figures), and in western Mongolia approximately 168,000 (1989 figures).

Information on native language use is harder to find. From 1926 to 1989 the percentage of Kalmyks claiming Kalmyk as their native language dropped from 99.3 percent to 90.0 percent, but the latter figure expresses ideals, not reality. Sociological investigation shows that the generation born around 1935 to 1955 spoke mostly "kitchen" Kalmyk, and those born after then often spoke little or no Kalmyk. In 1963 grade school "national classes," taught partly in Kalmyk, were discontinued and were revived only in 1993. The one Kalmyk language newspaper, *Khal'mag ünn* (Kalmyk truth), despite government subsidy, publishes irregularly, has a regular Russian-language section, and finds it hard to attract advertisers.

In Qinghai only those Upper Mongols living in Haixi, or less than 40 percent, actually speak their ethnic language, with the rest speaking Tibetan. In Qinghai, as in Kalmykia, there have been conscious programs of language revival since the 1980s. In Xinjiang virtually all the Oirat Mongols speak their own language.

DISTINCTIVE FEATURES

The Persian historian RASHID-UD-DIN FAZL-ULLAH in 1304 already noted the distinctive Oirat dialect. As found today, Kalmyk-Oirat phonology combines both archaic and progressive features. Archaic features include intervocalic labials already lost in Mongolian by the 14th century, for example in *kümn*, "person" (cf. Mongolian *khün*), and *öwr*, "one's own" (cf. Mongolian *öör*). Kalmyk-Oirat also preserves the forward articulation of the rounded vowels (Kalmyk *uul*, "mountain," is actually pronounced similarly to Mongolian *üül*, "cloud") and the *k* before front vowels, as in *ken*, "who" (cf. standard Khalkha *khen*).

In progressive features, Kalmyk-Oirat shares with Khalkha the splitting of the *ch* and *j* into *ts/ch* and *z/j* depending on the following vowel, although Kalmyk-Oirat *z* is a fricative, unlike the affricate *dz* of Khalkha. It also forms the accusative in *-ig* (cf. Mongolian *-iig*, but Buriat *-iiye*). Kalmyk-Oirat is particularly progressive in its palatalization of back vowels and has turned all diphthongs into long front vowels. Palatalization is accompanied by a switching of vowel harmony. Thus, *mörn*, "horse," in Kalmyk is a front word, while its Mongolian cognate *morĭ* is a back. Finally, like the old dialects of the western part of the MONGOL EMPIRE and Mogholi, Kalmyk-Oirat flattens noninitial rounded vowels, so that *dolo'an*, "seven," for example, develops not into *doloon* (Mongolian, Buriat), but rather *dolan*.

In morphology as well Kalmyk-Oirat shows a combination of archaic and progressive features. The ancient comitative case *-lugha* is preserved as *lä* (cf. Mongolian *tai*), and the old preverbal negative particle *es* is still used. In verb conjugations, however, Kalmyk-Oirat, like Buriat, has developed new personal conjugations from postposed pronouns: *yowlaw*, "I went" (from *yowla*, "went" + *bi*, "I"), *irläwdn*, "we came" (from *irlä*, "came" + *bidn*, "we").

In vocabulary the Oirat dialects show significant divergences. Kalmyk has an obvious heavy influence from Russian, but also a number of Turkish and even Caucasian words as well, while Upper Mongolian in Qinghai has some distinctive Tibetan words. Many of common Mongolian words have distinctive Kalmyk-Oirat forms sometimes shared with Buriat. Mongolian legends of the 17th century described how the Kalmyk-Oirat word for fermented mare's milk, *chigän* (cf. Mongolian *airag; see* KOUMISS), was one imposed on the defeated Oirats by MANDUKHAI SECHEN KHATUN (fl. 1475–1501).

SCRIPTS

Until the 20th century Kalmyk-Oirat was written in Kalmykia, Xinjiang, and for some purposes in western Mongolia with the CLEAR SCRIPT, a modified version of the vertical UIGHUR-MONGOLIAN SCRIPT. The 1920s were a time of script reform throughout the Soviet Union. In 1925 the Kalmyks adopted a Cyrillic script, while the Turkic peoples adopted the Latin script. In 1930 Latinization was made general Soviet policy for the non-Russian peoples, and the Kalmyks adopted a Latin script. With the encouragement of Russian nationalism under Joseph Stalin, the Cyrillic script was reintroduced to the Kalmyks in 1938. With the exile in 1943, Kalmyk language spent 13 years underground. Only after the return to Kalmykia in 1957 was a slightly modified Cyrillic script reintroduced, one still in use today.

The 1925 script pioneered most of the features that were to distinguish Cyrillic Kalmyk from Cyrillic Buriat or Mongolian: elimination of short, noninitial vowels and representation of noninitial long vowels by a single vowel, replacement of etymological diphthongs by long front vowels, separate letters for *j, ä,* and *ng,* and use of the "half i" (й) for the consonant *y* (*see* BURIAT LANGUAGE AND SCRIPTS; CYRILLIC-SCRIPT MONGOLIAN). In 1928 the letters representing *ä, ö, ü, j,* and *ng* were altered, and a new letter was introduced to represent *gh*. The subsequent 1930 Latin script and the 1938 and 1957 Cyrillic scripts represented Kalmyk phonology in basically the same way, although the Cyrillic scripts varied in the letters used to represent the non-Russian sounds before settling on the present system. Since 1991 the clear script has again been taught in Kalmyk schools in Russia.

See also MONGOLIAN LANGUAGE; MONGOLIC LANGUAGE FAMILY.

Further reading: György Kara, *Early Kalmyk Primers and Other Schoolbooks: Samples from Textbooks 1925–1930* (Bloomington, Ind.: Mongolia Society, 1997).

Kalmyks (Kalmucks) The Kalmyks on the Volga form the westernmost body of Mongolian peoples and the only Mongolian or Buddhist people in Europe. The Kalmyks originated as a branch of the Oirat, or West Mongols, people around the ALTAI RANGE and the Zünghar (Junggar) basin. The OIRATS dominated Mongolia in the 15th century and were known by the Turks as Qalmaqs. This term spread in the form "Kalmyk" to the Russians, who used it for all the Oirats, including those settled in the Caspian steppe after 1630. In the late 19th century the Oirats in Russia, and they alone, adopted as their self-designation the term *Kalmyk* (*Khalimag* or *Khal'mg*). The term *Kalmyk* is thus best restricted to the Volga Oirats.

SETTLEMENT

When Astrakhan on the Volga fell to Russian conquest in 1554, the Nogay Turks (*see* MANGGHUD) occupied the Caspian steppe. In 1608 Oirats of the Khoshud tribe first raided the Nogays. In 1630 KHOO-ÖRLÖG and his sons of the Torghud tribe became the first Oirats to occupy the Caspian steppe, with about 22,000 households. Later, under Khoo-Örlög's sons Shikür-Daiching (1644–61) and Puntsog (1661–69), the Khoshud prince Köndölöng Ubashi (brother of GÜÜSHI KHAN) led 3,000 Khoshud households to the Caspian, followed later by his nephew Ablai and his people. In 1677 the Dörböd Prince Solom-Tseren led 4,000 households of the Dörböd tribe to the Caspian. Oirats continued to arrive from the east through the 1680s. Meanwhile, Torghud camps moved west, reaching the Volga around 1648 and crossing it by 1656. At first the many new arrivals fought among themselves, but Puntsog's son AYUUKI KHAN (1669–1724) welded these disparate elements into a single confederation, about 40,000 to 50,000 households strong. (*On political, military, and cultural life in this period, see* OIRATS.)

THE KALMYK KHANATE

In 1655 Shikür Daiching first swore an oath of allegiance to the czar. These oaths, given in Russian with only a rough translation into Oirat, did not make the Kalmyk rulers subjects, although the demand for hostages, conceded by Shikür Daiching two years later, was seen as particularly humiliating. Under Ayuuki Khan the Kalmyks received greater respect from the Russians as well as a supply of muskets and cannons. When cooperative, the Kalmyks proved extremely effective allies of the czar against nomadic enemies, whether Crimean Tatars, Nogays, Bashkirs, or rebellious Cossacks.

In 1718 Peter the Great (1682–1725) built a series of forts from the Don to the Volga at Tsaritsyn (modern Volgograd) and established Astrakhan as a new province (*guberniia*). With the new Russian control of the steppe, the governor of Astrakhan tried to impose his candidate for ruler on the Kalmyks. A compromise allowed Ayuuki's weak son, Tseren-Dondug (r. 1724–35), to be enthroned at the cost of an oath of allegiance, this time written in Oirat and imposed on all the nobility (*noyods*) and petty officials (*zaisangs*). Official pressure toward Christian conversion became strong. Only in 1735, when the Russian authorities dismissed Tseren-Dondug and enthroned his independent-minded but able nephew Dondug-Ombo (r. 1735–41), did internal peace return to the Kalmyks.

Under Dondug-Dashi (r. 1741–61), however, more subtle Russian political and socioeconomic pressure increased. Dondug-Dashi had to revise the 1640 MONGOL-OIRAT CODE to deal with the increasingly common cases involving Russians, Cossacks, Nogays, and other outsiders. Colonization along the Volga deprived the Kalmyk herds of their chief spring pastures. By 1744 10,000 Kalmyk households had lost all their herds, and 6,400 were employed in fisheries. As Russian frontiers moved farther away, the Kalmyks were pressured to commit more troops to far-off European campaigns, where there was little prospect of booty. Catherine the Great (1762–96) greatly increased the tempo of colonization, while instituting reforms to strip Dondug-Dashi's son viceroy Ubashi (r. 1762–71—he was not enthroned as khan) of his remaining real power and independence.

By 1771 viceroy Ubashi and the great Torghud nobles as well as the Khoshud princes descendants from Köndölong Ubashi fled east in an effort to reoccupy Zünghuria, now emptied by the Qing conquest (*see* FLIGHT OF THE KALMYKS). The warm winter kept the Volga from freezing, and 11,198 households, about one-fourth of the Kalmyks, were trapped on the western side, joined by a small number of households that deserted Ubashi and turned back.

IN IMPERIAL RUSSIA

With the emigration of the core of the Torghud and Khoshud nobility, the Dörböd princes became the Kalmyks' de facto spokesmen. Throughout the rest of 1771 the Russian authorities placed garrisons of loyal Kalmyk and Cossack guards among the Dörböd nobles (TAIJI, *noyod; see* NOYAN), who were suspected of wanting to follow the other Kalmyks. On October 19, as Tsebeg Ubashi (d. 1774), the senior Dörböd chief, and the remaining Torghud leaders were sent under detention to St. Petersburg, Empress Catherine abolished the position of Kalmyk khan, or viceroy, making all the *taijis* separately subject to the Astrakhan governor. Catherine implemented her plan to turn the old *zarghu* (council or court) into a semilegislative body, with the nobles electing *zaisangs* (officials) from the three tribes and one lama from the monasteries.

In 1786 Catherine's favorite, P. S. Potemkin, abolished the *zarghu* and in its place proposed a Kalmyk quartermaster's office chaired by a Russian. Subsequently, 4,880 Dörböds under Prince Ekrem Khapchukov (d. 1799) fled to the Don, becoming the "Greater" (*Iki*) Dörböds, as opposed to the "Lesser" (*Bagha*) Dörböds, who remained. The emperors Paul (1796–1801) and Alexander I (1801–25) reversed Catherine's assimilationist policies and revived the *zarghu*, albeit under the supervision of a Russian *pristav* (police commissioner). A Lesser Dörböd prince, Chüchei Tundutov, was made viceroy from 1801 to his death in 1803. The rivalry between the Lesser Dörböds and the Greater Dörböds, who migrated to the steppe around Lake Manych-Gudilo after 1800, proved intractable, however. In 1805 the *pristav* ordered the Dörböd households to choose their own lords: 3,302 chose Chüchei's son Prince Erdeni Tundutov, and only 609 chose Ekrem's brother, Ghabung-Sharab (d. 1809). Thus, the "Lesser" Dörböds now outnumbered the "Greater" Dörböds.

Alexander's policy of accommodation also extended to the Buzava Kalmyks of the Dörböd tribe, who had settled under Baakhan and Baatur *taiji*s near Cherkassk in 1699. In 1806 they were formally included within the Don Cossacks as three units (*ulus*) and 13 "hundreds" (*zun*; Russian, *sotnia*). From 1812 to 1814 three all-Kalmyk regiments, each about 500 strong, and 2,000 Buzava Kalmyks fought in the Russian army against Napoleon all the way to Paris. One regiment of baptized Kalmyks from Stavropol' lost half its men.

Russian officials frequently criticized the *zarghu* for keeping few records and deciding cases in the interests of the nobility. By 1821 the governor of Astrakhan had restricted its jurisdiction to civil cases of less than five rubles. In 1822, however, the new *pristav*, A. V. Kakhanov, convened at Zinzili an assembly of Kalmyk noblemen, lamas, and judges in the *zarghu* to revise the Mongol-Oirat Code. Under Kakhanov's supervision Erdeni Tundutov and Serbe-Jab Tümen (1774–1851), a Khoshud prince and veteran of the Napoleonic wars, drew up a revised code. Despite opposition from the Russian officials in Astrakhan and the Greater Dörböd ruler, Ochirai Zanjin Ubashi Khapchukov (d. 1834), the Zinzili decrees were promulgated by imperial decree in 1828.

In the latter half of the 19th century the Kalmyks of Astrakhan—Lesser Dörböds, KHOSHUDS, and TORGHUDS—remained overwhelmingly nomadic, although pasture shortages diminished the total head of livestock from 2.5 million in 1803 to 453,000. Herdless Kalmyks became hired herders for wealthier Kalmyks, grooms for wealthy Ukrainian or Russian farmers, or worked in the fisheries or salt industries. Under Alexander III (1881–94) the government specified the nomadic territories, giving each Kalmyk male 30 *desiatina*s (81 acres) to encourage cultivation. Kalmyks generally rented these plots to non-Kalmyk peasants. Armenian merchants who exploited the lack of competition to sell goods at grossly inflated prices dominated the Kalmyk steppe trade. The nobility, formed in Russian gymnasia (high schools) and imperial cavalry regiments, frequently adopted European lifestyles, including experimentation with agriculture and improved stock breeds. The Buzava Kalmyks moved into sedentary stock breeding and farming as their allotted land was

The Khoshud Khural, a Buddhist temple, was built to commemorate the Kalmyks who fought against Napoleon in the Russian army. *(Lithograph from the 1840s)*

gradually reduced from 100 *desiatina*s (270 acres) in 1846 to 10 *desiatina*s (27 acres) just before World War I. The Greater Dörböd *ulus*, which had been assigned to the new Stavropol' province (*guberniia*) in 1861, was also pushed into farming by heavier land pressure from immigrant farmers and Nogay Turks.

Dondug-Dashi's laws in the 1740s and the Zinzili decrees of 1822 prescribed punishments for commoners and petty officials who did not teach their sons the written language. Many *manji*s (young lamas; Mongolian, *bandi*) studied in the monasteries but then withdrew to take up family duties before taking higher degrees. Among the Buzava a two-year Buddhist parochial school was opened in 1838, but by 1890 only four such schools existed. Among the Volga Kalmyks, Russian authorities established in 1847 a system of six-year elementary schools and a two-year middle school in Astrakhan. The inclusion of compulsory Christian education, however, kept all but wards of the state out of these schools.

Lamas formed a major part of the population, among both the Volga and the Buzava Kalmyks. In 1800 the Greater Dörböds, for example, were counted at 7,795 laymen, 47 *zaisang*s (commoner officials), and 1,615 lamas. Only after 1798 did the Russian authorities permit the construction of Buddhist monasteries and temples. The Khoshud Khural (monastery; Russian, *khurul*) in Kharabalin district, built to commemorate the Kalmyk dead in the war against Napoleon, adapted Russian architecture for Buddhist purposes. Kalmyk Buddhist sculpture was crude, but *thangka* painting was relatively developed; neither departed from the Indo-Tibetan canons of religious portraiture. The monastic hierarchy among the Buzavas and the Astrakhan Kalmyks was headed by a *bagshi* (teacher/master) lama confirmed by the Russian authorities.

Despite their complete isolation from Tibet and their kinsfolk to the east from the 1740s onward, the Kalmyks maintained their Buddhist and Oirat literary traditions. The copying, preservation, and instruction in the more accessible Buddhist literature and sciences—scriptures, edifying tales, devotional poems, astrology, and medicine—occupied most of their attention, as the higher sciences were inaccessible due to the lack of teachers. Significant works include the *Dörbön Oyiradiyin tüüke* (History of the four Oirats), written by the Khoshud nobleman Baatur Ubashi Tümen from 1801 to 1820 as a continuation and updating of Ghabang-Sharab's 1737 *History of the Four Oirats*, and the anonymous *Khalimag khaadiyin tuuji* (History of the Kalmyk khans), covering the time from Khoo-Örlög to Ubashi's flight in 1771.

NATIONAL REVIVAL

The last decades of the 19th century saw the Kalmyks begin to aspire toward achievement in the wider Russian society. The legal privileges of the nobility were abolished in 1892, eliminating the remaining Astrakhan Kalmyk administrative autonomy. The government school system increased by 1914 to 31 schools attended by 679 pupils. Among the Buzava, whose material culture and economy were identical to their Cossack neighbors, an even more dramatic increase in the number of parochial schools for boys and, for the first time, for girls, occurred: from four in 1890 to 37 in 1915 (*see* NEW SCHOOLS MOVEMENTS). A small Kalmyk intelligentsia formed, composed especially of Russian-educated schoolteachers. Discontent focused on remaining restrictions on non-Russian education and the division of the Kalmyks under Astrakhan, Stavropol', and Don Cossack administration. The election of the princes Tseren David Tundutov of the Lesser Dörböds and S.-D. Tümen of the Khoshud to the Russian Duma in 1906 and 1907 affirmed the continuing influence of the nobility.

Connections with the rest of the Mongolian and Buddhist worlds were also revived. Kalmyks made regular pilgrimages to Khüriye (modern ULAANBAATAR) from 1880. The surreptitious pilgrimage of Baaza-Bagshi Menkejuev (monastic name Lubsang-Sharab, 1846–1903) to Tibet in 1891–94 and the visits by the Buriat lama AGWANG DORZHIEV revived the scholarly study of Buddhism. The 1916 didactic poem *Chiknä khujr* (Ornament

Kalmyk princess Ölzätä Tundutov (Lesser Dörböd), seated with her elbow on the table, and her entourage, 1892. Her husband was Tseren David Tundutov. *(Courtesy estate of G. J. Ramstedt and WSOY)*

of the ear) by Boowan Badma (1880–1917) showed the vitality of traditional Buddhist literary genres.

The 1905 revolution saw the first signs of Kalmyk political activism with the short-lived organization "Banner of the Kalmyk Populists" (*Khal'mg tangghchin tug*), active in 1907–08. The removal of restrictions on non-Russian education after 1905 promoted the further development of the new intelligentsia. With the overthrow of the czar in 1917, Kalmyk intellectuals and activists put forward conflicting demands either for merger with the Don Cossack host or for an ethnically based autonomy. From November 1917 Kalmyks in Astrakhan began the first Kalmyk weekly, *Öördiyin zanggi* (Oirat news), with a benediction (*yöräl*; see YÖRÖÖL AND MAGTAAL) by Boowan Badma and the folklorist Nomto Ochirov (d. 1960) on the masthead.

Only after the Bolshevik seizure of power in Astrakhan on February 7, 1918, did the Communists find any recruits among the Kalmyks. The succeeding civil war destroyed the Buzava Kalmyk community, the great majority of whom fought with the Cossacks for the Whites. With the victory of the Red Army early in 1920, numerous massacres of Kalmyk refugees occurred, and about 1,500 went into exile in Europe. The Buzava community, 32,283-strong in 1897, was reduced to 10,750 by 1920, and the Kalmyks as a whole dropped from 190,600 in 1897 to 133,500 in 1926. The Kalmyks remained an almost entirely rural population, with only 1.3 percent living in cities.

SOVIET RULE AND EXILE

With the establishment of Soviet rule throughout Kalmykia, the Kalmyk territory was organized into a Kalmyk Autonomous Region (*oblast'*) on November 4, 1920, with its capital in the neighboring city of Astrakhan. The borders were expanded to include the Greater Dörböd *ulus* near Lake Manych-Gudilo, and the remnants of the Buzava and other isolated Kalmyk bodies were moved into the Kalmyk region in 1922–25. Given the paucity of Kalmyk Communists—the first regional conference of the Communist Party opened only in February 1921—the few pre-1921 Kalmyk Red Army commanders and intellectuals such as Vasilii Alekseevich Khomutnikov (1890–1945) and Anton Amur-Sanan (1888–1940) were swiftly promoted. The Soviet army also rapidly organized a volunteer international unit under Kharti Badievich Kanukov (1883–1933) to accompany the Red Army into Mongolia in 1921–25. Not until 1927, however, were Kalmyks subjected to conscription.

The traditional CLEAR SCRIPT was replaced in 1925 by the Cyrillic script, as some Kalmyk intellectuals had proposed before the revolution. Schooling was established in the Kalmyk language through the fourth year, and programs were initiated for the elimination of the common diseases tuberculosis and syphilis. In 1927 the Kalmyk region's capital was moved from Astrakhan to ELISTA (Kalmyk, Elstä). A number of monasteries still operated,

and in 1925 Lubsang-Sharab Tepkin (b. 1875), who had spent 10 years in Tibet, was elected by the Kalmyk clergy as *shajin lama*.

Collectivization beginning in 1929, and the Stalinist purges inflicted great hardship on the Kalmyk people, despite the symbolic elevation of the Kalmyk Autonomous Region to the status of Autonomous Soviet Socialist Republic (ASSR) in October 1935. By 1937 the Kalmyks were completely sedentarized. From 1928 to 1935 resistance to collectivization caused the number of livestock to drop by about half, while the Kalmyk population itself showed basically no increase from 1926 to 1939. Kalmykia's percentage of Kalmyks dropped from 75.6 percent in 1926 to 48.6 percent in 1939. In 1930 the first of a series of waves of repression struck Buddhist monasteries. Lubsang-Sharab Tepkin was arrested in 1931, and the last monastery was closed down in 1939. Stalin's purges also carried away native Communists such as Amur-Sanan.

Despite the progress during the 1920s in building schools in the republic, Kalmyk educational rates remained poor. Only 25.9 persons per thousand had completed secondary education, a rate lower not only than the Russians' (81.4 per thousand), but also the BURIATS' (46.4). In 1926 only 12.2 percent of the Kalmyks were literate, and of them only one-quarter in Kalmyk rather than Russian. Literacy reached 59.2 percent in 1939, but the three greater or lesser script changes for Kalmyk from 1928 to 1938 made it likely that most were literate in Russian.

During WORLD WAR II Kalmyk soldiers formed the Soviet Red Army's 189th Kalmyk Cavalry Regiment and the 110th Kalmyk Detached Cavalry Division. As Soviet troops abandoned Kalmykia, bands of Kalmyk deserters began seizing control. In late 1942 German troops occupied Elista and other parts of Kalmykia. As in many other areas of the Soviet Union, they were welcomed by Kalmyk locals, often even Communist Party members, as liberators from the Soviet regime. Exiles such as Prince N. Tundutov encouraged support for the Germans. When the Germans evacuated Kalmykia in January 1943, more than 3,000 Kalmyks in the Kalmyk Cavalry Corps followed them, fighting rear-guard actions against the Soviet Red Army from Kalmykia to Poland. Others worked as manual laborers. About 250 of these displaced Kalmyks survived the war and joined the surviving prewar exiles in France and the United States.

In Kalmykia, sporadic attacks on the returned Soviet authorities continued through the summer of 1943. Heeding accusations from the local Russian party cadres that the Kalmyks were hereditarily disloyal to the regime, the Soviet government on December 27, 1943, abolished the Kalmyk ASSR, and in a military operation lasting four days exiled the entire Kalmyk civilian population to Western and Central Siberia, Central Asia, and Sakhalin Island. The many thousands of Kalmyk soldiers in the

Red Army were demoted to labor battalions until the end of the war, when they were demobilized to join their families in exile.

Housing, when they arrived, was often nonexistent and food rations not paid, while the climate and work were completely unfamiliar. An estimated 16,017 Kalmyks perished directly in the deportation and aftermath, and the total population decreased from 134,400 in 1939 to 106,000 in 1959. All cultural monuments of the Kalmyk people, with the sole exception of the Khoshud Khural, with its Russian patriotic theme, were razed, and the Kalmyks were expunged from the Soviet public consciousness.

During the exile, Kalmyks were restricted to special settlements (*spetsposelenie*). Under the regulations for perpetual exile formalized in 1948, these special settlers had to register once a month with the security police and could not travel more than three kilometers from their place of residence without prior permission. Roadblocks around the settlements checked for violators.

At first special settlers lived in tents as apartments were built. Work was limited to manual labor; Kalmyks in Siberia worked in fisheries and logging. Schooling was only slowly provided and in Russian only. Virtually no Kalmyks received any higher education before the relaxation of the special regime in 1953, and few even then.

REHABILITATION AND REVIVAL

As part of de-Stalinization, the system of special registration was relaxed in 1955. On January 7, 1957 the exile of the Kalmyks was revoked, and the Kalmyk Autonomous Region was restored within most of its previous frontiers. The exiles were not allowed to claim lost property, however, and temporarily had to be housed in tents and barracks until new housing was built. The next year Kalmykia was again made an ASSR. Since their return, the Kalmyks have grown to be 45 percent of Kalmykia's population. During the postexile period the Kalmyks for the first time in the 20th century entered a period of relatively normal demographic and economic growth, with the population of Kalmyks reaching 174,000 in 1989. The restored Kalmyk population was much more urban than before the exile, with more than 20 percent living in cities. The Kalmyks are one of Russia's few minorities that are not distinctively rural in population. By 1970 44.3 percent of Kalmyks lived in towns of more than 15,000, higher than the percentage of Kalmyks in the republic as a whole.

Despite the rehabilitation, a shamed and frightened silence precluded discussion of the 13-year exile both in public and, for many, in private as well. Kalmyk identity focused on events in a Russian patriotic narrative: the first oaths of allegiance to the czar in 1659, the Kalmyk participation in Russia's defense against Napoleon, Pushkin's verses on the Kalmyks, and Lenin's Kalmyk grandmother. Interest in Kalmyk culture and folklore focused particularly on the JANGGHAR epic rather than the more controversial Buddhist past. Not surprisingly after the exile, the Kalmyks had relatively low educational achievement (29.8 percent with higher or secondary education, compared to 50.8 percent for Russians and 42.7 percent for Buriats) and a mediocre representation in skilled professions (92 of 1,000 Kalmyks, compared to 135 for Russians and 157 for Buriats, 1970 figures). Even so, modern Kalmyk literature, which had developed on Russian models since the 1920s, achieved maturity in the distinguished poems of David Kugul'tinov (in Kalmyk, Kögltin Dawa, b. 1922), well known in Russia, Mongolia, and other countries.

In the late 1980s pluralism and glasnost' (openness) began in Kalmykia as in other non-Russian areas of the Soviet Union in protests over environmental policy. Concern about destruction of pasture lands led to public demonstrations against the Volga-Chograi canal project, which was canceled in spring 1989. The transfer of AIDS to 75 children and 16 adults in a children's hospital in Elista, Russia's only mass outbreak of AIDS, focused attention on the often dangerously low quality of public services. Films and literary works publicly raised the issue of the scars of deportation and exile. Increased contact with the outside world also raised national consciousness. In August 1990 Kalmyk delegations from the United States and France visited Kalmykia for the first time, and since then contacts with the Kalmyk diaspora have become regular. The visit in August 1991 of the Dalai Lama and the Telo Tulku Rinpoche, an INCARNATE LAMA found among the American Kalmyks, gave vital impetus to the revival of Buddhism, which had begun locally in 1990. The suppressed claims for recognition of the exile period were finally met with Moscow's decree that victims could seek financial compensation and with the construction of a vast monument to the repressed near Elista.

Nationality classes in the Kalmyk language have been restored since 1991, and the clear script is also taught as a topic. Connections have been restored with the Oirats of Xinjiang. The Kalmyk Republic treats both Kalmyk Buddhism and Russian Orthodoxy as state religions. The theory of "enlargement of didactic units" for math education, developed by the Kalmyk professor of pedagogy Purvä M. Erdniev, is officially encouraged as a Kalmyk contribution to educational science. The annual summer festival, "Jangghariad," with ARCHERY, javelin-throwing, WRESTLING, and HORSE RACING on a 35-kilometer (21 mile) course has been revived.

Politically, the weakening of central control led the Kalmyk ASSR on October 18, 1990, to a symbolic declaration of sovereignty. With the breakup of the Soviet Union and the fall of Communist Party rule, Kalmykia was proclaimed the KALMYK REPUBLIC, or *Khal'mg tangghch* (Kalmyk Nation), on February 20, 1992, but genuine secession from Russia was never seriously contemplated. In 1994 the so-called Steppe Code renounced secession and recognized Kalmykia's integration within Russia. After several delays a charismatic nonparty Kalmyk millionaire and CHESS enthusiast of Buzava background, Kirsan N. Ilümzhinov (Iliumzhinov, Ilyumzhinov, b. 1962), won election as president of the new republic on April 11, 1993. Ilümzhinov's model of a new corporatist state was at first wildly popular with the Kalmyks despite charges in Russian liberal newspapers of gross corruption and intimidation of the press. Since 1999, however, significant opposition has emerged.

See also CLOTHING AND DRESS; DAMBIJANTSAN; DANCE; EPICS; JEWELRY; KALMYK-OIRAT LANGUAGE AND SCRIPTS; MUSIC; RELIGION; WEDDINGS; WHITE MONTH; YURTS.

Further reading: Fred Adelman, "Kalmyk Cultural Renewal" (Ph.D. diss., University of Pennsylvania, 1960); Sandji Balykov, *A Maiden's Honor: A Tale of Kalmyk History and Society,* trans. David Chavchavadze (Bloomington, Ind.: Mongolia Society, 1990); Sandji Balykov, *Stronger than Power: A Collection of Short Stories,* trans. David Chavchavadze (Bloomington, Ind.: Mongolia Society, 1990); Arash Bormanshinov, "Who Were the Buzâva?" *Mongolian Studies* 10 (1986–87): 59–87; Stephen A. Halkovic, Jr., *Mongols of the West* (Bloomington: Indiana University, 1985); Hans S. Kaarsberg, *Among the Kalmyks of the Steppe,* trans. John R. Krueger (Bloomington, Ind.: Mongolia Society, 1996); Michael Khodarkovsky, *Where Two Worlds Met: The Russian State and the Kalmyk Nomads, 1600–1771* (Ithaca, N.Y.: Cornell University Press, 1992); Aleksandr M. Nekrich, *The Punished Peoples,* trans. George Saunders (New York: W. W. Norton, 1978); Paula Rubel, *Kalmyk Mongols: A Study in Continuity and Change* (Bloomington: Indiana University, 1967); N. L. Zhukovskaia, "Republic of Kalmykia: A Painful Path of National Renewal," *Russian Social Science Review* 34 (1993): 80–96.

Kangyur *See* BKA'-'GYUR AND BSTAN-'GYUR.

Kanjur *See* BKA'-'GYUR AND BSTAN-'GYUR.

Kara Balgassun *See* ORDU-BALIGH.

Kara Khitay *See* QARA-KHITAI.

Kashmir Kashmir was repeatedly ravaged by Mongol armies, but Kashmiri Buddhist monks received a rich welcome at the courts of the Mongol khans. While the sultanate of Delhi ruled northern India (Hindustan to Islamic writers), the vale of Kashmir in the Himalayas, with its capital at Srinagar, was the only major Hindu-Buddhist kingdom in northern India. Sometime after 1235 Huqutur, a *tümen* (10,000) commander based in Qonduz (Afghanistan), invaded Kashmir, stationing a Mongol DARUGHACHI (overseer) there for several years. Around the same time, a Kashmiri Buddhist master the Mongols called Otochi (physician) and his brother Namo arrived at the court of ÖGEDEI KHAN (1229–41). GÜYÜG Khan (1246–49) employed Otochi as a court physician, while MÖNGKE KHAN (1251–59) made Namo chief of all Buddhist monks.

By that time the Kashmiris had revolted, and Möngke appointed Sali of the TATARS to replace the deceased Huqutur, sending Otochi as envoy and *darughachi* to Kashmir. The Kashmiri king killed Otochi when he entered Srinagar; Sali invaded again, killing the king and deporting vast numbers of captives for himself and for HÜLE'Ü (1256–65), the Mongol ruler in Iran. In 1273 the new Kashmiri king Lakshmanadeva consented to dual investiture by the Il-Khan in the Middle East and the great khan in East Asia. Kashmiri *baqshis*, or Buddhist masters, received warm welcomes among the Mongol rulers in Iran and China. While Sali and his descendants paid allegiance to Hüle'ü, the QARA'UNAS of Afghanistan, as independent freebooters, were friendly to the less orderly CHAGHATAY KHANATE of Central Asia. In 1320 a Qara'una Mongol named Dulucha, based in Kandahar, invaded with 60,000 men and demanded tax and tribute. Although the Kashmiri king, Suhadeva (1300–20), paid the tax, Dulucha plundered the kingdom and enslaved vast numbers of men. The Tibetan Rinchana (Rin-chen) invaded the weakened kingdom that same year and, having converted to Islam, began the Islamization of Kashmir.

See also BUDDHISM IN THE MONGOL EMPIRE; INDIA AND THE MONGOLS.

Further reading: Karl Jahn, "A Note on Kashmir and the Mongols," *Central Asiatic Journal* 2 (1956): 176–180.

Kazakhs While Muslim and Turkic speaking, the Kazakhs emerged as a people from the breakup of the MONGOL EMPIRE and have been in constant contact, both warlike and peaceful, with Oirats and Khalkha Mongols. Today they form Mongolia's largest non-Mongol minority.

ORIGINS

The Kazakh aristocracy reckons its descent from Toqa-Temür, the 13th son of CHINGGIS KHAN's son JOCHI (d. 1225?). The descendants of Toqa-Temür seized power over the BLUE HORDE in modern Kazakhstan under Urus Khan (d. 1377) but were driven east by the Uzbeks (Özbegs) under the rival Shibanid line in the mid-15th century. Urus Khan's descendants became *qazaqs*, "freebooters," around the modern Xinjiang-Kazakhstan border. (Kazakh is simply the Russian pronunciation of *qazaq*, a term that also gave rise to the designation Cossack.) Under Qasim Khan (d. 1523) the Kazakhs rose to power again and eventually drove both the Uzbeks and the rulers of MOGHULISTAN south to the oasis cities of Mawarannahr (Transoxiana) and the Tarim Basin.

Kazakh tribal and CLAN NAMES show their mixed origins. JALAYIR, Qunghrat, Manghit, Dughlat (Dogholad) and, of course, Chinggisid Qiyat clan names are of Mongolian origin (*see* BORJIGID, MANGGHUD, QONGGIRAD). The Nayman, Kerey, Qara-Qitay, Tangut, and Arghin (Arghun) clans are descended from conquered steppe peoples of the MONGOLIAN PLATEAU subjugated by the Mongols and brought west with the Mongol conquest (*see* KEREYID, NAIMAN, ÖNGGÜD, QARA-KHITAI, and XIA DYNASTY). QAR-LUQS, QIPCHAQS, and Qanglis were the native Turkish tribes of the area. Other tribal names are of obscure origin. The Kazakh language is a dialect of Common Turkish and shares with Tatar, Baskir (Bashkurt), and other Turkish languages of the Qipchaq family the change of initial *y-* to *j-* or *zh-* (thus *zheti,* "seven," and *zhīl,* "year," not *yeti* or *yīl*).

WARS WITH THE OIRATS

From their emergence in the 15th century the Kazakhs faced the OIRATS (whom they, like all Turkish peoples, called KALMYKS) on their eastern frontier. During the 16th century the Kazakhs pushed the Oirats north toward southern Siberia, but in the 17th century the Oirats conquered Züngharia (Junggar Basin) and the Ili Valley and attacked the Kazakhs. Under TSEWANG RABTAN KHUNG-TAIJI (b. 1663, r. 1694–1727) and Galdan-Tseren (r. 1727–45) the Oirats' Zünghar principality smashed the Kazakh confederation and drove the Kazakhs north and west in what was long remembered in Kazakh folklore as the "Barefoot Flight" (*Aqtaban Shubirindi*). By this time the Kazakhs were divided into three *zhüz* (100s, called "hordes" in Russian): the Great (Ulu) Zhüz in eastern and southeastern Kazakhstan, the Middle (Orta) Zhüz in central, northern, and southern Kazakhstan, and the Lesser (Kishi) Zhüz in western Kazakhstan.

The wars with the Oirats left a strong impression on the Kazakhs, Kyrgyz, and other Islamic peoples of the Inner Asian steppes. The Kazakhs had become Muslim in the 14th century, and after the Oirats converted to a peculiarly militant form of Tibetan-rite Buddhism around 1580–1615, their conflict became not just a struggle for livestock, territory, and honor but also on both sides a religious war against unbelievers. In Kazakh and Kyrgyz epics the hero's enemy is always a Kalmyk (i.e., Oirat).

EXPANSION EAST

As the Manchu QING DYNASTY (1636–1912) destroyed the crumbling Zünghar principality in 1752–59, Kazakhs migrated westward to occupy Oirat lands. The Ili Valley was settled by the Great Zhüz and the Zünghar (Junggar) Basin by the Kerey, Nayman, and Waq tribes of Middle Zhüz. The Qing dynasty granted the Kazakhs in Xinjiang titles as *teizhi* (from Mongolian *TAIJI*) and collected tribute from them. As Russia subdued and settled Kazakhstan from 1730 to 1864, more Kazakhs migrated into the less crowded Xinjiang pastures. The Kazakhs, having greater mobility, better weapons, and better Russian-language skills than did the XINJIANG MONGOLS, dominated border trading and smuggling.

By 1862 Kerey Kazakhs of the Middle Zhüz first appeared in western Mongolia's Khowd frontier. The Qing court granted them provisional recognition there in 1882. Legal disputes continued as the Kazakh population advanced at the expense of the indigenous ALTAI URIYANGKHAI.

During the 20th century Kazakhs began moving into pastures in Barköl, Gansu, and even Qinghai on the Tibetan plateau. The Kazakhs generally kept the upper hand in frequent clashes with the original Oirat Mongolian inhabitants. In 1949 the new Chinese Communist administration began fixing separate settlements for the Kazakhs and the Mongol nomads. The Kazakhs' higher birthrate continues to increase their share of the population even in Mongol autonomous units.

KAZAKHS OF MONGOLIA

In July 1912 a Kerey Kazakh leader, Sükirbay, on behalf of 400 families requested that the Kazakhs be allowed to stay in newly independent Mongolia. This request was granted and land set aside for a Kazakh banner in modern BAYAN-ÖLGII PROVINCE. Other Kazakh bands, however, continued to ignore the border between Mongolia and Xinjiang, now under the Republic of China, roughly defined in 1913. Even the recognized Kazakhs had tense relations with the local western Mongols, who accused them of horse theft and raiding.

After Mongolia's 1921 REVOLUTION the Kazakhs were organized into two banners. In 1940 Mongolia's maximum leader, MARSHAL CHOIBALSANG, (r. 1936–52), after visiting KHOWD PROVINCE, created a new province, Bayan-Ölgii, in predominantly Kazakh areas. The provincial administrative council consisted of seven members, five Kazakh and two Altai Uriyangkhai. The new province facilitated Mongolia's interventions as a Soviet proxy among northern Xinjiang's Kazakhs from 1942 to 1946. Kazakhs also form the majority in Khowd Sum just north of KHOWD CITY.

In the postwar period the population of Kazakhs in Mongolia rose from 36,700 (4.3 percent in 1956 to 120,500 (5.9 percent) in 1989. Kazakh (in the Cyrillic script) was used in all grades of general schooling and for some official purposes in Bayan-Ölgii as well. Distinguished Kazakhs in Mongolia included the Kazakh-language poet B. Aqtan (1897–1976), the Turcologist B. Bazylhan (b. 1932), and the union leader and political reformer Q. Zardyhan (b. 1940). Kazakhs were also recruited for the coal mines of Nalaikh (near ULAAN-BAATAR). Compared to the overall population, Kazakhs in 1989 were slightly overrepresented in both white-collar and working-class positions; collective herders were only 26.4 percent of the nationality's population. Mongolia's Kazakh nomads are famous, however, for their custom of FALCONRY with golden eagles.

In 1991, during the disintegration of the Soviet bloc, Bayan-Ölgii's unemployment rate hit 18.9 percent, and large numbers of Mongolian Kazakhs responded to the newly independent Kazakhstan's call for migration back to the homeland. The population of Bayan-Ölgii dropped from 101,000 in 1991 to 75,700 by 1993. By 2001 Kazakhstan figures showed 63,900 Mongolian Kazakhs had crossed the border from Mongolia at least once, and 5,000 had become Kazakhstan citizens. The Mongolian Kazakhs, however, generally did not fit well into Kazakhstan's sedentary and Russified lifestyle. Large numbers eventually returned to Bayan-Ölgii, whose population had rebounded to 94,600 by 2000. Grade school education in Bayan-Ölgii continues to be conducted in Kazakh, with most textbooks supplied from Kazakhstan.

See also BOROTALA MONGOL AUTONOMOUS PREFECTURE; HAIXI MONGOL AND TIBETAN AUTONOMOUS PREFECTURE; KHOBOGSAIR MONGOL AUTONOMOUS COUNTY; SUBEI MONGOL AUTONOMOUS COUNTY; XINJIANG MONGOLS.

Further reading: Uradyn Erden Bulag, "Dark Quadrangle in Central Asia: Empires, Ethnogenesis, Scholars, and Nation-States," *Central Asian Survey* 13 (1994): 459–478.

Ked-Buqa (Kitbuqa, Ketbugha) (d. 1260) *Commander of the Mongol forces at the Battle of 'Ain Jalut*

A court *ba'urchi* (steward) of the NAIMAN tribe, Ked-Buqa was dispatched to conquer Girdkuh and the other fortresses of the "Assassins," or ISMA'ILIS, in Quhistan (eastern Iran) in 1252. Ked-Buqa and 5,000 men assaulted several fortresses from May 1253 to November 1254 and put Girdkuh under siege but were unable to achieve decisive success.

In May 1256, with the arrival of a much larger force under HÜLE'Ü (r. 1256–65), Ked-Buqa ravaged the Isma'ili city of Tun (between Qayen and Tabas) before commanding the left wing of Hüle'ü's successful advance on the Isma'ili heartland in the Elburz Mountains (September–November 1256). In Hüle'ü's campaign against Baghdad (1257–58) he also commanded the left, sacking citadels in Luristan and Khuzistan before converging on Baghdad.

In Hüle'ü's invasion of Syria, Ked-Buqa served as the vanguard, with 10,000 Mongols and 500 Georgian and Armenian auxiliaries, taking Damascus's surrender (February 14, 1260) and subduing citadels in Lebanon and Jordan. As a Christian, he supported local Christian interests. Ked-Buqa met the advance of Qutuz, the sultan of MAMLUK EGYPT (1259–60), at 'Ain Jalut (near modern Bayshan, September 3, 1260). Refusing to retreat before Qutuz's much larger army, Ked-Buqa was captured and executed, and Qutuz captured his family in Lebanon. Admiring Ked-Buqa's defiance, Hüle'ü rewarded his surviving relatives richly.

See also 'AIN JALUT, BATTLE OF.

Kelüren *See* KHERLEN RIVER.

Kentei *See* KHENTII PROVINCE.

Kerait *See* KEREYID.

Kereyid (Kerait, Kereit) This khanate in central Mongolia was a major power in Mongolia during the time of CHINGGIS KHAN. The territory of the Kereyid was centered on the Black Forest of the TUUL RIVER. To the west lay the NAIMAN, to the north lay the MERKID along the SELENGE RIVER, and to the east and northeast lay the MONGOL TRIBE. To the south it bordered on the GOBI DESERT, beyond which was the Tangut XIA DYNASTY in Northwest China and the Jurchen JIN DYNASTY in North China.

EARLY HISTORY OF THE KEREYID

The Kereyid tribe seems to have originated as a branch of the Tatar tribe. Later Chinese editors called those TATARS nomadizing in the later Kereyid territory Zubu; the origin of this term is obscure. In 924 Abaoji, founder of the Kitan's Liao dynasty in North China, defeated the Zubu and made them tributary. The KITANS established many forts in cities in what was later the heartland of the Kereyid khanate, but the Zubu/Tatars continued to raid Kitan territory.

From 1189 to 1100 Chinese records speak of a Zubu chieftain, Mogusi, who united the tribes and attempted to throw off Kitan power, but whom the Kitans eventually defeated, captured, and executed. In 1125, however, the Kitans themselves were overthrown by the Jurchen, who founded the Jin dynasty, and the Zubu or Kereyid recovered their independence and the territory once occupied by the Kitans.

"Mogusi" is undoubtedly the same figure known as the Kereyid's Marqus-Buyruq Khan in RASHID-UD-DIN's FAZL-ULLAH's history, who adds that his wife avenged herself on the Tatar tribesmen who had assisted the Kitan generals. Marqus's line thus survived the Kitan attacks, and Marqus's descendant Qurjaqus-Buyruq Khan, built a powerful khanate despite wars with the Merkid and the Tatars (a term from then on applied solely to tribesmen allied with the Jin in northeast Inner Mongolia).

The language of the Kereyid, as of their Zubu/Tatar predecessors, is unclear. There are many Turkic names and titles among the Kereyid (as there are among the Mongols proper), but the historical record does not suggest a sharp language gap between the Mongols and the Kereyid, and most historians have concluded that the Kereyid court was either bilingual or predominantly Mongol speaking. Certainly after their conquest the Kereyid were treated as part of the larger Mongol people.

The Kereyid were wealthier and more advanced in political organization than the Merkid and the Mongols.

The Kereyid khan's court was a sumptuous gold palace-tent (ORDO) with golden vessels and a special staff. Kereyid princesses received dowries of up to 200 servants. The khan also had crack forces of ba'aturs, "heroes," and a 1,000-man day guard, institutions Chinggis Khan would later imitate. Finally, although many of the Kereyid were still tribally organized, already some of the Kereyid bore as their only clan name albatu, "subjects," which indicates break-down of the clan system. There is, however, no definite evidence of writing at the Kereyid court.

The ruling family of the Kereyid adhered to Christianity of the Syriac-rite Church of the East (known as Nestorians). Syriac historians record the conversion of a Kereyid king in 1007, who, having lost his way, was rescued by a vision of St. Sergius after agreeing to convert. After inquiring of Christian merchants (probably UIGHURS), the Kereyid king sent for the bishop of Merv (Mary) and was baptized. While some have doubted whether the word "Kereyid" is an interpollation in the accounts, Marqus and Qurjaqus were certainly Christians; their names (from "Marcus" and "Cyriacus") are sufficient proof of that. Moreover, Kereyid princesses formed the main Christian influence on the Mongol royal family.

The Christian conversion also highlights the importance of international contacts for the Kereyid. Turkestani merchants were regular guests at the Kereyid court. Also regular guests were envoys from the Jin dynasty of North China. Diplomatically, the Kereyid were hostile to their eastern neighbors, the Naiman khanate, the Merkid tribe to the north, and the Tatars in the east. Against the Naiman, they allied with the QARA-KHITAI Empire in Turkestan and the Tangut XIA DYNASTY in northwest China.

THE KEREYID AND CHINGGIS KHAN

After the death of Qurjaqus-Buyruq Khan, the Kereyid khanate declined. Qurjaqus-Buyruq had given his sons, numbering 40 by some accounts, their own appanages. The result was repeated conflict. The eldest son, Toghril, faced serious opposition after killing several of his brothers, yet with the aid of YISÜGEI BA'ATUR, a Mongol chieftain and the father of Chinggis Khan, Toghril Khan secured his throne and preserved Kereyid unity and power. The price, however, was deep-seated opposition even within his own court.

Years after the death of Yisügei Ba'atur, Toghril Khan sponsored Yisügei's son Temüjin (later Chinggis Khan) as khan of the Mongols. Together the two pursued assaults on their traditional enemies: Tatars to the east, Merkid to the north, and Naiman to the east. Chinggis Khan also helped Toghril regain the throne after another outbreak of fraternal hostility. In one attack on the Tatars in 1196, Toghril and Chinggis Khan had joined a Jin dynasty expedition, and the Jin granted Toghril the title ONG (Prince) KHAN. Over the next few years, as Chinggis Khan grew in power, Ong Khan's son Ilqa Senggüm grew increasingly jealous of his influence. When Chinggis Khan requested that the families become QUDA, or marriage allies, Ilqa Senggüm fashioned a plan to decoy Chinggis's Khan's Mongols and destroy them. Although the plan was revealed to Chinggis Khan, the Kereyid and their allies in the MONGOL TRIBE were victorious at the Battle of Qalaqaljid Sands in spring 1203.

Ong Khan's triumph was only temporary, however, as his anti-Chinggis Mongol allies caused turmoil that summer. In autumn 1203 Chinggis Khan decoyed the Kereyid with a bogus message that his brother was deserting to them. In the ensuing Battle of Jeje'er Heights, the Kereyid were defeated and conquered. Ong Khan fled west, abandoned by his men, where he was killed by Naiman frontier guards. Ilqa Senggüm fled south with his men to the Tangut Xia dynasty but later revolted and escaped west to Turkistan, where the chief of Kucha (Kuqa) city executed him.

THE KEREYID IN THE MONGOL EMPIRE

After their defeat the Kereyid became subjects of the Mongols, and Chinggis Khan took over the golden palace-tent of Ong Khan. At first Ong Khan's younger brother Ja'a-Gambu supported Chinggis Khan, and his people were preserved from pillaging, but within a year he had revolted and took his people to join the Naiman. With their defeat in 1204 Ja'a-Gambu's people were divided.

Chinggis Khan took many of the Kereyid princesses for himself and his sons, and through them Kereyid manners and beliefs, particularly Syriac-rite Christianity, entered the Mongol ruling class. SORQAQTANI BEKI, daughter of Ja'a-Gambu and mother of MÖNGKE KHAN, and TOGHUS KHATUN, Ong Khan's granddaughter and the principal wife of HÜLE'Ü Khan, were only two of the more famous of these Kereyid queens. Kereyid men also played a role in the empire, mostly as scribes and civil officials. CHINQAI and Bulghai, chief scribes under ÖGEDEI KHAN and Möngke Khan, had Kereyid connections. Under the Mongols' YUAN DYNASTY the Kereyid were included within the ranks of the Mongols and thus received preferential treatment.

While the Kereyid soon disappeared as a corporate body in the MONGOL EMPIRE, scattered Kereyid descendants are found widely. The Kereyid clan name is found among the ORDOS and Baarin Mongols of Inner Mongolia as well as among the KHALKHA of northern Mongolia. Under the form "Kerey" it is also found as a major tribe of the Middle Horde of the Kazakhs. The nobility of the TORGHUDS, a tribe of the OIRATS, traditionally traced their ancestry to Ong Khan as well. While this claim is most likely legendary, the very name Torghud means "day-guards," and the Torghuds may well be descendants of the Kereyid imperial guard.

Further reading: Erica C. D. Hunter, "The Conversion of the Kerait to Christianity in A.D. 1007," *Zentralasiatische Studien* 22 (1989/1991): 142–163; Isenbike Togan, *Flexibility and Limitation in Steppe Formations: The Kerait Khanate and Chinggis Khan* (Leiden: E. J. Brill, 1998).

Ke'rqin *See* KHORCHIN.

Kerülen *See* KHERLEN RIVER.

keshig (*kezig, keshik*) The *keshig* (from Turkish *kezig,* shifts, rotations) was not just the imperial guard of the MONGOL EMPIRE and its successor states, but also a forum for inculcating Mongol values in the hostages taken from tributary chiefs and officials. The earliest analogue of the Mongol *keshig,* or imperial guard, lies in the ORDO system of the Inner Mongolian KITANS. Under the Kitan Liao dynasty (907–1125) each emperor had a separate *ordo,* or camp, with a "heart and belly guard" of 10,000 to 20,000 households assembled from the ruling Kitans as well as Chinese and other peoples. The members of this guard, particularly the non-Kitans, were the emperor's private slaves, but their proximity to him gave them high status. After the emperor's death they guarded his mausoleum while his successor recruited a new *ordo* and guard. While the Liao system was not followed by the succeeding JIN DYNASTY (1115–1234), the 12th-century KEREYID Khanate on the Mongolian plateau possessed a 1,000-man body of day guards (*turghaq*) and presumably a corresponding number of sentries, or night guards. As the little-known Kereyid institution supplied the immediate predecessor of the Mongol *keshig,* and the Mongol *keshig* closely resembled the Liao *ordo* system, it is likely the Kereyid guard was modeled on that of the Liao.

Immediately after CHINGGIS KHAN's conquest of the Kereyid in 1203, he created a guard (*keshig*) of 80 sentries, or night guards (*kebte'ül*) and 70 day guards (*turghaq*) and a force of 1,000 *ba'atur*s, or "heroes," to serve in battle as a crack vanguard and in peace as day guards. After Chinggis Khan's coronation in 1206 the *keshig* expanded to a total of 10,000. The night guards grew to 1,000, the quiver bearers to 1,000, and the day guards to 7,000, while the vanguard *ba'atur*s remained at 1,000. Captains of 100s and 1,000s were expected to send two relatives each, together with five to 10 retainers and mounts, to serve as *keshigten* (members of the *keshig*). Chinggis Khan also encouraged likely volunteers from the captains of 10 and ordinary soldiers; they were allowed three retainers.

The *keshig* was merged with the household establishment of Chinggis's *ordo,* or palace-tent, whose staff the night guards supervised. The day guards, including cooks (*ba'urchi*), doorkeepers (*e'üdenchi*), and grooms (*aqtachi*), performed their tasks during the day under the supervision of stewards (*cherbi*). At night the night guards lay beside the tent of the khan and took turns standing sentry at the door. During the day the elite night guards also supervised the preparation and serving of food and wine for the khan and the care of the tent carts. Night guards never left the presence of the khan they were serving and also assisted the "great judges" (*yeke* JARGHUCHI) in resolving lawsuits. When nomadizing, the night guards camped around the center, while the *ba'atur*s held in the front and the day guards and quiver bearers held the right and left. The entire *keshig* was divided into four companies, each of which served three-day shifts under four shift commanders.

The *keshig* guarded the emperor from the dangers of assassination and poisoning and during war served as the heavily armed great center (*ghool*) of the army. Commanders in the *keshig* were senior to those commanding equivalent units in the outer armies, yet members of the *keshig* were also, paradoxically, hostages. The younger brothers and sons of the higher commanders served as guarantors of the good behavior of their fathers and brothers. From the beginning Chinggis Khan insisted that foreign rulers desiring to submit send sons or younger brothers to be enrolled as *keshigten*. After long service these hostages often became loyal supporters of the Mongol imperial cause. Many Mongol commanders, such as SÜBE'ETEI BA'ATUR, CHORMAQAN, and BAIJU, first served in the *keshig* before commanding separate armies.

Since the *kesig* was Chinggis Khan's personal appanage or property (*emchü*), his sons did not inherit it. Instead, the old *keshigten* continued to serve at the deceased emperor's palace-tent (*ordo*) while the new emperor recruited a new *keshig* from among his own appanage and/or foreign subjects. ÖGEDEI KHAN (1229–41), for example, recruited many *keshigten* from Korea. In practice, later emperors more often than not "recycled" old *keshigs*. GÜYÜG Khan (1246–48), for example, took half of Ögedei Khan's *keshig* for himself.

The reforms of QUBILAI KHAN (1260–94), founder of the Mongol YUAN DYNASTY in China, restricted the functions of the *keshig*. A new imperial bodyguard (Chinese, *shiwei qinjun*), at first entirely Han (North Chinese) in composition but later strengthened with Qipchaq, Ossetian, and Russian units, replaced the *keshig* as the emperor's military bulwark. Qubilai did not recruit his own full-scale *keshig* until 1263. However, once organized, the *keshig* handled the imperial board and entertainments, and its political importance was undiminished. Qubilai put three of the four shifts of the *keshig* under clan descendants of three of Chinggis's "four steeds" (Boroghul's Üüshin clan, BO'ORCHU's Arulad, and MUQALI's JALAYIR) and showed great favor to these families. The senior grand councillor (*chengxiang/chingsang*) usually supervised the fourth shift, nominally the emperor's personal shift. Hostages from among Chinese officials served in the *keshig,* and *keshigten* were preferred as judges. All four shift heads signed the decrees (JARLIQ) of the emperor. Unlike the non-Mongol imperial bodyguards, which in 1323 and 1328–29 overthrew reigning emperors, the Yuan emperors could rely on their personal *keshig*, but the financial cost was high. *Keshigs* expanded to sometimes 15,000 men, and from 1292 they all received rations and a stipend. In 1329 a one-time gift to the *keshig* members is estimated to have expended one-ninth of total government revenues. To reduce the cost, in 1331 the *keshigs* of several deceased emperors were reduced to 700–800 men.

When HÜLE'Ü (1256–65) founded the IL-KHANATE in Iran, he organized a *keshig* on the Chinggisid model governing the khan's household, supplying judges, and serving as the great *ghool*, or army center. Abagha Khan (1265–81) also recruited *keshig* for his son Arghun, viceroy in eastern Iran, to stiffen its defense. The Il-Khans also retained the *keshig's* dual role of holding hostages and enculturing non-Mongols. Hüle'ü, for example, recruited *ba'aturs* from the nobility of GEORGIA and Armenia, while Qutlughshah, a high Mongol nobleman of the MANGGHUD clan, and RASHID-UD-DIN FAZL-ULLAH, a Persian high official who began as a Jewish physician, shared a close relationship as men who had served on the same shift, or *keshig*. GHAZAN KHAN (1295–1304) created several new units, mostly of Mongols, for the army center, but they did not eclipse the political or military significance of the *keshig*. As in the Yuan, the commanders of the four shifts were chosen largely by family. The Suldus, Mangghud, and Jalayir clans generally had a place, but men of other clans also commanded *keshig* shifts. The khan appointed one of these four, "the commander of the commanders" (Arabic *amir al-umara'*) to be his chief Mongol commander. Either this chief commander or the vizier held the khan's vermilion seal, while three *keshig* commanders, or *ulus* emirs (commanders of the realm), added their black seals to all edicts.

In the CHAGHATAY KHANATE and the two wings of the GOLDEN HORDE (each of which had its own *keshig*), the power of these four *ulus* emirs (also called in Turkish *qarachi beys*, commoner, i.e., non-Chinggisid, commanders) and their "commander of commanders" (*beglerbegi* in Turkish) exceeded even that under the Il-Khans. By the 14th century the *ulus* emirs in these khanates monopolized the titles of sultan's deputy and vizier and controlled the khan's vermilion seal. The khans even lost the ability to choose their own shift commanders. Thus, while the Chaghatay khan Kebeg (1318–26) recruited a personal *keshig* (known later as Kebeg's *injü*, or personal appanage), by 1360 the emirs of the Arulad, Jalayir, Qa'uchin, and Barulas clans monopolized the Chaghatayid *keshig* command. Similarly, after the Golden Horde broke up, four tribes, clearly descendants of the *keshig*, occupied the military core of each of its small 15th-century successor states. In CRIMEA the collective approval of the

qarachi beys of the four clan was necessary for any action, particularly in foreign policy. The head of the leading Shirin clan held the title *bash-qarachi*, "chief of the *qarachis*," and at times made and deposed the Chinggisid khans. Thus, the *keshig*, which in the beginning was the personal appanage of the khan, in time came to control the khan as its puppet.

After the Yuan emperors fled from China back to Mongolia in 1368, there is no clear information on the *keshig*, yet the survival of certain clan and tribal names, including the KHORCHIN ("quiver bearers") and Kheshigten (from *keshigten*) of Inner Mongolia and the TORGHUDS (from *turgha'ud*, "day guards") among the OIRATS, indicates that many *keshig* units survived as coherent communities. The Kheshigten, currently a banner of Inner Mongolia, were long associated with the Latter Yuan (1368–36) emperors' personal appanage of CHAKHAR and may be descendants of the *keshig* of Mongolia's 16th-century emperors.

See also ARGHUN AQA; BAYAN; BOLOD CHINGSANG; CHABUI; EL-TEMÜR; HARGHASUN DARQAN; INDIA AND THE MONGOLS; *JARLIQ*; LIAN XIXIAN; *NÖKÖR*; ÖCHICHER; QARA'U-NAS; *QUDA*; TA'ACHAR; *TAISHI*; TUTUGH; YELÜ AHAI AND TUHUA.

Further reading: Ch'i-ch'ing Hsiao, *Military Establishment of Yüan Dynasty* (Cambridge, Mass.: Harvard University Press, 1978); Halil Inalcik, "The Khan and the Tribal Aristocracy: The Crimean Khanate under Sahib Giray I," *Harvard Ukrainian Studies* 3–4 (1979–80): 445–466; Uli Schamiloglu, "The Qaraçi Beys of the Later Golden Horde: Notes on the Organization of the Mongol World Empire," *Archivum Eurasiae Medii Aevi* 4 (1984): 283–297.

Ketbugha   *See* KED-BUQA.

khaan   *See* KHAN.

khadag (*khadak, khata, hadag*)   The *khadag* is a ceremonial silk scarf that accompanies all gifts to a respected person on ritual occasions in Mongolia. Derived from Tibetan *kha-bdags*, "square weavings," the *khadag* in 19th-century Lhasa was a square piece of silk sent with or without a small gift before visits as a kind of calling card. Today among the Mongols, the *khadag* is a long, narrow bolt of coarse silk, usually light blue or white. In blessings (*see* YÖRÖÖL AND MAGTAAL) the *khadag* is called the "best of goods" and its length compared to an endless life. When gifts are presented, they are placed on a *khadag* draped over both hands (gifts in Mongolia are always given with both hands). *Khadags* can also be presented to elders during greetings, such as in the WHITE MONTH (lunar new year).

See also RELIGION.

Khafungga (Hafeng'a, Ha-feng-a) (1908–1970) *Leader of the 1945 eastern Inner Mongolian nationalist movement* Khafungga (Chinese name Teng Xuwen) was the eldest of seven children of Rinchinjamsu (Teng Haishan), commander of the banner militia in KHORCHIN Left-Flank Middle banner (Horqin Zuoyi Zhongqi). In 1930 Khafungga attended MERSE's Northeast Mongolian Banners' Normal School in Shenyang, where his poems and speeches attracted admiration. Khafungga was fluent in Chinese and Japanese as well as Mongolian and was known for his intelligence and gentleness.

In summer 1931 the Comintern agent Temürbagana (1901–69) inspired Rinchinjamsu to organize an antiwarlord army and secretly recruited Khafungga and his sister's new husband, Asgan (Li Youtong, 1908–48), into the Inner Mongolian People's Revolutionary Party (IMPRP). After their army was taken over by pro-Japanese Mongols, all three became officials in Japanese-occupied Manchukuo while covertly spreading pro-Soviet, pan-Mongolist ideas. From 1941 Khafungga served as Manchukuo's cultural attaché in Tokyo, where he helped sponsor an association of Mongol students. Reassigned to Wang-un Süme (modern Ulaankhot/Ulanhot) in eastern Inner Mongolia in summer 1945, Khafungga began making serious anti-Japanese plans.

With the Soviet declaration of war on Japan, Khafungga launched a coup d'état in Wang-un Süme (Ulanhot) on August 11, 1945, and proclaimed the revived IMPRP's aim of a revolutionary pan-Mongolian republic. From then until spring 1946 Khafungga was the most popular leader and chief organizer of the East Mongolian nationalist movement, assisted by Asgan and Temürbagana. Instructed in an audience with Mongolia's MARSHAL CHOIBALSANG to cease pan-Mongolist agitation and cooperate with the Chinese Communists, Khafungga and Temürbagana put themselves under ULANFU's Chinese Communist–controlled front organization in April 1946. Khafungga joined the Chinese Communist Party and from then until 1954 served as Ulanfu's deputy in the Inner Mongolian government. He was, however, excluded from Inner Mongolia's top party leadership. Meanwhile, Asgan commanded Inner Mongolia's army until his death of encephalitis on January 31, 1948.

After the Communist victory in 1949, a new Inner Mongolian government was chosen in 1954. Khafungga was demoted to be only one of seven deputy chairmen, assigned to education. Khafungga chaired governmental committees on eliminating illiteracy (January 1953 on), introducing the Cyrillic script (July 1955 on), and science (March 1958 on). The rejection of Cyrillicization by China's premier Zhou Enlai in March 1958 damaged Khafungga's political standing (*see* CYRILLIC-SCRIPT MONGOLIAN). In 1964 he was transferred from the Inner Mongolian government to the People's Political Consultative Congress in Beijing, a sinecure for obsolescent officials.

When the Cultural Revolution inspired an attack on Ulanfu's policy, Khafungga's past made him an obvious target, and he was returned to Ulaanhot to be tormented and humiliated in struggle sessions until his death in 1970. He is still widely admired in the eastern Inner Mongolian countryside.

See also INNER MONGOLIA AUTONOMOUS REGION; INNER MONGOLIANS; JAPAN AND THE MODERN MONGOLS; "NEW INNER MONGOLIAN PEOPLE'S REVOLUTIONARY PARTY" CASE.

Further reading: Christopher P. Atwood, "The East Mongolian Revolution and Chinese Communism," *Mongolian Studies* 15 (1992): 7–83.

Khalkha (Halh, Qalqa) The Khalkha Mongols are the major subethnic group (*yastan*) of the independent State of Mongolia, or Outer Mongols. They number 1,610,400, or 78.8 percent, of Mongolia's population (1989 figures). Khalkha dialect is the standard language of Mongolia. The native Khalkha are virtually the sole ethnic group in Mongolia's vast rural interior; only in the border areas are other ethnic groups significant. While Chinese and Russians have been a large part of Mongolia's urban population, the Khalkha are also the only Mongolian subethnic group with a long urban tradition.

ORIGINS

The origins of the modern Khalkha can be traced to the second half of the 15th century, when they were one of the SIX TÜMENS (or six great confederations) making up the Mongols reunited under BATU-MÖNGKE DAYAN KHAN (r. 1480?–1517?). Divided into two groups, the Southern (*Öbör*) Khalkha became the ancestors of the Baarin (Bairin) and Jarud BANNERS (appanages) of eastern Inner Mongolia; only the Northern (Aru) Khalkha are the ancestors of today's Khalkha.

Dayan Khan assigned the Northern Khalkha to his youngest son, Geresenje Jalair Khung-Taiji (1513?–48). Geresenje divided the Khalkhas' 14 chief clans among his seven sons, forming the Northern Khalkha into seven OTOGs (camp districts). By the early 18th century a Mongolian chronicle listed 1,154 descendants of Geresenje, who were divided into a right (west) flank, led by descendants of Ashikhai Darkhan Khung-Taiji (b. 1530), Geresenje's eldest son, and a left (east) flank, led by descendants of Noonukhu Üizeng (b. 1534), his third son.

From 1567 until the early 17th century the Khalkhas warred incessantly on the OIRATS to their west, reaching the Irtysh valley in their raids. Noonukhu's son ABATAI KHAN (1554–88) and Ashikhai's grandsons Laikhur Khan (b. 1564) and Sholoi Ubashi Khung-Taiji (1567–1623?) led these campaigns. Laikhur and Abatai were acclaimed as khans, and their descendants bore the hereditary titles of Zasagtu (Ruling) and Tüshiyetü (Supporting) khans, respectively.

In 1581 Abatai Khan invited a lama from HÖHHOT to the Khalkha and converted to Buddhism (*see* SECOND

CONVERSION). In 1585 he built the great monastery ERDENI ZUU. In 1639 the left-flank Khalkha nobility recognized the son of the Tüshiyetü Khan Gömbö-Dorji (fl. 1639–55), the grandson of Abatai Khan, as an INCARNATE LAMA, the FIRST JIBZUNDAMBA KHUTUGTU. After this first Bogda (Holy One), known as Zanabazar (1635–1723), returned from study in Tibet in 1651, he became the supreme authority among the Khalkha.

The left-flank princes were relatively unified. All devout worshipers of the Bogda, they belonged to either the Tüshiyetü Khan's family or that of Sholoi Makhasamadi Setsen Khan (1577–1652), descendant of Geresenje's fourth son. The right flank, however, had four branches of Geresenje's family and lacked a single charismatic authority. Even among Ashikhai's descendants, the descendants of Sholoi Ubashi Khung-Taiji, ruling the KHOTOGHOID Khalkha, rarely obeyed their cousins, the Zasagtu Khans.

AS AN INDEPENDENT POWER

In 1655 the Khalkhas made peace with the rising QING DYNASTY, which had conquered Inner Mongolia in 1634–36. The Qing granted the title of ZASAG (or jasag, ruler) to eight Khalkha chiefs, who agreed to present a symbolic annual tribute of one white camel and eight white horses (the so-called tribute of nine whites) in return for gifts and trade relations. In 1682 11 zasags received trade rights, including the Bogda.

In 1640 the Khalkha Mongols had made peace with the Oirats, each side renouncing attacks and committing themselves to punish violators of the peace. Eventually, disputes within the right-flank Khalkhas broke up this concord, however. In 1662 after the Khotoghoid ruler murdered the Zasagtu Khan, the Khalkha left-flank nobles, led by the Tüshiyetü Khan Chakhundorji (Gömbö-Dorji's son, r. 1655–99), intervened, incidentally seizing many of the Zasagtu Khan's subjects.

Over the next 15 years the Zasagtu Khans unsuccessfully attempted to recover their lost subjects peacefully, allying with the Oirats and the Dalai Lama to press their case against Chakhundorji and his brother the Bogda. Chakhundorji refused all compromise, however, and in 1687 attacked the Zasagtu Khan. Finally, the Oirats under GALDAN BOSHOGTU KHAN (1678–97) of the Zünghar tribe invaded Khalkha in 1688, pillaging and burning temples. Chakhundorji, the Bogda, scores of thousands of left-flank Khalkhas, and even many right-flank Khalkhas fled to Inner Mongolia, appealing to the Qing for protection. After considerable hesitation, the Qing emperor Kangxi (1662–1722) accepted the Khalkha request for protection. On May 30, 1691, the Khalkhas officially submitted to the emperor at the great DOLONNUUR ASSEMBLY.

KHALKHA MONGOLS UNDER THE QING

Qing armies defeated the ZÜNGHARS in 1690 and 1696. Galdan died in 1697, and the Bogda returned to Khalkha in 1701. At the time of the Dolonnuur Assembly, Khalkha was reorganized into 34 BANNERS (appanages), each headed by a zasag. The Qing government recognized the Bogda as the symbolic head of all Khalkha and recognized the three khans, the Tüshiyetü Khan, the Setsen Khan, and the Zasagtu Khan, as the titular heads of three AIMAGS (provinces).

In 1725 the Qing court separated the princes of a junior line of Tüshiyetü Khan as a fourth aimag. This new aimag's titular head, equal in rank with the three khans, was the Sain Noyan (Good Nobleman). The number of banners was increased to 53. From 1724 to 1741 the Qing created a formal military and civil structure for the four provinces of Khalkha. Militarily they were headed by "assistant generals" (tusalagchi jangjun), and in civilian affairs the banners were grouped in LEAGUES (chuulgan), headed by captains general. Since the assistant generals and captains general were rotated among the banner heads, the khans lost any real power over their provinces. In 1765 the number of Khalkha banners was finally fixed at 86.

As the nobility were divided, the JIBZUNDAMBA KHUTUGTU's institutional authority increased. The Khalkhas all saw themselves as special shabi, or "disciples," of the Bogda. The Bogda's personal estate, the GREAT SHABI, (or lay disciples), became, in effect, a fifth province exempt from normal taxation and military requisition. His great monastery, located on the TUUL RIVER from 1779 on, became Khüriye, now modern Mongolia's capital, ULAANBAATAR. After CHINGGÜNJAB'S REBELLION in 1756–57, during which the SECOND JIBZUNDAMBA KHUTUGTU died, the Qianlong emperor (1735–96) ordered the next Bogda to be found in Tibet. From then on all the Bogdas were Tibetan in origin. While the nobility resented this, the devotion of ordinary Khalkhas did not diminish.

The Khalkhas exemplified many trends of Mongolian life under the late Qing. Socially and culturally, Buddhism and the Buddhist arts reached great heights, the petty Chinggisid nobility, or TAIJI, multiplied in numbers, the titled aristocracy increased their power and wealth, and clan structure broke down. Economically, imported Chinese goods virtually wiped out rural farming and handicrafts industries, turning the Khalkha into specialist livestock producers, while moneylending and international trade concentrated wealth among a declining population. One unique feature of Khalkha society in contrast to the other Mongols was the existence of a genuine Mongolian urban culture in Khüriye, not just of lamas but also of teamsters, butchers, carpenters, and other proletarians making a living around the city's monasteries and the Chinatown.

THE KHALKHAS IN INDEPENDENT MONGOLIA

With the 1911 RESTORATION of Mongolian independence and the suppression of Inner Mongolian's independence movement, Khalkha became the center of the only independent Mongolian state. While the Jibzundamba Khutugtu and the Khalkha aristocracy ruled the new theocratic regime, influence was also shared with Inner Mongolian and Buriat advisers and the mostly Khalkha class of urbanized officials and employees. Tensions with the western Mongols, led by the DÖRBÖD, led to significant discontent, a trend that continued after 1921.

The administrative reorganization of 1931 abolished the traditional four Khalkha provinces while diluting the subethnic homogeneity of the western (Oirat) Mongolian, DARKHAD, and DARIGANGA districts. The GREAT PURGE of 1937–40 hit BURIATS, INNER MONGOLIANS, and Chinese disproportionately hard, helping "nativize" Mongolia's intelligentsia and working class. The adoption of a Cyrillic script based on the Khalkha dialect and the development of education and mass media brought central Khalkha's linguistic and cultural standards to the most distant borders.

In the postwar period the percentage of Khalkha in Mongolia's population increased from 75.6 percent in 1956 to 77.5 percent in 1979 due to the overwhelming tendency of those with mixed origin to identify as Khalkha. Thus, the Khalkhas remain very much the sociological norm in Mongolian society, to which other ethnic groups conform. While the 1990 DEMOCRATIC REVOLUTION brought freedom for ethnic groups to organize as well as interest in Mongols beyond the frontier, the new democratic constitution strengthened majoritanianism, while economic liberalization has only enhanced Ulaanbaatar's dominant role in culture and society. Both these developments indicate that the Khalkhas' demographic and sociological dominance in Mongolia will only grow.

See also CLOTHING AND DRESS; EPICS; FAMILY; FOLK POETRY AND TALES; JEWELRY; LITERATURE; MUSIC; MONGOLIAN LANGUAGE; *NAADAM*; RELIGION; THEOCRATIC PERIOD; WEDDINGS; YURT.

Further reading: Fang Chao-ying, "Tsereng." In *Eminent Chinese of the Ch'ing Period (1644–1912)*, ed. by Arthur W. Hummel (Washington, D.C.: U.S. Government Printing Office, 1943); Junko Miyawaki, "The Qalqa Mongols and the Oyirads in the Seventeenth Century," *Journal of Asian History* 18 (1984): 136–173; Hidehiro Okada, "Outer Mongolia in the Sixteenth and Seventeenth Centuries," *Ajia Afurika Gengo Bunka Kenkyu* 5 (1972): 69–85; Herbert Harold Vreeland III, *Mongol Community and Kinship Structure* (New Haven, Conn.: HRAF Press, 1957).

Khalkha jirum (modern, Khalkh juram)

This law code, first enacted in 1709, applied to the GREAT SHABI, the JIBZUNDAMBA KHUTUGTU's personal estate, until the 20th century.

The Khalkha jirum, or "Khalkha Regulations," were enacted first in 1709. The MONGOL-OIRAT CODE of 1640 was nullified by the Khalkhas' surrender to the Qing

dynasty at the DOLONNUUR ASSEMBLY (1691), yet the Qing code for the Inner Mongolian BANNERS was not applicable. The Khalkha jirum was thus enacted by the Tüshiyetü Khan, Dorji-Erdeni-Akhai (r. 1702–11), and the ERDENI SHANGDZODBA, or estate manager of the Jibzundamba Khutugtu, with the other dignitaries of Khalkha's Tüshiyetü Khan AIMAG. From 1736 on the Setsen Khan and from 1745–46 the Zasagtu Khan nobility participated in revisions, thus acknowledging its authority.

As originally enacted, the law had seven articles and 194 sections. From 1718 to 1770 17 amendments were made to the code. The seven original articles cover supply of provisions for the "Gegeen" (the Jibzundamba Khutugtu), government messengers and nobility; premeditated murder; theft; marriage engagements, bridewealth, and dowries; fugitives and intruders; the prerogatives of the Gegeen; limitations on killing animals; death, bodily harm, or loss caused by noblemen's "jokes"; lies; assaults; lost cattle or other things; injuries from mad dogs, mad people, or trip-wired crossbows; public drunkenness; desecrating graves; wolves; disputes over wells and campsites; Chinese and Russian merchants; military preparedness; hospitality; witnesses in criminal cases; and relations of parents and children. The amendments usually added details to previously covered material but sometimes introduced new topics, such as rules on trade, limitations on alcohol consumption, and rules for HORSE RACING.

The Khalkha jirum codified the preeminent role of the Gegeen and evidenced the effort to enforce Buddhist norms, as reflected in the limitations on hunting, funerary sacrifices, liquor consumption, and cutting trees around the Gegeen's camp. The basic penalty was the livestock fine, most often counted in multiples of nine, but enslavement (or conversely deprivation of subjects) and confiscation of all property were also common penalties. Flogging, various forms of confinement, and hobbling were rather less common. The death penalty was applied only to assaults on monasteries and to certain forms of robbery.

From 1728 the Qing's Mongolian code (*see* LIFAN YUAN ZELI) began to applied to Khalkha Mongolia, although at first only as interpreted by Mongolian judges. After 1789 the Khalkha jirum no longer applied except to the Great Shabi, or personal subjects of the Jibzundamba Khutugtu. Even there, however, serious cases always and even minor cases sometimes were adjudicated according to the Qing codes. During this period the Ulaan khatsartu (Red covers), a body of precedents decided according to the Khalkha jirum, was compiled.

Further reading: Valentin A. Riasanovsky, *Fundamental Principles of Mongol Law* (1934; rpt., Bloomington: Indiana University, 1965).

Khalkhin Gol   *See* KHALKHYN GOL, BATTLE OF.

Khalkhyn Gol, Battle of (Khalkhin Gol, Nomonhan)

At the Battle of Khalkhyn Gol (May–September 1939), a heavily armored Soviet force crushed a Japanese force on disputed territory in Mongolia's Tamsagbulag salient.

In January 1935 began the first of a series of border incidents between Japanese and Inner Mongolian troops and those of the MONGOLIAN PEOPLE'S REPUBLIC. In 1936–37 Mongolia and the Soviet Union signed a military alliance, and 30,000 Soviet troops entered Mongolia. The frontier between Inner Mongolia (then Japanese occupied) and the Mongolian People's Republic had never been demarcated, and wide disputes remained. The Battle of Khalkhyn Gol (called Nom-un Khan or Nomonhan by the Japanese) centered on the Khalkha (Halh) River's right (eastern) bank, claimed by both sides.

In May, after clashes between border guards, 2,000 Japanese troops attacked 1,000 Mongolian and Soviet troops dug in on the right bank but were pushed back. Late in June both Soviet and Japanese air forces bombed air bases deep in the other's territory. On July 2 the 15,000-man-strong 23rd Division under Lieutenant General Komatsubara Michitaro (1886–1940) and the Inner Mongolian Khinggan Division assaulted Soviet forces on the right bank and at Mount Bayan Tsagaan (Bain-Tsagan) in undoubted Mongolian territory. The Bayan Tsagaan offensive was destroyed, and by July 25 the Japanese advance was halted, while several officers of the Khinggan Division deserted to the enemy. On August 20 the Soviet commander Georgii K. Zhukov (1896–1964) counterattacked with four Red Army rifle divisions and five mechanized brigades. The three Mongolian cavalry divisions under his command on the right and left flanks took heavy casualties. By August 31 the Japanese, completely outclassed in artillery and armor despite reinforcement with three new divisions, had been crushed. Total Japanese casualties were almost 20,000 out of 60,000 to 70,000 soldiers. The Soviet troops stopped at Mongolia's claimed frontier, and a cease-fire was signed on September 16. After the Soviet victory the Japanese avoided future border incidents, and a Soviet-Japanese nonaggression treaty was signed in May 1941.

See also JAPAN AND THE MODERN MONGOLS; SOVIET UNION AND MONGOLIA; WORLD WAR II.

Further reading: Alvin D. Coox, *Nomonhan: Japan against Russia, 1939* (Stanford, Calif.: Stanford University Press, 1985).

Khamnigan *See* EWENKIS.

khan (*qan, khan; qaghan, qa'an, kagan, khaan*)

This monarchic title, ubiquitous among the Mongolic and Turkic peoples, occurs in various forms, meaning "king," "emperor," or "sovereign." The earliest steppe peoples known to use the title *khan* were the XIANBI and their descendants, the ROURAN and the Avars, who from the second century B.C.E. to the sixth century C.E. moved east from Inner Mongolia to Europe. From 550 on the Turkish empires all titled their supreme ruler *qaghan*. The Mongolic KITANS were the only Inner Asian people to abandon this title in their own language, replacing it with the Chinese *huangdi*, or emperor, in 916.

From the earliest Turkish sources, the word *khan* is found in two forms with an uncertain etymological relationship: *qan* and *qaghan*. They are related to *qatun* or KHATUN, "queen, empress." In Old Turkish in the Runic and Uighur scripts, *qaghan* is used as a title, while *qan* is more abstract, meaning "sovereign, monarch," yet as the -*gh*- in *qaghan* weakened, the two converged in pronunciation, so that by the 11th century the lexicographer Mahmud al-Kashghari registered only *khan*. As Islamic titles were adopted, the title *khan* in the Turco-Iranian Middle East came to mean not a sovereign (who in the Turco-Iranian Islamic world bore the title *sultan* or *shah*) but a high-ranking provincial governor. In South Asia it has degenerated to a mere honorific title.

It appears that 12th-century Mongolian followed later Turkish usage in using only *qan*, for example, in the title *gür-qan*, "universal khan." Chinggis himself (r. 1206–27) bore the title *qan*, as is demonstrated by coins and the few surviving documents from his life. His son ÖGEDEI KHAN, however, revived the title *qa'an*, the equivalent of the old Turkish *qaghan*. This title, which became Ögedei's posthumous reign name, was seen as having greater dignity than *qan*, and from then on CHINGGIS KHAN's title was retroactively written in Mongolian as Chinggis Qa'an. During the subsequent decades *qan* became a title used for the subordinate khan, such as those of the IL-KHANATE and the GOLDEN HORDE, while *qa'an* was reserved for the emperor ruling in the east. *Qan*, as in Old Turkish, also retained the abstract meaning of "sovereign, monarch."

In later Mongolian usage *qan* as a title disappeared, leaving *qa'an* (now pronounced *khaan*) as the only title for any monarch and *qan* (now pronounced *khan*) as the abstract term for sovereign or monarch, especially in the plural *khad*. From around 1550 to 1634 the distinction between the supreme khan, or emperor of the Mongols, and a minor one was marked by giving the former a dynastic title, such as Dai Yuwan (or Dayun) Khaan, "Emperor of the Great Yuan (of the Mongols)," or Daiming Khaan, "Emperor of the Great Ming (of China)," and the latter the title simply of *khaan*. While the dynastic *khaan*s were so by heredity, other *khaan*s had, as it were, only a lifetime khanship, which their descendants had to reinforce each generation either through military achievements or through blessings from the Dalai Lama.

The title *khan* is also used by the Manchus of the Manchu-Tungusic language family. When the Manchu QING DYNASTY conquered the Mongol Northern Yuan, the Qing emperor distinguished himself from the remaining Mongol khans not only by his dynastic title as emperor of the Great Qing (Daiching Khaan), but also by a special title, Bogda Khaan, "Holy Khan." (This title was also adopted by the JIBZUNDAMBA KHUTUGTU when he became the last theocratic monarch of newly independent Mongolia in 1911.) Even so, the Qing in their official documents also revived the term qan/khan for a subordinate ruler. Thus, the three (later four) khans of Khalkha were always written khan, not khaan, further emphasizing their subordination to the Holy Khaan of the Great Qing. In pronunciation, however, there was no difference between the two; khan as a title was actually pronounced khaan.

In modern times khaan in Mongolian is used for emperors (e.g., that of Japan), while the borrowed Chinese title wang is used for kings such as those of Spain and Jordan. The term khan is no longer used in political terminology.

See also ALTAIC LANGUAGE FAMILY.

Further reading: Igor de Rachewiltz, "Qan, Qa'an, and the Seal of Güyüg," in Documenta Barbarorum, ed. Klaus Sagaster and Michael Weiers (Wiesbaden: Otto Harrassowitz, 1983), 273–281.

Khanbaligh   See DAIDU.

Khanddorj, Mijiddorjiin   See KHANGDADORJI, PRINCE.

Khangai Range
The main body of the Khangai Range runs northwest to southeast through west-central Mongolia, with the ridges at an average height of 3,000 meters (9,800 feet) above sea level. In Mongolian khangai means mountainous forest steppe, which the northern Khangai exemplifies. The southern slopes facing the Gobi, however, are drier and scored by seasonal rivers. Branch ranges north of the main range, such as the Bulnai and Tarwagatai, run east–west or northeast. The highest peak in the Khangai and the only one with perpetual snow is Otgon Tenger (4,021 meters; 13,192 feet). The Khangai's high ridges receive about 400–500 millimeters (16–20 inches) of precipitation annually and are the source of many of Mongolia's major rivers. Rivers flowing northeast (including the ORKHON RIVER, and the Tamir, Khünüi, Chuluut, and Ider Rivers) join the SELENGE RIVER and eventually drain into the Arctic. Those flowing south (including the Zawkhan, Baidrag, Tüi, and Ongi) drain either into the GREAT LAKES BASIN or disappear in the GOBI DESERT.

See also ANIMAL HUSBANDRY AND NOMADISM; BAYANKHONGOR PROVINCE; CLIMATE; ENVIRONMENTAL PROTECTION; FAUNA; FLORA; HORSES; MONGOLIAN PLATEAU; NORTH KHANGAI PROVINCE; SOUTH KHANGAI PROVINCE; ZAWKHAN PROVINCE.

Khangdadorji, Prince (Mijiddorjiin Khanddorj; Khangda Dorji) (1870–1915) The leading planner of the 1911 Restoration and the first foreign minister in theocratic Mongolia

Khandadorji succeeded as prince of Daiching Zasag banner (modern northern Bulgan) in 1892. From 1897 he was consultant to Tüshiyetü Khan AIMAG's assistant general and from 1900 to 1911 assistant general himself. He joined the Khalkha princes' 1899 remonstrance to the Qing court against granting gold MINING concessions to foreigners. In 1904 he invited the Thirteenth Dalai Lama to his seat at Wang-un Khüriye (modern Bulgan) and sent his son to escort the Dalai Lama to Beijing. There the Qing authorities, suspicious of Mongolian-Tibetan ties, accused the boy of a crime and executed him. From 1910 Khangdadorji served as an official in the new army-training and colonization offices in Khüriye. In July 1911 Khangdadorji organized the secret meeting that planned the 1911 RESTORATION of Mongolian independence, joined the secret delegation to get Russian aid, and on his return was appointed to the Provisional Administrative Office for Khüriye Affairs. In December he became foreign minister of the newly independent Mongolia. In January and February 1913 he negotiated in St. Petersburg a loan of 2 million gold rubles for 20 years as well as military assistance. Later the prime minister Namnangsürüng (1878–1919) eclipsed his role in foreign affairs. He died on February 26, 1915.

See also THEOCRATIC PERIOD.

Khar Balgas   See ORDU-BALIGH.

Kharachin (Harqin, Harchin, Qaracin, Kalaqin)
Once the leaders in Inner Mongolia's secular education and reform movement, the Kharachin are now almost completely Chinese speaking. Traditionally the Kharachin were part of Josotu league (chuugulgan), containing three Kharachin banners as well as two Tümed banners (not to be confused with the Höhhot Tümed to the west). Most of Josotu's former territory is now included in Liaoning province in Manchuria. Inner Mongolia's current Kharachin banner is the former Kharachin Right Banner. Its 1990 population was 357,000, of which one-third were Mongol. Manchus, descendants of servants brought by imperial princesses married to Kharachin princes, form more than 7 percent of the population. Liaoning's Kharachin Left-Flank (Harqin Zuoyi) Mongol Autonomous county (former Kharachin Left Banner) had a population of 372,393 in 1982, of which 43,928 (11.8 percent) were Mongol. Living interspersed among Chinese in farming villages, the Kharachin are everywhere in the minority. Mongolian-language abilities declined rapidly after 1910, and today Kharachin learn Mongolian only as a second language for reasons of ethnic pride. Reregistration of people with mixed Mongol-Chinese ancestry as Mongols expanded Kharachin banner's ethnic Mongol percentage from 24.6 percent in 1982 (82,439 persons) to more than 33 percent in 1990.

The Kharachin have a purely agricultural lifestyle, although the rugged terrain allows only 17 percent of Kharachin banner's 3,155 square kilometers (1,218 square miles) and 22 percent of Kharachin Left Flank's 2,238 square kilometers (864 square miles) to be cultivated. The principal crops are millet, corn, and sorghum supplemented by cotton and tobacco in Kharachin Left-Flank. Pigs accounted for 44 percent of Kharachin banner's 291,000 livestock (1984) and 61 percent of Kharachin Left-Flank's 269,000 head in 1983.

In 1389 the MING DYNASTY established the Döyin, or Uriyangkhan Guard (see THREE GUARDS), in northeastern Inner Mongolia. The Uriyangkhan rulers were reckoned descendants of CHINGGIS KHAN's companion Jelme of the Uriyangkhan. After 1448 the guard was resettled nearer to the Ming border in later Josotu league territory. Meanwhile, the Kharachin, descendants of the MONGOL EMPIRE's Qipchaq guards (see QIPCHAQS), formed part of the Yüngshiyebü Tümen (see SIX TÜMENS), inhabiting present-day Chakhar territory. Around 1600 Kharachin migrating east merged with the Uriyangkhan Mongols. Submitting to the Manchu QING DYNASTY in 1626, this mixed people was organized into three Kharachin BANNERS (appanages) in Josotu league, each ruled by a ruler of the old Uriyangkhan lineage.

From the 18th century Kharachin bannermen began dividing up their fields and employing Chinese immigrants as tenants. Prince Güngsangnorbu (1871–1931) of Kharachin Right expanded modern education among the Mongols, first in his banner and after 1912 in Beijing. While Kharachins dominated the Republic of China's Mongol bureaucracy and the early Mongol nationalist intelligentsia, their banner lands were excluded from the Japanese-supported autonomous Khinggan provinces in 1933–45. After 1945 the Chinese Communists set up new Kharachin banner governments, likewise kept outside Inner Mongolia. In 1955 Kharachin Right Banner was transferred to Inner Mongolia as Kharachin banner, and Kharachin Center banner was abolished. Kharachin Left Banner, left in Liaoning, was converted to an autonomous county in October 1957.

See also FARMING; FUXIN MONGOL AUTONOMOUS COUNTY; INJANNASHI; INNER MONGOLIA AUTONOMOUS REGION; INNER MONGOLIANS; MONGOLIAN LANGUAGE; NEW SCHOOLS MOVEMENTS.

Further reading: Sun, E-tu Zen, "Results of Culture Contact in Two Mongol-Chinese Communities," *Southwestern Journal of Anthropology* 8 (1952): 182–210.

Kharachin Left-Flank Mongol Autonomous County
See KHARACHIN.

khatun (*qatun, khatan*)   The term *khatun* is used in Mongolian for the wife of any sovereign or noble; it thus combines the meanings of "empress," "queen," and "lady" without distinction. The term *khatun* first appeared as *qasun* among the XIANBI, a people in Inner Mongolia, from the second century B.C.E. to the fourth century C.E. It appears to be etymologically related to the titles *qaghan/qan*, "KHAN, sovereign," which appear alongside it. It is found subsequently among virtually all the Turkic and Mongolic peoples. In contemporary Turkish *hatun* means simply "lady" or "wife, woman." During the MONGOL EMPIRE *qatun* (later pronounced *khatun* and written *khatan* today) was reserved for the wife of the sovereign or emperor, while princesses (whether daughters of khans or wives of princes) were called *beki*. (For reasons that are obscure, this term is the same as that for shaman or chief.) Under the Qing dynasty (1636–1912) the title *khatun* was extended to wives of all the Chinggisid nobility (TAIJI), no matter how poor. This usage continued until the 20th century.

See also ALAQAI BEKI; ALTAIC LANGUAGE FAMILY; BÖRTE ÜJIN; CHABUI; Ö'ELÜN ÜJIN; INJE; MANDUKHAI SECHEN KHATUN; OGHUL-QAIMISH; *ORDO*; SORQAQTANI BEKI; TÖREGENE.

Khentii province (Hentiy, Chentej, Kentei)   One of the original provinces created in Mongolia's 1931 administrative reorganization, Khentii province lies in Mongolia's northeast. It has a long frontier with Russia's Chita district. All of Khentii's territory was included within KHALKHA Mongolia's prerevolutionary Setsen Khan province. After 1920 Buriat Mongols settled heavily along the province's northern frontier. Khentii's 80,300 square kilometers (31,000 square miles) occupy the wooded mountains of the KHENTII RANGE in the northwest and the steppe land to the east and south. The famous ONON RIVER and KHERLEN RIVER cross this province, which contains what is considered to be the site of Deli'ün Boldaq, CHINGGIS KHAN's birthplace, as well as the famous mountain Burqan Qaldun. The population has risen from 34,800 in 1956 to 71,400 in 2000. The 1,471,400 head of livestock include relatively high numbers of CATTLE (218,000 head) and HORSES (192,800 head). From 1960 to 1990 Khentii was a leading agricultural area, although at present arable agriculture is only a shadow of its former importance. Khentii contains most of Mongolia's fluorspar mines at Berkh, Khajuu-Ulaan, and Bor-Öndör, as well as tin mines at Modot. Khentii's capital, Öndörkhaan, has a population of 15,500 (2002).

See also AWARGA; BURIATS OF MONGOLIA AND INNER MONGOLIA; CHOINOM, RENTSENII; LHÜMBE CASE; TSERINDORJI.

Khentii Range (Hentiy, Chentij, Kentei)   The Khentii Range runs southwest to northeast from northeast Mongolia into the Chita Region of Russia. The mountains are smooth and rounded, with steeper slopes to the northwest. High peaks include Asralt Khairkhan (2,800 meters, or 9,186 feet, above sea level) and Khiidiin Saridag (2,675 meters, 8,776 feet) northeast of ULAAN-BAATAR and Burun Shibertuy (2,519 meters, 8,264 feet) in southern Chita. None is permanently snow covered. The Khentii Range is one of Mongolia's wettest regions, with more than 500 millimeters (20 inches) of precipitation annually. The range divides the Arctic, Pacific, and Gobi inland drainage basins. Rivers flowing west into the SELENGE RIVER and thence to the Arctic include the TUUL RIVER and the Yöröö (Yeröö) and Chikoy Rivers; those flowing east into the Amur and the Pacific include the ONON RIVER, the KHERLEN RIVER, and the Ingoda River. The Khentii Range contains the famous peak of Burqan Qaldun (Burkhan Khaldun), which was CHINGGIS KHAN's heartland, usually identified with modern Khentii Khan Mountain (2,362 meters, 7,749 feet) between the head-waters of the Kherlen and the Onon.

See also AGA BURIAT AUTONOMOUS AREA; ANIMAL HUS-BANDRY AND NOMADISM; CENTRAL PROVINCE; CLIMATE; ENVIRONMENTAL PROTECTION; FAUNA; FLORA; KHENTII PROVINCE; MONGOLIAN PLATEAU; SELENGE PROVINCE.

Kherlen River (Herlen, Kelüren, Kerülen) The Kherlen River rises from the KHENTII RANGE in north-eastern Mongolia and flows east into Hulun (Khölön or Dalai) Lake in northeastern Inner Mongolia. Hulun Lake in turn drains into the Ergüne (Argun') and then the Amur River and finally into the Pacific. The Kherlen River is 1,254 kilometers (779 miles) long but shallow and nowhere navigable. Industrial and residential uses—the river flows past Baganuur coal mine and Öndörkhaan, Choibalsang, and Altan Emeel towns—have taxed water resources and degraded water quality. Originally pronounced "Kelüren," the -l- and -r- under-went metathesis, forming Kerülen, which formed, according to regular sound changes, the modern Kherlen. The Kherlen and the ONON RIVER together defined the original homeland of the MONGOL TRIBE, and AWARGA, the main archaeological site associated with CHINGGIS KHAN, is near the Kherlen headwaters. A South Chinese ambassador in 1236 claimed to have seen Chinggis Khan's tomb between the Kherlen River and the nearby mountains.

Khingan Range   *See* GREATER KHINGGAN RANGE.

Khinggan league (Hinggan) Khinggan league lies in eastern Inner Mongolia. The league covers 59,800 square kilometers (23,090 square miles) of territory and had a 1990 population of 1,524,064, of whom 587,929 (39 per-cent) were Mongol. The territory has three Mongol BAN-NERS (two KHORCHIN and one Jalaid) and one Chinese county. The capital is Ulaankhot (Mongolian "Red Town," also spelled Ulanhot). The Mongols of Jalaid ban-ner number 150,100 (40 percent of the banner's total

population) and have a mixed agropastoral economy. (*On the Khorchin banners, see* KHORCHIN.)

Ulaankhot, formerly Wang-un Süme (Prince's Tem-ple), formed around a Buddhist monastery in Khorchin Right-Flank Front banner (Horqin Youyi Qianqi). Under the Japanese occupation (1931–45) Wang-un Süme became the center of the autonomous Mongol Khinggan provinces, and a temple of Chinggis Khan was built there (*see* CHINGGIS KHAN CONTROVERSY). From 1945 to 1949 Wang-un Süme became the center of Mongol nationalist and Chinese Communist activity. The Inner Mongolian Autonomous Government was proclaimed in 1947. The town was renamed Ulaankhot in 1948. In 1949 Inner Mongolia's government seat was moved to Zhangjiakou. In 1990 Ulaankhot had a population of 229,100, of whom 52,300 were Mongol.

See also INNER MONGOLIA AUTONOMOUS REGION; INNER MONGOLIANS; JALAYIR.

Khitan   *See* KITANS.

Khō Örlökh   *See* KHOO-ÖRLÖG

Khobogsair Mongol Autonomous County (Hobok-sair) A Mongol autonomous county in northern Xin-jiang, China's Uighur autonomous region, Khobogsair county occupies the valley of the Hobok (medieval Qobaq) River as it flows from the Sair Mountains on the Kazakhstan frontier southeast into the utterly barren Gurbartünggüt Desert. The Mongol inhabitants are OIRATS, or western Mongols, related to Russia's KALMYKS.

The county covers more than 30,000 square kilome-ters (11,500 square miles) of steppe and desert. Adminis-tratively, it is part of Tarbagatai (Tacheng) district, a subdistrict of the Ili Kazakh Autonomous Prefecture. The total population in 1999 was 50,942, of which 16,349 (32.4 percent) were Mongols. Other ethnic groups include KAZAKHS (28 percent) and recently immigrated Chinese (37 percent). In 1982 the county's 13,029 Mon-gols were 36.8 percent of the population; Chinese immi-gration and a higher Kazakh birthrate account for the decrease in the percentage since then. Khobogsair is still predominantly a pastoral area, with 1,272,700 hectares (3,144,800 acres) of usable pasture. Only 6,680 hectares (16,510 acres) are farmed.

Under the Qing the Torghud Mongols of Khobogsair were organized as BANNERS (appanages) in the Ünen-Süzügtü North Route league. Khobogsair had an esti-mated 500,000 head of livestock in 1943, but clashes and pillage associated with the Kazakh-led Ili Revolution reduced the county's herd to 90,000 head in 1949. After the Chinese People's Liberation Army's occupied Xinjiang in 1949, Khobogsair was made an autonomous county in 1954, at which point Mongols were 58 percent of the population. Although the total herd reached 269,244 in

1957, collectivization in 1958 and antipastoral, anti–private-ownership policies kept numbers stagnant until 1979. In 1999 Khobogsair had 442,500 head of livestock and produced 4,700 metric tons (5,181 short tons) of meat, 5,597 metric tons (6,170 short tons) of DAIRY PRODUCTS, 588 metric tons (648 short tons) of wool, and 16.75 metric tons (18.46 short tons) goat hair.

See also FLIGHT OF THE KALMYKS; TORGHUDS; XINJIANG MONGOLS.

Khökhkhot   *See* HÖHHOT.

Khölön Buir   *See* HULUN BUIR.

khöömii   *See* THROAT SINGING.

Khoo-Örlög (Khō Örlökh, Kho-Urlük) (d. 1644)
Torghud leader who first led the Oirats to settle on the Volga, thereby founding the Kalmyk people
Around 1606–08 Khoo-Örlög was the TAISHI, or ruler, of about 4,000 Torghud households divided into five *uluses* nomadizing south of Tara in western Siberia. Around 1615 he moved northwest, occupying the Ishim and Tobol River areas and marrying a sister of a local Siberian Tatar chief. Meanwhile, the Oirat chief Chöökür of the Khoshud tribe raided the Turkish-speaking Nogay nomads (*see* MANGGHUD) on the Caspian steppe as early as 1608.

When Chöökür and his uterine brothers, the "Five Tigers" (*see* TÖRÖ-BAIKU GÜÜSHI KHAN), began a savage feud, Khoo-Örlög moved south and west to avoid involvement. From 1630 to 1635 Khoo-Örlög and his six sons appeared on the steppe between the Aral and the Emba, driving the Nogays toward CRIMEA. By this time Khoo-Örlög and his sons had 22,000 households.

In 1640 Khoo-Örlög attended the great assembly of OIRATS and Mongols and made that assembly's MONGOL-OIRAT CODE law for his TORGHUDS. Shortly afterward the Torghud moved west of the Ural Mountains, annexing the remaining Nogays on the Volga. In 1643–44 Khoo-Örlög and his sons crossed the Volga in force, but Khoo-Örlög's 10,000-strong force was shattered, and Khoo-Örlög was killed by a body of Caucasus mountaineers armed with harquebuses and aided by Nogay cavalry.

Khorazm (Khwarazm, Khwarizm, Khorezm)
The region of Khorazm was the center of the leading empire in Iran and Turkestan at the time of CHINGGIS KHAN. The Khorazmian dynasty, founded in 1097–98, reached its peak in 1218, just before being crushed by the Mongols. Located on the western bank of the Amu Dar'ya (Oxus) River as it flows into the Aral Sea, Khorazm's chief city and capital in the 13th century was Urganch (Urgench, Gurganj, or Ürünggechi). The people of Khorazm, known in classical antiquity as Chorasmia, were literate and spoke an Iranian dialect. By the ninth century C.E. the Khorazmians had converted to Islam and become famous traders, their merchants linking Eastern Europe with the Middle East. Turkish tribes were expanding south and west, and the Khorazmians adopted the Turkish language by the 12th century.

RISE OF THE DYNASTY
In 1138 Atsiz, the first Khorazm-Shah, rebelled against the Seljük Turks then ruling Iran and western Turkistan. His grandson Sultan Tekish (1172–1200) submitted to QARA-KHITAI suzerainty in the east but expanded his rule west to Hamadan and north to the Syr Dar'ya River. Tekish's son Sultan 'Ala'ud-Din Muhammad (1200–20/21) defeated the Ghuri dynasty of Afghanistan and expanded the empire to the shores of the Persian Gulf and Caspian Sea. Finally, in 1209 he revolted against the Qara-Khitai and seized the great cities of Bukhara and Samarqand. Dividing the Qara-Khitai empire in agreement with Küchülüg, a NAIMAN adventurer from Mongolia, by 1213 Sultan Muhammad had pushed his frontier east to Otrar on the Syr Dar'ya River. Thinking the eastern frontier secure, he turned to campaigns in Afghanistan and western Iran.

The empire of Khorazm, like many medieval Iranian dynasties, was built on a duality of Turk, the tribal warrior class, and Tajik (or Iranian), the tax-paying peasants and city dwellers. The Turkish ruling class of warriors depended on the Tajik bureaucrats, landholders, merchants, and Islamic clergy for finances and the maintenance of social order. While themselves Muslim, the Khorazm shahs' military core was the mostly non-Islamic Qangli Turks of present-day Kazakhstan. Sultan Muhammad's own mother, Terken Khatun, was a Qangli whose word held great weight with her son.

CLASH WITH THE MONGOLS
Meanwhile, the Mongols under Chinggis Khan (Genghis, 1206–27) conquered Küchülüg and opened relations with Sultan Muhammad. Embassies had been exchanged when Sultan Muhammad, campaigning in the Syr Dar'ya area, clashed with Mongol troops under Chinggis Khan's son JOCHI and SÜBE'ETEI BA'ATUR, who were pursuing Toqto'a of the MERKID tribe. Shortly thereafter, the governor of Otrar, Inalchuq Qadir Khan, with Sultan Muhammad's approval, massacred a large Mongol trade mission and confiscated its goods (*see* OTRAR INCIDENT). Informed of the Otrar massacre, Chinggis Khan demanded the life of Qadir Khan in exchange, but Qadir was Terken Khatun's kinsman, and the sultan killed these envoys, too. Chinggis then prepared a campaign of extermination against the Khorazm-shahs and their people.

Alarming stories spread of the Mongol soldiers' extraordinary hardiness, their great numbers, and their conquest of the legendary "Altan Khan," or Jin emperor, of North China. Court astrologers reported that any offensive move would be inauspicious. Thus, Sultan Muhammad took a purely defensive position and distributed his reputed 400,000 soldiers, which actually considerably outnumbered the Mongols, among the garrisons of Otrar, Fanakat, Bukhara, Samarqand, and other fortresses on the eastern frontier, while he himself retired south of the Amu Dar'ya River. He also ordered his mother and wives to leave Khorazm for central Iran. Thus, Chinggis Khan's armies found no one contesting their control of the whole Transoxiana countryside. The Mongols simply bottled up the Khorazmian troops in the walled cities and reduced them one by one.

MONGOL CONQUEST

Reaching Otrar first, the Mongols took it after a five-month siege. As the seat of the original massacre of Mongol merchants that started the war, all its inhabitants, civilian and military alike, were massacred along with Inalchuq Qadir Khan. Meanwhile, Chinggis Khan dispatched his eldest son, Jochi, with an army on the right to reduce the cities along the lower Syr Dar'ya and dispatched another army on the left to reduce those in the Ferghana valley. He himself advanced with the bulk of the army on Bukhara and Samarqand. When Bukhara surrendered on February 15, 1220, and Samarqand on March 16, 1220, only the Qangli garrisons in the fortified citadels were completely massacred. The cities were, however, plundered, and mass levies of inhabitants were herded against the walls of unconquered cities as cannon fodder. Each city paid tribute and received a DARUGHACHI, or overseer. Yelü Ahai, a Kitan, was appointed "Great Darughachi" in Bukhara, supervising all of Mawarannahr (Transoxiana) (see YELÜ AHAI AND TUHUA).

The surrender of Samarqand shook Sultan Muhammad, then in Balkh; it had been expected to hold out for months if not years. His son Jalal-ud-Din Mengüberdi offered to lead the Khorazmians on a counteroffensive, but Sultan Muhammad rejected this plan. With the news of the surrender of Samarqand, even the Qangli guardsmen of his mother's clan attempted to assassinate him. Sultan Muhammad escaped west to Nishapur, all will to fight gone, and spent spring 1220 drowning his despair in dissipation.

After conquering Samarqand, Chinggis Khan summered in uplands near Bukhara and dispatched JEBE and Sübe'etei with three *tümens* of cavalry (each nominally numbering 10,000) to find and destroy the sultan. Crossing the Amu Dar'ya in May 1220, they reached Balkh, which promptly surrendered. They appointed a *darughachi* and followed the sultan's trail west. Everywhere, they spared the cities that surrendered, placing *darughachis* and moving on, and massacred everyone in towns that resisted. Capturing Terken Khatun and the sultan's family, they almost caught Sultan Muhammad in the Zagros Mountains in southwest Iran before he fled north to an island on the Caspian Sea, where he died in winter 1220–21. Jebe and Sübe'etei continued north around the Caspian Sea and back to Mongolia.

Before long, the cities that had surrendered to Jebe and Sübe'etei killed their *darughachi*s and revolted. As the autumn weather cooled, Chinggis Khan began the second, most brutal, phase of the war. He sent out his vanguard under Toquchar to cross into eastern Iran and northwest Afghanistan and crush those he now took as incorrigible rebels. Chinggis sent his middle sons, CHA'ADAI and Ögedei, to join Jochi, and they destroyed Khorazm's capital, Urganch (April 1221). He himself stormed the city of Termiz on the Amu Dar'ya, crossed the river, and annihilated the great city of Balkh, where the Mongol *darughachi* had been killed. Meanwhile, his youngest son, TOLUI, destroyed Merv (Mary) in March 1221, Nishapur (Neyshabur) in April 1221, and Herat after an eight-month siege. In all six cities the craftsmen were deported and all other inhabitants massacred.

Meanwhile, Sultan Muhammad's son Jalal-ud-Din, after several narrow escapes, reached Ghazni in Afghanistan in February 1221. Rallying his father's commanders, he defeated a force of three *tümens* of Mongols (each nominally numbering 10,000) led by SHIGI QUTUQU at Parwan in the Hindu Kush (see PARWAN, BATTLE OF). Soon afterward, however, quarrels broke up Jalal-ud-Din's army, and as Chinggis Khan moved up with his full force, Jalal-ud-Din had to retreat. Finally, in November 1221 he gave battle with his back to the Indus River. The Mongols destroyed his army and killed his commanders, and Jalal-ud-Din swam across the Indus River into India. (See INDIA AND THE MONGOLS.)

Unable to cross the river, Chinggis Khan moved upstream to Peshawar, while Ögedei turned back to raze Ghazni. The Indian climate and disease enervated the Mongol army, and they were weighted down by booty and captives, 10 or 20 to each soldier. After the army had recovered and the excess captives were massacred, Chinggis Khan moved back up into the Hindu Kush. He and the main Mongol armies stayed in Afghanistan until spring 1223, when they returned to Mongolia. In this third stage of the war, clashes were constant, but resistance was disorganized and episodic. Mountain fortresses in Afghanistan were painfully besieged and their defenders slaughtered. The account of MASTER CHANGCHUN, the Taoist who visited Chinggis Khan in 1222–23, describes "bandit" attacks and conflagrations in the suburbs of Samarqand and attacks on the pontoon bridge over the Amu Dar'ya. Historical sources say very little about this plebeian guerrilla resistance, which must have been widespread.

THE PURSUIT OF JALAL-UD-DIN

Armies were also sent in pursuit of Jalal-ud-Din, who had recruited men to his standard among the Turk and Afghan soldiery in India. In 1224 he escaped through

Baluchistan back to western Iran, where the surviving Khorazmian commanders were regrouping. In the succeeding years he attempted to create a new empire in western Iran and Greater Armenia, fighting the rulers of GEORGIA, Seljük TURKEY, and the many petty fortress-states in KURDISTAN. When Ögedei Khan succeeded his father in 1229, he sent CHORMAQAN with three *tümens* (each nominally numbering 10,000) to destroy Jalal-ud-Din. In August 1231 they caught up with him, and he escaped alone, only to be killed by a Kurdish mountaineer. His turbulent Khorazmian troops, mostly Qangli Turks, fled south, where many were recruited into local armies.

KHORAZM IN THE MONGOL EMPIRE

In the Islamic world the brutal conquest of Khorazm left an enduring image of the Mongols as inhuman and irresistible conquerors. Chinggis Khan attempted to win over defectors as he had done so successfully in North China yet gained no significant support among Khorazmian commanders. Thus, no Khorazmian general in the service of the khans later looked back on the arrival of Chinggis Khan as the beginning of a brilliant career, as many Kitan and Chinese commanders did. Perhaps for this reason, Mongol accounts of the conquest seem curiously flat, as if numbed by three years of virtually uninterrupted victories and massacres.

Chinggis Khan gave Khorazm proper, along with Otrar and the cities on the Syr Dar'ya, to his oldest son, Jochi, as his appanage, and QONGGIRAD and ÖNGGÜD clansmen settled its pastures. Jochi appointed the Önggüd Chin-Temür as its first *darughachi*. The capital, Urganch, slowly recovered but remained in the shadow of Bukhara and Samarqand until 1260. After that year Bukhara and Samarqand declined due to repeated civil war and misrule by the Chaghatay khans, descendants of Cha'adai, Chinggis's, second son. Hostilities between the CHAGHATAY KHANATE and the Mongol rulers of Iran and China also blocked east–west trade, and Khorazm, part of the Jochids' GOLDEN HORDE, replaced the Transoxiana cities as the hub of Central Asian international commerce. The massive export of horses from the Caspian steppe to India also passed through Khorazm (*see* INDIA AND THE MONGOLS). When MUHAMMAD ABU-'ABDULLAH IBN BATTUTA visited Urganch in 1333, he found the crowds in the marketplace so dense he could not enter. The governor of Khorazm was one of the most important emirs of the Golden Horde, and as the Mongol ruling class had converted to Islam, the Mongol governors enjoyed intimate relations with the city's civil elite. Khorazm shared in the international crisis of the late 14th century. After the Golden Horde broke up, the Qungrats (Qonggirad), a lineage of Mongol descent, ruled Khorazm. Urganch had declined, and the Qungrat dynasty made its capital at Khiva until the Russian conquest in the 19th century.

Central Asian captives dwelling among the Mongols in the east (called Sarta'ul, or in modern Mongolian Sartuul) were eventually assimilated into the Mongolian people. In the 16th century the Sartuul formed one of the 14 clans of the Khalkha, and the Sartuul clan name is still widespread in Mongolia. It is also found among the Monggoljin Mongols of FUXIN MONGOL AUTONOMOUS COUNTY in Liaoning. In 1721 many Sartuul were left on the northern side of the newly demarcated Qing-Russian frontier, thus becoming part of the BURIATS in Russia.

See also MASSACRES AND THE MONGOL CONQUEST.

Further reading: W. Barthold, *Turkestan down to the Mongol Invasion*, rev. ed., trans. T. Minorsky (London: Luzac, 1968); 'Ala-ad-Din 'Ata-Malik Juvaini, *History of the World Conqueror,* 2 vols., trans. John Andrew Boyle (Cambridge, Mass.: Harvard University Press, 1958); Minhaj-ud-Dîn Abû-'Umar-i-'Usman [Juzjani], *Tabakat-i-Nasirî,* 2 vols., trans. Major H. G. Raverty (1881; rpt., Calcutta: The Asiatic Society, 1995).

Khorchin (Horqin, Horchin, Qorcin, Ke'rqin) The Khorchin Mongols are the most numerous of the Inner Mongolian subethnic groups. Their territory is in eastern Inner Mongolia, east of the GREATER KHINGGAN RANGE and along the Taor and Shara Mören (Xar Moron/Liao) Rivers.

The Khorchin Mongols traditionally belonged to Jirim league (*chuulgan*), with Gorlos, Dörbed, and Jalaid banners. Khorchin was divided into left (southern) and right (northern) flanks, each with three banners. Today CHINESE COLONIZATION and administrative reorganization have left four banners only, together covering a total of 63,689 square kilometers (24,590 square miles). They are inhabited by about 1,500,600 people, of whom 938,800, or almost 62 percent, are Mongol (1990 figures). Most Khorchins in this area speak their own distinct dialect of Mongolian, but a substantial minority speak only Chinese.

Arable agriculture, based mostly on corn, millet, *gaoliang* sorghum, and buckwheat, supplies more than two-thirds of the Khorchin banners' total agricultural sales. Livestock, 2,935,000 in number, include 1,225,000 sheep and goats; most of the rest is divided roughly equally between cattle and pigs (1990 figures). Wild vegetation is either couch grass steppe or dunes with pea bush, willow, and sagebrush thickets. Khorchins frequently leave their overcrowded steppes to become officials, teachers, soldiers, or migrant herders elsewhere in Inner Mongolia.

HISTORY

The Khorchin are descended from the semiagricultural Mongols of the Fuyu (Üjiyed) Guard around modern Qiqihar, who surrendered to the MING DYNASTY in 1389 (*see* THREE GUARDS). Ruled by descendants of CHINGGIS KHAN's younger brother Qasar, these Khorchins began allying in 1612 with the rising Manchus. The later

Farming family in Khorchin, left flank, middle banner, 1988. They are sitting on a *kang,* or heated living/sleeping platform. Note the moral maxims in Mongolian on the wall. *(Courtesy Christopher Atwood)*

emperors of the Manchu QING DYNASTY (1636–1912) rewarded the Khorchin nobles highly for this early loyalty. Frequent intermarriage between the Khorchins and Manchus influenced Khorchin customs and gave them powerful patrons in court. The great Kangxi emperor (1662–1722) was devoted to his Khorchin grandmother who raised him.

In 1891 the anti-Mongol Jindandao ("Golden Pill Way") rebellion among Chinese peasants drove many thousands of farming Monggoljin Mongols into Khorchin lands where they became tenant farmers for the native Khorchin (*see* FUXIN MONGOL AUTONOMOUS COUNTY). After 1900 both Chinese education and CHINESE COLONIZATION spread among the Khorchins. The song of the doomed 1929 insurrection led by Gada Meiren (1893–1931) against the brutal dispossession of the Khorchin Mongols for Chinese settlement is still widely sung. After the Japanese occupation of 1931 the Khorchin replaced the KHARACHIN as the most numerous and energetic proponents of secular learning and reform among the Mongols. While the Chinese Communists were able to win over most of the Khorchin Mongol nationalist intelligentsia after 1945, rural class struggle and the civil war of 1946–48 were very bloody and divisive. Since then the Khorchins and other east Mongols have been a powerful faction within Inner Mongolia's Chinese Communist Party apparatus.

After 1946 Khorchin territory was divided into Jirim league to the south and KHINGGAN LEAGUE to the north. In 1999 Jirim league was renamed TONGLIAO MUNICIPALITY.

See also DÖRBED MONGOL AUTONOMOUS COUNTY; FARMING; FRONT GORLOS MONGOL AUTONOMOUS COUNTY; INNER MONGOLIA AUTONOMOUS REGION; INNER MONGOLIANS; KHAFUNGGA; MONGOLIAN LANGUAGE; NEW SCHOOLS MOVEMENTS; WEDDINGS.

Further reading: "Child Birth and Child Training in a Khorchin Mongol Village," *Monumenta Serica* 25 (1966): 406–439; "Family and Kinship Structure of the Khorchin Mongols," *Central Asiatic Journal* 9 (1964): 277–311; "The Lama Temple and Lamaism in Bayin Mang," *Monumenta Serica* 29 (1970): 659–684; Pao Kuo-yi [Ünensechen], "Marriage Customs of a Khorchin Village," *Central Asiatic Journal* 9 (1964): 29–59.

Khorezm · *See* KHORAZM.

Khoshuds (**Khoshuud, Hoshut, Qoshot, Qoṣot**) The Khoshuds are a tribe of Oirat Mongols. (Oirat tribes were not consanguineal units but political-ethnic units, composed of many *yasu*, "bones," or patrilineages.) The Khoshuds' ruling Galwas "bone," were the OIRATS' only Chinggisids, claiming ancestry from Chinggis's brother Qasar. The Khoshud were most likely formed from diverse THREE GUARDS Mongols deported by the Oirat ruler ESEN (r. 1438–54) in 1446–47. (The name is written *Khoshuud* in Cyrillic-script Mongolian, *Khoshoud* in the Clear Script, and *Khoshud* in Cyrillic-script Kalmyk.)

The Khoshud first appeared in the 1580s and by the 1620s were the most powerful Oirat tribe, taking the lead in the SECOND CONVERSION of the Oirats to Buddhism. In 1636 TÖRÖ-BAIKHU GÜÜSHI KHAN led many Khoshuds to occupy Kökenuur; the Khoshuds from the great majority of the Tibetan plateau's almost 80,000 UPPER MONGOLS. About 10 years later his brother Köndölöng Ubashi migrated to the Volga, joining the KALMYKS. Many Khoshuds remained in the Oirat homeland of Zungharia under Ochirtu Tsetsen Khan (fl. 1639–76).

After GALDAN BOSHOGTU KHAN of the Zönghar tribe deposed Ochirtu Tsetsen Khan, the Khoshud chief Khoroli deserted to the QING DYNASTY with his people in 1686, receiving ALASHAN as his territory. Alashan's Khoshud Mongols numbered 36,900 in 1990. The Khoshud remained, however, a major tribe of Zünghar principality until its annihilation by the Qing in 1755. In 1771 Volga Khoshuds joined the FLIGHT OF THE KALMYKS back to Zungharia and were resettled by the Qing around Bosten Lake. They numbered around 12,000 in 1999.

Another small body of Khoshuds, associated with the "New" Torghud, was formed into a separate banner in western Mongolia (Bulgan Sum, Khowd). Today they are officially registered as Torghud.

The Khoshud *ulus* remains numerous in Kalmykia; its princes of the Tümen family were influential until 1917. The Khoshud traditionally occupy the lower Volga region.

See also BAYANGOL AUTONOMOUS PREFECTURE; KALMYK REPUBLIC; SUBEI MONGOL AUTONOMOUS COUNTY; ZAYA PANDITA NAMKHAI-JAMTSU.

Further reading: Slawoj Szynkiewicz, "Ethnic Boundaries in Western Mongolia," *Journal of the Anglo-Mongolia Society* 10 (1987): 11–16.

Khoshuud *See* KHOSHUDS.

Khotgoid *See* KHOTOGHOID.

Khotoghoid (**Khotgoid, Khotoghoit, Altyn Khans**) This branch of the Khalkha Mongols was formed from OIRATS and other peoples in northwestern Mongolia who had been subjugated by the KHALKHA prince Sholoi Ubashi Khung-Taiji (1567–1623?) and his descendants.

Born the second-ranking Khalkha right-flank (western) prince after his cousin Laikhur Khan (b. 1564), Sholoi Ubashi Khung-Taiji inherited territory in northwest Mongolia. Like Laikhur Khan, he campaigned incessantly against the Oirats. Subjugated Oirats of the Khotoghoid tribe came to form a large part of his people. After 1600 Sholoi expanded his domain to include the Uriangkhai of Tuva and the Kyrgyz of Khakassia. Hearing about Sholoi from the Kyrgyz as the Altyn czar (Golden Emperor), Russian Cossacks made contact with him in 1616. Hoping for firearms and Russian assistance against the Oirats, Sholoi provisioned and guided the Russian envoys to China. As the Russian refused to assist his continuing campaigns against the Oirats, however, he broke off relations in 1620. In perhaps 1623 Sholoi launched an expedition to the Irtysh River, where the united Oirats fighting under the leadership of Baibaghas Khan (d. 1630) of the KHOSHUDS killed him. The tale of this defeat is told in the 17th-century Oirat tale *Mongghol-un Ubashi Khung-taiji-yin tughuji* (Tale of the Mongol Ubashi Khung-Taiji). (The date of this defeat is given as 1587 in the text, but this must be wrong; 1623 is more likely.) His son Ombo-Erdeni (1623?–52, d. 1659) succeeded him.

In 1662 Ombo-Erdeni's son Lubsang-Rinchin Taiji (r. 1652–67) killed the Zasagtu Khan (Laikhur's grandson). The shocked Khalkha noblemen joined to punish him, driving him north into Tuva. In 1667 the Oirat ruler Sengge captured Lubsang-Rinchin there and plundered his people. After GALDAN BOSHOGTU KHAN's Oirat invasion of Khalkha in 1688, Lubsang-Rinchin's nephew Gendün Daiching (d. 1697) surrendered first to Russia and then to Galdan before submitting to the Qing in 1694. The Qing divided the Khotoghoid territory into four BANNERS (appanages) under Gendün Daiching and his family in modern northern ZAWKHAN PROVINCE and southwest KHÖWSGÖL PROVINCE. Gendün Daiching's third-generation successor, Chinggünjab (1710–57), led a rebellion in 1756–57 and was executed (*see* CHINGGÜNJAB'S REBELLION). In 1764 the Qing authorities separated most of the Khotoghoid princes' MINGGHAD subjects and made them an independent banner near KHOWD CITY. The four banners remained, however. Today the Khotoghoid are considered Khalkha Mongols.

Khoton *See* KHOTONG.

Khotong (**Khoton, Hoton**) The Khotong are a small subethnic group, or *yastan*, in Uws province. The Mongolian Khotong actually call themselves "Uighurs" and were deported by the ZÜNGHARS from the Central Asian cities of Osh and Bukhara and the neighboring Kazakh and Kyrgyz. ("Khotong" is the Mongol designation for Muslim oases dwellers and in Inner Mongolia designates the Hui, or Chinese-speaking, Muslims.) As enslaved prisoners of war, the Khotong followed their lord, the DÖRBÖD prince Tseren Ubashi, when he surrendered to the Qing in 1753 and received land near Ulaangom in modern UWS PROVINCE.

The Khotong delivered yearly 40 sacks of wheat and sent 11 laborers every summer to the prince's palace, where they also herded and worked flour mills. They were, however, free from any public duties. By the turn of the 20th century the Khotong lived in yurts and spoke the Dörböd dialect of Oirat Mongolian. Even so, they avoided intermarriage with the Dörböds and maintained fossilized Central Asian Turkish and Koranic phrases in prayers. The *molda*s (from *molla*, Islamic clergyman) performed religious ceremonies and placed written Koranic verses in the YURT where the Mongols placed Buddhas. Mountaintop OBOO sacrifices were practiced, although the victims were slaughtered in the Islamic fashion. While losing the use of their native Turki, the Khotong resisted using written Mongolian and so became essentially illiterate.

After the 1921 REVOLUTION and emancipation the 2,000 or so Khotong, with a reputation for diligence in manual labor, rapidly improved their living standards but still avoid Mongolian written culture. Only 6.6 percent of the 6,100 Khotong in 1989 were employed in white-collar positions, by far the lowest of any Mongolian ethnic group.

Kho-Urlük *See* KHO-ÖRLÖG.

Khowd city (Hovd, Kobdo, Qobdu, Jargalant)   Khowd was the administrative capital of the western Mongolian frontier under the QING DYNASTY (1636–1912). Situated on the Buyant River flowing east from the ALTAI RANGE to the Khar Us Lake, Khowd is dry, with only 127.4 millimeters (5.02 inches) average annual precipitation. The river has long been used for irrigation, however. The population of 26,000 (2000 figure) is about 85 percent KHALKHA, descendants of the local garrison and newcomers, but includes significant minorities of Chinese, KAZAKHS, ÖÖLÖDS, MINGGHADS, ALTAI URIYANGKHAIS, and others. American atlases frequently misidentify Khowd City as Dund-Us.

The Oirat ruler GALDAN BOSHOGTU KHAN established a farming colony in the Khowd area in 1685. In 1718 the Qing authorities settled 1,000 TÜMED Mongols from Höhhot in Inner Mongolia on the Khowd River as an agricultural colony. Chinese exiles were also settled there. In 1731 the site was moved downstream toward Khar Us Lake, and a Qing general was stationed there with a garrison of Chinese Green Standard soldiers. After this new site was flooded out, the garrison was moved to Khowd's current site in 1762, and walls were built. Chinese and

Khalkha soldiers supplied the garrison by farming. From 1754 one and from 1838 two AMBANs (Qing high officials, always ethnically Mongol or Manchu) and a subordinate staff administered both the town and the Khowd frontier, which covered today's western Mongolia, Russia's Altay Republic, and northern Xinjiang.

Khowd was rebuilt a few years after being sacked by Turkestani rebels in 1871. By the late 19th century Khowd had three centers: the garrison, called Sang-un Khota; the Chinese trading town, or Maimaching; and the Tügeemel Amurjuulagchi, or Yellow Temple. The Maimaching was the commercial center of western Mongolia and was served by nine major Chinese firms and more than 50 minor ones. A Russian consulate was established in 1905.

Mongolian independence forces sacked Khowd on August 7, 1912, destroying the Qing garrison and looting the Chinese shops. Khowd remained the largest town in western Mongolia, but the separation of UWS PROVINCE and BAYAN-ÖLGII PROVINCE from KHOWD PROVINCE diminished the city's role. In 1931 the city was renamed Jargalant, but the old name was restored by 1959. The city reached 17,500 inhabitants in 1979 and had a small diesel generator and local industries. In the 1970s and 1980s Khowd was used again as a place of exile for dissidents and resident aliens of Chinese and Inner Mongolian ancestry.

Khowd province (Hovd, Chovd, Kobdo)   One of the original 13 provinces created in the 1931 administrative reorganization, Khowd lies in western Mongolia. The province straddles the ALTAI RANGE, extending northeast into the GREAT LAKES BASIN and southwest into the Trans-Altai GOBI DESERT. Mongolian independence forces seized this area, the core of the Khowd frontier administration under the QING DYNASTY, in 1912 (*see* 1911 RESTORATION). The theocratic regime made the DÖRBÖD BANNERS (appanages) in modern UWS PROVINCE separate provinces, but in 1923 the whole western frontier was again unified as Chandamani Uula province, with its capital at Ulaangom in Dörböd territory. In 1931 the former Dörböd banners were again separated from Khowd as Uws province, but several districts traditionally part of KHALKHA Mongolia's Zasagtu Khan province were added to Khowd province. In 1940 the Kazakh-dominated western marches were separated from Khowd as Bayan-Ölgii. Khowd has a long frontier with Xinjiang in China.

The ethnic map of Khowd was drawn by the Qing dynasty after the conquest of the ZÜNGHARS in 1755–57. Around the garrison city of Khowd, the Qing settled Höhhot TÜMED from Inner Mongolia, Khalkhas, and Chinese troops as farmers to feed the garrison; their descendants today are considered Khalkhas. Around the garrison additional Oirat groups were settled with service obligations toward the garrison: ÖÖLÖDS and MINGGHADS to the north, ZAKHACHIN to the south, and ALTAI URIYANGKHAI to the west. In the southwest independent princely banners of TORGHUDS and KHOSHUDS were settled. In the late 19th century KAZAKHS immigrated and settled Khowd Sum, on the city's western outskirts.

Khowd province's 76,100 square kilometers (29,380 square miles) straddle the Altai Range and border several of Mongolia's highest peaks. North of the Altai Range lies the Great Lakes Basin, with the freshwater Khar Us and Khar Lakes and the salt Dörgön Lake. Khowd's Trans-Altai Gobi includes part of the Great Gobi Nature Preserve and many rare Gobi animals. The population of 42,300 in 1956 has grown to 87,800 in 2000. Livestock numbering 1,836,300 graze the province's pastures (2000 figure). Khowd's agricultural tradition has continued on a small scale; the province produced 8 percent of Mongolia's potato harvest in 2000. The provincial capital of Khowd has 26,000 inhabitants (2000 figures).

See also FARMING; THEOCRATIC PERIOD.

Khöwsgöl, Lake (Hövsgöl, Chövsgöl, Khubsugul)
Located among the taiga forest and mountains of far northern Mongolia, Lake Khöwsgöl is 136 kilometers (85 miles) long but only 36.5 kilometers (22.7 miles) wide at its greatest width. Its surface area of 2,620 square kilometers (1,012 square miles) is second in Mongolia to LAKE UWS, but with a depth of 262 meters (860 feet), Khöwsgöl contains 380.7 cubic kilometers (91.3 cubic miles) of water, more than eight times that of Uws. Its exceptionally clear water is fed by more than 90 rivers and drained by the EG (Egiin Gol) RIVER; the lake's name may be Turkish in origin, from Kök Su Köl, "Blue Water Lake." From 1913 on steamships have plied the lake carrying products between Khatgal at the lake's southern end and Khankh at the northern end and thence to nearby Siberia. In 1992 the area around Khöwsgöl was made a national park.

See also BAIKAL, LAKE; ENVIRONMENTAL PROTECTION; KHÖWSGÖL PROVINCE; MONGOLIAN PLATEAU.

Khöwsgöl province (Hövsgöl, Chövsgöl, Khubsugul)
One of the original provinces created in Mongolia's 1931 administrative reorganization, Khöwsgöl is the farthest north of Mongolia's provinces and has a long frontier with the Buriat and Tuvan Republics in Russia.

Khöwsgöl's northern territory includes the area of the DARKHAD, who were "lay disciples," or subjects, of the JIBZUNDAMBA KHUTUGTU (*see* GREAT SHABI). Surrounding the Darkhad were the Khöwsgöl Nuur Uriyangkhais, mostly TUVANS in origin. Originally part of Tannu Uriyangkhai province, the Darkhad and Uriyangkhai were reorganized in 1925 as Delger Yekhe Uula province. Khöwsgöl's southern half contains most of its population and is made up of territory from KHALKHA Mongolia's prerevolutionary Sain Noyan and Zasagtu Khan provinces. That of Zasagtu Khan is part of the KHOTOGHOID Khalkha

territory. In the northeast also reside immigrant Buriat Mongols. Khöwsgöl's Tuvans include the DUKHA (called Tsaatan in Mongolian), Mongolia's only reindeer herders.

Khöwsgöl's territory of 100,600 square kilometers (62,370 square miles) is marked by high parallel ridges and deep valleys. The northern ranges are among Mongolia's wettest, averaging more than 500 millimeters (20 inches) annually and many rivers, such as the EG RIVER, the Tes River, and the Shishigt River originate there. Most notable is the deep and clear LAKE KHÖWSGÖL. Khöwsgöl's population rose from 58,200 in 1956 to 119,800 in 2000, making it Mongolia's most populous province. Khöwsgöl contains Mongolia's second-largest herd of 2,269,600 head (2000 figures), with especially large numbers of HORSES (229,300 head), CATTLE (416,500 head), and SHEEP (944,900 head). Khöwsgöl's capital, Mörön, has a population of 26,800 (2002 figure).

See also BUDDHISM, CAMPAIGN AGAINST; BURIATS OF MONGOLIA AND INNER MONGOLIA; JALKHANZA KHUTUGTU DAMDINBAZAR; SHIRENDEW, BAZARYN.

Khoyar Yosu *See* "TWO CUSTOMS."

Khubilai *See* QUBILAI KHAN.

Khubsugul *See* KHÖWSGÖL PROVINCE.

khung-taiji *See* TAIJI.

Khunnu *See* XIONGNU.

Khutugtai Sechen Khung-Taiji (1540–1586) *Initiator of the Second Conversion to Buddhism in southwest Inner Mongolia*
Ruling the Üüshin and Besüd clans at Yekhe Shiber in today's Üüshin (Uxin) banner of ORDOS, this Chinggisid nobleman plundered the Torghud on the Irtysh River (1562). In 1566 Khutugtai Sechen Khung-Taiji brought home from another campaign in Kökenuur a lama, Wachir Tümei, whom he made his chief adviser. An intimate of his cousin ALTAN KHAN, he represented Ordos in the western Mongols' 1571 treaty with China. Already skillful in Buddhist language, he gave up horsemeat after a vision of a wrathful Buddhist deity. In 1574 Khutugtai and his son again plundered the OIRATS in the Altai, and in 1576–78 he represented Ordos among the western Mongols invited by bSod-nams rGya-mtsho (1543–88), the Third Dalai Lama, to Mongolia. The Dalai Lama declared him the incarnation of an ancient patron of the Buddha and gave him the title Chogchas-un Jirükhen (Heart of the Assemblages). Laws attributed to him prohibited the killing of animals or servants at lords' funerals and the making of an *ongghon* (spirit figurine) in the lords images and sacrificing to them. He also circulated

the CHAGHAN TEÜKE, which presented an idealized picture of Buddhist government. In 1580, angered over the delay of a higher title and stipend promised by China the year before, Khutugtai plundered 21 towns along the Shaanxi-Gansu frontier. Special rewards from China followed regularly thereafter. While meeting the Dalai Lama in 1585, he achieved a powerful meditation state and vowed to keep peace with his fellow Ordos noblemen. After his death in 1587, his wife, Sechen Beiji, received frequent awards from China until 1607. Ancestor of southern Üüshin's nobility, he was worshipped by them at his grave until the 20th century.

Khwarazm   *See* KHORAZM.

Khwarizm   *See* KHORAZM.

Kiakhta   *See* KYAKHTA CITY.

Kiev, siege of   The siege of Kiev, which ended on December 6, 1240, with the sack of the city, was the final great blow in the Mongol conquest of Russia.

On the eve of the Mongol invasion, Kiev was, despite political turmoil, still the mother-city of Russia (including Ukraine and Belarussia); whichever prince held Kiev became great prince of all Russia. After the Mongols under CHINGGIS KHAN's grandson BATU (d. 1255) destroyed several cities of northern Russia—Ryazan', Vladimir, Torzhok, and Kozel'sk—in 1238, the Mongols turned their attention to the steppe. In 1239 they advanced against southern Russia, taking Pereyaslavl' and Chernihiv (Chernigov) south and north of Kiev. In 1240 Batu's cousin MÖNGKE KHAN (1209–59), inspecting Kiev from across the Dniepr, sent an envoy summoning Prince Michael of Chernihiv, then holding Kiev, to surrender. Michael fled to Hungary, and no prince dared take command in the city; a commander of a 1,000 (*tysiatskii*), Dmitro, marshaled the final resistance.

After Batu crushed the "Black Caps" (Qipchaq Turkish allies guarding Kiev's southern approaches), the entire Mongol army camped outside Kiev under his command. Batu set up catapults near the southeast "Polish Gates," where tree cover extended almost to the walls, and began several days of bombardment. On the eighth day the walls were breached, and hand-to-hand combat followed on the walls, where a Mongol arrow wounded Dmitro. The Mongols held their positions when night fell, while Dmitro and the Kievans walled the Church of the Blessed Virgin for a last stand. The next day, as the Mongols assaulted the church, the people crowded into the upper chambers, and the walls collapsed. The population was butchered, although Dmitro was spared for his bravery.

JOHN OF PLANO CARPINI, who visited the town in 1246, described the surrounding countryside as littered with skulls and bones and the town itself reduced to scarcely 200 houses. He found a Mongol commander of a 1,000 and several nobles there. No Russian prince made his seat there, leaving Kiev, unlike other Russian cities, with no buffer against direct Mongol rule.

See also MASSACRES AND THE MONGOL CONQUEST; MILITARY OF THE MONGOL EMPIRE; RUSSIA AND THE MONGOL EMPIRE.

Further reading: George A. Perfecky, trans., *The Galician-Volynian Chronicle* (Munich: 1973).

kinship system   In the MONGOL EMPIRE wealthy Mongol men were organized into exogamous, patrilineal clans. By the 19th century the patrilineal clans were visibly breaking down. While in some areas matrilineal clans resulted, among most of the Mongols the stem family had become the main form of family life by the opening of the 20th century. Urban Mongols today live mostly in nuclear families.

CLANS AND MARRIAGE ALLIANCE

In the empire period the Mongols were famous for their genealogical knowledge and their use of that knowledge to place one another socially. At the time of CHINGGIS KHAN his BORJIGID clan was made up of sublineages linked by genealogies reaching back 11 generations. Only the dominant members in a Mongolian clan (*oboq* or *omoq*, modern *owog*) generally shared the same "bone" (*yasu*), or patrilineage. Many or most of the poorer subjects and slave members came from other clans or were not Mongol at all.

Each clan had a "personality" well known to other Mongols. The clans were also distinguished by common worship of their ancestors, by dedication (*ongghola-; see* ONGGHON) of different-colored livestock, and by different cattle brands (*tamagha*, modern *tamga*). They were also associated with different wild animals, although a full-blown totemic system seems absent. The medieval Mongolian system of kinship terms has features of what anthropologists call the Omaha system, after the American Indian tribe. This system emphasizes the unity of the patrilineage and its difference from one's mother's relatives.

Mongolian patrilineages were strictly exogamous, and the alliance relations formed by these relations were equally as important as the clans in structuring society. As in other exogamous Asian societies, conception was seen as a merger of the paternal semen/"bone" (*yasu*, modern *yas*) and the maternal blood/"meat" (*miqa*, modern *makh*). Patrilineages had a common "bone" and could not intermarry, although distantly related clans (traditionally at least 11 generations apart) could be and often were made "foreign" (*qari*, modern *khari*) and so became appropriate marriage partners.

The Mongol marriage system among the clan leaders was sometimes based on what anthropologists call "generalized exchange" (each patrilineage gave its women to one patrilineage and received them from another), in which the wife-giving lineage holds higher status than the wife-taking lineage (hypogamy). This arrangement was still found among the 19th-century BURIATS, where no single lineage held sway. Under the empire and even before, however, the dominance of the Borjigid lineage led to marriage alliances being formed bilaterally with other lineages. The resulting system thus resembled the anthropological "restricted exchange" (two patrilineages exchanging women in successive generations), except that the Borjigid maintained such restricted exchange with many lineages (*see* QUDA). Among the KITANS of Inner Mongolia, the alliance of the ruling Yelü and the allied Shimo clans approximated "restricted exchange" even more closely.

BREAKDOWN OF CLAN SOCIETY

Clan society remained strong among the Mongols through the 16th century. By the 19th century, however, genealogical knowledge past three or four generations had become rare among the KHALKHA Mongols and the INNER MONGOLIANS. Rules of exogamy were reinterpreted to prohibit marriage with near relatives on either the father's or the mother's side. Related men were addressed as "brother" (*akh/düü*) and women as "sister" (*egch/düü*) (younger sister), regardless of whether the relation was on the female or male side. Only the Borjigid TAIJI class (the nobility) retained any corporate clan structure and systematic genealogical knowledge.

However, the cultural vocabulary of patrilineal groupings formed by a territory, cult of a protector deity, consecrated animals, local landmarks, distinct cattle brands, and exogamy remained. Usually, these now began to be redefined as marking a local SUM, or subbanner district, with the cult attached to the OBOO (cairn) and open to all resident men. MATRILINEAL CLANS arose in the 19th-century Gobi, laying claim to clan territory and worshipping a single Buddhist protector god.

Among the Buriat Mongols of southern Siberia, however, patrilineal kinship and clan structures remain remarkably strong even today. Many know their patrilineal ancestors back 12 generations, and virtually everyone can trace a kinship network of more than 100 people. Among the Daurs and BARGA Mongols of northeastern Inner Mongolia as well, clans (called *khala* from the Manchu term) still function. Among the OIRATS of western Mongolia the clan structure is more visible than among the Khalkha but less so than among the Buriats or Barga and Daurs.

Several reasons can be proposed for this disintegration of clan structure among the Khalkha and Inner Mongolians. After 1500 the expansion of the Borjigid (Chinggisid) clan replaced the local non-Borjigid clan leadership. Manchu administration by BANNERS formalized this Borjigid dominance and further extended state institutions, leaving no role for non-Borjigid clan institutions.

The spread of Buddhism may also have played a factor by eliminating the worship of clan spirits (*ongghon*) and by weakening marriage. Since, however, the Buddhist New Bargas and Khori Buriats maintain clan institutions, religious changes appear to be secondary compared with the institutionalized Borjigid rule in the banners.

See also CLAN NAMES; FAMILY.

Further reading: David F. Aberle, *Kinship System of the Kalmuk Mongols* (Albuquerque: University of New Mexico Press, 1953); Roberte Hamayon, "Abuse of the Father, Abuse of the Husband: A Comparative Analysis of Two Buryat Myths of Ethnic Origin." In *Synkretismus in den Religionen Zentralasiens,* ed. Walther Heissig and Hans-Joachim Klimkeit (Wiesbaden: Harrassowitz, 1987), 91–107; Herbert Harold Vreeland, III, *Mongol Community and Kinship Structure* (New Haven: HRAF Press, 1957); Slawoj Szynkiewicz, "Kinship Groups in Modern Mongolia," *Ethnologia Polona* 3 (1977): 31–45.

Kin Tartars   *See* JIN DYNASTY.

Kitan language and script   The Kitan language, while still only imperfectly known, appears to belong to the Mongolic language family. Kitan syntax is clearly Altaic in type, with adjunct-head and subject-object-verb word order. (*On the Kitan people, see* KITANS.) Kitan language had two scripts, both written, like Chinese, in columns from right to left. Examples of both are extant today. The first, "large" script was created in 920 and was basically logographic (i.e., one character per word). A small number of Chinese characters were directly adopted into this new Kitan writing, but most were different from Chinese. It is unclear how, if at all, case endings were expressed. This large script, which presumably contained thousands of characters, is still undeciphered.

After learning the language of Uighur envoys who arrived in 925, the emperor's brother Yelü Diela was inspired to create a new Kitan script, which "though fewer in number covered everything." About 370 characters have been identified of this new "small" script. Some are logograms only, but the characters for single-syllable words are frequently used as syllabograms (i.e., for their phonetic value, not their meaning), thus reducing the number of logograms necessary and enabling case endings to be written. When used as syllabograms, the characters are assembled into box-shaped composite characters. The meaning and/or pronunciation of only about 130 characters is currently known.

The extant Kitan script sources include epitaphs, tomb and stupa inscriptions, and short inscriptions on mirrors, seals, and so on, with datable examples from 1055 to 1150. Kitan books included original poetry and legal codes, histories, and administrative compendia translated from Chinese. Small fragments from Turpan (Xinjiang) show Kitan writing on paper.

Of the known Kitan words, most of the basic vocabulary is clearly Mongolian: *tau*, "five" (cf. Middle Mongolian *tabu*); *jau*, "hundred" (cf. MM *ja'u*); *taula*, "rabbit" (cf. MM *taulai*); *mogho*, "snake" (cf. MM *moghai*); *deu*, "younger brother" (cf. MM *de'ü*); *ewul*, "cloud" (cf. MM *e'üle*); *po*, "time" (cf. MM *hon*, "year"); *sair*, "month" (cf. MM *sara*); *nair*, "day" (cf. MM *nara*, "sun"); *uwul*, "winter" (cf. MM *ebül*); *sheu-*, "dew" (cf. MM *si'üderi*); *m.ng.*, "silver" (dots indicate uncertain vowels; cf. MM *mönggö*); *kuichi*, "arriving" (cf. MM *kürchü*); *g.n.-*, "to mourn" (cf. MM *ghuni-*). However, a number of terms have no cognates in any Altaic language; *shi-*, "nine"; *i.r.*, "name"; *ai*, "year"; *jurgu*, "gold"; *m.o*, "big"; *m.n.*, "divine"; *m.u.-*, "holy"; *chishideben*, "filial piety." The political terminology shows numerous Chinese and Turkic terms.

Many peculiar Kitan words may, in fact, be old Mongolic words that in Middle Mongolian (the language of the MONGOL EMPIRE; *see* MONGOLIAN LANGUAGE) and its descendants were replaced by Turkic forms. Thus, the Middle Mongolian equivalents of Kitan *jurgu*, "gold," and *hasho*, "iron," are derived from the Turkic *altun* and *temür*. The Kitan word for "blue," while not fully readable, appears to be totally different from the Turkish-Middle Mongolian *köke*, "blue," and to share the same *-'an* ending of native Mongolian color words.

Phonologically, Kitan was considerably more progressive than was Middle Mongolian in the loss of certain short vowels, softening of the intervocalic *-b-*, palatalization of vowels, and transformation of vocal harmony from a primarily front-back distinction to a high-low distinction. Even so, it retains the initial *p-*, which in Middle Mongolian had become *h-* or simply disappeared.

After the fall of the Kitans' Liao dynasty in 1125, the Kitans under the succeeding Jin dynasty (1115–1234), both officials and common people, maintained their language. The Kitan language and script were also used in the QARA-KHITAI ("Black Kitan") dynasty (1131–1213) in Turkestan. The Jurchens introduced their own script in 1120 on the model of the Kitan large script, reforming it in 1145 on the model of the Kitan small script. The Kitan small script was widely used under the Jin, and translations from Chinese were frequently made from earlier Kitan translations. In 1191, however, the Jin banned the further use of Kitan. Kitan was still spoken widely by the time of the Mongol conquest (1211–15). The Kitan language was no longer used officially under the Mongols, however, and appears to have rapidly declined in favor of Mongolian and, to a lesser degree, Chinese.

See also ALTAIC LANGUAGE FAMILY; MONGOLIC LANGUAGE FAMILY.

Further reading: György Kara, "Kitan and Jurchen," in *The World's Writing System,* ed. Peter Daniels and William Bright (Oxford: Oxford University Press, 1996), 230–238; Fengzhu Liu, "Seventy Years of Kitan Small Script Studies," *Studia Orientalia* 87 (1999): 159–170.

Kitans (Khitan, Old Turkish Qitañ, Chinese Qidan)

The Kitan people of eastern Inner Mongolia founded the Liao dynasty (907–1125) that united Manchuria, Mongolia, and the borderlands of North China. What is known of the Kitan language shows it to be an independent branch of the Mongolic family, less influenced by Turkish than is modern Mongolian.

ORIGINS AND EXPANSION

According to Chinese histories, the Kitans originated from the Yuwen branch of the southern XIANBI. By the sixth century the Kitans dwelled along the Laoha River in southeastern Inner Mongolia. They were divided into eight clans that elected a common chief for a three-year term at an assembly (QURILTAI). Around 600 the Dahe family chiefs submitted to the Türk Empire and in 628 to China's Tang dynasty (*see* TÜRK EMPIRES). In 745 the Yaolian clan overthrew the Dahe and declared themselves *qaghan* (KHAN, emperor). They were allied 755 on with the UIGHUR EMPIRE (744–840) and the autonomous Chinese warlords in Hebei. The position of *qaghan* remained elective, however, at least formally. With the fall of the Uighur Empire, many UIGHURS fled to the Kitans. The Uighur Shimo (later sinicized to Xiao) clan later became marriage allies with the imperial Yila (later renamed Yelü) clan (*see* QUDA).

Under Qinde (reign title Hendejin Qaghan, 901–07) of the Yaolian, the Kitan began to expand. With Hendejin Qaghan's death, Abaoji, chief of the Yila clan and successful veteran of many campaigns, was elected *qaghan* in 907. Abaoji, who knew Chinese, built his power not only on military prowess but on his family's iron and salt works, which he expanded with captive labor.

Encouraged by his Chinese settlers, Abaoji refused to submit to reelection when his three-year period as *qaghan* was over. Executing recalcitrant chiefs and subduing rebellions of his ambitious brothers, in 916 he proclaimed himself *huangdi* (Chinese for emperor), and the title "khan" disappeared from Kitan life. In 918 he built a new capital, Shangjing, on the Inner Mongolian steppe (near modern Lindong). In 947 his second son and successor, Deguang (posthumous reign name Taizong, 927–47), flush with ambitions to conquer North China, changed the dynastic name from the ethnically limited Kitan (Chinese, Qidan) to the supraethnic Liao. In their own language, however, the dynasty was called the Daur Gurun (Daur Dynasty), a term that was inherited by their provincial descendants, the modern Daurs.

Under Hendejin and Abaoji the Kitans had conquered the closely related Qai (Chinese, Xi) tribes living to their south in the mountainous lands between modern Inner Mongolia and Liaoning. From 927 on the Qai lived under their own prince and paid tribute, but around 997 the Qai were integrated into the Liao system, and in 1006 the Qai prince's residence was made the city of Zhongjing, "Central Capital."

While early Kitan contacts with sedentary peoples were through deported captives, Abaoji eventually conquered Parhae (Bohai, 698–926), a Confucian realm centered around modern Yanji in eastern Manchuria, in 926. Abaoji's second son deported the Parhae ruling class to a new capital, Dongjing ("Eastern Capital," modern Liaoyang), but Parhae remained semiautonomous until a failed revolt in 1029.

From 905 on the Kitan were generally allied with the Shanxi-based Shatuo (or ÖNGGÜD) Turkish regimes. In 937 Deguang extorted from weak Shatuo rulers 16 prefectures, including Yanjing (modern Beijing), which became the Kitans' Nanjing ("Southern Capital"). Nevertheless, a Kitan invasion of North China in 947 ended, despite the sack of Kaifeng, in a fiasco. In 979 the new ethnic Chinese SONG DYNASTY (960–1279) conquered the Liao's last Shatuo client state in Shanxi and then invaded the Liao. The invasion was defeated, but the struggle continued until 1004, when a Liao counterattack bogged down at Shanyuan (near modern Puyang) on the Huang (Yellow) River. In the subsequent treaty the Song paid annual reparations of 200,000 bolts of silk and 100,000 taels of silver, but otherwise the two dynasties treated each other as equals and maintained the status quo.

Despite repeated invasions, the Liao were unable to control either Korea's Koryŏ dynasty (918–1392) or the XIA DYNASTY (1038–1227). Both agreed, however, to pay tribute to the Liao, from 1120 for Korea and from 1153 for the Xia.

KITAN RULE IN MONGOLIA

From the fall of the Uighurs in 840, central Mongolia had remained anarchic. Abaoji advanced toward Mongolia with his conquest of the "Black-Cart" SHIWEI (probably around modern SHILIIN GOL) in 907, famed for their carts and metalworking. From 912 Abaoji attacked the Wugu/Yuguli (probably Uighur remnants) in southeastern Mongolia and HULUN BUIR, and from 916 he attacked the diverse tribes of southwestern Inner Mongolia. A massive expedition in 924 completed the conquest. Despite frequent rebellions, the Kitans maintained their hold on both Inner Mongolia and eastern and central Mongolia throughout the dynasty.

Kitan with his horse, from a tomb painting, 11th century. The man's figure is 153 centimeters high. *(Courtesy Inner Mongolia Museum, Höhhot)*

Mongolia and central and northeastern Inner Mongolia came under the Kitans' northern administration, which administered primarily the Kitan people themselves. Thus, administration of the tribes of the KHERLEN RIVER valley, the Wugu, and the closely associated Eight Dilie (Töles?) followed those institutions used among the Kitans. Tribes were administered by a Kitan *senggüm* (*xiangwen*, from Chinese *xianggong*, lord chancellor), assisted by a *lingqu* (*lingwen*, from Chinese *linggong*, lord director) and staff. The more distant TATARS (renamed Zubu by later editors) of central Mongolia, ancestors of the later KEREYID Khanate, were ruled either by an *ong* (prince, from Chinese *wang*) or by a *taishi* (Chinese grand preceptor) and paid irregular tribute. In 1093 a Tatar chief, "Mogusi" (i.e., Marquz, r. 1089–1100), launched a massive rebellion against Liao rule, which was suppressed only in 1102. With the pacification of these rebellions, the Wugu and Dilie tribes and many Tatar refugees were deported closer to Liao lands.

The main Kitan garrisons in Mongolia were at Hedong (Züünkherem ruins in Mörön Sum, Khentii) on the Kherlen in Dilie territory and at Zhenzhou (Chintolgoi ruins in Dashinchilen Sum, Bulgan) in Tatar territory. Both areas had walled citadels with small garrisons that fed themselves on herds and farming. Kitan-period walls, coins, and inscriptions have also been found in Sükhebaatur and Middle Gobi provinces.

IMPERIAL INSTITUTIONS

The Kitan ancestor legend involved a man riding a white horse who met and married a woman in a cart drawn by a gray ox. This focus on an exogamous couple paralleled the dual organization of the Kitan ruling class, which was formed by the Yila, or Yelü, clan and the Shimo (sinicized as Xiao) clan. All the emperors were Yila and all the consorts were Xiao; all imperial princesses married Xiao men. The Kitans throughout their dynasty had two grand councilors: a Yila one in the south and a Xiao one in the north.

The Liao administered the northern part of their realm through a kind of semibureaucratic, semitribal structure, ranked according to genealogical and ethnic distance from the emperor: 1) the Yila clan itself, administered in households according to their distance from the imperial line; 2) the Xiao clan and the Yaolian clans; 3) the 34 inner tribes, including Kitans, Qai, Jurchens, Turks, Tanguts in Inner Mongolia, and Hejen/Nanai peoples on the Sungari; and 4) the 10 outer tribes, in eastern Mongolia, Jilin, and the Korean frontier. Each had its tribal chiefs and also a specified complement of officials, not necessarily drawn from the tribe in question.

The Kitan development of the ORDO institution weakened the power of the outer clans. Each emperor created an *ordo,* which combined the traditional palace-tent of the ruler (*ordo* in the strict sense), with a "heart and belly guard" recruited from prisoners of war and the people of the empire. Abaoji's *ordo* totaled 15,000 households. Although after 950 new *ordos* were generally "recycled" from old *ordo* personnel, the total *ordo* population reached perhaps 80,000 households and could supply 50,000–60,000 mounted soldiers. The other military forces of the empire were the Kitan and Qai tribesmen (perhaps 90,000 households), the Chinese (about 480,000 households), and Parhae (about 90,000 households) militiamen. Despite its large number of sedentary soldiers, the Kitan army proved ineffective at siege warfare.

In the three generations after Abaoji, the Kitan royal family moved away from the Inner Asian tradition of lateral succession to the primogeniture required by Chinese tradition, with the first noncontroversial succession taking place in 969. Abaoji's empress, Chunqin (Empress Dowager Yingtian), refused to sacrifice herself on Abaoji's grave, as Kitan tradition demanded, and became the first of several powerful Xiao empress dowagers. Ruizhi (Empress Dowager Chengtian, d. 1009), for example, ably organized the counterattack against the Song.

Local administration in nontribal areas took place through routes attached to the five capitals, each of which was governed by a regent of the imperial clan. In 947 the central administration at Shangjing was divided into northern and southern regions (not to be confused with the dual Yila-Xiao division still in effect within the northern region). The southern region ruled the Chinese and Parhae subjects. Officials of the southern region wore Chinese dress, while those of the north wore Kitan dress. After 1055 all wore Chinese dress for important functions, although the lower-ranked northern officials still wore Kitan dress at other times. At first the legal system was also dual, with customary Kitan law for the northerners and Tang law for the southerners. After 983, with the translation of the Tang code into Kitan, Chinese legal influence increased, a policy formalized by the unified law code of 1036. The Kitans implemented a Confucian exam system for ethnic Chinese, but it never gave access to high office.

KITAN LIFESTYLE AND CULTURE UNDER THE LIAO

Hunting and pastoralism remained the principal Kitan lifestyle through the dynasty's end. The emperor and his court moved among four seasonal *nabo* (camps) distributed between the lower Laoha, the GREATER KHINGGAN RANGE, and the Nanni (Nen) River. In 1086 the Liao's total horse herd reached 1 million, and shortage of pasture caused hardship. In 1188 the herd composition in the area was as follows: 32 percent horses, 59 percent sheep and goats, 9 percent oxen; that under the Liao was probably similar. Pigs were virtually unknown among the Kitans although common among the Qai. Ceramic "cockscomb pots" that imitate leather satchels illustrate the popularity of pastoral fashions, even among urbanized Kitans.

Kitan pottery cockscomb pot, 24.5 centimeters high *(Courtesy Inner Mongolia Museum, Höhhot)*

Kitan language was used throughout the dynasty, and under Abaoji two new scripts were created to write Kitan. Kitan cultural activity included poetry, painting, and Buddhism (entirely in the Chinese tradition), but there was little interest in CONFUCIANISM. Twice the court fed all the realm's monks: 50,000 of them in 942 and 360,000 in 1078. Kitans regularly sent at least one son to a monastery. Even so, traditional Kitan rituals continued, including monthly worship of the sun and annual worship of the dynastic progenitors at the sacred Muye Mountain near the Laoha-Shara Mören (Xar Moron) confluence. Shamans were an honored part of society. Kitan coronations included unique rituals such as the "rebirthing ceremony," in which the emperor was symbolically reborn as a baby, and the "firewood investiture," in which a dragon-embroidered rug was burned to announce the emperor's accession.

Archeologists have identified 200 Kitan settlements within Inner Mongolia. The capital, Shangjing, had a perimeter of seven miles and walls of pounded earth that even today are 6–10 meters (20–33 feet) high and 12–15 (40–50 feet) wide at the base. Within the city open space was kept for yurts. The city was divided into two halves, a northern one for the Kitans and the imperial family and a southern one for the Chinese and Parhae. Although the Kitan imperial tombs have long since been looted, murals depicting historical scenes have survived.

Originally, the Kitans, like the Shiwei, exposed dead bodies in trees for three years until the flesh rotted and then buried the bones. Under the Liao the Kitans practiced both cremation and direct burial, from contrasting Buddhist and Chinese influences. Both funerary urns for cremated remains and tombs for burial have been found in the shape of a YURT. While many later burials show strong Song influence, funerary masks show the persistence of earlier, possibly XIONGNU (Hun), burial customs.

THE FALL OF THE LIAO AND THE KITANS UNDER JURCHEN AND MONGOL RULE

The last two Liao emperors displayed the passivity and suspicion born of seclusion. From 1065 the imperial favorite, Yila Yixin (d. 1083), dominated the court, having the empress executed and the heir apparent first disgraced and then murdered. In 1114, when a tributary Jurchen chief, Wanyan (Onging) Aguda (b. 1068, posthumous reign name Jin Taizu 1115–23), defeated a Liao army and declared himself emperor of the JIN DYNASTY (1115–1234), no adequate response was forthcoming. By 1118 a Parhae rebellion gave Aguda the entire east. In 1120 Aguda sacked Shangjing and desecrated the Liao tombs and by 1122 had taken all the other capitals. Meanwhile the emperor wandered western Inner Mongolia with a few fugitive loyalists; he was finally captured in 1125. Yila Dashi, one of the remaining Liao partisans, fled in 1124 to Mongolia, eventually founding the QARA-KHITAI ("Black Kitan") dynasty (1131–1213) in Turkestan.

The succeeding Jin dynasty was deeply suspicious of the Kitans yet could not avoid employing them. The Kitan officials, particularly members of the Yelü and Xiao (Shimo) families, were far more literate than were the Jurchen. Kitan writings were not only the basis for the new Jurchen script but were also the intermediary in translating Chinese works. The Kitans and Qai were also indispensable to the Jin cavalry. Common Kitans and Qai were employed in "herds" (*qunmu*) under the supervision of Jurchen commissioners of herds. In this capacity they supplied most of the dynasty's horses. Widespread Kitan rebellions in 1159–64, sparked by total mobilization orders for war with the Song, were met with the execution of all surviving members of the Liao imperial family. These rebellions, in which five out of the nine "herds" deserted to the rebels, devastated the Jurchen imperial stud farm, which did not recover for 20 years.

The rise of CHINGGIS KHAN (Genghis, 1206–27) offered the Kitans a new opportunity for revenge. Chinggis Khan himself acknowledged that Kitan discontent with Jurchen rule was a vital factor in his success. Kitan soldiers became an important part of North China's TAMMACHI garrison under Chinggis's viceroy MUQALI. Except for the 1212 rebellion of Yelü Liuge in Manchuria, the

Kitans had no ambition to set up their own state, instead encouraging Chinggis Khan to set up more formal institutions of rule in North China. Ironically, some Kitan advisers, such as YELÜ CHUCAI, acquired notoriety as partisans of the institutions of the Jin dynasty, which they had served.

Under QUBILAI KHAN (1260–94) and his successors the role of the Kitans declined. While Chinggis Khan had treated the Kitans differently from the Jurchen, under the YUAN DYNASTY ethnic class system they were included not among the privileged Mongol or SEMUREN categories, but among the North Chinese, along with the Jurchen, Koreans, and Han (ethnic Chinese). With the growing literacy of the Mongol aristocracy, Kitans were no longer needed as intermediaries.

With the fall of the Yuan dynasty in China in 1368, the Kitans disappeared as an ethnic group, assimilated by the Mongols and the Chinese. The Yelü surname appears among Inner Mongolia's Monggoljin (Fuxin) and JUU UDA areas, both near the ancestral Kitan lands. The Daurs have also preserved both the old dynastic name and certain features of the Kitan language and may be, in part, descendants of northern provincial Kitans.

See also DAUR LANGUAGE AND PEOPLE.

Further reading: Sechin Jagchid, "Kitan Struggles against Jurchen Oppression—Nomadism versus Sinicization," in *Essays in Mongolian Studies* (Provo, Utah: David M. Kennedy Center for International Studies, Brigham Young University, 1988), 34–50; Adam Kessler, *Empires beyond the Great Wall: The Heritage of Genghis Khan* (Los Angeles: Natural History Museum of Los Angeles County, 1993); Denis Twitchett and Klaus-Peter Tietze, "The Liao," in *Cambridge History of China*, vol. 6, *Alien Regimes and Border States, 907–1368*, ed. Herbert Franke and Denis Twitchett (Cambridge: Cambridge University Press, 1994), 43–153; Karl Wittfogel and Feng Chiasheng, *History of Chinese Society: Liao* (Philadelphia: American Philosophical Society, 1949).

Kitbuqa See KED-BUQA.

Kiyad See BORJIGID.

Kjachta See KYAKHTA CITY.

Kobdo See KHOWD PROVINCE.

Köden See KÖTEN.

Kökechü See TEB TENGGERI.

Kökenuur See UPPER MONGOLS.

Kökeqota See HÖHHOT.

Kongrat See QONGGIRAD.

Korea and the Mongol Empire After decades of desultory invasions, Korea became an important Mongol client state in 1260. At the time of the Mongol conquest, Korea was ruled by the Koryŏ dynasty (918–1392). Occupying all the peninsula south of roughly the 40th parallel, the dynasty paid tribute to the JIN DYNASTY (1115–1234) while closely imitating the forms and ranks of a Chinese dynasty. In 1170 the military caste had overthrown civil rule, and from 1196 the military Ch'oe family maintained control over the king. The Ch'oe family overawed the armed Buddhist monks and built up its own armed retinue that replaced the traditional military. Policy making and civil appointments occurred in the Ch'oe household only.

In 1216 a massive body of Kitan freebooters, pressed by the Mongols, crossed into Korea from Manchuria. In January 1219 a Mongol detachment appeared, demanding an alliance with the Koreans against these KITANS. The Koreans submitted, and the Kitans were hunted down. In 1224 a Mongol envoy was killed in obscure circumstances, and Korea stopped paying tribute. In September 1231 ÖGEDEI KHAN (1229–41) dispatched Sartaq to subdue Korea and avenge the dead envoy. After the Mongols ravaged the peninsula, Korea agreed to accept Mongol overseers (DARUGHACHI). When Sartaq withdrew for the summer, however, Ch'oe U (r. 1219–49) ordered all the darughachis murdered and moved the court from Kaegyŏng (modern Kaeŏng) to Kanghwa Island, safe from the Mongols who lacked a navy.

A standoff lasted until 1260. Willing to send tribute, however massive, the Ch'oe regime adamantly opposed accepting any darughachis, sending a royal hostage, or relocating the capital to Kaegyŏng. The Mongols, in response, sent Sartaq back in 1232, until he was slain by a Buddhist monk-soldier's arrow, and later dispatched Tanggud (1235–36), Ebügen (Amukan, 1247–48), Prince Yekü (1253–54), and Jalayirdai (1254–55). The government did not resist the Mongols but gathered the peasantry into the mountain fortresses and islands to wait out the raids. In 1241 the Koreans sent as hostage a distant collateral member of the royal family, Wang Sun (1224–83). By the 1250s, however, this stalemate began to be unsupportable: 206,800 captives had been taken in Jalayirdai's 1254 razzia alone. Famine and despair forced peasants to surrender to the Mongols, who began fortifying Üiju (near modern Sinŭiju) and established a chiliarchy office at Ssangsŏng (modern Yŏnghŭng) with local Korean officials. Ordering defectors to build ships, the Mongols began attacking the coastal islands from 1255 on. In the Liaodong Peninsula the Mongols formed Korean defectors into a colony of eventually 5,000 households, first under the defecting official Hong Pogwŏn (1206–58) and then under Wang Sun, enfeoffed as prince of Shenyang in 1266.

In 1258 the Ch'oe clan retainer Kim Injun (a.k.a. Kim Chun) overthrew the Ch'oe family, ostensibly in the name of restoring the king. The new regime sent the crown prince Wang Chŏn (posthumous reign name Wŏnjong, 1260–74) to the Mongol court as a hostage and promised to return to Kaegyŏng. After his father's death in 1259 QUBILAI KHAN (1260–94) sent back the now strongly pro-Mongol crown prince to take over the government. In June 1260 Wŏnjong was officially enthroned at Kanghwa. Qubilai released some prisoners and recalled the troops, but Kim Injun repeatedly delayed the government's return from Kanghwa. In 1269 Im Yŏn overthrew Kim Injun and briefly deposed Wŏnjong. In response the Mongols supported a rebellion of Korean officials in the northwest and set up a directly administered Dongning (Tongnyŏng) prefecture at modern Pyongyang. In 1270, as the Mongols mobilized for another invasion, the Three Patrols (sambyŏlch'o), the military government's army, overthrew the Im family, and the officials finally moved back to Kaegyŏng. The Three Patrols themselves feared reprisals, however, and revolted, fleeing first to Chin Island and then to Cheju Island. Not until 1273 did a mostly Korean force land on Cheju and defeat them.

After 1270 Korea became a fully integrated client kingdom of the YUAN DYNASTY. Wang Sim (posthumous title Prince Ch'ungnyŏl, 1274–1308), who succeeded Wŏnjong in 1274, had received Qubilai's daughter Qutlugh-Kelmish as a wife, and his reign began a wholesale Mongolization of the Korean court that continued to the middle of the 14th century. Official protocol was demoted to that of a subordinate principality, and Korean rulers made lengthy stays at the Mongol Yuan court, both before and after their coronation. In 1280 Qubilai reorganized Korea as the Zhengdong (Chŏngdong) Branch Secretariat. Intended at first for the purpose of organizing an expedition against Japan, this secretariat continued to the end of the dynasty. The Korean prince served as grand councillor (chengxiang or chingsang), but the secretariat's managers (pingzhang) were appointed by the Yuan. In 1300 Manager Körgüz proposed abolishing Korea's court ritual and official hierarchy as inappropriate for a mere province, but his initiative was eventually rejected. In 1313 Prince Ch'ungnyŏl's son Wŏn (posthumous title Prince Ch'ungsŏn) abdicated his title as king of Korea and received instead a Yuan court appointment as prince of Shenyang, thus starting a rival branch of the royal line in Liaoning.

The later Mongol emperors, particularly Qubilai, had a great admiration for Korean culture, considering it in many ways superior to that of China. In 1275 the Mongol court began requisitions of Korean seamstresses and concubines for the court. In 1341 one such concubine, Madame Ki, became the empress of the last Yuan emperor, Toghan-Temür (posthumous title Shundi, 1333–70) and the mother of his successor. During the 15th and 16th centuries the post imperial Mongols frequently raided Korea and took many slave women from there. By the 16th century these interactions had turned into a Mongol legend of CHINGGIS KHAN's three-year dalliance with his Korean queen Qulan (historically a MERKID).

Korea also became a Mongol military base. Several myriarchy commands (none with anything near the full complement of 10,000 soldiers) were established in Korea. The Koreans had to join the campaigns against Japan, supplying 770 fully manned ships and 5,000 soldiers in 1274 and 900 ships and 10,000 soldiers in 1281. Korean shipwrights also largely built the Yuan navy that conquered the Song, while the prince of Shenyang led his Koreans against NAYAN'S REBELLION in 1287. After 1273 the Yuan also took over the royal stud farm on Cheju Island. Prince Ch'ungnyŏl eventually recovered formal control over the northwestern Dongning prefecture (1290) and Cheju (1294), but the myriarchy commands there remained autonomous.

The rebels that rose up against the Yuan dynasty after 1351 twice even attacked Korea (1359 and 1361). King Kongmin (r. 1351–74) abolished the Zhengdong Branch Secretariat, executed the relatives of Empress Ki, and began the recovery of Ssangsŏng. In 1368 he enthusiastically recognized the new MING DYNASTY in China. After Kongmin's murder in 1374 the military leader Yi In-im turned violently against the Ming and supported the Yuan, which still held Manchuria until 1387. Yi In-im was overthrown in 1388, and Yi Sŏng-gye, founder of the new Chosŏn (Yi) dynasty (1392–1910), cut off relations with the fugitive Mongol court.

See also EAST ASIAN SOURCES ON THE MONGOL EMPIRE; JAPAN AND THE MONGOL EMPIRE; MANCHURIA AND THE MONGOL EMPIRE.

Further reading: W. E. Henthorn, *Korea: The Mongol Invasions* (Leiden: E. J. Brill, 1963).

Körgüz (Görgüz) (d. 1242/3) *Uighur scribe who reorganized the Mongol administration of eastern Iran*

Born in Barligh of Uighuristan (near modern Qitai), Körgüz was orphaned at an early age. After studying the UIGHUR-MONGOLIAN SCRIPT, he borrowed the price of a horse and rode to the ORDO (palace-tent) of JOCHI (d. 1225), CHINGGIS KHAN's eldest son. Beginning as a herdsman, he rose to become the page of a Mongol chief and finally the chief scribe and tutor of Jochi's children. Jochi assigned Körgüz to the retinue of Chin-Temür, then serving as DARUGHACHI (overseer) first in KHORAZM and then in Khorasan (northeastern Iran). Around 1234 Chin-Temür sent Körgüz to ÖGEDEI KHAN (1229–41), where his glib tongue pleased the emperor. Chin-Temür died in 1235/6, and the khan made Körgüz governor in Iran. His effective administration caused jealousy among other officials, who demanded Chin-Temür's son Edgü-Temür be appointed in his place. A long lawsuit followed at the court in QARA-QORUM, which was finally resolved in Körgüz's favor. In 1239 he returned to Khorasan. He rebuilt the city of Tus and began extending civilian administration westward to the lands under CHORMAQAN. Raised with a Christian name (Körgüz is "George"), he became a Buddhist but finally converted to Islam. Later, in a quarrel, he spoke disrespectfully of the recently deceased CHA'ADAI, Chinggis Khan's second son. For this lèse-majesté, the empress-regent TÖREGENE ordered him arrested and executed by stuffing his mouth with stones.

See also PROVINCES IN THE MONGOL EMPIRE.

Köse Daği, Battle of (Köse Dagh)

On June 26, 1243, the Mongols decisively defeated the Turkish army at Köse Daği, opening Anatolia to Mongol rule. While the sultanate of Rum in Seljük TURKEY was cautiously friendly to the Mongols from their arrival in the Caucasus in 1231, from 1240 on the Mongols began probing its frontier. Realizing a full-scale invasion was imminent, Kay-Khusrau tried to build up a strong army, hiring mercenaries from Aleppo, the Greeks, the Crusader knights, and Iraq's Shi'ite Arab tribes. Other regional powers, the Ayyubid governors of Mayyafariqin (near modern Silvan) and Homs and Baron Constantine of LESSER ARMENIA, promised assistance but without any real intention of fighting. Kay-Khusrau's own Turkish army was strengthened by knights from GEORGIA, a princess from which country he had married. The core of the Mongol army, commanded by BAIJU, was three tümens (10,000s) of TAMMACHI troops, some purely Mongol and others UIGHUR and Turkestani with Mongol officers. Unlike the Turkish army, however, they had been fighting together for more than a decade and had strong group cohesion. The Mongols also made use of cavalry from Georgia and Greater Armenia. Troop sizes are hard to estimate, but Kay-Khusrau's army certainly outnumbered the Mongols.

The two armies met by Köse Daği Mountain, about 80 kilometers (50 miles) northwest of Sivas, and Kay-Khusrau gave battle before all the promised contingents had arrived. After a day of hard fighting in which the Georgian knights on both sides pushed back their opponents, the diverse units of the Turkish army suddenly disintegrated, forcing the sultan to flee with his wife and children to Ankara. Baiju, wary of a feigned retreat, waited a day before allowing his men to plunder the camp. Due to the delay, he was not able to capture Kay-Khusrau. The sultan's Persian vizier, Muhazzab-ud-Din, agreed to surrender as a vassal, and the Mongols withdrew, but Rum would trouble the Mongols until 1261.

See also MILITARY OF THE MONGOL EMPIRE.

Köten (Köden, Go-dan) (fl. 1235–1247) The first Mongol prince to patronize Tibetan Buddhism

The second son of ÖGEDEI KHAN (r. 1229–41) by his principal wife, TÖREGENE, Köten was ordered in 1235 to subdue northwest China's southern Gansu province. Köten won over the local ÖNGGÜD strongman Wang Shixian, a die-hard holdout for the former JIN DYNASTY, and advanced south into Sichuan, sacking Chengdu in November 1236. On his return in 1239, Köten received his appanage in the area of Liangzhou (modern Wuwei) in the former XIA DYNASTY, or Tangut territory of northwest China. The Xia rulers had been familiar with central Tibet and its lamas, and in 1240 Köten dispatched a Tangut, Dor-ta DARQAN (freeman), with an army to subjugate central Tibet and secure a lama-preceptor. Once there, he smashed two monasteries before receiving news of an appropriate lama, Sa-skya Pandita (1182–1251). In 1244 Köten sent an escort to Sa-skya (modern Sa'gya) to bring him to his court. Meanwhile, Ögedei had died, and Töregene began persecuting Ögedei's former officials. The high officials CHINQAI and Mahmud Yalavach (see MAHMUD YALAVACH AND MAS'UD BEG) sought refuge with Köten, who protected them in pursuance of his own ambition to succeed his father. At the QURILTAI of 1246, however, the other princes considered Köten too sickly and elected his elder brother GÜYÜG instead. Returning to Liangzhou in 1247, Köten found Sa-skya Pandita waiting for him. Köten took instruction from Sa-skya Pandita, who sent letters urging the monasteries in Tibet to submit to the Mongols. Köten's illness grew worse after the quriltai. Some accounts say he died soon after, while others indicate he lived until 1253.

koumiss (airag, qumyz)

Koumiss is fermented mare's milk, the national drink of Mongolia from ancient times to the present. The name koumiss comes from the Turkish name qumiz (qimiz in Kazakh) for the same drink. In the MONGOL EMPIRE the drink was called esüg in Mongolian; today it is called airag among the Khalkha but chigee in Inner Mongolia, chigän among the KALMYKS and OIRATS, and segee among the BURIATS.

Mares are milked at least four times daily in Mongolia from late May–early June to late July–early August. Several mares are tied to a line fixed into the ground with pickets and milked with their foals nearby to get the milk flowing. Traditionally, men do the milking, and all the equipment is kept on the men's, or right, side of the YURT. With the opening of the mare-milking season and the tying up of the first foals, herders offer aspersions of the first fruits of mare's milk to the 99 gods (see TENGGERI) and anoint their foals, while a speaker offers a blessing (yörööl; see YÖRÖÖL AND MAGTAAL). When the mares are released, wealthy horse herders may organize games (NAADAM). This ceremony was called julag in ORDOS, where it was traditionally held on a large scale on the 15th of the fifth lunar moon.

Once the milk is collected, some culture is put in the milk and it is churned in a vast sack, or sometimes today in a wooden butter churn. In all, 90 pounds of mare's milk should be churned about 4,500 times as it froths and foams until the butter is skimmed off and the fermentation is brought to the desired level. To get the proper fermentation, the vessel used must be clean and the temperature closely controlled.

The resulting liquid is turbid and white and has a low alcohol content, rather less than that of beer. As described by the 13th-century traveler WILLIAM OF RUBRUCK, the taste is at first sour like vinegar, but with an aftertaste like almonds. The fat content of koumiss is about 1.5–2.3 percent; the protein content is about 1.8–2.2 percent; and it is high in vitamins A, B$_{12}$, B$_2$, B$_1$, and C, with small amounts of vitamin E. It was traditionally taken for chronic lung diseases, coughs, stomach complaints, scurvy (naturally enough with its high vitamin C content), dropsy, gout, and in recent years has been used as treatment for hardening of the arteries, heart disease, high cholesterol, high blood pressure, and tuberculosis.

Koumiss has a natural tendency to sour quickly and separate into a clear liquid and turbid white lees. While this tendency is not desired today, in the 13th and 14th centuries, the clear liquid was separated and allowed to ferment further. The resulting alcoholic drink, called *qara-qumiz* (black, i.e., clear, koumiss) in Turkish, was a delicacy for the khans and nobles. It is also used today in shamanist ceremonies.

Today koumiss is also made from cow's milk and camel's milk by a similar process. In Inner Mongolia the standard Khalkha Mongolian name *airag* usually refers to fermented cow's milk, and only *chigee* means fermented mare's milk. Fermented mare's milk is, however, still everywhere preferred.

See also DAIRY PRODUCTS; FOOD AND DRINK.

Further reading: Henry Serruys, *Kumiss Ceremonies and Horse Races: Three Mongolian Texts* (Wiesbaden: Otto Harrassowitz, 1974).

Kubla   *See* QUBILAI KHAN.

Kublai   *See* QUBILAI KHAN.

Kulikovo Pole, Battle of   Dmitrii Donskoi's pyrrhic victory over the Golden Horde armies on September 8, 1380, was hailed as the end of the Tatar Yoke, despite the Russians' later defeats. In 1380 Emir Mamaq (Mamay) of the Qiyat (Kiyad) clan controlled the steppe from the Volga to the Dnieper. Facing repeated insubordination from Moscow's Grand Prince Dmitrii (1362–89), Mamaq hired Genoese, Circassians, and Ossetian (Alan) mercenaries and allied with Prince Oleg of Ryazan' and Grand Prince Jogaila (Jagiello) of Lithuania to punish Dmitri. As Mamaq's troops reached the upper Don, Dmitrii advanced with the troops of Moscow and its allied cities to Kolomna. Since Jogaila's formidable army was late for the rendezvous, two of Dmitrii's allied princes, Andrew of

Polatsk and Dmitrii of Bryansk, proposed immediate advance. Crossing the Oka and the Don, the Muscovites faced a roughly equal number of TATARS across a 11-kilometer (7-mile) front at Kulikovo Pole ("Snipe's Field," halfway between Lipetsk and Tula). Dmitrii placed an ambush in a forest by the Don under his cousin Prince Vladimir Andreevich of Serpukhov. Battle began in the afternoon, and after an hour the Russians were visibly weakening, with Dmitrii stunned by a blow and out of combat. Late in the afternoon, however, Vladimir's fresh troops charged out of ambush, putting Mamaq and his guard to flight. The exhausted Russians made a short pursuit and captured Mamaq's camp and baggage train. Jogaila retreated hastily, and Oleg of Ryazan' fled to Lithuania.

Sofony of Ryazan's *Zadonshchina* (Beyond the Don) was only the first of many works to celebrate the victory, and Dmitrii was given the title Donskoi ("of the Don"). No reliable estimates of the size of the armies or their casualties exist, but losses on both sides were extremely heavy. Ironically, the heavy Russian losses left Moscow too weak to resist when TOQTAMISH invaded in 1382. Nevertheless, this battle, in which Mamaq sought the assistance of mercenary infantry and was defeated by the mostly on-foot Russians, showed the passing of the dominance of Tatar cavalry in the western steppe.

See also GOLDEN HORDE; MILITARY OF THE MONGOL EMPIRE; RUSSIA AND THE MONGOL EMPIRE.

Further reading: Serge A. Zenkovsky, ed., *The Nikonian Chronicle,* Vol. 3; *From the Year 1241 to 1381* (Princeton, N.J.: The Kingston Press, 1986): 264–302.

Kuo Tao-fu   *See* MERSE.

Kurdistan   Although HÜLE'Ü crushed the local Turkish and Kurdish dynasties in 1358–62, communal strife continued under Mongol rule.

Kurdistan was famed for its inaccessible fortresses and the turbulent Kurdish and Turkmen tribes who supplied troops for armies all over the Middle East and plundered even pilgrims going to Mecca. Nevertheless, Kurdish and Turkmen dynasties often came to power in the neighboring lowland cities. Early in the 12th century the Turkmen dynasty of the Artuqids conquered the upper Tigris River valley, around Diyarbakır city in modern southeast Turkey, while separate branches of the Turkish Zangid family ruled Mosul on the middle Tigris and Aleppo in Syria. Later, Irbil in the east came under the Kurdish Begteginid family, while the Kurdish Ayyubid dynasty, founded by the famous Salah-ad-Din (Saladin, 1171–93), conquered Egypt and Syria. Seeking new recruits, the Ayyubids expanded back into Kurdistan, weakening the Zangids and Artuqids.

The arrival in 1225 of Jalal-ud-Din Mengüberdi's Khorazmian troops, in flight from the Mongols, threw

Kurdistan into still greater turbulence. When the Mongol commander CHORMAQAN drove out the Khorazmians in 1231, Mosul and Irbil recoiled into the orbit of the 'ABBASID CALIPHATE in Baghdad. In 1232 the last Begteginid bequeathed Irbil to Baghdad, and in Mosul the freedman and vizier Badr-ad-Din Lu'lu' (1233–61) received the caliph's blessing to depose the last Zangid ruler, becoming Baghdad's intimate ally. From 1238 to 1255 the Mongols under Chormaqan and his successor, BAIJU, raided Kurdistan repeatedly. Mosul submitted in 1244, sending envoys to the Mongol assemblies (QURILTAI) that elected GÜYÜG Khan (1248) and MÖNGKE KHAN (1251). The Ayyubid ruler of Mayyafariqin (near Silvan), Malik Kamil, and his cousin in Aleppo, Malik Nasir Yusuf, also sent envoys to Möngke Khan, who imposed overseers (DARUGHACHI) and a census on the Diyarbakır area.

When Hüle'ü (1256–65), founder of the Mongol IL-KHANATE, destroyed the caliphate and invaded Syria, this apparent submission disintegrated. Outraged by the attack on the caliphate, Malik Kamil crucified his Mongol darughachi and tried to persuade Malik Nasir Yusuf of Aleppo to join the defense of Baghdad. During the SIEGE OF BAGHDAD (January–February 1258), Hüle'ü dispatched his son Yoshmut to invest Mayyafariqin. The Mongols starved the defenders out after two years and executed Malik Kamil. Invading Syria, the Mongols overthrew Malik Nasir Yusuf in 1259–60 before being driven back by the new Mamluk rulers of Egypt. During the Egyptian counteroffensive the Artuqid ruler in Mardin, Malik Sa'id, also rebelled. His son Muzaffar-ad-Din, however, surrendered the city, and Hüle'ü made him governor of Mardin.

After initial hesitation the aged Badr-ad-Din Lu'lu' in Mosul had accepted a Mongol darughachi, sent his son, Malik Salih, with troops to the siege of Baghdad and the invasion of Syria, and personally attended Hüle'ü's court, thus rising high in Hüle'ü's esteem. After Badr-ad-Din died in 1261, however, his other sons fled to MAMLUK EGYPT, while Malik Salih in Mosul massacred the Christian residents and rebelled. The city fell in summer 1262, and the Mongols butchered all but the craftsmen. Organized resistance in Kurdistan thus ceased. While bands of Kurdistan's dissident tribes, Türkmen, Kurdish, and Arab Bedouin, periodically defected to Egypt, the Artuqids proved loyal and in 1297 received Diyarbakır (Amid) and in 1303 the Mosul area as well.

The region of Irbil and Mosul was the center of the Assyrian (Nestorian) Christians. Soon after Baghdad's fall, an Assyrian official seized Irbil from Kurdish freebooters in Mongol employ. Under Hüle'ü the Mongols honored the Christians, even making the local bishop governor of Jazirah (Cizre) from 1262 to 1267. Up to 1295 Mosul and Irbil usually had Christian governors, but faced with periodic communal rioting, court intrigue, and rivals ever willing to promise higher taxes, the Mosul governors, whatever their religion, became notorious for corruption and tyranny. When GHAZAN KHAN (1295–1304) made Islam the state religion, Mosul passed under Muslim governors, but Irbil, garrisoned by Assyrian soldiers, remained under a Muslim-Christian condominium until 1310, when relations finally broke down. With the khan's acquiescence, the local Kurds and Arabs massacred the Assyrian Christian population. With the breakup of the Il-Khanate in 1335, Kurdistan passed into the sphere of the Mongol JALAYIR dynasty under Hasan Buzurg, and the Artuqids again were caught in wars between Mongol and Türkmen tribal dynasties.

See also CHRISTIANITY IN THE MONGOL EMPIRE; ISLAM IN THE MONGOL EMPIRE; MASSACRES AND THE MONGOL CONQUEST.

kuriltai See QURILTAI.

Kyakhta city (Kiakhta, Kjachta, Hiagt)

This double city on the border of Mongolia and Siberia was a center first of Russo-Chinese trade and then Russo-Mongolian trade until the building of the TRANS-MONGOLIAN RAILWAY. Kyakhta today is a small town of 18,307 persons (1989) in the SELENGE RIVER valley along the main highway between ULAANBAATAR and ULAN-UDE. Industries include shoemaking, lumber, and food processing. Buriat Mongols constitute about one out of five residents. Monuments include the old Kyakhta merchants' guesthouse, the V. A. Obruchaev Local Museum (dating to 1850), and several fine churches. Altanbulag on the Mongolian side of the frontier is a small SUM center with fewer than 5,000 people.

Kyakhta (Mongolian, Khiagt, Buriat, Khyaagta) is named for the Kyakhta stream alongside of which grows couch grass (*khiag/khyaag*). Originally Kyakhta was made up of three towns: the trading site of Kyakhta proper on the Russian side, the Russian administrative town of Troitskosavsk next to Kyakhta, and Maimaching (from Chinese *maimaicheng*, trading town, but often called Khiagt in Mongolian) on the Mongolian side. Russian Kyakhta and Troitskosavsk were amalgamated in 1935 as Kyakhta.

HISTORY

In 1727 the Kyakhta treaty fixed the Russo-Qing dynasty frontier and established Kyakhta as the official site of Russo-Chinese border trade. The small Kyakhta fort was built on June 14, 1728, and Troitskosavsk village grew up outside it, while Chinese merchants built Maimaching south of the border. In 1862 the population of Kyakhta-Troitskosavsk together reached 5,430, and in 1850–60 the average annual trade turnover at the border station reached more than 30 million rubles. Troitskosavsk was a center of the Russian and Buriat Cossack hosts along the Siberian-Mongolian frontier and had a surprisingly active intellectual life, nourished by Russian political exiles. Maimaching was a small Chinese trading town with two

Chinese-style temples. It was administered by a Manchu *zarguchi* (judge; *see* CHINESE TRADE AND MONEYLENDING).

With the establishment of the Russo-Chinese railway link through Manchuria in 1900, Russo-Chinese trade through Kyakhta dried up. Even so, Troitskosavsk remained a center of Russo-Mongolian trade and of education for Mongolians and BURIATS, many of whom played a role in Mongolia's 1921 REVOLUTION. Troitskosavsk saw the Mongolian People's Party's first conference in March 1921 and was GENERAL SÜKHEBAATUR's base for the Mongolian partisans' attack on Chinese-occupied Maimaching. Burned down in the battle, Maimaching was rebuilt as Altanbulag and flourished as a center of Soviet-Mongolian trade, with a leather-goods factory and a distillery owned by an African-American woman. In 1931 Altanbulag became the capital of SELENGE PROVINCE (then called Gazartariyalang).

In 1937 the railway from Ulan-Ude reached the small settlement of Naushki, west of Kyakhta. In 1949 the line was completed via Sükhebaatur town in Mongolia to Ulaanbaatar. Sükhebaatur town replaced Altanbulag as Selenge's provincial capital, and although Kyakhta-Altanbulag remained the automotive border-crossing spot, the city never regained its former importance. In 2003 Altanbulag was made a free zone to encourage trade.

Kyakhta Trilateral Treaty

The Kyakhta Trilateral Treaty of 1915 among Russia, China, and Outer Mongolia replaced the internationally unrecognized independence of Mongolia from 1911 with a recognized status as a state under Chinese suzerainty whose autonomy from China was guaranteed by special Russian rights.

Although Russian support had been an essential precondition of the 1911 RESTORATION of Mongolian independence, the Russians desired a formal treaty recognizing their privileges there. Rebuffed by China, Russia first negotiated an agreement with Mongolia on October 21, 1912, in which Russia undertook to assist "Mongolia" in guarding its "autonomy." The precise boundaries of "Mongolia" and the nature of its "autonomy" were left unspecified. After Mongolian troops, with Russian assistance, occupied substantial areas of Inner Mongolia (*see* SINO-MONGOLIAN WAR), the Chinese agreed to a joint Russo-Chinese declaration of November 5, 1913 (October 23, old style) that defined "Outer Mongo-

lia" as an autonomous area under Chinese suzerainty. By summer 1914 the complete failure of the Mongolian government's attempts to secure wider international recognition forced it finally to join the Russo-Sino-Mongolian Trilateral Conference, which opened at the border town of Kyakhta on September 8, 1914 (August 26, old style). The interior minister Da Lama Dashijab headed the Mongolian delegation. China had appointed the governor of Heilongjiang, Bi Guifang (b. 1865), and the diplomat Chen Lu (1878–1939), while Russia's delegation was headed by the autocratic Aleksandr Iakovlevich Miller, the diplomatic agent in Khüriye.

Throughout the conference Miller held the upper hand, repeatedly threatening to close the conference if the Chinese and Mongolians did not agree to his demands. Dashijab was recalled from the Mongolian delegation under Russian and Chinese pressure because of his refusal to compromise on independence. The final treaty, signed on June 7, 1915, canceled the cherished symbols of Mongolia's sovereignty, although the Mongolians did not have to recognize explicitly those of the Republic of China. Autonomous Outer Mongolia retained DARIGANGA but lost not only Inner Mongolia but also HULUN BUIR, which was to be a separate "Special Region" under Chinese suzerainty. (A separate Russo-Chinese treaty on November 6 regulated its status). Economically, Russia had its rights to build telegraph and railroad lines in Mongolia confirmed, along with the right of duty-free trade. Chinese traders, however, had to pay a 5 percent transit duty at the Mongolian frontier. The one significant concession to China was the permission to station a high commissioner in Khüriye and deputy high commissioners in KYAKHTA CITY, ULIASTAI, and KHOWD CITY, each with a 50-man consular guard.

Although unhappy with the treaty, both China and Mongolia signed. The Chinese had in 1914 rejected very similar terms from the British at the Simla Convention on the status of Tibet, but under pressure from Japan they now needed Russian amity. Ironically, the Mongolian anger at Russia's diplomatic pressure allowed China's first high commissioner, Chen Lu, to lay much of the groundwork for the REVOCATION OF AUTONOMY in 1919.

See also THEOCRATIC PERIOD.

Kypchaks

See QIPCHAQS.

L

lamas and monasticism From 1600 to 1940 lamas and monasteries formed a major part of Mongolian society, influencing not just religion but also culture, economy, society, and politics.

NUMBER OF LAMAS AND MONASTERIES

The name *lama* (Tibetan, *bla-ma*), or "high one," is a translation of the Sanskrit *guru*, while ordinary monks are *khuwarag*. While "lama" was thus properly a title for high monks, in popular Mongolian usage, the term *lama* is used whenever the clerical state is contrasted to the lay.

In KHALKHA in 1918 census figures show that 105,577 men, or 44.6 percent, of the male population were registered as lamas. In one Khalkha banner lamas reached as much as 71 percent of men, yet of these it was estimated only a third, or 15 percent, actually lived in monasteries. The rest had been educated in monasteries and so bore the status of lamas yet returned to the steppe in their late teens to settle down with wives and children. In Mergen Wang banner (modern East Gobi) only 118 lamas out of 2,384 men holding the status actually lived in monasteries.

Numbers of lamas elsewhere appear to have been smaller. Fragmentary statistics from other Mongol lands show lamas, whether in monasteries or on the steppe, ranging from 17 percent (ÜJÜMÜCHIN, 1945) to 20 percent (New BARGA in 1945 and the KALMYKS in 1800) of the male population. A Japanese survey in KHORCHIN found 6 percent living in monasteries. In general, it appears unlikely that actual monastery residents before 1921 anywhere much exceeded 20 percent of the male population. Ironically, efforts in the 1920s to strip married lamas of their privileges may have caused an increase in the number of monastery residents, which reached about 25 percent of the male population in 1925.

A meaningful number of monasteries and temples is likewise difficult to ascertain, since they ranged so widely in membership. A 1930 survey found 1,243 temples in Inner Mongolia, and researchers have counted 941 in Mongolia proper (Outer Mongolia), but the vast majority were only empty assembly halls except during great *khurals* (assemblies). One count found about 170 significant monasteries in Mongolia proper in 1820.

Nunneries did not exist in Mongolia, and marriage was virtually universal among women of sound mind and body. Pious old widows or the occasional unmarried women often took the *ubasanja* vows and received an *abishig*, or consecration, equivalent to the *ubashi* vow for men, abstaining from killing, sexual immorality, stealing, lying, and drinking. After that they could advance to the grade of *chibagantsa* (modern *chawgants*), shave their heads, and wear a brown-colored robe. They did not, however, live in communities. Such women had a hard life and were often seen as ill omened, especially for small babies and children.

EDUCATION AND DAILY LIFE

Virtually all Mongolian lamas were dedicated to the calling by their parents as children. The rare lamas who took vows as adults were called *shine lamas* (new lamas) and had a reputation as trouble-making vagabonds. The initial vow of *ubashi* was originally intended for laymen but in Mongolia was usually immediately followed by initiation as *bandi* (Sanskrit, *vandya*), or novice. This initiation took place around age four or five at home, and it was not until the initiant was seven to 10 years of age that he actually entered a monastery, although he wore a robe and shaved his head.

Once in the monastery, a monk's life consisted of three stages. As a *bandi,* from seven or 10 to 15 or 17 years of age, the monk memorized the daily liturgy and performed the liturgies he had mastered at the *khurals.* Most *bandi*s paid for their keep by acting as a servant, and many lama-tutors beat them severely. Most *bandi*s left the monastery in their late teens and took up a householder's life; only a minority went on to the *getsül* degree. Once ordained as a *getsül* (Tibetan, *dge-tshul*), usually from ages 15 to 30, the students became real monks and had no stated duties other than participation in the daily services. They had only a meager income from their participation in the common services but much free time to go on pilgrimages to other monasteries. Studious *getsül*s could become *gelong*s (Tibetan, *dge-slong,* equivalent to Sanskrit, *bhikshu*), or fully qualified monks. *Gelong*s were widely sought by the laity to perform services at homes and public functions and so had better incomes and less free time than *getsül*s.

A lama's regular income came from the alms given by the laity for the religious services performed either together in the temple or, more lucratively, in patrons' own YURTS. Alms given during regular services were divided among participants in equal shares. Better-off lamas also owned their share of family herds, which were cared for either by the family or by hired herders. In only a few imperially supported temples did the lamas receive salaries, and that very irregularly.

The status of married *bandi*s living outside the monasteries was ambiguous. The Kalmyk ruler Dondug-Dashi (r. 1741–61) ordered that lamas who refused to leave their wives must not be allowed to participate in the assemblies, or perform services for individual persons and must be used in secular duties. This law was not, however, enforced. In Khalkha the secular authorities were very uncomfortable with any limits on boys entering the monasteries but certainly could not afford to allow almost half the male population to be exempt from secular duties. Thus, a compromise was made: Householder lamas continued to be in some sense lamas and participated in the great assemblies but paid taxes and performed postroad and other duties.

DRESS

Codes of monastic discipline required lamas to wear their distinctive dress at all times. Traditional distinctions of rank and ceremony were also made. For monks of the dGe-lugs-pa, or "Yellow Hat" order, which meant the vast majority of Mongolian lamas, the color scheme was based on the superiority of yellow, the order's distinctive color, over the red of other Tibetan lamas. The basic lama's dress consisted of a calf-length skirt, or *bangzal,* belted with a cloth sash, a sleeveless waistcoat opening in the front (*tsamtsa*), and a "toga" (*orkhimji*) wrapped over the left shoulder and under the right arm. The toga's color was brown for a *bandi,* red for a *getsül,* and yellow for a *gelong.* The higher lamas going to assemblies wore a sleeveless yellow cape, or *jangchi,* over their toga. Wearing of trousers under the skirt (as laymen and -women did) was seen as a serious fault.

On the street or going to the assemblies, lamas wore either a high hat tilted forward with a fringe in back or a pointed cap with a soft turned-up brim around the back. Street hats often followed a form said to have been designed by the FIRST JIBZUNDAMBA KHUTUGTU, Zanabazar, with a cloth *vajra* (powerbolt) on top and a higher front brim. Other required accessories included a *chabri,* or pocket flask, for holy water and a rosary of 108 beads.

SPECIALIZED ROLES

Intellectual activities in the monasteries were mostly carried on in the *tsanid* (Tibetan, *mtshan-nyid*) faculties, and even there only by a small minority. Such faculties were found only in the larger monasteries (see GANDAN-TEGCHINLING MONASTERY). The topics included general philosophy and logic, the *sutras,* monastic discipline, medicine, astrology, and the tantra, which was seen as the most difficult. The *tsanid* pupils who had completed their studies received the *gebshi* (Tibetan, *dge-bshes*) degree before taking competitive examinations leading to the *gabju* (Tibetan, *dka'-bcu*) degree. The most advanced *tsanid* courses were in Tibet, however, and those who made pilgrimages to study there could receive more respected degrees: *rabjamba* (Tibetan, *rab-byams-pa*) for *tsanid* studies in Tibet, *doramba* (*mdo-rams-pa*) for study at Bla-brang monastery (modern Xiahe), *agramba* (*sngags-rams-pa*) for Tantric studies in Tibet, or finally *lharamba* (*lha-rams-pa*) for defending one's degree in Lhasa's most prestigious debates.

Some monks engaged in periodic meditation retreats, setting up their yurts at some remote place and performing meditation for 30 or 49 days. A much smaller number of *dayanchi*s (from Sanskrit *dhyana,* meditation) devoted themselves to permanent contemplation in special hermitages. They held no services and had only a skeleton hierarchy to support the full-time *dayanchi*s. *Gürtümbe* lamas were media for possession by deities. Such lamas foretold the future as oracles, and were exempt from normal rules of monastic discipline (see CHOIJUNG LAMA TEMPLE).

ORGANIZATION OF MONASTERIES

Mongolian temples and monasteries began either as a temple (*süme*) to house an image, a hermitage (*kheid*) for the meditation of a holy lama, or as a true monastery (*zuu/juu* in southwest Inner Mongolia, *khüriye* in Khalkha and eastern Inner Mongolia, and *datsang* in Buriatia). Since many temples and hermitages grew and many monasteries declined, however, the names often did not fit their actual status.

Regardless of the actual name, monasteries all had roughly the same hierarchy. A *shiregeetü*, or "enthroned" lama, presided over all *khural*s. In larger monasteries a separate *tsorji* (Tibetan, *chos-rje*) handled daily administration, and in the largest monasteries a third official, the *khambo* (Tibetan, *mkhan-po*) lama, or abbot, exercised general supervision. A precentor, or *umdzad* (Tibetan, *dbu-mdzad*), led the reading of the services, and several proctors, or *gebkhüi* or *gesgüi* (Tibetan, *dge-bskos*) enforced discipline.

The greatest monasteries, often with a resident INCARNATE LAMA, were supported by "lay disciples," or ecclesiastical serfs (*shabi*, plural *shabinar; see* GREAT SHABI), who were, on average, the wealthiest Mongolian commoners. Taxes from the *shabi* and patrons' gifts gave many monasteries large treasuries, or *jisa* (modern *jas*), while the BANNERS (appanages) handled all building and upkeep in banner-supported monasteries. A treasurer (*nirba*, Tibetan, *gnyer-pa*) and secretary (*donir*, Tibetan, *mgrom-gnyer*) managed all monastery property. The Qing authorities required the appointment of a *da lama* (head

lama) and a *demchi* (steward) to supervise each officially registered monastery, but these lamas usually acted as mere assistants for either the proctors (*gebkhüis*) in the religious administration or the treasurer on the business side.

INFLUENCE OF MONASTICISM

The influence of monasticism resulted in a widespread "Tibetanization" of Mongolian culture (*see* TIBETAN CULTURE IN MONGOLIA). Economically, the monasteries included the largest enterprises in Mongolia and may have contributed to the concentration of wealth. At the same time, however, the system of almsgiving and the leasing of monastic herds could possibly have redistributed wealth from well-to-do benefactors to lamas and poorer herders. The lamas had an ambivalent relation with Chinese firms, dependent on many of their services yet also resenting their silent challenge to the primacy of Buddhist values in Mongolia (*see* CHINESE TRADE AND MONEYLENDING). The withdrawal of the *shabinar* from state duties, while beneficial for them,

Badgar Juu Monastery (Chinese, Wudang Zhao) in Inner Mongolia's Baotou municipality, 1985. This dGe-lugs-pa ("Yellow Hat") monastery was originally founded in Ordos. It was moved to its present location, and the first buildings begun in 1749. It was granted official recognition by the Qing court in 1756 and at its height housed 1,200 monks. *(Courtesy Christopher Atwood)*

increased the burden on the state commoners (*see* SOCIAL CLASSES IN THE QING PERIOD).

A large part of the lamas' influence on Mongolian society ironically came from householding lamas who left the monasteries in their late teens and married. Their instruction in Tibetan letters contributed to the widespread use of Tibetan script for writing Mongolian (*see* TIBETAN LANGUAGE AND SCRIPT). Since *bandi*s who left the monasteries could not formally marry their wives or give bridewealth, their children bore their mothers' CLAN NAMES. Thus, monastic education helped disintegrate the Mongolian clan system already weakened by one-clan BORJIGID rule and accelerated the emergence of MATRILINEAL CLANS in the Gobi.

The usual charges linking monasticism to economic decline and population decrease do not fully accord with available evidence. Since the actual monastic population was around 10 percent of working population, it is unlikely that it was a crippling drain on the rural labor force, especially as common monks often worked as carpenters, dyers, tailors, and so on. In any case, the anecdotal evidence all points to a rural labor surplus, not a shortage. Figures from the latter half of the 19th century consistently show herd size decreasing more rapidly than the population, indicating that problems in animal husbandry were driving population decline, not the other way around (*see* ANIMAL HUSBANDRY AND NOMADISM). Thus, while the monasteries may indeed have limited population growth, it seems likely that the check on population growth exemplified in widespread monasticism was an adaption to economic decline and not its cause.

MODERN MONASTICISM

After the great persecutions (*see* BUDDHISM, CAMPAIGN AGAINST), the monastic life reestablished at Gandan-Tegchinling Monastery in Mongolia in 1944 was funded differently from that in the past. Following a proposal first made by TSYBEN ZHAMTSARANOVICH ZHAMTSARANO in 1905 and officially implemented by AGWANG DORZHIEV as head of the Russian Buddhist community from 1927, private property among the lamas was prohibited. All lamas lived on stipends from the monastery administration, which itself was funded solely by contributions from believers. Lamas were also forbidden from performing ceremonies outside the monastery. Since the number of lamas was so small, however, the stipends proved adequate. Similar policies were followed in the few monasteries left under the hard-line communion in Buriatia and Inner Mongolia.

Monks lived as married men, and the area around Gandan-Tegchinling was a lama's town with lamas and their families living in yurt-courtyards. Children were no longer allowed to enter monastic life until they were 18. The incarnate lama institution was abolished and leadership in the monastery invested in a *khamba lama*, or abbot. Informants for the security organs were so common that the famous writer BYAMBYN RINCHEN jokingly called the new lamas the "Green Hat" order (Mongolian security services had uniforms trimmed in green).

Since 1990, with establishment of religious freedom, the limitations on private services and religious education have been revoked. A new religious school has been opened in the old GESER temple east of Gandan-Tegchinling where boys in clerical habit learn the services and receive a general education. Kushok Bakula Rinpoche (b. 1926), a Ladakhi incarnate lama serving as the Indian ambassador to Mongolia, has also funded a large new monastic school campus in ULAANBAATAR, Betüb-Danjai-Choinkhorling.

One innovation in the new monasticism is the organization of formal nunneries. The Fourteenth Dalai Lama, who has taken a deep personal interest in Mongolian Buddhism, has also pushed the Mongolians to reestablish a celibate monastic order. Meanwhile, a lay Buddhist group, led by the Mongolian academician and literary historian D. Tserensodnom, has advocated using a Mongolian rather than Tibetan liturgy. The future of these proposals remains to be seen.

See also DANSHUG; DIDACTIC POETRY; DUGUILANG; EDUCATION, TRADITIONAL; HÖHHOT; JANGJIYA KHUTUGTU; JIBZUNDAMBA KHUTUGTU; MEDICINE, TRADITIONAL; SHANGDZODBA; TSAM.

Further reading: Arash Bormanshinov, *Lamas of the Kalmyk People: The Don Cossack Lamas* (Bloomington, Ind.: Research Institute for Inner Asian Studies, 1991); Robert James Miller, *Monasteries and Culture Change in Inner Mongolia* (Wiesbaden: Otto Harrassowitz, 1959); Pao Kuo-yi [Ünensechen], "The Lama Temple and Lamaism in Bayin Mang," *Monumenta Serica* 29 (1970): 659–684; Aleksei M. Pozdneyev, *Religion and Ritual in Society: Lamaist Buddhism in Late 19th-Century Mongolia,* trans. Alo and Linda Raun (Bloomington, Ind.: Mongolia Society, 1978).

"Lament of Toghan-Temür" Spoken in the persona of the last Yuan emperor, the versified "Lament of Toghan-Temür" (r. 1333–70) bewails the loss of DAIDU and SHANGDU, the two Yuan-era (1271–1368) capitals of the Mongols in China. Two early forms of the poem appear in Lubsang-Danzin's ALTAN TOBCHI (Golden summary, c. 1655) and another in SAGHANG SECHEN'S ERDENI-YIN TOBCHI (Precious summary, 1662). Chroniclers of the 18th century often rewrote the *Altan tobchi* version. Since the *Altan tobchi* and the *Erdeni-yin tobchi* share a number of lines without their authors having consulted the other, the poem must date back still earlier. In the first-person poem in the *Altan tobchi*, Toghan-Temür describes the beauty of Daidu and Shangdu and expresses his loneliness at their loss ("like a new calf left behind on his land"). The second poem in the *Altan tobchi*, written in the third person, adds a more explicit dynastic context, emphasizing how the state and city won by the divine CHINGGIS KHAN and the bodhisattva QUBILAI KHAN had been lost to the Chinese. Mentioning the "precious jade seal" the khan had carried away in his sleeve, the poem concludes with a prayer that the khan's lineage might last for 10,000 generations and that the Buddhist religion left behind in Daidu might flourish again in a later generation. This popular poem expressed the Mongols' regret at the passing of imperial splendor and the continuing hope for continuity with the lineage of Chinggis Khan.

See also LITERATURE; 17TH-CENTURY CHRONICLES.

Further reading: Hidehiro Okada, "An Analysis of the Lament of Toghon Temür," *Zentralasiatische Studien* 1 (1967): 55–78.

laws *See* ALTAN KHAN, CODE OF; 1924 CONSTITUTION; 1940 CONSTITUTION; 1960 CONSTITUTION; 1992 CONSTITUTION; JARGHUCHI; JASAQ; KHALKHA JIRUM; LIFAN YUAN ZELI; MONGOL-OIRAT CODE; QUTUQU, SHIGI.

lCang-skya *See* JANGJIYA KHUTUGTU.

leagues The Mongolian leagues under the QING DYNASTY (1636–1912) were a midlevel administrative organ that transmitted appeals and orders between the banners and the central government.

In 1674 the Qing dynasty court ordered annual assemblies of the 49 BANNERS' rulers, noblemen, and staff, in the presence of an imperial commissioner to review their military preparedness. Inner Mongolia's six leagues (*chuulgan*, Chinese, *meng*) received their names from the six meeting places assigned for each of these assemblies. Most of the leagues corresponded roughly to the previous *tümens* (*see* SIX TÜMENS).

By 1751 the leagues met triennially in the presence of an official of the LIFAN YUAN (Court of Dependencies). The Lifan Yuan appointed for each a league captain general (*chuulgan-u daruga*) and deputy captain general (*ded chuulgan-u daruga*). Once appointed, the captain general normally served for life and was succeeded by his deputy, although he could be dismissed for misconduct. The captain general had to hold the rank of duke (*güng*) or above and in practice was always a banner ruler (ZASAG). Once appointed, he received ex officio the rank and salary of a prince, which made the post very attractive to lower-ranking *zasag*s. The captain general's primary role was 1) to serve as a place of appeals from the banner courts, 2) to report to the Lifan Yuan on local conditions, and 3) to transmit its directives to the banners.

After 1691 the numerous KHALKHA (Outer Mongolian) banners, despite being divided into 4 AIMAGS (provinces), had no higher administrative authority. From 1724 to 1741 the Qing appointed one banner *zasag* as "assistant general" (*tusalagchi jangjun*) in each Khalkha Mongol *aimag*. In 1728 the league system was established concurrently for Khalkha. Thus, by 1741 each Khalkha *aimag* was simultaneously a league. Tüshiyetü Khan *aimag*, for example, under an assistant general, was at the same time Khan Uula league under a league captain general. While in Inner Mongolia the league captain general simply used his banner staff, in Khalkha both the assistant general and the captain general had an office (*jisiya*, modern *jasaa*) with a small staff. From 1755 to 1823 the DÖRBÖD banners of western Mongolia, the TORGHUD and KHOSHUD banners of Xinjiang, and the UPPER MONGOLS' banners were successively organized into leagues.

After 1921 Mongolia's revolutionary government replaced league with the *aimag*. Completely new *aimag*s were created in 1931. After 1947 the Inner Mongolian Autonomous Region was divided into units called *aimag* (province) in Mongolian but *meng* (league) in Chinese. Their internal administrative structure bore no resemblance to the old leagues, however. From 1983 to 2001 JUU UDA, Jirim, and Yekhe Juu (ORDOS) leagues were successively transformed into municipalities, a measure intended to stimulate economic growth but opposed by nationalist-minded INNER MONGOLIANS.

Left Hand, Princes of the *See* BLUE HORDE.

leftist period The leftist phase in Mongolia (1929–32) was a time of radical experimentation and enthusiasm that brought economic disaster and finally civil war.

The leftist turn in Mongolia was directly related to Joseph Stalin's collectivization movement in the Soviet Union as well as to the increasingly tense international climate in northeast Asia. At the SEVENTH CONGRESS OF THE MONGOLIAN PEOPLE'S REVOLUTIONARY PARTY (October 23–December 11, 1928), Moscow's Communist International (Comintern) installed a new Mongolian leadership composed mostly of uneducated rural officials and recently graduated students. These inexperienced and dogmatic young officials were, in fact, led by Comintern advisers. Despite warning signs, the Eighth Congress of the People's Revolutionary Party (February 21–April 2, 1930) only accelerated the leftward turn.

The leftist movement strongly influenced culture. Speeches and propaganda plays constantly attacked "cruel feudalists, shrewd lamas, greedy Chinese traders, and foreign capitalists and generals." In January–February 1929 a new "Writers' Circle" formed to write stories for the revolution. The group encouraged Mongolian writers to turn to realistic prose stories, a new genre in Mongolia. A new Latin script was unveiled in February 1930 to replace the traditional UIGHUR-MONGOLIAN SCRIPT, although only in 1932 did a modified Latin script begin to be used widely. The Mongolian lunar new year (*Tsagaan sar*) was banned as a feudal and religious holiday, although celebration continued. Spending on literacy, hospitals and public health, and public entertainment shot up.

In the first year the party and government organs were purged of "class enemies" and generally unsatisfactory

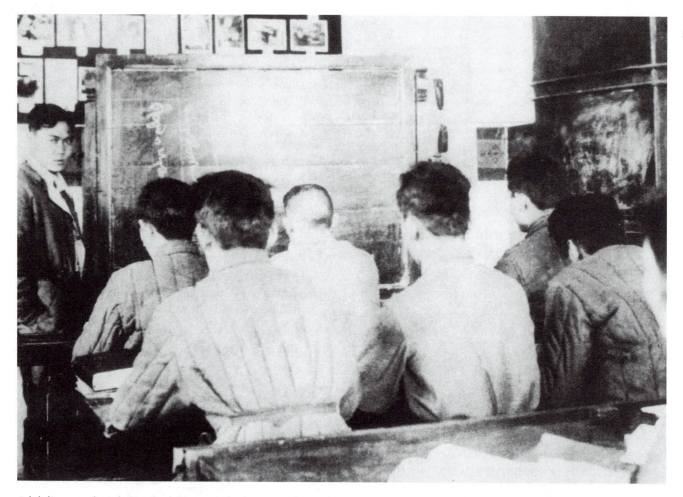

Adult literacy class during the leftist period. The text in the Uighur-Mongolian script denounces feudal reactionaries. *(From XX Zuun Mongolchuud: 2000)*

members. Party membership dropped from 15,269 in 1928 to 12,012 in 1929, while 238 of the 934 ULAANBAATAR city officials were dismissed. Once the party was purged, however, the ambition to draw in the "poor and middle *arad*s (commoners or herders)" generated a frantic expansion of the party to 42,000 members in 1932.

From 1929 to 1932 9.7 million tögrögs worth of property was confiscated from 1,022 aristocrats and 114 high lamas. The entire nobility (TAIJI were about 5 percent of the total population) was disenfranchised. The monasteries as an institution and eventually religious belief as a whole were attacked. The *jisa* (modern *jas*), or monastic herds, were reduced from 3.3 million head in 1929 to 0.39 million head in 1930. The government also imposed a head tax on lamas in lieu of military service. In spring 1930 collectivization began, and by the end of the year 29.7 percent of the poor and middle-class herders had been nominally collectivized. The collectives were a complete failure, and the number of livestock plummeted from about 24 million in 1930 to 16.2 million in 1932.

The leftist policies enforced a state monopoly on foreign trade and expelled all non-Soviet foreigners, giving the Soviet Union an almost complete monopoly on Mongolian trade. By 1932 total imports reached only half of estimated demand. After the windfall of confiscations, newly introduced income taxes could not make up for the loss of customs revenues, and the 39-million-tögrög budget of 1932 had a 12-million-tögrög shortfall. Covering the deficit with paper money led to rampant inflation.

The leftist policies bred widespread resistance. In Ulaanbaatar and the regime's other power centers, the population expressed its discontent passively. In the countryside emigration began on a large scale from late 1930; at least 7,542 households, or more than 30,000 persons, emigrated to China. Eventually insurrections threatened the very state's existence. In March 1930 the lamas of Ulaangom and Tegüsbuyantu Monasteries in Dörböd territory began a DUGUILANG-style resistance, which was suppressed with hundreds of arrests and scores of executions. On April 11, 1932, another far more serious rebellion broke out in KHÖWSGÖL PROVINCE'S Rashaant Sum. The rebels, inspired by apocalyptic legends of the hidden Buddhist kingdom of Shambala, appealed to the Panchen Lama (then in China) and organized a formal military command. Garnering widespread support, they conducted ferocious reprisals against government agents. By May 12 the regular army had to be called in to crush the rebellion with machine guns, armored cars, and bombers.

Late that month Joseph Stalin bypassed the Comintern and dispatched his personal envoys to report on the situation. Based on their report, which blamed the rebellion squarely on the leftist policies, on June 10 Stalin wired his men, ordering them to reverse the leftist policies and dismiss any Mongolian official who still embraced them. This they did at the Third Plenum of the party's Central Committee (June 29–30), inaugurating the NEW TURN POLICY. The rebellion was largely suppressed by July, with thousands executed, and in November special economic aid from the Soviet Union was sent and an amnesty for survivors proclaimed to win back the regime's popular support.

See also ARMED FORCES OF MONGOLIA; REVOLUTIONARY PERIOD.

Legdan *See* LIGDAN KHAN.

Lesser Armenia The kings of Lesser Armenia in Cilicia made a strategic decision in 1242 to ally with the Mongols. While they remained true to this alliance for decades, the kingdom eventually suffered greatly in the wars with Egypt.

While not an Armenian homeland, the plain of Cilicia was settled by many Armenian noblemen and their dependents. By 1100 the Rubenids in the east and the Het'umids in the west dominated the region. Deftly handling the outside powers—the Byzantine Empire, the sultanate of Rum in central TURKEY, the Frankish (Latin Christian) Crusaders in Antioch and Cyprus, and Muslim sultans in Syria—Levon I (1199–1219) of the Rubenid family was crowned king of Armenia in 1199 in the new capital of Sis (modern Kozan). French law, dress, and names powerfully influenced the Armenian nobility. The lower classes were mostly Greek and Armenian with Turkish nomads and Italian merchants. Levon died without a son, and the regent, Baron Constantine (Konstendin) of the Het'umid family, married his son Het'um I (1230–69) to Levon's daughter Zabel, starting the Het'umid dynasty.

In 1243 Baron Constantine promised to Sultan Ghiyas-ad-Din Kay-Khusrau of Rum an alliance against the Mongol commander BAIJU but later reneged. When Ghiyas-ad-Din lost the Battle of Köse Dağı, the Het'umids submitted to the Mongols. Constable Smbat, Het'um I's older brother, traveled four years to and from an audience first with BATU on the Volga and then with Great Khan GÜYÜG (1246–49) in Mongolia. From Eastertide 1252 to September 1256 King Het'um I himself stayed at the court of MÖNGKE KHAN (1251–59) and at the court of his brother HÜLE'Ü (1256–65), the founder of the Mongols' Middle Eastern Il-Khan dynasty. Due to Armenia's voluntary surrender, Constable Smbat received a Mongol wife, and the kingdom was spared a DARUGHACHI (overseer) and the Mongol census and tax. The port of Ayas became the main outlet for European trade with Tabriz, the IL-KHANATE capital. The Het'umid dynasty eagerly encouraged and participated in Il-Khanid campaigns against MAMLUK EGYPT, partly to recover Jerusalem for Christendom but also to fulfill the traditional Cilician Armenian aim of annexing Antioch (Antakya). The Mongol defeat at 'Ain Jalut (1260) and the subsequent Egyptian reconquest of Syria were thus bitter disappointments.

In 1266 Sultan Baybars (1260–77) of Mamluk Egypt advanced into Cilicia. Rejecting Baybars' offer of alliance, Het'um sought assistance from the Mongol commander in Rum. Before the Mongol army arrived, however, the Egyptians had defeated the Armenians and ravaged the whole country, burning the capital at Sis. Het'um soon abdicated in favor of his son Levon II (1269–89), who had been held captive in Egypt for two years. Raids from Egypt and pro-Egyptian Turkmen culminated in Baybars' second invasion in 1277. Again the Mongol response was too late, and Abagha Khan's (1265–82) long-awaited Mongol counteroffensive of 1281–82, in which Levon joined, was a miserable failure. Under Arghun Khan (1284–91) the Il-Khans used Levon as an intermediary to reopen an alliance with the Frankish powers. The Il-Khans' continued attempts to conquer Egypt ensured that Lesser Armenia's diplomatic and military importance continued even after GHAZAN KHAN (1295–1304) converted the Il-Khanate to Islam.

Despite the anti-Christian persecutions early in his reign, Ghazan Khan confirmed the immunities of the Christian church in Lesser Armenia and to a limited extent in Greater Armenia as well. Even so, Mongol control was increasing and in 1303, after the defeat of Ghazan's campaign against Egypt, in which King Het'um II (1289–1307) personally participated, 1,000 Mongol troops were stationed in Lesser Armenia. The garrison was soon drawn into the kingdom's internal struggles. In 1307 the Mongol *darughachi* Bulargi, with the support of the Armenian nobility hostile to Het'um II's pro-Roman policy, put him and other members of the royal family to death.

Little is known of the final three decades of Mongol rule in Lesser Armenia. The last Il-Khan, Abu-Sa'id (1316–35), made peace with Egypt in 1323. While still subject to the Mongols, the Armenian authorities began to travel directly to Egypt to negotiate payment of tribute in return for temporary cessation of raids. The Karaman (Laranda) Turkmen to the northwest also became aggressive. After the fall of the Il-Khanate, the Het'umid line ceased in 1341, and Egypt conquered Lesser Armenia in 1375.

See also 'AIN JALUT, BATTLE OF; CHRISTIAN SOURCES ON THE MONGOL EMPIRE; CHRISTIANITY IN THE MONGOL EMPIRE; GEORGIA.

Further reading: Ani Atamian Bournoutian, "Cilician Armenia," in *The Armenian People from Ancient to Modern Times,* ed. Richard G. Hovannisian (New York: St. Martin's Press, 1977), 273–292.

Lhümbe Case

The Lhümbe Case of 1933 led to more than 400 arrests for involvement in a concocted Japanese spy ring.

In early July 1933 an internal security agent, Danzin, in Norowlin Sum, KHENTII PROVINCE, who had been involved with the local cooperative chairman, Tsebegjab, in a love triangle, manufactured a letter implicating Tsebegjab as a key member of a Japanese plot to take over Mongolia. The accusation dovetailed with the long-held suspicions of the Soviet authorities about the loyalties of the Buriats who had fled the Russian Revolution to settle in northeast Mongolia.

Within two weeks Tsebegjab's case had chain-reacted into scores of arrests of "counterrevolutionaries" and "Japanese spies" in Khentii province. Tsebegjab's coerced testimony also led on June 22 to the arrest of more than 30 ULAANBAATAR officials, including the disgraced former prime minister Jigjedjab (Ts. Jigjidjaw, 1894–1933) and a current top party leader, Lhümbe (J. Lhümbe, 1902–34), who had fallen out with Prime Minister GENDÜN. Gendün's security chief, Namsarai (D. Namsrai), who had earlier chaired the commission to sentence antigovernment rebels, actively guided the investigation. Another wave of arrests occurred in EASTERN PROVINCE. From the beginning Soviet instructors, both Russian and Buriat, and their Mongolian pupils used systematic torture and coached testimony to expand the list of those implicated. Most of those convicted were sentenced at show trials in December 1933. Eventually, 60 persons were executed, 257 were imprisoned, and 126 were deported to the Siberian labor camp in Kolyma. Of those imprisoned or executed, 251 were BURIATS; 141 of those arrested were ordinary officials, 22 were security agents, and 149 were herders. Lhümbe himself refused to admit his guilt, even after torture in Moscow, and was returned to Mongolia and executed on June 30, 1934.

See also BURIATS OF MONGOLIA AND INNER MONGOLIA; GREAT PURGE; JAPAN AND THE MODERN MONGOLS; NEW TURN POLICY.

Lian Xixian (Lien Hsi-hsien) (1231–1280)
An Uighur raised in China and one of Qubilai's highest-ranking and most insistent promoters of Confucianism

The family of Lian Xixian were old officials in the Uighur kingdom. Lian's father, Bül-Qaya (1197–1265, sometimes erroneously written as Buyruq-Qaya), was enrolled as a hostage in CHINGGIS KHAN's KESHIG (imperial guard) in 1215. He served in the Khorazmian campaign with distinction and was granted a high-born Kitan woman of the defeated QARA-KHITAI as a wife. After Chinggis's death Bül-Qaya served in Yanjing (modern Beijing) as judge and inspector general. Chinggis's daughter-in-law SORQAQTANI BEKI became his patron, and his personal appanage grew to 30 households and shops, gardens, and fields in Zhongshan (modern Dingxian).

In 1231 Bül-Qaya became Yanjing South Route surveillance commissioner (*Lianfangshi*). Already enamored of Confucian civilization, he took the "Lian" of his office as surname, becoming Lian Xiaoyi (Filial and Righteous), while his second son, born on January 26 of that year, he named Lian Xixian. Lian Xixian early assimilated Confucian ethics, pleading as a child with his father to show mercy to an impoverished criminal, but once as an adolescent in his father's absence personally flogging family servants who showed disrespect to his mother.

In 1250 Lian Xixian accompanied his father on a visit to the Mongolian camp of Sorqaqtani Beki's son Qubilai. Qubilai admired the young man and added him to his entourage, giving him the nickname "Lian Mengzi" from his enthusiasm for the Confucian philosopher Mencius (Chinese, Mengzi). Compared to Qubilai's Chinese Confucians, Lian was robust and an excellent marksman, which won him credit among the prince's Mongol companions.

From 1254 to 1257 Qubilai appointed Lian Xixian to head the newly created Pacification Commission in Jingzhao (modern Xi'an), where he concentrated on enforcing existing decrees from ÖGEDEI KHAN's reign (1229–41), limiting interest to an amount equal to the principal and emancipating all Confucian scholars held in slavery. In 1257 MÖNGKE KHAN sent his governor of North China, 'Alam-Dar, and his deputy, Liu Taiping, to investigate charges of embezzlement and withholding tax revenues against the Pacification Commissions. Despite the two investigators' inability to document any corruption, the Pacification Commissions were abolished.

During winter 1259–60, after Möngke's death, Lian Xixian help gather support for Qubilai's election as great khan. In July 1260 QUBILAI KHAN appointed Lian the pacification commissioner of Shaanxi and Sichuan, provinces where Qubilai's rival ARIQ-BÖKE had already appointed Liu Taiping as civil administrator. Lian Xixian and his colleagues executed Liu Taiping, won over several wavering generals, and pushed through an all-out mobilization of men and materiel to expand the pro-Qubilai army, despite hardship wrought by years of military operations and a severe drought. Meanwhile, the Song still menaced Mongol-held Sichuan, and Lian had to battle several proposals to simply abandon the province.

In March 1262 Lian Xixian was promoted to manager (*pingzhang*) in the central Secretariat with supervision over Shaanxi and Sichuan, and in 1263 he returned to the capital. Lian Xixian now tried to push Qubilai toward curtailing the hereditary privileges of the conquest class. In his 1265 inspection tour of Shandong, he concentrated on punishing abuses of power by princely appanage holders. Nevertheless, his most serious opponent was not the old servants of the dynasty but a raising Turkestani fiscal expert, AHMAD FANAKATI. In 1264 Lian's criticism provoked Qubilai to reverse a major expansion in Ahmad's authority; yet, in 1268, as Lian sought to set up a censorate, he had to fight Ahmad again.

Lian Xixian also promoted Confucian principles by example, mourning his Kitan mother's death with ostentatious grief, refusing to perform the Buddhist fasting, which Qubilai, on advice of the Tibetan lama 'Phags-pa, had enjoined on his court, and adopting a stern and serious attitude in all discussions of state business. This principled refusal to compromise his sense of Confucian duty eventually damaged his relations with his sovereign, and after a minor dispute in 1270 Qubilai dismissed him.

In 1274 Qubilai once again sought Lian Xixian, appointing him to investigate abuses of power by Mongol appanage holders in Manchuria. In 1275, at the urgent insistence of Ariq-Qaya (1227–87), an Uighur general garrisoning the area, Qubilai appointed Lian Xixian head of the branch secretariat at Jiangling (modern Shashi) in Hubei, recently conquered from the Song. During his three years there, he saw the task as one of civilizing the Song "barbarians," inculcating sound Confucian principles and Yuan loyalism, and demilitarizing Mongol administration. Since his dismissal, Lian Xixian had been in poor health, and in 1277 he was recalled to SHANGDU for convalescence. Despite, or perhaps because of, his great support by the Confucian lobby and the heir apparent, JINGIM, Qubilai did not appoint him to any influential post before his death on December 11, 1280.

See also CONFUCIANISM.

Further reading: C. C. Hsiao, "Lien Hsi-hsien," in *In the Service of the Khan: Eminent Personalities of the Early Mongol-Yuan Period (1200–1300)*, ed. Igor de Rachewiltz et al. (Wiesbaden: Otto Harrassowitz, 1993), 480–499.

Liegnitz, Battle of (Legnica)

At the Battle of Liegnitz (today Legnica) in western Poland, the Mongols decisively defeated the armies of Poland and the Teutonic Knights on April 9, 1241.

As the Mongols invaded Hungary, a separate column under Hordu (CHINGGIS KHAN's senior grandson) and "Peta" (perhaps Baidar, CHA'ADAI's son) attacked Poland. While a detachment pillaged northern Poland, the column's main force drove through southern Poland, ambushing a Polish army (March 18) and sacking the capital of Cracow (Kraków) (March 24). Wrocław (Breslau) came under siege, but the Mongols broke off when news came that Wenceslas, king of Bohemia, was marching to the aid of Henry the Pious (r. 1238–41), the Polish duke of Silesia. The Mongol army reunited, and Henry the Pious marched out from his castle of Liegnitz with an army of feudal levies from Poland and Moravia, knights of the Templar, Hospitaller, and Teutonic orders, and an infantry of Silesian miners of Bavarian origin under Duke Boleslaw Szepiolka. The Mongols advanced in a narrow column to minimize their front and encourage Henry to attack. Once Henry had committed all his cavalry, the Mongols in the rear fanned out and showered the Polish flanks with arrows. Explosive shells fired by Mongol catapults further disoriented the Poles, and the Polish army was routed. Henry and Boleslaw Szepiolka were killed. The Mongols, after skirmishes with Wenceslas's Bohemian troops, rode through Moravia to rendezvous with the troops in Hungary.

See also CENTRAL EUROPE AND THE MONGOLS; MILITARY OF THE MONGOL EMPIRE.

Lien Hsi-hsien *See* LIAN XIXIAN.

Lifan Yuan

The Lifan Yuan (literally, Court of Administration of the Dependencies, commonly translated Court of Colonial Affairs) was the organ of the QING DYNASTY (1636–1912) charged with administering first the Mongols and later all the empire's Inner Asian dependencies.

The Lifan Yuan was originally created in 1636 as the Mongol Department (Manchu, Monggo jurgan, Mongol, Monggol jurgan). In 1638 it was renamed the Lifan Yuan, or in Mongolian the Court of Administration of the Autonomous Mongolian States (Gadagadu Monggol törö-yi zasakhu yabudal-un yamun), with a mandate to handle all affairs relating to the autonomous Mongol BANNERS. As the Qing dynasty's Inner Asian empire expanded, so did the court's competence. Until 1861 the court also handled relations with Russia and the dynasty's other northern and western neighbors.

Under the emperors Hong Taiji (1627–43), Kangxi (1662–1722), and Yongzheng (1723–35) the Lifan Yuan was of capital importance, frequently headed by princes of the blood and included in the highest imperial deliberations. Later, with the pacification of Inner Asia, its importance declined. The senior directors were all Manchus or Mongols (from either the EIGHT BANNERS or from the nobility of southeast Inner Mongolia), with only a single low-ranking office manager position reserved for a Chinese-martial bannerman. Of the top 68 offices, 43 were reserved for Mongols, but the highest offices and department heads were Manchus.

By 1761 the Lifan Yuan was divided into six bureaus (Mongolian, *kheltes*, Chinese *si*) handling: 1) Inner Mongolia; 2) reception of Inner Mongolian princes; 3) reception of KHALKHA's princes and supervision of Mongolian and Tibetan INCARNATE LAMAS; 4) Khalkha, Oirat, and CHAKHAR Mongols, the selection of AMBANs, and Russian relations; 5) administration of justice for Mongols; and 6) Xinjing. To assist its administrative duties, the Lifan Yuan ran schools for Mongolian language both in the UIGHUR-

MONGOLIAN SCRIPT and the CLEAR SCRIPT and in Tibetan. The records of the Lifan Yuan were invaluable in compiling the numerous monuments of Qing colonial historiography and geography still used by researchers today.

In 1906 the Lifan Yuan was renamed the Lifan Bu, or Ministry of Dependencies. Since Xinjiang had been made a province in 1884, the Republic of China renamed it the Mongolian and Tibetan Affairs Bureau in 1912. Promoted to a department in 1914 and a commission in 1928, the organization still exists in Taiwan. Its attached Mongolian and Tibetan school was the training ground for two generations of nationalist Inner Mongols and the precursor of the current Nationalities University in Beijing.

Further reading: Chia Ning, "The Lifanyuan and the Inner Asian Rituals in the Early Qing (1644–1795)," *Late Imperial China* 14 (1993): 60–92.

Lifan yuan zeli

The Lifan yuan zeli (Laws and regulations of the Court of Dependencies) was the final form of the law codes drawn up for Mongolia by the LIFAN YUAN under the Manchu Qing dynasty (1636–1912).

The first Qing code for Mongolia was issued in 1643 as the Menggu lüli, "Mongolian code" (Mongolian: Monggol-un tsaaza bichig), the earliest extant edition of it is that of 1696. As was traditional in Mongolia, punishments were still mostly cattle fines and included payments to the victim. The 1696 code, however, introduced from Chinese law several provisions on aggravation or mitigation of offenses and specified methods of execution.

Under the Qianlong emperor (1736–96) Chinese legal distinctions of intent were applied consistently, CATTLE fines and compensation for the victims disappeared, and compulsory imperial review of capital sentences was introduced. Corporal punishment became pervasive, and penal exile was introduced. The changes culminated in the 1789 Menggu lüli and the final displacement in KHALKHA Mongolia of the native KHALKHA JIRUM code. From 1790, if an applicable statute could not be found in the Menggu lüli, then the general Qing code, the Daqing lüli, would be applied. As a result, Mongolian law began to converge rapidly on the law of China. In 1811 the Lifan Yuan began a complete revision of the 1789 code that was issued in 1817 under the title Lifan yuan zeli. The new code was much larger than its predecessors, yet already by 1818 a new edition was needed. It was issued in 1826 with 1,554 articles.

Like previous codes, the Lifan yuan zeli included both administrative regulations and criminal law. Subjects covered included the composition of the Lifan Yuan; the BANNERS and their rulers' ranks, prerogatives, and salaries; AMBANS; imperial herds; census regulations; farming; public granaries; taxation; imperial audiences in Beijing; seals; marriages; funerary sacrifices; memorial tablets; famine relief; military preparedness; LEAGUES; postroads (see JAM); border guards; murder and manslaughter; robbery; theft; desecration of graves;

sumptuary legislation; kidnapping and slavery; perjury and judicial procedure; sentencing regulations; pardons and amnesties; game laws and nature preserves; assault; arson; spreading epizootic diseases; INCARNATE LAMAS; administration of Tibet; and Russian embassies and commercial missions.

In 1811 the Lifan Yuan formalized the process of applying the Daqing lüli wherever the Lifan yuan zeli was silent, which reduced the need for a new Mongolian code. Still, revised editions of the Lifan yuan zeli were issued in 1843, 1891, and 1908. In practice Mongolian courts applied both the Lifan yuan zeli and the Daqing lüli rather inconsistently. Qing law was the basis for the incomplete legal code of Mongolia's independent theocratic government published in serial form from 1914 on. After the 1921 REVOLUTION, however, European and Soviet legal concepts rapidly replaced Qing law.

Further reading: Mamoru Hagihara, "Mongol Law of Qing Dynasty and Judgement System in Mongolia, 17–19th Century," *Bulletin of Kobe University of Mercantile Marine* 1 (2000): 195–200; Dorothea Heuschert, "Legal Pluralism in the Qing Empire: Manchu Legislation for the Mongols," *International History Review* 20 (1998): 310–324; Valentin A. Riasanovsky, *Fundamental Principles of Mongol Law* (1934; rpt., Bloomington: Indiana University, 1965); Masao Shimada, "Studies in the Effectivity of the Ch'ing Mongol Laws." in *Proceedings of the 35th Permanent International Altaistic Conference*, ed. Chieh-hsien Ch'en (Taipei: Center for Chinese Studies Materials, 1993), 437–441.

Ligdan Khan (Ligden; Chinese, Lindan; Tibetan, Legs-Idan) (b. 1588, r. 1604–1634) *The last emperor of the Northern Yuan dynasty, whose rule generated violent opposition*

His father, Mangghus Mergen Taiji, having died early, Ligdan succeeded his grandfather Buyan Sechen Khan (b. 1555, r. 1593–1603) as khan of the Great Yuan with the reign title Khutugtu. At the time, the great khan's CHAKHAR people occupied the upper Shara Mören (Xar Moron) valley. Ligdan at first allied with princes of the southern KHALKHA (modern Baarin [Bairin] and Jarud bannermen) in raiding China and in 1620 received an annual subsidy from the Ming of 40,000 taels of silver. By 1614, however, the Jarud and KHORCHIN nobles had become QUDA (in-laws) with the rising Manchus to the east. In 1620, after an exchange of contemptuous letters, Ligdan and the Manchu khan Nurhachi (b. 1558, 1616–26) broke off relations, but his three-day siege of the Khorchin nobleman (NOYAN) Uuba in 1625 was broken by Manchu assistance.

Ligdan aimed at centralizing Mongolian rule. He appointed two officials, at least one of whom was a non-Chinggisid, to rule the eastern and western *tümens* (confederations) and organized a special court nobility and a corps of 300 *baaturs* (heroes). Ligdan allied with TSOGTU

TAIJI of the northern Khalkha to revive the old Sa-skya-pa order of Qubilai's time, inviting that order's Sharba Khutugtu to be his priest. Sharba Khutugtu installed in his capital an image of Mahakala that had supposedly been presented to the famous Sa-skya-pa monk 'Phags-pa (1235–80) by QUBILAI KHAN. By making use of earlier translation work, in 1628–29 Ligdan compiled a complete Mongolian translation in manuscript of the bKa'-'gyur, in the colophons of which he proclaimed himself "Chinggis Khan," "god of gods," "Indra," and so on. He also built a capital at Chaghan-Khota (near modern Lindong) and temples at Khüriye (Hure).

By 1627, however, the other *tümens* were in full revolt. Princes ruling the Sünid, ÜJÜMÜCHIN, and Abagha (Abag) revolted and moved northwest. In alliance with the Three Western Tümens and the south Khalkha, they attacked Ligdan at Zhaocheng. The allies were defeated, and in 1628–29 Ligdan raided Xuanfu (modern Xuanhua), Datong, and Yansui (modern Yulin). Hoping he would check the Manchus, the Ming increased his annual subsidy to 81,000 *taels* silver. In 1632 Nurhachi's son Emperor Hong Taiji (1627–43) and his southern Khalkha and Khorchin allies launched a massive expedition against Ligdan, who with his Mahakala image, wives, sons, and Chakhar people retreated west into ORDOS. Starvation ruled in the Three Western Tümens' overburdened pastures. Ligdan made himself yet more unpopular by seizing the wife of Erinchin Jinong (b. 1600, r. 1627–56) and taking the EIGHT WHITE YURTS, or shrine of Chinggis Khan, with him to Kökenuur (Qinghai). In 1634 he died of smallpox at Shara Tala (in modern Tianzhu country, Gansu). In June 1635 his sons and wives surrendered to Hong Taiji's generals at Toli in Ordos, and in 1636 the Mahakala image was enshrined in the Manchu capital of Mukden (modern Shenyang).

See also NORTHERN YUAN DYNASTY.

Ligden   *See* LIGDAN KHAN.

Lindan   *See* LIGDAN KHAN.

Li Tan's Rebellion   The rebellion of Li Tan in 1262 against Mongol rule was rapidly suppressed but led to a court purge and changes in Mongol administration.

The adoptive son of a Chinese bandit general in Mongol service, Li Quan (d. 1231), Li Tan won high praise in the years 1258–61 from MÖNGKE KHAN (1251–59) and QUBILAI KHAN (1260–94) for his campaigns against the Song in northern Jiangsu. Li Tan, however, felt unsupported by the khans and in violation of Mongol policy fortified his base at Yidu. In February 1262 Li arranged the escape of his son, who was a hostage at Qubilai's court, and contacted the Song court.

On February 22 he revolted, handing over frontier cities to the Song and massacring their Mongol garrisons.

Li Tan immediately moved north to secure Yidu, yet, as Qubilai's adviser Yao Shu (1203–80) predicted, he did not press on to the capital but instead attacked neighboring Shandong cities. Qubilai, occupied with ARIQ-BÖKE'S opposition in Mongolia, ordered an emergency mobilization of loyal Chinese forces in Henan, Hebei, and western Shandong to converge on the rebels.

Meanwhile, Li Tan's father-in-law Grand Councillor Wang Wentong, the designer of the dynasty's paper currency, was implicated and executed on March 14. Qubilai's commanders soon besieged Li Tan's forces at Ji'nan. On August 6 Li Tan tried to drown himself but was captured and executed. While short lived, Li Tan's Rebellion pushed Qubilai to separate military and civilian powers in North China.

Further reading: H. L. Chan, "Li T'an," in *In the Service of the Khan: Eminent Personalities of the Early Mongol-Yuan Period (1200–1300)*, ed. Igor de Rachewiltz et al. (Wiesbaden: Otto Harrassowitz, 1993), 500–519.

literature   While developing through close contact with other Asian literatures, prerevolutionary Mongolian literature is pervaded by distinctive themes and poetical characters drawn from historical legends and folk poetry. The distinctive range of foreign influences—it is the only literature in Asia equally fertilized by both Indo-Tibetan and Chinese influences—also adds to the flavor of prerevolutionary Mongolian literature. Modern Mongolian literatures have developed under strong Russian (Mongolia) and Chinese influence (*see* INNER MONGOLIANS), but through their ongoing links to premodern traditions they have preserved a distinct character. Little of Mongolian literature has yet been adequately translated into English or other European languages.

On the literature of other Mongolian groups, see BURIATS; KALMYKS; UPPER MONGOLS; XINJIANG MONGOLS.

LITERATURE OF THE MONGOL EMPIRE

Mongolian literature begins with perhaps its greatest monument, the *SECRET HISTORY OF THE MONGOLS*, written around 1252, only a few decades after the adoption of the UIGHUR-MONGOLIAN SCRIPT. Although other historical works were written in Mongolian in this period, none has survived except in translation, and, judging from the translations, none has the literary quality of the *Secret History* (*see* MONGOLIAN SOURCES ON THE MONGOL EMPIRE). A powerful narrative, the work is in prose with poetic passages that often incorporate proverbial material. The author eschews abstraction or self-consciously literary mannerisms for a laconic narration and vivid images from steppe life. The story portrays the betrayal, cruelty, loyalty, and love that accompanied the rise of CHINGGIS KHAN (Genghis, 1206–26) and his family to absolute power among the Mongols with strikingly subtle characterizations.

From about 1260 to 1350 many foreign literary and scholarly works were translated into Mongolian. Much of this translation work was done by non-Mongols, particularly UIGHURS. Of these works only the many Buddhist translations and the *Classic of Filial Piety*, an elementary Confucian text, became part of the later Mongolian literary tradition. Extant works also include a translation of the Persian Alexander Romance, and sources mention many translations from Chinese histories. Around 1300 Sonom-Gara was the first of many Mongols to translate the TREASURY OF APHORISTIC JEWELS, a Tibetan work of didactic aphorisms. The great Buddhist translator CHOSGI-ODSIR (fl. 1307–21) is the author of the earliest extant Mongolian devotional poetry. (*see* BUDDHISM IN THE MONGOL EMPIRE; CONFUCIANISM).

LEGENDS AND POEMS OF THE CHINGGIS KHAN CULT

The fall of the Mongol YUAN DYNASTY in China in 1368 and the return of the great khans to Mongolia set the state for the next era in Mongolian literature. With the *Secret History* and other historical works lost or preserved only in obscure manuscripts, new narratives about Chinggis Khan arose in the early 16th century linked to the EIGHT WHITE YURTS, the center of the worship of Chinggis Khan. Other stories, such as the "LAMENT OF TOGHAN-TEMÜR" and the tales of MANDUKHAI SECHEN KHATUN, told of how the Mongols lost their capital in China and fought to defend the rule of Chinggis Khan's descendants against Oirat usurpers. Wise sayings and stories with morals were also attributed to Chinggis Khan. Some of these stories, such as the "Tale of Quiver-Bearer Arghasun" and the "Lament of Toghan Temür," were incorporated later in the 17th-CENTURY CHRONICLES, while others, such as the "Story of How the Three Hundred Tayichi'ud Were Conquered," circulated independently. The written prayer texts used in the Eight White Yurts' cult of Chinggis Khan and the oldest texts in the FIRE CULT and in the prayers to heaven (TENGGERI) appear to have been fixed around this time.

BUDDHIST LITERATURE

The SECOND CONVERSION of the Mongols to Buddhism opened a new era of translation. From 1578 to 1749 several teams of Mongolian translators worked to translate the two immense collections of Tibetan Buddhist scriptures and canonical commentaries, the bKa'-'gyur and bsTan-'gyur. This work gave the Mongols access to the entire body of Indian Buddhist literature, including Dandin's influential *Kavyadarsha*, or treatise on poetics. Many translators followed the example of Chosgi-Odsir in the 14th century and appended devotional verses to their colophons or postscripts.

Indian story collections were among the most popular of the new Buddhist translations. The SUTRA OF THE WISE AND FOOLISH, a collection of stories about the Buddha's previous lives, was first translated around 1586. The more secular stories of King Kirshna and his *Thirty-Two*

Wooden Men were translated in 1686, and translations of later stories in the cycle followed. *The Tale of the Bewitched Corpse* was another popular Indian story cycle. Popular Tibetan works included the biography and *Hundred Thousand Songs* of Mi-la-ras-pa (Milarepa), translated in 1618, and the free Mongolian adaption of the GESER epic, which appeared in 1716.

As in the empire period, historical literature occupied a large part of early Buddhist writings. The JEWEL TRANSLUCENT SUTRA, written in 1607, is a versified history of ALTAN KHAN, who initiated the Second Conversion. Later 17th-century chronicles gather together the historical material on Chinggis Khan and his successors; of these, the ERDENI-YIN TOBCHI has the highest literary and historical quality. Hagiographies are an important genre: Parajana-Sagara's *Chindamani erikhe* (Rosary of wishing jewels, 1739) gives a readable and lively account of how the Buddhist missionary Neichi Toin (1557–1653) confronted shamans in eastern Inner Mongolia.

DIDACTIC POETRY in Mongolian began with translations from Tibetan and Sanskrit exemplars. The *Oyun tülkhigür* (Turquoise key), attributed to Chinggis Khan, is more likely a Mongolian adaption of this early tradition dating from the 17th century. The THIRD MERGEN GEGEEN, Lubsang-Dambi-Jalsan (1717–66), wrote many widely copied hymns and liturgies for uniquely Mongolian deities. By adapting Tibetan forms to the MONGOLIAN LANGUAGE, he gave strong impetus to Mongolian-language didactic poetry, a major genre of poetry through the early 20th century.

LITERATURE IN THE NINETEENTH CENTURY

In the 19th century the genres of chronicles, hagiographies, devotional hymns, and didactic poetry continued. The poems of "General Lu" (Lubsangdondub, 1854–1909) in KHALKHA and Ishidandzanwangjil (1854–1907) and Kheshigbatu (1847–1917) in ORDOS were particularly well known.

The *üge*, or "sermon," genre used the speeches of animals or inanimate objects to teach Buddhist lessons. The poet KHUULICHI (Storyteller) SANGDAG used this genre to speak more widely about the feelings of the lonely and marginalized in society.

Buddhist poetry in all genres reached its height in the works of DANZIN-RABJAI (1803–56). In 1831 Danzin-Rabjai also composed an original opera based on the Tibetan religious novel *Tale of the Moon-Cuckoo* (1737, Mongolian translation, 1770). This opera, in addition to the TSAM performances then begun in Mongolia, marked the beginning of Mongolian theater.

The 19th century also saw a growing vogue for CHINESE FICTION in translation. The first novels to be translated had Buddhist themes, but from the 19th century historical and romantic fiction became popular. In southeastern Inner Mongolia the family of INJANNASHI wrote Mongolian masterpieces of both Chinese-style poetry and fiction. Injannashi's *Khökhe Sudur* became famous for its romantic rewriting of the rise of Chinggis Khan as well as the preface's profound critique of contemporary attitudes to ethnicity.

MODERN MONGOLIAN LITERATURE

In Mongolia the literature after the 1921 REVOLUTION was dominated by drama based on Beijing opera and dealing with historical and propagandistic themes. Most of these plays have now been lost, with the exception of those by BUYANNEMEKHÜ (1902–37). The surviving poetry is mostly composed of patriotic songs and anthems. One of the first postrevolutionary prose works was the account of the 1921 Battle of Tolbo Nuur by the political leader DAMBADORJI.

From the 1920s the Philology Institute (later Mongolia's ACADEMY OF SCIENCES) began sponsoring translations of foreign literature, as well as reprinting classic pieces of Mongolian literature and Asian literature in traditional Mongolian translation. TSYBEN ZHAMTSARANOVICH ZHAMT-SARANO, NATSUGDORJI (1906–37), TSENDIIN DAMDINSÜREN, and BYAMBYN RINCHEN translated short stories and novels from German, Russian, French, English and other languages. After WORLD WAR II the volume of translations increased greatly.

The formation of the leftist Writer's Circle in 1929 brought many more writers into literature and encouraged the writings of short stories, beginning with "The Rejected Girl" (*Gologdson khüükhen*) by Ts. Damdinsüren (1908–86). The poet Natsugdorji, who had been excluded from the group as a TAIJI (petty nobleman), wrote several of the era's best-known short stories and poems, while Buyannemekhü continued as a poet and playwright. The GREAT PURGE of 1937–40 destroyed Buyannemekhü as well as many other notable authors.

In 1948 the First Congress of Mongolian Writers met with about 74 delegates. This marked the professionalization of Mongolian literature. Literary criticism also first appeared around this time as a discipline separate from creative writing. B. Rinchen (1905–79) published Mongolia's first novel, combining folklore, historical documents, and imaginative characters to re-create the 1921 Revolution in his trilogy *Üriin tuyaa* (Rays of dawn, 1951–55, revised 1971). The most popular novels remain historically based, such as Ch. Lodoidamba's *Tungalag Tamir* (The clear Tamir, 1961), and S. Erdene's *Zanabazar* (1989). Mongolian writers produce poetry, narrative poems, short stories, novels, European-style plays, and film scripts. Poetry remains, however, the form of literature with the highest public visibility, and its practitioners, including RENTSENII CHOINOM (1936–79), OCHIRBATYN DASHBALBAR (1957–99), D. Uriankhai, and L. Dashnyam have often played the role of controversial public intellectuals.

INNER MONGOLIAN LITERATURE

Between 1911 and 1945 Inner Mongolian authors associated with the eastern Inner Mongolian NEW SCHOOLS MOVEMENTS produced many essays advocating secular education and enlightenment. The KHORCHIN Mongol Kheshingge (1888–1950) wrote lyrics in the Chinese style. The first Inner Mongolian modern prose work was "Struggling in a Sea of Suffering" (*Gashigun-u dotorakhi telchilegchi khemekhü üliger*, 1940) by Rinchinkhorlo (1904–63) of Khüriye (Hure) banner, who also translated an American detective story from Japanese into Mongolian. The Chakhar romantic poet and essayist Saichungga (later known as NA. SAINCHOGTU, 1914–73) pioneered modern secular Inner Mongolian poetry during the Japanese occupation (1937–45).

After 1947 many young Inner Mongolians were recruited for propagandistic writing for the eastern Inner Mongolian cavalry and autonomous governments under Chinese Communist auspices. Saichungga, having changed his name to Sainchogtu, returned from a stay in ULAAN-BAATAR and joined them. The works of the leading authors in Inner Mongolia before the Cultural Revolution (1966–76), such as those of the poet Bürinbekhi (b. 1928), the novelist A. Oddzar (b. 1924) of Baarin (Bairin), Malch-inhüü (Malqinhu, b. 1925) of Liaoning province, and the playwright T. Damrin (b. 1926) of Jilin province, all bore the marks of this propagandistic origin. Reprinted works of Mongolia's Natsugdorji and the Buriat playwright Khotsa Namsaraiev (1889–1959) also served as models for revolutionary literature. The poets benefited from that genre's long Mongolian tradition and their works were technically of far higher quality than those of short stories and novels. Some writers, such as Malchinhüü, have written about Mongolian topics but only in Chinese.

After the Cultural Revolution, during which literary activity had been impossible, the surviving senior authors began writing again with a freer choice of topics. Young authors began pursuing more daring topics. One controversial work was Batumöngke's (b. 1951) novella *Üdeshiyin dulagan* (Evening warmth, 1984), whose main character, "Nose" Lodon's, responds to his humiliations in the Cultural Revolution in ways modeled on the title character of the great Chinese author Lu Xun's work *The True Story of Ah Q* (1921).

See also FOLK POETRY AND TALES; MONGOLIAN PEOPLE'S REPUBLIC; PROSODY; REVOLUTIONARY PERIOD; THEOCRATIC PERIOD.

Further reading: Charles R. Bawden, *Mongolian Traditional Literature: An Anthology* (London: Kegan Paul International, 2002); Ts. Bold and D. Natsadorj, eds., *Some Short Stories from Mongolia* (Ulaanbaatar; State Publishing House, 1988); Gombojab Hangin, "Batumöngke's 'Qamar Lodon'—A New Period in Inner Mongolian Literature," *Journal of Asian and African Studies* 27 (1984): 163–171; Malqinhu [Malchinhüü], *On the Horqin [Khorchin] Grassland* (Beijing: China Literature Press, 1988); Punsek [Pungsug], "The Golden Khingan Mountains," *Chinese Literature* 4 (1954): 106–154; Henry G. Schwarz, ed., *Mongolian Short Stories* (Bellingham, Wash.:

Center for East Asian Studies, 1974); Dojoogyn Tsedev, ed., *Modern Mongolian Poetry* (Ulaanbaatar: State Publishing House, 1989).

Liu Bingzhong (Liu Ping-chung) (1216–1274) *An eccentric Buddhist monk and specialist in divination and geomancy who introduced Qubilai Khan to Confucian principles and scholars*

Liu Bingzhong's ancestors served the Kitan Liao dynasty (907–1125) and the Jurchen JIN DYNASTY (1115–1234) as Confucian officials. When MUQALI conquered North China, he appointed Liu Run civil and military chief of Xingzhou (modern Xingtai). Run's son Liu Bingzhong received a typical Confucian education and in 1228 was taken by the Mongols to Xingzhou as hostage for his father's good behavior. In 1233 Liu Bingzhong began serving as a low-level scribe but soon fled this degrading service. Taking his Dhyana (Zen) ordination as Zicong, he later wandered to Datong. Meeting Dhyana Master Haiyun there in 1242, he followed him to the court of the prince Qubilai. Qubilai took a great fancy to the monk and kept him at his camp when Haiyun returned to China. Although Liu was a monk, he had great interest in Confucian divination texts, such as the *Classic of Changes* (*I Ching*) and the works of Shao Yong (1011–77). Qubilai believed implicitly in Liu's profound understanding of Heaven and Earth, and Liu Bingzhong began the process of familiarizing Qubilai with Confucian ideas and inviting Confucian scholars to the Mongol camp.

While Liu Bingzhong returned to Xingzhou to mourn his father, Qubilai's brother MÖNGKE KHAN was elected khan (1251) and Qubilai appointed to supervise North China. Xingzhou, which before the Mongol conquest had 10,000 households, had dropped to 500–700 households through war and maladministration. Liu, appalled by the conditions he saw in Xingzhou and excited by Qubilai's new influence, wrote a long memo-rial introducing the history of Confucian governance and proposing that Qubilai, while not a sovereign, still implement comprehensive reforms. Qubilai appointed Confucian officials in Xingzhou, and Liu followed Qubilai's entourage in his 1253 campaign against Dali (YUNNAN) and his 1259 campaign against the Song. Constantly repeating "Heaven and Earth love life" and "the Lord Buddha's heart lies in mercy," he significantly moderated Qubilai's practice of warfare. In 1256 Qubilai planned a new city in Inner Mongolia, Kaiping (later SHANGDU), for which Liu Bingzhong selected a site with excellent *fengshui*.

In 1260, with the election of Qubilai as great khan, Liu Bingzhong saw his plans for a Confucian administration bear fruit. QUBILAI KHAN ordered Liu to create a new court ritual that would combine Chinese experience with the traditions of the Mongols. Chinese-style year titles and the dynasty title Yuan were all chosen by Liu. In 1267 he also selected a new site for Yanjing (modern Beijing), which was renamed DAIDU and made the main capital. Despite his high court role, Liu continued to dress and act as an unworldly, rustic monk. In 1264 a more conventional Confucian minister, Wang E, memorialized that while Liu should receive the high honorific title of grand guardian (*taibao*), he should also accept a proper court title, wear proper clothes, and marry. Qubilai followed the memorial, but Liu's marriage with a high official's daughter was never consummated. He died in Shangdu in 1274 while meditating in a Buddhist monastery.

See also BUDDHISM IN THE MONGOL EMPIRE; CONFUCIANISM.

Further reading: H. L. Chan, "Liu Ping-chung," in *In the Service of the Khan: Eminent Personalities of the Early Mongol-Yuan Period (1200–1300)*, ed. Igor de Rachewiltz et al. (Wiesbaden: Otto Harrassowitz, 1993), 245–269.

Liu Ping-chung *See* LIU BINGZHONG.

M

Magsarjav, Sandagdorjiin *See* MAGSURJAB.

Magsurjab (Sandagdorjiin Magsarjav, Maksorjab) (1878–1927) *Major military commander under the theocratic, White Russian, and revolutionary regimes*

Magsurjab's father was a *sula* (unassigned) duke in Itegemjitü Zasag banner (modern Khutag-Öndör Sum, Bulgan). Born in July 1878, Magsurjab was tutored by the ZASAG (banner ruler) Ganjuurjab. Afterward, he farmed and served as clerk in the banner administration. Around age 30 he also began serving in the AIMAG administration, and during the 1911 RESTORATION of Mongolian independence he was representing the Sain Noyan *aimag* servicing the Qing garrison in KHOWD CITY. After fleeing the garrison in January 1912, he was appointed by the new Mongolian government to join the attack on Khowd in May 1912. He distinguished himself in his command of the final assault on August 5 and was given high titles. From 1913 to 1916 he battled Chinese forces and Chinese and Mongolian bandits on the southern frontier and was promoted to prince and given half of Itegemjitü Zasag banner. On September 11, 1920, the new Chinese authorities arrested him. Released from prison on February 4 by the victory of the White Russian commander BARON ROMAN FEDOROVICH VON UNGERN-STERNBERG, he was made minister of the army and commander in chief of all Mongolian troops in the baron's government on February 21, 1921. After scattering the Chinese troops in Choir Monastery, he was appointed to pacify the west. Soon disillusioned with the senseless violence of the Whites, on July 22, 1921, he killed 24 Russians and their Buriat commander, Wandanov, outside ULIASTAI. Magsurjab joined the new Soviet-supported revolutionary government in Khüriye in August, aiding the pursuit of the White Russian remnants from Khowd to Ulaangom in September–November 1921. He served as deputy minister of the army and then from December 1922 as army minister until his death on September 3, 1927. In 1924 he had renounced all his titles of nobility and joined the MONGOLIAN PEOPLE'S REVOLUTIONARY PARTY.

See also REVOLUTIONARY PERIOD; THEOCRATIC PERIOD.

Further reading: Kh. Choibalsan, "A Brief History of the People's Indomitable Hero Margsarjav," in *Mongolian Heroes of the Twentieth Century*, trans. Urgunge Onon (New York: AMS Press, 1976), 105–142.

Mahmud Yalavach (fl. 1218–1252) **and Mas'ud Beg** (d. 1289) *Father and son who served as chief administrators in Turkestan and North China under the great khans*

Little is known of the background of Mahmud Yalavach, except that he was a caravan trader from KHORAZM. Sometime before 1218 he must have entered the service of CHINGGIS KHAN, for in that year the Mongol ruler sent him with several other Turkestani merchants to serve as envoys to Sultan 'Ala'ud-Din Muhammad, the Khorazm-Shah. Delivering his message, he returned and fortunately did not attend the second Mongol mission, which was slaughtered by the Khorazmian governor of the city of Otrar (*see* OTRAR INCIDENT). During the ensuing invasion Mahmud, variously known as al-Khwarazmi, "The Khorazmian," or Yalavach, "Messenger," was appointed overseer (DARUGHACHI) of those spared in Ghazni in Afghanistan.

In 1229 the newly elected ÖGEDEI KHAN appointed Mahmud Yalavach the first governor (*sahib-divan*) of

Transoxiana, Turkestan, and Uighuristan and YELÜ CHU-CAI that of North China. Mahmud Yalavach won favor with Ögedei through lavish entertainments and through cultivating his love of stories of heroic generosity. Like Yelü Chucai, Mahmud freed civilian households from military levies and commuted unpredictable "contributions" (*qubchiri*) into a fixed silver tax. In 1238–39 he managed to stop the Mongol armies from exterminating the inhabitants of Bukhara, who had just risen in an abortive revolt. Muslim writers give him and his son Mas'ud Beg high praise for their administration.

In 1240, as Ögedei became entranced by the possibility of much higher revenues in North China, he replaced Yelü Chucai with Mahmud Yalavach who received the title "great judge," (*yeke* JARGHUCHI in Mongolian), leaving Mahmud's son, Mas'ud Beg, the governor of Turkestan and Uighuristan. At the same time he appointed 'Abd-ur-Rahman, a favorite of Empress TÖRE-GENE, chief tax collector in North China. After Ögedei died in 1241, Töregene tried to arrest Yalavach, whose influence she had long resented, but the governor fled to Köten, Ögedei's son, in northwest China. In his place Töregene elevated 'Abd-ur-Rahman and Yang Huaizhong, a Chinese clerk. Mas'ud Beg likewise fled to the court of BATU. Töregene's son GÜYÜG, however, supported Mahmud Yalavach and Mas'ud Beg, and after being elected khan in 1246 he returned them to their old positions: Mahmud as governor of North China based in Yanjing (modern Beijing), and Mas'ud Beg as governor of Turkestan and Uighuristan with his seat in Besh-Baligh. Güyüg's early death in 1248 did not affect their positions: They supported the election of MÖNGKE KHAN (1251–59) and at first remained high in favor.

Despite a good reputation in Muslim circles, Mahmud was not popular in North China. Mongol administrative methods inspired by Turco-Islamic usage, such as tax farming, tax payments in silver, and merchant-official partnerships, were unpopular innovations, and Mahmud's foreign origin made these practices more galling. With Möngke's election Chinese Confucian-trained opponents of these methods found a patron in his brother Qubilai (1215–94). In 1252 Qubilai criticized Mahmud over his cavalier execution of suspects during a judicial review. When Qubilai's Chinese protegé, Zhao Bi, attacked Mahmud for his presumptuous attitude toward the throne, Möngke dismissed the Khorazmian, who apparently died soon after.

Mas'ud Beg remained as the governor of Turkestan and Uighuristan until Möngke's death in 1259. When civil war broke out between Qubilai and his brother ARIQ-BÖKE, Mas'ud naturally opposed Qubilai. Ariq-Böke kept him in Mongolia until 1264, when he sent him to Alghu (r. 1260–65/6), khan of the CHAGHATAY KHANATE, or realm, to try to restore relations with them. Alghu employed Mas'ud Beg again as *sahib-divan* in Transoxiana. After the death of Alghu, he served Baraq Khan (r. 1266–71) as vizier, or prime minister. Baraq's rule in

Transoxiana began with widespread plunder of the peasantry, doing damage that Mas'ud in 1269–70 could only partially restore. After 1271 Mas'ud and his sons served QAIDU (1236–1301), who proved less destructive than Baraq. Mas'ud Beg had endowed one of the largest *madrasas* (Islamic schools) in Bukhara, but it was burned in an Il-Khan invasion in 1273.

See also CENSUS IN THE MONGOL EMPIRE; PROVINCES IN THE MONGOL EMPIRE.

Further reading: Th. T. Allsen, "Mahmud Yalavač, Mas'ud Beg, 'Ali Beg, Safaliq, Bujir," in *In the Service of the Khan: Eminent Personalities of the Early Mongol-Yuan Period (1200–1300)*, ed. Igor de Rachewiltz et al. (Wiesbaden: Otto Harrassowitz, 1993), 122–135.

Maksorjab   *See* MAGSURJAB.

Mamluk Egypt   The armies of Mamluk Egypt checked the Mongol advance in the Middle East and sapped the strength of the Mongols' IL-KHANATE. During the early Mongol conquests the fractious Ayyubid dynasty (1171–1260), founded by the Kurdish Salah-ad-Din (Saladin, 1138–93), collectively controlled Egypt, the Levant, and much of KURDISTAN. At first Kurds formed the dynasty's military core, but Sultan as-Salih Najm-ad-Din Ayyub (1240–49) exploited the flood of enslaved QIPCHAQS generated by the Mongol conquest to create a regiment of trained military slaves, or Mamluks. After his death in 1250, these Mamluks overthrew as-Salih's son, founding a new Mamluk regime (1250–1517). The royal Mamluks were Qipchaq slaves bought by the sultan, converted to Islam, trained in war, and then emancipated at their majority to serve as soldiers in the sultan's regiment. These highly trained royal Mamluks were supplemented by Mamluks of the sultan's emirs, Kurdish and other freebooters, and bedouin auxiliaries. The Mamluk core combined Inner Asian fighting skills with a strong pride in defending Islam and the orthodox caliphate (*see* 'ABBASID CALIPHATE).

After HÜLE'Ü (r. 1256–65) destroyed the Baghdad Caliphate (1258) and founded the Mongol Il-Khan dynasty, the Egyptian Mamluks under Sultan Qutuz (1259–60) crushed a Mongol force at 'Ain Jalut (in Palestine). Qutuz was murdered soon after, and it was left to his successor Baybars (1260–77) to create the ideological, diplomatic, and military foundation for defense against the Mongols. He settled an 'Abbasid heir in Cairo as caliph and symbol of Mamluk legitimacy. From 1262 he also exchanged envoys with Berke (1257–66), Muslim Mongol khan of the GOLDEN HORDE, expressing Mamluk hostility to Hüle'ü and emphasizing their common faith. Threats from their Mongol rivals prevented the Il-Khans from focusing forces on the Mamluks.

To warn of Mongol attacks, postroads and beacon towers linked the frontier fortresses of al-Bira (modern

Birecik), al-Rahba, and ʿAin-Tab (modern Gaziantep) to Egypt. In summer, when the heat forced the Mongol troops to evacuate the lowlands, Syrian troops—Kurds, Turkmen, and Arab Bedouins, occasionally aided by mamluks—raided the Mongol frontier in LESSER ARMENIA, Malatya, Diyarbakır, and Mosul. These raids especially focused on Armenian and Assyrian Christian targets. Meanwhile, tribal groups impatient with Il-Khan rule, whether Kurds, Turkmen, or even Mongols, often defected to the Mamluks. Baybars personally led large-scale raids into Lesser Armenia (1266) and Seljük TURKEY (1277). After 1277 the local Karaman Turkmen, based in the Taurus Mountains and Laranda, collaborated with Egypt in raiding both Lesser Armenia and Mongol-held Turkey.

The Mongol Il-Khanate's strategy in response was inconsistent and ineffective. Up through 1305 the Il-Khans fruitlessly sought alliance with Latin Christendom. Unlike the Mamluk sultans, the Mongol khans rarely campaigned personally in Syria. Thus, a 1281 Mongol advance was defeated at Homs due to inexperienced leadership and poor communication. Significantly, the one campaign personally led by a Mongol khan, that of GHAZAN KHAN (1295–1304) in 1299–1300, was the war's only resounding Mongol success. Even so, Ghazan evacuated with most of his troops in spring, and the Mamluks recovered the lost territory.

The Mamluks made no response to the naive peace offers of the Il-Khan Sultan Ahmad (1282–84), the Il-Khan's first Muslim ruler, but after Ghazan's accession Mamluk raids declined. In 1312 the Mamluk governor of Aleppo, Qarasonqur, fled to the Il-Khan's Sultan Öljeitü (1304–16), briefly reviving the Mongol war party. Threatened by the defection, Mamluk sultan an-Nasir Muhammad (1310–40) recognized the dangers of continued war, and when the Mongol commander in chief CHUBAN became regent for the young khan Abu-Saʿid (1317–35), peace was concluded in 1323. Despite Chuban's fall in 1327, the peace was confirmed by the two courts' mutual execution of exiles, including Chuban's son Temürtash and Mamluk defector Qarasonqur. Abandoned by the Mongols, Lesser Armenia made a separate peace in 1325, paying 50,000 gold florins annually to Egypt. As an Islamic realm, the Il-Khanate angled unsuccessfully from 1318 for support in Mecca, even sending an elephant to accompany the pilgrimage caravan in 1330. With the Il-Khans' fall in 1335, the Mamluks solidified their power in the former frontier zone and prospered as trade between Europe and India gravitated toward the Red Sea.

See also ʿAINT JALUT, BATTLE OF; BYZANTIUM AND BULGARIA.

Further reading: Reuven Amitai-Preiss, *Mongols and Mamluks: The Mamluk-Ilkhanid War, 1260–1281* (Cambridge: Cambridge University Press, 1995); Charles Melville, "'The Year of the Elephant': Mamluk-Mongol Rivalry in the Hejaz in the Reign of Abu Saʿid (1317–1335)," *Studia Iranica* 21 (1992): 197–214.

Manchuria and the Mongol Empire Only slowly subdued by Mongol armies, Manchuria supplied falcons, pearls, and other native products.

At the time of the Mongols, southern Manchuria (modern Liaoning), while ethnically diverse, was subject to regular Chinese-style civil administration. A substantial Han (ethnic Chinese) population coexisted with seminomadic KITANS, who had earlier founded the Liao dynasty (907–1125). North of them, along the Sungari (Songhua) River, lay the heartland of the Jurchens of the JIN DYNASTY (1115–1234), then ruling North China. Although Manchuria was the original heartland of the Jin dynasty, the migration of Jurchens to North China as soldiers left the Jurchen presence there rather weak.

In the north the Liao and the Jin dynasties gathered tribute from the so-called Water Tatars (Chinese, *Shui Dada*, Mongolian, *Usu Irgen* or *Usu Mongghol*). These included the Üjiyed (Chinese, Wuzhe) and Gilemi, ancestors of today's Manchu-Tungusic Nanai and Hejen nationalities (also called Hezhe, Golds, or Fish-Skin Tatars), who fished and hunted martens, otters, and seals along the lower Amur, and the Ghilyaks, whose lifestyle was similar to the Üjiyed but who spoke a Paleo-Asiatic language.

In 1211 as the Mongols invaded, the Jin government ordered that two Jurchen families be billeted with each Kitan family to keep watch. In 1212 a Kitan, Yelü Liuge, revolted in central Manchuria (near modern Changchun and Siping), his forces soon swelling to more than 100,000. When Mongol envoys arrived, Yelü Liuge swore loyalty to the MONGOL EMPIRE and fought off repeated Jin attacks by Puxian Wannu, the chief Jurchen general in Manchuria. However, in 1215, after the Jin rulers abandoned the north, Puxian Wannu himself set up his own Eastern Xia, or Jurchen, dynasty in eastern Liaoning. Both Yelü Liuge and Puxian Wannu had audiences with CHINGGIS KHAN (Genghis, 1206–27) and left hostages, yet by 1218 Yelü Liuge's Kitans had revolted against both him and the Mongols and were fighting a combination of Puxian Wannu's forces, the Koreans whose border towns they had occupied, and a Mongol force sent to bring order to the area. The Mongol force soon withdrew, and conditions remained chaotic.

In 1226 Yelü Liuge's widow visited Chinggis Khan's court again, and the next year his hostage son Xuedu was returned and made commander in chief of Guangning in western Liaoning. Puxian Wannu, however, did not submit, and ÖGEDEI KHAN (1229–41) dispatched Prince GÜYÜG and the general Tangghud with TAMMACHI troops (long-term garrison armies, largely non-Mongol) to dispose of him. By 1233 the pacification of southern Manchuria was complete.

Under Ögedei's reign the Mongols subdued the Water Tatars in the northern part of the region sometimes after 1233. In 1237 conditions seem settled enough for Ögedei to demanded harem girls, sparking unrest that was harshly suppressed. At the beginning of the Mongol YUAN DYNASTY (1271–1368) the area was put under the Helan Prefecture Water Tatars Route, with five myriarchies (10,000 household militia units) controlling the lower Songhua and Amur Rivers and the Pacific coast. In 1330 the total taxable population was recorded as 20,906 households.

During the conquest many princes and noblemen, particularly MUQALI and Chinggis's younger brothers Temüge Odchigin and Belgütei, received large appanages in various parts of Manchuria, delaying the implementation of regular civil administration. Descendants of the fraternal princes strongly supported QUBILAI KHAN's coronation in 1260, but the younger generation, led by Belgütei's descendant Nayan, desired more independence. Nayan's failed rebellion in 1287–88 pruned the fraternal lines and led to the creation of a Liaoyang Branch Secretariat covering Manchuria.

The Mongols' main interest in northern Manchuria was in the white and gray falcons that flew across the Sea of Okhotsk to roost at the mouth of the Amur. By 1297 they had created a special Üjiyed-Gilemi myriarchy on the lower Amur to handle enforcement of the falcon tribute and maintain dogsled post stations for tribute collectors. Demand for falcons was onerous from the beginning, and the Water Tatars rebelled in 1346. The rebellion was suppressed and the myriarchies reorganized in 1354. After the MING DYNASTY (1368–1644) expelled the Yuan from China proper, a Mongol commander, Naghachu, continued to hold southern Manchuria. Naghachu surrendered to a large Ming force in 1387, but the Ming solidified control only under the Yongle (1402–24) emperor.

See also FALCONRY; HUNTING AND FISHING; KOREA AND THE MONGOL EMPIRE; NAYAN'S REBELLION; THREE GUARDS.

Mandukhai Sechen Khatun (Wise Empress Mandukhai) (b. 1449?) *Empress who helped reestablish Chinggisid supremacy and overthrow Oirat rule*

Mandukhai was the daughter of Chorosbai-Temür Chingsang (Grand Councillor) of the ÖNGGÜD clan of the TÜMED Mongols. Married to Manduul Khan (1473–79), she bore two daughters and was preferred to his childless Oirat wife. Manduul's death left the throne without an heir. His grandnephew Bolkhu Jinong died in flight a few years later, but a seven-year-old boy was brought to the regent, Mandukhai, with the claim that he was Bolkhu Jinong son, Batu-Möngke. Mandukhai, then 33 years old, rejected the powerful suitor Üne-Bolod of the KHORCHIN and insisted on marrying Batu-Möngke as a true Chinggisid. She enthroned him as BATU MÖNGKE DAYAN KHAN (1480?–1517?) at the shrine of Eshi Khatun (that is, SORQAQTANI BEKI) in CHAKHAR. Later, she defeated the OIRATS, bringing the prince along "in a box," as the

chronicles state; the *Shira tughuji* attributes various Oirat folk practices to her punitive decrees. She participated in later attacks on the Oirat, during one of which she was pregnant with Dayan Khan's twin sixth and seventh sons. Mandukhai's giving birth to seven sons and only one daughter was seen as confirmation of her decision to marry a true Chinggisid. With Dayan Khan she later went to the EIGHT WHITE YURTS (the shrine of Chinggis Khan) in ORDOS to be re-enthroned, but they had to flee a Chinese attack and went to the KHERLEN RIVER (1501). She was apparently dead by 1510.

Mangghud (Mangudai: Turkish Manghit)   One of the major clans in CHINGGIS KHAN's army, the Mangghud were particularly important in the GOLDEN HORDE and its successor states.

The *SECRET HISTORY OF THE MONGOLS* and RASHID-UD-DIN FAZL-ULLAH (drawing on Mongol oral histories) both describe the Mangghud as a branch of the ruling Niru'un or Kiyad lineage, closely associated with the Uru'ud, but the two sources' exact genealogies differ. Two bodies of Mangghuds joined the conquest elite under Chinggis Khan. The first was under Jedei Noyan, whose father was killed by his Mangghud clansmen hostile to Chinggis. Raised in his BARGA (Barghu) mother's clan, Jedei, with his brother Doqolqu Cherbi (Steward), joined Chinggis Khan. The victorious Chinggis enslaved the hostile Mangghuds and gave them to Jedei Noyan as his 1,000. Doqolqu Cherbi commanded a 1,000 in the KESHIG (imperial guard).

According to the *Secret History* another body of Mangghuds under Quyildar Sechen formed, with the Uru'uds, part of Chinggis's crack vanguard troops famed for their military discipline. Quyildar himself died of wounds suffered at the defeat of Qalaqaljid Sands (1203), and his orphans were treated with special favor. After that defeat the 2,300 Uru'ud and Mangghud remained loyal, forming half of Chinggis's people. Rashid-ud-Din was familiar with this version yet also knew of another version in which only Quyildar and a few companions were loyal while the bulk of the Mangghud opposed Chinggis.

With the division of Chinggis's people, Mangghuds of both groups were distributed among the various appanages. Chinggis assigned the 1,000 under Quyildar's son Möngke-Qalja (along with the Uru'ud) to MUQALI's TAMMACHI (garrison) army assigned to North China. Under ÖGEDEI KHAN Möngke-Qalja received an appanage in Dongping. One branch of Jedei Noyan's descendants was assigned to the *tammachi* armies in Afghanistan, ancestors of the later QARA'UNAS. From there they entered the service of the Il-Khans. GHAZAN KHAN's commander in chief (*beglerbegi*), Qutlughshah, was one of them.

In the Golden Horde around KHORAZM, the Mangghud and QONGGIRAD formed the two main clans. Under Edigü (Edigei, d. 1420), the Manghit (as written in the

Turkish language they had adopted) displaced the Qonggirad as ANDA (sworn brothers) and QUDA (marriage allies) of the BLUE HORDE (the Golden Horde's eastern half) khans. Edigü eventually deserted his Chinggisid sovereign, TOQTAMISH (fl. 1375–1405), serving after 1395 as *beglerbegi* (commander in chief) for a succession of Jochid puppet rulers, while his son Nur-ad-Din held the Manghit base between the Volga and the Emba Rivers. After Edigü's death his descendants served as *beglerbegis* and *anda-quda* for the contending Jochid sovereigns, while the main clan body, said to number 200,000 warriors, remained around Saraychik. From the time of Edigü's grandson Musa (fl. 1455–1502), the Manghit lords (*beg/biy*) dominated the Black Sea–Caspian steppe in the middle 16th century as independent potentates. These Manghit appear in Russian, Crimean, and Ottoman Turkish sources as "Nogays," after a certain Noghay, but any connection to the 14th-century Jochid prince NOQAI/Noghay is uncertain. Bodies of Manghit tribesmen followed *biys* of Edigü's family into CRIMEA by 1523 and into the Uzbek horde, which had occupied Mawarannahr (Transoxiana) by 1512. In Crimea they were (under the name Mansur-oghlan) one of the major clans, and in Mawarannahr the Manghit founded their own dynasty at Bukhara from 1753 to 1920.

With the Kalmyk invasion of the 1620s, the Nogay-Manghits were driven out of the Volga River basin. The largest body settled in northern Dagestan, and another group settled in Khorazm (around the modern town of Mangit). Those in Dagestan now form the Nogay nationality (estimated population 60,000–80,000), while those in Khorazm are a major component of the Karakalpak people. Manghits are also found among the TATARS, Bashkirs (Bashkurt), and KAZAKHS. Everywhere the Manghits have preserved tales of the heroic liege Edigü and his tyrannical master Toqtamish.

On the MONGOLIAN PLATEAU Mangghuds are found in eastern KHALKHA (Mongolia proper) and in Baarin (Bairin) banner of eastern Inner Mongolia.

Further reading: Yu. Bregel, "Mangit," in *Encyclopaedia of Islam*, 2d ed., vol. 6, 417–418; Vadim V. Trepavlov, *The Formation and Early History of the Manghīt Yurt* (Bloomington: Indiana University, Research Institute for Inner Asian Studies, 2001).

Manghit   *See* MANGGHUD.

Mangudai   *See* MANGGHUD.

Mangu Khan   *See* MÖNGKE KHAN.

Maodun   *See* MODUN.

Mas'ud Beg   *See* MAHMUD YALAVACH AND MAS'UD BEG.

Masqud Beg   *See* MAHMUD YALAVACH AND MAS'UD BEG.

massacres and the Mongol Conquest   Wholesale massacres, particularly after a city was taken by storm, were a recurrent feature of medieval warfare, engaged in by most of the Mongols' enemies. Mongol massacres stood out, however, for their systematic character. When a city was taken by storm, the regular Mongol precedent was to order all the inhabitants of the defeated city out into the surrounding plain and to assign a specified number to each Mongol soldier. Craftsmen, including physicians, astronomers, and sometimes actors and clergy, were separated out. While the inhabitants were outside the city, the Mongol army would enter the city and pillage it, killing all they found hiding there. Sometimes sympathetic clergy were allowed to use churches, mosques, or temples as places of refuge. Having numbered the defeated, the Mongol soldiers, if so ordered, would dispatch their victims with an ax. Even if the inhabitants were generally spared, each soldier would levy a number of able-bodied men to serve as cannon fodder against the next city. The craftsmen would almost always be spared and divided among the commanders and princes to be deported and serve as slaves. At Zhongdu (modern Beijing) in 1215 and Baghdad in 1251 the population seems to have been too large to move out into the plain, so the victors simply entered the city and massacred as they pleased for a week or so.

Mongols generally massacred in those cities that had surrendered and then rebelled again, where their envoys had been killed, or where the resistance was particularly fierce. Occasionally, as at Bamiyan and Nishapur (Neyshabur), where missiles from the defenders' mangonels killed relatives of CHINGGIS KHAN, all the living creatures, including the craftsmen and even the dogs and cats, were destroyed. In rural areas where the Mongols faced persistent guerrilla resistance, they would form their soldiers in a hunting ring, or *nerge*, up to 150 kilometers (100 miles) wide and comb through the land, slaughtering all they found.

The precedent for these wholesale massacres was the 1202 conquest of the TATARS. Convinced that these hereditary foes of the Mongols would never become obedient, Chinggis Khan ordered all those taller than a Mongol cart's linch-pole, male and female alike, massacred. Due to the tenacious resistance, Chinggis Khan and his generals repeatedly massacred cities during the conquest of the JIN DYNASTY in North China (1211–23) and KHORAZM (1219–23). Likewise, the sieges in Eastern Europe from 1236 to 1242 and those of HÜLE'Ü in southwest Asia from 1256 to 1262 were mostly concluded by massacres. In China, local officials in Mongol service began to alter Mongol policy toward the defeated. Chinggis Khan's ethnic Tangut (Mi-nyag) commander Chagha'an dissuaded him from several massacres in 1226–27. During the final annihilation of the Jin in 1234, YELÜ CHUCAI convinced ÖGEDEI KHAN to spare the Jin capital of Kaifeng (*see* KAIFENG, SIEGE OF), and under QUBILAI KHAN in China the conquest of the Song in 1274–76 took place with few wholesale massacres.

The death toll of Mongol massacres is difficult to estimate. Persian historians estimate the death toll in cities such as Herat and Nishapur (Neyshabur) at more than 1.5 million, but these estimates seem to exceed considerably the possible populations of these cities. Hüle'ü claimed that his Mongol soldiers killed 200,000 people in Baghdad (1258). In North China, under the previous Jin dynasty (1115–1234), a census of 1207 found 7.68 million households, while the Mongol census of the same territory in 1236 found only 1.83 million households. While the Mongol census certainly involved a major undercount, the figures plainly demonstrate a demographic catastrophe. Much population loss took place as a result of the anarchy of the invasion and subsequent Mongol misrule. Persian and Chinese writers claim that this maladministration was even more damaging than the conquest themselves. Thus, by 1330 cities such as Samarqand and Bukhara, where the civilian population was not massacred, were in decline under the unreformed Mongol rule of the CHAGHATAY KHANATE, while Urganch city in Khorazm, which suffered wholesale massacre, was flourishing under the more effective Mongol administration of the GOLDEN HORDE.

See also ARTISANS IN THE MONGOL EMPIRE; BAGHDAD, SIEGE OF; CENSUS IN THE MONGOL EMPIRE; KIEV, SIEGE OF; MILITARY OF THE MONGOL EMPIRE; ZHONGDU, SIEGES OF.

matrilineal clans   The anthropologically unusual situation of matrilineal pastoral nomadic clans emerged in the Gobi during the 19th century.

By the 19th century the traditional Mongolian patrilineages, outside the ruling BORJIGID (Chinggisid) lineage, were disintegrating. Monasticism brought about unbalanced sex ratios, and even householding lamas could not formally marry or pass their clan membership to their sons. In many areas of the GOBI DESERT matrilineal lineages of varying degrees of cohesion replaced the old patrilineages. Called *deedüül*, from *deedes* (ancestors), these lineages were named after male apical ancestors, four or five generations before the 1950s.

Despite the male apical ancestor, membership in these lineages was transmitted solely through the female line, and daughters, not sons, stayed in their family of origin. Formal marriage on the Mongolian pattern, with the giving of bridewealth and virilocal residence, was unknown, and even long-term uxorilocal cohabitation was not common, replaced by brief liaisons or visiting marriage, in which the man would spend the days in his sisters' YURT and nights with his woman in her yurt. Few children had close relations with their fathers. Headship of the matrilineage passed to a son who resided in his mother's yurt, and a man's wandering days often ended by returning to the maternal yurt to take up lineage headship on the death of a brother or mother's brother.

Each matrilineage retained a distinct territory (*nutag*) with a cairn (OBOO). Matrilineages, like Mongolian patrilineages and clans elsewhere, also had their own *tamga* (cattle brand) and consecrated animal, marked with *seter*, or strips of cloth. The lineage maintained a main family yurt with a particular fierce Buddha as guardian (*sakhius*). Before the 1950s lineages contained large joint families with up to 20 persons and more than 1,000 head of livestock. Division of such joint families did not, however, end membership in the lineage.

In the 1950s the matrilineal lineages declined. Progressive taxation of private herds, intended to promote collectivization, broke up the joint families, antireligious pressure forced the lineage cult underground, and increasing familiarity with the outside world introduced both the traditional Mongolian concept of patrilineal kinship and the modern ideal of the nuclear family. *Khot-ails* (camps) are still mostly formed on a matrilateral kinship basis, however. With democracy and DECOLLECTIVIZATION after 1990, the old matrilateral clans have partially revived their prestige as part of local tradition, but the bilateral model of modern Mongolian kinship is still strong.

See also CLAN NAMES; FAMILY; KINSHIP SYSTEM; LAMAS AND MONASTICISM.

Further reading: Tomasz Potkanski and Slavoj Szynkiewicz, *The Social Context of Liberalisation of the Mongolian Pastoral Economy* (Brighton, 1993).

mausoleum of Chinggis Khan   *See* EIGHT WHITE YURTS.

medicine, traditional   Before 1900 the principal Mongolian methods for treating the physically and emotionally sick included: 1) shamans and shamanesses; 2) special healing by bone setters, or *bariach*; 3) a wide variety of unsystematized cures, including foods, herbs, heated stones, and so on; and 4) the elaborate system of Tibetan medicine combining empirical observation with a multifaceted theory of human bodily and psychological operations. (*For more on the first and second methods, see* BARIACH *and* SHAMANISM.)

A number of folk remedies have a long history on the MONGOLIAN PLATEAU. Common Mongolian foods are traditionally believed to have curative properties. The famous 1330 cookbook for the Mongol court in China by the Uighur Hu Sihui (Qusqi) classifies foods according to their nourishing qualities and recommends the many varieties of mutton soup among "red foods" (meat) and fermented mare's milk, or KOUMISS, among "white foods" (DAIRY PRODUCTS).

The XIANBI, an early steppe people, are said to have used both hot stones and moxibustion, and hot stones are still believed to cure ills when applied locally. The skins or warm rumen of freshly slaughtered animals are also believed to cure diseases; in 1269 QUBILAI KHAN had his feet treated for gout by wearing boots made from the skin of a large fish. The ultimate example of this practice was the use of fresh human organs. This method was used by a Mongol prince, Quli, in Armenia around 1260. ALTAN KHAN may have planned such a treatment in 1580, although some sources say it was with a horse's body; in any case a Buddhist cleric intervened, curing him with prayer.

In the MONGOL EMPIRE the khans actively sought all varieties of medicine. Physicians were among those exempt from taxes and always spared in massacres (*see* ARTISANS IN THE MONGOL EMPIRE.) CHINGGIS KHAN (Genghis, 1206–27) had a Chinese physician, Liu Zhonglu, and in 1262 QUBILAI KHAN created a Chinese-style Palace Medical Service. He also commissioned the Nepalese artist ANIGA to revise a chart of Chinese acupuncture and moxibustion points on the body. In 1270 he created a Muslim Medical Office to dispense Middle Eastern medicines. Meanwhile, among the Mongols in the Middle East two Jewish doctors, SA'D-UD-DAWLA and RASHID-UD-DIN FA'ZL-ULLAH, rose to high power as physicians at the khan's court.

TIBETAN MEDICINE

After the fall of the Mongol Empire Buddhist medical knowledge dominated the Mongols' medicine. This knowledge was vital in the SECOND CONVERSION of the Mongols to Buddhism from 1575 on. In conversion accounts lamas frequently converted both nobles and even shamans by their effectiveness in healing with prayer. Medically, the Tibetan lamas vaccinated against smallpox, which since the 1550s had been ravaging the Mongols. In nomadic Mongolia smallpox was often contracted by adults with devastating effects, so that the Tibetan live-virus technique, using pus scraped from pox sores, was worth the risk to children.

Tibetan Buddhist medicine is based on the fundamental text the *Four Roots* (Tibetan, *rGyud bzhi*; Mongolian, *Jud-shi* or *Dörben ündüsü*), said to have been rediscovered or authored by gYu-thog Yon-tan mGon-po (1112–1203). Even as Buddhism was spreading in Mongolia, the Tibetan medical system was reorganized by the Fifth Dalai Lama's regent (*sde-srid*), Sangs-rgyas rGya-mtsho (r. 1679–1703), who sponsored the now authoritative commentaries on the *Four Roots* and created a series of 79 paintings illustrating the *Vaidurya sngon-po*. Sangs-rgyas rGya-mtsho also created the first unified monastic medical college in Tibet.

Tibetan medicine, like Greek, Indian, and Chinese medicine, views the body as a system of interrelated phases, or humors. Illness is caused by imbalance in humors, and treatment primarily consists of weakening the excess humor. Karmic and demonic causes of disease are also accepted and need to be dealt with by appropriate religious and/or exorcistic means. The *Four Roots* uses the Indian Ayurvedic humors of bile (*bad-kan*, Mongolian, *batgan*), phlegm (*mkhris-pa*, Mongolian, *shar*, yellow), and wind (*blung*, Mongolian, *khii*), and the Greek conception of wind and phlegm as cold humors and blood and bile as hot humors. In treatment, the pride of place is taken by Indian herbal remedies with Chinese moxibustion also used. As in Chinese medicine, taking the pulse is the dominant diagnostic tool. While surgery is theoretically known, it is virtually never used.

While some monastic physicians in traditional Mongolia, called *sutra* doctors, relied purely on the Tibetan classics, others adopted Mongolian and Chinese medicine in varying degrees. Some, such as Chorji Mergen (fl. 1728), who focused on healing external wounds, were predecessors of the modern BARIACH, or "bone setters." The great Tu (Monguor) lama and polymath Sum-pa mKhan-po Ishi-Baljur (Ye-shes dPal-'byor, 1704–87) incorporated many Mongolian folk remedies in his medical works while being the first to link bubonic plague to marmots (*see* BLACK DEATH; TU LANGUAGE AND PEOPLE). The Mongolian lay Tibetologist DUKE GOMBOJAB (fl. 1692–1749) chaired a translation project that produced a comparative Sanskrit, Tibetan, Chinese, and Turkish materia medica, although his work was later criticized by *sutra* doctors, who felt he had misunderstood some Tibetan terms. The ORDOS INCARNATE LAMA and physician Ishidandzanwangjil (1854–1907) used poetry to explain medical ideas in Mongolian.

TRADITIONAL MEDICINE IN THE MODERN ERA

The encounter between Tibetan and Western medicine began in Russia. While Russian doctors denounced what they saw as the quackery of many lama physicians, the Buriat physician Pëtr A. Badmaev (1856–1920) became a court physician for the last czar in St. Petersburg. While

Mongolian doctor wrapping Tibetan-style powdered medicines in Shiliin Khot, Inner Mongolia, 1987. The labels on the bottles are all in Tibetan. *(Courtesy Christopher Atwood)*

himself a Christian, Badmaev published an unabridged translation of the *Four Roots* in Russian in 1902. The great Buriat Mongolian lama AGWANG DORZHIEV (1853–1938) brought a set of Sangs-rgyas rGya-mtsho's 79 medical paintings to Buriatia to his new Atsagat Medical College there; it is now one of the three extant copies in the world.

In the 20th century the Soviet government in Russia used discrediting Buddhist medicine as a key to winning over its Kalmyk and Buriat Mongol populace. From 1921 on in Mongolia proper as well, Buddhist physicians were accused of charlatanism and were denounced. The death of the revolutionary hero GENERAL SÜKHEBAATUR in 1923 was blamed on poisoning by jealous lamas. Eventually, the virtual annihilation of the monasteries almost destroyed Tibetan medicine in Mongolia. The new medical system built in Mongolia after 1940 was entirely European in content. Even so, in Buriatia the priceless set of 79 illustrations was rediscovered in 1958 and became the core of scholarly research on the Tibetan medical tradition, although its religious origins still had to be played down. In 1968 an institute devoted to the study of Tibetan medicine was created.

The Chinese Communist government, however, followed the policy of pairing Western medicine with a modernized Chinese medicine. In Inner Mongolia a Chinese-Mongolian medical college was created in 1953, and in 1959 a separate Mongolian medical faculty was created. That same year the *Four Roots* and Sangs-rgyas rGya-mtsho's commentaries were published in Mongolian for the first time, although with the religious material completely cut. Mongolian folk remedies, acupuncture, and modern anatomy were also added to Mongolian medicine. Despite the translations, prescriptions were still written in Tibetan. Mongolian doctors in Inner Mongolia have a good reputation for healing liver diseases.

Since 1990 traditional medicine has rapidly revived in Mongolia and Mongol areas of post-Communist Russia. The revival was spurred not only by religious freedom but also by the economic crisis, which made imported Western medicines hard to obtain and expensive.

See also LAMAS AND MONASTICISM.

Further reading: Thomas T. Allsen, *Culture and Conquest in Mongol Eurasia* (Cambridge: Cambridge University Press, 2001); John F. Avedon, et al., *The Buddha's Art of Healings: Tibetan Paintings Rediscovered* (New York: Rizzoli International Publications, 1998); C.R. Bawden, "Supernatural Element in Sickness and Death according to Mongol Tradition, Parts I and II," *Asia Major* 8 (1961): 215–257 and 9 (1962): 153–178; Tseren Korsunkiyev, *Ancient Oirat Books about Oriental Medicine* trans. John R. Krueger, (Bloomington: Indiana University, Research Institute for Inner Asian Studies, 2001); Ruth Meserve, "On the History of Medicinal Plant Research in Mongolia," in *Remota Relata,* ed. Juha Janhunen and Asko Parpola (Helsinki: Finnish Oriental Society, 2003), 155–167.

Menggeser Noyan (d. 1253) *Chief judge during the accession of Möngke Khan, who executed the purge of the khan enemies*

The clan of Menggeser Noyan (Commander Menggeser) of Jait JALAYIR had served CHINGGIS KHAN's father, YISÜGEI BA'ATUR, and remained loyal to Chinggis Khan even during the khan's orphaned childhood. Menggeser served Chinggis's son TOLUI at the siege of Fengxiang (1231) and Tolui's son MÖNGKE KHAN during the great western campaign of 1236–41, winning favor by forwarding all booty to the princes and keeping nothing for himself. GÜYÜG Khan (r. 1246–48) made him a judge (JARGHUCHI). After Güyüg died Menggeser strongly supported the candidacy of Möngke as khan, threatening to behead Bala, an Uighur scribe who opposed him. On his coronation Möngke immediately appointed Menggeser supreme judge. When it was revealed that Güyüg's branch of the imperial family was staging a coup, Menggeser captured the plotters before they realized the plot had been discovered. Möngke put Menggeser in charge of interrogating and executing all malcontents. During the purge, which lasted through fall 1252, Möngke relied on Menggeser implicitly, not reviewing the sentences until after their execution. In fall 1253 Möngke appointed Menggeser a commander of 10,000 for the coming China campaign, but he died that winter.

Mengü Khan *See* MÖNGKE KHAN.

Mergen Gegeen, Third, Lubsang-Dambi-Jalsan (Dambijaltsan) (1717–June 7, 1766) *Liturgist, lyricist, translator, and incarnate lama who dedicated his life to making Buddhism truly Mongolian*

A son of the ordinary herder Lubzang from Urad Left-Duke banner (modern Urad Zhongqi) was enthroned as the Third Mergen Gegeen (INCARNATE LAMA of Mergen) in 1721. He presided over Mergen Kheid Hermitage in the Muna Uula Mountains of Urad Right-Duke banner (modern Urad Qianqi), with the monastic name Lubsang-Dambi-Jalsan. The Third Mergen Gegeen's life's work was to create a Mongolian liturgy for the full cycle of Buddhist service. In addition to the complete Indo-Tibetan liturgy, the Mergen Gegeen added liturgies for the worship of fire and the local Muna Uula Mountain in the temples, as well as for lay-oriented festivals dedicated to Mongolian deities: The OBOO (local cairn), CHINGGIS KHAN, the banner standard, and the WHITE OLD MAN. Similar Mongolian themes were even more widespread in his "81 Songs" on devotional topics, many still sung today. The Mergen Gegeen also composed widely imitated didactic poems, exhorting listeners to strive to repay the kindness of the Buddhist and secular authorities. To encourage literacy he wrote rhymed primers of the Mongolian alphabet. He also wrote the *Altan tobchiya* (Golden summary), a Mongolian-language history of Buddhism in India, Tibet, and Mongolia.

In his liturgy the Third Mergen Gegeen departed from the previous approach of wiping out the *ongghon* (shaman spirits) and replacing them with Buddhist deities. Instead, following Tibetan precedent, he wanted to see the old *ongghons* put under oath to protect the superior Buddhist faith. While frustrated by the persistence of bloody sacrifices even at the *oboo*, the Mergen Gegeen's aim was to make Buddhism, now unassailably dominant, more truly Mongolian and to preserve into the future a version of the pre-Buddhist past, suitably transformed by Buddhist ethics. Thanks to his work the monasteries of Urad Left-Duke banner continue to hold Mongolian-language services to the present.

See also EIGHT WHITE YURTS; FIRE CULT; FOLK POETRY AND TALES; MONGOLIAN RELIGION.

Merkid (Merkit) The Merkid tribe in northern Mongolia tenaciously resisted the rise of CHINGGIS KHAN. In the mid-12th century the Merkid occupied the land along the lower SELENGE RIVER, between where it meets the ORKHON RIVER and the Khilok River. To the north lived the BARGA (Barghu) people, to the south was the KEREYID Khanate, and to the southeast lay the perennially divided Mongol clans. The Merkid presumably spoke a Mongolic language. Like the rest of the people on the Mongolian plateau, they were nomads, but since captives among the Merkid were made to pound grain, presumably some agriculture was practiced. In their religion the Merkid seem to have been shamanist; at least one chief bore the title Beki, which referred to a chief shaman. The Merkid were divided into many clans and had no khan. The Uduyid and U'as clans were dominant, but at least four others are known.

The Merkid first appear in the records of the Kitans' Liao dynasty in North China. In 1096–97 they joined Marqus, chief of the Zubu (Kereyid) tribe, in an attack on the Liao dynasty. In 1129 Merkid tribesmen joined a Kitan adventurer in founding the QARA-KHITAI dynasty in Turkestan. After this event Merkid history again becomes obscure.

The Merkid grudge against Chinggis Khan went back to his father's time. When the Merkid tribesman Chiledü was leading home his bride, Ö'ELÜN ÜJIN, the Mongol YISÜGEI BA'ATUR kidnapped her and took her for his own. Later, after Yisügei died and when his son Temüjin (Chinggis Khan) had just married his bride BÖRTE ÜJIN, three Merkid chiefs, including Toqto'a Beki of the Uduyid, led 300 soldiers to attack Temüjin's camp in revenge. They kidnapped both Börte and Yisügei's second wife, giving Börte to Chiledü's younger brother. Temüjin escaped, however, and sought the aid of JAMUGHA, the main chief of the Mongols, and Toghril, khan of the Kereyid. These allies welcomed an opportunity to spoil the Merkid, and they recovered Temüjin's family.

In succeeding years Chinggis Khan and Toghril Khan (later named ONG KHAN) repeatedly raided the Merkid.

Toqto'a Beki in turn made alliance with the NAIMAN khan in western Mongolia, marrying a Naiman woman. When Jamugha and Chinggis Khan fell out, the Merkid joined a league of the TATARS, the Naiman, and the OIRATS as well as many Mongol clans in acclaiming Jamugha khan.

In 1204, having defeated his old ally Ong Khan, Chinggis Khan attacked the Naiman. Toqto'a Beki supported the Naiman, but they were defeated, and in the same year Chinggis conquered the Merkid at the Battle of Qaradal Huja'ur. Toqto'a and his sons fled west to the remnants of the Naiman in the ALTAI RANGE. After Mongol raids in 1206 and 1208 Toqto'a Beki lay dead, and his sons fled west to the Turkic Qangli and Qipchaq peoples in modern Kazakhstan.

While Toqto'a's sons and followers fled west, the bulk of the Merkid submitted to the Mongols and were allowed to continue as a tribe. In 1216, however, when Chinggis Khan was returning from the conquest of North China, the Merkid again revolted, attacking the Mongols in their home camp, or *a'uruq*. Chinggis sent his great general SÜBE'ETEI BA'ATUR against the rebels, and after a desperate resistance the Merkid were conquered. This time they were slaughtered and the remnants divided up as slaves among the Mongols. Their former territory was taken over by the Suldus. Sübe'etei followed up this campaign around 1218 with a successful raid on the QIPCHAQS between the Volga and Ural Rivers, killing Toqto'a's sons.

After these victories the Merkid lost their corporate identity. One Merkid woman, OGHUL-QAIMISH, became a wife of GÜYÜG Khan and served as regent from 1248 to 1251. Few Merkid men received high posts in the early MONGOL EMPIRE, but BAYAN (1281?–1340) and his nephew TOQTO'A served as grand councillors of the Mongols' YUAN DYNASTY from 1335 to 1356. Descendants of the Merkid, under the clan name Merged, are found today in ORDOS (southwest Inner Mongolia) and in KHENTII PROVINCE of Mongolia.

Merkit *See* MERKID.

Merse (Guo Daofu, Kuo Tao-fu) (1894–1934?) *A Daur Mongol intellectual and nationalist of wide talents who became disillusioned with revolutionary activity after the failed insurrection of 1928*

Born in Mekhertü Ail (in modern HULUN BUIR's Ewenki Autonomous banner), Merse was the son of a wealthy Daur rancher and official of the Gobol clan. After being educated in Manchu and Mongolian in Hailar and attending a Chinese high school in Qiqihar, Merse studied Russian in Beijing. After being baptized a Christian in 1917, a bandit attack on his hometown forced him to leave school. From then on he and Fumingtai (revolutionary alias Buyangerel, 1898–1938), a Daur relative by marriage, promoted education in Hulun Buir. Merse designed a Latin script for the Daur language. The two also joined the Buriat-led 1919 pan-Mongolist DAURIIA STATION MOVEMENT. Merse married two Daur women, Xujie and Soujie (probably sisters), and had several daughters.

Inspired by Mongolia's 1921 REVOLUTION, Merse, who was no longer a Christian, created with Fumingtai successively a student union, a local branch of the Mongolian People's Party (later MONGOLIAN PEOPLE'S REVOLUTIONARY PARTY), and a cooperative to finance revolutionary activities in 1923–25. Among Chinese he wrote and spoke widely, attacking China's neglect and exploitation of the Mongols and advocating reform.

In December 1924 Merse linked up with a mostly KHARACHIN group of all-Inner Mongolian nationalists led by Bai Yunti (1894–1980). At a party congress on October 13–27, 1925, Merse became secretary, under Chairman Bai Yunti, of the People's Revolutionary Party of Inner Mongolia (PRPIM), fighting for Mongol autonomy and supported by the Communist International (Comintern). In 1927 Merse and Bai split over tactics, and Merse relocated to ULAANBAATAR, becoming secretary of the Mongolian trade unions. Appointed the Inner Mongolian party's acting chairman in November, Merse (with Fumingtai) followed Comintern instructions to launch an insurrection in Hulun Buir in July 1928. By September the insurrection had been bloodily suppressed, while promised aid from Mongolia and the Comintern never materialized. Merse made peace with the Manchurian authorities, while his former comrades returned to Ulaanbaatar.

Now strongly critical of the Soviet Union and of Mongolia as a puppet state, Merse returned to educational activities, opening a normal school for Mongols in Mukden (Shenyang) and writing books and articles advocating genuine Han (ethnic Chinese)-Mongol cooperation and equality. In September 1931, when Japan invaded Manchuria, Merse returned to Hulun Buir to rally resistance. Entering the Soviet consulate in Manzhouli to request assistance, he was arrested on December 11 and tried by Soviet security organs in 1934 for counterrevolutionary activities. His sentence and fate are unknown.

See also INNER MONGOLIANS; KHAFUNGGA; NEW SCHOOLS MOVEMENTS.

Further reading: Christopher P. Atwood, *Young Mongols and Vigilantes in Inner Mongolia's Interregnum Decades, 1911–1931* (Leiden: E. J. Brill, 2002); Uradyn E. Bulag, *The Mongols at China's Edge: History and the Politics of National Unity* (Lanham: Rowman and Littlefield, 2002); Kuo Tao-fu [Guo Daofu/Merse], "Modern Mongolia," *Pacific Affairs* 3 (August 1930): 754–762.

mGon-po-skyabs   *See* GOMBOJAB, DUKE.

Middle Gobi province (Middle Govi, Dundgov')

Middle Gobi province was carved out of South Gobi in 1941 and lies in south-central Mongolia. Its territory is entirely in KHALKHA Mongolia's prerevolutionary Tüshiyetü Khan province. The province is 74,700 square kilometers (28,840 square miles) in area, but despite its name is only partly gobi (habitable desert); the northern half is dry steppe. Small mountain ranges dot the province's landscape. Middle Gobi's population of 24,600 in 1956 grew to 51,300 in 2000. The number of livestock reached 2,105,200 head in 1999, but they were devastated by the ZUD (winter disaster) of spring 2000 and fell by the end of that year to only 1,282,800 head. SHEEP (663,800) and GOATS (441,400) form the great bulk of the animals. The capital, Mandalgowi, has a population of only 14,500 (2000 figure), the second-smallest of any provincial capital.

See also BUYANNEMEKHÜ.

Middle Mongolian   *See* MONGOLIAN LANGUAGE.

military of the Mongol Empire

The Mongol military of the 13th century combined the characteristic strength of nomadic warriors with the siege warfare capabilities of sedentary armies, as well as a vision of comprehensive warfare unique in the Middle Ages. (*On the later Mongolian armies, see* NORTHERN YUAN DYNASTY; OIRATS; TUMU INCIDENT; ZÜNGHARS. *On the modern Mongolian military, see* ARMED FORCES OF MONGOLIA.)

The Mongol army inherited many centuries of military development. The warriors of the earliest nomadic empire in Mongolia, the XIONGNU, had only simple saddles, no stirrups, and a bow inferior to that of their Chinese enemies. By the sixth century Byzantine descriptions of the Avars describe the full panoply of the heavily armored Inner Asian cavalryman: wooden saddle and iron stirrup giving a strong seat on an armored horse for shots with a powerful composite bow, numerous remounts and flocks of sheep accompanying the warriors, and characteristic tactics involving ambushes, sudden appearance and disappearance, and feigned retreats followed by a volley of arrows and a sudden charge. Over the centuries these tactics time and time again devastated inexperienced armies not familiar with nomadic tactics. Inner Asian armies were, however, frequently ununified, weak against fortifications, and useless at occupying and garrisoning the territory of defeated lands. The Mongols stood out by combining the strengths of Inner Asian cavalry with effective siege and occupation capabilities.

The MONGOL TRIBE before the rise of CHINGGIS KHAN (Genghis, 1206–27) was extremely poor. Later sources claim that their stirrups were of wood and their arrowheads of bone; iron stirrups marked a great chief. Unfortunately, little is known in detail of their equipment and strategies at the time. In Inner Mongolia and Manchuria the Liao dynasty (907–1125) of the Inner Mongolian KITANS and the Jurchens' JIN DYNASTY (1115–1234) had brought Inner Asian cavalry techniques and equipment to perfection, and once the Mongols unified the MONGOLIAN PLATEAU and invaded the Jin, they must have rapidly reequipped their armies with the excellent equipment later observers noted. The following is a description of Mongolian military organization at its height, from roughly 1220 to 1260.

OCCASIONS AND AIMS OF MONGOL WARFARE

Despite their reputation as insatiable conquerors, the Mongols themselves believed that all their campaigns had a clear justification. For Chinggis Khan in particular, war was a personal vendetta against willfully defiant rulers. After his unification of Mongolia, all Chinggis Khan's campaigns were justified in one of three ways: 1) avenging past attacks by the enemy on Chinggis's ancestors; 2) punishing those who gave refuge to defeated enemies of the Mongols; and 3) punishing those who executed Mongol envoys. Once defeated, the most hated enemy rulers were given derisive nicknames, such as Jirumtu, "The Righteous," Shidurghu, "The Upright," or Xiaosi, "Little Slave."

By the time of Chinggis's grandson GÜYÜG Khan (1246–48), the Mongols had begun to proclaim an explicit ideology of world conquest. When the papal envoy JOHN OF PLANO CARPINI arrived at the Mongol court to protest Mongol attacks on the Catholic kingdoms of Central Europe, Güyüg stated that these people had slain Mongol envoys in the time of Chinggis Khan and of his son ÖGEDEI KHAN (1229–41). He also claimed that "from the rising of the sun to its setting, all the lands have been made subject to me. Who could do this contrary to the command of God?" Submission was now demanded of unconquered peoples all over Eurasia without any pretense of prior offense against the Mongols.

Full submission to the Mongols meant agreeing to seven demands: 1) the ruler's personal attendance at court; 2) dispatch of sons or younger brothers as hostages; 3) a census; 4) a supply of soldiers for further Mongol conquests; 5) payment of tribute; 6) appointment of a Mongol DARUGHACHI (overseer); and 7) maintenance of the JAM (postal relay). Still, the Mongols rarely demanded the full rigor of submission from peoples far away or on the border of hostile powers.

Before going to war the Mongols always sent envoys to demand surrender. Faced with defiance, the envoys would formally announce their hostility along the following lines: "If you should not believe our letters and the command of God, nor hearken to our counsel, then we shall know for certain that you wish to have war. After that we do not know what will happen, God alone knows." Before any campaign was undertaken, favorable omens had to be sought by SCAPULIMANCY (burning a sheep's shoulder blades). From the time of Chinggis Khan victory in war had become the seal of divine approval of the righteousness of the Mongol conquests. Mongol khans and officials repeatedly pointed to the Mongol victories as proof both that their enemies were wicked people and that God (or heaven) had willed the rule of the Mongols.

The Mongol way of warfare stood out from that of their sedentary contemporaries as well as from other nomadic peoples in its single-minded focus on conquest as the sole war aim. Once provoked to war, the Mongols aimed not for plunder, annexation of disputed territory, or receipt of tribute, but rather for the complete subjugation of the enemy ruler, who would be either destroyed with his whole family or enrolled as a subordinate executor of Mongol administration.

Despite this single-minded focus on conquest, the Mongols repeatedly concluded treaties with states who proved too large or powerful to be absorbed in one campaign. These treaties, however, the Mongols considered merely temporary, and they felt free to resume the conquest of these states without warning at any time. Not until the YUAN DYNASTY withdrew from Vietnam in 1294 and the Middle Eastern IL-KHANATE made a permanent peace with MAMLUK EGYPT in 1323 did the Mongol successor states formally renounce their ambitions of total victory.

THE SOLDIERS: WEAPONRY, TRAINING, REWARDS

The core of the Mongol army was its cavalry. Mongolia possessed great herds of HORSES, and each Mongol cavalryman thus went on campaign with at least two and usually four to seven remounts, so that horses ridden one day would be allowed to rest for a few days afterward. The Mongolian horse is small, about 12 to 13 hands high, but admirably hardy and usually well trained. Mongols rode geldings almost exclusively because of their strength, docility, and quietness, an especially important point in ambushes. Mongolian saddles, then as now, were built on wooden cores with a high pommel and cantle and weighed 3.5–4.5 kilograms (eight to 10 pounds). Horses were, if it could be afforded, shod with iron or wooden shoes. While on the road, the Mongols did not allow the horses to eat or drink but waited until the evening and let the horses cool off before putting them to pasture. To whip a horse in the face and to eat before seeing to one's horses' needs in the evening were capital offenses.

The Mongol cavalry's main weapons were first the bow and arrow and second the sword. A full-size Mongolian composite bow made of sheep's horn and wood had a normal range of about 325 meters (350 yards) but could reach more than 530 meters (575 yards) with a strong archer under optimal conditions. Each cavalryman carried two bows, or at least one good one. The Mongols had a wide variety of arrows, most tipped with a pointed iron head, but some with v-shaped points designed to inflict slicing wounds, some with holes that produced whistling sounds to serve as guides for others to follow, and also camel-bone arrowheads to stun, not kill. Each warrior carried two or three quivers of these various types. The wealthy had a light scimitar and sometimes one or two lances or halberds. Clubs or maces served the poorer soldiers for hand-to-hand combat.

Defensively, the Mongols wore armor in accordance with their wealth. The wealthiest had scale or chain mail made of iron, those of middling rank had leather armor, and the majority (six or seven out of 10, according to one estimate) had little or no armor. Leather armor was sewn from pieces and, hanging from iron shoulder plates, reached from the neck to the thigh. Separate strips were tied over the arms and legs. Wealthier Mongols also armored their horses down to the horse's knees or fetlocks in the usual steppe and East Asian style, usually with sewn leather but occasionally with iron, and always with an iron head plate. Helmets were iron on top, with leather neck pieces. The most common kind of shield was almost one meter (three feet) wide and half again as tall and made of light wood (willow or bamboo) as available, but it was used mostly by sentries on guard. Heavy iron-reinforced shields were used to protect the vanguard when they dismounted to deliver either a particularly accurate or particularly powerful volley of arrows.

Each Mongol soldier also carried rope for drawing siege engines; an ax (rarely used in battle), and files for sharpening arrows. Leather sacks of varying sizes were used to keep their equipment dry when fording rivers; the commanders had sacks large enough to sit on and row with oars.

On large-scale campaigns intended to occupy new territory, the main body of the army would move with their families and their gers (yurts) and herds. The mounts fed on grass, and mare's milk and sheep's meat supplied the army. If the food ran short, they would hunt and eat small game. Those going on long expeditions demanding speed took only a small tent and two leather flasks of up to 4.5 kilograms (10 pounds) of qurud (modern khuruud), a kind of dried cheese (see DAIRY PRODUCTS). This they supplemented with blood bled from their horses.

The skills of the Mongolian soldiers were honed by their lives. Babies in the cradle would be tied to saddles and followed their mothers; by their third or fourth year they would sit in the saddle and begin to practice shooting with small bows and arrows. The great hunts developed war skills: Just like a campaign, they began with dispatching scouts to inspect the game and proceeded with the mobilization of men through the DECIMAL ORGANIZATION, strictly enforced rendezvous, and coordinated movement in a circle often scores of kilometers wide to concentrate the animals in a single spot to be killed.

All Mongol men aged 15 and older served as soldiers and received no pay. War booty was, however, a vital incentive. From the beginning Chinggis Khan insisted that the destruction of the enemy be completed before the soldiers seized booty for themselves, and this rule was strictly enforced. Once the battle was over, booty would be divided among all soldiers according to their merits and demerits, leaving shares for the great khan, imperial family, and commanders (NOYAN). While planned retreat was a routine maneuver, those guilty of retreat against orders were cowards and either executed or drafted into ba'atur (hero) units that were routinely assigned the most risky assaults. Several observers noted that in reporting on their battle experiences, the Mongol soldiers showed the most extraordinary honesty, informing on themselves to their commander even about faults deserving death and meekly accepting execution. Nevertheless the Mongol soldiers were by no means automatons. Their tactics and strategy depended almost entirely on exploiting the initiative of autonomous groups of cavalrymen often operating far from any watching eye. Obedient to their commanders to a degree that frightened observers from China to Europe, the Mongol soldiers behaved in battle not as passive instruments but as active partners in the venture of world conquest.

MOBILIZATION, ORGANIZATION, AND COMMAND

The Mongol armies generally preferred to campaign in the winter and rest during the summer. Even during long expeditionary campaigns, the main body of men and horses would rest during the summer, especially in the Middle East, China, or India, where the summer heat was particularly oppressive (see INDIA AND THE MONGOLS; MAMLUK EGYPT; SONG DYNASTY). Campaigns were discussed at the summer QURILTAI, and active preparation, particularly reconditioning the horses, began in autumn. The Mongols disliked fighting in either the late spring, when the horses were weak due to exertion and poor fodder, or in the full summer, when they were fat and out of condition (qadaq).

To mobilize their armies the Mongols used the famous decimal organization. All Mongols were divided into 10s, 100s, and 1,000s. For each campaign the khan would command that every unit, either in a particular area or over the whole empire, provide a certain number out of 10 (usually one to three) to meet at a rendezvous point. With the order transmitted on notched sticks down the chain of command, the relevant commanders of 10 would each select the requisite number from their unit to serve and dispatch them to the designated point. Failure to appear at the right time was a capital offense. Knowing the number of 10s specified in the original order, the commander of the campaign could thus know the exact size of his task force. In deciding the time of rendezvous and choosing commanders, the Mongols again took omens by scapulimancy and trusted the resulting decisions implicitly as the decision of heaven.

Total Mongolian manpower was a tightly guarded secret, but estimates under Chinggis Khan range from 95,000 in 1206 to 129,000 at his death. Since the 1,000s averaged only half strength, this would indicate an available manpower of 50,000–75,000 at most. On Chinggis's early campaigns, such as those in North China and against KHORAZM, he seems to have used most of his available soldiers. Allies and local recruits (particularly in China) also swelled the ranks. Eventually, subject peoples were also brought into the decimal organization so that several field armies totalling as many as 100,000 or 200,000 were used against South China in 1258–59 and in 1273–76. Even so, many of the most famous Mongol exploits were achieved by quite small task forces. JEBE and SÜBE'ETEI A'ATUR commanded only three *tümen*s (nominally 30,000 men) on their legendary sweep around the Caspian Sea; CHORMAQAN subdued the Caucasus with the same number; and Uriyangqadai (1199–1271) and AJU rode from YUNNAN, subdued Vietnam, and crossed hundreds of kilometers of hostile Song territory in 1258–59 with 13,000 men, only 3,000 of whom were Mongol.

Mongols armies were deployed in a great center (*ghol,* modern *gol*) and two wings. When the khan personally joined battle, his bodyguards, or KESHIG, held the center. This force, consisting of 10,000 men, was particularly well armored and had a vanguard of 1,000 *ba'atur*s, or heroes, chosen for their prowess. Great commanders received special guards (*qabiqchi*) for the duration of their campaigns, to which they could add their *ger-ün kö'üd* (houseboys) or personal slaves. Command of the right and left wings, both for the nation as a whole and for the commanders' task forces, was highly prestigious and usually fixed by hereditary precedent based on past service.

As a sign of Mongolian battlefield professionalism, the chief commander, whether a khan or a great *noyan* (commander), rarely participated personally in battle. Instead, he and his family and retinue occupied a command post that gave a view of the battlefield. This command was marked by a banner specially designed for each commander, in addition to a parasol if the great khan was commanding. The Mongols did, however, recognize the value for morale of leading from the front, and crown princes and wing commanders often fought in the forefront. As in all East Asian armies, advance was signaled by a kettledrum set up by the command post and retreat signaled by a gong.

Since their tactics emphasized ambush, the Mongols themselves were constantly on guard against the same methods. The army carefully chose upland sites with good visibility for night camps. Camps were pitched in broad daylight, so that the surrounding area could be carefully inspected. Sometimes, though, fires would be lit, and after dark the army would move to a different spot, leaving the fires behind as a decoy. Tent sites were well spaced, so that grass within the camp was left for the horses, of which two for each soldier would be kept on hand and saddled through the night. The commander camped with his tent facing south or southeast and with his men to the left, right, and behind him. The commander's name was the sentries' password.

Armies on the move were screened on all four sides by scouts reconnoitering scores or even hundreds of kilometers beyond the main force. Such scouts paid special attention to capturing locals with information about roads, topography, cities, enemy movements, provisions, fodder, and the like. The scouts also attacked enemy soldiers but scrupulously avoided the distraction of pillage. At night the scout parties camped in a circle with the unit commander and the horses in the center. To avoid noise, the sentries used special pieces of wood in place of passwords. Long-distance coordination between units was achieved by mounted messengers. Mongol scouts were extremely effective: Mongol armies rarely, if ever, suffered ambush, and they usually knew the battlefield and their enemy far better than their opponents did.

MONGOL STRATEGY AND TACTICS

Mongolian strategy generally emphasized forcing an engagement with the enemy's main body of troops. Once the Mongols mastered siege warfare techniques (see below), they could deal with an enemy dispersed in fortresses, but they usually preferred to begin the conquest of a new enemy with a victory in open battle and then besiege the remaining citadels. Despite their small numbers, Mongol invasions took place on vast fronts, and they relied on their messengers and superior mobility to converge suddenly on the enemy's main force. The simultaneous invasion of Central Europe in 1240–41 by several columns operating on a front stretching from the Danube to the Vistula was only the most extraordinary example of this.

While scouts and special task forces pursuing foreign rulers avoided the distraction of pillage, plunder was an important part of general Mongol strategy. Once the main body of the army entered enemy territory, raiding parties were sent out to plunder, focusing especially on captives and livestock. Captives were useful as cannon fodder, and livestock formed the Mongols' provisions. These depredations weakened the enemy and helped provoke the decisive battle for which the Mongols were looking.

By the 1240s, however, the Mongols found themselves engaged on several fronts and possessing forces too small to advance everywhere. Thus, in areas such as KURDISTAN in the west and on the frontier with the Song dynasty in the east, local Mongol commanders reverted to the nomadic tradition of repeated razzias. While incapable of destroying the enemy, these raids weakened their opponents until major forces could be dedicated to the front in question.

Mongol battlefield tactics were designed to produce decisive victories and inflict such high casualties as to prevent the enemy from recovering. Following East Asian practice, the Mongols cut off the ears of dead enemies to get an accurate body count. A common way to achieve this decisive victory was to lure the enemy away from their base by a brief attack, followed by a feigned retreat of several days' duration. If the enemy followed, the Mongols, after giving battle at a place of their own choosing, would then be able to wipe out the defeated soldiers as they fled back to their base.

Mongol armies were almost always outnumbered by their enemies, who often fought behind battlefield fortifications. Thus, a key tactical precept was never to attack until the enemy's formation was disorganized. The most common tactic to produce this disorganization was an immediate attack followed by a quick withdrawal. The advancing enemy's disorganized lines would then be vulnerable to a sudden counterattack. In the 1204 Battle of Keltegei Cliffs against the NAIMAN and in 1241 at Liegnitz in Poland, the Mongols used a more complex strategy to achieve this aim. The Mongols first approached in a tight array, called the *qaraghana* march after the dense and thorny pea shrub (*Caragana*), thus minimizing their front to enemy arrows. Once the battle began, they rapidly fanned out in a "lake" array, surrounding the enemy and shooting arrows to disorganize their ranks. Once the enemy's disorganization was complete, the armored vanguard formed up and charged the enemy in the "chisel fight." When the enemy was behind fortifications or proved impervious to the previous techniques, the Mongols would stampede cattle or drive captives against them. When heavily outnumbered, the Mongols would create an impression of numbers by setting up dummy figures on extra horses, use cattle to create clouds of dust that could be confused for reinforcements, or light extra fires at night. Setting extra fires could also cover a nighttime retreat. The Mongols, unlike their enemies, preferred to fight in cold weather, and one unusual tactic was using a magical *jada* (Turkish, *yai*) stone to bring on snow and disorganize the enemy. Mongol and Chinese sources state that the Mongols broke Jin armies with this technique in 1232.

Once the enemy's main force had been defeated, the Mongols often faced sustained guerrilla resistance from remnant enemy troops, bandits, escaped prisoners of war, and armed civilians. In this case, when the enemy was numerous but disorganized and weakly armed, the Mongols applied the principles of the great hunts directly to war. The troops would deploy over a wide front covering over a hundred kilometers. As the wings advanced, they would gradually converge in a circle, driving before them everyone within their reach, civilian and military alike. When the circle was closed and tightened, all inside would be killed. This *nerge* (hunting circle) formation was used to great effect in Galicia in 1240–41, in Yunnan in 1254, and by MÖNGKE KHAN against Mongol malcontents in 1251.

SIEGE WARFARE AND OCCUPATION

The Mongol military would have had only the temporary successes of other nomadic armies had it not been for the speed with which it absorbed the techniques of siege warfare. Mongol tribes in the forest-steppe built wooden palisades when on the defensive. In their early campaign against the XIA DYNASTY in 1205 and 1209 and against the Jin in 1211–12, Mongol generals had to rely on surprise to capture walled cities, but by 1213 the Mongols were successfully besieging prepared citadels in North China. Chinggis Khan appointed a BARGA (Barghu) Mongol, Ambaghai, the chief of the Mongols' engineer corps, and he began to train a multiethnic force of 500. Artillery soon became an integral part of Mongolian military techniques, and Ambaghai's force by the time of the campaigns in Central Asia had expanded to a *tümen* (nominally 10,000). Artillery was used primarily in siege warfare but also on the battlefield and in naval warfare. While small rivers could be forded by swimming, the Mongols relied on pontoon bridges to cross large rivers. In 1218 Chinggis Khan appointed Zhang Rong (Chang Jung, 1158–1230), the leader of his military engineers. Completing a sturdy pontoon bridge across the Amu-Dar'ya in less than a month, Chinggis gave Zhang the title of *usuchi* (marine) and made him commander of a permanent multiethnic artillery and marine unit.

The Mongols adopted the usual elements of medieval siege warfare. In any siege they first erected a *chapar,* or circumvallation, to keep in the attackers and then dug saps toward the enemy walls. Sappers dug under mantlets armored against the defenders' projectiles. The Mongol assault parties approaching the walls fired crossbows and defended themselves with special linked shields. Walls were battered with trebuchets and other mangonels which were dug into pits for protection and fired large stones. Where stones were unavailable locally, as, for example, in the SIEGE OF BAGHDAD in 1258, they were imported or trees were cut down for ammunition. While they preferred direct assault through breached walls, the Mongols were familiar with night attacks, tunneling under the walls, and diverting watercourses to flood cities. Starvation brought down otherwise impregnable fortresses, such as Zhongdu (modern Beijing) and Kaifeng. During sieges the Mongols constantly dispatched envoys to demand the surrender of the city, frequently promising safe conduct. Once the siege had begun, however, the Mongols saw no obligation to keep such promises. The massacres that frequently followed sieges were the grimmest part of the Mongol conquest.

The Mongols eagerly adopted new artillery technology and counted catapult operators among the craftsmen almost always exempted from any massacres of defeated soldiers. In their last-stand defense of 1232–34, Jin dynasty generals began firing exploding cast-iron shells, and by 1240 the Mongols themselves were hurling such exploding shells against Kiev and the armies of Hungary and Poland. Burning naphtha was also hurled at enemy

The Mongols besieging a city, from an illustrated version of Rashid-ud-Din's *Compendium of Chronicles (Courtesy Staatsbibliothek zu Berlin—Preussischer Kulturbesitz, Orientalabteilung)*

cities to set them aflame. The Mongols exchanged artillery technology between China and the Middle East. Under Ambaghai 1,000 Chinese mangonel operators and naphtha throwers participated in the siege of the Isma'ili fortresses in northern Iran, while in 1272 in the siege of the great Song citadel of Xiangyang the Mongols' Uighur general, ARIQ-QAYA, brought in especially powerful catapults and their operators from Iraq. The world's earliest known cannon, dated 1282 and found in Heilongjiang province in Mongol-held Manchuria, attests to the Mongols' continued experimentation with siege weaponry.

Siege was medieval warfare's most deadly operation, and the Mongols reduced the cost to themselves by using prisoners of war as cannon fodder. After taking one town, the Mongols would levy young men from the city, assigning up to 20 men to each Mongol soldier, and would use them in assaulting the next town: filling in moats, digging saps and artillery pits, and making the first assault on breached walls. Such levies sometimes served in the Mongol army for years, forcing the Mongols to levy provisions for them from the conquered territories. When the Mongols began drafting soldiers from the sedentary peoples, this need for levies became more acute. When HÜLE'Ü set out for Persia in 1256, for example, not only were all pastures reserved for the Mongol cavalry, but the subject lands had to supply one *taghar* (305 kilograms or 675 pounds) of flour and half a *taghar* of wine per soldier, in addition to a heavy monetary tax.

Once the Mongols pacified a given area, they drafted laborers to break down all remaining city walls. Although the Mongols proved effective at siege war, they recognized its high cost in lives and saw their great advantage in open fields. Mongol garrison camps stayed outside the cities. Should an insurrection occur, the local *darughachi* (overseer) would send out messengers, and the Mongol soldiers would converge on the city. From Armenia to China large areas were also emptied of cultivators to provide pasture for the garrisons' livestock as well as hunting for the khans. In the Middle East the Mongols adopted the traditional pattern of nomadizing from the mountain pastures in the summer to the lowlands in the winter, but in China they became mostly sedentary ranchers.

END OF THE MONGOL WAY OF WARFARE

Despite the division of the Mongol world empire in 1260 into four separate khanates, the distinctive Mongolian military tradition continued for several decades. In the Mongol Yuan dynasty in China, effective assimilation of Chinese naval techniques allowed the generals Aju, Ariq-Qaya, and BAYAN CHINGSANG to lead a mixed Sino-Mongolian army down the Chang (Yangtze) River in the complete conquest of the Song dynasty in 1276. Most Mongol wars from 1260 on, however, were civil wars, and the Mongolian strategic aim of total victory proved inapplicable to civil war among rulers who were all descendants of Chinggis Khan. By the 1290s all the Mongol successor states had become deeply influenced by the political concepts of their subject peoples. While the adoption of such concepts stabilized the regimes financially and politically, they proved incompatible with the Mongolian concept of unlimited expansion and the treatment of subjects as cannon fodder. The natural tendency of the decimal units, more or less hereditary from the start, to become uneven in size and resources impeded full mobilization. Finally, as the Mongolian aristocracy expanded and the memory of the charismatic early khans faded, the former unity of vision broke down into factionalism and insubordination. Thus, the strategic clarity, the brutally effective tactics, total mobilization, and the unified command of the Mongol army at its peak all declined. The Mongol successor dynasties on the Black Sea–Caspian steppe, in Central Asia, and in Mongolia proper continued to wage war successfully in the Inner Asian fashion for several centuries more but never attempted to duplicate the strategic vision of Chinggis Khan and his immediate successors.

See also 'AIN JALUT, BATTLE OF; ARCHERY; CENSUS IN THE MONGOL EMPIRE; HUAN'ERZUI, BATTLE OF; HUNTING AND FISHING; JUYONGGUAN PASS, BATTLES OF; KAIFENG, SIEGE OF; KIEV, SIEGE OF; KÖSE DAĞI, BATTLE OF; KULIKOVO POLE, BATTLE OF; LIEGNITZ, BATTLE OF; MASSACRES AND THE MONGOL CONQUEST; *TAMMACHI*; XIANGYANG, SIEGE OF; ZHONGDU, SIEGES OF.

Further reading: Nicola di Cosmo, ed., *Warfare in Inner Asian History (500–1800)* (Leiden: E. J. Brill, 2002).

Mingat *See* MINGGHAD.

Ming dynasty As successor of the Mongol YUAN DYNASTY, the ethnic Chinese Ming dynasty (1368–1644) had multifaceted relations with the Mongols. The Ming employed numerous Mongol troops in the capital and along the borders yet had to deal with the constant problem of border defense. This article describes Chinese-Mongol relations during the Ming: (*For the general history of the Mongols in this period, see* NORTHERN YUAN DYNASTY.)

FOUNDING OF THE DYNASTY

Zhu Yuanzhang (b. 1328, reigned as Hongwu emperor, 1368–98) founded the Ming dynasty in Nanjing in 1368 out of the chaos of the late Yuan rebellions. On September 14, 1368, Zhu Yuanzhang's generals entered the Yuan dynasty capital, DAIDU, as the Mongol emperor Toghan-Temür (1333–70) and his court fled north. Daidu (Great Capital) was renamed Beiping (Northern Pacification). The victorious advance carried Ming armies through Gansu and into Inner Mongolia, where they captured the emperor's family in 1370. In 1372, however, the Yuan crushed the Ming armies in the Mongolian heartland, checking the Ming advance.

Yuan armies still held the frontier region of Inner Mongolia and had the loyalty of commanders and princes of Manchuria and YUNNAN. In 1382 Ming armies conquered Yunnan. From 1387 to 1390 Ming generals established new garrisons in southeast Inner Mongolia, induced the Mongol commander in Manchuria, Naghachu, to surrender, captured another Yuan emperor's family at Buir Lake, and formed the THREE GUARDS in northeast Inner Mongolia from several captured Mongol princes and commanders (NOYAN).

Despite these successes, the Ming founder could not force the Yuan emperors in Mongolia to give up their imperial pretensions. The Mongol emperors still preserved the Yuan seal, to which they clung as an ultimate symbol of legitimacy. Attempts to induce Mongol surrender by sending back captured crown princes proved fruitless.

After Zhu Yuanzhang's death, his youngest son, Zhu Di, seized the throne and declared himself the Yongle emperor (1402–24). Originally stationed in southeast Inner Mongolia, his troops included Mongol soldiers from the Three Guards. After his accession he rewarded them by opening horse fairs in 1407, at which the Ming state purchased army mounts for cloth, silk, and other goods. In 1421 he moved the capital north to Beiping, now renamed Beijing. Finally, Yongle removed the frontier garrisons in Inner Mongolia, creating a vacuum of power. It is scarcely surprising that the rumor spread among the Mongols that Yongle was really Toghan-Temür's son and a Mongol.

Yongle continued his father's struggle to subdue the Mongols. After 1388 incessant fratricidal struggle among the Yuan princes meant the Yuan was no longer a credible dynastic rival. Yongle led imperial armies deep into Mongolia in 1410, 1414, 1422, and 1423, but only the first of these expeditions was aimed (in part) at a Yuan emperor. The others were all against non-Chinggisid kingmakers, whether among the Mongols or the OIRATS, a closely related people to the northwest.

MONGOLS IN THE MING

The Ming founder's policy toward the Mongols and the Mongol legacy was ambivalent. (Legends of a general Chinese massacre of the Mongols during the mid-autumn festival, with messages spread by moon cakes, have no historical foundation.) The new dynasty immediately restored classical standards of education and began referring to the unsubmissive Mongols as "barbarian slaves," yet Zhu Yuanzhang encouraged Mongol desertions to his camp and proclaimed his intention to treat such surrendered Mongols fairly. Mongols served in "Tatar" (the usual Ming word for Mongols) units, accompanied by their wives and children. Since the Ming adopted the Yuan institution of a hereditary caste of military households, the integration of Mongol households was relatively easy. Mongols became as much as a fourth of the metropolitan guard units.

While these Mongols adopted Chinese dress and hairstyle as a sign of loyalty, they maintained their language and much of their pastoral way of life for a century or more. As late as 1465 special Mongolian-speaking officials were assigned to Nanjing to handle the guardsmen there. Land grants to surrendered Mongols were used both to pasture livestock, especially the "Tatar" cavalry's horses, and for farming. Despite claims by disgruntled Chinese officials, the Tatar soldiery remained loyal throughout the dynasty.

The Ming also had a number of loosely controlled garrisons beyond the frontier, composed of surrendered Mongols. The Three Guards of northeast Inner Mongolia eventually were resettled to the south and are the ancestors of many of southeast Inner Mongolia's Mongols. The Chigil Guard in Gansu became part of the Yellow Uighurs, the modern Yogur nationality in Gansu. Finally, Mongol and ÖNGGÜD "aboriginal officers" (tusi) near Xining formed the nucleus of the current Tu (Monguor) nationality.

THE TRIBUTARY SYSTEM, 1424–1454

From Yongle's time until 1454 Ming policy was to engage the Mongols and Oirats (who became dominant on the plateau from 1423 on) through tribute, the granting of titles, and the generous treatment of defecting Mongols. Eventually, even the Yuan emperor Togtoo-Bukha (titled Taisung, 1433–52) sent tribute missions. This TRIBUTE SYSTEM was, in fact, a form of trade, allowing the Mongols and Oirats access to grain, silk, iron kettles, and other everyday and luxury goods. Indeed, the often 2,000-man-strong tribute missions from the Oirats contained many merchants from Hami, Turpan, and Samarqand. At the same time, the discontinuation of tribute missions supplied a stick to punish recalcitrant nomads. However, as a form of politically structured foreign trade, the Mongols and Oirats constantly used violence or the threat of violence to improve their bargaining position.

The tribute system remained in operation through the 15th century yet became less effective after the TUMU INCIDENT of 1449, in which the Oirat ruler, ESEN Taishi (r. 1438–54), captured the Ming's Zhengtong emperor (1436–49, re-enthroned as Tianshun, 1457–64). The Ming's Inner Mongolian buffer zone completely collapsed, the Three Guards were dispersed before resettling closer to the border, and the Mongols swarmed into the strategic ORDOS region south of the Huang (Yellow) River. The extensive migrations made any centralized policy hard to maintain. Esen's sons did not maintain his close ties with the Central Asian oasis states, whose merchants had formed a large part of his embassies. Without buyers to the west, the Mongols proved less interested in paying "tribute," even though the Ming remained basically willing to receive it until at least 1504.

Despite the frequency of raids, there was little chance of the Mongols overthrowing the Ming. Even formidable commanders such as Esen proved completely unable to take fortified cities. The Ming installed cannons in their towers as early as 1449, and many Ming strategists considered firearms to be the key to defeating the nomads, although they never made effective offensive use of them. The Mongol raids on China generally began in the fall, while the Ming counterattacked in the spring or summer, when Mongolian horses were out of condition. The Ming's major successes came either by trapping the more mobile Mongols against fixed points (lakes, walls, etc.) or by attacking the Mongolian base camps with their women and children, forcing the soldiers to come to their defense.

BORDER POLICY, 1454–1571

By 1472 court officials, unwilling to accept the Mongol occupation of Ordos, proposed to drive the Mongols out of the area. A Shaanxi administrator, Yu Zijun (1429–89), who understood the small likelihood of success, took advantage of a local Ming victory to build an adobe wall in 1473–74 along the northern border of Shaanxi, the first branch of the Great Wall. The wall proved successful in reducing raids, but Ming statesmen continued to advocate military offensives they did not have the finances or soldiery to achieve.

Frontier raids reached a new level of scale under BATU-MÖNGKE DAYAN KHAN (1480?–1517?). His reign marked a resurgence of the Chinggisid ideology, and his mission in 1488 was the first in decades to use the title "Great Khan of the Great Yuan." After 1500 the Mongols' growing military and dynastic confidence suspended their interest in paying tribute. By the time their interest revived in 1541, the Ming's Jiajing emperor (1522–67) was adamantly opposed to receiving it. The emperor briefly supported instead a plan for conquering Ordos, proposed by a frontier general, Zeng Xian (1499–1548), and the grand secretary Xia Yan (1482–1548), but eventually rejected it and executed its authors. While tribute and military policy were both blocked, wall building took their place. Weng Wanda (1498–1552), responsible for the key Datong-Xuanfu (modern Xuanhua) sector, built the most elaborate and complex system of walls.

BORDER POLICY, 1571–1644

ALTAN KHAN (1508–82) of the TÜMED (around modern Höhhot) took the most active interest in opening tribute relations. A junior grandson of Dayan Khan, Altan Khan spent his long life looking for alternative sources of legitimacy. Serious epidemics, which hit the unexposed Mongols when they came in contact with Chinese, also caused hardship. Even after Altan Khan burned the suburbs of Beijing in 1550, he immediately requested tributary relations. Many Ming officials believed that the Mongols were raiding only out of hunger and advocated opening relations. Under severe pressure the Jiajing emperor opened horse markets for a year and then closed them.

After Jiajing's death, however, the grand secretary Zhang Juzheng (1525–82) adopted a plan of Wang Chonggu (1515–89) to open not tributary relations,

which had proven hard to control, but frontier horse fairs from 1571. At these fairs the Ming government bought horses from Mongols for the Chinese army with cloth, kettles, and other goods. Mongol noblemen presenting goods were entertained, and each fair was assigned to particular noblemen. Private trade was allowed but taxed. At first the trade was limited to a few fairs a year, but eventually it grew to many large and small fairs operating year round. Altan Khan was enfeoffed as prince of Shunyi.

In Tümed, at least, the fairs did exactly what the advocates of peace said they would. From 1571 the frontier's military and financial situation improved dramatically. The fairs did not work so well in Ordos, where instead of one Tümed prince, the Ming had to deal with four dozen or so smaller princes only nominally unified under a titular ruler. Even so, everywhere the fairs were opened the scale of raids declined.

In the eastern frontier, however, the Yuan great khans, ruling only the CHAKHAR tribe now, appear to have continued their objection to relations with the Ming under any form. In fact, by controlling the Three Guards, now resettled along the Inner Mongolian–Liaoning frontier but still part of the tribute and horse fair systems, the Yuan khans could indirectly trade with China without recognizing its sovereignty. From 1595 to 1615 a renewed bout of raiding, carried out by the Chakhar khans and their Three Guards allies, affected the eastern frontier, although Ordos also showed unrest. Continuing the logic of the peace policy, the Ming responded by carrot and stick methods: temporarily cutting off horse markets and restoring them when the leaders involved proved more reasonable. Meanwhile, wall building continued.

By 1619 the appearance of the Manchus, a powerful new force in the northeast, caused the Ming to see the Chakhar khans as allies. Having begun through the Three Guards to receive trading rights in the east, Ligdan Khan by 1620 was receiving 40,000 *taels* of silver annually as a subsidy. As the other Mongols revolted against Legdan's attempt to centralize control over them, the Ming only increased his subsidy as he attacked the Tümed and Ordos Mongols to the west. The Ming themselves fell to peasant rebellions, and the empire was conquered by the Manchus' QING DYNASTY in 1644.

See also MOGHULISTAN; TU LANGUAGE AND PEOPLE; UIGHURS; YOGUR LANGUAGES AND PEOPLE.

Further reading: Hok-lam Chan, *China and the Mongols: History and Legend under the Yüan and Ming* (Aldershot, Hampshire: Ashgate, 1999); Henry Serruys, *Mongols and Ming China: Customs and History* (London: Variorum Reprints, 1987); ———, *Sino-Mongol Relations during the Ming*, vol. 1, *Mongols in China during the Hung-wu Period (1368–1398)* (Brussels: Institut belge des hautes études chinoises, 1980); Arthur Waldron, *The Great Wall of China: From History to Myth* (Cambridge: Cambridge University Press, 1990).

Mingghad (Myangad, Mingat) The Mingghad are a subethnic group or *yastan* in northern Khowd province. The name *mingghad* means "thousands" and apparently has arisen several times independently in post-Chinggisid Inner Asia.

The ancestors of the western Mongolian Mingghads appeared in 1695 along the Kem River in Tuva as tributaries, along with a body of Bashgid (i.e., Bashkir) and Kirgis (i.e., Kyrgyz) people, to the KHOTOGHOID of western KHALKHA. In 1764, due to the Mingghads' complaints about mistreatment from their lord, Dorjitseden (r. 1737–64), they were detached from the Khotoghoids and settled on the east of the Khowd River (modern Myangad Sum, KHOWD PROVINCE).

There, along with the ÖÖLÖDS settled on the other side of the river, they performed special corvée services for the Manchu garrison at the Khowd fortress. The Mingghads elected their own banner *da* (commandant general). They shared the Tügemel Amurjuulagchi Temple (popularly called Shara Süme or Yellow Temple) on the Buyantu River with the Öölöds, jointly inviting either the Jalkhanza or the Narobanchin khutugtus (*see* INCARNATE LAMA) when the incumbent passed away. The Mingghads were divided into three "bones" (*yasu*)—Mingghad proper, Bashgid, and Kirgis—which were strictly exogamous.

After 1912 the Mingghad resisted successfully when the theocratic government tried to make the banner rulership hereditary. Their population of 3,537 in 1916 has grown slowly, reaching only 4,800 in 1989. Mingghad is still found as a clan name in the old Khotoghoid territories (northeast UWS PROVINCE and southwest KHÖWSGÖL PROVINCE) and in Tuva.

See also KHOWD CITY; THEOCRATIC PERIOD.

mining Poor transportation and initial investment costs kept mining only a small part of the Mongolian economy until after 1970, when it became the country's main export earner.

Around 550 C.E. the founders of the Türk Empire were said to be iron miners in the ALTAI RANGE, and MARCO POLO in the late 13th century mentioned the mining of asbestos from Tuva. Modern mining in Mongolia started with the Mongolor Company, which began mining gold in 1906 despite local Mongolian opposition. From 1907 to 1913 Mongolor mined 771 kilograms (1,697 pounds) of gold. In 1915 Russian investors also opened up Nalaikh Coal Mine, which by 1920 had a capacity of 1,500 metric tons (1,653 short tons) annually. In both, the workforce was primarily Chinese. In 1921 these enterprises were nationalized. Soviet geological expeditions surveyed the country in 1930–31. Production at Nalaikh increased from 869 metric tons (958 short tons) in 1922 to about 150,000 in 1940, and in 1938 a narrow-gauge railway connected Nalaikh to ULAANBAATAR.

After WORLD WAR II two Soviet-Mongolian joint-stock companies, Sovmongolmetall and Mongolneft', were established in 1949 to exploit Mongolia's mineral wealth. The former mined fluorspar, tin, and uranium in Choibalsang province (now EASTERN PROVINCE) and SÜKHEBAATUR PROVINCE, where the metals could be shipped out on the Choibalsan-Borzya Railway built for military purposes in World War II. Profits were shared equally between the Mongolian and Soviet governments. Mongolneft' pumped and refined oil from the Züünbayan field in EAST GOBI PROVINCE; Mongolia received 5–6 tögrögs per metric ton of oil and 20 percent of profits. Both companies proved disappointing, and in 1957 the Soviet Union donated its shares to Mongolia. By 1958 major mining commodities included coal (472,900 metric tons; 521,283 short tons), fluorspar (32,200 metric tons; 35,494 short tons), crude oil (35,400 metric tons; 39,022 short tons), and lime (17,300 metric tons; 19,070 short tons). Production was almost solely for the domestic market, however. Coal production reached 1,999,300 metric tons (2,203,850 short tons) in 1970, with a new mine in Sharyn Gol opening in 1964. Subsidized Soviet oil, however, made Züünbayan's oil uneconomical; production fell to 4,500 metric tons (4,960 short tons) before being stopped in 1969.

Only in the 1970s did mining became a major branch of the economy, thanks to a single enterprise, the ERDENET CITY mine, producing molybdenum and copper concentrate. Coming into operation in 1978, the mine, operated by the Soviet-Mongolian joint-stock company Erdenet Ore-Dressing Plant, produced in 1990 4,208,000 metric tons (4,638,525 short tons) of molybdenum concentrate and 354,100 metric tons (390,328 short tons) of copper concentrate at 35 percent purity, accounting for 74 percent of Mongolia's total mining output. To supply the plant's vast consumption of energy, Ulaanbaatar's no. 4 power plant was constructed. To fuel it coal production was expanded to 7,147,500 metric tons (7,878,768 short tons) annually by bringing into production the vast Baganuur field. These three new enterprises—Baganuur, no. 4 power plant, and Erdenet—constitute what is still Mongolia's major industrial base despite their dependence on imported equipment, spare parts, and diesel fuel. In the east a Mongolian-Czechoslovak company, Monczechoslovakmetall (established in 1979), and a Mongolian-Soviet company. Mongolsovtsvetmet (now Mongolrostsevmet), mined fluorspar, tungsten, uranium, and aluminum. Unprocessed fluorspar production reached 455,900 metric tons (502,544 short tons) in 1990, and fluorspar concentrate 118,900 metric tons (131,065 short tons). In 1988 mining products first topped 40 percent of Mongolia's exports. When annual gold production was made public in 1991, it was 722.5 kilograms (1,593 pounds).

The collapse of the Soviet economy and the opening of Mongolia in 1990 changed somewhat the structure of the Mongolian mining economy, but not its importance; it now employs more than 18,000 persons. Since 1995 the total output of Mongolia's mining has increased absolutely, in percentage of all industrial production (55.7 percent in 2000), and in its edge over other manufacturing branches in value added per person. Mongolia's shares in Erdenet and Mongolrostsvetmet remain state owned, although the Russian shares were transferred to the privately owned company, Zarubezhtsevmet, Inc. The Mongolian government now holds the controlling interest in the Erdenet joint venture. Concerns over corruption in the plans to privatize Erdenet played a large role in the troubles of the Democratic Coalition administration from 1996–2000, and the plans have been shelved.

Higher oil prices and Western technology and investment have made Züünbayan and other oil fields economical again; production reached 65,220 barrels in 2000. Another mining branch revitalized by foreign investment has been gold, with production in 2000 reaching 11,808 kilograms (26,032 pounds), although it dropped by 11.8 percent in 2001. All gold must be sold to the Central Bank, making it an important revenue source. Coal production, meanwhile, has declined to around 5 million metric tons (5.5 million short tons) annually. After serious problems in the transition, Erdenet's present production, all of which is exported, is 450,000–480,000 metric tons (496,000–529,000 short tons) of copper (at 27 percent purity) and 2,800,000 metric tons (3,086,000 short tons) of molybdenum concentrate (at 50 percent purity). Recent rebuilding promises to increase this output significantly. After an initial drop, flourspar production reached 733,500 metric tons (808,545 short tons) in 2000. Important newly exploited deposits include the zinc deposit at Tömörtiin Owoo near Sükhebaatur province's Baruun-Urt, to be developed with Chinese capital, the gold deposits of Bornuur in Central Province, and the new gold and copper deposits discovered in Oyuu Tologoi in SOUTH GOBI PROVINCE both to be developed by Canadian companies. Ferrous metals, lead, silver, and especially rare earths are all potentially exploitable, although transportation remains a key bottleneck.

See also AGA BURIAT AUTONOMOUS AREA; ARTISANS IN THE MONGOL EMPIRE; BAOTOU; BURIAT REPUBLIC; HAIXI MONGOL AND TIBETAN AUTONOMOUS PREFECTURE; INNER MONGOLIA AUTONOMOUS REGION; KALMYK REPUBLIC; UST'-ORDA BURIAT AUTONOMOUS AREA; WUHAI.

Modogoiev, Andrei Urupkheevich (1915–1989)

Chief official during the Brezhnev years who presided over the industrialization and Russification of Buriatia

Born on January 13 in the Zagatui *ulus*, or village, of the Kuda area (in modern Bayandai district of Ust'-Orda), Andrei Modogoiev studied accounting in Irkutsk. He worked first as an accountant for the livestock procurement office of Yeravna (Buriat, Yaruuna) district in the Buriat-Mongolian Autonomous Soviet Socialist Republic and then for several higher offices in ULAN-UDE.

Modogoiev's rise as a party apparatchik began in November 1941 with his election as first secretary of the Communist Youth League's Buriat Regional Committee. He worked as the first secretary of the KYAKHTA District Party Committee and in 1957 was instructor in the party school attached to the Communist Party's Central Committee in Moscow. In 1960 he returned to Ulan-Ude as the chairman of the Buriat ASSR's Council of Ministers (i.e., premier). From 1962 on he was concurrently the first secretary of the Buriat Regional Party Committee.

Closely associated with the Soviet ruler Leonid Brezhnev, Modogoiev remained in power until Brezhnev's death, when Moscow's new leaders retired him. Like other Soviet ethnic party bosses, Modogoiev supported cultural Russification—in 1970 Buriat-language classes were eliminated in schools—while favoring a network of rural-origin officials of his own ethnic group. He also used his influence to create a research center for the study of traditional bioactive substances, headed by the dissident Buddhist scholar Bidiyadara Dandaron (1914–74), although he could not prevent Dandaron's arrest in 1972.

See also BURIAT REPUBLIC; BURIATS; UST'-ORDA BURIAT AUTONOMOUS AREA.

Modun (Maodun, Modu) (r. 209–174 B.C.E.)

Xiongnu (Hun) leader who founded Mongolia's first unified steppe empire

Modun was the eldest son of Touman, Shanyu (ruler) of the XIONGNU. Hoping to make his son by a favored concubine his successor, Touman dispatched Modun as a hostage to the Yuezhi nomands in Gansu. Modun escaped, and Touman, appreciating his ability, made him a commander of 10,000. In 209 B.C.E. Modun led a band of horse archers trained to unquestioning obedience to murder his father and seize the throne. Modun paid tribute to the seminomadic eastern Hu (*see* XIANBI) but attacked them when they demanded some of his land in the GOBI DESERT. He then subdued various South Siberian tribes. Having recovered Inner Mongolia, Modun extorted from the new Han dynasty's emperor Gaozu (256–195) a Han princess and a treaty of *heqin* (peace and friendship) with the Xiongnu (198). Sometime before 176 Modun drove out the Yuezhi from Gansu and conquered Kroraina (modern ruins at Loulan, near Lop Nuur) and other towns of the Tarim Basin. His son and successor, Jizhu (reign name Laoshang, 174–60), continued Modun's campaign against the Yuezhi, killing their king and making his skull into a goblet. Modun's biography by the Chinese historian Sima Qian (145–89) highlights Modun's regard for loyalty and land as the basis of rule.

Mogholi language and people

The Mogholi people in Afghanistan, descendants of the Negüderi QARA'UNAS, preserved into the 20th century their now almost extinct Mongolic language.

ORIGINS

The Mogholis stem from the Negüderi group of the Qara'unas, who from 1270 on occupied the province of Sistan along the modern Iranian-Afghan border (including the Helmand and Farrah watersheds). The two known Mogholi CLAN NAMES, Burghut and Arghun, are found elsewhere only in the Jochid BLUE HORDE and presumably arrived with the NOYAN Negüder (fl. 1238–62), who was a Jochid retainer. Conquered by TIMUR in 1383, the Negüderis appear as a nomadic people in 16th- and 17th-century histories; Babur (1483–1530) noted that some of them still spoke Mongolian in his day.

LANGUAGE

Mogholi language is one of the most conservative Mongolic languages, fully preserving diphthongs such as *i'a-*, *a'u-*, and so on (for example, *nioldu-*, "to glue," *qalöun*, "hot," *köun*, "son"), and the unbroken *-i-* (for example, *miqon*, "meat," *shira*, "yellow"). On the other hand, the initial *h-*, preserved in Mongolic languages such as Daur and Tu, had disappeared. Another conservative feature is the preservation of the *q* and the back *ï* (for example, *qudol*, "falsehood," *qïtqei*, "knife," *qïmsun*, "fingernail"); in most other Mongolia languages *q* has changed to either *x* or *k*, and in all others *ï* has merged with *i*. This conservatism is probably related to the Turkic and Iranian environment. Iranian influence also seems responsible for the frequent change of *a* to *o* (for example, *ghol*, "fire," *soin*, "good"). Given the fragmentary knowledge of Mogholi and the dialect of Middle Mongolian spoken in the western khanates, it is hard to find any clear similarities between the two. In a few cases, however, Mogholi shares the flattening of noninitial *o* found in the western khanates (for example, *quana*, "it dries," from *qo'o-*; cf. *qo'osun*). In morphology Moghol is fairly conservative but like some other Middle and New Mongolian languages has created personal conjugations through postposed pronouns (for example, *irambi*, "I come," *iranchi*, "you come," *iramda*, "we come") (*see* ALTAIC LANGUAGE FAMILY; MONGOLIC LANGUAGE FAMILY).

DISTRIBUTION AND TRADITIONAL LIFE

By 1800 the Mogholis (Persian for Mongols) lived solely in mountain valleys in Afghanistan's Ghorat province, south of Teywarah (Teyvareh) and east of Por Chaman (Parjuman). Sunni Muslims, they had a somewhat Mongolian appearance. Mogholis began emigrating due to land pressure from their Afghan (Pashtun) and Teymanni neighbors, forming several villages near Herat by 1815 and others near Maymaneh (Maimana) and Pol-e Khomri (Pul-i Khumri) by 1935. In the Ghorat, where they lived in scattered villages practicing irrigation agriculture, Moghol social life was relatively egalitarian, with widespread landownership. During the summer the Mogholis lived with their herds in black goat-hair YURTS of the Afghan (Pashtun) type in outlying fallow fields to fertilize them. The remembered clan division into the western Burghutis and the eastern Arghunis played no role in everyday life. The Mogholis of Herat were sharecroppers, while those in Pol-e Khomri were seminomadic. The total number of Mogholis by 1954 was perhaps several thousand persons.

MODERN CHANGES

By the time detailed linguistic investigation was undertaken, the Mogholi language was rapidly declining. Although mostly a kitchen language used in private, Mogholi poetry written in the Arabic script has been preserved. By the 1950s only the Herat Moghols still spoke Mogholi fluently and that only at home, while in the Ghorat they spoke Dari Persian and in Maymaneh and Pol-e Khomri, Pashtun. Only a few elders there could remember Mogholi phrases. Even in Herat virtually all sophisticated vocabulary, including all numbers over five, was Dari Persian. Since then Mogholi has rapidly declined as a spoken language even in Herat. Their fate in Afghanistan's wars since 1978 is not clear, and their language seems likely to be on the verge of extinction.

See also HAZARAS; MONGOLIC LANGUAGE FAMILY.

Further reading: H. F. Schurmann, *Mongols of Afghanistan: An Ethnography of the Moghols and Related Peoples of Afghanistan* (The Hague: Mouton, 1962).

Moghulistan The eastern successor state of the Chaghatayid dynasty, ruling the steppes north of the Tianshan Mountains until 1508, long retained Mongolian language and customs. In the chaos of the CHAGHATAY KHANATE breakup after 1338, the QARA'UNAS, based in the south, and the previously obscure Mongol clan of Dughlat (Dogholad), based in the east, emerged as the main power contenders. In 1347 Emir Bolaji of the Dughlat sought out and enthroned Tughlugh-Temür (1329–62), a last descendant of the Chaghatay Ulus's Esen-Buqa Khan (1309–18). Tughlugh-Temür converted to Islam and briefly occupied Samarqand. After his death Emir Bolaji's brother, Qamar-ud-Din, deposed Tughlugh-Temür's son and seized the throne (1365–92). This non-Chinggisid usurpation and repeated invasions by TIMUR (Tamerlane), who had founded a new dynasty in the central Chaghatayid lands, threw Moghulistan into chaos. Eventually, Bolaji's son, Emir Khudaydad (fl. 1363–1446), set another of Tughlugh-Temür's sons on the throne and submitted to Timur. The restoration of the Chaghatayid dynasty and the death of Timur in 1405 stabilized Moghulistan; Kashgar was recovered around 1433–34 and Tashkent around 1486.

The term *Moghul Ulus*, used by the Moghuls themselves, meant simply "Mongolian realm or people" and expressed the Moghuli's pride in their ancestry. (The widely used Moghulistan, "land of the Moghuls," is properly geographical and not political.) The Timurids and the Moghuls were rival successors of the Chaghatay Khanate; the Timurids called the Moghuls *jete* (bandits), while the Chinggisid Moghuls despised the Timurids as *qara'una*s (half-breeds) and insubordinate commoners. Decrees (*JARLIQ*) were written in Mongolian exclusively to the end of the 14th century, and Mongolian was spoken at court through the reign of Sultan-Mahmud Khan (1487–1508). MING DYNASTY (1368–1644) records call the realm Ili-Baligh, "Ili-City."

Like other Mongol realms, Moghulistan was structured into right and left wings and a center. The emir of the Dughlats, who held the center, received the title of *ulus-begi* (commander of the realm), and the status of *DARQAN* (exempt) and khan's *QUDA* (in-laws) in every generation. From the time of Emir Sayyid-Ali (d. 1458), the emirs dwelt in Kashgar, while the junior members (*mirza*) controlled other cities of the Tarim Basin. The Kashgar population was divided into civilian households, or *tümen* (10,000, from the units in the old 13th-century Mongol census) and military households, or *qa'uchin* ("old" armies). Other classes were the *aimaq* (tribes), or Moghul nomads, and the urban learned class.

Moghulistan included most of modern Xinjiang as well as Kyrgyzstan, the Ferghana valley, and adjacent parts of Kazakhstan. The rulers nomadized in the pastures north of the Tianshan and through the mountain passes into the Aksu area. The area south of the Tianshan (the Ferghana valley, the Tarim Basin, and the Ysyk Köl), dominated by oasis agriculture, constituted the Mangalai Sübe, or "Facing the Sun," and was granted to the Dughlat. Turpan (Turfan) and Hami were not originally part of the Moghul realm. Tributary under Ways Khan (1417–32), Turpan became an integral part of the realm in 1487–88, and Mansur Khan (1508–43) conquered Hami from the Ming in 1513. Ming records show Buddhist clergy in Turpan and Hami emigrating to Gansu around 1437 and 1473, respectively, due to Moghuli raids and domestic Islamization.

The legend of the Sufi Arshad-ud-Din's conversion of Tughlugh-Temür to Islam became the realm's founding charter. Arshad-ud-Din's descendants, keeping his tomb in Kucha (Kuqa), were titled "great *khoja*s" (descendants of Muhammad). However, even late in his life Tughlugh-Temür invited Tibetan Buddhist clerics, and Mongol rituals, such as worshiping the battle standard, continued at court at least through 1508. The historian Mirza Haydar Dughlat (1499–1551), an embittered emigré whose Persian-language *Tarikh-i-Rashidi* (c. 1533) is the major source on Moghuli history, admired the unsuccessful efforts of Yunus Khan (1472–87), raised as an emigré at the Timurid court, to force sedentarization and Islamic law on the Moghuls.

After 1508 the Moghuls lost first the Ferghana valley and then the Ili region to the KAZAKHS. Although Moghuli rule continued in Turpan and Yarkand, the Moghuls rapidly lost their Mongolian language and customs after losing the Ili Valley. In the Tarim Basin Sufi *khoja*s of the Naqshbandi order eventually deposed the Moghul khans, but the Chaghatayids in Turpan surrendered to the QING DYNASTY (1636–1912) in 1689 and maintained their rule there and in Hami as local princes until the 20th century.

See also ESEN; NORTHERN YUAN DYNASTY; OIRATS; YOGUR LANGUAGES AND PEOPLE.

Further reading: Mano Eiji, "Moghulistan," *Acta Asiatica: Bulletin of the Institute of Eastern Culture* 34 (1978): 46–60; Kim Ho-dong, "The Early History of the Moghul Nomads: The Legacy of the Chaghatai Khanate," in *The Mongol Empire and Its Legacy*, ed. Reuven Amitai-Preiss and David O. Morgan (Leiden: E. J. Brill, 1999), 290–318; W. M. Thackston, trans., *Mirza Haydar Dughlat's Tarikh-i-Rashidi: A History of the Khans of Moghulistan*, vol. 2 (Cambridge, Mass.: Harvard University, 1996).

money, modern Until 1911 Mongolia used a wide variety of currencies, some common to the QING DYNASTY of which Mongolia was a part and some peculiar to itself. The standard Mongolian tögrög was introduced in 1925 and has, despite bouts of serious inflation, been in use continuously since then.

THE QING DYNASTY AND THEOCRATIC PERIOD

From the disintegration of the MONGOL EMPIRE's successor states in the mid-14th century to the 18th century it is not known what currency, if any, was used in Mongolia. In the late 18th and 19th centuries silver ingots were used as they had been in China since the Middle Ages (*see* YASTUQ). The largest ones were the fifty-tael *yüwembüü* (Cyrillic, *yömbüü*, from Chinese *yuanbao*, "main treasure"), shaped like the bottom of a boot or a boat and weighing about 1.86 kilograms (4.1 pounds). Also circulating were Spanish and Mexican silver dollars, called *yangchiyan* (Cyrillic, *yanchaan*, from Chinese *yangqian*, "foreign money"), weighing about 24 grams (0.85 ounces). Within the capital city, blocks or loads of brick TEA were the principal fractional currency. The treasuries of nine great monasteries issued paper notes called *teize* (Cyrillic, *tiiz*, from Chinese *tizi*, "signature"). Those issued by the ERDENI SHANGDZODBA (the treasury of the JIBZUNDAMBA KHUTUGTU) circulated from at least 1870 to 1908–09. Chinese-style square-hole cast copper coins (*zoos*) were rarely used.

During the THEOCRATIC PERIOD (1911–21) the newly independent Mongolian government did not issue its own currency, despite the chartering of a Russian-financed National Bank in 1915. In 1913 the government made the Russian gold ruble note the legal currency, while tea blocks and silver ingots and coins remained the primary money used in the marketplace.

The Russian Revolution made the gold ruble worthless, ushering in a period of financial chaos. Mongolia's

Chinese occupation government from 1919 to 1921, the succeeding White Russian government, and the revolutionary government in KYAKHTA all issued short-lived banknotes. None of these currencies alleviated the desperate shortage of reliable money, which was part of the collapse in trade in Mongolia from 1920 to 1923.

MONEY IN INDEPENDENT MONGOLIA

In 1925 the joint Soviet-Mongolian Bank of Trade and Industry created a new tögrög (Uighur-Mongolian tögörig, "round") currency. The new currency was based on a tögrög of 18 grams (0.63 ounces) of 22.2 carat silver. To win confidence the paper bills were completely convertible to silver coins. Small copper fractional currency, or möngö (silver) were also introduced. All other currencies were withdrawn. During the LEFTIST PERIOD (1929–32) the government cancelled convertibility amid rampant inflation.

A new design for paper bills and base metal fractional coins (möngö) was issued in 1939 with the portrait of General SÜKHEBAATUR, now enshrined as the founder of the Mongolian People's Republic. Slightly new versions were introduced to take account of the beginning of Cyrillicization and the new seal (1941), the completion of Cyrillicization (1955), and another new seal (1966). The latter issue added the government palace and electrification on the 20-, 50-, and 100-tögrög denomination bills.

The massive inflation from 1991 to 1995 that accompanied the market transition resulted in the disappearance of the möngö as their metal value came to exceed their face value. New bills have been issued in denominations up to 10,000 tögrögs with new designs: a horse, General Sükhebaatur in traditional Mongolian dress, and CHINGGIS KHAN. A new fractional currency of 100, 200, and 500 tögrögs has also been introduced.

MONEY IN INNER MONGOLIA

Inner Mongolia, after being incorporated into the Republic of China in 1911, used the same diverse combination of moneys as in China. In HULUN BUIR the local semiautonomous government in 1919 issued its own bills, called "Mongol money." In Japanese-occupied Inner Mongolia PRINCE DEMCHUGDONGRUB's autonomous government issued through the Mongol-Border Bank (Mengjiang yinhang) a new currency in 1938. Called "camel money" from the main design on the bills, the bills were bilingual, with the main matter in Chinese and some subsidiary inscriptions in Mongolian. From 1947 to 1949 the Chinese Communist–backed Inner Mongolian Autonomous Government also issued its own currency with bilingual inscriptions. Since 1949 Inner Mongolia has used the money of the People's Republic of China.

See also MONEY IN THE MONGOL EMPIRE; PAPER CURRENCY IN THE MONGOL EMPIRE; YASTUQ.

money in the Mongol Empire The MONGOL EMPIRE adopted the Chinese silver ingot as a unified money of account, while issuing paper money in China and coins in the western areas of the empire. Before the Mongol Empire neighboring realms in Inner Mongolia and Turkestan used various forms of money. The Uighur kingdom of Turpan (Turfan) and the Kitan Liao dynasty (907–1125) in Inner Mongolia used cloth bolts (*see* UIGHURS and KITANS). Uighur monetary bolts were four cubits long and a span in breadth and were stamped with the seal of the Uighur khan. Every seven years the strips were washed and restamped. After about 975 the Liao dynasty began importing Chinese-style copper coins from the SONG DYNASTY (960–1279) in China and coining their own copper cash. After the fall of the Liao and the rise of the Jurchen people's JIN DYNASTY (1115–1234), the Jin mostly used Song dynasty coins supplemented by paper currency. In South China the Song had begun using paper cash as the principal currency after 1160.

Although the Mongols conquered North China beginning in 1211, they did not at first issue local currency. As the rump Jin dynasty's paper currency entered an inflationary spiral and copper cash began flowing back to the Song in South China, parts of North China reverted to silk bolts for money. Under ÖGEDEI KHAN (1229–41) the Mongol administration began circulating paper currency backed by silk reserves. At the same time, the Mongols also began collecting taxes directly in silver and adopted the ding, or silver ingot, weighing 50 taels about 2.2 kilograms (almost five pounds), as a money of account (*see* YASTUQ). Under QUBILAI KHAN (1260–94) the Mongol YUAN DYNASTY in China issued a unified paper currency backed by silver reserves. Despite chronic inflation after 1272, the paper currency, supplemented by old cash and limited issues of new copper cash, served as the principal means of exchange until after 1345, when rebellions, economic crisis, and fiscal mismanagement destroyed public confidence in the bills.

In the western realms of Turkestan and Iran the Mongols began sponsoring coinage almost immediately after the conquest. Heavily debased silver dirhams (silver coins) were struck in the name of CHINGGIS KHAN (Genghis, 1206–27) in Afghanistan, and local Mongol commanders issued silver coins in GEORGIA and Azerbaijan during the 1240s. Under MÖNGKE KHAN (1251–59) Mongol coinage increased substantially, with gold and debased silver coinage in Central Asia and silver and copper coins for Georgia, Iran, and the BULGHARS on the Volga.

In the steppe cloth bolts continued to be used as currency from Mongolia to the Black Sea, while in the forest zone, from Russia to eastern Siberia, squirrel skins and other pelts functioned as money (*see* SIBERIA AND THE MONGOL EMPIRE). Money did, however, penetrate the steppe: The Mongol capital of QARA-QORUM has yielded large numbers of Song coins, and Yuan dynasty paper currency has been found in Mongolia and Siberia.

With the division of the Mongol Empire the western successor state of the IL-KHANATE in Iran, the CHAGHATAY

KHANATE in Central Asia, and the GOLDEN HORDE each began its own coinage. While theoretically bimetallic, a silver shortage in the Islamic world had eliminated genuine silver currency since 1000. The Mongol conquest, coinciding with an increased supply of European silver, brought genuine silver coinage back into use in the Islamic world. The Il-Khans and their local vassals, who straddled the trade routes linking European silver and African gold to Indian goods, coined in gold and silver with relative purity until 1287, when a trade downturn slashed bullion reserves and led to a fiscal crisis. A 1294 attempt to introduce paper currency into the IL-KHANATE was a miserable failure. Fiscal reforms and a trade revival enabled GHAZAN KHAN (1295–1304) to inaugurate a unified bimetallic currency throughout the realm, including the highly sought gold "Ghazani dinars," and succeeding Il-Khans maintained a fine currency to the dynasty's fall in 1335.

In the Golden Horde a strong silver currency was maintained from around 1260 on, although internally the *sum* (Italian, *sommo*), or ingot, weighing a tenth of a *yastuq*, remained the major currency. The Chaghatay Khanate's silver coinage began somewhat later (1269–70), stimulated by the same trade to the East through CRIMEA. Both realms shared in the economic downturn of 1287, but in the Golden Horde coinage revived in 1304–05. Only under the Chaghatayid khan Kebeg (1318–26) did wealth from both trade and raids on India result in a high-quality silver dirham. From 1339 the Golden Horde benefited from the breakdown of the Il-Khanate to became a major route for Mediterranean trade with the East, until civil wars in the Horde and economic decline in the Mediterranean and China cut off the trade after 1381.

See also INDIA AND THE MONGOLS; MONEY, MODERN; PAPER CURRENCY IN THE MONGOL EMPIRE.

Further reading: Bruce G. Lippard, "The Mongols and Byzantium, 1243–1341" (Ph.D. diss., Indiana University, 1983); A. P. Martinez, "The Use of Mint-Output Data in Historical Research on the Western Appanages," in *Aspects of the Altaic Civilization*, ed. Denis Sinor (Bloomington: Indiana University, 1990), 87–126.

Monggoljin *See* FUXIN MONGOL AUTONOMOUS COUNTY.

Möngke Khan (Mengü, Mangu, Mongka) (b. 1209, r. 1251–1259) *Third successor of Chinggis Khan, who began a new line, reformed administration, and extended Mongol conquests*

MÖNGKE'S EARLY LIFE

Möngke was born on January 10, 1209, the eldest son of CHINGGIS KHAN's teen-aged boy TOLUI and his wife of six years, SORQAQTANI BEKI. TEB TENGGERI, the powerful shaman who would soon lose his life in a challenge to Chinggis Khan's new dynasty, saw in the stars a great future for the child and bestowed on him the name Möngke, "eternal." Tolui and Sorqaqtani Beki gave up their first child to Tolui's brother, Ögedei, who had his childless third wife, Angqui, raise him.

In August–September 1230 Möngke went to war for the first time, following ÖGEDEI KHAN and Tolui into battle against the JIN DYNASTY in North China. In 1232 his father, Tolui, died. Ögedei returned Möngke to his father's ORDO (palace-tent), now under the control of Möngke's widowed mother, Sorqaqtani Beki. Following Mongol custom, Möngke inherited at least one of his father's wives, Oghul-Qoimish, the daughter of Qutuqa Beki of the Oirat tribe. WILLIAM OF RUBRUCK observed that Möngke had loved her deeply and gave special favor to her elder daughter, Shirin, but Oghul-Qoimish was dead by the time of his coronation.

Möngke's mother, Sorqaqtani Beki, was a Christian, and from William of Rubruck's description, Armenian and Assyrian Christian priests had a significant influence over all of Möngke's major wives. Möngke himself, however, evinced no more than a polite respect for Christianity. Möngke reacted to the diverse religious currents in the empire with a renewed devotion to Mongol traditions. Both William of Rubruck and Chinese sources agree that he never took any important action without consulting the omens found in burnt shoulder blades (*see* SCAPULIMANCY.)

In 1235 Ögedei dispatched Möngke along with his own son GÜYÜG, CHA'ADAI's son Büri, and several of the Jochid princes headed by BATU (d. 1255) to attack the QIPCHAQS, Russians, OSSETES, and other peoples of Eastern Europe. Möngke made the most of this opportunity. One episode, found in several histories, formed the centerpiece of narratives justifying Möngke's rise, just as similar episodes of heavenly intervention did in the histories of Chinggis Khan. When the most formidable Qipchaq chief, Bachman, fled to an island in the Volga delta, a heavenly wind dried out the land between the island and the mainland. Möngke and his soldiers rushed out, captured Bachman, and returned just as the water flowed back. Möngke also engaged in hand-to-hand combat in the sieges of the Russian cities. He participated in the conquest of Kiev and led the long siege of the Ossetian (Alan) city of Magas. While Güyüg and Büri let their relationships with Batu deteriorate into open ridicule, Möngke, as chief man in the Toluid family, preserved good relations with Batu and the Jochids, a fact that would prove crucial to his later rise to khan.

When Ögedei recalled Möngke and Güyüg in winter 1240–41, Toluid's son had become one of the leading Mongol princes. In 1246, when Temüge Odchigin, Chinggis Khan's sole remaining brother, tried to seize the throne and rule without confirmation by a QURILTAI (assembly), the new khan, Güyüg, entrusted the delicate task of trying Odchigin to him and Hordu, Chinggis Khan's senior grandson. When Güyüg died in 1248 without leaving an heir with the experience and influence to secure the throne, Möngke emerged as one of the main contenders.

THE TOLUID REVOLUTION AND MÖNGKE'S ENTHRONEMENT

Late in Güyüg's reign, when he and Batu seemed headed for confrontation, Tolui's widow Sorqaqtani Beki had warned Batu of Güyüg's hostile intentions, thus establishing the Jochid-Toluid alliance against the Ögedei and Cha'adaid lines. After Güyüg's death Batu became the clear leader among the Mongol princes despite the gout that kept him bedridden.

Batu called a *quriltai* (assembly) in his own territory (at Ala-Qamaq or Alaq-Toqraghu). Sorqaqtani Beki sent Möngke, while other attendees included leaders of the families of Chinggis Khan's brothers as well as several important generals. Güyüg's sons, Khoja and Naqu, attended briefly but then left. Thereafter, the only remaining representatives of the Ögedeid and Cha'adaid families were outsiders with little influence in their families. Güyüg's widow, the regent OGHUL-QAIMISH, sent the Uighur scribe Bala as her delegate.

The *quriltai* rejected the idea that only descendants of Ögedei could be khan and first offered the throne to Batu. Rejecting it, Batu instead nominated Möngke. Despite vehement objections from Bala, the *quriltai* approved Möngke. One supporter of Möngke, MENGGESER NOYAN, threatened to execute anyone who opposed Batu's choice.

Given its location outside the Mongolian heartland and its limited attendance, the *quriltai* was of questionable validity. The supporters of Möngke tried to get the regent Oghul-Qaimish and the main Ögedeids and Cha'adaids to attend a formal *quriltai* at Ködö'e Aral in the ONON RIVER-KHERLEN RIVER heartland, but they refused. Möngke's supporters went ahead anyway, and on July 1, 1251, the delegates at Ködö'e Aral elected Möngke great khan. Only a few Ögedeid and Cha'adaid princes acknowledged Möngke as khan: mostly sons by lesser wives and Qara-Hüle'ü, a grandson of Cha'adai who had been deposed from rule over the family by Güyüg. Meanwhile, Ögedei's grandson Shiremün and Güyüg's son Naqu moved toward the *quriltai* site with covert plans for an armed attack. By chance, one of Möngke's falconers, searching for a stray camel, entered the conspirators' camp, discovered the preparations for the attack, and gave the news to Möngke. The khan dispatched Menggeser Noyan, his chief judge (*JARGHUCHI*), with an armed escort to investigate. The conspirators were intimidated into abandoning their plan and brought to Möngke's court. Meanwhile, Bala, the Uighur scribe, arranged with the king in Uighuristan a combined anti-Muslim pogrom and anti-Möngke uprising, but this plan, too, was thwarted,

Under Möngke's active supervision, Menggeser Noyan now began a thorough purge of the opposition.

Lasting until the final executions of Oghul-Qaimish and CHINQAI in summer and winter 1252, the purge was extended over all the empire. Estimates of the officials and Mongol commanders executed range from 77 (RASHID-UD-DIN FAZL-ULLAH) to more than 300 (William of Rubruck). Most of the princes of the blood involved in the conspiracy, however, were given some form of exile or house arrest. The Mongol general Eljigidei in the Middle East and Cha'adai's son Büri were handed over to Batu and executed. The only pause came when Möngke's mother, Sorqaqtani Beki, fell ill during the purges; to prolong her life an amnesty was declared for those condemned at that time. Her death early in 1252, along with the purges, left Möngke and Batu the two authorities in the empire.

MÖNGKE'S CONQUESTS

Since the 1242 conclusion of the great campaign in Eastern Europe, the Mongols had not significantly expanded their empire. Even before the conclusion of the purges, Möngke set in motion several campaigns that had been planned earlier. One place in which Möngke did not resume the Mongol conquests was in Eastern Europe. Batu emerged from the Toluid revolution as a virtual coemperor in the west with Möngke. Old and ill, Batu was evidently satisfied with his territory and wary of having troops of princes and soldiers from other lines cross his lands to the front. Thus, Möngke's conquests were all directed to East Asia and the Middle East. In his first plans of 1252 he chose Korea and the Dali kingdom in modern YUNNAN as the main targets in the east and India, the fortresses of the ISMA'ILIS, and the 'ABBASID CALIPHATE in Baghdad as the main targets in the west, assigning generals to each.

Against Korea he assigned Jalayirtai Qorchi. Working together with Korean commanders who had joined the Mongols, he ravaged Korea, but the king on Kanghwa Island still refused to submit. Another general, Qoridai, also launched an attack that ravaged Tibet and induced leading monasteries there to submit to Mongol rule.

Ögedei and Güyüg had found Mongol advances against South China's SONG DYNASTY foiled by the Chang (Yangtze) River. Möngke decided to outflank the Song by attacking Dali (in modern Yunnan) to the southwest and assigned this campaign to his brother Qubilai and Uriyangqadai (1199–1271), the son of SÜBE'ETEI BA'ATUR. Marching through the Sino-Tibetan borderlands, Qubilai took Dali city in January 1254. Left as garrison commander, Uriyangqadai reduced the neighboring peoples to submission and in winter 1257–58 beat the Trân dynasty rulers of Vietnam into temporary submission.

Its inaccessible fortresses in the Elburz mountains of northern Iran and daring attacks of the *fida'is* (fedayeen, or warriors of the faith) had generated a mystique of invincibility about the Isma'ili theocratic state in Alamut. The Mongols were also wary of the 'Abassid Caliphate's religious charisma. Preparations for the war against the two Middle Eastern enemies were therefore very extensive. Möngke put his brother HÜLE'Ü in overall charge of all military and civil affairs in the Iran area, and Hüle'ü set out in May 1253. Once operations began in earnest in fall 1256 the two realms proved hardly a match for the Mongols. The Isma'ili leader, Rukn-ud-Din, surrendered in January 1257, while the caliph in Baghdad surrendered in February 1258. Both were executed with their generals, officials, and scores of thousands of their people.

Meanwhile, in July 1256 Möngke decided on all-out war against the Song dynasty. He would campaign personally in Sichuan, while his brother Qubilai would attack in Hubei. Again, long preparation ensued, and Möngke first attacked Song positions in Sichuan in March–April 1258. Military operations, while generally successful, were prolonged. Meanwhile, Qubilai was still proceeding through North China toward the Song frontier. During the lunar new year celebrations (January 25, 1259), Möngke decided to stay in the south through the coming hot summer instead of retiring north as was the Mongol custom. The result was as his companions feared: Möngke died of fever before the walls of Chongqing on August 11, 1259.

MÖNGKE'S ADMINISTRATION

Möngke did not act according to the Turco-Mongol ideal of freehanded generosity but instead followed a more calculating and centralized model of rule. Unlike Ögedei, who gave his high officials free rein to initiate policy, Möngke drafted his own decrees and kept close watch on their revision. Möngke limited gifts to the princes, converting them into regular salaries, and tried to reverse the practice of making extravagant payments in return for *tangsuqs* (rarities). He deprived the ORTOQ merchants of their semiofficial status, making them subject to taxes and prohibiting them from using the official postal relay system. This measure, too, hurt the Mongol nobles, who were virtually all involved as silent partners in *ortoq* firms. He also repeatedly punished those generals and princes, including his own son, who allowed their troops to plunder civilians without authorization.

In administration Ögedei had given high position to North Chinese, and Güyüg had relied heavily on UIGHURS. Möngke Khan still used such officials but relied on Islamic officials more than any great khan before him. His chief judge, Menggeser, was of a Mongol family long in the service of Chinggisids, while the chief scribe, Bulghai (d. 1264) was a Christian, probably of KEREYID origin. Even so, of the 16 chief provincial officials listed in the YUAN SHI, nine were certainly Muslim and none Chinese. He reappointed Güyüg's three supreme provincial administrators, all Muslim: Mahmud Yalavach in North China, Mas'ud Beg in Turkestan, and ARGHUN AQA in Iran and vicinity (see MAHMUD YALAVACH AND MAS'UD BEG). Rumors spread that at the behest of Batu's brother Berke, Möngke

had made the Islamic profession of faith before his coronation.

Reports on local conditions convinced Möngke that the *qubchiri* (contribution) system of allowing local army units simply to demand what they wanted from the neighboring population needed to be commuted into a fixed poll tax collected by imperial agents and forwarded to the needy units. Initially, the maximum rate was fixed at 10–11 gold dinars in the Middle East and 6–7 *tael*s of silver in China. Protests from the landlord classes reduced even this relatively low rate to 6–7 dinars and 4 *tael*s. Subsequently, officials such as Arghun Aqa raised the top rate on the wealthy to 500 dinars. In practice, the reform of the *qubchiri* did not lighten the tax burden and probably made it more regressive, yet it did make the payments more predictable and evened out the burden on areas along popular routes. Along with the reform of the tax system and the postroads, Möngke counted the entire empire in a single census for the first and last time. The application of this census and the regressive silver tax to remote areas, such as Novgorod, which hitherto had been little affected by Mongol demands, caused riots that were rapidly crushed.

After the purges of the Ögedeids, Möngke eliminated their traditional *ulus*, or territory, in the Emil and Qobaq (Emin and Hobok) valleys, assigning to acquiescent members of the family new territories either in Turkestan or in northwest China. In another move to consolidate his power, Möngke gave his brothers Qubilai and Hüle'ü supervisory powers in North China and Iran, respectively. While Möngke's officials in Iran, led by Arghun Aqa, developed cordial relations with Hüle'ü, Qubilai's entourage had frequent conflicts with Möngke's administrators in North China. Although Möngke also appointed Cha'adaids and Jochids to join Hüle'ü's expedition to Iran, the creation of what became new khanates led to tensions that after Möngke's death sparked the final breakup of the empire.

When William of Rubruck met Möngke Khan in 1253, his most beloved wife, Oghul-Qoimish (not to be confused with Güyüg's widow), had been dead for several years. His youngest wife, Chübei, who had accompanied him on his last campaign to China, died a month after Möngke at the base camp at the Liupanshan Mountains. Thus, after Möngke's death there was no empress of stature to serve as regent, a fact that hastened the disintegration of the empire.

See also APPANAGE SYSTEM; BUDDHISM IN THE MONGOL EMPIRE; CENSUS IN THE MONGOL EMPIRE; CHRISTIANITY IN THE MONGOL EMPIRE; INDIA AND THE MONGOLS; ISLAM IN THE MONGOL EMPIRE; KIEV, SIEGE OF; KOREA AND THE MONGOL EMPIRE; PROVINCES IN THE MONGOL EMPIRE; RELIGIOUS POLICY IN THE MONGOL EMPIRE; RUSSIA AND THE MONGOL EMPIRE; TAOISM IN THE MONGOL EMPIRE; TIBET AND THE MONGOL EMPIRE; WESTERN EUROPE AND THE MONGOL EMPIRE.

Further reading: Thomas T. Allsen, *Mongol Imperialism: The Policies of the Grand Qan Möngke in China, Russia, and the Islamic Lands, 1251–1259* (Berkeley: University of California Press, 1987).

Mongol Empire From 1206 to 1260 CHINGGIS KHAN and his sons and grandsons built the Mongol Empire into the largest land empire in history. At its greatest extent as a unified empire in 1259, it included all of present-day Mongolia, Central Asia, Tibet, Afghanistan, Iran, Iraq, Armenia, Georgia, Azerbaijan and Ukraine, most of Siberia, European Russia, and Turkey, and the northern and western parts of China. After the breakup of the empire into successor Mongol states in 1260, the Mongols in the East completed the conquest of China and added Korea and northern Burma to their rule. Mongol rule in the major sedentary states such as Persia and China fell in the 14th century, but Mongol khans descended from Chinggis Khan continued to rule the Inner Asian steppe and the oasis cities of Central Asia until the 18th century. This entry surveys the history of the Mongol Empire from its beginnings until its split into separate successor states in 1260.

THE MONGOL EMPIRE'S RISE AND CONQUESTS

The Mongol Empire began with the unification of the tribes on the MONGOLIAN PLATEAU by Chinggis Khan. Born under the name Temüjin, the son of a chieftain of the MONGOL TRIBE, he suffered a difficult childhood after his father was poisoned. Alliances with traditionally dominant powers, particularly ONG KHAN of the KEREYID Khanate in Mongolia, made Temüjin an important player in Mongolian politics. A falling out with Ong Khan nearly destroyed Temüjin's power, but, in a series of lightning campaigns from 1203 to 1205, he defeated Ong Khan, conquered his Kereyid tribe, and unified Mongolia. In 1206, Temüjin was crowned khan of the "Great Mongol Empire" (*Yeke Mongghol Ulus*) at a QURILTAI (great assembly) and assumed the name Chinggis Khan.

Succeeding campaigns by Chinggis Khan from 1211 to his death in 1227 drove the JIN DYNASTY in North China south of the Huang (Yellow) River, wiped out the QARA-KHITAI Empire, which held a loose rein over the oasis cities of Turkestan (modern Xinjiang, Kyrgyzstan, and adjacent areas), and destroyed the Muslim dynasty of KHORAZM, which ruled the area of modern Uzbekistan, Afghanistan, Turkmenistan, and most of Iran. His final campaign was undertaken against the Tangut people's XIA DYNASTY that ruled northwest China. In all these campaigns Chinggis Khan preferred to bring local rulers into tributary relations, often cemented by intermarriage with the Mongol ruling house. Nevertheless, when fighting those whom Chinggis considered hereditary enemies of the Mongols, such as the Jin rulers, or when cities or tribes had killed Mongol envoys or rebelled after accepting Mongol governors, Chinggis and his lieutenants would order wholesale slaughter of the offending population. Such massacres were particularly devastating in the campaigns in northern China, in Khorasan in eastern Iran, and in Chinggis's final campaign against the Xia dynasty in northwest China.

After the death of Chinggis Khan his third son, ÖGEDEI KHAN, succeeded to the throne, according to his father's will. Ögedei (r. 1229–41) immediately set in motion campaigns intended to wipe out all the Mongols' remaining foes. To the southeast he ordered the final campaign to destroy the Jin, who had retreated south of the Huang (Yellow) River. In the southwest he sent CHORMAQAN to eliminate Jalal-ud-Din, son of the last ruler of Khorazm, who was organizing resistance in western Iran, TURKEY, Armenia, and GEORGIA. To the northeast he sent troops against the QIPCHAQS of the Caspian–Black Sea steppe, who had harbored refugees from Chinggis's unification of Mongolia and resisted his generals. The Russian (including Belarussian and Ukrainian) principalities were allied with the Qipchaqs and had killed envoys of Chinggis, and since the king of Hungary took Qipchaq refugees into his service, the third campaign expanded into a general assault on central and eastern Europe, one that reached the Adriatic Sea before returning to the Mongol homeland on Ögedei's death.

Succession struggles prevented the renewal of conquests during the regency of the empress TÖREGENE, the reign of her and Ögedei's son GÜYÜG (r. 1246–48), and the regency of Güyüg's empress, OGHUL-QAIMISH. Oghul-Qaimish's regency was overthrown in a coup d'état that brought MÖNGKE KHAN, son of TOLUI, Chinggis Khan's youngest son, to the throne. Möngke (r. 1251–59) reignited the engine of Mongol conquest. In the east he launched campaigns of conquest against Korea, the SONG DYNASTY ruling South China, and Tibet, all of which had suffered Mongol raids under Ögedei. To the west he sent his brother HÜLE'Ü to destroy the strongholds of the ISMA'ILIS (an Islamic sect known as the "Assassins") in the mountains of northern Iran, as well as the 'ABBASID CALIPHATE in Baghdad, the titular suzerains of the Islamic world. These campaigns were mostly successful, and the Mongol Empire reached its greatest extent as a unified realm, although Möngke died before his campaign against the Song could reach a conclusion.

RULE AND ADMINISTRATION OF THE MONGOL EMPIRE

At the head of the empire was the "Great Khan" (Qa'an), a title first adopted by Ögedei (*see* KHAN). The Mongols had traditionally elected their ruler at a great assembly (QURILTAI) of the leading clan heads, and this practice continued throughout the empire and in all its successor states. While only descendants of Chinggis Khan were eligible to rule, the empire never adopted any fixed succession rule, a fact that led to repeated

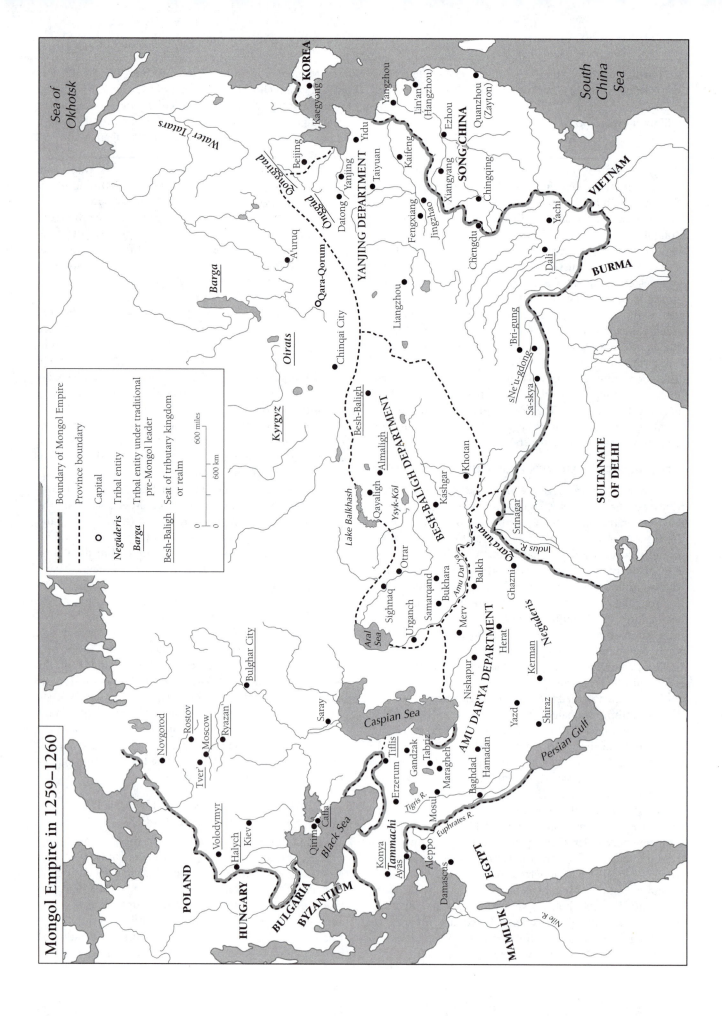

Mongol Empire in 1259–1260

Legend

Boundary of Mongol Empire
Province boundary
● Capital
Negüderis Tribal entity
Barga Tribal entity under traditional pre-Mongol leader
Besh-Baligh Seat of tributary kingdom or realm
○ Capital

600 miles
600 km

Sea of Okhotsk

KOREA
Kaegyong

Water Tatars

Beijing
A'uruq

Barga

Qara-Qorum
Chinqai City

Oirats

Kyrgyz

Datong
Yanjing
Yidu
Taiyuan
Liangzhou

YANJING DEPARTMENT

Fengxiang
Jingzhao
Kaifeng
Lin'an (Hangzhou)
Yangzhou
Ezhou
Quanzhou (Zayton)

SONG CHINA

Xianyang
Chengdu
Chingqing
Dali
Yachi

VIETNAM

BURMA

Bri-gung
sNe'u-gdong
Sa-skya

SULTANATE OF DELHI

Besh-Baligh
Almaligh

BESH-BALIGH DEPARTMENT

Kashgar
Khotan

Lake Balkhash
Qayaligh
Ysyk-Köl

Srinagar

Qara'unas

Indus R.

Otrar
Sighnaq
Urganch
Samarqand
Bukhara
Amu Dar'ya
Merv
Balkh
Ghazni

Aral Sea

Herat

Negüderis

AMU DAR'YA DEPARTMENT

Nishapur
Kerman
Yazd
Shiraz

Caspian Sea

Saray

Bulghar City

Novgorod
Rostov
Moscow
Tver'
Ryazan'

Persian Gulf

Tiflis
Erzerum
Gandzak
Tabriz
Maragheh
Baghdad
Hamadan

Tigris R.
Mosul
Euphrates R.

Volodymyr
Halych
Kiev

Qirim
Caffa
Black Sea

POLAND

HUNGARY

BULGARIA

BYZANTIUM

Konya
Tammachi
Ayas
Aleppo
Damascus

EGYPT

MAMLUK

Nile R.

South China Sea

strife. The emperor's person was protected by a KESHIG, or imperial guard, which served as a training corps and crack military force. From Chinggis Khan's time scribes recorded the khans' and princes' wise sayings (*bilig*) and these, together with the empire's written decrees, formed a body of precedents, or JASAQ, which came to function as a sort of constitution of the empire. Any violation of these precedents by the khans could lead to widespread opposition.

From the beginning of his rise, Chinggis sponsored a new Mongol aristocracy. Those who had supported him early on were given high positions that they handed on to their descendants. Meritorious servants had regular Mongol subjects and also received grants of captive artisans and settled peoples all over the empire. These benefits were also given to members of the ruling family, which quickly grew to staggering size. Compared to other Turco-Mongol states, the Mongol Empire was a family affair. The Mongol commoners showed deep deference to the Chinggisid family, and despite their often serious divisions, members of the ruling family showed an impressive forbearance toward one another. Even after the breakup of the dynasty, defeated Chinggisid rivals were only rarely killed, and relatively few khans met their death at the hands of subjects. At the same time, the large Mongol aristocracy, which insisted on sharing both the administration and the revenue of the empire, constituted a constant enemy of centralization and fiscal restraint.

According to Mongolian custom, wives of great men were the keepers of the palace-tents (ORDO) both during their husbands' lives and afterward and were invited to all the great assemblies of the empire. As keepers of the *ordo*s they also had a recognized right to receive tax moneys and in-kind supplies from appanages to provision the *ordo*s and their staff in suitable style. Thus, while not given formal positions of power, the women of both the imperial clan and the QUDA (marriage ally) clans were full-fledged and influential members of the new Mongol aristocracy.

The nomadic peoples of the Mongolian plateau served the empire and its new aristocracy both as taxpayers and soldiers, receiving in return a share of the booty. They were divided according to a cell-like DECIMAL ORGANIZATION (10s, 100s, 1,000s, 10,000s), which made it easy to pass demands down the chain of command. Toward the sedentary people, the Mongols at first had little organized policy, but eventually they imposed the census and the decimal organization on them as well. From the beginning significant numbers of sedentary peoples were also incorporated into the Mongol military, as common soldiers and specialists in artillery and other branches.

The Mongols administered the empire through a simple bureaucracy. In Chinggis Khan's time the Mongols adopted the vertical, alphabetic UIGHUR-MONGOLIAN SCRIPT, and the chief judge (JARGHUCHI) and scribe at the khan's court were always UIGHURS or Mongols. Those rulers who surrendered to the Mongols would send sons or brothers as hostages to the Mongol court and receive imperial overseers (DARUGHACHI) to guard Mongol interests. They also supplied troops for the Mongol conquests and paid taxes based on a Mongol census. The Mongols divided the wealthiest zone of their realm, whether directly ruled or tributary, into three departments: Yanjing (North China), Besh-Baligh (Turkestan), and Amu Dar'ya (Persia), each of which had a single supreme official (either Chinese, Turkestani, or Mongol) supervising its tax payments and administration. Local affairs were administered by the conquered peoples. A postroad system (JAM) kept communications open between the far-flung outposts of the empire.

While Chinggis Khan retained his ancestors' mobility, he did build a sort of fort in northeast Mongolia, called A'uruq, or "base camp" (*see* AWARGA). Ögedei built a large capital in central Mongolia called QARA-QORUM, which for a few decades became a center of Eurasian commerce. Other princes, princesses, and officials built palaces and colonies throughout the Inner Asian steppe. All these areas were settled primarily by people deported from the conquered areas: artisans, farmers, and postroad workers. After the breakup of the empire, the rulers of the successor states also founded such cities in their domains, such as Saray in the GOLDEN HORDE and Soltaniyeh in the IL-KHANATE (*see* SARAY AND NEW SARAY). Even so, the Mongol khans long retained their nomadic customs, making regular circuits through seasonal camps and palaces.

FINANCE IN THE MONGOL EMPIRE

Lavish gift giving to Mongols and subjects alike held a central position in the political system of the Mongol Empire, as it did in all Turco-Mongol Empires. From the time of Chinggis Khan, those who suffered in war expected to be rewarded richly. The importance of generosity was particularly great, since Chinggis Khan strictly prohibited individual soldiers from seizing loot for themselves, a precedent followed in the empire. His successor, Ögedei Khan, took his generosity to extremes, developing a reputation for reckless prodigality. Ögedei and his successors hoped such generosity would encourage the empire's warriors, draw able men from all over the world to the court, circulate back to the people the booty seized in conquest, and give the emperor a glorious reputation among his subjects and foreigners and in heaven. While many later rulers followed this pattern of heedless liberality, others, such as Möngke, attempted to turn gifts into budgeted annuities.

While much of the wealth of the Mongol rulers came from battle plunder, a regular tax system soon became necessary. Mongol nomads did pay taxes supplying milk and other pastoral products to their captains and to the ruling family, but such supplies were far from meeting the needs of the court or the army. The Mongols continued most of the existing tax payments in the various regions they conquered but added on top of them *qubchiri* (contributions), a special tax to meet the immediate needs of the Mongol rulers and their army. With regard to this *qubchiri*, Mongol financial policy oscillated between two distinct principles: either use messengers bearing tablets or badges of authority (PAIZA) to simply seize what was needed from the civilians, or turn the *qubchiri* into a regular tax, payable in silver to the treasury of the emperor, who would in turn forward it to the army and the aristocracy according to a regular budget. Ögedei and Müngke tried hard to implement the *qubchiri* as a regular silver tax, but under the regents and Güyüg's reign the empire fell into a virtual anarchy of messengers bearing badges and demanding goods. This oscillation continued in the successor states.

The Mongols never imposed a unified currency on the empire as a whole but quickly adopted and produced local currencies, including Chinese paper money. However, Mongol financial practice everywhere encouraged a silver standard. As the main unit of account for their central treasury, the Mongols adopted the Chinese silver ingots, or *ding*, called YASTUQ in Uighur and weighing 50 taels (2.2 kilograms or almost 5 pounds). In the Islamic areas silver always predominated over gold in Mongol coinage. The Mongols borrowed the Turco-Persian practice of ORTOQ, "partners," in which the Mongol rulers and aristocrats loaned silver from the treasury at interest to merchants and moneylenders as capital. They also preferred to collect taxes by tax farming, in which agents would bid for the right to collect taxes in a given area, with a share going to the collectors as profit. The result in many cases was bidding wars between tax farmers, which led to dramatic tax increases. Many writers lamented that such financial practices were more ruinous even than the conquest itself.

CULTURAL AND RELIGIOUS POLICY IN THE UNIFIED EMPIRE

The Mongol rulers made no attempt to impose a common culture on the empire. This attitude of cultural pluralism toward their subject peoples was exemplified in the Mongols' famous policy of religious tolerance. One of the clearest legacies of Chinggis Khan, the Mongol policy of religious tolerance was based on the view that all worthy religions were, in fact, praying to the same god, the great eternal god the Mongols called TENGGERI. God or heaven (*tenggeri* means both) had granted world rule to Chinggis and his successors. The Mongol rulers presented the clergy of the recognized religions—Christianity, Buddhism, Taoism (Daoism), and Islam—a deal: In return for their prayers to God for the Mongol rulers, the rulers would grant the clergy equal status and exemption from military service and taxes. Everywhere, socially dominant clergies accepted this deal, and saw their influence expand.

Mongol tolerance was not complete, however. Some Mongol rulers, such as CHA'ADAI, Chinggis Khan's second son, tried to enforce certain Mongol practices, such as a distinctive method of slaughtering without shedding blood and a prohibition against soiling water by washing clothes or bodies, particularly in the summer. These two rules ran afoul of Islamic laws on slaughtering and ablutions and caused serious tensions. The Mongols also pressured the Chinese in their major garrison cities to adopt the distinctive Mongol style of head shaving.

Certain religious groups were also seen as anti-Mongol or subversive and hence eliminated. The Isma'ilis, or "Assassins," a sect of Shi'ite Muslims, had assassinated Mongol officials, and the Mongols eventually responded by destroying their stronghold in Alamut in modern Iran in 1256. The Dhutaists and other sects of Buddhism in China were at first denied recognition and sporadically persecuted by the Mongol authorities. Later anti-Buddhist polemics distributed by the Taoists were also banned by the Mongols. In all these cases the Mongols were also following the lead of the established religious authorities, who expected the rulers to crush heretical and antisocial sects.

Finally, the Mongols did not extend recognition to clergy who did not have state power. Zoroastrian fire priests in Persia, Manichean clergy in Turkestan, and Jewish rabbis were not given any recognition by the Mongols before 1260, although they were not persecuted. Under Chinggis Chinese CONFUCIANISM was not treated as a religion, but Ögedei founded a temple of Confucius in his capital, and later QUBILAI KHAN would extend to Confucian scholars the same privileges and immunities as the Buddhist and Taoist clergy.

In the successor states Mongol khans would become strong adherents of either Islam or a mixture of Confucianism and Tibetan Buddhism. By 1260 already one local khan, Berke in the northwest, was a Muslim. Even after the rulers' conversion, however, the Mongol aristocracy often resisted linking public policy to personal religious beliefs.

BREAKUP OF THE UNIFIED EMPIRE

By the time of Möngke's death in 1259, differing branches of the Chinggisid family had developed clear spheres of influence in differing areas. The descendants of JOCHI, Chinggis's oldest son, had received the western part of the empire as their appanage, while Cha'adai, Chinggis's second son, had received Turkestan. Möngke Khan granted his brothers, Qubilai and Hüle'ü, jurisdiction over North China in the East and the Middle East in the West, respectively. Hüle'ü's position in the Middle East caused resentment among the descendants of Jochi, who considered that their claims to that area were being ignored. Similarly, the descendants of Cha'adai felt constricted between Qubilai in the East and Hüle'ü in the West. When Möngke's death led to a civil war in North China and Mongolia between his two brothers, Qubilai and ARIQ-BÖKE, the other branches of the Chinggisid family used the interregnum to assert their own claims. By 1265 four independent regimes had emerged: the Golden Horde in the northwest, ruled by the descendants of Jochi; the Il-Khanate in the Middle East, ruled by Hüle'ü; the Chaghatay Khanate in Central Asia; and the realm of Great Khan Qubilai, later called the YUAN DYNASTY (1206/1271–1368), in North China and Mongolia. Despite intermittent warfare over the next few decades, none of these four realms was able either to reunite the empire or even to alter significantly the balance of power. While the other realms would usually acknowledge the titular preeminence of the Yuan dynasty's great khans in the East, in practice each remained completely independent. (*For subsequent events, see* CHAGHATAYID KHANATE; GOLDEN HORDE; IL-KHANATE; YUAN DYNASTY.)

THE MONGOL EMPIRE IN MEDIEVAL HISTORY

It is customary to see the Mongol Empire as a brief historical interlude that left no impact on Eurasian history. Certainly its legacy was not in proportion to its size or comparable to that of the Roman, Arab, or European colonial empires, yet its influence on contemporary medieval history was substantial. (*On the issue of Mongol influence on the history of specific peoples, see the articles mentioned above on the successor states.*) By 1300 the areas conquered by the Mongols had recovered from their devastation, and tax policies, while still heavily regressive, were no longer destructive of economic development. The latter half of Mongol rule coincided with the height of medieval east-west trade linking Europe, Persia, Turkestan, India, Southeast Asia, and China. Travelers and writers such as MARCO POLO, RASHID-UD-DIN FAZL-ULLAH, and MUHAMMAD ABU-'ABDULLAH IBN BATTUTA responded to this cosmopolitan environment by expanding their intellectual horizons far past earlier limits, thus permanently altering the worldview of European, Islamic, and, to a lesser degree, East Asian civilizations. The extraordinary events of the conquest led to some of the most brilliant historical and travel writing of the Middle Ages. Although these expanded horizons contracted again dramatically after the catastrophes of the mid-14th century, they left effects that bore fruit in the Tunisian historian Ibn Khaldun's pathbreaking conception of world history and the voyages of the Chinese explorer Zheng He and, later, Columbus. Ironically, it was the cross-cultural transmission of another novelty—the BLACK DEATH—in which the Mongols inadvertently seem to have played a crucial role, that brought this Indian summer of their rule to an end.

See also APPANAGE SYSTEM; ARTISANS IN THE MONGOL EMPIRE; CENSUS IN THE MONGOL EMPIRE; CENTRAL EUROPE AND THE MONGOLS; CLOTHING AND DRESS; *DARQAN;* FOOD AND DRINK; INDIA AND THE MONGOLS; *JARLIQ;* KHAN; KOREA AND THE MONGOL EMPIRE; MANCHURIA AND THE MONGOL EMPIRE; MILITARY OF THE MONGOL EMPIRE; MONEY IN THE MONGOL EMPIRE; *NOYAN;* PAPER CURRENCY IN THE MONGOL EMPIRE; PROVINCES IN THE MONGOL EMPIRE; RELIGIOUS POLICY IN THE MONGOL EMPIRE; RUSSIA AND THE MONGOL EMPIRE; SIBERIA AND THE MONGOL EMPIRE; SOCIAL CLASSES IN THE MONGOL EMPIRE; *TAMMACHI;* TIBET AND THE MONGOL EMPIRE; WESTERN EUROPE AND THE MONGOLS.

Further reading: Thomas T. Allsen, *Culture and Conquest in Mongol Eurasia* (Cambridge: Cambridge University Press, 2001); Reuven Amitai-Preiss and David O. Morgan, *Mongol Empire and Its Legacy* (Leiden: E. J. Brill, 1999); Rene Grousset, *Empire of the Steppes: A History of Central Asia,* trans. Naomi Wallford (New Brunswick, N.J.: Rutgers University Press, 1970); Peter Jackson, "The Dissolution of the Mongol Empire," *Central Asiatic Journal* 22 (1978): 186–243; David Morgan, *Mongols* (Oxford: Basil Blackwell, 1986); H. F. Schurmann, "Mongol Tributary Practices of the Thirteenth Century," *Harvard Journal of Asiatic Studies* 19 (1956): 304–389.

Mongolia, State of The only independent state for the Mongol peoples and for many decades the only independent state in Central and Inner Asia, the State of Mongolia lies between China and Russia. Its borders have been roughly fixed at their present form since 1915, although there was great controversy over Mongolia's status until after WORLD WAR II. Ethnically, Mongolia's 2.4 million people are overwhelmingly ethnic Mongols speaking one or another Mongolian dialect. All of the Mongols are traditionally Buddhist, although some also have active traditions of SHAMANISM. Non-Mongols include the KAZAKHS (about 5 percent of the population) in the far west, who are Turkic-speaking Muslims, and small numbers of Chinese and Russian immigrants. Among the Mongol ethnic groups, the KHALKHA, at 79 percent, form the overwhelmingly dominant group. Other main Mongolian subgroups include the various Oirat ethnic groups in the west (about 7.5 percent) and the BURIATS in the northeast (1.7 percent).

With the 1911 RESTORATION of Mongolian independence from China's QING DYNASTY, the country entered its THEOCRATIC PERIOD. This period ended in disaster, with Mongolia fought over by Chinese and White Russia troops. The 1921 REVOLUTION began Mongolia's REVOLUTIONARY PERIOD, which ended with the GREAT PURGE (1937–40) and the destruction of Buddhism, solidifying the new regime as a Communist dictatorship. Called the MONGOLIAN PEOPLE'S REPUBLIC from 1924 to 1992, Mongolia received massive Soviet aid that created a new industrial and largely urbanized society. In 1990, however, the collapse of the Soviet bloc sparked the 1990 DEMOCRATIC REVOLUTION, which led to the adoption of the 1992 CONSTITUTION and the renaming of the country to simply the State of Mongolia.

MONGOLIAN GEOGRAPHY IN WORLD COMPARISON

The State of Mongolia lies in eastern Inner Asia. The country's territory covers 1,566,500 square kilometers (604,830 square miles), roughly the size of Texas, Oklahoma, New Mexico, and Arizona or Germany, the Low Countries,

France, Spain, and Portugal combined. The country is roughly lens shaped and has a 3,485-kilometer (2,165-mile) land border with Russia and a 4,673-kilometer (2,904-mile) border with China. As a landlocked country sandwiched between two great powers, modern Mongolia has always faced serious threats to its independence.

The country stretches between latitudes 52°09" and 41°35", or roughly from the latitude of Cleveland to that of Saskatoon or Rome to London, yet Mongolia's capital, ULAANBAATAR, whose climate is close to the country's average, has temperature extremes similar to those of Fairbanks, Alaska. As in many cold weather areas, vegetation is relatively abundant despite a level of precipitation similar to that of Tucson or Tehran. Mongolia's average altitude is 1,580 meters (5,184 feet) above sea level.

The State of Mongolia is the most sparsely populated independent country in the world. In 2000 the total population of 2,407,500 persons was distributed at just over 1.5 persons per square kilometer (3.9 per square mile). By comparison, Australia has 2.3 persons per square kilometer (6 per square mile) and Wyoming 1.8 per square kilometer (4.7 per square mile) (see CLIMATE; FAUNA; FLORA; MONGOLIAN PLATEAU).

GOVERNMENT AND POLITICS

Since the 1990 Democratic Revolution and the adoption of the 1992 Constitution, Mongolia has made the transition from Soviet-style communism to a democratic and pluralist society with a market economy. Mongolia's 1992 Constitution guarantees basic democratic freedoms and unlike those in the previous constitutions, these guarantees are observed in practice. Demonstrations are a routine aspect of political life, and there are no prisoners of conscience. The major newspapers and some cable television channels are now privately owned and represent a range of views. (*On the formal structure of the state, see* 1992 CONSTITUTION.) Mongolia's foreign policy is formally one of neutrality and nonalignment, although in reality since 1991 it has been closely aligned with the Western countries (see FOREIGN RELATIONS).

Given Mongolia's small population and unicameral legislature elected at one time by a first-past-the-post system, Mongolian elections have seen wild fluctuations in party strength in each election. In 1992 the Mongolian People's Revolutionary Party (MPRP), the former Communist Party then in transition to becoming a democratic party, received 72 of 76 seats in the Great People's Khural. In 1996, however, the opposition Democratic Coalition received 50 of 75 seats, while in 2000 the MPRP again won 72 of 76 seats. In 1993 and 1997 Mongolian voters used the presidential elections, which take place one year after the parliamentary elections, to check these lopsided mandates, although in 2001 the MPRP candidate also won the presidency.

The Mongolian party system is still dominated by the MPRP, whose base is older, more rural, and culturally conservative voters than the other parties. This rural base has given the MPRP a continued lock on local government; even in 1996, 52 percent of local deputies were MPRP members, and in 2000 the number rose to 89 percent. Several new parties emerged from the 1990 Democratic Revolution, of which the Democratic Party was the largest. After the failure of the 1992 election, the Democratic Party and several smaller parties merged to form the National Democratic Party (NDP). In 1996 they formed a winning Democratic Coalition with the Social Democrats (a smaller party formed in 1990), but shortly before the 2000 election the coalition broke up, and they campaigned separately. In 2000 the NDP gained only one seat and the Social Democrats none; instead, two new parties, the Civic Courage-Republican Party led by S. Oyuun (b. 1964), the sister of the slain democratic leader SANJAASÜRENGIIN ZORIG, and the New Democratic Socialist Party shared the other three non-MPRP seats. The NDP and the Social Democrats have now merged into a new Democratic Party, and discussions are proceeding with the New Democratic Socialist Party.

The chief issue in Mongolian elections has been economic management. Generally, the MPRP is seen as having a more statist approach, while the Democrats represent free-market liberalism. The new parties in the 2000 parliament see themselves as moderates between these two extremes. In fact, while the 1992–96 MPRP administration of Prime Minister P. Jasrai (b. 1933) was relatively slow in PRIVATIZATION, the 2000 MPRP administration of Nambaryn Enkhbayar (b. 1958) has mostly continued the free-market policies of the Democratic Coalition, including controversial land privatization. The freedom of action of Mongolia's government is limited by harsh economic constraints and the priorities of donor countries and international aid organizations.

The new elite of Mongolia is a continuation of the late socialist elite created by massive urbanization from the 1960s on. Most of the leaders of the MPRP and the democratic movement were educated in the Soviet Union or Eastern Europe, which, regardless of their often humble rural origins, made them part of the socialist elite. One important division in this elite was and remains that between the managers, who mostly stayed with the MPRP, at least at first, and the intellectuals (academics, writers, and artists), who led the democratic movement. Another difference is age, with the MPRP leaders being mostly born before and the democratic movement leaders mostly after 1955.

Despite the continuity in elites, government corruption has, at least in popular impression, become a much more serious problem since the democratic transition. (An accurate assessment of high-level corruption before 1990 is, of course, virtually impossible to obtain.) Scandals associated with banking and later privatization have touched all sides of the political spectrum, but particularly the democratic movement leaders. As is typical after

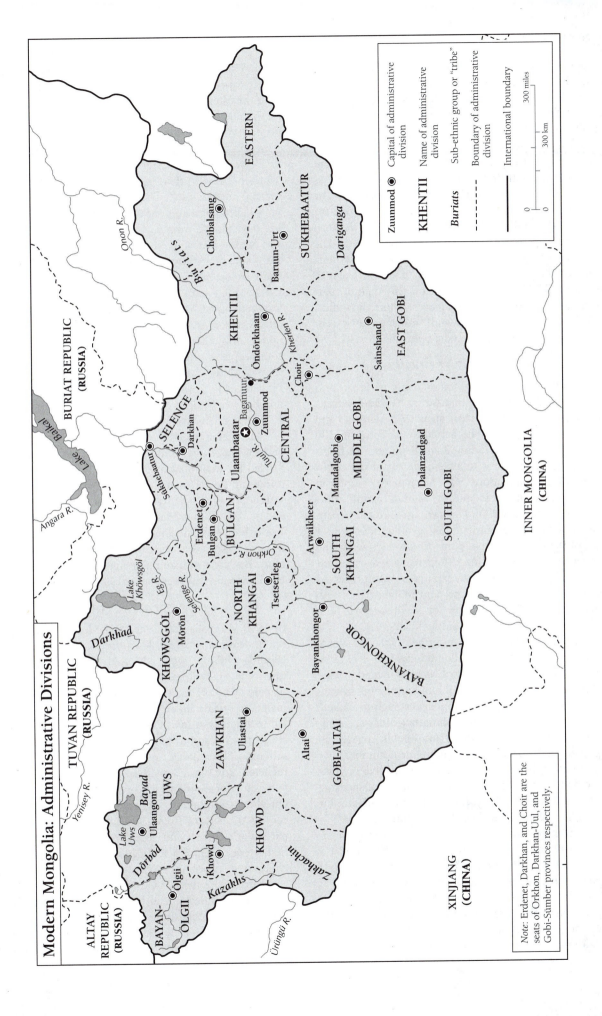

Modern Mongolia: Administrative Divisions

ALTAY REPUBLIC (RUSSIA)

TUVAN REPUBLIC (RUSSIA)

BURIAT REPUBLIC (RUSSIA)

INNER MONGOLIA (CHINA)

XINJIANG (CHINA)

Lake Baikal

Angara R.

Yenisey R.

Onon R.

Urüngü R.

Lake Uws

Bayad

Ulaangom

Dörböd

Ölgii

Khowd

Kazakhs

Zakhachin

Darkhad

Lake Khöwsgöl

Eg R.

Selenge R.

Mörön

Lake Uws

BAYAN-ÖLGII

KHOWD

UWS

ZAWKHAN

Uliastai

Altai

GOBI-ALTAI

KHÖWSGÖL

NORTH KHANGAI

Tsetserleg

Bayankhongor

BAYANKHONGOR

SOUTH KHANGAI

Arwaikheer

Sükhebaatur

Erdenet

Bulgan

BULGAN

Orkhon R.

Darkhan

SELENGE

Ulaanbaatar

Tuul R.

Zuunmod

Bagannuur

CENTRAL

Mandalgobi

MIDDLE GOBI

Choir

Sainshand

SOUTH GOBI

Dalanzadgad

Buriats

Choibalsang

EASTERN

Baruun-Urt

SÜKHEBAATUR

Dariganga

KHENTII

Öndörkhaan

Kherlen R.

EAST GOBI

Legend:

Zuunmod ◉ Capital of administrative division

KHENTII Name of administrative division

Buriats Sub-ethnic group or "tribe"

‒ ‒ ‒ Boundary of administrative division

—— International boundary

0   300 miles

0   300 km

Note: Erdenet, Darkhan, and Choir are the seats of Orkhon, Darkhan-Uul, and Gobi-Sumber provinces respectively.

the toppling of authoritarian governments, Mongolia has experienced a serious crime wave. From 1990 to 2000 the rate of violent crimes increased from 1.5 per 1,000 adults to 2.5, while that of property crimes increased from 1.8 per 1,000 to 3.6.

Radical opposition to the post-1990 democratic regimes comes from a vocal minority of vehement nationalists and cultural conservatives. Some, such as G. Boshigt (b. 1942), are disillusioned supporters of the 1990 democracy movement who see the hoped-for Mongolian cultural renaissance threatened by a cheap sensationalist pop culture and the privileges of the Communist-era "red aristocracy" replaced by new market inequalities. The distinguished poet OCHIRBATYN DASHBALBAR (1957–99) was elected on this type of platform in the 1992 and 1996 parliaments. While the radical nationalists denounce poverty and embrace statist economic policies, no genuine Marxist opposition exists.

LIFESTYLE AND ECONOMY

The Mongolian population is today a mix of urban and rural. In 2000 the capital, ULAANBAATAR, had 32.7 percent of the population, other urban areas 24.5 percent, and rural areas 42.8 percent. The agricultural sector, mostly nomadic herders but including a small number in farming, hunting, and forestry, totals 49 percent of the country's working population. Of Mongolia's employed persons, 14 percent are in mining, manufacturing, utilities, or construction, and 36.7 percent are in retail, repair, and other services. The agricultural sector produces 33.4 percent of the country's gross domestic product, while the industrial sectors account for 19.7 percent and trade and services 48.7 percent. The main exports are semiprocessed mineral products, such as copper and molybdenum, textiles such as CASHMERE, and raw or semiprocessed furs, skins, and hides (see ECONOMY, MODERN; MINING).

Most urban Mongols live in either high-rise apartment blocks (privatized as condominiums in 1997) or in fenced YURT courtyards (privatized as fully owned private land in 2003). Since 1990 a small number of large private houses have also been built. Appliances such as radios, televisions, refrigerators, and washing machines are common among the urban dwellers. Households engaged in Mongolia's traditional nomadic herding now number only 34.6 percent of the country's total; most still live in yurts and nomadize regularly. A small number of herding households have electricity provided by a generator or windmill, and about 17 percent have motorcycles.

The average annual income in Mongolia was estimated in 1998 as the purchasing power equivalent of US $1,356, somewhat more than that of the Philippines but well below that of either the former Soviet Union or of Asia's newly industrialized countries. Income has dropped significantly from the estimated $1,640 in 1990 due to the general economic crisis of the former Soviet bloc, although there has been a modest recovery since 1995. This economic decline has hit the small cities and towns especially hard, while the capital and rural areas have weathered it more successfully. About one-third of the population lives below the poverty line. The distribution of income, as measured by the Gini index number of 33.2 (1995 figure), is rather more egalitarian than in Russia, China, or the English-speaking democracies, but somewhat less so than in Japan or the western European social democracies.

Despite the economic crisis, Mongolian life expectancy has risen slowly from 63.7 years in 1990 to 65.1 in 1998. The main causes of death are cardiovascular problems and cancer; respiratory diseases, which used to be the main cause, have declined sharply since 1980. In the 1980s Mongolians married quite young (average age 20 for women and 24 for men), and in 1990 the total fertility rate was 4.5 children. During the transition, with economic difficulties and the legalization of abortion and contraception, the average age at first marriage rose two years and the fertility rate plummeted to 2.2 children. Probably due to the aggressive promotion of breast-feeding, however, infant mortality has dropped from 63.4 per 1,000 live births in 1990 to 35.4 in 2000.

Medical services were funded directly from the state budget under the communist government but are now funded by a national medical insurance system with premiums and copayments. Tibetan medicine, BARIACH (bone setters), and other traditional medicines have revived widely. While quantitative indicators of the health network show some decline, the quality of health care seems to have increased in the transition, and health care is one of the few areas of material living standards in which more people see improvement since 1990 than see decline.

EDUCATION AND CULTURE

By 1990 Mongolia had a universal education system based on 10 years of general education (from ages eight to 18). Herding children were educated in boarding schools at district (SUM) centers. Adult literacy was estimated at 96.5 percent by 1989, and there was no significant gap between male and female literacy. Since then the budget crisis has led to a deterioration in educational facilities and teacher-student ratios and to the introduction of fees for boarding schools. The change in the economy has not been reflected in the curriculum, leading to a mismatch between education and job opportunities. As a result, the enrollment of children eight to 18 dropped from 98 percent to 87 percent from 1990 to 2000. This has affected particularly boys, and female students now dominate higher education. Since 2000, however, the percentage of children in school has again swung upward.

During the democracy movement years the Mongolian press was dominated by party publications that discussed political questions and exposed the dark side of the communist era. By the mid-1990s the party publications had mostly folded due to lack of reader interest and were replaced by the commercial press. The state-run newspaper, *Ardyn erkh,* replaced the MPRP newspaper *Ünen,* "Truth," as the main newspaper in 1990. Ownership of *Ardyn erkh* and the other state-owned paper, *Zasgiin gazryn medee,* "Government News," was transferred to their staffs by the Democratic Coalition government in 1998–99. Now renamed *Ödriin sonin,* "Daily News," and *Zuuny medee,* "Century News," these two publications are the main newspapers, although after the MPRP's victory in 2000 *Ünen* has again increased its readership. There are still state-owned television and radio channels, but a number of privately owned television and radio broadcast channels and television cable channels are also available, including many foreign channels. In the capital television, with very cheap cable service, is the most widely used medium, while in the countryside radio is the only regular source of news.

Since 1990 there has been a tremendous revival in interest in pre-1921 Mongolian culture. CHINGGIS KHAN has become the premier national icon, treated with a combination of deep reverence and crass commercialization. Television programs, particularly during the time of the WHITE MONTH (lunar new year) and the NAADAM (national day celebrations), frequently feature historical dramas and brief introductions to Mongolian traditional culture, from games with sheep astragali to throat singing to Buddhist devotional poetry. Mongolia's Buddhist culture and legacy have also been revived both by individual believers and by state patronage of Mongolian cultural monuments, such as the statue of the Buddhist deity Migjid-Janraisig at GANDAN-TEGCHINLING MONASTERY (*see* LITERATURE; RELIGION).

Since 1990 Western and Asian popular culture, including music of various genres (Asian pop, folk rock, heavy metal, hip-hop, and so on), video games, pornography, and the Internet have spread widely in Mongolia. Scores of thousands of Mongolians, mostly from the capital, have emigrated to developed countries to seek opportunity. Mongolians both old and young often deplore the ignorance and neglect of youth toward their country's cultural heritage. Nevertheless filial piety has always been a deep ethical value of the Mongols, and songs of appreciation for one's mother are still very popular and widely sung with deep emotion.

See also ARMED FORCES OF MONGOLIA; MONGOL ZURAG.

Further reading: Martha Avery, *Women of Mongolia* (Boulder, Colo.: Asian Art and Archaeology, 1996); Ole Bruun and Ole Odgaard, eds., *Mongolia in Transition* (Richmond, Surrey: Curzon Press, 1996); Uradyn E. Bulag, *Nationalism and Hybridity in Mongolia* (Oxford: Oxford University Press, 1998); Keith Griffin, ed., *Poverty and the Transition to a Market Economy in Mongolia* (London: St. Martin's Press, 1995); *Human Development Report Mongolia 2000* (Ulaanbaatar: Government of Mongolia and United Nations Development Program, 2000); Jill

Lawless, *Wild East: Travels in the New Mongolia* (Toronto: ECW Press, 2000); National Statistical Office of Mongolia, *Mongolian Statistical Yearbook 2000* (Ulaanbaatar: National Statistical Office, 2001); Ricardo Neupert, *Urbanization and Population Redistribution in Mongolia* (Honolulu: East-West Center, 1994).

Mongolian language Mongolian, spoken by perhaps 4.5 million people, is the national language of Mongolia and a regional language of Inner Mongolia in China. It is by far the largest and most important language in the Mongolic family and has a written history dating back to the 13th century. While Mongolian sometimes is said to include the closely related Buriat and Kalmyk-Oirat languages, they are not included in this discussion (*see* BURIAT LANGUAGE AND SCRIPTS *and* KALMYK-OIRAT LANGUAGE AND SCRIPTS).

DIALECTS AND DISTRIBUTION

Mongolian has numerous dialects, some of which shade into the Kalmyk-Oirat and Buriat languages to the west and north. Mongolian, together with Kalmyk-Oirat and Buriat, form the New Mongolian subfamily within the larger MONGOLIC LANGUAGE FAMILY. Modern Mongolian evolved in the 17th–18th centuries from Middle Mongolian, the medieval form of the language.

The dialects included within Mongolian proper can be divided into two main groups, the central Mongolian dialects and the east Mongolian dialects. The central Mongolian dialects include Mongolia's main dialect, KHALKHA. The Khalkha in Mongolia number 1,610,400, or 78.8 percent of the country's population (1989 figures) and show certain dialectal variations, although these do not impede communication. Mongolia's DARIGANGA (28,600, or 1.4 percent, DARKHAD (14,300, or 0.7 percent), and ÜJÜMÜCHIN (2,100 in Mongolia) also speak central Mongolian dialects.

In Inner Mongolia the central Mongolian dialects can be divided into 1) the Gobi group (Abaga, Sönid, eastern ULAANCHAB, and ALASHAN), which is phonologically virtually identical to southern, or Gobi, Khalkha, although Alashan dialect shows Oirat features; 2) the CHAKHAR group (Chakhar, Üjümüchin, Kheshigten, and Urad); and 3) ORDOS, which mixes Chakhar and Oirat features. Excluding Inner Mongolian districts where the Mongols have lost their language, Mongols in the Gobi area number 203,000, in the Chakhar group area 184,000, and in Ordos 102,000.

Inner Mongolia and Manchuria's east Mongolian dialects differ substantially from the central Mongolian dialects, and some are, in their pure form, virtually incomprehensible to Khalkha speakers. These dialects can be divided into 1) the JUU UDA group, which is the closest to central Mongolian; 2) the Josotu group (including the now virtually extinct KHARACHIN dialect and the living Monggoljin, or Fuxin, dialect); 3) the KHORCHIN group (including Jarud); and 4) the Far Eastern group (including Jalaid, DÖRBED, and Gorlos). Excluding districts where Mongolian has been mostly replaced by Chinese, Mongols in the Juu Uda area number 402,000 and the Khorchin areas 1,014,000. The Far Eastern and Josotu groups are mostly spoken in China's Manchurian provinces and number perhaps 235,000 and 175,000 speakers, respectively (based on 1990 figures).

OFFICIAL DIALECTS AND LANGUAGE STATUS

In Mongolia central Khalkha (i.e., the dialect spoken around the capital, ULAANBAATAR), written in the Cyrillic script, is the official national language. As the national language, it is spoken by non-Mongol immigrants, by urban populations all over the country, and to an increasing degree even by non-Khalkha rural populations. Although standard Inner Mongolian is based on the Chakhar dialect of Plain Blue banner (Zhenglanqi), in reality the sheer numbers and relatively high educational levels of the Khorchin and Juu Uda Mongols have given a strong east Mongolian cast to the spoken language of educated INNER MONGOLIANS. It is written in the UIGHUR-MONGOLIAN SCRIPT.

The most characteristic phonological feature separating Khalkha from standard Inner Mongolian is the split of middle Mongolian affricates *ch* and *j* into *ch/j* before *i* and *ts/dz* (conventionally written *z*) before other vowels. Thus, middle Mongolian *jam*, "road," and *jima*, "way, manner," become *dzam* and *jam* in Khalkha but *jam* and *jäm* in standard Inner Mongolian. This Khalkha split is shared with Kalmyk-Oirat and Buriat, although it is realized in a different way.

Compounding these differences in pronunciation are those in vocabulary: Compare Khalkha (*niisekh*) *ongots* and Inner Mongolian *niisgel* for "airplane," Khalkha *toglokh* and Inner Mongolian *naadakh* for "to play," Khalkha *olon* and Inner Mongolian *ärwin* for "many," and so on. Russian loanwords in Khalkha and Chinese loanwords in Inner Mongolian add to the contrast. The usage of verb forms, particularly in the past tense, is also different, although the differences have not been adequately described.

In Inner Mongolia and Manchuria Mongolian language is being transmitted to the next generation primarily in rural areas, whether herding or farming. In urban environments children generally do not achieve fluency. Mongolian-language publishing and writing are heavily subsidized in China, and in the Mongol-dominant rural areas Mongolian is used for official purposes at the SUM (township) and sometimes banner (county) level, yet the lack of jobs for persons trained in Mongolian is blighting the prospects of Mongolian-language education in Inner Mongolia.

Language planning in both Mongolia and Inner Mongolia is concerned primarily with the creation of technical terminology. In both areas the aim of using Mongolian neologisms rather than loanwords is officially promoted, but in Inner Mongolia in particular such neologisms frequently exist only on paper. In Mongolia the source of loanwords in recent years has switched from Russian (*oochirlo-*, "to stand in line," from Russian *ócher,* "queue, line," *siliiser,* "pipe-fitter, repairman" from Russian *slésar'*), to English (*menajment,* "management," *ii-meil,* "e-mail"). As seen from these examples, loanwords, once established, are generally transformed according to vowel harmony based on the stressed vowel, which is treated as long. This phenomenon is also seen in Inner Mongolia, particularly with dialect loanwords such as Khorchin *piijii,* "airplane," from Chinese *feiji,* and SHILIIN GOL (*süüder*) *joolokh,* "to take a photograph," from Chinese *zhao* (*xiang*). Formal language planning in Mongolia and Inner Mongolia generally rejects these "Mongolized" loanwords in place of native Mongolian neologisms.

VOWEL HARMONY

The vowel system of Khalkha and standard Inner Mongolian maintains a two-way vowel harmony. The basic distinction is of back vowels (*a, o, u*) and front vowels (*e, ö, ü*), with *i* as neutral. The first syllable of a word establishes it as front or back, which constrains all subsequent vowels to be from the same category (except that *i* can appear in back words). Central Mongolian dialects also harmonize high (*o, ö*) and low (*a, e, u, ü*) vowels. High vowels cannot appear in words that begin with a low vowel, although long low vowels may appear in words beginning with high vowels. Case endings thus appear in at least two and as many as four vowel-harmonic forms, as shown by the past marker *-laa* in four verbs: *yawlaa,* "went," *khonoloo,* "spent the night," *elslee,* "joined, entered," and *törlöö,* "gave birth."

Compared to Middle Mongolian and Kalmyk-Oirat, the Mongolian rounded vowels have moved far back, so that what are conventionally rendered as *o, u, ö,* and *ü* are in fact ɔ, ɷ, ɵ, and ʉ. Khalkha and standard Inner Mongolian also show to a moderate degree the general New Mongolian trend toward palatalization of back vowels, particularly *a* and *o,* in the vicinity of *i*. This produces front vowels that are, in fact, still treated as "back" in vowel harmony. Palatalization strengthens to the east (Khorchin) and west (Kalmyk-Oirat) and is weakest in dialects such as Ordos and central Khalkha, midway between the two.

East Mongolian and Chakhar share with Buriat the Manchurian areal tendency to change *e* to ə and split *ö* into *ü* or ə. These changes with Inner Mongolian's strong palatalization of all back vowels in the vicinity of *i* transform the simple front-back opposition of other Mongolian languages into a center versus back/front opposition. At the same time, Middle Mongolian's consonantal reflection of vowel harmony disappears completely in Inner Mongolia with the merger of velar stop

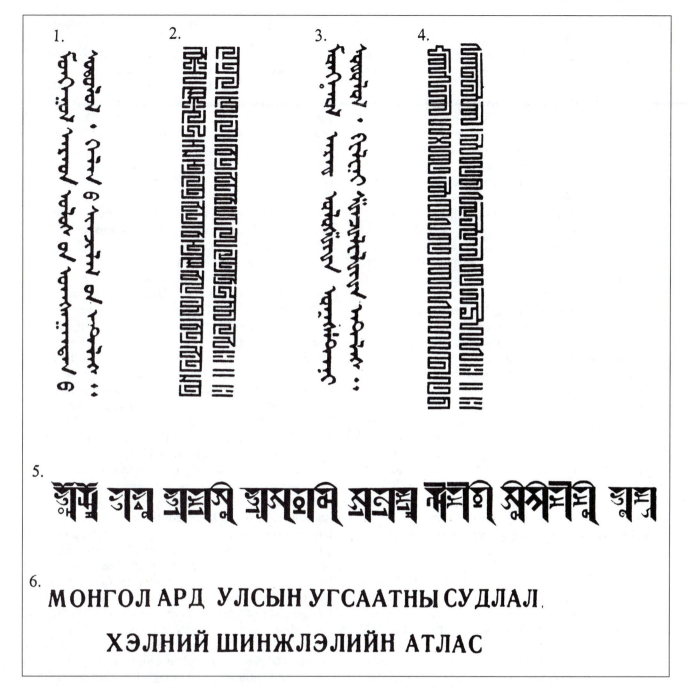

Scripts of the Mongolian language. 1) Duighur-Mongolian script, 2) Square Script, 3) Clear Script, 4) Ornamental version of the Uighur-Mongolian script, 5) Soyombo Script, 6) Cyrillic-script Mongolian *(From B. Rinchen,* Mongol Ard Ulsyn ugsaatny sudlal, khelnii shinjleliin atlas *[1979])*

allophones *g/gh* and *k/q* into *g* and *h*, respectively (in Khalkha *g/gh* are still distinct in prevocalic positions).

As in all New Mongolian languages, *u* diphthongs have been merged into long vowels, giving Mongolian phonemic vowel length as shown by minimal pairs such as *uul* (from *a'ula*), "mountain," and *ul* (from *ula*), "sole." The only surviving diphthongs are formed by back vowels or *ü* in combination with *i*, but these, too, show a tendency to merge into long vowels, palatalized or not. Short

noninitial vowels are sharply reduced, creating in effect a three-way length distinction of long, initial short, and noninitial short vowels.

AGGLUTINATION

Modern Mongolian is an agglutinative language, indicating grammatical relations by "gluing" one or more discrete endings onto the word root. Thus *khüükhdüüdeesee,* "from one's own children," breaks down into *khüükhed,* "child" + *üüd* PLURAL + *ees*, "from" + *ee* SUBJECT-POS-SESSIVE. There is no agreement (e.g., in gender or number) between nouns or adjectives and no subject-verb agreement (except in the imperative), and multiple nouns can be governed by a single final ending. In these aspects Modern Mongolian seems to be subject to East Asian areal influences, as Middle Mongolian retained traces of natural gender and agreement and Buriat and Kalmyk-Oirat have developed subject-verb agreement. Although some Middle Mongolian noun declensions and converb forms have been simplified (locative *-a*, dative *-da*, and dative-locative *-dur* have merged to dative-locative *-d/-t*) or have been replaced in Khalkha and standard Inner Mongolian by other forms (thus, the Middle Mongolian comitative *-lu'a*, "with," by *-tai*, and contemporal converb *-maghcha*, "as soon as," by *-nguud*), modern Mongolian in general has maintained complex declension and conjugation systems.

As an Altaic language, Mongolian generally uses verb endings called converbs in place of conjunctions and uses verbal nouns to form relative clauses. Modern Mongolian shows certain changes in the use of these forms. Khalkha and standard Inner Mongolian share with Buriat the elimination of preverbal negation by means of the particles *ülü* and *ese* with finite verb forms and their replacement by postverbal negation through adding *güi* (from *ügüi*, "without") to verbal noun forms. Thus, instead of Middle Mongolian *ese idebei*, "didn't eat," Modern Mongolian has *ideegüi* (Khalkha) or *idsengüi* (standard Inner Mongolian). In conditional and concessive clauses as well, verbal nouns with special particles (conditional *bol*, concessive *ch*) often replace converbs. In Khalkha verbal nouns frequently replace even affirmative finite verbs.

SCRIPTS

Around 1204 CHINGGIS KHAN adopted the Uighur script for his new MONGOL EMPIRE. His grandson QUBILAI KHAN tried to promote a new Tibetan-based SQUARE SCRIPT, but after the expulsion of the Mongols from China in 1368 Mongolian was again written solely in the Uighur-Mongolian script until 1932. The SOYOMBO SCRIPT, designed by Zanabazar in 1686, was more for ornamental inscriptions than for real use. A literary language called Classical Mongolian, written in the Uighur-Mongolian script, developed in the 17th century, which preserved many features of Middle Mongolian. Due to the monastic educational system, Mongolian was also written with Tibetan letters in the 19th and early 20th centuries.

In 1932 a Latin script was briefly adopted in independent Mongolia during the LEFTIST PERIOD of 1929–32. In 1940 a renewed Latinization movement was proposed but in 1941 superseded by Cyrillicization. The transfer to the Cyrillic script was not formally completed until 1950, however. In Inner Mongolia, after a brief experiment with the Cyrillic script in 1955–58, the Uighur-Mongolian script in a standardized postclassical orthography using modern inflectional endings has been used as the official script.

See also ALTAIC LANGUAGE FAMILY; CYRILLIC-SCRIPT MONGOLIAN; TIBETAN LANGUAGE AND SCRIPT.

Further reading: Robert I. Binnick, *Modern Mongolian: A Transformational Syntax* (Toronto: University of Toronto Press, 1979); Rita Kullmann and D. Tserenpil, *Mongolian Grammar*, 2d ed. (Hong Kong, 2001); John C. Street, *Khalkha Structure* (Bloomington: Indiana University, 1963); N. N. Poppe, *Grammar of Written Mongolian* (Wiesbaden: Otto Harrassowitz, 1954).

Mongolian People's Party, Third Congress of At this congress, which took place from August 4 to September 1, 1924, the "noncapitalist development" line was affirmed, and its opponent, GENERAL DANZIN, was shot.

From 1923 General Danzin, as de facto government leader, had aimed to restore Mongolia's natural trade links with China and to compromise with the Chinese firms on the issue of unpaid private debts. The dogmatism of many Russian and Buriat advisers, especially ELBEK-DORZHI RINCHINO, a Buriat Mongol member of the party's presidium, irked General Danzin as well as the prime minister, TSERINDORJI, and the party chairman "Japanese" Danzin (1875–1934; no relation to General Danzin, nicknamed from his visit to Japan in 1916). In April 1924 the two Danzins had denounced Rinchino as an enemy, yet Tserindorji patched up the quarrel.

In the congress's opening sessions Danzin defended the government's record, as the young party presidium member DAMBADORJI criticized its penny-wise, pound-foolish economizing and Rinchino dazzled the delegates with long speeches full of Soviet jargon. On August 26 Danzin absented himself from the sessions, later claiming plots against him were afoot in the army. The same day the youth league members of the Khüriye (modern ULAAN-BAATAR) branch entered to accuse their national leaders Babasang (1899–1924) and BUYANNEMEKHÜ, of stifling the youth league's revolutionary actions in collusion with Prime Minister Tserindorji. That night the delegates ordered Danzin's arrest and investigation. On August 30 Danzin and Babasang were executed, the one for plotting with Chinese capitalists and the other for making the youth league a rival party as Rinchino, noncapitalist development, and the principle of one-party autocracy triumphed. "Japanese" Danzin was demoted to ambassador to Moscow. Choibalsang replaced Danzin as commander in chief, and Dambadorji replaced "Japanese" Danzin as party chairman. Tserindorji's presence was considered important in calming the conservative populace, and he remained prime minister.

See also CHOIBALSANG, MARSHAL; MONGOLIAN PEOPLE'S REVOLUTIONARY PARTY; MONGOLIAN REVOLUTIONARY YOUTH LEAGUE; REVOLUTIONARY PERIOD.

Further reading: *Mongolia: Yesterday and Today* (Tianjin, n.d.).

Mongolian People's Republic Mongolia's official name from 1924 to 1992, the Mongolian People's Republic was founded as a revolutionary socialist regime, deeply dependent both materially and spiritually on the Soviet Union.

After the 1921 REVOLUTION the revolutionaries first established a constitutional monarchy that lasted until 1924. With the death of Mongolia's theocratic ruler in May 1924 (*see* JIBZUNDAMBA KHUTUGTU, EIGHTH), a people's republic with a new constitution was proclaimed in November (*see* 1924 CONSTITUTION). For the next 16 years radical social and intellectual change, Soviet control, and foreign tensions wracked the Mongolian People's Republic. After the horrific GREAT PURGE and the destruction of Buddhism (*see* BUDDHISM, CAMPAIGN AGAINST), the new state became stabilized as a communist dictatorship under MARSHAL CHOIBALSANG (1895–1952), Joseph Stalin's hand-picked man in Mongolia. (*For a survey of Mongolia from 1921 to 1940, see* REVOLUTIONARY PERIOD.) The Mongolian People's Republic was renamed the State of Mongolia in 1992 as a result of the 1990 DEMOCRATIC REVOLUTION. (*For Mongolia's contemporary situation, see* MONGOLIA, STATE OF.)

INTERNATIONAL STATUS AND FOREIGN RELATIONS

By 1940 Mongolia's status was still the same as in 1921: Dependent on the Soviet Union, Mongolia was treated as a breakaway territory by China and was ignored by other powers. As Choibalsang had hoped, WORLD WAR II generated a breakthrough in formal recognition. In 1945, as a condition of the Sino-Soviet Friendship Treaty, China's ruler, Chiang Kai-shek, agreed to recognize Mongolia, conditional on a plebiscite. In February 1946 China officially recognized Mongolia's independence. Efforts to become a member of the UNITED NATIONS were, however, stymied by emerging Soviet-American tensions and Mongolia's own diplomatic inexperience.

The Communist victory in China's civil war (1946–49) opened a new stage in Mongolia's international status. By 1960 Mongolia was a full member of the Communist bloc, with embassies in and active relations with not only China and the Soviet Union but also Eastern Europe, North Korea, North Vietnam, and neutral nations such as India. In 1961 Mongolia was finally admitted to the United Nations. The opening of diplomatic relations with Great Britain, France, and other West European countries soon followed, and those with Japan were achieved after difficult negotiations in February 1972. Even so, Mongolia's foreign policy remained slavishly dependent on the Soviet Union.

While Mongolia's formal diplomatic ties expanded, the security environment changed radically with the switch from the SINO-SOVIET ALLIANCE of the 1950s to the SINO-SOVIET SPLIT of the 1960s and 1970s. Mongolia now became the Soviet Union's frontline against its Chinese rival. The U.S. opening to the People's Republic of China in 1972 was thus of ambiguous significance. While it eliminated the issue of Chiang Kai-shek's obstructionism, Soviet fear of the potential U.S.-China alliance prevented any U.S.-Mongolia normalization.

The easing of Sino-Soviet tensions in 1985 and the breakup of the Soviet bloc in 1990 allowed Mongolia to establish relations with the United States in 1987 and South Korea in 1990, thus virtually completing Mongolia's quest for recognition. At the same time, the favorable conditions allowed Mongolia to become for the first time genuinely nonaligned and to pursue an independent foreign policy (*see* FOREIGN RELATIONS; SOVIET UNION AND MONGOLIA).

GOVERNMENT

In formal structure the Mongolian People's Republic was a democratic republic in which all positions were open to talent and in which regular elections decided the nation's top leadership. In reality, while upward mobility in society was real, the government structure oscillated between one-man rule and oligarchy. In general, the 10 or so members of the Politburo, or Political Bureau (Uls töriin towchoon), of the MONGOLIAN PEOPLE'S REVOLUTIONARY PARTY (MPRP) were the supreme authority. Choibalsang had ruled the Politburo with unquestioned authority until his death in 1952, but his hand-picked successor, YUMJAAGIIN TSEDENBAL (1916–91), had to share power with his colleagues until about 1964, when he managed to reestablish his dominance. Tsedenbal was deposed in 1984 through Soviet intervention when advancing senility made his slavish devotion to Russian ways an embarrassment. His successor, JAMBYN BATMÖNKH (b. 1926), presided over an increasingly aged oligarchy until the Democratic Revolution of 1990 toppled the Communist regime.

The MPRP's central committee, which slowly swelled to 90 or so members, contained all the chief figures in government. Meeting several times a year and in the 1950s and 1960s still the scene of serious debate, it was the closest thing to an open forum of the national elite. The top government organ was the council of ministers (Said naryn Zöwlel) or cabinet, headed by a chairman (*darga*) equivalent to a premier or prime minister. Until 1974 the republic's maximum leader held this position. As in the Soviet Union, state control of the diversifying economy multiplied the number of cabinet-level ministries, which reached 42 by 1981. The MPRP congresses and the Great People's Khural or legislature, ostensibly the supreme organs of party and government power, met only twice under Choibalsang's rule and under Tsedenbal were convened every five years for solely symbolic sessions. The eight-member presidium of the Great People's Khural performed certain routine government tasks, and its chairman was titular head of state. After 1974 this position, along with that of general secretary of the party's central committee, became the mark of the supreme leader. All these organs were chosen in pro forma elections with only one candidate; the sitting party branches actually chose the candidates.

Ideology was pervasive in the Mongolian People's Republic. Socialism, "proletarian internationalism" (i.e., a pro-Russian and pro-Soviet viewpoint), and a formulaic Marxism-Leninism were written into the 1960 CONSTITUTION as obligatory articles of faith for the whole citizenry. The regime required of its people repeated public affirmation that the Communist governments of Mongolia and the Soviet Union were the acme of human history. Compared even to other communist societies, such as in Eastern Europe, the limits of public discourse in Mongolia under Tsedenbal were extremely narrow. Mongolia's linguistic and cultural isolation, its defensiveness over the China threat, and its steadily increasing material prosperity helped keep dissent well within manageable limits. Nevertheless, many writers, academics, and party leaders such as BYAMBYN RINCHEN (1905–79), DARAMYN TÖMÖROCHIR (1921–85), and RENTSENII CHOINOM (1936–79) suffered verbal attacks, exile, and/or imprisonment for implicitly criticizing the regime's exaggerated Russophilia, its denial of Mongolian identity, and its refusal to honestly confront the crimes of the Great Purge era.

Local administration in Mongolia was highly centralized. After 1940 the country was divided into 18 provinces roughly equal in size and without any historical identity. They and the capital, ULAANBAATAR, had elected local administrations that were strictly controlled by the centralized party and government apparatus. Rural administration was merged after 1960 with the negdels, or herding collectives, while urban administration was often a passive bystander to the actions of the large factories that reported directly to their relevant ministries and hence were effectively beyond the reach of local government. In cases such as the Erdenet Soviet-Mongolian joint-stock company, the powerful managers were actually Soviet expatriates.

While income disparities in Mongolia were relatively low compared to those of many other countries, the ruling class enjoyed many tightly guarded privileges, such as entrance into the No. 2 Clinic attached to the Government Palace and to a network of special shops accessible only by special identification card, exemption from paying utilities or rent, and state-paid vacations abroad (i.e., in the Soviet Union or Eastern Europe) twice a year.

ECONOMICS AND FINANCE

The Mongolian People's Republic after 1940 saw the creation of a modern economy in Mongolia. In 1986 tögrögs the gross social product rose from 960 million tögrögs in 1940 to 17.75 billion in 1990. In per capita terms, this meant a sixfold increase in social product. The composition of the economy also changed. In 1959 the countryside was collectivized, and in the early 1960s a mechanized arable agriculture sector was created. Industrialization,

which began in 1934 with Ulaanbaatar's Industrial Combine, accelerated in the 1960s and in the 1970s was joined by the creation of a massive new mining sector. Railroad, motor, and airplane transportation led to the abolition of the traditional ulaa, or postroad, corvée duty in 1949. Thus, from 1940 to 1990 the composition of the Mongolian economy changed fundamentally. Herding and arable agriculture's share of the total social product declined from 64 percent to 15.7 percent, while industry and MINING's share rose from 12.7 percent to 49 percent. The percentage of the labor force employed in herding and arable agriculture declined from 69.9 percent in 1960 to 39 percent in 1990. (Exactly comparable figures for 1940 are not available, but the percentage of those in herding and farming was around 85 percent.) The industrial and mining labor force expanded from 14 percent in 1960 to 26.5 percent in 1990.

After 1960, and particularly after 1975, Soviet and Eastern European aid, both direct and indirect, reached vast proportions. In 1990 the total value of outstanding Soviet loans reached 10 billion "transferable rubles," a kind of trade counter used within the Soviet bloc; the real value of this debt in hard currency as well as the actual significance of Soviet aid has been the subject of deep and continuing controversy between Mongolia and Russia. Two-thirds of these loans were directed toward investment in agriculture, infrastructure, energy, housing, health, science, and culture. The other third was directed to cover Mongolia's chronic massive trade imbalance with the Soviet Union. Other forms of aid included the supply of whole factories, joint-stock companies for vast new investments in the transportation and mining sectors, and Soviet technical specialists. While the quality and exact value of these investments is controversial, the importance of foreign aid for the Mongolian People's Republic's development is not in doubt.

The Mongolian People's Republic began to plan economic growth with FIVE-YEAR PLANS in 1948. Only with collectivization in 1959 was the entire economy brought under state control. The planning process focused not only on raising the overall national income but on developing a diversity of new sectors as well as on spreading industrialization evenly over the whole country. Efficiency was a secondary concern. At the same time, the massive Soviet assistance was devoted primarily to developing raw materials industries, particularly in mining. As a result, the Mongolian economy by 1990 had competitive mining and animal husbandry sectors along with very inefficient light-industrial, construction, mechanized arable agriculture, and material supply and repair sectors. Factories and construction enterprises in the provinces were particularly uncompetitive.

The economic changes and massive foreign aid also fundamentally altered the Mongolian People's Republic's finances. From 1948 to 1989 direct taxation of the populace virtually disappeared, falling from 23 percent of the budget to less than 1 percent. Foreign loans and aid, however, jumped from a negligible 4.1 percent to 24 percent. Sales taxes, customs revenues, and resale profits on sales of goods through state trade organizations remained the main source of income, but taxes on industrial profits rose in importance. Moreover, much of the resale and sales tax revenues now amounted to foreign subsidy, as the artificially low prices of imported Soviet goods allowed the government to profit on resale while avoiding consumer discontent. In expenditures, defense and administrative costs declined from 49 percent of the budget in 1948 to only 13 percent in 1989. In 1948 social and cultural expenses (education, health, social security, etc.), at 27 percent of the budget, predominated over "material" expenses (agriculture, industry, housing, etc.), with 16 percent of expenditures, but the opposite was true in 1989: The material sector took 47 percent and the social-cultural expenses 39 percent of the budget.

With the growth in the economy and massive foreign assistance, living standards also saw some improvements. Real per capita income expanded 65 percent from 1965 to 1988. From 1970 to 1990 the percentage of households with a television rose from 6 percent to 41 percent, while that of households with a refrigerator rose from 2 percent to 35 percent. Meanwhile, fees for utilities and rents in state-owned apartments remained fixed, becoming in effect a steadily increasing subsidy for the urban population. Despite the universal health care and pension system instituted after collectivization, the quality of health care appears to have been quite low. In 1964–65 the government claimed a life expectancy of 65 years, and that infant mortality had dropped to 70 per 1,000 live births. Later figures show that in 1960 the life expectancy was actually 47 years, which by 1980 had risen to 58; 1990 infant mortality was 73 per 1,000 live births. Unhealthy habits impeded improvements in public health. Respiratory disorders were by far the leading cause of death, and by 1990 fewer than half of mothers were breast-feeding their children.

SOCIAL CHANGE

The major social change in the Mongolian People's Republic was the postwar population boom and the advance of urbanization. From around 1947–49 in the eastern and southern provinces and about five years later in the western provinces, fertility rates showed a dramatic increase related to the creation of special clinics to eliminate venereal diseases and improve women's health, the provision of stovepipes to reduce smokiness in yurts, and the inculcation of a strongly pronatalist policy. From the late 1940s to 1960 the annual population growth rate jumped from zero to almost 3 percent, where it remained until 1990. Mongolia's population went from 759,200 in the 1944 census to 2,044,000 in the 1989 census. This baby boom resulted in a very youthful population, with more than 55 percent of the population 19 or under in 1979.

Much of the surging new population moved to the cities. From the 1956 census to that of 1989, the urban percentage increased from 21.6 percent to 57 percent, which, combined with the total population growth, caused Mongolia's urban population to explode from 183,000 to 1,166,100. While Ulaanbaatar was the only significant city in 1956, by 1989 the new industrial-mining towns of DARKHAN CITY and ERDENET CITY had sprung up. Heavy investment in housing kept the unplanned YURT districts around the cities and towns at manageable proportions, and in Ulaanbaatar the middle and upper classes were mostly living in high-rise apartments by 1990.

The constitutions of the Mongolian People's Republic had proclaimed male-female equality since 1924, and the Mongolian government also saw women's labor as an important part of the solution to the country's perennial labor shortage. The male-female literacy gap was largely resolved in the 1950s, and in 1979 women were 50 percent of all secondary school graduates and 34 percent of those with at least some higher education. In 1992 73 percent of working-age women were in the labor force compared to 79 percent of men. In 1987, at the height of the industrial boom, women had an unemployment rate triple that of men, but overall rates were still very low. Women's education, employment, the housing shortage, and availability of pensions all stoked a trend toward smaller family size, and despite the prohibition on contraception and abortion, the total fertility rate dropped from a maximum of 8 in 1963 to 4.5 in 1990.

EDUCATION, CULTURE, AND THE ARTS

Under the Mongolian People's Republic Mongolian cultural life was pushed firmly in a European direction. The switch from the traditional UIGHUR-MONGOLIAN SCRIPT to the Cyrillic alphabet was completed by 1950 and ensured that the large new cohort of Mongolians would not have direct access to the literary monuments of the past. Official statistics put literacy among those aged nine to 50 rising from 24 percent in 1940 to 60 percent in 1947 and 95 percent in 1956, a rate that was maintained until 1990. By the mid-1950s the once sharp male-female gap in literacy had been essentially eliminated. Since the rural population remained largely nomadic, a boarding school for herders' children had to be established in every SUM center.

Mass media also reached an increasingly large public. By 1970 35 percent of households had a radio and 6 percent a television; the average person saw eight movies per year. In 1985 radios were in 51 percent of households and televisions in 30 percent, while the average person saw 10 movies. Television and radio were owned by the state, while the main newspaper (Ünen, "Truth") was put out by the MPRP. At the mass level Mongolian culture under the people's republic focused around a limited number of stereotyped socialist-realist themes: the national liberation struggle, the illiterate but wise old herdsman, the unshakeable Soviet-Mongolian friendship, the antifascist war, the peace movement, the unmasking of the spy, the smiles of innocent children, the romantic artist, the girl on a tractor, and the heroine mother.

From the 1940s, the Mongolians began producing their own successful examples of European arts and entertainment. This included the full-length feature film (*Tsogtu Taiji*, 1945), the Mongolian State Circus (opened in 1941), and European style opera, symphonies, and ballet. A few Western-style popular music groups formed in the 1960s. Meanwhile, the assimilation of Marxism-Leninism, while shot through with tendentious dogma, opened to Mongolian intellectuals in the 1950s many aspects of European social science and historiography. The search for national identity was also visible in the developing of the neo-traditional MONGOL ZURAG (Mongolian painting) genre, which flourished in the late 1950s and 1960s.

At the same time, the government and the intelligentsia waged a covert struggle over the issue of nationalism. The CHINGGIS KHAN CONTROVERSY began with the Politburo's aggressive attack on intellectual trends in 1949, parallel with attacks on GESER and other non-Russian epic heroes in the Soviet Union itself. De-Stalinization from 1956 to 1963 promised significantly greater freedom, but in 1956 intellectuals who had been encouraged to air their criticisms were suddenly slapped down by the Mongolian ruler Tsedenbal, and in 1959 the scholar B. Rinchen was publicly attacked as a nationalist. In 1963 Tsedenbal delivered a series of blows against Chinggis Khan, the frank treatment of the Great Purge in the film *Tümenii neg* (One in a million), and revisionist trends in Marxism-Leninism. Later in 1969 he attacked abstract art, professors such as Sh. Gaadamba and TSENDIIN DAMDINSÜREN who encouraged too much free thinking among their students, and in 1979–80 scholars who criticized the overemphasis on Russian and who used Chinese historical sources. As a result, the 1970s and 1980s were culturally and academically a barren era in which approved classics were honored but new approaches stifled. Not until the new era of "openness" began in 1986 did Mongolia's cultural life return to the themes first broached in the late 1950s and early 1960s.

See also ARMED FORCES OF MONGOLIA; COLLECTIVIZATION AND COLLECTIVE HERDING; ECONOMY, MODERN; LITERATURE; NAMES, PERSONAL.

Further reading: Academy of Sciences, MPR, *Information Mongolia* (Oxford: Pergamon Press, 1990); Tsedendambyn Batbayar, *Modern Mongolia: A Concise History* (Ulaanbaatar: Offset Printing, Mongolian Center for Scientific and Technical Information, 1996); D. Dashpurev and S. K. Soni, *Reign of Terror in Mongolia, 1920–1990* (New Delhi: South Asian Publishers, 1992); Alan J. K. Sanders, *Mongolia: Politics, Economics, and Society* (Boulder, Colo.: Lynne Rienner, 1987); State Statistical Office of the MPR, *National Economy of the MPR for 70 Years* (Ulaanbaatar: State Statistical Office, 1991).

Mongolian People's Revolutionary Party   Beginning as the Mongolian People's Party and dedicated to restoring Mongolian independence from the Chinese, the Mongolian People's Revolutionary Party (MPRP) was gradually transformed into an imitation of the Soviet Communist Party. After 1990, however, the party changed again into a nonideological party in a democratic and market-oriented Mongolia.

ORIGINS

The Mongolian People's Party began as the union of two conspiratorial groups formed in late 1919 in response to the REVOCATION OF AUTONOMY. The larger group, led by GENERAL DANZIN, was composed of petty officials in the theocratic government, and the smaller group, led by BODÔ, was composed of several former lamas and other commoners (*see* 1921 REVOLUTION).

Danzin's and Bodô's groups came together to found the Outer Mongolian People's Party on or around June 25, 1920. The party's aims, as expressed in its early documents, were to protect the Mongolian religion and nation, to restore Mongolian independence, and to conduct reforms to improve the poor commoners' lives. From the beginning the party sought Russian help and showed no fear of Soviet Russia.

Once the party began organizing on Russian territory, Buriat Mongols there joined the party, adding to its sophistication and leftist tendencies. From March 1–3, 1921, 26 party members convened at Troitskosavsk (in modern KYAKHTA CITY) and elected Danzin party chairman, while approving a manifesto drafted by the Buriat member TSYBEN ZHAMTSARONOVICH ZHAMTSARANO. (This meeting was designated the party's First Congress in 1924.) The manifesto called for restoring Outer Mongolia's equality as an independent state with other nations but also advocated eventual pan-Mongolian unification, possibly within a progressive, confederated China. Customs incompatible with the times would be abolished, but the party was willing to work with other friendly parties.

Buriat and Russian advisers had been calling the party the People's Revolutionary Party, but Danzin insisted that the word *revolutionary* was too controversial, although the manifesto spoke of applying the "firm principles of a revolutionary party." Only in March 1925, after Mongolia had been declared a people's republic, did the party become the People's Revolutionary Party.

After the revolutionaries were installed in power, the party was still small, numbering only 225 at the beginning of 1922 and 799 a year later. Danzin, the major national leader, resigned his position as party chairman in December 1921, and the party's central committee functioned more as a talk shop than a real decision-making body. Meanwhile, the MONGOLIAN REVOLUTIONARY YOUTH LEAGUE, organized in fall 1921, functioned as the leftwing opposition. Only in July–August 1923, with the party's First Congress (later renumbered as the Second), was a formal party constitution adopted. Rapid expansion brought party membership to around 3,000 at the beginning of 1924.

In August 1924, at the party's Third Congress, a new principle of one-party rule was enforced with executions, subordinating the youth league to the party's leadership. Under ELBEK-DORZHI RINCHINO and Dambadorji, the party finally became the real center of power. When the Communist International (Comintern), the Moscow-based league of Communist and anticolonial parties, appointed a formal representative to the party, the party's presidium became Moscow's chief transmission route for its policies in Mongolia.

AS A RULING PARTY, 1924–1940

At the Fourth Congress of the Mongolian People's Revolutionary Party (September 1925), the Comintern representatives imposed a new party program. This second party program rejected pan-Mongolism, calling instead for cooperation first with the Soviet Union and then with people's parties in Tuva, China, Korea, Japan, and elsewhere. Members were to "totally liquidate the remnants of the yellow and black [that is, clerical and lay] reactionaries," remove counterrevolutionaries and exploiters from government, and struggle for the "real people." The program also called for the extension of public education, literacy, clubs, state-owned factories and banks, farming, cooperatives, hospitals, and an eight-hour workday.

Dambadorji's leadership adopted a cautious attitude toward implementing this ambitious program, and in autumn 1928 he was overthrown by the Comintern delegation. The leftist leaders who came to power in 1928 purged members of "exploiting" class backgrounds or habits from the party, reducing membership from 15,810 at the beginning of 1929 to 12,019 a year later. The subsequent LEFTIST PERIOD (1929–32) ventured beyond the 1925 program into collectivization and open attacks on religion. By 1932 the party ranks were swelled to more than 40,000 in an effort to recruit the poor herders, women, and other unrepresented groups. With the failure of the leftist policies, the NEW TURN POLICY (1932–36) under Prime Minister GENDÜN cut down the party ranks to less than 10,000 by 1933, and local branches were temporarily suspended. The following GREAT PURGE of 1937–40 drowned the old party in blood and created a new one under MARSHAL CHOIBALSANG (r. 1936–52), the only party leader of the 1921 generation to survive.

With the Great Purge and the destruction of the monasteries (see BUDDHISM, CAMPAIGN AGAINST), a new party program was needed. The 1940 party program highlighted Mongolia's "noncapitalist development," by which Mongolia was, with assistance from the Soviet Union, jumping directly from feudalism to socialism. The 1940 program also affirmed the teachings of Marx-Engels-Lenin-Stalin as "the only true science." It also formally committed the party to careful but intensive antireligious propaganda and voluntary collectivization.

From August 1921 the party center had issued a weekly journal under many names, finally settling in April 1925 on Ünen (Truth), imitating the Soviet Union's Pravda. During the 1930s it moved to a daily format. In March 1924 the party began a short educational course with 60 students training for one month. A year later it was expanded into the Central Party School, and by 1927 its programs were expanded to three years. By 1941 it had graduated more than 1,000 students.

PARTY LEADERSHIP AND ORGANIZATION

From 1923 to 1928 party congresses had occurred yearly and entertained relatively frank debate. From 1930 to 1960 only six congresses were held, each time to ratify key decisions a year or two after they had been made. From 1961 the party congresses became purely symbolic events, held every five years to coincide with those of the Soviet Union and the formulation of the FIVE-YEAR PLANS.

Despite the party congresses, at no time did the party's membership actually exercise control over the leadership. While the congresses supposedly elected the Central Committee, which in turn elected a small standing body called either the presidium or (after 1940) the political bureau (or Politburo), all elections were decided beforehand by the existing leaders. Before 1929 the party's titular head was a chairman assisted by a secretary and deputy, elected by the Central Committee. In late 1928 the Comintern replaced them with three equal secretaries to weaken the party's ability to resist its directives.

From 1924 to 1936 no single person dominated the party, and the party's real ruling organ, the presidium, was the ultimate decision-making body, where top leaders hammered out their differences. After the Great Purge, however, Choibalsang exercised unchallenged one-man rule. The new position of general secretary of the Central Committee was given to his designated successor, YUMJAAGIIN TSEDENBAL. After Choibalsang's death the party returned to the collective rule of the Politburo, with Tsedenbal as first among equals. By 1964, however, Tsedenbal had ousted his rivals and established another period of one-man rule that lasted until his own dismissal in 1984. After his dismissal JAMBYN BATMÖNKH succeeded him as general secretary until the 1990 DEMOCRATIC REVOLUTION. Under Tsedenbal and Batmönkh the party grew increasingly geriatric. By 1990 50 percent of the Central Committee members were beyond retirement age, and one-third had been members of the Central Committee uninterruptedly since 1965.

AS A RULING PARTY, 1940–1990

From 1952 to 1986 the party membership increased from about 3.5 percent to 4.6 percent of the population. Party membership was the precondition for advancement into high managerial positions. The party's newspaper, Ünen, and other journals, the Central Party School, and facilities throughout the country made it a pervasive presence. In all large social organizations (collectives, or *negdels*, factories, universities, cities, etc.) the unit's regular head (as a rule a party member, too) worked in tandem with a party secretary, who ran that unit's party branch. This dual organization secured greater top-down control, although open conflict between the two leaders was not common.

With collectivization of the herds completed in 1959, a fourth program was adopted at the party's Fifteenth Congress (June 1966). This program opened with a thoroughly mythological description of the party's history as inspired by the "Great Socialist Revolution of October," led by the "outstanding revolutionary GENERAL SÜKHE-BAATUR," assisted by the "victorious proletariat of the Soviet Union," guided by meetings with "the great revolutionary Lenin," following the "Marxist-Leninist general line," and so on. The current task was "developing the material-technical base of socialism"; hence, economic development and increasing social services were accorded the primary position. This program served the party until 1990.

To build its prestige in the Soviet bloc, the MPRP encouraged the study of Marxism-Leninism and increased the number of workers in the party. The party founders, Danzin and Bodô, were already dead when the first work of Marxism-Leninism, the *Communist Manifesto* (1925), was translated into Mongolian by the Buriat Ishidorji. Only in 1946 was a Marxist-Leninist section organized in the ACADEMY OF SCIENCES, and in 1955 an Institute of Party History was attached to the MPRP's Central Committee. The first large body of Marxist works translated into Mongolian, Joseph Stalin's collected works, was completed in 1954 but fell out of favor with de-Stalinization in 1963. Lenin's complete works were translated only in 1967, in language often unreadably literal.

From around 1950 to 1970 a new group of intellectual Marxists emerged, including DARAMYN TÖMÖR-OCHIR, L. Tsend, Ts. Lookhuuz, and Sh. Agwaandondow, who approached the party's history and contemporary social issues from a fresh reading of the Marxist classics. As with the "revisionist" movement in Eastern Europe emerging at the same time, such approaches soon carried them outside party orthodoxy, and they were all exiled or imprisoned by Tsedenbal. From then on Marxism-Leninism was restricted to approved party formulas.

The effort to turn the MPRP into a party of workers, as befitted a communist party, had similarly superficial results. In 1925 the closest the capital ULAANBAATAR's 421 party members had to a worker were two artisans. In 1941 the party's membership was 47.5 percent white-collar workers, 46.0 percent herders and farmers, and only 6.5 percent workers, a percentage that changed little by 1951. Under the rule of Tsedenbal (r. 1952–84), there was a concerted effort to proletarianize the membership.

Workers rose to 26.6 percent of the party in 1961 and 32.6 percent in 1981. This growth came at the expense of the rural population, which fell to 17.5 percent of members in 1981 but did not, however, in any sense increase the real influence of workers on decision making.

THE MPRP IN DEMOCRATIC MONGOLIA

On March 12–14, 1990, the MPRP's Politburo, including general secretary J. Batmönkh, facing serious demonstrations and no longer supported by the Soviet Union, resigned and promised to allow free elections. From May the MPRP renounced its previous state subsidy of 30 million tögrögs, became self-financing, and had to adapt from being a selective vanguard party to drumming up mass support. Nevertheless it still had formidable financial and institutional advantages in the July 1990 elections and won an overwhelming majority. Despite this victory, the MPRP formed a coalition government with the new democratic parties, both to deflect anger at the inevitable economic crisis caused by the rupture in Soviet aid and to keep Western donor countries interested in Mongolia. In June 1992 a relatively conservative MPRP slate won 71 of 76 seats in the new unicameral legislature under the 1992 CONSTITUTION. To the consternation of more liberal party leaders, the MPRP's victory was so crushing that no coalition was feasible.

Ideologically, the party's think tanks, all trained in Marxism-Leninism, proposed a variety of new models, ranging from the "Asian tiger" model of export-led development under authoritarian government, to the Indian Congress Party's tradition of extended one-party leadership within democratic forms, to appropriating the ancient Indian Buddhist philosopher Nagarjuna's idea of the "Middle Way" to argue for moderated democratization.

The party's new electoral base was the conservative three western provinces (BAYAN-ÖLGII PROVINCE, KHOWD PROVINCE, and UWS PROVINCE) and to a lesser degree the Khalkha countryside, while its weakness was in the cities. The party's campaign strategy was to welcome multiparty democracy and PRIVATIZATION but to picture itself as more experienced, more responsible, and more patriotic than its young urban rivals. In 1993, however, the party's old guard overreached. Having rejected incumbent president P. Ochirbat (b. 1942) as candidate for his relatively liberal line, the party could not stop his victory on the Democratic Coalition ticket. Finally, in 1996, after a lackluster response to a serious outbreak of wildfires, the MPRP government was swept out of power by the Democratic Coalition in June.

Four years out of power completed the MPRP's separation from government. In 1997 the MPRP regained the presidency with the defeat of P. Ochirbat by N. Bagabandi (b. 1950). The internal conflicts in the Democratic Coalition along with the accusations of corruption and massive

ZUD (winter disasters) all gave the MPRP a sweeping victory in the parliament in 2000, carrying even the city and youth vote. Bagabandi was reelected president a year later. The MPRP has, however, continued the policy of privatization and the generally pro-Western foreign policy.

See also MONGOLIA, STATE OF; MONGOLIAN PEOPLE'S PARTY, THIRD CONGRESS OF; MONGOLIAN PEOPLE'S REPUBLIC; MONGOLIAN PEOPLE'S REVOLUTIONARY PARTY, SEVENTH CONGRESS OF; REVOLUTIONARY PERIOD.

Mongolian People's Revolutionary Party, Seventh Congress of

At the Seventh Congress (October 23–December 11, 1928), Moscow's Communist International (Comintern) delegation mobilized radical students and young rural delegates to overthrow the DAMBADORJI leadership.

In August 1927 the Buriat Comintern agent Matvei Innokent'evich Amagaev (1897–1939) began denouncing the Mongolian party chief Dambadorji as a rightist with dangerous plans for relations with China and Japan. Students returning from Moscow found the leadership ignoring their proposals. The *khödöö*, or "countryside," faction of officials, led by Badarakhu (Ö. Badrakh, 1895–1941) of the DÖRBÖD and GENDÜN, resented the ULAANBAATAR-bred multilingual officials (in 1925 96 of Ulaanbaatar's 421 party members knew a foreign language) who held sway in Dambadorji's *khota,* or "city," faction and charged them with preferring old feudals to poor and oppressed rural herders.

From spring 1928 the Comintern issued increasingly serious threats to abandon the Mongolians unless they changed course. Fearing international isolation, the party presidium was already coming to heel by July. On September 22, 1928, Amagaev and a Czech lawyer, Bohumír Šmeral, led a Comintern delegation to Mongolia for the upcoming congress. Now the presidium hoped only to appease the Comintern. Even before the congress began, Dambadorji was admitting errors.

The actual congress thus was somewhat anticlimactic despite the delegates' frequently raucous behavior. The well-coached delegates hammered home the theme that the Dambadorji regime had talked left and walked right. The final resolutions called for a comprehensive intensification of class struggle, vast new programs of social and cultural construction, and direct entry into socialism. Behind the scenes the Comintern delegation selected all the new leaders of Mongolia. The party chairmanship was abolished, and three equal secretaries were selected: Gendün, Badarakhu, and the Moscow-educated student Eldebwachir (B. Eldew-Ochir, 1905–37). To appease the traditionalists, AMUR and Choibalsang were retained in the government. The congress thus initiated the disastrous LEFTIST PERIOD of 1929–32.

See also CHOIBALSANG, MARSHAL; MONGOLIAN PEOPLE'S REVOLUTIONARY PARTY; REVOLUTIONARY PERIOD.

Mongolian plateau While no longer a political or ethnographic unity, the Mongolian plateau is a distinct geographic and environmental area. Including the independent State of Mongolia and neighboring areas of Transbaikalia and Inner Mongolia, the plateau occupies the eastern part of the great Eurasian steppe zone, just southeast of the geographical heart of Asia.

Traditionally Mongolia was the area between the ALTAI RANGE and GREATER KHINGGAN RANGE in the west and east and between the Yin Shan Mountains and LAKE BAIKAL to the south and north. Today the independent State of Mongolia occupies the heart of this region. The plateau's southern and eastern reaches are the traditional HULUN BUIR, SHILIIN GOL, and ULAANCHAB regions of Inner Mongolia in China, while its northeastern section includes the BURIAT REPUBLIC and Aga steppe in Russia's Transbaikal region. The Tuvan basin and the Russian Altay in Siberia and ALASHAN in Inner Mongolia also share links to this plateau. Defined in this way, the Mongolian plateau occupies more than 3.3 million square kilometers (1.27 million square miles).

TOPOGRAPHY

The Mongolian plateau can be divided into two large zones: the mountains to the north and west and the plains to the south and east. The mountains consist of several ranges: the ALTAI RANGE, the KHANGAI RANGE, and the KHENTII RANGE in Mongolia proper, the Tannu Ola (Tagna Uul) and the Sayan defining the northwestern Tuvan basin, and the Khamar-Daban, Ulan-Burgasy, Barguzin, Yablonovyy, Daur, Onon, Mogotuy, and other ranges in the Transbaikal region. The Altai and Khangai Ranges are by far the highest, with some perpetually snowcapped peaks over 4,000 meters (13,000 feet) high. They and the Sayan define several high basins: the Tuvan basin in Russia's Tuvan Republic, the Darkhad basin in far northern Mongolia, and the GREAT LAKES BASIN of western Mongolia. The Khentii and the Transbaikal Ranges define a series of valleys running southwest to northeast. Around Lake Baikal the relief is sharp, with high mountains and deep valleys, but in the Khentii and eastern Transbaikalia the slopes are gentler. The mountains have relatively higher rainfall and are mostly wooded, while the large basins are mostly desert steppe.

The plains are generally over 1,000 meters (3,300 feet) above sea level in the southwest but slope down to little more than 500 meters (1,600 feet) above sea level in the northeast. The southwest, consisting of the GOBI DESERT of southern Mongolia and Ulaanchab and the Alashan Deserts of far southwestern Inner Mongolia, is broken by many isolated massifs, while Mongolia's eastern plain, extending into Hulun Buir, eastern Shiliin Gol, and the Aga steppe in Russia, is largely flat. The Helan Shan and Yin Shan Mountains separate the Gobi and Alashan Deserts from the Huang (Yellow) River valley, while the Greater Khinggan Range separates the eastern plains from

Manchuria. To the south and west the plains are mostly sandy or gravelly gobi, while the north and east are grassy steppe with water-logged basins. A line of terrain less than 1,000 meters (3,280 feet) above sea level running roughly along the southern border of Mongolia proper divides the Gobi into north-flowing (Inner Mongolia) and south-flowing (Mongolia) drainage areas.

SURFACE WATER

The Khentii and Khangai separate the Arctic and Pacific drainage basins to the north and northeast from the Central Asian blind drainage basin. Within this vast basin the Altai and its southern spurs separate the Great Lakes Basin and the Valley of the Lakes to the northeast from the Zünghar (Junggar) Basin to the southwest. Western Mongolia contains many lakes fed by streams flowing from the Khangai and the Altai. Some are fresh, but most, such as LAKE UWS, are salt. Smaller salt lakes fed by groundwater and small rivers dot the Gobi. The largest are Alashan's Gashuun (Gaxun) and Sogoo (Sogo) Lakes, fed by the Ruo River flowing north from the Tibetan plateau.

Hulun Buir, the Aga steppe, and northeastern Mongolia are drained by the ONON RIVER, KHERLEN RIVER (Kelüren), Khalkha River, and Hailar River, which eventually flow into the Amur River and the Pacific Ocean. These rivers generally carry only small volumes of water. The Hulun Buir steppe is named from two freshwater lakes, the Buir Nuur (covering 615 square kilometers, or 237 square miles) and the Hulun Nuur (Khölön, or Dalai, covering 2,210 square kilometers, or 853 square miles). These lakes lie at 583 and 539 meters (1,913 and 1,768 feet) above sea level, respectively, and both average about eight meters (26 feet) in depth.

Lake Baikal's drainage basin covers north-central Mongolia and western Transbaikalia. This area includes the largest rivers of Mongolia and Buriatia, particularly the SELENGE RIVER and its tributaries. The much smaller Barguzin (Buriat, Bargazhan) and Upper Angara flow into the central and northern Baikal. LAKE KHÖWSGÖL, the Selenge's ultimate source, is the deepest lake of Mongolia proper, while Baikal is the deepest lake in the world. The shores of Lake Baikal, at 456 meters (1,496 feet) above sea level, are the lowest area of the Mongolian plateau. The Tuvan and Darkhad basins are drained by the Yenisey River and its affluents and the Russian Altai (the Altay Republic, or Gorno-Altay) by affluents of the Ob' River, all flowing ultimately into the Arctic.

POLITICAL AND ETHNIC GEOGRAPHY

Politically, the Mongolian plateau today is divided between Mongolia, Russia, and China. Mongolia, with an area of 1,566,500 square kilometers (604,830 square miles), had a population in the 1989 census of 2,044,000 people, which ethnically was more than 90 percent Mongol. The largest minority is the KAZAKHS of far western BAYAN-ÖLGII PROVINCE.

Before 1000 C.E. the plateau was dominated by Turkic peoples. Today Turks are significant only in the northwest in Russia's Tuvan and Altay Autonomous Republics and in Mongolia's westernmost province, Bayan-Ölgii. These three areas together cover 308,800 square kilometers (119,230 square miles) and have a population of almost 594,000, of which 356,000, or 60 percent are TUVANS, Khakas, Altays, Kazakhs, and other Turkic peoples (1989 figures). The balance of the population includes Russians in Tuva and the Altay Republic and ethnic Mongols in Bayan-Ölgii.

China's Inner Mongolian Autonomous Region, which includes the southern part of the plateau as well as the ORDOS plateau, the CHAKHAR area, and much of western Manchuria, covers 1,183,000 square kilometers (456,760 square miles) and had in 1990 a population of 21,626,000, of which only 16 percent were Mongols. Counting only those areas within the Mongolian plateau in the strict sense, the population was about 2,343,000, of whom 473,000, or 20 percent, were Mongols or allied nationalities (Daurs, EWENKIS, etc.). Several districts along the frontier of Mongolia, however, such as the BARGA, ÜJÜMÜCHIN, Abaga (Abag), and Sönid, have Mongol majorities.

In Transbaikalia the Buriat Republic and the Chita region together have an area of 782,800 square kilometers (302,240 square miles) and a total population 2,314,200 (1989). Of these, 310,400, or 13 percent, are Buriat Mongols. Buriatia and Chita can also be seen as the southwestern extension of the east Siberian uplands. While certain rural districts, particularly Chita's AGA BURIAT AUTONOMOUS AREA and Buriatia's Kizhinga and Kurumkan districts, have Buriat majorities, the population overall is fairly urbanized.

The differing ethnic percentages between Mongolia and the neighboring Chinese and Russian areas also correspond to differences of population density. The most barren area is the Gobi, where densities drop to 0.6 (1.6 per square mile) in Alashan and even below 0.3 persons per square kilometer (0.8 per square mile) in Mongolia's SOUTH GOBI PROVINCE. Mongolia as a whole in 1989 had 1.3 people per square kilometer (3.4 per square mile), and Tuva and the Altay Republic 1.9 (4.9 per square mile). The bordering area of Inner Mongolia (excluding Alashan) had 3.9 persons per square kilometer (10.1 per square mile), and Transbaikalia had 3.0 persons per square kilometer (7.8 per square mile).

See also CLIMATE; DAUR LANGUAGE AND PEOPLE; FAUNA; FLORA; FOSSIL RECORD; INNER MONGOLIA AUTONOMOUS REGION; MONGOLIA, STATE OF.

Further reading: Academy of Sciences, MPR, *Information Mongolia* (Oxford: Pergamon Press, 1990), 6–33.

Mongolian Revolutionary Youth League The Mongolian Revolutionary Youth League, founded in August

1921, functioned as a virtual left-wing opposition party in 1921–24 and as the shock troops of the antireligious campaign in 1929–32, before being tamed as the feeder organ for the ruling MONGOLIAN PEOPLE'S REVOLUTIONARY PARTY. The All-Mongolian Revolutionary Youth League was organized on August 25, 1921, by several Irkutsk-trained Russian-language interpreters, including then deputy commander in chief Choibalsang. Membership was restricted to those aged 15 to 25. The youth league immediately won a reputation as a radical force, cutting off married women's hair ornaments as a feudal custom, arresting counterrevolutionaries, trying practitioners of feudal customs such as wife beating, and so on. At the same time the youth league's Beijing-opera style theater performances were very popular. Politically, the league, through Choibalsang, was linked to his mentors Prime Minister BODÔ and GENERAL SÜKHEBAATUR, but only the former received the blame for the less popular actions.

Soviet encouragement nourished the league against the more conservative Mongolian People's Party (later renamed the Mongolian People's Revolutionary Party). Moscow's chief "Mongolia hand," the Siberian party boss B. Z. Shumiatskii, sent a youth league delegation to Moscow's "Congress of the Toilers of the Far East" (January 1922). By June 1923 the Communist International of Youth, working through a former army trainer, Alexei G. Starkov (alias "Zorigtu," b. 1899), was demanding that the Mongolian People's Party recognize the league's independence as a separate political body. The party leaders, such as GENERAL DANZIN, tried to calm the league by cultivating its leaders, including Babasang (1899–1924) and BUYANNEMEKHÜ. In 1924 ELBEK-DORZHI RINCHINO executed Babasang, who had become unpopular in the league ranks, and used the execution to emphasize the youth league's subordination to the party. As the party moved left, the Soviet Union no longer supported the league's independence and recalled Starkov.

During the LEFTIST PERIOD (1929–32), however, the youth league again became important as the frontline of attack on the old society. The league formed ideological brigades to attack the "feudals," transfer livestock to the poor, and carry on collectivization. More important, the youth league, which once again became semi-independent, criticized "feudals" and "opportunists" within the party on the basis of both their customs and their habits and on their connections. The league, which numbered 8,000 in 1930, expanded to 27,000 in 1932. This number, barely half that of the party, shows that far from forming a broader stratum from which the party drew selected members, the league was still functioning something like a rival, more radical, party.

The conservative NEW TURN POLICY, formulated in response to the insurrections against the leftist policy, reduced the youth league to only 6,100 members. From 1940 the youth league was gradually reduced to a feeder for the party. As party membership became more selective, the upper age limit of league enrollment was raised from 25 to 35, while the percentage of party members admitted as students declined from 40.2 percent in the 1940s to a negligible 3.4 percent in 1976–80. By the 1980s the youth league's membership reached 280,000, more than three times that of the party, and included more than half the young herders and the overwhelming majority of working-class youth.

The Young Pioneers was founded on May 8, 1925, as a branch of the league for children under 15. In 1930 its membership hardly exceeded 800, but with the final subordination of the youth league, its membership expanded to almost 6,300 in 1940, and by 1975 it was more than 250,000.

The Youth League lent its facilities to the movement that became the 1990 DEMOCRATIC REVOLUTION. After declaring its independence from the party, the Youth League won nine seats in the 1990 elections for the multiparty Great People's Khural. Torn by dissension over its future course, the Youth League soon disintegrated. A conservative faction allied to the MPRP has won title to its extensive facilities.

See also CHOIBALSANG, MARSHAL; DAMBA, DASHIIN; TSEDENBAL, YUMJAAGIIN; ZORIG, SANJAASÜRENGIIN.

Mongolian script *See* UIGHUR-MONGOLIAN SCRIPT.

Mongolian sources on the Mongol Empire While providing little information on later reigns, Mongolian chronicles are the source, directly or indirectly, for most of our knowledge of the history of CHINGGIS KHAN. Mongolian history writing, like Mongolian writing itself, begins with the MONGOL EMPIRE. During the 13th century at least two separate chronicles covering Chinggis Khan and ÖGEDEI KHAN were written. One, the SECRET HISTORY OF THE MONGOLS, was probably written in 1252. The other, now found only in a Chinese translation titled SHENGWU QINZHENG LU (Campaigns led by the lawgiving warrior), seems to be the text of the Mongolian-language *Veritable Records* (*shilu*) of Chinggis Khan and then Ögedei Khan, written by Sarman (also written Sarban) (1288) and by Sarman and Uru'udai (1290), respectively. Of these two texts, the *Secret History* was an "insider" account that emphasized the role of Chinggis Khan's family and his companions (NÖKÖR). The only source to give a connected account of Chinggis's youth before his first battle with JAMUGHA at Dalan Baljud, it nevertheless contains numerous obvious inaccuracies, particularly connected with the biographies of *nökör*s, such as MUQALI, SHIGI QUTUQU, and SÜBE'ETEI BA'ATUR. Its chronology of the conquests outside Mongolia is particularly confused. The *Veritable Records,* by contrast, was more of an official history that omitted both discreditable events and the stories of the companions and family members. For the latter part of Chinggis Khan's reign and that of Ögedei's, however, it supplies valuable evidence on affairs in North China in a terse, annalistic style.

The YUAN DYNASTY's Hanlin and Historiography Academy, staffed by Mongols, kept the *Secret History* and the *Veritable Records,* and "outsiders" were not permitted to see either. The records were, however, transmitted to the Mongol rulers of Iran. There, GHAZAN KHAN (1295–1304) allowed RASHID-UD-DIN FAZL-ULLAH to use the *Altan debter* (Golden record), "which is always kept in the khans' treasury by great officers," for his COMPENDIUM OF CHRONICLES. This *Altan debter*'s exact identity is unclear, but certainly the *Veritable Records* formed Rashid-ud-Din's primary source on Chinggis Khan.

Histories of Chinggis Khan's companions were also composed in the 13th century. Both Rashid-ud-Din and the YUAN SHI incorporate, for example, parallel texts on BO'ORCHU, Chagha'an, Sübe'etei, and others that have obviously been translated from Mongolian. Mongolian-language historical writing continued in the 14th century in the Mongol Yuan dynasty of China. Veritable records were composed for the successors of QUBILAI KHAN, eventually covering 13 reigns. Except as translated into Chinese and incorporated in the *Yuan shi*'s basic annals, however, they have not survived.

Scribes such as Tatar-Tong'a and Shigi Qutuqu had been recording Chinggis Khan's judgments (JASAQ) and issuing decrees (JARLIQ) since 1204, yet only fragments of Mongol imperial archives have survived. The oldest document written in Mongolian, found near Nerchinsk and called the "Stone of Chinggis Khan," dates to around 1226 and records a 335-fathom bow shot by Chinggis's nephew Yisüngge. Throughout the Mongol Empire, a number of decrees granting tax exemptions to religious institutions and meritorious ministers have been found. Due to their importance for their possessor, such exemption decrees were carefully preserved, both written on paper and inscribed on stone, in the territory of all four successor states of the empire and occur both in Mongolian and in translation into the other languages of the empire—Chinese, Persian, Tibetan, and Russian. (Later *jarliq*s from the western khanates are in Turkish.) While useful for preserving Mongol chancellery formulas, they are not of tremendous independent historical value. Other stone inscriptions include several Sino-Mongolian bilingual inscriptions from 1335 to 1362 recording the achievements of civil officials of the Mongol Yuan dynasty, and the famous hexalingual (Sanskrit, Tibetan, SQUARE SCRIPT Mongolian, Uighur, Chinese, and Tangut) inscription at Juyongguan Pass, north of Beijing, glorifying the Yuan emperors as bodhisattvas. While offering insight into Confucian and Buddhist influence on Mongolian royal ideology, they supply little new historical data.

See also LITERATURE.

Further reading: Shugdaryn Bira, *Mongolian Historical Writings from 1200 to 1700,* trans. John R. Krueger (Belingham: Western Washington University, 2002).

Mongolic language family   In addition to Mongolian, the national language of Mongolia, the Mongolic language family includes a number of regional and local minority languages in Russia and China and one, Mogholi, in Afghanistan. All the living Mongolic languages are closely related and clearly derive from Middle Mongolian, the language of the 13th-century MONGOL EMPIRE.

LANGUAGES, DIALECTS, AND CLASSIFICATION

The Mongolic languages can be divided into two groups: 1) the New Mongolian languages including MONGOLIAN LANGUAGE proper, Kalmyk-Oirat, Buriat, and the East Mongolian dialects of eastern Inner Mongolia; and 2) the peripheral languages, including Daur in Manchuria, Dongxiang, Tu, Eastern Yogur, and Bao'an in northwest China, and Mogholi in Afghanistan. Historically, the New Mongolian languages have been in continuous contact, making dialectal distinctions fuzzy. Thus, distinguishing languages from dialects among the New Mongolian speeches is somewhat arbitrary. Since the "peripheral" languages lost contact with the main body of Mongolian speakers after the fall of the Mongol Empire in the 14th century, they are now clearly distinct both from Mongolian and from one another.

Within Russia and Mongolia the New Mongolian dialects are written using three separate Cyrillic scripts: Kalmyk, Buriat (based on the Khori dialect), and Mongolian (based on the KHALKHA dialect). These dialect divisions correspond roughly, but not exactly, to the political divisions of the Buriat and Kalmyk Republics of Russia and independent Mongolia. In China all New Mongolian dialects have been classified as Mongolian, yet Barga-Buriat–type dialects exist in northeastern Inner Mongolia and Kalmyk-Oirat–type dialects in Xinjiang, Gansu, and Qinghai (Kökenuur). Moreover, the dialects of eastern Inner Mongolia and Manchuria form a family at least as divergent from Khalkha as are Buriat or Kalmyk. For historical reasons, however, this East Mongolian dialect family has never had a separate written language. Throughout China, with the partial exception of Xinjiang, standard Inner Mongolian is the dominant dialect. Standard Inner Mongolian is written in the UIGHUR-MONGOLIAN SCRIPT and based on the CHAKHAR dialect, one easily intercomprehensible with Khalkha.

Using 1989–90 census figures and a very loose definition of language competence, Mongolia, Inner Mongolia, and Manchuria have up to 5 million Mongolian speakers; Kalmykia and western Mongolia and Xinjiang, Gansu, and Qinghai in China have up to 510,000 Kalmyk-Oirat speakers; and southern Siberia, northeast Mongolia, and northeast Inner Mongolia have almost 475,000 Barga-Buriat speakers. A definition of speakers based on language regularly spoken in most social contexts would show rather smaller numbers, particularly for Buriat.

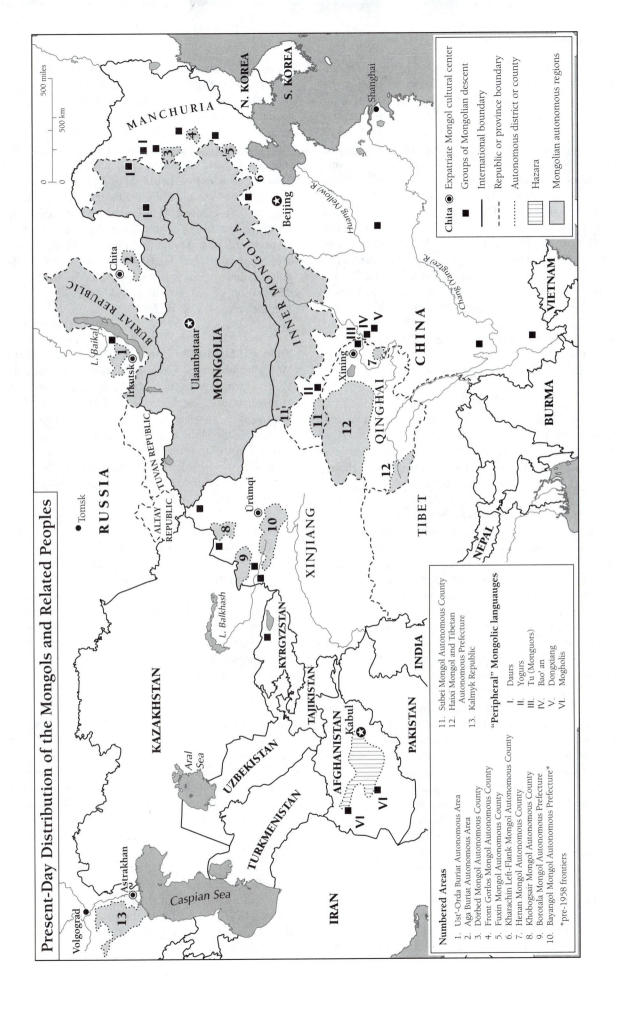

Present-Day Distribution of the Mongols and Related Peoples

Numbered Areas
1. Ust'-Orda Buriat Autonomous Area
2. Aga Buriat Autonomous Area
3. Dorbed Mongol Autonomous County
4. Front Gorlos Mongol Autonomous County
5. Fuxin Mongol Autonomous County
6. Kharachin Left-Flank Mongol Autonomous County
7. Henan Mongol Autonomous County
8. Khobogsair Mongol Autonomous County
9. Borotala Mongol Autonomous Prefecture
10. Bayangol Mongol Autonomous Prefecture*

11. Subei Mongol Autonomous County
12. Haixi Mongol and Tibetan Autonomous Prefecture
13. Kalmyk Republic

"Peripheral" Mongolic languuages
I.   Daurs
II.   Yogurs
III. Tu (Monguors)
IV.   Bao'an
V.   Dongxiang
VI.   Mogholis

*pre-1958 frontiers

Legend:
Chita ■ — Expatriate Mongol cultural center
⊙ — Groups of Mongolian descent
── International boundary
──── Republic or province boundary
········ Autonomous district or county
Hazara
Mongolian autonomous regions

RUSSIA · Tomsk · Volgograd · Astrakhan ⊙ · Caspian Sea · Aral Sea · KAZAKHSTAN · UZBEKISTAN · TURKMENISTAN · L. Balkhash · KYRGYZSTAN · TAJIKISTAN · AFGHANISTAN · Kabul ✪ · IRAN · PAKISTAN · INDIA · NEPAL · BURMA · VIETNAM · TIBET · XINJIANG · Ürümqi ⊙ · QINGHAI · Xining ⊙ · CHINA · Beijing ✪ · Huang (Yellow) R. · Chang (Yangtze) R. · Shanghai · INNER MONGOLIA · MONGOLIA · Ulaanbataar ✪ · BURIAT REPUBLIC · Chita ⊙ · L. Baikal · Irkutsk ⊙ · MANCHURIA · N. KOREA · S. KOREA · TUVAN REPUBLIC · ALTAY REPUBLIC

500 miles
500 km

The "peripheral" languages can be divided into two isolates, Daur and Mogholi, and the four languages of the Gansu-Qinghai subfamily. Daur is spoken primarily in northeast Inner Mongolia and near neighboring Qiqihar city; an estimated 95 percent of the nationality's 121,357 (1990 census) speak the language. Mogholi was spoken in the Herat and Ghorat areas of Afghanistan by a few thousand persons, and it is unclear if it survived the wars following the Communist coup d'état of 1978. Of the Gansu-Qinghai family, Dongxiang (Santa) in western Gansu is the largest "peripheral" language, with more than 95 percent of the nationality's 373,900 (1990 census) members speaking the language. About 60 percent of the 191,600 Tu (Monguor) people living around Xining city speak the Tu language. By contrast, less than 30 percent of the 12,300 Yogurs speak Eastern Yogur (a somewhat larger percentage speak the Turkic Western Yogur). Many of the 12,200 Bao'an in western Gansu speak Chinese, but since a certain number of Tu speak Bao'an, the total number of speakers is perhaps 10,000.

HISTORY

The prehistory of the Mongolic family is related to the question of its affiliation with the larger ALTAIC LANGUAGE FAMILY, including the Turkic and Manchu-Tungusic languages. Many distinguished linguists, such as Nicholas Poppe and Gustav Ramstedt, have considered all these languages to be part of one genetic family. In recent years the theory that the Altaic family was formed through convergence due to prolonged contact has gained currency. If this is the case, one must posit several strata of both Turkic-Mongolic contact and Mongolic-Manchu-Tungusic contact, with loanwords generally moving west to east. The still imperfectly deciphered Kitan stands out among the Mongolic languages by being phonologically progressive yet lacking many Turkic words found in Middle Mongolian.

The history of the main body of Mongolic languages can be divided into a hypothetical Ancient Mongolian, formed on the Mongolian steppe before the 12th century; Middle Mongolian, recorded in the 13th to 16th centuries; and New Mongolian, which includes modern Mongolian (in the narrow sense), Barga-Buriat, Kalmyk-Oirat, and the East Mongolian dialects. The progression from Ancient Mongolian to Middle Mongolian was marked by transformation of a reconstructed initial p- to initial h- (e.g., reconstructed *pon*, "year," to attested *hon*) and the disappearance of intervocalic -g- and -gh- (e.g., *segül*, "tail," and *baraghun*, "right," to *se'ül* and *bara'un*). Middle Mongolian still retained traces of natural gender (*jirin* as feminine "two" versus *qoyar*, feminine past in -*bi* versus -*bai*/-*bei*, etc.), which have been lost in all extant Mongolic languages.

The phonetic evolution of Middle Mongolian into New Mongolian saw the following processes: 1) the disappearance of the initial h- (e.g., *hon* to *on*); 2) the merging of the diphthongs produced by the disappearance of -g-/-gh- into long vowels (*se'ül* to *süül* and *bara'un* to *baruun*); 3) retrogressive assimilation of first-syllable -i- or "breaking of the -i-" (e.g., *chidör*, "hobble," to *chödör*); 4) palatalization of back vowels when followed by -i-, forming a long or short secondary front vowel (e.g., *sayin*, "good," and *mori(n)*, "horse," to Kalmyk *sään* and *mörn*); and 5) transformation of q- and often k- and medial -b- into spirants (e.g., *qa'aqu*, "to close," to *khaakh*). The loss of the initial h- and elimination of all -u diphthongs are the chief diagnostic features that separate the New Mongolian language from both Middle Mongolian and the peripheral languages. In many respects the East Mongolian dialects are the most progressive, particularly in palatalization. In Fuxin (Monggoljin) dialect spirantization proceeds to the actual elimination of intervocalic -k-/-q- (e.g., *jakidal*, "letter," to *jeedel*, and *ekilekü* to *iileh*).

SCRIPTS

Kitan and Middle Mongolian are the two earliest attested Mongolic languages. Kitan inscriptions from the 11th and 12th centuries are still imperfectly deciphered. Middle Mongolian, the lineal ancestor of the extant Mongolic languages, is, however, quite well known through works in the Uighur-Mongolian script and SQUARE SCRIPT preserved from 1226 on, glossaries of Mongolian words into Chinese, Turkish, Persian, Armenian, and other languages, and phonetic transcriptions prepared in the MING DYNASTY (around 1400).

From 1600 on writing revived among the Mongolians. A classical language was formed, which to a certain extent concealed the ongoing transformation of Middle Mongolian into modern Mongolian. Writing appears among the Kalmyk-Oirats in the CLEAR SCRIPT in the 17th century, among the BURIATS in the Uighur-Mongolian script in the 18th century, and among the Daurs in the Manchu script in the 19th century. Linguistic description of Kalmyk, Buriat, and Mongolian dates to the 19th century. The other Mongolic languages were not written or described until the 20th century.

See also BAO'AN LANGUAGE AND PEOPLE; DAUR LANGUAGE AND PEOPLE; DONGXIANG LANGUAGE AND PEOPLE; KALMYK-OIRAT LANGUAGE AND SCRIPTS; MOGHOLI LANGUAGE AND PEOPLE; ROURAN; TU LANGUAGE AND PEOPLE; XIANBI; XIONGNU; YOGUR LANGUAGES AND PEOPLE.

Further reading: György Kara, "Late Medieval Turkic Elements in Mongolian," in *De Dunhuang à Istanbul: Hommage à James Russel Hamilton*, ed. Louis Bazin and Peter Zieme (Turnhout, Belgium: Brepols, 2001), 73–119; Juna Janhunen, *The Mongolic Languages* (London: Routledge, 2003); Hans Nugteren, "On the Classification of the 'Peripheral' Mongolic Languages," in *Historical and Linguistic Interaction between Inner-Asia and Europe*, ed. Árpád Berta and Edina Horváth (Szeged, Hungary: University of Szeged, 1997), 207–216; Nicholas Poppe, *Introduction to Mongolian Comparative Studies* (Helsinki: Suomalais-Ugrilainen Suera, 1955).

Mongol-Oirat Code (*Mongghol-Oirad tsaaji*) The Mongol-Oirat Code was issued around September 20 (fifth day of the eighth moon), 1640, at a great assembly called by the Zasagtu Khan Subadai of the KHALKHA Mongols. Other participants included the Khalkha Tüshiyetü khan Gömbö-Dorji and the Oirat rulers Erdeni Baatur Khung-Taiji (r. 1634–53), TÖRÖ-BAIKU GÜÜSHI KHAN, and KHOO-ÖRLÖG. The INCARNATE LAMA Manjushri Khutugtu of the Sa-skya order was also present.

The purpose of the assembly was to unify the Khalkhas and OIRATS, after decades, even centuries, of animosity. The first provision of the 120 provisions in the code therefore prescribed collective action by all the signatories against any person who "destroys this state (*törö*)," provisions that worked against Lubsang-Rinchin Taiji (*see* KHOTOGHOID) but failed to resolve the war between GALDAN BOSHOGTU KHAN (1678–97) and Chakhundorji (r. 1655–99). Further provisions established the requirement of notification of the approach of an enemy, return of fugitives from other nobles, respect and provisions due officials, and the postroad system. Family law is also detailed, specifying the authority of fathers and mothers over sons, daughters-in-law, and slaves and prescribing amounts of bridewealth and dowry and penalties for breaking engagements, elopements, and other offenses. The interest of the confederation as a whole in marriage was clearly expressed in the rules specifying that every 40 households must marry out four girls per year and that any girl unmarried by age 20 must be reported to the authorities. After these coherent sections followed a series of almost random provisions. Notable are the provisions enforcing respect for the Buddhist clergy and prohibiting either inviting shamans to practice or offering funerary sacrifices. The code also specifies rules for collective hunts parallel to those for war. Capital punishment was levied only for crimes of war: failing to report or assist against an enemy invasion or abandonment of one's prince in battle. While flogging, confinement, and mutilation were occasionally prescribed, the vast majority of punishments were CATTLE fines reckoned in "nines."

Among the Khalkha the war with Galdan and the 1709 proclamation of the KHALKHA JIRUM (Khalkha regulations) voided the code, yet among the Oirats it long remained in force. Galdan added provisions in 1678 strengthening the requirements of collective responsibility, while Dondug-Dashi (1741–61) of the Volga KALMYKS added a wide variety of provisions. Further modified by the Zinzili Decrees of 1822, the code remained in force among the Volga Kalmyks until the abolition of the nobility's authority in 1892.

See also ALTAN KHAN, CODE OF.

Further reading: John R. Krueger, "New Materials on Oirat Law and History, Part One: The Jinjil Decrees," *Central Asiatic Journal* 16 (1972): 194–205; Valentin A. Riasanovsky, *Fundamental Principles of Mongol Law* (1934; rpt., Bloomington: Indiana University Press, 1965).

Mongol tribe At the time of the rise of Chinggis Khan, the term *Mongol* meant only one particularly fractious and warlike tribe nomadizing along the ONON RIVER and KHERLEN RIVER in northeastern Mongolia. After CHINGGIS KHAN founded his empire, this tribe gave its name to the other peoples of the plateau, while the tribes' common speech came to be called the MONGOLIAN LANGUAGE. This entry describes the Mongol tribe proper, before the rise of Chinggis Khan.

THE EARLY MONGOLS IN CHINESE RECORDS

The origin of the Mongols may be the SHIWEI, a people or group of peoples found in Chinese records in northern Manchuria from the fifth century on. During the time of China's Tang dynasty (618–906), a tribe of the Shiwei called the Mengwu appear east of the GREATER KHINGGAN RANGE, perhaps the first appearance of the name *Mongol*. Many etymologies of this word have been attempted by Mongols as well as by foreigners, but none has proved convincing.

The Mongols, now called Menggu in Chinese, reappear in 1084 as one of the more distant tribes paying tribute to the Kitan Liao dynasty. Chinese writers linked them to the Shiwei and described them as originally having lived purely by hunting. Like other people in Manchuria, they were said to have dressed in fish skins. As the Mongols crossed the Greater Khinggan Range going west, they became not just hunters but pastoralists and often traded with the neighboring peoples, including the dynasties in North China. The KITANS and after them the Jurchen, however, prohibited the export of iron, and the Mongols had to make do with stirrups of wood and arrows of bone.

The Menggu were not the exclusive ancestors of the Mongols. Clans that later joined the Mongol tribe appearing independently in Chinese records include the Jajirad (first reported in 1093) and the QONGGIRAD (first reported in 1129). As the nucleus of the Mongols moved onto the MONGOLIAN PLATEAU, Chinese observers lumped them as TATARS (Dadan).

After the fall of the Kitans in 1125 and the rise of the Jurchens' JIN DYNASTY (1115–1234), the Mongols became a leading steppe tribe. From 1139 to 1146 the Mongols leagued with malcontents within the Jin frontiers and repeatedly defeated the Jin forces, capturing numerous forts and frontier towns. The Jin dynasty secured peace only in 1147 by giving the Mongols generous gifts of CATTLE, SHEEP, grain and beans, and various silk stuffs.

Mongol oral histories told of the powerful Mongol khans who threatened the Jin. Qabul Khan, his cousin Hambaghai Khan, and Qabul's son Qutula Khan ruled in succession until about 1164, when Qutula died in battle with the Tatars, a tribe allied with the Jin. Earlier, the

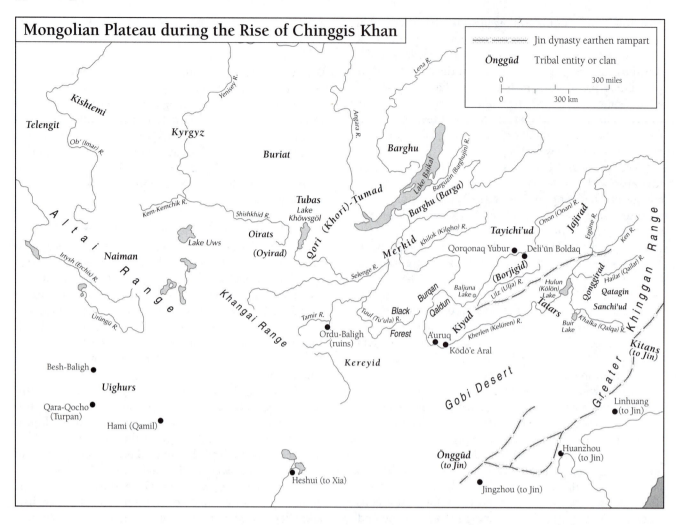

Mongolian Plateau during the Rise of Chinggis Khan

Jin dynasty earthen rampart

Önggüd   Tribal entity or clan

0   300 miles

0   300 km

Kishtemi

Telengit

Ob' (Imar) R.

Kyrgyz

Yenisey R.

Angara R.

Lena R.

Buriat

Barghu

Lake Baikal

Barguzin (Barghujin) R.

Altai Range

Irtysh (Erchis) R.

Naiman

Lake Uws

Ürüngü R.

Kem-Kemchik R.

Shishkhid R.

Tubas
Lake
Khöwsgöl

Oirats

(Oyirad)

Qori (Khori)-Tumad

Merkid

Barghu (Barga)

Selenge R.

Khilok (Kilgho) R.

Tayichi'ud

Qorqonaq Yubur

Onan (Onan) R.

Jajirad

Ergüne R.

Ken R.

Deli'ün Boldaq

Khangai Range

Tamir R.

Tuul (Tu'ula) R.

Black

Forest

Burqan

Baljuna
Lake

Qaldun

(Borjigid)

Ulz (Ulja) R.

Kiyad

Hulun
(Kölön)
Lake

Kherlen (Kelüren) R.

Tatars

Qonggirad

Hailar (Qailar) R.

Qatagin

Sanchi'ud

Khalka (Qalqa) R.

Buir
Lake

Greater Khinggan Range

Kitans
(to Jin)

Ordu-Baligh
(ruins)

A'uruq

Ködö'e Aral

Kereyid

Gobi Desert

Linhuang
(to Jin)

Besh-Baligh

Uighurs

Qara-Qocho
(Turpan)

Hami (Qamil)

Önggüd
(to Jin)

Huanzhou
(to Jin)

Heshui (to Xia)

Jingzhou (to Jin)

Tatars had captured first Hambaghai Khan and then Qabul Khan's eldest son, Ökin Barqaq, and handed them over to be nailed to a wooden mule by the Jin rulers. Under these blows the early Mongol Khanate disintegrated. The Chinese envoy Zhao Gong described the Jin rulers as mounting yearly expeditions against the Mongols, which they called "thinning the ranks." From 1160 to 1190 the victories of the Jin and their tribal allies filled the North China markets with Mongol slaves. Even so, the Mongol rulers regularly paid tribute to the Jin dynasty, really a form of state-subsidized trade (*see* TRIBUTE SYSTEM). Chinggis Khan discontinued this tribute only in 1210.

SOCIAL STRUCTURE OF THE MONGOL TRIBE

Thanks to the *SECRET HISTORY OF THE MONGOLS* and RASHID-UD-DIN FAZL-ULLAH'S *COMPENDIUM OF CHRONICLES*, the internal structure of the Mongol tribe is relatively well understood. The clans in the Mongol tribe belonged to two moieties, the Niru'un and the Dürlükin. The Dürlükin were ordinary Mongols, while the Niru'un (backbone) were the rulers. The 20 or so Niru'un clans belonged to one lineage, the Kiyad, and thus, according

to Mongolian rules of exogamy, had to marry among the Dürlükin moiety. The interrelations of the 15 or so known Dürlükin clans are less clear, but they were called the Negüs lineage and sought wives among the Niru'un. The long genealogy in the *Secret History of the Mongols* includes only the Niru'un Mongols, not the Dürlükin clans.

The Mongol lineages practiced ancestor worship, and participation in the sacrifices was tantamount to membership in the tribe. Exclusion from participation in the sacrificial meat, whether due to suspicion of illegitimacy or to intraclan feuds, marked the creation of a new lineage fragment.

Many Negüs clans—for example, the Qonggirad, Olqunu'ud, Ikires, Qongqotad, and Arulad—were free people, building their fortunes on marriage alliances with particular ruling lineages. Such marriage allies called each other QUDA (affines). A long poem in the *Secret History* painted an idealized portrait of the Qonggirad people putting their trust not in war but in their beautiful daughters, who they would give to the khans in marriage, and in the wealth of their sons, who would receive the daughters of khans.

Many Negüs lineages, however, lost their freedom and became servants of the Kiyad. This could happen through poverty, in which families would sell their children, or through conquest. Generations serving a different clan weakened the subjects' original lineage identity, partially incorporating them into the new clan. The recurring pattern in which sharpshooting, lineage-proud, Kiyad falconers subjugated herding men of unclear lineage and took their beautiful women may reflect actual events but must be read principally as an ideology of conquest justifying Kiyad rule.

The same legends reflected the ruling Kiyad lineages' belief in its heaven-destined right to rule. The first ancestor of all the Kiyad was a bluish wolf "having a destiny from Heaven above." Later, a Kiyad widow, ALAN GHO'A, gave birth to three sons fathered by a man from heaven. Of these, the youngest, Bodonchar, while seemingly a fool, showed his superior destiny through conquest. Finally, Bodonchar's fourth-generation descendant Qaidu demonstrated his right to rule by conquering the JALAYIR, who had attacked the Mongols. His descendants, the BORJIGID in the narrow sense, monopolized the position of khan. Again, such stories were charters of rule for particular lineages over the Mongols.

CHINGGIS KHAN'S RISE AND THE MONGOL TRIBE

Qaidu's great-grandson was Qabul Khan, the first figure in Mongol oral history whose existence can be surmised from non-Mongol sources. At the time of Qabul Khan and his successors, the ruling Borjigid lineage had further divided into several sublineages. Of these, the TAYICHI'UD lineage of Hambaghai Khan was more independent. The clans of Qabul Khan's descendants included the Yürkin, the Changshi'ud, and the Kiyad (in the narrow sense). This last was headed by YISÜGEI BA'ATUR, the grandson of Qabul Khan and the father of Chinggis Khan. The khans of the Mongol tribe were elected at assemblies (QURILTAI), and the position was not hereditary, although only Qaidu's descendants were eligible.

After the Jin and Tatar destruction of the first Mongol khanate, the Tayichi'ud became the dominant group. Other groups with an uncertain claim to membership in the Borjigid, such as the Jajirad clan of JAMUGHA, ascended to positions of importance. (The Borjigid claimed that the father of the Jajirad ancestor was not Bodonchar but really his Uriyangkhan slave boy.)

The descendants of Qabul Khan thus at first welcomed the rise of Chinggis Khan, beginning in the mid-1180s. As Jin and Tatar pressure diminished, Chinggis Khan reasserted Borjigid supremacy against both Tayichi'ud cousins and the Jajirads. Over the next 15 years, however, Chinggis Khan's strict discipline alienated his senior relatives. Chinggis crushed some allied clans, such as the Yürkin, while others deserted his camp. Eventually,

Chinggis's inner circle came to consist solely of his immediate family and his "companions" (NÖKÖR) from Negüs lineages, who gave him complete loyalty. The old Borjigid aristocracy turned to Jamugha, chief of the Jajirad lineage, who was proclaimed *gür khan* (universal khan) by an alliance of the Tayichi'ud and other Kiyad (in the broad sense) clans together with several free Negüs clans. From 1201 on, under repeated blows from Chinggis Khan, the coalition crumbled. The free Negüs clans allied with Chinggis, and the Kiyad clans were either crushed or fled for refuge with other peoples on the Mongolian plateau. With Chinggis's reunification of the Mongolian plateau in 1204, the remaining Kiyad clans submitted.

After Chinggis Khan's reunification of the Mongols, the name *Mongol* came to be applied to all the tribes and khanates of the Mongolian plateau. The bilateral organization of Niru'un and Dürlükin and the aristocratic concept of collective Borjigid rule were transformed into a monarchic idea of Chinggis and his descendants alone as the heavenly destined rulers, yet ideas such as the importance of lineage, the *quda*-relation, and the link of war and hunting to rule continued as a legacy of the Mongol tribe into the new empire.

See also FALCONRY.

Mongol *zurag* Mongol *zurag* is a style of modern Mongolian painting using the traditional mineral-paint medium for nonreligious, frequently folkloric themes. The medium of Mongol *zurag* is taken from traditional Tibeto-Mongolian *thangka* paintings and consists of mineral paints or crushed lac (scale bugs) suspended in an animal-fat size, similar to European gouache. The paintings are done on cotton scrolls. Precursors to Mongol *zurag* include Buddhist paintings of processions and sacred places and folk art, including manuscript illustrations, furniture, and playing cards. "BUSYBODY" SHARAB'S scenes of Mongolian life in the 1910s were the first major examples of nonreligious art painted in mineral paints on a cotton medium.

After the 1921 REVOLUTION painters such as Sharab and Sonamtsering (Sonomtseren) began to use the mineral paints on a cotton medium for portraits in a strongly photographic and European-influenced style. Much of the painting of this era has not survived. In the two decades after 1940, oil painting done in the socialist-realist style dominated Mongolian art, yet the painting *Old Hero* (1942) by D. Manibadar used mineral paints for an approved folkloric theme, in this case recalling Mongolia's heroic traditions during WORLD WAR II.

The real flourishing of Mongol *zurag* began in the late 1950s, with the great success of the *Old Fiddler* (1958) by ÜRJINGIIN YADAMSÜREN (1905–87). In the 1960s the genre's basic themes and styles were established. Themes included the collective farm life (with or without signs of modern progress), scenes of the 1921 Revolution, emblematic figures of the Mongolian past, and scenes of old Mongolian life. Religious themes such as E. Pürewjal's *Geser Khan En Route* (1960) and M. Khaidaw's *White Old Man* (1961) were frowned on. The pictures of CAMELS (1968, 1971) by D. Sengetsokhio (b. 1917) are perhaps the most popular and widely reproduced examples of Mongol *zurag*. While some, such as Ts. Minjuur's (b. 1910) *Nomadizing* (1967) and P. Tserendorj's (b. 1910) *Wedding Customs* (1967), used shading in ways relatively close to European realistic painting, most followed Yadamsüren in using flat swaths of bright but cool colors. Many works, such as D. Damdinsüren's (b. 1909) 1966 *Games* and *Tsam in Khüriye* and Ts. Dawaakhüü's *Festivities at a Cooperative* (1979), ignore perspective and follow the layout of older Buddhist painters; others, such as B. Gombosüren's (b. 1930) *The New Masters of the State Have Come* (1963) and Ts. Jamsran's *Mongol Woman* (1968), boldly display geometric perspective. A few examples, such as Damdinsüren's *Mother's Glory* and D. Urtnasan's *Mandukhai the Wise Queen* (1982), explicitly exploit Buddhist iconographic forms for secular national topics. Urtnasan's *Mandukhai* is also notable for its black-ground *nagtang* iconic technique traditionally used for fierce protector deities (*dogshid*).

Since 1989 young Mongol *zurag* painters have turned to overtly religious and nationalist topics. The FIRE CULT, the OBOO (sacred cairn), scenes from the SECRET HISTORY OF THE MONGOLS, images of CHINGGIS KHAN, and shamans have all joined the themes of livestock, countryside life, and emblematic Mongol figures. At the same time Mongol *zurag* has become less strictly representational and more symbolic.

See also BUDDHIST FINE ARTS; REVOLUTIONARY PERIOD; THEOCRATIC PERIOD.

Further reading: N. Tsultem, *Development of the Mongolian National Style Painting "Mongol Zurag" in Brief* (Ulaanbaatar: State Publishing House, 1986).

Monguor   *See* TU LANGUAGE AND PEOPLE.

morin huur   *See* HORSE-HEAD FIDDLE.

Muhi, Battle of   While hard fought, the Battle of Muhi on April 11, 1241, ended in total victory for the Mongols over the Hungarian army. The Mongols crossed the Carpathians into the Hungarian plain in winter 1240–41 under the direction of the Mongol general SÜBE'ETEI BA'ATUR. CHINGGIS KHAN's grandson BATU (d. 1255), with his brother Shiban in the vanguard, advanced through the Veretski Pass (between modern Mukacheve and Stryy), while his cousin Büri (son of CHA'ADAI) attacked the Saxons of Transylvania and Böchek (son of TOLUI) ravaged Wallachia and the Banat.

King Bela IV (1235–70) of Hungary had been attempting to expand royal power since his coronation, and the nobility suspected him deeply. When Bela ordered a kingdomwide mobilization in February 1241, the nobility blamed him for provoking the war and refused to cooperate. Shiban's vanguard soon reached Pest (Budapest east of the Danube), but Sübe'etei ordered a feigned retreat to lure the Hungarians out. Bela took the bait, and the Hungarian nobility rallied to what now seemed a winning cause.

After two days the Mongols camped on the wooded high ground east of the Sajó River at Muhi (downstream from modern Miskolc), while Bela penned his troops in a corral of carts on the western bank. The numbers, double that of the Mongols, and the quality of the Hungarian cavalry worried the Mongols, and before the battle Batu went to a hilltop alone to plead with heaven for victory. Sübe'etei planned for Batu, assisted by the commander Boraldai, to assault the bridge over the Sajó, while he would cross the river downstream and surprise the enemy from the rear. After midnight Shiban led the Mongol vanguard to attack the bridge defended by Bela's brother Koloman (Kálmán). Hungarian valor matched Mongol expectations, and Batu lost more than 30 of his *ba'atur*s (heavily armed vanguards) before retreating. Eventually Mongol catapults firing explosive bombs disoriented the defenders, and the Mongols took the bridge.

Meanwhile, high water delayed the building of Sübe'etei's pontoon bridge downstream, and his force did not arrive until around 7:00 A.M. The Hungarians withdrew into their corral, and as the Mongols showered the corral with arrows and explosive bombs, the general Boroldai stormed the royal pavilion. The Mongols deliberately left their circle open and first isolated stragglers, and then the whole body fled westward while Mongol scouts hunted them down as they ran. The king and Koloman escaped, but Koloman later died of his wounds. The spoils included a good part of the royal treasure as well as the seal and the king's tent, which Batu later used to entertain European envoys. Batu and the princes were dismayed with their losses and advocated retiring, but Sübe'etei insisted the Mongols press their advantage to the Danube.

See also CENTRAL EUROPE AND THE MONGOLS; MILITARY OF THE MONGOL EMPIRE.

Mukhali   *See* MUQALI.

Mulahidah   *See* ISMA'ILIS.

Muqali (1170–1223) *One of Chinggis Khan's earliest nökörs, or companions, and his regent in North China*
Muqali belonged to the JALAYIR clan, which for many generations had been hereditary servants of the aristocratic BORJIGID rulers of the Mongols. His father, Gü'ün-U'a, was a servant of the Yürkin branch of the Borjigid but deserted them for CHINGGIS KHAN's Kiyad branch. Gü'ün-

U'a gave his son Muqali to the young Chinggis as a personal slave. Along with BO'ORCHU and other "companions" (NÖKÖR), Muqali shared in the hardships of Chinggis Khan's rise to power. At Chinggis Khan's coronation in 1206 Muqali and Bo'orchu received command of the left and right wings of the army, respectively, and they were made one of the "four steeds" (along with Boroghul and Chila'un).

During the conquest of the JIN DYNASTY in North China, Muqali commanded the charge that brought victory in Chinggis's decisive battle with the Jin at Huan'erzui (February 1212). In 1214 he commanded the Mongol forces that subdued the Jin armies in Liaoning, or southern Manchuria. After three years of campaigning he became more familiar with Chinese ways of warfare and developed a staff in which surrendered locals of Kitan ethnicity played a major role. In 1217, as Chinggis Khan was leaving North China to deal with unrest in Mongolia and Turkestan, he appointed Muqali his viceroy of the North China plain, granting him the Chinese titles "prince of state" (Chinese, guo wang, Mongolian, gui ong) and "grand preceptor" (taishi) and allowing him to use the nine-tailed banner, which he himself had raised in 1206. The core of the viceroy's TAMMACHI, or garrison army, was his own Jalayir clan and four other clans, the QONGGIRAD, Ikires, MANGGHUD, and Uru'ud, totaling about 13,000 men. The Önggüd tribe, numbering 10,000 and ruled by Chinggis's daughter ALAQAI BEKI as regent, was also under his command. Around this core locally recruited armies, Han (ethnic Chinese), Tangut, and Kitan, were attached to the Mongol tribes.

Over the course of the next seven years, Muqali waged a brutal but increasingly effective campaign to crush all remaining resistance in North China's Shanxi, Hebei, and Shandong provinces. Early on in his campaign in Liaoning, he had come to accept the Chinese practice of enrolling defeated generals and their soldiers into his force, yet he also made liberal use of the Mongol practice of wholesale massacre when confronted by stubborn resistance. By this time the Jin Empire had been driven south of the Huang (Yellow) River and no longer dared openly challenge Mongol armies in the Hebei plain yet held fortresses in Shandong and Shaanxi provinces. The Jin and the SONG DYNASTY in South China also engineered defections among generals who had surrendered to the Mongols. Within his base of Shanxi and Hebei provinces, Muqali dealt with the local chiefs and bandits resisting the chaos of the Mongol invasions with the time-tested techniques of counterinsurgency: concentrating the rural population in fortified villages, destroying all life and property outside these strategic hamlets, and rewarding strongmen who surrendered with ranks and titles. Under his rule Mongol tribal and tammachi garrisons and high-ranking surrendered commanders, such as YAN SHI, ZHANG ROU, and the Shii family (see SHII TIANZE), ruled their districts as virtually private kingdoms.

Muqali's chief problem lay in his small numbers. Chinggis Khan had taken the bulk of the Mongol cavalry west to conquer KHORAZM, leaving Muqali few resources to hold North China, a problem masked from his enemies only by his cavalry's extraordinary mobility, accurate intelligence, and awesome reputation. Even so, due to the small size of his troops he could not attempt more than occasional booty hunting expeditions in the Jin strongholds of Shaanxi and Henan.

Muqali died in 1223. His son Bo'al (sometimes erroneously written Boro) and later descendants succeeded to the title of prince of state and commanded forces in the completion of the conquest of North China, but they did not have anything comparable to Muqali's viceregal position. His later descendants became strong proponents of Confucian principles of rule and opponents of exploitative government practices.

See also HUAN'ERZUI, BATTLE OF; MANCHURIA AND THE MONGOL EMPIRE; MASSACRES IN THE MONGOL EMPIRE.

Further reading: Igor de Rachewiltz, "Muqali, Bôl, Tas, An-t'ung," in *In the Service of the Khan: Eminent Personalities of the Early Mongol-Yuan Period (1200–1300)*, ed. Igor de Rachewiltz, et al. (Wiesbaden: Otto Harrassowitz, 1993), 3–12.

music Mongolia's richly diverse musical traditions form one of the most distinctive and appealing parts of its folk culture. While there have been ensembles in the past, traditionally instruments were performed solo or to accompany a singer. Mongolian music uses pentatonic scale forms and is generally monophonic. Monastic musicians used a traditional Tibetan notation by the 18th century, but lay musicians have used European notation only since the 20th century.

SONGS

Singing is the main musical art of the Mongols and is divided into two types, the long song (urtyn duu; Kalmyk, ut dun) and the short song (bogino duu), although there are many intermediate forms. The first category is called the long song due to the extreme length of word and melodic phrases, which are drawn out with an abundance of ornamentation, such as glissandos, tones of indefinite pitch, and trills, and with no regular beat. Singers in a single song may cover a range of up to three octaves through the use of a powerful falsetto. In the classic KHALKHA style wide intervals of thirds and fourths are often used in succession, and the melodic contours have been compared to hills with a short, profusely ornamented ascent and a long rolling descent. Among the OIRATS and KALMYKS long songs are somewhat less "long" than among the Khalkha and INNER MONGOLIANS. The long song is usually accompanied by a fiddle (khuur) or less often a transverse flute (limbe).

Short songs have a much less unusual signing style, and the lyrics are often important. Time is usually duple or quadruple, rarely triple, a feature that fits the mostly disyllabic nature of Mongolian PROSODY. While the long songs are sung impassively, short songs are sometimes sung with vivid facial expressions and mime. This is particularly true of the *khariltsaa duu*, or dialogue songs, which may be sung by several people but more often by one singer under different voices for the different parts. Short songs may be accompanied but are, of course, frequently sung alone.

Mongolian songs cover virtually every topic: religious exhortation, recalling ancient heroes, praise and blessing of horses, mountains, and other beauties, thwarted love, lullabies, mothers' and fathers' kindness, and comic songs of promiscuous lamas or frustrated sexual desire. Dialogue songs and songs with comic topics are always short songs, but long songs can have many topics. The Mongols, in classifying their long songs, traditionally adopted the Tibetan distinction of "state songs" (*töriin duu*, from Tibetan *rgyal-po'i glu*, king's songs) and "popular songs" (*tügeemel* or *jiriin duu*, from Tibetan *'bangs-kyi glu*, commoners' songs). The most important of the "state songs" is *Tümnii ekh*, "Beginning of Ten-Thousand," which opens any *nair*, "feast," or athletic NAADAM games and calls on the listeners to remember the preciousness of human birth and devotedly to serve the church and state. After the 1920s, the words were rewritten to emphasize devotion to the Mongolian Peoples's Republic and its great hero GENERAL SÜKHEBAATUR. Sometimes the "state songs" were divided into (Buddhist) church and state subcategories. The famous THROAT SINGING was traditionally sung only in northwestern Mongolia and had rather low status. Songs were traditionally sung alone; choral singing was introduced in political songs only from the first half of the 20th century.

INSTRUMENTS

Traditional Mongolian lay instruments include the following categories: 1) bowl-, box-, and tube-bodied fiddles; 2) lutes; 3) flutes and pipes; and 4) zithers and dulcimers. Buddhist services are accompanied by percussion instruments and shawms. The most important of these instruments is undoubtedly the fiddle. Lutes and flutes are more widely distributed, but zithers and dulcimers were traditionally more urban and sometimes used orchestrally. In the middle ages shawms were used in non-Buddhist music.

Most Mongolian fiddles are spike fiddles, that is, the neck extends through the box and is fixed through the box's lower edge. A virtually obsolete two-string fiddle, the "ladle-fiddle" (*shanagan khuur*), was, however, carved from one piece of wood like the Kazakh *qobiz* fiddle. Traditionally, the front of the sound box is made of skin, not wood, and horse or *matar* (crocodile) heads are carved on the scroll, as they are in Tibet. The instrument is fingered by pushing the string with the finger, nail, or knuckle, not by pressing it against the neck. Fiddles are generally used for accompanying singers but sometimes are played solo.

The most common fiddle has a box-shaped body and two horsehair strings tuned in fifths. It was called a *khili khuur*, "bow fiddle," in Inner Mongolia, but due to the horse head commonly carved on its scroll it is now known as the HORSE-HEAD FIDDLE. The *ikil* of western Mongolia's Oirats is a version of the *khili khuur* without a horse-head scroll. The other main type, the tube-bodied fiddle, is different in virtually every regard: It has vertical, not horizontal, tuning pegs and four silk strings (also tuned in fifths) in two harmonizing pairs. The strings pass not over a bridge but through a high metal ring. The bow has two strings that pass between the strings and are thus attached to the fiddle. Finally, it is played kneeling, while the horse-head fiddle is played sitting. The instrument is called a *dörben chikhi-tei khuur*, "four-eared fiddle," in Inner Mongolia and a *khuuchir* in Khalkha.

Mongolian lutes occur in three forms, the *towshuur*, which is more like the horse-head fiddle but plucked, the KAZAKHS' two-string *dombra*, with a triangular body and movable frets, and the three-string fretless *shanz* or *shudraga* with an oval body. These instruments are used especially among the Oirats of western Mongolia, Xinjiang, and Kalmykia, where they accompany dances. The *dombra* (Kalmyk, *dombr*) is used only by the Kalmyks among the Mongolian-speaking people, and the *towshuur* also accompanies epic singing among western Mongolia's Oirats. The *shanz* is a Chinese instrument (Chinese, *sanxian*; Japanese, *shamisen*) adapted by the western Mongolian Oirats but also used in ULAANBAATAR and Inner Mongolia.

Mongolian wind instruments occur in two types: the transverse flute, or *limbe*, used among the Mongols and Inner Mongolians, and the vertical flute, or *tsuur*, used among the Oirats, TUVANS (were it is called *shuur*), and

Lamas performing in a yurt during the White Moon (lunar new year) services, Bandida Gegeen Monastery, Shiliin Khot, 1987 *(Courtesy Christopher Atwood)*

Kazakhs (*sibizghi*) and occasionally among the ORDOS Mongols. The *limbe* has six finger holes and other holes that affect the timbre. By contrast the *tsuur* is a simple tube with four holes used to amplify the overtones of throat singing.

The Mongolian zither, or *yatga,* is formed of a rectangular box with a convex cover and movable bridges. Strings were traditionally made of goat gut, horsehair, or silk. The instrument is similar enough to the Chinese *zheng* and Japanese *koto* that Mongolian players can play on the latter, if necessary, although the Mongolian examples are constructed slightly differently. Strings range from 12 to six, and they are plucked with a plectrum while the left hand may press the strings to produce a glissando. The *yoochin,* or dulcimer (from Chinese *yangqin*), has a trapezoidal body and brass strings and is played with wooden hammers. It is played while sitting at a table. Both these instruments were patronized primarily by the court and demanded too much specialized training to be played well by countryside musicians.

Of the many Buddhist instruments used in ritual, the only ones used in other musical contexts are the shawms, or *bishgüür,* the great copper trumpets (*büree* and *ükher büree*), the latter up to nine feet long, and the drums and gongs. The *büree* (Middle Mongolian, *büriye*) was used in the Mongol army in the 16th century to give the signal for battle. Buddhist chant is distinctive for its strongly rhythmic character, which influenced Mongolian prosody and perhaps indirectly Mongolian songs. The chanting proceeds on distinct notes, but the orchestral music, while often impressive, has no recognizable melody. This music is, however, played according to notation. One monastery in central Khalkha used *gür* (Tibetan, *mgur*), or religious long songs, for certain services, and these had a written notation dating back to the late 18th century.

HISTORY

While Mongolian music undoubtedly has a long history, most of it cannot be traced due to lack of documentation. In particular, while instrumental forms such as the "ladle fiddle" have sometimes been traced back to the XIONGNU (Huns) of the second century B.C.E., and the Mongol khans are recorded as having played a lute-type instrument, the more central singing art cannot be documented.

Under the MONGOL EMPIRE, CHINGGIS KHAN (1206–26) adopted for his court the music of the Tangut XIA DYNASTY (1038–1227), while his son ÖGEDEI KHAN allowed court musicians of the Jurchen JIN DYNASTY (1115–1234) to be gathered to preserve their music. QUBILAI KHAN (1260–94) expanded the court music, incorporating that of the Chinese SONG DYNASTY as well as foreign instruments. These included a wind organ with 90 pipes played with a bellows, a "wooden peacock" that waved peacock feathers as it played, a *qobuz,* or Kazakh-style bowl-bodied lute, and a fiddle with a carved dragon head, presumably a predecessor of Mongolian string instruments.

Traditional Mongolian music was influenced by the introduction of Buddhist music from Tibet in the 16th century and Chinese Beijing opera in the 19th century. Tibetan lhamo-style opera was also performed in Alashan and the Gobi (*see* DANZIN-RABJAI). In 1914, Mongolia's newly independent theocratic government formed a military brass band with Russian aid.

From the first years after the 1921 REVOLUTION, Mongolian folk music was recognized by urban artists and government officials as a great cultural repository. At the same time, European classical music was introduced into Mongolia from the 1940s on. Milestones were the European-style opera (*Uchirtai gurwan tolgoi,* Three fateful hills, 1942) by B. Damdinsüren and B. F. Smirnov, the symphony (*Minii nutag* My homeland, 1955) by L. Mördorj (1919–97) and the ballet (*Gankhuyag,* 1957) by S. Gonchigsumlaa. The Mongolian State Circus opened in 1941. Western popular music began to be performed in the late 1960s, with *estrad* music, a combination of jazz and folk rock, played by the two approved bands, Soyol Erdene ("Culture Jewel") and Bayan Mongol ("Rich Mongolia"). From then on Mongolian music can be seen as having four trends: amateur folk music, professional folk music, European classical music, and popular music.

Professional folk music has been institutionalized in Mongolia since 1951 in the State Folk Song and Dance Ensemble. In this process instruments were selected and often modified to give them a stronger, more stable sound. The *yatga* and *yoochin* were revived in a new symphonic context, combining fiddles of various sizes, great temple trumpets, flutes, and other instruments. Thus, the context of folk music has completely changed, losing its earlier religious, ethnic, and political context while gaining in virtuosity.

See also FOLK POETRY AND TALES; LITERATURE.

Further reading: Carole Pegg, *Mongolian Music, Dance, and Oral Narrative* (Seattle: University of Washington Press, 2001); Henning Haslund-Christensen, ed., *Music of the Mongols,* Part I, *Eastern Mongolia* (Stockholm: Trycheri aktiebologet Thule, 1943).

Recordings: Altai-Khangai, *Gone with the Wind* (Window to Europe, 1988); Badma Khanda, *In a Song—My People's Soul* (Badma Seseg Records, 2000); *Tsahan: Masterpieces of Kalmyk Traditional Music* (OOO "Kailas," 2001); *White Moon: Traditional and Popular Music from Mongolia* (Pan Records, 1992).

Myangad *See* MINGGHAD.

N

naadam (*nadom, nadamu*) The *naadam* (Uighur-Mongolian, *nagadum*), or "games," of modern Mongolia and Inner Mongolia is the modern form of the ancient Mongolia summer festival.

ORIGINS

The Mongolian calendar from the 13th century had both winter (the WHITE MONTH, or lunar new year) and summer (KOUMISS aspersions and the great QURILTAI) celebrations. While WRESTLING, HORSE RACING, and ARCHERY were all popular games, no texts directly link games at this time to the celebrations.

At least since the 17th century communal summer religious ceremonies have always concluded with competitions of the "three manly games" (*eriin gurwan naadam*). Such summer ceremonies include aspersions of koumiss at the opening of the mare-milking season, OBOO (cairn) worship, and the DANSHUG ritual, in which lay patrons present a mandala to INCARNATE LAMAS. All these rituals were carried out by both large and small groups.

The largest of these was the great triennial *danshug* for the JIBZUNDAMBA KHUTUGTU held in Khüriye (modern ULAANBAATAR) by all four AIMAGS (provinces) of the KHALKHA. Called the "Danshug Games of the Seven BANNERS [of Khalkha]" (Dologan khoshigun-u danshug nagadum/Doloon Khoshuuny danshig naadam), it was first celebrated in 1697 and became a major event in Khalkha life. The "three manly games" on this occasion, and especially wrestling, became the focus of intense rivalries between localities and especially between the clerical and lay estates. At these vast games as many as 1,012 wrestlers and 3,000 horses took part. Another *danshug* supported by the GREAT SHABI, or the Jibzundamba's personal subjects, and with athletes from Khalkha's two eastern *aimags* took place annually.

MODERN TIMES

In 1912, after the 1911 RESTORATION of Mongolian independence, the *danshug* games were moved to the last lunar month of summer (July–August) and held annually for all the subjects of the state, not just the Khalkha. The *danshug* games thus became the great celebration of the new nation, at which all the local nobility gathered to express devotion to the Jibzundamba Khutugtu, the new head of state.

In April 1922, after the 1921 REVOLUTION, the new government limited the religious *danshug* ceremony before eliminating the public ceremony altogether in 1923. *Naadams* connected with minor religious holidays continued until the destruction of Buddhism in the 1930s. In 1922 GENERAL SÜKHEBAATUR ordered that army games be held on July 11, the anniversary of the revolution's victory. The purely secular meaning attached to the games and the fixing of their date according to the European calendar were new; previously, the religious rituals occurred either on a fixed lunar date or more usually on an astrologically determined date. After 1924 the country's national holiday was fixed for July 11, and the army games became the "National Holiday Naadam" (*ulsyn ikh bayar naadam*), celebrating the success of the 1921 Revolution and the achievements of the new state. The rivalry between the clerical and lay estates continued and became more dangerous; after a lama won the 1937 wrestling competition in the midst of the antireligious campaign, he was arrested and sentenced to 15 years in prison.

In the postwar period wrestling and archery events were moved from the fields to stadiums built outside the major cities and towns. (Mongolian cross-country horse racing still necessarily takes place in the fields). During the Communist period the "three manly games" themselves were carried on in a traditional manner, but the attendant opening ceremonies in the capital resembled Soviet political celebrations, with parades of military units and weapons. Representatives of social organizations held red banners and portraits of Marx, Lenin, and Sükhebaatur as they marched past government and party leaders on the reviewing stand next to the tomb of Sükhebaatur and MARSHAL CHOIBALSANG.

Since the 1990 DEMOCRATIC REVOLUTION the review in the capital at the tomb of Sükhebaatar and Choibalsang has continued, but only the color guard, equipped with new, traditional-looking uniforms, parades. The white (or peaceful) horsehair standard is now placed in the stadium for the wrestlers to salute before and after matches. (A black, or warlike, standard also exists and would presumably be used in time of war.) Actors re-create personalities in Mongolia's premodern history. Personal attendance is no longer compulsory, and many Mongolians in the capital prefer to watch the games on television. Smaller *naadam*s are held in provincial and *sum* (district) centers; the small ones involve more than 100 athletes and the large ones about 1,000.

In Inner Mongolia *naadam*s are celebrated on a variety of regional and local occasions in July or August, although there is no regular all-regional *naadam*. In Buriatia an annual *sur-kharbaan* (archery) festival has been held on the first Sunday in July in ULAN-UDE since 1924, although wrestling and horse racing are also practiced. Smaller *sur-kharbaan*s are held locally as well. Since 1990 the games among the Buriats and Kalmyks have been called after their epic heroes, thus Geseriad among the Buriats and Jangghariad among the Kalmyks. The Kalmyks add javelin throwing and the Daurs field hockey to the three manly games.

See also CALENDAR AND DATING SYSTEMS; REVOLUTIONARY PERIOD; THEOCRATIC PERIOD.

Further reading: Iwona Kabzińska-Stawarz, *Games of the Mongolian Shepherds* (Warsaw: Institute of the History of Material Culture, Polish Academy of Sciences, 1991); Henry Serruys, *Kumiss Ceremonies and Horse Races: Three Mongolian Texts* (Wiesbaden: Otto Harrassowitz, 1974).

Naiman The Naiman was probably the most powerful Mongolian khanate during the rise of Chinggis Khan. The word *Naiman* means eight in Mongolian, referring to the number of clans, or lineages, contained in it. Despite this name, virtually all the names and titles found among the Naiman indicate that they spoke a Turkish language.

The Naiman appear to be the same as the Nianbage or Nianba'en found as a distant tribe in Kitan records of the 11th century. They became a major tribe in the 12th century, straddling the ALTAI RANGE. At its height it stretched from QARA-QORUM in the east past the Irtysh River in the west and bordered the Zunghar (Junggar) basin and the UIGHURS to the south and the Siberian Kyrgyz (in the modern Minusinsk basin) to the north.

Due to the barrier of the Altai, the Naiman Khanate was often divided in two, each half ruled by a brother. In the early history of the Naiman, RASHID-UD-DIN FAZL-ULLAH speaks of rivalry between two brothers, Narqiz-Tayang and Anyat Khan. At other times, however, the two halves were united. Around 1160 the Naiman seem to have reached the apogee of their power with the united rule of Inancha Bilge Khan. He divided the realm between his two sons, Buyruq Khan and Tayang Khan, but by 1204 Tayang Khan ruled both sides of the Altai again.

CULTURE

The Naiman were nomadic and similar in customs to the Mongols, but their khanate had a higher level of organization. Unlike the Mongols, the Naiman had a single ruling dynasty, frontier guards, a throne, and a seal kept in 1204 by a Uighur scribe, TATAR-TONG'A. The court was presumably literate. Thus, the Naiman despised Chinggis's Mongols as bad-smelling savages unfit to rule the MONGOLIAN PLATEAU.

The religious beliefs of the Naiman varied. Episodes of the *SECRET HISTORY OF THE MONGOLS* show the Naiman rulers as practicing rainmaking and other shamanistic rituals. Rashid-ud-Din reports that one khan was able to milk both female demons and wild animals of the wastelands. Nevertheless, Tayang Khan's son Küchülüg, was raised a Christian, and WILLIAM OF RUBRUCK reported that the Naiman were Christian. A Syriac rock inscription and cross in KHOWD PROVINCE (Mönkhkhairkhan Sum), while not yet professionally deciphered, testifies to early Christian activity in Naiman territory.

HISTORY

At the time of the rise of CHINGGIS KHAN, the rivalry of the KEREYID and Naiman Khanates was a constant of Mongolian political life. Under Inancha Bilge Khan the Naiman dominated the Kereyid, but after his death the balance switched the other way. Against the Kereyid, the Naiman cemented marriage alliances with the Merkid to the north. When the Kereyid khan Toghril, or ONG KHAN backed Chinggis Khan (Temüjin) as khan of the Mongols, the Naiman supported Chinggis's rival, JAMUGHA. In 1202 Ong Khan and Chinggis Khan together attacked Buyruq Khan and drove him west. Ong Khan and Chinggis fell out, however, and Buyruq Khan's Naiman, under the general Kögse'ü-Sabraq, rallied the remains of the tribe and defeated Ong Khan. Kögse'ü-Sabraq joined his people to those of Tayang Khan, reunifying most of the Naiman. In 1204, after Chinggis conquered the Kereyid, Tayang Khan, egged on by his wife and stepmother, Gürbesü, attacked the Mongols, but was defeated and killed at the Battle of Keltegei cliffs, and Chinggis Khan took Gürbesü as a concubine.

Tayang's son Küchülüg fled to join his uncle Buyruq in the western steppes, but in 1206 Mongol troops captured Buyruq. Küchülüg found refuge among the QARA-KHITAI. Küchülüg gathered the remnants of the Naiman tribe and with their help usurped the Qara-Khitai throne, ruling until his capture and execution by the Mongols in 1218.

THE NAIMAN IN THE MONGOL EMPIRE

After the conquest a few Naiman men achieved high positions: the JARGHUCHI (judge) Qadaq under GÜYÜG Khan, the Il-Khanid general KED-BUQA, and the warlord Chagha'an-Temür of the late Yuan. Naiman women were considered beautiful, and the imperial family often took them as wives. One, TÖREGENE, actually became regent of the empire in 1242–46. In the YUAN DYNASTY class structure among the Mongols in the East, the Naiman were not included within the ranks of Mongols but combined with the Muslim, Uighur, Tangut, and other peoples in the second-rank SEMUREN, or "various sorts," category.

Eventually, the bulk of the Naiman seem to have moved into the Jochid BLUE HORDE in present-day Kazakhstan. The Naiman clan, or lineage, thus came to form an important clan among the descendants (in whole or part) of that horde: the Kazakhs, Bashkir (Bashkort), and Kyrgyz. In the Northern Yuan (1368–1634) the Naiman were one of the eight OTOGS (camp district) of the CHAKHAR. After 1636 this otog was made a banner in southeastern Inner Mongolia (see JUU UDA). The Naiman clan name is found there and elsewhere in southeastern Inner Mongolia, as well as among the KHALKHAS of west-central Mongolia.

names, personal Mongolian personal names have gone through two "naming revolutions." In the first, traditional Mongolian names were replaced by Tibetan names, while in the second, Tibetan names were replaced by new Mongolian names rather different from those before the first naming revolution.

Generally, the Mongols, unlike the Chinese, have only one personal name, which remains the same throughout their lives. While clan organization remained important among the Mongols into the 17th century (and among the Buriat Mongols even today), CLAN NAMES were not linked with the personal name in a family name system. While the personal name of the living ruler was not originally tabooed, as in China, the names of deceased rulers were tabooed for several generations. Even today, people feel very uncomfortable speaking their parents' name in their hearing, and in the past this prohibition was even stronger.

TWELFTH TO FOURTEENTH CENTURIES

The most common category of Mongol names were those of auspicious or (for boys) manly things, such as the number nine (yisü), gold (altan), eternity (möngke), excess (hüle'ü), blue (köke), white (chagha'an), health (esen),

firmness (batu), stability (toqto'a), bulls (buqa, for men), iron (temür), steel (bolad), black (qara), hardness (berke), and so on. The number nine (yisü) is particularly common and can be found in many forms (yisügei, yisüder, yisüngge, yisülün, yisünjin, yisüi, etc.) and compounds (yisü-buqa, nine-bulls, yisü-möngke, nine-eternity, yisün-to'a, ninth-number, yisün-temür, ninth-iron, etc.) Such names were often combined with suffixes used only for personal names, such as -dai, -ge/gei, and -der for boys and -jin, -tani, and -lun for girls. (The -jin in CHINGGIS KHAN's original name, Temüjin, is not the feminine suffix but a derivation from the occupational suffix -chin in Temürchin, "blacksmith.") Apart from those formed by feminine suffixes, girls were frequently given male names. Checheg, "Flower," is one of the few distinctive girls names.

Other names were based on either conquests or clan names. Thus, we find Mongols named Qashi (Hexi, or the XIA DYNASTY), Qurumsi (KHORAZM), Asudai (OSSETES, or Alans), Orus (Russia), and Majar (Magyar, or Hungary). Clan names could be combined with the -dai suffix for boys' or -jin for girls' names to form personal names: Mangghudai, Targhudai, Eljigidei, Baya'ujin, Monggholjin, and so on. Frequently, such clan-based personal names were not from the person's own clan. Thus, Targhudai was actually a TAYICHI'UD, and Mangghudai actually a Tatar, and so on.

One finds a number of degrading or inauspicious names among the Mongols of this time, such as Sorqaqtani, "Pox girl," obviously an attempt to fool the smallpox spirit into thinking it had already afflicted her. Other names appear to express frustration, such as the not-uncommon girls' name Oghul-qaimish (Turkish, [We] Were Searching for a Boy), while the name Jochi, "Guest," indicated doubts about the child's paternity. Others such as Bujir-Ebügen (Filthy Old Man) or the later Ghazan (Persian, "Kettle") and Kharbanda (Persian, "Muleteer") are more likely to be the result of the practice noted by MUHAMMAD ABU-'ABDULLAH IBN BATTUTA of Mongol mothers naming their children after the first thing they saw after childbirth. This may also account for some of the conquest and clan names: A subject of the conquered people or a member of the Mongol clan may have appeared in the camp just at the time of birth.

The Mongols at this time frequently used purely Turkish names (Jelme, Qutlugh, Arghun, Abishqa, Oghul-Qaimish, etc.). Later, as the Mongols spread out to Eurasia, names in other languages became common, either because the word for that thing had entered the MONGOLIAN LANGUAGE (such as Ghazan or Kharbanda, above, or toghus, peacock) or from a desire to use a prestigious foreign language. This later practice was connected with the adoption of foreign religions.

Before and during the imperial expansion, Christian names were found among the KEREYID and ÖNGGÜD tribes. Occasional Chinese names were already in use among the Önggüds and UIGHURS, and later some Mongolian parents requested Chinese Taoist priests and Buddhist monks to bestow a name. From the 1250s Sanskrit, Uighur, and Tibetan Buddhist names (Manggala, Ananda, Gamala, Wachir, Irinchin, Dorji, etc.) granted by Tibetan teachers became common in the royal family and the aristocratic clans. In the west some Mongols took Islamic names after they converted, although many kept their Mongolian names.

After the 1368 expulsion of the Mongols from China, the Sanskrit names in the imperial family soon disappeared. Christian names appeared occasionally before disappearing. Turkish names also declined, leaving primarily the auspicious Mongolian names similar to those in the early empire, although "nine" (*yisü*) and "bull" (*buqa*) names become rare after 1500.

SEVENTEENTH TO TWENTIETH CENTURIES

With the beginning of the SECOND CONVERSION to Buddhism in 1575, however, a naming revolution took place in Mongolia. From 1635 on the vast majority of Mongols had Buddhist names, usually Tibetan but sometimes Sanskrit or from the traditional Mongolian Buddhist terminology. A number of Mongolian-language names survived, particularly with more pacific elements designating peace (Engkhe, Amur), happiness (Jirgal), long life (Nasu), and blessing (Ölzei, Kheshig).

Buddhist names were granted according to several different principles. The most common for laymen are based on the Tibetan or Sanskrit names of powerful deities: Damdin/Damrin (Hayagriva), Dulma/Dari (Tara), Gombo (Mahakala), Chagdur/Shagdur (Vajrapani), Jamsrang (Beg-tshe), Jamyang (Manjushri), etc. Another type of Buddhist name derives from the Tibetan days of the week, themselves named after the Sun, Moon, and five visible planets (Nima, Dawa, Migmar, Lhagba, Pürbü, Basang, Bimba). Another astrological scheme divides the months' days into five classes, each under an element: Dorji (power bolt), Rinchin (jewel), Badma (lotus), and Sangjai (Buddha). (For some reason the fourth class, Liji, was never used.) The suffixes -*jab* (Tibetan, *skyabs*, "protecting") and -*sürüng* (Tibetan, -*srung*, "guarding") were commonly added to these Buddhist names. Finally, some names, particularly for monks, were based on Tibetan words for desired qualities or aspects of the religion: Lubsang, "good intellect," Agwang, "powerful in speech," Danzin "instruction keeper," Dashi/Rashi, "blessed." A number of Buddhist terms exist in multiple forms transmitted from Old Uighur, Tibetan, and Sanskrit: thus, Wachir/Ochir, Dorji, and Bazar all mean "power bolt," while Erdeni, Rinchin, and Radna all mean "jewel."

A distinctive type of Mongolian name that flourished in this period and is still common in the countryside is the avoidance name, designed to avert misfortune from the boy child: Nergüi, "No Name," Enebish, "Not This," Terbish, "Not That," Muu'Ökhin, "Bad Girl," Khorkhoi, "Worm," Gölgöö, "Puppy."

At the same time, the conquest of the Mongolian peoples by the Manchu and the Russian Empires resulted in a limited influence from these languages. In eastern Inner Mongolia Manchu names with the adjectival suffix-*ngga* based on desired moral qualities became common: Saichungga, Khafungga, Khuturingga. After 1911 such names were no longer given. Among the non-Buddhist western BURIATS Russian names became dominant in the 19th century, although often pronounced in strange ways: *Roman* became Armaan, and Vasilii became Bashiila or Bashil.

MODERN NAMES

The Communist overthrow of Buddhism in the 20th century resulted in a second naming revolution, which replaced Tibetan names with new Mongolian ones. Mongolian names became more frequent in the 1930s and 1940s but were still the minority. A local study of names in KHOWD PROVINCE found that of those born before 1950, only 35 percent had Mongolian names and 52 percent Tibetan and Sanskrit ones (the rest were unclassified local names). By 1972 in the capital, ULAANBAATAR, about 85 percent of kindergarten children had Mongolian names, with the remainder being Tibetan and Sanskrit. Percentages of Mongolian names in the countryside remained lower: A local study of children named from 1978 to 1995 in SÜKHEBAATUR PROVINCE found 65 percent with Mongolian names. The most common purely masculine elements are Bat (Firm), Baatar (Hero), Bayar (Joy), Sükh (Axe), and Bold (Steel), while the most common purely feminine elements are Tsetseg (Flower), Tuyaa (Ray), Chimeg (Ornament), Bolor (Crystal), and Naran (Sun). Elements found in both boys' and girls' names include Mönkh (Eternal), Erdene (Jewel), Enkh (Peace), and Jargal (Happiness). The Tibetan element maa functions as a feminine adjective, so that while Soyolt, "Cultured," is a boy's name, Soyolmaa is a girl's.

This second naming revolution began even earlier in eastern Inner Mongolia, where Mongolian names increased after 1911, becoming dominant after 1945. While many elements are similar to those in Mongolia proper, Inner Mongolian boys' names more frequently use adjectives ending in -*tu*: Gereltü (Shining), Chogtu (Glorious), Bayartu (Joyous), Chenggeltü (Rejoicing). Inner Mongolians rarely use the -maa ending, however. In addition to those in use in Mongolia, Tana, "Pearl," and -*khuwar* (from Chinese *huar*, "flower") are also common feminine elements. From 1900 to 1945 Inner Mongolians frequently bore two names, a Chinese name and a Mongolian name, which often had no connection in sound or meaning. This practice, extremely confusing for historians, was replaced after 1945 by using Chinese characters to render the sound of the Mongolian names.

Outside Mongolia proper Russian and Chinese names have become common. Among the Buriats perhaps half of younger adults have Russian personal names. In

Kalmykia, as among other Oirat peoples, there are many unusual non-Mongolian, non-Buddhist names, sometimes borrowed from the neighboring Turkic peoples. In Inner Mongolia perhaps 10 percent of younger adults, mostly from eastern Inner Mongolia, have Chinese names. These names, however, tend to use a distinctive and rather narrow range of Chinese characters.

See also PATRONYMICS.

Further reading: Wonsoo Yu, "Names of the Dariganga **Sum** Children," *Han-Mong kongdong haksul yŏn'gu* 4 (1995): 93–181.

Natsugdorji (Dashdorjiin Natsagdorj) (1906–1937)
The founder and most widely read author of modern Mongolian literature

Born in Darkhan Zasag banner (modern Bayandelger Sum, Central province) to the heavily indebted TAIJI (petty noble) Dashidorji, Natsugdorji lost his mother, Pagma, in his seventh year. His father, a scribe, had the boy tutored by a colleague from his ninth year. As a young teenager Natsugdorji served as a clerk in the army ministry. After the 1921 REVOLUTION he became the private secretary of GENERAL SÜKHEBAATUR and in April 1922 an assistant in the Party Central Committee. From 1923 to 1925 Natsugdorji served as secretary first in the Central Committee and then in the party's Military Commission, an extraordinary responsibility for one still under 20. Simultaneously, he helped found youth organizations: the Revolutionary Youth League in 1921 and the Young Pioneers in 1925. He participated in the league's *shii jüjig* (Beijing opera–style plays) productions and wrote the lyrics of the Pioneers' anthem "Song of the Pioneers."

In 1925 he left government to study, first at Leningrad's Military-Political Academy (1925–1926) and then at the University of Berlin's journalism school and Leipzig University (1926–29), where he studied with the German Mongolist Erich Haenisch. Natsugdorji's wife, Pagmadulma, entered the Leipzig Higher School for Women. In 1929 the new leftist government recalled all students studying outside the Soviet Union. Natsugdorji on his return was excluded from the revolutionary "Writers' Circle" as a disenfranchised *taiji* but did work in a succession of journalistic and research positions. He translated several books and stories from German originals or translations, including MARCO POLO's travels, the Mongolian history by the czarist adviser to Mongolia Ivan Ya. Korostovets, and "Gold Bug" by Edgar Allan Poe. He was imprisoned in 1932 for celebrating the lunar new year (Tsagaan Sar) and was released only after almost a year with the advent of the NEW TURN POLICY. Meanwhile, his marriage to Pagmadulma collapsed, and he married a Soviet German woman, Nina Chistikova. In 1935 Nina Chistikova was deported to Leningrad (St. Petersburg) with their daughter, Anandaa-Shir for overstaying her visa. In 1936 Natsugdorji was again imprisoned. He was a heavy drinker, and on July 13, 1937, he was found in a coma on the streets of Ulaanbaatar and died without regaining consciousness.

Only a few works by Natsugdorji before his stay in Germany are extant, although a now-lost play, *Monggol-un ügeigüü ail-un khöbegün* (Son of a Mongolian proletarian family, 1924) won an award. In Germany Natsugdorji wrote several poems whose theme is summed up in the widely quoted final lines to "Traveling to a Far Land to Learn": "From lands that geese cannot attain by wing / The child of man returns, in his bosom jewels enfolding." His first prose sketch, "May Day in a Capitalist Country," expressed his admiration of the working-class movement in Germany and his shame that supposedly revolutionary Mongolia could not muster the same spirit.

Natsugdorji's main period of productivity came from 1929 to his death. His poems generally follow traditional alliterative structure and a relatively strict isosyllabic PROSODY. The rhythm and phrasing of his poem "My Homeland" (*Minii nutag*, 1932), a staple of patriotic education to the present, strongly recall traditional praise songs. During his imprisonment in 1932, he wrote on candy wrappers poems of longing for his wife, for the beauties of nature, and for freedom. Other poems he wrote for programmatic purposes such as promoting hygiene and modern medicine. Natsugdorji's stories are more sketches than plot-driven narratives. His famous "Young Old-Timer" (*Khuuchin khüü*, 1930) painted a schematic yet vivid picture of the isolation and changelessness of the steppe, while "Tears of the Reverend Lama" (*Lambuguain nulims*) presents a sympathetic portrait of a lama from the countryside arriving at GANDAN-TEGCHINLING MONASTERY and falling desperately in love with a fickle Chinese prostitute. Later poems and stories written during the New Turn period show a more romantic attitude toward the herders' life. The opera *Three Fateful Hills* (*Uchirtai gurwan tolgoi*), presented in beautiful verse strongly reminiscent of folk poetry, has the common revolutionary theme of a young couple's love thwarted by tyrannical lords. Its originally tragic ending was rewritten after Natsugdorji's death to accord with revolutionary optimism.

See also LITERATURE; REVOLUTIONARY PERIOD.

Nauruz   *See* NAWROZ.

Nawroz (Nauruz) (d. 1297) *Mongol commander in the Middle Eastern Il-Khanate who engineered Ghazan Khan's rise and converted him to Islam*

As the son of ARGHUN AQA, the governor of Khorasan (eastern Iran), Nawroz enjoyed a youth of wealth and power, which nourished his unpredictably violent and obstinate personality. He shared with his wife, Abagha Khan's daughter Toghanchuq, a deep Muslim faith, and they were very close. In 1289 Nawroz, afraid of being implicated in the fall of the vizier BUQA, rose in rebellion with his *tümen* (10,000) of QARA'UNAS against Arghun's son and viceroy in Khorasan, GHAZAN KHAN (1271–1304). After crossing the Amu Dar'ya to join QAIDU's forces, Nawroz invaded Khorasan in 1291; his subsequent three years of pillage devastated the region.

In winter 1294–95, at Toghanchuq's urging, Nawroz returned to his allegiance to Ghazan. During Ghazan's bid for the throne from that May on, Ghazan relied implicitly on Nawroz's skillful use of guile and disinformation, first to disarm Baidu's suspicions and then to sow treason and fear in his camp. Once Ghazan accepted Nawroz's urgings to convert to Islam, Nawroz arranged vital support from the Islamic clergy and even contacted the Il-Khans' Egyptian enemy. By October 4 GHAZAN KHAN had entered the capital, Tabriz, where, at Nawroz's instigation, he proclaimed the destruction of all Buddhist temples, churches, and synagogues.

Ghazan made Nawroz nominally chief commander and vizier of the empire, but to remove him from court dispatched him east to Khorasan to deal with a renewed invasion there. In summer 1296 Nawroz returned to court without authorization to see Toghanchuq, who died in July. Over the objections of his old commanders, Ghazan pardoned this disobedience and allowed Nawroz to return to Khorasan again. In March 1297 rivals at court used Nawroz's earlier contacts with MAMLUK EGYPT to charge him with treason, and on March 17 Ghazan ordered Nawroz's family executed. Nawroz fled to Herat, whose ruler handed him over to Ghazan's men for execution on April 14, 1297. After 1335 Nawroz's clansmen ruling the Ja'un-i Ghurban tribe again achieved influence in Khorasan.

Nayan's Rebellion

The rebellion of Nayan in 1287 expressed the dissatisfaction of the Mongol princes and the Manchurian and eastern Inner Mongolian populations under the long reign of QUBILAI KHAN. Quickly suppresed, it led to the extension of provincial rule to Manchuria.

Nayan was a fourth-generation descendant of Belgütei, CHINGGIS KHAN's half-brother (some sources confuse him with another Prince Nayan, the descendant of Chinggis's brother Temüge Odchigin). The older generation of the descendants of Chinggis Khan's four brothers who held appanages in Manchuria and eastern Mongolia had given vital support to Qubilai Khan in 1260, but their children felt both neglected and threatened by the advance of bureaucratization. Nayan, who instigated the revolt, was about 30 years old, a freehanded and popular prince whose support included virtually all the fraternal lines and Manchuria's native Jurchen and "Water Tatars," who had suffered famine in 1287.

Despite widespread support, Nayan's Rebellion was crippled by early detection and timid leadership and lacked coordination with Qubilai's foreign enemy, QAIDU. Once the court detected the planned rebellion in May–June 1287, Qubilai set out personally with his Chinese and Ossetian guards under a Jurchen general, Li Ting (d. 1304), while a larger Mongolian force under Öz-Temür (1242–95) was being mobilized. The two sides clashed on July 14, and Nayan's 60,000 green soldiers soon withdrew behind their carts despite their advantage in numbers. That night Li Ting began a bombardment and attacked, putting the rebels to flight. Öz-Temür and Li Ting then pursued Nayan, who was eventually captured and executed. Meanwhile, on July 24 the rebel prince Shigtür invaded the Chinese districts in Liaoning but was defeated within a month.

Widespread but uncoordinated risings of Nayan's supporters continued until winter 1288–89 but were ruthlessly repressed. As a result of the rising, Qubilai approved the creation of the Liaoyang Branch Secretariat on December 4, 1287, while rewarding loyal fraternal princes. Continuing famine was addressed with tax remissions and special grain transports.

See also MANCHURIA AND THE MONGOL EMPIRE.

Nei-Ren-Dang Case *See* "NEW INNER MONGOLIAN PEOPLE'S REVOLUTIONARY PARTY" CASE.

"New Inner Mongolian People's Revolutionary Party" Case (Nei-Ren-Dang Case)

From 1968 to 1969 opponents of Mongol autonomy in Inner Mongolia implicated hundreds of thousands of persons and killed at least 22,900, the vast majority ethnic Mongols, for involvement in a fabricated "New Inner Mongolian People's Revolutionary Party" (abbreviated in Chinese as Nei-Ren-Dang) Case.

In spring 1946 the Chinese Communist Party (CCP), led in Inner Mongolia by ULANFU, took over a strong pan-Mongolist nationalist movement in eastern Inner Mongolia led by the Inner Mongolian People's Revolutionary Party (IMPRP). Created with Soviet and Mongolian aid in 1925, this party had revived in August 1945 after Japan's surrender. While the IMPRP's leaders agreed to Communist demands to dissolve the party, the last grassroots cells were, in fact, disbanded only in fall 1947. From 1949 Inner Mongolia's CCP propagandists attacked the IMPRP's legacy, even though former IMPRP leaders held high governmental positions. In 1956 Ulanfu had to reassure former IMPRP members that they need not give further "confessions" of their errors.

In 1966 Ulanfu was dismissed as part of the Cultural Revolution in China. After a year of violent political struggle, a new leadership imported from Beijing under the military man Teng Haiqing was installed in Inner Mongolia on November 1, 1967, with a mission to cleanse Inner Mongolia of supposed traitors and class enemies. Meanwhile, Han (ethnic Chinese) cadres, particularly new immigrants, hoped to secure their advance by destroying Mongol autonomy. Old members of the IMPRP had, of course, already been "struggled" (targeted in public sessions of verbal and physical abuse), often to death, but in winter 1967–68 an ambitious Mongol writer and Cultural Revolution activist, Ulaanbagana, began charging that a "New IMPRP" still existed as a secret pervasive Soviet-Mongolian spy organization. In April 1968 Teng Haiqing arrested eight top Mongols as alleged ringleaders. On April 25, 1968, after 18 hours of unbearable interrogation, Batu, the vice president of Inner Mongolia University, confessed the existence of the "New IMPRP," although he quickly retracted his confession and refused to sign it. From April 26 the anti-"New IMPRP" campaign was begun.

By June victims were regularly giving interrogators hundreds of names, and an entire fictitious party structure with organizational charts, a seal, a flag, and so on was "uncovered." In HULUN BUIR interrogators uprooted a "United Nationalities Party," and in ALASHAN's Ejene banner a "TORGHUD People's Party." While persecutors included Mongols such as Teng Haiqing's deputy Wu Tao and Ulaanbagana, the basic ethnic thrust of the persecution is undeniable. In the local military units every ethnic Mongol officer above regimental level was implicated, and in the Orochen Autonomous Banner literally every single Orochen man, woman, and child was implicated in an "antiparty renegade clique." In the more than 90 percent Mongol Tug Commune in Ordos's Üüshin banner, 1,926 of 2,961 members, or 71 percent of the adults, were accused; 270 were maimed in some way, 116 made into partial or total invalids, and 49 killed. Although more than 70,000 victims were targeted in ULAANCHAB, where the Mongol population was less than 40,000, the Han targets were associated with Mongols and were supportive of Ulanfu's autonomy policy. The final death toll, according to official accounts, was 22,900 killed and 170,000 injured or crippled. Official figures on those arrested range from 346,000 to 750,000.

In October 1968 China's premier, Zhou Enlai, asked Teng to investigate possible abuses, but this casual intervention had no effect. A meeting in Beijing on February 4, 1969, attended by Zhou Enlai and all the other top leaders except Mao Zedong himself, completely vindicated Teng Haiqing and Wu Tao's approach.

Nevertheless, on May 22, after Mao had criticized excessive persecutions in general terms, Teng Haiqing was forced to make a confession of having committed abuses. In July Inner Mongolia was partitioned, removing the east and west from Teng's jurisdiction. Finally, in December Teng, Wu Tao, and the other leaders were dismissed, and Inner Mongolia was put under a new Han armyman from Beijing. Only on April 20, 1978, however, was the "New IMPRP" Case officially acknowledged to have been fabricated. To the present none of the top leaders responsible has been punished. In 1987 Ulaanbagana

was tried and sentenced to prison for 15 years, although the judges noted with dissatisfaction that he was by no means the principal culprit.

The "New IMPRP" Case radicalized Inner Mongolian youth, causing many to reject their elders' Chinese Communist loyalism. The absence of any serious reckoning among the Chinese leadership and the public with this legacy of injustice is still a deeply held grievance.

See also INNER MONGOLIA AUTONOMOUS REGION; INNER MONGOLIANS; KHAFUNGGA.

Further reading: William R. Jankowiak, "The Last Hurrah? Political Protest in Inner Mongolia," *Australian Journal of Chinese Affairs* 19/20 (1988): 269–288; W. Woody, *Cultural Revolution in Inner Mongolia: Extracts from an Unpublished History,* trans. Michael Schoenhals (Stockholm, Stockholm Center for Pacific Asian Studies, 1993).

New Policies The New Policies (Chinese, *Xin zheng,* Mongolian, *Shine zasag*), initiated in 1901, were a comprehensive effort by the QING DYNASTY (1636–1912) to modernize society and government. In Inner Asia the New Policies' emphasis on assimilating the frontier raised violent opposition.

By 1901 China's final dynasty, the Qing, had been repeatedly humiliated. Following the dynasty's defeat in the Sino-Japanese War (1894–95), the European powers scrambled for spheres of influence, while the fiasco of the 1900 anti-foreign Boxer movement led to the Boxer Protocols that imposed a massive indemnity and humiliating sanctions on China's government. In response, the dowager empress Cixi (1835–1908) finally supported a comprehensive reform program modeled on Meiji Japan.

Avoiding direct confrontation with foreign powers, the Qing used indirect means to strengthen the dynasty's Mongolian and Tibetan borderlands against Russian and British encroachment. The centerpiece was state-directed agricultural colonization of the steppe (*see* CHINESE COLONIZATION), which would finance modernizing agencies and lead to the integration of these areas as provinces.

In April 1902 the Qing government appointed the Manchu bannerman Yigu (d. 1926) the new commissioner for colonization in central and western Inner Mongolia. Yigu demanded that banners open vast new areas for cultivation and canceled the numerous deals private land developers (*dishang*) had previously made with the Mongolian banners, appropriating the traditional rents and fees for the provincial and local governments as a means of financing New Policies reforms. The Mongolian banners thus lost both control over and financial benefit from colonization.

In CHAKHAR, where the banner chiefs were appointed officials, the policy was pushed through with little overt opposition. The dukes and princes of ORDOS (Yekhe Juu) and ULAANCHAB leagues were less amenable. By 1903 the court had appointed Yigu head of the LIFAN YUAN (Court of Dependencies) and *jiangjun* (general in chief) of Suiyuan (*see* AMBAN) to increase his authority, and he replaced the stubborn prince of Khanggin (Hanggin) with the more pliable grand duke of Üüshin (Uxin) as the head of Yekhe Jun league. In 1908, however, Yigu was impeached and dismissed for abuse of authority. Still, 613,000 hectares (1,513,000 acres) of land had been opened for cultivation. In Jirim (for eastern Inner Mongolia) the Manchurian provincial authorities opened 4,540,000 *shang* (the amount of land plowed in a day) from 1903 to 1911.

HULUN BUIR, in Russia's sphere of influence, was a particularly sensitive area. The local banner administration was not considered secure and in 1908 was placed under the Chinese circuit intendant of the railway town Hailar. Chinese troops also replaced the border guards. Climate defeated colonization attempts, but mines were opened.

KHALKHA (Outer Mongolia) was in a similarly strategic situation along Russia's Siberian frontier, and the court proposed in 1906 to convert it, too, into a Chinese province. The *amban*s in Outer Mongolia all protested the risks and likely futility of such a procedure. In November 1909 Sandō (b. 1875) was appointed the new "Manchu" *amban* in Khüriye (actually he was a Mongol bannerman from Hangzhou; *see* EIGHT BANNERS). Urged by the central government, in Khüriye (modern ULAANBAATAR) and KYAKHTA he expanded the garrison with a new army training office and created offices to sponsor modernization. His colleagues in ULIASTAI CITY and KHOWD CITY did the same. They also began prospecting for minerals and preparing for vast colonization schemes to lay the essential economic foundation for assimilation and forestall Russian advances. More than 5 million hectares (13 million acres) were set aside for colonization.

Opposition to the New Policies was immediate and widespread at both official and popular levels. In 1906 the court rebuked the Ulaanchab league captain general for open insubordination. In Ordos "circles" (*DUGUILANG*) expressed popular protest against the New Policies. Revolts broke out in Jalaid, Monggoljin (modern Fuxin), Front Gorlos, and Jüüngar (Jungar) banner. All were suppressed, although one rebel leader, Togtakhu Taiji (1863–1922), found asylum with his band in Russia. In April 1910 a riot broke out in Khüriye that led to the looting of Chinese shops. From 1900 the EIGHTH JIBZUNDAMBA KHUTUGTU had secretly been in contact with the Russian administration, and in fall 1911, with the Qing facing revolts in China, the JIBZUNDAMBA KHUTUGTU overthrew the *amban*s and restored Mongolian independence. In January banner troops in Hulun Buir converged on Hailar and overthrew Chinese rule, announcing allegiance to independent Mongolia.

See also 1911 RESTORATION.

Further reading: Roger DesForges, *Hsi-liang and the Chinese National Revolution* (New Haven, Conn.: Yale University Press, 1973); Sechin Jagchid, "The Yigu Episode and Its Repercussions," in *Opuscula Altaica*, ed. Edward H. Kaplan and Donald W. Whisenhunt (Bellingham: Western Washington University Press, 1994), 349–370; Mei-hua Lan, "Chinese 'New Administration' in Mongolia," in *Mongolia in the Twentieth Century: Landlocked Cosmopolitan*, ed. Stephen Kotkin and Bruce A. Elleman (Armonk, N.Y.: M. E. Sharpe, 1999), 39–58; G. Navaangnamjil, "A Brief Biography of the Determined Hero Togtokh," in *Mongolian Heroes of the Twentieth Century*, trans. Urgunge Onon (New York: AMS Press, 1976), 43–76.

New Schools movements The New Schools movements among the BURIATS, KALMYKS, and INNER MONGOLIANS created a new intelligentsia in each of these regions in the late 19th and early 20th centuries.

The new schools used Russian or Chinese in the curriculum and exposed Mongolian students to elementary geographical and scientific knowledge. Unlike the old banner schools (*see* EDUCATION, TRADITIONAL), they taught the MONGOLIAN LANGUAGE with a view to comprehension, not just penmanship. The movement opened new horizons professionally and intellectually and prepared students for higher schools in St. Petersburg, Tokyo, and Beijing. The initiative for these new schools came not from obstructive Russian or Chinese officials, but from Mongol philanthropists, usually of the nobility or local leadership.

FORERUNNERS

Russian- or Chinese-language education was available in certain Mongol areas in the 19th century, but was limited in approach and accessibility. By 1890 most of the six public schools among the Transbaikal Buriats, such as the Russo-Mongolian Military Academy in Troitskosavsk (in modern KYAKHTA), where DORZHI BANZAROVICH BANZAROV studied, served the Buriat Cossacks. While that school taught both Mongolian and Russian, arithmetic, and geography, graduates were required to use their skills in Cossack units. Among the Kalmyks the Buzava Cossacks developed a Russian- and Kalmyk-language school system with Buddhist instruction in 1838. Most Russian schooling for the Buriats and Kalmyks, however, was intended to Christianize the students and was unpopular.

For most Inner Mongolians Chinese-language instruction was legally forbidden until 1910. Only the CHAKHAR, HÖHHOT TÜMED, and HULUN BUIR bannermen could learn Chinese as members of the EIGHT BANNERS system (an institution something like the Cossacks of the Russian Empire). Until the NEW POLICIES of 1901 even these Chinese schools had a purely Confucian curriculum.

PIONEERING SCHOOLS

Sakhar Khamnaev, *taisha* (Uighur-Mongolian, *TAISHI*) of the Barguzin Buriats, founded the first Buriat secular school for non-Cossacks in 1844. Khamnaev, who was an able writer of both Russian and Buriat and was familiar with all the schools in St. Petersburg, attended personally to the school's difficulties and paid the tuitions of deserving poor students. In 1884 Aga Buriat leaders cooperated to open a gymnasium (high school) in Chita later attended by many Buriat scholars. The Buriat court physician Pëtr A. Badmaev (1856–1920) tried to found a gymnasium for Buriat students in St. Petersburg in 1895, but the school disbanded rather than accept required Christian doctrine classes.

In Inner Mongolia Prince Güngsangnorbu (Prince Güng) of KHARACHIN Right Banner (1871–1931) privately funded from his own princely budget three schools: Chongzheng Academy for boys (1902), Shouzheng Military Academy (1903), and Yuzheng Girls Academy (1903). All three academies used Mongolian and Chinese and had distinguished Chinese and Japanese academics and educators on the teaching staff. In 1906 five graduates were sent to Japan for further education. Later, in 1912, Prince Güng founded the Mongolian-Tibetan School in Beijing as a publicly funded school offering a modern secondary education in Chinese to Inner Mongolian students. From 1906 to 1915 other local leaders, such as Prince Amurlinggui of KHORCHIN Left-Flank Rear banner (Horqin Zuoyi Houqi), the Jasag Lama Agwangbaldan of Khüriye (Hure) banner and Yue Shan, adjutant in Kheshigten (Hexigten) banner, founded similar schools in their banners with free tuition. Meanwhile, the Chakhar, Höhhot Tümed, and Daur schools modernized their curricula.

ACHIEVEMENTS

In Russia Buriat and Kalmyk education expanded greatly after 1890. By 1914 68 schools operated in Kalmyk lands, 37 among the Buzava Kalmyks of the Don Cossack horde, and 31 under the Ministry of Education among the larger body of Kalmyks. In the latter schools Buddhist religious instruction was substituted for Christian, and Kalmyk was used for instruction only from 1911. In 1911 the eastern Buriats had 64 schools, 36 under the Ministry of Education and 28 under the Russian Orthodox Church. Total enrollment among the Transbaikal Buriats was 2,082, of which 18 percent were girls. Despite this enrollment, female literacy remained very low.

In Inner Mongolia by 1931, the three eastern leagues, Jirim, JUU UDA, and Josotu, maintained 137 lower elementary schools and 19 higher elementary schools. Chakhar had 12 lower elementary schools, and Hulun Buir had six lower and one higher elementary school. The Höhhot Tümed had five lower and one higher elementary school. There were also several normal schools, including the Northeastern Mongol Banners Middle School, founded in 1929 by the Daur educator MERSE. Inner Mongolia's western leagues of ULAANCHAB, SHILIIN GOL, ORDOS, and ALASHAN combined had only four public elementary schools (excluding traditional scribal schools).

The rapid progress of Soviet education after 1920 in Buriatia and Kalmykia and of Japanese and Chinese Communist education in Inner Mongolia after 1931 was built on the achievement of early pioneers. The movement also influenced Mongolia proper after its independence in 1911. The first public school opened by the theocratic government in 1912 was staffed entirely by Buriats (see THEOCRATIC PERIOD). In the 1920s hundreds of nationalist Inner Mongolian students, graduates of the new schools, went to Mongolia, where they staffed new schools and other cultural institutions.

Despite the generosity of the pioneering upper-class educators, many of the graduates of the new schools turned against their mentors. By 1905 the younger Buriat intelligentsia was breaking with the old *taisha* class and arguing for democratic socialism. In 1923 many of the younger Mongols in Beijing's Mongolian and Tibetan School joined the Communist movement and the Inner Mongolian People's Revolutionary Party and denounced the school's founder Prince Güng as a reactionary.

NEW SCHOOLS AND BUDDHISM

While the Buriat New Schools movement was associated with the idea of reforming Buddhism, that in Inner Mongolia kept its distance from Buddhism and often became violently anticlerical. Buriat and Kalmyk educators, both religious and lay, shared their hostility to the Russian Orthodoxy officially imposed by the czarist government. Buddhism was thus a bulwark of national identity, to be reformed but not destroyed. The writer TSYBEN ZHAMTSARANOVICH ZHAMTSARANO proposed in 1905 that the monasteries promote general education with a fund formed from the confiscation of the lamas' religiously dubious private property. From 1917 the Buddhist cleric AGWANG DORZHIEV cooperated in monastic reforms with the liberal Buriat Mikhail N. Bogdanov (1878–1920) and the socialist ELBEK-DORZHI RINCHINO.

In Inner Mongolia the author INJANNASHI (1837–92), while not involved in education, had a tremendous impact on educators with his attacks on the narrow-minded hypocrisy of the lamas. Still, he proposed in place of narrow sectarianism not secularism, but a kind of Confucian-Buddhist spirituality. The schoolteacher Rinchinkhorlo (1904–63) from Khüriye banner published Inner Mongolia's first novella in 1940, about two boys sucked into the monasteries, one of whom escaped and found deliverance in a secular Chinese-Mongolian school. In it he emphasized that he was not against religion, but asked only that it be voluntarily adopted. However, from the 1920s on most "Young Mongols" believed Buddhism and the Qing regime had cut off the Mongols from the world, reduced their population, and weakened their fighting ardor, thus causing the decline of the Mongols from the glory days of CHINGGIS KHAN.

The new schools spread this anticlerical ideology widely.

See also RELIGION.

Further reading: Sechin Jagchid, "Prince Gungsangnorbu and Inner Mongolian Modernization," in *Essays in Mongolian Studies* (Provo, Utah: David M. Kennedy Center for International Studies, Brigham Young University, 1988), 207–233.

New Turn policy   The New Turn policy (*Shine ergilteyin bodolga / shine ergiltiin bodlogo*), adopted from 1932 to 1936, reversed the leftist policies of 1929–32 and advocated growth in privately owned herds, religious toleration, and budgetary retrenchment.

With the bloody insurrection of April 1932 against the Mongolian government, the Soviet ruler Joseph Stalin intervened personally to change Mongolia's far-left course. At the Third Plenum of the MONGOLIAN PEOPLE'S REVOLUTIONARY PARTY's Central Committee in June 1932, the policies of the LEFTIST PERIOD were repudiated as mechanical imitations of Soviet policies that were completely unsuited to nomadic Mongolia. Two of the three party secretaries, the uneducated Dörböd Badarakhu (Ö. Badrakh, 1895–1941) and the Soviet-educated Shijiye (J. Shijee, 1901–41), were blamed for the debacle, while the third, GENDÜN (P. Genden, 1892–1937), was promoted to prime minister. In 1933–34 several remaining leftists, including Lhümbe (J. Lhümbe, 1902–34) and the 1930–32 prime minister, Jigjedjab (Ts. Jigjidjaw, 1894–1933), were executed as Japanese spies in the fabricated LHÜMBE CASE.

Under the New Turn policy Mongolia returned to the situation before 1929, when a troika of strong government, military, and party leaders ruled the country. Gendün was the prime minister, MARSHAL DEMID was the commander in chief, and Lubsangsharab (D. Luwsansharaw, 1900–40) was the party chief. In contrast to the leftist period, the government dominated the party, and Gendün was Mongolia's undisputed maximum leader. Moscow's Communist International no longer supervised Mongolia, and Gendün dealt directly with Stalin and his entourage.

The campaign against Buddhism was reversed, imprisoned lamas were released, and publicity given to freedom of religion. Those officials, including Gendün himself, who were personally religious no longer hid the fact. In one year 27,000 lamas returned to the monasteries. Strictly religious articles were made tax exempt, although heavy taxes were still maintained on other monastic property. Gifts to the monasteries were again allowed. Qualified amnesties were also given to the remaining participants in antigovernment insurrections, and several thousand emigrés were enticed to return. A purge and voluntary withdrawals dropped the Mongolian People's Revolutionary Party's membership from a high of

Mongolia's leaders under the New Turn policy: (left to right) Commander in Chief Demid, Prime Minister Gendün, and Mongolian People's Revolutionary Party chairman Lubsangsharab *(From Tsedendambyn Batbayar,* Modern Mongolia: A Concise History *[1996])*

42,000 in 1932 to only 7,976 in 1934, while the youth league, which had been the main center of offensive anticlericalism, was thoroughly reorganized.

In the economy the more than 800 collectives were immediately disbanded. The Mongolian state budget was reduced from a projected 39 million tögrögs in 1932 to 33 million (1933), while the total livestock tax was reduced from 4.3 million in 1931 to 1.8 million in 1933. The Soviet Union also assisted in reviving the Mongolian economy. Certain Mongolian commercial debts were canceled, others were bundled into long-term loans, and special attention was paid to moving imported consumer goods from the Russian border into the countryside. Even so, 10 million tögrögs of income had to be covered by loans from the Soviet Union. As a result of these reforms, livestock numbers, which had dropped from about 24 million in 1930 to 16.2 million in 1932, reached 22.6 million by 1935.

Culturally, the Latinization campaign that finally got underway in 1932 was hastily abandoned. Writers and grammarians such as Shagja (S. Shagj, 1886–1938) concentrated rather on reforming and developing the UIGHUR-MONGOLIAN SCRIPT so that it could be the writing system for a modern nation. Several large-scale cultural projects, such as an only partially completed history of Mongolia, TSYBEN ZHAMTSARANOVICH ZHAMTSARANO's ethnography of Mongolia, and the atlas of the Russian geographer Andrei Dmitrievich Simukov (1902–42), all combined modern scholarship with a respect for Mongolia's heritage.

While Stalin fully supported economic liberalization, he believed the lamas formed a state within a state that must not be tolerated a moment longer than necessary. In November 1934 he began urging Gendün to eliminate them. In January 1935 occurred the first of many clashes on Mongolia's disputed frontier with Japanese-occupied Manchuria. Faced with Gendün and his allies' apparent insouciance, Stalin came to believe that the Mongolian leaders were not genuinely interested in stopping Japan. While direct threats during winter 1935–36 forced the Mongolians to comply, Stalin had MARSHAL CHOIBALSANG appointed head of the new Interior Ministry in February 1936, and in the next month Gendün was dismissed. Militarization, the GREAT PURGE, and the destruction of Buddhism followed.

See also REVOLUTIONARY PERIOD.

Noin-Ula   *See* NOYON UUL.

nökör (nöker)   *Nökörs* (modern Mongolian *nökhör*), or "companions," were the Mongol khans' most intimate servants, eating and drinking at their table and guarding their lives in battle. Their politicomilitary role resembled the "house carls" in early medieval English society and the "companions of the Prophet" in early Islam. (The spelling *nöker* is a western dialect form). In the MONGOL TRIBE before the rise of CHINGGIS KHAN (Genghis, 1206–27), leaders from branches of the BORJIGID lineage (TAYICHI'UD, Yürkin, Changshi'ud, and Chinggis's own Kiyad) fought for preeminence. While these leaders expected the support of their near kin, they sought to draw to themselves unrelated able young men who would give them loyal service. Most is known about the *nökörs* in the rise of Chinggis Khan, and a vital theme in all the accounts of his rise derived from Mongol sources is how the khan found such companions and won their loyalty.

Nökörs were most often of low birth. The rival ruling clans of the Mongols all had lineages subject for generations to their rule. Leaders often took outstanding young men of these subjects as *nökörs*. Early in Chinggis's career, for example, an old man of the Uriyangkhan, which had been subject to Chinggis's family for several generations, gave his son Jelme as a personal slave to Chinggis, to saddle his horses and open his door. Jelme later saved his lord Chinggis's life by taking care of him when he was wounded in a battle with the Tayichi'ud. Once when Jelme was slaughtering an ox for Chinggis's table, he helped rescue Chinggis's boy, TOLUI, from a Tatar who snuck into the camp to kill him. In 1206 Chinggis Khan made Jelme a commander of a thousand and DAR-QAN (immune to taxes and punishments). Other *nökörs*, such as BO'ORCHU, came from independent but nonruling tribal groups, joining Chinggis of their own free will. Some, such as Chila'un of the Suldus, whose clan was subject to the Tayichi'ud, became disaffected with their lords and fled to join Chinggis. When a leader defeated a rival clan, the rival group's subject peoples could sometimes become *nökörs* of the victorious leader. Thus, Gü'ün-U'a of JALAYIR, subject to the Yürkin clan, gave his son MUQALI to Chinggis and Jebke to Chinggis's brother

Qasar to guard their thresholds. Jebke brought a small child, Boroghul, of the Üüshin lineage, also subject to the Yürkin, to be raised by Chinggis Khan's mother.

From early in his career Chinggis Khan used his *nökörs* for tasks both personal and public. They served as quiver bearers, stewards, cup bearers, cooks, shepherds, YURT keepers, and grooms as well as envoys, commanders, and advisers. Chinggis grouped them into several lists of four, such as the "four steeds" (Bo'orchu, Muqali, Boroghul, Chila'un), who were his supreme commanders and supervised the imperial guard (KESHIG), and the "four dogs" (Qubilai Noyan, Jelme, JEBE, SÜBE'ETEI BA'ATUR), who commanded his crack troops. From the "four foundlings" (Güchü, Kököchü, Shigi SHIGI QUTUQU, Boroghul), raised from infancy by Chinggis's mother, and his four councillors (Üsün, Ghunan, Kökö-Chos, and Degei) he assigned advisers to counsel his brothers and sons.

The ranks of *nökörs* were not restricted to Mongols, and among those to whom Chinggis Khan declared his undying fidelity in the BALJUNA COVENANT (1203) were Muslims, KITANS from North China, UIGHURS, and Tanguts. After his conquest of North China, local defectors such as Liu Bolin, Shimo Ming'an, and even a one-time hostage, Nianhe Zhongshan, joined the khan's inner circle (*see* SHIMO MING'AN AND XIANDEBU). In his campaign against KHORAZM, however, Chinggis was unable to recruit *nökörs*.

After Chinggis Khan the striking upward mobility of the early empire disappeared as the *nökörs* of Chinggis's time formed aristocratic families. Only princes such as QAIDU, who had no firm base of support, had to rely on able men from a wide variety of families, thus reproducing the situation of Chinggis's rise. In later Mongolian history, too, the solidification of princely privilege and the decline of military activity after 1700 resulted in the disappearance of the *nökör* as an institution. In the 20th century *nökör* came to be used to mean "comrade" in a variety of nationalist and communist movements.

nomadism   *See* ANIMAL HUSBANDRY AND NOMADISM.

Nomonhan   *See* KHALKHYN GOL, BATTLE OF.

Noqai (Noghay, Nogay) (d. 1299) *Commander and elder statesman in the Golden Horde who challenged the authority of its khans*

Junior cousin of the GOLDEN HORDE khans, Noqai commanded Berke Khan's (1257–66) forces against the Mongols' Middle Eastern IL-KHANATE in 1262–63 and 1265 and raided Thrace in 1264. Under Berke's successor, Mengü-Temür Khan (Möngke-Temür, 1267–80), Noqai, holding the steppe between the Dnieper and the Danube, began independent foreign relations, sending envoys to MAMLUK EGYPT, forming marriage alliances with Byzantium and the

Il-Khanate, and raiding Bulgaria and Serbia. With Mengü-Temür's death he began openly to oppose the khan's policies. From 1284 he supported peace with the YUAN DYNASTY and Il-Khanate despite Töle-Bugha Khan's (1287–91) war policy. In Russia he supported his own candidates and policies among the rival prince, coming into open conflict with the khan's court on the Volga. In 1291 Noqai assisted the prince Toqto'a in overthrowing Töle-Bugha.

RASHID-UD-DIN FAZL-ULLAH presents Noqai first as a brave general but later as a wily old politician. He self-consciously promoted Mongol ways. In 1272, when Byzantine envoys presented rich brocades, Noqai slyly asked if they could ward off lightning bolts, prevent headache, or promote good health before praising the practicality of the dog skins his people wore. (Noqai means "dog.") Indeed, Noqai's subjects, including many Russians, Vlachs (Romanians), and OSSETES (Alans), began to adopt "Tatar" (Mongol) dress and "Tatar" language.

Noqai's religious beliefs apparently followed his diplomatic needs; in a letter to Egypt in 1270–71 he claimed to have converted to Islam, yet in 1288 he presented Buddhist relics to the Il-Khan Arghun. One of Noqai's wives, Yailaq, regularly visited a Franciscan convent in Qirim (Staryy Krym) and was baptized a Catholic. After Toqto'a ascended the throne, Noqai married his daughter Qiyat to Yailaq (no relation to Noqai's wife), a Buddhist and son of the QONGGIRAD tribe commander Salji'udai. Noqai's daughter Qiyat, after her marriage, converted to Islam (Noqai had evidently not raised her as a Muslim), keeping her faith despite bullying from her Buddhist in-laws.

Noqai and Salji'udai soon had bad relations, and Toqto'a sided with his commander against the overmighty Noqai. Noqai refused Toqto'a's invitations to attend the court on the Volga, and in winter 1298–99 Toqto'a's and Noqai's armies met on the Dnieper but turned back without fighting. The following year Noqai attacked Toqto'a, who after several battles emerged victorious; Noqai died in the final battle.

Noqai's son Jöge escaped to Bulgaria, where he briefly became czar. In the mid-14th century Muhammad Khoja Beg, son of Yailaq of the Qonggirad, patronized a Khorazmian Turkish poet. He may perhaps have been the son of Noqai's daughter Qiyat and her Qonggirad husband Yailaq. In any case, the oft-assumed linkage between Noqai and the later Nogay people of the Manghit (see MANGGHUD) clan is very uncertain.

See also BYZANTIUM AND BULGARIA; GOLDEN HORDE.

Northern Yuan dynasty Established with the flight of the Mongol great khans from China, the Northern Yuan emperors from 1368 to 1634 maintained their claim to Chinggisid legitimacy, yet were only sporadically able to make that claim effective. (*On the Northern Yuan dynasty's relations with China, see* MING DYNASTY.)

THE RETURN TO MONGOLIA

The early history of the Northern Yuan is known almost entirely from records of the rival Ming dynasty (1368–1644). As the Ming armies converged on the Yuan capital, DAIDU, in September 1368, the Mongol emperor Toghan-Temür (posthumous titles Shundi or Uqa'atu, 1333–70) and his court fled out the northern gate and established a temporary capital in Inner Mongolia at Yingchang (on Dalai Nuur Lake, near modern Shiliin Khot/Xilinhot). Toghan-Temür's sons Ayushiridara (posthumous title Biligtü, 1370–78) and Toghus-Temür (posthumous title Uskhal, 1378–88) were both almost captured by Ming armies in 1370 and 1388, respectively, and fled farther north.

The Northern Yuan rulers held tenaciously to their title of emperor (or great KHAN) of the Great Yuan (*Dai Yuwan khaan*). For at least part of this period, the Yuan khans also retained a Chinese-style court organization. In the 15th century the old Yuan's high titles appear repeatedly: the three honorific ranks TAISHI (grand preceptor), *taifu* or *taiwei* (grand mentor), *taibao* (grand guardian), and the offices of right and left grand councillor (*chingsang*) and director (*zhiyuan*) of the Bureau of Military Affairs. Chinese-style titles of nobility, such as Esen's rank of "prince of Huai," were also given by the Yuan court. At least through the mid-15th century the Yuan proclaimed Chinese reign titles (*nianhao*).

As the title customarily granted the most honored official, *taishi* became the usual title for the regent who ruled in the name of the emperor, equivalent to the *beglerbegi* in the later GOLDEN HORDE (*see* KESHIG). From the time of CHINGGIS KHAN the OIRATS had been QUDA (marriage allies) to the khans. Eventually, the position of *taishi* and *quda* of the khan came to be a prerogative of the Oirats, so that in the later 15th century even *taishi*s of non-Oirat origin were treated as Oirats. Given the power of the *taishi*s, the Chinese soon designated the Yuan khans "little princes" (*xiao wangzi*), an eloquent expression of their degraded status.

The most important remaining sign of the khans' authority was the seal. Mongol legends speak of Toghan-Temür bringing it in his sleeve out of Daidu. Chinese records show that usurpers captured the seal several times; whether it was the same one each time is unknown. In 1442 a Mongol envoy berated the Koreans: "You have submitted to the . . . Great Ming who has ascended the throne in a city built by men, while you despise the Mongol emperor to whom heaven has bestowed the jade seal." Evidently, the legend that Chinggis Khan was born with a jade seal in his hand was already current.

THE MONGOL-OIRAT CONFLICT

In 1388 Yisüder, a descendant of Qubilai Khan's brother ARIQ-BÖKE, murdered the emperor Toghus-Temür, initiating a complex period of usurpation and conflict. On one side stood the Oirats in the northwest, first under

Möngke-Temür (fl. 1400) and by 1403 under three chiefs, Mahmud (d. 1417), Taiping (d. 1426), and Batu-Bolod. The Oirats drew to their side the descendants of Ariq-Böke and other princes who had been relegated to Mongolia during the Yuan. Against them stood Arugtai (d. 1434) of the Asud, active from 1403 on in HULUN BUIR. The Asud (OSSETES) had been an important unit in the Mongol imperial guard in the Yuan, and Arugtai apparently spoke for the old Yuan court.

Another force was the line of ÖGEDEI KHAN, which under the Yuan had lived in China's Gansu area but were expelled along with the Yuan. The khan Guilichi (murdered 1408), reigning with Arugtai as his commander in 1400, had his base in southwest Inner Mongolia at Ejene (see ALASHAN) and was apparently an Ögedeid. Farther to the west were the Chinggisid khans of MOGHULISTAN, based in modern Xinjiang, and TIMUR and his dynasty beyond them. Arugtai's new khan after Guilichi, Bunyashiri (Öljeitü, r. 1408–12), came from Temür's court in Samarqand in 1405, whence he had fled in opposition to the Oirats.

Under Yongle (1402–24) the Ming dynasty intervened aggressively against any overpowerful leader, exacerbating the Mongol-Oirat conflict. In 1409 Bunyashiri and Arugtai crushed a Ming army, so that in 1410 Yongle attacked the two on the KHERLEN RIVER. In 1412 Mahmud of the Oirats killed Bunyashiri, enthroning an Ariq-Bökid, Dalbag (1412–14). Arugtai appealed to the Yongle emperor, who in 1414 defeated Mahmud. With Mahmud's death in 1417 Arugtai became dominant again, and Yongle campaigned against him in 1422 and 1423, ending when news of Arugai's defeat by the Oirats arrived. From Yongle's death, however, Mahmud's son Toghoon Taishi (d. 1438) built up power without interruption. In 1433 Arugtai was pushed east of the GREATER KHINGGAN RANGE, where he subjugated the Ming-allied Mongols in the THREE GUARDS. Finally, after a great defeat in 1434, Arugtai fled west to the Muna Uula Mountain (west of Baotou), where Toghoon killed him. Arugtai's khan, Adai (1426–38), another Ögedeid based in Ejene, made a last stand there before succumbing.

Toghoon died in the very year of his final victory over Adai. His son ESEN Taishi (r. 1438–54) brought the Oirats to the height of their power. In the west he drove back the Moghulistan rulers, while to the east he destroyed the Three Guards and the Jurchen. In 1449 he captured the Ming emperor, bringing about a wholesale collapse of the Ming defense line. The Three Guards streamed south to the Shara Mören (Xar Moron) valley, while they and fragments of virtually every other Mongolian group poured into the Huang (Yellow) River bend and ORDOS. Esen ruled as the taishi for the khan Togtoo-Bukha (reign name Taisung, 1443–52), but after punishing his restive Chinggisid khan in winter 1451–52, Esen took the title khan himself, the first non-Chinggisid to do so. Esen was, however, soon over-thrown by his own chingsang (grand councillor) of the right, Alag.

From Esen's death to 1481 the Oirats ceded power among the Mongols to taishis of obscure origin. Bolai Taishi (fl. 1457–66) seems to have inherited Esen's titles and men but belonged to the KHARACHIN, descendants of the YUAN DYNASTY's Qipchaq KOUMISS brewers. After a period of domination by Muulikhai Ong, a descendant of Chinggis's half-brother Belgütei and closely allied to the Three Guards, there appeared three taishis, Beg-Arslan (d. 1479), Ismayil (d. 1486), and Iburai (perhaps from Ibrahim, d. 1533), all active in the Ordos (Huang [Yellow] River bend) area. Most Mongolian sources call them Uighurs, and Beg-Arslan and Ismayil certainly had ties to the Uighur oasis-city of Hami. The Uighur otogs (camp districts; see OTOG) among the TÜMED and Ordos along the Huang (Yellow) River seem to have been the power base for these western adventurers.

The importance of the Huang (Yellow) River bend increased when the EIGHT WHITE YURTS, or the shrine of Chinggis Khan, moved there around 1450. Perhaps from Adai's reign on (1426–38), khans were crowned before the shrine. The Chinggisid ruler of the shrine, the jinong, a title first seen in 1452, became under Bayan-Möngke Bolkhu Jinong (fl. 1470–79) an important figure. The death of the Oirat taishi Toghoon at the height of his power in 1438 was turned into an illustration of the shrine's power. In the Mongolian chronicle ALTAN TOBCHI (c. 1655), Toghoon decided to become great khan before the Eight White Yurts but was supernaturally slain, thus proving that only descendants of Chinggis could be khans.

RELIGION AND CULTURE IN THE EARLY NORTHERN YUAN

Despite later Mongolian stories that the "TWO CUSTOMS" of religion and state were lost in 1368, "state preceptors" (guoshi/güüshi) or Buddhist chaplains were active from at least 1407 to 1452. Tibetan monks were particularly active among the Chigil Mongols in the Ming guards of western Gansu. Hami, which had close ties to the Oirats, kept a significant Buddhist population until the 1470s. At the same time, Islam had a significant presence, particularly among the Oirats. Both Esen Taishi and Bunyashiri Öljeitü Khan converted to Islam, one to marry the sister of a Moghul khan and the other during his stay at Temür's court in Samarqand. Finally, both Mar-Hasia, who held high office under the khans from 1388 to 1403, and the khan Mar-Körgis (c. 1455–65/7) have Syriac names that attest to some continuing Christian cultural influence.

No works of literature survive from the earlier Northern Yuan, but a few letters testify that the Yuan khans preserved the UIGHUR-MONGOLIAN SCRIPT. The survival of 13th-14th century manuscripts into the 17th century also demonstrates that Buddhist translations the

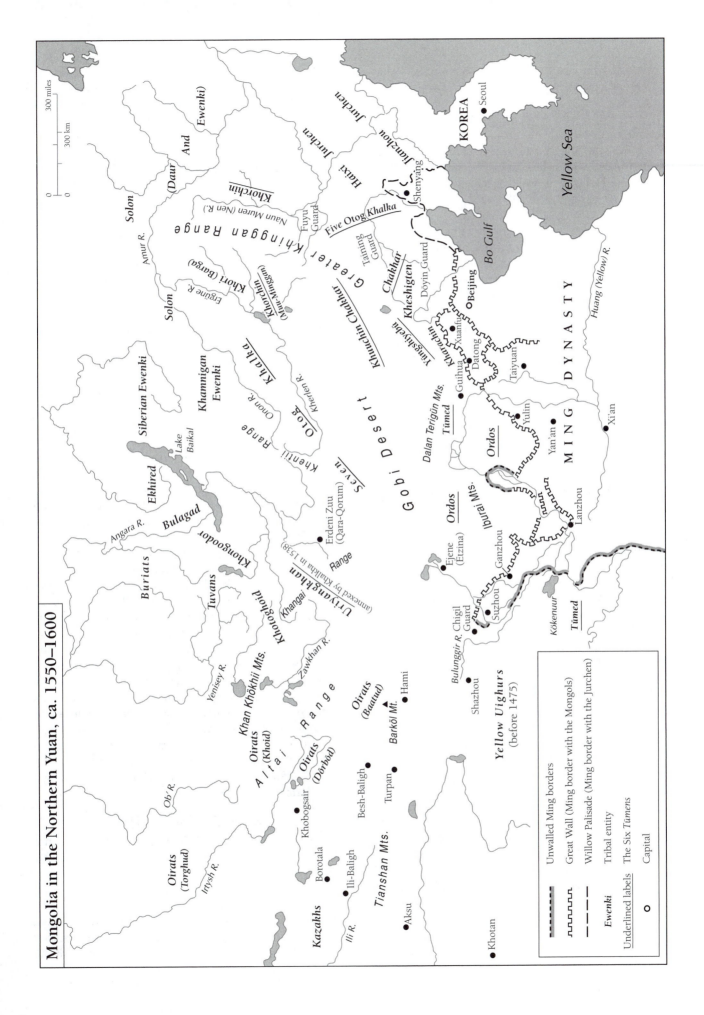

Mongolia in the Northern Yuan, ca. 1550–1600

Legend:

- Unwalled Ming borders
- Great Wall (Ming border with the Mongols)
- Willow Palisade (Ming border with the Jurchen)
- *Ewenki* — Tribal entity
- Underlined labels — The Six Tümens
- O — Capital

Labels on map:

Seoul, KOREA, Yellow Sea, Bo Gulf, Shenyang, Jianzhou Jurchen, Haixi Jurchen, Khorchin, Solon, And Ewenki (Daur), Amur R., Fuyu Guard, Naun Muren (Nen R.), Five Otog Khalka, Greater Khinggan Range, Khori (Barga), Khorchin (Mu-Minggan), Taining Guard, Khuuchin Chahar, Chakhar, Döyin Guard, Kheshigten, Beijing, Yingshyebu, Xuanhua, Guihua, Khwachin, Datong, Taiyuan, MING DYNASTY, Huang (Yellow) R., Dalan Terigün Mts., Tümed, Ordos, Yulin, Yan'an, Xi'an, Lanzhou, Ordos, Iburai Mts., Ganzhou, Suzhou, Köke nuur, Tümed, Ejene (Etzina), Chigil Guard, Bulunggir R., Shazhou, Yellow Uighurs (before 1475), Khotan, Aksu, Ili R., Tianshan Mts., Turpan, Ili-Baligh, Borotala, Khobogsair, Besh-Baligh, Barköl Mt., Hami, Oirats (Baatud), Oirats (Dörböd), Oirats (Khoid), Altai Range, Khan Khökhii Mts., Oirats (Torghud), Irtysh R., Ob' R., Kazakhs, Yenisey R., Khotoghoid, Khangai, Uriyangkhan (annexed by Khalkha in 1538), Range, Zawkhan R., Tuvans, Khongoodor, Buriats, Bulagad, Angara R., Lake Baikal, Ekhired, Siberian Ewenki, Khamnigan Ewenki, Khalkha, Otog, Khentii Range, Onon R., Kherlen R., Seven, Erdeni Zuu (Qara-Qorum), Gobi Desert, Solon

Scale: 300 miles / 300 km

SECRET HISTORY OF THE MONGOLS and other works, including were still read and copied.

DAYAN KHANID RESTORATION

From around 1480 MANDUKHAI SECHEN KHATUN (fl. 1473–1501), the widow and regent of the Great Khan Manduul, ruled with a boy said to be son of the *jinong* Bokhu, who had died in exile. Mandukhai and this boy, BATU-MÖNGKE DAYAN KHAN (1480?–1517?), presided over a revival of the Chinggisid legacy.

At first the new rulers operated with the *taishi* system. After driving Ismayil Taishi out of Ordos in 1483, Dayan Khan and Mandukhai appointed *taishi*s to rule the Huang (Yellow) River Mongols: Qorqada'un (fl. 1490–91, probably Esen's son) and then Iburai (d. 1533). The khan and khatun themselves generally stayed among the CHAKHAR to the east. In 1508 Dayan Khan appointed his own second son *jinong*. When Iburai killed him and revolted, Dayan Khan crushed the southwestern Mongols at Dalan Terigün in 1510. Making his third son, Barsu-Bolod (1484–1521), *jinong* at the Eight White Yurts, Dayan Khan abolished the position of *taishi* along with other Yuan court titles such as *chingsang*.

Dayan Khan reorganized his Mongols into the SIX TÜMENS, which functioned both as military units and as tribal administrative bodies. The Ariq-Bökids and Ögedeids had disappeared, and the tribes ruled by descendants of Chinggis Khan's brothers were allied. Geographically, Dayan Khan's rule was concentrated in Inner Mongolia. In Mongolia proper the ONON RIVER–KHERLEN RIVER region was settled by the northern Khalkha and the KHANGAI RANGE region by the Uriyangkhan. Under Dayan Khan these two groups were attached to the South Khalkha of eastern Inner Mongolia's Shara Mören (Xar Moron) valley and the Döyin Uriyangkhan of the Three Guards, respectively. After the northern Uriyangkhan chiefs turned hostile, they were conquered in 1538 and mostly annexed by the northern Khalkha.

POLITICAL AND MILITARY ORGANIZATION

During Dayan Khan's life he enforced requisitions on the Six Tümens through *noyad* (officials; see NOYAN), yet granted his own sons, or TAIJI, and their subjects immunity. Thus, the *tümens* all hoped to receive a *taiji*. By 1540 new regional circles of Chinggisid *taiji*s, descended from Dayan Khan, and local *tabunang*s, or sons-in-law (marriage allies) of the *taiji*s had emerged in all the former Dayan Khanid domains. The title "Great Khan of the Great Yuan" and control over the Chakhar descended by primogeniture, but the great khans soon had only symbolic control over the other Six Tümens. The title *jinong*, with titular authority over the Three Western Tümens, descended by primogeniture from Dayan Khan's second son, Barsu-Bolod, but the *jinong*, too, lost power to collateral lines. Daraisun Küdeng Khan (1548–57) had to grant titles of "khan" to his powerful cousins Altan (1508–82),

ruling the Tümed, and Bayaskhal (1510–72), ruling the Kharachin. Despite this decentralization there was a remarkable concord within the new Dayan Khanid aristocracy, and intra-Chinggisid rebellion or civil war remained unknown until the reign of LIGDAN KHAN (1604–34).

Against China the Northern Yuan fielded a purely cavalry army. The troops along the border of China at least were generally well armored, with mail, helmets, and horse armor of iron. Weapons consisted of bows, swords, and halberds. One Chinese border official spoke of the Mongols fighting in three-man teams, with a halberdier in the center, a bowman on the right, and a swordsman on the left. When crossing the Great Wall, which was mostly made of rammed earth, a vanguard of up to 1,000 men would also carry pickaxes to break down the wall. The walls of small towns were scaled with hooks on poles. The Northern Yuan army, unlike that of the empire, had no artillery and could not take large towns (see MILITARY OF THE MONGOL EMPIRE).

As in the MONGOL EMPIRE campaigns began in late autumn, after the HORSES had been put into training. The khan or *taiji* prepared large campaigns by sending around to his people over several months a messenger with a baton to call an assembly. As in the Mongol Empire, failure to arrive at the rendezvous was a grave offense. At the rendezvous a horsehair standard was set up, to which a prisoner would be sacrificed at the beginning and end of the campaign. Soldiers appeared at the rendezvous with their families, oxen, and yurts, which would be left behind at a base camp. Advance was in the form of a V, like a wild geese formation, with the khan in front. Large horns, or *büriye*, like those later used in monasteries, were used to signal the advance. As in the empire, booty was handed up through the *taiji*s to the khan, who then distributed it according to the soldiers' merits.

The tactics of the Mongol cavalry were similar to those of the empire period: feigned retreat, ambush, misdirection, and so on. Traditional tactics used to defeat a strong enemy included blowing the *büriye* horns and stampeding cattle to disorganize enemy ranks or using weather stones (*jada*) to make snowstorms. At the Battle of Dalan Terigün in 1510, the Three Western Tümens put their forces in the "bow-key" formation, so that Dayan Khan formed his men into 61 "butting bull" formations, although the meaning of these terms can only be guessed at.

RELIGION AND CULTURE

The decentralized peace of the Dayan Khanid restoration was based on religious and cultural unity created by the Chinggisid cults. Under Dayan Khan two different shrines, that of Chinggis Khan in Ordos (the Eight White Yurts) and that of Eshi Khatun (The First Lady, i.e., Qubilai Khan's mother SORQAQTANI BEKI) in Chakhar, formed the center of the right and left Three Tümens, respectively. The Yuan khan guarded the Eshi Khatun shrine, while the *jinong* guarded the Eight White Yurts. The khan himself, however, had to be enthroned before the Eight White Yurts, thus necessitating accord with the *jinong*. One or both shrines might accompany the Mongols to war on major campaigns.

The Chinggisid revival among the Mongols was expressed in a few surviving literary works, particularly the recently rediscovered *Chinggis Khaghan-u altan tobchi* (Golden summary of Chinggis Khan), which described the life of Chinggis Khan in legends that emphasized his sole claim to sovereignty. Legends about the fall of the Yuan and the struggle of the Chinggisids against the Oirat usurpers were probably also written at this time and formed the bulk of the later 17TH-CENTURY CHRONICLES. The ritual text *Bogda Chinggis Khaghan-u takil-un sudur oro-shi-ba* (Sutra of the offerings to Holy Chinggis) describes how the Yuan khan should present the animal and liquor offerings of the Chakhar to the Chinggis Khan shrine. The introductory Buddhist formulas show, however, that Buddhism still had some influence.

RENAISSANCE AND FALL OF THE NORTHERN YUAN

From 1540 on a series of smallpox epidemics and droughts struck the Mongols near the frontier, causing serious hardship. These disasters stimulated the Mongols' need for trade and, lacking that, plunder from China. In 1571 Ming China finally opened trade and tribute relations with the Three Western Tümens (Ordos, Tümed, and Yüngshiyebü/Kharachin). Through the tribute and horse markets, Altan Khan's capital, Guihua (modern HÖHHOT), became the conduit for Chinese trade not only locally but for the caravan trade through the northern Khalkha lands, the Oirats, and to the Central Asian oases (*see* TRIBUTE SYSTEM).

The large-scale SECOND CONVERSION to Buddhism, begun in the Three Western Tümens from 1575 on, built on the decentralized amity of the Chinggisids and the revival of caravan trade. Tümen Jasagtu Khan (b. 1539, r. 1558–92) appointed a Tibetan Buddhist chaplain of the Karma-pa order. In 1580 the northern Khalkha also proclaimed their leading Dayan-Khanid prince a khan, and in 1585–86 this prince, ABATAI KHAN, also joined the Buddhist conversion. The conversion sparked large-scale literary works, such as the CHAGHAN TEÜKE (White History) and the JEWEL TRANSLUCENT, and legal works (*see* ALTAN KHAN, CODE OF).

The rise of Nurhachi (b. 1558, r. 1616–26) in Manchuria eventually destroyed the Northern Yuan. From 1612 to 1615 Nurhachi made marriage alliances with the princes of KHORCHIN and Jarud Mongols in eastern Inner Mongolia, and in 1624 the southern Khalkha (north of modern Chifeng) and Khorchin made a formal alliance with the Manchus. Resenting this suborning of his nominal subjects, the Chakhar great khan Ligdan unsuccessfully attacked the Khorchin in 1625. Ligdan now made attempts to centralize authority, appointing his officials over the *tümen*s (confederations) and forming an elite military band to coerce opposition. He also began to oppose the dGe-lugs-pa ("Yellow Hat") order that had dominated the Second Conversion, promoting instead the older orders of Yuan times. The result was a massive rebellion of the Mongols in 1628. Ligdan defeated their combined armies at Zhaocheng in west-central Inner Mongolia, but in 1632 he fled a large Manchu punitive expedition. Reaching Ordos, he deposed the *jinong* and took the Eight White Yurts with him to Kökenuur, thus attacking the other pillar of the Dayan Khanid restoration. Ligdan died in 1634, and his sons surrendered to the Manchus in 1635, ending the Northern Yuan.

Further reading: Carney T. Fisher, "Smallpox, Salesmen, and Sectarians: Ming-Mongol Relations in the Jiajing Reign (1522–67)," *Ming Studies* 25 (1988): 1–23; M. Honda, "On the Genealogy of the Early Northern Yuan," *Ural-Altaische Jahrbücher* 30 (1958): 232–248; Hidehiro Okada, "The Chakhar Shrine of Eshi Khatun," in *Aspects of Altaic Civilization III*, ed. Denis Sinor (Bloomington: Indiana University, 1990): 176–186; Hidehiro Okada, "The Khan as the Sun, the Jinong as the Moon," in *Altaica Berolinensia: The Concept of Sovereignty in the Altaic World*, ed. Barbara Kellner-Heinkele (Wiesbaden: Otto Harrassowitz, 1993): 185–190; Dmitrii Pokotilov, *History of the Eastern Mongols during the Ming Dynasty from 1368 to 1634* (1947; rprt., Philadelphia: Porcupine Press, 1976); Henry Serruys, *Mongols and Ming China: Customs and History* (London: Variorum Reprints, 1987).

North Hangay *See* NORTH KHANGAI.

North Khangai province (North Hangay, Arhangai, Archangaj, Ara Khangai) One of the original provinces created in the administrative reform of 1931, North Khangai lies in west-central Mongolia. Made up almost entirely of KHALKHA Mongolia's prerevolutionary Sain Noyan province, two BANNERS (appanages) of ÖÖLÖDS were also included in its territory, although they have been assimilated to the Khalkhas. The province's area is 55,300 square kilometers (21,350 square miles). It covers the northern slopes of the KHANGAI RANGE and is watered by the headwaters of the ORKHON RIVER, Tamir River, and others. The population has grown from 60,300 in 1956 to 97,500 in 2000. North Khangai had 2,216,100 head of livestock in 2000, the third-highest in the country. In 2000 the number of HORSES (273,500 head) and horned CATTLE (428,600 head) was the highest in the country. About half the horned cattle are yaks or *khainag* (yak-cattle crossbreeds). Although sown acreage was among Mongolia's highest in 1990, arable agriculture has collapsed almost completely since then. The territory of North Khangai was the center of the TÜRK EMPIRES and the UIGHUR EMPIRE. The province's capital, Tsetserleg, was originally the monastery town Zaya-yin Khüriye, headed by the Khalkha Zaya Panditas. Its population in 2000 was 18,500. The town is one of Mongolia's wettest (350.5 millimeters, or 13.80 inches, annually), with one of the most equable climates.

See also DANZIN, GENERAL; DEMID, MARSHAL.

noyan (**noyon**)   The word *noyan* has throughout Mongolian history signified those not of the ruling lineage who are entrusted by the sovereign, or KHAN, with higher office. Its specific designation at any one time flows from the particular character of Mongolian authority at the time. In the MONGOL EMPIRE the commanders of the decimal units (10s, 100s, 1,000s, and 10,000s) were all *noyan*, although in practice the title was reserved for the higher ranks. *Noyan* (plural *noyad*) were thus above the ordinary Mongols but below the *uruq* (seed), or descendants of CHINGGIS KHAN (Genghis, 1206–27) and his brothers. Since the main task of these *noyad* was war, *noyan* acquired the connotation of "commander," equivalent to the Arab and Persian *emir* and the Turkish *bey/beg*. Chinese dictionaries, however, also gave its equivalent as *guanren*, "official."

During the QING DYNASTY (1636–1912) the sovereign rulers in Beijing entrusted rule in Mongolia to the descendants of Chinggis Khan, who were thus called *noyan*. Since this Mongolian ruling class was now purely hereditary and Mongolia was mostly at peace, *noyan* in this epoch acquired the connotation of "nobleman." After 1921 the word *daruga/darga*, "boss," "head," replaced the aristocratic *noyan* as the term for officials.

See also SOCIAL CLASSES IN THE MONGOL EMPIRE; SOCIAL CLASSES IN THE QING PERIOD.

Noyon Uul (**Noin-Ula**)   Located in Batsümber Sum (Central province) north of ULAANBAATAR, Noyon Uul is the richest known XIONGNU (Hun) grave site. Discovered in 1912, the graves were excavated by P. K. Kozlov (1924), S. A. Teploukhov and G. I. Borovka (1924–25), A. D. Simukov (1927), and Ts. Dorjsüren (1954–55). The site contains 212 graves of varied status from the first century B.C.E. and the first century C.E. Under the grave mound the largest burial chamber measures 13 meters (43 feet) long, 12 meters (39 feet) wide, and 9 meters (30 feet) deep. The graves typically have double coffins with

Griffon attacking a moose. Felt carpet, from Noyon Uul, first–second centuries *(From* Mongolian Arts and Crafts *[1987])*

bodies oriented to the north, ceramic jugs placed between the inner and outer coffin at the northern corners, and sometimes a bronze cauldron with the remains of a funerary horse sacrifice. Other remains include typical Xiongnu grave goods: bronze mirrors, iron arrowheads, knives, and bridles. The larger graves also show remains of embroidered silk coffin linings, hats, boots, felt saddle cloths with appliqué patterns of fighting beasts in the ANIMAL STYLE, votive cloth flags, copper pestles, and fragmentary gold ornaments (unfortunately, all the richer tombs have been robbed). Other decorative goods include a silver plaque decorated with the figure of a yak in a landscape very different in style from the ANIMAL STYLE. Fragmentary wool cloth, tapestries, and embroidery from Syria, Bactria, and Sogdiana as well as abundant Chinese silk and lacquer ware show the extent of Xiongnu foreign relations.

See also ALTAIC LANGUAGE FAMILY.

obo   *See* OBOO.

oboo (*owoo, ovoo, obo*)   The *oboo* is a cairn that served as a border marker, a site of sacrifices to the local deities, and a physical manifestation of the link between the land and the men who occupy it.

The *oboo* (meaning simply heap), situated on a mountain or hilltop or at least a rise with auspicious configuration, is an ubiquitous feature of the Mongolian landscape today among all the Mongolian peoples: BURIATS, OIRATS, KALMYKS, UPPER MONGOLS, KHALKHA, INNER MONGOLIANS, Daurs, Tu, and Yogurs. Some *oboo*s are simply round heaps of stones, but branches and prayer flags (*khei mori*) are often stuck into the cairn. In the absence of stones, *oboo*s can be made almost entirely of branches. *Oboo*s associated with a strongly Buddhist cult are built in three stages and have 12 smaller heaps extending out in the cardinal directions around them, in imitation of the continents around the world mountain Sumeru (Mongolian, Sümber) of Buddhist cosmology. During sacrifices ropes are tied from the *oboo*'s peak to the ground, and small coloured flags (*dartsag*) are draped from the ropes.

Since the 18th century at least, virtually every male-based social group—BANNERS and *SUM*, clans (if they existed), colleges (*AIMAG*) of lamas—has had its own *oboo*, which is the sign of its connection to the land. In addition to these large formal *oboo*s, smaller temporary *oboo*s can also have a small-scale cult. Among the Daurs there also exist women's *oboo*s to bring rain to the vegetable plots. Travelers passing an *oboo* are expected to circumambulate it clockwise and to add a stone to it.

Regardless of the exact religious complexion of those performing the ritual, *oboo* sacrifices are everywhere strikingly similar. Formal worship is always performed in the summer, on a date determined by astrological calculation, and is intended to ensure seasonable rainfall and fertile livestock. Only adult men are allowed to participate in or even watch the ceremony (men are banned from the Daur women's *oboo*s). The deities worshiped include the various *tenggeri* (gods), the dragons (*luu*) who control the rains, the "master of the land" (*gazar-un ezen* or *sabdag,* from Tibetan *sa-bdag*), or shaman spirits among still shamanic peoples such as the BURIATS and Daurs. Buddhist *oboo* worship also invokes the powerful fierce bodhisattva Vajrapani (of whom CHINGGIS KHAN was believed to be an emanation body). Either a lama or a respected lay elder presides over the ritual, never a shaman, even if the deity worshiped is a shaman spirit. A small table is set up by the *oboo*'s southern side for the offering of prayers. Offerings of sacrificial meat are placed on the *oboo,* and liquor and water are poured on the stones. Most of the meat is eaten by the members of the group sponsoring the sacrifice, but the bones are left at the *oboo.* Worship opens and closes with a triple clockwise circumambulation, and athletic competitions follow the ritual. Skulls of beloved HORSES are also placed on the *oboo* after their death.

The texts used by Mongolian lamas for setting up Buddhist *oboo*s and performing the offerings were written by the THIRD MERGEN GEGEEN (1717–66). In them the Mergen Gegeen criticized the blood sacrifices and gluttonous feasting and merrymaking that accompanied the *oboo* sacrifice, but despite his admonition and that of later authors of Buddhist didactic poetry, meat was still widely used even in lamas' offerings.

Since the time of the Buriat scholar DORZHI BANZAROVICH BANZAROV (1822–55), the *oboo* has been interpreted as a remnant of SHAMANISM within Mongolian Buddhism. However, not only is the Mongolian *oboo*

Oboo, Khentii province, 1991 *(Courtesy Christopher Atwood)*

essentially identical in form and cult to the Tibetan cairn, or la-rtse, in fact no known source before the 16th- to 17th-century SECOND CONVERSION to Buddhism even mentions the colorful and now-ubiquitous cult. (*Oboo*s are occasionally mentioned, but only as markers.) Thus, one might suggest that this cult is, like the GESER epic, an aspect of imported Tibetan Buddhist culture that, while in certain tension with stricter Buddhist ideas, has spread even to those Mongolian peoples who rejected Buddhism. In all Mongolian lands *oboo* worship was suppressed during times of Communist antireligious propaganda; however, today it is again one of the most prominent aspects of revived religious practice, as drivers drive around roadside *oboo*s for quick blessings and local officials once again participate in the cult.

See also DAUR LANGUAGES AND PEOPLE; KHOTONG; TU LANGUAGE AND PEOPLE; YOGUR LANGUAGES AND PEOPLE.

Further reading: C. R. Bawden, "Two Mongol Texts concerning Obo-Worship," *Oriens Extremus* 5 (1958): 23–41.

Ocean of Story   *See* SUTRA OF THE WISE AND FOOLISH.

Öchicher (1247–1311) *Mongol aristocrat of the Yuan dynasty who overthrew Sangha and commanded the final defeat of Qaidu and Du'a's partisans*

A descendant of Boroghul, one of CHINGGIS KHAN's "Four Steeds," Öchicher entered the court of QUBILAI KHAN in 1279 as head of a KESHIG shift and from 1281 as head of the Palace Provisions Commission. In 1291, as *keshig* chief, Öchicher received from one of his guardsmen, an official for the powerful and controversial finance minister SANGHA, incriminating data on Sangha's sale of offices. Once Sangha was executed, Öchicher received his vast personal estate as a reward. While appointed with HARGHASUN DARQAN to administer Huguang province, Öchicher stayed at the capital, where he personally supervised the *keshig* guards in digging the Tonghui Canal to DAIDU (modern Beijing). Emperor Temür (1294–1307) treated Öchicher as an elder statesmen and in 1301 dispatched him to QARA-QORUM to assist his brother Prince Gammala (1263–1302) in pacifying the threat from QAIDU KHAN and Du'a Khan. Although Qaidu defeated the Yuan dynasty forces in 1301, he died of wounds, and Du'a (d. 1308) made peace with the Yuan. While he never achieved the final surrender of either Qaidu or Du'a's successors, Öchicher basically neutralized them by skillfully exploiting their divisions and reviving military farms up to the ALTAI RANGE. From 1308 to his death he served, again with Harghasun, as grand councillor in the new Qorum Branch Secretariat administering the Mongolian heartland.

Ö'elün Üjin (Hö'elün) (fl. 1162–1210) *As mother of Chinggis Khan, Ö'elün was seen as a paragon of heroic motherhood, raising her sons in great adversity.*

Ö'elün Üjin (Lady Ö'elün) came from the Olqunu'ud lineage of the QONGGIRAD clan. Betrothed to a MERKID tribesman, the Mongol chief YISÜGEI BA'ATUR and his brother kidnapped her and made her Yisügei's principal wife. Ö'elün bore Yisügei four sons and one daughter. The eldest son was Temüjin, the future CHINGGIS KHAN. (While her name is given as Ö'elün in the Chinese transcription of the *Secret History of the Mongols,* earlier sources such as RASHID-UD-DIN indicate that Ö'elün is the correct spelling.)

When Temüjin was nine years old hostile Tatar tribesmen poisoned Yisügei, leaving Ö'elün a widow (c. 1171). The TAYICHI'UD clan, Yisügei's rivals for leadership of the whole MONGOL TRIBE, then rallied most of Yisügei's clan followers. Ö'elün was abandoned on the steppe with her five children, Yisügei's minor wife, Sülchigei, her two sons, and a certain number of retainers. The *SECRET HISTORY OF THE MONGOLS* celebrates her subsequent heroism in raising her children all alone, although it exaggerates her isolation.

Ö'elün identified completely with her husband's lineage and passed on to her sons her hatred of the

Tayichi'ud. As the children got older she tried to stop the rivalry between the two sets of half-brothers, although her sons eventually murdered one of Sülchigei's. O'elün helped Temüjin by raising orphaned children as "companions" (NÖKÖR) for him. After Temüjin was crowned as Chinggis, she had to defend her second son, Qasar, against accusations of disloyalty stemming from TEB TENGGERI, a shaman (c. 1210). She died soon after.

Ögedei Khan (Ögödei, Ögetei, Ugedey) (b. 1186, r. 1229–1241) *Successor of Chinggis Khan, who expanded the empire and reformed administration*

Under Ögedei Khan the Mongols completed the conquest of North China and expanded the empire into the Middle East, the Qipchaq steppe, and the Russian principalities (modern European Russia and Ukraine). At the same time Ögedei created written regulations for many of his father's new institutions and began the process of adapting Mongol rule to sedentary institutions and ideas in North China and Turkestan. His generosity and flexibility established a new model for Mongol emperors, one that would compete with his father's legacy of severity and rigor.

EARLY LIFE AND CORONATION

Ögedei was the third son of BÖRTE ÜJIN (Lady Börte), CHINGGIS KHAN's principal wife, and participated in the turbulent events of his father's rise. At age 17 he experienced the disastrous defeat of Qalaqaljid Sands (1203). Wounded and lost on the battlefield, he was rescued by one of Chinggis Khan's companions (NÖKÖR), Boroghul. Although already married, in 1204 his father gave him TÖREGENE, the wife of a defeated MERKID chief. Töregene bore him five sons, and despite her plain appearance she was extremely able. She eventually came to have great influence on her husband.

After Chinggis was proclaimed emperor in 1206, Ögedei received four or five 1,000s (the sources differ) of the JALAYIR, Besüd, Suldus, and Qongqotan clans as his appanage. The Jalayir commander, Ilügei, had been Ögedei's tutor, and he, his son Danishmand, and his younger brother Eljidei formed Ögedei's intimate circle. Ögedei's territory occupied the Emil and Qobaq Rivers (Emin and Hobok, near modern Tacheng).

Chinggis Khan allowed his three elder sons, JOCHI, CHA'ADAI, and Ögedei, to campaign independently for the first time in November 1211 against the JIN DYNASTY in North China. In autumn 1213 Chinggis sent the three elder sons to ravage the land south through Hebei province and then north through Shanxi before linking up with their father at Yanjing (modern Beijing).

During the campaign against KHORAZM Ögedei and Cha'adai butchered the people of Otrar after a five-month siege (winter 1219–20), before joining Jochi to besiege the capital of Urganch, slaughtering the entire population in 1221. Only the artisans were spared, and the three

sons divided them among themselves. When they returned to their father, he berated them for not giving him a share, until CHORMAQAN and other of Chinggis's quiver bearers placated the emperor's wrath. Chinggis then sent Ögedei against Ghazni. Despite its surrender, Ögedei massacred all but the craftsmen.

Fraternal rivalry emerged over the discussion of the succession. Jochi was widely suspected of being the son of the Merkid man who had kidnaped his mother shortly after her marriage to the young Chinggis. Even so, the emperor had always treated Jochi as his presumptive heir. According to the SECRET HISTORY OF THE MONGOLS, before the expedition against Khorazm in 1219, the empress Yisüi insisted that the emperor, then in his 50s, designate an heir. An ugly scene followed in which Cha'adai accused Jochi of being a bastard. After the two brawling sons were separated, Cha'adai suggested as a compromise that Ögedei be chosen. Jochi agreed, and Chinggis confirmed their choice, making Ögedei his successor.

Chinggis died in August 1227, and Jochi had died a year or two earlier, removing any possible source of conflict. Cha'adai continued to support his younger brother's claim; the alliance of the Ögedeid and Cha'adaid families

Ögedei Khan (1229–1241). Anonymous court painter *(Courtesy of the National Palace Museum, Taipei)*

was a constant of Mongolian politics for the next eight decades. Ögedei's younger brother TOLUI held the regency until 1229, when a great QURILTAI met at Ködö'e Aral on the KHERLEN RIVER. After ritually declining three times, Ögedei was proclaimed Qa'an, or "Great KHAN" of the Mongols, on September 13, 1229.

MILITARY EXPANSION

Unlike his father or his younger brother Tolui, Ögedei took relatively little personal interest in campaigning. After his coronation, he participated personally in only two seasons of campaigning. Depending on the extraordinary commanders nurtured by Chinggis Khan, however, he presided over conquests far beyond what his father had achieved. Ögedei participated in the campaigns against the rump Jin dynasty. At the end of summer 1230, responding to the Jin's unexpected defeat of the Mongol general Doqulqu, the khan went south to Shaanxi province with Tolui, clearing the area of the Jin forces and taking the city of Fengxiang. After returning north for the summer, Ögedei and Tolui again campaigned against the Jin redoubt in Henan from October 1231 on, cutting through territory of South China's Song (Sung) dynasty to assault the Jin's rear. By late February 1232 the Jin ruler was besieged in his capital of Kaifeng, and Ögedei soon departed for Mongolia, leaving the final conquest to his generals. In the event, the Jin dynasty held out for two full years more (see KAIFENG, SIEGE OF).

Ögedei's attempt to subjugate the kingdom of Korea met with less success. He dispatched Sartaq there in 1231; the Korean king temporarily submitted but then rose up and killed the Mongol overseers (DARUGHACHI) and fled to Kanghwa Island. As Sartaq was campaigning against them, he was hit with a stray arrow and died.

At the same time, Ögedei completed Chinggis's conquests in the Middle East. Jalal-ud-Din Mengüberdi, son of the last ruler of Khorazm, had been trying to build a new base in western Iran, but Mongol operations in that area had driven him off and secured the surrender of Isfahan in 1229. Jalal-ud-Din having fled to the area of GEORGIA, Armenia, and TURKEY, Ögedei dispatched Chormaqan to put an end to him. Chormaqan advanced rapidly and harried Jalal-ud-Din's increasingly small band, until Jalal-ud-Din was killed in August 1231 by a Kurd in the mountains. Chormaqan and his Mongols then set about reducing the citadels of the Armenians and the Georgians.

In 1234 after returning to Mongolia, Ögedei held another quritlai, announcing plans for conquest of the Koreans, the SONG DYNASTY in South China, and the QIPCHAQS and their allies in the west, all of whom had killed Mongol envoys. The campaigns against the Song, commanded by Ögedei's sons, KÖTEN in the west and Köchü in the east, penetrated deep into Song territory but did not deliver any decisive blow. In 1240 Köten dispatched a subsidiary expedition to Tibet, which was the Mongols' first contact with that land.

The campaign against the Qipchaqs and their allies was the largest. To it Ögedei assigned many princes of the imperial family, including his own sons GÜYÜG and Qadan, BATU (d. 1255), the son of Jochi, who held the empire's northwestern area as his appanage, and Tolui's son Möngke. Expert guidance was provided by Chinggis's famous general SÜBE'ETEI BA'ATUR. Facing a divided enemy, the Mongols swept all before them. By 1240 the Turkish Qipchaq tribes of the Caspian–Black Sea steppe, the BULGHARS and their capital (in modern Tatarstan), the various Russian principalities, the Qipchaqs of CRIMEA, and the Ossetian (Alan) capital of Magas had all fallen. Despite these spectacular successes, the Mongol camp suffered dissension. At several points Batu, head of the Jochid line, had been stymied by tough resistance, and Ögedei's son Güyüg and Cha'adai's son Büri ridiculed him for his weakness. Ögedei recalled Güyüg and Möngke in winter 1240–41, but the advance into Eastern Europe continued under the command of Qadan, Batu, and Sübe'etei, culminating in the nearly simultaneous defeats of the Poles, Czechs, and Teutonic Knights at Liegnitz and of the Hungarians at Muhi (April 1241). Only the news of Ögedei's death, reaching Batu's camp in 1242, prompted a withdrawal.

BUILDING IMPERIAL INSTITUTIONS

In his administration of the empire, Ögedei's reign was marked by a paradox: The same emperor who began the bureaucratization of Mongol administration was engaging in the most extravagant acts of reckless generosity. Actually, Ögedei needed bureaucratic administration to supply the gifts with which he could fulfill his image as the openhanded khan of Turco-Mongol ideals.

Ögedei took his administrators from three cultures: 1) the largely Christian eastern Turk circle, represented by CHINQAI, a Uighur Christian scribe with KEREYID ties; 2) the Islamic circle represented by two Khorazmians, Mahmud Yalavach and his son Mas'ud Beg (see MAHMUD YALAVACH AND MAS'UD BEG); and 3) the North Chinese Confucian circle, represented by YELÜ CHUCAI, a Kitan scholar and lay Dhyana Zen devotee, and Nianhe Zhongshan, a Jurchen. Conflicts often erupted between Mahmud Yalavach and Yelü Chucai. Yelü Chucai encouraged Ögedei to institute a traditional Chinese system of government, with taxation in the hands of government agents and payment in kind or in a government-issued currency. Mahmud Yalavach promoted a system in which the government would delegate tax collection to tax farmers, who would bid for the privilege and collect payments in silver. The Mongols mostly followed Yalavach's proposals. Since North China did not use silver as currency, ORTOQ merchants and moneylenders (mostly Uighur and Turkestani), working with capital supplied by Mongol aristocrats, loaned at high interest the silver needed for tax payments. This caused great hardship, a fact not relieved by ineffectual imperial decrees limiting interest.

From 1229 to 1240 Mahmud Yalavach administered Turkestan, while Yelü Chucai administered North China. In both areas the Mongols conducted a census (although on differing principles), pacified the population, suppressed banditry, and encouraged the redevelopment of agriculture. In both areas, however, the new centralized administration had to adjust to the existence of large appanages ruled by members of the Mongol imperial family and aristocracy, which were largely autonomous. Yelü Chucai also had to share power with SHIGI QUTUQU, one of Chinggis Khan's "four foundlings," whom Ögedei appointed chief judge (JARGHUCHI) in North China in 1234. In Iran, beyond the Amu Dar'ya River, Ögedei appointed first Chin-Temür, variously described as a QARA-KHITAI or an ÖNGGÜD, and then KÖRGÜZ, a low-born Christian Uighur who later converted to Islam. Körgüz, in particular, proved to be an efficient and honest administrator.

Ögedei also refined his father's Mongol institutions. He codified rules of dress and conduct during the *quriltai*s. Throughout the empire he created postroad (JAM) stations with a permanent staff, who would supply the post riders' needs and were exempt from other taxes. Where necessary he dug wells to ease travel. He decreed that within the decimal units one out of every 100 sheep of the well-off should be levied for the poor of the unit, and that one sheep and one mare from every herd should be forwarded to form a herd for the imperial table.

Ögedei built the city of QARA-QORUM in 1235, assigning different quarters to Islamic and North Chinese craftsmen, who competed to win the emperor's favor. In the Chinese ward there was a Confucian temple and an observatory, which Yelü Chucai used to create and regulate a calendar on the Chinese model.

PERSONALITY AND STYLE OF RULE

In describing his sons, Chinggis Khan saw Ögedei's chief characteristic as courtesy and generosity. Despite the continued carnage of the Mongol conquests, Ögedei tried to live up to this assessment. He kept peace among the branches of his family, criticizing his own son Güyüg and Cha'ada's son Büri for not respecting their nephew Batu. The mysterious death of Tolui in 1232 seems to have affected him deeply, although whether his grief included some remorse for having contributed to his younger brother's death is hard to say.

Ögedei desired to win the support of both the Islamic and the North Chinese sections of his empire, employing members of both as high officials. The result, intended or not, was a constant rivalry between the two peoples, a rivalry that deflected animosity away from the Mongols and onto each other. This rivalry was accentuated by the cost of Ögedei's heroic generosity; the constant outflow from the treasury, principally to the west, had to be made up by taxes, principally on North China. By 1240 Ögedei had replaced Yelü Chucai with Mahmud Yalavach and handed taxes over to 'Abd-ur-Rahman, who promised to double the annual payments of silver.

Ögedei eventually fell victim to alcoholism. From 1235 he had became an increasingly heavy drinker of both Mongol KOUMISS and Turkestani grape wine. Cha'adai entrusted an official to watch his habit, but Ögedei managed to drink anyway. When he died at dawn on December 11, 1241, after a late-night drinking bout, Chinese officials blamed the grape wine forwarded to the feast by 'Abd-ur-Rahman, while others blamed the sister of Tolui's widow, who had arranged the feast. The Mongol aristocrats recognized, however, that the khan's own lack of self-control had killed him, and they squashed any investigation into his death. Ögedei had nominated his grandson Shiremün as his heir, but Empress Töregene became regent.

See also APPANAGE SYSTEM; BUDDHISM IN THE MONGOL EMPIRE; CENSUS IN THE MONGOL EMPIRE; CENTRAL EUROPE AND THE MONGOLS; CHRISTIANITY IN THE MONGOL EMPIRE; CONFUCIANISM; INDIA AND THE MONGOLS; ISLAM IN THE MONGOL EMPIRE; KOREA AND THE MONGOL EMPIRE; MANCHURIA AND THE MONGOL EMPIRE; PAPER CURRENCY IN THE MONGOL EMPIRE; PROVINCES IN THE MONGOL EMPIRE; RELIGIOUS POLICY IN THE MONGOL EMPIRE; RUSSIA AND THE MONGOL EMPIRE; SIBERIA AND THE MONGOL EMPIRE; TAOISM IN THE MONGOL EMPIRE; TIBET AND THE MONGOL EMPIRE; WESTERN EUROPE AND THE MONGOL EMPIRE.

Ögetei Khan   *See* ÖGEDEI KHAN.

Oghul-Qaimish (regent, 1248–1251, d. 1252) *Second empress-regent in the Mongol Empire, whose reign ended with the coronation of Möngke and her execution for alleged sorcery.*

Nothing is known of Oghul-Qaimish's early life, except that she was a member of the MERKID tribe, which had been conquered by CHINGGIS KHAN in 1204 and virtually wiped out as a separate people in retaliation for its revolt of 1216–19. She was given as a wife to GÜYÜG, son of ÖGEDEI KHAN and grandson of Chinggis Khan, probably in the aftermath of that rebellion. Oghul-Qaimish bore Güyüg two sons, Khoja and Naqu. She is not known to have had any influence on her husband's policies before his death.

Güyüg died while camping at Qum-Sengir in Turkestan. Oghul-Qaimish brought his remains to his ORDO (palace-tent) in his appanage in the Emil-Qobaq region (around modern Tacheng). Despite her suspicion of Güyüg's motives, BATU (d. 1255), head of the senior Jochid line, allowed Oghul-Qaimish to serve as regent. Güyüg's chief officials, the scribes CHINQAI and Bala, and his former tutor and judge, Qadaq, remained with her at the *ordo*, which became the de facto capital of the empire. While Chinqai and Qadaq were Christians, often criticized by Muslim historians for their anti-Islamic posture,

Oghul-Qaimish is said to have spent her time with the native Mongol shamans (bö'e; Turkish, qam) and paid little attention to imperial affairs. Unlike TÖREGENE, her mother-in-law and forerunner as regent, she had no discernible political agenda. Her sons, Khoja and Naqu, together with their nephew Shiremün, son of Ögedei's son Köchü, spent their time attempting to secure the election of one of their number to the throne. In this endeavor their primary support came from Yisü-Möngke, head of the Cha'adaid family.

One of the few public affairs of Oghul-Qaimish's regency was the embassy from Louis IX of France. An envoy, claiming to be from Güyüg but probably acting on his own, had offered Louis IX, crusading against Egypt, an alliance against the Muslims to take Jerusalem. The king sent his own envoys in reply, but after she received his envoys at her ordo on the Emil (Emin) River, Oghul-Qaimish sent them back with presents and letters announcing the usual Mongol demand for submission.

In 1249 or 1250 Batu hosted a QURILTAI (assembly), which selected Möngke, son of Tolui, as khan. Oghul-Qaimish sent Güyüg's Uighur clerk, Bala, to that assembly with a demand that Shiremün be elected khan. The nobles rejected Bala's proposal and insisted that disobedience to Batu's advice would be punished. Oghul-Qaimish refused to recognize this decision, as did most of the other Ögedeid and Cha'adaid princes. She continued her passive resistance to the new turn of events, refusing, with her son Khoja, to come when the scribe Shilemün summoned her, her sons, and Shiremün to a second quriltai on the KHERLEN RIVER in July 1251, which officially proclaimed MÖNGKE KHAN.

Her second son, Naqu, and Shiremün proceeded to the quriltai and attempted to overthrow Möngke. When the conspiracy was discovered, scribe Shilemün was again dispatched to summon Oghul-Qaimish and Khoja. Khoja obeyed, and like the other hostile princes was exiled to the South China front. Oghul-Qaimish again refused, still insisting that the transfer of the empire away from the line of Ögedei was invalid. In summer 1252 Möngke had her and Qadaqach (Shiremün's mother) arrested and their hands stitched in rawhide. MENGGESER NOYAN, Möngke's chief judge (JARGHUCHI), had Oghul-Qaimish stripped naked, questioned, and executed by being wrapped up in felt and flung into a river. In the eyes of Möngke her crime was not only rebellion but witchcraft. The khan described her to WILLIAM OF RUBRUCK as "more vile than a dog," "the worst kind of witch," who had destroyed her family by her "sorcery." Since all our knowledge stems from Toluid sources, it is difficult to say what truth, if any, lies behind these accusations.

Ögödei Khan   See ÖGEDEI KHAN.

Oirad   See OIRATS.

Oirats (Oyirad, Oirad, Oyrat, Oyrot, Western Mongols)   The Oirat people, while definitely a part of the broader Mongolian world ethnically and linguistically, have played an ambiguous role in Mongolian history, sometimes challenging the Mongols for leadership, sometimes forming independent states, and sometimes being incorporated by the Mongols. Their relation to the Mongols can thus be roughly compared to the relations of the Austrians to the Germans or the Ukrainians to the Russians.

Contemporary communities of Oirat ancestry or cultural affiliation include the KALMYKS of Russia, numbering 174,000 (1989); the XINJIANG MONGOLS, numbering 138,000 (1990); the western Mongols, mostly in Mongolia's UWS PROVINCE and KHOWD PROVINCES, numbering 168,400 (1989); the UPPER MONGOLS of Qinghai, numbering 72,000 (1990); the Khoshud and Torghud Mongols of ALASHAN, numbering 41,900 (1990); the Mongols of Gansu's SUBEI MONGOLIAN AUTONOMOUS COUNTY, numbering 4,200 (1999); and the Yekhe Minggadai of Fuyu county, Heilongjiang, numbering 2,400 (1988).

Oirat speech is a distinctive dialect or language of the Mongolian family. Today it is strongly influenced by standard Mongolian everywhere except in Kalmykia and Xinjiang. These are also the only two regions where a distinctive Oirat script, either Cyrillic Kalmyk or the traditional CLEAR SCRIPT, is used.

IN THE MONGOL EMPIRE

In 1202 the Oirats were ruled by Qutuqa, who bore the title beki, meaning "clan elder" and "shaman" (see SHAMANISM). The Oirats occupied eastern Tuva and Khöwsgöl, with their center along the Shishigt River. Qutuqa Beki submitted to CHINGGIS KHAN's son JOCHI in 1207 and was made a myriarch, or commander of a tümen (nominally 10,000). Qutuqa's two sons received Chinggis's daughter Checheyiken and Jochi's daughter Holuiqan in marriage (see SIBERIA AND THE MONGOL EMPIRE).

The Oirats continued as one of the most prominent QUDA (marriage ally) families in the MONGOL EMPIRE. Every branch of the Chinggisid family received Oirat women in marriage, and virtually every known descendant of Qutuqa bore the title kürgen (son-in-law of the imperial family). The Oirats were particularly prominent in the Middle Eastern IL-KHANATE, whose founder, HÜLE'Ü (1217–65), married two Oirat women in succession. An Oirat tümen under the Il-Khans' kürgens (son-in-laws) settled in the area of Diyarbakır in modern Turkey. This tümen deserted as a block in 1296 to MAMLUK EGYPT when GHAZAN KHAN favored their local Turkmen rivals, but by 1336 'Ali-Padshah, a member of the Oirat ruling family, was again a contender for power in the disintegrating Il-Khanate. ARGHUN AQA, an able but low-born Oirat, became governor of Khorasan (eastern Iran) and founder of a prominent Oirat family there.

Closer to their homeland, the Oirat chiefs maintained strong ties to the families of Jochi's sons Hordu (*see* BLUE HORDE) and BATU. They also were *quda* to QUBILAI KHAN's brother ARIQ-BÖKE (d. 1266) and his descendants, whose territory bordered on the Oirats'. During Ariq-Böke's bid for the throne, Oirats formed a large part of his army. With Ariq-Böke's defeat, the Oirat commanders entered the victor, Qubilai Khan's service, but by around 1279 common Oirats were joining rebellions against Qubilai. Little is known of the Oirats from then until the expulsion of the Mongols from China in 1368.

THE FOUR OIRATS

Strongly folkloric accounts in the 17TH-CENTURY CHRONICLES say the Oirats began to challenge the Mongols' Chinggisid rulers in the reign of Elbeg (c. 1394–99). The Mongolian chronicles evidence the Mongols' bitter hostility to the Oirat usurpers, whom they say had become "foreign enemies" (*khari daisun*). These sources oppose the "Four Oirats," or the Oirats' four *tümens* (nominally 10,000), to the SIX TÜMENS of the Chinggisid Mongols. Despite the universal currency of the term *Four Oirats* among Mongols and Oirats and numerous explanations by both traditional and modern historians, no consensus has been reached on the identity of the original four Oirat tribes.

Elbeg's supposedly pivotal reign unfortunately falls within a gap in contemporary Chinese records. However, by 1412 Chinese records do speak of an Oirat chief, Mahmud, deposing a Mongol khan. Mahmud's son and grandson, Toghoon (d. 1438), and ESEN (r. 1438–54), brought the Oirats to the height of their power over the Mongols, with Esen even assuming the title of khan in 1452. Esen and his predecessors had close relations with MOGHULISTAN to the west, in which their own clan, the Choros, was prominent. During their rise the Oirats occupied northwest Mongolia. Barköl and the Irtysh were the western limits of their settlement. The Oirats' Turkish neighbors always called them Qalmaq, a term of uncertain origin, which became Kalmyk in Russian.

Up to the 16th century the major Oirat tribes were the Khoid, the Baatud, the TORGHUD, the DÖRBÖD (ruled by chiefs of the Choros clan), the BARGA, the BURIATS, and the KHOSHUD. The origins of these groups are extremely diverse. The Khoid chiefs claimed descent from Qutuqa Beki, and thus were the original Oirats. The Baatud (heroes) were the Khoids' vanguard force. The Barga and Buriats around Lake Baikal were part of the Oirat confederation from the 15th century to about 1625. The Torghud were descendants of the KEREYID tribe in central Mongolia. The Choros clan shared the Uighur ancestry legend of birth from a female sacred tree and may have been of Uighur ancestry. The Khoshud

tribe's ruling Galwas lineage claimed descent from Qasar, Chinggis Khan's younger brother; the tribe itself formed around THREE GUARDS refugees from eastern Inner Mongolia deported by Esen in 1446–47. Not only were the Oirats as a whole of diverse origin, each tribe was formed from many *yasu* (bones), or patrilineages. Modern counts among the Dörböd tribe, for example, have found 40 to 60 such different *yasu*. Thus, only the smallest units of social organization were actually based on common ancestry.

The unifying factor in the early Oirat confederation was lack of Chinggisid ancestry, which disqualified its chiefs from the title of khan and the claim of sovereignty. The Mongol chronicles recount an elaborate story of how Toghoon Taishi tried to seize the throne, relying on his holy ancestress (the Choros's sacred tree), but was defeated by the power of the Mongols' holy ancestor Chinggis. Thus, the Oirats, like the JALAYIR, Suldus (*see* CHUBAN), Barulas (*see* TIMUR), and MANGGHUD clans in the post-Chinggisid world, could rule only as the *quda* (marriage allies) of Chinggisid emperors. The supreme Oirat chief bore the Chinese title TAISHI (the highest honorific rank in the Mongols' YUAN DYNASTY) as the regent who actually ruled in the name of the khan.

The Oirats under Esen depended heavily on their Islamic connections. The lineage of Esen and his ancestors, the Choros, was probably Uighur and in any case hailed from Moghulistan. Esen married the sister of a Moghuli khan, and the frequency of Muslim names among the Oirats of this period (Mahmud, Abdullah, 'Ala'ud-Din, etc.) is striking. In the 1440s and probably earlier Oirat tribute missions regularly included merchants from Hami, Turpan, and Samarqand (*see* TRIBUTE SYSTEM). From 1441 on a Muslim, Pir-Muhammad, and his assistant, Hajji-Ali, headed Esen's tribute missions. Apparently, the Samarqandi and Turpan-Hami merchants played the same role with the Oirats that the Sogdians had with the TÜRK EMPIRES and the UIGHURS with the Mongols.

The death of Esen in 1454 broke up the Oirats' role as patrons of Turkestan-China trade. One of Esen's non-Muslim sons moved west, launching devastating attacks on Moghulistan and the Uzbeks. It was a sign of the times that Pir-Muhammed by 1457 had decided to stay in China, while tribute envoys suddenly declined. Mongolian chronicles still speak of "Oirat *taishis*" bullying Chinggisid rulers, but most of these *taishis* appear to have been adventurers with little or no relation to the Oirats as a people. By 1510 BATU-MÖNGKE DAYAN KHAN unified the Mongols and abolished the position of *taishi*, Oirat or otherwise. From 1552 to 1628 ALTAN KHAN, KHUTUGTAI SECHEN KHUNG-TAIJI, Sholoi Ubashi Khung-Taiji (*see* KHOTOGHOID), and other princes of southwest Inner Mongolia and KHALKHA repeatedly looted the Oirats living in the Irtysh, Barköl, and Altai regions.

OIRAT REVIVAL

The Oirats revived in the early 17th century. After Altan Khan's death in 1582, raids from southwest Inner Mongolia ceased. The Oirat confederation crushed the Khalkha invader Sholoi Ubashi Khung-Taiji perhaps around 1623. In 1640 the Oirats and the Khalkha made peace and formed an alliance, issuing a new code, the MONGOL-OIRAT CODE, to regulate their relations. The alliance ratified the Oirat's partial adoption of Chinggisid titles. By 1640 the title *taishi* was almost wholly replaced by *khung-taiji* (Russian, *kontaisha*), or its abbreviated form TAIJI. Derived from Chinese *huang-taizi,* "crown-prince," and originally containing the idea of Chinggisid blood, *khung-taiji* became the title of great Oirat rulers, while the lesser nobility of the Oirats became *taiji*. *Quda* ties remained important but served mainly to link the members of the Oirat confederation to one another rather than the Oirats to Chinggisid Mongols.

The Oirats also participated in the SECOND CONVERSION of the Mongols to Buddhism. Led by the Khoshud nobility, the Oirats invited Tibetan high lamas and dispatched their sons to Tibet for training as monks. By 1640 the Oirats had emerged as the chief defenders of the Dalai and Panchen Lamas from all their rivals, both inside and outside Tibet. The conversion to Buddhism energized with a revival of culture. The Oirats, who had previously made only occasional use of the UIGHUR-MONGOLIAN SCRIPT, adopted in 1648–49 the CLEAR SCRIPT designed by the cleric and scholar ZAYA PANDITA NAMKHAI-JAMTSU (1599–1662).

As Oirat power expanded, their tribal and territorial distribution changed. The Baatud tribe disintegrated, as did the remaining Barga-Buriat elements; those Buriats around the Baikal had no further connection with the Oirats. By 1640 the Oirats had occupied most of the fertile pastures south and west of the Zünghar (Junggar) basin as well as their traditional Barköl and Irtysh lands. They also expanded northwest along the Yenisey, Ob, and Irtysh Rivers as far as the Russian Cossack settlements of Tara and Tobolsk. KHOO-ÖRLÖG led the Torghud from western Siberia to the Volga in 1630. In 1636–37, at the invitation of the Dalai Lama, the Khoshud under TÖRÖ-BAIKU GÜÜSHI KHAN occupied Kökenuur on the Tibetan plateau.

By 1642, if not before, the Khoshud rulers, who reckoned their descent from Chinggis Khan's brother Qasar, took the title khan. The Dalai Lama also granted this title to totally non-Chinggisid rulers, such as GALDAN BOSHOGTU KHAN of the Choros (1678) and AYUUKI KHAN of the Torghud (1690). Both Galdan and Ayuuki were Khoshud on their mother's side and so could possibly claim Chinggisid ancestry. Still, the title *khan* was never strictly hereditary among the Oirats and always required some external validation: at first from the Dalai Lama but by the mid-18th century from the QING DYNASTY or Russia.

THE OIRATS AT THEIR HEIGHT

By 1690 three different Oirat confederations, or states, had emerged. In Tibet the Khoshuds, with some Khoids and Torghuds, formed the khanate of Tibet under the descendants of Güüshi Khan (*see* UPPER MONGOLS). Straddling the Volga, the Torghuds, with some Dörböds and Khoshuds, formed the Kalmyk Khanate under Khoo-Örlög's descendants. The Kalmyks numbered at their height 40,000–50,000 households. In the Oirat homeland of Zungharia, the ZÜNGHARS, an offshoot of the Dörböd also ruled by the Choros, displaced the Khoshud in 1676. The Zünghar principality included the Zünghars, Dörböds, Khoshuds, and Khoids (with some attached Torghuds) and is said to have numbered 200,000 households. From this time until 1771 the Oirats remained powerful players in Inner Asian politics.

The Kalmyk and Zünghar confederations were similar in many ways. Both were divided into tribes (AIMAG), which themselves were conglomerations of exogamous *yasun* (bones, or patrilineages). The khan or *khung-taiji* was assisted by an office (*yamu*) or court (*zarghu*) composed of four chief officials, variously called ministers (*tüshimed*), judges (*zarghuchis; see* JARGHUCHI), or *zaisangs* (from Chinese *zaixiang,* grand councillor). These were commoner retainers of the ruler's tribe. The Zünghar ruler GALDAN-TSEREN (r. 1727–45) expanded the council by adding six *zarghuchis* to assist the four *tüshimed*.

The people were assigned to appanages (*ulus* or *anggi*) controlled by a nobility (*noyod* or *taiji; see* NOYAN) of the tribes' particular ruling "bones." Below the *noyods* were the *tabunangs,* or sons-in-law or those who had married women of the *noyod* lineages. The positions of "four ministers," or "judges," were restricted to such *tabunangs* of the ruler. Below them were minor functionaries: standard bearers, trumpeters, aides-de-camp (*kiya*), and so on.

Each appanage was divided into *otogs* (a camp district composed of several clans and usually with 3,000 to 6,000 households; *see* OTOG). The *otogs* were divided into groups of 40 households, and they in turn into 20s. Each of these units had officials: *zaisangs, demchis,* and *shülengges,* respectively. These local officials were all accounted commoners. Commoners without office were divided into the "good" (*said*), the "middle," and the "base."

While Oirat *noyods* frequently resisted the khan, insubordination among the commoners to their noblemen was virtually unknown. Every household was assigned both to its particular unit and to that unit's assigned territory. Local officials were responsible for keeping their people in line and reporting external or internal disorder. The commoner officials were required to assemble periodically at the palace-yurt (*örgöö*) of their *noyon,* and *otog* elders had to assemble the *demchis;* failure to appear was subject to a fine. Government was maintained almost entirely by in-kind contributions. The commoners were required to give food, mounts, and other necessary supplies to government messengers and "feed" their own nobles, *tabunangs*, and the high officials.

MILITARY

The Oirat khanates excelled among contemporary Inner Asian peoples in the use of muskets and cannons. During both the 1688 invasion of Khalkha and the 1723 campaign against the KAZAKHS, firearms, both small and heavy, gave them the margin of victory. Despite Russian bans on export of firearms, the Kalmyk Ayuuki Khan could muster 3 cannons and 4,000 muskets in 1682. From 1697 on the Kalmyks as Russian allies received a regular supply of gunpowder and bullets from Russia as well as the use of cannons during war. Supplying Russian firearms to the Zünghars was still banned, however. Bukharan merchants and Zünghar trade missions frequently evaded these bans, and raids on Siberia also supplied firearms. The Zünghar ruler Galdan-Tseren in 1733 asked the Russians in vain for a military alliance and blacksmiths to make cannons to use against the Qing. In 1744 he captured and used Russian gunsmiths, carpenters, and blacksmiths. Even so, demand remained high for sabers, lances, bows and arrows, armor, and helmets, and these edged weapons were still the mainstay of the Oirat armies.

COMMERCE

From the time of Toghoon Taishi in the 15th century to the loss of independence, the Oirats maintained symbiotic relations with Turkestani Muslim merchants (cf. the ORTOQ of the empire period). Due to their military prowess, China and (after 1600) Russia tried to buy off Oirat raids by allowing Oirats to participate in "tribute" and duty-free trade missions to China and Siberia subsidized by their hosts (*see* TRIBUTE SYSTEM). The nobles delegated much of the actual trading to Samarqandi (15th century) or Bukharan (17th–18th century) merchant clients who joined Oirat missions. Both Chinese and Russian hosts frequently protested the size of these 2,000–3,000-man trade missions.

While the anarchy among the Oirats in the mid-16th century led to frequent raids on trade caravans, the restoration of order in the 17th century revived trade with Siberia, Turkestan, and China. Bukharan merchants also peddled goods through the steppe and at fairs, such as at the Yamysh salt lake (near Maykain). The Oirats' major export was horses, along with other livestock. Red fox, ermine fur, and lambskin were also welcomed in China and Siberia. Oirats sold to the Bukharans rhubarb and slaves, usually Russian, Chinese, or Mongol. In return for these goods, Bukharans sold a variety of thick cotton cloth, *kamka,* or silk damask, flour, smuggled Siberian weapons, coins, beads, combs, needles, fine Siberian furs, and other luxury products. The formation of monasteries also promoted commerce. Patrons and monastic treasurers in Züngharia regularly made visits to China to sell horses and purchase religious articles.

RELIGION AND CULTURE

Cultural life among the great Oirat khanates was dominated by Buddhism. The Buddhist belief among the Oirats, surrounded by the Muslim Turks, was peculiarly militant and focused on the Dalai Lama in Tibet, whose name itself was a common religious prayer. The biography of the great monk-scholar Zaya Pandita Namkhai-Jamtsu vividly illustrates the aristocratic Buddhist milieu. A nobleman might donate up to 10,000 horses for a single religious service or requisition his subjects to become *bandi* (novices) or lay servants in the monasteries. The clergy and their "disciples" were protected from both violence and state duties. Novices who had married without taking the major vows were probably common although legally discouraged. The monasteries were mostly nomadic, although in 1638 a Zünghar ruler requested pigs from Russia to give to the monasteries.

At its height the Kalmyk chief lama's estate of *shabinar* (disciples, or serfs), for example, reached 3,000–4,000 households. Galdan-Tseren organized the entire clergy into nine *jisai* (Mongolian, *jisiya*), with 9,000 lamas and 10,600 households of *shabinar.* To improve the clergy, he requisitioned 500 pupils, each with two yurts, three servants, two horses, and 100 sheep to be trained by a respected Tibetan lama. One special *otog*, or camp district, named *Altachin*, "goldsmiths," was dedicated to making Buddhist images.

The ethos of later Zünghar Buddhism was exemplified by Lubzang-Puntsog (fl. 1707–17), a noble-born lama and student of the famous Tibetan scholar 'Jam-byangs bZhad-pa (1648–1721) in Lhasa. A Torghud tale pictures him as a lineage-proud and petty-minded disciplinarian. Galdan had installed three holy images, which he had brought from Tibet, in three new monasteries in Zungharia, but on his return Lubzang-Puntsog consolidated them into a college (*datsang*) solely for the higher study of the Vinaya (monastic discipline). He expelled 3,500 of Galdan's 5,000 monks, giving the Zünghar monks an excellent reputation for discipline. At the same time, Lubzang-Puntsog became notorious in Tibet in 1717 for persecuting the traditional and unscholarly rNying-ma-pa (Old Order).

While Tibetan language and scriptures were diligently studied in the monasteries, for civil purposes the Kalmyks and Zünghars used Oirat Mongolian in Zaya-Pandita's clear script, in which a number of diplomatic letters have survived in Russian archives. Large numbers of Buddhist translations are mentioned, but the only surviving historical works from before the loss of independence are Zaya Pandita's hagiography *Sarayin gerel* (Light of the moon), written in Zungharia around 1690, and *Emchi* (Physician) Ghabang-Sharab's *Dörbön Oyirodiyin töüke* (History of the four Oirats), written in Kalmykia in 1737. Unlike earlier Mongolian histories, this last is not a chronological narrative but rather a treasury of genealogy, wise sayings, and episodes left by the heroes of Oirat independence, written as the Kalmyks fell into subjection to Russia. This distinctive genre of historical highlights was continued in the work of the same name by the Kalmyk nobleman Baatur Ubashi Tümen from 1801 to 1820, and in the *Khoo-Örlögiyin töüke* (History of Khoo-Örlög, late 18th century) and *Mongghol ug ekiyin töüke* (History of the origin of the Mongols, 1825), both written in Xinjiang. Another interesting monument of Oirat intellectual activity consists of two detailed and comparatively accurate maps drawn by a Zünghar cartographer in 1742 and taken to Europe by a returning Swedish captive.

DISINTEGRATION OF THE OIRATS

The reign of Galdan Boshogtu Khan (1678–97), which seemingly marked the height of Oirat power, also led to the first permanent rifts in Oirat solidarity. In 1686 a Khoshud prince fled Galdan's rule and surrendered with his people to the Qing. This group was resettled as Alashan (Alxa) banner in southwest Inner Mongolia. The Khoshud of Kökenuur and Tibet also suspected Galdan's intentions and accepted Qing protection in 1697. They finally lost all independence in 1724 (*see* UPPER MONGOLS). In 1697 and 1702 Zünghar nobles with their subjects surrendered to the Qing; they were eventually resettled as widely scattered ÖÖLÖD banners. In 1704 a party of 500 Kalmyk pilgrims to Tibet, led by the Ayuuki Khan's junior cousin Arabjur (d. 1716), was unable to return home. The Qing authorities resettled them in Ejene (Ejine) banner in far western Inner Mongolia.

The Kalmyks came under Russian suzerainty from the death of Ayuuki Khan in 1724, a development accentuated by the rupture of relations with the Zünghars in 1727. From 1749 the Zünghars began to disintegrate. Most of the Dörböds surrendered to the Qing in 1753 and were resettled in modern-day UWS PROVINCE of western Mongolia. A body of Khoids who surrendered in 1755 was resettled in Heilongjiang as the Yekhe Minggadai of Fuyu. The Zünghars proper were, however, crushed after rebelling under AMURSANAA. Most of the current-day Mongols of Xinjiang are descended not from them but from the Torghud and Khoshud Kalmyks who fled increasing Russian control in 1771 (*see* XINJIANG MONGOLS). The modern Torghuds of KHOWD PROVINCE in Mongolia had fled first from the Qing conquest of Zungharia in 1755 to Russia, and then from Russia with the Kalmyks back to the Qing in 1771. They were resettled in Bulgan Sum, Khowd province. The remaining Kalmyks, mostly Dörböds, but also Khoshuds and Torghuds, came under strict Russian sovereignty after 1771.

By 1775 the various Oirat peoples were almost completely isolated from one another. Connections were partly revived in the late 19th and early 20th centuries, but the revolutionary governments of the Soviet Union, Mongolia, and China again cut off connections from around 1930 to 1990. With increasing liberalization the Oirats have again been able to renew their connections, although their remoteness and poverty within their respective countries still severely hinder cultural and personal interchange.

See also ALTAI URIYANGKHAI; BAYAD; KALMYK-OIRAT LANGUAGE AND SCRIPTS; MINGGHAD; ZAKHACHIN.

Further reading: Todd Gibson, "A Manuscript on Oirat Buddhist History," *Central Asiatic Journal* 34 (1990): 85–97; Junko Miyawaki, "The Nomadic Kingship Based on Marital Alliances: The Case of the 17th–18th Century Oyirad," in *Proceedings of the 35th Permanent International Altaistics Conference,* ed. Chieh-hsien Ch'en (Taipei: Center for Chinese Studies Materials, 1993), 361–369; Junko Miyawaki, "Political Organization in the Seventeenth-Century North Asia," *Journal of Asian and African Studies* 27 (1984): 172–179; Hidehiro Okada, "The Origin of the Dörben Oyirad," *Ural-Altaische Jahrbücher,* n.s. 7 (1987): 181–211.

old script *See* UIGHUR-MONGOLIAN SCRIPT.

Ölöt *See* ÖÖLÖD.

Ömnögov' *See* SOUTH GOBI.

Onan *See* ONON RIVER.

ongghod *See* ONGGHON.

ongghon (*ongghod, onggon, ongon, ongod*)   The word *ongghon* (singular) or *ongghod* (plural) indicates any material thing (including an animal) within which dwells a spirit of the dead. The term is thus used for graves, sacred places, or animals dedicated to a spirit and also refers to the spirit inhabiting the thing. It referred especially to small figurines kept by pre-Buddhist Mongol families, which were made as material supports for the ancestor spirits so that they could be fed.

Medieval travelers and modern ethnographers describe the *ongghon* figurines as a universal phenomenon in the native Altaic and Siberian religions. Only roughly anthropomorphic, they could be made of silk, felt, wood, sheet metal, or bronze. Particularly among the BURIATS they often took the form of animals and other symbolic figures painted on silk in red. In later times *ongghon*s were sometimes hung in boxes or pouches from the YURT roof; three or so might be kept in a box 20 by 30 centimeters (8 by 12 inches). Shamans also attached *ongghon* housing their familiar spirits to their costumes.

The role of ordinary household *ongghons* was to give success in the chase or animal husbandry and to prevent sickness. This they did only as long as they were regularly "fed" by smearing their mouths with butter, first fruits of milk, and aspersions (*satsal*) before each meal. Travelers in the 13th century described each tent of a respected Mongol as having several *ongghon*. Above the master and mistress's place was hung an *ongghon* representing Nachighai, the general protector of growth and abundance. (In the 18th century this deity was usually known as Mother Emegeljin.) Two others were kept on the yurt wall above the master's and mistress's place at the back of the yurt. Two more were kept near the door on the men's and women's side of the yurt. These included a figure shaped like an udder to bless the milking of mares (men's work) and SHEEP and CATTLE (women's work).

In the empire period travelers saw old women assembling to make silk *ongghon* with great reverence, and today ordinary people still make their own *ongghons*. An *ongghon* of an ancestor is made only after three years after death, when the soul has, with the full disintegration of the body, joined the spirit world. When an *ongghon* is made specifically to propitiate a harmful spirit subdued by a shaman, as in case of illness, then the shaman must make or consecrate it. Some seem to have descended from father to son, while others were passed from mother to daughter. The greater chiefs (captains of 100 and above and members of the royal family) had special carts where *ongghon* were kept. The *ongghons* of CHINGGIS KHAN were also kept by his descendants in special carts (*see* EIGHT WHITE YURTS).

During the SECOND CONVERSION (1575–1655) Buddhist missionaries saw the *ongghon* as the heart of the shamanist religion and called on all converts to throw them into great piles to be burned; their continued possession was banned. By the 19th century *ongghons* were common only among the Buriats but could sometimes be found in eastern Inner Mongolia, ORDOS, and among the KALMYKS and OIRATS.

See also ALTAIC LANGUAGE FAMILY.

onggon   *See* ONGGHON.

Önggüd (Shatuo, White Tatars, Tenduc) Important allies of CHINGGIS KHAN and later marriage allies of the Yuan emperors, the Önggüd first appear in Chinese records as the Shatuo (Chinese, Sandy Gravel) tribe of the West Türk confederation. In the seventh century they settled around the Barköl area (eastern Xinjiang) under the protection of China's Tang dynasty (618–907). As the Tang weakened, Shatuo chiefs served the dynasty as allies. By the ninth century the Shatuo were dispersed in small settlements over North China, from Taiyuan in Shanxi province, through southwest Inner Mongolia, to Gansu.

While the Tang dynasty fell to peasant rebels, Li Ke-yong, a Shatuo chief who had received the Tang dynasty's Li surname, built up a military force of 10,000 Shatuo cavalrymen. In 923 Li's son defeated the peasant rebels' new dynasty and became emperor of a revived Tang dynasty. The dynasty was thoroughly Chinese in organization, but the Shatuo retained their Turkish language and culture. Shatuo generals overthrew the Li family and founded the Latter Jinn dynasty (937–47) and the Latter and Northern Han (947–79) dynasties. The main Shatuo colonies that settled in Lintao (Gansu province) and Yanmen (Daixian, in northern Shanxi) eventually submitted to the Northern SONG DYNASTY (960–1126).

With the rise of the TATARS in Mongolia, the Shatuo tribe was called "White Tatars" in distinction to the Mongolian "Black Tatars." When the Jurchen JIN DYNASTY (1115–1234) drove the Song out of North China, they recruited the White Tatars as tribal auxiliaries. A White Tatar notable, Buguo, in Yanmen, was made *digid-quri,* or hereditary chief, with the task of guarding the Jin's frontier fortifications. From this time on the Mongols called these people the "Önggüd," supposedly from the word *önggü,* or wall. The Jin titled the Önggüd forces "Tiande Military Prefecture" (Tiande Jun), which in medieval pronunciation became MARCO POLO's Tenduc.

By this time the Önggüd, or White Tatars, had been converted to the Syriac-rite Christianity of the Church of the East (the Nestorians), as is attested in widespread names such as Ioqanan (John), Sirgis (Sergius), and Körgis (George). This conversion was almost certainly related to Uighur Christian merchants following trade routes from Turkestan through Inner Mongolia to North China. Marco Polo describes "Tenduc" as a mixed agropastoral area, famed for its camlets of white camel hair. The non-Turkish majority followed Chinese religions, and there was also a Muslim trading minority called Arghuns.

In 1205 the khan of the NAIMAN in western Mongolia called on the Önggüd *digid-quri,* Ala-Qush, to attack the rising Chinggis Khan. Ala-Qush instead revealed the Naiman plan to Chinggis Khan, sending an envoy with a gift of wine, a delicacy previously unknown to the Mongols. When Chinggis invaded the Jin dynasty in 1211, Ala-Qush supported him, and Chinggis bestowed his daughter ALAQAI BEKI on Ala-Qush's son. This departure from the Önggüd's pro-Jin tradition caused a revolt, and Ala-Qush and his son were murdered. After the revolt was put down, Alaqai ruled the Önggüd as regent for several underage princes until the time of GÜYÜG Khan (1246–48).

The Önggüd rulers after Alaqai Beki regularly received imperial princesses; Körgis (r. 1264?–98) received two daughters of QUBILAI KHAN as wives. Active in fighting the incursions of QAIDU KHAN and his allies, Körgis was eventually captured and executed by Qaidu's forces in 1298. Shortly before his death, Körgis converted from the Church of the East to the Roman Catholic Church, but after his death the opposition of the nobility kept the Önggüd in the Church of the East.

After 1221 many Önggüd were resettled in KHORAZM, where they served as governors and as QUDA (marriage partners) for the Jochid princes. A fragment of the Arghun clan achieved importance in the Jochid BLUE HORDE and formed part of the KAZAKHS and the Mogholis (see MOGHOLI LANGUAGE AND PEOPLE.)

Several Önggüd sites, including their major center at Olon-Süme and many tombs, have been excavated in the ULAANCHAB, HÖHHOT, and SHILIIN GOL areas of modern Inner Mongolia. The artifacts, including gold brocaded clothing, golden stemmed cups, a BOQTA (married woman's headdress), and tomb murals, show a wealthy Sino-Mongolian material culture. Seated "STONE MEN" funerary statues may also be associated with them.

After the expulsion of the Mongols from China in 1368, the Önggüd (or Enggüd) became an OTOG (camp district) of the TÜMED Mongols settled around modern Höhhot; the famous queen MANDUKHAI SECHEN KHATUN was of this clan. Descendants of the Shatuo in Lintao (Gansu) are also found among the Tu (Monguor) people in modern Qinghai (see TU LANGUAGE AND PEOPLE).

Ong Khan (Toghril, Wang Khan) (d. 1203) *Khan of the Kereyid khanate in central Mongolia and Chinggis Khan's first patron*
Ong Khan, born Toghril, was a son of the KEREYID khan Qurjaqus-Buyruq Khan. Under Qurjaqus-Buyruq Khan the KEREYID Khanate faced fierce opposition from the MERKID tribe to the north and the Tatar tribe to the east. As a child Toghril was captured once by the Merkid and once, with his mother, Ilma Khatun, by the TATARS. Qurjaqus-Buyruq defeated his enemies but willed that after his death the khanate be divided among his sons. After his death the Kereyid khanate was riven by family conflict. Toghril soon killed his two half-brothers. His uncle Gür-Khan drove Toghril out of the khanate, but Toghril recovered the throne with the help of Toqto' a Beki of the Merkid and YISÜGEI BA'ATUR of the Mongols, with whom he become ANDA (blood brother).

Around 1180 Yisügei's orphaned son, Temüjin (later CHINGGIS KHAN), sought Toghril's support against the Merkid. Toghril helped Temüjin and supported him as khan of the Mongols. Subsequently, the two campaigned together against the Tatars, the Merkid, and the NAIMAN. When Erke-Qara, another of Toghril's brothers, received Naiman help and drove Toghril off the throne, Temüjin assisted him to regain power. In 1196 he and Temüjin assisted the Jurchen JIN DYNASTY in North China against the Tatars, and the Jin emperor gave Toghril the title Ong (Prince) Khan.

Around 1201 Ong Khan forced his younger brother, Ja'a-Gambu to flee to the Tangut XIA DYNASTY in north-west China. Ja'a-Gambu later joined with Temüjin and helped him gather Kereyid warriors to his standards. Even so, Ong Khan's alliance with Temüjin held.

In 1203 Temüjin proposed a marriage alliance with Ong Khan. Ong Khan's son and heir Ilqa Senggüm, worried that Temüjin might usurp the throne, prompted his father to pretend agreement and use the marriage to attack Temüjin. The plan was revealed, but the Kereyid allied with anti-Temüjin Mongols defeated Temüjin anyway at Qalaqaljid Sands (spring 1203). In the aftermath Ong Khan's Mongol allies tried to seize the throne, and Temüjin counterattacked that autumn, defeating Ong Khan at the Battle of Jeje'er Heights (autumn 1203). Ong Khan fled and was killed by Naiman frontier guards.

To European writers such as MARCO POLO, Ong Khan, ruler of the Christian Kereyid tribe, was Prester John, the legendary Christian ruler in the East. In Mongol histories, however, Ong Khan shows no trace of any Christian belief or identity.

Despite the turbulent struggles of his youth, the *SECRET HISTORY OF THE MONGOLS* portrays the mature Ong Khan as a lax and indecisive ruler, cruel to his brothers, excessively indulgent to his son, and almost wholly dependent on Mongols such as Yisügei and Temüjin (Chinggis) for his success. Nevertheless, the emphasis on Ong Khan's bad character cannot hide the fact that his patronage was the major factor in Chinggis's early rise.

ongod See ONGGHON.

ongon See ONGGHON.

Onon River (Onan) The Onon River flows northeast from the KHENTII RANGE in northeast Mongolia through Russia's Chita district and along the southern border of the AGA BURIAT AUTONOMOUS AREA. Merging with the Ingoda (Buriat, Yengüüd), it forms the Shilka River, which in turn merges with the Ergüne (Argun') to form the Amur River, emptying into the Pacific Ocean. The Onon is 808 kilometers (502 miles) long but not navigable. Together with the KHERLEN RIVER (Kelüren), it defined the original homeland of the MONGOL TRIBE. CHINGGIS KHAN's coronation took place at Ködö'e Aral, near the headwaters of the Onon.

Ööld See ÖÖLÖD.

Öölöd (Eleuths, Ölöt, Öelet, Ööld) The original significance of the widely used tribal name *Öölöd* among the Oirat Mongols is unclear. QING DYNASTY (1636–1912) records, however, use the term as a euphemism for the hated word *Zünghar*. (*On the Öölöds before their surrender to the Qing dynasty, see* ZÜNGHARS.)

In 1697 and 1702 two relatives of the Zünghar GAL-DAN BOSHOGTU KHAN (1678–97), Danjila (d. 1708) and Rabdan (d. 1703), surrendered to the Qing. Their people were organized as two "Öölöd" BANNERS and given pastures in modern northern BAYANKHONGOR PROVINCE. In 1731 500 households fled back to the Zünghars, and the remaining Öölöds were deported to HULUN BUIR. In 1761, with the annihilation of the Zünghars, part of these Öölöds were resettled in eastern NORTH KHANGAI PROVINCE.

Those who remained in Hulun Buir (northeast Inner Mongolia) formed a directly administered banner along the Imin and Shinekhen Rivers. Under Japanese administration (1932–45) some Öölöds were resettled to the east around modern Yakeshi city. The Öölöds of North Khangai and Hulun Buir have been thoroughly "Mongolized."

In 1764, after an Öölöd duke again tried to flee west, his people were resettled on the Khowd River (modern Erdenebüren Sum, Khowd province) as a directly administered banner that, along with the MINGGHADS, supplied corvée services for the Khowd garrison. These Öölöds alone have preserved their Oirat dialect and folkways. Khowd's Öölöds numbered 3,770 in 1929, 4,900 in 1956, and around 9,100 in 1989; 3,774 live in Erdenebüren Sum (1997 figures) and 3,000 in KHOWD CITY.

Those Zünghars remaining in Xinjiang were also renamed Öölöds. Under the Qing dynasty 30 of the 148 Mongol sumus (SUM) in Xinjiang were Öölöd. In 1999 the predominantly Öölöd Mongols of Tekes and Zhaosu counties numbered 18,000, and those of Tacheng and Emin, 7,000.

See also KHOWD PROVINCE; XINJIANG MONGOLS.

Orchon   *See* ORKHON RIVER.

ordo (horde, *hordu, orda*)   The word *ordo* refers to the great palace-tents and camps of the Mongol princes and emperors, which served as the nucleus of their power. By a strange evolution, it has come to be used in English for a disorganized mob of people. It is found in Mongolian in many forms, sometimes with the initial h- and sometimes without. *Orda* is a dialectal variant common in the western khanates.

The term *ordo* or *hordu* first appears in eighth-century Turkish Runic inscriptions designating a palace-yurt. Each *ordo* belonged to a single KHATUN (lady or empress), which meant that in the polygamous Inner Asian society each lord, or khan, held several *ordos*. The Liao dynasty (907–1125), founded by the seminomadic KITAN of eastern Inner Mongolia, further developed the *ordo* institution by uniting it with a specially recruited multiethnic bodyguard, numbering 10,000 to 20,000 soldiers and their families. The Liao, however, adopted the Chinese practice of having only one principal wife, so that each emperor possessed only one *ordo*.

The impoverished MONGOL TRIBE of the 12th century knew *ordos* only as objects of plunder among their richer MERKID, KEREYID, and NAIMAN neighbors. When CHINGGIS KHAN (Genghis, 1206–27) conquered the Kereyid Khanate of central Mongolia, he inherited the Kereyid khans' *ordo*, golden flagons, servants, and guards. Known generally as the Shira Ordo, "Yellow *Ordo*," due to its gold-plated doors, threshold, and pillars, it became the great throne room of the realm and could hold several hundred people. When a Mongol lady married, she received a large number of her father's subjects, or INJE, to which would be added her husband's maids and houseboys (*ger-ün kö'üd*), either inherited slaves or prisoners. According to WILLIAM OF RUBRUCK, BATU (d. 1256, grandson of Chinggis Khan) had 26 *khatuns*, each of whom had one great YURT and up to 200 smaller yurts. The chief yurts were arranged in a line by seniority from west to east, and each great yurt was followed by its attendant smaller yurts. William of Rubruck and other European writers called the camp as a whole the *ordo*, whence the term *horde* (from the alternate pronunciation *horda*) for a great congregation of nomadic peoples. In fact, however, *ordo* referred to each particular *khatun's* camp, and so what Rubruck saw was actually 26 *ordos*.

The *ordos* were legal and economic corporations. ÖGEDEI KHAN (1229–41) and his successors granted their mothers, wives, and daughters appanages in sedentary districts all over the empire. Thus, when HÜLE'Ü (1256–65) went to Iran, he left his second wife, Qutui Khatun, behind with her *ordo* but took with him a maid of that *ordo* who had borne Hüle'ü a son. Hüle'ü assigned to the concubine a new yurt and a share in all his booty. When Qutui Khatun finally arrived in Iran all the concubine's property automatically reverted to Qutui Khatun's *ordo*, which also received a regular stipend from districts in KURDISTAN worth 100,000 gold dinars annually. The *khatuns* throughout the empire increased their incomes by investing their silver with ORTOQ (partner) merchants, who invested it or loaned it out on interest. The Mongol YUAN DYNASTY in China curbed the *ordo's* autonomous control over their appanage villages, while GHAZAN KHAN (1295–1304) in the Middle Eastern IL-KHANATE prohibited their participation in moneylending, but in both realms the corporate character of the *ordo* remained.

Ordos survived the death of either the *khatun* or the khan. Upon remarrying the khan could install a new wife in the *ordo*. After the khan died, his successor frequently remarried the *ordo's khatun* if she was not his mother. Astute use of this tactic could build up a very large *emchü*, or personal property, for the khan. Geikhatu Khan (1291–95) in Iran, for example, married two brides with new *ordos*, but after his coronation he married four widows of his predecessors, acquiring their *ordos*, three of which dated to his grandfather Abagha Khan's (1265–82) time. Widows controlling the *ordos* often became formidable political figures. The Mongol Yuan emperor

Temür (1294–1307) bestowed new guards and assets on his mother, Kökejin's (Bairam Egechi), *ordo,* renamed the Longfugong Palace. Kökejin and her successor remained powers behind the throne until 1328. While large palatial tents continued to be called *ordo*s, the social institution they represented does not seem to have survived the fall of the MONGOL EMPIRE.

See also APPANAGE SYSTEM; EIGHT WHITE YURTS.

Ordos (Urdus, Erduosi; Yekhe Juu, Ih Ju, Yike Zhao)

The Ordos Mongols inhabit a dry plateau south of the Huang (Yellow) River in China's Inner Mongolian Autonomous Region. Famous as guardians of the EIGHT WHITE YURTS of CHINGGIS KHAN, they have a distinguished literary and scholarly tradition extending to the present.

The name *Ordos* means "palace-tents" and refers to the shrine of Chinggis Khan. As a league under the QING DYNASTY (1636–1912) it was named Yekhe Juu, "Great Monastery," referring to the Wang-un Juu Monastery in Dalad where the league's nobles met. This name was used until 2001, when Yekhe Juu was renamed Ordos municipality.

After 1949 Yekhe Juu/Ordos had an area of 86,400 square kilometers (33,360 square miles). The plateau's elevation ranges from 850 to 2,000 meters (2,790–6,560 feet) above sea level. The total population in 1990 was 1,198,912, of which 141,020 (12 percent) were Mongolian. The four western and southern BANNERS of Khanggin (Hanggin), Otog, Otog Front (Otog Qianqi), and Üüshin (Uxin) have almost 75 percent or Ordos's territory but only 387,300 inhabitants, of whom 93,900, or 24 percent, were Mongols. Most rural Mongols here live in majority-Mongol districts, and the vast majority still speak Mongolian.

In 1990 Ordos had 4,973,000 head of livestock, of which 4,400,000 were sheep and goats and 49,000 horses. Much of Ordos is covered by the Khöbchi Desert in the north and the Muu Usu Desert in the south. Characteristic vegetation is thickets of sagebrush (*Artemisia*), willows, and pea bushes (*Caragana*).

The maze of rivers and canals in the Hetao (River Bend) region northwest of the Huang (Yellow) River's great bend was originally included within Ordos's Dalad and Khanggin banners. Easily irrigable, its 6,553 square kilometers (2,530 square miles) had 974,300 inhabitants and only 16,700 Mongols in 1990. Hetao is now part of Bayannuur league.

HISTORY

The Ordos plateau was the original heartland of both the XIONGNU (Hun) nomads (209 B.C.E. to 91 C.E.) and the Tangut XIA DYNASTY (1038–1227). Mongols first settled Ordos in the wake of the TUMU INCIDENT in 1449, bringing with them the Eight White Yurts, or shrine of Chinggis Khan. By 1470 Ordos was counted one of the Mongols' SIX TÜMENS, and Ordos's *jinong* (viceroy), as

ruler of the Eight White Yurts, was the titular leader of the Three Western Tümens. In 1510 the Chinggisid ruler BATU-MÖNGKE DAYAN KHAN (1480?–1517?) conquered Ordos and installed his son Barsu-Bolod Sain-Alag (d. 1521) as *jinong*. While the Ordos dialect and folkways show some similarities to the OIRATS, their CLAN NAMES are mostly of the Mongols proper.

Barsu-Bolod was the ancestor of all Ordos's Chinggisid nobility. The title of *jinong* descended to his sons by primogeniture but retained only nominal authority. The incessant raids from Ordos into China sparked the beginning of the Great Wall (*see* MING DYNASTY). The Ordos noble KHUTUGTAI SECHEN KHUNG-TAIJI (1540–86) helped initiate the SECOND CONVERSION of the Mongols to Buddhism, while his great-grandson SAGHANG SECHEN (b. 1604) wrote one of Mongolia's most famous chronicles.

In the civil war that ended the reign of LIGDAN KHAN (1604–34) first he and then the armies of the Qing dynasty occupied Ordos. After the rebellion of Jamsu in 1649, the Qing court divided Ordos into six banners (appanages), to which a seventh was added in 1736.

During the 19th century Ordos DUGUILANG (circle) movements attacked princely misrule and encroaching CHINESE COLONIZATION. The celebrated poet and singer Kheshigbatu (1847–1917) of Üüshin lampooned the *duguilang*s' enemies. The *duguilang*s organized violent but futile resistance to Christian missionaries in 1900 and then to the Qing dynasty's NEW POLICIES after 1903. After the establishment of the Republic of China in 1912, Ordos remained an isolated district ravaged by bandits and sullenly hostile to contemporary Chinese culture. By this time the Hetao and the northeastern Dalad, Jüüngar (Jungar), Wang, and Jasag (modern Ejin Horo) banners had been almost completely covered by agricultural colonization, leaving only a few sites surrounding temples and Chinggis Khan's shrine still virgin steppe there.

During the Sino-Japanese War (1937–45) the Japanese encroached along the Huang (Yellow) River, while tenuous Chinese Communist influence spread north from Yan'an. Ordos fell to Chinese Communist armies in 1949–50. In 1954 the Communist government returned to Ejen Khoroo (Ejin Horo) the shrine of Chinggis Khan, which had previously been removed by the Nationalists to Qinghai province to keep it out of Japanese hands. A new mausoleum was built in 1956, and Wang and Jasag banners combined as Ejen Khoroo banner. In Inner Mongolia today the Ordos Mongols are seen as the most religious.

See also 17TH-CENTURY CHRONICLES; DIDACTIC POETRY; INNER MONGOLIA AUTONOMOUS REGION; INNER MONGOLIANS; LITERATURE; MONGOLIAN LANGUAGE; WUHAI.

Further reading: Hong Jiang, *The Ordos Plateau of China: An Endangered Environment* (Tokyo: United Nations University Press, 1999); Antoine Mostaert, "Matériaux ethnographiques relatifs aux Mongols ordos," *Central Asiatic Journal* 2 (1956): 242–294; Antoine

Ruins of Ordu-Baligh *(From N. Tsultem,* Mongolian Architecture *[1988])*

Mostaert, "Ordosica," *Bulletin of the Catholic University of Peking* 9 (1934): 1–96.

Ordu-Baligh (Khar Balgas, Karabalghasun, Kara Balgassun)   The city of Ordu-Baligh was completed under Bayan-Chor (Moyanchuo, 747–59) as the capital of the UIGHUR EMPIRE. An Arab visitor, Tamim ibn Bahr, described the city in 821 as a great town, with 12 large iron gates, markets, craft quarters, and extensive agricultural suburbs. In the center was a walled palace crowned with a golden YURT that could hold 100 people and was visible for kilometers. The population, including many Sogdians and Chinese, were mostly Manichean in religion. The ruins of Ordu-Baligh, now called Khar Balgas (Black Ruins) in Khotont Sum, (North Khangai), were excavated by D. A. Klements and W. W. Radloff in the late 19th century and by D. Bukenich (1933–34) and S. V. Kiselev and Kh. Perlee (1949). Parts of the citadel towers still stand 14 meters (46 feet) high. Outside the palace citadel a Manichean temple contained a fragmentary trilingual (Old Turkish, Sogdian, Chinese) inscription. The 1949 excavations also found a bronze smithing area with iron implements, wax, and flat and cast pieces of bronze, together with Chinese copper coins dated to 840. Mortars and pestles were found in large numbers, but all of them were broken, apparently a testimony to the destruction wrought by the Kyrgyz sack of the city in 840.

   See also ARCHAEOLOGY; RUNIC SCRIPT AND INSCRIPTIONS.

Orhon   *See* ORKHON RIVER.

Orkhon province   *See* ERDENET CITY.

Orkhon River (Orhon, Orchon)   The longest river entirely in Mongolia, the Orkhon rises in the KHANGAI RANGE and flows northeast to empty into the SELENGE RIVER near the northern border town of Sükhebaatur. Major tributaries rising from the KHENTII RANGE and draining into the Orkhon include the TUUL RIVER, Kharaa River, and Yöröö (Yeröö) River. The drainage area of the 1,124-kilometer-long Orkhon is 132,000 square kilometers (50,970 square miles). Along the Tamir, a tributary of the upper Orkhon, in the Khangai Range was the site of the Ötüken Forest, the sacred center for the XIONGNU (Huns), the TÜRK EMPIRES, and the UIGHUR EMPIRE. The upper Orkhon valley itself contains many major historical sites, including Old Turkish Runic inscriptions (*see* RUNIC SCRIPT AND INSCRIPTIONS), the Uighur capital ORDU-BALIGH, the Mongol imperial capital QARA-QORUM, and the 16th-century Buddhist temple ERDENI ZUU. In modern times MINING and logging have degraded water quality.

ortoq (partners) *Ortoq,* or "partner," merchants engaged in commerce and moneylending with capital supplied by the Mongol Empire's imperial treasury or the private treasuries of the empire's great aristocrats.

By the 11th century Middle Turkish *ortoq,* "partner," meant commercial partners who pooled their capital and shared their profits according to agreed-upon percentages. This relation was eventually to become the model for ties between nomadic rulers and Central Asian merchants. Long-range caravan commerce had played a vital role in all the steppe empires of Inner Asia. Sogdian merchants from Samarqand and Bukhara had a symbiotic partnership with the rulers of the first Türk Empire (552–659), serving as scribes, religious preceptors, and ambassadors in return for the rulers' promotion of their trade with China, Iran, and Byzantium. In the 10th and 11th centuries a partnership of Uighur merchants based in Turpan (in modern Xinjiang) and the KITANS' Liao dynasty (907–1115) in Inner Mongolia dominated Inner Asia. After the Manchurian Jurchen people overthrew Kitan rule, conquered North China, and founded their own JIN DYNASTY (1115–1234), Turkestani Muslims began to join the UIGHURS in long-distance trade among North China, Inner Mongolia, and Central Asia.

Even before uniting the Mongols, CHINGGIS KHAN (Genghis, 1206–27) had drawn into his entourage merchants such as the Uighur CHINQAI, who had traded extensively in North China and Mongolia, and Hasan, from the Muslim "Arghun" minority among the Inner Mongolian ÖNGGÜD tribe. These foreign merchants provided him with valuable intelligence on the Jin dynasty and the realms to the west. By 1218 merchants from Bukhara, KHORAZM, and Otrar were serving Chinggis Khan as diplomats. In that year Chinggis Khan ordered his family and commanders (NOYAN) each to chose eligible non-Mongol clients from their retinue, supply them with capital, and send them together as a trade party to the realm of the sultanate of Khorazm, then ruling Central Asia and Iran (*see* OTRAR INCIDENT).

Under ÖGEDEI KHAN (1229–41) and GÜYÜG Khan (1246–48) *ortoq* businesses flourished. These *ortoq* kept the great palace-tents (*ordo*) of the Mongol rulers supplied with clothing, grain, and other provisions. Uighur administrators also invested tax monies to stretch official budgets. As agents of the ruling Mongolian aristocracy, *ortoq* merchants received tablets of authority (PAIZA) exempting them from taxes and allowing them to use the official JAM, or postroad system. *Ortoq* merchants, unlike other civilians, were allowed to bear arms freely, and their losses to banditry had to be made up by the local population. Following Chinggis Khan's precedent, his successors encouraged foreign merchants, whether Hansa traders entering Russia or Indians from Lahore going to Central Asia, to take advantage of these privileges. *Ortoq* relations frequently took the form of exchanging gifts, the merchants presenting pearls and other *tangsuqs* (precious rarities), and the Mongols in return presenting their partners with war booty to invest in trade. The Mongol nobles and ladies, when lacking money on hand to invest, frequently paid their partners with drafts drawn on their distant appanages in China, Central Asia, or Iran, thus allowing enormous debts to accumulate.

The *ortoq* merchants used their capital both for long-range commerce and for moneylending. In North China, where most of the *ortoq*s were Uighurs or Central Asian Muslims, the Mongols' introduction, for the first time in China's history, of a silver tax created a strong demand, driving interest rates on silver loans to 100 percent per year. Once the silver tax was paid, it was then available to be given to an *ortoq* and lent out again, with a share of the interest again accruing to the Mongol rulers. By 1240 usury was causing great hardship in North China, and Ögedei Khan ineffectually decreed that total interest was never to exceed the principal. *Ortoq* merchants also served as tax farmers, managing the collection of taxes for a profit from collection over quotas.

Aware of how the unregulated *ortoq* system was overtaxing the *jam* and causing the flight of civilians, MÖNGKE KHAN (1251–59) attempted to limit the main abuses. In 1253 he appointed officials to supervise the *ortoq.* In his reform of the tax and *jam* systems, he ordered all *ortoq*s to pay both commercial and *qubchiri* taxes. He also strongly discouraged the presentation of *tangsuqs.* By paying large outstanding debts to *ortoq* merchants, however, he demonstrated their interests were still being considered.

In the Mongol YUAN DYNASTY in China, the vacillations of Möngke's policy were continued. In 1263 QUBILAI KHAN (1260–94) reiterated that *ortoq* merchants were subject to taxes, but this edict was widely ignored. The institution of a paper currency probably reduced interest rates on silver, but after 1272 depleted bullion reserves led to new silver-denominated commercial taxes. In 1268 an office, eventually titled the Quanfusi, or "Office of Market Taxes," was set up to supervise all *ortoq*s. Despite attempts at abolition by Confucian-oriented Mongol aristocrats opposed to the whole idea of *ortoq,* the office continued until 1311. With the Mongol conquest of South China, the *ortoq* merchants expanded their sphere of operations to the SOUTH SEAS. In 1286 maritime trade was put under the Quanfusi, and *ortoq* merchants were given a monopoly on overseas commerce in metals and slaves. Late in his reign Qubilai began discouraging the presentation of *tangsuqs* and curtailed the possession of arms by *ortoq* merchants, measures that were revoked after his death. The abolition of the Quanfusi in 1311 came not from opponents of *ortoq,* but from SEMUREN (Central and West Asian) officials who opposed any regulation of *ortoq* whatsoever. The high point of *ortoq* operations came under Yisün-Temür (titled Taidingdi, 1323–28), whose Muslim-dominated administration exempted Christians and Muslims from any corvée payments and guaranteed the fantastic payments promised by the Mongolian nobility in return for *tangsuqs*. The coup d'état of 1328 reversed these policies, and the new regime, by contrast, granted exemption from the commercial tax only to Buddhist and Taoist monasteries in 1330.

In Mongol Iran *ortoq* merchants also flourished. After HÜLE'Ü's 1258 conquest of Baghdad, he appointed a Khorazmian client, Ali Ba'atur, the overseer (DARUGHACHI) of the city, with special oversight of the *ortoq*s and the artisans. Hüle'ü and his successor, Abagha Khan (1265–81), ignored Möngke Khan's regulations and ordered their officials not to interfere with *ortoq*s in any way, and *ortoq* commerce once again flourished. As the Mongols did not enforce the Islamic prohibition of usury, many with no mercantile background, often Jews and Assyrian Christians, flocked to borrow money, buy *tangsuqs*, and become *ortoq*. GHAZAN KHAN (1295–1304), however, as part of his program of Islamization and financial reform, prohibited both usury and the loan of government funds, thus destroying the *ortoq* institution. The Mongol *khatun*s and their *ordo*s were now financed directly through dedicated taxes.

In the GOLDEN HORDE, despite its early Islamization, the institution of *ortoq* continued. The fragmentary data show that in Russia, too, *ortoq* merchants as tax farmers loaned money to local authorities unable to pay their tax quotas. Russian sources of the 15th century describe the *ordobazarets*, or "ordo camp merchants," who inhabited the bazaars following the *ordo* palaces.

In the 15th to 18th centuries the OIRATS (West Mongols) built a relationship with the merchants of Samarqand and Bukhara strongly reminiscent of the early Mongol Empire's relations with the Turkestani merchants.

See also APPANAGE SYSTEM; JEWELRY; POLO, MARCO; SOCIAL CLASSES IN THE MONGOL EMPIRE.

Further reading: Thomas T. Allsen, "Mongol Princes and Their Merchant Partners," *Asia Major* 3, 2 (1989): 83–126; Elizabeth Endicott-West, "Merchant Associations in Yüan China: The *Ortogh,*" *Asia Major* 3, 2 (1989): 127–153.

Ossetes (Alans, Asud)

Many Ossetes on the steppe between the Black and Caspian Seas were brought into the MONGOL EMPIRE, some being deported as far as China.

Others, protected in the Caucasus Mountains, were never entirely subdued.

The Ossetes, known in Europe as the Alans and now living on the border of Russia and Georgia, were a branch of the ancient Sarmatians, first appearing in the first century C.E. Defeated by the Huns in 371, most Ossetes moved into the Caucasus, while others remained along the northern coast of the Caspian Sea. An Ossetian chief dwelling at the Caucasus fort of Magas converted his people to Christianity around 900–25, and they remained mostly Christian thereafter. By the 13th century the Ossetes of the Caucasus were farmers living in independent villages constantly at war with one another.

The first contact with the Mongols occurred in 1223, when SÜBE'ETEI BA'ATUR and JEBE came north through Derbent and attacked the Caucasian Ossetes. The Mongols returned in 1229, but the Volga and Caspian Ossetes resisted until winter 1236–37. In autumn 1239 GÜYÜG, MÖNGKE KHAN, and other Mongol princes advanced into the Caucasus and sieged Magas. The Mongols cut roads for their siege engines through the thick forests and after a three-month siege captured the fortress, killing all 2,700 defenders. Other Ossetian forts remained defiant, and the Mongols kept guard posts along the Caucasus passes to block their raids. In 1277 Mengü-Temür (1267–80), khan of the GOLDEN HORDE, took another major Ossetian mountain fort.

Möngke and other princes brought back Ossetian (Mongolian, *Asud*) prisoners with them to the east. In 1272 QUBILAI KHAN (1260–94), emperor of the Mongol YUAN DYNASTY in China, organized an Asud guard of 3,000 soldiers. By 1309 the number had expanded to 30,000. The Catholic archbishop in DAIDU (modern Beijing) counted these Ossetian soldiers among his flock. The guard helped subdue NAYAN'S REBELLION (1287) and also fought in the coup d'état of 1323 that enthroned Yisün-Temür (Taidingdi, 1323–28). Ossetes served as the Yuan's crack soldiers into the 1350s and followed the Mongol khans back into Mongolia in 1368. During the 15th and 16th centuries assimilated Asud formed part of the Yüngshiyebü *tümen* in central Inner Mongolia. The Asud clan is found today in Aru Khorchin (Ar Horqin) banner of eastern Inner Mongolia.

See also BULGHARS; CHRISTIANITY IN THE MONGOL EMPIRE; NORTHERN YUAN DYNASTY; QIPCHAQS; RUSSIA AND THE MONGOL EMPIRE.

otog (otoq, otok)

The basic unit of Mongol sociopolitical life from the 15th and 16th centuries on, the *otog* was replaced by the banner and SUM system in the Mongolian BANNERS under the QING DYNASTY (1636–1912). It was, however, retained in the ecclesiastical estates and other areas.

The *otog* (Middle Mongolian, *otoq*) was unknown in the period of the MONGOL EMPIRE. It first appeared in the

15th century. In addition to its administrative meaning, the word also means a "hunting camp" or a "hearth." In this last meaning it maybe related to the Turkish *ot*, "fire." The meaning thus appears to be of a body of people gathered around a single hearth.

By the turn of the 16th century the Mongols were divided into the SIX TÜMENS, each of which in turn was divided into many *otog*s, totaling 54. As the *otog*s frequently combined or divided clans, they were evidently supposed to be roughly equal in size. After the reign of BATU-MÖNGKE DAYAN KHAN (1480?–1517?) the *tümens* were divided among his sons and the *otog*s among his grandsons. The frequent identity between the number of *otog*s in a *tümen* and the number of grandsons inheriting them indicates that the count of *otog*s as we have it now was probably fixed after, not before, this repartition.

The OIRATS also maintained a system of *otog*s at this time. After the reorganization of GALDAN-TSEREN (r. 1727–45) the Zünghar principality's directly administered core was divided into 14 "old" and 16 "new" *otog*s. Ranging from 500 to 6,000 households in size, they averaged almost 3,600 households. The names of the *otog*s were sometimes clan or ethnically based (e.g., Telengit, Tsokhur) but were often occupational (e.g., Buuchin, "musketeers"). They were each headed by one to five officials called *albachi zaisang*, or "tax officials."

The Qing dynasty abolished the *otog* organization, replacing it with banners (*khoshuu*) and "arrows" (*sumu*; modern *sum*), yet the *otog* remained in ecclesiastical estates, such as the GREAT SHABI of the JIBZUNDAMBA KHUTUGTU and the organization of the TAIJI, or Chinggisid nobility, within the banners. The term is occasionally used among the BURIATS as well.

See also APPANAGE SYSTEM.

Otrar Incident (Utrar) The Otrar Incident, in which a delegation of the Mongols' merchant partners was massacred without provocation by a local governor, provoked CHINGGIS KHAN's war on Muslim Central Asia.

By 1216 the new empires of Mongolia under Chinggis Khan (Genghis, 1206–27) and of KHORAZM under Sultan 'Ala-ud-Din Muhammad (r. 1200–20/1) had divided the QARA-KHITAI Empire between them. Chinggis Khan deputed three Muslim merchants in his service to announce his desire for peace with Sultan Muhammad and to present rich gifts. The envoys met the sultan early in 1218 as he was returning from a western campaign. The Khorazm shah needed information about the new power and dispatched his own envoys to Mongolia as merchants opened private trade.

In autumn 1218 Sultan Muhammad, campaigning in the north, ran across a Mongol army pursuing fugitive MERKID tribesmen. Despite the outnumbered Mongols' attempts to appease him, the sultan attacked. An inconclusive battle followed, but the skill of the Mongol cavalry combined with his envoys' reports of the Mongol conquest of North China made Sultan Muhammad very uneasy.

At that point Chinggis Khan sent a large delegation of Muslim ORTOQ (partner) merchants to Khorazm, numbered in the sources at either 100 or 450. The delegation arrived in winter 1218–19 at Otrar on the Syr Dar'ya (in modern Kazakhstan, between Turkestan and Shymkent). The frontier governor, Inalchuq Qadir Khan (or Inal Ghayir Khan), a cousin of Sultan Muhammad's mother, coveted the delegation's rich goods and sent a message to Sultan Muhammad charging the merchants with spying. Sultan Muhammad agreed to their arrest, and Inalchuq put them to death, seizing the goods for himself.

When the sole survivor reached Mongolia and reported to Chinggis Khan, he sent three envoys, two Mongols and a Khorazmian, to demand that Inalchuq be handed over as restitution. Sultan Muhammad refused—due to Inalchuq's influence in the realm he could do no other—and then killed the envoys. This final act infuriated Chinggis Khan, who prayed to heaven for success in a righteous campaign and began war against Khorazm. In the end Otrar's population was massacred and Inalchuq executed in the khan's presence outside Samarqand.

See also MAHMUD YALAVACH AND MAS'UD BEG.

Outer Mongolia *See* MONGOLIA, STATE OF.

overtone-singing *See* THROAT SINGING.

ovoo *See* OBOO.

Övörchangaj *See* SOUTH KHANGAI PROVINCE.

Övörhangai *See* SOUTH KHANGAI PROVINCE.

Owenk'e *See* EWENKIS.

Oyirad *See* OIRATS.

Oyrot *See* OIRATS.

Özbeg Khan (Uzbek) (r. 1313–1341) *Khan who made Islam the ruling religion of the Golden Horde*
Özbeg's father, Toghrilcha, was a leader in the junta that overthrew Töde-Mengü (1280–87). Later, however, Toghrilcha's brother, TOQTO'A Khan (1291–1312) overthrew the junta and promoted Buddhism.

Converted to Islam by Ibn 'Abd-ul-Hamid, a Bukharan *sayyid* (descendant of the prophet) and sheikh (Sufi master) of the Yasavi order, Özbeg seized power from his base in KHORAZM after Toqto'a's death. He killed a number of emirs and Buddhist clerics who opposed Islamization of the Mongols, and to commemorate his rule he built a splendid mosque at Qirim (modern Staryy Krym in CRIMEA) in 1314. Özbeg honored Ibn 'Abd-ul-Hamid as Sayyid Ata (Sayyid Father), making him hereditary *naqib* (marshal) with the right to drink first of KOUMISS and tutor for his second son, Janibeg. Özbeg made Qutlugh-Temür, who had assisted his rise, commander in chief (*beglerbegi*), but by 1332 Qutlugh-Temür had been transferred to rule Khorazm and 'Isa Beg became commander in chief. Following Mongol practice Özbeg married his father's wives, which the Islamic clergy allowed, as their husband had been an unbeliever.

Özbeg pursued an aggressive policy toward the IL-KHANATE and Byzantium. Domestically, despite his suspicion of Moscow's growing power, Özbeg gave his sister Könchek to Iurii of Moscow, allowing her to be baptized. Repeated provocations from Moscow's rival city Tver', including the capture and suspicious death of Könchek, eventually pushed Özbeg to side with Moscow and make Iurii's brother, Ivan I, grand prince of Russia (1332–41).

Sayyid Ata and the clergy preferred Janibeg, but following primogeniture Özbeg's elder son, Tïnibeg, succeeded him in 1341. With the clergy's support, Janibeg murdered Tïnïbeg and seized the throne as khan (r. 1342–57).

See also BYZANTIUM AND BULGARIA; GOLDEN HORDE; ISLAM IN THE MONGOL EMPIRE.

Further reading: Devin DeWeese, *Islamization and the Golden Horde: Baba Tükles and the Conversion to Islam in Historical and Epic Tradition* (University Park: Pennsylvania State University Press, 1994).

P

paiza The Mongol *paiza* was a badge or tablet that gave the bearer authority to demand goods and services from civilian populations. The Mongol *paiza* system combined the *pai,* or "tablet," and the *fu,* or "tally," systems of China. In the traditional Tang dynasty (618–907) system preserved by the Liao (907–1125), a limited number of silver *pai* or *paizi,* issued only in emergencies, gave the bearer the right to use the official postroad, while "goldfish tallies," divided into left and right halves, authenticated mobilization orders. Troops could be mobilized only when the emperor dispatched a half to match that held by the commander. Under the JIN DYNASTY postroad tablets, ranked as gold, silver, and wooden, were given permanently to the heads of militias' decimal units. While the goldfish shape was replaced by a golden tiger, the tally system was otherwise unchanged.

CHINGGIS KHAN (Genghis, 1206–27) seems to have adopted the tablet and tally system within a year or two of invading the Jin, and the form of Mongol *paizas* (modern *paiz,* from Chinese *paizi*) copied the Jin tablets and tallies closely. There were four ranks, golden tiger, gold (actually gilded silver), silver, and wood, all worn on the bearer's belt. The silver and gold *paizas* were basically rectangular in shape with rounded ends and a hole toward the upper end. The tiger-head *paizas* were round and surmounted by a tiger's head and a ring. The Mongolian *paiza* inscription, however, granted far more comprehensive authority than did the Jin or Liao: "By the power of eternal Heaven, by the protection of the great blessedness [of Chinggis]," and on the back, "Whoever has no reverence [some add: for the decree of so-and-so] shall be guilty and die."

The Mongols did not distinguish between tallies and tablets; bearers kept all badges permanently and even transferred them to others. Commanders of decimal units, overseers (DARUGHACHI), tributary rulers, honored clerics, ORTOQ merchants, meritorious soldiers, and hordes of envoys all received them. Only the accompanying JARLIQ, or warrant, specified the reason for conferring the *paiza.* Members of the ruling family also made and granted *paizas* to their servitors. While technically the *paiza* and *jarliq* simply entitled the bearer to use the postroads, in practice the higher badges gave virtually unlimited power over life and property. The Persian historians 'ALA'UD-DIN ATA-MALIK JUVAINI and RASHID-UD-DIN FAZL-ULLAH paint a vivid picture of provincial officials and envoys, all armed with *paizas* and *jarliqs,* engaged in unending wars over jurisdiction.

After Chinggis's time strong rulers aimed to limit both the power and the number of *paizas* in circulation. ÖGEDEI KHAN (1229–41) prohibited the nobility from issuing *paizas* and *jarliqs,* but in the long interregnum following his death, the Mongol nobility again issued them freely. Even orders to recall all old *paizas* and *jarliqs* proved ineffective, as the badges, undated and of unchanging form, could easily be concealed and used again. MÖNGKE KHAN (1251–59) prohibited merchants from using *paizas.* QUBILAI KHAN (1260–94) divided the golden tiger tablet into three ranks and added a new category of gerfalcon *paiza,* conferred only on active-duty officers, which gave the right to use special "gerfalcon" postroads. In the IL-KHANATE, GHAZAN KHAN (1295–1304) canceled all old *paizas,* requiring their holders to exchange old ones for new. The new *paizas,* fashioned in two ranks, contained the names of the bearers on them to prevent them from being transferred and were to be turned in at the end of the official's term. Nevertheless, even strong advocates of regular procedures found that the *paiza* system, in the hands of loyal and able servants, readily cut through bureaucratic knots. Thus, the crisis-filled beginning of Qubilai Khan's reign juxtaposed repeated injunctions for officials not to arbitrarily levy goods or troops with continued issuance of high-ranking *paiza*s in large numbers to favored commanders, who used them as rewards for their officers.

The QING DYNASTY (1636–1912) also maintained a postroad system in Mongolia and issued "postroad riding certificates" (*ulaa unukhu temdeg*). Like the old Chinese tablets, however, they were specified for a particular office and, while still open to abuse, were reserved more strictly to actual postroad use. Still, the reputation of messengers was not good; a proverb in the Mongolian genre "THREES OF THE WORLD" describes messengers thus: "In government, a messenger is rough / In metals, a file is rough / In a hole, a hedgehog is rough."

palaces of the Bogda Khan By 1911 the Bogda Khan (Holy Khan), or JIBZUNDAMBA KHUTUGTU, had four palaces. Only one, the Green, or Winter, Palace, has survived. The Dechingalba Temple was originally built by the SECOND

JIBZUNDAMBA KHUTUGTU in 1739, with four *dugang*s (assembly halls) for the four tantras. It was expanded by the Fourth Jibzundamba in 1807–09. The architecture was a distinctive Mongolian departure on a Chinese design. The Bogda lived within the yellow-walled compound (hence its common name, Yellow Palace) in two yurts, one wooden and one felt. In 1892 the temple burned down but was rebuilt. It was located in East Khüriye, just north of modern-day central ULAANBAATAR. After 1911 it was the seat of the theocratic government.

The other palaces were all built south of the city, between the Selbe River and the TUUL RIVER. Gunggade-jidling, or "White Temple" was to the west and was built by the Fifth Jibzundamba (1815–42) in a Tibetan style. After 1928 it was for several years the party school for the MONGOLIAN PEOPLE'S REVOLUTIONARY PARTY. The Khaisu-tai Labrang Palace (also called the Brown, or Summer, Palace) to the east was built around the turn of the 20th century by the EIGHTH JIBZUNDAMBA KHUTUGTU (1870–1924). Within its courtyard the Bogda pastured his herds of pet animals, including an elephant.

Sharabpeljailing, the Green, or Winter, Palace, was built from 1893 to 1906 by the Tezhan firm. Its chief hall is dedicated to the maharajas, or deities, of the four quarters. In 1905 a two-story white European-style building

The Andingmen Gate, built from 1912 to 1919 in front of the Bogda Khan's Green Place to commemorate Mongolian independence *(From N. Tsultem,* Mongolian Architecture *[1988])*

was added. From 1912 to 1919 the monumental Andingmen (Mongolian, *Amugulang Engkhe-yin Khagalga*), or "Gate of Peace and Stability," was constructed in front of the palace by the same Tezhan firm. Pictures on the gate show episodes from the GESER epic and the Chinese novel *Journey to the West*. This palace, which was well known in Mongolia for housing the Eighth Bogda's stuffed animals, curios, mechanical devices, and other objects of general interest, was made a museum in 1924.

See also THEOCRATIC PERIOD.

Pao-an   *See* BAO'AN LANGUAGE AND PEOPLE.

Pao-tou   *See* BAOTOU.

papacy   *See* WESTERN EUROPE AND THE MONGOLS.

paper currency in the Mongol Empire   Travelers such as MARCO POLO and MUHAMMAD ABU-'ABDULLAH IBN BATTUTA considered the Mongol YUAN DYNASTY's use of paper currency as one of the marvels of the world. The SONG DYNASTY (960–1279) and JIN DYNASTY (1115–1234) in China began issuing paper bills (*chao*) at first to supplement and then to replace copper coins. Lack of financial discipline began to eat into the Jin currency after 1190 and the Song currency after 1210, and the death throes of both dynasties were accompanied by a hyperinflationary spiral. After conquering North China the Mongol administration issued local bills from 1227 on. These bills had limited circulation and expired after two or three years, and the Mongol administration did not accept them as tax payments, insisting on silver. Such locally issued currencies continued until 1261.

In August 1260 QUBILAI KHAN (1260–94), under the advice of Wang Wentong (d. 1262), LIU BINGZHONG, and others created China's first unified paper currency with bills that circulated throughout the realm with no expiration date. To guard against devaluation, this Zhongtong (Chung-t'ung) currency was fully convertible with silver and gold, and the government accepted tax payments in paper currency. The currency's 10 denominations were given in copper cash equivalents from 10 coins to two strings of 1,000 coins each. Two strings of paper money were exchangeable for one tael of silver and 15 strings for 1 tael of gold. The YASTUQ, or ding, a silver ingot worth 50 taels, was retained as the money of account. The Mongol currency was printed on one side in black ink only, at first by wooden blocks on coarse cloth. In 1276 the mints shifted to more durable copper blocks and mulberry-bark paper. Used bills were replaced for a 3 percent fee for ink and labor.

Currency emissions were kept small at first, but from 1273 to 1276 war against the Song in South China and Japan made emissions of paper currency explode from 110,000 *ding* to 1,420,000 ding. With the conquest of the Song, its bills were taken out of circulation at the confiscatory rate of 50 to 1, and convertibility was canceled until 1282. From then on chronic inflation replaced the slight deflation that marked the 1260s. Fragmentary data show rice prices rising from 1276 to 1308 at around 12–13 percent a year. Fiscal indiscipline—government expenditures routinely exceeded revenues by 40 percent or more—was this inflation's most obvious cause, yet the Yuan's currency emissions also correlated closely with Eurasian silver supply trends visible elsewhere, indicating that currency managers did make a serious effort to keep currency issues in line with silver reserves.

Outside observers understood nothing of paper money's complex financial underpinnings, considering it almost a species of magic. In 1294, facing a fiscal crisis, the Mongol khan in Iran, Geikhatu (1291–95), and his vizier, Sadr-ud-Din Zanjani (d. 1298), consulted with BOLAD CHINGSANG, the Yuan's representative in Iran, and attempted to introduce unbacked paper currency (called *chao* from the Chinese). Massive popular resistance forced its abandonment after a few weeks.

In 1287 Qubilai's minister SANGHA introduced a new currency, the Zhiyuan (Chih-yüan) bills, to deal with the budget shortfall. The new nonconvertible currency was also denominated in copper cash. Officially, the Zhongtong bills were now devalued to 20 percent of the value of a Zhiyuan bill of the same denomination. In fact, however, the Zhongtong currency circulated at equal or even greater value, probably due to the fact that after 1304 it became convertible to silver again. Another experiment in 1309 tried to remove the Zhongtong currency from circulation at only 4 percent of its original value and to introduce new silver-denominated and nonconvertible Zhida (Chih-ta) bills and copper coins. This initiative was abandoned after 1311 in favor of printing Zhongtong and Zhiyuan currency again. After 1321 emissions declined, and prices stabilized. After plague, flooding, and climate change brought massive economic dislocation in the 1330s and 1340s, however, the minister TOQTO'A tried to finance his hugely ambitious program of reconstruction with a new unbacked Zhizheng (Chihcheng) currency in 1351. The renewed emission of currency combined with massive revolts that crippled revenues forced the Yuan into a hyperinflationary spiral, driving paper currency out of use by 1359 or so.

See also MONEY IN THE MONGOL EMPIRE.

Further reading: Peng Xinwei, trans. Edward H. Kaplan, *A Monetary History of China* (Zhongguo Huobi Shi) (Bellingham: Western Washington University Press, 1994), 2: 458–536.

Parwan, Battle of   (Perwan, Parvan)   At the Battle of Parwan in Afghanistan in spring 1221, a Central Asian Turkish army defeated the Mongols. The victory temporarily raised hopes of driving out the Mongols, but it soon evaporated in internal dissensions.

In February 1221 Jalal-ud-Din Mengüberdi (d. 1231), son and heir of the sultan of KHORAZM, came to Ghazni in Afghanistan intending to revive resistance to CHINGGIS KHAN's invasion. Malik Khan (Amin Malik, d. 1221) of Herat was already in Ghazni with 50,000 pagan Qangli Turks. After the arrival of Jalal-ud-Din, famous for his bravery, local Ghuri warriors rallied to his banner, as did Saif-ud-Din Ighraq with 40,000 warriors of the Muslim Khalaj Turks.

In spring 1221 Jalal-ud-Din advanced to Parwan in the Hindu Kush mountains, defeating a small detachment of Mongols. A week later Chinggis Khan dispatched SHIGI QUTUQU with three *tümens* (nominally 30,000) cavalry. Jalal-ud-Din ordered the army to dismount, so that the men would fight without thought of flight. Taking the center, he put Ighraq on the left and Malik Khan on the right. Malik Khan's 10,000 men on the right slowly pushed the Mongols to their base in hard fighting. The next day the Mongols set figures on their spare remounts to make their numbers look greater, but the ruse did not fool Jalal-ud-Din. The third day Mongol *ba'aturs* (heroes) charged Ighraq's left wing. Ighraq's men, on foot again, fired their arrows, and the Mongols feigned flight. Jalal-ud-Din beat the drums to mount, Ighraq's men charged, but the Mongols suddenly turned and charged again, killing 500. Just then Jalal-ud-Din personally rode up and put the Mongols to flight. Large numbers of Mongols were captured, and Jala-ud-Din killed them by nailing stakes into their ears.

Unfortunately for Jalal-ud-Din's cause, Malik Khan struck Ighraq in a dispute over booty, and when Jalal-ud-Din proved unable to discipline the turbulent Qangli Turks, Ighraq and his men deserted the army. Chinggis Khan soon moved up his whole army, and Jalal-ud-Din, unable to resist, retreated to the Indus.

patronymics In Mongolia the practice of using a patronymic, or one's father's name, began in Buriatia and was introduced by the government into Mongolia in the 1930s. Today patronymics are seen as inadequate and are being supplemented by the revival of ancient clan names. The use of patronymics among the Mongolian peoples began among the 19th-century BURIATS of southern Siberia. Buriats created Russian-style surnames, not from their own clan names, but simply from their fathers' given names. The patronymics eventually became fixed surnames, although they remained flexible well into the Soviet era.

In Mongolia proper the government used only personal names until around 1934, when a patronymic system (designated *owog*, clan) was introduced on administrative forms to resolve confusion among people with the same names. From 1943 the initial syllable of patronymics began to be widely used with names in all formal writing. This gave way with Cyrillicization in 1950 to the use of the initials. The introduction of patronymics had to overcome strong resistance from the population due to the traditionally strict prohibition on children mentioning their parents' names in public.

When speaking in Mongolian, the patronymic, if needed, is used in the genitive (possessive) form with the patronymic first (e.g., Dorjiin Baatar, Dorj's Baatar, or D. Baatar). In writing for foreign audiences, however, the genitive is often dropped and the order reversed. Titles are always attached to the name, never the patronymic (thus Doctor Baatar, not Doctor Dorjiin).

In 1997 Mongolia's government decided that even the combination of patronymics and names left too many people with the same names. The genuine ancient *owogs*, or CLAN NAMES, were to be revived, with the patronymic functioning as a middle name. (Thus, if Dorjiin Baatar's clan name was BORJIGID, he would be Borjigid Dorjiin Baatar.) This new reform has run up against the problem that most Mongols do not know their clan names.

Mongolia's patronymic system was sometimes imitated in Inner Mongolia from 1947 on, although it never became official.

See also NAMES, PERSONAL.

petroglyphs Found throughout the territory of Mongolia and Inner Mongolia and dating from all periods, petroglyphs (paintings or carvings on stone) form a survey of the lifestyles and beliefs of the peoples inhabiting the MONGOLIAN PLATEAU. They are, however, difficult to date, especially as favored sites were used for several millenia.

Art in Mongolia, as in Europe and Siberia, began in the Upper Paleolithic (40,000–14,000 years ago). Pictures of Ice Age animals have been found in Mongolia at Khoid Tsenkher (Mankhan Sum, Khowd) and elsewhere. In the Mesolithic (11,000–8,000 years ago) and Neolithic (5000–1500 B.C.E.) considerably cruder animal figures were usually carved in outline. Cattle were commonly represented in these periods, often with a circle or even a whole calf inside the body. Horses, elk, and ibex are also common. Hunting scenes are rare, but faces and standing male and female figures occur frequently.

The Bronze and early Iron Ages (around 1500–500 B.C.E.) were the "golden age" of Mongolian petroglyphs, both carved and painted in red ocher. Bichigtiin Am (Bayanlig, Bayankhongor) is perhaps the richest site. The most common theme is ibex and elk being hunted by men with bows and arrows and assisted by dogs. Wolves, foxes, sheep, boars, camels, and other game appear regularly, but cattle are rarer. Stylized elk identical to those on ELK STONES are found as well as less-stylized elk with high-standing horns. Carefully rendered two-wheeled chariots drawn by two (or occasionally three) horses are separate from hunting scenes. Figures lead or ride horses and occasionally camels. Ocher rock paintings often show a square outline filled with dots (corrals? lineage grave sites?), with flying birds and stick figures leading quadrupeds (horses? dogs?) nearby. Figures of mounted archers hunting presumably postdate the eighth century B.C.E.

Later petroglyphs, while usefully illustrating aspects of material culture—headgear, Mongol yurts (*ger*), carts, armored cavalrymen, composite bows—lack the rich composition of the Bronze Age sites. Finally, in the Buddhist era monks often wrote *Om Mani Padme Hum* and other inscriptions over rock drawings. Abstract designs probably related to lineage brand markings are common throughout the history of Mongolian petroglyphs.

See also HUNTING AND FISHING; PREHISTORY.

Further reading: Esther Jacobson, Vladimir Kubarev, and Damdinsürengijn Tseevendorj [*sic* for Tseveendorj], *Répertoire des pétroglyphs d'Asie centrale*, vol. 6, *Mongolie du Nord-ouest: Tsagaan-Salaa/Bago Oigor* (Paris: De Boccard, 2001) [in English].

'Phags-pa Lama (hP'ags-pa Lama) (1235–1280) *Tibetan Buddhist cleric who designed a new script for Mongolian and began Tibet's priest-patron relation with the Mongols*
'Phags-pa Lama, scion of the powerful 'Khon family in central Tibet, which had controlled both the monastery and secular rule in the Sa-skya (modern Sa'gya) district, was born on March 26, 1235, in the Ngam-rings (modern Ngamring) district of western Tibet. Originally named Blo-gros rGyal-mtshan, he was later known as 'Phags-pa Lama (Noble Guru). When the Mongol prince KÖTEN summoned the boy's uncle Sa-skya Pandita (1182–1251) to his appanage in Liangzhou (modern Wuwei) in 1244, Sa-skya Pandita brought with him both 'Phags-pa and 'Phags-pa's younger brother Phyag-na rDo-rje (1239–67).

In 1253, after the death of Köten and Sa-skya Pandita, the prince Qubilai summoned 'Phags-pa and Phyag-na rDo-rje to his court. On June 21, 1255, 'Phags-pa received his monastic vows, and three years later he played a major role in a Buddhist-Taoist debate before Qubilai. That same year 'Phags-pa gave Qubilai and his wife CHABUI the first of three Tantric Hevajra initiations of the Sa-skya order.

Elected khan in 1260, QUBILAI KHAN appointed 'Phags-pa as state preceptor (Chinese, *guoshi*) with a jade seal on January 14, 1261, and he served both as the emperor's personal chaplain and head of all Buddhist monks. 'Phags-pa was chosen for this position not due to any established leadership in Tibet—the Sa-skya-pa were only one of many Tibetan monastic orders—but due to his intellectual ability, familiarity with the Mongol world, and loyalty to Qubilai.

In June 1264 Qubilai sent 'Phags-pa and Phyag-na rDo-rje back to Tibet, granting 'Phags-pa authority over all the Buddhist clergy in Tibet while investing in Phyag-na rDo-rje, now prince of Bailan and husband of a Mongol princess, secular rule in dBus-gTsang, or central Tibet. Other orders were disgusted by 'Phags-pa's Mongolian clothes and manners, and after Phyag-na rDo-rje's sudden death in 1267 the traditionally unruly 'Bri-gung-pa order revolted. 'Phags-pa returned to Qubilai's court at SHANGDU as Mongol troops cowed the 'Bri-gung-pa into submission and reinstalled regular Mongol rule.

Once at court, Qubilai charged 'Phags-pa with designing a new script that could render all the scripts of the empire, particularly Chinese and the Uighur script used for writing Mongolian. 'Phags-pa based his new SQUARE SCRIPT on Tibetan and presented it to the emperor on March 17, 1269. As a reward Qubilai promoted 'Phags-pa to the position of imperial preceptor (Chinese, *dishi*).

'Phags-pa spent the next years mostly at Lintao, in northwest China. In spring 1274 he finally resigned his position as imperial preceptor to his younger half-brother Rin-chen-rGyal-mtshan (1238–79) and returned to central Tibet with a large escort. Delayed in the high mountains near the source of the Huang (Yellow) River, he arrived at Sa-skya late in 1276. In 1277 he called the Council of Chu-mig (modern Qumig, near Xigazê) in 1277, which he asked a master of the rival bKa'-dams-pa order to chair, to restore peace between the various orders of Tibetan monks. He died on December 14, 1280. 'Phags-pa's family held the Imperial Preceptorate until his nephew Dharmapalarakshita's death in 1287. From 1320 on memorial halls to 'Phags-pa were constructed by imperial order over all the empire.

'Phags-pa wrote many works in Tibetan, in particular several handbooks of Buddhism intended for the Mongol royal family. His *Shes-bya rab-gsal* (Elucidation of the knowable), written for the crown prince JINGIM, was translated into Chinese (1306) and later included in the Chinese Buddhist canon. Excerpts were also incorporated as a chapter in the later Mongolian-language Buddhist handbook *Chikhula kereglegchi* (What it is important to know, c. 1600). This work promoted the concept of the Mongol dynasty as successor to a long line of Buddhist rulers in India and Tibet. As a Sanskritist he also promoted the study and imitation of Sanskrit canons of poetry in Tibet.

In subsequent Tibetan and Mongolian historiography, 'Phags-pa appears as the first Tibetan cleric to establish the "priest-patron" relation with an Inner Asian or Chinese ruler and one who secured the high-level autonomy of Tibet under Mongol rule. In fact, however, 'Phags-pa was a rather unambitious scholarly monk, loyal to the Mongol rulers but uncomfortable in his position as Qubilai's viceroy in Tibet.

See also BUDDHISM IN THE MONGOL EMPIRE; RELIGIOUS POLICY IN THE MONGOL EMPIRE; TIBET AND THE MONGOL EMPIRE; *TREASURY OF APHORISTIC JEWELS*; TWO CUSTOMS.

Further reading: Agata Bareja-Starzyńska, "A Brief Study of the Mongolian Transmission of the Buddhist Treatise *Śes bya rab gsal* by 'Phags pa bla ma Blo gros rgyal mtshan," in *Tractata Tibetica et Mongolica*, ed. Karénina Kollmar-Paulenz and Christian Peter (Wiesbaden: Otto Harrassowitz, 2002), 13–20; Constance Hoog, *Prince Jin-gim's Textbook of Tibetan Buddhism* (Leiden: E. J. Brill, 1983); L. Petech, "'P'ags-pa," in *In the Service of the Khan: Eminent Personalities of the Early Mongol-Yuan Period (1200–1300)*, ed. Igor de Rachewiltz et al. (Wiesbaden: Otto Harrassowitz 1993), 646–654.

'Phags-pa script   *See* SQUARE SCRIPT.

plebiscite on independence   In the plebiscite of October 20, 1945, the Mongolian people voted unanimously for independence from China.

Based on the Yalta accords of February 1945 between the United States, Britain, and the Soviet Union, the Chinese ruler Chiang Kai-shek was forced in the Sino-Soviet Friendship Treaty of August 14 to recognize Mongolian independence within its current frontiers. The one face-saving condition was that the Mongolian people should confirm their desire for independence with a plebiscite. From August 30 the Mongolian government began a massive campaign for a successful plebiscite, eventually holding 13,000 mass meetings. On October 20 the plebiscite was conducted, with Li Fazhang, China's deputy interior minister as observer. The logistics of assembling the people for voting and reporting the results proved quite formidable, as Mongolia's ruler MARSHAL CHOIBALSANG demanded full counts by 12 noon in the countryside and 8 P.M. in the towns. In open balloting—all voters had to sign their names or affix thumbprints—the Mongolian people voted 483,281 to 0 for independence from China. On January 6, 1946, the Chinese government recognized the results as valid, and on February 13 the Chinese foreign minister and a Mongolian delegation headed by the deputy secretary of the party's Central Committee, Ch. Sürenjaw, exchanged formal recognition. Nevertheless, diplomatic relations were never actually established, and outstanding issues, particularly the border, were never settled.

Poland   *See* CENTRAL EUROPE AND THE MONGOLS.

Polo, Marco (1254–1324) *Italian merchant and traveler who gave the most famous account of Asia and East Africa at the time of the Mongol Empire*
Marco Polo was born in 1254 into a well-to-do Venetian merchant family. In 1260 Marco's father, Niccolò, and his brother Maffeo, traveled through Soldaia (in Crimea) to the court of Berke, khan of the GOLDEN HORDE. By presenting *tangsuq*s (rarities, in this case jewels), they received goods and capital from Berke and became semiofficial ORTOQ (partner) merchants traveling through Bukhara to "Cambalu" (DAIDU, modern Beijing) and the court of QUBILAI KHAN (1260–94).

Being by their own account the first Latins Qubilai had ever seen, the khan sent them back with a PAIZA (badge of authority) to seek more men from the pope. Reaching Venice in 1269, the Polos waited for a new pope to be elected. Delayed several years, they eventually returned to Qubilai, accompanied only by Niccolò's son Marco, whom they had picked up in Venice.

The Polos then spent more than a decade in China, where they were members of the SEMUREN (various sorts) class, below the Mongols but above the local Chinese. By his own account Marco served the khan on missions to YUNNAN and the Indian Ocean, gratifying Qubilai Khan's hunger for fascinating stories of those far-off places. In 1289 Qubilai appointed the Polos to accompany Kökejin as a new bride for the Il-Khan Arghun (1284–91) in Iran. Traveling by sea, they found Arghun Khan dead and so took the bride to his son Ghazan in Khorasan.

The Polos finally returned to Venice in 1295. Marco was captured while commanding a Venetian war galley in 1296 and imprisoned in Genoa. There he met a Pisan romance writer, Rustichello, to whom he narrated his experiences. Rustichello wrote Marco's account in Franco-Italian, adding many elements of medieval romance writing and entitling the whole *Le Divisament dou monde* (The description of the world). After his release Marco Polo returned to Venice. Despite his travels, he does not seem to have achieved any great wealth, and his will passed on only a few souvenirs of his time in the East.

The *Description of the World* is organized around three itineraries Marco Polo actually traveled: 1) the Polos' 1276–79 route east from LESSER ARMENIA through Iran and Afghanistan to "Cambalu"; 2) Marco's route from "Cambalu" to Yunnan; and 3) the Polos' 1289–91 route from "Cambalu" to the port of Zaiton (modern Quanzhou) and from there by sea to Java, southern India, and Iran. Along each route, however, numerous digressions describe places such as KASHMIR, the Mongolian heartland, Japan, Socotra, and Zanzibar, which Marco Polo never visited personally. A final chapter describes Russia and Siberia with romanticized incidents from the history of the western khanates.

Since the Polos traveled as *ortoq* merchants and envoys using the Mongol JAM (postroads) and escorts, it is not surprising that Marco Polo's account of the "Tartars" (Mongols) is extremely favorable. As a jumble of first-, second-, and third-hand material retold without the aid of notes many years later, the historical value of the descriptions is uneven. Boasts of having participated in the siege of Xiangyang (modern Xiangfan) and having been governor of Yangzhou, easily refuted by Chinese records, have damaged his reputation, yet Marco Polo at his best has a genius for vivid description and supplies invaluable historical information.

From the beginning the *Description of the World* was immensely popular in Europe. More than 150 manuscripts exist in many languages, and the textual history is extremely confused. In 1307 Marco Polo himself abridged and translated the text into French, and Tuscan Italian and Latin abridgements were also made during his life. The so-called Z, or Toledo, manuscript in Latin contains many additional passages shared with the first printed edition of Giovanni Ramusio (1539). Whether these additions go back to Polo himself is disputed. The influence of Marco Polo on European knowledge of the East was immense; Christopher Columbus was only one of those inspired by his account.

See also CHRISTIAN SOURCES ON THE MONGOL EMPIRE; WESTERN EUROPE AND THE MONGOLS.

Further reading: A. C. Moule and Paul Pelliot, *Description of the World* (1938; rpt., New York, 1976); Paul Pelliot, *Notes on Marco Polo,* 3 vols. (Paris: Librairie Adrien-Maisonneuve, 1959, 1963, 1973); Igor de Rachewiltz, "Marco Polo Went to China," *Zentralasiatische Studien* 27 (1997): 34–92.

Polovtsi *See* QIPCHAQS.

prehistory Stone Age sites have been found over much of the territory of Mongolia. While graves and settlements from the Bronze Age onward are generally concentrated in the *khangai* (wooded mountain) zone of Mongolia, Stone Age sites are generally found in the *gobi* and steppe zones.

LOWER AND MIDDLE PALEOLITHIC

Possibly the earliest stone tools in Mongolia are found in the Tsagaan Agui cave (Bayanlig Sum, Bayankhongor). The date of these tools is, however, controversial; some archaeologists date them to strata from 700,000 years before the present (BP), when the climate of Mongolia was relatively favorable. Others regard their presence as intrusive and date them to higher strata from around 300,000 years BP.

The next datable tools in Mongolia, those of Yarkh Uul (Gurwansaikhan, Middle Gobi), are dated to 300,000 years BP. The industries are dominated by handax forms similar to the Acheulian of Europe and Africa but quite different from the pebble industries of East, South, and Southeast Asia. The Moiltyn Am (Kharkhorin Sum, North Khangai) site, however, shows chopping tools characteristic of South and Southeast Asia, together with remains showing the Levallois technique of using prepared cores, which developed among the Acheulian industries to the west.

The Mousterian industries of the Middle Paleoithic are represented at Orkhon-7 (Kharkhorin Sum, North Khangai), Otson Maanit (South Gobi), Chikhen Agui cave (Bayan-Öndör Sum, Bayankhongor), and other sites, dated at 60,000 and 38,000 years BP. The Otson Maanit industries include bladed flakes, retouched round scrapers, small hand axes, and triangles, many struck with soft hammers of wood or bone. No early hominid remains have been found in Mongolia, but the above industries are elsewhere associated with *Homo erectus*, archaic *Homo sapiens* (or *Homo heidelbergensis*), and *Homo neaderthalensis*.

UPPER PALEOLITHIC AND MESOLITHIC

The Upper Paleolithic industries, associated with modern *Homo sapiens* and found in the cold climate of the last glaciation (dated 40,000–14,000 years BP), not only show more specialized and standardized flakes and blades but also, at Rashaan (Batshireet Sum, Khentii) and Khoid Tsenkher (Mankhan Sum, Khowd), the earliest Mongolian art: ocher paintings and carvings of wooly rhinoceroses, mammoths, ibexes, ostriches, bison, and camels. Human and animal figurines and shelters have been found at the South Siberian site of Mal'ta, near Usol'ye Sibirskoye, and willow basketwork at Jalainuur (Djalai-nor, Zhalainuor) in northeast Inner Mongolia.

Microlithic industries characteristic of the Mesolithic appear relatively early in Mongolia, with unrecalibrated radiocarbon dates of 11,000–8,000 years BP. At Moiltyn Am the transition from Upper Paleolithic to Mesolithic shows both primitive-looking pebble tools and small scrapers, awls, and points, an assemblage similar to the Ordosian assemblage of southwestern Inner Mongolia, exemplified at Shara Usu Gool (Sjara-osso-gol, modern Wuding River), and to the post-Mal'ta Siberian site of Afontova-Gora on the Yenisey.

NEOLITHIC

The Neolithic in Mongolia (5000–1500 B.C.E.) shows considerable continuity in chipped-stone industries with the Mesolithic. Characteristic of both periods are the "Gobi cores" that are retouched and used as scrapers after having flake tools removed from them. Arrowheads of several types and rarer large spearheads and bone knives set with flint blades were the culmination of chipped-stone industries in Mongolia. Cultivation of millet and wheat brought into use querns, mortars, pestles, and other ground-stone articles. Pottery decorated with lines, waves, stripes, and rope impressions appeared as did bone fishing harpoons. Hearths and semisubterranean dwellings and a number of early Neolithic gravesites have been found near Choibalsang city, at Baruun Ölziit, Norowlin, Tamsag, and the Kherlen Bridge. Tightly doubled-up bodies were placed facing west in narrow pits and covered with ocher. Ornaments included pearl and deer-and marmot-teeth necklaces, bone and shell plates of various forms, and bracelets. A unique find from Norowlin is an oval bone plate with a schematic human face. Nephrite goods in eastern Mongolia show trade links to Tuva's Sayan Mountains.

BRONZE AGE

The MONGOLIAN PLATEAU is richly supplied with the copper and tin deposits needed to make bronze. Slab (or stone-cist) graves, PETROGLYPHS, and ELK STONES mark archaeologically the distinctive Bronze Age culture of Mongolia, Transbaikalia, and Tuva, dated from the 13th to the eighth centuries B.C.E. Bodies were buried lengthwise in the soil with flagstones on the head and chest. Around the grave, in a 2 by 3 meter (7 x 10 feet) rectangle, was erected a fence of slabs. Finally, a memorial stone might be erected at the site. Fields of such slab graves marked major gravesites, but all known slab graves have been looted. Remaining grave goods include sprinklings of ocher, Neolithic-style flint blades, remains of livestock including one or more horses, pottery, necklaces, inlaid ornaments, and remnants of hearths, perhaps connected to the funerary meal and/or a commemorative bonfire. Pottery includes tripods modeled on Chinese Bronze Age *li* vessels, while helmets and ring-pommel bronze knives show important links to Bronze Age Inner Mongolia and the Karasuk culture of Khakassia. Contemporary petroglyphs show two-wheeled chariots and livestock but mostly archers hunting ibex or elk on foot. Elk imagery has been linked to the cult of a deer goddess.

IRON AGE

The transition to the Iron Age took place from the eighth to fifth centuries B.C.E. along with the refinement of horse-riding technology to permit mounted ARCHERY. Mobility increased, transforming transhumance into long-distance pastoral nomadism. Northwest Mongolia's Iron Age culture, as exemplified at Chandmani Uul (Ulaangom Sum, Uws), was identical to the Uyuk culture of Tuva and similar to the Tagar culture of Khakassia. In contrast to the slab grave culture, burials were collective and diverse in form. The approximately 300 graves of Chandmani Uul show four types: 1) large pyramidal stone barrows; 2) stone barrows without a coffin; 3) small stone coffins; and 4) log-walled barrows. Only examples of the last type, invisible from the surface, have been relatively undisturbed. Each burial chamber contains up to 10 bodies, men, women, and children together, doubled up tightly with their heads to the west. Ceramic vessels, bronze cauldrons, animal bones, hearth sites, and elk stones show continuity with Bronze Age funerary practices. Articles of bronze, iron, and bone include daggers; battleaxes; arrowheads; knives; awls; belt and saddle-girth buckles; harness plates; mirrors; gold and tin earrings; necklaces; stone, deer- and marmot-teeth pendants; wooden bowls and plates; and wool, felt, and leather clothes. Glass beads from the Near East show western trade links, and the bronzes furnish fine examples of the ANIMAL STYLE.

Although the Iron Age burials have been seen as evidence of a warlike, patriarchal aristocracy, this description appears more appropriate for the Scythian-Sarmatian culture to the west. Except for the Arzhan site in Tuva, Tuvan and Mongolian Iron Age graves are not grouped around a single chief, and while grave goods differ by age and sex, the distinction is not strict. Not until the emergence of the XIONGNU around 210 B.C.E. does the aristocratic chief accompanied in death by slaves and family appear in Mongolian ARCHAEOLOGY.

See also ANIMAL HUSBANDRY AND NOMADISM; FUNERARY CUSTOMS.

Further reading: Ignace Bourgeois et al., *Ancient Nomads of the Altai Mountains: Belgian-Russian Multidisciplinary Archaeological Research on the Scytho-Siberian Culture* (Brussels: Royal Museums of Art and History, 2000); Esther Jacobson, *Burial Ritual, Gender, and Status in South Siberia in the Late Bronze-Early Iron Age* (Bloomington, Ind.: Research Institute for Inner Asian Studies, 1988).

privatization Privatization in Mongolia was carried out very rapidly by means of vouchers from 1991 to 1995. During this period the private sector's share of the economy rose from 10 percent in 1990 to 63.7 percent in 1995. Further privatization by auction of several large enterprises, apartments, and residential and farmland (but not pastures) followed.

VOUCHER PRIVATIZATION

With the 1990 DEMOCRATIC REVOLUTION the new Mongolian government created a plan for rapid privatization of existing enterprises. The plan was developed by the head of the State Privatization Commission, D. Ganbold (b. 1957), a Moscow-trained economist and founder of the National Progress Party. It was ratified by the Law on Privatization passed on May 22, 1991. Privatization for the nonagricultural sector was envisioned in two parallel processes: For small enterprises (shops, handicrafts, etc.) the aim was to enable individuals with entrepreneurial abilities and interest to gather enough capital to buy them outright, and for large enterprises (factories, supermarkets, hotels, etc.) the aim was to create a dispersed stock ownership while allowing for a continuity of management. Twenty large enterprises, in utilities, transport, communications, and research, were reserved for continued state ownership.

Each citizen of Mongolia born before May 31, 1991, received two types of vouchers, three pink vouchers with a nominal value of 1,000 tögrögs each, and one blue voucher with a face value of 7,000 tögrögs. At the same time the government-owned daily *Ardyn erkh* (*Democracy* or *People's power*) published basic information on all the assets being privatized to guide citizens in their investments. The pink vouchers were transferable, so that persons willing to take on ownership could buy them from citizens uninterested in the opportunity. This phase was called "small privatization." The blue vouchers were nontransferable, although they could be grouped within a household. These blue vouchers were usable only to bid on larger enterprises that would be auctioned off by the government at the Mongolian Stock Exchange, which had been created in January 1991 under the Hungarian-trained economist N. Zoljargal (b. 1964). This phase, called "large privatization," began in February 1992.

Considering the scale of the task, privatization went remarkably smoothly. By the end of 1993 764 large and 2,440 small enterprises had been privatized, and by the end of 1994 the total reached 4,483 enterprises worth 20 billion tögrögs. Essentially the entire adult population, 1.1 million citizens, participated. While the privatization law allowed for mutual funds, only 2 percent of all vouchers were traded through them. The aim of dispersed ownership was achieved only too well, some companies ending up with more than 20,000 shareholders. Citizens showed a strong attraction for enterprises they worked in, so that employee ownership averaged 44 percent in large enterprises. In small privatization citizens preferred cooperatives rather than sole proprietorships. By 1993 the country's 4,332 economic entities included 449 shareholding companies, 1,099 limited liability companies, 1,869 cooperatives, and 905 sole proprietorships. The end of voucher privatization was marked in August 1995, when the Mongolian Stock Exchange opened a secondary securities market with cash trading. While rural privatization was organized on the same legal framework, in practice it functioned as a separate procedure in which only cooperative (*negdel*) members participated largely under rules set by their own membership (*see* DECOLLECTIVIZATION).

THE SECOND WAVE OF PRIVATIZATION

Despite the relatively smooth implementation, policy makers worried about the excess dispersal of ownership and the lack of real accountability on the part of company management. At the end of the process, the state still held 62 percent of the ownership of larger enterprises, with ownership concentrated in energy, infrastructure, and utilities. Even where it did not have the majority share, it still exercised the predominant influence on corporate direction.

Since 1995 the government has turned to auctions and to a lesser extent to sales of shares on the stock exchange as the primary methods for privatizing those remaining state assets not planned for continued state ownership. Foreign direct investment was encouraged in this process. The new Democratic Coalition government accelerated privatization in 1997, and from 1996 to 2000 a total of 942 enterprises and assets were privatized for a value of US $65 million. In this phase of privatization accusations of corruption have become serious. An offer for the State Department Store made in February 1996 was canceled after accusations of insider trading, while from 1998 on privatization of the colossal Erdenet ore-dressing plant was bogged down in accusations of corruption and Russian mafia influence (49 percent of the shares were held in Russia). These accusations contributed to the Democratic Coalition's defeat at the polls in 2000, but the new MONGOLIAN PEOPLE'S REVOLUTIONARY PARTY (MPRP) government has continued the privatization program.

HOUSING AND LAND PRIVATIZATION

While at first it was thought apartments might be privatized through the voucher system, in February 1997 the Democratic Coalition government passed a law, over the veto of President N. Bagabandi (of the opposition MPRP), simply giving apartments to their current residents. That year 25,000 apartments were privatized, and the figure eventually reached 83,169 apartments, or 98.3 percent of the total. Condominium associations manage the apartment blocks. This program, along with rural decollectivization that distributed the herds to the herders, has been one of the most popular parts of the privatization agenda.

Although both the 1992 CONSTITUTION and Mongolian tradition block the privatization of rangeland, privatization of urban plots and farmland was an important part of the original reform program. Although allowed under the constitution, fears of foreigners buying up Mongolia prevented land privatization from being passed until 2002. In June 2002 the MPRP government passed a land privatization law that allowed Mongolian citizens to receive free of charge on May 1, 2003, land that they had personally improved for residential and nonpastoral economic use. Land is to be owned and assigned per family, with smaller limits for urban families and larger limits for rural families. All are allowed additional small vegetable plots. Large agricultural plots of up to 100 hectares are to be assigned to experienced farmers only. New property taxes are also to be instituted. Since those already living in YURT-courtyards would become owners, those with resources scrambled to develop residential and agricultural land. However, opposition politicians led protests demanding that the law be reworked to make residential holdings reflect family size and to have farmland holdings assigned randomly. The protests did not, however, reverse the government's policy.

See also ECONOMY, MODERN; MONGOLIA, STATE OF.

prosody Poetry in Mongolian is primarily governed by alliteration, in which the two or more successive lines have the same first syllable. While often irregular, alliteration usually groups the lines into couplets or quatrains, sometimes grouping up to eight lines. The alliteration itself is often only approximate. In written poetry one also finds purely visual alliteration, using the ambiguities of the UIGHUR-MONGOLIAN SCRIPT to create first syllables that look the same even though they have a different pronunciation.

Folk poetry usually has seven to eight syllables per line, with a cesura after the fourth syllable. While the rhythm usually seems irregular when written, the frequent dropping or extension of vowels usually makes the verse completely isochronic in performance. While the MONGOLIAN LANGUAGE has phonemic vowel length, such length plays no role in Mongolian prosody, which is dependent rather on the regular equivalence of the length of the metrical units as spoken or sung, something that does not follow vowel length. Normally, the syllables group themselves into two-syllable and three-syllable feet, with the first syllable longest. Three-syllable feet are found most often at the end of the line.

In later Tibetan-influenced Buddhist didactic poetry and liturgy, the natural first-syllable stress in Mongolian pronunciation is used for an isosyllabic metrical prosody. The most regular form has four trochees followed by a cesura and two trochees and a dactyl. Although Mongolian poets were familiar with the complex composition rules and paraphrasings prescribed in the *Kavyadarsha* of the ancient Indian literary critic Dandin, these rules were by no means the sine qua non of Mongolian poetry as they were in Tibet.

Modern Mongolian poetry has used both folk poetry prosody based on isochronic lines and the Tibetan-style prosody based on isosyllabic lines, although the former tends to predominate. Free verse forms have also become common, although most poetry still alliterates. The Communist-era poet-laureate D. Sengee (1916–39) experimented with Russian-influenced iambic meter but found few imitators.

See also FOLK POETRY AND TALES; LITERATURE.

Further reading: György Kara, "Stave Rhyme, Head-Rhyme, and End-Rhyme in Mongolian Poetry," in *Altaic Affinities, Proceedings of the 40th Meeting of the Permanent International Altaistic Conference (PIAC), Provo, Utah (1997)*, edited by David B. Honey and David C. Wright, Indiana University Uralic & Altaic Series, Vol. 168 (Bloomington: Indiana University, Research Institute for Inner Asian Studies, 2001), 267–280; John R. Krueger, *Poetical Passages of the Erdeni-yin tobči: A Mongolian Chronicle of the Year 1662 by Sagang Sečen* (The Hague: Mouton, 1961).

provinces in the Mongol Empire

provinces in the Mongol Empire The current provinces of China date back, in their rough outlines, to the branch secretariats established by the Mongol YUAN DYNASTY after its conquest of all China.

With the initial Mongol pacification of North China under MUQALI (1170–1223), local Han Chinese and Kitan administrators under Mongol rule set up "branch departments of state affairs" (*xing shangshu sheng*). Such early departments were set up first in Xijing (modern Datong) and Zhongdu, or Yanjing (modern Beijing) and later in Dongping and Hezhong (near modern Yongji). Given the chaotic conditions of the time, they carried on little but military and paramilitary functions.

ÖGEDEI KHAN (1229–41) abolished these branch secretariats and divided the pacified areas of North China (roughly modern Hebei, Shanxi, Shandong, and south-central Inner Mongolia) into 10 routes (Chinese, *lu;* Mongolian, *chölge*) for taxation purposes. At the same time Ögedei divided the whole empire's wealthier areas into a Yanjing administration, covering north and northwest China, and a Besh-Baligh (near modern Qitai) administration, covering Central Asia from Hami to the Amu Dar'ya. Late in Ögedei's reign a third Amu Dar'ya administration was organized to administer pacified Afghanistan and Iran. The Chinese called these three administrations Branch Secretariats (*xing zhongshu sheng*). Under MÖNGKE KHAN (1251–59) they were renamed Branch Departments of State Affairs. Each administration had one to four chiefs, with two or three senior assistants.

In 1260 QUBILAI KHAN (1260–94), who at first controlled only North China, reorganized the Yanjing Department of State Affairs as his secretariat (*zhongshu sheng,* abbreviated *sheng*), the central bureaucratic organ of his state. In North China the secretariat controlled 10 Pacification Commissions covering the area of Ögedei's original 10 routes together with Shaanxi and Henan. In Shaanxi and Sichuan, which faced multiple military emergencies, he organized a Branch Secretariat (*xing zhongshu sheng,* abbreviated *xingsheng* but usually called simply *sheng* by foreigners). This use of branch secretariats for emergency situations was the origin of the subsequent Yuan regional administrative system. In the following decades branch secretariats were repeatedly created and dissolved in Shaanxi, Sichuan, Gansu, and Henan, depending on military vicissitudes. With the final conquest of South China, military emergencies dissipated, but the branch secretariats had proven their utility, and those in the areas outside the dynasty's North China base were retained.

By 1299 the borders of the Yuan dynasty's nine branch secretariats and the one central secretariat were fixed. While several secretariats, such as YUNNAN, Gansu, and Shaanxi, were relatively similar to modern provinces, others, such as Henan and Jiangxi, were much larger, and Liaoyang, Jiangzhe, and the Central Secretariat combined several modern provinces. Only the Mongolian heartland and Tibet remained outside the rule of branch secretariats. In 1312 Mongolia was reorganized as the Lingbei Branch Secretariat.

The Central Secretariat in the capital, DAIDU (modern Beijing), had two grand councillors (*chengxiang* or *chingsang*) and four managers (*pingzhang* or *pingjang*), but after 1286 two managers alone headed the branch secretariats. These managers were either Mongols or SEMUREN (Central and West Asian immigrants). Although the Central Secretariat controlled appointments, the branch secretariats had wide autonomy in their ordinary operations, handling taxation, garrison troops, transportation, and other aspects of rule. Local administration was based on counties (*xian*) and urban administrations under metropolitan and rural prefectures (*fu* and *zhou*), which in turn were usually supervised by 185 or so routes (*lu*), headed by a commander (*zongguan*) and a *DARUGHACHI*. Up to 24 surveillance commissioners and many pacification commissions (*xuanweisi*) and/or myriarchy commands in strategic or unruly areas exercised overlapping jurisdiction.

After the outbreak of widespread rebellions in 1351, the provincial governments underwent another bout of repeated reorganizations before the fall of the dynasty in 1368. The succeeding MING DYNASTY built on the Yuan precedent and divided its territory into *sheng*s (now translatable simply as provinces) very similar to China's current provinces.

See also APPANAGE SYSTEM; ARGHUN AQA; BAYAN; HARGHASUN DARQAN; KÖRGÜZ; LIAN XIXIAN; MAHMUD YALAVACH AND MAS'UD BEG; MANCHURIA AND THE MONGOL EMPIRE; ÖCHICHER; QARA-QORUM; SAYYID AJALL; YELÜ CHUCAI.

qa'an See KHAN.

qaghan See KHAN.

Qahar See CHAKHAR.

Qaidu Khan (1235–1301) *Heir of Ögedei who defied Qubilai Khan and took over the Chaghatay Khanate, dominating Central Asia for three decades*

Qaidu was the son of Qashi (or Qashidai), heir apparent of ÖGEDEI KHAN (1229–41). Qashi inherited his father's alcoholism and died early. Qaidu's mother, Sebkine, was of the Turco-Mongolian Mekrin mountaineers of the eastern Tian Shan. Qaidu was raised first by one of CHINGGIS KHAN's empresses and then in his senior relative Möngke's ORDO (palace-tent). In 1251 MÖNGKE was elected khan (1251–59) and purged the Ögedeids. He spared Qaidu and gave him Qayaligh (near modern Taldyqorghan in Kazakhstan). As early as 1256, however, Qaidu showed signs of discontent.

Perhaps in reaction to his father's and grandfather's excess, Qaidu was a teetotaler, eschewing even KOUMISS. Qaidu adhered to the native Mongol religion, rising before dawn to meditate and bowing down to the sun several times daily. He and his able daughter Qutulun (MARCO POLO's Ay-Yaruq, d. 1306) had unusually close relations, which gave rise to rumors of incest. While at war with virtually all the Mongol rulers, Qaidu rarely took the offensive, preferring to exploit his enemies' missteps.

When MÖNGKE KHAN's brother QUBILAI KHAN (1260–94) secured his throne, he insisted Qaidu come personally to court. Upon Qaidu's refusal, Qubilai insti-

gated the Chaghatay khan Baraq (1266–71) to attack him. Baraq defeated Qaidu in 1268, but after the GOLDEN HORDE khan Mengü-Temür (1267–80) sided with Qaidu, the three, Baraq, Qaidu, and Mengü-Temür, came to an agreement, swearing an alliance at Talas (spring 1269) and charging Qubilai with having abandoned the old Mongol JASAQ (laws) and *yosun* (customs) for Chinese institutions. After Baraq's defeat by the IL-KHANATE and his subsequent death, Qaidu was elected khan of a revived Ögedeid house (September 1271) and seized control over the Chaghatay Khanate. Despite revolts by dissatisfied Chaghatayid princes, Qaidu won the loyalty of Mas'ud Beg (d. 1289), the CHAGHATAY KHANATE's most experienced administrator (*see* MAHMUD YALAVACH AND MAS'UD BEG). Meanwhile defections from Qubilai's Yuan dynasty swelled Qaidu's army. In 1274 an Ögedeid prince, Hoqu, in Gansu deserted to Qaidu. In spring 1277 several sons of ARIQ-BÖKE and Möngke, then garrisoning in Almaligh (near modern Huocheng) for Qubilai, rebelled and imprisoned Qubilai's son Nomuqan and his chief minister, Hantum. The rebellion gave Qaidu control of Almaligh and a large force under Ariq-Böke's son Mingliq-Temür; he shared the hostages with Mengü-Temür Khan.

In response Qubilai and his YUAN DYNASTY strengthened the garrisons in Uighuristan and the Tarim basin. Only after finally driving out the dissident Chaghatayids and appointing Baraq's son Du'a (1282–1307) the Chaghatay khan did the merged Chaghatayid-Ögedeid Khanate expand. Du'a served as Qaidu's spearhead, capturing Besh-Baligh (near modern Qitai, 1286) and forcing Yuan armies to evacuate the Tarim Basin (1288–89). Although he failed to take full advantage of NAYAN'S REBELLION in 1287, Qaidu defeated a major Yuan army in the KHANGAI RANGE in 1289, briefly occupying QARA-QORUM. Later Nawroz's 1289 rebellion in Khorasan facilitated Du'a's 1295 invasion of Mazandaran in eastern Iran.

This expansion cost Qaidu his support from the Golden Horde. In 1283–84 Mengü-Temür's successors returned Nomuqan as a peace overture to the Yuan, and Qaidu felt obliged to return Hantum as well. By 1288 Qubilai's envoys were in contact with Qonichi, khan of the BLUE HORDE, the Jochid khanate along Qaidu's northern frontier. When Qonichi died Qaidu and Du'a supported a rival prince, Köbeleg, in a protracted civil war against Qonichi's son Bayan (fl. 1299–1304), the candidate of Toqto'a (1291–1312), khan of the Golden Horde. From 1298 on Bayan insistently advocated a unified attack of the Mongol khanates of Qaidu and Du'a.

In 1293 Qubilai's general TUTUGH counterattacked, clearing Qaidu's forces out of Tuva, and in 1296 defections gave the Yuan the Baarin *tümen* (10,000) on the Ob River. From 1300–01 the Yuan forces under Prince Haishan and Tutugh's son Chong'ur attacked Qaidu's main force in the ALTAI RANGE. Although vastly outnumbered and ill, Qaidu won a victory at Qaraqata (September 4–5, 1301, near Zawkhan River) but died soon after.

Qaidu had groomed his son Orus as his successor, but Du'a elevated Chabar (d. 1328) instead. Orus, Qutulun, and Hoqu's son Tökme (d. 1308) opposed Du'a, and by 1306 Qaidu's armies and children were deserting either to the Il-Khanate or the Yuan. Chabar's surrender to Emperor Haishan in 1310 ended the independent Ögedeid Khanate.

See also ÖCHICHER; SIBERIA AND THE MONGOL EMPIRE.

Further reading: Michal Biran, *Qaidu and the Rise of the Independent Mongol State in Central Asia* (Richmond, Surrey: Curzon Press, 1997).

Qalqa *See* KHALKHA.

qan *See* KHAN.

Qaracin *See* KHARACHIN.

Qara-Khitai (Qara-Kitan, Kara Khitay, Caracathay)
The Qara-Khitai Empire (1131–1213) dominated Turkestan during the rise of the Mongols and pioneered some early Mongol institutions. The empire appeared out of the wreckage of the Liao dynasty (907–1125), which had dominated Manchuria, Mongolia, and northernmost China for two centuries. The Liao dynasty had been founded by the KITANS, a seminomadic people of eastern Inner Mongolia who spoke a language related to but not identical to Mongolian. When the Liao dynasty was overthrown by the rival Jurchen people of eastern Manchuria, Yelü Dashi, a Kitan of the Liao ruling family, escaped north into Mongolia. In 1129 he rallied both the men of the Kitan garrisons stationed there and of the tribes surrounding them to build up a core of supporters. He gained support of the UIGHURS of Qara-Qocho (modern Turpan), and in 1133 he founded his capital, Ghuzz-Ordo, on the Chu River (near Bishkek in modern Kyrgyzstan). In 1141, after crushing the Seljük Turks in the Battle of Qatawan, he made KHORAZM and Mawarannahr (roughly, modern Uzbekistan and Tajikistan) and the Tarim basin tributary. As a member of the Liao imperial family, he proclaimed a revived Liao dynasty. The KITANS were called Khitayans by the Turks, and they called his new empire the Qara-Khitai, or "Black (i.e., commoner) Kitans," to distinguish them from the earlier Liao dynasty in the east.

The Qara-Khitai state was very loosely organized. The ruling core, numbering perhaps 40,000 families, lived a seminomadic life in the steppe around Ghuzz-Ordo. The formal structure of government was that of a Chinese dynasty, but military- and clan-based Kitan institutions also had great importance. The Kitans were Buddhist in the Chinese tradition. Most of their subjects were Muslim, although the Uighurs were mostly Buddhist, and there were Christian communities in Ghuzz-Ordo and elsewhere. The tributary states governed their own affairs under the supervision of overseers, called *jianguo* in Chinese, *shahna* in Persian, and *basqaq* in Turkish. The Kitan rulers made no attempt to impose their language or religion on their subjects.

THE MONGOL CONQUEST

When CHINGGIS KHAN unified the Mongolian Plateau in 1204, refugees from the MERKID and NAIMAN tribes spilled west across the ALTAI RANGE. Further campaigns in 1206 and 1208 sent the refugees farther into Qara-Khitai territory. One refugee, Küchülüg, son of the Naiman khan Tayang, came to Ghuzz-Ordo in 1210. After winning the favor of the last Liao emperor, Yelü Zhilugu, Küchülüg proposed to collect the Naiman and Merkid refugees to strengthen the regime. Instead, he conspired with 'Ala'ud-Din Muhammad, the sultan of Khorazm, to rebel against Qara-Khitai rule and divide the regime between them. The Kitans defeated Küchülüg's refugee force but were in turn defeated by the Khorazm shah's armies, and chaos ensued. In 1211 Küchülüg captured Zhilugu during his autumn hunt in Kashghar. The adventurer ruled in Zhilugu's name until the emperor's death in 1213, marrying Zhilugu's stepdaughter and converting to Buddhism.

Meanwhile, from 1209 on the Buddhist Uighur ruler in Qara-Qocho and the Muslim rulers of the cities of Qayaligh (near modern Taldyqorghan in Kazakhstan) and Almaligh (near modern Huocheng in Xinjiang), all weary of heavy Qara-Khitai demands, had submitted to Chinggis Khan. The Uighur ruler and Arslan Khan of Qayaligh went to Mongolia in person in 1211 and received Mongol princesses as tokens of their alliance.

As the Qara-Khitai regime crumbled, Küchülüg crushed resistance in Kashghar and Khotan, the only cities left to the empire apart from Ghuzz-Ordo itself. In Khotan he forced the Islamic population to embrace Buddhism, martyring an Islamic cleric. In 1217 Chinggis Khan returned from his campaigns in North China and dispatched his cavalry vanguard under JEBE to destroy Küchülüg. The Kitan ruling elite supported Jebe against the usurper, and Küchülüg fled south into the Pamir Mountains. In 1218 shepherds in Badakhshan seized him and handed him over to Jebe, who beheaded him, while Kashghar and Khotan surrendered to the Mongols.

QARA-KHITAI IN THE MONGOL EMPIRE

The Mongols employed a certain number of Qara-Khitai Kitans as scribes and administrators, but the main contribution of the Qara-Khitai to Mongol rule was the model of a steppe-centered empire loosely controlling sedentary peoples through tributary rulers supervised by overseers (*shahna*s or *basqaq*s), with control that did not interfere with the local peoples' religion or customs. Chinggis Khan seems to have preferred this sort of rule, and the *shahnas*/*basqaq*s were the institutional prototypes for the Mongol DARUGHACHI system. The submission of Khotan and Kashghar was immediately followed by the first-known proclamation of the Mongols' policy of religious toleration. While the Kitan model of decentralization would later prove impractical in most cases, the institution of *darughachi*s and the principle of cultural and religious toleration became main planks of Mongol imperial policy.

After the empire's division the Qara-Khitai heartland, with most of the ethnic Kitans, came under the Jochid BLUE HORDE. The (Qara-) Qitay clansmen found among the modern Uzbek, Kazakh, Karakalpak, and Bashkir (Bashkort) nationalities are their descendants.

See also QARLUQS.

Qara-Kitan   *See* QARA-KHITAI.

Qara-Qorum   Begun in 1235, Qara-Qorum served as the capital of the empire only until 1260 but for the next 100 years or so remained the administrative center for Mongolia.

From 1235 to 1238 ÖGEDEI KHAN constructed a series of palaces and pavilions at stopping places in his annual nomadic route through central Mongolia. The first palace, Wan'angong (Palace of Ten-Thousandfold Peace), and its irrigated garden were constructed by North Chinese artisans. Ögedei regularly stayed at the Wan'angong for a month in March and April and again briefly in the summer. The emperor urged his relatives to build residences nearby and settled the deported craftsmen from China near the site, thus starting the city of Qara-Qorum. Its mud walls were completed in summer 1251.

Even at its height, under MÖNGKE KHAN (1251–59), Qara-Qorum was, said the visitor WILLIAM OF RUBRUCK,

Stone turtle at Qara-Qorum, 13th–14th centuries. The turtle originally carried a stela with an inscription. *(From N. Tsultem,* Mongolian Sculpture *[1989])*

no more populous than the village of St. Denis in France. As found in the 1948–49 excavations of S. V. Kiselev, the city was about 1.6 kilometers (0.99 miles) east to west and 2.4 kilometers (1.49 miles) north to south, with the Wan'angong palace in the southwest corner of the city. The population settled in two districts, one of Chinese craftsmen and the other of Muslims, mostly merchants. Markets were in the Muslim sector and outside the four gates. Chinese farmers grew grains and vegetables, but the city depended on imports of foodstuffs from North China. William of Rubruck noted there were 12 "pagan temples," that is, Buddhist and Taoist monasteries, two mosques, and a church. Ögedei's minister YELÜ CHUCAI had built a Confucian temple and observatory in 1233, apparently in Qara-Qorum or its vicinity.

The 1948–49 excavations of the palace quarter found all the palaces built on raised platforms of pounded earth and sand and connected by raised walkways. The Wan'angong, floored with green tiles, measured about 55 by 45 meters (180 by 148 feet) and had six rows of seven wooden pillars resting on granite pedestals. Glazed green, red, and dark blue tiles and molded dragons and other animals ornamented the roof. Palace frescoes had mostly Buddhist themes and were painted in a style reminiscent of Uighur and XIA DYNASTY art. Excavated houses were warmed with Chinese-style *kang*s, or warming stoves. The "House at the Crossroads" contained smithies in which steel was forged with blasts driven by waterwheels connected to a canal from the ORKHON RIVER. Metal items found included axle boxes for the YURT carts, three-footed cauldrons, scissors, sickles, plowshares, pickaxes, arrowheads, and spearheads. Pottery kilns produced finely glazed Cizhou, Junyao, and Liuli pottery as well as celadon. Large numbers of cast copper coins, almost all of the SONG DYNASTY (960–1279), were found.

After 1260 Qara-Qorum became the center for ARIQ-BÖKE's resistance to QUBILAI KHAN (1260–94). Qubilai, whose base was North China, blockaded the city, which led to starvation. By 1263 Ariq-Böke was confiscating goods even from the religious leaders, but Qubilai's victory in 1264 reopened trade with China. In 1289 as QAIDU KHAN again challenged Qubilai's control of Mongolia, the Mongol general BAYAN CHINGSANG established a Pacification Commission and a Chief Military Command there. More than 100,000 bushels of grain were budgeted annually to supply the city. In 1307 the Pacification Commission was elevated to a Branch Secretariat (effectively a provincial government) based at Qorum. With a massive infusion of cash, refugees were resettled and farms and workshops reopened. In 1312 the city's Chinese name, Helin (pronounced in the Middle Ages as Holum) was changed to Hening (Peaceful and Pacified).

In 1370 after the Mongol rulers fled from China, Ayushiridara Khan (1370–78) reestablished his capital at Qara-Qorum. Sometime after 1400 wars between the Northern Yuan emperors (1368–1636) and the OIRATS finally ruined Qara-Qorum. In 1585 the ruins of the town were reused to build the new monastery ERDENI ZUU. Today Qara-Qorum (Kharkhorin in modern Mongolian) is a state farm with irrigation-based agriculture as well as a cultural and tourist site. Mongolians revere two stone turtles, Qara-Qorum's only visible remains, for their healing powers.

See also ARCHAEOLOGY.

Qara'unas A mixed group of Mongols on the frontier of India, the Qara'unas were turbulent but valued for their fierceness by both the Chaghatayid and Il-khanid states. ÖGEDEI KHAN (1229–41) first dispatched Mongol TAMMACHI troops to garrison the area of Afghanistan facing the sultanate of Delhi in Hindustan. Each branch of the imperial family sent non-Chinggisid commanders (NOYAN) of their own entourage. Thus, CHA'ADAI sent Dayir Ba'atur (d. 1241–42) of the Qongqotan, and BATU sent Negüder (fl. 1238–62). Ögedei and his successors gave command of these two *tammachi tümens* (10,000s) to two Toluid *noyans*, first Mönggetü Sa'ur of the Besüd, and then Sali of the TATARS, with campgrounds in Taloqan and Qonduz (northeast Afghanistan). Military campaigns against Hindustan and KASHMIR yielded vast numbers of slaves. Most were sold, but intermarriages with captive Indian women produced by about 1270 a new generation who were called Qara'unas, from Mongolian *qara*, "dark."

MARCO POLO claimed they also learned the famous magical techniques of Kashmir and Tibet.

When MÖNGKE KHAN dispatched his brother HÜLE'Ü (r. 1256–65) to Iran, he ordered Sali and his units to serve Hüle'ü. By 1261, however, Negüder Noyan, acting on the orders of Batu's brother Berke (1257–66), was opposing Hüle'ü in Sistan. The next year Berke's partisans in Hüle'ü's entourage escaped east to Ghazni, where they merged with Negüder's troops. Eventually, the Chaghatayid Alghu Khan (1261–66) intervened, inciting the *noyans* to arrest Sali. By around 1275 a junior Chaghatayid prince, Mochi, ruled the Qara'unas in the area of Ghazni. (A Chaghatayid prince Tegüder, is, through an erroneous reading as Negüder, often confused with the Negüder Noyan of Sistan. In fact, Prince Tegüder had nothing to do with the Qara'unas.)

Despite these setbacks, the IL-KHANATE were able to recruit three *tümens* of soldiers among Sali's Qara'unas. Around 1262 Hüle'ü recruited for his son Abagha (1234–82), then viceroy in Khorasan, a KESHIG (royal guard) one *tümen* strong of Qara'unas under the command of Mönggetü's son. When Abagha became khan, he brought this Qara'una *tümen* west with him. After Abagha's death this Qara'una *tümen*, governed by TA'ACHAR of the Suqai'ud Baarin, became a turbulent independent force in Il-Khanid politics. As khan Abagha recruited another *keshig* for his own son Arghun (1260–91), who replaced him as viceroy of Khorasan. A third *tümen* of Qara'unas, under the commander NAWROZ, existed by 1284. Nawroz's 1289 rebellion broke up these two *tümens* into small bands, some loyal, some rebellious. Arghun's son Ghazan (1271–1304), first as viceroy of Khorasan and then as khan, reunified the Qara'unas in Khorasan and in the west under Sali's son Uladu.

In addition to using the services of Toluid-aligned Qara'unas, the Il-Khans vainly tried to control the Chaghatayid-aligned Qara'unas. After defeating a Chaghatayid invasion in 1270, Abagha Khan installed a dethroned Chaghatay khan, Mubarakshah (r. 1266), over the Negüderis (Negüder's old troops in Sistan) and reinstalled Mubarakshah's son over them in 1279. Even so, Chaghatayid-aligned Qara'una and Negüderi forces continued to raid Fars and Kerman in southern Iran until about 1300.

After 1300 the Chaghatay khans solidified their control over the Qara'unas nomadizing between Qonduz and Ghazni. From 1292 on raids on India resumed, and soon Du'a Khan (1282–1307) replaced Mochi's Muslim son 'Abdullah with his own sons, first Qutlugh-Khoja and then Esen-Buqa. From then on the Chaghatay khans appointed either a crown prince or a great emir (commander) as Qara'una viceroy. Thus, under Du'a's sons Kebeg (1318–26/7) and Eljigidei (1327–30) their brother Tarmashirin ruled the Qara'una. When Tarmashirin became khan (1331–34) he appointed over the Qara'unas his commander in chief, the giant Emir Burundai

(Boroldai) of the Oronar, whom MUHAMMAD ABU 'ABDUL-LAH IBN BATTUTA described as a pious Muslim who gave alms to Sufi brethren and kept the roads safe.

From 1306 on, as dissension weakened the Chaghatayids, Il-Khan Sultan Öljeitü (1304–16) settled dissident Chaghatayid and Ögedeid princes in Khorasan and by manipulating internecine conflicts briefly reoccupied Sistan and subdued the Negüderis in the east. In the backlash against Il-Khanid expansion, however, previously loyal Toluid Qara'unas fell under the influence of the resettled Khorasan Chaghatayids. Bektüt, the son of Uladu, joined the Chaghatayid prince Yasa'ur (1288–1320)'s rebellion in 1318–20. By this time the former Qara'unas of Nawroz had probably reformed as the Ja'un-i Ghurban (Three from a Hundred) near Tus. After the 1335 disintegration of the Il-Khanate the southward migration of the core Chaghatayid tribes intensified as the Qara'unas absorbed tribes from both the Chaghatayid and former Il-Khanid realms.

In 1346–47 the Qara'una emir Qazaghan (perhaps of Tibetan origin) overthrew the Chaghatayid Qazan Khan and controlled the khanate through puppet khans until his assassination in 1257/8. He and Burundai's son having married sisters, Qazaghan took over Burundai's *tümen* while rallying the southern Chaghatayid tribes in Khorasan and the upper Amu Dar'ya. Qazaghan's son 'Abdullah was murdered after attempting to move his base from the upper Amu Dar'ya to Samarqand. 'Abdullah's nephew Emir Husain rebuilt the Qara'unas' influence until he was defeated in 1369 by his former friend and rival TIMUR (Tamerlane, 1336?–1405) of the northern Chaghatayid Barulas tribe.

Temür gave the Qara'unas, still one of his empire's most powerful components, to his Barulas commander in chief (*amir al-umaara'*) Chekü. Chekü's son Jahanshah inherited this still-considerable "army of Qonduz and Baghlan," the term that now replaced the derogatory "Qara'una." The more isolated Negüderis of Sistan also came under Timür's rule in 1383. As late as Babur's time (1483–1530) significant communities among both the "army of Qonduz and Baghlan," by then called Hazaras, and the Negüderis, ancestors of today's Mogholi people, still spoke Mongolian.

See also HAZARAS; INDIA AND THE MONGOLS; MOGHOLI LANGUAGE AND PEOPLE.

Further reading: John Andrew Boyle, "The Mongol Commanders in Afghanistan and India according to the *Tabaqat-i Nasiri* of Juzjani," *Islamic Studies* (Islamabad) 2 (1963): 235–247; Hirotoshi Shimo, "Qaraunas in the Historical Materials of the Ilkhanate," *Memoirs of the Research Department of the Toyo Bunko* 35 (1977): 131–181.

Qarluqs

The Qarluq, a small nomadic Turkish tribe on the upper Irtysh River, participated in the Uighur rebellion of 742 that overthrew the Türks' Ashina dynasty. The Uighur khans soon drove the Qarluqs west until they occupied the Chu and Ili valleys, between the Tianshan Mountains and Lake Balkhash (*see* TÜRK EMPIRES; UIGHUR EMPIRE). The local sedentary population there spoke Sogdian, a language of the Iranian family. By 900 the Assyrian Christian Church of the East had churches in the area, but in the 10th century military pressure and commercial penetration won many converts to Islam. Several Qarluq clans also began to farm.

By the early 13th century the Muslim Qarluq khan held Qayaligh City (near modern Taldyqorghan in Kazakhstan) as a vassal to the Buddhist QARA-KHITAI (1131–1213). Resenting the Qara-Khitai's increasingly burdensome rule, the Qarluq khan, Arslan, submitted peacefully when CHINGGIS KHAN's (Genghis, 1206–27) commander, Qubilai Noyan of the Barulas clan, appeared in the area. In spring 1211 Arslan Khan went to Mongolia for an audience. Chinggis, planning the conquest of North China, could not immediately assist his new ally but granted him an imperial princess as a wife. Meanwhile, a Qarluq bandit, Ozar, had seized the cities of Almaligh (near modern Huocheng in Xinjiang) and Bolad (Fulad, near modern Bole in Xinjiang) from Qara-Khitai rule. He, too, submitted to Chinggis Khan and was to receive a Mongol princess as a bride. Although the Qara-Khitai captured and killed Ozar, Chinggis finally overthrew the Qara-Khitai in 1216 and restored Ozar's son Siqnaq Tegin to Almaligh. When Chinggis Khan went to war against KHORAZM in 1219, Arslan Khan and Siqnaq Tegin joined his campaign; Arslan Khan's 6,000 Qarluq troops joined the Mongols in the two lengthy sieges in northeast Afghanistan.

Before his death Chinggis Khan gave the Qarluq region to his second son, CHA'ADAI, as his territory. For fiscal purposes ÖGEDEI KHAN (1229–41) assigned the area to the Besh-Baligh province or department under Mahmud Yalavach (*see* MAHMUD YALAVACH AND MAS'UD BEG; PROVINCES IN THE MONGOL EMPIRE). The Qarluq vassals coexisted with Cha'adai and his family and the governor at Besh-Baligh until 1252. In that year, after purging his enemies, MÖNGKE KHAN (1251–59) gave Qayaligh to QAIDU KHAN (1236–1301), the grandson of Ögedei. In compensation, Arslan's son received the city of Özgön in the Ferghana valley, beginning a southwestward movement of the Qarluqs. QUBILAI KHAN occupied Almaligh from 1268 to 1276, when a princely rebellion gave control once again to Qaidu. After Qaidu's death Almaligh again became the Chaghatayid (Cha'adaid) capital.

Visitors to Almaligh in the 13th century noted the apple orchards and irrigated fields that grew cotton, while Qayaligh drew attention for its thronging markets. Religiously, the population was mostly Muslim, particularly the Qarluq nomads, but significant colonies of Uighur Buddhists, Assyrian Christians, Manicheans, and Chinese Taoists also existed. Qayaligh and Almaligh fell victim to the BLACK DEATH and the general crisis of the mid-14th century and were in ruins before 1400. Moving southwest, the Qarluqs appear in Transoxiana in the 15th century and today in northwest Afghanistan.

Further reading: Peter Golden, *An Introduction to the History of the Turkic Peoples: Ethnogenesis and State-Formation in Medieval and Early Modern Eurasia and the Middle East* (Wiesbaden: Otto Harrassowitz, 1992).

qatun See KHATUN.

Qidan *See* KITANS.

Qing dynasty (Ch'ing) China's last dynasty, the Qing dynasty (1636–1912) originated among the Inner Asian Manchus, and by both persuasion and force it extended its sway over almost all the Mongolian peoples. While Qing rule is often excoriated as a period of stagnation and decline, it saw the creation of most of Mongolia's traditional literary and folk cultural heritage.

ORIGINS AND CONQUEST OF INNER MONGOLIA

The Qing dynasty originated among the Jurchen people of Manchuria (present-day Northeast China), who had earlier founded the JIN DYNASTY (1115–1234). After the Mongol YUAN DYNASTY fell in 1368 (*see* MANCHURIA AND THE MONGOL EMPIRE), the Jurchen became tributary to the MING DYNASTY (1368–1644) in 1387. Like the Mongol THREE GUARDS to their east, they enjoyed the rights both to present "tribute" (really a form of state-subsidized trade) and to participate in horse fairs. While the Jurchen had earlier had their own script modeled on the Kitan script (*see* KITAN LANGUAGE AND SCRIPT), it went out of use sometime after 1525. Mostly living by farming, the Jurchens were also fully part of the Inner Asian horse-archer and hunting culture. The Qing founder, Nurhachi (b. 1558, r. 1616–26), sometimes emphasized his Jurchen people's difference from the Mongols, telling eastern Inner Mongolian chiefs in 1619 that since the Mongols were pastoralists and the Jurchens farmers they were two different people. At other times, however, he also stated that compared to the Chinese and the Koreans, the Jurchen and Mongolian clothes and way of life were as one and only their language different. This ambivalence between East Asian and Inner Asian identity would remain with the Qing almost to its end.

In 1583 Nurhachi succeeded his father, Taksi, who had been treacherously killed by the Ming, as head of the Aisin (Golden) Gioro clan (*hala*) near the (ethnic Chinese) Han-settled Liaodong area (modern Liaoning). During Nurhachi's rise he alternately allied and battled with the rival Jurchen tribes and the Mongols of both the KHORCHIN and southern KHALKHA (later eastern Inner Mongolia's JUU UDA league) *tümens*. In 1593 he defeated a Khorchin-Jurchen "league of nine tribes." From 1612 Khorchin and southern Khalkha chiefs contracted marriage alliances with Nurhachi and presented tribute. In 1616 Nurhachi proclaimed himself "bright KHAN" (*genggiyen han*) of the revived Jin dynasty, and in 1621 he conquered Liaodong.

In 1624 the Khorchin under their senior chief Uuba (d. 1632) revolted as a block against the suzerainty of LIGDAN KHAN (1604–34), the last emperor of the NORTHERN YUAN DYNASTY (1368–1634), and allied with Nurhachi. From 1626 to 1629 the Three Guard Uriyangkhan (later the KHARACHIN) and the southern Khalkha did the same with Nurhachi's son and heir, Hong Taiji (b. 1592, r. 1627–43). In 1632 Hong Taiji and his eastern Mongolian allies launched a grand expedition against the CHAKHAR. Ligdan fled to ORDOS and then Kökenuur (Qinghai), where he died of smallpox. In 1635 his sons led Ligdan's Chakhar people to surrender to Hong Taiji's armies. In that year and the next Hong Taiji renamed his people the "Manchus" and his dynasty the Qing (Pure) and organized all of Inner Mongolia into BANNERS (appanages).

Mongolian cultural influence on the early Manchus was very important. The scholars of the early Manchus were the *baksi* (from Mongolian *bagshi*), who knew both the Mongolian and the Chinese languages. In 1599 Erdeni and Gagai *baksi*s adopted the UIGHUR-MONGOLIAN SCRIPT to write Manchu. From around 1620 to 1633 other *baksi*s such as Dahai, Kara, and Kûrchan extended contemporary ideas on reforming the Mongolian script to create a new Manchu script. Hong Taiji was closely familiar with the *bilig*s (wise sayings) of CHINGGIS KHAN, which he quoted to his entourage.

Both Nurhachi and Hong Taiji viewed their empire as in part a successor to the Mongol Northern Yuan Dynasty. The proclamation of the revived Jin dynasty in 1616 was preceded by marital alliances with Mongol rulers, and that of the Qing on May 15, 1636, was preceded by the submission of all Inner Mongolia. Ligdan Khan's sons brought to Hong Taiji's capital, Mukden, the "precious jade seal," which Mongolian legend said had been born in the hands of Chinggis Khan, and the Mahakala image of QUBILAI KHAN's chaplain 'PHAGS-PA LAMA (1235–80). They also presented Ligdan's two queens, who Hong Taiji made his senior wives alongside his three Khorchin queens. Imperial titles and reign years were all proclaimed in Manchu, Mongolian, and Chinese, a practice that continued to the end of the dynasty.

The early oaths of alliance of the Khorchins and Uriyangkhan (Kharachin) in 1624 and 1628 were both sealed with an offering of a white horse, a black ox, and a bowl of liquor. After the coronation of 1636, the relation was no longer one of equal alliance, but rather one in which the emperor (*Bogda Khaan*, Holy Khan in Mongolian) gathered around him both inner (Manchu) and outer (Mongol) noblemen, to whom he granted titles as princes and dukes and who in return strove to win commendation through meritorious service. The new

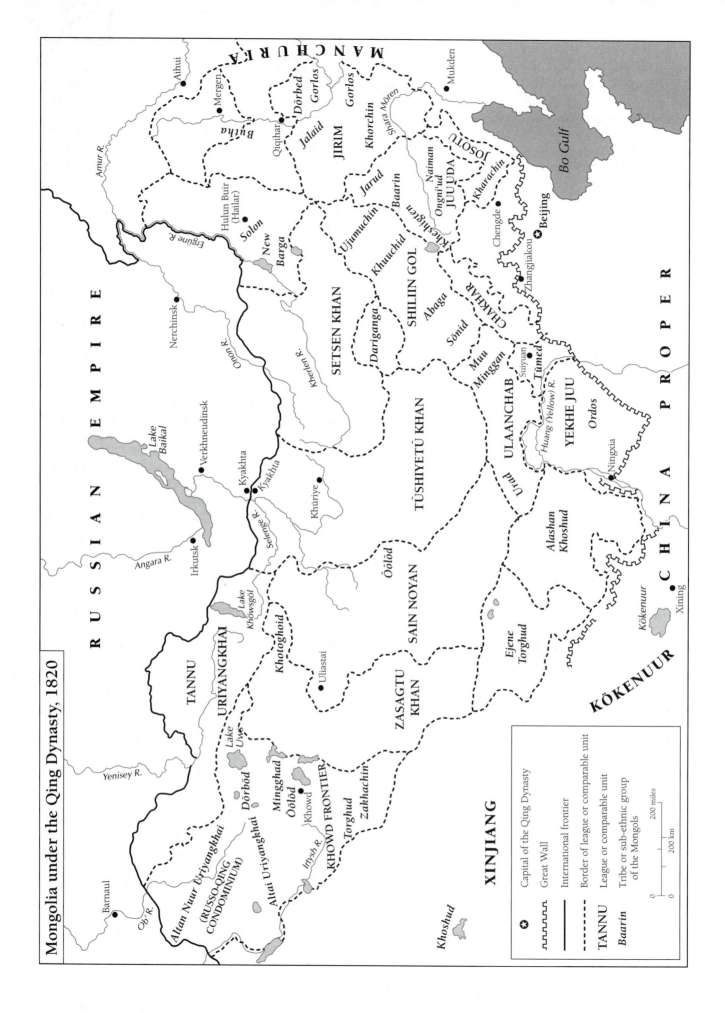

Mongolia under the Qing Dynasty, 1820

RUSSIAN EMPIRE

MANCHURIA

CHINA PROPER

KÖKENUUR

XINJIANG

Amur R.
Aihui
Mergen
Qiqihar
Butha
Dörbed
Gorlos
Jalaid
Gorlos
JIRIM
Khorchin
Shara Mören
Mukden
Bo Gulf

Hulun Buir (Hailar)
Solon
New Barga
Ergüne R.
Jarud
Baarin
Ujumuchin
Naiman
Ongni'ud
JUUDA
Kharachin
JOSOU
Khüshigten
Chengde
Beijing

Nerchinsk
Onon R.
Kherlen R.
SETSEN KHAN
Khuuchid
SHILIIN GOL
Abaga
CHAKHAR
Zhangjiakou

Lake Baikal
Verkhneudinsk
Dariganga
Sönid
Muu Minggan
Suiyan
Tümed
ULAANCHAB
YEKHE JUU
Ordos

Irkutsk
Angara R.
Kyakhta
Kyakhta
Selenge R.
Khüriye
TÜSHIYETÜ KHAN
Ural
Huang (Yellow) R.
Ningxia

Lake Khöwsgöl
Öölöd
SAIN NOYAN
Alashan Khoshud
Kökenuur
Xining

TANNU
URIYANGKHAI
Khotoghoid
Uliastai
Ejene Torghud

Lake Uws
ZASAGTU KHAN

Yenisey R.
Dörböd
Mingghad
Öölöd
Khowd
Torghud
Zakhachin
KHOWD FRONTIER

Barnaul
Ob R.
Altan Nuur Uriyangkhai (RUSSO-QING CONDOMINIUM)
Altai Uriyangkhai
Irtysh R.

Khoshud

Legend

⊛ Capital of the Qing Dynasty
〰 Great Wall
— International frontier
--- Border of league or comparable unit
TANNU League or comparable unit
Baarin Tribe or sub-ethnic group of the Mongols

200 miles
200 km

emperor promised to treat the Mongols and Manchu princes equally. Likewise, the direction of marriage alliance changed. At first it was the Khorchins who honored the Manchu emperors and nobles with their sisters and daughters. After 1636 the honor went the other way, and Mongols were eager to become *efu* (imperial sons-in-law) of the Manchu emperors.

Hong Taiji also constructed the institutions by which the Qing would rule the Mongols until 1911. Already the Manchu army had been organized into eight banners, each named after the color of its battle standard. From 1622 more and more Mongol noblemen and subjects were directly attached to the Manchu armies. In 1635 Hong Taiji organized these units into EIGHT BANNERS, parallel to the earlier Manchu Eight Banners units. A year earlier he had dispatched two commissioners to survey Inner Mongolia, define the Mongols' traditional territories, and confirm submissive noblemen in their rule. The nobilities' appanages were renamed banners (*khoshuu*) but unlike the Eight Banners largely retained their traditional structure. At each banner's head was a hereditary, and usually Chinggisid, ZASAG, or ruler. To supervise these autonomous banners he created in 1636 the Mongolian Department, soon renamed the LIFAN YUAN (Court of Dependencies). From 1638 Hong Taiji had been hearing appeals from Mongols, and in 1643 he promulgated the Qing's earliest law code for the Mongols (*see* LIFAN YUAN ZELI).

SHUNZHI AND KANGXI, 1644–1722

In 1644 the regent Dorgon led the Manchu forces to victory against rebels fighting over the corpse of China's Ming dynasty. In Beijing he proclaimed Hong Taiji's son by his first Khorchin wife, Empress Xiaozhuang (1613–88), the new Shunzhi emperor (personal name Fulin, r. 1644–61). After the conquest of China the Qing began to see itself more as a successor of the Ming than as an Inner Asian state. Inner Asian Buddhism remained important, but with Shunzhi's reception of the Fifth Dalai Lama in 1653, the Sa-skya-pa sect with its connotations of Mongol Yuan legitimacy was replaced by the Dalai Lama's up-and-coming dGe-lugs-pa (Yellow Hat) order (*see* TWO CUSTOMS). In 1659 the Lifan Yuan was put under the Board of Rites, which normally handled foreign envoys, thus downgrading Mongolian ties.

In 1635–37 the northern Khalkhas of Mongolia proper sent missions to open "tribute" relations. Khalkha raids on Inner Mongolia, the rebellion of the SHILIIN GOL prince Tenggis in 1646, who received Khalkha assistance, the rebellion of the prince Jamsu in Ordos in 1649, and the defection of the Khalkha ruler Bondar with his subjects to the Qing in 1653 all complicated relations. In 1655, however, the Khalkha became regular tributaries of the Qing. In return for an oath of allegiance and a tribute of "nine whites" (one white camel and eight white horses), the Khalkha princes received gifts and also the right to engage in trade. The Qing enfeoffed eight Khalkha noblemen as *zasags* (rulers) of eight Khalkha banners. In reality, however, "tribute relations" meant only a subsidized trading relationship and a forswearing of active hostilities. Beyond the Khalkhas, the OIRATS, too, were allowed to present "tribute," receiving "gifts" in return (*see* TRIBUTE SYSTEM).

After Shunzhi's death the regent for his son, the Kangxi emperor (personal name Xuanye, 1662–1722), immediately restored the high rank of the Lifan Yuan. Kangxi had a strong personal interest in Inner Asia, but from 1673 to 1681 he was occupied with a great rebellion in China and the 1675 rebellion of Ligdan's grandson Burni in Chakhar. After the suppression of Burni's rebellion the Chakhar aristocracy was stripped of its rights, and its banners were integrated into the Eight Banners system under an appointive official hierarchy.

By 1681, when the Qing was again at peace, GALDAN BOSHOGTU KHAN (b. 1644, r. 1678–97) of the Zünghar tribe of the Oirats had overthrown the previously dominant Khoshud tribe, something Kangxi had publicly censured. The Oirats had been bound in a collective security agreement with the Khalkhas since 1640 (*see* MONGOL-OIRAT CODE) and this agreement now brought both them and the Qing into the quarrel between the Khalkhas' Tüshiyetü Khan Chakhundorji (r. 1655–99) in the east and the Zasagtu Khan Tsenggün (r. 1670–86) in the west. Eventually, Chakhundorji attacked Tsenggün's young son, provoking Galdan to undertake a full-scale invasion of Khalkha in spring 1688. Pushed by events, Kangxi accepted the full submission of Chakhundorji, his brother, the great INCARNATE LAMA the FIRST JIBZUNDAMBA KHUTUGTU (1635–1723), and the Khalkha nobility at the DOLONNUUR ASSEMBLY in 1691, but not until 1694 did he prepare for a final war on Galdan. In 1696 and 1697 Kangxi personally participated in the expedition against Galdan's weakening forces until the news came of Galdan's death by disease in April 1697.

Galdan's overreaching pushed several blocks of Mongols into the Qing orbit. The Khalkhas were now organized into 34 banners, this time under tight control from Beijing. The UPPER MONGOLS of Kökenuur (Qinghai), mostly Khoshud Oirats, had resented Galdan's usurpation and submitted to Qing suzerainty in 1697. Several Khoshud and Zünghar princes in the Oirat heartland of Zungharia also deserted and were resettled in ALASHAN and central Khalkha, respectively (*see* ÖÖLÖD). In 1715 border conflicts in Khalkha with Galdan's rival and successor, TSEWANG-RABTAN (r. 1694–1727) led to the second Qing-Zünghar war. Kangxi defended the Qing positions in Khalkha, Hami, and Turpan while using conflicts over the Dalai Lama to install Qing troops in Lhasa in 1720.

The struggle with Galdan also invigorated Kangxi's religious policy. Trained in piety by his beloved Khorchin grandmother Empress Xiaozhuang, who had raised him after his parents' early deaths, he was profoundly impressed by the First Jibzundamba Khutugtu, who remained at his court from 1691 to 1701. Kangxi created the position of JANGJIYA KHUTUGTU as the supreme authority over all Inner Mongolian monasteries and sponsored the publication of both a special red-letter Tibetan bKa'-'gyur (Buddhist canon) and a Mongolian version in 1720. The emperor also transmitted his devotion to his sons, such as Prince Yunli (Kheng-ze, 1697–1738), who developed his own coterie of nonsectarian Buddhists and wrote two Buddhist treatises in Mongolian. While Manchu patronage of Mongolian Buddhism has often been seen as a cynical but effective act of realpolitik, in Kangxi's case his undoubted sincerity helped win over many of the most prestigious noble families.

RESISTANCE AND SOCIAL CHANGES, 1723–1796

Despite the Qing's strong position among the Mongols at Kangxi's death, serious opposition developed under his son and successor, the Yongzheng emperor (personal name Yinzhen, r. 1723–35). The 1723–24 rebellion of Lubsang-Danzin of the Upper Mongols of Kökenuur drew in not only many Mongol princes but also vast numbers of Tibetan nomads and monks. In 1724 the surviving Upper Mongol nobles were organized into banners, and their former Tibetan subjects were organized as independent tribes. In Khalkha, during the deep incursions of the Zünghar ruler GALDAN-TSEREN (r. 1727–45) in 1731–32, the Zasagtu Khan Tsewangjab (r. 1703–32) abandoned his army rather than fight and had to be cashiered; almost two-thirds of a Khalkha detachment sent to ERDENI ZUU deserted; previously surrendered Öölöds defected back to the invaders; and unspecified disturbances roiled Setsen Khan AIMAG. Although most of the Khalkha princes remained loyal and fought off the invaders, the cost of sustaining the war evidently bore heavily on them.

Throughout his empire the Yongzheng emperor vigorously centralized his rule, and he did the same in Inner Asia. Inner Mongolia was already tightly controlled, but in Khalkha he created the office of assistant general to be filled by loyal Khalkha princes, organized the princes there into LEAGUES, split off Sain Noyan *aimag* from Tüshiyetü Khan *aimag*, and appointed new AMBANS and generals in chief for Kökenuur, Lhasa, and Khalkha. His 1727 treaty of Kyakhta with Russia sacrificed traditional Khalkha claims over the Buriat Mongols but secured him a firm and well-policed northern frontier. He also strengthened the border by settling Daur, Ewenki (Solon), BARGA, and Öölöd bannermen in HULUN BUIR, a fertile pasture at the strategic point where Khalkha, Manchuria, and Russia met.

Yongzheng realized the strain in Khalkha and did not follow up his victories against the Zünghars. His son, the Qianlong emperor (personal name Hongli, r. 1735–96), confirmed this cease-fire with an official peace treaty in 1739. In 1753, however, with the political disintegration of the ZÜNGHARS, Qianlong mustered a massive army that in 1755 effortlessly occupied the Zünghar heartland with the assistance of the defecting Oirat nobleman AMURSANAA. When Amursanaa rebelled, the Zünghars were almost exterminated, while Qianlong resettled Chakhars, Solons, and Shibes (a Manchu-related people) in Xinjiang. The FLIGHT OF THE KALMYKS from the Volga back to Xinjiang in 1777 was taken by Qianlong as the ultimate confirmation of the rightness of his policies, which brought virtually all the Mongolian people under Qing rule.

The collapse of the Zünghars coincided with the ZUD (winter disasters) and smallpox in Khalkha, and provisioning the Qing expeditionary forces had been very expensive. In 1756 the public debt of the Khalkha leagues and banners to Chinese merchant companies amounted to 155,700 taels of silver. Chinese merchants had entered Mongolia with Kangxi's armies in 1696, and the opening of KYAKHTA on the border as an entrepôt for the Russian trade in 1728 had increased the attractions of commerce in Mongolia. Despite Qing efforts to limit mercantile activity, debts to Chinese traders were already serious by mid-century. In that year, widespread hardship and Qianlong's execution of a Khalkha prince sparked the widespread and uncoordinated unrest known as CHINGGÜNJAB'S REBELLION. Numerous executions were followed by serious efforts from the court to liquidate the Mongols' debt to Chinese merchants.

Through his intimate relationship with his classmate and chaplain the Second Jangjiya Khutugtu Rolbidorji (1716–86), Qianlong became the Qing emperor most deeply involved in Buddhist practice. Precisely due to his own high initiations, however, Qianlong confidently directed Buddhist affairs with an eye to increasing his dynasty's authority. The emperor began to control the SECOND JIBZUNDAMBA KHUTUGTU's movements, and after the death of the Second Jibzundamba Khutugtu in 1758, whose loyalty had wavered in Chinggünjab's Rebellion, he ordered all future incarnations of his lineage found in Tibet. In 1793 he sent a golden urn to Lhasa to be used in a random drawing to decide the final candidates for the highest incarnations. Qianlong's reign also saw the final multiplication of banners in Khalkha to 86 and the replacement of Mongolian legal principles by Chinese. In 1781, as a reward to the Mongols, Qianlong decreed that all of their princes would inherit their titles in perpetuity.

By this time the Manchu emperor was being regularly identified in texts, popular songs, and religious art as an incarnation of the bodhisattva Manjushri, traditionally the special protector of China. He was thus on a level with the Dalai Lama, the incarnation of Avalokieshvara, the protector of Tibet, and Chinggis Khan the incarnation of Vajrapani, the protector of Mongolia. The cult site of Wutai Shan Mountain in Shanxi, also associated with Manjushri, became a major pilgrimage destination for the

Mongols; its attractiveness was increased by the frequent residence there of the Jangjiya Khutugtu. The capital of Beijing was also identified in both political ritual and song as the mandala (a geometrical representation of a "Buddha field," or perfected world) of the Buddha Vairochana.

SOCIAL AND ECONOMIC DRIFT, 1796–1862

With the retirement of Qianlong in 1796 and his death three years later, the heroic phase of the Qing Empire passed. The traditional incarnate lama leadership also declined. None of the Jibzundamba Khutugtus between 1813 and 1870 reached 30 years of age, nor did any of the Dalai Lamas between 1804 and 1876. This left the Third Jangjiya Khutugtu (1787–1846) and the Fourth Panchen Lama (1781–1854) as the most active figures in Mongolia and Tibet.

The new Jiaqing emperor (personal name Yunyan, r. 1796–1820) reversed his predecessor's restrictions on Chinese trade in Mongolia, allowing merchants to trade on the spot in the Mongolian banners. In 1811 the minister of the Lifan Yuan advocated the compilation of a new law code, one that resulted in the 1819 promulgation of the *Lifan Yuan zeli*. The long peace saw the apex of wealth of the religious institutions in Khalkha and new construction at Erdeni Zuu, Khüriye (*see* ULAANBAATAR), and elsewhere. From the 1776 introduction of the full Mahakala services in Erdeni Zuu to the 1811 inauguration of TSAM dances in Khüriye's main monastery, Nom-un Yekhe Khüriye, virtually all the institutions and services current in Tibet were introduced into Khalkha's monasteries. In the 1830s the Qing government took significant steps to limit the expansion of the clerical estate.

During the succeeding period, from 1820 to 1850, for the first time published figures give a picture of demographic and economic trends in one of Khalkha's four *aimags* (provinces). Figures for Setsen Khan province show the lay population rising from about 106,000 in 1828 to 130,000 in 1835 and dropping to 124,000 in 1841. Livestock figures for the same years, however, show a sharp drop, from 1,820,000 head to 1,320,000 and then 1,225,000. Figures from the Jibzundamba Khutugtu's personal herd and for the herd of his subjects, while difficult to interpret, show peaks around 1773–78 and 1794–97 and declines thereafter. The cause of this decline is unclear but is probably linked to increasing the indebtedness of Mongolia as a whole, which led to higher offtake of livestock to China proper. At the same time, influences from the consistent cooling trend in Mongolia from around 1780 to 1870 cannot be excluded (*see* CLIMATE).

Traditional status distinctions began to be blurred. The position of the petty nobility (the TAIJI class) declined sharply, while the banner officials, who were often commoners, expanded their wealth. The economic position of the state commoners remained stagnant at the bottom,

lower even than that of the *taijis*' "serfs" (*khamjilga*) and far lower than the wealthy ecclesiastical subjects (*shabi*).

After 1840 the troubles of the Qing court with European gunboats and the Taiping rebellions drew Qing attention away from Inner Asia. At one point of financial embarrassment during the Opium War (1840–42), the Qing court was reduced to paying the Mongolian *zasags*' regular salaries in silver-plated copper ingots. From the period of the death of the Third Jangjiya (1846) and the Fourth Panchen (1854) to about 1890, none of the great incarnate lamas in Tibet and Mongolia were of age. Despite this lack of strong leadership, the Mongols remained loyal to the Qing dynasty. The Khorchin prince Senggerinchin (known to the British as Sam Collinson, 1811–65) led a Mongol volunteer cavalry against the Chinese Taipings from 1853, against the invading British-French army at Tianjin in 1859, and against the Nian rebels until his death in battle. The celebration of his battles in the Khorchin folksong "Seng Wang" (Prince Seng) showed the strength of popular Qing loyalism.

SOCIAL AND ECONOMIC DECLINE, 1862–1901

In 1868–70 bands of Hui (Chinese-speaking Muslim), rebels from Gansu, and Turkestani rebels from Xinjiang entered Alashan (Alxa), Ordos, the Khowd frontier, and western Khalkha, seizing livestock and burning monasteries and sanctuaries. Turkestani rebels besieged KHOWD CITY and sacked ULIASTAI before being stopped on the road to Khüriye, while small bands reached as far at Mergen Wang banner (modern East Gobi province) and almost 150 kilometers within (100 miles) of Ulaanbaatar. Swarms of beggars testified to the devastation of the decade. The ravages of the Muslim rebels were succeeded by the security issue of Russian expansion. In 1860 a Russian consulate was opened in Mongolia. Already in 1862 a Russian government commission publicly announced that Russia should strive for a natural evolution of Mongolia away from Qing control and into Russian hands. Thus, Qing military mobilization in Mongolia, begun in response to the Muslim rebellion, continued in response to the chronic Russian threat.

Muslim raids, cattle murrain, the cost of Qing expenses for fortifications, and the permanent garrisoning of soldiers in Khüriye may have been responsible for the steady decline in livestock and population figures in the decade after 1864 for the Jibzundamba Khutugtu's estate and the GREAT SHABI (his personal subjects). While the population of beggars later declined, population and livestock numbers continued to drop. Figures for Setsen Khan show the lay population having declined from 122,000 in 1841 to 90,000 in 1907. While this population decline has often been blamed on monasticism, the Mongolian herd size declined even faster than the population, suggesting that monasticism was not the cause of economic decline but a response to it. The already staggering indebtedness of the Mongols to Chinese merchants and moneylenders made it impossible for them to halt the growing export of animals and animal products generated by China's entry into the world market for wool.

NEW POLICIES AND REVOLT, 1901–1911

After the Qing dynasty's disastrous defeat at the hands of Japan in 1894–95, Beijing faced the possibility of imminent partition by the powers. Europeans and Japanese divided the empire into spheres of influence within which each power had preferential rights in the construction of railways and in forming direct relations with the local government. Mongolia, Inner and Outer, fell at first entirely into the Russian sphere. The Trans-Siberian Railroad was extended through the Hulun Buir district and northern Manchuria as the Chinese Eastern Railway in 1900. With the outbreak of the anti-Christian Boxer movement, the Russians occupied all of Manchuria and began cultivating friendly princes in eastern Inner Mongolia. The Russian advance into Korea, however, provoked the Russo-Japanese War of 1904–05. Southeastern Inner Mongolia immediately moved into the Japanese sphere, although a formal division of spheres was not achieved until 1912.

After the Boxer movement was crushed in 1900 and a crippling indemnity imposed on Beijing, the Qing court moved in a radically new direction. The NEW POLICIES (*Xinzheng*) in Inner Asia completely reversed the previous policy of keeping Mongols and Chinese separate. CHINESE COLONIZATION, which had been proceeding all along the Inner Mongolian border since the 18th century, was suddenly taken over and vigorously promoted by the Qing government. New schools, hygiene bureaus, army units, and schools were all to be established and paid for by the proceeds of colonization and the opening of mines, either by Qing or foreign investors.

The Mongols strongly resisted these policies. The approval of government-sponsored Chinese colonization seemed to mark the death knell of the Mongols as a people. In Tibet as well the New Policies caused violent opposition, eventually driving the Dalai Lama into exile in India. Opposition included bureaucratic obstruction and protests from the Khalkha princes, popular *DUGUILANG* movements in Ordos, insurrections in eastern Inner Mongolia, and riots in the streets of Khüriye.

Even where the substance of the policies was not objectionable, the court put them in the hands of *ambans* and new frontier officials, effectively stripping the Mongolian banners of their autonomy. In southeast Inner Mongolia Prince Güngsangnorbu (1871–1931) and others responded by creating their own modern-style schools and police bureaus, funded and controlled by their own banners with Japanese assistance. However, the Qing government refused to recognize officially such locally controlled New Policies (*see* NEW SCHOOLS MOVEMENTS).

Most significantly, the Jibzundamba Khutugtu, who had appealed to the Russian government for protection in 1900, began to conspire with his Khalkha nobility, ecclesiastical officials, and emigré Inner Mongolian dukes and princes on an approach to Russia. By August 1911 the last *amban* in Khüriye, Sandô (b. 1875), had become aware of the Khutugtu's plans, yet the Qing dynasty's position in Mongolia was too weak and the incarnate lama's prestige too high for him even to attempt punishment.

On October 10 a republican Chinese uprising broke out against the Qing in Wuchang (modern Wuhan) in central China. The Jibzundamba Khutugtu exploited the uncertainty to call Mongolian troops into Khüriye, while the Russians shipped weapons to their consulate. Although the Qing defeated uprisings in northern China, the Khalkhas declared independence from the Qing on December 1 and enthroned the Jibzundamba Khutugtu as the new Bogda Khan, "Holy Emperor," on December 29.

Meanwhile, in Inner Mongolia the princes waited to see whether the Qing court would survive. Modernizing eastern Inner Mongolian princes such as Güngsangnorbu were skeptical that a Tibetan cleric could deliver the kind of modernization Mongolia needed. They would have preferred to remain with a rump Qing state including Manchuria and Mongolia, yet a south Chinese republic was ethnically and politically anathema as well. Other Inner Mongolian princes eagerly supported the Khalkha declaration of independence. By January 1912 the Qing court's chief general, Yuan Shikai, was negotiating with the republicans. On February 12, 1912, he forced the last Qing emperor, Puyi (the Xuantong emperor, 1909–12), to abdicate and recognize the republican regime. Most of the Inner Mongolian princes and commoners as well supported union with Khalkha, while Prince Güngsangnorbu and others vainly pursued the idea of a Qing restoration with Japanese assistance. Within a few months Yuan Shikai forced all the Inner Mongolian banners to submit to the Republic of China, leaving invasion from Mongolia as their only option for independence.

LEGACY OF THE QING

By the 1920s the "Young Mongols" in Mongolia and Inner Mongolia and the Chinese nationalists were united in excoriating Manchu rule as a period of evil and regressive tyranny. The Qing were seen from the hindsight of 300 years as pursuing a planned policy of imperial expansion in Mongolia. The Manchus were blamed for cynically encouraging Buddhism to sap the Mongols' morale and to decrease their numbers. The animosities and misunderstandings among Mongols of various groups were denounced as fruits of the Qing's "divide and rule" policy, exemplified in the banner system. The policy of preserving the Mongols' separation was treated as a deliberate device to keep the Mongols stupid and ignorant of the outside world.

However, few of the extreme accusations against Qing policies hold up to critical scrutiny. Caution more than aggressiveness marked the Qing's dealings with the Ligdan Khan, the Khalkha Mongols, and the Zünghars. Once involved in all-out war, the Qing armies were ruthless and thorough in crushing opposition. Nevertheless, in each new theater it took literally decades of conflict to provoke the final decision to pursue total conquest. Religiously, the Qing court's support for grassroots monasticism was more nominal than real, and the emperors focused on increasing Mongolian martial abilities, not weakening them. Moreover, the most active religious policy was pursued precisely by emperors such as Kangxi and Qianlong, who acted as devout Buddhist initiates, not cynical manipulators. The banner system grew out of the already existing rule by a decentralized confederation of Chinggisid nobility. While undoubtedly designed to maintain Qing control, it was not a radical deviation from the pre-Qing political order. While the later part of Qing rule saw clear demographic and economic decline, that must be balanced against both the maintenance of peace and the just as clear prosperity of the late 18th–early 19th centuries.

Virtually all the policies and attendant social problems found among the Mongols in 1900 were also found among the Manchu peoples of Manchuria and the Buriats and Kalmyks of Russia. The Qing dynasty's system of legal and social separation was seen as the best way peacefully to integrate hierarchical, kinship-oriented, and barely monetized peoples like the Mongols into a larger, socially mobile, impersonal, and commercialized polity like China's. Rulers have independently invented analogous systems many times, from the Jesuit mission communities of Paraguay to the Speransky reforms in Siberia. While often far from ideal in their results, critics have generally offered few real alternatives.

See also ANIMAL HUSBANDRY AND NOMADISM; CHINESE TRADE AND MONEYLENDING; *JAM*; JIBZUNDAMBA KHUTUGTU, EIGHTH; KINSHIP SYSTEM; LAMAS AND MONASTICISM; LITERATURE; SOCIAL CLASSES IN THE QING PERIOD; *SUM*; TIBETAN CULTURE IN MONGOLIA; XINJIANG MONGOLS.

Further reading: Christopher P. Atwood, "'Worshiping Grace': The Language of Loyalty in Qing Mongolia," *Late Imperial China* 21 (2000): 86–139; C. R. Bawden, *The Modern History of Mongolia* (1969; rpt., London: Kegan Paul International, 1989); Nicola D. Cosmo and Dalizhabu [Darijab] Bao, *Manchu-Mongol Relations on the Eve of the Qing Conquest: A Documentary History* (Leiden: E. J. Brill, 2003); Evariste-Régis Huc and Joseph Gabet, *Travels in Tartary, Thibet, and China, 1844–1846*, trans. William Hazlitt (1928; rpt., New York: Dover, 1987); Hidehiro Okada, "The Yuan Seal in Manchu Hands: The Source of the Ch'ing Legitimacy," in *Altaic Religious Beliefs and Practices*, ed. Géza Bethlenfalvy et al. (Budapest: Research Group for Altaic Studies, 1992), 267–271; A. M. Pozdneyev, *Mongolia and the Mongols*, ed. John R. Krueger, trans. John Roger Shaw and Dale Plank (Bloomington: Indiana University, 1971).

Qipchaq Khanate   *See* GOLDEN HORDE.

Qipchaqs (Kypchaks, Comans, Polovtsi) A sprawling, disunited tribal confederacy, the Qipchaqs formed the base population of the Mongol GOLDEN HORDE.

The Qipchaqs first appeared around 750 as a Turkish tribe occupying the ALTAI RANGE. Later they moved west and joined the Kimek confederacy in western Siberia. Beginning around 1017 tribes fleeing the growing Kitan Empire in Mongolia pushed the Qipchaqs south and east. From 1070 until the rise of the Mongols, the Qipchaqs dominated the vast steppe from central Kazakhstan to the Danube River. The Qipchaqs had no unified state and never attempted to conquer their settled neighbors. Instead, clans, each under its own chief, either raided their neighbors or served them as mercenaries. Qipchaq warriors buttressed rulers in Bulgaria, Hungary, and GEORGIA, as did the Qangli (eastern Qipchaqs) in KHORAZM. Russia and CRIMEA, being less unified, suffered more from Qipchaq raids, although interethnic marriage among the chiefly families occurred there, too. Christian influence on the western Qipchaqs was significant, but most adhered to their native religion.

The first Mongol contact with the Qipchaqs came after 1216, when Qodu, a defeated chieftain of the Mongol MERKID tribe, took refuge among the Ölberi chiefs by the Ural Mountains. The Ölberi rejected CHINGGIS KHAN'S (Genghis, 1206–27) demand to surrender the fugitive, and the khan dispatched SÜBE'ETEI BA'ATUR, who raided the Qipchaqs and killed Qodu before returning. After the Mongols' great campaign against Khorazm, Sübe'etei and JEBE again swung north through Derbent to reconnoiter the territory. After they defeated the Qipchaqs of the Kuban steppe, the western Qipchaq leader Köten (Kotian, Kötöny) received aid from his Russian son-in-law Mstislav of Halych, but Jebe and Sübe'etei crushed the combined Russian-Qipchaq army at Kalka River (May 31, 1223) before turning east. Meanwhile, Chinggis Khan had assigned to JOCHI, his eldest son, the conquest of the Qipchaqs. Jochi (d. 1225?) subdued the Qangli by 1224 but refused to move west, angering his father.

In 1229 Chinggis's son ÖGEDEI KHAN (1229–41) sent Kökedei and Sönidei to conquer the Qipchaqs and other people along the Volga River and in the Ural Mountains, such as the BULGHARS, Saqsin, and Bashkir (Bashkort). The Mongol force proved too small for the fierce resistance of the Qipchaq chief Bachman, and in 1235 Ögedei mobilized a much larger expedition headed by his nephews BATU (son of Jochi) and Möngke and his son Güyüg together with Sübe'etei. Some Ölberi Qipchaq chiefs surrendered and joined the Mongol army, but most fled the area; some joined Bachman's guerrilla resistance. Möngke finally captured Bachman's island base in the Volga delta in winter 1236–37. By autumn 1238 other princes had conquered the Qipchaqs of Crimea and the Ukrainian steppe. Köten led a large number of Qipchaqs in flight to Hungary, which the Mongols invaded next. Qipchaq chiefs in the Caucasus resisted until 1242.

Batu and the sons of Jochi divided up the entire Qipchaq steppe among them. Batu on the Volga headed the "Princes of the Right Hand," west of the Ural River, while his elder brother Hordu headed the "Princes of the Left Hand," in the old Qangli territory. Together they formed what Russian historians termed the GOLDEN HORDE but which Islamic sources always call the Qipchaq *ulus* (realm). Under ÖZBEG KHAN (1313–41) the Jochids became Muslim, yet as late as 1330 MUHAMMAD ABU-'ABDULLAH IBN BATTUTA considered the Qipchaqs primarily Christian. The merging of the Muslim Mongols and the Turkic Qipchaqs eventually produced a new Turkic-speaking, Islamic, nomadic people, commonly called the TATARS. Their modern descendants include the Crimean, Astrakhan, and Siberian Tatars, the Kazakhs, the Nogays, and the Karakalpaks.

After Jebe's and Sübe'etei's campaigns Qipchaq prisoners served the Mongols in North China as warriors and as horse herders for the khans, known also as Qarachi from their task of making clarified fermented mare's milk (Turkish, *qara-qumiz*). Under QUBILAI KHAN (1260–94) TUTUGH (1237–97), an Ölberi Qipchaq, won distinction in battles against QAIDU KHAN, and the Qipchaqs were gathered under his command as a special guards corps. Qangli guards were also formed in 1308–09. The Qipchaq guards achieved great political power, and Tutugh's grandson EL-TEMÜR led the 1328 coup d'état that put Tuq-Temür (titled Wenzong or Wen-tsung, 1328–32) on the throne. These Qipchaq guards retreated to Mongolia with the Yuan emperors in 1368, and under the name KHARACHIN (the modern plural of Qarachi) they nomadized in central Inner Mongolia.

See also BULGHARS; CENTRAL EUROPE AND THE MONGOLS; KALKA RIVER, BATTLE OF; OSSETES; RUSSIA AND THE MONGOL EMPIRE; "STONE MEN."

Further reading: Th. T. Allsen, "Prelude to the Western Campaigns: Mongol Military Operations in the Volga-Ural Region, 1217–1237," *Archivum Eurasiae Medii Aevi* 3 (1983): 5–24; Peter B. Golden, "Nomads in the Sedentary World: The Case of Pre-Chinggisid Rus' and Georgia," in *Nomads in the Sedentary World*, ed. Anatoly M. Khazanov and André Wink (Richmond, Surrey: Curzon Press, 2001), 24–75.

Qiu Chuji *See* CHANGCHUN, MASTER.

Qiyat *See* BORJIGID.

Qobdu *See* KHOWD CITY.

Qonggirad (Unggirad, Qunqirat, Qunghrat, Kongrat)
The Qonggirad were the classic example of a Mongol clan building its fame and fortune as marriage partners of the Mongol great khans. The Qonggirad as a great QUDA (in-law) clan became powerful and influential in the Mongol YUAN DYNASTY and the GOLDEN HORDE. (The alternate form *Unggirad*, without the initial Q-, may be a pronunciation influenced by Manchurian languages.)

The Qonggirad first appear in Chinese records in 1126. In the succeeding years Qonggirad attacks often troubled the JIN DYNASTY (1115–1234) in North China. At first the Qonggirad were not part of the MONGOL TRIBE, and legends spoke of ancient hostility between them and the Mongols. Qabul Khan, the Mongol khan around 1140, however, took a Qonggirad as his principal wife, and Qabul Khan's sons allied with their mother's clan in its feud with the Tatar tribe. In the end the Qonggirad clans came to be an important component of the Mongol tribe.

The Qonggirad people in the broad sense contained many sublineages, descended in legend from three sons. The eldest son fathered the Qonggirad in the strict sense (or Bosqur clan), the second son fathered the Ikires and Olqunu'ud clans, and the third son fathered four other clans. The Qonggirad clans all lived along the GREATER KHINGGAN RANGE, stretching north to the Ergüne (Argun') River.

CHINGGIS KHAN'S father, YISÜGEI BA'ATUR, seized as a wife Ö'ELÜN ÜJIN of the Olqunu'ud clan. He first thought to marry his son to an Olqunu'ud girl, but in the end married him to a Bosqur Qonggirad girl, BÖRTE ÜJIN. Despite Yisügei's death soon after, Börte become Chinggis's principal wife. Chinggis later married his sister and his eldest daughter to Botu of the Ikires and married his fifth daughter to an Olqunu'ud.

Despite these marriages, most of the Qonggirad clans allied early on with Chinggis's enemies. In the years leading up to 1201, they supported JAMUGHA of the Jajirad clan, possibly seeking to break BORJIGID hegemony over the Mongol tribe. Qonggirad hostility was also blamed on Chinggis's brother Qasar, who had unwisely plundered them.

In 1203, when Chinggis Khan's uncles and cousins had turned against him and ONG KHAN had defeated him, the Qonggirad and the Ikires suddenly rallied to Chinggis's standard. The support of these Qonggirad clans in 1203 gave Chinggis much needed numbers, and he honored their chiefs highly. In 1227 Börte's younger brother Alchi Noyan was titled "imperial maternal uncle," and a decree was issued by Chinggis and Börte's sons that in every generation a Qonggirad girl would be made an empress and a Qonggirad boy would be granted an imperial princess. This pattern continued virtually to the end of the Yuan dynasty. Chinggis Khan gave his daughter Temülün to Alchi Noyan's son Chigü and sought Qonggirad princesses for his son JOCHI and grandson Qubilai.

In 1214, after the invasion of North China, Chinggis Khan gave the land of south-central Inner Mongolia to the Qonggirad tribes as their appanage. Alchi Noyan, with a more gentle reputation than the brutal MUQALI, became commander of a *tümen* (10,000) in North China. Under QUBILAI KHAN (1260–94) the Qonggirads build two cities, Yingchang and Quanning, on their appanage. Alchi Noyan's daughter and Qubilai's chief wife, CHABUI, was very influential. Qubilai's son JINGIM also married a Qonggirad wife, Bairam-Egechi (Kökejin). Despite Jingim's early death, his wife retained great influence over Qubilai, became regent after his death, and secured the succession to her son Temür (titled Chengzong, 1294–1308). The ORDO (palace-tents and associated estates) of Kökejin became a center of power for the next few decades. In the succession struggles that followed Temür's death, powerful Qonggirad empresses such as Targi (d. 1322) and Budashiri exercised a dominant role. The coup d'état of 1328, however, that enthroned Tuq-Temür (titled Wenzong, 1330–33), son of a Tangut empress, injured Qonggirad influence, which ended with the fall of Budashiri in 1340.

The Qonggirad also played a powerful role in the Golden Horde. Chinggis's oldest son, Jochi, had two Qonggirad queens, and their sons Hordu and BATU both married Qonggirad princesses, as did most of their descendants. Settled in KHORAZM, the clan (called Qunghrat in Turkish) retained its local power throughout the Golden Horde's turbulent disintegration. The so-called Sufi dynasty of Qunghrat emirs dominated Khorazm from 1364 to as late as 1464, submitting alternately to Timurid and Jochid rule. After a period of direct Jochid rule by the local 'Arabshahid dynasty (1511–c.1700), Qunghrat emirs in Khiva (late medieval Khorazm), holding the title *inaq*, "companion," ruled through Jochid puppet khans until 1804, when they assumed the title of khan themselves. The Qunghrat today are an important clan among the Karakalpaks of Khorazm as well as the KAZAKHS and Uzbeks.

After the expulsion of the Yuan dynasty from China, the Qonggirad lost their role in Mongolia as imperial consorts and became widely scattered. In 1371 a body of Qonggirads and Olqunuds on the ORDOS plateau of southwestern Inner Mongolia surrendered to the Ming. Their descendants formed an *OTOG* (camp district) of the TÜMED *tümen*. Another Qonggirad *otog* belonged to the southern KHALKHA *tümen* of eastern Inner Mongolia (*see* JUU UDA); their descendants are in modern Jarud banner. The Olqunu'ud branch is scattered over Khalkha territory. The Qonggirad also appear as a clan of the small Turko-Mongolian Yogur nationality in Gansu. Finally, Börte's Bosqur sublineage may be preserved as the Boskochaina clan among the Daur in northeastern Inner Mongolia (*see* DAUR LANGUAGE AND PEOPLE.

Further reading: C. E. Bosworth, "Kungrat," in *Encyclopaedia of Islam*, 2d ed., Vol. 5 (Leiden: E. J. Brill, 1960 on) vol. 5, 391–392; Hidehiro Okada, "The Chinggis Khan Shrine and the Secret History of the Mongols." In *Religious and Lay Symbolism in the Altaic World and Other Papers*, ed. Klaus Sogaster and Helmut Eimer (Wiesbaden: Otto Harrassowitz, 1989), 284–292.

Qorcin *See* KHORCHIN.

Qošot *See* KHOSHUDS.

Qubilai Khan (Khubilai, Kublai, Kubla) (b. 1215, r. 1260–1294) *Reformer of Mongol institutions and conqueror of South China who established Mongol rule over a unified China*

As the Mongol emperor in China who welcomed MARCO POLO, Qubilai Khan became a legend in Europe. Despite his fame for adopting Chinese institutions, Qubilai was the only Mongol khan after 1260 to win new conquests, and when he died in 1294 his closest advisers were all Mongols of old aristocratic families.

CHILDHOOD AND YOUTH

Qubilai Khan was the second son of TOLUI, CHINGGIS KHAN's youngest son, and of SORQAQTANI BEKI, a KEREYID princess. When Qubilai was born, Chinggis Khan said, "All of our children are of a ruddy complexion, but this child is swarthy like his [Kereyid] maternal uncles. Tell Sorqaqtani Beki to give him to a good nurse to be reared." Sorqaqtani Beki chose as Qubilai's nurse a Tangut woman, whom Qubilai later honored highly.

As was common in the Mongol imperial family, Qubilai's first marriage was arranged when he was very young. His most beloved wife and life's companion was his second wife, CHABUI (d. 1284), of the QONGGIRAD and mother of his sons JINGIM (1243–85), Manggala (d. 1280), and Nomoqan (d. 1301).

Sorqaqtani Beki followed the Christian Church of the East, yet Qubilai's Tangut nurse, for whose soul he often sponsored prayers, possibly nourished Qubilai's belief in Buddhism. Around 1242 Qubilai invited Haiyun, the leading Buddhist monk in North China, north to his ORDO in Mongolia. Qubilai made Haiyun's attendant LIU BINGZHONG his permanent adviser. Qubilai soon added the Shanxi scholar Zhao Bi (1220–76) to his entourage, even telling Chabui to sew clothes personally for him. Accounts such as Zhang Dehui's *Lingbei jixing* (Notes on a journey north of the ranges, 1248) established Qubilai's reputation as a Mongol prince sincerely interested in sagely governance.

VICEROY OF NORTH CHINA

The coronation of Qubilai's brother Möngke as khan in 1251 catapulted Qubilai to a high position. Qubilai received the viceroyalty over North China and moved his *ordo* south to central Inner Mongolia, which was his home base for the next decade or more. Along with conquering the Dali kingdom in YUNNAN in southwestern

China (winter 1253–54), Qubilai built the new city of Kaiping (later SHANGDU) and allowed his Confucian entourage to begin a series of experiments in government. Conflict with MÖNGKE KHAN's regular administration stymied these innovations. In 1252 Qubilai and Zhao Bi forced out the long-time Khorazmian official Mahmud Yalavach (*see* MAHMUD YALAVACH AND MAS'UD BEG), but in 1257 Möngke ordered Qubilai's new Pacification Commission abolished.

Already suffering from gout, Qubilai was attracted by the abilities of Tibetan monks as healers. In 1253 he exploited his new rank to order 'PHAGS-PA LAMA (1235–1280), a Tibetan monk of the Sa-skya-pa order, to join his entourage. 'Phags-pa also bestowed on Qubilai and Chabui a Tantric Buddhist initiation. In 1258 Qubilai presided over a Buddhist-Taoist debate in Kaiping and judged that the Taoist clergy were guilty of defaming Buddhism.

On campaign on the Chang (Yangtze) River, Qubilai received news of Möngke's death in September 1259. Fearing to return home empty-handed, he vainly besieged Ezhou (modern Wuhan) and Yuezhou, but by December Qubilai had to retreat, leaving the besiegers in

Qubilai Khan (1260–1294). Anonymous court painter
(*Courtesy of the National Palace Museum, Taipei*)

Ezhou and Yuezhou to extricate themselves as best they could; large numbers of Mongols surrendered.

CORONATION AND CIVIL WAR

After easily eliminating all opponents from the Hebei-Shandong-Shanxi-Inner Mongolia area, Qubilai's Chinese staff eagerly encouraged him to ascend the throne, and virtually all the senior princes and great commanders (NOYAN) resident in North China or Manchuria also supported Qubilai's candidacy. On April 15, 1260, a hand-picked QURILTAI at Kaiping containing supporters of Qubilai from all the Chinggisid and fraternal lines except that of JOCHI elected Qubilai khan. A month later Möngke's old officials elevated Qubilai's brother ARIQ-BÖKE as khan near QARA-QORUM.

The following civil war was fought on four fronts. First in Shaanxi and Sichuan, where Möngke's army was still stationed, Qubilai had to seize control of the civil administration and win over or defeat units of Möngke's army sympathetic to Ariq-Böke. This was achieved by autumn 1260 largely through the efforts of his Uighur official LIAN XIXIAN (1231–80). Second, on the homefront already exhausted by Möngke's campaign, revived pacification commissions staffed by Confucian officials drafted every available man and horse, rebuilt fortifications, and manned the strategic passes. Despite LI TAN'S REBELLION in 1262, Qubilai was able to rely on the loyalty of his North Chinese generals and officials. Third, Qubilai personally led two Sino-Mongolian armies to Mongolia in autumn 1260 and autumn 1261, but both invasions proved indecisive, while losses in the cold to both armies were massive. Fourth, Qubilai eventually defeated Ariq-Böke by winning over Alghu, the Chaghatayid khan in Turkestan, and HÜLE'Ü in the Middle East, depriving Ariq-Böke's base of its economic foundation. Ariq-Böke surrendered to Qubilai at Kaiping on August 21, 1264, and was pardoned, although at least 10 of his chief supporters were executed.

QUBILAI AND HIS OFFICIALS

Until around 1275 Qubilai relied heavily on the Chinese advisers from his days as a prince in both civil and military roles and appreciated the knowledge of those he often called "you fellows who read books." New court rituals designed by Liu Bingzhong established an arena in which the Chinese officials felt more comfortable. Qubilai's rebuilding of Yanjing (modern Beijing) as his new capital, DAIDU, begun in 1267, and his proclamation of a Chinese dynastic name, Yuan, in December 1271 marked the culmination of the Confucian period of governance.

At the same time, however, tensions grew. When Qubilai founded a censorate in 1268, he was chagrined to find that his first choice, the Chinese Confucian Zhang Dehui (1197–1274), refused to serve as long as Qubilai did not bind himself with a formal law code. Eventually, he turned to a Mongol nobleman, Öz-Temür, to fill the position. Qubilai's dismissal of Lian Xixian in 1270, together with the deaths of Liu Bingzhong (1274), Shii

Tianze (1275), Zhao Bi (1276), and Dong Wenbing (1278), ended Qubilai's early reliance on Chinese officials. When Qubilai heard that Lian in exile was still reading books, he said, "We have certainly been taught to read books, but if you read them and are not willing to have them applied, what is the use of reading a lot?"

Replacing the Chinese comrades of his youth, Qubilai turned to non-Chinese officials offering technical skills. From 1262 one of Chabui's ORDO servants, AHMAD FANAKATI (d. 1281), ran the government monopolies. Qubilai admired his undoubted abilities, yet Chinese colleagues loathed his nepotism and corruption. In 1281 an abortive coup d'état killed Ahmad, and the subsequent revelation of the scale of his corruption shocked and embittered Qubilai. In 1286 the Tibetan SANGHA became the empire's chief fiscal officer. After Ahmad's fall Qubilai was less trusting, and five years later Sangha was executed for corruption.

With Sangha's execution, Qubilai came to rely wholly on younger Mongol aristocrats, descendants of the NÖKÖRS (companions) of Chinggis Khan. Qubilai loved the hunt and the pageantry and feasting at the *quriltais* of the Mongols, and these Mongol aristocrats shared that world with him. Despite relying on princes and *noyans* (commanders) of his own generation to defeat Ariq-Böke, Qubilai had kept them out of central administration. To the younger generation of *noyans*, however, he gave high positions in both the bureaucracy and the royal family. Hantum (1245–93) of the JALAYIR and BAYAN CHINGSANG (1236–95) served as grand councillors (*chengxiang* or *chingsang*) from 1265; Öz-Temür (1242–95) of the Arulad headed the censorate from 1275; and ÖCHICHER (1247–1311) headed the palace establishment from 1281. Hantum, Öz-Temür, and Öchicher also supervised KESHIG, or imperial guard, shifts, thus overseeing Qubilai's daily life. Hantum was the son of Chabui's elder sister, and Qubilai married Bayan Chingsang to Hantum's sister. These officials sympathized with the Confucians and strongly opposed the financier cliques.

Qubilai and Chabui's eldest son, Dorji, was sickly and died young. Qubilai early groomed Jingim as his successor, making him titular director of the Secretariat and head of the Bureau of Military Affairs from 1263 on. Nomuqan was sent out to garrison the frontier at Almaligh (near modern Huocheng in Xinjiang) in 1271, and Manggala was given a fief in Shaanxi in 1272. In 1273 Qubilai formally designated Jingim heir apparent.

A final part of Qubilai's entourage was religious leaders. In 1260 Qubilai made 'Phags-pa his state preceptor (*guoshi*) and head of all Buddhist monks in China. 'Phags-pa's primary appeal to Qubilai seems to have been intellectual, and after 1264 'Phags-pa spent only two years (1269 and 1274) at court. In his place 'Phags-pa recommended the lama Dam-pa Kun-dga'-grags (1230–1303), whose magical accomplishments greatly impressed Qubilai.

Jingim, at least, sought Buddhist names for his children, and despite occasional criticism from Qubilai's Confucian advisers, Buddhism permeated court life.

FOREIGN CONQUESTS AND OPPOSITION IN THE MONGOL HEARTLAND

Qubilai's first foreign conquest was Korea. After the reigning king died in 1259, Qubilai used the Korean king's son and heir, Wang Chŏn (titled Wŏnjong, 1260–74), a hostage at the Mongol court, to bring Korea into submission. Despite the necessity for later military interventions there, Qubilai saw this as a triumph of peaceful Confucian conquest through virtue. The pacification of Korea gave the Mongols a significant maritime force, and Qubilai drew on Korean shipbuilding heavily during his campaigns against Japan and Song China. The first Mongol-Korean expedition against Japan ended in failure in 1274, and Qubilai turned to opportunities in South China.

After the fall of the great fortress of Xiangyang (modern Xiangfan) in 1273, Qubilai's Uighur general ARIQ-QAYA and the Mongol general AJU proposed the final conquest of the Song. In the following court debate there was significant opposition, although the opponents' names are not recorded. Most likely the Confucian party opposed the Song expedition, just as it had the 1274 expedition against Japan. Qubilai appointed Bayan Chingsang and Aju his commanders and ordered 100,000 soldiers drafted. Qubilai's primary concern from the beginning was to preserve the tremendous wealth of South China from possible destruction by the Mongol armies. He thus gave command of the final advance on the Song capital of Lin'an (modern Hangzhou) to Bayan Chingsang, whose diplomatic finesse he trusted. In March 1276 Lin'an and most of the Song imperial family surrendered; operations to 1279 were in the nature of mop-up.

The victorious campaign against the Song, however, coincided with disaster on the northern frontier. There, an Ögedeid prince, QAIDU KHAN (1236–1301), had from 1269 rallied an alliance of the CHAGHATAY KHANATE and the GOLDEN HORDE and raided the YUAN DYNASTY's possessions in Mongolia and East Turkestan (modern Xinjiang). In spring of 1277 Möngke Khan's son Shiregi rebelled, kidnapping Prince Nomuqan and Hantum Noyan and turning them over to the Golden Horde and Qaidu, respectively. Unrest from Shiregi's rebellion briefly spread as far as Yingchang in Inner Mongolia, but by February 1278 Bayan Chingsang and the Qipchaq general TUTUGH had driven Shiregi's partisans west of the ALTAI RANGE.

QUBILAI'S LATER YEARS

Jingim's Confucian education distanced him from his father's later court, dominated by Ahmad and Sangha. After Chabui died in 1281, Qubilai married her Qonggirad cousin Nambui and began to withdraw from direct contact with his advisers, issuing instructions through her. In 1284 the Golden Horde sent back Nomuqan and induced Qaidu to return Hantum. Nomuqan expressed his resentment that Jingim had been made heir apparent, and Qubilai banished him to the north again. When an official in the south proposed in 1285 that Qubilai abdicate in favor of Jingim, only Jingim's sudden death at age 42 averted a crisis between father and son. After Jingim's death, however, Qubilai remained very close to Jingim's widow Bairam-Egechi (also known as Kökejin), and in 1293 Jingim's third son, Temür (b. 1265, titled Chengzong, 1294–1307), was proclaimed heir apparent.

Despite the gesture of peace from the Golden Horde, hostilities on the frontier increased. In 1285 Qubilai's Central Asian rival Qaidu destroyed an army at Besh-Baligh, and Qubilai evacuated the Tarim Basin. In 1287 the princes of the fraternal lineages in Manchuria, headed by Nayan, rebelled. Warned in advance, Qubilai, now grossly overweight, took to the field to defeat NAYAN'S REBELLION, riding on a palanquin born by elephants. With the death of Nayan, Qubilai returned home, but scattered rebellions continued until 1289. From 1286 on Qaidu also began regularly raiding Mongolia; his brief occupation of Qara-Qorum brought Qubilai out of his palace for the last time, but Qaidu was long gone by the time he arrived at Qara-Qorum. Supply and morale among the defenders were poor; in 1292 Bayan Chingsang had executed soldiers for refusing to advance. Qubilai replaced Bayan Chingsang with Öz-Temür and ordered Qipchaq troops under the aggressive general Tutugh to occupy Kem-Kemchik (Tuva) and attack Qaidu's positions. This advance would eventually break the back of Qaidu's opposition, but only after Qubilai's death.

In the South Seas Qubilai overrode repeated warnings from experienced officials and put together a vast second expedition against Japan, which was likewise destroyed by storms. A small maritime invasion of Champa in 1281 and a massive land-sea invasion of VIETNAM in 1284–88 both failed. Simultaneous invasions of BURMA (Myanmar) (1282–87) and a smaller seaborne expedition against Java (1292–93) also brought no lasting gains.

Domestically, several quixotic campaigns of religious repression against Taoists and Muslims marked the later years of Qubilai's reign. This late anti-Islamic attitude also influenced his diplomacy, leading him to support the Buddhist Arghun over the Muslim Sultan Ahmad in the IL-KHANATE's succession conflict of 1282–84.

QUBILAI'S CHARACTER AND SIGNIFICANCE

On the lunar new year's day (January 28, 1294) Qubilai was too ill to hold the customary ceremonies. Having ruled as great khan for 34 years, Qubilai was now something of a relic from an earlier era. Seeking an old companion to comfort him in his final illness, the palace staff could chose only Bayan Chingsang, more than 30 years his junior. On February 18 Qubilai died, and two days later his funeral cortege set out for the burial place of the khans in northeast Mongolia.

Qubilai's seizure of power in 1260 pushed the MONGOL EMPIRE in a new direction. In his contest with Ariq-Böke, Ariq-Böke stood for continuity with Möngke's self-conscious Mongol nativism. Qubilai was rather a new ÖGEDEI KHAN, magnanimous and willing to experiment with non-Mongol ideas. Qubilai's controversial election, at first supported by no one outside North China and Manchuria, accelerated the breakup of the MONGOL EMPIRE. At the same time, Qubilai's willingness to formalize the Mongol realm's symbiotic relation with North China gave the Mongol Empire a cultural and administrative brilliance that impressed the world.

Despite the vast amount of information about Qubilai's reign and administration, his ultimate beliefs and character remain enigmatic. Even as a prince, Qubilai excelled at making people of diverse backgrounds believe that he shared their deepest desires, inspiring very different people to devoted service. Only Chabui shared with him these varied personalities. Apart from her he preferred to surround himself with men who either by background or by age were unlikely to penetrate into the inner sanctum of his thought. Officials who pressed Qubilai too insistently for commitment to one vision, such as Lian Xixian, eventually found their access cut off and not restored until they recognized the emperor's right and obligation to be an emperor of all persuasions.

See also KOREA AND THE MONGOL EMPIRE; JAPAN AND THE MONGOL EMPIRE; SOUTH SEAS.

Further reading: Morris Rossabi, *Khubilai Khan: His Life and Times* (Berkeley: University of California Press, 1988).

quda This term, used for marriage allies or two men whose children have married each other, marked a key political relationship in Mongolian society and politics.

At the time of the empire, the Mongols were organized into patrilineal lineages. These lineages were strictly exogamous. Thus, parents had to contract marriage alliances for their children with other lineages. Once two lineages contracted such a tie, the two sets of fathers would call each other *quda,* or "marriage allies" (modern Mongolian, *khud*); *qudaghui* (modern, *khudgui*) was used by the mothers. Preferably, the tie was reciprocal, so that a father of one lineage, having received a bride for his son in a second lineage, would give a bride to someone in the second lineage. This sort of exchange could go on for generations.

Thus, for example, CHINGGIS KHAN (Genghis, 1206–27) gave his sister Temülün to Botu of the Ikires clan. Botu's son Sorqaq received as a bride Altu, the daughter of Köchü, the son of Chinggis's son Ögedei. Meanwhile, Ula'adai, Botu's son, gave his daughter Qutuq-tai to Möngke, the son of Chinggis's son TOLUI. Sorqaq's son Jaqurchin married Yisünjin, the daughter of Alchidai, the son of Chinggis's brother Qachi'un. Several generations later this intermarriage continued. The chief wife of Emperor Shidebala (titled Yingzong, 1320–23) was an Ikires princess, Sügebala, whose father was Ashi, son of Jaqurchin's son Qurin; her mother was Ili-Qaya, the daughter of Emperor Temür, son of JINGIM, son of Tolui's son Qubilai. Given the Mongol practice of polygamy and the lack of Chinese concern about contracting marriages in higher or lower generations, the *quda* established an extraordinarily complex web of relations.

When a bride of noble family went to her new home, she would be given from her father's subjects an INJE, or dowry, of maidservants to accompany her. In ruling families this *inje* included menservants as well and numbered in the 100s. The *quda* relationship thus brought about substantial and repeated exchanges of subject populations as well.

Even before the rise of Chinggis Khan, all the contenders for leadership of the Mongols were branches of the BORJIGID lineage. As a result, the theoretically reciprocal relation of *quda* became a way for nonruling but wealthy clans to be attached to the warlike ruling clans as clients. While theoretically Chinggis could have established *quda* relations with any non-Borjigid lineage, he generally preferred to do so with the ruling families of semiautonomous tribes and peoples who surrounded the MONGOLIAN PLATEAU rather than with his intimate servitors. Only a few leading generals, such as SÜBE'ETEI BA'ATUR and CHORMAQAN, received imperial princesses. To the east the QONGGIRAD, the Ikires, and the Olqunuds, to the northwest the OIRATS, and to the south the ÖNGGÜD tribes all became firm *quda* relations of the Borjigid, ties that lasted through the YUAN DYNASTY to 1368. Those lineage chiefs who received Chinggisid princesses bore the title of *kürgen*, "son-in-law." The Chinggisids also used the *quda* alliance as a preferred method to tie friendly non-nomadic peoples to the realm. Chinggis Khan established *quda* relations with the UIGHURS and the Muslim QARLUQS of Almaligh (near modern Huocheng in Xinjiang). After Korea surrendered to the Mongols in 1260, QUBILAI KHAN and his descendants established *quda* relations with the ruling Wang family of the Koryö dynasty.

While during the Yuan dynasty the khans preferred to keep the ranks of *quda* separate from those of the generals and ministers, in the three western khanates (the CHAGHATAY KHANATE, the GOLDEN HORDE, and the IL-KHANATE) and their successors, the same families that dominated the KESHIG, or imperial guard, also came to dominate the ranks of the khan's *quda*. The Qonggirad were represented in these ranks in several khanates, and the Oirats were *quda* to the Il-Khans, but other families, such as the Barulas and the Suldus, also held this position. By the 15th century the leading *bey* (chief or lord), or *beglerbegi*, often monopolized the right to marriage exchange with the khan. In the Chaghatay Khanate TIMUR Kürgen (son-in-law), the famous Tamerlane, of the Barulas lineage, reduced his father-in-law to a puppet and opened the way for his sons to replace the Chinggisid line in that khanate.

After the expulsion of the Yuan from China in 1368, the Chinggisid rulers of the Mongols found themselves in a similar situation with the Oirats, who forced them to continue in *quda* relations. Repeatedly, Chinggisid khans came into conflict with their *quda* partners among the Oirats. During the Mongol-Oirat wars of the 15th century, the Mongol rulers responded by reemphasizing the higher call of blood and lineage over marriage affinity, an emphasis reflected in chronicles such as the ERDENI-YIN TOBCHI and the ALTAN TOBCHI. When BATU-MÖNGKE DAYAN KHAN (1480?–1517?) decisively defeated the Oirats and reunified the Mongols proper in the east, he divided the Mongol peoples among his sons. Since the Mongol peoples (with the exception of the Oirats and BURIATS) mostly came to be ruled by Dayan Khan's descendants, the role of *quda* relations declined in intra-Mongol politics. The revived Chinggisid aristocracy descended from Dayan Khan's sons preferred to contract marriage with the more prominent of their own subjects rather than with those outside their power. Called *tabunangs*, these sons-in-law of the new Chinggisid aristocracy formed an important, although definitely subordinate, part of the Mongol ruling class.

The Manchus of the QING DYNASTY (1636–1912), who conquered Inner Mongolia in 1636 and received the submission of KHALKHA (Outer Mongolia) in 1691, shared a social structure of exogamous patrilineages with the Mongols and also used marriage ties to secure allies. In this case, however, it was the Mongols who became "son-in-law" people. Mongol aristocrats, particularly from the KHARACHIN and KHORCHIN Mongols in eastern Inner Mongolia, often received Manchu princesses. These princesses, according to Manchu and Mongol custom, came with *inje*, or a human dowry. These dowry servants, usually from Beijing, helped spread Chinese customs among the Mongols.

During the Qing dynasty the monopoly of local authority by an almost purely Borjigid aristocracy caused a decline in clan structures and exogamy among the commoners. Only the Kharachin and Monggoljin (Fuxin) banners in the southeast of Inner Mongolia retained their non-Borjigid nobles and thus became favored marriage partners for the Borjigid nobility. By 1900 Mongol commoners were even beginning to forget their CLAN NAMES. Even so, among commoners the idea of two groups exchanging brides retained its importance. Oftentimes it was reinterpreted as an exchange not between clans or lineages but between BANNERS or *sumus* (local administrative districts). In this sense it can still be found today among some rural Mongols.

See also FAMILY; KINSHIP SYSTEM; WEDDINGS.

Further reading: Hirotoshi Shimo, "The Central Organization of the Il-Khanate Governments." In *Proceedings of the 35th Permanent International Altaistics Conference,* ed. Chieh-hsien Ch'en (Taipei: Center for Chinese Studies Materials, 1993), 443–446.

qumyz See KOUMISS.

Qunghrat See QONGGIRAD.

Qunqirat See QONGGIRAD.

quriltai (*quriltay, kuriltai*) The *quriltai* was a grand assembly at which the Mongol ruling class elected their khans, planned campaigns, and distributed rewards.

In the 13th and 14th centuries the Mongol rulers held annual *quriltai*s during the sixth lunar month (late June or early July) and at the WHITE MONTH, or lunar new year (late January or early February). Those in the summer, when the mares were milked and the horses fattened, were the more splendid occasions, sometimes lasting two months. The greatest assemblies brought together under a single pavilion the entire ruling class: princes and princesses of the blood, imperial sons-in-laws, captains of 1,000 and of 10,000 and their ladies, and scribes and stewards and their wives. Each participant was allowed 10 followers. One observer estimated the attendance at the summer coronation *quriltai* of 1246 at 5,000. Governors of the conquered peoples and envoys of foreign nations remained outside the pavilion and were allowed in only by special invitation. Entrance and seating followed strict order. According to Mongol custom, the great palace-tents (ORDO) faced south, and the lords sat in descending seniority on the right (western) side, while the ladies sat facing them on the left (eastern) side. Approach to the hitching posts (*kirü'ese*) outside the pavilion, where the horses with their valuable trappings were tied, was also strictly regulated.

At the summer *quriltai*s, often held at the Shira Ordo, or "Yellow Palace-Tent," all present wore a different color every day, but at the new year's *quriltai* they wore white only. The emperor's KESHIG or imperial guard served liquor, carved the meat, and guarded the door. Singing and elaborate rituals of toasting accompanied the day-long drinking of KOUMISS and wine. Those attending brought gifts and rarities (*tangsuqs*), while the emperor bestowed on the guests suits of baldachin (gold brocade) and other colors for the occasion as well as gold ingots and raw fabrics.

When a coronation *quriltai* had decided on a candidate, a senior prince of the right hand (representing the families of Chinggis's sons JOCHI and CHA'ADAI) and of the left hand (representing the families of CHINGGIS KHAN's brothers) led him to the throne, while another senior prince offered a cup of ÖTÖG, or offering wine. All but the emperor removed their hats and slung their belts around their necks as a sign of obedience. Clergy of the various religions of the empire offered prayers for the KHAN and the realm. Coronation and new year's *quriltai*s were followed by full prostrations of all present before the khan.

The early MONGOL TRIBE in the mid-12th century undoubtedly held regular summer *quriltai*s, although the rituals differed. The *quriltai* at the Branching Tree of Qorqonaq valley, a tributary of the ONON RIVER, was legendary. Following the powerful Qutula Khan's election, he danced with his people until his pounding feet dug a ditch to his knees. The *quriltai* of 1201 that raised JAMUGHA to the throne swore a covenant of unity over a sacrificed stallion and mare.

Little is known of the ceremonial during the *quriltai* that elected Chinggis Khan emperor in 1206. He displayed a new nine-footed banner, and some say that seven Mongol clan chiefs lifted him up on a piece of black felt. RASHID-UD-DIN FAZL-ULLAH states that this coronation *quriltai* was held at the new year, not in the summer. The 1229 *quriltai* that enthroned his son ÖGEDEI KHAN established regular rituals, including prostration of all relatives to the new emperor, which were further codified in 1234.

In later generations coronation *quriltai*s proved particularly controversial. The Mongols had no rule of succession, and *quriltai*s considered a wide range of Chinggisid princes. The prolonged feasting and drinking aimed to produce frank discussion and eventual consensus. Since the aim of the election was to discern which candidate was truly destined by heaven to rule, the decision had to be unanimous, putting strong pressure on dissidents to support the majority. Once a candidate was chosen, he usually demanded written guarantees (*möchelge*) from the princes that they would abide by the choice. After the controversial election of MÖNGKE KHAN in 1251, *quriltai* organizers frequently faced the choice of either following the *quriltai* with a purge of opponents or restricting it to supporters only.

The successor states maintained the *quriltai* institutions. In the YUAN DYNASTY under QUBILAI KHAN (1260–94), the *quriltai*s grew more frequent and more splendid, with assemblies added to celebrate the emperor's birthday as well as each lunar month. The western khanates observed the summer and new year's *quriltai*s even after converting to Islam, which has its own lunar calendar. Drinking of koumiss and mead also continued, although some khans prohibited grape wine. Some of the later Islamic successor states excluded women, with the exception of the khan or sultan's immediate family, from the *quriltai*s. The *quriltai* disappeared from the historical record after the 14th century. The later Mongol NAADAM was also a seasonal assembly with a religiopolitical focus, but it was not called a *quriltai* or modeled on it.

See also CALENDARS AND DATING SYSTEMS; FOOD AND DRINK.

Mongol khan and his *khatun* (lady) enthroned at the *quriltai*. From an illustrated version of Rashid-ud-Din's *Compendium of Chronicles* (Courtesy Staatsbibliothek zu Berlin—Preussischer Kulturbesitz, Orientalabteilung)

Further reading: Ron Sela, *Ritual and Authority in Central Asia: The Khan's Inauguration Ceremony* (Bloomington, Ind.: Research Institute for Inner Asian Studies, 2003).

Qutuqu, Shigi (1178?–1260) *Tatar captive and first chief judge of the Mongol Empire*

The SECRET HISTORY OF THE MONGOLS and RASHID-UD-DIN FAZL-ULEAH agree that Shigi Qutuqu was found as a small child in a Tatar camp after a successful attack by the Mongols. They differ, however, on when this happened (1196 or the early 1180s) and on whether it was Chinggis's mother, Ö'ELÜN ÜJIN, or his wife BÖRTE ÜJIN who adopted him. Chronology indicates Rashid-ud-Din is correct. Shigi Qutuqu trained early on in writing. In 1215, when Zhongdu, the capital of the JIN DYNASTY in North China, surrendered to the Mongols, he was sent to make a complete record of the booty for CHINGGIS KHAN, who praised his scrupulous devotion (*see* ZHONGDU, SIEGES OF). The *Secret History of the Mongols* states that Chinggis Khan made Shigi Qutuqu his chief scribe, chief judge, and overseer of all sedentary cities at the great QURILTAI in 1206, but this account must refer to some later event. Accompanying Chinggis Khan on his campaign against KHORAZM, Shigi Qutuqu was defeated by Jalal-ud-Din Mengüberdi at Parwan in Afghanistan. After Chinggis's death Shigi Qutuqu also participated in TOLUI's campaigns against the Jin in North China in 1230–31. In 1234 ÖGEDEI KHAN appointed Shigi Qutuqu chief judge (JARGHUCHI) for North China, responsible for enforcing taxation and other laws. Arriving at Yanjing (modern Beijing), Shigi Qutuqu ordered another census of North China, completed in 1236. The SONG DYNASTY envoy Xu Ting considered Shigi Qutuqu's taxation oppressive, but the Confucian scholar Zhang Dehui later praised Shigi Qutuqu as a model civil official, and Rashid-ud-Din notes that he encouraged suspects not to incriminate themselves out of fear of punishment. His court practice formed the basis for judicial procedures all over the empire.

See also CENSUS IN THE MONGOL EMPIRE; *JARLIQ*; *JASAQ*.

Further reading: P. Ratchnevsky, "Šigi Qutuqu," in *In the Service of the Khan: Eminent Personalities of the Early Mongol-Yuan Period (1200–1300)*, ed. Igor de Rachewiltz et al. (Wiesbaden: Otto Harrassowitz, 1993), 75–94.

R

Rashid-ud-Din Fazl-ullah (Rashid al-Din, Rashid ad-Din) (1247–1318) *Vizier of the Mongols in Iran and world historian*

Rashid-ud-Din was born in Hamadan, Iran, the son of a Jewish pharmacist, and was trained as a physician. In 1295, as Rashid-ud-Dawla, he served as steward to the court of Geikhatu Khan (1291–95) but eventually absconded when financial chaos made his task impossible. Later Rashid-ud-Din was sharing shifts in the Mongol prince Ghazan's KESHIG (household guard) with a Mongol commander, Qutlughshah. By 1297 GHAZAN KHAN (1295–1304) was in power, Qutlughshah was his chief commander, and Rashid-ud-Din was at court hearing the petitions of the Christian patriarch MAR YAHBH-ALLAHA. Rashid-ud-Dawla's name change to Rashid-ud-Din probably marks his conversion to Islam, although a late Arab biographical source dates his conversion to his 30th year. His history shows the exaggerated contempt of a would-be landed gentry for the ambitious Jewish "hucksters" who had flourished before 1295 as *ortoq* agents of the Mongol nobility. Rashid-ud-Din leaned toward the rationalist Mu'tazili school of Islam, and court intriguers later denounced his commentary on the Koran as a Jew's philosophical falsification of the word of God.

In 1298 Rashid-ud-Din's superior, Sadr-ud-Din Zanjani, was executed, and Rashid-ud-Din became the second-ranked vizier in the empire, under Sa'd-ud-Din Savaji. Rashid-ud-Din and his sons served GHAZAN KHAN as his most trusted and intimate stewards. Ghazan Khan commissioned Rashid-ud-Din to write a complete history of the Mongols, giving him unprecedented access to confidential Mongolian records. Under Ghazan Khan's brother Sultan Öljeitü (1304–17) Rashid-ud-Din com-

pleted his history and was commissioned to add the chronicles of all the known world, thus creating the first truly multicivilization history, the *Jami' al-tawarikh,* or *COMPENDIUM OF CHRONICLES*. Receiving a supposed million gold dinars as a reward, he invested it in wasteland he improved through his agronomic expertise. Chief of his investments were several tax-exempt pious foundations (*waqf*) and especially his tomb complex at Rab'-i Rashidi, outside Tabriz. Here, through the production of illuminated and illustrated manuscripts, including the *Compendium*, Rashid's patronage greatly advanced the Persian miniature tradition. Rashid-ud-Din's generosity to petitioners was widely praised.

In 1312 Öljeitü executed Sa'd-ud-Din, and Rashid was accused of leading a Jewish clique that had poisoned Ghazan Khan. Rashid's youthful new colleague as vizier, Taj-ud-Din 'Alishah, began to intrigue against him and under Abu-Sa'id (r. 1317–35) brought accusations of having poisoned Öljeitü. Rashid's Mongol patron, Emir Sevinch, died, and Rashid was dismissed in 1317 and executed in 1318, as Mongol soldiers looted Rab'-i Rashidi. After Taj-ud-Din's death Rashid's son Ghiyas-ud-Din Muhammad revived the family's fortunes, serving Abu-Sa'id as vizier.

religion   The two main organized religions in Mongolia have been SHAMANISM and Buddhism. Shamanism was dominant at the court of the MONGOL EMPIRE and among the Mongols up to around 1575. From 1260 on Tibetan Buddhism also became an important influence on Mongolian religious life, coexisting with shamanism. After 1575 a new wave of persecution from the dGe-lugs-pa, or "Yellow Hat" Buddhists, progressively drove shamanism out of central Mongolia. By the beginning of the 20th century only the Daurs, western BURIATS, DARKHAD, and a few other peripheral peoples were still predominantly shamanist.

At the same time, a large number of lay rituals have shown substantial continuity from the time of the Mongol Empire to the present. While these rituals, including libations of mare's milk to heaven (TENGGERI), the FIRE CULT, and the worship of standards are often interpreted as "shamanist survivals," these cults are best seen as a separate "elders' religion" (Caroline Humphrey's term), distinct from shamanism and Buddhism but antagonistic to neither. Buddhism aims to improve one's reincarnation through building merit and ultimately to cease the round of incarnation and achieve birthlessness through detachment from all desire, and shamanism aims to embody spirits nursing grudges for insults done in the past so that they can be propitiated and reconciled with the living. The "elders' religion," however, aims to show forth and celebrate the social orders of clan, neighborhood, family, and state and to give them eternal and cosmic status. Since both shamanism and Buddhism recognize and accept these social groups, both are compatible with the "elders' religion."

In the 20th century Communist persecution harshly repressed all forms of Mongolian religious life (see BUDDHISM, CAMPAIGN AGAINST; INNER MONGOLIANS; KALMYKS). Since 1985 traditional religious practice has revived. The new religious scene differs, however, from the prerevolutionary era in the presence of new ideals of religious tolerance and secular government. In Mongolia proper, particularly in the capital, ULAANBAATAR, evangelical Christianity is also a significant new factor in religious life.

BUDDHISM AND SHAMANISM

Under the Mongol Empire and the succeeding YUAN DYNASTY (1206/71–1368) the shamans, organized in a hierarchy under the *beki*, or senior clan leader, handled the rituals of the ancestral temple and the seasonal festivals. Clergy of other religions, such as Buddhism and Christianity, also participated. From the time of QUBILAI KHAN (1260–94) Tibetan Buddhism became the dominant influence on the court, but judging from personal names and other pieces of evidence it was less influential on the ordinary Mongols in China than were native traditions or even CONFUCIANISM. Certainly the Buddhists did not repress the shamanist court ceremonies. Coexistence of court Buddhism with shamanism continued at least into the 15th century, if not longer (see BUDDHISM IN THE MONGOL EMPIRE; RELIGIOUS POLICY IN THE MONGOL EMPIRE).

The SECOND CONVERSION of the Mongols to Buddhism, which began around 1575, introduced a new, fiercely exclusivist view of Buddhism's rightful role in society. Missionaries of the new dGe-lugs-pa, or "Yellow Hat" order, founded by Tsong-kha-pa (1372–1419),

eschewed the previous compromises of the other orders and tried to destroy shamanism completely. Shamanist ONGGHON figurines were burnt in great bonfires. Friendly Mongolian rulers championed the "TWO CUSTOMS" idea of mutually supportive church and state. The dGe-lugs-pa monasteries became the single most influential institution for educating the Mongols.

By the mid-18th century shamans were difficult, if not impossible, to find in most of Mongolia. Less exclusivist approaches toward the native religion began emerging that viewed conversion as a process of converting the local spirits and putting them under oath to protect the superior Buddhist faith. The THIRD MERGEN GEGEEN, Lubsang-Dambi-Jalsan (1717–66), composed a whole liturgy of prayers to specifically Mongolian deities and spiritual powers: local mountains, CHINGGIS KHAN and his standards (see EIGHT WHITE YURTS), the WHITE OLD MAN, the OBOO and fire cult, and so on.

The conflict between shamanism and Buddhism was joined again in the late 18th and 19th centuries among the eastern Buriats in southern Siberia. The 19th-century Buriat chronicles, written by Buddhist partisans, record that from the 1780s shamanism was steadily driven back by literacy and more effective medicine, especially the live-virus smallpox vaccine long taught in monasteries. By 1819 shamanist, *ongghon* figure were being burned among the Buriats as well. At the same time, the method of putting local spirits, such as mountains, under oath to protect Buddhism was also being applied to take over and Buddhicize traditional cult sites.

In the 20th century Buddhism went from achieving the height of its power under the EIGHTH JIBZUNDAMBA KHUTUGTU from 1911 to 1921 to suffering virtual destruction under the Communist regime from 1936 to 1944. Similar campaigns were waged in Mongol areas of Russia and China. The period of persecution improved Buddhism's relations with shamanism. In Buriatia some Buddhist clergy even recommend that those with peculiar illnesses see shamans for treatment. At the same time, other lamas and devout Buddhist laymen, whether among Buriats, KHALKHA Mongols, or Inner Mongolians, often look askance at shamanists and avoid contact with shamanic spirits.

THE "ELDERS' RELIGION"

Regardless of whether an area is Buddhist or shamanist, shamans no longer handle the local calendrical and life-cycle rituals that form the traditional "elders' religion." Today these rituals are carried out either by lamas or by lay elders known for their command of the old traditions and the ability to speak the traditional blessings well. They are called by different names in different places: *khadashan übegen* (old man of the cliffs) or *medelshe akhamad khün* (knowledgeable elders) among the Buriats, *khondon* (KHORCHIN), *khonjin* (ORDOS), or *baksh* (teacher) among the Daurs. Details of the cults of the elders religion vary from region to regions, but they are everywhere broadly similar both to one another and to the ancient rituals of the Mongol Empire and before.

From the ancient TÜRK EMPIRES through the Mongol Empire, the peoples of Mongolia worshiped "Eternal Heaven" (*möngke tenggeri*) and "Mother Earth," named in ancient Mongolian prayers Mother Etüken. In later centuries Eternal Heaven had a varying relation with the "99 gods/heavens" divided into two camps, white to the west and red to the east, sometimes being one of the 99, sometimes the head of all of them, and sometimes a sort of summation of them.

Another important cult was what the *SECRET HISTORY OF THE MONGOLS* calls the "masters and sovereigns of land and water" (*ghajar usun-u ejed khad*), especially associated with mountains and large bodies of water. Chinggis Khan daily worshiped and prayed to Mt. Burqan Qaldun in the KHENTII RANGE of his homeland, where he had taken refuge from his enemies. In recent centuries both the Buddhist church, the secular rulers in the BANNERS (appanages), and the QING DYNASTY (1636–1912) AMBANs conducted regular worship of the major mountains. Another form of this worship is that at the *oboo*, or cairn, where both the masters of the land and the dragons that inhabit atmospheric water are worshiped. While the mountains are often seen as sons or messengers of the upper heaven(s), the waters are linked to the underworld gods, ruled by Erlig Khan. Hunters viewed game as gifts from the "Lord of the Forest" (*see* HUNTING AND FISHING).

Since clans occupied particular areas and buried or exposed their dead there, mountains and trees at the vicinity of such an ancestral spot (called *barisa* by the Buriats) also became associated with ancestral lineages. The horse sacrifice (*tailgan*) to the ancestors was one aspect of the elders' religion that the Buddhists virtually always opposed. (An exception was at the shrine of Chinggis Khan in Ordos.) Thus, in Buriatia places where the *tailgan* sacrifice took place would be replaced by a clan *oboo* cult with mutton or sometimes bloodless offerings.

Within the family the fire cult and the *ongghons* formed two parts of the ancient Inner Asian elders' religion. Curiously, among the Turkish Inner Asian nomads the Muslim missionaries extirpated the fire cult (perhaps due to its similarity to the rival religion of Zoroastrianism) but long tolerated the *ongghons*, while the Buddhist missionaries destroyed *ongghons* but encouraged the fire cult.

The larger political structures were embodied in the cult of the standards, large spears planted vertically with knotted horsehair tails tied below the spearhead. These standards were often worshiped in black (war) and white (peace) forms. In the Qing dynasty every banner (local district) also kept its own trident standard. During the 1911 RESTORATION prisoners of war were even sacrificed to these war standards.

MODES OF WORSHIP

Traditional lay religion in Mongolia has a common vocabulary of worship of both ancient Inner Asian and Buddhist origin. Many such practices evidently stem from the ancient Eurasian traditions.

The most ancient and powerful of these forms of worship were human and horse sacrifices. The former is, of course, defunct, and the horse sacrifice is still practiced regularly only among the western Buriats. Cooked sheep continue to be offered to the household Buddhas on the eve of the WHITE MONTH (lunar new year) and in *oboo* worship, even if performed for a monastery. Another ancient Eurasian custom encouraged under Buddhism was the practice of dedicating horses and other livestock to the ancestral or local spirits. Once dedicated, such livestock wandered freely, were not sold or ridden, and could be killed only for sacrifice. Originally called *ong-ghola-* (to make into an *ongghon*, or sacred vessel), it was renamed in Buddhist Mongolia *seterle-* (to decorate with *seter*, or colored strips, from Tibetan *se-ter*).

The practice of decorating sacred things with strips of cloth is ancient. At the election assembly (QURILTAI) of Qabul Khan, decades before Chinggis Khan, the great lone tree there was dedicated with colored strips of cloth. As in Tibet, colored cloth strips (*dartsug*, from Tibetan *dar-lchog*) or whole KHADAG scarves are still used to dedicate all sorts of sacred and protected things: Buddhist temples, *oboo*s, grave sites, clan burial spots, or *barisa*, wrestlers, horse-head fiddles, hats, and so on. The ultimate form of such strips is the *kheimori* (modern *khiimori*), or "wind horse" or prayer flag, printed with Tibetan prayers surrounding a horse carrying the *chindamani* (wishing jewel).

Liquid offerings are made by aspersions or sprinkling (Inner Mongolian, *sachul*, Khalkha, *tsatsal*, Buriat, *sasal*). Usually offered to heaven and all the 99 deities without distinction, such aspersions are made before drinking any liquor with the ring finger of the right hand in the four directions. In large outdoor ceremonies special ladles with nine built-in cups are used so that the 99 aspersions can be performed conveniently. Spoken blessings are made concrete in an anointing (*milaa-/myalaa-*): horses with KOUMISS, or fermented mare's milk, and children and yurts with butter. Fire is "anointed" by pouring butter or sheep fat on it.

While running water is pure, its purity is passive and sullied by contact with dirt. Fire, however, is actively pure and is still used for purification. Shamans also use a burning juniper (*arts*) branch for purification. Fire is also used to send things to the dead. In this sense, burning powdered juniper or incense are used in Buddhist worship as an offering (Mongolian, *sang* or *ubsang*, from Tibetan *bzang*).

Movement around sacred places is always clockwise, or as the Mongols call it, *naran züg* (sun direction), following the movement of shadows inside the YURT. Only when carrying a corpse from the yurt is counterclockwise motion prescribed. This is another aspect in which Buddhist patterns were already congruent with traditional Inner Asian patterns. Another form of clockwise motion was the beckoning motion (*dallaga*) of the upward-facing hands, summoning good fortune. This motion is accompanied by the repeated cry of *khurui*.

The Mongolian calendar of worship has long been divided into two basic seasons: the winter of meat (red food), the White Month, hunting, and EPICS, and the summer of dairy products ("white food") milk aspersions, the three manly games, and the *oboo* offering. In the pre-Buddhist period, ancestral sacrifices took place in all seasons but with different characters. Although several calendars and astrological conceptions were at work, all were lunar-solar in nature and involved timing with the seasons, the moon, and the major stars (*see* ASTROLOGY; CALENDARS AND DATING SYSTEMS.)

Ritual activities are also governed by powerful numbers and color dualities. The most important number is 9, or in its multiplied form 99. Other important numbers are 5, linked with the five directions (including center) and five colors, 12, linked to the 12-ANIMAL CYCLE, and 7, linked to the five visible planets with the sun and moon. Colors are organized into dualities: white versus black (noble versus base), white versus red (milk versus meat), and yellow versus black (Buddhist versus lay). White and nine are often used to express the acme of pure offerings.

Finally, the verbal forms of prayers, addresses, blessings, and praises (*see* YÖRÖÖL AND MAGTAAL) all share certain features: groups of alliterative lines with seven or eight syllables with a parallel grammatical structure and meaning (*see* PROSODY). The content of such prayers frequently shows a combination of cosmic scale and repetitive description. The form of these addresses parallels the function of the "elders' religion": to celebrate the firm, eternal nature of the social groups involved.

MODERN RELIGION

Despite the persecutions of the Communist era, the prerevolutionary religious scene of the distinctive Mongolian regions is reemerging. Everywhere the "elders' religion" has shown paradoxical strength and weakness. During the Communist era much of its practice was treated as "folklore" and hence preserved, albeit in bowdlerized form. In the post-Communist era it has gained immense prestige from its role as a repository of Mongolian tradition. At the same time, the way it is embedded in the pastoral cycle and closed clans or local communities makes it seem irrelevant to some urban and socially mobile Mongols.

In Russia Buddhism has long been a bulwark of national identity for the Buriats and Kalmyks. Today one commonly finds committed devotion to Buddhism (or shamanism among the Buriats), even among Buriat and

Kalmyk intellectuals who cannot speak their own languages, while observance of traditional rituals at *oboo*, *barisa*, and other traditional religious sites is widespread, sometimes even attracting Russian patronage as well. The Russian state currently encourages all traditional faiths both as a reaction to the Communist past and to combat what are seen as divisive missionary sects. This encouragement also makes devotion to the Mongolian religions a politically and socially safe way of expressing ethnic identity.

In Inner Mongolia the anticlerical and anti-Buddhist current begun in eastern Inner Mongolia in the late 19th and early 20th centuries is still strong (*see* NEW SCHOOLS MOVEMENTS). Many nationalist intellectuals believe Buddhism was responsible for weakening and pacifying the Mongols and diminishing their population. Inner Mongolian scholars often write with deep bitterness about the Buddhist clergy's attempts to influence Mongolian traditions and, for example, turn Chinggis Khan into "nothing but a Lama-Buddhist deity." Thus, while a limited Buddhist revival has occurred in Inner Mongolia as well, few of the intelligentsia and virtually none of the large Chinese-speaking Mongol minority are believers.

In independent Mongolia from 1990 to 2000 opinion polls showed the number of those who considered themselves believers in some religion rose from 30 percent to 70 percent. Of those 70 percent, Buddhists account for 80 percent. Monastic education has been revived, and young child-lamas in their religious garb in the street are a cherished sign of the new freedom for Mongolia's Buddhists. Shamanism has also been revived, both in traditional form among the Buriat and Darkhad ethnic groups and in a kind of synthetic neoshamanism in the capital. While the intense anti-Buddhist feeling frequently found in Inner Mongolia is rare, shamanism's comparatively greater antiquity and "Mongolness" has attracted much attention. Since 1990 traditional community and family rituals, such as sacrificing at *oboos*, making aspersions to Heaven, observing the White Month (lunar new year), and worshiping the household fire, have become mass phenomena once again in both cities and the countryside, although devotion is less widespread than among the Mongols of Russia. At the same time, Christian missionary efforts have also met a strong response from Mongolia's urban population. Polls show 7 percent of the population now consider themselves Christian, despite the high dropout rate among converts. The Christian population is mostly young, urban, female, and almost exclusively low-church evangelical in belief.

See also BARIACH; BUDDHISM IN THE MONGOL EMPIRE; DAUR LANGUAGE AND PEOPLE; FUNERARY CUSTOMS; JIBZUNDAMBA KHUTUGTU; LAMAS AND MONASTICISM; RELIGIOUS POLICY IN THE MONGOL EMPIRE; TU LANGUAGE AND PEOPLE.

Further reading: E. P. Bakaeva, "Buddhism in Kalmykia (Excerpts)," *Anthropology and Archeology of Eurasia* 39, no. 3 (winter 2000–2001): 11–85; C. R Bawden, "Notes on the Worship of Local Deities in Mongolia," in *Mongolian Studies,* ed. Louis Ligeti (Budapest, 1970), 57–66; ———, "An Oirat Manuscript of the 'Offering of the Fox,'" *Zentralasiatische Studien* 12 (1978): 7–34; Krystyna Chabros, *Beckoning Fortune: A Study of the Mongol Dalalga Ritual* (Wiesbaden: Otto Harrassowitz, 1992); Walther Heissig, *Religions of Mongolia,* trans. Geoffrey Samuel (Berkeley: University of California Press, 1980); Caroline Humphrey, *Shamans and Elders: Experience, Knowledge, and Power among the Daur Mongols* (Oxford: Oxford University Press, 1996); Magdalena Tatar, "Two Mongolian Texts concerning the Cult of the Mountains," *Acta Orientalia* 30 (1976): 1–58; N. L. Zhukovskaia, "Neo-Shamanism in the Context of the Contemporary Ethno-Cultural Situation in the Republic of Buryatia," *Inner Asia* 2 (2000): 25–36; N. L. Zhukovskaia, "Revival of Buddhism in Buryatia: Problems and Prospects," *Anthropology and Archeology of Eurasia* 39, no. 4 (spring 2000–01): 23–47.

religious policy in the Mongol Empire

In return for the prayers of their clergy, the Mongol khans extended tax exemptions and favor at court to the major religions of the empire.

Mongol religious policy developed from the political theology of CHINGGIS KHAN (Genghis, 1206–27) and his successors, who believed firmly that "Eternal Heaven" (*möngke tenggeri*), or God (the Mongols used TENGGERI for the Islamic and Christian God as well) governed all human affairs and had given world rule to the Mongols. The great religions of Eurasia, specifically Buddhism, Christianity, Taoism (Daoism), and Islam, all worshiped this same God, who listened to the prayers of holy men from all these religions. Thus, in return for the clergies' prayers, he granted them and their dependents exemption from all taxes. The Mongols khans, confident in their obedience to "heaven," at first sought primarily the worldly blessings of long life, prosperity, and victory in war.

After Chinggis Khan overthrew the rival shaman TEB TENGGERI around 1210, he reorganized the Mongols' native shamans (*bö'e*, Turkish, *qam*) under a timid supporter, Old Man Üsün. The shamans served the court through divination and suppressing hostile magic. After the death of Chinggis Khan, his tomb and tent also became the site of a religious cult, something continued by his descendants to the present (*see* EIGHT WHITE YURTS). These cults and divination were still practiced at court, and the Mongols occasionally demanded that conquered leaders participate. It is unknown if the shamans also received tax exemptions.

By the 1203 BALJUNA COVENANT Chinggis's entourage included Muslims, Christians, and Buddhists. Intermarriage with the KEREYID and ÖNGGÜD royal families after 1203–05 brought intimate contact with Christian peoples, yet there is no evidence of an explicit religious policy that early. Anti-Islamic persecutions had contributed to the fall of the QARA-KHITAI Empire in Turkestan, and in 1218 the victorious Mongols announced that "each should abide by his own religion." Since it is always the first religion mentioned in Chinese edicts of exemption, Buddhism was probably the first religion to receive official status. In 1219, on the recommendation of his viceroy in North China, MUQALI, Chinggis Khan ordered two Dhyana (Zen) Buddhist monks made DARQAN (tax exempt) because they "truly were speakers to Heaven." From 1220 MASTER CHANGCHUN, a Taoist priest, was summoned to an audience and made both *darqan* and head of all the monks of China, causing controversy with the Buddhists. No specific decrees are known for Christian and Muslim clergy, but in 1219 Chinggis Khan spared Samarqand's chief Islamic clergy and their dependents from the general pillage, and in 1222 he was inquiring about the traditions of Muhammad's life. Such encounters defined Chinggis's legacy to his descendants in religious policy.

In later contacts other religions were added to the policy, although the list of the first four religions remained canonical. ÖGEDEI KHAN (1229–41) took great interest in CONFUCIANISM. Confucian scholars, along with physicians and diviners, were exempted from taxation, while those enslaved in the conquest were freed, policies that were continued in the Mongol YUAN DYNASTY in China. However, the Confucians were only occasionally listed in the edicts along with Buddhism or Taoism. Judaism, Manicheism, Zoroastrianism, and other minority religions of the Middle East were not recognized at first, although the Il-Khans and possibly the Yuan later accorded exemption to Judaism.

Despite this policy of tolerance, Mongol rulers did erratically enforce on non-Mongols their prohibition on bathing in summer and their peculiar customs of slaughtering and levirate marriage. The first two directly contradicted Islamic observances, while the third shocked most Christian peoples. Chinggis's second son, CHA'ADAI (d. 1241/2), proved notoriously rigorous in Central Asia in enforcing these rules. If convinced that a given religion was dangerous, the Mongols had no compunction about suppressing it; MÖNGKE KHAN decreed the extermination of the Islamic ISMA'ILIS ("the Assassins") in 1257 and allowed his brother Qubilai to proscribe certain anti-Buddhist Taoist writings in 1258. In 1264 QUBILAI KHAN (1260–94) ordered religious establishments to pay the grain and commercial taxes, and late in his reign he showed a strong streak of intolerance, decreeing the death penalty for those practicing Islamic-Jewish ritual slaughter or circumcision in 1280 and prohibiting all Taoist writing except the *Daodejing* (*Tao Te Ching*) in 1281. In 1291 he prohibited *yin-yang* fortune-tellers from contacting imperial princes, lest they encourage sedition. All but the last of these decrees was later revoked, however.

As the MONGOL EMPIRE began to divide and interaction with other cultures became more intense, many khans personally adopted various religions. Abagha Khan of the IL-KHANATE (1265–82) was baptized a Christian, and Berke Khan (1257–66) and Sultan Ahmad (1282–84) in the Il-Khanate embraced Islam, yet none of them withdrew patronage from clergy of other religions. In the Yuan dynasty Qubilai Khan made the Tibetan Buddhist 'PHAGS-PA LAMA his state preceptor and directed government patronage to Tibetan Buddhist monasteries. The Yuan emperor Ayurbarwada (titled Renzong, 1312–21), while reinstating the examination system in 1315, made Zhu Xi's philosophy the official school of Confucianism. Nevertheless, after the revocation of Qubilai's later repressive measures, the general Mongol religious policy continued in the Yuan to the end of the Yuan dynasty. Even after the coup d'état of 1328, when sentiment against SEMUREN (Central and West Asian immigrants) grew, the Buddhist and Taoist monasteries merely received special exemptions from the commercial tax (tamgha) in 1331. In the western khanates, however, the adoption of Islam eventually resulted in the proscription of Buddhism, officially sponsored iconoclasm, and the reduction of Christianity to the subordinate status traditional in Islam. This happened first in Iran under GHAZAN KHAN (1295–1304), then in the GOLDEN HORDE under ÖZBEG KHAN (1313–41), and lastly in the CHAGHATAY KHANATE in Central Asia under Tarmashirin (1331–34).

See also ASTROLOGY; BUDDHISM IN THE MONGOL EMPIRE; CHRISTIANITY IN THE MONGOL EMPIRE; CLOTHING AND DRESS; FOOD AND DRINK; ISLAM IN THE MONGOL EMPIRE; RASHID-UD-DIN FAZL-ULLAH; RELIGION; SA'D-UD-DAWLA; SCAPULIMANCY; SHAMANISM; SOCIAL CLASSES IN THE MONGOL EMPIRE; TAOISM IN THE MONGOL EMPIRE; TIBET AND THE MONGOL EMPIRE.

Further reading: Francis Woodman Cleaves, "The Rescript of Qubilai Prohibiting the Slaughtering of Animals by Slitting the Throat," *Journal of Turkish Studies* 16 (1992); 67–89; Elizabeth Endicott-West, "Notes on Shamans, Fortune-tellers and *Yin-Yang* Practitioners and Civil Administration in Yüan China," in *The Mongol Empire and Its Legacy*, ed. Reuven Amitai-Preiss and David O. Morgan (Leiden: E. J. Brill, 1999), 224–239.

Republic of Mongolia   *See* MONGOLIA, STATE OF.

1911 Restoration

The 1911 Restoration secured Mongolia's independence from the Manchu QING DYNASTY (1636–1912) and the succeeding Republic of China (1912–49) and made the country a theocratic monarchy under Mongolia's great incarnate lama, the EIGHTH JIBZUNDAMBA KHUTUGTU (1870–1924).

By the late 19th century, there was a growing feeling that the Qing dynasty was not only uninterested in but actively out of sympathy with Mongolia's Buddhist social

order, led by the Bogda (Holy One, the Khutugtu's usual title among Mongols). The Bogda began to think of Russia as a possible protector for Mongolia's traditional religion and society. His first appeal for Russian aid in 1900, as the Qing court embarked on the disastrous Boxer adventure, was met, however, with counsels of patience.

In March 1910 the new AMBAN Sandô arrived in Khüriye to implement the NEW POLICIES. While there was support for some aspects of modernization, the New Policies' centerpiece of state-sponsored agricultural colonization was anathema. In July 1911, during the regular DANSHUG offerings ceremony, the Bogda secretly consulted with the top princes and lamas of the KHALKHA Mongols and secretly dispatched PRINCE KHANGDADORJI, Da Lama Tserinchimed, and the Inner Mongolian official Haishan (1857–1917) to appeal to St. Petersburg for protection. Although the Bogda informed the Russian consul V. N. Lavdovskii of this decision on July 28, the delegation did not follow his advice to delay. On August 16 the delegation presented their petition to Russia's foreign minister.

The Russian government did not accept the proposal of Mongolian independence but informed the Chinese government of the Mongols' mission and Russia's opposition to the New Policies. It also decided to strengthen the consular guard in Khüriye by 800 men, thus vastly outnumbering the Manchu *amban* (imperial resident) Sandô's 130-man garrison. By August 24 Beijing informed Sandô what had transpired, but he did not feel secure enough to crack down on the Mongols.

In October and early November the Qing's position in Mongolia deteriorated on every side. The delegation to St. Petersburg returned to Mongolia, a republican rebellion broke out in central China on October 10, and in early November the Russian government transferred 15,000 single-shot Berdan rifles with 7,500,000 rounds of ammunition to the Mongols. On November 13 the Khalkhas set up a Provisional Administrative Office for Khüriye Affairs, and on November 28 4,000 militiamen from eastern Khalkha were ordered to converge on Khüriye. Finally, on December 1 the formal declaration of independence from the Qing dynasty was issued. Sandô took asylum in the Russian embassy and was deported back to China on December 4.

On December 29 (16th of the 12th lunar month) the Bogda was enthroned in a vast YURT covered with yellow silk and blue designs as the new Holy Emperor (Bogda Khagan), the Qing emperor's traditional title. Added, however, was the title "dual ruler of religion and state," which expressed the theocratic nature of the new government. His consort, Dondugdulma, was enthroned as the White Tara (the great female bodhisattva) and "mother of the nation." From November 13 the use of Qing reign years for dating was discontinued, and now, following East Asian imperial custom of reign-titles, 1911 was proclaimed year one of Olan-a Ergügdegsen, or "Elevated by the Many," the title of the first Indian monarch Mahasammata in Buddhist legend (*see* CALENDARS AND DATING SYSTEMS). While the new government enjoined its subjects to respect the property of peaceful Chinese merchants, commoners and soldiers in the west and the countryside spontaneously looted and burned many shops.

When first declared, the new state controlled only eastern Khalkha. Soon the HULUN BUIR bannermen who had driven Chinese troops out of Hailar (January 2) and Manzhouli (January 22) were incorporated, and on January 12 the Qing officials in ULIASTAI surrendered. Meanwhile, revolutionaries in China declared a republic on January 1, 1912, and the last Qing emperor abdicated on February 12.

The garrison in KHOWD CITY proved more stubborn than that in Uliastai, and in May 1912 the JALKHANZA KHUTUGTU DAMDINBAZAR (1874–1923) was ordered to pacify the west. From August 5 to 7 the 2,000 Mongolian soldiers under the Barga GRAND DUKE DAMDINSÜRÜNG and the Khalkha Duke MAGSURJAB victoriously stormed the city. Meanwhile, officials of the imperial herds of DARIGANGA petitioned to join the new country on March 3 and were officially confirmed in early July. On the other hand, an effort in August to take over Inner Mongolia's Jirim league by Togtakhu Taiji and Prince Utai ended in failure. The conquest of Khowd thus rounded out the territory of the new state.

See also THEOCRATIC PERIOD.

Further reading: Thomas E. Ewing, *Between the Hammer and the Anvil? Chinese and Russian Policies in Outer Mongolia, 1911–1921* (Bloomington: Indiana University, 1980); Mei-hua Lan, "The Mongolian Independence Movement of 1911: A Pan-Mongolian Endeavor" (Ph.D. diss., Harvard University, 1996); Tatsuo Nakami "A Protest against the Concept of the 'Middle Kingdom': The Mongols and the 1911 Revolution," in *The 1911 Revolution in China: Interpretive Essays*, ed. Etō Shinkichi and Harold Z. Schiffrin (Tokyo: University of Tokyo Press, 1984), 129–149; Urgunge Onon and Derrick Pritchatt, *Asia's First Modern Revolution: Mongolia Proclaims Its Independence in 1911* (Leiden: E. J. Brill, 1989).

Revocation of Autonomy In 1919 Outer Mongolia's autonomous government, led by a faction of lay nobles, petitioned to revoke its autonomous status. This act discredited the traditional authorities and led to the formation of Mongolia's first political party. The KYAKHTA TRILATERAL TREATY of 1915 had given Russia the position of guaranteeing Outer Mongolia's autonomy, but the Russian Revolution, beginning in March 1917, plunged Russia into anarchy. Threats from war-torn Russia several times prompted the Chinese high commissioner Chen Yi to pressure the vacillating Mongolian government into accepting troops in Mongolia beyond the Kyakhta Trilateral Treaty limits. Rumors of a Bolshevik invasion in

April 1918 brought two battalions into Mongolia in September. More serious threats from the Buriat-led pan-Mongolist DAURIIA STATION MOVEMENT, sponsored by the notoriously violent White (anticommunist) Russian Cossack commander Grigorii Semenov, led the upper house of the Mongolian parliament, composed of high nobles and banner *zasags*, to ask for Chinese protection and troops on August 13, 1919.

The August debate in the parliament revealed the existence of a powerful faction of nobles in favor of thoroughly revising the government of Mongolia. After 1915 the GREAT SHABI, or personal subjects of Mongolia's theocratic ruler, the JIBZUNDAMBA KHUTUGTU, or Bogda (Holy One), had exploded in size, leaving steadily fewer and poorer commoners to fulfill state duties. Meanwhile, the nobles felt excluded by the Bogda's favorites. Chen Yi and the Chinese government assiduously courted the disgruntled nobility with honors and promises. By October 1 Chen Yi and Mongolia's leading secular officials had drawn up 63 articles for a new regime in Mongolia that prohibited Chinese colonization or the conversion of Mongolia into a province, yet put the nobility directly under the Chinese high commissioner and eliminated Russia's role. On October 19 the Bogda sent an envoy directly to Beijing to oppose this proposal, but it was approved by the Chinese parliament on October 28.

On October 29 a Chinese frontier general, "Little" Xu Shuzheng (1880–1925), arrived in Mongolia from Beijing with the 6,000-strong mixed brigade requested on August 13. Xu, who had the Chinese president's backing, canceled Chen Yi's cautious approach and advocated modernizing Mongolia, encouraging colonization, and exploiting its natural resources. On November 15, with troops threatening to arrest the Bogda, the upper house yielded to force and voted to petition for the revocation of Mongolia's autonomy, and the government confirmed the petition two days later. Xu was officially confirmed on December 1 as the supreme authority in Mongolia, replacing Chen Yi. The Bogda's secret appeals to the American legation went unanswered, and on January 1, 1920, the Bogda and his officials publicly swore allegiance to the Republic of China. Opponents formed several groups that merged in June to form the secret Mongolian People's Party and begin the 1921 REVOLUTION.

See also BADMADORJI; JIBZUNDAMBA KHUTUGTU, EIGHTH; THEOCRATIC PERIOD.

Further reading: Thomas E. Ewing, *Between the Hammer and the Anvil? Chinese and Russian Policies in Outer Mongolia, 1911–1921* (Bloomington: Indiana University, 1980).

1921 Revolution In the 1921 Revolution the Soviet Red Army installed in power in Mongolia a government whose revolutionary reforms fed off the popular anger and disillusionment with both the REVOCATION OF AUTONOMY by the Chinese and the violence of BARON ROMAN FEDOROVICH VON UNGERN-STERNBERG'S White Russian occupation.

SOCIAL ORIGINS OF THE REVOLUTIONARIES

The 1921 revolutionaries were creatures of Mongolia's capital, Khüriye (modern ULAANBAATAR), and the post-1911 theocratic government. They were virtually all commoners, often without any secure social position (several were illegitimate children), whose parents or they themselves had migrated to the city to make a living. There they were employed in the new government offices as army officers, customs officials, telegraph operators, interpreters, and bureaucrats, both civil and monastic. Several had connections to the Russian consulate and knew the Russian language, and a few had been to Europe or Japan. All were under 40, and all owed what social position they had to Mongolia's autonomy. Another group involved in the revolutionary activities from the beginning were Buriat Mongols from southern Siberia. These BURIATS had had experience in Mongolia after 1911 working for Russian diplomats and expeditions.

FORMATION OF THE EARLY "PARTIES"

The 1921 Revolution grew out of three different "factions," or *nam* (the word was later used for parties) that formed in opposition to the threatened Revocation of Autonomy, which was publicly discussed from August 1919 on. The "officials' faction" (*tüshimed-un nam*, also called the East Khüriye Group), founded by Danzin, Dindub (Ö. Dendew, 1882–1922), and Dogsum (D. Dogsom, 1884–1941), was composed of lower-level officials in the theocratic government, many of whom were in the parliament's lower house. The "commoners' faction" (*arad-un nam*, also called the Consulate Terrace Group), founded by BODÔ, Choibalsang, and Chagdurjab (D. Chagdarjaw, 1880–1922), was a discussion group linking Mongols employed at the Russian consulate and their friends. Bodô, its leader, was friendly with a Bolshevik-leaning mechanic at the consulate, M. Kucherenko (d. 1921). The Bogda (Holy One), or EIGHTH JIBZUNDAMBA KHUTUGTU (1870–1924), Mongolia's theocratic ruler, called together the "nobles' faction" (*noyad-un nam*), including MAGSURJAB, the Jalkhanza Khutugtu, and others, with the aim of appealing to the United States or Japan.

From the beginning the officials' and commoners' factions mixed nationalist and antiaristocratic goals. The role of the aristocrats and the Upper House in the abolition of autonomy had discredited the old ruling class. A spring 1920 poster written by Dogsum used Confucian language to call for the election of banner rulers. There was no opposition to Buddhism, however. Indeed, in 1919 the officials' faction's members swore to defend the Mongolian religion and people before the fierce "Red Protector" (Jamsrang, or Beg-tshe) in ABATAI KHAN'S old shrine. Many were personally religious, although all, even the lamas such as Chagdurjab, preferred life outside the monasteries.

APPEAL TO SOVIET RUSSIA

From the night of November 15, when the parliament's Upper House voted to abolish autonomy, the officials' group made fruitless appeals to the Bogda and the (anti-Bolshevik) Russian consul for assistance. By March to April 1920 the "officials' faction" had linked up with the "commoners' faction" and local Bolsheviks in Khüriye. In January 1920 the Red Army occupied Irkutsk, and in June the two factions merged as the "People's Party of Outer Mongolia" and contacted Bolshevik representatives from Irkutsk.

On July 26 the Bogda, disappointed with the possibilities of aid from elsewhere, finally gave the People's Party a stamped appeal to Soviet Russia. Seven delegates traveled to Irkutsk to ask for assistance: Danzin, Dogsum, and Sükhebaatur from the "officials' faction" and Choibalsang, Bodô, Chagdurjab, and Losal (D. Losol, 1890–1940) from the "commoners' faction." They met both local Soviet leaders and Buriats such as TSYBEN ZHAMTSARONOVICH ZHAMTSARANO, and ELBEK-DORZHI RINCHINO. While Bodô and Dogsum returned to Khüriye to organize the party, Danzin, Changdurjab, and Losal went to Omsk and then Moscow to pursue the request for aid. Sükhebaatur and Choibalsang, left behind in Irkutsk, helped the Buriats in the Siberian Communist Party design propaganda for Mongolia.

Meanwhile, in Khüriye the Chinese police arrested the leaders of both the People's Party and the "nobles' faction" in September. When the White Russian commander Baron Roman F. Ungern-Sternberg invaded Mongolia with a call to free the land from the Chinese, several members of the People's Party, including Bodô and Dogsum, eventually joined his forces. On February 4 the baron marched into Khüriye and released the imprisoned anti-Chinese conspirators, while the Chinese fled north to the border town of KYAKHTA CITY. The baron formed a new government from the "nobles' faction."

BATTLE FOR KYAKHTA

In early November Moscow's Communist International promised military aid to Danzin and company. Danzin returned to Irkutsk, while the others moved on to the border town Troitskosavsk (in modern Kyakhta) with their Buriat allies, where they began recruiting partisans from frontier pickets and BANNERS (appanages) along the border. They were still poorly armed but were drilled intensively by Soviet instructors. On the night of March 17 Sükhebaatur, a former platoon commander in theocratic Mongolia's army, led 400 Mongolian partisans in an assault on the Chinese at the Mongolian border town of Kyakhta. After tough fighting the 2,000–2,500 dispirited

Chinese soldiers fled. The revolutionaries made the smoking ruins of Kyakhta (renamed Altanbulag) their center. Elected at an assembly on March 1–3, the new leadership troika was Danzin as party chairman, Sükhebaatar as commander in chief, and Chagdurjab as provisional prime minister. During the preparations the partisans used the letter from the Bogda to aid their recruitment, and in the siege raised both yellow (Buddhist) and red (revolutionary) flags.

DESTRUCTION OF THE WHITES

With the Chinese gone, the conflict now involved Soviet Russia and the People's Party on one side, which proposed comprehensive reforms and the gradual elimination of hereditary privileges, and Ungern-Sternberg's Whites with the Bogda, the "nobles' faction," and a few People's Party members on the other. Dogsum and Bodô, however, had escaped to rejoin their comrades in Altanbulag. In April Bodô replaced Chagdurjab, who had a reputation as an overly sociable lightweight, as provisional prime minister, and the People's Party sent representatives to the northern KHÖWSGÖL PROVINCE and the western DÖRBÖDS to widen the struggle.

From June 5 to 13 a mixed ethnic force of Ungern-Sternberg's troops, 5,000 strong, attacked Altanbulag but were driven back by the 700 Mongolian partisans and Russian reinforcements. Finally, on June 28 a Red Army force of over 13,000 directly invaded Mongolia, taking Khüriye on July 6. In western Mongolia separate Red Army columns entered Mongolia around Khöwsgöl and the Khowd frontier to destroy the 4,000 remaining Whites. Magsurjab, of the "nobles' faction" switched sides and massacred the White Russians outside Uliastai on July 21, and a revolutionary government was formed among the Dörböds in July. A small Red Army force composed of volunteers from the KALMYKS remained in Ulaanbaatar until 1925, despite Chinese protests.

THE NEW REGIME

The revolutionaries enthroned the Bogda as the "constitutional monarch" on July 11, the day celebrated as National Day in Mongolia. From then on a steady stream of reforms were enacted, directed at abolishing the Qing social hierarchies and separating religion and state. While the old "nobles' faction" joined the new regime enthusiastically, the revolution remained an affair principally of Khüriye, viewed with great skepticism by the rural elites. Within the revolutionary ranks violent controversies soon broke out. As early as April some Mongolian officials complained that Russian advisers were interfering in government business. In fall and winter 1921 conflicts developed around the unpredictable Bodô, which ended with his execution as well as that of Chagdurjab, Dindub, and other party founders on August 31, 1922. Despite these conflicts, the new regime steadily built up rural support through school-

ing, demobilized veterans, youth leagues, and especially by economic expansion, which brought increasing prosperity until 1930.

See also ARMED FORCES OF MONGOLIA; CHOIBALSANG, MARSHAL; DANZIN, GENERAL; JIBZUNDAMBA KHUTUGTU, EIGHTH; REVOLUTIONARY PERIOD; SÜKHEBAATUR, GENERAL; THEOCRATIC PERIOD.

Further reading: Thomas E. Ewing, *Between the Hammer and the Anvil? Chinese and Russian Policies in Outer Mongolia, 1911–1921* (Bloomington: Indiana University, 1980); Hiroshi Futaki, "A Re-examination of the Establishment of the Mongolian People Party Centring on Dogsom's Memoir," *Inner Asia* 2 (2000): 37–62; Urgunge Onon, ed., *Mongolian Heroes of the Twentieth Century* (New York: AMS Press, 1976).

revolutionary period From 1921 to 1940 successive waves of revolutionaries wrestled in an extremely turbulent period with issues of modernization, the role of religion, the rise of Japan, and dependence on the Soviet Union. Not until the creation of the Choibalsang dictatorship by 1940 was the revolutionary period succeeded by a stable Communist-style government. (*For subsequent developments, see* MONGOLIAN PEOPLE'S REPUBLIC.)

INTERNATIONAL STATUS

After the 1921 REVOLUTION Mongolia reverted to the same uncertain status as after the 1911 RESTORATION of independence: claiming independence but treated by China and other powers as a rebellious province. Even more complicated was the fact that neither China nor many of the other powers had yet recognized Mongolia's patron, Soviet Russia. In its own program, the Mongolian People's Party spoke both of pan-Mongolian unification and of joining a loosely confederated China. However, the first was a distant aspiration and the second only a concession to Russian concerns.

On September 14, 1921, the new prime minister, BODÔ, announced Mongolia's independence to the world. On November 5, 1921, in a relatively simple "agreement" (the Russians deliberately did not use the word *treaty*), Soviet Russia recognized Mongolia's "people's government" as the sole legitimate government. Even so, influential "China hands" in Soviet diplomacy preferred to court China at Mongolia's expense. On May 30, 1924, in a treaty with China, the Soviet Union received recognition in part for recognizing Chinese sovereignty (i.e., full control) over Mongolia. In spring 1925 the last Soviet troops were removed from Mongolia. In fact, the Soviet authorities were confident that China was too weak to recover Mongolia.

Mongolia proved unable to develop formal relations with countries outside the Soviet Union. Visits in 1921–22 by the American consul in Zhangjiakou ended in fiasco as his interlocutor, Bodô, was executed as a supposed traitor. Unofficial links with outside powers, however, grew steadily. From 1923 to 1933 Mongolia covertly supported Inner Mongolian revolutionaries. From 1924 to 1927 Mongolia was also allied with the Soviet-aligned Guomindang or Nationalist Party in China, while the Soviet-supported Chinese warlord Feng Yuxiang maintained an office in ULAANBAATAR from 1925 to 1928. Mongolian students and technicians studied in Germany from 1926 to 1929. Nevertheless, the attempts by the Mongolian leader DAMBADORJI to open relations with Japan in 1926–28 led the Soviet Union to consider him a dangerous "rightist."

After 1929 the leftist policy enforced on the Mongolian government by Moscow's Communist International (Comintern) closed down all these ties with non-Soviet countries. The June 17, 1929, Soviet-Mongolian Agreement laid the basis for an almost complete Soviet monopoly on Mongolian trade. The Japanese invasion of Manchuria and Inner Mongolia widened from 1931 to 1937, and border incidents from 1935 snowballed into an undeclared war (*see* KHALKHYN GOL, BATTLE OF). On March 12, 1936, Mongolia signed the Protocol on Mutual Assistance with the Soviet Union, and the Red Army reentered Mongolia's territory. Not until 1946, after Mongolia had joined the Red Army's destruction of Japanese forces, did China recognize Mongolia's independence.

GOVERNMENT

From 1921 to 1924 Mongolia was a constitutional monarchy, with the Bogda Khan (Holy Emperor; *see* JIBZUNDAMBA KHUTUGTU, EIGHTH) as the head of state. Although draft constitutions were prepared, the Comintern and the more radical Mongols feared that a constitution would lock the government into an excessive conservative legal framework. After the Bogda's death in May 1924, Mongolia was made a people's republic in November with a new constitution written by the government's Soviet legal adviser. The 1924 CONSTITUTION confirmed Mongolia as a secular state and abolished the old hereditary estates. At the same time, however, it designated a new category of "exploiting classes" (old aristocrats, monks, rentiers), who were separated from the "real people" and disenfranchised. These provisions were not consistently applied until 1929.

The constitution's formal government structure did not, however, have anything to do with the real power relations, which throughout this period are best described as the rule of a revolutionary conquest elite. Before the rise of MARSHAL CHOIBALSANG in 1936, this elite was not dominated by one man nor was power vested in one particular position. Top leaders were all members of the presidium of the MONGOLIAN PEOPLE'S REVOLUTIONARY PARTY's Central Committee, a seven- to 17-man body that met weekly. The top leader, however, could hold various positions: prime minister, party chairman, or commander in chief of the military.

The Mongolian power elite in this period can be divided into roughly four groups: 1) the 1921 revolutionaries, city-bred commoners who served as clerks, students, and petty officials in the theocratic period, called the "city" (*khota;* Russian, *khoton*) faction after 1925; 2) patriotic officials, older, higher officials under Qing and theocratic governments supplying institutional continuity; 3) the rural (*khödöö;* Russian, *khudon*) faction, uneducated commoners who entered political life through organizing rural party, youth league, and cooperative cells after the 1921 Revolution; and 4) students with no work or study experience under the old regime, but who graduated from party or military schools after 1921. In 1928–29 the rurals and the students linked to overthrow the remaining 1921 revolutionaries, and they ruled Mongolia until the GREAT PURGE annihilated all four groups and created a new elite.

The Mongolian leaders were an extraordinarily youthful lot: Until Marshal Choibalsang's rise not a single leader (the "patriotic officials" functioned as career bureaucrats, not political leaders) reached age 40 in office. Frequently, they began by ranting Soviet slogans in their early 20s yet were sobered by officeholding into pragmatic national-minded rulers in their 30s, at which point Soviet pressure would bring in a new group of slogan shouters.

Until 1924 the Soviet influence on Mongolian policy was exercised through individual advisers, many of whom were ethnic BURIATS. ELBEK-DORZHI RINCHINO, a Buriat member of the presidium and chairman of the party's military commission, at times was a virtually dictator. After 1925 Soviet influence was formalized through the Communist International, whose delegation in Mongolia virtually ran the country in the LEFTIST PERIOD from 1929 to 1932. After the leftist debacle in 1932 Joseph Stalin's Politburo (the Soviet Communist Party's ruling organ) assumed direct supervision over Mongolia, punctuated by Stalin's semiannual meetings with the Mongolian leaders in Moscow.

ECONOMY AND FINANCE

The first decade of the new regime saw sudden growth in herds and population. Available figures show livestock increasing from 9.6 million in 1918 to 13.8 million in 1924 and approximately 24 million in 1930. Population rose from about 540,000 in 1918 to 651,700 in 1925 and 727,400 in 1930. While the statistical evidence is somewhat equivocal, the impression of observers is that this increase was also reflected in growing foreign trade. This growth was the foundation for the stability of the regime, regardless of the conflicts among the men at the top.

The attempt at collectivization, begun in late 1930, reversed these positive trends. The number of livestock collapsed from 24 million to 17.6 million in 1933, while the population, due to emigration and civil war, declined to 723,600 in 1935. While the cancellation of collectivization and the NEW TURN POLICY allowed livestock to increase to 22.6 million head in 1935 and 26.2 million in 1940, the catastrophic Great Purge and the liquidation of the lama population kept the population stagnant, reaching only 725,500 in 1940. The antifeudal campaigns and progressive livestock taxes equalized wealth, making Mongolia, pastorally speaking at least, a "middle-class" country. Mongolian statistics measured animals in *bod*, a unit equivalent to one horse or cow, three-fourths of a camel, five sheep, or seven goats. In 1927 the 6 percent of households with more than 101 *bod* held 41.7 percent of the livestock, while the 63.7 percent with less than 20 *bod* owned only 14.4 percent. By 1939 the 4.3 percent of households with more than 101 *bod* held only 18.8 percent, and the 41.4 percent of households with less than 20 *bod* held 14.0 percent. The rural middle class with 21–100 *bod* made up 54.3 percent of the population and held 67.2 percent of the livestock.

Despite this growth there was little industrialization of the Mongolian economy. In 1932 total industrial production was 3.5 million tögrögs, of which 2.4 million came from the recently collectivized handicrafts workers, largely Chinese, while only 1.1 million came from state-owned factories, mostly mines. In 1931 plans were made to develop a significant light industrial plant. Delayed by the crisis of 1932, the Ulaanbaatar Industrial Combine began operation in 1934 as a Soviet-Mongolian joint-stock company, processing animal products to produce washed wool, shoes, felt, and leather goods and containing its own heat and power station. This combine, the Khatgal wool-washing plant, and other smaller factories elevated the production of state-owned factories to 12.8 million tögrögs in 1935 and 53.7 million in 1940. The laicization of the lamas supplied 5,543 new members to the craft cooperatives, whose output jumped to 23.3 million tögrögs in 1940. Through the 1930s the ethnic composition of the workers and artisans was nativized. In 1927 only 26 percent were Mongolian, in 1935 about half, and by 1940 87.7 percent of the 33,100 workers were Mongolian. The balance was Chinese and to a lesser degree Russian.

The leftist period affected finance as well. Up until 1928 customs receipts made up 40–50 percent of the budget, while direct taxation, mostly on livestock, took in 10–15 percent. During the leftist period these percentages almost reversed. Deficit spending covered the more than doubling of the budget from 1928 to 1931, until the crisis of 1932 forced drastic retrenchment. In this crisis bonds and a state lottery were temporarily used to raise money for needed military expenditures. In the succeeding New Turn Policy customs receipts (almost wholly from trade with Russia), direct taxes, and sales and excise taxes supplied the bulk of revenues in roughly equal parts. During the final phase of the antireligious persecution, taxes on lamas and monastic funds became major revenue sources as well. The lack of fundamental change in the economy was reflected in the maintenance of the *ulaa*, or the traditional postroad corvée duty, with posts every 48 kilometers (30 miles) until 1949.

CULTURE, ARTS, AND EDUCATION

The crisis of 1919–21 put an end to the last flowering of Buddhist art and architecture in Mongolia. After 1921 the court painter "BUSYBODY" SHARAB, for example, famous for his guru portraits, switched to posters and cartoons lampooning the greed and treason of the old feudal classes. Party pamphlets, journals, and textbooks not only expounded immediate political tasks but also published in translation Marx's and Engels' shorter works and classics of general European and American culture. Up to 1928 the Revolutionary Youth League was a major center of literary production, particularly Beijing-opera-style plays and propagandistic songs and anthems by BUYAN-NEMEKHÜ, NATSUGDORJI, and others. The more traditional "patriotic officials" such as Jamyang (O. Jamiyan, 1864–1930), Shagja (S. Shagj, 1886–1938), Batuwachir (Ch. Bat-Ochir, b. 1874) and the Buriat TSYBEN ZHAMT-SARANOVICH ZHAMTSARANO (1881–1940) founded the "Philology Institute" (Sudur bichig-ün khüriyeleng), the precursor of the modern ACADEMY OF SCIENCES, and focused on the collection and publication of traditional Mongolian works directed to a lay audience as well as newer textbooks. The combination of a traditional family-based loyalism toward the new government with a secular, antimonastic trend created a peculiarly Confucian cast to conservative thought in this era, exemplified by Batuwachir's didactic treatise *Mandukhu naran-u tuyaga* (Rays of the rising sun).

The leftist period marked a revolutionary break in culture as well as in economics and government. The regime's conservative supporters were silenced, and some, such as Zhamtsarano, were deported to Russia. The formation of the "Writers' Circle" (Zokhiyalchid-un bülgüm) in January 1929, a precursor of the later official Writers Union, sparked a tremendous expansion of revolutionary literature and the opening of new genres, particularly short stories. The creation of revolutionary literature continued during the New Turn policy, although during that time Shagja and other conservatives again criticized slavish imitation of European cultural forms.

The leftist period also saw a vast expansion in the government budget devoted to education, mass culture, and entertainment. The share of the budget for cultural-educational expenditures jumped from 11 percent in 1928 to 23 percent in 1929. The number of public schools and students rose from 40 students in one school in 1921 to 24,341 students in 331 grade schools in 1940. Only with the destruction of the monasteries did the public school system acquire a monopoly.

In a special "Cultural Offensive" in 1930–31 about 28,100 adults were taught to read and write, 20,000 of whom were in the provinces. Female literacy remained extremely low, and even in this campaign only 8,100 were female. Among the lamas, most of whom could at least recognize the Tibetan alphabet and many of whom used it freely to write Mongolian, about 20,000 were taught the Mongolian script in 1935–37. By 1940 20.8 percent of the population was literate in Mongolian.

In medicine proponents of the Tibetan and European methods violently denounced each other, with only a few, like Zhamtsarano, urging the selection of the best from both. With only 27 European-trained doctors and 81 paramedical personnel in 1930, however, Tibetan medicine was the only alternative for most of the population. By 1940, with the elimination of the lamas, 108 doctors and 923 paramedical staff had to serve the entire nation's medical needs.

Particularly for the educated and urban youth, the whole "feel" of life was changing with the rapid adoption of European customs. Students studying in Russia learned new ways of dressing, new foods, new sports, and new ways of entertainment, which they carried home with them (see CLOTHING AND DRESS). Movie theaters were also opened in the early 1930s, and a craze for social dancing swept the young people during the height of the Great Purge. Despite these changes, ULAANBAATAR in 1940 still looked physically much like the same as in 1921; the great construction projects that would utterly transform the urban landscape began only after 1945.

See also ANTHEM; ARMED FORCES OF MONGOLIA; FLAGS; MONEY, MODERN.

Further reading: Baabar [Bat-Erdene Batbayar], *Twentieth-Century Mongolia*, ed. C. Kaplonski, trans. D. Sühjargalmaa et al. (Cambridge: White Horse Press, 1999); Tsedendambyn Batbayar, *Modern Mongolia: A Concise History* (Ulaanbaatar: Offset Printing, Mongolian Center for Scientific and Technical Information, 1996); Owen Lattimore and Fukiko Isono, *The Diluv Khutagt: Memoirs and Autobiography of a Mongol Buddhist Reincarnation in Religion and Revolution* (Wiesbaden: Otto Harrassowitz, 1982); Ma Ho-t'ien, *Chinese Agent in Mongolia*, trans. John de Francis (Baltimore: Johns Hopkins University Press, 1949); Robert A. Rupen, *Mongols of the Twentieth Century*, 2 vols. (Bloomington: Indiana University, 1964); Shagdariin Sandag and Harry H. Kendall, *Poisoned Arrows: The Stalin-Choibalsang Mongolian Massacres, 1921–1941* (Boulder, Colo.: Westview Press, 2000).

Rinchen, Byambyn (Rintchen, Yü. Rinchen)

(1905–1979) *Multitalented author and scholar who ran afoul of the party for his national sentiment and criticism of ideological obscurantism*

Although ethnically KHALKHA of the Yüngshiyebü clan, Rinchen's grandfather Bimba fled ZUD (winter disaster) and enrolled in Russia's Buriat Cossacks. His mother was a descendant of the famous Khalkha prince TSOGTU TAIJI. After 1911 Rinchen's father, Radnajab (1874–1921), became a border official in Mongolian KYAKHTA (modern Altanbulag) and supported both the pan-Mongolist 1919 DAURIIA STATION MOVEMENT and the 1921 REVOLUTION.

Born in Troitskosavsk (in modern Kyakhta) on December 21, 1905, Rinchen learned Mongolian and Manchu before he entered the Russian school there from 1914 to 1920. (Early on, Rinchen used the Russian-style surname Bimbaev from his grandfather's name and sometimes his full name, Rinchendorji.) From 1923 to 1927 Rinchen studied at the Oriental Institute in Leningrad (St. Petersburg) and worked at the Philology Institute (later Institute of Sciences) after his return. Writing poetry from 1923, he joined the leftist "Writers' Circle" in 1929, publishing his anticlerical poem "For the Yellow Parasites" (*Shira khubalza nar-tu*). In 1931 Rinchen married the Buriat Ochiryn Ratna (Russian, Maria Ivanovna Oshirov, b. 1900), former wife of an arrested Buriat specialist Dashi Sampilon. They had three daughters and one son, Rinchenii Barsbold, who became one of Mongolia's leading paleontologists.

On September 10, 1937, he was arrested by order of MARSHAL CHOIBALSANG as a "pan-Mongolist Japanese spy." Spared execution by chance, he was released on March 30, 1942, at Choibalsang's own behest and became an editor at *Ünen* newspaper with TSENDIIN DAMDINSÜREN, with whom he had many disagreements. From 1944 until his retirement he worked at the State University, the State Publishing House, and the ACADEMY OF SCIENCES.

Rinchen was a poet, essayist, short story writer, novelist, and translator. His 1944 screenplay for the film *Tsogtu Taiji* (*Tsogt Taij*) won a state award. His most famous work was his trilogy *Üriin tuyaa* (Rays of dawn, 1951–55, revised 1971), Mongolia's first published novel set during the 1921 Revolution. *Lady Anu* tells of GALDAN BOSHOGTU KHAN's resistance to the Qing invaders, while the children's novel *Zaan Zaluudai* (1966) tells a story of Stone Age clans. In 1947 he translated the *Communist Manifesto* into Mongolian. A poem ostensibly on QUBILAI KHAN's SQUARE SCRIPT criticized in Aesopian language the government's abandonment of the traditional UIGHUR-MONGOLIAN SCRIPT.

As a scholar, Rinchen wrote on numerous topics of MONGOLIAN LANGUAGE and LITERATURE. He also edited many works of Mongolia's premodern literature. His publication of shamanistic (1959–75) and general folkloric (1960–72) texts, which he had been collecting since 1928, was criticized both for its content and for its publication in revisionist West Germany. He organized the First International Congress of Mongolists in 1959, the first Mongolian forum to invite non-Soviet bloc scholars.

In 1948 Rinchen had criticized the work of a Soviet adviser at the Mongolian State University, and in 1949 the party Politburo first attacked him for nationalism. This accusation was repeated in 1959, citing *Tsogtu Taiji's* excessive admiration of feudal characters, Rinchen's poetically expressed distaste for Russian urban life, and his praise for prerevolutionary cultural achievements shown in his 1959 travelogue about Hungary. The third volume of his *Grammar of Written Mongolian*, published in 1967, was recalled and destroyed again for its expression of nationalism. Another attack in March 1976 also posthumously attacked his parents and brother. In these later criticisms, which hastened his death from cancer, academic rivals such as Sh. Gaadamba eagerly supplied the party ideologues with ammunition.

Rinchen's wit and practical jokes made him a legendary scourge of pompous officials and arrogant Russians. Nevertheless, to the end of his life he believed in the 1921 Revolution, and his scholarly work shows both admiration of the great Russian tradition of Mongolistics and a defensive reaction to Soviet denigration of Mongolian culture. According to his wishes, his coffin was lined not with the Russian-style black or red cloth but with the auspicious Mongolian white, with the outside covered in green and the lid in blue, symbolizing heaven over the Mongolian steppe.

See also BURIATS; MONGOLIAN PEOPLE'S REPUBLIC; SOVIET UNION AND MONGOLIA.

Further reading: B. Rinchen, *Lady Anu* (Ulaanbaatar: State Publishing House, 1980).

Rinchino, Elbek-Dorzhi (R. Elbegdorj) (1888–1938)

Buriat pan-Mongolist revolutionary who became the virtual dictator of Mongolia from 1922 to 1925

Born on May 16, 1888, in Khilgana village in northern Barguzin (Buriat, Bargazhan) district to an unwed mother, Bubei Balagano, Elbek-Dorzhi in his third year was adopted by his stepfather Rinchin, an elder of Ekhired (Russian, Ekhirit) Buriat origin. After graduating from the Barguzin primary school, Rinchino pursued a technical education in Verkhneudinsk (modern ULAN-UDE), Troitskosavsk (near KYAKHTA), and Tomsk. From 1908 to 1914 he attended the school of law of St. Petersburg University with a stipend from the Ekhired clan association.

From 1903 to 1913 Rinchino participated in illegal revolutionary student groups and was imprisoned briefly in fall 1907. He also wrote on cultural topics under the pen name "Alamzhi Mergen," the hero of a Buriat epic poem. He revised AGWANG DORZHIEV's new Buriat script with Nikolai Amagaev (1868–1932) in 1910 and published a two-volume collection of Barguzin folk poetry (1911). In 1915–16 he joined the Russian Economic-Statistical Expedition to Mongolia before heading the statistical department of the cooperatives of Transbaikal province.

After the czar's abdication in March 1917, Rinchino became a leader in the Buriat National Committee (Russian abbreviation, *Burnatskom*). As a student he had joined Bolshevik, Menshevik, and left-wing populist organizations by turns, and this lack of party loyalty continued. In April 1917 he joined the Social Revolutionary Party's Maximalist group but left it in the fall. At first he opposed the Bolsheviks, but by summer 1918 he was organizing Buriat Red Guards for the Soviet regime. After the Whites took Siberia, Rinchino became a chief mover in the 1919 pan-Mongolist DAURIIA STATION MOVEMENT of the White Russian half-Buriat Cossack leader Grigorii M. Semenov. By April 1919 Rinchino had joined the Bolshevik guerrillas again, and immediately after the Red Army's return to Verkhneudinsk he was recognized on March 17, 1920, as chairman of a revived pro-Bolshevik Burnatskom.

Always interested in exporting revolution to Mongolia, in summer 1920 Rinchino linked up with the Khalkha Mongolian revolutionaries coming to Soviet Russia for aid against the Chinese occupation (*see* 1921 REVOLUTION). From then on Rinchino transferred his interest from Buriatia to Mongolia. Until May 1921 he chaired the Mongolian-Tibetan department in Irkutsk, a committee successively part of the Siberian Communist Party apparatus and then of the Communist International (Comintern). By this time he had married Mariia Nikiforovna Namm, a western Buriat graduate of the Irkutsk gymnasium. They had two daughters, Yenok and Erjima (1921–81), and a son, Sanandar (d. 1946).

After the installation of the new regime in Mongolia, Rinchino became chairman of the military committee, a member of the economic committee, and a member of the Mongolian People's Party's presidium. While in Mongolia Rinchino was not an agent of Comintern policy but a rather erratic implementer of his own vision of a radical pan-Mongolist republic. Rinchino at first supported Danzin and General SÜKHEBAATUR against BODÔ, who was executed in 1922. By 1924, however, GENERAL DANZIN had become wary of Rinchino's flamboyant revolutionary rhetoric, while Rinchino believed Danzin to be collaborating with Chinese merchants. During the party's Third Congress (August 1924), Rinchino allied with DAMBADORJI and Choibalsang to execute Danzin and his allies, enforcing the principle of one-party rule and "noncapitalist development," a slogan he was the first to popularize.

After the congress Rinchino was riding high in Mongolia. Nevertheless from fall 1924 he had constantly to fend off criticism from the Comintern's first official representative, the Kazakh Turar R. Ryskulov (1894–1938). The disagreements came to a head over Rinchino's advocacy of an adventurous pan-Mongolist policy in Inner Mongolia. The Comintern recalled both to Russia and entrusted a Balagan Buriat, Matvei I. Amagaev (1897–1939), with eliminating pan-Mongolism in the Mongolian party.

From 1925 Rinchino taught political economy in Moscow, first at the Institute of Red Professors and then at the Communist University of the Toilers of the East. Rinchino was arrested on July 19, 1937, in the first wave of the GREAT PURGE as a pan-Mongolist (now treated as a criminal offense) and a Japanese spy and executed a year later, on June 23.

See also BURIAT LANGUAGE AND SCRIPT; BURIATS; MON-GOLIAN PEOPLE'S PARTY, THIRD CONGRESS OF; NEW SCHOOLS MOVEMENTS; REVOLUTIONARY PERIOD.

Rintchen   *See* RINCHEN, BYAMBYN.

rJe-btsun Dam-pa   *See* JIBZUNDAMBA KHUTUGTU.

Rouran (Jou-jan, Ruanruan, Juan-juan)   The Rouran were a powerful steppe empire from the later fourth century to 552. The Rouran appear to have been a mix of Wuhuan (War or Avar) and XIONGNU (Hun) peoples. Chinese accounts describe the empire's dynastic ancestor as an emancipated slave of the Eastern Hu who fled from the land of the Tabghach (Tuoba) clan of the XIANBI in south-central Inner Mongolia around 310. The slave's band became the nucleus of a new people. The dynasty's original family name was Mugulü, meaning "bald" (cf. Mongolian *muqur*, "cropped, bobtailed"), but it was later changed to Rouran. Later the Tabghach, now ruling North China, contemptuously renamed them Ruanruan, "wriggling insects."

"Eastern Hu" was a general Chinese term for the Xianbi and the Wuhuan originating in eastern Inner Mongolia. Since the Rouran dynasty is linked with the War/Avars of Europe, whose name corresponds to the medieval pronunciation of modern Chinese "Wuhuan," the Rouran dynasty was presumably Wuhuan in origin. Little is known directly of their language, but they used the title *qaghan,* "khan." Since the Eastern Hu as a whole appear to be of Mongolic ancestry, the Rouran, too, were presumably Mongolic in language. The name Rouran (medieval Chinese *ñzhu-ñzhän*) resists any convincing etymology.

By the time of the khan Shilun (r. 402–10), the Rouran dominated the Mongolian steppe from Korea to Yanqi in the Tarim Basin and from the Tabghach's frontier in Inner Mongolia to the Turkish "High-Carts" (Chinese, Gaoju) of Siberia. The Tabghach's Northern Wei (386–528) dynasty attempted to weaken the Rouran both by invasion and by allying with rival tribes, particularly the High-Carts and their allies the Tiele (Töles?). Eventually, under their chief Afujiluo (fl. 490–520), the Tiele became a serious danger to the Rouran. After the revolt of the Northern Wei border garrisons, the last Rouran ruler, Anagui (520–52), allied with the weakened dynasty, receiving a Tabghach princess. When the Wei split into two regimes, the ethnically Xianbi Yuwen regime in Shaanxi and the Han (ethnic Chinese) Gao regime in Hebei, the Rouran allied with the Gao family. In 545 the Yuwen family allied with the Ashina clan in the ALTAI RANGE, which in 552 overthrew Rouran rule and founded the TÜRK EMPIRES.

From 434 on the Rouran had intervened in the Central Asian oases, supporting the Heftalite dynasty (per-haps of Khion/Xiongnu ancestry) to outflank the Tiele and High-Carts. From the late fifth century the ethnic term *War* appears in close association with *Hun* among both the Heftalites and the Oghur Turks on the Volga. It was these War, apparently western outliers of the Rouran confederacy, who after the Turkish conquest invaded the Black Sea steppe. Under Baianos Khaganos (Mongolian, Bayan Qaghan, that is, Rich Khan, fl. 562–82) they formed the Avar Empire (c. 568–796) based in Hungary, which was finally destroyed by Charlemagne.

See also ALTAIC LANGUAGE FAMILY; MONGOLIC LAN-GUAGE FAMILY.

Further reading: Peter Golden, *An Introduction to the History of the Turkic Peoples: Ethnogenesis and State-Formation in Medieval and Early Modern Eurasia and the Middle East* (Wiesbaden: Otto Harrassowitz, 1992).

Ruanruan   *See* ROURAN.

Rum, Sultanate of   *See* TURKEY.

runic script and inscriptions   The Old Turkish runic script (the similarity to German runes is entirely superficial) was the first extant script to be developed for an Altaic language. Examples are found in all but easternmost Mongolia and in Tuva, Khakassia, and around Ust'-Orda, but not in Transbaikalia. It probably developed from the Sogdian script as a rectilinear form suitable for carving. What seems to be the earliest known example, that of Ereen Kharganat (Bugat Sum, Bayan-Ölgii), discovered in 1990, has been dated to the period of Tang rule in Mongolia (630–82). Runic inscriptions are often found with "STONE MEN" in funerary complexes and near petroglyphs.

The earliest extensive inscription in the runic script is that of the famous minister Toñuquq (Bayantsogt Sum, Central province, dated to 715). In it Toñuquq, from a Türk family long resident in China, records how Ilterish (682–91) and Qapaghan (691–716) *qaghans* (see KHAN) built the second Türk Empire. The next major inscriptions are those of Bilge Qaghan (716–34) and his brother Kül Tegin (Khashaat Sum, North Khangai), which record their far-flung campaigns. Taken together, these inscriptions evoke a consciously nativist vision of Türk rule in the Ötüken land, with harmony between older and younger and nobles (*begler*) and commoners (*qara budun,* black people). That of Toñuquq especially denounces the Türks' previous slavery to the deceitful Chinese, who had set the juniors against their elders.

The inscription of the Uighur *qaghan* Bayan-Chor (Moyunchuo, 747–59) records his father's and his own founding of the UIGHUR EMPIRE, campaigns against hostile Turkish tribes, and his building of a city on the SELENGE RIVER. An early ninth-century fragmentary runic inscription from the Uighur capital, ORDU-BALIGH (Khotont Sum, eastern North Khangai), has not been studied, but the better-preserved Chinese and fragmentary Sogdian parallels show it recorded the conversion of the Uighurs to Manicheism and subsequent military campaigns. The Süüjiin Dawaa inscription (Saikhan Sum, Bulgan province) records an elderly Uighur aristocrat's satisfaction with his great fame, rich horse herds, well-married daughters, and many grandsons and expresses his hopes that his sons will serve their *qaghan* well.

The only extant book in runic script is the *Irk Bitig*, an Old Turkish book of omens discovered in Dunhuang, probably dating from the Uighur Empire. Others, including Buddhist and Manichean translations, certainly existed.

The runic script was also used to write Old Turkish in the Kyrgyz Empire in Khakassia. Inscriptions appear on funerary monuments, cliffs, and grave goods and appear to date to the ninth century.

See also ALTAIC LANGUAGE FAMILY; ARCHAEOLOGY; TÜRK EMPIRES.

Further reading: Talât Tekin, *A Grammar of Orkhon Turkish* (Bloomington: Indiana University, 1968); Talât Tekin, *Irk Bitig: The Book of Omens* (Wiesbaden: Otto Harrassowitz, 1993).

Russia and the Mongol Empire

Russia and the Mongol Empire The Mongol conquest of the Russian duchies ironically led to the emergence of Muscovy as the center of a new united Russian state. At the time of the Mongol invasions the Russians, or East Slavs (including the Ukrainians and Belarussians), were ruled by princes (or dukes, *kniazi*) of the Riurikid family, dating back to the ninth century. Since no system of primogeniture existed, the number of new appanages (*udel*) multiplied steadily. Politically, the unifying institution was the grand duchy, that is, the special title of grand prince (or grand duke, *veliki kniaz'*), which accrued, after 1169, to the possessor of the city of Vladimir in the northeast. However, this position of grand prince had no set rule of succession, leading to complex family politics. The real unity of the Russian land, surrounded by Catholic, Muslim, and pagan neighbors, was provided by the Orthodox Church, conducting its services in Old Church Slavonic and headed by the metropolitan in Kiev. Economically, the Russian duchies had ceased coinage in the 12th century, using furs for money instead. The largest city, Novgorod, which traded Russia's furs, falcons, and lumber to the Baltics, had an estimated 22,000 persons.

THE CONQUEST

The Russians first collided with the Mongols (or TATARS, as the Russians always called them) through their Turkish-speaking Qipchaq (Polovtsi or Cuman) allies. When SÜBE'ETEI BA'ATUR and JEBE led a reconnaissance force of three *tümen*s (10,000s) through Qipchaq territory in 1223, the latter appealed to allied southwest Russian princes, who joined the QIPCHAQS, slaying the Mongol ambassadors. Sübe'etei and Jebe crushed the Russian-Qipchaq force on the Kalka River (May 31, 1223).

Thus, in 1235 ÖGEDEI KHAN added the Russians to the list of targets of the Mongols' great Western campaign. As usual, the Mongols campaigned principally in the winter. The main Mongol force, headed by the Jochid princes BATU and Hordu, the future great khans GÜYÜG and Möngke, and several others, arrived at Ryazan' in December 1237. Once Ryazan' refused to surrender, the Mongols sacked it and stormed through the northeastern district of Suzdalia, sacking its cities and defeating Russian field forces before leaving that summer. Among the casualties was Grand Prince Iurii (1217–38), killed on the River Sit' (March 4, 1238). The Mongols reappeared in southern Russia in 1239, sacking Pereyaslavl' (March 3) and Chernihiv (Chernigov, October 18). Finally having smashed the Russians' Qipchaq allies, the Black Caps, the full Mongol army sacked Kiev (December 6, 1240), Halych (Galich), and Volodymyr (Vladimir) before passing on to Central Europe. Throughout the campaign the Russians showed neither unity of purpose nor any sense of the enemy they were facing. No Russian princes surrendered to the Mongols, but most fled when it became clear resistance was futile.

MONGOL RULE AT ITS HEIGHT

When Batu, son of JOCHI and grandson of CHINGGIS KHAN, established his gold-hung ORDO (palace-tent) along the lower Volga, he followed Mongol precedents and required all Russian rulers personally to attend his court to inherit their thrones. From then on "going to the (Golden) Horde" (a word derived from the variant pronunciation *horda* of *ordo*) became a regular part of the Russian princes' lives. Before 1259 several princes even made the vast journey to Mongolia itself, including Iaroslav (1190–1246), who died there, poisoned, his entourage believed. These audiences demanded delicate negotiation of religious and communal boundaries. The Russian clerics viewed common Mongol foods such as marmots and KOUMISS as unclean, a prohibition reflected in the chronicles' excoriation of the "impure" and "accursed raw-eating Tatars." Another issue was the ceremony of purification by fire with its attendant religious ceremonies, required of all those received in audience by the khan. In 1245 Daniel of Halych (d. 1264) performed the purification and drank fermented mare's milk at Batu's *ordo* without incident, but Michael of Chernihiv in 1246 refused the purification and was martyred. Such incidents soon became rare as the Jochid lords and the Russian princes adjusted to each other.

Daniel of Halych and Iaroslav's son Alexander (1220–63) illustrate two of the possible responses to the Mongol conquest. Daniel toyed first with the idea of allying with Hungary and Poland and converting to Catholicism. Then he allied with still-pagan Lithuania. In the end, abandoned by all, he fled as the Mongols invaded

Lithuania and destroyed the Russian fortifications in Halych and Volyn (1259–60). By contrast, Alexander Nevskii fought the Swedes (1240) and Teutonic Knights (1242) while at the same time winning the grand ducal throne from his brother Andrew in 1251 by submission to the Mongols.

From 1270 on the northern Russian princes appealed to the Mongol *basqaq*s (overseers) and troops to assist their particular ambitions. By the 1280s the emergence of the Jochid prince NOQAI west of the Dnieper as a challenger to the khan on the Volga encouraged a bloody rivalry between Alexander Nevskii's sons Dmitrii (r. 1276–94) and Andrew (r. 1281–1304) for the position of grand prince. Four times between 1281 and 1293 armies from the khan plundered Suzdalia on behalf of Andrew, while Noqai's armies backed Dmitrii. A similarly protracted feud broke out from 1278 to 1294 between brothers claiming the ducal throne of Rostov as well.

Eventually, many princes developed close relations with the Mongols, spending years at a time "at the Horde" and participating in the Horde's wars. Several Russian princes received Mongol princesses as wives; even after the Horde's Islamization the brides were always baptized before marriage. Following Mongol precedents, the khans granted complete tax exemption to the Orthodox Church and all its estates. In the church liturgy prayers for the "czar" (king/emperor) on the steppe replaced those for the "czar" in Byzantium. By the 1280s the khans also began to use the church hierarchs, particularly the metropolitan (who after 1240 resided at Vladimir in the northeast) and the bishop of Saray, as mediators between hostile princes. While the princes soon accepted Mongol rule as inevitable, Russian popular assemblies (*veche*) could still react unpredictably to Tatar envoys and/or troops entering Russian cities, rising up in Novgorod (1258), in several cities of Suzdalia (1262), in Rostov (1289), and in Tver' (1327).

Numerous Russians also lived within the GOLDEN HORDE territories, in Saray and other cities on the Volga and on the steppe. Russian captives, along with Hungarians, OSSETES, and others, served in the *ordo*s of their masters; many escaped and lived as bandits. Life on the steppe was hard for Christians, since the ban on eating Mongol food created a difficult choice between being a Christian and staying alive. Russians also served as levies in the Horde's armies, and some appear to have reached high positions; in 1327 one Fedorchuk commanded the army dispatched by ÖZBEG KHAN (1313–41) to suppress the rebellion in Tver'. In the YUAN DYNASTY Russians taken captive during the first conquest to the east were even formed into a guards units in DAIDU (modern Beijing) in 1330.

While the Mongols worked through client rulers, they also established independent organs of rule. *Basqaq*s (*see* DARUGHACHI) were appointed as supervisors to all the major cities and princes, with the "great *basqaq*" (*veliki baskak*) assigned to the grand prince of Vladimir. The

Mongols conducted three censuses in the Russian lands: one in 1245–46 in the south and two in 1255–59 and 1273–74 covering the east and north. On the basis of this census, Russian households were enrolled in the DECIMAL ORGANIZATION and divided (exclusive of Novgorod) into 46 *tümens*, each nominally 10,000 households. As elsewhere in the MONGOL EMPIRE, subjects of the church were not included in the census. Servants directly attached to the Mongol *ordo*s and postroad personnel were exempt from other taxes. The district of Tula, for example, was assigned to Taidula Khatun, wife of Özbeg.

At first the Mongols treated the Russians much like Siberian peoples, demanding furs, including sable and polar bear skins, from every person counted in the census (*see* SIBERIA AND THE MONGOL EMPIRE). This demand for skins intensified the northern fur trade. By 1257 urban customs tax, or *tamga* (Mongolian, *tamagha*), and the *iam* (Mongolian, JAM), or postroad taxes, were also organized. Passing envoys and falconers were also free to levy contributions. The Mongols entrusted collection to tax farmers, at first Muslim merchants but later the princes themselves. In either case tax farming led in Russia, as elsewhere, to bidding wars between rival farmers for the right to collect the tax. People flocked to tax-exempt patrons, especially the Orthodox Church, but also ironically to the tax-exempt ORTOQ merchants who served as tax farmers. In 1284, for example, controversy arose when two cities near Kursk built by the Muslim *basqaq* (overseer) and tax farmer Ahmad drained population from the neighboring cities.

DECLINE OF MONGOL RULE

In the 14th century the Horde's authority over the Russian lands slowly eroded. In southern Russia the reunification of Poland under Casimir the Great (1333–70) led to the conquest of Halych in 1349. The Lithuanian grand prince Algirdas (Olgierd, 1341–77) defeated three princes of the Horde at the Battle of Blue Water in 1363, securing overlordship over all the Russian princes in the Dnieper watershed. While northeastern Russia remained under Mongol rule, Moscow became the dominant power. Abetted by the metropolitan, who had moved to Moscow in 1325, Alexander Nevskii's grandson Ivan Kalita (Moneybags) defeated his rivals in Tver' and secured the patent as grand prince (1331–41). The Horde would not accept Muscovite unification of all the old territory of Vladimir-Suzdalia, however, and ordered the princes of Tver', Suzdal, and Ryazan' to collect taxes separately; eventually they, too, were granted the title grand prince. Not until 1375 did Grand Prince Dmitrii Donskoi (1362–89) force Tver' to accept Muscovite supremacy.

With the rise of regional powers in northeast Russia, *basqaq*s disappeared, replaced by "messengers" (Russian, *posoly*, Mongolian, *elchi*) shuttling between the Horde and the Russian cities. The collection of taxes and postroad operations were taken over by the grand princes, eliminating the role for non-Russian merchants. Taxes were reduced to a single payment (*vykhod*), now paid in silver, with Muslim moneylenders involved only in granting interest-bearing loans to cover any temporary arrears. In 1389 Moscow's tribute payment was 1,000 rubles (a ruble equaled 100 grams, or 3.53 ounces, of silver); the amounts had probably been considerably higher in the 13th century. Islamization under Özbeg (1313–41) affected relations surprisingly little; the Orthodox Church's privileges were fully confirmed, and Özbeg allowed his sister to be baptized before marriage to Ivan Kalita. However, the disintegration of the Golden Horde after 1359, meaning the Russian princes had to deal with several rivals at once, changed the balance of power. Originally, the princes of Suzdalia had assembled personally at the Horde to receive patents of office, but from 1362 on they preferred to send representatives to request their patents rather than risk the chaos reigning on the steppe.

From his victory over Tver' in 1375, Dmitrii Donskoi pursued a controversial program of confrontation with the chaotic Golden Horde. In 1374 in Nizhnii Novgorod, his agents countenanced a popular riot against Tatar envoys and soldiers, and in 1378 he defeated a Tatar detachment on the Vozha (near Ryazan'). This contest ended with Dmitrii's pyrrhic victory over Emir Mamaq (Mamay, d. 1381) at the BATTLE OF KULIKOVO POLE (September 8, 1380). By 1382 TOQTAMISH had defeated Mamaq, reunited the Golden Horde, and sacked Moscow (August 26, 1382), still weakened by the heavy casualties of Kulikovo Pole. From 1389 to 1433 Moscow's tribute rose to 5,000 and then 7,000 rubles.

Even so, Toqtamish was unable to reestablish the old Tatar yoke and had to reconfirm Dmitrii as grand prince. While Moscow was hesitant about again confronting Tatar forces, turmoil in the Horde prevented anything more than fitful reassertion of its authority over Moscow. Toqtamish himself was overthrown by his Central Asian patron TIMUR (Tamerlane) in 1395. Subsequently, the kingmaker Edigü (Edigey) of the Manghit (MANGGHUD) clan besieged Moscow (December 1408) and compelled Grand Prince Vasilii I (1389–1425) to "go to the Horde" in 1412—but for the last time. Vasilii II (1425–62) received patents from the khan Ulugh-Muhammad (1419–45)—again, the last grand prince to do so. Ulugh-Muhammad's reign saw the breakup of the Horde, and by 1453 his son Kasim headed a new Tatar czardom at Kasimov subservient to Moscow. Ivan III (1462–1505) unified all the Russian lands not under Lithuania and took the title "czar" (king-emperor). The standoff in 1480 on the Ugra River (near Kaluga), in which Ivan faced down Khan Ahmed (fl. 1451–80) of the Great Horde, who was demanding restoration of tribute and patent relations, merely confirmed the end of Mongol-Tatar rule over Russia. Nevertheless, raids from the Golden Horde's successor states would continue, and Moscow would continue to buy peace with "payments" for a century or more.

MONGOL LEGACY IN RUSSIA

The question of the Mongol influence on Russia is vast and controversial. The Mongol conquest and ensuing "Tatar yoke" have been held responsible for many "Asiatic" features of Russian life, such as the autocracy under the czars, isolation from the development of the Renaissance, seclusion of women, and more generally poverty and backwardness. The 20th-century Eurasianist school, on the other hand, saw the Russian Empire as the legitimate successor of the khans and thus as playing a unique world role as an empire melding Asia and Europe. While many of these claims are vague and difficult to substantiate, certain areas of clear impact can be seen.

The initial conquest and the subsequent campaigns and tribute demands undoubtedly damaged Russian material life. Numerous luxury craft skills, such as cloisonné enamel, filigree, and niello, disappeared, while building crafts declined and church construction stopped. Revival occurred earlier in Novgorod, but only after the middle of the 14th century in eastern Russia. The eastern trade, which was reviving on the eve of the conquest, underwent another depression until the 14th century.

Mongol influence on Russian Christianity was paradoxical. While the conquest destroyed many religious institutions, the Horde's complete tax exemption of the church later expanded both the numbers and the influence of monasteries. The frequently unpleasant contact with non-Christian rulers increased the church leaders' isolationism and Russian national feeling. Nevertheless, church scribes under the later czars ironically translated the Mongol-era *yarlyks*, or patents (*see JARLIQ*), in a vain attempt to defend the privileges and immunities they had received from the Horde.

Numerous specific administrative terms and practices in Russia can be traced to those of the Horde. Attempts to link czarist autocracy to imitation of the khans, however, do not take into account the aristocratic nature of the Golden Horde and other Mongol successor states, which actually resembled in their political dynamics the Kievan appanage system more than the czarist autocracy. Likewise, arguments that base autocracy on the struggle against the "Tatar yoke" ignore the equal success of the aristocratic Lithuanian regime in fighting the Tatars. However, Mongol rule undoubtedly weakened the role of the *veche*, or popular assemblies, in the Russian cities, which were far more hostile to the Mongols than were the princes. Similarly, the bidding wars between the Russian princes for the right to farm the tribute undoubtedly strengthened their collective control over the commoners. Once the grand princes acquired the right to collect the tribute themselves, they also imposed heavier payments on subordinate princes rather than on their own crown lands.

Finally, the Mongols' unification of the steppe under Chinggisid rulers supplied a model that czars from Ivan III on consciously used in their relations with the khans of the steppe. Ivan the Terrible's (1533–84) conquest of the Golden Horde successor states of Kazan' (1552) and Astrakhan (1554), and his successors' subjugation of Tyumen' (1582–96), CRIMEA (1783), and the Kazakh khans (1730–1824), all ruled by Jochi's descendants, made the czar, known to the Mongols as the White Khan (*tsagaan khaan*), the virtual successor of the Golden Horde. Likewise, the Mongols' imposition of a fur tax on the Russians supplied the model for the same tax (*yasak*, from Uighur-Mongolian *yasaq*/JASAQ) that would lead the Cossacks to the shores of the Pacific. Thus, the Mongol Empire nurtured in Russia the same practices that would ultimately make the once fractured and subjugated Russia Mongolia's powerful and unified neighbor.

See also APPANAGE SYSTEM; CENSUS IN THE MONGOL EMPIRE; CHRISTIAN SOURCES ON THE MONGOL EMPIRE; CHRISTIANITY IN THE MONGOL EMPIRE; KALKA RIVER, BATTLE OF; KIEV, SIEGE OF; SARAY AND NEW SARAY.

Further reading: John Fennel, *Crisis of Medieval Russia, 1200–1304* (London: Longman, 1983); Charles J. Halperin, *Russia and the Golden Horde: The Mongol Impact on Medieval Russian History* (Bloomington: Indiana University Press, 1985); ———, *Tatar Yoke* (Columbus, Ohio: Slavica, 1985); Donald G. Ostrowski, *Muscovy and the Mongols: Cross-Cultural Influences on the Steppe Frontier, 1304–1589* (Cambridge: Cambridge University Press, 1998); Michel Roublev, "The Mongol Tribute according to the Wills and Agreements of the Russian Princes," in *Structure of Russian History: Interpretive Essays*, ed. M Cherniavsky (New York: Random House, 1970), 29–64; George Vernadsky, *Mongols and Russia* (New Haven, Conn.: Yale University Press, 1953).

Russia and Mongolia   Once a subject of the MONGOL EMPIRE, Russia from the beginning of the 17th century again came in contact with Mongolian peoples in its expansion into Siberia. (*On the Russians and other East Slavic peoples under Mongol rule, see* RUSSIA AND THE MONGOL EMPIRE.) The Buriat Mongols of southern Siberia came under Russian rule in the 17th century, while the Kalmyks along the Volga were gradually reduced to subject status through the course of the 18th century. (*On Russian rule over these peoples, see* BURIATS and KALMYKS.) Russian diplomatic relations with the ZÜNGHARS of today's Xinjiang and the KHALKHA of Outer Mongolia continued until these Mongolian peoples were brought under the sway of the Manchu Qing Empire. Russian interest in Outer Mongolia increased in the 1860s, leading to Russian support for the 1911 RESTORATION of Mongolian independence.

The Russian Revolution and the creation of a Soviet-supported regime in Mongolia during the 1921 REVOLU-TION marked a new stage in Russia's relations with independent Mongolia, marked by a pervasive Soviet Russian influence on every aspect of Mongolia's internal life. (*On Soviet political influence on Mongolia, see* SOVIET UNION AND MONGOLIA). With the transition from communism and the breakup of the Soviet Union, Mongolia's cross-border trade, investment, and cultural connections with the new Russian Federation remain close, although they are now only a single part of Mongolia's multifaceted foreign relations.

DIPLOMATIC RELATIONS, 1606–1758

From the Russian conquest of the remnants of the Mongol GOLDEN HORDE, the czars treated all Eastern peoples through a system of tribute remarkably similar to China's TRIBUTE SYSTEM. In this system all Asian chiefs desiring relations with Russia had to take an oath of allegiance to the czar and pay *yasak*, or tribute, while their envoys to Moscow had to kowtow before the czar. Although Russia did not really control any part of Inner Asia until the late 18th century, many steppe chiefs made submission to receive the rich gifts the Russian envoys gave them as well as to gain the right to trade duty free as guests in the Siberian forts, both for themselves and for their merchant clients from the Central Asian oasis cities. Thus, as in China, the tribute system functioned actually as a kind of state-subsidized foreign trade. However, Russian disregard for the existing claims of Inner Asian peoples over the Siberian natives caused frequent conflict.

Czarist Russia's first diplomatic contact with Mongolian-speaking peoples came in 1606–07, with emissaries between the OIRATS (West Mongols) and the *voevoda* (Cossack military governor) of Tomsk. In 1608 the Tomsk *voevoda*, on orders of the czar, also initiated contact with the "Altan Khan" (Golden Khan) of western Khalkha's KHOTOGHOID principality. In 1629 the *voevoda* of Yeniseysk began to collect *yasak* from the Buriat Mongols, and in 1646 a Cossack expedition pushing beyond Buriatia visited the court of the Setsen Khan of eastern Khalkha. The Cossacks were motivated both by rumors of gold and silver mines and by the czar's command to find new ways to China, which Russian envoys had first reached in 1617–18, led by representatives of the Khotoghoid prince.

By 1644 Beijing came under the new Manchu QING DYNASTY, which had pacified Inner Mongolia on the Khalkhas' southern border in 1636. At first wavering between opening tribute relations with Russia or the Qing, in 1655 the Khalkha princes became tributaries of the Qing, largely due to resentment at Russian encroachments on their northern Buriat and Khalkha Mongolian subjects. In 1666 the Khalkha began attacking Cossack forts. These attacks were stopped only by the massive invasion of Khalkha in 1689 by the ZÜNGHARS (the main Oirat tribe). The Khalkha leaders sought Qing protection, while the Russians strengthened their frontiers and received many Khalkha refugees.

When order returned to Qing-controlled Khalkha after 1697, the Khalkha no longer challenged Russian control in southern Siberia, but conflicts over refugees were constant. Unofficial Russian trade with the Khalkha flourished, supplying animals for the official caravan trade to China vital to supplying Siberian settlements. In 1727 Russia negotiated with the Qing court in Beijing the Kyakhta and Bura treaties that together demarcated the frontier, created procedures for repatriation of refugees, and restricted Sino-Russian trade to the new border town of KYAKHTA and to official missions to Beijing. The border between Mongolia and southern Siberia was guarded by Khalkha and Buriat Cossack border guards. For almost 200 years contact between the peoples on the border was limited.

After the 1755–58 destruction of the Zünghars, a more open frontier was created in western Mongolia and Xinjiang. Here border guards were stationed well back from the limit of Qing control, leaving a buffer zone north of it in KHÖWSGÖL PROVINCE, Tuva, Altay, and modern-day eastern Kazakhstan. In Khöwsgöl and Tuva Qing political control was clear, but there was no military presence. Altay and eastern Kazakhstan were a kind of no-man's land where the natives paid tribute to both powers.

RUSSIAN INTERESTS, 1860–1911

From 1727 to the mid-19th century Russian contact with the Mongols was not intensive. Official trade and diplomatic caravans had some contact with the Mongol nobility both along the route from Kyakhta to Beijing and in Beijing itself, and Russian scholars and missionaries made many pioneering discoveries. Such contacts were closely monitored by the Qing authorities.

With the Chinese Qing Empire facing European attacks and internal rebellions, in 1854 the ambitious new governor general of Siberia, Nikolai N. Murav'ev (later Murav'ev-Amurskii, 1808–81), proposed that with the likely overthrow of the Qing, Russia would be able to take over Mongolia naturally. Russian policy makers responded that in the event of the fall of the Qing, Mongolia should become independent and thought that direct annexation would be unduly provocative to the other European powers.

In 1860 the Treaty of Beijing, which gave Russia vast tracts of territory in Manchuria and the Altay-Kazakhstan buffer zone, also gave Russia the right to trade in and station a consul in Khüriye (modern ULAANBAATAR). In 1881 the Treaty of St. Petersburg allowed Russia to open consulates in ULIASTAI and KHOWD CITY and to trade duty free throughout Mongolia. After the Sino-Japanese War (1894–95) and the scramble for concessions in China, all of the Qing Empire north of the Great Wall became Russia's sphere of influence. From 1900 Russian troops actually occupied Manchuria, HULUN BUIR, and eastern Inner Mongolia as Russia cultivated Inner Mongolian princes. The defeat by Japan in the Russo-Japanese War (1904–05)

and 1905 Revolution forced a withdrawal of Russian troops and brought southeastern Inner Mongolia into the Japanese sphere.

Meanwhile, the new consul in Khüriye, Yakov Parfen'evich Shishmarëv (1833–1915), served from 1861 to 1905 and by the time of his retirement had become one of the leading men in the town, familiar with all the Mongol elite. Russia opened a post office in Khüriye and in 1897 operated a telegraph line from KYAKHTA CITY to Zhangjiakou, by the Great Wall. The Russo-Asiatic Bank, a state-controlled bank with French and Belgian investors, began operations in Mongolia, including a subsidiary in Mongolor, headed by Baron Victor von Grot (b. 1863), which began gold mining in 1907. Culturally, in 1903 a Russian club with a balalaika orchestra opened in Khüriye, serving a Russian population of 600, and the von Grots' red mansion in Khüriye became a local landmark.

Even so, Russia's role in Mongolia fell far short of its ambitions. The consulates allowed in the 1881 treaty were not actually opened until 1905 (Khowd) and 1908 (Uliastai). Despite duty-free trade rights, the completion of the Trans-Siberian and Chinese Eastern Railroads diverted transit trade away from Mongolia to Manchuria. Russian exports through Mongolian border stations declined sharply from 1899 to 1909, to be replaced by goods (both Chinese and European) sold by Chinese merchants. Russian merchants in Mongolia were increasingly limited to the purchase of unprocessed animal products. Advocates of Russian mercantile expansion argued strongly for encouraging Mongolian secession as the only possible way to exclude Chinese merchants.

RUSSIA AND THEOCRATIC MONGOLIA, 1911–1919

When secession actually came, however, it was too soon for Russian convenience. In 1900 the Bogda, or "Holy One," Mongolia's great INCARNATE LAMA (see JIBZUNDAMBA KHUTUGTU, EIGHTH), appealed to Russia for assistance in secession but was told to wait. In summer 1911 the Bogda and a group of Khalkha and Inner Mongolian aristocrats again appealed to the Russian consul V. N. Lavdovskii for assistance. Despite Lavdovskii's counsel of patience, the Mongols again sent a delegation to St. Petersburg. The Russian Foreign Ministry used the appeal to protest China's new Sinicization policies while not supporting secession outright, until the October 10 uprising against the Qing in China suddenly gave the Russians the cover they needed to support the 1911 RESTORATION.

Russian support for Mongolia was by no means unconditional, however. Russian policy makers had to balance their ambitions in Mongolia with the reactions of both China and the European powers. Since the treaty system binding China presupposed the inviolability of the 1911 frontiers, czarist diplomats opened negotiations with China not on the basis of recognizing Mongolia's independence but on the basis of Chinese suzerainty over an autonomous Outer Mongolia. Mongolia hoped to unify all the Mongols of the Qing Empire, but this, too, was scotched by St. Petersburg. In 1914–15 the Russians convened a trilateral conference at Kyakhta, in which both Mongolia and China were forced to give in to Russian demands, the Mongols having to forgo real independence and pan-Mongol unification and the Chinese having to forgo actual control over Mongolia and accept Russian commercial privileges.

In return for its ambiguous support of Mongolian autonomy, Russia received confirmation of its duty-free trade rights in Mongolia. Concessions were granted to the Russians in Khüriye and Khowd. Chinese mercantile activity was damaged, and Russian exports did receive a boost. In 1914, in connection with a Russian loan of 1 million gold rubles amounting to almost half the Mongolian government's central budget, a financial adviser, S. A. Kozin, was appointed to control all payments from the Mongolian state budget. Railroad concessions were granted in the same year. The gold ruble was made the official currency, and in May 1915 a Mongolian National Bank headed by the Russian D. P. Pershin was chartered with the exclusive right to issue banknotes.

Although the KYAKHTA TRILATERAL TREATY seemingly achieved all the aims of czarist Russian policy—complete control over Mongolia without antagonizing the European powers—it actually marked the high point of Russian control. Economically, World War I from 1914 on made it impossible for Russia to meet the Mongolian demand for goods or to make more than small investments in the Mongolian economy. While the former consul Ya. P. Shishmarëv had been well liked—one of the Mongolian requests in 1911 was to reappoint him as consul—his successors made little secret of their low regard for the Mongolians. Russian prestige in Mongolia plummeted as a result of the unpopular Kyakhta treaty and still further due to the Russian Revolution and civil war. In 1918 the Russian adviser was expelled from Mongolia, and the Mongolian National Bank was closed before it issued a single banknote. Inflation made the gold ruble worthless by 1919. In that year the Chinese high commissioner in Mongolia, whose office was created by the Kyakhta treaty, convinced the Mongolians to accept voluntarily the REVOCATION OF AUTONOMY, ending Russia's special role in Mongolia.

RUSSIAN CULTURE AND ETHNIC RUSSIANS IN MONGOLIA

The following White Russian and Red Army occupations of the capital in 1921 returned Mongolia to the Russian sphere of influence. During the succeeding decades it was the new Soviet Russian culture that influenced Mongolia. Russian drivers, mechanics, workers, and artisans played an important role in Mongolia's embryonic working class. In 1924 Russian members of the Mongolian Trade Unions (which then included many white-collar workers) totaled

1,000, or 25 percent. Subsequently, however, the number of Russian workers (this time not including white-collar workers) in Mongolia's principal production sites declined to 17.1 percent in 1932 and 2.2 percent in 1938. Other parts of Mongolia's Russian population included a small number of farmers (some of whom were Old Believers) and wives of Mongolian students who had studied in the Soviet Union. Total ethnic Russian numbers were reported in the 1956 census as 13,400, or 1.6 percent of the population. Later figures show the population at 8,900 in 1963 but as high as 22,100 in 1969. It is unclear whether these figures counted advisers and other temporary residents.

Apart from the political influence of the Soviet system, Russification of Mongolian life proceeded in both high and low culture. In high culture area after area of European culture was transplanted into Mongolia in specifically Russian forms: ballet, classical music, opera, the circus, cinema, neoclassical architecture, oil painting, heroic statuary, and so on. In low culture hundreds of small features of daily life, from clothing and interior decorating to language and entertainment, reflect Russian culture. The Mongolians also assimilated much of the Russian view of their own Asian heritage and culture.

RUSSIA AND MONGOLIA, 1991 ON

From 1980 on the entire Soviet bloc showed increasing economic problems, which became a massive crisis by 1990. Instead of subsidizing Mongolia to protect its great-power status, the Soviet Union began demanding repayment of loans. In March, in the midst of the Mongolian 1990 DEMOCRATIC REVOLUTION, the Soviet press publicized Mongolia's total debt to the Soviet Union as 9.5 billion "convertible rubles," or 4,570 rubles for every Mongolian. (The actual value of the "convertible ruble," which was a money of account used only for international transactions within the Soviet bloc, remains controversial.) This sudden turn to debt collection helped push Mongolia into a pro-Western foreign policy, a move confirmed when the Soviet Union demanded all international transactions be carried out in hard currency beginning on January 1, 1991. From 1990 to 1991 the Soviet Union's role in Mongolia's total trade turnover dropped from 77.8 percent to 66.8 percent.

The turmoil associated with the disintegration of the Soviet Union in fall 1991 and the formation of the Russian Federation kept Russia from paying more than passing attention to Mongolian affairs, despite the January 1993 treaty on friendly relations. One important area of controversy was the PRIVATIZATION of the Russian shares in the several Soviet-Mongolian joint-stock MINING companies, which, like the Russian privatization program in general, has been plagued with accusations of corruption and influence of organized crime. The role of Russia and the former Soviet Union in Mongolian trade continued to shrink. Previously, the copper-molybdenum concentrate of Erdenet mine had been sold to Kazakhstan, but after 1995 China became the main buyer. In 1999 Russia reached a low of 23 percent of Mongolia's total trade turnover. (The share of Mongolia's trade held by other former Soviet bloc nations is negligible.)

Since the inauguration of the new president, Vladimir Putin, in 1999, Russia has attempted to reconstruct its former prestige. Putin responded to Mongolian president N. Bagabandi's 1999 state visit to Moscow with a visit to Mongolia in November 2000, the first top Soviet/Russian leader to do so since 1974. Putin signed a pact recognizing Mongolia's nuclear-free status and pledging to rebuild Russo-Mongolian trade. Russia has proposed that Mongolia's debt to the former Soviet Union be converted into shares in Mongolia's state-owned enterprises as a method of boosting Russo-Mongolian economic ties. Despite these steps, Mongolia has remained aloof from the tentative new Russo-Chinese alliance embodied in the Shanghai Cooperation Organization, a joint-security forum of China, Russia, and the former Soviet Central Asian countries formed in 2001.

See also FOREIGN RELATIONS; MONGOLIA, STATE OF; THEOCRATIC PERIOD.

Further reading: Elena Boikova, "Russians in Mongolia in the Late 19th-Early 20th Centuries," *Mongolian Studies* 25 (2002): 13–29; Elizabeth Endicott, "Russian Merchants in Mongolia: The 1910 Moscow Trade Exhibition," in *Mongolia in the Twentieth Century: Landlocked Cosmopolitan,* ed. Stephen Kotkin and Bruce A. Elleman (Armonk, N.Y.: M. E. Sharpe, 1999), 59–68; Michael Khodarkovsky, *Russia's Steppe Frontier: The Making of a Colonial Empire* (Bloomington: Indiana University, 2002); Tatsuo Nakami, "Russian Diplomats and Mongol Independence," in *Mongolia in the Twentieth Century: Landlocked Cosmopolitan,* ed. Stephen Kotkin and Bruce A. Elleman (Armonk, N.Y.: M. E. Sharpe, 1999), 69–78.

S

Sa'd al-Dawlah   *See* SA'D-UD-DAWLA.

Sa'duddawla   *See* SA'D-UD-DAWLA.

Sa'd-ud-Dawla (Sa'd al-Dawlah, Sa'duddawla) (d. 1291)
Jewish physician whose rise and fall as vizier of Arghun, khan of the Middle Eastern Mongols, brought prosperity and then ruin to his people
Stemming from an Iranian Jewish family of physicians from Abhar (near Qazvin), Sa'd-ud-Dawla entered the IL-KHANATE'S administration in 1284 as deputy to the DARUGHACHI (overseer) of Baghdad. Other officials, threatened by his ability, removed him from the scene by arranging his summons to the court of Arghun Khan (1284–91) as a physician. There Sa'd-ud-Dawla, intrigued with a Mongol retainer, Ordu-Qaya (d. 1291) and proposed to recover 5 million gold dinars in back taxes from Baghdad.

Appointed Baghdad's auditor general on June 6, 1288, with Ordu-Qaya the city's garrison commander, the two returned to the khan next spring with the promised sum. In June 1289 Sa'd-ud-Dawla was appointed *sahib-divan* (chief of administration, or vizier), placing his family in governorships in Baghdad, Fars, Diyarbakır, and Tabriz. Sa'd-ud-Dawla destroyed the remaining members of the Juvaini faction and other Muslim rivals and strictly controlled spending by the great Mongol commanders (*NOYAN*). Jews and, to a lesser degree, Christians briefly dominated the Il-Khanid bureaucracy. To guard against the *noyans'* hostility, Sa'd-ud-Dawla assigned key garrison commands to Ordu-Qaya and a few other low-born Mongol supporters and appointed his brother, also a physician, to guard the khan's health.

In 1290 an Indian Buddhist monk's sulfur and mercury alchemical regime led, despite the best efforts of Sa'd-ud-Dawla's brother, to Arghun's paralysis. Seizing the opportunity, TA'ACHAR, Qunchuqbal, and other *noyans* murdered the comatose khan before executing Sa'd-ud-Dawla, Ordu-Qaya, and their clique on April 2–3, 1291. Sa'd-ud-Dawla's estate was pillaged, and massive anti-Jewish riots broke out in Isfahan and Baghdad.

See also JOVAINI, 'ALA' UD-AIN ATA-MALIK AND SHAMS-UD-BIN MUHAMMAD.

Sagaalgan   *See* WHITE MONTH.

Sagang Sechen   *See* SAGHANG SECHEN.

Saghang Sechen (Sagang Sechen, Sanang Sechen, Ssanang Ssetsen) (b. 1604)
Author of the *ERDENI-YIN TOBCHI* (Precious chronicle), Saghang Sechen was the great-grandson of the Buddhist prince KHUTUGTAI SECHEN KHUNG-TAIJI, inheriting his rule at Yekhe Shiber (modern southern Üüshin/Uxin banner). As a child in 1614, he participated in the consecration of a Shakyamuni Buddha commissioned by Boshugtu Jinong (1565–1624, the titular ruler of ORDOS), and received, in light of his ancestry, the title *sechen khung-taiji*, "wise prince." As a young official he joined Boshugtu's 1622 negotiations with Chinese frontier officials in Yulin. In 1627 he proclaimed the enthronement of Erinchin Jinong (1600–56) and with the new *jinong* received a Buddhist initiation. Compelled with Erinchin to serve in LIGDAN KHAN'S army during his 1632 occupation of Ordos, Saghang Sechen befriended some disaffected CHAKHAR men and deserted, sheltering Erinchin at Yekhe Shiber

from Ligdan's wrath until 1634. After Ligdan's death and Erinchin's restoration, Saghang was honored with the title *Erke sechen khung-taiji*, "beloved wise prince," and given the right to hold the vanguard in the army and the center in the hunt. Nothing else is known of his life except that he later moved to northern Üüshin, where his grave and descendants were found. In 1662 he completed the *Erdeni-yin tobchi*. Offerings were made to him both at his grave and at that of his great-grandfather Khutugtai Sechen Khung-Taiji.

Saichungga *See* SAINCHOGTU, NA.

Sainchogtu, Na. (Sayincogtu; Saichungga, Sayičungga) (1914–1973) *Leading Inner Mongolian poet and diarist under Japanese occupation, he converted to the Communist cause in 1947*
Sainchogtu was born on March 23, 1914, in Chakhar's Plain Blue banner (Qahar Zhenglanqi), in the herding family of Nasundelger and his wife Degjima; his original name was Saichungga. Familiarized with letters and Mongolian oral poetry by his relatives, Saichungga attended a banner school and became a banner clerk before being selected by the Japanese "Good Neighbor Society" in 1936, first for education in a Japanese-run Chakhar school and then for study in Japan. Graduating from the Teacher's College of Tokyo Oriental University in 1941, he returned home and taught in the girls' school in Sönid Right Banner (Sonid Youqi) sponsored by PRINCE DEMCHUGDONGRUB.

Saichungga's early works include the poem collection *Sedkhil-un khani* (The thought's companion, 1941), the diary of a summer vacation in Inner Mongolia, *Elesü mangkhan-u ekhe nutug* (Motherland of sands and dunes, 1942), and the collection of letters and essays in *Man-u Monggol-un mandukhu daguu* (Song of our Mongolia rising, 1945). His poems expressed his longing for release and the purification of Mongolia in romantic imagery of chaste maidens, courageous youths, and nature. His prose writings passionately denounced superstition, poverty, and abuse of power without explicitly raising larger political issues.

Saichungga welcomed the Soviet-Mongolian invasion of August 1945. After the failure of pan-Mongolian unification he studied at the Sükhebaatur Party Cadres' School in ULAANBAATAR. As Saichungga eagerly absorbed Communist Party history, his poetry became strongly political. In November 1947 he returned to Inner Mongolia, then torn by the Chinese Communist-Nationalist civil war. Saichungga changed his name to Na. Sainchogtu and worked successively for the *Inner Mongolian People's Daily*, the propaganda committee of the Communist Party's Inner Mongolian branch, and the secretariat of the China's Writers' Union. Sent to the countryside for re-education in 1958–60, he joined the Chinese Communist Party in 1959.

Sainchogtu published poems steadily until 1966, and was acknowledged as Inner Mongolia's leading author, publishing collections such as *Man-u khüchürkheg dagun* (Our powerful song, 1955) and a poetic record of his return to his home banner (1962). The widely acclaimed poem *Khökhe torgan terlig* (Blue silk robe, 1954) praised the new romantic freedoms for women. His only novel was *Khabur-un nara Begejing-eche* (The spring sun is from Beijing, 1956), and in 1957 he published a 1,200 line narrative poem, *Nandir Sümbür khoyar* (Nandir and Sümbür), on the trials of two young lovers during collectivization.

Sainchogtu was attacked and tormented during the Cultural Revolution (1966–76) and finally exiled to Shanghai. He began writing poetry again in 1971 but died on May 13, 1973.

See also INNER MONGOLIANS; JAPAN AND THE MODERN MONGOLS; LITERATURE; NEW SCHOOLS MOVEMENT.

Further reading: Christopher P. Atwood, "A Romantic Vision of National Regeneration: Some Unpublished Works of the Inner Mongolian Poet and Essayist Saichungga," *Inner Asia* 1, no. 1 (1999): 3–43; Gombojab Hangin, "Na. Sayinčoүtu's (Sayinčungүa) Works: The Period of Nationalistic Realism," in *Tractata Altaica*, ed. Walther-Heissig (Wiesbaden: Otto Harrassowitz, 1976).

Sai Dianchi *See* SAYYID AJALL.

Sai Tien-ch'ih *See* SAYYID AJALL.

Sanang Sechen *See* SAGHANG SECHEN.

Sangdag, Khuulichi *Early 19th-century poet whose mastery of the "speech" (üge) genre voiced a sense of powerlessness before fate and oppression*
Little is known of Sangdag's life. He was from Mergen Wang (Tüshiyetü Khan's Left Wing Middle) banner (modern East Gobi province) and was a contemporary of DANZIN-RABJAI (1803–56). Late in his life he become a *kiya* (aide-de-camp) for a prince. His nickname, *khuulichi*, is not the modern "lawyer" but rather "storyteller." Sangdag's extant works are 13 short poems in the *üge*, or "speech," genre. The style is close to spoken language, and the PROSODY is relatively free. In it animals or inanimate things speak out their complaints. Lama *üge* authors Agwang-Khaidub (1779–1838) and Ishisambuu (1847–96) used the genre to chastise the hypocrisies of their fellow monks and urge better behavior. Sangdag's *üge* poems mostly adopt the voice of some animal or thing trapped into decline by circumstances or others' power: melting snow, a tumbleweed in the wind, a camel cow and calf separated when the mother is sent on caravan, a wolf caught in a tightening hunting circle. These speeches resonated with impoverishment, family breakup, and the

subjection of the Gobi commoners. The speech of the pet dog, reciting its duties in attacking anyone who approaches his master and yet complaining of the blows and bad food it receives, recalls contemporary denunciations of aides-de-camp who encouraged princely misrule.

Sangha (Sang-ko, Sengge) (d. 1291) *Notorious Tibetan official whose strict measures to deal with financial crises late in Qubilai's reign caused widespread dissatisfaction*
Sangha (the spelling Sengge of his Chinese name, Sangge/Sang-ko, is erroneous) was born in the Tibetan bKa'-ma-log tribe on China's Sichuan frontier. A pupil of the Buddhist miracle worker Dam-pa Kun-dga'-grags (1230–1303), he knew Tibetan, Chinese, Mongolian, and Uighur and first entered the Mongol court around 1268 as interpreter for the imperial preceptor 'PHAGS-PA LAMA. Sangha later became estranged from Dam-pa Kun-dga'-grags, whom he would persecute once he came into power.

With 'Phags-pa Lama's frequent absences, Sangha became the effective head of the Buddhist bureaucracy under QUBILAI KHAN (1260–94). When 'Phags-pa Lama died in Tibet in 1280, Sangha was dispatched to Tibet with 7,000 Mongol troops. After executing the chief administrator in Tibet, Kun-dga' bZang-po, in 1281, Sangha assigned his troops as Tibet's first permanent Mongol garrison. On his return Sangha served in 'Phags-pa's place as head of the bureaucracy administering Buddhist monks throughout the empire and secular affairs in Tibet. In 1288 several offices were combined under Sangha as the Commission for Buddhist and Tibetan Affairs (Xuanzheng Yuan).

Through his supervision of Buddhist monasteries, which traditionally controlled large investments, Sangha became involved in both economic and personnel issues. In December 1284 he recommended Lu Shiyong to Qubilai Khan as right grand councillor with the assurance that government income could be multiplied 10 times. Despite Lu Shiyong's disgrace in May 1285, Sangha's influence was not impaired.

On March 19, 1287, after two years of unprecedented emissions of paper currency, Qubilai adopted Sangha's controversial proposal to devalue the convertible Zhongtong currency and issue in its place a new, nonconvertible Zhiyuan currency. To administer financial affairs, Qubilai appointed Sangha manager (*pingzhang*) for a revived Department of State Affairs alongside the existing secretariat. On December 11 Sangha was promoted to grand councillor of the Department of State Affairs.

Despite the devaluation of the Zhongtong currency, Sangha understood the importance of silver backing for the paper currency. His term in office, from 1287 to 1291, coincided with the beginning of a decade-long shortage in the Eurasian silver supply. In 1289 Sangha ordered the quotas for the commercial tax, payable in silver, increased to a total of 450,000 ding (*yastuq*), a 10-fold increase over the 1270 quota. He invested in silver production in YUNNAN province and confiscated gold and silver still circulating in South China. To increase the international trade that ultimately formed China's main source of silver and was largely in the hands of Muslims, Sangha convinced the khan to revoke his prohibition on Muslim slaughtering.

Despite these measures, the massive spending of previous years could not be sustained. Sangha's four years in office were occupied with an obsessive search for expenses to eliminate, inefficient officials to dismiss, and tax exemptions to revoke. As with other financially strapped Chinese regimes, he also practiced the sale of offices on a large scale. Sangha curtailed the independence of the censorate. The results, while very unpopular, were successful. Emissions of paper currency, which had reached more than 2 million guan in 1285–86, were kept to 500,000 guan from 1290 on. Particularly unforgivable to the regular officialdom was his judicial murder of policy opponents. Lavish Buddhist ceremonies at court and his own accumulation of a large estate only increased opposition.

Early in 1291 several Mongol and Turkish officials impeached Sangha. The final blow came in March, when two high Mongol aristocrats, ÖCHICHER and Öz-Temür (Örlüg Noyan), intervened against Sangha, accusing him of corruption. After a debate in the emperor's presence, Sangha was disgraced and executed on August 17. The Department of State Affairs was abolished and Sangha's coterie dismissed or executed. Several of his stricter measures of economy were revoked, but Sangha's restoration of financial discipline lasted under his successors for the next 10 years.

See also BUDDHISM IN THE MONGOL EMPIRE; PAPER CURRENCY IN THE MONGOL EMPIRE; TIBET AND THE MONGOL EMPIRE.

Further reading: H. Francke, "Sangha," in *In the Service of the Khan: Eminent Personalities of the Early Mongol-Yuan Period (1200–1300)*, ed. Igor de Rachewiltz et al. (Wiesbaden: Otto Harrassowitz, 1993), 558–583.

Santa   *See* DONGXIANG LANGUAGE AND PEOPLE.

Saray and New Saray   Built along the Akhtuba River running parallel to the lower Volga, these cities served successively as the capitals of the GOLDEN HORDE. The first town of Saray (at modern Selitrënnoye, about 100 kilometers [60 miles] north of Astrakhan) was begun by BATU (d. 1255). The town flourished in the first half of the 14th century before entering decline. The city extended for 3 or 4 kilometers (1.9–2.5 miles) on a bluff over the Akhtuba. Apparently spared destruction by TIMUR, the city remained settled at least until the early 15th century. The khans generally wintered around Saray and summered on the steppe.

During MUHAMMAD ABU 'ABDULLAH IBN BATTUTA'S visit in 1323, Saray was a vast city with many inhabitants. The Muslim population was served by 13 mosques. Each ethnic group—Mongols, OSSETES, QIPCHAQS, Circassians, Russians, and Greeks—as well as foreign merchants—Egyptian, Syrian, Iraqi, Iranian, and Italian—had its own quarters and bazaars. Inscriptions in Turkish (in Arabic and Uighur script), Persian, and Arabic testify to the range of languages spoken. The absence of pig bones and the rarity of Christian art indicate the public predominance of Islam, but tomb figurines cut out of bronze or iron sheets show the coexistence of native religious practices.

The second town of Saray (at modern Kolobovka, formerly Tsarev, about 85 kilometers [40 miles] east of Volgograd), called New Saray (Saray al-Jadid) on coins, was first built in 1332. It flourished as the capital from 1341 on until it was sacked in 1395, effectively disappearing. (The designation of New Saray as Saray-Berke is erroneous; Saray Berke is actually old Saray.) Built on a floodplain, New Saray's walls were constructed in 1361, amid the Golden Horde's "Great Troubles." They enclosed a space about 1.6 by 1.0 kilometers (1.0 by 0.6 miles).

Houses in both cities ranged from simple dugouts heated by braziers to large walled manors dominated by multiroom houses with tiled walls, *kang*s (sleeping platforms heated by flues), *tandur*s (ovens for baking flat bread), and wash basins. Remains of yurts were found in a few manor houses. In several cases semidugout houses were gradually improved and filled in as slave artisans upgraded their status. In the 1350s and 1360s many large manor houses were divided and occupied by poorer residents. In New Saray traces of Timur's sack of 1395, including unburied and decapitated skeletons, were found.

See also CHRISTIANITY IN THE MONGOL EMPIRE; RUSSIA AND THE MONGOL EMPIRE.

Further reading: German A. Fedorov-Davydov, *Silk Road and the Cities of the Golden Horde*, trans. Aleksandr Naymark, (Berkeley: Zinat Press, 2001); ———, *Culture of the Golden Horde Cities*, trans. H. Bartlett Wells (Oxford: B.A.R., 1984).

Sawma, Rabban   *See* YAHBH-ALLAHA, MAR.

Sayičungga   *See* SAINCHOGTU, NA.

Sayincogtu   *See* SAINCHOGTU, NA.

Sayyid Ajall (Sai Dianchi, Sai Tien-ch'ih) 'Umar Shams-ud-Din (1218–1279) *Muslim administrator who integrated Yunnan into China proper*
'Umar Shams-ud-Din's usual Persian name, Sayyid Ajall, was an honorary title for descendants of Muhammad, while the Chinese Sai Dianchi derives from Mongolian

Sayid Elchi (Sayyid the Envoy); he inherited both titles from his Bukharan grandfather, who first joined Mongol service. 'Umar Shams-ud-Din first served ÖGEDEI KHAN (1229–41) as DARUGHACHI (overseer) in Inner Mongolia and Shanxi and JARGHUCHI (judge) in Yanjing (modern Beijing) and then MÖNGKE KHAN (1251–59) as governor in Yanjing and commissary for the Sichuan campaign. In 1264 QUBILAI KHAN appointed Sayyid Ajall head of the branch secretariat of Shaanxi and Sichuan. Sayyid Ajall expanded the population and economy as he carefully moved Mongol-held Sichuan, still threatened by unconquered Song strongholds, from military to civilian rule. In 1273 Qubilai appointed Sayyid Ajall manager (*pingzhang*) of the new branch secretariat in YUNNAN (Qarajang). First conquered in 1254, Yunnan had been a virtually independent kingdom under the Mongol prince Toqur. Buttressed by Qubilai's confidence, Sayyid Ajall mollified Toqur by giving him a voice in administration but steadily enforced civilian rule. Sayyid Ajall's civilizing mission combined Islam and CONFUCIANISM; he built halls of both teachings while promoting wet-rice cultivation, literacy, arranged marriages, and burial (rather than cremation). Sayyid Ajall's sons Nasir-ad-Din (d. 1292), Husain (d. 1310), and Mas'ud all served as managers of the Yunnan secretariat, continuing Sayyid Ajall's policies. Nasir-ad-Din also campaigned successfully in BURMA (Myanmar) and VIETNAM.

See also ISLAM IN THE MONGOL EMPIRE.

Further reading: P. D. Buell, "Saiyid Ajall," in *In the Service of the Khan: Eminent Personalities of the Early Mongol-Yuan Period (1200–1300)*, ed. Igor de Rachewiltz et al. (Wiesbaden: Otto Harrassowitz, 1993), 466–479.

scapulimancy   Divining by reading the cracks in burnt bones, an almost universal practice in ancient Eurasia, was the major method of divination in the MONGOL EMPIRE and was practiced until recent times. While in ancient Shang China tortoise shells were burned by a piece of hot iron, the Mongols always used sheep scapula, or shoulder blades, and simply placed them in a fire. The great khans of the Mongol Empire used scapulimancy to divine the will of heaven (TENGGERI) before virtually every decision. CHINGGIS KHAN carried a charred sheep pelvis as an amulet. This divination was performed by the khans themselves, by shamans (*bö'e*, modern *böö*), and sometimes by foreign divination experts, such as YELÜ CHUCAI (1190–1244). The inquirer first had to whisper to the shoulder blade, and then the blade was burned. A straight vertical crack meant yes, and a horizontal crack or splintering meant no. Today shamans follow up the reading of the blade's cracks with a shamanic session to ask the ONGGHONs (spirit figurines) for further information about the inquirer's troubles.

Scapulimancy continued in Buddhist Mongolia. The great Tu (Monguor) lama and scholar Sum-pa mKhan-po Ishi-Baljur (Ye-shes dPal-'byor, 1704–87) wrote a text on the topic based on what he knew of the practice among the ÖÖLÖD Mongols. In it he notes that a shoulder blade from a freshly slaughtered, healthy, white sheep had to be washed and censed with juniper and/or incense. In a room, the diviner prayed alone to the Buddhist deities and recited a *dharani* (sacred spell) several times before placing the bone in the fire. The resulting cracks were interpreted according to a complex division of the bone into areas along its edges and along the central spine. The cracks' lengths, colors, and positions were all considered, allowing much room for the diviner's interpretation of the event. Evil omens were to be dealt with by having the appropriate scriptures recited by a lama.

Scapulimancy was still practiced widely in the late 1930s in Inner Mongolia and is practiced today by shamans among the DARKHAD, ZAKHACHIN, and other western Mongolian groups. It has given way to ASTROLOGY in modern urban milieus.

See also MILITARY OF THE MONGOL EMPIRE; RELIGION; TU LANGUAGE AND PEOPLE.

Further reading: C. R. Bawden, "A Tibetan-Mongolian Bilingual Text of Popular Religion," in *Serta Tibeto-Mongolica*, ed. Rudolf Kaschewsky, Klaus Sagaster, and Michael Weiers (Wiesbaden: Otto Harrassowitz, 1973), 15–32; Ágnes Birtalan, "Scapulimancy and Purifying Ceremony," in *Proceedings of the 35th Permanent International Altaistic Conference*, ed. Chieh-hsien Ch'en (Taipei: Center for Chinese Studies Materials, 1993), 1–10.

seal In the Mongolian constitution of 1924 the SOYOMBO SYMBOL on a lotus served as the state seal of the new MONGOLIAN PEOPLE'S REPUBLIC. In late 1939 the Mongolian leader MARSHAL CHOIBALSANG presented to Joseph Stalin a proposed new seal for Mongolia in a typical Soviet style: sheaves of wheat forming a circle around a sunburst with a red star on the top and the name of the country on a ribbon at the bottom. Stalin, interested in Mongolia as a source of animal products, insisted the seal have a herder on a horse surrounded by busts of animals. The seal approved in the 1940 CONSTITUTION followed his recommendation and replaced the wheat sheaves with a geometric scroll and pasture grass. In the 1960 CONSTITUTION the aspirations to symbolize a modern economy returned; the wheat sheaves were restored, the animal busts removed, and an industrial cogwheel added at the bottom. The Soyombo symbol was, however, added to the star. In 1992, with the new democratic constitution, the seal was transformed by Buddhist symbolism. The ribbon at the base became a lotus, the cogwheel became a dharma wheel intertwined with a KHADAG (scarf), the wheat sheaves became a swastika-based scroll (with a Buddhist, not racial, meaning), and the "three jewels" replaced the star. The horse became a *khii mori* (wind horse), or symbol of good fortune, carrying the Soyombo symbol over a blue surface symbolizing the sky.

Second Conversion The Second Conversion refers to the Buddhist missionary movement from 1566 to around 1650, through which Buddhism became the sole authorized religion among the Mongols. The Second Conversion followed what the movement's missionaries believed to be a period of apostasy after the fall of the YUAN DYNASTY in 1368. (*For the earlier spread of Buddhism, see* BUDDHISM IN THE MONGOL EMPIRE). Although Tibetan-rite Buddhism lost its preeminent role after 1368, occasional Mongol requests for Buddhist scriptures and ritual items from China show contact with Tibetan-rite Buddhist clerics through the 15th century. Meanwhile, Mongolian expansion in Kökenuur and Tibet, which began in 1510 and accelerated after 1533, opened direct links with Tibetan Buddhism.

PROGRESS OF THE CONVERSION

The major Mongolian histories treat (KHUTUGTAI SECHEN KHUNG-TAIJI (1540–86) of the ORDOS Mongols and ALTAN KHAN (1508–82) of the TÜMED as the initiators of the links to Tibetan Buddhism. After initial contact with lamas, these two led the nobility of southwest Inner Mongolia in 1575 to invite bSod-nam rGya-mtsho (1543–88), leader of the aggressive new dGe-lugs-pa (Yellow Hat) order of Tibetan Buddhism. Their meeting in Kökenuur in 1576 began the Second Conversion, marked by the dominant role of the dGe-lugs-pa order, the proscription of Mongolian native religious practices, the creation of a new monastic body, the installment of venerable Buddhist images, and the translation of scriptures.

From 1585 to 1588 the Third Dalai Lama personally toured southwest Inner Mongolia. In 1585 a ruler of KHALKHA (Mongolia proper), ABATAI KHAN (1554–88), learned about Buddhism from a party of merchants from the Tümed region and began building a temple. The next year he personally visited the Dalai Lama at Altan Khan's capital, Guihua (modern HÖHHOT). To the east the CHAKHAR became officially Buddhist with the invitation of a Karma-pa (Red Hat) chaplain by Tümen Jasagtu Khan (b. 1539, r. 1558–92).

East of the Chakhar Altan Khan's preceptor, Ashing Lama, later spread the faith from 1600 to 1630 among the Baarin (Bairin) and KHARACHIN before founding a monastery at Khüriye (Hure). Among the Ongni'ud and KHORCHIN, a Oirat monk trained in Tibet, Neichi Toin (1557–1653), together with his 30 pupils, served as a Buddhist missionary from around 1629 to 1652, transforming a tenuous official acceptance of Buddhism into a more profound conversion.

Among the OIRATS the official establishment of Buddhism began when Baibaghas Baatur Noyan (d. 1630) of the Khoshud invited Tsaghan Nom-un Khan (King of the White Dharma). In 1615 the Oirat lords all agreed to send one son to Tibet to become a monk. Still, there must have been some earlier contact with Buddhism, as Neichi Toin went to Tibet to become a monk as early as 1580.

METHODS AND EXPERIENCES OF CONVERSION

Mantras and numbered categories, such as the Three Jewels, the "six syllables" *om mani padme hum,* and the eightfold restraint (moral rules), transmitted basic instruction. Neichi Toin and his patrons rewarded anyone who memorized the mantra of the fierce protector deity Yamantaka. Neichi Toin was later accused of freely giving out Yamantaka initiations to commoners and was recalled from the mission field by the Manchu emperor on advice of the Fifth Dalai Lama in 1652. Key political leaders, both male and female, everywhere received the Tantric Hevajra initiation.

Conversion narratives suggest varied patterns for individual conversion. Neichi Toin rejected the world when he saw the death throes of a pregnant wild ass he and his friends had shot. Altan and Abatai converted after successful campaigns had confirmed their leadership; they saw reestablishing the "TWO CUSTOMS" (*khoyar yosu*) of religion and state as a way of confirming their success. Miracles, healings, and supernatural contests played a role. Reading Mongolian translations of Buddhist hagiographies and viewing the splendor of mandalas and other Tantric rituals are also mentioned as strengthening weak faith. Although not treated in detail in the sources, it seems clear that women played the leading role in promoting conversion; virtually every strong male adherent can be linked to a devout woman, either his wife or a blood relative.

INSTITUTIONALIZING BUDDHISM

The Second Conversion was fiercely intolerant of the native Mongolian religion. The *JEWEL TRANSLUCENT SUTRA* (1607) boasts that under Altan Khan "the mad and stupid shamans were annihilated and the shamanesses humiliated." Khutugtai Sechen Khung-Taiji prescribed harsh penalties for funerary blood sacrifices, making or sacrificing to an ONGGHON (spirit figurines), or striking a monk. Instead, yurts were to have six-armed Mahakalas worshiped with fasting and bloodless offerings, and funerals were to be marked by almsgiving. In Khorchin government messengers accompanied by Neichi Toin's disciples collected enough *ongghon*s to fill a YURT, all of which were burned. Later codes, such as the 1640 MONGOL-OIRAT CODE, reduced unrealistically severe penalties to more practical livestock fines but kept the prohibitions on shamanist activity.

Apart from these laws, few other Mongolian practices were directly banned. Human sacrifice disappeared rapidly. Individual hunting and the eating of horse flesh were discouraged, but collective public hunts continued and were enshrined in the Mongol-Oirat Code. Strikingly, the EIGHT WHITE YURTS, or shrine of CHINGGIS KHAN, with its blood sacrifices, remained an integral part of government even in a Buddhist utopia such as the *CHAGHAN TEÜKE* (White history).

This new exclusivist vision of dGe-lugs-pa Buddhism also targeted the older orders still found in eastern and northern Mongolia. The Fifth Dalai Lama (1617–82) told an eminent Mongolian lama returning from education in Tibet: "If you propagate the Old Teaching in the Mongol lands it will only bring bad luck! If anybody else tries to spread them, you must stop him!" dGe-lugs-pa exclusivism won ardent champions among the Oirats and the Tu (Monguors). Warring constantly with Muslim powers, the Oirats zealously defended the Dalai Lama (*see* ZÜNGHARS; UPPER MONGOLS; KALMYKS). The small group of Mongolic-speaking Tu people in China's northwest borderlands found in the international dGe-lugs-pa hierarchy their only avenue to high office (*see* TU LANGUAGE AND PEOPLE).

On the positive side, institutionalizing Buddhism involved planting on Mongolian soil the Three Jewels: the dharma (i.e., scriptures), the Buddha (i.e., images and teaching lineages), and the *sangha* (i.e., monasteries). All these activities depended on noble patronage. Many translated scriptures were still extant from the 14th century, and from 1592 to 1607 translators in Altan Khan's Guihua city (modern HÖHHOT) completed the translation of the bKa'-'gyur, or Tibetan collection of the Buddha's words. Copying, consecrating, and installing scriptures crowned the establishment of monasteries, yet noncanonical hagiographies and handbooks were more important in actual conversion.

The nativization of the Buddha in Mongolia involved installing Buddha images and relics and establishing lines of teaching lineages and INCARNATE LAMAs. Thus, after the first meeting with Altan Khan, the Dalai Lama sent Manjushri Khutugtu, an incarnate lama, to live in Guihua, and in 1586 Nepalese craftsmen completed a Shakyamuni image. The Third Dalai Lama sent images and relics home with Abatai to the Khalkha. Many of the missionary lamas, such as Neichi Toin and the First Zaya Pandita of Khalkha, Lubsang-Perenlai, posthumously founded incarnation lineages in Mongolia.

Establishing monasteries was the final part of institutionalizing the conversion. In 1578 Altan Khan and the Tümed nobility dedicated 108 of their sons to the monastic life, while in 1615 the Oirat chiefs agreed to dedicate one son each. In Khorchin the nobility dedicated great numbers of Chinese and Korean prisoners of war as monks. Building a monastery and donating livestock, undoubtedly with attached herding households, completed the formation of the *sangha*. Quality was another matter, however. In 1602 the Tibetans insisted that Guihua, by then the leading monastic center among the Mongols, simply had no fit teachers to educate the FOURTH DALAI LAMA. Not until the 18th century, long after the initial conversion, did Mongolian scholars begin to win respect in Tibetan eyes.

See also BKA'-'GYUR AND BSTAN-'GYUR; NAMES PERSONAL; RELIGION; TIBETAN CULTURE IN MONGOLIA.

Further reading: Damchø Gyatsho Dharmatâla, *Rosary of White Lotuses,* trans. Piotr Klafkowski (Wiesbaden: Otto

Harrassowitz, 1987); Walther Heissig, "A Mongolian Source to the Lamaist Suppression of Shamanism," *Anthropos* 48 (1953); 1–29, 493–536.

Secret History of the Mongols   The *Secret History of the Mongols* (*Mongghol-un ni'ucha tobchiyan*) contains not only the most vivid and frank account of the rise of CHINGGIS KHAN but is also the landmark beginning of Mongolian literature.

TOPIC AND STYLE

Divided by its early editors into 10 chapters and two chapters of continuation, the work begins with a genealogy tracing the lineage of Chinggis Khan (Genghis, 1206–27). The history then gives a complex, episodic narrative of Chinggis's childhood, his rivalry with JAMUGHA, and his dependence on an increasingly unreliable patron, ONG KHAN of the KEREYID Khanate, climaxing with Ong Khan's 1203 betrayal of Chinggis and Chinggis's defeat of all his Mongolian rivals. The first dated event in the history is the 1201 election of Jamugha as KHAN of an anti-Chinggis confederacy. With Chinggis Khan's coronation of 1206 the text records numerous judgments (JASAQ) rewarding his companions (NÖKÖR) and establishing his KESHIG (imperial guard). The 10 chapters conclude with the defeat of Chinggis's last domestic rival, the once-supportive shaman TEB TENGGERI. The two chapters of continuation describe incidents in Chinggis's great campaigns in China and the Middle East, the dispute among Chinggis's sons over the succession, and Chinggis's death. The coronation of his son ÖGEDEI KHAN follows, with his conquests and new institutions, concluding with a curious "testament" of Ögedei describing his four good deeds and four faults.

The *Secret History of the Mongols* is written in prose but with numerous long and short passages in alliterative verse, much like the Icelandic sagas. While it is often compared to an epic, it differs greatly from the known Mongolian oral EPICS. The close similarity between the *Secret History* and the lost Mongolian chronicle preserved in Chinese translation as the SHENGWU QINZHENG LU show that the *Secret History* is, in intention at least, likewise a chronicle. It is, however, considerably less reliable than the *Shengwu* on chronology.

MAIN THEMES

The main theme of the *Secret History* is the rise of Chinggis Khan, which was destined by heaven. The signs of Chinggis's predestined rise begin with his first forefather, Blue Wolf, and continue through his defeat of Teb Tenggeri. In differing ways Jamugha and Ong Khan both serve as antiexamples of leadership. Jamugha is clever, glib, and easily bored, while Ong Khan is lazy, disloyal to kin, and easily swayed by bad advice. However, the *Secret History* author puts in the mouths of both the conviction that Chinggis is the destined khan of the Mongols. It is

hard not to see in such passages a response to an implicit charge against Chinggis of bad faith toward his two first patrons.

The *Secret History* does not, however, glorify Chinggis Khan as a superhuman figure. In fact, it contains numerous shocking and humiliating episodes that all other chroniclers, Mongol or foreign, omitted, from his youthful fear of dogs to his murder of his brother Begter. Instead, the *Secret History* links Chinggis's rise to the strength of his family, especially his mother Ö'ELÜN ÜJIN and his wife BÖRTE ÜJIN, both of whom at key points give him lifesaving advice. The theme of brotherly unity is also stressed. The other pillar of Chinggis's regime is his companions, whom he gathers to himself through his rise. Here, too, Ö'elün plays an important role, raising four foundlings to serve as extra brothers for her son. One exception to this rhetoric of family unity is the contempt shown toward the second wife of Chinggis's father YISÜGEI BA'ATUR, the mother of Chinggis's half brothers Belgütei and Begter.

COMPOSITION

The original title of the work is not clear. The present text contains the title *Secret History of the Mongols* (*Mongghol-un ni'ucha tobchiyan*). At the head of the text is another title, however, the *Origin of Chinggis Khan* (*Chinggis qa'an-u huja'ur*), which would serve as a good description of the initial 10-chapter text. The name *Secret History* stemmed from the high secrecy with which its very frank account of Chinggis's origin was treated. Even RASHID-UD-DIN FAZL-ULLAH used at most only occasional snippets of the work. In May 1331 the compilers of an administrative encyclopedia in Mongol China were refused access to the *Secret History* because "the Tobchiyan's episodes involve prohibited secrets and must not be allowed to be copied by outsiders."

To the present no consensus has formed on the date of the *Secret History*. The text as it now stands is dated to the year of the mouse, which could be 1228, 1240, or 1252. Since the surviving text ends with the reign of Ögedei Khan (1229–41) almost complete, the text as a whole is most commonly dated to 1240. However, anachronisms in the section on Ögedei indicate 1252 as the earliest possible date for the history if it is considered as a unitary text. Since the editors divided the surviving text into 10 chapters and a continuation, however, some treat the continuation as an interpolation, leaving only the material up to the death of Teb Tenggeri (c. 1210) as the original *Secret History* text. Even in this case, anachronisms within the smaller text make it flatly impossible to date before 1228. There is, however, close continuity in language and themes between the 10-chapter text and the two-chapter continuation, particularly in the exaggerated role ascribed to SHIGI QUTUQU and the denigration of MUQALI. If the text is, as it seems, a unity, then 1252 is the most likely date, since the accession of QUBILAI KHAN in

1260 introduced new issues that are not at all reflected in the text.

The author of the original *Secret History* is unknown. The author was certainly an "old Mongol," uninterested in sedentary societies or conquests. The *Secret History*'s partisanship for Shigi Qutuqu and denigration of Muqali and Belgütei, whose descendants were Shigi Qutuqu's rivals as viceroy of North China and *JARGHUCHI*, suggest as author a clerk who had apprenticed with Shigi Qutuqu. The glorification of Mother Ö'elün suggests links to the surviving entourage in her *ORDO*, or palace-tent, as well.

TRANSMISSION OF THE TEXT

After the fall of the Mongol YUAN DYNASTY in China, the MING DYNASTY's Bureau of Interpreters used the *Secret History* and other texts as language-instruction material for its interpreters, who needed only to speak, not write, Mongolian. The *Secret History* was thus transcribed from the original UIGHUR-MONGOLIAN SCRIPT into a Chinese phonetic transcription and supplied with an interlinear and running translation. The full text, including the transcription, which virtually no Chinese could read, was scrupulously preserved in a few copies until its final publication by Ye Dehui in 1908. Succeeding scholarship by F. W. Kotwicz, Erich Haenisch, Paul Pelliot, F. W. Cleaves, Igor de Rachewiltz, Yekhe-Minggadai Irinchen, and others has reconstructed the original Uighur-script text. In 1934 the Mongolian Institute of Science published the sole extant Uighur-script copy of the *Secret History*, containing about three-fourths of its life of Chinggis Khan, incorporated in the 17th-century Mongolian chronicle *ALTAN TOBCHI* of Lubsang-Danzin. The 1934 reprinting was, however, rather sloppy, and the accuracy of the preserved Mongolian text was not appreciated until a facsimile version was published in 1990. The 1947 publication of TSENDIIN DAMDINSÜREN's literary paraphrase into modern CYRILLIC-SCRIPT MONGOLIAN began the reintroduction of the Mongolian people to this almost lost monument of their literature, and since 1989 the *Secret History* has become a focal point of national unity for Mongolia and a symbol of ethnic pride for Mongols the world over.

See also LITERATURE; MONGOLIAN SOURCES ON THE MONGOL EMPIRE; 17TH-CENTURY CHRONICLES.

Further reading: Francis Woodman Cleaves, trans., *Secret History of the Mongols.* (Cambridge, Mass.: Harvard University Press, 1982); Igor de Rachewiltz, trans., *The Secret History of the Mongols: A Mongolian Epic Chronicle of the Thirteenth Century* (Leiden: E. J. Brill, 2003); ———, "Some Remarks on the Dating of the *Secret History of the Mongols*," *Monumenta Serica* 24 (1965): 185–205.

Selenge province (Selenga) One of the original provinces created in Mongolia's 1931 administrative reorganization, Selenge was originally named Gazartariyalang, or "Farmland," referring to its most distinctive economic activity. After being merged with Central province in the early 1950s, Selenge was reestablished in 1959 and by 1961 was expanded to its present extent. Selenge has a long frontier with the BURIAT REPUBLIC in Russia. The newly built DARKHAN CITY was removed from the province's jurisdiction in 1962.

The province's current territory is entirely contained within KHALKHA Mongolia's prerevolutionary Tüshiyetü Khan province. Before 1921 Chinese and Russians dwelt as farmers in the countryside and as traders and artisans in the border-town of KYAKHTA CITY (modern Altanbulag). To this day the province has a reputation for being "mongrel" (*erliiz*). Buriat Mongols also immigrated into the border districts after 1920.

The province's 41,200 square kilometers (15,910 square miles) cover branches of the wooded KHENTII RANGE and Büren Range surrounding the broad valleys of the SELENGE RIVER, ORKHON RIVER, Kharaa River, and Yöröö (Yeröö) River. Selenge's population of 42,700 in 1969 has expanded to 100,900 in 2000, making it the third most populous province. The TRANS-MONGOLIAN RAILWAY was built across the province from the border town of Sükhebaatur to Ulaanbaatar in 1949.

Selenge has the smallest number of livestock of any rural province, only 654,500 head, although the number of cattle (108,500 head) is relatively high. Selenge is the center of Mongolian agriculture, however, and during the collectivization era was unique in being almost completely covered with state farms rather than collectives. In 2000 Selenge produced 54 percent of Mongolia's wheat, 15 percent of its potatoes, and 20 percent of its vegetables.

Originally, the province's economic center was the border town of Kyakhta (renamed Altanbulag in 1921). Nearby Sükhebaatur city (23,400 inhabitants in 2002) replaced Altanbulag after 1937 as the gateway to Russia and the provincial capital, when a Russian railway reached Naushki, just across the border. Selenge's other main city is Züünkharaa, on the Trans-Mongolian Railway, with 17,200 people (2002).

See also BURIATS OF MONGOLIA AND INNER MONGOLIA; CHINESE COLONIZATION; FARMING.

Selenge River (Selenga) The Selenge is Mongolia's only navigable river. Its watershed of 447,060 square kilometers (172,610 square miles) covers much of north-central Mongolia and most of south-central Buriatia in Russia.

The Selenge is formed by the confluence of the Ider, rising in the KHANGAI RANGE, and the Delgermörön (or Mörön), rising in the mountains west of LAKE KHÖWSGÖL. Its main tributaries include the EG RIVER (Egiin Gol) and ORKHON RIVER in Mongolia and the Jida (Buriat, Zede), Chikoy (Buriat, Sükhe), Khilok (Buriat, Khyolgo), and Uda (Buriat, Üde) in Russia's BURIAT REPUBLIC before it empties into LAKE BAIKAL. After the confluence with the

Uda, the Selenge carries 910 cubic meters (32,136 cubic feet) of water per second. From Lake Baikal to the Ider headwaters the Selenge-Ider system is 1,453 kilometers (903 miles) long.

The Selenge valley is navigable up to Selenge Sum (Bulgan province), north of Erdenet. Cargo ships first plied the river between Mongolia and southern Siberia in 1909. ULAN-UDE, the capital of Buriatia, is the largest city in the Selenge valley, with 370,400 inhabitants in 2000.

Seljüks See TURKEY.

se-mu-jen See SEMUREN.

semuren (se-mu-jen)

Under the Mongols in China the semuren constituted a class of immigrants lower than the Mongols in status but above the indigenous Chinese.

Throughout their empire the Mongols employed various peoples outside their own homeland both as officials and privileged ORTOQ (partner) merchants. In China these immigrants included UIGHURS (mostly Buddhists), Turkestani Muslims, and Middle Easterners (Muslim and occasionally Christian). Early in Mongol rule these immigrants were effectively tax exempt and shared in the privileges of the Mongol ruling class. Ordinary immigrants soon lost their tax exemption, but other privileges remained.

During the YUAN DYNASTY in China QUBILAI KHAN imitated the four-class system of the Jin dynasty by formalizing the division of the population into four classes: Mongols, semuren, Han (North Chinese), and southerners. Semuren, meaning "various sorts," designated all peoples who immigrated from the west of China. Two Sino-Inner Asian border peoples, the Tanguts and the ÖNGGÜD, along with the NAIMAN of the Mongolian plateau, were also considered semuren, but the KITANS and Jurchens were assigned to the Han, or North Chinese, category along with the Koreans.

The semuren shared with the Mongols a number of rights. After 1270 these two groups monopolized the top administrative positions. The lower positions of DARUGHACHI (overseer) and surveillance commissioner were also restricted to Mongols or semuren of good family. When the examination system was revived in 1315, each ethnic class had an equal quota, which, given their small numbers, gave the semuren and the Mongols a tremendous advantage. Judicially, the semuren, like the Mongols, retained the right to bear arms and to defend themselves if attacked. Criminals of both classes were exempt from tattooing. Slave ownership, a sign of privilege rare among the Chinese, was common among all semuren, although not so much as among Mongols.

Within the class of semuren each group had a distinctive occupational profile. Uighurs, Tanguts, and the Önggüd all played a major role in the civil bureaucracy due to their literacy and familiarity with Chinese culture. Many became passionate advocates of CONFUCIANISM. QIPCHAQS, Qangli, QARLUQS, OSSETES, and Russians formed ethnic units within the imperial guard; these units allowed the Qipchaqs and Qangli to play major political roles. Tibetans were mostly Buddhist clerics, while Turkestanis and Middle Easterners, both Muslim and Christian, served as ortoq merchants, financial officials, physicians, astronomers, and artisans.

With the fall of the Yuan dynasty in 1368, the semuren lost their privileged positions, and most eventually assimilated into the Chinese. Only the Muslims, having a group identity buttressed by religion, remained distinct, forming the nucleus of the Hui (Chinese-speaking Muslim) nationality today.

See also AHMAD; ANIGA; ARIQ-QAYA; BAO'AN LANGUAGE AND PEOPLE; CHOSGI-ODSIR; DONGXIANG LANGUAGE AND PEOPLE; EL-TEMÜR; LIAN XIXIAN; 'PHAGS-PA; POLO, MARCO; SANGHA; SAYYID AJALL; TUTUGH.

Further reading: Chen Yuan, *Western and Central Asians in China under the Mongols: Their Transformation into Chinese*, trans. Chien Hsing-hai and L. Carrington Goodrich (Los Angeles: Monumenta Serica, 1966); Igor de Rachewiltz, "Turks in China under the Mongols: A Preliminary Investigation of Turco-Mongol Relations in the 13th and 14th Centuries." In *China among Equals: The Middle Kingdom and Its Neighbors, 10th–14th Centuries,* ed. Morris Rossabi (Berkeley: University of California Press, 1983), 281–310.

shahna See DARUGHACHI.

shamanism

Shamans, both male and female, were the traditional clergy of the Mongols up to the 16th century despite having sometimes to coexist with clergy of other religions. Persecuted by the Buddhists during the SECOND CONVERSION after 1575, they disappeared from many areas of Mongolia, particularly in the central steppe area of KHALKHA and central Inner Mongolia. Even so, shamanism remains the dominant religion among the western BURIATS, Daurs, Old BARGA, and DARKHAD and is also strong among the Khori Buriats. Shamans can also be found less commonly among the Selenge Buriats, eastern INNER MONGOLIANS, and western Mongolian OIRATS.

SHAMANISM IN THE MONGOL EMPIRE

Among the tribes of 12th-century Mongolia, shamans functioned both not only as healers and spirit mediums, but as regular clergy with their own ranks, and even as powerful chiefs.

Under the MONGOL EMPIRE the khans kept a whole college of male shamans (Mongol, *bö'e;* Turkish, *qam*) who specialized in various functions. Some made astrological observations and could predict eclipses. SCAPULI-MANCY and astrology were used to appoint favorable and unfavorable days for nomadizings, make decisions about wars, and divine the sources of troubles. Shamans presided over the regular calendrical ceremonies, such as the aspersions to heaven (TENGGERI) at the opening and closing of the mare milking season. Shamans supervised the purification by fire of gifts intended for the great lords and of anything that had been in the presence of the dead (see FIRE CULT). During war others performed weather magic with the *jada* stone and brought snowstorms and extreme cold. Only some shamans performed the meat offering and drummed the famous shamanic seances that are now essential for any shaman. It was undoubtedly these shamans who visited the sick and dying and made ONGGHON figures to propitiate spirits causing sickness.

Female shamans (*idughan*) performed roles at court, but they seem to have been less important. They certainly participated in the fire purification ceremonies. A Russian chronicle mentions a witch (evidently a shamaness) commanding a Mongol force at Ryazan'.

The chief of the shamans was the *beki*, who was also the genealogical senior member of a clan or tribe. Before CHINGGIS KHAN the *bekis* in some tribes, such as the MERKID, Oirats, and Dörben, were, in fact, the real chiefs; the chief of the Oirats was a powerful weather magician. (The term *beki* also meant "princess"; the connection between these two titles in uncertain.) The *bekis* wore white clothes, rode a white horse, and would be seated highest in the assembly and receive the offerings of the other chiefs. The *beki* himself served the *ongghon*, or spirit figurines, of the ancestors of the clan's ruling lineage.

In the MONGOL TRIBE the *bekis* were important but not great chiefs. The *bekis* Sacha and Quchar of the Mongols' ruling Kiyad (or BORJIGID) lineage helped Chinggis in his rise but then deserted him, so that in 1206 he appointed a new beki, "Old Man Üsün," from the Baarin line, a senior branch but by a different mother. While the other shamans stayed behind the great khan's palacetent, the *bekis* camped in front of it, and the KHAN made offerings to him on ritual occasions. The khan also performed divination by scapulimancy and prayed to heaven on his own account. Genealogy alone could not assure shamanic charisma. During Chinggis's rise to around 1210, the most influential shaman was not a *beki* but the powerfully supernatural TEB TENGGERI of the junior Qongqotan lineage.

The college of shamans at the imperial and princely courts played a powerful political role behind the scenes. According to observers such as WILLIAM OF RUBRUCK, the shamans were always ready to account for untoward events by leveling accusations of witchcraft, particularly against women. Certainly during the later succession conflicts there were frequent accusations of witchcraft, which the shamans were capable of performing, detecting, and averting. The involvement of shamans in the death of TOLUI, Chinggis Khan's youngest son, has also been seen as a case of politically motivated murder.

The relations of the shamans with the clergy of non-Mongol religions varied. Under the great khans of the Mongol Empire and in the YUAN DYNASTY (1206/1271–1368), Christian priests of the Assyrian Church of the East (the Nestorians) performed calendrical rituals alongside the shamans; after 1260 Tibetan Buddhist monks joined shamans at the ancestral temple worship. At the court of the Il-Khans and the other western khanates, divination and astrology seem to have been monopolized by the *baqshis* (teacher), a name usually used for Buddhist monks, and the shamans were not very important. With Islamization these *baqshis* disappeared or, in the GOLDEN HORDE and its successor states, left the court to practice among ordinary herders. Today among the KAZAKHS shamans are called *baqsi*, a direct descendant of the Mongol-era *baqshi*.

RECENT SHAMANISM

From the 18th century much more information exists on shamanism. Accounts of Buddhist missionary activity in the 16th and 17th centuries supply little new information about shamanism, save that the title of *beki* was replaced by that of *jaarin* and that leading shamans still rode white horses and had some form of organization. From the 18th century, however, both ethnographic accounts and the use of texts emanating from shamanist circles allow shamanism to be described in more detail.

Shaman functions, even among the non-Buddhist peoples, are much more limited than during empire times. Astrology is no longer a shamanistic practice, and shamans play no role in casting horoscopes for babies, or arranging marriages and funerals. Calendrical ceremonies, such as the first fruits of mares' milk and the OBOO ceremony in high summer, are also off-limits to shamans. Instead, shamans now specialize in healing and have a very ambivalent relation to the larger clan structure.

In shamanism souls or spirits are believed to be detachable from the body both during and after life. If the soul leaves the body during life, serious illness or misfortune may result, while if a person has died through violence or unfair treatment, the deceased soul can become vengeful and cause illness. To heal the victim the shaman begins a seance by calling down the spirits of his or her instruments, then making a meat offering to the spirits, followed by a dance with a drum. During this dance the shaman is possessed by a powerful ancestral spirit, thus becoming an *ongghon*. This possession is clear from the noticeably different voice, gait, personality, and often extreme endurance and strength the medium exhibits while the possession lasts. This powerful ancestral spirit frequently gives oral instructions identifying the problem, translated by an assistant. At the same time, however, the shaman's trance is often seen as the shaman him-or herself traveling on the drum to find the problem. The problem

Ongghons in felt, metal, and wood and a shaman hat with antlers, Buriat United Museum, Ulan-Ude *(From* Mongolian Arts and Crafts *[1987])*

usually involves some fault on the part of the victim that provoked a supernatural punishment from the offended spirits, and the solution consists in ritually making up the fault. Often, however, the shaman's ancestral spirit must subdue the offending spirit before it accepts the ritual reparation.

The shaman costume and equipment are a crucial part of his or her work. Generally based in the past on a leather caftan, the shaman's cloak is a melange of extraordinarily complex elements intended both for symbolic purposes and to create an impressive magical effect. All costumes contain a mirror to reflect any evil and to allow the shaman to view the unseen. Many have snake figures hanging from the armpits or back. The hat is usually crowned by antlers tied with *khadags*, or ceremonial scarves. Among the Buriats the face is covered by a fringe, and a skull cap is decorated with eyes. The shaman's large handheld drum is made of goatskin.

To become a shaman one must have an ancestral spirit (Buriat, *udkha*) on either one's father's or mother's side. The powerful ancestor spirit chooses a descendant through a shaman's sickness, a strange disease that sometimes resembles insanity and that cannot be cured until the person agrees to become a shaman and receives initiation as a shaman. The Khori Buriats have a system of ranks achieved through participation in a *shanar*, or initiation ceremony, which can be repeated up to nine times.

The ancestor spirits of shamans, who are buried at mountains and other landmarks (called *barisa* in Buriat),

are closely associated with, although not the same as, the masters or sovereigns of the land (*gazar-un ezed/khad*), who inhabit these same areas, and with the ultimate clan ancestors, such as "Lord Bull" (*Bukha Noyon*) of the Ekhired-Bulagad Buriats and Tsagaadai and the Tsankhilan of the widespread Sharanuud clan. These masters of the land are linked to the 99 gods (*tenggeri*), of whom they are children or messengers. Clan ancestors and shaman tutelary spirits, especially female ones, may also be associated with household gods such as the fire (*see* FIRE CULT) or with Mother Emegeljin, the name for the main *ongghon* in the YURT.

Many shamans among the Mongols operated, however, with an almost completely Buddhist cosmology. They are sometimes distinguished from the less Buddhist influenced shaman as yellow opposed to black (from the Buddhist "Yellow Faith") or as white opposed to black. Among the Khori Buriats white-side and black-side shamans coexist as two different traditions often practiced by a single shaman. While the black-side shamans use a drum and have an antlered cap, the white-side shamans hold a dragon-headed staff (like that of the WHITE OLD MAN), ring a bell, and use the Buddhist *om mani padme hum* chant. Their cap has eyes and fringe over the face but no antlers. Shamans among the KHORCHIN wear a special five-sided hat borrowed from the services of the fierce Buddhist protector deities.

MODERN SHAMANISM

At first the revolutionary changes of the 20th century strengthened shamanism. Among the Buriats the 1905 revolution in Russia weakened the power of the eastern Buriat upper class, which had supported the suppression of shamanism and the imposition of Buddhism. The czarist policy of official Christianization in western Buriatia was also crippled by the revolution.

From 1929 on, however, collectivization and antireligious attacks in Buriatia caused the death and imprisonment of many shamans. In Mongolia the GREAT PURGE struck the Buriats of Mongolia hard and swept away many shamans. In Russia a renewed wave of antireligious persecution around 1960 targeted, among others, Siberian shamans. In Inner Mongolia persecution of shamans was sharpest from 1958 to 1962 and from 1964 to 1979.

Since the religious revival of 1990 in Buriatia and Mongolia, shamanism has revived among the Buriats in particular as well as among the Darkhad. While shamanism today is most widespread among the Buriats, the traditional knowledge was not as well preserved there as among the Buriats of Mongolia and Inner Mongolia. Khori Buriat shamans have gone to their kinsmen in Mongolia or the Buriats of Inner Mongolia to receive training. Buriat shaman costumes today usually do not include the leather caftan but instead consist of the Buriat-style *deel,* or robe (*see* CLOTHING AND DRESS), worn with the shaman's hat and equipment.

See also BANZAROV, DORZHI; *BARIACH*; DAUR LANGUAGE AND PEOPLE; RELIGION; RELIGIOUS POLICY IN THE MONGOL EMPIRE; TU LANGUAGE AND PEOPLE; YOGUR LANGUAGES AND PEOPLE.

Further reading: Mircea Eliade, *Shamanism: Archaic Techniques of Ecstasy* (New York: Bollingen Foundation, 1964); Caroline Humphrey, *Shamans and Elders: Experience, Knowledge, and Power among the Daur Mongols* (Oxford: Oxford University Press, 1996); Jorma Partanen, "A Description of Buriat Shamanism," *Société Finno-Ougrienne* 51, no. 5 (1941): 1–34; Virlana Tkacz, with Sayan Zhambalon and Wanda Phipps, *Shanar: Dedication Ritual of a Buryat Shaman in Siberia* (New York Parabola Books, 2002).

Shangdu (Shang-tu, K'ai-p'ing, Xanadu) Shangdu, QUBILAI KHAN's summer city, became the inspiration for the English poet Samuel Taylor Coleridge's famous poem *Xanadu*. In 1256 Prince Qubilai built Kaiping in Inner Mongolia (near modern Zhenglan Qi), where he was elected great khan in 1260. During the ensuing war with ARIQ-BÖKE, Kaiping became Qubilai's military headquarters, while Yanjing (modern Beijing) served as his supply center. Kaiping was built in three quadrangles: the outer city of about 2,200 meters (7,200 feet) square, the large imperial city abutting the outer city's southwest section, and the smaller palace city, slightly north of the imperial city's center. Buddhist monasteries marked each corner of the imperial city. To the north the outer city's wall enclosed a well-watered hunting park, where Qubilai built a collapsible cane palace (Coleridge's "stately pleasure dome"). Ordinary residents occupied the outer city's southwest district and the suburbs outside the gates. In 1263 Kaiping was renamed Shangdu (Upper Capital). In 1272 Yanjing, now renamed DAIDU (Great Capital), became the preeminent capital, but Shangdu retained its importance. The khan and a skeleton administrative staff resided there from May to September each year, conducting formal audiences at the Da'an Hall and performing rituals of sprinkling KOUMISS to heaven (TENGGERI) from the khan's herds of white horses. Shangdu was the site of all the election assemblies (QURILTAI) through 1328. During the rebellions at the end of the Yuan dynasty, a column of rebels burned Shangdu in winter 1258–59. Garrisoned by the succeeding MING DYNASTY (1368–1644), Shangdu was abandoned around 1430.

See also "LAMENT OF TOGHAN-TEMÜR."

Shangdzodba, Erdeni (Erdene Shandzowa) The treasurer, or Erdeni Shangdzodba (Tibetan *shan-mdzod-pa*), of the JIBZUNDAMBA KHUTUGTU headed the single most powerful economic institution of prerevolutionary Mongolia. A *shangdzodba* was a general term for both the estate and the steward of an INCARNATE LAMA; that of the Jibzundamba Khutugtu was distinguished by the honorific Erdeni, "Precious."

The Jibzundamba Khutugtu's Shangdzodba existed at least as early as 1709, when it helped issue the law code KHALKHA JIRUM. It administered the secular affairs of the Khutugtu's "clerical and lay disciples," while an abbot, or *khambo lama*, administered purely religious affairs in Khüriye (see ULAANBAATAR). From 1723 the QING DYNASTY court issued seals to the Shangdzodba. In 1767 the position of *da-lama* was created to assist the Shangdzodba in administering the GREAT SHABI (the Khutugtu's personal subjects).

At its height from 1800 to 1865, the Erdeni Shangdzodba directly controlled 55,000–90,000 head of the Khutugtu's livestock, 90,000–115,000 "lay disciples" (serfs) in the Great Shabi with their personal herds, and significant farmland. All these figures later declined, particularly the herd numbers, presumably sold to pay debts to Chinese firms; a single such payment in 1900 reached 50,000 *taels*. From 1868 to 1909 the Shangdzodba also printed its own paper money (*tiiz*). It established monastic courses in various scripts (Mongolian, Tibetan, Sanskrit) and *thangka* painting as well as primary schools in the Great Shabi.

During the THEOCRATIC PERIOD (1911–21) the Great Shabi grew rapidly, and the Erdeni Shangdzodba was made a separate ministry. Shangdzodba BADMADORJI became prime minister from 1915 to 1919, while the Interior Ministry was headed by his *da-lama*, Tseringchimed (1872–1914).

After the 1921 REVOLUTION the Shangdzodba in 1923 was transformed into the elective administrator of the Great Shabi as an administrative unit. In 1925, with the confiscation of the Jibzundamba's property, the position of Shangdzodba was abolished.

See also JIBZUNDAMBA KHUTUGTU, FIRST.

Shang-tu *See* SHANGDU.

Sharab, "Busybody" (Balduugiin Sharav) (1869–1939) *Court painter who transformed the traditional Mongolian guru portraits before going on to create revolutionary cartoons and portraits*

Sharab (or Lubsang-Sharab) was born the illegitimate son of Norjun, daughter of Balduu, in Zasagtu Khan banner (northeast Gobi-Altai province). His first tutor as a Buddhist iconographer was Jantsan, a locally famous *dogshin* (fierce) Buddha painter and sculptor.

Sharab left for Khüriye (modern ULAANBAATAR) at age 22. He ran with a crowd of wild Tibetan lamas and gambled heavily. He painted furniture and *üichüür* (playing cards) but soon got a reputation as an untaught genius at painting portraits "more alike than a photograph," painted either from life or memory. The Bogda (Holy One) commissioned several portraits of himself and his consort. Sharab several times dropped the portraits to go off on gambling sprees, and the Bogda nicknamed him "Busybody (Marzan) Sharab."

Sharab mastered pencil and *tush'* (a thick Russian ink) and was inspired by both photographs and Chinese ink paintings. His guru portraits combined mineral paints with ink and Buddhist canons and symbolism with realism. Like contemporary photographs, they often contain a clock, an icon of modernity. His paintings of the Green and Brown Palaces of the Bogda and of the *Koumiss Festival* and *Autumn* pushed two traditional Buddhist genres, the portrait of a holy place (Sharab also painted Lhasa) and the portrait of animal and human life in the wheel of samsara, in the direction of ethnographic realism.

After the 1921 REVOLUTION Sharab became a printer, designing the masthead for periodicals such as the army magazine *Uriya* as well as Mongolian paper currency, medals, and other works. He illustrated printings of translated works such as Daniel Defoe's *Robinson Crusoe* and the traditional Indian *Tales of the Bewitched Corpse*. He also painted portraits of Lenin, GENERAL SÜKHE-BAATUR, Prime Minister TSERINDORJI, and other foreign and domestic revolutionaries. His last known work was a glossary of folk designs and decorative motifs produced in 1935.

The value of Sharab's works was not recognized in the years after the persecution of Buddhism. Few of his works have survived, many only in retouched or copied form.

See also JIBZUNDAMBA KHUTUGTU, EIGHTH; REVOLUTIONARY PERIOD; THEOCRATIC PERIOD.

Further reading: C. R. Bawden, trans., *Tales of an Old Lama* (Tring, U.K.: Institute of Buddhist Studies, 1997); N. Tsultem, *Development of the Mongolian National Style Painting "Mongol Zurag" in Brief* (Ulaanbaatar: State Publishing House, 1986).

Shatuo   *See* ÖNGGÜD.

Shav'   *See* GREAT SHABI.

sheep   Sheep are economically the most important part of Mongolian pastoral nomadism and thus play the same foundational role in Mongolian civilization as does rice in Japan and corn in Mexico. Mutton is Mongolia's main meat; sheep milk is used for TEA and cheeses; sheepskins line winter clothes; and sheep wool forms the felt covering Mongolian yurts. In 2000 Mongolia had a total of 13,876,400 sheep, or almost six per person.

Traditional Mongolian sheep have massive, fat-filled tails, floppy ears, and coarse or semicoarse wool. Annual wool yields range from 1–1.4 kilograms (2.2–3.1 pounds) for ewes to 1.6–2.0 kilograms (3.5–4.4 pounds) for rams. In recent decades the amount of wool supplied annually per head of sheep has ranged from around 1.2 kilograms (2.7 pounds) in 1960 to around 1.4–1.5 kilograms (3.1–3.3 pounds) in later decades. Mongolian sheep are sheared mostly in late spring but sometimes in fall as well. The main use of the wool is for felt, although in the 20th century raw wool has became an important export commodity.

Sheep are also milked, and ewes produce about 36–39 kilograms (79–86 pounds) of milk over a milking season of 45–60 days. In milking sheep, two or three families camp at a short distance from one another, with one taking all the lambs and the other taking all the ewes. This separation prevents the lambs from exhausting the milk during the day. Such partners are called *saakhalt ail*, a term now used in Mongolia for neighbors.

Mongolian mutton has a strong taste whose exact properties are influenced by its pasture. In the WHITE MONTH (lunar new year) a whole sheep is boiled and dressed on a platter. Called *shüüs*, "nutrition" (or in some dialects of Inner Mongolia *bükhüli*, whole), it is surmounted by the head and the fat tail, which is a delicacy offered to honored guests.

Sheep are generally herded together with GOATS in Mongolia, since the goats' greater initiative can be valuable in finding the sheep good grazing and dealing with bad weather and predators. For this reason traditional counts did not distinguish sheep and goats. A unique, early census in 1188 shows sheep and goats together accounted for 59 percent of the animals kept in eastern Inner Mongolia. In the 19th century, as the number of horses declined, that of sheep, GOATS, and CATTLE increased. In eastern Mongolia in 1835 sheep and goats formed 64 percent of the total herd. In 1924 Mongolia had 10,649,200 sheep and goats, forming 77 percent of the total herd. By 1929 sheep alone were 67 percent and goats another 15 percent of Mongolia's livestock, as herders responded to the powerful export demand for wool.

The subsequent removal of Mongolia from the world market lowered the demand for sheep, whose numbers throughout the 1950s remained around 12.6–12.8 million, or 54–56 percent of all livestock. During the succeeding decades sheep numbers increased by 1990 to 15,083,000 head, or 58 percent, while wool production rose from 15,200 metric tons (16,755 short tons) in 1960 to 21,100 (23,259 short tons) in 1990 and mutton and goat's meat from 96,200 metric tons to 132,300 (106,042 to 145,836 short tons). Despite the reopening of the Mongolian economy after 1990, the demand for wool was low compared to that for CASHMERE, and sheep numbered only 15,191,300 head (45 percent of all livestock) in 1999 before two disastrous winters in 2000 and 2001 sharply cut their numbers. Sheep are herded all over the country, but have particularly high numbers in ZAWKHAN PROVINCE, SOUTH KHANGAI PROVINCE, and CENTRAL PROVINCE. EASTERN PROVINCE's herd is unusually heavy in sheep, while they are unusually few in SOUTH GOBI

PROVINCE, BAYANKHONGOR PROVINCE, and GOBI-ALTAI PROVINCE.

In China and Russia the governments pushed herders in ethnic Mongol regions to focus on sheep to feed the textiles industry. In 1947 in Inner Mongolia sheep numbered 3,426,000, or 43 percent of the Mongols' traditional "five livestock" (HORSES, cattle, CAMELS, sheep, goats). By 1965 the number of sheep shot up to 20,174,000 (49 percent). By 1990, as the absolute numbers of livestock showed only a moderate increase, those of sheep soared further to 27,343,000, or 60 percent. The dominance of sheep was even more extreme in Russia's BURIAT REPUBLIC, the AGA BURIAT AUTONOMOUS AREA, and the KALMYK REPUBLIC. In Russia desertification, an end to centralized planning, and a general economic depression brought a partial shift back toward subsistence-oriented herding. A similar or even greater ecological disaster seems ongoing in Inner Mongolia, but the Chinese authorities have not yet reconsidered the stress on commercialized sheep ranching.

State-directed commercial sheep farming has also involved the creation of fine-haired and semifine-haired sheep breeds, such as Mongolia's Orkhon semifine-wool breed, Inner Mongolia's Aohan and Ordos fine-wool breeds, and the Transbaikal fine-wool breed. Karakul sheep have also been introduced into the Mongolian Gobi and Inner Mongolia's ORDOS, ALASHAN, and BAYANNUUR LEAGUE areas.

See also ANIMAL HUSBANDRY AND NOMADISM; DAIRY PRODUCTS; DESERTIFICATION AND PASTURE DEGRADATION; FOOD AND DRINK.

Further reading: B. Minzhigdorj and B. Erdenebaatar, "Why Mongolians Say Sheep Herders Are Lucky," *Nomadic Peoples*, 33 (1993): 47–50; Ts. Namkhainyambuu, *Bounty from the Sheep: Autobiography of a Herdsman*, trans. Mary Rossabi (Cambridge: White Horse Press, 2000).

Sheng-wu ch'in-cheng lu *See* SHENGWU QINZHENG LU.

Shengwu qinzheng lu (*Sheng-wu ch'in-cheng lu*; Campaigns of Genghis Khan) The *Shengwu qinzheng lu* is a Chinese translation of the lost Mongolian chronicle that also formed a basic source for RASHID-UD-DIN FAZL-ULLAH's COMPENDIUM OF CHRONICLES (c. 1304) and the first chapter of the Chinese YUAN SHI (1370).

The *Shengwu* text as we have it today begins with the birth of CHINGGIS KHAN and continues to the death of his son ÖGEDEI KHAN in 1241. The Mongolian original, however, probably had chapters on the history of Alan Gho'a, Bodonchar, and the subjugation of the JALAYIR, accounts preserved in the *Compendium of Chronicles* and the *Yuan shi*. Compared to the SECRET HISTORY OF THE MONGOLS, the *Shengwu* is much more an official history, burying discreditable incidents of Chinggis's early history, such as his murder of his brother Begter and the rape of his wife BÖRTE ÜJIN. It gives little emphasis to Chinggis's family or companions (NÖKOR). Its chronology and its account of the conquest of North China are, however, far more accurate.

The Mongolian original was apparently the text known as the *Shilu* (Veritable records), presented to QUBILAI KHAN (1260–94) by his minister of education Sarman (or Sarban) in 1288. The khan demanded revisions of the later reigns, and revised records on Ögedei were presented by Sarman and an assistant, Uru'udai, in 1290. These records appear to have been originally composed in the SQUARE SCRIPT but were later at Sarman's request allowed to be transcribed into the UIGHUR-MONGOLIAN SCRIPT. A final version of the first five reigns' *Veritable Records* was presented in 1303. The veritable records of Qubilai and his successors were later compiled in much greater detail, but they do not survive except as incorporated in the *Yuan shi*. The reason for the name change from *Veritable Records* to *Campaigns Led by the Lawgiving Warrior* (that is, Chinggis) is unclear.

The translation into Chinese of the *Shengwu*, together with that of the YUAN DYNASTY's *Shisan chao shilu* (Veritable records of the thirteen reigns), was rushed through in 1369 as part of the succeeding MING DYNASTY editors' compilation of YUAN SHI (*History of the Yuan*). By comparison with parallel passages in Rashid-ud-Din, the Chinese translators can be demonstrated to have misunderstood the Mongolian at several points. Many of the Mongolian names were further mangled in transmission, leaving many difficult problems to be worked out by Wang Guowei, Paul Pelliot, and others. Overshadowed by the more dramatic and better preserved *Secret History*, the *Shengwu* has not received the attention it deserves as a monument of Mongolian historiography.

Shera Yogur *See* YOGUR LANGUAGES AND PEOPLE.

Shigi Qutuqu *See* QUTUQU, SHIGI.

Shih-mo Hsien-te-pu *See* SHIMO MING'AN AND XIANDEBU.

Shih-mo Ming-an *See* SHIMO MING'AN AND XIANDEBU.

Shih T'ien-tse *See* SHII T'IEN-TSE.

Shih-wei *See* SHIWEI.

Shii Tianze (Shih T'ien-tse) (1202–1275) *Chinese general who helped conquer North China for the Mongols and helped defend Qubilai Khan's rule*
When the Mongols invaded the JIN DYNASTY (1115–1234) then ruling North China, the Shii family of Yongqing county in northern Hebei was a wealthy

landlord family, unintellectual but used to taking the lead in famine relief and assisting persons of quality in distress. When the great Mongol general MUQALI reached Hebei in 1213, the clan patriarch, Shii Bingzhi (1150–1220), led several thousand to surrender to the Mongols. Muqali married the patriarch's daughter, and Bingzhi's eldest son, Tianni (1187–1225), joined Muqali's army, receiving a golden tiger PAIZA in 1215. In 1220 the Jin dynasty general Wu Xian surrendered the major city Zhending (in Hebei province) to Muqali, who made Tianni garrison commander for West Hebei along with Wu Xian. Five years later Wu Xian revolted and killed Tianni. The Mongols confirmed Tianze, then in Yanjing (modern Beijing), in his elder brother's command and helped him retake Zhending, driving Wu Xian south and pacifying West Hebei by 1226.

In 1229 ÖGEDEI KHAN made Shii Tianze one of the first three Chinese myriarchs (commander of 10,000), and Shii joined both the final campaign against the Jin dynasty and the first, inconclusive Mongol campaigns against the Song. Shii's advocacy also secured limitations on interest paid on silver loans and a clearer separation of civil and military households among the Han (ethnic Chinese). More cultured than most of his Chinese military colleagues, Shii cultivated modest literary achievements in his middle age, studying the famous history *Zizhi Tongjian* (Comprehensive mirror in aid of government) of Sima Guang (1019–86) and trying his hand at poetry and vernacular drama.

In 1252 MÖNGKE KHAN, on the advice of his brother Qubilai, made Shii Tianze expeditionary commissioner for Henan and added Weyzhou to his appanage. Since 1244 Qubilai had interviewed many scholars from Zhending and was familiar with Shii. Shii's new alliance with Qubilai involved him in the rivalry between Möngke's officials, led by 'Alam-Dar, and Qubilai's. Thus although Shii was serving with Möngke's army in Sichuan when the khan died (August 1259), he immediately threw his support behind Qubilai.

On QUBILAI KHAN's coronation in 1260 he rewarded Shii with 15,000 taels of silver, military and civil control of Henan, and a position as grand councillor in the new Secretariat (1261). Shii participated in the battle of Shimu'ultu Na'ur (Mosquito Lake, November 1261) against Qubilai's brother and rival ARIQ-BÖKE and commanded the suppression of LI TAN'S REBELLION (1262). By this time rivals suggested the Shii family's combined civil-military power was no less threatening than Li Tan's. Qubilai at one point even contemplated interrogating Shii Tianze, but Shii wisely ordered his family members in 1262 to choose military or civilian posts. In one day they resigned 17 military commands.

In the central government, however, Shii became vice commissioner in the Bureau of Military Affairs in 1264 while still holding his position as grand councillor in the Secretariat. Clashes over fiscal policy with the articulate

and ingenious AHMAD FANAKATI showed Shii in a bad light, and Qubilai dismissed him in 1268. Even so, he gave Shii a large role in the siege of Xiangyang (modern Xiangfan) and command of the final attack on the Song. Due to illness, however, BAYAN CHINGSANG replaced him, and he died on March 5, 1275. His sons and cousins held a wide variety of high offices until the 1320s.

Further reading: C. C. Hsiao, "Shih T'ien-tse," in *In the Service of the Khan: Eminent Personalities of the Early Mongol-Yuan Period (1200–1300)*, ed. Igor de Rachewiltz et al. (Wiesbaden: Otto Harrassowitz, 1993), 27–45.

Shiliin Gol (Shili-yin Gool, Xilingol, Xilinguole)

Traditionally the most isolated and nomadic area of China's INNER MONGOLIA AUTONOMOUS REGION, Shiliin Gol league now includes part of the old CHAKHAR district as well.

Before 1958 Shiliin Gol referred to the ÜJÜMÜCHIN, Abaga (Abag), and Sönid banners along the border of KHALKHA (Outer) Mongolia. In 1990 these banners, along with the new cities of Shiliin Khot (Xilinhot) and Ereenkhot (Erlian or Erenhot), had an area of 174,100 square kilometers (67,220 square miles) and a population of 407,000, of which 181,100, or about 45 percent, were Mongol. The countryside is almost entirely devoted to animal husbandry and has 5,651,200 head of livestock, of which 4,727,400 are SHEEP and GOATS. Shiliin Gol's Mongols are nomadic or seminomadic, supplementing YURTS with mud-brick houses. Mining, including coal and oil, is the other important industry. In 1958 Shiliin Gol and Chakhar leagues merged; in 1990 the resulting administrative unit had an area of 200,600 square kilometers (77,450 square miles) and a population of 888,047, of which 254,797, or less than 30 percent were Mongol.

HISTORY

In the 16th century the banners of modern Shiliin Gol were part of the Chakhar *tümen*. In 1627 many princes, including those of Sönid, Üjümüchin, and Ongni'ud, revolted against Chakhar's LIGDAN KHAN (1604–34) and fled north to Khalkha. In 1637, after the new Manchu QING DYNASTY (1636–1912) had defeated Ligdan, they and other former Chakhar princes submitted to the Qing and received territory in modern Shiliin Gol, The Ongni'ud were renamed Abaga and Abaganar (uncles) banners; their rulers were descendants of CHINGGIS KHAN's brother Belgütei. Shiliin Gol was eventually organized into a league (*chigulgan*) with 10 BANNERS (appanages): two each of Üjümüchin, Khuuchid, Abaganar, Abaga, and Sönid. (The Khuuchid banners were merged with Üjümüchin after 1945.)

Although the Shiliin Gol banners were forced into submission to the Republic of China in 1915, they remained virtually untouched by the modern Inner Mongolian nationalist movement. However, Sönid Right Banner's PRINCE DEMCHUGDONGRUB (Prince De, 1902–66) became leader of Inner Mongolia's autonomous movement after 1933 and led central Inner Mongolia, including Shiliin Gol, under the Japanese occupation of 1937–45. The modest educational initiatives under Prince De's rule were destroyed first by the Soviet-Mongolian invasion and subsequent plunder, and then by a savage civil war between pro-Chinese Communist Mongols under ULANFU and anticommunist guerrillas led by the Buriat refugee Irinchindorji. The Communists executed the last rebel leaders in 1952.

After 1952 the new city Shiliin Khot developed at the old Bandida Gegeen Hermitage (Beizi Miao) as an administrative center, while Saikhan Tal and Ereenkhot developed as railway towns on the TRANS-MONGOLIAN RAILWAY. In 1982 Shiliin Khot's built-up area had a population of about 66,200, while Saikhantala had 20,500 and Eriyenkhota more than 7,200 inhabitants. Drought and locusts hit Shiliin Gol hard from 1999 to 2002, drawing attention to serious desertification and pasture degradation. By January 2002, 14,691 Mongol herders had been relocated from the Shiliin Gol steppes as part of the Chinese government's "ecological migration" (*shengtai yimin*) program.

See also INNER MONGOLIANS; MONGOLIAN LANGUAGE.

Further reading: Ou Li, Rong Ma, and James R. Simpson, "Changes in the Nomadic Pattern and Its Impact on the Inner Mongolian Steppe Grasslands Ecosystem," *Nomadic Peoples* 33 (1993): 63–72.

Shili-yin Gool *See* SHILIIN GOL.

Shimo Ming'an (1164–1216) **and Xiandebu** (Shih-mo Ming-an and Hsien-te-pu) (fl. 1216–1230) *Kitan defectors who served Chinggis Khan as strategists and officials in North China*
Shimo Ming'an, from a prominent Kitan family, lived in Fuzhou, Inner Mongolia. Under the JIN DYNASTY (1115–1234) he served as envoy to the northern nomads, becoming acquainted with CHINGGIS KHAN. In 1212, at the BATTLE OF HUAN'ERZUI, the Jin commander sent him as messenger to denounce the Mongol invaders. After the battle Shimo Ming'an announced his desire to serve the Mongols and helped subjugate the area of Xijing (modern Datong). Chinggis Khan wished to rest after these border victories, but Shimo Ming'an warned him that Jin resources, once mobilized, were inexhaustible and encouraged him to invade the North China plain, where military skills had long ago atrophied. In 1215 Shimo Ming'an won merit in the siege of the Jin capital, Zhongdu (modern Beijing), always striving to moderate Mongol treatment of the defeated. Chinggis Khan appointed him DARUGHACHI (overseer) and JABAR KHOJA administrator of the city. When Ming'an died in 1216, his eldest son, Shimo Xiandebu, succeeded him. Xiandebu's administration was marred by brigandage and rebellions. After Chinggis Khan's death in 1227, YELÜ CHUCAI

reformed the administration and denounced Shimo Xiandebu's administration as brutal and corrupt. Xiandebu appealed to the Mongol royal family, but the new emperor, ÖGEDEI KHAN, backed up Yelü Chucai. Xiandebu was dismissed in 1230.

See also ZHONGDU, SIEGES OF.

Shinekhen Buriats *See* BURIATS OF MONGOLIA AND INNER MONGOLIA.

Shirendew, Bazaryn (Shirendyb, Shirendev) (1912–2001) *High-ranking official in culture and education and long-term president of the Academy of Sciences*
Shirendew was born on May 14, 1912, the sixth of 13 children, in Dalai Choinkhor Wang banner (modern Shine Ider Sum, Khöwsgöl). In 1923 Shirendew was made a lama but ran away twice until his father hired him out as a herder. In 1928 Shirendew became a student of Choisdoo, the local party representative, who first started him on the path of becoming a cadre. After political schools and practicums in collectivization and struggle, Shirendew from 1932 attended a special Mongolian preparatory cause in Verkhneudinsk (modern ULAN-UDE) and then the Irkutsk Pedagogical Institute. While there he married a Russian woman, Zina. They had two sons and a daughter.

In 1941, on his return to Mongolia, he was made a "referent," or reference assistant, digesting news, information, and books for MARSHAL CHOIBALSANG. In 1945–46 he interpreted for Choibalsang at several meetings with Joseph Stalin. From 1944 to 1948 he served as secretary of the party Central Committee's propaganda department until he was blamed for continued popular dissatisfaction with government policies and dismissed. He maintained his position in education, however, serving as rector of the Mongolian State University (1944–54) and minister of education (1951–54).

After Marshal Choibalsang's death in 1954 Shirendew became a full Politburo member and first deputy prime minister. While chairing the special commission for reevaluating the Stalin-era purges, the maximum leader, YUMJAAGIIN TSEDENBAL, tried to arrest him as a spy. Warned by the party general secretary, DASHIIN DAMBA, Shirendew withdrew from government work and defended a doctorate in Far Eastern studies at the Soviet Academy of Sciences in 1957–60. In July 1960 he became head of Mongolia's Institute of Sciences and Higher Education, which was expanded into the ACADEMY OF SCIENCES in 1961. Shirendew's efforts to make it a genuine scientific academy pursuing original research in all fields conflicted with Tsedenbal's agenda of having the academy simply apply the results of Soviet research to Mongolia. With Tsedenbal's increasing authoritarianism, the party Politburo dismissed Shirendew from all positions in 1981, and shortly afterward his wife, Zina, died. In 1991, after democratization, the MONGOLIAN PEOPLE'S REVOLUTIONARY PARTY reversed its criticism, and Shirendew published his memoirs and a historical novel about the 1921 REVOLUTION before his death on March 8, 2001.

See also MONGOLIAN PEOPLE'S REPUBLIC; SOVIET UNION AND MONGOLIA.

Further reading: Bazaryn Shirendev, *Through the Ocean Waves,* trans. Temujin Onon (Bellingham: Western Washington University Press, 1997).

Shiwei (Shih-wei)   The Shiwei, although little known, have been considered the ancestors of the Mongols. The Shiwei first appear in Chinese records in the fifth century occupying the HULUN BUIR, Ergüne (Argun'), Nonni (Nen), middle Amur, and Zeya watersheds; they were divided into five to 20 tribes. They collected scanty harvests of wheat and millet and kept pigs, dogs, oxen, and a small number of horses, but no sheep. Sable skins were their chief articles of trade. Wintering in marshy lowlands and summering in mountains, they lived in huts of bent branches covered by skins or pelts or in trees in the summer to escape mosquitos. Burial was by exposure on arboreal platforms. Their language is variously described as similar to Kitan and Qai (Chinese, Xi), that is, Mongolic, or as similar to Mohe (Malgal or Mukri), that is, Manchu-Tungusic.

The first Türk dynasty (552–630) installed *tudun*s, or governors, over the Shiwei and collected tribute. From 631 to at least 850, despite occasional conflicts, they presented sable skins to the Tang. One Shiwei tribe, living south of the Ergüne and Amur Rivers, was called (in Chinese) "Mengwu," that is, Mongghol. Some scholars believe they and other Shiwei moved west from 850 on to become ancestors of the steppe Mongols. Other Shiwei who stayed in the forest have been identified as ancestors of the EWENKIS. While the earlier Shiwei did not know ironworking, a later "Black-Cart" Shiwei tribe, probably living in east-central Inner Mongolia, were master ironworkers. The KITANS conquered these and other Shiwei from 885 to 905.

See also ALTAIC LANGUAGE FAMILY; MONGOLIC LANGUAGE FAMILY.

Siberia and the Mongol Empire   The demand for falcons and furs from the "Peoples of the Forest" brought Mongol conquerors north to the Arctic.

The peoples of the Mongolian steppe had long maintained intimate relations with the peoples of the Siberian taiga (forest). They called those in the forest "People of the Forest" (*Oi-yin Irged*), but this term covered a wide range of peoples, many of whom were little different from the steppe Mongol people. The BARGA (Barghu), east of Lake Baikal, were like the Mongols except for keeping reindeer. Others, such as the "Forest" Uriyangkhai, lived in wigwams of birchbark, detested

sheep, excelled in sledding, skiing, and reindeer herding, and tried to have as little as possible to do with the steppe Mongols (*see* ALTAI URIYANGKHAI; TUVANS). While the tribes around LAKE BAIKAL were Mongolic speaking, those to the west spoke Turkic, Samoyedic, or Kettic (Paleo-Siberian) languages.

In 1207 CHINGGIS KHAN (Genghis, 1206–27) sent his eldest son, JOCHI, to subjugate the forest tribes from the Barga east of the Baikal to the Bashkirs (Bashkort) near the Urals. He then organized the Siberians into three *tümen*s, or 10,000 households. Chief Qutuqa Beki of the OIRATS, dwelling in the Shishigt valley, surrendered, and Chinggis made him a myriarch (commander of a *tümen*) and gave his daughter Checheyiken to Qutuqa's son. The Yenisey Kyrgyz of Khakassia (ancestors of the modern Khakas and of uncertain relation to the Kyrgyz of modern Kyrgyzstan) also surrendered and were numbered as a *tümen*. Chinggis gave the Telengit and Tölös along the Irtysh River (ancestors of the modern Altay nationality) to an old companion, Qorchi, of the Baarin clan. Together with Qorchi's original three Ba'arin 1,000s, this made Qorchi commander of a third Siberian *tümen*. Other peoples, such as the BARGA, Tumad, BURIATS, and Khori in the east, the Keshtimi in the center, and the Bashkirs to the west, were organized in separate 1,000s.

For tribute, gerfalcons and furs were the chief things the Mongols valued in Siberia, although Kyrgyz horses were also famous. Since gerfalcons nested only near the Arctic Ocean, the Mongols and their tributaries made regular expeditions all the way to the northern shores of Siberia. The Mongol khans did not regard this tribute as enough, however, and regularly demanded labor service and harem girls from the forest peoples. A Tumad rebellion broke out in 1217, when Chinggis Khan allowed Qorchi to seize 30 Tumad maidens. Dense forest and narrow mountain paths covered their territory along the Angara, and the Tumads captured Qutuqa Beki and killed Boroghul, one of Chinggis Khan's "four steeds," before Dörbei the Fierce of the Dörbed clan smashed them and freed Qutuqa Beki.

Despite the cold, Chinggis Khan settled a successful colony of Chinese craftsmen and farmers at Kem-Kemchik in the Tuvan basin. As the empire broke up in 1260, the Yenisey Kyrgyz and the colony at Kem-Kemchik became objects of contention between QUBILAI KHAN (1260–94) of the Mongol YUAN DYNASTY and his enemies. In 1262 ARIQ-BÖKE, cut off by Qubilai's blockade, tried to use the colony at Kem-Kemchik as his base. After Ariq-Böke's defeat Qubilai Khan sent a Chinese official, Liu Haoli, with a new batch of colonists to serve as judge of the Kyrgyz and Tuvan basin areas in 1270. From 1275 on, however, QAIDU KHAN, another rival, occupied central Siberia. In 1293 Qubilai's Qipchaq general TUTUGH reoccupied the Kyrgyz lands, severing one of Qaidu's important supply bases. From then on the Yuan controlled central Siberia.

Western Siberia came under the eastern, or BLUE HORDE, of the GOLDEN HORDE. Ruled by the descendants of Jochi's eldest son, Hordu, this area was isolated and conservative. In the swamps of western Siberia, dogsled JAM (post) stations were set up to facilitate collection of tribute in sable, ermine, black fox, and other furs. With the breakup of the by-then Islamic and Turkish-speaking Golden Horde late in the 14th century, a Siberian khanate was formed with its center at Tyumen' (from Mongol *tümen*, 10,000). The non-Chinggisid Taybughid dynasty (probably KEREYID in origin) vied for rule with the descendants of Shiban, Jochi's fifth son, until Russian Cossacks drove out the last Shibanid khan, Kuchum, in 1582. Qorchi's Baarin *tümen*, moving south to the Tianshan Mountains and assimilating nomads from the Blue Horde, formed the nucleus of the modern Kyrgyz of Kyrgzstan. Even today, the Kyrgyz's dominant clan, the Taghai, is named after Qorchi's son.

Further reading: Allen Frank, *The Siberian Chronicles and the Taybughid Biys of Sibi'r* (Bloomington, Indiana University, 1994).

Sinkiang   *See* XINJIANG MONGOLS.

Sino-Mongolian War

The Sino-Mongolian War of 1913 ended inconclusively, with the Mongolian army forced to withdraw from Inner Mongolia by Russian pressure. After the 1911 RESTORATION of Mongolian independence, eventually 35 of the 49 banners (appanages) of Inner Mongolia expressed some form of support. On August 20, 1912, after receiving arms from the Mongolian government, the eastern Inner Mongolian Prince Utai (c. 1859–1920) of KHORCHIN Right-Flank Front Banner (Horqin Youyi Qianqi) attacked Chinese towns in Jirim territory but by September 12 had retreated in disorder to Outer Mongolian territory. Togtakhu Taiji's simultaneous attack on Chinese towns was also defeated.

After receiving a promise of immediate supply of Russian arms and trainers in January 1913, the Mongolian government on January 23 ordered the neighboring Inner Mongolian SHILIIN GOL and ULAANCHAB leagues to mobilize 2,000 troops, and in February the commanders set out from Khüriye (ULAANBAATAR). In summer 1913 the troops advanced toward Linxi, Dolonnuur (Duolun), Zhangjiakou (Kalgan), Guisui (HÖHHOT), and the Urad banners. Virtually all the commanders were Inner Mongolian: the Monggoljin (modern Fuxin) bandit Babujab (d. 1916), GRAND DUKE DAMDINSÜRÜNG of New Barga (Xin Barag), and others. The soldiery was a core of KHALKHA and Inner Mongolian militiamen supplemented by many mixed Chinese and Mongolian bandits who fought for the Russian rifles and pay supplied by the Mongolian government. The five columns totaled about 7,000–8,000 men with rifles and five cannons.

At their furthest advance the Mongolian soldiers occupied Linxi, Kheshigten (Hexigten) Banner, Jingpeng, the outskirts of Dolonnuur (modern Duolun), Pangjiang, Erfenzi, Batu-Khaalga (Bailingmiao), Dashetai, and Ulaan Oboo. The lack of artillery was their great weakness. The armies' base camps in Shiliin Gol and Ulaanchab were open steppe areas with few resources, and lack of ammunition and provisions from Mongolia caused hardship to the soldiers and frequent pillaging of the locals. One Mongolian commander, Duke Nasun'arbijikhu of Khorchin Left-Flank Rear (Horqin Zuoyi Houqi), deserted to the Chinese in the middle of the campaign.

Despite the mission of the Sain Noyan Khan Namnangsürüng (1878–1919) to St. Petersburg in October, Russia refused to support Mongolia's war against China and on October 28 sent a telegram ordering the campaign to stop. This threat and the cold and shortage of supplies finally forced the Khalkha and BARGA militiamen and commanders to withdraw. This withdrawal was formalized in 1915 by the KYAKHTA TRILATERAL TREATY. The locally recruited soldiers were disbanded and sent home with their rifles to trouble western Inner Mongolia as *duli* (independence) bandits for years to come. Babujab refused to recognize the treaty, and his band disturbed the Sino-Mongolian frontier until 1917. The Sino-Mongolian War left Mongolia with a burdensome debt to Russia, payments of which reached 332,000 gold rubles in 1916, more than a fifth of the total central government expenditures.

See also THEOCRATIC PERIOD.

Further reading: Tatsuo Nakami, "Babujab and His Uprising: Re-examining the Inner Mongol Struggle for Independence," *Memoirs of the Research Department of the Toyo Bunko* 57 (1999): 137–153.

Sino-Soviet alliance

The Sino-Soviet alliance from 1949 to 1960 reduced Mongolia's border tensions and offered the prospect of Chinese economic assistance but did not challenge the country's fundamentally pro-Soviet orientation.

The Sino-Soviet alliance was formed after the Chinese Communist ruler Mao Zedong proclaimed the People's Republic of China on October 1, 1949. The alliance became strained when the Russian leader Nikita Khrushchev gave his famous de-Stalinization speech on February 24–25, 1956, criticizing Joseph Stalin. Relations grew more strained during the Chinese Great Leap Forward (1958–61), when Mao Zedong rejected the Soviet development strategy and became hostile after the Soviet Union abruptly recalled all its advisers in China in 1960.

While the younger members of Mongolia's government were optimistic about relations with the new China, Mongolia's ruler MARSHAL CHOIBALSANG (1895–1952) had no such confidence. Informed by Stalin, he knew that even before proclaiming his new government in 1949 Mao Zedong had vainly requested that the Soviet Union allow the reunification of Inner and Outer Mongolia as part of the People's Republic. Thus, despite mutual recognition on October 6, 1949, there was no warmth. Choibalsang felt insulted by the choice in July 1950 of an Inner Mongolian revolutionary, rather than a real diplomat, as China's first ambassador.

In 1952, after Choibalsang's death, Sino-Soviet-Mongolian relations warmed considerably, and the new Mongolian premier YUMJAAGIIN TSEDENBAL visited Beijing in October. On September 15, 1952, the Soviet Union, Mongolia, and China signed an agreement to build the TRANS-MONGOLIAN RAILWAY, which entered operation on January 1, 1956. A Sino-Mongolian economic assistance agreement of early 1955 allowed Chinese guest workers to enter Mongolia and, if they so chose, to reside permanently and apply for Mongolian citizenship. Chinese workers built roads, bridges (including ULAANBAATAR's Peace Bridge over the Dund Gol River), a hydroelectric power plant at Kharkhorin (ancient QARA-QORUM), and apartment blocks in Ulaanbaatar. The number of workers reached 13,150 in May 1961, although most left in 1962–63. Still, Chinese monetary assistance was smaller than that of the Soviet Union, while China's share of Mongolian trade did not begin to match that of the Soviet Union. Secure between two friendly powers, Mongolia let defense spending fall to less than 6 percent of its budget in 1958, compared with more than 36 percent a decade earlier.

Connections with Inner Mongolia also became important. The Chinese Communists' Inner Mongolian leader ULANFU led large delegations to Mongolia in 1954 and 1958. In spring 1957 Mongolia opened a consulate in the Inner Mongolian capital of HÖHHOT, and many families were reunited. The prestige of Mongolian culture remained high in Inner Mongolia, and from 1955 to 1958 Inner Mongolia planned to introduce CYRILLIC-SCRIPT MONGOLIAN in place of the UIGHUR-MONGOLIAN SCRIPT.

Despite the announced friendship and high-level delegations, Sino-Mongolian ties were not close. Mongolia's independence was, despite China's explicit recognition, a standing contradiction to the doctrine, elsewhere so tenaciously asserted, of the indivisibility of China, by which was meant the territory of the QING DYNASTY. In 1954, with Khrushchev's first visit, and in 1956, after the de-Stalinization speech, Mao repeated his request to reunify the Mongolias under China. Symptomatically, cooperation in a project to write a new Mongolian history broke down in 1958. Wherever contact between Inner Mongolian or Mongolian populations took place, the governments competed to make their own Mongols look better off.

With the deterioration in Sino-Soviet relations, China tried to woo Mongolia in 1960 with a large loan, a visit from Premier Zhou Enlai, and a promise of assistance in building a steel plant. China never really had a chance of replacing Soviet patronage, and Mongolia in the 1960s joined Soviet denunciations of Maoism.

See also CHINA AND MONGOLIA; SOVIET UNION AND MONGOLIA.

Sino-Soviet split   The rupture of the previous SINO-SOVIET ALLIANCE in 1960 and the increasingly hostile relations between Mongolia's two giant neighbors pushed Mongolia into a materially profitable dependence on the Soviet Union.

In 1960 Sino-Mongolian relations ostensibly flourished, with Chinese premier Zhou Enlai's visit to Ulaanbaatar on May 27–June 1 and the signing of a Treaty of Friendship and Mutual Assistance. Zhou Enlai wooed Mongolia with the promise of a loan of 200 million rubles, a steel plant, and a new batch of Chinese guest workers. Despite the speculation of some outside "Mongolia watchers," there was never any "pro-Chinese" lobby in the Mongolian government. Mongolian premier YUMJAAGIIN TSEDENBAL took the loan but refused the steel mill and the additional Chinese workers. (The Chinese loans were immediately matched by much more generous Soviet ones). Meanwhile, as Sino-Soviet ties deteriorated, Mongolia quietly liquidated outstanding issues. In May 1962 existing Chinese guest workers began departing, leaving only 12 of the 32 planned projects completed. Aiming to isolate India for its intransigence, China conceded virtually every controversial issue to Mongolia in the border treaty signed on December 26, 1962, during Tsedenbal's last visit to Beijing. Even so, Tsedenbal pointedly made a toast to the Soviet Union at the state dinner. Border demarcation was completed in June 1964.

In June 1964 Mongolia's leadership publicized its criticism of China's policy, while in the next month the supreme Chinese leader, Mao Zedong, complained to Japanese journalists of how the Soviet Union's domination of Mongolia had stolen it from China. In reaction to this threat, the Mongolian government renewed its lapsed 1946 Friendship Treaty with the Soviet Union in 1966 and added a secret defense agreement that allowed for the creation of Soviet military bases in Mongolia. In the first two years of China's Cultural Revolution (1966–76), expatriate Chinese Red Guards staged demonstrations in ULAANBAATAR and several times attacked the Mongolian embassy and diplomats in Beijing. Chinese border incidents with both the Soviet Union and Mongolia culminated in armed Sino-Soviet clashes in 1969. In 1979 the Soviet leadership pushed Tsedenbal to accept more Soviet troops to put pressure on China, which was then attacking VIETNAM. By 1980 the Soviet troops in Mongolia reached 65,000, and the Mongolian military was expanded to 36,500, with a well-equipped air force.

Beginning in September 1973 Tsedenbal publicized Mao's repeated efforts to annex Mongolia and attacked the Maoists' supposed glorification of CHINGGIS KHAN. Mongolian scholars were mobilized to analyze the Maoist heresy and document its oppression of INNER MONGOLIANS and Tibetans. In 1981–83 Tsedenbal deported or resettled in the countryside Mongolia's remaining Chinese citizens, even ethnic Mongol refugees from the Cultural Revolution. In February 1980 the Politburo exiled several historians simply for using Chinese sources in their professional work. Bizarre but widely accepted rumors that all the Inner Mongolians had been forced to marry Chinese reinforced the Mongolians' sense of themselves as the only pure-blood true Mongols left.

Economically, Mongolia benefited substantially from the Sino-Soviet split. Tsedenbal skillfully used Mongolia's position as a frontline state to extract development assistance from the Soviet leader Leonid Brezhnev in the form of soft loans, training, and indefinite maintenance of a massive trade deficit. Mongolia's importance to the Soviet Union was underlined by Soviet ruler Leonid Brezhnev's state visits in 1966 and 1974.

With the close of the Cultural Revolution in 1976 and its repudiation by the Chinese ruler Deng Xiaoping in 1979, the Sino-Soviet conflict became purely geopolitical. The partial withdrawal of Soviet troops in 1987 led to normalization of relations among China, Mongolia, and the Soviet Union in 1989 and full troop withdrawal by 1991.

See also CHINA AND MONGOLIA; CHINGGIS KHAN CONTROVERSY; SOVIET UNION AND MONGOLIA.

Six Tümens   The Six Tümens appeared as an organizational framework for the Mongols near the end of the 15th century. The term *tümen* originally came from the Mongolian DECIMAL ORGANIZATION and meant "10,000" households. This number was merely nominal from the beginning and by the 15th century had lost any numerical meaning. During the career of BATU-MÖNGKE DAYAN KHAN (1480?–1517?) the expression *Six Tümens* referred to the whole Mongol people, as opposed to the Four Tümens of the OIRATS. According to Mongolian legend, emperor Toghan-Temür (1333–70) managed to take only 10 of the Mongols' 44 *tümens* back with him to Mongolia. When the four Oirat *tümens* separated in the first half of the 15th century, only six Mongol *tümens* were left.

The Six Tümens were divided into two wings, right and left, each with three *tümens*. The ruler of the Three Western Tümens, or *jinong* (viceroy), administered the EIGHT WHITE YURTS, or shrine of CHINGGIS KHAN and hence had to be a Chinggisid. The Three Eastern (or Left) Tümens, Dayan Khan's original power base, were the CHAKHAR, the KHALKHA, and (depending on the source) either the Uriyangkhan or the KHORCHIN. (After their 1538 rebellion the Uriyangkhan were removed from the rank of *tümen*.) The Three Western (or Right) Tümens were the ORDOS, the TÜMED (or Monggoljin), and the Yüngshiyebü, which formed a single *tümen*, with the Asud (OSSETES) and KHARACHIN. Each *tümen* was divided into OTOGS (camp districts), and the *tümens* and *otogs* fought together as units in battle. The number of *otogs* in the *tümens* followed a conventional schema: Chakhar and Ordos, eight; Tümed and Khalkha, 12; Yüngshiyebü and Khorchin, seven. Thus, there were, in theory, 54 *otogs* in the whole Mongol people. The *otogs* were defined by clans, but by no means exactly. One clan in a *tümen* might constitute several *otogs*, while many other *otogs* consisted of two or three clans. Moreover, *otogs* of the same clan name were sometimes in different *tümens*.

After Dayan Khan reunited the Six Tümens in 1510, he divided them among his sons. Again, the division was not exact: His third son, Barsu-Bolod, received all three western *tümens*; the Khalkha were divided among two sons; the Khorchin and Uriyangkhan remained under their previous rulers, and so on. The next generation divided the *otogs* among their children, and so on. In this way the Six Tümens, originally non-Chinggisid clan confederations, became (with the exception of the Uriyangkhan and the Khorchin) family circles of Chinggisid noblemen. Migrations and the Manchu conquest reorganized the *tümens* in the 17th century, but several of them survived more or less intact to become, under new names, the LEAGUES of later Inner Mongolia.

See also APPANAGE SYSTEM.

Further reading: Hidehiro Okada, "The Fall of the Uriyangqan Mongols," *Mongolian Studies* 10 (1986–87): 49–57.

social classes in the Mongol Empire   The unification of the Mongolian plateau by CHINGGIS KHAN (Genghis, 1206–27) centered the social hierarchy around him and his family. The *SECRET HISTORY OF THE MONGOLS* nicely defines the ruling class of the empire by listing those who participated in the election assembly (QURILTAI) of Chinggis's successor: his and his brothers' 1) sons, 2) daughters, 3) their sons-in-law, and 4) the captains of 10,000 and 1,000.

MONGOL CLASS STRATIFICATION

Before the unification of the MONGOL EMPIRE several branches of the dominant BORJIGID lineage, all descended from the legendary ancestress ALAN GHO'A, competed for leadership. The lineage of the sovereigns (*qad*, khans; *see* KHAN) was white, the honored color, while the commoners were *qarachus*, "black ones," and *bo'ol*, "slaves." With unification only Chinggis Khan and his brothers—the sons of YISÜGEI BA'ATUR—formed the new ruling lineage. Known as the *altan uruq*, "golden seed," or *uruq*, "seed," the *uruq* expanded enormously; the Persian historian 'ALA'UD-DIN ATA-MALIK JUVAINI estimated in 1257 that it already numbered 20,000 (presumably including wives, minor children, and household slaves).

Given the Mongolian rule of exogamy, members of the *uruq* always married commoners. Borjigid daughters (*ökid*) received dowries of subject peoples and sometimes appanages in their own right, and their husbands, as *kürgen*, "sons-in-law," of the ruling family, formed the third stratum in the ruling class. The Chinggisids generally reserved this reciprocal QUDA (marriage ally) relation to particular clans, particularly the QONGGIRAD, but it varied with each branch.

Chinggis Khan promised his favored "companions" (NÖKÖR) of non-Borjigid ancestry that their descendants would be honored "unto the seed of the seed," and they founded the great families of nonimperial blood. They served as commanders (NOYAN) of 10,000s and 1,000s and supervised the KESHIG, or imperial guard, and the palace-tent (ORDO), or household of the khan. Great *noyans* were hereditary, and the *keshig* was recruited from the sons and younger brothers of the decimal unit commanders. Captains of 100s and 10s, while technically *noyans*, were not counted part of the ruling class, and their offices were not hereditary. They and ordinary Mongols (*irgen*, subjects, *haran*, commoners, or *dürü-yin kü'ün*, simple people) were distributed all over Eurasia in the service of the empire.

Only the general outline of economic relations among these classes is clear. ÖGEDEI KHAN (1229–41) ordered for his table one milch mare, one milch cow, and one sheep for slaughter annually from every 100 animals. The other members of the imperial family and the *noyans* likewise received regular tribute of mares (and presumably other livestock) from their subjects. The mares so received were put out to herders, who delivered every third day's produce to their lords; BATU in the GOLDEN HORDE had a herd of 3,000 such mares. Despite the lack of direct evidence, the imperial family and the *noyans* doubtless required of their subjects the same labor services delivered by ordinary Mongols to their lords in the 19th century—herding, collecting dung for fuel, felt making, household chores, and so on (*see* SOCIAL CLASSES IN THE QING PERIOD). Each lord directed the nomadizations of his subjects and undoubtedly used the best pastures, but to see in this some implicit property in land would be inaccurate.

Although the rise of Chinggis Khan destroyed the old ruling class and replaced it with his own family and *nökörs*, once the new regime was in place social mobility was very limited. The khans did encourage commoners to volunteer for the *keshig*, and they, with other able houseboys (*ger-ün kö'üd*, or Turkish, *ev-oghlan*), had some chance of finding a patron and being promoted, usually to a scribal or civil administrative position.

Outside observers were struck by the extraordinary docility toward authority in Mongolian society. Contrary to common stereotypes of "turbulent nomads," European, Chinese, Armenian, and Islamic observers all found the 13th-century nobility unusually obedient to their khans and the commoners still more obedient to the nobility. *Uruq* could not be tried or harmed except by other members of the *uruq*, and non-*uruq* rarely dared to resist princes, even when they were fugitives or dissidents. The extraordinary multiplication of the imperial family and the eventual transformation of the great *noyan* families from a service nobility into a proud and self-reliant aristocracy lessened this cohesion in time. Still, the Armenian

knight Hetoum wrote in 1307, "To their lords [the Tartars] be more obedient than any other nation."

CLASS STRATIFICATION AND THE CONQUEST

Over and above this internal class stratification, the ruling class establishments also drew in the sedentary areas as subjects. In their conquests the Mongols regularly deported artisans and divided them up as "houseboys" (*ger-ün kö'üd*) of the noble families. The higher-ranking aristocracy also received cities or towns in conquered lands as appanages. The aristocracy's right to issue tablets (PAIZA) that gave their bearers the ability to use the JAM, or postroads, and demand requisitions gave them leverage over merchant partners, or ORTOQ, to whom they lent money and fine goods as capital for caravan trading and usury.

Thus, most needs of the ruling class were supplied from their own far-flung estates. Princes, princesses, and great *noyans* received grain, cotton, and silk from appanages in the southern territories as well as mares' milk from their Mongol subjects and furs from the northern forest peoples. Mongols not in the ruling class, however, traded grains and fabrics for live sheep and skins with the Turkestani, Uighur, and North Chinese peddlers who plied the steppe. In winter the poor wore dog-or goatskin coats and lined their trousers with cotton or coarse wool, while the wealthy wore forest furs or foxskins and lined their trousers with silk stuffing.

Conquest offered both advantages and disadvantages to the Mongol commoners. War booty included slaves whose labor permanently enriched their masters' families. In one county of South China in 1330, Mongol families had on average 15 slaves, while Chinese families had none. At the same time, preparing military equipment and losing manpower to campaigns could impoverish Mongol households. To address this problem, Ögedei Khan ordered that each decimal unit transfer one sheep per 100 to its own poor. Under QUBILAI KHAN (1260–94) the government began regularly sending relief and remitting the taxes of distressed Mongols. The Mongols practiced debt slavery, and by 1290 in all of the successor states Mongol commoners were selling their children into slavery. Seeing this as damaging to both the manpower and the prestige of the Mongol army, Qubilai Khan forbade the sale abroad of Mongols in 1291, and GHAZAN KHAN (1295–1304) in Iran budgeted funds to redeem Mongol slaves.

COLLABORATOR CLASSES IN THE EMPIRE

Everywhere the Mongols granted their favored collaborators among the conquered peoples *paizas* (tablets, or badges of authority) and *jarliqs* (patents or writs) granting tax exemption, the right to use the postroads (*jam*), and to bear arms, and in practice a virtually unlimited right to seize requisitions from those who did not possess such tablets and patents. Mongols granted these rights to clergy of the four favored religions (Buddhism, Christianity, Taoism, and Islam) as well as to physicians, astrologers, and (in China) Confucian scholars. The other major components of the collaborator class were the *ortoq* (partner) merchants, who received capital from the Mongol aristocracy for their trading and moneylending operations. Finally, in choosing administrators for pacified lands, the Mongols generally drew on the existing landholding nobility or scholar-official classes that in differing forms dominated Eurasia.

The Mongols altered the existing ruling classes by their deliberate policy of employing ethnic outsiders in a hierarchy of reliability. The Mongols favored certain groups who had surrendered early, particularly the UIGHURS, and preferred to employ potentially unreliable groups outside their own homelands. *Ortoq* merchants and non-Mongol overseers (DARUGHACHI) were usually either immigrants or local ethnic outgroups. Thus, in China they were Uighurs, Turkestani or Iranian Muslims, and Christians, while in Iran they were Uighurs, Assyrian Christians, Jews, or Turkestani Muslims. Foreigners from outside the empire entirely, such as the Polo family, were everywhere welcomed. Combined with the Mongol preference for Uighur scribes and for Buddhist clerics from KASHMIR or Tibet, the Mongols thus nurtured a distinctive multiethnic and parvenu ruling milieu that often aroused the deep disgust of the traditional landed upper class. In Iran Islamization dealt a strong but not fatal blow to this new milieu, but in China it lasted until the fall of the dynasty.

In China Qubilai Khan codified this hierarchy of reliability by dividing the population into four classes: 1) Mongol; 2) SEMUREN (literally "various sorts"), a catchall term for western immigrants into China, especially Uighurs and Turkestani Muslims; 3) Han, including North Chinese, KITANS, Jurchens, and Koreans; and 4) southerners (*nanren*), including all subjects of the former Song Empire. In Iran Uighurs, Assyrian Christians, Jews, and Turkestani Muslims played the role of *semuren*, although the traditional Persian-speaking Sunni Muslim ruling class retained more of their leading role than did the Confucian gentry in China.

The Mongols everywhere abolished inheritance taxes, and the use of government tax funds for commercial capital in the *ortoq* system compounded the concentration of wealth. While frequently careless of the safety of individual members of the landed classes, the Mongols, particularly after adjusting to being rulers in their lands, relied relatively heavily on commercial taxes and little on the more evenly applied land taxes. What fragmentary evidence exists, particularly in the Middle East, suggests that these policies and the conquest itself substantially increased the concentration of wealth.

See also ANIMAL HUSBANDRY AND NOMADISM; APPANAGE SYSTEM; ARTISANS IN THE MONGOL EMPIRE; FALCONRY; HISTORY; RELIGIOUS POLICY IN THE MONGOL EMPIRE.

social classes in the Qing period   The development of Mongolian classes under the Qing dynasty (1636–1912) was conditioned by the power of the Chingissid aristocracy, the military system of the Qing rulers, and the Buddhist monastic system.

CONCEPTS OF HIERARCHY

In Mongolian thought under the QING DYNASTY as expressed in sources from the 17TH-CENTURY CHRONICLES to praises and blessings for sprinkling mares' milk and WEDDINGS, CHINGGIS KHAN was the founder and culture hero of Mongolia. His descendants, the TAIJI class, were the only full members of the Mongolian community. The *taiji*s ruled not in view of any special function but simply because of their descent. Government being the rule of one lineage over another confirmed by conquest, the *taiji*s were exempt from rule, that is, from taxation, corvée labor, and corporal punishment. This relation of *taiji* and subject was symbolized by the colors white (noble) and black (common).

The heaven-mandated state, or *törö*, was embodied in the seal that authenticated state documents. The greatest seal was that of the Qing emperor in Beijing. As an additional sign of their legitimacy the Qing emperors also held that of the Mongol YUAN DYNASTY, which was surrendered to them in 1635. Locally, the rule of Mongolia's almost 200 banner rulers was embodied in the seal worshiped at the "opening the seal" ceremony around the 20th day of the WHITE MONTH (lunar new year).

In Buddhist social thought the essential division was that between monk and householder. The monk was supported by the alms of the householder, and the giving of alms earned merit for the householder. This relation of monk and householder was symbolized by the colors yellow (monastic) and black (lay).

Finally, the political concepts of hierarchy were buttressed by the familial and gender hierarchies of parents over children, elders over younger, and men over women. All these hierarchies were expressed both in daily ritual and in the popular literature, such as the *Treasury of Aphoristic Jewels* and Buddhist didactic poetry. Authorities delivered undeserved kindness (*achi*, *kheshig*) to those below them and deserved sincere striving in return.

LEGAL STATUS DISTINCTIONS

Each of the hierarchical relations noted above was embodied legally in various status categories among the Mongols. Although few comprehensive statistics from the Qing period have been gathered, data from the early 20th century can be used with caution.

The banner officials, the numerically smallest of these dominant strata, held privilege by virtue of representing the power of the emperor. They formed 0.8–1.6 percent of the laity. While the top banner officials, the ZASAG and his one or two administrators, were always *taiji*s, the categories otherwise had no necessary overlap: Many banner officials were commoners, and many *taiji*s, even of ducal or princely rank, were *sula* (not in government service).

The *taiji*, as noted above, represented Chinggis Khan. Figures from eastern KHALKHA from 1841 and 1918 show the *taiji* occupied 9.0–10.5 percent of the lay male population. Elsewhere, in western Khalkha's Zasagtu Khan province and in a KHORCHIN banner of eastern Inner Mongolia, comparable figures were 16.4 percent and 18.2 percent.

In 1918 Khalkha's monks were counted at 44.6 percent of the male population. In fact, only about 35,000 lamas, or 15 percent of males, actually lived in the monasteries. The other two-thirds of those registered as lamas lived as householders, only performing services during the greater *khurals* (assemblies). Lamas numbered 14.2 percent of the banner membership in a typical Khorchin banner.

In Khalkha the commoners were divided into three categories: the *sumu arad*, or state commoners (*see* SUM), also called the *albatu* (taxpayers), serving the banner office and Qing state; the *khamjilga* (serfs), serving the *taijis*; and the SHABI (lay disciples), serving the monks (*see* GREAT SHABI). These bodies numbered 41–49 percent, 30–33 percent, and 5–7 percent of the lay population, respectively. Of course, all laymen, not just the *shabi*, gave alms to the monasteries, and in Inner Mongolia the category of *shabi* was very small. There, too, the *khamjilga* and state commoners were not divided; statistics in a Khorchin banner simply show commoners, soldiers, and postroad staff together totaling 65 percent of the laity.

Numerous legal disputes developed over the boundaries of these categories. Householding lamas were frequently impressed into state duties, although theoretically they were exempt. Since the remaining commoners would have to shoulder identical duties with a smaller population, state commoners resisted the *taijis*' gift of commoners as *shabi* or their illegal appropriation of commoners as *khamjilga*. They also resisted the banner rulers' frequent attempts to treat all the banner people as their personal *khamjilga*, forcing them to pay the rulers' debts, do personal service in their palaces, and so on.

A number of banner residents did not enter into the status system. Bastard sons, who numbered 7 percent of Khalkha's male population in 1918, were not assigned to any status. Chinese slaves (Mongolian, *bool*, Manchu, *booi*), particularly common in eastern Inner Mongolia (10.3 percent of the laity in one Khorchin banner), were either purchased or taken as prisoners of war from campaigns against rebels under the Qing. Frequent intermarriage with the Manchu house also made dowry servants (INJE) arriving in the train of Manchu princesses from Beijing relatively numerous in eastern Inner Mongolia. Reserved for only the *zasags*, these servants, numbering 4.4 percent of the laity, were a rough parallel to Khalkha's *khamjilga*.

PROPERTY AND LABOR

Herd statistics from Khalkha's Setsen Khan *aimag* from 1835 and 1841 demonstrate the tremendous wealth of the *zasags* and the INCARNATE LAMAS, whose private herds averaged 1,500–2,500 sheep, 500–800 horses, and 300 cattle. In Khalkha's Setsen Khan province in 1835, the 27 *zasags* and high lamas, together with the monastic treasuries, or *jisa* (modern *jas*), combined held 19 percent, 16 percent, and 12 percent of the *aimag*'s SHEEP, HORSES, and CATTLE. In Khalkha in 1918 the titled nobility and high lamas held 23 percent, 18 percent, and 23 percent, respectively. Relatively, the state commoners were the poorest of all, with an average 20–21 sheep per household, while the *khamjilgas* had 26 sheep per household and the *taijis* 49–57 per household. The banner officials and *shabi* in 1841 had almost double the average herd of the *taijis*.

Despite these differences among status groups, inequality in herds was not wholly or even primarily a matter of legal status. Figures combining all the wealthy households, including commoners, show that in Alashan (Alxa) in 1947 the wealthiest 25 percent held 60.4 percent of all livestock, while the poorest 25 percent held only 3.6 percent. Less complete figures suggest equal or greater inequality elsewhere. These percentages did not change significantly in Inner Mongolia after China's Communist government abolished "feudal" status relations.

Labor for working large herds was secured in three ways: 1) a patriarchal form in which a poorer family camped with the richer (and/or higher status) one, giving labor to the rich family in return for access to its resources; 2) an absentee herding form in which the owner or institution placed herds out with a herder in return for a specified return; and 3) contract labor from transient men from outside the community.

The first was the sort of relation supposed to exist between *taijis* and *khamjilga*. *Khamjilgas* traditionally camped near their *taijis* and performed pastoral and domestic tasks for them. By 1900 or so both in Inner Mongolia and Khalkha, however, poor or positionless *taijis* could rarely require these services, and even influential *taijis* usually offered some kind of informal compensation to their *khamjilgas*. Relations between wealthy commoners and poor families who camped with them (called *zarutsa-yin ail*, hired households, in Khalkha, *saalin-u ail*, milking households, in CHAKHAR, and so on) resembled these *taiji-khamjilga* ties, except that they involved fewer outward signs of respect, few, if any, purely domestic tasks, and no element of compulsion. Either way, the patron and client lived in intimate contact with each other, and their exact reciprocal obligations were unspecified.

The banner rulers' and temples' vast herds were invariably divided up and leased to herders. Terms varied widely. For example, in Alashan (southwest Inner Mongolia) shepherds kept the milk and wool, while the owners received the young. More commercialized arrangements near Khüriye (modern ULAANBAATAR) required of the herders 15 *jing* (9 kilograms, or 20 pounds) of butter per cow and one fathom of felt per 15 sheep, commutable into TEA units. Even with a herd owner's private *shabi* or *khamjilga,* incentives for good management were always provided. Herders found these contracts very desirable. Buddhist institutions viewed leasing their herds as a merit-building activity to help the poor, and *zasags* used it as a way to reward well-regarded subjects. Even so, lawsuits, often over blame for large losses, were frequent.

Finally, men from outside the community could be hired to perform designated short-term tasks. In relatively uncommercialized northwest Khalkha these tasks were limited to leading caravans of CAMELS, driving animals to monasteries, and farming monastery-owned fields. Near Khüriye and in Inner Mongolia, however, Chinese or Mongol laborers would be hired for the full range of pastoral activities, particularly during the busy seasons, or else to perform the *alba,* or state-duties, as substitutes for wealthy commoners. They were paid in cash, animals, or a designated share of the product (especially shorn wool), but rarely if ever became intimate with their employers.

See also ANIMAL HUSBANDRY AND NOMADISM; CHINESE COLONIZATION; CHINESE TRADE AND MONEYLENDING; HISTORY; MONEY, MODERN; SOCIAL CLASSES IN THE MONGOL EMPIRE.

Further reading: C. R. Bawden, "Remarks on Land Use Control in Later Ch'ing Dynasty Outer Mongolia," in *Proceedings of International Conference on China Border Area Studies,* ed. Lin En-shean (Taipei: Mongolian and Tibetan Affairs Commission, 1984), 547–603; Š. Rasidondug and Veronika Viet, trans., *Petitions of Grievances Submitted by the People (18th–beginning of the 20th century)* (Wiesbaden: Otto Harrassowitz, 1975).

Solon *See* DAUR LANGUAGE AND PEOPLE; EWENKIS.

somon *See* SUM.

Song dynasty (Sung) The conquest of South China's Song dynasty under QUBILAI KHAN (1260–94) was the Mongol Empire's last great military achievement.

The founders of the Song dynasty (960–1279) reacted against the powerful satraps that broke up the great Tang dynasty (618–907) by keeping military and civil powers rigidly separate and concentrating the armies in the capital. The neo-Confucian revival and the examination system exalted the civil scholarly ideal over martial virtues. Not surprisingly, the Song dynasty, after uniting the Chinese heartland, proved unable to defeat rival non-Chinese dynasties. First the KITANS' Liao (907–1125) and then the Tanguts' Western XIA DYNASTY (1038–1237) forced the Northern Song (960–1127) to recognize their independence and pay tribute. The greatest humiliation came in 1127, when the Jurchens' JIN DYNASTY (1115–1234), having overthrown the Liao, sacked the Song capital of Kaifeng and occupied North China, forcing Song loyalists to enthrone a new emperor in Lin'an (modern Hangzhou). Despite prosperity, indicated by a population that reached perhaps 60 million, an increasingly embittered culture of revanchism gripped the Southern Song (1127–1279).

THE SONG AND THE MONGOLS

In 1211, when CHINGGIS KHAN invaded North China, the Song was exhausted from a humiliating defeat in the Kaixi War (1205–08) it had deliberately provoked against the Jin. In 1217 the Jin court, having taken refuge south of the Huang (Yellow) River, began encroaching on Song territory. The Song thereupon began its own intervention in the savage proxy war the Jin and the Mongols were waging in the anarchic province of Shandong. The Mongols decisively defeated this fruitless eight-year effort by the Song to recover the north in 1225.

On his death in 1227 Chinggis Khan bequeathed a plan to attack the inaccessible Jin capital by passing through Song territory, but arranging this plan with the Song proved difficult. At least one Mongol ambassador was killed in uncertain circumstances. Before receiving any reply, Mongol troops marched through Song territory to enter the Jin's redoubt in Henan from the south. In December 1233 Song forces finally advanced into Henan with men and supplies to assist the Mongols in the siege of the last Jin emperor.

This belated cooperation did not advance peace between the Mongols and the Song. In 1234 ÖGEDEI KHAN (1229–41) declared war on the Song again, claiming that the murder of a Mongol ambassador and continuing border incidents showed hostile intent. In a series of winter razzias from 1235 to 1245, mixed Mongol-Chinese armies reached Chengdu, Xiangyang (modern Xiangfan), and the middle Chang (Yangtze) River, yet heavy losses due to climate and the sheer numbers of the Song troops always forced withdrawals. The only permanent gain was Chengdu. In the Huai River area the watery terrain favored the Song, and the MONGOL EMPIRE's commanders, mostly Chinese, remained on the defensive.

In 1256 MÖNGKE KHAN (1251–59) proposed the final conquest of the Song by means of simultaneous attacks in Sichuan, Xiangyang, and Ezhou (modern Wuhan). Despite the massive preparations, coordination was weak. Möngke entered Sichuan in autumn 1258 with two-thirds of the Mongol strength, but progress against the well-prepared defenses was very slow. Prince Ta'achar and Möngke's brother Qubilai, with one-third, likewise proved unable to take their objectives before the khan's death of disease near the defiant city of Chongqing forced a general withdrawal.

The Song dynasty's effective defense stemmed from able border commanders such as Lü Wende (d. 1270) and Zhang Shijie (d. 1279), who operated autonomously from the stifling central control of the Song court. Together they anchored the Song's defense on three major

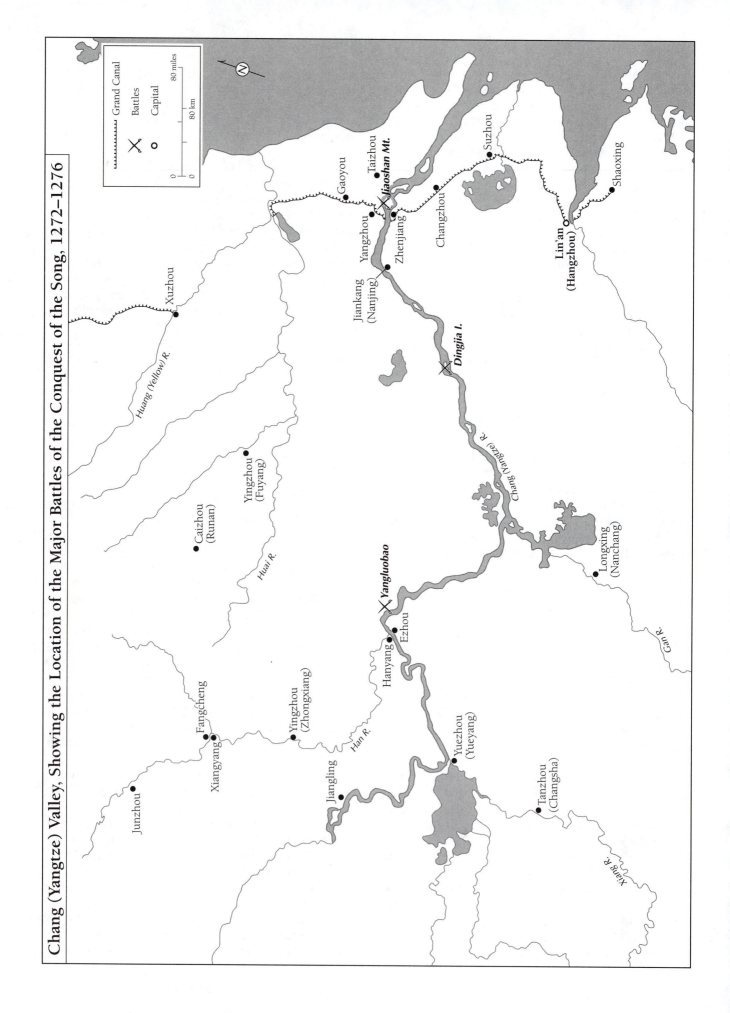

Chang (Yangtze) Valley, Showing the Location of the Major Battles of the Conquest of the Song, 1272–1276

Grand Canal
Battles
Capital

80 miles
80 km

N

Xuzhou

Huang (Yellow R.)

Caizhou (Runan)

Yingzhou (Fuyang)

Huai R.

Junzhou

Fangcheng

Xiangyang

Yingzhou (Zhongxiang)

Han R.

Jiangling

Yuezhou (Yueyang)

Tanzhou (Changsha)

Xiang R.

Hanyang

Ezhou

Yangluobao

Chang (Yangtze) R.

Longxing (Nanchang)

Gan R.

Dingjia I.

Jiankang (Nanjing)

Zhenjiang

Yangzhou

Jiaoshan Mt.

Taizhou

Gaoyou

Changzhou

Suzhou

Shaoxing

Lin'an (Hangzhou)

buttresses: the Chongqing and Hezhou (modern Hechuan) fortresses in Sichuan, the Xiangyangfu-Fancheng double city on the Han River, and Yangzhou in the lower Chang (Yangtze). The width of the Chang (Yangtze) and the vast Song navies linked these fortresses into a formidable defense system. Nevertheless, central strategy remained weak. In 1259 the Song emperor Lizong (r. 1224–64) appointed Jia Sidao (1213–75), the brother of his favorite concubine, grand councillor. While revanchist accusations of appeasement lacked substance, strident attacks on Jia Sidao's missing Confucian credentials and his notorious dissipation paralyzed the Song defense. The death of Lizong in 1264 delivered the throne to the crippled emperor Duzong (r. 1264–74), who was content to maintain Jia Sidao in office.

At first Qubilai Khan (1260–94) took a defensive stance in the South even after repeated frontier incidents and Jia Sidao's detention of Qubilai's ambassador Hao Jing. Li Tan, one of Qubilai's Chinese generals in Shandong, defected to the Song in 1262, but his rebellion was soon crushed. In 1268, however, AJU and Liu Zheng (1213–75), a Song defector who initiated Mongol navy construction, began the siege of the Xiangyang-Fancheng fortress. Lü Wende, commanding the defense of the Middle Chang (Yangtze), had died in 1270, and Lü's officers did not work well with Jia Sidao's replacement, Li Tingzhi (d. 1276). After the Mongols broke into Fancheng, Xiangyang surrendered in 1273, breaking the first link in the Song defense.

Aju reported to the khan a definite weakening in Song defenses, and after a long debate in March 1274 Qubilai launched a full-scale offensive with 100,000 men, appointing BAYAN CHINGSANG commander. In the same year Emperor Duzong died, throwing the Song into a regency under Empress Dowager Xie Qiao (1210–83). The Song posture thus remained passive. Once the Mongol YUAN DYNASTY troops and navy reached the Chang (Yangtze), Aju and Bayan Chingsang moved east, while the Uighur general ARIQ-QAYA moved west. The Yuan navy, built by Korean and Jurchen shipwrights, defeated the Song flotillas at Yangluobao (January 12, 1275) and Dingjia Isle (March 19) despite Jia Sidao's personal arrival at Dingjia Isle with 100,000 men. The surrender of key cities crowned this debacle. Empress Xie exiled Jia Sidao, and he was soon murdered. Under the loyalist Zhang Shijie's command, a 10,000-ship Song flotilla was annihilated by Aju's smaller Yuan force at Jiaoshan Mountain (July 26).

Despite desperate Song peace missions, the Mongol offensive resumed in November 1275. Aju besieged Li Tingzhi in Yangzhou, and Ariq-Qaya advanced into Hunan while Bayan and Dong Wenbing (1218–78) converged on the Song capital of Lin'an. Now patriotic militias commanded by fanatic loyalists such as Wen Tianxiang (1236–83) came to the fore. Resistance became stiffer, resulting in Bayan's massacre of the inhabitants of Changzhou in December 1275 and mass suicide of the defenders at Tanzhou (modern Changsha) in January 1276. When Bayan and Dong Wenbing camped outside Lin'an in February 1276, the Empresses Dowager Xie and Quan Jiu (1241–1309) surrendered with the underage emperor and the imperial seal. On March 28 Mongol troops peacefully entered the Song capital.

Even so, Chongqing and Hezhou in Sichuan, Li Tingzhi in Yangzhou, and most of the far southern provinces still held out. In February Empress Dowager Xie had secretly sent the child emperor's two younger brothers to Fuzhou (in Fujian). There, die-hard loyalists such as Zhang Shijie and Wen Tianxiang gathered. For the next two years Wen Tianxiang fought advancing Yuan forces in the mountainous Fujian-Guangdong-Jiangxi borderland, while Zhang Shijie guarded the two successive boy emperors at sea. The northern strongholds fell one by one: Yangzhou (August 1276), Chongqing (March 1277), and Hezhou (February 1279). On February 2, 1279, Wen Tianxiang was captured and taken to Beijing to be executed in 1283. On March 19, 1279, Yuan marines crushed Zhang Shijie's forces at Yaishan Island in the Canton harbor. Zhang drowned, and a civil official, Lu Xiufu (1238–79), leaped into the sea with the last Song emperor. Thousands more followed him in suicide.

The influence of the Song on the Mongol Yuan dynasty was surprisingly slight. Despite the thousands of loyalist suicides, the Mongol conquest of South China did not cause the massive dislocation and depopulation that had engulfed North China. Demographically and economically, the newly won territories dwarfed the old. The southerners were the lowest ranked in the Yuan status hierarchy, and by the time of the conquest Mongol government forms had long been set. Perhaps the greatest influence was the eventual adoption by the Mongol court of Song neo-CONFUCIANISM as the guiding ideology of its examination system in 1315.

See also BUDDHISM IN THE MONGOL EMPIRE; EAST ASIAN SOURCES ON THE MONGOL EMPIRE; LI TAN'S REBELLION; TAOISM IN THE MONGOL EMPIRE; XIANGYANG, SIEGE OF.

Further reading: Richard L. Davis, *Wind against the Mountain: The Crisis of Politics and Culture in Thirteenth-Century China* (Cambridge, Mass.: Harvard University Press, 1996).

Sonombaljiriin Buyannemekh *See* BUYANNEMEKHÜ.

Sorqaqtani Beki (d. 1252) *The mother of Möngke and Qubilai Khans and the ancestress of the Mongol ruling family in East Asia and the Middle East*
Sorqaqtani Beki (Princess Sorqaqtani) was the daughter of Ja'a Ghambu, the younger brother of ONG KHAN, ruler of the KEREYID Khanate. When CHINGGIS KHAN conquered the Kereyids in 1203, he gave Sorqaqtani Beki as a bride to his son TOLUI, then little more than 10 years old. She

bore Tolui their first son, Möngke, in 1209. In 1215 she bore her second son, Qubilai, and then HÜLE'Ü (1217), and ARIQ-BÖKE.

When Tolui died prematurely in 1232, ÖGEDEI KHAN made Sorqaqtani Beki chief of Tolui's *ulus*, or appanage. From then on she ranked as one of the major personages in the empire. The Persian historians 'ALA'UD-DIN ATA-MALIK JUVAINI and RASHID-UD-DIN FAZL-ULLAH, writing in the service of her descendants, picture her as a woman of exemplary prudence and wisdom. Her control over Tolui's appanage, which included the bulk of the Mongols and widespread districts in North China and Iran, gave her great power. Their accounts have been doubted as mere conventional panegyric, yet JOHN OF PLANO CARPINI, at the Mongol court in 1246, before the elevation of her son to khan, says she was more renowned than any Mongol woman except TÖREGENE and more powerful than any Mongol noble except BATU (d. 1255).

Religiously, Sorqaqtani, as a Kereyid, was raised a Christian in the Church of the East and kept to that faith until her death. Even so, she also financed the construction of a *madrasa* (Islamic school) in Bukhara and gave alms to both Christians and Muslims. She played the main role in instructing her sons, and they all seem to have inherited her ecumenical piety, although they were quite diverse in their eventual beliefs.

On the death of Ögedei in 1241, the MONGOL EMPIRE entered a prolonged period of uncertainty over the succession. Sorqaqtani Beki spoke for the Toluids in all these conflicts, but until late in GÜYÜG's reign she avoided making any steps that could be construed as partisan. When Güyüg Khan (r. 1246–48) moved the court west, however, she warned Batu that the khan intended to attack him, thus cementing an alliance with Batu against Ögedei's heirs. After Güyüg's sudden death, she sent her eldest son, Möngke, to Batu's QURILTAI (assembly), where Batu chose him as the next khan. In the ensuing controversies and purges, Sorqaqtani played an active role in assisting MÖNGKE KHAN to secure his power. In February or March 1252 she fell ill and died.

After Sorqaqtani's death she eventually became the subject of a long-lasting cult. In 1335 it was reported to the Mongol court that Sorqaqtani Beki was enshrined in a Christian church in Ganzhou (modern Zhangye), and sacrifices were ordered to be offered there. By around 1480 a cult was conducted at the ORDO (palace-tent) of Eshi Khatun (the First Lady), that is, Sorqaqtani, kept by the CHAKHAR Mongols. This *ordo* appears to have been moved to Ordos in the 17th century, where the cult was continued to the 20th century (*see* EIGHT WHITE YURTS).

soum *See* SUM.

South Gobi province (South Govi, Ömnögov')

Created in the 1931 administrative reorganization, South Gobi is Mongolia's largest (165,400 square kilometers, 63,860 square miles), most sparsely populated (barely one person per four square kilometers, or per 1.5 square miles), and southernmost province. It has a long frontier with southwestern Inner Mongolia in China.

Its territory was the southern part of KHALKHA Mongolia's prerevolutionary Tüshiyetü Khan and Sain Noyan provinces. While mostly desert and gobi (habitable desert), several low ranges, such as the Gurwan Saikhan Range, traverse the area, moderating the otherwise dry and relatively hot climate. Most of Mongolia's major dinosaur fossils have been found in this province.

Its population of 20,200 in 1956 has grown to 46,900 in 2000. The province's total herd of 1,489,600 head includes 92,800 CAMELS, accounting for almost 30 percent of Mongolia's total. The number of GOATS, 868,700 head, is second only to BAYANKHONGOR PROVINCE and GOBI-ALTAI PROVINCE. The capital, Dalanzadgad, has a population of 14,200 persons (2000 figures).

See also CASHMERE; DINOSAURS; GOBI DESERT; MATRILINEAL CLANS; MINING.

South Hangay *See* SOUTH KHANGAI PROVINCE.

South Khangai province (South Hangay, Övörhangai, Övörchangaj, Ubur Khangai)

Created in 1931, South Khangai province lies in west-central Mongolia, straddling the border of KHALKHA Mongolia's prerevolutionary Sain Noyan and Tüshiyetü Khan provinces. The province has an area of 62,900 square kilometers (24,290 square miles), extending from the wooded southeastern slopes of the KHANGAI RANGE into the GOBI DESERT. In Kharkhorin Sum, near the province's northern frontier, are the ruins of the Mongol imperial capital, QARA-QORUM, and Khalkha's first monastery, ERDENI ZUU.

The province's total population has grown from 49,900 persons in 1956 to 113,000 in 2000, the second-highest of any province in Mongolia. The total herd of livestock reached 2,956,600 in 1999, the largest ever in a Mongolian province, but it was reduced by the severe ZUD (winter disaster) of 1999–2000 to 2,159,000 by the end of 2000. Cattle were struck particularly hard, dropping from 296,000 head to 174,800. South Khangai still has Mongolia's second-largest sheep herd, with 1,059,000 head. The relatively large-scale arable agriculture of 1960–90 proved almost completely unable to weather economic liberalization. South Khangai's capital, Arwaikheer, was formed around Üizeng Zasag banner's Arbai-Kheere-yin Khüriye Monastery. In 2000 the town's population reached 19,100.

See also GENDÜN; JIBZUNDAMBA KHUTUGTU, FIRST.

South Seas

With the conquest of South China, the Mongols entered actively into the commerce, diplomacy, and wars of the South China Sea and the Indian Ocean.

In 1278 QUBILAI KHAN (1260–94) appointed Mangghudai (d. 1290) of the TATARS, a general in the conquest of the Song, to handle overseas trade. As head of the Maritime Trade Supervisorate in Zaytun (modern Quanzhou), which MARCO POLO called perhaps the world's most flourishing port, Mangghudai followed the Song regulations, levying a 10 percent tax on high-priced commodities and 6.7 percent on bulk goods. Merchants going abroad had to register their ships and declare their destinations, with deviations allowed only in emergencies. By 1293 six additional ports, from Shanghai in the north to Canton in the south, had Maritime Trade Supervisorates.

The court actively funded overseas expeditions, issuing government capital to privileged ORTOQ merchants. However, mercantilist anxieties showed in the prohibition on the export of metals, both precious and base; foreign merchants had to sell their goods for paper currency (chao). Foreign policy and prestige considerations prohibited the export of slaves and weapons and occasioned temporary embargoes against hostile states. Desire to profit by a government-carrier monopoly and vague worries over luxury exports led in 1285, 1303, and 1320 to prohibitions on all foreign trade by private domestic merchants. None lasted long, and in any case foreign merchants were never affected.

In 1278 Mangghudai's colleague Sodu (d. 1284) of the JALAYIR dispatched edicts to 10 South Seas kingdoms, from Cham-pa in present-day south-central VIETNAM to Quilon on India's southwest coast, demanding submission. By long-standing practice the South Seas realms were accustomed to paying nominal tribute to China, receiving investitures and gifts in return. Now, demanding that their rulers attend his court, Qubilai in January 1280 dispatched Sodu to Cham-pa and a Canton DARUGHACHI (overseer), Yang Tingbi, to Quilon. By 1286 Yang Tingbi had reached India's Maabar and Quilon coasts several times, collecting eager professions of nominal submission of rulers from Kerala to Malaya. Cham-pa had, however, turned hostile, and in December 1282 Sodu led a maritime invasion with 5,000 men. The Yuan troops occupied the capital, Vijaya (near modern Qui Nho'n), but the king, Jaya Indravarman IV (1266–c.90), retreated to the mountains. Stymied by this withdrawal, Sodu eventually sailed home in March 1284, just as Aq-Taghai (1235–90) embarked with another 5,000 men on a fruitless mission to reinforce him. Sodu's subsequent plan to invade Cham-pa through Vietnam resulted only in his death and a 10-year quagmire for the Mongol YUAN DYNASTY. In 1293 Ighmish (fl. 1266–1311), an Uighur envoy and Fujian high official with experience in Champa (1281), Vietnam (1284), and Maabar (1287), led an expedition against Java with 20,000 men. Ighmish occupied the capital, Kediri, but was soon driven out.

Qubilai's successor, Temür (1294–1307), abandoned the aim of conquering the South Seas and, content with only nominal tribute, received envoys from previously hostile Siam and Cambodia. The account of the Yuan's 1296 envoy to Cambodia by the envoy Zhou Daguan (Chou Ta-kuan), is a major source on Cambodian history and society.

The Mongol IL-KHANATE in Persia also bordered the Indian Ocean. Trade between India and the Middle East passed through Hormoz, a port city theoretically tributary to the Il-Khans but effectively independent. From the reign of Abagha on (1265–81) the sea route from Zaytun to Hormoz was favored for embassies between the Il-Khans and the Yuan. Marco Polo and MUHAMMAD ABU-'ABDULLAH IBN BATTUTA left vivid accounts of the South Seas commerce and diplomacy.

See also INDIA AND THE MONGOLS; TRIBUTE SYSTEM.

Further reading: Janet L. Abu-Lughod, *Before European Hegemony: The World System A.D. 1250–1350* (Oxford: Oxford University Press, 1989); David Bade, *Khubilai Khan and the Beautiful Princess of Tumapel* (Ulaanbaatar: A. Chuluunbat, 2002).

Soviet Union and Mongolia While Russia had been a patron of Mongolian independence since 1911, the conservative society of theocratic Mongolia resisted making reforms according to foreign models. From 1921 on, however, Soviet Russia became not only the foreign patron but also the model of revolution, social transformation, and modernization for Mongolia's revolutionaries. Despite the resistance of many Mongolian leaders, the Soviet Union molded every aspect of Mongolian life up to its own collapse in 1991. This article describes the influence of Soviet Russia (1917–22/24) and then the Soviet Union (1922/24–91) on Mongolia in political, ideological, and economic spheres. (*For Russian relations with Mongolia before 1917, for Russian cultural influence on Mongolia in the Soviet period, and for Russian relations with Mongolia after 1991, see* RUSSIA AND MONGOLIA.)

SOVIET INTERESTS IN MONGOLIA

Internal documents and journalistic pieces from the first decades of the Soviet-Mongolian relationship consistently enumerate Moscow's main interests in Mongolia: 1) as a place to showcase Soviet Russian ideology and benevolence; 2) as a buffer zone protecting Siberia; 3) as an animal products and mineral supplier; and 4) as a transit point for communication with China. While later assessments were far less frank, these four lines of interest can be seen operating throughout the Soviet-Mongolian relation until the collapse of the Soviet Union in 1991. While the first of these items remained relatively constant, the composition of Mongolia's exports changed sharply, as did the Soviet Union's relationship with Mongolia as either a buffer zone (defensive) or a transit point (expansive).

EARLY SOVIET DIPLOMACY AND CHINA'S INNER ASIAN QUESTION

From 1920, when Soviet Russia first reestablished its presence in Siberia and received an appeal from the Mongolian People's Party for assistance against China, Soviet

Russia's key dilemma was how to balance its interests in Mongolia with its desire to woo China. The Chinese regarded China's claims to the 1911 frontiers (including Manchuria, Mongolia, Xinjiang, and Tibet) as inviolable and the 1911 RESTORATION of Mongolian independence as part of unequal treaties, while Soviet Russia hoped to woo China by touting its renunciation of unequal treaty privileges.

Thus, while Russia's "China hands" in the foreign service and the Communist International (Comintern) preferred to sacrifice Russia's interests in Mongolia for greater influence in China, the "Mongolia hands" in the Siberian party apparatus preferred to forgo the uncertain Chinese alliance for the certain benefits of a friendly Mongolia. In spring and summer 1921, with the occupation of Mongolia by anticommunist White Russian forces, the "Mongolia hands" won the debate, and the Soviet Red Army was sent south to occupy Khüriye (modern ULAANBAATAR), setting the Mongolian People's Party in power (see 1921 REVOLUTION).

Since the Russian intervention was not against China but against the widely distrusted White Russians, Soviet diplomats were able to finesse the issue of Mongolia in their negotiations with China. In May 1924 the new Sino-Soviet treaty recognized Chinese sovereignty (i.e., full control) in Mongolia, all the while knowing that the Chinese government, divided among jealous warlord factions, was incapable of enforcing its claims. From this time until 1945, while the Chinese government would periodically protest manifestations of Mongolia's independence, these protests had no real bearing on Sino-Soviet relations. Due to Moscow's nominal recognition of China's theoretical claim to Mongolia, however, Soviet agreements with Mongolia were always "agreements" or "protocols" and never treaties, and its diplomats in Mongolia were "political representatives," not ambassadors. Although the Mongolian government found these concessions to Chinese claims galling, they had little recourse except to accept the assurances of Moscow's men in Mongolia that Moscow's concessions were purely nominal.

INTERNATIONAL CONTEXT

From 1923 to 1927 Soviet interests in Mongolia were expansive. Allying with the Nationalist (Guomindang) Party in Canton, the warlord Feng Yuxiang in China's northwest, and pan-Mongolist nationalists in Inner Mongolia, the Soviet Union armed and funded a multifaceted campaign against Beijing's warlord government and foreign concessions in China. Mongolia served this coalition as a land conduit for weapons, Soviet advisers, and Chinese and Inner Mongolian students and as an advertisement for postrevolutionary progress.

In April 1927, however, the Guomindang leader, Chiang Kai-shek, turned against the Soviet Union. From 1928, when Chiang unified China, Mongolia's role for the Soviet Union thus became defensive, although it was also

a highly secret base for infiltration into China of persecuted Chinese Communists and Inner Mongolian revolutionaries. This defensiveness continued after Japan's occupation of Manchuria in 1931 and was heightened by clashes along the Mongolian-Manchurian frontier from January 1935 on. Both Japan and the Soviet Union viewed relations in the context of their deep ideological hostility, and while internal documents show both had a primarily defensive strategy, each believed the other to harbor aggressive aims. In 1939 the massive Battle of Khalkhyn Gol established Soviet dominance on the frontier and led eventually to the Soviet-Japanese Non-Aggression Pact of May 1941.

In the last days of WORLD WAR II, the Soviet Union, with Mongolia in tow, declared war on Japan and invaded Japanese-occupied Inner Mongolia and Manchuria. The Soviet Union's power now forced Chiang Kai-shek to recognize formally Mongolia's independence in 1946 (see PLEBISCITE ON INDEPENDENCE), thus freeing Soviet-Mongolian relations from its previous limbo. Despite this recognition, Mongolia's only real contact in China was with Inner Mongolian supporters until the Chinese Communist victory of 1949 paved the way for a decade of SINO-SOVIET ALLIANCE. Joining this alliance, Mongolia's role as a buffer was replaced by a new role as transit point between two allied powers (see TRANS-MONGOLIAN RAILWAY.) From 1960, however, the growing SINO-SOVIET SPLIT made Mongolia once again a buffer protecting Siberia from dangers to the south. The thawing of frozen Sino-Soviet and Sino-Mongolian relations from 1987 was eventually overtaken by the end of the Communist system and the breakup of the Soviet Union.

During periods of high tension the Soviet Union has stationed troops in Mongolia. In 1921–25 they were principally in the capital, in 1936–56 mostly in the east, and in 1966–90 along the southern frontier.

FORMAL ALLIANCES

Mongolia's formal treaties with the Soviet Union and Soviet-type organizations began with the November 5, 1921, agreement on mutual recognition. Trying to avoid inflaming Chinese public opinion, this agreement did not mention mutual defense, the continued presence of Soviet troops, or economic assistance, all of which proceeded on an unpublicized basis.

One issue that threatened to damage Soviet-Mongolian relations was that of Tuva. Administered with Outer Mongolia under the Qing, the area had been virtually annexed by czarist Russia in 1914 and settled by 8,100 Russians. In August–October 1921, after a very confused period of conflict, the TUVANS and the now Sovietized Russian settlers created a separate Tuvan government. Mongolia's leaders agreed to recognize this government only on August 15, 1926.

In 1924, after the Third Congress (see MONGOLIAN PEOPLE'S PARTY, THIRD CONGRESS OF), the Mongolian People's Party (soon renamed the People's Revolutionary Party) became a formal member of the Communist International (Comintern), the Moscow-based league of world Communist and "People's Revolutionary" (i.e., non-Communist but anticolonial) parties. Up to 1922 the Mongolian revolutionaries had dealt primarily with the local Siberian branch of the Russian Communist Party. From 1924 to 1932 the Comintern's Eastern Department in Moscow became the chief organ for Soviet diplomacy and interference in Mongolia. Its permanent representatives to the Mongolian party and special delegations to the Mongolian party congresses played a decisive role during the LEFTIST PERIOD from 1929 to 1932 (see MONGOLIAN PEOPLE'S REVOLUTIONARY PARTY, SEVENTH CONGRESS OF). When the failure of the Comintern's policies threatened the Soviet position in Mongolia, Soviet leader Joseph Stalin intervened personally and ordered the Comintern to reverse its policies there. From then on the general direction of Soviet-Mongolian relations was handled directly by the two countries' top leaders.

The first general state-to-state agreement since 1921 was a secret Soviet-Mongolian agreement of June 27, 1929, binding each party to give preferential treatment to the other in foreign trade. With the rise of Japan the Soviet Union became willing for the first time to make a formal alliance with Mongolia. During the first of the many summit meetings between Stalin and the Mongolian leaders, in this case Prime Minister GENDÜN (r. 1932–36), a verbal "gentlemen's agreement" was concluded on November 27, 1934. Only after Gendün's fall did the two countries formalize this as a Mutual-Defense Protocol (March 12, 1936). Hoping to deter Japan, this protocol was the first agreement to be widely publicized by the Soviet and Mongolian press, provoking a predictable but pro forma Chinese protest.

In 1946, after China recognized Mongolian independence, Mongolia and the Soviet Union renewed their military alliance, this time in a formal Treaty of Friendship and Mutual Assistance, with a concurrent economic and cultural treaty on February 27. When the treaty lapsed after 10 years, it was not renewed, as the Sino-Soviet alliance had rendered it moot. The frequent meetings between Stalin and Mongolia's ruler MARSHAL CHOIBALSANG (r. 1936–52) were not repeated in the 1950s as Mongolia's importance waned.

In 1966, however, during Leonid Brezhnev's visit to ULAANBAATAR—the first by any Soviet ruler—a 20-year Treaty of Cooperation, Friendship, and Mutual Aid was signed on January 15. The published treaty's provisions about military measures were supplemented by secret defense-related protocols directed against the Chinese threat. Mongolia's June 1962 entry into the Council of Mutual Economic Assistance (Comecon, or CMEA), the organization integrating the Soviet Union's economy with that of its East European satellites, marked the broadening of bilateral Soviet-Mongolian ties into multilateral ties with the Soviet bloc as a whole. In 1986 the 1966 treaty was automatically renewed for 10 more years, although the Soviet foreign minister Eduard Shevardnadze in Ulaanbaatar pointedly noted the improvement in Sino-Soviet relations. With the breakup of the Soviet Union in 1991, the previous system of political relations had to be rebuilt.

Given Mongolia's profound dependence on the Soviet Union, Mongolians had several times proposed that Mongolia join the Soviet Union, yet Soviet leaders, wary of accusations from China, were not supportive. In the late 1920s, radical western Mongols, such as the DÖRBÖD Badarakhu (Ö. Badrakh, 1895–1941) and the KHOTONG Lagan (L. Laagan, 1886–1940), resented KHALKHA dominance and proposed that western Mongolia and Tuva together join the Soviet Union. In the 1940s and early 1950s the Soviet-trained technocrats under Choibalsang repeatedly questioned whether socialism could be built in Mongolia without joining the Soviet Union. The procurator B. Jambaldorj raised the possibility in 1944, when Tuva joined the Soviet Union, and DARAMYN TÖMÖR-OCHIR and YUMJAAGIIN TSEDENBAL raised it again late in Choibalsang's life. Choibalsang himself violently opposed such ideas, but after his death the Mongolian Politburo in 1953 approved unification, only to be rebuked by V. M. Molotov for their "simple-minded error." In the mid-1970s the Soviet ruler Leonid Brezhnev sounded out his Mongolian counterpart. Tsedenbal about this issue. By then, however, the very success of Mongolian industrialization with Soviet aid had decreased Mongolia's perceived need for unification, and the issue was dropped.

ECONOMIC TIES: TRADE, AID, AND INTEGRATION

An important aim of the Soviet Union in Mongolia had been the supply of animal products and minerals to Siberia. For the first 40 years of the relationship, the trade of minerals remained only potential, but Mongolia soon began exporting animal products to the Soviet Union. From 1922 to 1930 the Soviet Union went from being a minor player to securing a complete monopsony on Mongolia's exports of wool, furs, hides, and live cattle. More slowly, but also largely complete by 1930, the Soviet Union monopolized Mongolia's imports. This monopsony/monopoly position was acquired by the Mongolian government's support of Soviet trade organs and Mongolian cooperatives, both of which traded exclusively with the Soviet Union. The Soviets worked in Mongolia through joint-stock companies focused on trade (Stormong, 1927–32, and Monsovbuner, 1932–34), banking (Mongolian Trade and Industrial Bank, 1924–35), and transportation (Mongoltrans, 1929–36). All these companies were eventually transferred to Mongolia.

The advance of the Soviet trade monopoly in 1928–30 resulted in a shortage of consumer goods previously imported from China. A Soviet delegation in 1932 credited this shortage with being a factor in the revolts.

Stalin ordered that the terms of trade be improved for Mongolia. At the same time, the fledgling Mongolian industrial plants beginning in 1933–34 with Soviet assistance actually increased the need for spare parts, electrical goods, and other inputs. As a result, by 1935 the chronic deficits first arose that would characterize Mongolia's trade with the Soviet Union from then on. Once the lamas had been destroyed and Choibalsang installed as unchallenged dictator, Stalin in 1940 demanded Mongolia sell 30,000 metric tons (33,069 short tons) of sheep wool, 1,000 metric tons (1,102 short tons) of camel hair, and 1,000 metric tons (1,102 short tons) of CASHMERE at low prices. Mongolia's actual 1940 production of these items was 10,600, 2,000, and 100 metric tons, respectively (equal to 11,680, 2,205, and 110 short tons). He also asked Mongolia to increase its herd, then at 26 million, to 200 million head.

While such demands proved impossible, World War II succeeded in reversing Mongolia's trade deficit with the Soviet Union as the German invasion devastated the Soviet economy and the Mongolian government mobilized the population to supply its ally. In 1942 exports to the Soviet Union exceeded imports by 122 percent. In the postwar period the deficits reappeared and expanded through the 1950s. Despite the expansion of coal mining and the establishment of a small petroleum industry, as late as 1958 98 percent of Mongolia's exports were still animal products or live animals.

The Brezhnev-Tsedenbal years completely transformed the Soviet-Mongolian economic relationship. Aid promised in the 1966 treaty came to supply 40 percent of Mongolia's investment capital, financing projects all over the country. Investment in mining finally realized the Soviet dream of making Mongolia a major mineral supplier, as mineral exports rose from 0.6 percent of Mongolia's exports in 1965 to 39.2 percent in 1985. The great bulk of this was supplied by the massive copper-molybdenum mine at ERDENET CITY, which came on line in 1978–81 as the centerpiece of Soviet aid. With the development of extractive industries, however, Mongolia's imports of machine technology, petroleum, trucks, and other goods again increased, so that imports from the Soviet Union regularly exceeded exports by 30–45 percent. Mongolia's foreign debt to the Soviet Union accumulated relentlessly, although Brezhnev's belief that Mongolia would eventually join the Soviet Union meant that repayment was not seriously expected.

STUDENTS AND ADVISERS

Exchange of people was an essential part of the Soviet-Mongolian relationship. In this exchange the Soviet Union sent advisers and trainers, while the Mongols sent students to the Soviet Union. Soviet instructors worked with the Mongolian partisans from the very beginning, and after the formation of the new government virtually every office had its Soviet personnel. By 1927 Soviets living in Mongolia reached 2,679, many of whom were workers. In 1924 the Mongolian army had 14 trainers, but the Mutual-Aid Cooperatives, responsible for wool purchases, employed 273 Russians. Controversies over the advisers centered first on their generally low quality, which even Soviet sources acknowledged, and second over the hiring of experts from the 15,000 or so Buriat refugees from the Russian Revolution in Mongolia (see BURIATS OF MONGOLIA AND INNER MONGOLIA).

The exchange of Mongolians educated in the Soviet Union, particularly at the Communist University of the Toilers of the East (known by its Russian acronym KUTV) and at the Red Army academy in Tver proved more effective than advisers in transmitting Soviet influence in Mongolia. Returned students were essential in implementing the leftist policy line of 1929–32. The special classes for Mongolians, BURIATS, and KALMYKS at the Oriental Institute in Leningrad nurtured many of Mongolia's later authors and scholars. The Mongolian Rabfak (from Russian *Rabochii fakul'tet,* or workers school) in ULAN-UDE from 1930 to 1941 furnished at Soviet expense 166 Mongolians with a middle school education as preparation for higher education in Russia; graduates included the academician BAZARYN SHIRENDEW, while Tsedenbal graduated from a similar program in Irkutsk (see DAMDINSÜREN, TSEDIIN; RINCHEN, BYAMBYN; YADAMSÜREN, ÜRJINGIIN).

The post–World War II baby boom and the vast expansion of the industrial economy supplied a similarly vast increase in the number of students studying in the Soviet Union. By 1981–82 almost 10,300 Mongolian students were studying in 362 separate Soviet research institutes, universities, colleges, professional middle schools, and technical schools. Knowledge of Russian became a prerequisite for any sort of responsible position in Mongolia. By 1990 virtually the entire ruling class of Mongolia had received education in the Soviet Union or in Eastern Europe (see BATMÖNKH, JAMBYN; DASHBALBAR, OCHIRBATYN; ZORIG, SANJAASÜRENGIIN).

During the mid-1930s the number of Soviet advisers increased from 81 in 1935 to 205 in 1936. The previous economic focus of Soviet advisers changed, and military advisers increased to 110 in 1936 and 681 in 1939. A more sinister class of advisers trained the security organs in counterespionage, with a focus on the use of torture to fabricate ever-expanding spy cases. Several cases in the early 1920s, such as that of BODÖ in 1922, were clearly fabricated by Soviet advisers, but the security services were reigned in after 1925 until the outbreak of the much larger LHÜMBE CASE in 1933. From 1937 to 1940 Soviet security advisers assisted Mongolians from lowly investigators up to Marshal Choibalsang himself in creating thousands of cases and snaring tens of thousands of victims in a far-off theater in Stalin's war against his own society. Encouraged by Choibalsang's compliance, many advisers began to give edicts on subjects far beyond their competence.

From 1940 to the mid-1960s Soviet academics and artists working in Mongolia opened up field after field of academic research. The chief physics, chemistry, and biology professors at Mongolian State University's founding in 1942 were all Russian; up to the 1980s more than 400 Soviet academics had taught at the school. Soviet geological, botanical, paleontological, and archaeological surveys became the training ground for Mongolia's first specialists in those disciplines (*see* ARCHAEOLOGY; DINOSAURS.) Circus, cinema, classical music, and ballet all eventually became nativized in Mongolia through Soviet advisers in Mongolia and Mongolian students studying in the Soviet Union.

The vast expansion of Soviet aid swelled the number of Soviets working in Mongolia. In the 1980s an estimated 32,000 Soviet civilians in addition to the 75,000 military personnel lived in Mongolia. Those in Ulaanbaatar had a network of special apartments, stores, buses, and clubs that kept them almost completely isolated from the Mongolians. Popular resentment of the Soviet presence broke out over a Soviet bus's collision with a Mongolian one in 1979, but it was immediately squelched by the authorities. The Russian-language grade school no. 23 in Ulaanbaatar, founded in 1965, became the favored school for the children of the elite, due to both its high academic standards and its language of instruction.

IDEOLOGY AND SYMBOLISM

In the early years of Soviet-Mongolian relations symbolic exchanges of delegates, telegrams, demonstrations, memorial services, and membership in Moscow-based internationals, such as the Communist Youth International, the Profintern, or Red International of Trade Unions, and so on, stimulated solidarity with the international revolutionary cause. The Mongolian painter "BUSY-BODY" SHARAB's portraits of V. I. Lenin and other world revolutionary leaders, painted from photographs, were placed in congresses and offices. Themes of "Lenin" and "October" began appearing in works by authors such as NATSUGDORJI and BUYANNEMEKHÜ from 1931 on.

With the rise of Choibalsang the growing cult of the leader in Mongolia was matched with a similar cult of Stalin and Lenin. Stalin's statue was erected in 1949 in front of the Stalin State (or National) Library, and in 1950–54 his complete works were published. Lenin received his own statue and Mongolian-language complete works in 1954 and 1967, respectively. The subject of the meeting of Lenin and GENERAL SÜKHEBAATUR (which may or may not have happened and was certainly not a one-on-one interview) was first treated by the painter D. Choidog (1917–56) in 1942 and became a stock theme of Mongolian art.

The emphasis on the theme of Soviet-Mongolian friendship was carried to baroque excesses under

A Meeting with Lenin by A. Sengetsokhio, painted in 1967 in the Mongol *zurag* style. Lenin's meeting with Sükhebaatur was a favorite theme of art during the Communist era. *(From* Orchin Uyeiin Mongolyn Dürslekh Urlag *[1971])*

Tsedenbal (r. 1952–84). Publicity focused on events such as the March 22–30, 1981, joint Soviet-Mongolian space flight of the Soviet cosmonaut Vladimir A. Zhanibekov and his Mongolian partner, J. Gürragchaa. Its perfect expression was a children and youth's encyclopedia, which devoted one volume to Mongolia after 1921, one volume (under the name "A Great Friendship") to the Soviet Union after 1917, and a third volume to the rest of human civilization.

LEGACY

Given its pervasive character, it is difficult to separate the Soviet legacy in Mongolia from that of post-1921 Mongolia as a whole. The most important aspect of Soviet influence on Mongolia was the degree to which its advocates, both Soviet and Mongolian, fused independence from China, modernization, Communist ideology, and Soviet-Russian culture into one inseparable package, insisting that rejecting one would lead to rejecting all four. Mongolian attempts to break apart this package and separately evaluate its contents were repeatedly squelched, until the collapse of the Soviet empire made the issue moot.

See also ARMED FORCES OF MONGOLIA; 1990 DEMOCRATIC REVOLUTION; ECONOMY, MODERN; FOREIGN RELATIONS; KHALKHYN GOL, BATTLE OF; MINING; MONGOLIAN PEOPLE'S REPUBLIC; MONGOLIAN PEOPLE'S REVOLUTIONARY PARTY; MONGOLIAN REVOLUTIONARY YOUTH LEAGUE; REVOLUTIONARY PERIOD; THEOCRATIC PERIOD.

Further reading: Christopher P. Atwood, "Sino-Soviet Diplomacy and the Second Partition of Mongolia, 1945–1946," in *Mongolia in the Twentieth Century: Landlocked Cosmopolitan,* ed. Stephen Kotkin and Bruce A. Elleman (Armonk, N.Y.: M. E. Sharpe, 1999), 137–161; Tsedendambyn Batbayar, "Stalin's Strategy in Mongolia, 1932–1936," *Mongolian Studies* 22 (1999): 1–17; Bruce A. Elleman, "Final Consolidation of the USSR's Sphere of Interest in Mongolia," in *Mongolia in the Twentieth Century: Landlocked Cosmopolitan,* ed. Stephen Kotkin and Bruce A. Elleman (Armonk, N.Y.: M. E. Sharpe, 1999), 123–136; Irina Y. Morozova, *The Comintern and Revolution in Mongolia* (Cambridge: White Horse Press, 2002); Kyosuke Terayama, "Soviet Policies toward Mongolia after the Manchurian Incident," in *Facets of Transformation of the Northeast Asian Countries,* ed. Tadashi Yoshida and Hiroki Oka (Sendai: Center for Northeast Asian Studies, 1998), 37–66.

Soyombo script This script, designed by the First JIBZUNDAMBA KHUTUGTU, Zanabazar (1635–1723), in 1686, was used mostly for writing short ornamental Buddhist texts. The Soyombo script was apparently created as a way to write Mongolian with Sanskrit and Tibetan in a single script. Zanabazar also experimented with a "horizontal square script" (*khebtege dürbeljin üsüg*), a rare and imperfectly known script similar to 'Phags-pa Lama's SQUARE SCRIPT but written in horizontal rows, not columns. Before Zanabazar, all Mongolian scripts had been vertical, but Sanskrit and Tibetan were both written in rows. Zanabazar's horizontal scripts thus may have been intended to ease production of interlinear parallel texts. The Soyombo script was one of the lesser-used scripts taught in courses organized by the ERDENI SHANGDZODBA (the administrative office of the JIBZUNDAMBA KHUTUGTU's estate) in the late 19th and early 20th centuries. Only a few texts of any length are known, and none was originally written in the Soyombo script.

The name *Soyombo* derives from Sanskrit Svayambhu, "self-existing," and it was called in Mongolian the "brilliant self-existent script" (*öber-iyen bolugsan gegen üsüg*). The SOYOMBO SYMBOL was placed at the beginning of texts written in the script, displaying in several signs the union of skills in means and wisdom that generates the self-existing bliss of enlightenment.

The Soyombo script is, like the Tibetan and 'Phags-pa (square) script, a script of the Indic type. While fundamentally alphabetic, it is written in blocks of one syllable. Graphically, every syllable is based on a superscribed downward pointing solid triangle and a vertical beam on the right. The vowels are marked either above or below the triangle and the initial consonant is marked below the triangle. Syllable-final consonants are attached to the lower part of the vertical beam. As in all Indic scripts, an *a* is implied when no vowel is written. Diphthongs are indicated by vowel signs added outside the beam on the right, while long vowels are indicated by a slanting extension of the vertical beam. The resulting initial and final letters for Mongolian are conventionally counted at 59. The alphabet also includes 33 special signs for Sanskrit words and eight for Tibetan words.

Orthographically, the Soyombo script was, like other Mongolian scripts, not fully consistent. In general, it retains many Uighur-Mongolian forms characteristic of Middle Mongolian, such as the diphthongs and archaic verbal forms. Even so, it reflects KHALKHA pronunciation in distinguishing *ts* from *ch* and *dz* from *j* only by the absence or presence of an *i* following the consonant. Interestingly, Zanabazar also used this same etymological device to distinguish *s* from *sh*.

See also MONGOLIAN LANGUAGE.

Soyombo symbol Derived from Sanskrit *svayambhu,* "self-existent," the Soyombo symbol was designed by the FIRST JIBZUNDAMBA KHUTUGTU Zanabazar (1635–1723). On the top of the Soyombo and often used separately appear a sun disk and crescent moon surmounted by a three-pointed flame. The lower part of the Soyombo has the *arga-bilig* (skill-wisdom), or *yin-yang,* symbol (often interpreted as two fish). Framing it are two long vertical sidebars, while above and below are downward pointing triangles and short horizontal bars. The Soyombo rests on a lotus.

The Soyombo symbol was named after the famous Svayambhu stupa, or Buddhist reliquary, outside Katmandu city in Nepal. Since the 18th century, the crescent moon, sun disk, and flame have surmounted stupas in both Tibet and Mongolia. The EIGHTH JIBZUNDAMBA KHUTUGTU, as theocratic ruler of Mongolia (1870–1924), used the symbol on both Mongolia's flag and state SEAL. From there it has become the symbol of the independent Mongolian nation, found on all FLAGS since then, although without the lotus since 1940. Since 1990 the sun disk, crescent moon, and flame have been adopted on the flags of the BURIAT REPUBLIC and the AGA BURIAT AUTONOMOUS AREA, as well as by Mongolian, Buriat, and Inner Mongolian opposition political organizations.

While the full meaning of the original symbol is obscure, the sun and the moon and the *arga-bilig* symbol clearly refer to the union of wisdom (*bilig*), identified with the sun and the feminine principle, and the skillful means (*arga*) to teach that wisdom, identified with the moon and the masculine principle. The surmounted flame thus refers to the thought of enlightenment (*bodi sedkil*) generated by the union of feminine wisdom and masculine skill in means.

In 1945, when the anomaly of a Buddhist symbol on a Communist flag became disturbing, the scholar BAMBYN RINCHEN concocted for Mongolia's maximum leader MARSHAL CHOIBALSANG a secular explanation: the flame represents the people's glory, its three points their past, present, and future; the sun and moon, the people's eternity; the downward pointing triangles, the destruction of the people's enemies; the horizontal bars, the people's struggle for justice; the two fish, with their unblinking eyes, unceasing vigilance against enemies; and the vertical bars, that if the people remain united they will be firmer than a stone wall. While this explanation is obviously grossly anachronistic, it preserved the symbol and is now widespread in Mongolia.

See also SOYOMBO SCRIPT.

sports and games   *See* ARCHERY; CHESS; HORSE RACING; HUNTING AND FISHING; *NAADAM*; WRESTLING.

square script (**'Phags-pa Script**)   First designed by the Tibetan 'PHAGS-PA LAMA, the square script was designed as a universal script of the Mongol Empire yet was never widely adopted even for the MONGOLIAN LANGUAGE. In 1269 QUBILAI KHAN (1260–94) ordered 'Phags-pa Lama (1235–80), his state preceptor (*guoshi*), to create a new script for the Mongolian language. While the UIGHUR-MONGOLIAN SCRIPT, in use since the time of CHINGGIS KHAN (Genghis, 1206–27), was well adapted in many ways to the Mongolian language, certain peculiarities made it ambiguous, lacking any distinction between *t* and *d*, *k* and *g*, and so on. It was even less adequate for writing the Chinese names and terms increasingly common

in the empire's administrative documents or as a phonetic transcription to help Mongols learn Chinese. Qubilai thus commissioned 'Phags-pa to create a script that could represent the sounds of the empire's major languages, particularly Mongolian and Chinese.

'Phags-pa based his new alphabet closely on the Tibetan script, itself derived from an Indic script. While the Indian and Tibetan scripts were written in horizontal rows from left to right, however, 'Phags-pa arranged his alphabet in vertical columns, left to right, following the Uighur-Mongolian script. The forms of the letters were mostly taken from Tibetan, with a number of slightly altered letters added to cover Mongolian and Chinese sounds that did not exist in Tibetan. 'Phags-pa squared off most of the letters, thus giving rise to the modern Mongolian name of "square script" (*dörbeljin bichig*, modern Mongolian, *dörwöljin bichig*). In adapting basically Tibetan letters to Mongolian, 'Phags-pa made use of devices that had been pioneered centuries before in the writing of the Uighur language (phonetically similar to Mongolian) in the Brahmi script.

The orthography of square-script Mongolian shows a number of conventions borrowed from the Uighur script, particularly relating to the representation of vocal harmony. At the same time, it is an important witness to the phonology of 13th-century Mongolian. Unlike the Uighur-Mongolian script, for example, the square script distinguishes a closed e- from the more open one and marks the early Altaic initial h- that disappears in later Mongolian. Like the Chinese transcription of the SECRET HISTORY OF THE MONGOLS from around 1400, it also testifies to the widespread shifts between weak and strong stops in the dialect spoken among the Mongols in North China. The square script orthography for Chinese also furnishes an accurate representation of Chinese phonology in a stage between Middle Mandarin and modern Chinese. It does not, however, distinguish between tones.

After the script was presented to the court, Qubilai immediately decreed that all documents with the imperial seal be written in this "new Mongolian script," and schools were created to teach it (*see* CONFUCIANISM; EDUCATION, TRADITIONAL). Court records, including the Mongolian *Veritable Records* written by Sarman in 1288, were drafted in the script by the Mongolian Hanlin Academy. The new script rapidly replaced the Uighur-Mongolian script for Mongolian-language inscriptions on tablets of authority (PAIZA), cast-copper coins, and paper money, while a number of inscriptions of 'Phags-pa dating from 1276 to 1368 have been found. Even so, repeated decrees issued from 1271 to 1284 insisting that the bureaucracy use the square script show that passive resistance to the script change was widespread. Records of publication of a number of translated Chinese histories and Confucian works and fragmentary remains of books, including Buddhist translations and a birchbark verse found on the Volga, show there was at least a small readership of books in the square script. The majority of extant square-script documents, however, were written not in Mongolian but in Chinese and show the widespread use of the square script by Mongols and UIGHURS to read and write Chinese.

After the expulsion of the Yuan from China, the square script disappeared among the Mongols. As the *Hor-yig*, or "Mongolian script," it was still used for ornamental purposes on the Tibetan plateau, and handbooks of the script were block printed there until the 20th century. Often what is called the "Mongolian script," however, is actually simply squared-off Tibetan script and not genuine square script at all.

See also ALTAIC LANGUAGE FAMILY.

Further reading: Nicholas Poppe and John R. Krueger, *Mongolian Monuments in hP'ags-pa Script* (Wiesbaden: Otto Harrassowitz, 1957).

Ssanang Ssetsen   *See* SAGHANG SECHEN.

stag stones   *See* ELK STONES.

"stone men" (*baba*)   Stone figures formed a distinctive genre of funerary art during the Türk (552–742) and early Uighur (744–840) period. They cover the steppe from Mongolia to the Black Sea. About 400 such figures are known, of which about half are in Mongolia, primarily central Mongolia (around the sacred Ötüken forest) and the ALTAI RANGE (the old Türk homeland).

All the figures hold a cup to their chests with one or both hands; in the former case the left hand holds the pommel of a sword. The men are belted and bearded. Stone men occur in distinct funerary complexes often associated with Old Turkish inscriptions. Elaborate complexes consist of a templelike structure with walls, a ditch, and a figure of a seated man often with a seated woman, his wife, attended by standing or kneeling figures. Outside, to the east or southeast, extends a line of erect stones (*baba*), sometimes including schematic stone men. Ordinary complexes contain usually a single stone man in an enclosure defined by stone slabs and a line of *baba*s. Qipchaq *baba*s in the Black Sea steppe (11th and 12th centuries) are either male or female, often with exaggerated breasts and belly, and generally hold a cup with both hands to the chest or abdomen.

In southeastern Mongolia and north-central Inner Mongolia occur distinctive stone men seated on armchairs with one hand holding a stemmed cup and the other the figure's left knee. They are located southeast of mounds with remains of templelike structures. Many figures are naked and androgynous, with prominent male genitalia and breasts; none has a moustache or weapons. Others, however, are clothed and elaborately carved, often holding a rosary in their left hand. Details of hairstyle and clothing match those of the 13th-century MONGOL EMPIRE. Their

Seated "stone man." His clothing is typical of the Yuan era. *(From N. Tsultem,* Mongolian Sculpture *[1989])*

regional origin and dates suggest that they belonged to the ÖNGGÜD or possibly QONGGIRAD tribes and show the gradual transformation of funerary beliefs during the Yuan under Confucian and Buddhist influence. Stone men found with ELK STONES (Mongolia) or Scythian graves (Ukraine) may represent either early examples or more likely intrusive artifacts due to reuse of old grave sites.

See also FUNERARY CUSTOMS; QIPCHAQS; RUNIC SCRIPT AND INSCRIPTIONS.

Sübe'etei Ba'atur (Sübü'etei, Sübödei, Sübetei) (1176–1248) *Chinggis Khan's most formidable general, who campaigned in North China, Iran, Russia, and Hungary* Sübe'etei belonged to the Uriyangkhan clan. By CHINGGIS KHAN's time the clan had been subject to the khan's ancestors for five generations. As a blacksmith clan, the Mongols also ascribed supernatural powers to them. According to the YUAN SHI (more accurate here than the *SECRET HISTORY OF THE MONGOLS*), Sübe'etei was the son of Qaban, who joined Chinggis Khan's cause with 100 households at Baljuna in 1203 (*see* BALJUNA COVENANT).

Sübe'etei first fought for Chinggis in the decisive victory over the NAIMAN Khanate at Keltegei Cliffs (1204). In the conquest of North China's JIN DYNASTY, Sübe'etei was the first over the walls at the siege of the frontier town of Huanzhou (February 1212). His first independent campaign was against the MERKID of northern Mongolia, who had revolted in 1216. Sübe'etei subdued them and by 1218–19 had pursued the remaining Merkid deep into the Qipchaq steppe north of the Caspian Sea. This campaign made Sübe'etei the Mongols' expert on western peoples.

In May 1220, during his campaign against the Khorazm shah, Sultan 'Ala'ud-Din Muhammad, Chinggis Khan dispatched Sübe'etei together with JEBE and three *tümens* (nominally 30,000 men) to pursue the fleeing sultan and subdue the west. Racing forward, they captured 'Ala'ud-Din Muhammad's wife and treasures and blockaded him on an island in the Caspian Sea. With news of the sultan's death in winter 1220–21, Sübe'etei and Jebe pushed on, reconnoitering the west while scattering the remaining Khorazmian troops. This mission led them through western Iran into GEORGIA and Azerbaijan and through the Derbent Pass. Everywhere they placed overseers (*DARUGHACHI*) in cities that surrendered and slaughtered those who resisted. Passing into the Caspian and Black Sea steppes, they attacked the Alans (OSSETES) first, then the southern QIPCHAQS, and finally a force of Qipchaqs and Russians at Kalka River (May 31, 1223). The Mongol generals then rode east to Mongolia.

After this extraordinary campaign, never before attempted and never again repeated, Sübe'etei spent several years warring in China. From 1226 he commanded the western wing in Chinggis's final campaign of annihilation against the Tangut XIA DYNASTY in northwest China. In 1230 the new emperor ÖGEDEI KHAN dispatched him to rescue Doqolqu from the Jin armies ensconced in the strategic Tongguan Pass, but for the first time he was stymied. In 1232 Ögedei's brother TOLUI and Sübe'etei found an alternate route around the Jin fortifications, and in 1233–34 Sübe'etei victoriously besieged both the Jin capital, Kaifeng, and the Jin emperor's final refuge in Caizhou (modern Runan). Sübe'etei asked to exterminate the entire population according to Mongol practice, but Ögedei, influenced by his civilian adviser YELÜ CHUCAI, ordered the population spared.

In 1235 Ögedei dispatched Sübe'etei against the unsubdued Qipchaqs. On this great western campaign, which would carry the Mongols as far as Hungary, Sübe'etei mostly let the younger princes, such as BATU, GÜYÜG, and Möngke, take the lead. Still, he took over the siege of Torzhok after Batu's attack failed and played a crucial role in the battle on the Muhi River in Hungary (April 11, 1241). Batu later said, "Everything that we captured at that time is Sübe'etei's merit."

Subsequently, Sübe'etei retired as an immensely respected elder statesman until his death in 1248. Sübe'etei, along with Qubilai Noyan, Jebe, and Jelme, had proudly formed the "four dogs" of Chinggis Khan, a title that reflected their tenacious ferocity in the Mongol vanguard. In 1229 Ögedei bestowed the imperial princess Tümugen on Sübe'etei. JOHN OF PLANO CARPINI, who visited Mongolia in 1246, says that he was known simply as Ba'atur, "Hero." His son Uriyangqadai (1199–1271) and grandson AJU continued his martial reputation.

See also KAIFENG, SIEGE OF; KALKA RIVER, BATTLE OF; MUHI, BATTLE OF.

Further reading: P. D. Buell, "Sübötei Ba'atur," in *In the Service of the Khan: Eminent Personalities of the Early Mongol-Yuan Period (1200–1300),* ed. Igor de Rachewiltz et al. (Wiesbaden: Otto Harrossowitz, 1993), 13–26.

Subei Mongol Autonomous County (Su-pei)

Occupying two noncontiguous blocks in Gansu province, Subei Mongol Autonomous county has an area of 66,748 square kilometers (25,772 square miles). The southern block, in which is situated Dangchengwan, the county seat, occupies the valley of the Danghe River as it flows from the Tibetan plateau northwest into the desert near Dunhuang. The northern block occupies the desert from Mazong Shan Mountain to the Mongolian frontier, between Xinjiang and Inner Mongolia.

Subei's small Mongol population has increased from 3,834 in 1982 to 4,219 in 1999, at which time it formed 38 percent of the county's 11,215 people. The county's economic base is pastoralism, and it has 235,000 head of livestock but only 10,000 hectares (24,710 acres) of cultivated fields.

The Mongol population of Subei is mostly UPPER MONGOLS migrating from Kökenuur (Qinghai). From 1766 to 1897 bannermen from the Kökenuur Khoshud's Körlög Beile and Körlög Jasag BANNERS (in modern northeast Haixi) fled to the Serteng (in modern Aksay Kazakh Autonomous county, just west of southern Subei) and Danghe valleys to avoid first Tibetan and then Hui (Chinese-speaking Muslim) depredations. By 1940 the two valleys had 599 Mongol households and 250,000 livestock. Northern Subei was long a no-man's land haunted by refugees and adventurers such as DAMBIJANTSAN. In 1926 KHOSHUDS from Xinjiang (in modern Bayangol prefecture) and in 1931 TORGHUDS from Khobogsair settled the area, making about 90 families.

In 1940–41 invading Xinjiang KAZAKHS routed the Serteng and Danghe Mongols. The Chinese People's Liberation Army entered the area in 1949, restored order, and on July 29, 1950, made Subei a Mongol autonomous area. The 268 surviving Mongol households had only 20,724 livestock left. In 1953 it was decided to give Serteng to the now-pacified Kazakhs, reserving Danghe and Mazong Shan for the Mongols.

See also BAYANGOL MONGOL AUTONOMOUS PREFECTURE; HAIXI MONGOL AND TIBETAN AUTONOMOUS PREFECTURE; KHOBOGSAIR MONGOL AUTONOMOUS COUNTY.

Sübetei *See* SÜBE'ETEI BA'ATUR.

Sübödei *See* SÜBE'ETEI BA'ATUR.

Süchbaatar *See* SÜKHEBAATUR PROVINCE.

Sühbaatar *See* SÜKHEBAATUR, GENERAL; SÜKHEBAATUR PROVINCE.

Suiyuan *See* HÖHHOT.

Suke-Bator *See* SÜKHEBAATUR, GENERAL.

Sükhbaatar *See* SÜKHEBAATUR, GENERAL; SÜKHEBAATUR PROVINCE.

Sükhebaatur, General (Damdiny Sükhbaatar, Süh-baatar, Suke-Bator) (1893–1923) *Founder and first commander of the Mongolian armed forces; his role in the 1921 Revolution was later exaggerated to make him the revolution's sole leader*

Sükhebaatur's parents immigrated from Yosutu Zasag banner (modern Sükhebaatur Sum, Sükhebaatur) to Khüriye (modern ULAANBAATAR) in 1890, where his father, and later Sükhebaatur himself, worked as a manual laborer. The future commander was born on February 2, 1893. In 1907–09 he learned to read and write from the scholar official Jamyang (O. Jamiyan, 1864–1930).

General Sükhebaatur (seated left), his deputy Choibalsang (seated right), and his chief of staff Valentin A. Khuya (standing) (a Soviet), winter 1922. (*Photo from* Damdiny Sükhbaatar [1980])

After being mobilized as a soldier during the 1911 RESTORATION, he compiled a distinguished record commanding a machine gun platoon, despite leading a mutiny over poor living conditions. During this time, if not before, he learned a little spoken Russian. Discharged in 1918, he became a copy editor for the publication of Mongolia's law code. In 1913 he settled down with Yangjima, who lived near his family's first yurt-courtyard in Khüriye. They had one son, Galsang.

IN THE REVOLUTION

With the 1919 REVOCATION OF AUTONOMY Sükhebaatur made a living as a teamster for Russian and Tatar merchants in Khüriye, which joining the secret "officials' faction" led by Danzin and Dogsum (D. Dogsom, 1884–1941) aiming to restore Mongolian autonomy. In July 1920 the new Mongolian People's Party chose Sükhebaatur as one of the "first seven" sent to Soviet Russia to appeal for assistance against the Chinese. Once he crossed the border, Sükhebaatur cut off his queue and began wearing Russian-style clothing.

From November Sükhebaatur was sent to the border town of Troitskosavsk (in modern KYAKHTA) to begin recruiting Mongolian soldiers. On February 9, 1921, Sükhebaatur was designated commander in chief, and he built up a several-hundred-strong partisan force from frontier pickets and border banners. Assisted by a Soviet Red Army staff command, Sükhebaatur led them on the night of March 17–18 against the much larger Chinese garrison at Mongolian Kyakhta (modern Altanbulag) in his first victory as a commander. Sükhebaatur's family had been under surveillance first by the Chinese and then by the White Russians, but now Yangjima escaped to Altanbulag. Sükhebaatur's small force played only a secondary role in the Red Army's later victorious advance on Khüriye in June–July 1921.

IN THE NEW GOVERNMENT

In July 1921 Sükhebaatur was confirmed commander in chief and minister of the army in the new government and a member of the Military Commission with ELBEK-DORZHI RINCHINO and later MAGSURJAB. Sükhebaatur organized military reforms: establishing a 210-bed military hospital, a factory at Altanbulag to produce military uniforms, and a military academy. Proposals not implemented during his life included a universal conscription system, the replacement of the postroad duty with hired transport, and an eight-hour workday for all office workers. He also paid close attention to military intelligence.

Sükhebaatur joined Danzin (now party chief and finance minister) and the deputy foreign minister TSERINDORJI on the mission to negotiate the November 5 friendship treaty with Soviet Russia in Moscow. Sükhebaatur had long disliked Prime Minister BODÖ and on his return strongly supported his resignation.

In his lifetime Sükhebaatur had a great reputation among the Mongols for his battlefield courage and heroic demeanor. His main policy interests were in the building of a strong European-style military and the advocacy of severe measures against real or suspected counterrevolutionaries. Not religious, Sükhebaatur was a heavy drinker and chain smoker and from 1920 had frequent bouts of illness. At his death he was heavily in debt.

After completing a tour of the eastern frontier in November 1922, Sükhebaatur was replaced by Magsurjab as army minister while remaining commander in chief. On February 14, 1923, while inspecting the troops guarding against a counterrevolutionary plot allegedly timed for the WHITE MONTH (lunar new year), Sükhebaatar became ill. He was bedridden from the next day until his death on February 23. His death immediately occasioned suspicions of poisoning, which have continued to the present, although the only autopsy, done in Chita, considered a liver disease the likeliest cause of death. By the late 1920s Sükhebaatur was already becoming legendary, and his one-time deputy MARSHAL CHOIBALSANG later developed this legend into a myth of Sükhebaatur as the brilliant leader of the Mongolian revolution.

See also ARMED FORCES OF MONGOLIA; 1921 REVOLUTION; REVOLUTIONARY PERIOD; THEOCRATIC PERIOD.

Further reading: L. Bat-Ochir and D. Dashjamts, "Sükhbaatar the Supreme Hero," in *Mongolian Heroes of the Twentieth Century*, trans. Urgunge Onon (New York: AMS Press, 1976), 143–192; Owen Lattimore, *Nationalism and Revolution in Mongolia* (Oxford: Oxford University Press, 1955).

Sükhebaatur province (**Süchbaatar, Sühbaatar, Suke-Bator, Sükhbaatar**) Sükhebaatur province, lying in southeastern Mongolia, was carved out of Eastern (then Choibalsang and Khentii provinces in 1941. The province is named after GENERAL SÜKHEBAATUR, who was a native of the province. It has a long frontier with central Inner Mongolia in China.

The province's territory includes all the prerevolutionary DARIGANGA herd, an area that raised livestock for the Qing emperor in Beijing and that until 1912 was attached to CHAKHAR in Inner Mongolia. To the north and east it includes territory that belonged to KHALKHA Mongolia's prerevolutionary Setsen Khan and Tüshiyetü Khan provinces.

Its 82,300 square kilometers (31,780 square miles) belong to Mongolia's eastern steppe and are the site of several extinct volcanos. Its population of 30,700 in 1956 rose to 55,900 in 2000. Its total livestock population of 1,492,500 head is notable for the relatively high numbers of HORSES (192,200 head) and CATTLE (209,600 head). SHEEP, however, are the most numerous, at 717,300 head. The capital, Baruun-Urt, has 15,100 people (2000 figure);

somewhat less than half the city's inhabitant are of Dariganga Mongol origin.

See also DASHBALBAR, OCHIRBATYN; MINING.

sum (**sumu, somon, soum**) First introduced as a militia unit under the QING DYNASTY, the *sum* (Middle Mongolian, *sumu*) is now the basic unit of rural administration in both Mongolia proper and Inner Mongolia.

Sum or *sumu* translates the Manchu term *niru*, "arrow," and designated a militia company. Under the Manchus' Qing dynasty (1636–1912) the Mongol *sumus* were fixed as a unit of 150 households, each supplying one able-bodied man. The *sumu* was divided into three 50-man units that rotated with one unit on active duty and the other two on reserve. The *sumu* was headed by a company captain (*sumun-u janggi*) assisted by a lieutenant (*orolan khööegchi*) who supervised the active duty unit. *Sumus* were divided into 50s and 20s so called from the number of households. In large, sparsely inhabited areas such as KHALKHA and ALASHAN, the subdivisions were called *bag* (teams).

The Mongolian *sumus* were combined into BANNERS. The number of *sumus* per banner varied widely. Inner Mongolia's 49 autonomous banners averaged more than 25 *sumus* per banner, and one banner, Monggoljin (Fuxin), had 97. KHALKHA's 86 autonomous banners, on the other hand, averaged less than two *sumus* per banner, and none had more than 14. While membership in the *sumus* was hereditary, they were not territorial communities, and herders could pasture their flocks anywhere in the banner.

In 1931 Mongolia was redivided into 18 provinces each with 15 to 25 *sums*. In 1990 the slightly more than 300 *sums* had an average of 5,000 square kilometers (1,930 square miles) of territory and a little more than 2,500 persons each. *Sum* members are not allowed to pasture their flocks outside their *sum* except in case of emergency. Under collectivization, from 1960 to 1992, the *sums* were coextensive with either cooperatives (*negdels*) or state farms (*sangiin aj akhui*). The *sum* local administration was thus largely merged with the cooperative or state farm management (*see* COLLECTIVIZATION AND COLLECTIVE HERDING). Since DECOLLECTIVIZATION the *sums* have reemerged as a discrete, purely territorial administrative unit. Under collectivization the *sums* were divided into brigades, which have now been renamed *bags*.

In the INNER MONGOLIA AUTONOMOUS REGION *sumus* are the subbanner rural administrative unit in areas where Mongols are either the majority or a large minority. (Elsewhere the subbanner or county rural unit is the *xiang*, or township.) From 1958 to 1985 Inner Mongolian herding and agriculture were also collectivized, and the *sumu* was coextensive with the commune (*gongshe*). In Buriatia the term *somon* was adopted in 1923 as the lowest unit of rural administration, equivalent to Russian *selo* (settlement) and used until 1965, when the Russian term was reinstated.

Su-pei   *See* SUBEI MONGOL AUTONOMOUS COUNTY.

Sutra of the Wise and Foolish (*Ocean of Story, Üliger-ün dalai*)   Stories of Shakyamuni Buddha's earlier lives, called *jataka* in Sanskrit (*chadig* in Mongolian), have been a popular genre of literature in Mongolia as in all Buddhist countries. These stories often resemble beast fables but have been transformed to teach Buddhist ethical lessons. A Chinese translation from a lost Sanskrit original was translated into Tibetan as the *mDzangs-blun zhes-bya-ba'i mdo* (Sutra to distinguish the wise and foolish), or *mDo mdzangs-blun* (Sutra of the wise and foolish) for short, in 632. Other slightly differing Tibetan translations with 51 or 52 *jataka*s also circulated, however. Extant, more literary, Indian versions include Arya Shura's *Jatakamala* (Garland of *jataka*s, English translation, *Once the Buddha Was a Monkey*) and Somadeva Bhatta's *Ocean of Story* (Sanskrit, *Kathasaritsagara*). Shiregetü Güüshi Chorjiwa (fl. 1578–1618), while at ERDENI ZUU, first translated the 52-*jataka* version into Mongolian from Tibetan as *Shilughun onol-tu sudur* (Sutra of the simple and the experienced). Toin Güüshi at HÖH-HOT made another translation around the same time. In 1655 ZAYA PANDITA NAMKHAI-JAMTSU (1599–1662) translated the 51-*jataka* version using the Oirat CLEAR SCRIPT as *Medeetei medee ügeyigi ilghagchi kemekü sudur* (Sutra to distinguish the wise and foolish). Shiregetü Güüshi Chorjiwa's version remained the most common, being block printed separately in 1714 and 1728 as well as being included in the printed Mongolian scriptures (bKa'-'gyur). *Üliger-ün dalai* (Ocean of story), the block printed title, became the usual Mongolian name.

See also DIDACTIC POETRY; LITERATURE.

Further reading: Stanley Frye, trans., *Sutra of the Wise and Foolish* (Mdo mdzaṅs-blun) *or Ocean of Story* (Üliger-ün Dalai) (Dharamsala: Library of Tibetan Works and Archives, 1981).

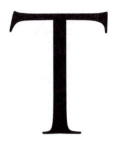

Ta'achar (Taghachar, Tājir) (d. 1296) *Mongol commander in the Middle Eastern Il-Khanate who overthrew three khans before being executed by his fourth khan, Ghazan Khan*

Ta'achar, of the minor Suqai'ud branch of the Baarin clan, served in the KESHIG (imperial guard) and ORDO (palace-tent) of Abagha Khan (1265–82) ruler of the Mongols in the Middle East. In 1281 Abagha deputed Ta'achar and Ordu-Qaya (d. 1291) to investigate charges against 'ALA'UD-DIN ATA-MALIK JUVAINI of withholding revenue. Under Abagha's brother Sultan Ahmad (1282–84) Ta'achar and Abagha's other intimate servitors—Qunchuqbal of the QONGGIRAD (d. 1296), Doladai of the TATARS (d. 1296), and Ordu-Qaya—formed a faction supporting the rival candidacy of Arghun, Abagha's eldest son. Imprisoned by Ahmad in January 1284, they were freed in July after BUQA enthroned Arghun.

Although Arghun made Ta'achar commander of his personal Qara'una *tümen* (10,000), Ta'achar resented Buqa's arrogance and tight control over state finances. Buqa fell in 1289, but the new vizier, SA'D-UD-DAWLA, now with Ordu-Qaya's support, continued this tight control. In 1291 Ta'achar's clique murdered the paralyzed khan (March 10) and then Sa'd-ud-Dawla and Ordu-Qaya.

After enthroning Arghun's brother Geikhatu and making Ta'achar's client Sadr-ud-Din Zanjani (d. 1298) vizier, the Mongol commanders (NOYAN) achieved freedom from financial oversight. Nevertheless, offended by Geikhatu's pederasty among the *keshig* pages, Tödechü jarghuchi (Judge Tödechü) of the Qongqotan conspired to enthrone Baidu instead. Geikhatu imprisoned Qunchuqbal and Doladai but entrusted Ta'achar with two *tümens* (10,000) to fight Baidu. Ta'achar seized control of the army, while the other conspirators escaped from prison. They killed Geikhatu on March 24, 1295.

The crown was forced on the easygoing Baidu, who knew his likely fate, and the kingdom was divided among the conspirators, with Ta'achar and Sadr-ud-Din receiving Anatolia and Diyarbakır. Even so, they resented Tödechü's receiving the wealthy city of Baghdad and Jamal-ud-Din Dastjerdani's receiving the ultimate prize of the vizierate. Thus, in May 1295 Ta'achar and Sadr-ud-Din secretly contacted the clique around Arghun's son Ghazan (1271–1304) in northeast Iran. When Ghazan and Baidu's armies met on September 26, Ta'achar's desertion gave the challenger victory. As agreed, GHAZAN KHAN made Sadr-ud-Din vizier, but Ta'achar was again relegated to Anatolia, where Ghazan had him discretely murdered in May 1296. Sadr-ud-Din Zanjani was executed two years later.

Taghachar *See* TA'ACHAR.

Ta Hsing-an Ling *See* GREATER KHINGGAN RANGE.

Taichuud *See* TAYICHI'UD.

taiji (tayiji, taij) The title *taiji* was the title of the nobility among the Mongols proper and the OIRATS from the 16th century. (It is not be confused with TAISHI, which is of completely different origin and significance.) The title originated from Chinese *taizi* (prince, son of the emperor) and was first used for the proliferating aristocracy composed of sons and descendants of CHINGGIS KHAN's descendant BATU-MÖNGKE DAYAN KHAN (1480?–1517?). By 1594 the Chinese observer Xiao Daheng was already treating these *taiji* as a kind of petty nobility between the king or sovereign and the common Mongols.

When the Manchu QING DYNASTY (1636–1912) reorganized Inner Mongolia into autonomous BANNERS (appanages), it confirmed most of the privileges of the Mongolian *taiji* class and extended the term to those local Mongol rulers claiming descent from Chinggis Khan's brothers. Even the completely non-Chinggisid nobility of the KHARACHIN and Monggoljin (modern Fuxin) banners were designated (within their banners) as *taiji*. At the same time, the mostly non-Chinggisid nobility of the Oirats in the 17th century adopted the title, which was preserved among the KALMYKS until the late 19th century. When the Qing conquered the Oirats, however, only the banner ZASAGs (rulers) received rights of nobility, while their petty nobility were entitled *zaisangs* and not given the privileges of *taiji*.

Under the Qing dynasty the *taiji* were all ranked based on their traditional prominence, seniority, and service to the dynasty. Below the titled nobility of princes and dukes, the ordinary *taijis* were graded in four ranks. In practice, the term *taiji* by itself often referred only to these lower nontitled nobility. The commoner population was either wholly (Inner Mongolia) or partially (KHALKHA Mongolia) assigned to the various *taijis*. The *taijis* and their ladies received domestic and pastoral services from their subjects. *Taijis* divided up their subjects among their sons and also bestowed subjects as dowry (INJE) along with their daughters. Qing law, however, removed their previous criminal jurisdiction and limited their exactions. Only *taijis* could be *zasags* or administrators (*tusalagchi taiji*).

The number of *taijis* proliferated compared to the commoners, reaching up to 42 percent of some banners, although the average in Khalkha was about 10 percent of the lay population. As the *taiji* class increased in size, many inherited no subjects and became *khokhi taijis*, "destitute taijis."

As descendants of Chinggis Khan or his brothers, the *taijis* bore the clan name BORJIGID or its synonym, Kiyad. The banner offices kept *taiji* genealogies, updated every three years. In many banners different families of *taijis* were represented, sons of different Dayan Khanid lines or of brothers of Chinggis Khan. Generally, *taijis* married commoners; husbands of *taiji* women received the rank of *tabunang*. By the 17th century intermarriage among the descendants of Chinggis Khan himself and those of his brothers was accepted, although some authors such as Rashipungsug (fl. 1774–75) criticized the practice.

The *taijis'* privileges were abolished in Kalmykia in 1892, in Mongolia in 1922–24, and in Inner Mongolia under the Japanese (1931–45). During the leftist period of 1929–32 in Mongolia, activists disenfranchised the *taiji*, confiscated their herds, and burned their genealogical records. In Inner Mongolia the Soviet invasion of 1945 and rural class conflict and herd reform supported by the Chinese Communists in 1946–52 led to similar measures.

Further reading: Junko Miyawaki, "Birth of the Khung-Tayiji Viceroyalty in the Mongol-Oyirad World," in *Altaica Berolinensia: The Concept of Sovereignty in the Altaic World*, ed. Barbara Kellner-Heinkele (Wiesbaden: Otto Harrassowitz, 1993), 149–155.

taishi (tayisi, taisha) The title *taishi* was used for distinguished non-Chinggisid rulers among the Mongols, OIRATS, and BURIATS. (It is not to be confused with TAIJI, a title of completely different origin and significance.)

Taishi in Chinese means "grand preceptor" and was used as a high honorific title. The Kitan Liao dynasty (907–1125) bestowed the title on prominent chiefs of the MONGOLIAN PLATEAU, thus making it a prestigious title among the KEREYID tribe and the MONGOL TRIBE in the decades before CHINGGIS KHAN (Genghis, 1206–27). In 1217 Chinggis Khan granted it to his viceroy in North China, MUQALI.

Under the Mongol YUAN DYNASTY (1206/71–1368) Emperor Temür (posthumous reign name Chengzong, 1294–1307) revived the time-honored Chinese practice of granting the court's three chief officials honorific titles: "grand preceptor" (*taishi*), "grand mentor" (*taifu*), and "grand guardian" (*taibao*). From then until the end of the dynasty, these titles confirmed the power of the top-ranking Mongol officials, usually of prestigious NÖKÖR (companion) families. They were never held by members of the royal family.

After the expulsion of the Yuan from China, the Mongol khans of the northern Yuan continued to grant these titles to their officials. After 1403 Arugtai Taishi (d. 1434) of the Asud clan (*see* OSSETES) became the first of many *taishi*s to reduce their khans to puppets. Under him and the Oirats Toghoon (d. 1438) and ESEN (r. 1438–54) the *taishi*s became the real rulers. As with the *beglerbegi*s of the western khanates (*see* KESHIG), a key privilege of the *taishi* was to be QUDA (marriage allies) with the khan. The title also entered the Chinggis Khan cult, in which a *taishi* headed the shrine's mock court (*see* EIGHT WHITE YURTS).

The Chinggisid revival under BATU-MÖNGKE DAYAN KHAN (1480?–1517?) drove out the Oirats and eliminated the *taishi*, replacing it with rule through princes (*taiji*) of his own blood. Among the Oirats the title of *taishi* continued to be used for the chiefs of the great tribes (conventionally numbered as four), even though they no longer were associated with Chinggisid khans. In the 17th century the Oirats slowly replaced *taishi* with *khan* or *khung-taiji*, while *taiji* (originally restricted to petty Chinggisid nobility) became used for lesser Oirat chiefs. Russian diplomats, familiar since 1600 with the term *taishi* (under the form *taisha*), confused it with the new *taiji*, so that *taisha* thus became the Russian translation for the Kalmyk-Oirat *taiji* (petty nobility).

Among the Buriats, who lacked centralized single-lineage rule, the term *taisha* (from *taishi*) was used, along with other administrative terms borrowed from older Oirat and early Khalkha usage, for the highest level of clan chiefs. While some *taishas* ruled a few hundred households, the head *taisha* of the Khori and Aga tribes had at least nominal authority over thousands.

Tâjir *See* TA'ACHAR.

Tamerlane *See* TIMUR.

tammachi *Tammachi* armies were dispatched by the Mongol khans as permanent garrison troops in sedentary lands. The term originated from the Chinese *tanma* (medieval pronunciation, *tamma*), "scout horse," used during the Tang dynasty (608–906). Succeeding dynasties used the term for escort or bodyguard soldiers.

After shattering the main armies of the JIN DYNASTY in North China, CHINGGIS KHAN (Genghis, 1206–27) appointed his old companion MUQALI his viceroy in China in 1217 and assigned him a *tammachi*. The 1,000-man vanguard was chosen two by two from each of the other 10 clans and tribes of the Mongols and so designated *Qoshiqul*, "pairs." Of the rest, 12,000 were from five semiautonomous clans of the MONGOL TRIBE: the Uru'ud, the MANGGHUD, the QONGGIRAD, the Ikires, and Muqali's own JALAYIR. These five clans came to be called the "Five Touxia," or "Five Appanages." Another 10,000 men were from the large Turkish-speaking ÖNGGÜD tribe in Inner Mongolia. Finally, an undetermined but large number came from local Kitan, Tangut, and Han (ethnic Chinese) troops who had deserted the Jurchen-dominated Jin dynasty. Although Muqali's *tammachi* soldiers were mostly discrete tribal units, the command was exceedingly diverse, and Muqali's leading lieutenants were from the TATARS, KEREYID, and Han.

ÖGEDEI KHAN (1229–41) formed new *tammachi* units and dispatched them to the frontiers. One *tammachi* of three (some sources say four) *tümens* (10,000s) was levied and put under CHORMAQAN, a member of Chinggis's bodyguard. This unit, like Muqali's, was also ethnically diverse, consisting of Sönid, Besüd, and Ghorolas clans of the Mongols, in addition to a *tümen* of men conscripted from Uighuristan, the cities of Turkestan, and Türkmen nomads. These men conquered and held the area of western Iran, the Caucasus, KURDISTAN, and Iraq. Another *tammachi* unit under Tangghud was dispatched to the border of Korea and Manchuria. MÖNGKE KHAN (1251–59) placed Sali of the Tatars in command of two *tümens* sent to northeast Afghanistan with a mandate to conquer India.

The *SECRET HISTORY OF THE MONGOLS* links the *tammachi* and *alginchi* (scouts) troops with the DARUGHACHIs, or overseers, as the pillars of Mongol rule over distant sedentary lands. The *darughachis* oversaw the local officials in the cities, while the *alginchis* and *tammachis* supplied the local military force to deal with any revolt. *Tammachi* armies were accompanied by their families and were expected to reproduce their ranks from generation to generation. Service as a *tammachi* was thus sometimes tantamount to exile. When Sali, on being assigned to conquer India and KASHMIR, asked the khan how long he would be there, Möngke replied, "You will be there forever." The *tammachi* commanders, appointed to frontiers far from the khan, had virtually unlimited power over their territories, appointing *darughachis* and collecting taxes freely.

As regular Mongol administration expanded out to the frontiers, the autonomy of the *tammachi* armies declined. Only Sali's *tammachis*, isolated on the border of India, retained their former independence, becoming the turbulent QARA'UNAS. Under Ögedei and Möngke Khans civil administrators gradually restricted the power of Chormaqan and his successor, BAIJU, of the Besüd. When Möngke's brother HÜLE'Ü (1256–65) arrived in western Iran with a vast army, Baiju first lost his autonomy and was later executed. While Chormaqan's son Shiremün enjoyed authority under Hüle'ü and his son, Abagha Khan (1265–81), most of his *tammachi* commanders were eventually disgraced and their units reduced to the status of the other Mongol units.

In North China the descendants of Muqali retained their high position but soon lost control of the *tammachi*. In 1236 Ögedei assigned new troops to the *tammachis* of North China and ordered them to garrison the major prefectural seats. In 1255 the *tammachi* households were demobilized. In the conflicts after Möngke Khan's death the heads of the "Five Touxia" clans all supported QUBILAI KHAN (1260–94), and in 1262 Qubilai ordered the *tammachi* men called up again, this time serving under the general military command. In 1284 the *tammachi* armies were transferred to the jurisdiction of JINGIM, the heir apparent. Jingim's mother and wife were the Qonggirad family, and the *tammachi* armies became the military foundation for the Qonggirad influence in the dynasty until the clan's decline in 1340.

Tammachi armies served to the end of the YUAN DYNASTY (1271–1368) primarily as garrisons in the Hebei, Shandong, and Shanxi areas of North China. Repeated levies of soldiers impoverished many *tammachi* households, and the government attempted unsuccessfully to encourage agriculture among them. In 1320 reports of *tammachi* households leasing their pastures in North China to provide equipment for their tour of duty show both their hardship and yet how their lives still revolved around pastures and military service.

See also INDIA AND THE MONGOLS; MILITARY OF THE MONGOL EMPIRE.

Further reading: Koichi Matsuda, "On the Ho-nan Army," *Memoirs of the Research Department of the Toyo Bunko* 50 (1992): 29–55.

Tanguts *See* XIA DYNASTY.

Tanjur *See* BKA'-'GYUR AND BSTAN-'GYUR.

Tannu Tuva *See* TUVANS.

Taoism in the Mongol Empire (Daoism)

While the Taoist adept Changchun won favor under CHINGGIS KHAN, Taoism suffered persecution under QUBILAI KHAN but was again honored by later Yuan emperors. At the time of the Mongol conquest of North China, Taoism was undergoing important changes. Under the JIN DYNASTY (1115–1234) a controversial new Taoist sect called Complete Realization (Quanzhen) spread from its cradle in Shandong. Its founders combined extraordinary ascetic powers, strict monastic organization, and a popular preaching style. At the time of the Mongol conquest, this school's MASTER CHANGCHUN (1148–1227) received invitations from the rival powers in North China, but Master Changchun accepted the summons of Chinggis Khan (Genghis, 1206–27) only, visiting him in Afghanistan. In return for his instruction, Chinggis bestowed on Changchun edicts making him and his temples DARQAN, or tax exempt, and appointing him chief of all the monks in China. In the hardship and chaos of the Mongol invasion, many laymen sought a living by joining tax exempt Complete Realization Taoist temples. Chinese settlers deported to cities such as Chinqai (*see* CHINQAI) and QARA-QORUM established Taoist temples in Mongolia and Central Asia. Changchun's disciples also took over large numbers of Buddhist temples.

This aggressive expansion brought resistance, and in 1230 Changchun's disciple Li Zhichang was briefly arrested for defaming Buddhism. Under ÖGEDEI KHAN (1229–41) the Buddhist-Confucian minister YELÜ CHUCAI secured equal treatment for Buddhism, Taoism, and CONFUCIANISM. In 1237 Yelü Chucai tried to limit the number of monks and control heretical teachings by using examinations to dismiss improper Taoist and Buddhist monks, yet marks of special favor to Complete Realization Taoism continued. Li Zhichang tutored the Mongol princes in Yanjing (modern Beijing), while Empress TÖREGENE sponsored a historic block printing of the complete Taoist canon in 1240–44. In 1251 MÖNGKE KHAN appointed Li chief of all Taoist priests. From 1255 to 1257, however, Li actively promoted in Qara-Qorum the Taoist view that Buddhism was only a barbarous form of Taoism. In 1258, after a debate in the presence of Möngke's brother Qubilai, this claim was officially declared refuted, and 237 temples were forcibly converted to Buddhism. When Qubilai became khan (1260–94), the controversy continued, until in 1281 Qubilai banned the newly printed Taoist canon, sparing only Laozi's *Dao De Jing* (*Tao Te Ching*).

In South China the leading school was the Celestial Master (Tianshi) sect, based at Dragon and Tiger Mountain (*Longhu Shan*) in Jiangxi. Southern Taoism was less ascetic, more cultured, and had a smaller following than the northern form. After his conquest of the south in 1276, Qubilai Khan summoned the Celestial Master to his capital, SHANGDU. After a favorable interview, the master returned south, leaving his disciple Zhang Liusun (d. 1322) behind at the court. Zhang was an able physician and won the favor of Qubilai's heir apparent, JINGIM (Zhenjin), who prevented enforcement of Qubilai's anti-Taoist edicts. In 1278 Qubilai appointed Zhang the patriarch of a new Mysterious Teaching (Xuanjiao) order, separate from that of the Celestial Masters. Under Zhang's advice he put southern Taoist temples under a government office staffed by literati, the Academy of Scholarly Worthies.

After Qubilai's death and the accession of Jingim's sons and grandsons, Taoism again received lavish patronage. Zhang Liusun's disciple Wu Quanjie managed prayer services at the coronation of Temür (titled Chengzong, 1294–1307). Temür made Zhang Liusun cochair of the Academy of Scholarly Worthies and appointed him to lecture on the *Zhuangzi*. The other branches of Taoism were not forgotten, however. In 1304 Temür invested the Celestial Master of Dragon and Tiger Mountain as head of the Orthodox Unity (Zhengyi) school. South Chinese Confucian scholars began using their friendship with influential southern Taoist clerics to advance at court, stimulating a close synthesis between Confucianism and Taoism in South China.

Zhu Yuanzhang (titled Ming Taizu, 1368–99), who overthrew Mongol rule and founded the MING DYNASTY, abolished the Mongol-created Mysterious Teaching order but left untouched the ascetic Complete Realization order in the north and the more flexible Celestial Master order in the south.

See also BUDDHISM IN THE MONGOL EMPIRE; EAST ASIAN SOURCES ON THE MONGOL EMPIRE; RELIGIOUS POLICY IN THE MONGOL EMPIRE.

Further reading: Li Chih-ch'ang, *Travels of an Alchemist,* trans. Arthur Waley (1931; rpt. New York: AMS Press, 1979); K'o-k'uan Sun, "Yü Chi and Southern Taoism during the Yüan Period," in *China under Mongol Rule,* ed. John D. Langlois, Jr. (Princeton, N.J.: Princeton University Press, 1981), 212–253.

tarqan *See* DARQAN.

Tartars *See* TATARS.

Tatars The tribal name *Tatar* served successively as a name for the nomads of Mongolia as a whole, for a Mongolia-speaking tribe in the HULUN BUIR area, for the Mongol conquerors as a whole, and for the Turkish-speaking Muslim peoples in the Russian Empire. The Tatar name first appears in the Turkic Kül-Tegin inscription of 731, in which the "Thirty Tatars" and the "Nine Tatars" are grouped with various peoples as enemies of the Türks (*see* TÜRK EMPIRES). The Tatars seem to have been east of the Türks' central Mongolian heartland, perhaps in the area east and southeast of LAKE BAIKAL, in what would later be the Mongol heartland.

The Tatars next appear around 842, when they submitted to the Kyrgyz Empire based in southern Siberia (modern Khakassia). After the decline of the unstable Kyrgyz Empire, the Tatars flourished. They appear regularly in the Chinese records as "Dadan" (derived from Tatar) and also in Persian and Islamic records. Ibn al-Athir described the Tatars and the KITANS in 1043 as the only nomads untouched by Islam. Around the same time Mahmud Kashghari, the Turkish lexicographer, described the Tatars as people who speak their own language but "also know Turkish." This presumably indicates that the Tatar were Mongolic speaking. By this time the Kitan Liao dynasty in North China and Manchuria had established its dominance over the MONGOLIAN PLATEAU. In 942 Kitan armies attacked and defeated several branches of the "Tatars," a term that Kitan inscriptions used for a wide variety of nomadic peoples of Mongolia.

Sources based on Mongol oral history, however, use the term *Tatar* only for a particular tribe in the modern Hulun Buir area of northeast Inner Mongolia. The Tatars, even in this narrow sense, numbered 70,000 households according to RASHID-UD-DIN FAZL-ULLAH. The tribe was divided into numerous clans, such as the Chagha'an (White) Tatar, the Alchi Tatar, and the Tutuqli'ud (Chiefly) Tatar. The JIN DYNASTY in North China enrolled the Tatars as *jüyin*, or border auxiliaries, receiving subsidies from the dynasty in return for joining Jin attacks on hostile tribes, especially the MONGOL TRIBE to their west. At times, however, the Tatars would threaten the Jin themselves and had to be attacked. Rashid-ud-Din describes the Tatars as courageous and savage warriors, like the Kurds and the Frankish Crusaders; if they had only been united, they would have been irresistible. Economically, the Tatars seem to have benefited from their relations with the Jin dynasty. The children of Tatar chiefs had silver cradles, gold nose rings, gold-embroidered silk clothes, and pearl-encrusted quilts. The Mongol chiefs, by contrast, were reduced to wooden stirrups and arrows of bone.

Apart from their internal feuds, the Tatars fought repeatedly against the Mongol tribe and the KEREYID Khanate. The feud with the Mongols was blamed on the Tatar shaman Chargil-Nudui, who had been invited to cure Sayin-Tegin, the QONGGIRAD brother-in-law of the Mongol Qabul Khan. When Sayin-Tegin died, the Qonggirad killed Chargil, and the Mongols backed them as allies. On later occasions, when the Tatars captured Mongol chiefs, they would hand them over to the Jin dynasty to be nailed to a wooden mule. Qabul's son Ökin-Barqaq and his successor, Hambaghai Khan, both died this way. In their battles against the Kereyid, the Tatars at one point captured the wife of the Kereyid khan and her son Toghril (later ONG KHAN).

One khan of the Mongols, Hambaghai, was captured after sending his daughter in marriage to a friendly clan of Tatars. Later, YISÜGEI BA'ATUR, another Mongol chief, was poisoned by a party of Tatars when coming home from the camp of his son's betrothed Qonggirad bride. This son, Temüjin (later CHINGGIS KHAN), was himself named in 1164 after a captive Yisügei had taken from the Tatars in battle. Chinggis Khan thus inherited the traditional Mongol feud with the Tatars.

Not until 1196, however, did Chinggis Khan get an opportunity for revenge. After 1190 the new Jin emperor had ceased the raids on the Mongols, and in 1196 his grand councillor, Wanyan Xiang, was dispatched to attack Me'üjin-Se'ültü, who had unified the Tatars around his fortress on the Ulz River. Wanyan Xiang sought the aid of Chinggis Khan's Kiyad Mongols, the Yürkin Mongols, and Toghril Khan's Kereyid Khanate. Chinggis and Toghril killed Me'üjin Se'ültü and seized rich booty. Later, the Tatars, under Jalin-Buqa of the Alchi Tatar, supported Chinggis Khan's rival, JAMUGHA, who was enthroned as a rival to Chinggis in 1201. Chinggis Khan dispersed this coalition and in autumn 1202 launched a campaign of annihilation against four major Tatar clans. The Mongols were victorious, and Chinggis Khan, remembering the long Mongol feud, decreed that all Tatars taller than a linch pole would be slaughtered and the small children enslaved. When the Tatars learned of this decision, they organized for a desperate last stand but were destroyed, and the sentence carried out. The Tatars disappeared as a corporate tribal body.

When the Mongols conquered Eurasia, Muslim and Chinese writers continued to call all the nomads of the Mongolian plateau Tatars, as they had since the 10th century. In western Europe this unfamiliar name was distorted further to "Tartar"; medieval writers punned that the name was appropriate for a savage people from Tartarus (that is, hell). The Chinese envoy Zhao Gong reported that in the 1220s the Mongols still accepted this term for themselves. The Mongols, however, soon came to object to this term and insisted that they be called Mongols. Eventually, the term *Tatar* went out of use among writers subject to the Mongols, but it continued to be used by Indians, Arabs, Russians, and Europeans. Through the Russian use of the term the people of the Turco-Islamic successor states of the GOLDEN HORDE came to refer to themselves as Tatars, although only a few leading families were of Mongol descent.

Despite the extermination of the Tatar tribe, a surprising number of Tatars achieved high office in the later MONGOL EMPIRE. SHIGI QUTUQU, a Tatar foundling, became chief judge (JARGHUCHI) of the Mongol Empire. Chinggis took two Tatar women, Yisüi and Yisülün, as his empresses, and several men from their family remained alive due to their intercession; Sali, Mongol conqueror of KASHMIR, was a descendant of one. Other Tatar clans who joined the Mongol aristocracy presumably started in the same way. Even so, the Tatars never again achieved independent influence, and the clan name *Tatar* is currently found only among the Monggoljin in southeast Inner Mongolia.

Tatar-Tong'a (Tatatungga) (fl. 1204–c. 1235) *First scribe at the Mongol court*

An Uighur scribe, Tatar-Tong'a first served at the court of the western Mongolian NAIMAN ruler Tayang Khan. (The spelling Tatatungga is an erroneous reconstruction from Chinese). After Tayang Khan's defeat by CHINGGIS KHAN at the Battle of Keltegei Cliffs in 1204, the Mongols captured Tatar-Tong'a as he wandered the battlefield with the state seal frantically looking for his sovereign. Chinggis Khan was impressed by the scribe's loyalty and brought him into his service. Under Tatar-Tong'a's influence Chinggis Khan also began to use a seal to authenticate official documents. He had Tatar-Tong'a teach the crown princes how to read and write the Uighur script, which, once adapted to the MONGOLIAN LANGUAGE, became the Mongol script still used today. When one of Tatar-Tong'a's pupils, Ögedei, became khan, he again put Tatar-Tong'a in charge of the imperial jade seal as well as the imperial treasuries. Ögedei asked Tatar-Tong'a's wife to serve as wet nurse for his son Qarachar. Tatar-Tong'a died in ÖGEDEI KHAN's reign; his sons all served in the court of QUBILAI KHAN.

See also UIGHUR-MONGOLIAN SCRIPT.

Tatatungga   *See* TATAR-TONG'A.

Ta-tu   *See* DAIDU.

Tayichi'ud (Taichuud)   The Tayichi'ud clan was one of the leading clans of the Mongols before CHINGGIS KHAN's rise and the main rivals of his youth. The second khan of the Mongols, Hambaghai Khan, was of the Tayichi'ud clan. After his death the Tayichi'ud became rivals of the Kiyad clans (the descendants of Hambaghai Khan's cousin and predecessor, Qabul Khan).

Like all Mongol clans, the Tayichi'ud consisted of a ruling lineage, the descendants of Charaqa Lingqum and their subject clans. Subject clans included the Suldus, Besüd, Targhud, and Je'üred. Later Mongol legend estimated the clan's total number at 300 households. The Tayichi'ud rulers were notorious for their divisions.

In 1172, when YISÜGEI BA'ATUR, a major Kiyad leader, died, the Tayichi'ud seized power away from his widow Ö'ELÜN ÜJIN. When Yisügei's son Temüjin (the future Chinggis Khan) reached adolescence, they captured him. Temüjin escaped with the aid of a Suldus family, and as he matured he nourished a deep hatred of the Tayichi'ud. Chinggis secured the allegiance of several Tayichi'ud subjects and at one point induced the whole Je'üred to defect.

The Tayichi'ud eventually supported JAMUGHA of the Jajirad clan as khan. In 1201 Chinggis Khan, having defeated Jamugha, finally defeated the Tayichi'ud and enslaved them. Few members of the Tayichi'ud later achieved prominence in the MONGOL EMPIRE. The Tayichi'ud clan name is currently found in southeastern Inner Mongolia.

tayiji   *See* TAIJI.

tea   Tea, almost always boiled with milk and salt, forms one of the chief foods of the Mongols. While the Mongols, of course, had to import their tea from China, the habit of drinking it appears to have been a Tibetan influence. From the Northern SONG DYNASTY (960–1127) on, Chinese tea was traded on a large scale to Tibetans and UIGHURS. In the 15th century only those Mongols in Gansu, ancestors of today's Yogur nationality and loyal Tibetan Buddhists, drank tea (*see* YOGUR LANGUAGES AND PEOPLES). Tea first came to the rest of the Mongols as part of Tibetan-rite Buddhist services; the first Mongolian requests to trade horses for tea with China in 1577–78 were connected with religious rites. By 1600, however, tea was becoming a regular part of the Mongolian diet.

In recent centuries "milk tea" (Uighur-Mongolian, *sü-tei chai*, Cyrillic, *süütei tsai*) has become the regular accompaniment of every meal and often the meal itself. Tea is boiled with water, milk, and salt in a large wok (*togoo*) with repeated ladling as it comes to a boil. Sometimes milk tea is made without any tea at all, only water, milk, and salt; this is called *khyarman tsai* and is mostly drunk in eastern KHALKHA, by youths, and in the summer. Milk tea is drunk throughout the year, although during the winter milk may run short so that plain tea with salt is sometimes drunk. Tea aspersions are made as offerings to heaven during the celebrations of the WHITE MONTH (lunar new year).

Milk tea often forms the whole morning meal, particularly in cold weather. Not only butter but also millet, rice, or flour is mixed into tea. In the morning cold meat is often heated up by being put in tea. The result is not so much tea as a kind of salty stew.

Under the QING DYNASTY the Mongols made tea with brick tea imported from the Hubei area in central China. Such bricks were even used as money in Khalkha Mongolia. After 1929 independent Mongolia's trade with China was restricted to the Soviet bloc, and the Mongols eventually changed their tastes to prefer black tea from GEORGIA in the Caucasus. The INNER MONGOLIANS still use Hubei brick tea.

See also CHINESE TRADE AND MONEYLENDING; FOOD AND DRINK; MONEY, MODERN.

Teb Tenggeri (Kökechü) (d. c. 1210) *Shaman who proclaimed Chinggis Khan's heavenly mission*

Teb Tenggeri's father, Münglig, was of the commoner Qongqotan lineage and a senior follower of CHINGGIS

Preparing tea inside a Mongolian yurt. Khöwsgöl Province, 1992 *(Courtesy Christopher Atwood)*

KHAN. He had seven sons. For his services Chinggis Khan later granted Münglig his widowed mother, Ö'ELÜN, in marriage. Münglig's middle son, Kökechü, was a powerful shaman able to walk naked in Mongolia's coldest winters and to make ice steam. The Mongols believed he rode into heaven on a gray steed. He is also said to have understood ASTROLOGY. His shamanist title, "Teb Tenggeri," means "Wholly Heavenly." His proclamation that Chinggis Khan was the heaven-destined ruler powerfully influenced the Mongols, and the title Chinggis was bestowed on him in 1206 by Teb Tenggeri. Around 1210 Teb Tenggeri and his brothers began to challenge Chinggis's family, attacking the khan's brothers Qasar and Temüge Odchigin while claiming that heaven might take the throne from Chinggis. Stiffened by his mother and wife, who saw the seven brothers of the Qongqotan as a threat to the dynastic succession, Chinggis allowed his brother (Qasar or Temüge—accounts differ) to kill Teb Tenggeri in a WRESTLING match, and the Qongqotan family declined in power. Chinggis Khan himself assumed the shamanic function of communicating with heaven.

See also SCAPULIMANCY; SHAMANISM.

Teh, Prince   *See* DEMCHUBDONGRUB, PRINCE.

Temple of Chinggis Khan   *See* CHINGGIS KHAN CONTROVERSY.

Temüder (d. 1322) *Notorious financial official who attempted to resolve the Mongol Yuan dynasty's chronic deficits with aggressive taxation*
A personal retainer of QUBILAI KHAN (1260–94), Temüder served in the palace provisions and postroad (JAM) administrations under Temür (1294–1307). During the interregnum of 1311 his patroness, Empress Targi of the QONGGIRAD, had Temüder briefly promoted to senior grand councillor. In 1314 Temüder was again promoted to the office and proposed an aggressive plan for fiscal retrenchment. The plan involved collecting salt and iron monopoly taxes a year in advance, a comprehensive land survey, and strict control over both the bureaucracy and the Mongol appanages. Although Emperor Ayurbarwada (1311–20) approved the plan, violent opposition blocked the cadastral survey. Despite this setback, government expenditures were cut significantly. In 1317 censors exposed numerous instances of personal corruption and

nepotism, forcing Temüder to flee to the ORDO (palace-tent) of Targi. Protests greeted Temüder's later appointment as tutor to the heir apparent until the heir's sudden death made the issue moot. In 1320, with Ayurbarwada's death, Empress Targi again made Temüder senior grand councillor. While Temüder's persecution of his opponents in the censorate alienated the new emperor, Shidebala (1320–23), Temüder remained in power until his death in 1322. Temüder's coterie, including his son Sonam, toppled Shidebala a year later, but the new monarch, Yisün-Temür (1323–28), executed Sonam.

Temür   *See* TIMUR.

Tenduc   *See* ÖNGGÜD.

tenger   *See* TENGGERI.

tenggeri (*tengri, tenger*)   *Tenggeri* refers to both heaven and, in older Mongolian, to God and the gods, although in modern KHALKHA Mongolian it usually means simply "sky."

The word *tenggeri* is a common Turco-Mongolian word possibly used as early as the XIONGNU (Huns), 2,000 years ago. It is found in Old Turkish as *tengri*, but in Mongolian appears as *tenggeri* (modern *tenger*), with the basic meaning of "heaven." According to the 11th-century Turkish lexicographer Mahmud al-Kashghari, *tengri* meant God (writing in Arab he wrote Allah), the sky, and anything huge and immense. Other Turkish texts used *tengri* for Christian, Hindu, and Zoroastrian gods.

Under the MONGOL EMPIRE Möngke Tenggeri (Eternal Heaven) was the center of the Mongolian civic religion. Below heaven was Mother Etüken (or Ötüken), the sacred forest of the TÜRK EMPIRES, now designating all the earth and protecting the Mongol ruling family. The ruling lineage of CHINGGIS KHAN (1206–26) was originally born "with a destiny from Heaven above," and heaven spoke to the Mongols, identifying their true sovereign both through miraculous signs and through shamans who divined by mantic trance and SCAPULIMANCY. During moments of crisis or great decision, Chinggis and his successors would go to a high hill, remove their hats, sling their belts around their necks in a sign of humility, and plead with heaven for victory for the Mongols. All decrees began with the formula "By the power of Eternal Heaven, by the fortune of the Khan." At the opening (late May–early June) and closing (late July–early August) of the mare-milking season, the great khans, accompanied by a shaman, offered to heaven, the ancestors (including Chinggis Khan), and other deities aspersions (*sachul,* modern *satsal* or *tsatsal,*) of fermented mare's milk (KOUMISS or *airag*) taken from herds of pure white HORSES.

The Mongols believed their "Eternal Heaven" to be the *tian* (Heaven) of Chinese religions, the Islamic Allah, and the Christian God. This claim, reflected in vocabularies and translation practices, was at the heart of the Mongolian religious policy, based on asking the clergy of many religions to pray to God/heaven for the khan. Muslim authors such as 'ALA'UD-DIN ATA-MALIK JUVAINI and RASHID-UD-DIN FAZL-ULLAH thus considered the Mongols basically monotheistic, despite the many local and household cults.

With the conversion to Buddhism, the Mongols followed the Uighur example and used the term *tenggeri* as the name of the Hindu gods (*deva*). (In writing, the Mongols used the archaic Uighur spelling *tngri*, written without vowels.) In Buddhism these gods are not the creators or ultimate objects of worship but instead constitute simply one of the six births, mightier and more blessed than the human birth, but just as much in need of enlightenment. In practice, they are seen simply as supernaturally powerful and wealthy patrons of the Buddhist dharma. Of these Indra, already identified by the UIGHURS with the Zoroastrian Ahura Mazda and written *Khormusta*, thus entered the Mongolian pantheon as the king of the gods.

In recent centuries Mongolian peoples have traditionally spoken of 99 gods (now pronounced *tenger*), of whom the 55 in the west are helpful and the 44 in the east are harmful. (The number 99 is related to the 33 gods headed by Indra in the Buddhist scriptures.) In ORDOS Khormusta/Indra is said to be chief of them all, while Myalaan Tenger (Anointing God) heads the western gods and Ataa Ulaan Tenger (Jealous Red God) the eastern; among the western BURIATS Khormusta heads the western gods and Ataa Ulaan Tenger the western, and Malaan (i.e., Myalaan) Tenger is over all. Among the KHORCHIN Bayan Chagaan Tenggeri (Rich White God) in the southwest opposes Irô Shoro Tenggeri (Omen-Fork God) in the northeast. Some clans, such as the Khatagin of Ordos, worship only the Jealous Red God. The Buriat GESER epic speaks of the war of the two camps and the defeat of the Jealous Red God by Khormusta, a conflict that has been linked to the moiety-based social structure based on marriage exchange (*see* KINSHIP SYSTEM; QUDA).

As in empire times, Eternal Heaven and the 99 gods are worshiped by Mongols annually at the opening of the mare-milking season with 99 aspersions of the first fruits of milk. Also, before dawn on the first of the WHITE MONTH (lunar new year), the Mongols burn incense, bow down before heaven, and sprinkle TEA, butter, and fried bread to the 10 directions. Prayers to Eternal Heaven, as the one who destines all things, are also given during fire worship (*see* FIRE CULT) and the dedication of a new YURT, seeking good fortune and happiness for one's children and protection from disease and violence.

Further reading: C. R. Bawden, "A Prayer to Qan Ataga Tngri," *Central Asiatic Journal* 21 (1977): 199–207.

tengri See TENGGERI.

Tengyur See BKA'-'GYUR AND BSTAN-'GYUR.

theocratic period (Autonomous, Bogd Khaan, Olnoo Örgögdsön)

The theocratic period began with the 1911 RESTORATION of Mongolian independence and ended with the turbulent period of the REVOCATION OF AUTONOMY, the White Russian restoration of independence, and the 1921 REVOLUTION that installed a Soviet-supported revolutionary government. Its distinguishing feature was the supreme role of the Bogda (Holy One) or EIGHTH JIBZUNDAMBA KHUTUGTU (1870–1924), who ruled as the head of both religion and state.

INTERNATIONAL STATUS

Like its southern neighbor the Republic of China (1912–49), theocratic Mongolia emerged from the fall of the QING DYNASTY in 1911–12. Both entities were thus bound by the treaty system that the world powers had created with the Qing dynasty after 1840. This treaty system prohibited the Chinese government from erecting barriers to international trade. To contain rivalries among the powers, it also enjoined all signatories—the major powers of Europe, as well as Russia, the United States, and Japan—to respect China's formal sovereignty over the entire territory of the late Qing, including Mongolia and Tibet. Even so, all were allowed to create spheres of influence, in which one or another power had preferential rights to finance railroads and telegraph lines and station garrison troops. Respect for China's formal sovereignty did not preclude foreign powers from dealing directly with local governments.

Thus, while the Mongolian government hoped to become independent and the Chinese government hoped to incorporate Mongolia as an integral part of China, the internationally recognized formula, ratified in the KYAKHTA TRILATERAL TREATY of 1915, was that Mongolia was an autonomous state within Chinese suzerainty but also in the Russian sphere of influence. The Russian Revolution of 1917–21 upset this formula by allowing the Republic of China to recover real control over Mongolia in 1919. In 1920–21, however, the White Russian commander BARON ROMAN FEDOROVICH VON UNGERN-STERNBERG drove out the Chinese before being himself driven out by the Soviet Red Army and its Mongolian partisan supporters. These changes were not recognized either by China or by the other powers, and the vexed question of Mongolia's status was bequeathed to the succeeding "people's government."

GOVERNMENT

The 1911 Restoration of Mongolian independence created an absolute monarchy under the Eighth Jibzundamba Khutugtu (1870–1912). He assumed the title of Bogda Khan (Holy Emperor), which had previously been borne by the Qing emperor, and like the Qing emperor proclaimed a reign title, making 1911 Year One of Olan-a Ergügdegsen (modern Olnoo Örgögdsön), "Elevated by the Many." The capital was named Neislel (Capital) Khüriye (modern ULAANBAATAR).

The new government consisted of five ministries: interior, foreign, finance, army, and justice. Except for the Interior Ministry, headed by Da Lama (monastic administrator of the GREAT SHABI) Tserinchimed (1872–1914), all the ministers were KHALKHA aristocrats. At first Tserinchimed functioned as the prime minister, but aristocratic opposition to clerical influence led in August 1912 to the creation of an office of prime minister, a position filled by the Sain Noyan Khan, Namnangsürüng (1878–1919). In September 1915 the prime minister's powers were greatly weakened, and another monk-bureaucrat, BADMADORJI (d. 1920), was put at the head of the Interior Ministry. Clerical domination of domestic administration thus increased.

Local government continued on the pattern of the Qing dynasty's BANNERS (appanages) and AIMAGS/LEAGUES, with their hereditary aristocracies. The four Khalkha and two DÖRBÖD leagues covered most of the territory. Far from restricting aristocratic privileges, the theocratic government extended them to areas where they had not previously existed (Dariganga, many Khowd banners, HULUN BUIR), and gave all high officials ranks of nobility. *Saids*, or viceroys, were appointed for KHOWD CITY, ULIASTAI, and KYAKHTA CITY (modern Altanbulag), but they had little influence and represented far less of a burden than the old Qing AMBANs.

The Bogda's personal estate and his Great Shabi, or personal subjects, were administered by a separate ministry headed by the ERDENI SHANGDZODBA, the Bogda's traditional steward. The Great Shabi, as the Bogda's personal subjects, did not pay taxes or perform military or corvée services for the state. After 1915 joining the Great Shabi became a profitable means of evading public duties, and the numbers climbed sharply. By 1918 about 15 percent of the population belonged to the Great Shabi.

Mongolian aristocrats had participated briefly in the late Qing parliament, and following a report by the Buriat adviser TSYBEN ZHAMATSARANOVICH ZHAMTSARANO (1881–1942), a bicameral advisory parliament was created in 1914. The upper house consisted of the titled nobility, INCARNATE LAMAS, and banner rulers, while the lower house consisted of officials and clerks in the various ministries. While neither elective nor controlling the cabinet, the parliament became a significant organ of public opinion.

FRONTIERS AND THE MILITARY

While the 1911 Restoration began among the Khalkha, the Bogda's ambition, shared by the top cabinet ministers, was to unify all the Mongolian BANNERS of the Qing dynasty into one state. This ambition was all the more important as many important officials and much of the soldiery on hand were Inner Mongolian emigrés. The aim was stymied both by Chinese military resistance and by diplomatic opposition from the powers, especially Russia. In 1912 the new government incorporated Hulun Buir, Dariganga, and the Khowd-Altai frontier districts. The Khowd-Altai frontier proved difficult to demarcate. On December 21, 1913, after repeated clashes, the Russian consul and China's Altay high commissioner divided the Altay district, leaving some ALTAI URIYANGKHAI Mongols on the Chinese side of the frontier. Despite the 1913 invasion of Inner Mongolia (*see* SINO-MONGOLIAN WAR), Russian pressure forced the Mongolian government at the 1914–15 Kyakhta Trilateral Conference to renounce both Hulun Buir and Inner Mongolia. Equally frustrating for the Mongols was the separation of Tuva (Tangnu Uriyangkhai) into an almost wholly Russian-controlled protectorate. Cossacks had entered Tuva in 1912, and in October 1914 the area was annexed to Russia's Yenisey province. By 1915 the current territory of the modern State of Mongolia was basically defined.

From 1911 to 1914 the theocratic government mobilized local banner troops, eventually building up a standing army of 10,000 men. The battles of the 1911 Restoration brought out a series of notable commanders, particularly GRAND DUKE DAMDINSÜRÜNG of BARGA and MAGSURJAB of Sain Noyan Khan province. To ensure central control the Bogda assigned oversight over the western and eastern borders to his fellow incarnate lamas the JALKHANZA KHUTUGTU Damdinbazar (1874–1923) and the Yegüzer Khutugtu Galsangdashi (1870–1930), respectively. Even so, in Khowd the Kalmyk adventurer DAMBI-JANTSAN (d. 1922) was virtually independent until his deportation by the Russians in 1914.

ECONOMY AND FINANCE

The economy of theocratic Mongolia showed only incremental change from that of the late Qing. The 1911 restoration caused frequent looting and violence against Chinese, and the expulsion of Chinese colonists brought about a decline in farming output. The theocratic government tried to revive agriculture with Mongolian farmers and to protect Chinese firms from looting. It appears that the official debts of the Mongolian leagues and banners to Chinese firms were not serviced, although private debts could still be collected. The damage done to Chinese firms brought on a temporary "goods famine" in Mongolia that Russian imports could not fill, particularly after the beginning of World War I. The role of British and particularly American firms in the wool export trade increased. In 1918 an American company established a motor-car service between Khüriye and Zhangjiakou (Kalgan). Russian firms had began gold mining in 1907, and Nalaikh coal mine was opened in 1915, although by 1918 mining and industry formed only an estimated 6 percent of the national income.

Financially, the expenses of the banners and *aimags*/leagues went on as before, not fully monetized, let alone budgeted, yet they are estimated at four times that of the central government. The abolition of the Manchu *amban*s significantly lightened the burden on the commoners, particularly in the west. The central government's revenues depended on internal and external customs revenues (600,000 rubles in 1916), despite the exemption of Russian firms. Telegraph and telephone fees (128,000 rubles) and user fees for pastures, timber, and livestock (123,000 rubles) were the only other significant items. Expenditures in the same year included the nobles' salaries (123,542 rubles), military training (157,000), and unspecified "central government administration" (573,714). This latter rubric covered the government's massively increased religious expenditures.

To cover Mongolia's war debt to Russia, 332,000 rubles were paid in 1916 and the considerable budget deficit was made up by funds from a 2-million-ruble loan contracted in January 1913. As these facts make clear, the Mongolian government was financially completely dependent on Russia. This leverage was used not only to force Mongolia to comply with Russian diplomatic and territorial ambitions but also to force Mongolia to give monopolistic railroad and telegraph concessions. After 1914, however, Russia was too involved in World War I to take advantage of these concessions.

The increase in Chinese influence from 1917 on brought in a trickle of Chinese settlers, and in 1919 Chinese firms again began demanding payment of official and nonofficial debts. The chaos in Russia, the catastrophic devaluation of the gold ruble, which had been made Mongolia's official currency in 1913, and the record glut in the wool markets caused by the post–World War I depression all delayed a return to the pre-1911 trade, until the savage conflicts of 1920–21 swept away such a possibility forever.

CULTURE AND THE ARTS

Culturally, the theocratic period saw both the culmination of late Qing trends and the advent of new trends that would continue into the 1920s. The decades between 1900 and 1920 in Khalkha were a barren period for original literature, particularly in comparison to Inner Mongolia. Translations of Chinese novels and the performing arts (unfortunately very poorly known) such as *tsam* and traditional Tibetan- or Chinese-influenced opera flourished. In the visual arts the projects sponsored by the Eighth Bogda—his "Green" and "Brown" palaces, the CHOIJUNG LAMA TEMPLE, the Migjid Janraisig Temple and statue, and the Andingmen Gate—marked the apex of Mongolian Buddhist architecture (*see* GANDAN-TEGCHINLING MONASTERY; PALACES OF THE BOGDA KHA). Overall, the artistic monuments reflect the cultural tone of the theocratic period: luxurious, sensuous, and hierarchical.

While other painters followed traditional *thangka*-painting canons, "BUSYBODY" SHARAB and Tsagan (White) Jamba adopted the new media of pencil drawings and ink. Tsagan Jamba's colored drawings portray Mongolian figures such as the deity Lhamo and the epic hero Dugar Zaisang, in ways influenced by Chinese novels. His chief interest, however, was in drawing livestock and game animals.

Public education began in Mongolia with the needs of the ministries. The first state-funded elementary school opened at the Foreign Ministry in March 1912 with 47 students. The teachers were all BURIATS attached to the Russian consulate. The government founded a telegraph school and a printing school, while the Russian consulate enrolled Mongols in its Russian-Mongolian Translators' School. At public expense 12 students were sent to gymnasia (high schools) in Irkutsk and Troitskosavsk (in modern Kyakhta). In 1915 a public middle school was added, the number of students expanded to 80, and the curriculum established as a definitely modern one. Finally, military training also involved basic education. The small number of graduates of these schools played a wholly disproportionate role in the subsequent revolutionary government.

A leading advocate of education, Tsyben Zhamtsarano, also founded the first movable-type press in Mongolia, the Russko-Mongol'skaia tipografiia (Russian-Mongolian Press). His *Shine Toli* (New mirror) journal, which began publication on March 6, 1913, was the first Mongolian-language periodical to be widely distributed. He also published many books and translations, some of which generated tremendous controversy.

A final aspect of the opening cultural horizons of the period was the Mongolian officials and private people who traveled abroad not only to Russia but also to Europe and Japan. Many of these private travelers later became leaders in the 1921 Revolution.

See also ANTHEM; ARMED FORCES OF MONGOLIA; FLAGS; MINING; MONEY, MODERN; SEAL.

Further reading: George A. Cheney, *The Pre-revolutionary Culture of Outer Mongolia* (Bloomington, Ind.: The Mongolia Society 1968); Thomas E. Ewing, *Between the Hammer and the Anvil? Chinese and Russian Policies in Outer Mongolia, 1911–1921* (Bloomington: Indiana University, 1980); Owen Lattimore and Fukiko Isono, *The Diluv Khutagt: Memoirs and Autobiography of a Mongol Buddhist Reincarnation in Religion and Revolution* (Wiesbaden: Otto Harrassowitz, 1982).

Three Guards The Three Guards were Mongol appanages that surrendered to the Chinese MING DYNASTY in the 14th century and later became the ancestors of many eastern Inner Mongolian peoples.

THE GUARDS SYSTEM

In 1389 the Ming Dynasty (1368–1644) set up three "loose-rein" (*jimi*) guards (*wei*) for Mongol chiefs on the eastern slopes of the Khinggan. The Uriyangkhan clan formed the Döyin (Chinese, Duoyan) Guard on the Chaor River, and the Mongolized Tungusic Üjiyed (Chinese, Wuzhe) formed the Fuyu Guard near modern Qiqihar. The Ming put two surrendered princes (Mongolian, *ong*, from Chinese *wang*) from the line of CHINGGIS KHAN's brothers over the Taining Guard; its people were called the Ongni'ud ("the ones with *ongs*/princes"). Commonly, however, but inaccurately, the Three Guards were all called Uriyangkhad (Chinese, Wuliangha[te], plural of Uriyangkhan) Guards.

As "loose-rein" guards, the Three Guards' chiefs participated in the Ming's "tribute" and horse fair systems, through which chiefs and ordinary guardsmen traded HORSES and other livestock, furs, ginseng, mushrooms, honey, and lumber for silk, satins, cotton, robes, cooking pots, and spades. The Three Guards did some of their own FARMING but in famine years also received grain in aid and exchange. If payments were unsatisfactory, however, the Three Guards frequently turned to raiding.

Within a few decades the rise of powerful Mongol rulers threatened the sustainability of the Three Guards system. From 1421 the powerful Arugtai Taishi of the Asud (d. 1434) took over the Three Guards and confiscated their seals. The Three Guards eagerly continued tribute relations with the Ming, but in face of their actual control by hostile Mongol powers the Ming was less tolerant of their raids, staging a massive counterattack in 1444. From 1446 to 1448 the powerful Oirat leader ESEN Taishi (d. 1454) smashed the Three Guards.

THE RESETTLEMENT OF THE THREE GUARDS

The Three Guards mostly fled south and were resettled along the modern-day Inner Mongolia–Liaoning frontier. Many Fuyu guardsmen remained in the north, however, along the Nen River and ONON RIVER; they became the KHORCHIN Mongols. Esen drove a body of Döyin Uriyangkhan to southwest Inner Mongolia, where they were known as Monggoljin. Finally, another body incorporated into the OIRATS became the Khoshud tribe. Rightly doubting the Three Guards' autonomy from the Mongol rulers, the Ming suspended the horse fairs in 1449. Facing Ming hostility, Three Guards commanders such as Kötei of the Üjiyed/Fuyu and Tölöögen (fl. 1470–88) of the Monggoljin/Döyin became active players in Mongol politics while joining raids from Shaanxi to Liaodong. Still, they sent tribute missions to the Ming, and in 1479 regular horse fairs resumed.

THE THREE GUARDS AND THE SIX TÜMENS

By 1495 the Three Guards became an important part of the Mongol reunification under BATU-MÖNGKE DAYAN KHAN (1480?–1517?) and were incorporated into his SIX

TÜMENS. The Üjiyed/Fuyu Guard, resettled in the south, formed part of the southern KHALKHA *tümen*. The Döyin formed the southern part of the Uriyangkhan *tümen*, which also included the northwestern Uriyangkhan in the KHANGAI RANGE. (The northwestern Uriyangkhan revolted and were largely wiped out in 1538; from then on the Uriyangkhan were not counted as a TÜMEN.) Meanwhile, the Monggoljin resettled in the southwest (around modern HÖHHOT) under Tölöögen's son Khooshai Tabunang and became key local allies for Dayan Khan's conquest of the western *tümens*. Nevertheless, however tension filled, the Three Guards' dual relationship with the Ming and the Mongols' revived NORTHERN YUAN DYNASTY continued.

Dayan Khan's western grandsons, ALTAN KHAN (1508–82) ruling the Monggoljin and TÜMED and Bayaskhal (b. 1510) ruling the KHARACHIN, both established QUDA (marriage ally) relations with the Döyin Uriyangkhan, and frequent movement between them resulted by the 17th century in the merger of large bodies of Tümed and Kharachin with the Döyin Uriyangkhan. Meanwhile, Daraisun Khan (1548–57) brought the Fuyu/Üjiyed and Training/Ongni'ud Guards under his direct control, and they collaborated in raiding China. Around 1586 Tümen Khan (b. 1539, r. 1558–92) made the Fuyu/Üjiyed chief Subakhai head of the southern Khalkha *tümen*.

Most of the Three Guards joined the great rebellion against LIGDAN KHAN in 1628. The succeeding Manchus made descendants of the Döyin chiefs rulers (*jasag*) of the Kharachin and Left Tümed (Monggoljin) BANNERS (appanages) in Josotu league. The Üjiyed were divided among other princes in JUU UDA league, but the Ongni'ud and their offshoot, the Abaga, became banners of Juu Uda and SHILIIN GOL leagues, respectively.

See also APPANAGE SYSTEM; FUXIN MONGOL AUTONOMOUS COUNTY; MANCHURIA AND THE MONGOL EMPIRE; TRIBUTE SYSTEM.

"Threes of the World"

"Threes of the World" (*yörtöntsiin guraw*) is a genre of oral poetry that expresses proverbial wisdom by linking three items found in the world with one common feature. The title is then derived from that common feature: "Three Roughs of the World," "Three Missings of the World," and so on. Each of the three descriptions forms one line, which must alliterate in the first syllable with the other two and is isosyllabic, with a fairly strict prosody. There are also a few examples of "Fours of the World." Sometimes the comparison brings out the peculiarity of something in the human world by means of comparisons in the natural world. Thus, "In government, a messenger is rough / In metals, a file is rough / In a hole, a hedgehog is rough." Sometimes the three illustrate a similar pattern in diverse examples of human life: "Without an arrow in the hunt is regret / Without (memorized) scriptures in the assembly for a lama is regret / Without skills in the in-laws' house for a girl is regret." Sometimes the three refer only to features of the natural world: "That the sky has no pillar is something missing / That the mountains have no belt is something missing / That the sea has no churning staff is something missing." The "Threes of the World" vividly express the range of Mongolian values and views of the natural and social world.

See also FOLK POETRY AND TALES.

throat singing (overtone-singing, *khöömii, höömii, xöömii*)

In throat singing the singer produces two or even three separate vocal lines at the same time. In the early 20th century it was found in the Mongolian world in far western Mongolia and Tuva only but in recent years has become popularized as an emblematic aspect of Mongolian music. The word is pronounced *khöömii* in modern Mongolian, *köömä* in Kalmyk-Oirat, and *khöömei* in Tuvan.

Western Mongolian and Tuvan throat singing usually involves producing a low drone over which by squeezing the larynx tightly, one or two high whistling sounds are produced as controlled overtones. In recent decades a number of different styles have been identified by performers and musicologists in Mongolia and Tuva. In Mongolia the styles are divided into "melodic" (*uyangyn*) throat singing and *kharkhiraa* (Tuvan, *kargyraa*). The latter, which has a sound described as a rushing waterfall, involves an exceptionally deep and powerful voice but is produced with an open throat and lacks the whistling overtone.

Throat singers often link the origin of their art to the sounds of nature, especially wind and water, and continue to find inspiration from the different sounds of different landscapes. The masterwork of throat singing, which every singer must be able to perform, is the "Praise of the Altai" (Altain magtaal; *see* YÖRÖÖL and MAGTAAL). Throat singing was traditionally restricted to men not only because of its physically exhausting character but also because of its link to the mountain cult, epic singing, and other aspects of patrilineal religious beliefs.

Something like throat singing is first described among the TÜMED of Inner Mongolia in the late 16th century. The musical concept of a low drone accompanied by a high whistling sound is found also in folksong duets and in the HORSE-HEAD FIDDLE accompaniment of the long song. The deep drone and the overtones link throat singing to both the epic-singing voice (*khailakh*; Kalmyk-Oirat *khäälkh*) and the *tsuur*, or vertical flute. The low drone of Tibetan Buddhist chants also produces overtones, yet performers distinguish it sharply from throat singing. Indeed, throat singing was in decline in the early 20th century, perhaps due to clerical disapproval. It was widespread only among the ALTAI URIYANGKHAI, BAYAD, KAZAKHS, and TUVANS of western Mongolia and the KHALKHA of Chandmani Sum (Khowd province). It was discovered by musicologists in the 1930s as an aspect of folk art first in Tuva and then in Mongolia. Since 1990 throat singing has become a major part of world MUSIC, and both Tuvan and Mongolian groups, such as Huun Huur-tu and Altai-Khangai, have achieved international recognition.

Recordings: Altai-Khangai, *Gone with the Wind* (Window to Europe, 1998); Huun Huur-tu, *Sixty Horses in My Herd* (Shanachie/Asia, 1994).

Tibetan culture in Mongolia   Mongolia's SECOND CONVERSION to Buddhism (c. 1565–1655) resulted in a strong influence of Tibetan culture, both literary and popular, on Mongolia. The spirit of Mongolia's Second Conversion to Buddhism was summed up in words attributed to ALTAN KHAN in 1578: "In short, everything in this country should be done in the way it is done in . . . Tibet." An important issue was the question of the language of Buddhist services. On the one hand, many strong personalities in the early conversion and after, such as Neichi Toin (1557–1653), the THIRD MERGEN GEGEEN (1717–66), and Prince To (Togtakhu-Törö, 1797–1878, ruling in modern Khalkhgol Sum, Dornod) insisted that the Mongols must have the Buddhist dharma in their own language. On the other hand, desire to introduce new or more complete services for Buddhist deities led to the frequent transplantation of Tibetan services to Mongolian monasteries. As a result, by the late 19th century only a few BANNERS conducted services in Mongolian, while the vast majority conducted them purely in Tibetan.

The original process of Tibetanization was first generated by long stays of Mongolian monks in Tibet. On their return to Mongolia they usually brought back texts, images, and memories of how things ought to be done. Powerful visitors, such as the FIRST JIBZUNDAMBA KHUTUGTU (1635–1723), would bring back artists, astrologers, precentors, and other specialists. Every INCARNATE LAMA discovered in Tibet brought to Mongolia large entourages of family, tutors, and servants. After 1750 ordinary Tibetan lamas also began making pilgrimages to Mongolia, where their prestige as Tibetans ensured favorable treatment from local patrons, although at the same time the "Tangut (Tibetan) Lama" became a stock figure of bawdy tales.

By the 19th century every known genre of Tibetan monastic culture was being practiced in Mongolia in both KHALKHA and Inner Mongolia. Scholars wrote in Tibetan on a full range of topics, from Buddhist history and hagiographies to Tibetan syntax and artistic canons. While Tibetan scholars still evinced a certain condescension toward Mongolian Buddhist scholarship, Mongolian writers enriched the range of Tibetan-language scholarship with works on new topics, such as the history of Chinese Buddhism (*see* GOMBOJAB, DUKE). Mongolian sculptors, *thangka* painters, and temple-banner seamstresses created works that European and American museums have mistaken as masterpieces of Tibetan art

(*see* BUDDHIST FINE ARTS). Mongolian monks wrote and performed Tibetan performing arts genres of TSAM dances, *gür* (tibetan *mgur*) songs and melodies in the style of Mi-la-ras-pa (Milarepa, 1040–1123), and *shabdan* poems to accompany the DANSHUG offering to revered incarnations.

Mongolian PERSONAL NAMES came to be overwhelmingly Tibetan Buddhist in origin, although pronounced with a distinctive Mongolian pronunciation. Tibetan letters were also used to write Mongolian (*see* TIBETAN LANGUAGE AND SCRIPT). Tibet's great GESER epic spread to Mongolia by 1716, when a Mongolian translation was printed in Beijing. Many subsequent versions were printed in both Mongolian and Tibetan. As late as 1928 more than two-thirds of literate men could recognize Tibetan letters.

Tibetan influence on Mongolian culture was not even. As one might expect, the UPPER MONGOLS of Kökenuur (Qinghai) were the most heavily influenced, adopting Tibetan dress and, for the majority, the Tibetan language. Nowhere else did Tibetanization proceed so far. It was stronger in KHALKHA, where Tibetan names of Buddhist deities and days of the week replaced the original Uighur-Mongolian ones, than in Inner Mongolia. The international frontier between the Qing Empire and Russia to some extent retarded Tibetan influence on the BURIATS and KALMYKS. Even so, in the later 19th century Buriat and Kalmyk lamas such as AGWANG DORZHIEV (1840–1938) and Baaza-Bagshi Menkejuev (1846–1903) managed to visit Tibet and on returning home attempted to imitate in their homeland what they had found there.

In the 20th century modernization movements led by Mongol intellectuals ascribed to Buddhism all that was backward in their society, a judgment sealed by Soviet- and Chinese-inspired antireligious persecutions. Tibetan personal names became less common in both Mongolia and Inner Mongolia and Tibetan language skills very rare. While lamas have preserved the Mongolian tradition of Tibetan learning and direct contacts with Tibetans have been revived all over the Mongolian world in the 1980s and 1990s, large-scale Tibetan influence on mass culture has not returned.

See also BKA'-'GYUR AND BSTAN-'GYUR; CHOIJUNG LAMA TEMPLE; DANCE; DANZIN-RABJAI; DIDACTIC POETRY; EDUCATION, TRADITIONAL; FOOD AND DRINK; FUNERARY CUSTOMS; JANGJIYA KHUTUGTU; JIBZUNDAMBA KHUTUGTU; KHUTUGTAI SECHEN KHUNG-TAIJI; MEDICINE, TRADITIONAL; MUSIC; TEA; TIBET AND THE MONGOL EMPIRE; *TREASURY OF APHORISTIC JEWELS*; TWO CUSTOMS.

Further reading: Sh. Bira, *Mongolian Historical Literature of the XVII–XIX Centuries Written in Tibetan*, trans. Stanley N. Frye (Bloomington, Ind.: The Mongolia Society, 1970); A. G. Sazykin and D. Yondon, "Travel-Report of a Buriat Pilgrim, Lubsan Midžid-Dordži," *Acta Orientalia* 39 (1985): 205–241.

Tibetan language and script From at least the late 17th century the Tibetan language and script came to dominate Mongolian monastic life and through education influence the secular world as well. Despite the tremendous effort from 1578 to 1749 made to translate the Buddhist scriptures and canonical treatises (*see* BKA'-'GYUR AND BSTAN-'GYUR) and many later works into Mongolian, by the 18th century the Buddhist services (*khurals*) were conducted purely in Tibetan in the vast majority of areas. At the highest levels this resulted in the formation of a major literature written in Tibetan by Mongols. Still, administration in the Mongolian BANNERS (appanages) was always carried out in the MONGOLIAN LANGUAGE, and in all but the most purely Buddhist or Tibetan fields, Mongolian lamas continued to study and write major works in Mongolian as well. The only nonmonastic school for Tibetan language maintained by the Qing government was the Tangut School under the LIFAN YUAN (Court of Dependencies) in Beijing, which trained clerks to handle Tibetan and Kökenuur affairs. Until 1785 the instructors, mostly Mongolian lamas, taught Mongolian and Manchu students.

In the YUAN DYNASTY Mongolian pronunciation of Tibetan was very conservative, simplifying only the initial consonant clusters. The modern Mongolian pronunciation of Tibetan, as used in services and to represent Tibetan personal names and terms, reflects not the Lhasa dialect now considered standard, but that of A-mdo (in Gansu, northern Qinghai, and northern Sichuan), with modifications enforced by Mongolian phonology.

Due to monastic education Mongolian was often written in Tibetan letters. Novices began with five to 10 years of memorizing the pronunciation of Tibetan prayers. Since 45 percent of KHALKHA's male population (1918 statistics) spent some years in the monasteries, although most left after memorizing the services, the monasteries created a large number of householders who knew the pronunciation of Tibetan letters but had never actually learned to read or write either Mongolian or Tibetan. Those who stayed in the monasteries to become monks learned Tibetan, but perhaps only one-tenth learned to read and write Mongolian. Thus, even many able lamas were unable to write in the UIGHUR-MONGOLIAN SCRIPT, although they were fluent in the Tibetan language and were able to translate it into spoken Mongolian.

Thus, some householders and many, if not most, lamas wrote Mongolian in Tibetan letters. Extant examples of this script include signs and advertisements appealing to a lama clientele, business correspondence between lamas, Tibetan-Mongolian dictionaries, and songs and benedictions written down by monastery-educated householders. In 1936 the Mongolian government produced a *Journal of the Lamas* (*Lama-nar-un sedkhül*) in Mongolian written in both the Uighur-Mongolian and the Tibetan scripts.

As a script only in private use, Tibetan-script Mongolian had no standardized orthography. Some examples follow the conservative UIGHUR-MONGOLIAN SCRIPT forms, while others closely reflect pronunciation. Poems and songs written according to pronunciation offer valuable evidence for PROSODY. Consonants were relatively easy to render, but Mongolian's seven vowels, each with its long and short forms (as opposed to Tibetan's five vowels), were either not distinguished clearly or were distinguished by various expedients with the '*a-chung* and *wazur,* two letters often not pronounced in Tibetan.

See also EDUCATION, TRADITIONAL; LAMAS AND MONASTICISM; TIBETAN CULTURE IN MONGOLIA.

Further reading: Stéphane Grivelet, "Preface," *The Journal of the Lamas: A Mongolian Publication in the Tibetan Script* (Bloomington, Ind.: Mongolia Society 2001), i–vi.

Tibet and the Mongol Empire The Mongol conquest of Tibet brought it for the first time under the rule of one of China's Inner Asian dynasties.

From the assassination of the last Tibetan emperor, Glang Dar-ma (836–42), to the time of the Mongol conquest, Tibet lacked any central government. Contemporary Chinese records divided the plateau into four areas: Tufan (Tibetan, mDo-smad), along the Qinghai-Gansu frontier; Xifan (Tibetan, mDo-khams), along the Sichuan frontier; Dafan (Tibetan, dBus-gTsang), or Central Tibet; and Xiaofan (Tibetan, mNga'-ris), or westernmost Tibet. Along the Chinese border Tufan and Xifan principalities flourished on the horse trade with China. In mNga'-ris and dBus-gTsang from 978 on, local chiefs sent Tibetan monks to Kashmir and India and invited gurus to revive Buddhism. Indian-trained Tibetan gurus formed new monastic lineages based around fortress-monasteries such as Rʷa-sgreng (near modern Lhünzhub, refounded in 1057) of the bKa'-gdams-pa order; Sa-skya (modern Sa'-gya, founded in 1073) of the Sa-skya-pa order; and 'Bri-gung (modern Zhigung, founded in 1179) and gDan-sa-thel (near modern Sangri, founded in 1198) of the multifarious bKa'-brgyud-pa order. The great monastic founders usually belonged to powerful landed families that controlled the monasteries from generation to generation. In northwest China the Tangut ruling family of the XIA DYNASTY (1038–1227) followed Tibetan-rite Buddhism and recruited bKa'-brgyud-pa clerics as *guoshi,* "state preceptors."

The earliest Mongol contact with ethnic Tibetans came in 1236, when a Tibetan chief near Wenzhou (modern Wenxian) submitted to the Mongols campaigning in Sichuan. In 1240 a Mongol border prince, KÖTEN, stationed at Liangzhou (modern Wuwei), sent a Tangut commander, Dor-ta Darqan, with a small force to dBus-gTsang. Dor-ta burned Rʷa-sgreng, killing about 500 persons. The bKa'-brgyud-pa monasteries of sTag-lung and 'Bri-gung, with their old link to the Xia, were spared. The 'Bri-gung abbot suggested the Mongols invite the Sa-skya-pa hierarch, Sa-skya Pandita. He complied but died in Liangzhou at 1251, leaving two nephews stranded among the Mongols.

Under MÖNGKE KHAN (1251–59) the Mongols advanced in both the Sino-Tibetan borderlands and dBus-gTsang. In 1251 the khan made Qoridai commander of the Mongol and Han troops in Tufan, and in 1252–53 Qoridai invaded dBus-gTsang, reaching as far as 'Dam (modern Damxung). Once the Central Tibetan monasteries submitted, the Mongol princes divided them as their appanages and sought the blessings of prominent lamas. Möngke Khan patronized Karma Baqshi (1204–83) of the Karma-pa suborder and the 'Bri-gung Monastery, while HÜLE'Ü, khan of the Mongols in the Middle East, sent lavish gifts to both 'Bri-gung and the Phag-mo-gru-pa suborder's gDan-sa-thel monastery. In 1253 Prince Qubilai summoned to his court the Sa-skya-pa hierarch's two nephews, Blo-gros rGyal-mtshan, known as 'PHAGS-PA LAMA (1235–80), and Phyag-na rDo-rje (d. 1267).

The fierce Song-Mongol battles for Sichuan and the civil war between QUBILAI KHAN (r. 1260–94) and ARIQ-BÖKE spilled over into the Tibetan borderlands, and the Xifan and Tufan borderlands were pacified only after the defeat of Ariq-Böke in 1264. In 1265 Qongridar ravaged the Tufan/mDo-smad area, and from 1264 to 1275 several campaigns pacified the Tibetan and Yi peoples of Xifan (mDo-khams) around Jiandu (modern Xichang). By 1278 myriarchies (commands of 10,000) and postroads reached through mDo-khams as far west as Litang.

At first Qubilai made 'Phags-pa Lama and Phyag-na rDo-rje the preferred instruments of his policy in Central Tibet. In 1264 the two returned to dBus-gTsang, with 'Phags-pa as the religious authority and Phyag-na rDo-rje as prince of Bailan and son-in-law (kürgen) of the imperial family. Despite 'Phags-pa's mastery of Buddhist learning, his Mongolian clothing and habits alienated many lamas. After Phyag-na rDo-rje's sudden death in 1267, the 'Bri-gung-pa order, whose leading lamas had supported Ariq-Böke over Qubilai, led an armed revolt against this Mongol-Sa-skya-pa domination. From 1267 to 1269 Mongol troops crushed the revolt and implemented regular Mongol rule in Tibet.

Further unrest continued in 1275–76, when 'Phags-pa returned to Tibet with a Mongol escort under Qubilai's son, Prince Auruqchi. After 'Phags-pa died in 1280 the Mongols' Tibetan official, SANGHA, entered Tibet with 7,000 troops and executed the Sa-skya administrator in 1281 on charges of poisoning 'Phags-pa. In 1290 Auruqchi's son and successor, Prince Buqa-Temür, again assaulted the 'Bri-gung Monastery, now openly allied with Qubilai's rivals in Turkestan. Only after this final assault, which cost 10,000 Tibetan lives, did resistance to Mongol rule cease.

Mongol administration in Tibet, as elsewhere, relied on many overlapping layers of authority. The *dishi*, or imperial preceptor, always a Sa-skya-pa lama and resident of DAIDU (modern Beijing), appointed a Sa-skya-pa monk as *dpon-chen* (great official) to concurrently administer Sa-skya lands and dBus-gTsang as a whole. The abbots and hierarchs at Sa-skya Monastery had influence but no direct political authority. The Commission for Buddhist and Tibetan Affairs (Xuanzheng yuan) in Daidu, one of whose two commissioners was nominated by the *dishi*, headed a parallel bureaucratic hierarchy. The commission supervised three Pacification Commission-Chief Military Commands (Xuanwei si-Du yuanshuai fu): that of Tufan, placed at Hezhou (modern Linxia), that of mDo-khams (Xifan), and that of dBus-gTsang at Sa-skya. Each had four to five commissioners; dBus-gTsang's Pacification Commission always included the *dpon-chen*. Finally, the descendants of Qubilai's son Manggala supervised Tufan from Shaanxi, while Manggala's half-brother Auruqchi and his descendants periodically toured dBus-gTsang.

After 1280 Sangha and Qubilai attempted to curtail Tibetan influence in the administration, employing UIGHURS over Tibetans and demoting 'Phags-pa's powerful 'Khon family. Emperor Temür (1294–1307) and his successors reversed the policies. The 'Khon family was again honored as *kürgen* (imperial son-in-law, in 1296), as *dishi* (1315 on), and finally as princes of Bailan (1322 on). After 1292 Tibetans gradually displaced the Uighurs in the bureaucracy.

Local administration in the eastern mDo-smad and mDo-khams borderlands with China was under Mongol-Chinese garrisons and local chieftains; western mDo-khams and mDo-smad had virtually no Mongol administration at all. In dBus-gTsang the 1268 census divided 37,203 registered households into 13 myriarchies, each with a hereditary myriarch (khri-dpon). The census takers established 27 postroad stations (JAM), with designated staff serving under the supervision of Mongol officials. The postroad system proved particularly onerous for the local population. Although the Tibetan and Yi tribes in mDo-khams used salt for money, dBus-gTsang used the Yuan's paper currency.

Mongol-Sa-skya rule in Tibet remained unquestioned into the 1330s, and the census was revised around 1335. However, an intractable border dispute emerged between the sNe'u-gdong (modern Nêdong) and the gYa'-tsangs myriarchies, each affiliated with monasteries of rival bKa'-brgyud-pa sublineages. The monk-myriarch Byang-chub rGyal-mtshan (1302–64) of sNe'u-gdong's Phag-mo-gru-pa sublineage eventually came into conflict with the Sa-skya-pa *dpon-chens* who supported gYa'-tsangs. Frequent interventions by extortionate Mongol officials and princes only exacerbated the conflict. Protesting his loyalty throughout, Byang-chub rGyal-mtshan twice defeated invasions by the *dpon-chen*'s forces (September 2, 1348, and April 19, 1349) before receiving the *dpon-chen*'s personal submission on

New Year's Day 1354. Although he abolished the Mongolized dress and customs of the Sa-skya administration, Byang-chub rGyal-mtshan avoided any open break with the Yuan, defusing accusations of disloyalty from the *dishi* at Daidu and receiving from the court the honorific title Tai Situ. In 1370 the Tufan pacification commissioner surrendered to the advancing MING DYNASTY (1368–1644) armies, and in 1372–73 the dBus-gTsang authorities, including Byang-chub rGyal-mtshan's successors, recognized the new dynasty.

Tibet's influence on the Mongols of the empire was primarily religious. Under Mongol patronage Tibetan lamas became a frequent sight from China to Azerbaijan. While its influence among the Middle Eastern Mongols was shattered by Islamic conversion (1295), in MOGHULISTAN and in the Mongols' YUAN DYNASTY in East Asia Tibetan-rite Buddhism remained a court religion into the 1360s. Although the Mongol conquest was far from bloodless, Tibetan writers showed little bitterness, presumably due to the Mongols' later generous patronage of Buddhism. Later writers saw the relationship between 'Phags-pa and Qubilai as one of "priest and patron" (*mchod-yon*), manufacturing a supposed donation of all authority in dBus-gTsang from Qubilai to his priest 'Phags-pa. While this grossly exaggerated 'Phags-pa's actual authority, it expressed the basically religious nature of the Mongols' interest in Tibet.

Mongol rule transformed Tibet politically creating the institutions that unified the country. Byang-chub rGyal-mtshan incorporated compliant members of the old myriarch (*khri-dpon*) aristocracy into his new ruling class of fortress chiefs (*rdzong-dpon*) and preserved many titles and institutions of Mongol rule. The continued unification of dBus-gTsang and the active relations of Tibetan lamas with the Ming dynasty after 1372, compared with the disintegration and isolation before the Mongol conquest, demonstrated the permanent nature of the changes Mongol rule made in Tibet.

Incorporation of Tibet in the MONGOL EMPIRE expanded Tibet's artistic and cultural repertoire. The Nepalese-influenced style created by ANIGA at the Mongol court continued under Ming patronage and influenced later Tibetan iconography. Tibetans also became aware of Chinese history, both through translations and consultations with Mongols, stimulating their own historical traditions. Earlier Tibetan historical writing had been limited to spiritual lives and lineages of limited scope; the Tibetan tradition of general history writing began in 1323 with Bu-ston's history of Buddhism.

See also BKA'-'GYUR AND BSTAN-'GYUR; BUDDHISM IN THE MONGOL EMPIRE; CENSUS IN THE MONGOL EMPIRE; EAST ASIAN SOURCES ON THE MONGOL EMPIRE.

Further reading: Herbert Franke, "Tibetans in Yüan China," in *China under Mongol Rule*, ed. John D. Langlois, Jr. (Princeton, N.J.: Princeton University Press, 1981): 296–328; Luciano Petech, *Central Tibet and the Mongols:*

The Yuan-Sa-skya Period of Tibetan History (Rome: Instituto Italiano per il Medio ed Estremo Oriente, 1990); Elliot Sperling, "Hülegü and Tibet," *Acta Orientalia* 44 (1990): 145–157.

Timur (Temür, Tamerlane) (1336?–1405) *Conqueror of Mongol ancestry who ravaged the lands from India to Turkey and founded the Timurid dynasty in Central Asia and Iran*

The son of Taraghai, member of a junior sublineage of the Barulas (Barlas) clan near Samarqand, Timur gathered a personal following of 40 to 300 horsemen through raiding and sheep stealing. (Timur is the Persian form of his Turco-Mongol name, Temür.) The Barulas were a prominent clan of Mongol ancestry in the CHAGHATAY KHANATE. Timur and his entourage remained nomads until his death, but he was thoroughly familiar with the Persian sedentary world. By this time all the western Chaghatayids were at least nominally Muslim. Parts of the Chaghatayid population still spoke Mongolian into the 16th century, but Timur, as far as is known, spoke only Turkish and Persian. The Uighur script, used extensively by the Mongols, remained the preferred script for writing Turkish until about 1450, when it was replaced by the Arabic script.

In 1334 the Khanate's eastern area of MOGHULISTAN (Mongol Land) had broken away, and in 1346–47 the southern clans, aligned with the QARA'UNAS, had seized power, leaving the northern Chaghatayid clans, such as the Barulas, caught between Moghulistan and the Qara'unas. From 1360, when the invading Moghul khan Tughlugh-Temür (1351–63) first made Timur chief of the Barulas clan, to 1369, when Timur finally defeated Emir Husain of the Qara'unas, Timur made his way between Moghulistan and the Qara'unas, allying now with one and now with the other. Having defeated and killed Emir Husain, Timur called a general assembly, or QURILTAI, to confirm his rule over the Chaghatay Khanate on April 9, 1370. By this time an injury or illness had deformed his right leg, giving him the Persian name Timur-i Lang, "Timur the Lame," whence Tamerlane.

Like previous contenders for power in the Chaghatay Khanate, Timur, who was not of Chinggisid blood, did not assume the title of KHAN. Instead, he married a Chinggisid princess, Saray Malik, daughter of the Chaghatayid Qazan Khan (1343–46), and set up an Ögedeid as puppet khan, taking the titles of *kürgen* (son-in-law) and emir (commander).

After becoming Chaghatayid commander Timur campaigned regularly northward against Moghulistan and the QONGGIRAD dynasty in KHORAZM. At the same time, he faced repeated rebellion among the independent-minded Chaghatayid clans, particularly the JALAYIR. Patient defeat of these revolts subdued them all by 1378–79, after which Timur's ambitions turned outward. The subjugation of

Khorasan and Mazandaran, completed by 1384, led to the first of his expeditionary campaigns against western Iran and the Caucasus in 1386–87. By now his chief rival was a one-time protégé, TOQTAMISH, ruler first of the BLUE HORDE and then of the reunified GOLDEN HORDE in the northern steppe. First sacking Urganch (1287), the capital of Toqtamish's allied country, Khorazm, Timur launched a "five-year campaign" (1392–96) against Baghdad's Jalayir dynasty as well as against western Iranian, Turkmen, and Georgian powers, culminating in the sack of Toqtamish's capital, New Saray, on the Volga and crippling Toqtamish's power. After a successful razzia against Delhi in 1398, Timur overrode the war weariness of his emirs to launch his "seven-year campaign" (1399–1404), defeating the armies of MAMLUK EGYPT in Syria (winter 1400–01) and the Ottomans in Turkey (July 1402). While Timur exercised forbearance with his Chaghatayid enemies, outside the khanate he used massacres and terror as policy, emulating earlier Persian and Indian rulers by building pyramids of skulls outside city gates. Timur's final plan was the conquest of Ming China, but he died in Otrar on the night of February 17, 1405.

Timur's original army was a hodgepodge of leftover Chaghatayid units: clans (Barulas, Jalayir, etc.), local soldiery created a century earlier under the Mongol census (called qa'uchin, old units), independent KESHIG (guards) tümens (nominally 10,000) that had outlived their khan, and the Qara'unas, an old TAMMACHI garrison. Timur did not disperse these traditional units but controlled them by changing their leadership, removing major cities such as Bukhara from their control, and eventually recruiting new armies outside the Chaghatay Khanate, especially local units from the defunct Mongol IL-KHANATE. Foreign troops and craftsmen—Indians, Persians, Arabs both settled and bedouin, and Turks— were deported and settled around Samarqand and Bukhara. By 1400 his own companions commanded about 13 tümens, while his sons commanded at least nine. Timur's sons' tümens were assembled from troops of all origins. The core of Timur's army was its Inner Asian cavalry, but he also valued Tajik (Iranian) infantry units. In an inscription he claims to have attacked Toqtamish in 1391 with 20 tümens, a statement that at the usual 40 percent nominal strength is plausible.

Like many Muslim Mongols, Timur claimed special affinity to the family of 'Ali, son-in-law of the prophet Muhammad. Like the Chinggisids, the Barulas tribe was descended from ALAN GHO'A, and on Timur's tombstone it was written that the man of light who impregnated her was a son of 'Ali. Timur kept many Islamic scholars and sheikhs (leaders of Sufi mystical orders) at his court. The Tunisian historian Ibn Khaldun, who met Timur at Damascus, described him as very intelligent and, despite his illiteracy, addicted to intellectual debate. Timur's personal tastes ran to the monumental, and his conquests brought booty and artisans from Turkey to India to the suburbs of Samarqand. He commissioned numerous masterpieces of architecture at Samarqand and his summer capital of Kish (modern Shakhrisabz).

Timur gave little power to his Persian divan (secretariat), and in 1403 he divided his realm among the houses of his four sons. Although like many Mongol rulers he appointed a grandson as his heir apparent, the surviving sons refused to recognize this appointment. After Timur's death his youngest son, Shahrukh (1377–1447), reunified the empire in 1409, but Khorazm had been lost to the Golden Horde and Iraq, Azerbaijan, and Armenia to the Jalayirids and the Turkmen. Shahrukh moved the capital to Herat and abandoned the pretense of Chinggisid rule, taking the title sultan. Praised by their subjects as benevolent rulers and great patrons of the arts and sciences, Shahrukh and his son Ulugh-Beg (1394–1449), Shahrukh's regent in Samarqand, could not defend the empire effectively. The illuminated manuscripts from the kitabkhana (royal library-atelier) of Shahrukh's son Baysonghur (1397–1434), the Turkish poems of Ali-Shir Nawa'i (d. 1567), and Ulugh-Beg's observatory at Samarqand and his astronomical chart are only three of the great cultural monuments from this era. After the deaths of Shahrukh and Ulugh-Beg, the Turkmen sacked Herat, and the Uzbeks, a new confederation formed out of the Golden Horde, invaded the south. Collateral lines maintained Timurid authority in Khorasan and Transoxiana until the Uzbeks occupied Herat in 1507. Zahir-ud-Din Babur (1483–1530), a fifth-generation descendant of Timur, fled to India, where he founded the famous Mughal (Mongol) dynasty (1526–1858) that continued the Timurids' melding of Turco-Mongol rule and Persian culture.

See also ISLAM IN THE MONGOL EMPIRE; SARAY AND NEW SARAY.

Further reading: Ruy Gonzalez de Clavijo, *Narrative of the Spanish Embassy to the Court of Timur at Samarkand in the Years 1403–1406,* trans. Guy le Strange (London: Hakluyt Society, 1859); Thomas W. Lentz and Glenn D. Lowry, *Timur and the Princely Vision: Persian Art and Culture in the Fifteenth Century* (Los Angeles: Los Angeles County Museum of Art, 1989); Beatrice Forbes Manz, *Rise and Rule of Tamerlane* (Cambridge: Cambridge University Press, 1989).

Toghus Khatun (Doquz, Toquz) (d. 1265) *The wife of Hüle'ü, the first Il-Khan, and patroness of Christians in the Middle East*

Toghus Khatun (Lady Toghus) was the granddaughter of ONG KHAN (d. 1203) of the KEREYID. After defeating Ong Khan, CHINGGIS KHAN gave Toghus to his youngest son, TOLUI, but the marriage was never consummated. As Tolui's son HÜLE'Ü was setting out for the Middle East, he married his stepmother, and she accompanied him on his campaigns against Baghdad (1257–58) and Syria (1259–60). Hüle'ü and Toghus had no children, but Hüle'ü respected her as a senior wife, accepting her intercession to protect the Christians of Baghdad, for example. Toghus, like other Kereyid princesses, was a Christian of the Assyrian Church of the East (Nestorians), and she kept in her ORDO (palace tent) a linen chapel-tent with a clapper to announce worship, while giving Christian instruction to the young and patronizing clergy of all denominations. Despite Hüle'ü's later turn to Buddhism, for which she often reproached him, she continued to intercede for his Christian subjects. She died on June 16, 1265, a few months after her husband, sincerely mourned by her Christian subjects. Her stepson Abagha (r. 1265–82) gave her *ordo* to his new queen, Toghus's niece, Tuqtani. The *ordo*'s chapel was in use past 1291, and the *ordo* and her Kereyid relatives remained influential to 1319.

See also CHRISTIANITY IN THE MONGOL EMPIRE.

Toli   *See* TOLUI.

Tolui (Toli, Tuluy) (1191?–1232) *Chinggis Khan's youngest son and father of two great khans, Möngke and Qubilai*
Although not involved in the battles of his father CHINGGIS KHAN's rise, Tolui was almost killed at age five by a hostile tribesman. In 1203 his father bestowed on Tolui as wife SORQAQTANI BEKI, the niece of the KEREYID's ONG KHAN; their first son, Möngke, was born in 1209. Chinggis Khan considered Tolui to be the best warrior among his sons. He first entered combat against North China's JIN DYNASTY in 1213, scaling the walls of Dexing with his brother-in-law Chigü. Tolui's first independent campaign came in 1221, when his father dispatched him to Khorasan in Iran. The cities in this area had revolted several times, and Tolui ordered total massacres at Merv (Mary) and Nishapur (Neyshabur). Tolui was with his father on his last campaign against the XIA DYNASTY, and after his father's death he supervised the empire until the election of his brother ÖGEDEI KHAN in 1229. As youngest son, he inherited as his appanage the undistributed part of his father's people, who occupied the center of Mongolia. Tolui campaigned with Ögedei and Möngke against the Jin dynasty, serving as both strategist and field commander. In 1232, with the Jin's defenses breached, Ögedei returned north, and Tolui died. 'ALA'UD-DIN ATA-MALIK JUVAINI says he died from alcoholism, yet Mongol sources say that when the vengeful spirits of North China brought Ögedei to the brink of death, Tolui volunteered to take his brother's place, drinking a potion brewed by the court shamans and dying shortly thereafter. Modern suspicions that the shamans poisoned Tolui with Ögedei's connivance cannot be proven.

Tömör-Ochir, Daramyn (1921–1985) *Mongolia's first prominent Marxist-Leninist, who was dismissed in 1962 for his defense of Chinggis Khan*

Orphaned as a child, Tömör-Ochir from age 15 hired himself out to shear wool and do other odd tasks before pursuing an education and becoming one of the early graduates of Mongolian State University. In 1950 Tömör-Ochir, as one of Mongolia's noted new intellectuals, signed his name to a collective letter questioning whether Mongolia could really build socialism without joining the Soviet Union. This letter led to an investigation by MARSHAL CHOIBALSANG and his more nationalist associates (YUMJAAGIIN TSEDENBAL, however, supported Tömör-Ochir). In 1953 Tömör-Ochir defended his master's degree in philosophy (that is, Marxism-Leninism) from Moscow State University and in 1957 received the title (rare in Mongolia's Soviet-based academic system) "professor."

In the early Tsedenbal years Tömör-Ochir became a member of the Politburo (the leading body) of the MONGOLIAN PEOPLE'S REVOLUTIONARY PARTY (MPRP), assisted in Tsedenbal's 1956 criticism of intellectuals, and wrote the 1959 article that attacked BYAMBYN RINCHEN for his "nationalism." Tsedenbal admired Tömör-Ochir's command of Marxism-Leninism, and in 1961 he was elected an academician in the ACADEMY OF SCIENCES. By this time, however, Tsedenbal began to see Tömör-Ochir as an unstable individualist being taken in by "nationalism." Certainly Tömör-Ochir's ideas were in flux; he now completely repudiated his previous support for unification with the Soviet Union and in 1962 sought to have his 1956 and 1959 criticisms withdrawn. Tömör-Ochir's party-historical textbook that frankly pointed out the non-Marxist nature of the early MPRP infuriated Tsedenbal. In 1962 Tömör-Ochir was one of several supporting the celebration of CHINGGIS KHAN's birth, which, when criticized by the Soviet Union, gave Tsedenbal the opportunity to dismiss him from the Politburo as a "nationalist" on September 10.

Tömör-Ochir asked for the chance to translate Karl Marx's *Das Kapital* into Mongolian but was instead made head of a construction office in BAYANKHONGOR PROVINCE. The office's poor performance was attributed to him, and he was expelled first from the party and then his job and returned to ULAANBAATAR, where he was jailed briefly. Exiled to KHÖWSGÖL PROVINCE, he returned to Ulaanbaatar for medical reasons before being sent to DARKHAN CITY in 1968, where, despite being under constant surveillance, he opened a museum, "Friendship," while his wife, Ninjbadgar, taught at the polytechnic institute. After Tsedenbal was ousted in 1984, his wife delivered an appeal to Ulaanbaatar for reconsideration of his case; while she was away, Tömör-Ochir was brutally murdered in his apartment. The murderer was never apprehended.

See also CHINGGIS KHAN CONTROVERSY; MONGOLIAN PEOPLE'S REPUBLIC; SOVIET UNION AND MONGOLIA.

Tongliao municipality   Tongliao city is a small city in southeastern Inner Mongolia with a metropolitan area population in 1982 of 225,400, of whom Mongols numbered 34,500. Tongliao municipality also administers five rural Mongol BANNERS and two Chinese counties, covering 59,500 square kilometers (22,970 square miles). In 1990 this area had 2,753,727 inhabitants, of whom Mongols were 1,160,851 (42 percent).

The city was originally founded as a Chinese county in KHORCHIN territory in 1914. It was reached by rail in 1921. In 1934, under Japanese occupation, Tongliao was transferred to form part of the autonomous Mongol Khinggan South province. In 1945–46 Tongliao became the center of Jirim league, and in 1949 the Chinese Communist government assigned Jirim league to Inner Mongolia. In 1999 Jirim league was renamed Tongliao Municipality.

See also INNER MONGOLIA AUTONOMOUS REGION.

Toqtamish (Tokhtamysh) (fl. 1375–1405) *Last strong ruler to unify the Golden Horde*
Toqtamish's father was a descendants of Toqa-Temür, one of the "princes of the left hand," or the BLUE HORDE, in modern Kazakhstan, and his mother was of the QONGGIRAD clan from near KHORAZM. At the time the Blue Horde was ruled by Urus Khan (d. 1377) and his sons, whose seat was at Sighnaq (near modern Chiili). By allying with the Chaghatayid conqueror TIMUR, Toqtamish succeeded after many reverses in taking control of the Blue Horde (spring 1377). Later, local chronicles speak of Toqtamish as defending four tribes (*el*)—Shirin, Baarin, Arghun, and Qipchaq—from the tyranny of Urus Khan. Once enthroned in Sighnaq, Toqtamish led his four tribes west to defeat Emir Mamaq (Mamay) of the Qiyat clan (1380) and reestablish GOLDEN HORDE rule over Russia by sacking Moscow (1382).

Eventually, Toqtamish turned against his old patron, Timur, to pursue the Golden Horde's old territorial claims in Azerbaijan (1385 and 1387), Khorazm, and the Syr Dar'ya region down to Bukhara (1388). Timur responded with a massive punitive expedition into Kazakhstan, which finally cornered and defeated Toqtamish's army near Orenburg (June 1391). Timur also wooed away Emir Edigü, leader of the Manghit (MANGGHUD) clan, from Toqtamish's camp. After rebuilding his power in the west, Toqtamish again invaded Azerbaijan (1394); Timur crushed his army again on the Terek (March 15, 1395) and sacked Saray and Astrakhan.

Toqtamish fled and for the next 10 years vainly sought allies to defeat Emir Edigü and regain the throne. His son Qadir-Berdi killed Edigü in 1420; Toqtamish's four clans eventually found rest in the CRIMEA and in Kazan under khans of collateral Toqa-Temürid descent.

See also RUSSIA AND THE MONGOL EMPIRE; SARAY AND NEW SARAY.

Further reading: D. DeWeese, "Toktamish," in *Encyclopaedia of Islam*, 2d ed., vol. 10 (Leiden: E. J. Brill, 1960 on): 560–563.

Toqto'a (Toghto, Tuotuo, T'uo-t'uo) (1314–1356) *Minister in the late Yuan dynasty who attempted ambitious plans of financial and economic renovation*
Toqto'a first rose to power among the Mongols in China as the nephew of BAYAN (1281?–1340), one of the leaders of the 1328 coup d'état and grand councillor from 1335 on. Toqto'a's father, Majardai (1285–1347), had given his son Toqto'a a Confucian education, and Toqto'a did not approve Bayan's anti-Confucian policy.

In March 1340 Toqto'a secured Bayan's dismissal, and in November Toqto'a became grand councillor. With Bayan's fall the Confucian examination system was immediately revived. In 1343 Toqto'a sponsored the long-delayed completion of the histories of the Yuan dynasty's immediate predecessors, the Song (960–1279), Liao (907–1125), and Jin (1115–1234), treating all three as legitimate dynasties. In 1244, however, an overambitious plan to divert the Yongding River to facilitate water transport to the capital of DAIDU (modern Beijing) generated heavy opposition, and Toqto'a resigned, joining his father in Gansu.

During the 1330s plague and famine devastated the Huai River area, while unrest appeared in South China, Manchuria, and the Sino-Tibetan borderlands. As Toqto'a was dismissed, massive flooding of the Huang (Yellow) River inundated 17 cities, putting the Grand Canal out of service and beginning the river's migration to a new channel north of the Shandong peninsula. Meanwhile, piracy made the sea route for transporting South Chinese grain to the capital increasingly risky. The new grand councillor, Berke-Buqa, had no effective response. In August 1249 Toqto'a was reappointed grand councillor.

Under Toqto'a's second administration he focused on the grain transport issue. In winter 1350–51 his attack on the pirate chief Fang Guozhen failed. With the support of Emperor Toghan-Temür (1333–70), Toqto'a advocated rerouting the Huang (Yellow) River back to its southern channel as a way to repair the Grand Canal. In April 1351 he began his great project, employing 150,000 civilian workers, 20,000 soldiers, and 1,845,636 *ding* (*yastuq*) of paper currency. Earlier issues of paper currency had been limited by silver reserves, but Toqto'a issued 2 million *ding* of unbacked paper currency to pay for labor and materials.

In May 1351 uprisings of sectarian "Red Turbans" rebels animated by Buddhist millenarian beliefs broke out in Yingzhou (modern Fuyang). The rebels spread and defeated successive attacks by guards units and volunteer armies, including one led by Toqto'a's brother Esen-Temür. Toqto'a did not lose his high position, however, and in 1252 assembled a "Yellow Army" of mostly Chinese volunteers, so-called for the color of their uniforms. On October 23, 1352, he retook the strategic city of Xuzhou after a six-day siege. Other provincial officials raised Chinese, Mongol, and Miao armies to attack the rebels. By winter 1353–54 the "Red Turban" movement was virtually extinct. Even so, piracy and the occupation of the Grand Canal at Gaoyou by the salt smuggler Zhang Shicheng still blocked grain shipments from the south and caused hunger in the capital. Toqto'a proposed another grand plan for rice farming in central Hebei, importing 2,000 South Chinese farmers and spending 5 million *ding* of currency, all the while assembling another army to attack Gaoyou and reopen the Grand Canal.

A court rival, Qama of the Qangli (d. 1356), exploited Toqto'a's absence to arrange his dismissal and banishment by imperial decree, just as the siege of Gaoyou was nearing victory. After Toqto'a's banishment on January 7, 1355, many of his units mutinied, and Zhang Shicheng exploited Yuan peace offers to seize the Lower Chang (Yangtze). Toqto'a, exiled to YUNNAN, was poisoned by Qama's agents on January 10, 1356.

Financially, Toqto'a's overambitious programs and the rebellions led Yuan paper currency into a hyperinflationary spiral. Even so, his dismissal on the very eve of success ended the last chance for the Yuan to suppress the rebellions and restore the dynasty.

Toquz *See* TOGHUS KHATUN.

Töregene (regent, 1242–1246, d. 1246) *Wife of Ögedei Khan and first empress-regent of the Mongol Empire*
Born in the NAIMAN tribe, Töregene was given as wife to Qudu, the eldest son of the MERKID chieftain Toqto'a Beki. When the Merkid were conquered by the Mongols in 1204, CHINGGIS KHAN gave her as a second wife to his third son Ögedei. While Ögedei's first wife had no sons, Töregene gave birth to five sons, including GÜYÜG, KÖTEN, Köchü, and Qashi, and she soon eclipsed all of Ögedei's other wives. Qashi (b.c. 1205) became Chinggis Khan's favorite grandson before his untimely death from alcoholism. During the reign of her husband ÖGEDEI KHAN Töregene, whose ability was acknowledged even by her enemies, gradually increased her influence but still resented Ögedei's officials and their policy of centralizing administration and lowering tax burdens. Her religious beliefs are unclear, although she did sponsor the reprinting of the Taoist canon in North China, and one of her favorites, Fatima, was an active Shi'ite Muslim who had been deported from the Shi'ite shrine city of Meshed. Through the influence of Fatima, a Muslim tax farmer, 'Abd-ur-Rahman, received the contract to collect taxes in North China in 1240.

When Ögedei died in December 1241, at first power passed to the hands of Möge, one of Chinggis's wives, who Ögedei had inherited. Ögedei had nominated his grandson Shiremün as heir, but he was universally regarded as too young. With the support of Ögedei's brother CHA'ADAI and her sons, in spring 1242, Töregene received the consent of the princes to act as regent until a QURILTAI (assembly) named a new khan. Beginning slowly at first, she soon turned this regency into a position of active power. Eventually she tried to arrest several of Ögedei's major officials. CHINQAI, his chief secretary, and Mahmud Yalavach, chief administrator in North China, fled to the ORDO (palace-tent) of her son Köten, while Mahmud's son Mas'ud Beg, chief administrator in Turkestan, fled to Batu's ordo (*see* MAHMUD YALAVACH AND MAS'UD BEG). In Persia she ordered KÖRGÜZ arrested and handed over to the family of Cha'adai, whom he had unwisely defied; they executed him. She replaced Körgüz with ARGHUN AQA, a Mongol official of the Oirat tribe. Töregene had friendlier relations with some of Ögedei's North Chinese officials and commanders, such as ZHANG ROU, who she ordered, with the Mongol general Chagha'an, to attack the SONG DYNASTY. Even so, under Fatima's influence she put the hated tax farmer 'Abd-ur-Rahman in charge of general administration in North China. These administrative changes, together with the lack of accountability, led the Mongol ruling class into a frenzy of extortionate demands for revenue.

Although Töregene desired her eldest son, Güyüg, to be the next khan, he delayed the calling of the *quriltai* for several years. Her second son, Köten, whose territory was in northwest China, opposed his mother's plans for Güyüg and desired to be elected khan himself. When Chinggis Khan's youngest brother, Temüge Odchigin, gathered his men and unsuccessfully tried to seize the throne, the princes realized the time had come to call the long-awaited *quriltai*. Köten's election bid was rejected, and with the support of Töregene and of the Toluids, Güyüg became khan in August 1246. Töregene retired west to Ögedei's appanage on the Emil and Qobaq Rivers (Emin and Hobok), and officials such as Chinqai were restored to power. After a few months Fatima was accused of using witchcraft to damage Köten's health, and when Köten died soon after Güyüg insisted that his mother hand Fatima over. Töregene threatened that if her son insisted on seizing her she would commit suicide to spite him. After a period of deadlock Güyüg's men seized Fatima, tortured her into confessing, and executed her. Töregene died soon after.

Torghuds (**Torghut, Torgut, Torguud**) The Torghuds are a component tribe of the Oirat Mongols. (Oirat tribes were not consanguineal units but politico-ethnic units composed of many *yasu*, or patrilineages.) The Torghud ruling dynasty traced its descent to ONG KHAN (d. 1203) of the KEREYID tribe, and while that claim appears to be legendary, the Torghud's name does derive from the Kereyid "day guards" (*turqa'ud*). (The name is written Torguud in Cyrillic-script Mongolian, Torghoud in the Clear Script, and Torghud in Cyrillic-script Kalmyk.)

The Torghud first appear as an Oirat tribe in the mid-16th century. The bulk of the Torghud migrated from Zungharia (northern Xinjiang) west to the Volga in 1630, forming the core of the KALMYKS. A few Torghud princes followed TÖRÖ-BAIKHU GÜÜSHI KHAN into Kökenuur, becoming part of the UPPER MONGOLS. In 1698 a Torghud Kalmyk nobleman on pilgrimage to Tibet with his family and 500 subjects was unable to return home. They were resettled by China's QING DYNASTY in Ejene, in far western Inner Mongolia (*see* ALASHAN). Ejene Torghuds numbered 5,000 in 1990.

In 1699 15,000 Torghud households returned from the Volga to Zungharia, where the Zünghar ruler TSE-WANG-RABTAN KHUNG-TAIJI attached them to the Khoid tribes. With the Qing conquest of the ZÜNGHARS in 1755, a body of these Züngharian Torghuds fled to Russia and were resettled among the Volga Kalmyks.

In 1771 most of the Kalmyks' Torghud princes and subjects migrated back to Zungharia, where they were resettled by the Qing dynasty as "Old Torghuds" (*see* XIN-JIANG MONGOLS). Mongols in Xinjiang's primarily Torghud counties today number more than 65,000 (1999). The Zungharian Torghuds returned together with their Kalmyk clansmen in 1771 and were resettled in western Mongolia (modern Bulgan Sum, Khowd province) as "New Torghuds." Large numbers of Torghuds also remained in Kalmykia, however. They traditionally inhabited the "Black Lands," the Caspian Sea shore, and the Volga area above the Khoshud lands.

In 1906 the Qing dynasty put western Mongolia's New Torghuds under the new Altai district, with its capital at Chenghua (modern Altay). In 1911–12 one New Torghud prince opposed Mongolian independence and fled to Xinjiang, taking the lamas and wealthy herders with him. The others were reincorporated into Mongolia's Khowd frontier. They numbered 4,700 in 1956 and about 10,200 in 1989.

See also AYUUKI KHAN; BAYANGOL MONGOL AUTONOMOUS PREFECTURE; BOROTALA MONGOL AUTONOMOUS PREFECTURE; HENAN MONGOL AUTONOMOUS COUNTY; KALMYK REPUBLIC; KHOBOGSAIR MONGOL AUTONOMOUS COUNTY; KHOO-ÖRLÖG; KHOWD PROVINCE; SUBEI MONGOL AUTONOMOUS COUNTY.

Torghut *See* TORGHUDS.

Torgut *See* TORGHUDS.

Torguud *See* TORGHUDS.

Töv *See* CENTRAL PROVINCE.

Trans-Mongolian Railway Completed in 1956, the Trans-Mongolian Railway cuts through Mongolia north to south and links ULAN-UDE in Russia to Jining in China. Chinese and Russians had long planned railways into Mongolia to secure control, while Mongolians desired a railway for development. In 1937 a railway was built from Ulan-Ude to Naushki on the Mongolian border, and in 1939, with Soviet assistance, a paved road was extended on to ULAANBAATAR. Delayed by WORLD WAR II, the Naushki-Ulaanbaatar line was completed in 1949. With the SINO-SOVIET ALLIANCE the Soviet Union, Mongolia, and China agreed to link Ulaanbaatar and Jining by rail; the line was formally opened by the Inner Mongolian leader ULANFU on January 1, 1956. The railroad was entirely built by soldiers of the Soviet Union's 505th Penal Unit in Mongolia, manned by Soviet soldiers imprisoned for surrendering to the Germans in World War II and other crimes. In 1958 the line transferred to diesel engines and automated switching. Branches off the railway were built to coal mines at Sharyn Gol (1963) and Baganuur (1982), the new ERDENET CITY (1975), and the fluorspar mine at Bor-Öndör (1987).

The 1,109 kilometers (689 miles) of the railway in Mongolia are managed by the Ulaanbaatar Railway Company, a Russian (formerly Soviet)-Mongolian joint-stock company. Railway transport in Mongolia, which also includes the unconnected Choibalsang-Borzya line built in 1938–39, carried 96 percent of Mongolia's total freight transportation and 55 percent of its total passenger traffic in 1998.

See also CHOIR; DARKHAN; EAST GOBI PROVINCE; ECONOMY, MODERN; SELENGE PROVINCE; SHILIIN GOL.

Treasury of Aphoristic Jewels The *Treasury of Aphoristic Jewels* was the most popular of the many Sanskrit and Tibetan didactic aphoristic works translated into Mongolian. The collection, entitled *Subhashitaratnanidhi* in Sanskrit and *Legs-par bshad-ba rin-po-che'i gter* in Tibetan, was written in Tibetan by the monk-scholar Sa-skya Pandita (Scholar of the Sa-skya Order) Kun-dga' rGyal-mtshan (1182–1251) before his summons to the Mongol court in 1244. While modeled on Sanskrit aphoristic verses and containing many allusions to Indian legends, only 35 of the 457 aphorisms are actually translations, close or loose, of Sanskrit originals. The aphorisms set forth the contrasting characters of the wise and the foolish and the importance of good lineage and dutiful rulers. Addressed to householders, the basic message was expressed in the final aphorism: "If one knows the deeds of this world well, by that one is also fulfilling the way of the Dharma [i.e., Buddhist religion]." It was familiarly known in Tibetan as the *Sa-skya legs-bshad,* or "Sa-skya's Aphorism," and in Mongolian as the *Subashida* (modern *Suwshid*), from Sanskrit *Subhasita,* "aphorisms."

The earlier translations into Mongolian by Sonom-Gara (c. 1300), ZAYA PANDITA NAMKHAI-JAMTSU (1599–1662), and the THIRD MERGEN GEGEEN LUBSANG-DAMBI-JALSAN (1717–66) were relatively literal, while that of Chakhar Gebshi (student of Buddhist philosophy) Lubsang-Tsültim (1740–1810) was a free translation in elegant verse. Lubsang-Tsültim also translated with additions of his own the *Subashida's* Tibetan commentary by Rin-chen dPal-bzang-po (1230–92), which explained the allusions to Indian legends. This commentary transmitted to the Mongols a skeletal knowledge of the Indian epics *Ramayana* and the *Mahabharata*. Lubsang-Tsültim's translation and commentary were block printed in 1778–79, reprinted in Inner Mongolia in the early 20th century, and published in Cyrillic transcription by TSENDIIN DAMDINSÜREN in 1958.

See also BUDDHISM IN THE MONGOL EMPIRE; DIDACTIC POETRY; LITERATURE; 'PHAGS-PA LAMA.

Further reading: James E. Bosson, *A Treasury of Aphoristic Jewels: The Subhasitaratnanidhi of Sa-Skya Pandita in Tibetan and Mongolian* (Bloomington: Indiana University, 1969).

tribute system   The tribute system was a China-centered way of looking at foreign relations that influenced Chinese-nomadic relations for almost 2,000 years. In their dealings with foreign peoples, Chinese officials traditionally tried to maintain the idea that the emperor was the sole "Son of Heaven." Thus, all foreign leaders were required to approach the emperor as subjects (*chen*), not as equal sovereigns. While the emperor was the world's only Son of Heaven, he was not to aspire to rule the distant peoples directly but instead to allow them, with their strange and barbaric customs, to continue under their accustomed rulers. It was expected, however, that the "virtue" (*de*), or charisma, of the emperor and of the realm he ruled would draw foreign chiefs or their envoys to the Chinese court, where they would present gifts as tribute. The emperor would then shower the chiefs with gifts in return to show his benevolence. Distinguished court titles and patents were additional signs of imperial favor. Nearer peoples would be more attracted and so could open such tribute relations regularly, while more distant ones would show up on the border only occasionally.

This ideal bore, however, only occasional relation to China's real foreign policy. In practice, tribute relations with the nomads, such as between the Han (202 B.C.E. to 220 C.E.) and the XIONGNU (Huns), the Tang (618–907) and the TÜRK EMPIRES and the MING DYNASTY (1368–1644) and the Mongols, were a method of trade, something the Chinese court well understood. "Tribute" items, such as HORSES and skins, were exchanged on specified schedules for "gifts" from the court. The trade was made all the more lucrative for the nomads in that the Chinese court often paid room and board for the envoys from the time of their entry into Chinese territory. This trade operated primarily to the benefit of the nomads who desired textiles (primarily silk), grains, iron kettles, and later, TEA. Since tribute was essentially a form of state-administered foreign trade, it was subject to constant political negotiation, with the threat of raids if the Chinese payments were not satisfactory.

The Mongols, after conquering China and founding the YUAN DYNASTY (1206/71–1368), faced the possibility of continuing the traditional tribute relations with Southeast Asia. At first, under QUBILAI KHAN, the Mongols tried to turn these loose tribute relations into the much tighter control sanctioned by Mongol precedents. This attempt failed, however, and subsequent emperors were content with continuing the traditional tribute system with Southeast Asia and the Indian Ocean.

The operations of the tribute system between China and the nomads is best documented under the Ming dynasty, when the Chinese dealt with Mongol and Oirat (west Mongol) envoys. Their tribute goods presented at the capital were principally horses but also included CAMELS and furs. The emperor responded to this tribute by giving rewards to the emissaries, which were determined by a fixed schedule. Thus, one ordinary horse was rewarded with two lined satin garments. Each member of the envoys, down to the servants, also received personal gifts, graded according to rank, and the envoys were feted at government expense throughout their stay. Finally, tribute missions under the OIRATS contained many merchants from the Central Asian oasis cities of Hami, Turpan, and Samarqand. Mongol and Oirat embassies sometimes numbered more than 2,000 men presenting 40,000 head of horses and camels. The Ming responded by attempting to limit the size and frequency of the embassies or by reducing the unit price. However, if dissatisfied with the payments, the nomads would raid to force better terms.

When the nomads were powerful, they could also force the Chinese into an alternative form of diplomatic relations, the *heqin* (peace and intermarriage) system. In this system, based on the relations between China's feudal states in the Zhou period (1122–256 B.C.E.), the nomadic ruler received the right to address the emperor as a kinsman, not a subject. Regardless of whether the kin term was a senior or junior one, it marked the equivalent of diplomatic equality. (The emperor's real relatives all formally addressed him as *chen*, subject.) To seal the alliance, the nomad ruler would receive a woman of the imperial family as wife. *Heqin* relations were always extremely controversial in China and never undertaken except under severe pressure. In the late imperial period, from the 14th century on, the dynasties in China refused any form of *heqin* system.

At certain periods the Chinese also opened horse markets for regular tributary powers, in which ordinary nomads could trade their horses at fixed prices. The horses were bought by the Chinese army and paid for according to fixed prices. Horse markets were reserved for close allies such as the THREE GUARDS and the HÖHHOT TÜMED after they made peace with the Ming.

While in theory contrary to the tribute system, Chinese military action was, in fact, a necessary complement to it. All of China's great dynasties, the Han (202 B.C.E. to

220 C.E.), the Tang (618–907), and the Ming (1368–1644), undertook expeditions into the steppe to search for and destroy hostile nomad leaders. The Chinese dynasties always linked attacks on nomadic rulers with attempts to entice rival rulers into regular tribute relations. This policy of "using the barbarians to control barbarians," backed by carefully chosen blows from Chinese forces, was pursued with varying effect by all the dynasties. The Han dynasty used this policy to break up the Xiongnu, the Tang used it to break up the Türk empires, and the JIN DYNASTY (1115–1234) used it against the MONGOL TRIBE in the days before CHINGGIS KHAN. The victims of this policy often felt outraged by what they saw as a perfidious and cowardly, but all too effective, policy.

See also BURMA; KOREA AND THE MONGOL EMPIRE; SOUTH SEAS; VIETNAM.

Further reading: Sechin Jagchid and Van Jay Symons, *Peace, War, and Trade along the Great Wall* (Bloomington: Indiana University Press, 1989); Alastair Iain Johnston, *Cultural Realism; Strategic Culture and Grand Strategy in Chinese History* (Princeton, N.J.: Princeton University Press, 1995); Henry Serruys, *Sino-Mongol Relations during the Ming*, vol. 2: *The Tribute System and Diplomatic Missions* (Brussels: Institute belge des hautes études chinoises, 1967) and vol. 3: *Trade Relations: The Horse Fairs (1400–1600)* (Brussels: Institute belge des hautes études chinoises, 1975).

Tsaatan *See* DUKHA.

Tsagaan Sar *See* WHITE MONTH.

Tsakhar *See* CHAKHAR.

tsam This sacred dance (from Tibetan 'cham) was part of the ceremony of the fierce (dogshid) deities in Mongolian monasteries.

Tsam (pronounced *cham* in Inner Mongolia) in its current form was created by the Tibetan rNying-ma-pa (Old Order) lama Chos-kyi dBang-phyug (1212–73). In the late 18th century it was introduced to ERDENI ZUU and in 1811 to Khüriye (modern ULAANBAATAR) in the choreography of the Fifth Dalai Lama (1617–82), and thereafter it spread very rapidly.

All the *tsam* figures wear large masks of papier-maché. The coral-inlaid masks of the deity Jamsrang (Beg-tshe), made by the late-19th-century craftsmen Tabkhai-Boro and Puntsug-Osor for the Khüriye *tsam*, are particularly impressive. Mongolian monasteries performed the *tsam* annually, preceded by an early morning service for the deity Yamantaka. After several introductory figures entered, including the comic *azar* (from Sanskrit *acarya*), or Indian pilgrim, 10 fierce deities (*dogshid*) successively came out and danced. The solemn dances consisted of slow bouncing or twirling on one foot or leaping from foot to foot, all the while brandishing swords and other attributes. Near the end the WHITE OLD MAN came out and performed comic antics, and then 32 "black-hat" lamas danced. At the conclusion, as all the figures were dancing, dough figures (*baling*) were destroyed to complete the exorcism of evils.

There were also *tsams* dedicated to Mother Tara and GESER. In southeastern Inner Mongolia's Aohan banner, *cham* developed into a kind of village procession of "blessings givers" (*khutugchin*), including the White Old Man and Monkey, Pigsy, and Sandy from the Chinese novel *Journey to the West* (*see* CHINESE FICTION). *Tsam* was outlawed in Mongolia after 1937, but has again begun to be performed on a small scale since 1990.

See also CHOIJUNG LAMA TEMPLE; DANZIN-RABJAI.

Tsedenbal, Yumjaagiin (1916–1991) *Modern Mongolia's longest-ruling leader, Tsedenbal, from 1952 to 1984, sought to make Mongolia in every way a loyal junior partner of the Soviet Union.*

Born on September 17, 1916, to an unwed mother in Bayan Chandamani Uula banner (modern Dawst Sum, Uws), Tsedenbal (originally named Tserenpil) was a DÖRBÖD Mongol. In October 1929 Tsedenbal was selected with 21 other students for a special Mongolian *rabfak* (preparatory school) in Irkutsk. In 1931 he joined the MONGOLIAN REVOLUTIONARY YOUTH LEAGUE. After graduating from the *rabfak*, he studied at the Institute of Finance and Economics in Irkutsk, graduating in July 1938. His fellow students remembered him as a loner, and in a note from 1943 he congratulated himself on his intolerance of social chitchat and carelessness in work.

Upon graduation the Mongolian students were invited to Moscow for sightseeing, where Tsedenbal was singled out for notice by the Soviet Communist Party Central Committee. In September 1938 he was returned to Mongolia and was employed as an instructor in the Finance Ministry's attached technicum. Recommended to Mongolia's ruler, MARSHAL CHOIBALSANG, by the Soviet intelligence officer and diplomatic representative Ivan Alekseevich Ivanov (1906–48), Tsedenbal became deputy finance minister in March 1939 and in December joined Choibalsang and Ivanov in meeting with Soviet ruler Joseph Stalin in Moscow. There, Choibalsang promised to arrest Mongolia's sitting party secretary, Basanjab (1904–40), and replace him with Tsedenbal, who had just joined the party. Thus, at age 24 Tsedenbal became the general secretary of the MONGOLIAN PEOPLE'S REVOLUTIONARY PARTY (MPRP) and the nation's number-two leader at the party's Tenth Congress in March 1940.

From then on Tsedenbal formed part of Choibalsang's inner circle, participating in several highly secret security cases. Even so, Tsedenbal shared none of Choibalsang's enthusiasm for pan-Mongolian unification, and around 1950 he supported the proposition advanced by several young officials that Mongolia would need to join the Soviet Union if it were to achieve socialism.

In 1947 Tsedenbal married Anastasia Ivanovna Filatova at the Savoy Hotel in Moscow. Despite the match's political implications, Tsedenbal was genuinely devoted to his wife, who assumed complete responsibility for their household, leaving Tsedenbal free to concentrate on his political career. At the same time, he was sometimes uncomfortable with her critical and domineering personality. Their two sons, Vladislav (Slavik) and Zorig, were registered as Soviet citizens. The family atmosphere and language were completely Russian, with vacations every summer in the Soviet Union. Anastasia, with her husband's consent, kept the children away from Mongolian children lest they "catch infectious diseases."

FIRST AMONG EQUALS, 1952–1964

After Choibalsang's death in January 1952, Tsedenbal allied with the second secretary DASHIIN DAMBA (1908–89?) to defeat the bid for power by the hard-line Ch. Sürenjaw, who was exiled to Moscow. Tsedenbal become "Chairman of the Council of Ministers," or premier, on May 27, 1952, and gave up the first secretaryship to Damba two years later. As premier Tsedenbal immediately visited Moscow and then Beijing, signing the

agreements that created the TRANS-MONGOLIAN RAILWAY and Sino-Soviet-Mongolian alliance (see SINO-SOVIET ALLIANCE). With Choibalsang out of the way, the Politburo formally approved joining the Soviet Union. Attending Stalin's funeral, Tsedenbal presented the request to the Soviet leadership, which rejected it and rebuked its originators.

Tsedenbal and Damba split over its response to Soviet ruler Nikita S. Khrushchev's famous speech criticizing Joseph Stalin in April 1956. At first, the Mongolian Politburo created a special commission headed by BAZARYN SHIRENDEW to reexamine cases from the Choibalsang period. While Damba supported the commission, Tsedenbal repeatedly blocked its work. In 1958 Tsedenbal secured Damba's dismissal, taking over his position as first secretary of the MPRP. In 1961–62, as Khrushchev intensified the de-Stalinization drive, a "Rehabilitation Commission" was appointed, but Tsedenbal here, too, criticized its work. In 1963 the Politburo banned the film *Tümnii Neg* (A million in one), which dealt with the purges. Due to Tsedenbal's stubborn resistance to de-Stalinization, a statue of Stalin remained in front of the Mongolian National Library until 1990.

In 1962–63 Tsedenbal expelled several rivals and critics from the MPRP on charges of "nationalism." He used the 1962 CHINGGIS KHAN CONTROVERSY to dismiss

Soviet ruler Leonid Brezhnev and Mongolia's Yumjaagiin Tsedenbal signing the Soviet-Mongolian defense treaty of 1966 *(From 50 Years of People's Mongolia [1971])*

his erstwhile Politburo allies, first DARAMYN TÖMÖR-OCHIR and then L. Tsend. At the same meeting three Central Committee members handling economic issues, Ts. Lookhuuz, B. Nyambuu, and B. Surmaajaw, argued that people's living standards were declining and criticized the party's "petit-bourgeois" attitude. They, too, were expelled from the party and exiled to rural areas. From 1966 on, when he received Leonid Brezhnev on the first visit of a Soviet leader to Mongolia and presided unchallenged over the MPRP's Fifteenth Congress, Tsedenbal was the undisputed leader of Mongolia.

TSEDENBAL'S REGIME AND HIS DECLINE

In his comments on Tömör-Ochir, Tsedenbal had stated that "new young forces must be drawn into leadership work," but his own policies accentuated the aging of the leadership. From 1963 on Tsedenbal and his cultural enforcer, "Horse-Headed" B. Lhamsüren, condemned area after area of new intellectual and social endeavor: abstract art, new appreciation of Buddhist literature, survey-based sociology, and so on. From 1966 to 1981 the Politburo remained remarkably constant in its composition. Khalkhas accused Tsedenbal of preferring Dörböds for high office. In 1974 he imitated Brezhnev in giving the office of premier to an underling (in this case JAMBYN BATMÖNKH) and taking for himself the office of head of state.

From 1966 Tsedenbal's conformist reverence for authority, boundless admiration of Soviet Russia, and determination to make Mongolia an "industrial-agricultural country" shaped the nation's policies, even if the industry involved was mostly semiprocessing of raw materials for the Soviet market. His great detestation of Tömör-Ochir sprang from the latter's irreverent criticism of the country's accomplishments since 1921, as if he, Tömör-Ochir, were Mongolia's first real Marxist-Leninist. In 1962 Tsedenbal proposed the slogan that mastering Russian, "the language of Lenin," was "a component of ideological education." In the late 1970s an attempt to conduct all higher education in Russian was only barely defeated. In a note written in 1963 Tsedenbal rejected Chinese suggestions that Mongolia, by being relegated to mining and light industry, was becoming a colony of the Soviet Union. "The development of the international socialist division of labor is a LAW," he fumed.

Around late 1973 Tsedenbal began to experience moments of memory loss that grew increasingly serious from 1975 on. Spells of dizziness also alarmed him. His wife, Anastasia Ivanovna, began a public career as chairwoman of Mongolia's Children's Fund while criticizing Mongolian leaders behind the scenes. By 1982 Tsedenbal's son Vladislav (Slavik) was drinking heavily, while Zorig accused his father of abdicating his fatherly role, of not teaching his sons Mongolian, and pushing everything onto their domineering mother.

In 1981, at the Eighteenth Party Congress, plaudits to "the best leader of party and state" filled the air. At the same time, Tsedenbal began attacking not only intellectuals but his cronies. In December 1983 Tsedenbal linked S. Jalan-Aajaw to the old 1963 Lookhuuz group and exiled him. By 1984 one-third of the Central Committee and almost half the ministry heads appointed in 1981 had been dismissed. After Brezhnev's death in 1982 the new Soviet leadership decided in November 1983 that Tsedenbal's increasingly erratic behavior was becoming a liability. On August 9, 1984, while Tsedenbal was vacationing in Moscow, the Kremlin doctor Chazov diagnosed Tsedenbal as suffering from overwork, and top Soviet leaders summoned Batmönkh and Tsedenbal's old crony D. Molomjamts, telling them Tsedenbal could no longer serve. On August 23 the Mongolian Politburo dismissed Tsedenbal from all positions.

RETIREMENT

After his dismissal Tsedenbal lived in lonely retirement in Moscow with his wife and sons. From 1988 increasing public criticism of "Tsedenbalism" embittered his last days, as his senility and Anastasia Ivanovna's overprotective rages increased. In March 1990, at the height of the peaceful 1990 DEMOCRATIC REVOLUTION, the MPRP Central Committee harshly criticized Tsedenbal's legacy and expelled him from the party while exonerating his old victims, such as Tömör-Ochir and Lookhuuz. Even more personally distressing to Tsedenbal, however, was the expulsion of Slavik, as a Soviet citizen, from the MPRP. Tsedenbal died in Moscow on April 21, 1991, and was buried in Ulaanbaatar. In 1997, as nostalgia for the economic security of the Communist era increased, Tsedenbal's titles and honors were restored.

See also MONGOLIAN PEOPLE'S REPUBLIC; SOVIET UNION AND MONGOLIA.

Tserendorj, Balingiin   *See* TSERINDORJI.

Tserindorji (Balingiin Tserendorj) (1868–1928) *Mongolia's respected foreign minister and prime minister in the theocratic and revolutionary periods*

Tserindorji was born on May 25, 1868, to a Chinese father and a Mongolian mother; they were subjects of the GREAT SHABI in Setsen Khan banner (in modern Öndörkhaan, Khentii). After serving as a Chinese translator in the Manchu AMBAN's office in Khüriye (modern ULAANBAATAR), in 1911 he joined independent Mongolia's Foreign Ministry, rising to deputy foreign minister in 1913 and participating in Prime Minister Namnangsürüng's 1913–14 mission to St. Petersburg and the 1914–15 Kyakhta Trilateral Conference (*see* KYAKHTA TRILATERAL TREATY). In December 1915 he became foreign minister, the first lay commoner to hold such high office. He was widely regarded as the only able man in the government after 1915. Tserindorji collaborated with Chen Yi's "soft" version of the REVOCATION OF AUTONOMY but was shunted aside under Xu Shuzheng's "hard" version.

In July 1921 the new revolutionary government appointed Tserindorji deputy foreign minister, and he helped negotiate the 1921 Friendship Agreement with Russia. In 1922 he became foreign minister and Presidium member of the party Central Committee. In October 1923, as part of GENERAL DANZIN's conservative retrenchment, he was named prime minister. Despite his criticism of blind faith in Soviet advice, he remained indispensable to the revolutionary regime as prime minister until his death on February 13, 1928.

See also MONGOLIAN PEOPLE'S PARTY, THIRD CONGRESS OF; REVOLUTIONARY PERIOD; THEOCRATIC PERIOD.

Tsevang-Rabtan *See* TSEWANG-RABTAN KHUNG-TAIJI.

Tsevan-Ravtan *See* TSEWANG-RABTAN KHUNG-TAIJI.

Tsewang *See* ZHAMTSARANO, TSYBEN ZHAMTSARA-NOVICH.

Tsewang Araptan *See* TSEWANG-RABTAN KHUNG-TAIJI.

Tsewang-Rabtan Khung-Taiji (Tsevang-Rabtan, Tsevan-Ravtan, Tsewang Araptan) (b. 1663, r. 1694–1727) *Ruler of the Zünghars whose daring intervention in Tibet brought Manchu rule there*
Tsewang-Rabtan at first served his uncle GALDAN BOSHOGTU KHAN (1678–97) as the ZÜNGHARS' commander against the KAZAKHS. In 1688, after the suspicious death of his younger brother, relations worsened, and Tsewang-Rabtan seized the Zungharian homeland while Galdan was invading KHALKHA. In 1694 the Dalai Lama's regent (*sde-srid*) Sangs-rgyas rGya-mtsho (r. 1679–1703) bestowed on Tsewang-Rabtan the title khung-taiji, the next-highest title to khan among the OIRATS. (He never received the title khan.) Like that of Galdan, Tsewang-Rabtan's foreign policy was built on defense of the Dalai Lama's office. From 1690, when he controlled Zungharia, Tsewang-Rabtan allowed the regent to dissuade him from joining the Qing assault on Galdan. In 1697–98 he married the daughter of the Torghud AYUUKI KHAN (r. 1669–1724). In 1699 Ayuuki's son Sanjib rebelled against his father and fled to Zungharia with 15,000 households, strengthening Tsewang-Rabtan's forces.

At first Tsewang-Rabtan cooperated with both the Qing emperor Kangxi (1662–1722) and Russia, throwing his largest forces against the Kazakhs in repeated raids from 1698 on. In 1715, however, the Qing attacked in the Altai, and Tsewang-Rabtan sent 2,000 men to seize Hami in response. At the same time, Tsewang-Rabtan turned against his QUDA (marriage ally), the Khoshud Lhazang Khan in Tibet, who had enthroned a new Sixth Dalai Lama. Responding to appeals from Lhasa's three great monasteries to depose the pretender, he sent his brother Tseren-Dondug with 6,000 men to occupy Lhasa in December 1717; Lhazang died in battle. The ZÜNGHARS made themselves hated by their attacks on non-dGe-lugs-pa (Yellow Hat) monasteries, attacks instigated by Tsewang-Rabtan's austere and intolerant chief monk, Lubzang-Puntsog. In 1719–20 the Qing expelled the Zünghars first from Tibet and then from Hami and Turpan. After the death of Kangxi, Qing pressure on the Zünghar temporarily lessened. Tsewang-Rabtan used this breathing space to launch a massive attack on the Kazakhs, forcing them into their disastrous "Barefoot Retreat" in winter 1723–24. After his death his son GALDAN-TSEREN succeeded him.

Further reading: Fang Chao-ying, "Tsewang Araptan." In *Eminent Chinese of the Ch'ing Period (1644–1912)*, ed. by Arthur W. Hummel (Washington, D.C.: U.S. Government Printing Office, 1943).

Tseween, Jamsrangiin *See* ZHAMTSARANO, TSYBEN ZHAMTSARANOVICH.

Tsogtu Taiji (1581–1637) *Poet, supporter of Ligdan Khan, and opponent of the Dalai Lama's "Yellow Hat" order*
Tümengken Tsogtu, usually known as Tsogtu Taiji (Prince Tsogtu), was a nephew of ABATAI KHAN (1554–88). From 1601 to 1617 he built six fortified monasteries; ruins of two, the "White Building" and the "Khar Bukh Ruins," are found today in modern Dashinchilen Sum (Bulgan province). Unlike the other KHALKHA nobles, including his own family, Tsogtu Taiji ardently supported the Yuan emperor LIGDAN KHAN (titled Khutugtu, 1604–34) and opposed the dGe-lugs-pa (Yellow Hat) order. Already in 1621 he felt isolated, particularly when his beloved paternal aunt was married to a prince of the "Ongni'ud" (here meaning Abaga, modern Abag), refugees in Khalkha from Ligdan's rule. His servants carved on a rockface a famous poem of longing for his aunt and a blessing for Ligdan in 1624 (in Delgerkhaan Sum, Central province). Eventually, Tsogtu Taiji fled south with his subjects, following Ligdan to Kökenuur. After Ligdan's death Tsogtu Taiji began attacking dGe-lugs-pa monasteries. When Tsogtu sent 10,000 men under his son Arslang against the Dalai Lama in Lhasa, Arslang switched sides and supported the Dalai Lama. The dGe-lugs-pa hierarch, the Fifth Dalai Lama (1617–82), summoned the Oirat GÜÜSHI KHAN TÖRÖ-BAIKU, whose 10,000 men in early 1637 crushed Tsogtu's 30,000 at Ulaan-Khoshuu; Tsogtu Taiji was killed. Mongolia's first successful feature film, whose screenplay was written by BYAMBYN RINCHEN, was entitled *Tsogtu Taiji* (1945).

Tula *See* TUUL RIVER.

Tu language and people (Monguor)

The Tu nationality are a farming people in northwest China numbering 191,624 in 1990. Their language is a separate branch of the Mongolic family, one with peculiar phonetic features and many Tibetan and Chinese loanwords.

ORIGINS

The Tu as a people formed in the early MING DYNASTY (1368–1644). When the Ming dynasty drove the Mongol YUAN DYNASTY (1206/71–1368) out of China's Gansu province, 16 local commanders near Xining surrendered in 1369–71 with their subjects and were made *tusi* (*t'u-ssu*), or "aboriginal officers." Of these 16, the most important were two Chinggisid princes and two commanders of the originally Turkic-speaking Lintao ÖNGGÜD. One other was Chinese and one Turkestani; the other 10 were called "Tu." While this word can mean simply "aborigines" in Chinese, it may have been used as an abbreviation for Tuyuhun, a branch of the probably Mongolic XIANBI, who settled in the area in the fourth century. In any case, during the Yuan the mixed, mostly Turco-Mongol, inhabitants around Xining had evidently begun using Mongolian on a wide scale and by the Ming dynasty came to call themselves "Mongols." They distinguished themselves as "White Mongols" (*chagaan Monggol*) from the still independent "Black Mongols" (*khara Monggol*) of Mongolia. The word *Mongol* is pronounced in the Minhe dialect as "Monguor," forming the origin of a common European and American designation for this nationality.

LANGUAGE

The Tu language forms the Gansu-Qinghai family within the MONGOLIC LANGUAGE FAMILY together with the Dongxiang, Bao'an, and (less certainly) Eastern Yogur languages. The vocabulary of Tu is mostly Mongolic in origin but has numerous Tibetan and Chinese elements, often for fairly basic vocabulary. Phonologically, Tu is the most aberrant language of the Mongolic family. Under the influence of A-mdo Tibetan, the language has lost all Altaic features, losing vowel harmony and developing through the loss of the first vowel many cases of word-initial consonant clusters and initial r-. Thus, Middle Mongolian *arbai*, "barley," *sayiqan*, "beautiful," and *ire-*, "come" developed in Tu (Huzhu dialect) into *shbaii*, *sgan*, and *re-*.

While Tu preserves some features of Middle Mongolian, it is not as conservative as Mogholi or Daur. Tu preserves the Middle Mongolian h- as f- (in the Huzhu dialect) or sh- (as in *foodə*, "star" and *shjauur*, "root"; cf. Middle Mongolian *hodu[n]* and *huja'ur*). However, regressive assimilation of the -i- (vowel breaking) is relatively advanced (cf. Tu *shira*, "yellow," *makha*, "meat," and *nudu*, "eye" to Middle Mongolian *shira*, *miqa*, and *nidü*), long vowels are widespread, and -u diphthongs fairly rare. Postverbal negation in *guaa* (cf. Mongolian *ügei/güi*) is also widely used. A number of other idiosyncratic phonological developments in Tu are not explainable by either the Tibetan sound environment or greater archaism.

The Tu language is divided into two quite different dialects, Huzhu and Minhe. Natives of Huzhu, Ledu, and Tianzhu counties speak Huzhu, while those of Minhe county speak Minhe. The Minhe dialect has no phonemic vowel length, has fewer initial consonants clusters, and simplifies syllable-final -l to -r and -m to -n or -ng. In phonology and vocabulary, Minhe is thus closer to Chinese and Huzhu to Tibetan.

All the Tu of Datong county, about 20 percent of the total nationality, now speak Chinese, and Chinese sources estimate only about 60 percent of the Tu as a whole speak the Tu language. A new Latin script was created for the previously unwritten language and began to be used in a limited way in the early 1980s.

HISTORY

The people of the 16 Tu tusis, or "aboriginal officers," totaling 11,000 households in the early Ming, served primarily as border wardens, protecting the frontier from Tibetan and Yellow Uighur (see YOGUR LANGUAGES AND PEOPLES) nomads. From 1509 to 1723 independent Mongol princes from Inner Mongolia and KHALKHA and the OIRATS occupied the Kökenuur area, forming the UPPER MONGOLS. The Tu *tusis* were repeatedly called up to resist Mongol raids on Ming territory. The *tusis* surrendered en masse to the new QING DYNASTY (1636–1912) in 1645, which multiplied the number of *tusis* to 23, but raids and rebellions during the turbulent dynastic transition continued.

At the same time, the Tu began to form links with the Mongols and the Tibetans. The Tu were, at the time of their surrender to the Ming, already Tibetan-rite Buddhists. A temple had been built at Qutan (in modern Ledu county), and Buddhist clerics were granted Ming titles. In 1604 the FOURTH DALAI LAMA, a TÜMED Mongol, encouraged the construction of the new dGon-lung (Ergulong) Monastery (Chinese, Youning Temple, in modern Huzhu county). From this monastery came three lineages of INCARNATE LAMAS: the JANGJIYA KHUTUGTU, the Tuguan Khutugtu, and Sum-pa Khutugtu. The Sum-pa mKhan-po (abbot of the Sumpa lineage) Ishi-Baljur (Ye-shes dPal-'byor, 1704–87) was one of the great polymaths of Tibetan Buddhism.

Despite imperial patronage of the high lamas, many Tu lamas joined the Upper Mongol prince Lubsang-Danzin's great rebellion against the Qing in 1723–24, although the *tusis* remained loyal. The rebellion and the Qing's savage reprisals devastated the Tu. A subsequent influx of Han (ethnic Chinese) and Hui (Chinese-speaking Muslim) settlers transformed Xining into a farming area.

TRADITIONAL SOCIETY, ECONOMY, AND RELIGION

The *tusi* was a hereditary officer, equivalent in rank to a Chinese county magistrate. The *tusi's* subjects served him with taxes and corvée but were exempt from any obligations toward the Chinese counties established in their territory. Each *tusi* took a Chinese surname, which was also adopted by his followers. Thus, the *tusi* institution became a kind of exogamous clan, ritually unified by the worship of the founding *tusi*. The real descendants of the original *tusi* formed a hereditary nobility that was exempt from taxes.

By the early 20th century the Tu were settled farmers, living in loosely clustered villages along the Huangshui and Datong River valleys growing barley, wheat, peas, rapeseed, colza, hemp, and potatoes. The Tu kept much livestock, however, and maintained their tradition of breeding fine horses. Tu caravaneers also frequently joined pilgrimages and caravans to Tibet. Emigration of Tu farmers to cultivate virgin lands on the Tibetan plateau broke up somewhat the close links between the *tusis* and their subjects. Close interaction with Tibetans and Chinese influenced culture and religion. Religious beliefs focused on the Buddhist monasteries but also on the household worship of heaven, mostly Taoist tutelary deities, and "black" and "white" shamans (*boo*).

MODERN HISTORY

With the overthrow of the Qing in 1912, the Tu feared the destruction of the *tusi* system that guaranteed their autonomy. In 1916 a number of Tu clerics and *tusis* participated in an unsuccessful Qing restoration movement. Only later, however, did the threat of forced assimilation become real. In 1929 the counties around Xining, previously part of Gansu province, were transferred to Qinghai, and in 1931 the *tusi* system was finally abolished. Qinghai's Hui (Chinese-speaking Muslims) warlord Ma Bufang (r. 1931–49) implemented universal conscription and a land tax designed to force inefficient farmers, such as the Tu, off productive lands and after 1938 prohibited Tu clothing and language in public.

The People's Republic of China reversed the policy of assimilation, Nationality policy officials designated *Tu* as the name of the nationality and Chinese scholars have tended to stress the Tu's Tuyuhun ancestry. The scattered distribution of the Tu has made territorial autonomy only nominal. Huzhu was declared a Tu nationality autonomous county in 1954, yet the county contained less than 35 percent of the total Tu population, and Huzhu's Tu were only 14.52 percent of the county's 156,024 people. Due to a high birthrate, the Tu's percentage in Huzhu had risen to 15.44 percent in 1982, yet Tu were still only 12 percent of administrative officials. In 1986 Minhe (1982 population 287,389), with about 23 percent of the Tu, and Datong (1982 population 336,327), with about 20 percent, were both made joint Hui and Tu autonomous counties.

See also ALTAIC LANGUAGE FAMILY; BAO'AN LANGUAGE AND PEOPLE; DONGXIANG LANGUAGE AND PEOPLE.

Further reading: Limusishlden and Kevin Stuart, ed., *Huzhu Mongghul Folklore: Texts and Translations* (Munich: Lincom Europa, 1998); Louis J. Schram, *Monguors of the Kansu-Tibetan Frontier,* 3 vols. (Philadelphia: American Philosophical Society, 1954–61); Henry Schwarz, *Minorities of Northern China: A Survey* (Bellingham: Western Washington University Press, 1984), 107–117; Kevin Slater, *A Grammar of Mangghuer: A Mongolic Language of China's Qinghai-Gansu Sprachbund* (London: Routledge Curzon, 2002).

Tuluy   *See* TOLUI.

Tumd   *See* TÜMED.

Tümed (Tumd, Tümet, Tumote)   A center of Mongol expansion in the 16th century under ALTAN KHAN, the Tümed Mongols were deprived of their aristocracy under the Qing dynasty. Completely sedentarized as farmers, many Tümeds became activists in the Chinese Communist Party. With few exceptions, Tümeds today speak Mongolian only as a second language for reasons of ethnic pride.

Tümed today has two banners, a Left Banner (Zuoqi) under HÖHHOT municipality and a Right Banner (Youqi) under BAOTOU municipality. Together they cover 4,996 square kilometers (1,929 square miles) and have 647,000 inhabitants, of whom only 37,800 are Mongols. A substantial number of Tümed Mongols also live in Höhhot's "Old Town" or Yuquan district and suburbs. Subsistence crops include naked oats, wheat, and potatoes, while cash crops include rape, sugar beet, linseed, and tobacco.

From the 11th to 14th centuries the Tümed plain was settled by the ÖNGGÜD tribe. After 1450 the Tümed (the 10,000s) formed one of the Mongols' SIX TÜMENS. The tribe achieved the height of its power as the appanage of the Chinggisid Altan Khan (1508–82). After surrendering to the rising Manchu Qing dynasty (1636–1912), the Tümed were put under Manchu officials as part of the EIGHT BANNERS system. In 1741 a special Salaachi (Salaqi) prefecture was created to administer the already numerous Chinese settlers. By the mid-19th century many Tümeds could not speak Mongolian, and CHINESE COLONIZATION intensified after 1900. ULANFU, a Tümed peasant's son, became the Chinese Communists' chief Mongol leader. The Communists occupied Tümed territory in 1949, and in 1954 Tümed territory was included in Inner Mongolia. Tümeds remain influential in the Inner Mongolian Communist apparatus even today.

See also FARMING; INNER MONGOLIA AUTONOMOUS REGION; INNER MONGOLIANS; NEW SCHOOLS MOVEMENTS.

Tümet *See* TÜMED.

Tumote *See* TÜMED.

Tumu Incident (T'u-mu) In the Tumu Incident of 1449, the Chinese emperor was captured by the Oirat (West Mongol) ruler ESEN Taishi as the Chinese frontier lines collapsed.

Responding in 1449 to reports of the Oirat ruler Esen's plans to invade China, the chief of the Chinese palace eunuchs, Wang Zhen, convinced the Zhengtong emperor (1436–49, reenthroned as Tianshun, 1457–64), to lead a punitive expedition against Esen.

The emperor and Wang Zhen set out from Beijing on August 4 supposedly with 400,000 troops and reached Datong on August 18. Unseasonable rains, restiveness in the Chinese ranks, and news of a crushing Mongol victory convinced Wang Zhen to abandon the punitive expedition and return to Beijing. On August 30, after the emperor set out from Xuanfu (modern Xuanhua) back to the capital, Esen annihilated the Chinese rear guard at Yao'erling. On September 1 the Mongols destroyed the remaining troops at Tumu, killing Wang Zhen and capturing the emperor.

Esen treated the emperor well, but his desire to use him to make the MING DYNASTY cooperate failed. Xuanfu and Datong refused to open their gates, and Wang Zhen's ignominious death broke the power of the eunuchs, bringing the emperor's brother and a war party to power. After briefly returning north, Esen fruitlessly besieged Beijing from October 27 to 31 with his captive in tow. The standoff continued until Esen returned the now ex-emperor without condition in September 1450. The Mongols did, however, exploit the crisis to seize the ORDOS pastures south of the Huang (Yellow) River.

Further reading: Frederick W. Mote, "The T'u-mu Incident of 1449," in *Chinese Ways in Warfare*, ed. Frank A. Kierman, Jr., and John K. Fairbank (Cambridge, Mass.: Harvard University Press, 1974): 243–272.

Tung-hsiang *See* DONGXIANG LANGUAGE AND PEOPLE.

T'ung-liao *See* TONGLIAO MUNICIPALITY.

Tungus *See* EWENKIS.

Türk Empires (Tujue, T'u-chüeh) The first literate empire on the Mongolian plateau, the Türk Empires initiated a period of both political and cultural expansion from 552 to 742.

The two Türk Empires were founded by the Ashina clan, who served as blacksmiths in the ALTAI RANGE for the ROURAN Empire. Most of the Türk khans' names and titles were not Turkish, however, indicating that the Ashina clan was of foreign origin. Chinese histories claim that the Ashina was of XIONGNU origin and fled persecution in North China in 439 before moving with 500 families northwest to the Rouran. Tokharian and Iranian terms and titles among the Ashina confirm their foreign origin and indicate they presumably resided first in the Turpan oasis before moving north to the Altai.

In 546 the Ashina chiefs opened relations with the Yuwen regime (Western Wei-Northern Zhou, 535–81) in northwest China. In 551, when the Ashina chief Bumin (d. 552/53) defeated a rebellion against the Rouran, he requested the hand of the Rouran emperor's daughter. Rejected as a mere blacksmith, Bumin conquered the Rouran, taking the title Illig Qaghan, or "Great Khan of the Realm." After Bumin's death Bumin's son Mughan (553–72) became Qaghan of the center, and Bumin's brother Ishtemi (552–75/76) became the Yabghu Qaghan on the western frontier. Under their leadership the Türks annihilated the Heftalite dynasty in the Central Asian oases by 556. Mughan's brother and successor, Taspar Qaghan (572–81), received a princess and annual gifts of 100,000 pieces of silk from the Yuwen regime in northwest China. From their earliest appearance in 546 the Türks were closely allied with the Sogdians of Bukhara and Samarqand, an Iranian people whose caravan trade spread from the cities of China to CRIMEA. This Türk-Sogdian symbiosis foreshadowed the later Mongol-Uighur symbiosis (*see* UIGHURS; ORTOQ).

After Taspar's reign the central Türk realm in Mongolia was riven by succession wars. Nivar (reign title Ishbara, 581–87) saved his throne from Tardu (fl. 576–603), the western Yabghu Qaghan, only by submitting to China, now under the Sui dynasty (581–617). In 594 Tardu made another attempt to reunify the central and western qaghanates, but a revolt of allied western tribes in 603 overthrew him. The rebellions at the end of the Sui gave the Türks temporary dominance, but China's reunification under the Tang (618–907) reestablished Chinese sway. In 630 the Tang emperor captured the unpopular Xieli Qaghan (620–30, d. 634), ending the Türk rule in Mongolia. In the west the influence of Tong Yabghu Qaghan (618/9–630) extended from India to the Caucasus, but a rebellion of the Qarluq tribe (627) and Tong's murder led to the western Türks' disintegration into their constituent clans, the On Oq "Ten Arrows." In 659 these, too, submitted to Tang rule.

CONCEPTS AND INSTITUTIONS OF RULE

The center of the Türk political system was the "Heavenly-commanded" qaghan (*see* KHAN), who owed his sanctity to his Ashina lineage identity. Like earlier and later steppe rulers, the Ashina believed their clan ancestor had been suckled by a wolf and had found refuge from

A "stone man" from the Türk era, Bayan-Ölgii province
(*From N. Tsultem,* Mongolian Sculpture *[1989]*)

enemies in a cave with his 10 brothers, of whom Ashina was the wisest. The Bugat (Bugut) inscription (Ikhtamir Sum, North Khangai) shows a wolf suckling a child, undoubtedly the Ashina ancestor.

The Ötüken mountain forest on the upper Tamir River was the Türks' sacred center, one they had inherited from the Xiongnu. On the Tamir's banks they worshiped heaven/God every fifth moon. In addition to heaven, the Türks also worshiped Umay, an earth goddess (cf. Mongolian *umai,* womb) and the spirits of *yir-sub,* "earth-water." The qaghan also annually returned to the ancestral cave with the lords to offer sacrifices (as did the earlier XIANBI).

Politically, the Türk khanate was bilateral, with the center at Ötüken and the western khanate at Suyab or Ordukent, near modern Tokmak. Far to the west, in the Caspian steppe, the Türks also ruled over the Oghurs, speaking a rather different Turkish language ancestral to Old Bulghar and modern Chuvash. This far-western branch eventually became the Khazar Khanate, whose Ashina lineage qaghans extended their rule to the Caucasus and Crimea and deeply influenced early Russia.

TÜRK CULTURE

Although Türk grave sites are common, no significant settlements have been found. Türk graves were marked by distinctive STONE MEN (Russian, *baba,* Mongolian, *khün chuluu*), or statues representing the deceased, his family, and the men he killed in battle. These latter would serve him as pages in the next world, just as HORSES in the funerary sacrifices would serve as mounts. Türkish artwork is not abundant, and what does exist is both less stylized and less powerful than the Scythian and Xiongnu ANIMAL STYLE. Stone men and petroglyphs show that Türk dress was quite similar to that of the Sogdians: long jackets with broad, pointed lapels and prominent mustaches for men. Well-equipped riders had chain or scale armor for themselves and their mounts and rode with stirrups.

The Türks spoke a dialect of Old Turkish belonging to the Oghuz family, close to modern Uighur, Uzbek, Türkmen, and Turkish, somewhat more distant from the Qipchaq family of Kazakh and Tatar, and quite far from the Oghur family of Chuvash and Old Bulghar. Although many other tribes also spoke close or identical dialects, the Türks' imperial prestige gave a single name to the whole family of dialects. The Türks were also responsible for first committing Turkish to writing. The earliest Türk inscription, the Bugat (Bugut, found at Ikh Tamir Sum, North Khangai Province) inscription of 589, was written in the Sogdian language and script, and the Türk court used the Sogdian language extensively. Even so, already under Taspar Qaghan (572–81) a Chinese monk translated a Buddhist sutra into Old Türkish, and attempts to write Old Türkish in Sogdian letters may go back to the fifth century. Later, the so-called Runic script developed from the Sogdian script specifically to write Old Turkish; the earliest extant example is from the mid-seventh century (*see* RUNIC SCRIPT AND INSCRIPTIONS).

THE SECOND TÜRK EMPIRE AND ITS FALL

By the 680s dissatisfaction with Tang rule seems to have been widespread. Qutlugh, an Ashina clansman, turned his small band into the nucleus of a revived Türk state based in Ötüken and took the reign name Ilterish (682–91). First his brother Bögö Chor (reign name Qapaghan, 691–716) and then his sons Bilge Qaghan (716–34) and Kül Tegin, who ruled as a duumvirate, rebuilt the Türk Empire, campaigning from the "Iron Gate" near Samarqand in the west to Shandong in the east and from Tibet in the south to the Siberian Bayirqu tribe in the north. After Bilge's death by poisoning in 734, the Türks were ruled again by minors until a coalition of Basmil (in the Tianshan), Qarluqs (in Zungharia), and Uighurs (to the north) overthrew the dynasty in 742. Independent rulers among the western On Oq lasted longer, although not of the Ashina dynasty. The last qaghans belonged to the Türgesh clan before the On

Oq and their land were overrun by the QARLUQS in 766. The second Türk Empire left as monuments the famous runic inscriptions of Toñuquq (fl. 681–716), a minister who served Ilterish, Qapaghan, and Bilge Qaghan, and of Bilge Qaghan and Kül Tegin.

See also ALTAIC LANGUAGE FAMILY; BULGHARS; QIPCHAQS; RELIGION; TRIBUTE SYSTEM; TURKEY; UIGHUR EMPIRE.

Further reading: Michael R. Drompp, "Supernumerary Sovereigns: Superfluity and Mutability in the Elite Power Structure of the Early Türks (Tu-jue)," in *Rulers from the Steppe: State Formation on the Eurasian Periphery,* ed. Gary Seaman and Daniel Marks (Los Angeles: Ethnographics Press, 1991): 92–115; Peter Golden, *An Introduction to the History of the Turkic Peoples: Ethnogenesis and State-Formation in Medieval and Early Modern Eurasia and the Middle East* (Wiesbaden: Otto Harrassowitz, 1992); Denis Sinor, "The Establishment and Dissolution of the Türk Empire," in *The Cambridge History of Early Inner Asia,* ed. Denis Sinor (Cambridge: Cambridge University Press, 1990): 285–316.

Turkey (Rum, Seljüks) The Mongols first reduced to tribute and then annexed the Seljük Sultanate in central Turkey. Turkish nomads poured into Anatolia after the Seljük Turks crushed the Byzantine army at Mantzikert (Malazgirt) in 1071. In 1081 a scion of the Seljük dynasty, Süleyman, founded the Rum Sultanate (from "Rome," the Arab word for Byzantium) at Iconium or Konya in modern Turkey. While the majority of Rum's population was still Greek and Armenian, the Seljük Turks made Islam the state religion and Persian the administrative language. Ironically, the sultans often found Greek, Armenian, and Georgian lords more reliable allies than the virtually ungovernable Turkmen nomads. By 1230 the Seljüks of Rum had reached the apex of their power. Having unified the Anatolian Turks and conquered the ports of Antalya and Sinop, the Seljüks grew rich in the flourishing world of Mediterranean commerce.

When the Mongols under CHORMAQAN appeared in western Iran, they initially accepted a Seljük offer of friendship and a modest tribute. Under Ghiyas-ad-Din Kay-Khusrau (1236–45/46), however, the Mongols began to pressure the sultan to go to Mongolia in person, give hostages, and accept a DARUGHACHI (overseer). Raids began in 1240, and Ghiyas-ad-Din gathered a motley army, including Greek, Crusader, and Kurdish mercenaries, to meet them. In June 1243 BAIJU, Chormaqan's successor, crushed the Seljük army at Köse Daği, and Ghiyas-ad-Din escaped to Ankara, while the Mongols plundered or took tribute from the eastern cities. Ghiyas-ad-Din's vizier sent envoys to sue for peace, but the sultan died before ratifying the agreement.

The subsequent Mongol domination of the Seljük Sultanate can be divided into four phases. In the first phase, from 1246 to 1261, Ghiyas-ad-Din's sons 'Izz-ad-Din Kay-Kawus (1246–61) and Rukn-ad-Din Qilich-Arslan (1249–65) struggled incessantly for the throne. 'Izz-ad-Din had received the throne in 1246, but his guardian foolishly sent Rukn-ad-Din to Mongolia as a hostage, hoping to dispose of him. Instead, GÜYÜG Khan (1246–49) ordered Rukn-ad-Din enthroned in 'Izz-ad-Din's place. A *darughachi* with 2,000 Mongol troops was sent to enforce this decision. 'Izz-ad-Din proved almost impossible to subdue, even after Baiju again crushed the Seljük armies at Aksaray (October 1256). The plan of HÜLE'Ü (1256–65), founder of the Mongol IL-KHANATE in the Middle East, to divide the kingdom likewise foundered.

In 1261 Rukn-ad-Din's Persian tutor, Mu'in-ad-Din, known as the Pervâne, "aide-de-camp," conspired with the local Mongol commander to drive 'Izz-ad-Din into exile. In this second phase, from 1261 to 1277, the sultans were reduced to puppets of the Pervâne, who ruled as the Il-Khans' loyal servant, thus retaining a certain amount of autonomy.

When the Sultan Baybars (1260–77) of MAMLUK EGYPT invaded Rum and temporarily occupied Kayseri in 1277, Hüle'ü's son Abagha Khan (1265–82) suspected the Pervâne of communication with the enemy and had him executed. In this third stage, Mongol princes were stationed permanently in Rum, which became the right wing of the Il-Khanate and a key strategic area. Financial integration was also completed, as the *tamgha* (commercial tax) was imposed on Rum.

By the time Geikhatu, the viceroy in Anatolia, became khan (1291–95), the expansion of the southwestern, Karaman dynasty (based at Laranda) had replaced Egyptian invasion as the main danger, and princely regents were discontinued. Rum came into the hands of powerful commanders and was a frequent seat of revolt, often with the assistance of the Karaman Turkmen: TA'ACHAR of the Baarin and Baltu of the JALAYIR in 1296, Sülemish of the OIRATS in 1299, and Temürtash of the Suldus from 1321 to 1327. Even nominal Seljükid rule lapsed in 1307/08, leading to the fourth stage of direct Mongol rule in the east and increasingly expansionist and hostile Turkmen principalities in the west.

Despite the heavy tax demands, Anatolia's economic expansion continued under Mongol rule. When MUHAMMAD ABU 'ABDULLAH IBN BATTUTA visited Turkey in 1332, he found a prosperous Muslim land with a significant Greek population. East of Aksaray the governor Artana, an urbane Muslim Mongol conversant in Arabic, ruled for the Il-Khans. In the southeast the Karaman dynasty, still aligned with Egypt, was expanding, while in the west independent Turkish emirs were slowly driving back the Greeks. When the Il-Khanate broke up in 1335, Artana founded his own dynasty; Anatolia remained disunited until the rise of the Ottoman Empire.

See also GEORGIA; KÖSE DAĞI, BATTLE OF; KURDISTAN; LESSER ARMENIA.

Tushi   *See* JOCHI.

Tutugh (Tutuha, T'u-t'u-ha) (1237–1297) *Qipchaq commander who proved Qubilai Khan's most effective commander in Mongolia*

Tutugh's father, a Qipchaq tribal leader, surrendered to MÖNGKE KHAN in 1237, and with his 100 followers served QUBILAI KHAN in the conquest of Dali and the campaigns against ARIQ-BÖKE. Enrolled in the imperial guard (KESHIG), the Qipchaqs supplied the khan's table with "black" KOUMISS (Turkish, *qara-qumiz*) and hence were called Qarachi (*see* KHARACHIN). In 1277–78 rebel princes kidnaped Qubilai's son Nomuqan, and Tutugh led the QIPCHAQS as part of the army against them. Tutugh's small force proved so effective that Qubilai transferred all enslaved Qipchaq households to his jurisdiction, and all their able-bodied men were made salaried guards. In 1286 the Qipchaqs became an independent imperial guard unit under the hereditary control of Tutugh's family. As guard commander Tutugh received vast estates in the suburbs of DAIDU (modern Beijing) for pasture and farms as well as new Mongol and Chinese recruits. In 1287–88 Tutugh's Qipchaqs effectively mopped up NAYAN'S REBELLION, enrolling all Qipchaqs captured among the enemy's subjects. Tutugh's forces, now numbering 19,000, garrisoned Mongolia, hunting moose in Siberia and raiding the hostile QAIDU KHAN's pastures in the ALTAI RANGE. In 1289 he rescued the future emperor Temür from capture by Qaidu's army. In 1293 he occupied Kem-Kemchik (Tuva), an important base for Qaidu. He died at the front, but his son Chong'ur helped defeat Qaidu and in 1314 led the Yuan armies deep into Central Asia. Later in the dynasty the Qipchaq guards became a powerful political force; his grandson EL-TEMÜR (d. 1334) became senior grand councillor from 1328 to 1333.

Tu'ula   *See* TUUL RIVER.

Tuul River (Tula, Tu'ula)   The largest tributary of the ORKHON RIVER and the main water source for Mongolia's capital, ULAANBAATAR, the Tuul is 819 kilometers (509 miles) long. It flows southwest from the KHENTII RANGE past Ulaanbaatar before turning north to drain into the Orkhon. The Tuul's total drainage area is 50,400 square kilometers (19,460 square miles). The *SECRET HISTORY OF THE MONGOLS* mentions the "Black Forest" on the Tuul (Tu'ula in Middle Mongolian) as the favorite camping grounds of ONG KHAN, ruler of the KEREYID Khanate and early patron of CHINGGIS KHAN. Never a very deep river, the Tuul has been seriously taxed by the growth of Ulaanbaatar; the river's water resources have lessened, and the lower Tuul's water quality has been significantly degraded.

Tuvans (Tyvans, Tuvinians, Tannu Uriyangkhai)   Originally a mixed Samoyed, Turkish, and Mongolian people, the Tuvans were administered as part of Outer Mongolia during the QING DYNASTY (1636–1912) and came under heavy Mongolian influence in their language, culture, and religion. While Tuva was annexed by Russia in 1914, small numbers of Tuvan speakers, including the reindeer-herding DUKHA, remained in Mongolia. The Tofalar and Soyot in Russia's Irkutsk and Buriat regions are also Tuvan in origin.

The Tuvan territory is geographically the northwestern part of the MONGOLIAN PLATEAU, and is drained by the upper Yenisey River. The central lowlands around the capital, Kyzyl, are classic steppe, while the uplands are occupied by larch pine mountain taiga and the northeast by a Siberian steppe of pine, spruce, and fir. The high ALTAI RANGE and the Tannu-Ola and Sayan Mountains are covered by alpine tundra.

ORIGINS AND EARLY HISTORY

The name *Tuva*, which is also found in dialect forms as Tuba, Toba, Tyva, Dyva, and Tofalar (with the plural *-lar* suffix), first appears in Chinese records as "Dubo" (then pronounced Duba/Tuba). They are described as isolated bands living in grass tents, eating lily roots, fish, birds, and animals and dressing in sable and deerskin. The rich had horses, but herding was not widely practiced. Dead bodies were given a "sky burial" in trees. They were ruled by the TÜRK EMPIRES and the UIGHUR EMPIRE (552–840), and many Tuvans today trace their ancestry to the UIGHURS.

In the 13th and 14th centuries, the "Tuba" reappear as a forest clan in the *SECRET HISTORY OF THE MONGOLS*. Other sources describe them as "Forest Uriyangkhai": isolated bands of hunters and reindeer herders living in birchbark tepees (*see* SIBERIA AND THE MONGOL EMPIRE). Again, nothing is known of their language. In the 16th and 17th centuries, the KHOTOGHOID KHALKHA conquered the "Uriyangkhai" of the Yenisey River basin, which passed into the hands of the ZÜNGHARS in the 1660s.

After the fall of the Zünghars to the Manchu QING DYNASTY in 1755, Tuva and northern KHÖWSGÖL PROVINCE were organized into the Tannu Uriyangkhai AIMAG (province) comprising the Kemchik, Tannu (Oyun), Salchak, Tozhu (Toja), and Khöwsgöl Nuur Uriyangkhai BANNERS as well as the territory of the DARKHAD in modern-day Mongolia. The Uriyangkhai banner rulers (Manchu *uheri-da*) were subject to the *jiangjun* (general in chief) in ULIASTAI (*see* AMBA). Other Tuvans were attached as SUM (a subbanner unit) to Khalkha Mongolian banners. All paid tribute in furs. Being outside the Qing dynasty's frontier pickets, Tannu Uriyangkhai was isolated from the main body of Khalkha Mongols.

Under this Manchu-Mongolian condominium the Tuvans became Buddhist. In the 1920s Tuva had 5,000 lamas in 30 monasteries and 1,000 shamans. The western Tuvans (about 80 percent of the population) inhabited steppes and mountain pastures and lived in yurts as live-stock herders, while the eastern Tuvans, or Tozhu, inhabited the taiga forest and lived in bark tepees as hunters and reindeer herders. The western Tuvans are mostly Turco-Mongolian in origin, with some Samoyed clans, while the Tozhu Tuvans are mostly Samoyed with a few Ket, or Turco-Mongolian, clans.

By the 19th century both eastern and western Tuvans spoke Tuvan, a conservative Turkic language overlaid with Mongolian phonetic and lexical influence seen in loanwords such as *saazïn*, "paper," from Mongolian *tsaas(an)*, and *salġin*, "wind," from Mongolian *salkh(in)*. The banner administration was carried on entirely in Mongolian, as was apparently much of the religious life; popular Buddhist prayers in Tuvan are still recited in Mongolian, not Tibetan.

SEPARATION FROM MONGOLIA

With the 1911 RESTORATION of Mongolian independence, the Tozhu, Salchak, and Khöwsgöl banners formally petitioned to be included in Mongolia. Only the head of Tannu banner appealed to czarist Russia for incorporation. Russian settlers poured in, and in 1914 the area of modern Tuva was incorporated into Russia de facto. The Khöwsgöl banners, together with the Darkhad, remained in Mongolia.

After pro-Soviet Russian settlers seized power in the Russian Civil War, Tuva was declared a people's republic in October 1921. The new nation had an area of 168,600 square kilometers (65,100 square miles) and a population in 1926 of 58,117 Tuvans and about 12,000 Russian settlers. At first Mongolian continued to be used as the official language, and many Tuvan leaders desired union with Mongolia. Mongolia recognized Tuvan independence only under pressure in 1926. In 1930–31 Tuva's old aristocratic and monastic classes were disenfranchised, and a new Latin script for writing Tuvan was introduced. Collectivization failed, however. Pro-Mongolian politicians were repeatedly executed for "pan-Mongolism."

Tuvans were conscripted into the Soviet Red Army during WORLD WAR II, and in 1944 the Soviet Union annexed Tuva as an autonomous region in the Russian Soviet Federated Socialist Republic (RSFSR). A Cyrillic script had been introduced for Tuvan in 1943, and Soviet-style collectivization was completed in 1954. In 1961 Tuva was promoted to the status of Autonomous Soviet Socialist Republic, still within the RSFSR. The percentage of ethnic Tuvans increased from 57 percent in 1959 to 60.5 percent in 1979, and full Russification was rare. With the disintegration of the Soviet Union the Republic of Tuva became a constituent republic of the Russian Federation. Ethnic Tuvans in Tuva numbered 198,448, or 64 percent of the republic's 308,557 people, in 1989. Border transit points have been opened with Mongolia, although livestock theft and unauthorized pasturing are significant problems.

TUVANS IN MONGOLIA

After 1914 small Tuvan-speaking populations remained in Mongolia and Xinjiang. Kök Monchak (Blue Button) and Soyon Tuvan clans had been incorporated among the mostly Mongolian ALTAI URIYANGKHAI banners under the Qing. In the division of the Khowd frontier in 1913 between Xinjiang and Outer Mongolia, many were left in northern Xinjiang. Today 1,500–2,000 villagers, officially considered Mongols, still speak Tuvan in northern Xinjiang's Akkaba (Habahe/Kaba county), Kanas, and Kom-Kanas (Burqin county) villages. The Tuvan speakers among Mongolia's Altai Uriyangkhai live in KHOWD PROVINCE's Buyant and BAYAN-ÖLGII PROVINCE's Tsengel Sum (totaling perhaps 2,100 persons). Since 1989 schooling in Tsengel has been conducted in Tuvan, with textbooks from the Republic of Tuva. In Buyant, however, Tuvan is not used in education.

After 1911 the three banners of the Khöwsgöl Uriyangkhai—Köwsgöl Nuur and South Shirkhid east of the lake and North Shirkhid west of the lake—remained in Mongolia. In 1931 they numbered 6,441 persons. CLAN NAMES demonstrate them to be mostly Tuvan in origin, and in the 1920s some still spoke Tuvan and lived in skin or birchbark tepees like the eastern Tuvans, although most had been Mongolized in speech and lifestyle. Today Tuvan speakers live in Tsagaan-Üür Sum and around Khankh and are called by the Mongols Uighur-Uriyangkhai. They call themselves, however, Dukha, thus allying them with the reindeer-herding Dukha or Tsaatan, a separate group of Tuvans in western Khöwsgöl. The Arig-Uriyangkhai (along the Arig River) are Mongolian speaking. Until recently all these Tuvan-origin groups were merged with the Altai Uriyangkhai in Mongolian censuses as "Uriyangkhai."

See also FARMING; HUNTING AND FISHING.

Further reading: Talant Mawkhanuli, "The Jungar Tuvans: Language and Identity in the PRC," *Central Asian Survey* 20 (2001): 497–517; Sevyan Vainshtein, trans. Michael Colenso, *Nomads of South Siberia* (Cambridge: Cambridge University Press, 1980).

Tuvinians *See* TUVANS.

twelve-animal cycle Originating in ancient China, the twelve-animal cycle was adopted by the early steppe empires and following them, the Mongols. It is now used widely in Mongolia for astrological and traditional dating purposes.

The twelve-animal cycle originated with the system of 10 heavenly stems and 12 earthly branches found in the early Chinese writings from the second millennium B.C.E The 10- and 12-year cycles, running concurrently, produce a larger 60-year cycle used to number both days and years. The original names for these two cycles are of obscure meaning. During the Han dynasty (202 B.C.E. to

220 C.E.), cosmological speculation linked the 10 earthly branches to the five phases (wood, fire, earth, metal, and water) and their associated colors (blue, red, yellow, white, and black) and the 12 earthly branches to 12 animals (mouse, cow, tiger, hare, dragon, snake, horse, sheep, monkey, chicken, dog, and pig). This produced the twelve-animal cycle. These equivalences were, however, never used for dating systems in China.

Under the TÜRK EMPIRES (522–742) the nomads of Mongolia adopted as their dating system the twelve-animal cycle but not the full 60-year cycle. This usage continued under the UIGHUR EMPIRE in Mongolia and after the UIGHURS resettled in modern Xinjiang. This usage was then taken up during the MONGOL EMPIRE and spread by the Mongols and their Uighur scribes into the farthest corners of the empire. It was used officially in Iran, for example, until 1925.

The twelve-animal cycle creates serious confusion when used to date isolated events—indeed, the date of composition of the SECRET HISTORY OF THE MONGOLS, dated only the year of the mouse (1228? 1240? 1252?, etc.), remains uncertain to this day for that reason. Uighur astronomers had long used the Chinese 10 heavenly stems, written phonetically in their Uighur script, for astrological purposes. In the mid-17th century the Mongolian historian SAGHANG SECHEN adopted these 10 stems in Uighur writing to produce a full 60-year cycle. Most authors, however, adopted the Tibetan system, which used the five phases combined with "male" and "female" to replicate the 10-stem cycle, or a later Mongolian system that used the five colors (associated with the five phases) with or without a female suffix to replace the 10-stem cycle. Thus, 1913, *gui/chou* year in Chinese, could be either *güi ükher* (*gui*/cow) year, *eme usun ükher* (female water cow) year, or *kharagchin ükher* (black-female cow) year. The final refinement to this system of numbering the 60-year cycles was taken by the Tibetans and a few Mongolian imitators, so that dates could be fixed without ambiguity.

As throughout East Asia, the twelve-animal cycle is used for astrological purposes, particularly to determine compatibility between marriage partners. The full cycle of 60 combinations is used by lama-astrologers for the days as well as years and is held to determine the name, spiritual affinities (i.e., which class of Buddhas they should worship), and other features of newborn children.

See also ASTROLOGY; CALENDARS AND DATING SYSTEMS; 17TH-CENTURY CHRONICLES; ZUD.

Further reading: Charles Melville, "The Chinese-Uighur Animal Calendar in Persian Historiography of the Mongol Period," *Iran* 32 (1994): 83–98.

"Two Customs" (*Khoyar Yosu*) This concept, along with the allied concept of "offering site and almsgiver" (or priest and patron), linked the Buddhist religion to imperial rule in Inner Asia. The "Two Customs" of Bud-

dhist religion (*shashin*) and monarchical rule (*törö*) established a mutually harmonious relation between the two fundamental orders of society, celibate monks and married householders. The monarch served as an "almsgiver" (*öglige-yin ejen,* from Tibetan *yon-bdag*) to the monks, who served as an "offering site" (*takhil-un oron,* from Tibetan *mchod-gnas*). The monarch also had the duty to ensure the discipline of the monastic community (*sangha*), expelling the unfit. From the Tangut XIA DYNASTY (1038–1227) on, the monarch would ideally receive an initiation into one of the great Tantric Buddhist deities following a preparatory course of study with fastings and meditations and would prostrate himself before his lama-teacher. While shocking to defenders of imperial prerogatives, this Tantric pupil-teacher relation was the acme of the "almsgiver–offering-site" relation. (Although the translation "two principles" has become common, the word *yosu* in Mongolian is always "custom," with its implication of past tradition.)

The advocates of this order saw the "Two Customs" and "offering site–almsgiver" relations as a perennial tradition that linked both genealogical lineages of monarchs and initiation lineages of Tantric masters. Some historical works argued implicitly and explicitly that the almsgivers had to be of Chinggisid lineage (for example, the JEWEL TRANSLUCENT SUTRA of 1607) and others that the offering site had to be the incarnate Dalai Lama of Tibet (for example, the Fifth Dalai Lama's history of Tibet). Others used the concepts as free-floating images that could be applied to any devout monarch and accomplished lama.

The term and concept of the "Two Customs" appeared explicitly in Mongolia with the SECOND CONVERSION of the Mongols (roughly 1575 to 1655). The CHAGHAN TEÜKE (White history) envisioned the "Two Customs" as a comprehensive system of government, with dignitaries divided into monastic and lay ranks and the monastic ones of distinctly higher rank. This utopian scheme was projected back to the time of the Yuan emperor QUBILAI KHAN (1260–94) and the Sa-skya-pa Tibetan cleric 'PHAGS-PA LAMA (1235–80) and their Yuan and Sa-skya successors. Histories of this era, such as the *Jewel Translucent Sutra* (1607) and the ERDENI-YIN TOBCHI (1662), explained how, although lost in the fall of the Yuan in 1368, ALTAN KHAN (1508–82) and KHUTUGTAI SECHEN KHUNG-TAIJI (1540–86) revived the "Two Customs." In reality, although Qubilai and 'Phags-pa had certainly established an "offering site/–almsgiver" relationship, including a Tantric initiation, Qubilai never granted the exclusive patronage of Buddhism and the autonomy for the "offering site" implied in the mature "Two Customs" concept. Even so, the Third Dalai Lama (1543–88) recognized Altan Khan as an incarnation of Qubilai and himself as an incarnation of 'Phags-pa, although Altan Khan was not the senior descendant of Qubilai Khan and the Dalai Lama was not a Sa-skya-pa monk, but a member of the new dGe-lugs-pa (Yellow Hat) order.

In the 17th century the concept of the "Two Customs" and "offering site and almsgiver" became an area of violent political contention. LIGDAN KHAN (1604–34), as Qubilai Khan's senior descendant, implicitly rebuked the claims of Altan Khan and the Dalai Lama by patronizing the Sa-skya-pa order and installing in his capital an image of Mahakala previously said to have been given to 'Phags-pa by Qubilai. In Tibet the Fifth Dalai Lama (1617–82) held that the Dalai Lamas were the rightful offering sites for all the Inner Asian rulers and that almsgivers such as Qubilai had always given administration of Tibet, as a religious country, to their offering sites. The chief point of the "Two Customs" was thus to ensure Tibet's autonomy under the Dalai Lamas. Oirat rulers in Kökenuur and Z̈ungharia, such as TÖRÖ-BAIKHU GÜÜSHI KHAN and GALDAN BOSHOGTU KHAN, cultivated the Dalai Lamas as a way to overcome their lack of Chinggisid ancestry.

The KHALKHA Mongolian Chinggisids focused their devotion on the local incarnation lineage of the JIBZUN-DAMBA KHUTUGTUS, whose first two incarnations were nobleborn Khalkhas. The Jibzundamba Khutugtu, as the offering site for an ever-expanding Chinggisid nobility, thus became the symbol, spokesman, and leader of the Khalkha Mongols.

The Manchus' QING DYNASTY (1636–1912), having defeated Ligdan Khan in 1634, at first emphasized their heaven-destined capture of the Mahakala image and the "precious jade seal," objects that embodied the holiness of the Sa-skya religion and Chinggisid state, respectively. With the Shunzhi emperor's meeting with the Fifth Dalai Lama in 1652, however, the Qing emperors explicitly stepped into Altan Khan's shoes as supreme "almsgiver" for the dGe-lugs-pa. Giving initiation to the Qianlong emperor in 1745, Rolbidorji (Tibetan, Rol-pa'i rDo-rje),

the second JANGJIYA KHUTUGTU, declared that he was 'Phags-pa Lama and Qianlong was Qubilai. Writers such as Damchoi-Jamsu Dharmatala in his *Rosary of White Lotuses* (1889) called the Manchu emperors, as the guarantors of monastic discipline, the "backbone" of the dGe-lugs-pa teaching. In southwest Inner Mongolia the Mongols looked to the Qing monarchs as defenders of their Buddhist society against Muslim bandits and Catholic missionaries.

The modernizing and sinicizing NEW POLICIES reforms at the end of the Qing forfeited them this role, and Mongolian independence in 1911 had as one of its key aims the protection of the "Two Customs" of Buddhist society and Chinggisid nobility. The EIGHTH JIBZUN-DAMBA KHUTUGTU (1870–1924) was enthroned as the "dual ruler of religion and state." Although the fall of the theocratic state in 1919 seriously damaged the prestige of the old order, even in the 1921 REVOLUTION songs that spoke of simultaneously raising the red flag of revolution and the yellow flag of religion showed the influence of "Two Customs" imagery.

See also DIDACTIC POETRY; JIBZUNDAMBA KHUTUGTU, FIRST; JIBZUNDAMBA KHUTUGTU, SECOND.

Further reading: Damchø Gyatsho Dharmatāla, trans. Piotr Klafkowski, *Rosary of White Lotuses* (Wiesbaden: Otto Harrassowitz, 1987); Samuel M. Grupper, "Manchu Patronage and Tibetan Buddhism during the First Half of the Ch'ing Dynasty," *Journal of the Tibet Society* 4 (1984): 47–75.

"Two Principles" *See* "TWO CUSTOMS."

Tyvans *See* TUVANS.

U

Ubsa Nurr   *See* LAKE UWS.

Ubur Khangai   *See* SOUTH KHANGAI PROVINCE.

Ugedey Khan   *See* ÖGEDEI KHAN.

Uighur Empire (Uyghur, Uygur, Uigur)   The Uighur Empire, which ruled Mongolia from 744 to 840, converted to Manicheism and built numerous cities and settlements in Mongolia.

ORIGINS AND RISE

The UIGHURS first appear as a tribe in the Toquz Oghuz, or "Nine Oghuz," confederation, linked by Chinese histories to the earlier "High-Carts" (Gaoju) and the vast "Tiele" (Töles?) confederation. These peoples were south Siberian and apparently Turkish speaking. During the sixth century, the Uighurs ruled the eight other Toquz Oghuz tribes and were themselves divided into 10 clans, of which the Yaghlaqar was the ruling one. By 552 at least one body of Uighurs was in the Transbaikal area, while another occupied the Altai-Tuvan region.

The Toquz Oghuz formed an important but turbulent subject population for the two TÜRK EMPIRES (552–630, 682–742). In 742, in cooperation with the Basmil near the Tianshan Mountains, and the QARLUQS in Zungharia, the Uighurs overthrew the second Türk Empire. Three years later the Uighurs drove out the Basmil and elevated Qulligh Boyla as the Qutlugh Bilge Kül Qaghan (744–47), establishing their capital, ORDU-BALIGH, in the ORKHON-RIVER-TAMIR region that had been the Türk Empire's sacred center.

Qilligh Boyla's son Bayan-Chor (Moyanchuo, reign title Bilge-Kül Qaghan, 747–59) drove his former Basmil and Qarluq allies west, securing the Besh-Baligh-Gaochang (modern Turpan) oases. He also began the Uighurs' alliance with China's Tang dynasty by crushing the An Lushan Rebellion (755–62) that threatened to overthrow the dynasty. As Bayan-Chor's son Bögü (reign title Tengri Qaghan, 759–79) stamped out An Lushan's last adherents in Luoyang, he was converted by a colony of Sogdian Manicheans. Accompanied by a Manichean priest, Ruixi, Bögü returned to Ordu-Baligh and declared Manicheism the state religion. In 779 Bögü's cousin Tun Bagha Tarqan, alarmed at the Sogdian dominance of Uighur policy, assassinated Bögü and seized the throne (reign name Alp-Qutlugh Bilge Qaghan, 779–89). The Tang alliance was renewed, but the Tibetan Empire delivered several humiliating defeats to Tun-Bagha's sons.

INSTITUTIONS AND CULTURE

The Uighurs appear at first to have inherited most of the institutions of rule found in the Türk Empires. Unlike the Türks, however, who followed lateral succession, the Uighurs preferred primogeniture. The qaghans (*see* KHAN) chose reign titles that show the influence of the Türk concepts of *qut,* "heaven-bestowed good fortune," and *bilge,* "wisdom," as the necessary attributes of good rule. A new feature of the later reign titles was the reference to *Ay Tengri,* "Moon God," and *Kün Tengri,* "Sun God," which may reflect the Manichean reverence for the sun and moon.

Like the Türks before them, the Uighurs ruled in a virtual symbiosis with the Sogdian merchants of Bukhara and Samarqand. Their attitude toward the Chinese, however, was very different from the Türk rulers' usually hostile stance. Facing a much weaker China, the Uighur rulers treated the Tang as a protectorate. In return for fighting rebels and Tibetans, the Uighurs expected vast sums of silk, as much as 230,000 bolts in a single year, and imperial princesses. Although the Uighurs also traded horses and presented "tribute goods" at the same time, the Tang found Uighur assistance very expensive, while Uighur troops were often as destructive as the rebels they were fighting.

Uighur culture changed dramatically with Bayan-Chor's forced conversion of his people to Manicheism. Manichean doctrines required strict vegetarianism of the elect priests, including the renunciation of KOUMISS. Bögü exhorted his people to "let [the country] with barbarous customs and smoking blood change into one where people can eat vegetables; and let the state where men kill be transformed into a kingdom where good works are encouraged." By 821 the Arab visitor Tamim bin Bahr at the capital, Ordu-Baligh, found the city's population primarily Manichean. Manicheism also adapted to Uighur life; Manichean hymns, for example, incorporated the Türk-Uighur reverence for Ötüken.

Unlike the Türks, the Uighurs were avid city builders. The first two qaghans built Bay-Baligh on the SELENGE RIVER (in Khutag-Öndör Sum, Bulgan) and the capital, Ordu-Baligh, with Sogdian and Chinese labor. The conquest of Besh-Baligh (near modern Qitai) and Gaochang also amplified the importance of farming for the Uighur state; cotton soon came to be one of the tribute products presented to China. An Uighur expatriate community in China dwelt in several cities served by Manichean temples. The Uighurs are particularly mentioned as moneylenders. At first these "Uighurs" were probably in large part the qaghans' Sogdian subjects, but ethnic Uighurs later played a major mercantile role.

While their own spoken dialect may have differed somewhat, the Uighurs adopted the written form of Old Turkish used in the Türk empires. Uighur inscriptions found in Mongolia show the primary use of the Türks' Runic script alongside a cursive adaption of Sogdian for Uighur, which after the fall of the empire became the Uighurs' main script.

FALL OF THE UIGHUR EMPIRE

In 795, when Tun Bagha's second son died without an heir, the commander in chief Qutlugh of the Ediz tribe seized the throne as Alp-Qutlugh Bilge Qaghan (795–805). Alp-Qutlugh took the Yaghlaqar surname but dispatched the true Yaghlaqar princes to China as hostages. It is not clear if the later Uighur qaghans were his descendants, but at some point the Yaghlaqar dynasty appears to have been restored. Under Alp-Qutlugh's successors the Tang grew increasingly resistant to Uighur demands, although the reappearance of the Tibet threat made them more cooperative in the 820s.

After 832 several qaghans were killed by their servitors. In 839 a massive snowfall devastated the Uighur herds, and in 840 a disaffected Uighur general led a force of 100,000 Yenisey Kyrgyz from Khakassia to sack Ordu-Baligh and slay the last qaghan. The Uighur ruling class fled to the Chinese border but were hunted down and captured by the Kyrgyz. Others found refuge among the KITANS in eastern Inner Mongolia, in the Uighur protectorate of Besh-Baligh and Gaochang (Turpan), and in the Gansu corridor under the Tibetans. In the diaspora Uighurs continued and expanded their involvement in caravan trade and moneylending while eventually abandoning Manicheism for Buddhism. The Uighurs of Uighuristan (Besh-Baligh and Turpan) later "tutored" the Mongols, just as the Sogdians had tutored them. Those of the Gansu corridor became the nucleus of the Yogurs, a partly Mongol partly Turkic people. The Uighar clan of Tuva and modern UWS PROVINCE of northwestern Mongolia appears to be a remnant of the original Uighurs of the plateau.

See also RELIGION; RUNIC SCRIPT AND INSCRIPTIONS; TRIBUTE SYSTEM; TUVANS; UIGHUR-MONGOLIAN SCRIPT; YOGUR LANGUAGES AND PEOPLES.

Further reading: Peter Golden, *An Introduction to the History of the Turkic Peoples: Ethnogenesis and State-Formation in Medieval and Early Modern Eurasia and the Middle East* (Wiesbaden: Otto Harrassowitz, 1992); Colin Mackerras, "The Uighurs," in *The Cambridge History of Early Inner Asia,* ed. Denis Sinor (Cambridge: Cambridge University Press, 1990), 317–342.

Uighur-Mongolian script (old script, vertical script, mongolian script, written Mongolian)

Ultimately stemming from the Aramaic script via Sogdian and Uighur, the Uighur-Mongolian alphabet was the medium of almost all Mongolia's written and literary heritage until the 20th century. Although replaced in Mongolia proper by the Cyrillic script in 1950, it is still used for daily purposes in Inner Mongolia and for scholarly and academic uses throughout the Mongolian world.

EARLY DEVELOPMENT OF THE SCRIPT

The official use of the Aramaic script, close to the Hebrew script, in the ancient Persian Empire (549–323 B.C.E.) brought it to the Sogdian city-states of Central Asia, which adopted it for the Iranian language. In the sixth to ninth centuries the Sogdians became merchant partners of both the TÜRK EMPIRES and the UIGHUR EMPIRE. As a result, the UIGHURS adopted the Sogdian script in a modified form.

As a Semitic-type script, Aramaic and Sogdian were traditionally written like Hebrew in separate letters in rows from right to left arranged from top to bottom. Under the Uighurs the script was eventually turned vertically so that it read in top-down columns arranged from left to right. The script also slowly developed into a cursive script, in which all the letters in a word were connected. This involved the simplification of forms and the further creation of initial, medial, and final forms of most of the letters. Vowels, originally mostly omitted, came to be more regularly written. Dots were introduced to distinguish *n* from *a/e*, *gh* from *q*, and *sh* from *s*, although they were often not used consistently. Even so, the script as adopted for Uighur contained many ambiguities that made it hard to use.

ADOPTION BY THE MONGOLS

By the beginning of the 13th century Uighur scribes were already being employed on the MONGOLIAN PLATEAU. When CHINGGIS KHAN's remote and completely illiterate MONGOL TRIBE conquered the more civilized NAIMAN Khanate in 1204, he took over the Uighur script and made the Uighur scribe TATAR-TONG'A a tutor for his children. Later an Uighur merchant, CHINQAI, became the khan's chief scribe. Throughout the subsequent MONGOL EMPIRE Uighurs dominated the scribal class.

The adaption of the Uighur script to Mongolian increased the already considerable number of ambiguities in the script. Uighur scribes writing in Mongolian conformed to a number of spelling rules appropriate for Uighur but not for Mongolian: only *t-* was written in the word-initial position and only *-d-* in the medial or final position. Uighur had no *j*, but instead of creating a new character *y-* was used in word-initial positions and *-ch-* used medially. This preserved a number of identical spellings for which Uighur had *y-* for Mongolian *j-* (for example, Uighur *yarliq* and Mongolian *jarliq*, decree), but again at the price of ambiguity.

Early Uighur-Mongolian was thus a very imperfect script, leaving many words open to multiple readings. An extra *i* was used to separate *ö* and *ü* from *o* and *u* and diphthongs were now usually distinguished if necessary by *ii*. The script's serious faults may be why QUBILAI KHAN in 1269 commissioned 'PHAGS-PA LAMA to create the SQUARE SCRIPT based on Tibetan. However, despite imperial promotion, the square script never replaced the Uighur-Mongolian script except for official purposes. After the expulsion of the Mongol YUAN DYNASTY from China in 1368, the Uighur-Mongolian script survived among the Mongols, but the square script did not.

DEVELOPMENT OF THE SCRIPT

With the cultural revival of the 17th century a number of reformers set out to correct the imperfections of the Uighur script. Comprehensive reforms resulted in the creation of a new script for the rising Manchu people of Manchuria and the CLEAR SCRIPT used among the OIRATS (West Mongols), yet even without such radical reforms, the Uighur-Mongolian script was greatly improved. In the middle of words, two different styles of writing *ch/j* were fixed as separate letters for the two consonants, although initial *y-* and *j-* remained generally undistinguished. Diacritical dots came to be used more consistently.

The accurate rendition of Sanskrit, Tibetan, and Chinese words was virtually impossible in the original Uighur script. In 1587 the great Buddhist translator Ayushi Güüshi (fl. 1578–1609) created a complete set of new *galig* (transcription) letters to render all the different letters of Sanskrit and Tibetan. In the 17th century a complete set of Chinese transcription letters was devised by the Manchus.

Classical Mongolian, as enshrined in official administrative documents of the 18th and 19th centuries, was thus far more readable than the preclassical Mongolian of the MONGOL EMPIRE. Given the constraints of Mongolian syllable structure and vowel harmony, only the ambiguities of *t/d*, *o/u*, *ö/ü*, word-initial *y/j*, and sometimes *a/e* remained, and they posed little problem for a fluent reader. Even so, orthography had not changed since the 13th century, and language change had made many of the spellings and forms, particularly in the case endings, obsolete. While colloquial forms and dialectal variations become frequent from the 18th century on, Mongolian scribes, who usually worked by dictation, developed an artificially archaic scribal pronunciation.

The Uighur-Mongolian script was originally written with a calamus cut diagonally and dipped in ink. The official administration under the Qing dynasty (1636–1912) used the Chinese brush, a practice maintained in independent Mongolia until 1929. Texts were printed with block prints (from a carved wooden block), not with movable type. The usual training in literacy emphasized penmanship, and regular stints as scribe in the local administration were required of all literate persons. To avoid this service, even many distinguished authors preferred not to become too able at writing and instead dictated to scribes. The existence of different letter forms depending on the preceding or following letter meant that the Uighur-Mongolian script was taught to students not so much as an alphabet but as a syllabary. Different areas used different orders of the letters in teaching, making alphabetized referencing inconvenient.

MODERN DEVELOPMENTS

The introduction of movable-type printing presses for Mongolian, first created in Russia for Christian missionary needs in the early 19th century, and typewriters in the 1920s highlighted some of the challenges in adopting a vertical, cursive script to modern writing technology. The first proposals for replacing the Uighur-Mongolian script came among the Buriat Mongols of southern Siberia after 1905, where many did not use the script and the speech was particularly divergent from the classical language (*see* BURIAT LANGUAGE AND SCRIPTS).

The effective impetus behind dropping the Uighur-Mongolian script was, however, political. The Buriat Latin script was introduced in 1931 during the Communist International's hard-left policies, and experiments were made in Mongolia proper at the same time with

Latinization, new orthography, and teaching the script purely as an alphabet. With the moderate NEW TURN POLICY (1932–34) in Mongolia, the grammarian and lexicographer Shagja (S. Shagj, 1886–1938) denounced these changes as distorting the script's fundamental nature, while he made the script more usable by standardizing orthography and the order of the alphabet and creating dictionaries and other reference works. Political demands eventually forced a decision to Cyrillicize in 1941, although the Uighur-Mongolian script in a semiclassical orthography was not actually phased out until 1950.

In Inner Mongolia the Japanese-educated KHARACHIN Temgetü (1887–1939) set the standard for movable-type printing with his 1923 typography. Following eastern Inner Mongolian handwriting style, he adopted a number of useful Manchu features, such as an initial *y* distinct from *j* and a distinction of *f* and *p* in foreign words. After WORLD WAR II these changes were incorporated into a new postclassical Mongolian, which systematically modernized the orthography for suffixes. Standardization of the alphabet facilitated the use of alphabetic referencing in dictionaries and reference works. This postclassical script is still the standard script for Mongolian in Inner Mongolia; a brief attempt in Inner Mongolia to switch to the Cyrillic in 1955–58 was canceled due to political considerations.

From 1989 the Uighur-Mongolian script underwent a renaissance in Mongolia proper. For a while plans were made to switch back to the "old script," but popular resistance proved too great to overcome in a democracy. The Uighur-Mongolian script, however, is now a required topic in Mongolia's secondary schools.

See also MONGOLIAN LANGUAGE.

Further reading: György Kara, "Mongolian Script," in *The World's Writing Systems,* ed. Peter Daniels and William Bright (Oxford: Oxford University Press, 1996), 545–548; Igor de Rachewiltz, "Some Remarks on Written Mongolian," in *Meng-ku wen hua guo chi hsüeh shu yen t'ao hui lun wen chi,* ed. Chün-i Chang (Taipei: Mongolian and Tibetan Affair Commission, 1993), 123–136.

Uighurs (Uyghurs, Uygurs, Uigurs) During the rise of the Mongols the Uighurs were Turkic-speaking people who lived in the oases of modern Xinjiang and served as the foremost teachers of literacy and administration for the Mongol Empire builders. The Uighurs first lived in northern Mongolia, where they formed an empire in the eighth and ninth centuries (*see* UIGHUR EMPIRE). After 840 the Uighurs fled the plateau due to economic hardship and invasion.

SETTLEMENT IN TURPAN

The Uighurs who fled the Mongolian plateau settled in two areas, Ganzhou in the Gansu corridor of northwest China and the oases of what came to be called Uighuristan in modern eastern Xinjiang. The Tangut XIA DYNASTY (1038–1227) in northwest China eventually conquered the Ganzhou Uighurs, who dwindled to became ancestors of the small Yogur nationality in contemporary China. Those of Uighuristan, however, maintained their autonomy for centuries, ruling from Hami (Qamil or Kumul) west to Aksu. Their capital was Qara-Qocho (Chinese, Gaochang) in Xinjiang's fertile Turpan oasis. The indigenous inhabitants of Uighuristan had been Hinayana Buddhists, and the Uighurs' ruling Yaghlaqar dynasty converted from Manicheism to Buddhism by at least 1000. Chinese cultural influence was of long standing in the area, and Mahayana Buddhist texts, translated from Chinese, influenced the Uighur Buddhists deeply. By 1200 the Uighurs were mostly Buddhist but also had a significant Christian community (Manicheism was almost extinct). Christian-Buddhist relations were traditionally harmonious, while the Muslim Turkestanis to the west were seen as both military threats and trade rivals. The Uighurs had long had trade connections with the Sogdians of Transoxiana and had adopted their alphabet from them, although they wrote it vertically, not horizontally.

The Uighurs dominated North China's trade with Central Asia. Relations with the KITANS, a Mongolic people in Inner Mongolia who founded the Liao dynasty (907–1125), were particularly cordial. In 1130, after the Jurchen people of Manchuria crushed the Kitans' Liao dynasty, the Uighurs became junior allies of the QARA-KHITAI Empire founded by a Kitan adventurer in Central Asia. Uighur trade in North China and Mongolia continued. Uighurs served as scribes and even imperial tutors for the Qara-Khitai and the NAIMAN Khanate in western Mongolia and traded with the KEREYID Khanate in central Mongolia.

UIGHURS AND THE MONGOL EMPIRE

By the time CHINGGIS KHAN united the Mongols in 1206, he had conquered both the Kereyid and the Naiman, and several Uighurs were already in his service, including TATAR-TONG'A and CHINQAI. By this time the Qara-Khitai overlordship had become onerous, and in 1209 the *iduq-qut* (or *idi-qut,* Holy Majesty, the Uighur royal title) Barchuq Art Tegin and the Uighur lords killed the Qara-Khitai representative and surrendered to the Mongols. In 1211 Barchuq visited Chinggis Khan in Mongolia and received high favor as the first sedentary ruler to submit to the Mongols. A Mongol princess was bestowed on the *iduq-qut,* the first of many intermarriages with the Mongol imperial clan. The Uighurs sent 10,000 troops to assist the Mongols on their campaigns against KHORAZM (1219–23) and the Tangut Xia dynasty (1226–27). Under the Mongols the capital was moved north to Besh-Baligh (near modern Qitai).

Uighurs won fame, however, not as soldiers but as clerks. Influenced by Tatar-Tong'a, Chinggis Khan adopted the Uighur script as the official Mongol alphabet.

By the time of his son ÖGEDEI KHAN (1229–41), both the khan and the princely establishments throughout the empire were employing Uighur scribes. Ambitious men all over Uighuristan found that employment under the Mongols was a ticket to wealth and fame. Uighur dominance of the scribal guild was so complete that numerous phonological peculiarities of the Uighur script were directly imported into the new Mongolian alphabet. Under Ögedei's son GÜYÜG Khan (1246–48) Uighur officials increased their dominance, sidelining the North Chinese and Muslims. The Uighurs, both Christian and Buddhist, came to see Muslim officials as their chief rivals for influence. After Güyüg died and his cousin MÖNGKE khan was elected (1251–59), a Buddhist Uighur scribe named Bala inveigled the *iduq-qut* Salindi into an anti-Möngke and anti-Islamic plot. The plot was discovered, and Salindi, Bala, and their confederates were publicly executed. Even so, the royal family remained high in the favor of the Mongols, although the predominance of Uighur scribes declined somewhat.

UIGHURS AND THE YUAN

With the breakup of the MONGOL EMPIRE, Uighuristan became a battle zone between the YUAN DYNASTY of QUBILAI KHAN (1260–1294), centered in North China, and his enemies. During the brief conflict between Qubilai Khan and his brother ARIQ-BÖKE from 1260–64, the *iduq-qut* stayed neutral. When QAIDU KHAN, a grandson of Ögedei, allied with the CHAGHATAY KHANATE to oppose Qubilai, the reigning *iduq-qut*, Qochqar, and the Uighurs strongly supported Qubilai. Qaidu and his allies were based northwest of Uighuristan, and around 1270 the *iduq-qut* moved his court from Besh-Baligh back to the more sheltered site of Qara-Qocho in the Turpan basin. In 1283, when Qochqar died, his son was still young, and Qubilai removed his seat from Qocho to Yongchang in northwest China, while Yuan commanders established garrisons and military farms in Uighuristan. Civil administration was reorganized on the Chinese pattern with a "Pacification Commission for Besh-Baligh, Qara-Qocho, and Vicinity." In 1286 the Yuan lost Besh-Baligh, and constant raids by Qaidu's forces prompted steady migration of those Uighur families with means away from Uighuristan and into China, a migration which the Yuan government attempted to counter with state-sponsored relief and assistance.

In China the Uighur community flourished, serving in every corner of the empire. LIAN XIXIAN, for example, son of a Uighur official in Yanjing (modern Beijing), and the general ARIQ-QAYA, son of a poor farmer, both achieved high position in Qubilai's administration. Among officeholders in the Yuan, Uighurs were outnumbered only by the Mongols themselves and the North Chinese. Many found no difficulty assimilating Chinese ideas and mastering the Confucian classics. Qubilai Khan nicknamed Lian Xixian "Lian Mencius" for his devotion to the works of the Chinese philosopher. Nevertheless, despite the frequent adoption of Chinese names and the eager assimilation of Chinese literary culture, these same Uighur clans preserved their language and a distinct social network of intermarrying Uighur families.

Buddhist Uighurs came strongly under the influence of the Tibetan Buddhism patronized by the Mongol court. Both Mongol and Uighur Buddhists eagerly read Uighur translations of Tibetan-language hagiographies and commentaries. Even CHOSGI-ODSIR, one of the great translators of Tibetan works into Mongolian, seems to have been Uighur in origin. In the western khanates—the GOLDEN HORDE, the CHAGHATAY KHANATE, and the IL-KHANATE—Uighur *baqshis* (teachers or masters) propagated Buddhism and were frequent rivals of Islamic clerics.

UIGHURS AND THE CHAGHATAYIDS

Sometime between 1295 and 1305 Uighuristan drifted into the orbit of the Mongol Chaghatay Khanate. Yuan-Chaghatayid tensions prompted a renewed effort at Yuan control in 1316, but by 1338–39 Besh-Baligh and Qara-Qocho were back again in the Chaghatay orbit. Turpan remained a semiautonomous vassal state, first of the Chaghatay Khanate and by 1420 or so of MOGHULISTAN (the eastern Chaghatay successor state). It was not, however, fully integrated into Moghulistan until the reign of Sultan Mansur (1504–43).

The Uighurs in Hami, however, came under a different dynasty. After the fall of the Yuan dynasty, Gunashiri (or Unashiri), a Buddhist Chaghatayid prince who had followed the Yuan emperors back into Mongolia, established himself in Hami by 1390. Submitting to China's MING DYNASTY in 1404, his dynasty maintained relations with the Ming and the OIRATS (West Mongols) until being overthrown in 1463. From 1467 the Ming repeatedly reinstalled relatives of the old dynasty, but Hami was finally conquered by Sultan Mansur of Moghulistan in 1513. Buddhists in Uighuristan maintained contact with the Ming, the Oirats, the Yellow Uighurs of Gansu (ancestors of the Yogurs), and Tibet until the final conversion to Islam. The last Buddhists fled to China around 1441 from Turpan and around 1473 from Hami.

After Hami submitted to the Oirats in the 1430s, the Uighurs also became active in southwest Inner Mongolia. A large body of Uighurs settled by the Huang (Yellow) River bend, and the Uighur chiefs Beg-Arslan (d. 1479), Ismayil (d. 1486), and Iburai (d. 1533) became major leaders of the western Mongols. The reunification of Mongolia under BATU-MÖNGKE DAYAN KHAN (1480?–1517?) put an end to these contacts, but the Uighurjin clan name is still found today in the ORDOS area of Inner Mongolia.

From Islamization until 1923 the term *Uighur* was used only locally for the Muslim Turkic-speaking peoples of Hami and Turpan. In 1923 it was chosen as a general designation for Xinjiang's Tarim Basin oasis dwellers.

See also ALTAIC LANGUAGE FAMILY; BUDDHISM IN THE MONGOL EMPIRE; CHRISTIANITY IN THE MONGOL EMPIRE; JARLIQ; UIGHUR-MONGOLIAN SCRIPT; YOGUR LANGUAGES AND PEOPLE.

Further reading: Thomas T. Allsen, "The Yüan Dynasty and the Uighurs of Turfan in the 13th Century," in *China among Equals: The Middle Kingdom and Its Neighbors, 10th–14th Centuries,* ed. Morris Rossabi (Berkeley: University of California Press, 1983), 243–280.

Ujimqin *See* ÜJÜMÜCHIN.

Üjümüchin (Ujimqin, Üzemchin, Wuzhumuqin) One of the banners (districts) of Inner Mongolia's Shiliin Gol, the Üjümüchin are known for the beautiful embroidered hems on their traditional Mongolian robes (*deel*). In 1945 a body of Üjümüchins emigrated to (Outer) Mongolia.

In 1949 the Üjümüchin and neighboring Khuuchid banners were merged. In 1956 this combined territory was again divided into two Üjümüchin banners. In 1990 the two Üjümüchin BANNERS had a combined population of 127,700, of which 83,700 were Mongols. In Mongolia the Üjümüchin *yastan* (subethnic group) numbered 2,100 in 1989 and were settled in Eastern Province's Sergelen Sum.

Üjümüchin was an OTOG (camp district) of the CHAKHAR *tümen* in the 16th century. Like the nobility of SHILIIN GOL's Khuuchid and Sönid banners, the princes of Üjümüchin were junior descendants of the Chinggisid Bodi Alag Khan (1519–47), grandson of BATU-MÖNGKE DAYAN KHAN. After fleeing LIGDAN KHAN's rule in 1627, the nobles of Üjümüchin surrendered to the new Manchu QING DYNASTY in 1637, and two of them were selected as *jasag*s (rulers; *see* ZASAG) of Üjümüchin Right and Left Banners.

Üjümüchin remained isolated despite incorporation into the Republic of China after 1915 and Japanese occupation after 1937. After the Soviet-Mongolian invasion of 1945 that ended WORLD WAR II, Üjümüchin Left Banner's young *jasag*, Minjurdorji, led 1,785 Üjümüchins to migrate to Mongolia.

See also FOLK POETRY AND TALES; GOMBOJAB, DUKE; INNER MONGOLIA AUTONOMOUS REGION; INNER MONGOLIANS; MONGOLIAN LANGUAGE.

Ulaanbaatar (Ulan-Bator, Urga) Beginning in the 17th century as a monastery town and the seat of the great INCARNATE LAMA, the JIBZUNDAMBA KHUTUGTU, Ulaanbaatar since 1911 has been the political, economic, cultural, and social center of Mongolia.

LOCATION AND ENVIRONMENT

Ulaanbaatar's physical environment is close to average for Mongolia. At 1,300 meters (4,265 feet) above sea level, it is situated near the border of the *khangai* (mountainous forest-steppe) and steppe zones. Average annual precipitation is 258.5 millimeters (10.18 inches), and average temperatures range from –22°C (–8°F) in January to 17° (63°F) in July. Ulaanbaatar is the coldest national capital in the world.

Ulaanbaatar lies in an east-west valley at the western edge of the KHENTII RANGE at the confluence of the Selbe River with the TUUL RIVER. The valley is bounded to the south by wooded Bogd Uul (Holy Mountain), which reaches 2,256 meters (7,402 feet) above sea level. Killing or cutting trees was forbidden anywhere around the camp of the Jibzundamba Khutugtu, and these prohibitions were strictly applied on Bogd Uul. Bogd Uul is currently a nature preserve inhabited by elk that until recently sometimes wandered the city's streets and parks.

The builtup area of Ulaanbaatar stretches along the Tuul's northern bank, expanding upstream and downstream and north into the valleys of the Tuul's tributary streams. Newer builtup districts are also expanding around the Buyant-Ukhaa airport south of the river. New districts are mostly made of YURT-courtyards (*ger khashaa*). In 1992 43 percent of the city's residents lived in such residences. The city's symbol, revived after the 1990 DEMOCRATIC REVOLUTION, is the legendary Garuda bird holding a snake in its claws and beak.

ADMINISTRATION, POPULATION, AND ECONOMY

The population of Ulaanbaatar is 786,500 (2000 figure). The population is, like Mongolia itself, more than 75 percent KHALKHA Mongolian. Immigrant groups, such as INNER MONGOLIANS, Chinese, and Russians, form about 8 percent of the population, while BURIATS and DÖRBÖDS each form about 5 percent.

Ulaanbaatar's administration has undergone a number of changes. The city's administrative area, including nearby steppe and coal mines, was expanded in 1957–59 from 188 square kilometers to 1,686 (73 to 651 square miles), and then to 2,058 square kilometers (795 square miles). In 1965 the city's administration was reorganized from 10 wards (*khoroo*) into four districts (*raion*; changed to *düüreg* in 1992), each with numbered wards (*khoroolol*). The number of districts later expanded with the city to nine. In 1992 the city administrative names were changed from those expressing communism and Soviet-Mongolian friendship to mostly traditional topographical and historical names. The number of districts was expanded to 12, and the city grew to 4,700 square kilometers (1,815 square miles). Of these districts, six—Sükhebaatur, Chingeltei-Uul, Bayangol, Songino-Khairkhan, Bayanzürkh, and Khan-Uul—cover the builtup area and have the overwhelming majority of the population.

With the opening of the Industrial Combine in 1934 to process animal products and its attendant thermal power station, Ulaanbaatar began developing as an industrial center. By 1969 62.9 percent of the city's population were workers. In 1985 Ulaanbaatar produced 46.8 percent of Mongolia's industrial output, with light industry (38.0 percent of total output), power (18.5 percent), and food processing (18.5 percent) the main sectors. After the withdrawal of Soviet aid in 1991, the city was hit hard by depression, shortages, and increases in poverty. It has, however, weathered the transition relatively successfully, expanding its share of Mongolia's total industrial sales from 38 percent (1992) to 47 percent (2000), while unemployment, already below the national average at 3.9 percent in 1992, dropped to Mongolia's lowest, at 2.8 percent in 2000. The privatized service economy has added numerous jobs, and since 1997 Ulaanbaatar has been in the midst of a renewed construction boom after an almost 10-year hiatus. Not surprisingly, Ulaanbaatar's share of Mongolia's growing population expanded very rapidly after 1990, from 25.9 percent in 1990 to 32.7 percent in 2000.

The satellite city of Nalaikh (11,300 people in 2002) developed around Mongolia's first coal mine (opened in 1915), with many KAZAKH workers brought in from the west. After the mines closed in 1992, unemployment locally reached 68 percent, but a new Chinese-financed oil refinery is expected to bring growth.

KHÜRIYE

Although Ulaanbaatar's founding is conventionally dated to 1639, this refers only to the enthronement of Zanabazar, the FIRST JIBZUNDAMBA KHUTUGTU. In 1654 the Bogda (Holy One) began a monastery, Nom-un Yekhe Khüriye (Great Monastery of the Dharma, officially called Rebu- or Baraibung-Gejai-Gandan-Shaddubling), in the KHENTII RANGE, which after many migrations became the core of Ulaanbaatar. Not until 1700 did the Bogda live there frequently, and not until 1741 was it his permanent seat. Despite having a wooden main hall, or Tsogchin, the monastery was still nomadic, moving through the western Khentii Range and eastern KHANGAI RANGE 14 times from 1719 to 1747. These moves, funded by the Bogda's personal subjects, the GREAT SHABI, became increasingly burdensome. From 1747 to 1779 the monastery moved four times before being fixed at its present place, with a population of 2,000 lamas. As a city developed around the monastery, Russian traders called it Urga, from Mongolian *örgöö*, "the palace-tent," but the Mongols called it Da Khüriye, "Great Monastery," (Chinese, *Kulun*).

After 1698 the monastery became a trading center where Russian and Chinese merchants exchanged goods.

Sükhebaatur Square, Ulaanbaatar, 1989. In the background, from left to right, are the Government Palace, the tomb of Choibalsang and Sükhebaatur, the statue of Sükhebaatur, and the State Printing Press. *(Courtesy Christopher Atwood)*

By the 1750s Russian and QING DYNASTY authorities shifted international trade to the KYAKHTA border towns, and the Chinese traders in Da Khüriye branched out to trade among the Mongols. A Chinatown, called Maimaching, was formed 5 kilometers (3 miles) east of the temple by Chinese merchants and moneylenders operating among the Mongols. In 1758 a Khalkha Mongolian aristocrat was appointed by the Qing court in Beijing as an AMBAN (imperial resident) to supervise the secular affairs of the Bogda's subjects. In 1761 another Manchu *amban* was appointed for the same purpose. In 1786 these *amban*s were made supervisors of Khalkha Mongolia's two eastern provinces, thus making Da Khüriye a major administrative center. A *zarguchi* (judge; *see* JARGHUCHI) was appointed to administer Maimaching, and he organized a watch of Chinese policemen over all the markets in the city, paid for by contributions from Chinese and (later) Russian merchants.

In 1809 new temples were begun for Nom-un Yekhe Khüriye's *tsanid* (higher Buddhist studies) faculty a few kilometers west of the monastery's main buildings. This was the beginning of GANDAN-TEGCHINLING MONASTERY, called West (Baruun) Khüriye. In 1836, irritated by the encroaching Chinese shops, the Bogda moved the entire monastery to West Khüriye. In 1855 the Nom-un Yekhe Khüriye Monastery and the Bogda's court moved back to the old site, now called East (Züün) Khüriye.

From this time on Da Khüriye was divided into three areas: East Khüriye, centered on Nom-un Yekhe Khüriye Monastery and the Bogda's private Dechingalba Temple (Yellow Palace; *see* PALACES OF THE BOGDA KHAN); GANDAN-TEGCHINLING MONASTERY to the west; and Maimaching to the east. After the Bogda moved back to East Khüriye, Chinese and Russian merchants began settling again around East Khüriye, just outside the open space left for the annual Maitreya procession to circumambulate the monastery. East Damnuurchin, on the eastern side of East Khüriye, thus replaced Maimaching as the city's major market district. South of East Khüriye and again outside the circumambulation route were the compound of the *amban*s, townhouses for visiting Mongol aristocrats, and the meat market. Between Maimaching and East Khüriye was the Russian consulate, established in 1860. North, in the upper Selbe valley, was Dambadarjiya Hermitage with 500 lamas. Nom-un Yekhe Khüriye had around 13,800 lamas from 1889 to 1910. Gandan-Tegchinling had more than 2,000 lamas in 1868, and Maimaching had about 1,800 inhabitants in 1876. Total population was estimated at 15,000–20,000 by 1900, although most of the populace was transient.

East Khüriye and Gandan-Tegchinling followed the traditional nomadic Mongolian monastery organization. Around a central palace for the Bogda, a great assembly hall (*tsogchin dugang*), monastic administrative offices, and some specialized temples (tantric, medical, etc.) were distributed among the yurt-courtyards of the lamas in a horseshoe-shaped ring open to the south. The lamas were divided into *aimag*s (parishes), 28 for East Khüriye and four for Gandan-Tegchinling, with each *aimag* occupying its own place in the great horseshoe-shaped ring and having its own meeting hall (*dugang*), a large yurt attached to a wooden building that held the Buddha images. The narrow streets were fronted by the high walls of the yurt-courtyards, with poles to tether HORSES. Maimaching, with wider but winding streets, was centered on the shops and houses of the Chinese merchants and moneylenders, often walled with mud brick. Around Maimaching's central commercial district were the yurt-courtyards of Mongols who worked mostly as teamsters and caravaneers. Mongols were also active in the lumber and carpentry trades.

A peculiarity of Khüriye's population was its sex imbalance. The lamas were all men (nuns, or *chibagantsa*, were mostly old women and not organized into institutions), and the Chinese merchants never brought their families to Mongolia. As a result, prostitution flourished, and sexually transmitted diseases were rampant. Most of the prostitutes were Mongols, some entering the trade voluntarily and others sold by their fathers. Lay Mongols immigrated to Khüriye in response to rural troubles. Already in 1830–35 the Bogda's administration recorded more than 3,000 lay Mongol subjects in the city, of whom some 180 were on relief. Hardships in the countryside in 1865–75 brought beggars swarming into the city, to which the Bogda's treasury, the ERDENI SHANGDZODBA, responded with a work relief program until conditions improved. Lay Mongol migrants to Khüriye maintained their home banner registration. Despite the absence of any sanitation system, the climate and the packs of roving dogs kept the town relatively clean.

FROM KHÜRIYE TO ULAANBAATAR

The 1911 RESTORATION of Mongolian independence graced Khüriye with several new monuments, including the Migjid Janraisig Temple at Gandan-Tegchinling, which towered over the city. The city's lay Mongol population expanded greatly, particularly south of East Khüriye, where two new districts, the Southeast Ward (Züün Emüne Khoriya) and the Southwest Ward (Baruun Emüne Khoriya), grew up around the old aristocratic town houses.

Telegraph lines had reached Khüriye soon after the Russian consulate was opened. Increasingly scarce *argal* (dried cattle dung) and lumber were gradually replaced as fuel by coal from the Nalaikh mine, opened in 1915. This mine, along with an electrical generator, a timber mill, a brick factory, and a printing shop, were funded by Russian and other investors. In 1919 the Chinese reoccupation of Mongolia brought a radio station to the hills northeast of the city. A number of Russian-style houses were built in Mongolia in the first two decades of the 20th century.

A central bus system was established in the early 1960s in Ulaanbaatar, in front of the two-story cooperative building, which in 1961 became the State Department Store and now is the Fine Arts Museum. *(From XX Zuun Mongolchuud: 2000)*

After the 1921 REVOLUTION and the death of the last Bogda in 1924, the city was designated in the 1924 CONSTITUTION the capital of the Mongolian People's Republic and renamed Ulaanbaatar Khot, "City of the Red Hero (or Heroes)"—exactly who was meant by the hero(es) was not specified. After the Bogda's death his palaces along the Tuul were confiscated by the state, but the revolutionaries otherwise made little mark on the city's public spaces before 1937, placing the new party and government offices in the Southeast Ward, away from the great square in front of the Bogda's Yellow Palace. In April 1925 regulations for registering lay Mongols as residents of Ulaanbaatar were created for the first time. By 1927 the city had 13,030 registered residents, although a 1925 estimate put lay Mongols at 14,750, lamas at 20,000, Chinese residents at 23,919, and other foreigners at 2,417, making a total of more than 61,000.

After 1925 more multistory European-style buildings began to appear, of which the Central Theater (built 1927, later burned), designed in the form of a yurt by the Hungarian Joseph Gelet, was the most distinctive. Popularly called the "Green Dome Theater," it was placed just south of the deceased Bogda's palace and housed sessions of the new legislature. During The LEFTIST PERIOD in 1929, more new constructions appeared in the heart of East Khüriye with the State Printing Press (1929) and Government Building (1930, the modern National Teachers Training University). In 1934 Mongolia's first Industrial Combine, a light industrial plant processing felt, shoes, leather, and skins, was opened southwest of the city beyond the Selbe with 1,183 workers.

The great break in Ulaanbaatar's history came, however, only with the annihilation of the monasteries and the dispersal of the Chinese community. The new regime's campaign against Buddhism entered its final stage in 1936, and in late 1939 Gandan-Tegchinling and Nom-un Yekhe Khüriye were closed and the surviving lamas laicized (*see* BUDDHISM, CAMPAIGN AGAINST; Gandan was later revived with 100 lamas). Suspect for their foreign ties, the Chinese who survived the GREAT PURGE avoided suspicion by assimilating. In 1944 Ulaanbaatar's population was only 35,456, barely half that of two decades earlier, and only 53 percent male. Having destroyed what it considered alien elements, the new regime could now build a secular, modern, and Mongolian metropolis on its ruins.

THE NEW ULAANBAATAR

The new Ulaanbaatar began with the conquest of the public space. In 1937–39 a new Sükhebaatur Square was created south of Nom-un Yekhe Khüriye, and the city streets and squares were named. Construction was delayed by WORLD WAR II, but from 1945 to 1950, with the aid of 12,318 Japanese prisoners of war and funds available with the coming of peace, a monumental city center was created on and around Sükhebaatur Square, including the Government Palace (built on the site of the "Green Dome Theater"), the Opera and Ballet Theater, a cinema (now the stock exchange), the Foreign Ministry, Mongolian National University, the National Public Library, and other buildings. The designs of this period emphasized neoclassical facades. Symbolic of the new regime were the statues of the leaders GENERAL SÜKHE- BAATUR, MARSHAL CHOIBALSANG, and Stalin and the tomb of Sükhebaatur and Choibalsang, designed by the Mongolian architect B. Chimid in imitation of Lenin's tomb.

The 1950s completed the foundation of a modern city as the population reached 118,387 in 1956. In 1953 Soviet architects drew up Ulaanbataar's first general city plan. Following a 1955 agreement with China, Chinese guest workers, eventually numbering 13,150 entered Mongolia (see SINO-SOVIET ALLIANCE). They paved the main street grid of central Ulaanbaatar and built several large reinforced concrete bridges. Chinese workers also built the first of the housing projects that transformed central Ulaanbaatar's living space. This first "50,000" of the 1950s and the Soviet-built "40,000" of the early 1960s, so-called from the square meters of living space planned, were low four-story buildings that echoed the neoclassical style. (Apartment blocks had first been built for the workers in the Industrial Combine and its power plant in 1940–45.) At the same time, a central water and plumbing system was first built in 1954–57, and a central heating system in 1959. In 1966 a central garbage disposal system was set up.

Further development of Ulaanbaatar was mostly a result of expansion of industry and population. The SINO- SOVIET SPLIT sent most of the Chinese guest workers home, preventing the reemergence of a new Chinatown. A milestone in Ulaanbaatar's demographic transformation was the change from a 52.7 percent male majority in 1957 to a 50.1 percent female majority in 1969. The number of persons living in yurt-courtyards declined from 65 percent in 1960 to 60 percent in 1970. In the 1970s and 1980s housing projects west of Gandan and near the old Russian consulate took on an increasingly gargantuan and impersonal character, while the percentage of those living in yurts dropped to 31.6 percent in 1984. The city's total population grew from 267,400 in 1969 to 584,400 in 1989, almost 27 percent of the country's total population. While the transition from a state- owned economy after 1990 caused a temporary break in this growth, Ulaanbaatar's superior infrastructure and cosmopolitan society have made it as welcoming to the market economy as it had been to the socialist economy.

See also BODÔ; BUYANNEMEKHÜ; DAMBADORJI.

Further reading: Robert A. Rupen, "The City of Urga in the Manchu Period." In *Studia Altaica*, ed. Julius von Farkas and Omeljan Pritsak (Wiesbaden: Otto Harrassowitz, 1957), 157–169; N. Tsultem, *Mongolian Architecture* (Ulaanbaatar: State Publishing House, 1988).

Ulaanchab (**Ulaantsav, Ulanqab, Wulanchabu**) Ulaanchab was one of Inner Mongolia's traditional six leagues under the Qing dynasty and mostly occupied the GOBI DESERT north of the Yin Shan Mountains. The original Ulaanchab BANNERS were Dörben Kheükhed (Siziwang), Darkhan, Muuminggan (now Darhan Muminggan Lianheqi), and the three Urad banners. All six are in the Gobi Desert except for Urad Front banner (Urad Qianqi), near the Huang (Yellow) River. The five Gobi banners occupy 90,983 square kilometers (35,129 square miles), with a total population of 483,600, of which only 65,000, or 13 percent, are Mongols (1990 figures). Ethnic Chinese dwell in densely populated farming villages along the banners' southern border, in small administrative centers, and some as pastoralists among the Mongols. Most of the 11,000 Mongols of Urad Front banner (Urad Qianqi) live on the unplowed slopes of Muna Uula Mountain surrounded by densely populated Chinese lowland farming villages. The overwhelming majority of the Mongols in Ulaanchab's traditional six banners speak Mongolian. The five Gobi banners together have 3,383,000 head of livestock, of which 92–95 percent are SHEEP and GOATS (1990 figures). The mining town of Bayan Oboo, in the middle of Darkhan- Muuminggan territory, has about 22,700 people but is administratively attached to BAOTOU municipality.

After 1958 Ulaanchab's original territory was divided. The three eastern banners were merged with Pingdiquan region around Jining, and the western Urad banners, renamed Bayannuur (Bayannur), merged with the Hetao region (see ORDOS) around Linhe. Both Pingdiquan and Hetao are farming areas south of the Yin Shan. Ulaanchab league as thus reconstituted covers 84,700 square kilometers (32,700 square miles) and in 1990 had a population of 3,171,294, of which Mongols were 84,344, or less than 3 percent. BAYANNUUR LEAGUE is likewise only 4 percent Mongol.

The original Ulaanchab steppe was the homeland of the ÖNGGÜD in the 12th to 14th centuries. From about 1500 on Urad (meaning craftsmen) and Muu-Minggan (meaning the bad 1,000) appeared as OTOGS (camp districts) of the ORDOS and TÜMED Mongols, respectively. In 1638, to forestall KHALKHA Mongolian raids from the north, the Qing dispatched to the area Mongol noblemen from the HULUN BUIR area with their subjects, some of whom were also named Muu-Minggan. These noblemen were descendants of CHINGGIS KHAN's brother Qasar and were related to the KHORCHIN nobles. They formed the ancestors of the Dörben Kheükhed, Muuminggan, and Urad rulers. In 1653 a Khalkha nobleman defected to the Qing with 1,000 households; they were resettled under his rule as Darkhan banner.

See also INNER MONGOLIA AUTONOMOUS REGION; INNER MONGOLIANS; MERGEN GEGEEN, THIRD, LUBSANG-DAMBI-JALSAN.

Ulaankhüü   *See* ULANFU.

Ulaantsav   *See* ULAANCHAB.

Ulaan-Üde   *See* ULAN-UDE.

Ulan-Bator   *See* ULAANBAATAR.

Ulanfu (Ulanhu, Wulanfu, Ulaankhüü; Yun Ze, Yün Tse) (1906–1988) *Long-time Communist activist, Ulanfu became the Chinese Communists' "man in Inner Mongolia" until being toppled during the Cultural Revolution.*
Born on December 23, 1906, into a declining Tümed Mongol farming family in Tabucun village, Yun Ze, as he was originally named, attended primary school in nearby Guisui (modern HÖHHOT) in 1919 and entered the Mongolian and Tibetan School in Beijing in 1923. Yun Ze had participated in demonstrations in Guisui, and in Beijing he joined the Socialist Youth League and in September 1925 the Chinese Communist Party. Unlike many of his friends, he did not join any pan-Mongolist organization. The next month he entered the Sun Yat-sen University in Moscow. Yun Ze spoke Chinese and fluent Russian but only broken Mongolian.

In June 1929 the Communist International (Comintern) sent him back to Inner Mongolia together with members of the Inner Mongolian People's Revolutionary Party to organize underground party cells. From 1933 his assignment changed to coordinating anti-Japanese sympathizers in various military organizations, such as PRINCE DEMCHUGDONGRUB's military forces and the Tümed local militia. From May 1937 he served in ORDOS under the alias Yun Shiyu as a political instructor in a Mongol unit in the anti-Japanese warlord Fu Zuoyi's army.

In 1938 he reported to Mao Zedong's Communist Party center in Yan'an for the first time and in March 1940 was transferred to Yan'an. Until 1945 he served as a teacher and committee member in the party center's fledgling nationality apparatus while undergoing reeducation during the Maoist Rectification Campaign. In April 1945 he was elected a candidate member of the party's Central Committee.

After Japan's surrender Yun Ze was assigned to neutralize the pan-Mongolist nationalist movements in Inner Mongolia. In October 1945, after his first successes, he organized the Federation of Inner Mongolian Autonomy Movements (FIMAM) as a front organization. From this time he bore the name Wulanfu in Chinese, which could be either Chinese for Russian Ulianov (Lenin's original surname) or for Mongolian Ulaanhüü (red son). In April 1946 he pressured the East Mongolian autonomous government, the most powerful in Inner Mongolia, to accept Chinese Communist leadership. Ulanfu led campaigns to attack landlords, exterminate anticommunist guerrillas, and support with cavalry and materiel the Communists' front against the Nationalists.

From 1947 to 1966 Ulanfu achieved unprecedented concentration of power as the chairman of the INNER MONGOLIA AUTONOMOUS REGION, secretary of its party committee, and commander and political commissar of its military region. After 1949 he also served in Beijing on top-level committees supervising defense, nationality policy, and North China party affairs. He became president of Beijing's Nationalities Institute (the new name of his old alma mater) and in 1957 of the new Inner Mongolia University.

While loyal to the Chinese Communist Party and opposed to secession, Ulanfu also actively promoted use of the MONGOLIAN LANGUAGE and delayed rural class struggle in the sensitive SHILIIN GOL and HULUN BUIR leagues. Both Chinese and East Mongols accused him of favoring his own TÜMED Mongols, especially after the HÖHHOT area was brought into Inner Mongolia in 1954.

In May 1966 Ulanfu's colleagues in the North China Bureau attacked his supposed policy of "class reconciliation" and accused him of making Inner Mongolia an "independent kingdom." Ulanfu was exiled but covertly protected from the worst torments inflicted on other exiled Mongols. In 1979, with Deng Xiaoping's rise and the repudiation of the Cultural Revolution, Ulanfu became a prominent official in Beijing, serving from 1983 as China's vice president. Meanwhile, his son Buhe (Bökhe) became chairman of Inner Mongolia from 1982 to 1992, and many other family members held high positions. Ulanfu's persecution in the Cultural Revolution increased his identification with the Mongols and his credibility as an advocate of nationality autonomy. After his death on December 9, 1988, a mausoleum and memorial were dedicated to him outside Höhhot in 1992, but his family was eased out of power.

See also INNER MONGOLIANS; "NEW INNER MONGOLIAN PEOPLE'S REVOLUTIONARY PARTY" CASE.
Further reading: Uradyn E. Bulag, *Mongols at China's Edge: History and the Politics of National Unity* (Lanham, Md.: Rowman and Littlefield, 2002).

Ulanhad   *See* CHIFENG MUNICIPALITY.

Ulanhot   *See* KHINGGAN LEAGUE.

Ulanhu *See* ULANFU.

Ulanqab *See* ULAANCHAB.

Ulan-Ude (Ulaan-Üde, Verkhneudinsk, Verchneudinsk)
Ulan-Ude is the capital and only large city in Russia's BURIAT REPUBLIC in southern Siberia. The city was founded at the confluence of the Uda River (Buriat, Üde) and SELENGE RIVER in an area of forest and steppe about 490 meters (1,608 feet) above sea level. Average daily temperatures range from –25.4°C (–14°F) in January to 19.4°C (67°F) in July, but temperatures as low as –51°C (–60°F) and as high as 38°C (100°F) have been recorded. Annual precipitation is around 246 millimeters (9.69 inches). The city was originally named Verkhneudinsk, or "Upper Uda" (Deede Üde in Buriat); the current name of Ulan-Ude, "Red Uda" (Buriat, Ulaan-Üde), was adopted in 1934.

POPULATION AND ECONOMY

Ulan-Ude's three urban districts cover 170 square kilometers (66 square miles). The city's population, which was 28,000 in 1926, had risen to 352,530 in the 1989 census; the estimate for 2000 was 370,400. Ulan-Ude thus contains 34 percent of the Buriat Republic's total population and 55 percent of the republic's urban dwellers. Ulan-Ude straddles both the Trans-Siberian Railway and the railway and automotive lines into Mongolia (*see* TRANS-MONGO-LIAN RAILWAY). River transport, of historical importance, is no longer used.

In the postwar period Ulan-Ude's economy was developed as a major industrial center, with more than 30 percent of industrial output consisting of heavy industries, another 30 percent of light industrial products, and 20 percent of processed foods. Construction and lumber-woodworking industries together totaled 5 percent of industrial output. Ulan-Ude also has three coal-fired thermal-electric power stations.

As the capital of the Buriat Republic, Ulan-Ude is a major educational, cultural, and scientific center. By 1970 Ulan-Ude had four institutes, or colleges of higher education—technical, pedagogical, agricultural, and cultural—as well as the Buriat branch of the Siberian division of the Russian Academy of Sciences (founded

Buriat Radio and Television Building near the Central Square of the Soviets, Ulan-Ude *(Courtesy Tristra Newyear)*

1966). Institutions of performing arts include theaters of Buriat and Russian drama, puppet theaters, dance theaters, and a folk song and dance theater, all with attached troupes. In 1995 the Buryat State Teachers Training Institute and the Ulan-Ude Branch of Novosibirsk State University were combined to form the Buriat State University.

In 1926 Ulan-Ude was an almost purely Russian town. Since then BURIATS have immigrated on a large scale. In 1989 they formed 21.1 percent of the population.

HISTORY

Ulan-Ude began in 1666 as the Cossack fort of Udinsk. Straddling the Russo-Chinese trade route through KYAKHTA, the fort grew rapidly into a town, and in 1783 Verkhneudinsk became a district (*uezd*) administrative center. In 1741 the Odigitrievskii Cathedral was begun, and in 1803 the Commercial Rows were rebuilt in stone. In the second half of the 19th century Verkhneudinsk acquired a comprehensive women's school, a duma and town council, a public library, two leather factories, and a vodka distillery. Until 1905, however, the town was still a place of exile.

In 1899 the city streets were illuminated with kerosene lamps, and in August the first train arrived at Verkhneudinsk on the Trans-Siberian Railway. By 1916 the city had almost 16,000 residents, of which 1,000 worked on the railroad and 282 in the 16 to 18 other industrial enterprises. The town had 28 schools of various sorts, two doctors, three dentists, five pharmacies, and two cinemas.

The Bolsheviks seized power in Verkhneudinsk on January 23, 1918, but the city fell to the Japanese intervention on August 20, 1918, before being retaken by the Red Army on March 2, 1920. From April to November 1920 Verkhneudinsk was the capital of the newly established Far Eastern Republic, a Communist-controlled buffer state between Soviet Russia and Japan. After the buffer state's capital was moved to Chita, Verkhneudinsk became in January 1922 the seat of its Buriat-Mongolian Autonomous Region. With the absorption of the republic into Soviet Russia, Verkhneudinsk became the center of the new Buriat-Mongolian (later Buriat) Autonomous Soviet Socialist Republic on May 30, 1923.

By 1939 Ulan-Ude had a population of 125,000 and several large industrial plants: a locomotive and railroad car repair plant, a glass plant, and a meatpacking combine. Many of these factories were developed with the import of laborers from European Russia, forming purely Russian districts in the city. During WORLD WAR II an aircraft factory was evacuated with its workers from Moscow to Ulan-Ude. After World War II Ulan-Ude's population reached 175,000 in 1959 and thereafter grew very rapidly as shipbuilding, machine tools, and construction materials industries were constructed.

Further reading: Balzhan Zhimbiev, *History of the Urbanization of a Siberian City* (Cambridge: White Horse Press, 2000).

Uliastai (Uliyasutai, Uliastay, Javhlant) The city of Uliastai, situated in west-central Mongolia, was the administrative center of Outer Mongolia under the QING DYNASTY (1636–1912). The capital of ZAWKHAN PROVINCE, it is located in the western KHANGAI RANGE at the confluence of the Chigistei and Bogd Rivers. Winter temperatures are frequently bitterly cold, reaching –45°C (–49°F). Current population is 24,300 (2000 figure).

Uliastai was founded in 1733 as the residence of the *jiangjun* (general in chief), the chief Qing administrator in Mongolia. Under him were stationed two AMBANs (one from the EIGHT BANNERS system and one a KHALKHA Mongol aristocrat), clerks, and garrisons of both Chinese Green Standard and Khalkha Mongol banner troops. In 1765 the city was rewalled with wooden palisades filled with brick, and in 1787 it was given a temple to the Chinese god of war, Guandi (identified in Mongolia with GESER). Burned in 1869 by Turkestani rebels, the town was soon rebuilt. In 1908 a Russian consulate was opened. In 1910 the town had about 200 Chinese and 1,000 Mongol residents. Outside the walls in the trading town were about 80 Chinese shops and five or six Russian ones.

On January 12, 1912, the Qing authorities surrendered to the new independent Mongolian government (*see* 1911 RESTORATION). Uliastai remained a strategic center for control of western Khalkha through the turbulent years leading up to the 1921 REVOLUTION. In 1931 the city was made the capital of Zawkhan province and renamed Jawkhlant (Javhlant); the old name was restored by 1959. By 1979 the population reached 15,400 and the city had acquired a diesel-powered electric generator and a few local factories.

Üliger-ün dalai   *See* SUTRA OF THE WISE AND FOOLISH.

Uliyasutai   *See* ULIASTAI.

Undur Gegeen   *See* JIBZUNDAMBA KHUTUGTU, FIRST.

Ungern-Sternberg, Baron Roman Fëdorovich von (1886–1921) *White Russian commander who won Mongolian independence from the Chinese but lost support by his senseless cruelty*
A Baltic German aristocrat, Baron Roman Fëdorovich von Ungern-Sternberg had his first experience in Mongolia in 1910 as a member of the Russian consular guard in Khüriye (*see* ULAANBAATAR). Serving in World War I on the Turkish front, he was commissioned an officer. After the 1917 revolution the half-Buriat Cossack Grigorii M. Semënov (1890–1945) assigned the baron to train Inner

Mongolian bandit troops and organize a multinational "Asiatic Cavalry Division"—Cossacks, BURIATS, INNER MONGOLIANS, Tibetans, Chinese, Japanese—to fight the Bolsheviks.

On October 2, 1920, as the Bolsheviks advanced east, the baron escaped and crossed over the Mongolian border with 900 men. His aim, shared by the EIGHTH JIBZUNDAMBA KHUTUGTU, Mongolia's theocratic ruler, was to build a new anticommunist base by freeing Mongolia from Chinese rule. After an unsuccessful siege from October 26 to November 7, his soldiers, now numbering 3,000, again attacked Khüriye from January 24 to February 4, 1921, this time successfully. On February 8 the baron issued an order for the city's 40 Jews and 80 alleged Russian and Mongolian Bolsheviks to be killed, often with great cruelty. On February 21 the Jibzundamba Khutugtu was enthroned and a new administration proclaimed. After waiting vainly for Mongolian reinforcements, the baron set out in late May to halt the Red Army advancing south. Defeated, he retreated west. On August 22 he was betrayed by his Mongolian soldiers and handed over to the Soviet authorities, who executed him on November 15.

See also DAURIIA STATION MOVEMENT.

Unggirad   *See* QONGGIRAD.

United Nations

Having first applied for membership in the United Nations (UN) in 1946, Mongolia was admitted in 1961, which was a milestone in the country's international recognition. After joining WORLD WAR II by declaring war on Japan on August 10 and receiving recognition from the Republic of China as an independent state on January 6, 1946, the MONGOLIAN PEOPLE'S REPUBLIC applied by telegram on June 24 for membership in the United Nations. On August 30 the Soviet delegate recommended admission, the Chinese delegate offered qualified support, but the British and American delegates vetoed Mongolia's admission due to doubts about its real desire or ability for full independence. A year later, when the Soviet Union again presented the Mongolian request, the Sino-Mongolian border clash at Baytik Shan (Baitag Bogd) led China to join Britain and the United States in rejecting Mongolia's application.

In 1955 an admission package of 18 nations, including Mongolia, was vetoed by China (that is, the Nationalist government on Taiwan) alone, while Britain supported admission and the United States abstained. The Soviet Union dropped Mongolia and Japan from the package, and the other 16 won admission, breaking a long-standing logjam in UN admissions and increasing the number of Asian and African members. After this disappointing vote Mongolia protested the rejection of its application on September 13, 1956, its first direct communication with the United Nations since 1946. Still, Mongolia's individual applications were rejected again in 1956 and 1957 with the veto of China and/or the United States.

In 1961 the Soviet Union linked the admission of Mauritania with that of Mongolia. Since Mauritania was part of a conservative African bloc being wooed by the United States, the United States abstained from voting, and China, under strong U.S. pressure, cast no vote, allowing both Mongolia and Mauritania to be recommended for admission by the Security Council on October 25 and approved by the General Assembly two days later. The actual Mongolian mission to the United Nations was opened in 1962, and membership in a number of international organizations—UNESCO, World Health Organization, United Nations Development Organization, the International Labor Organization—followed by 1968.

Following Mongolia's admission it was until around 1990 a reliable supporter of the Soviet Union, speaking for the Soviet bloc particularly on issues of peace and disarmament. Since 1990, with the breakup of the Soviet bloc, Mongolia as a small nation has advocated strengthening the international treaty regime and sought UN assistance in securing implementation of its rights as a landlocked nation to free access to the sea and international recognition of its 1992 declaration as a nuclear-free zone. The Mongolian ACADEMY OF SCIENCES has become the major participant in the UNESCO-organized International Institute for the Study of Nomadic Civilizations, founded in 1998.

See also FOREIGN RELATIONS.

Further reading: Sister Mary Aline Henderson, "United Nations Admission of the Mongolian People's Republic" (Ph.D. diss., Fordham University, 1971).

Upper Mongols

The Upper Mongols (Deedü Monggol) of Kökenuur played a major role in Sino-Mongol-Tibetan politics of the 17th and 18th centuries, but after loss of independence they became a small and largely Tibetanized population.

SETTLEMENT

Mongols on the Gansu-Kökenuur (modern Qinghai) frontier under the YUAN DYNASTY (1206/71–1368) submitted to the Ming (1368–1644) after 1368. They became the predecessors of the Yogur and Tu (Monguor) nationalities. The modern "Upper Mongols" stem from the Mongols and OIRATS who invaded Kökenuur in the 16th and 17th centuries. The first invasions began in 1509 with refugees from BATU-MÖNGKE DAYAN KHAN's unification of the Mongols. From 1559 to 1586 princes of the ORDOS and TÜMED Mongols invaded Kökenuur, subjugating the local Tibetan nomads and vastly increasing their followings.

In 1632 LIGDAN KHAN and TSOGTU TAIJI took refuge in Kökenuur from the rising QING DYNASTY (1636–1912). While the Ordos and Tümed Mongols supported the Dalai

Lama's "Yellow Hat" (dGe-lugs-pa) order, the newcomers leagued with its Tibetan opponents. The Fifth Dalai Lama (1617–82) appealed to the Oirats in Zungharia (Junggar Basin). TÖRÖ-BAIKHU GÜÜSHI KHAN, with a vanguard of 10,000 men, defeated all the Dalai Lama's enemies from 1637 to 1642 and was enthroned by the Dalai Lama as KHAN of Tibet (1642–55). Having conquered Tibet, Güüshi Khan divided the Tibetans of Kökenuur among his sons and brothers of the Khoshud tribe as well as among allied Torghud and Khoid noblemen. The king of Tibet himself nomadized in 'Dam-gzhung (modern Damxung) near Lhasa, where Mongols had lived at least since 1558. Güüshi Khan's son Dayan Ochir (1655–69) and grandson Gönchug Dalai Khan (1669–98) succeeded him as khan at 'Dam-gzhung. Meanwhile, the Kökenuur nobility, organized into right and left wings, was under the senior prince, who held as regent for the khan the title Dalai Khung-Taiji. In 1685 the Dalai Khung-Taiji promulgated a law code for the Kökenuur confederation.

INNER ASIAN POLITICS

In 1652–53 representatives of Güüshi Khan accompanied the Fifth Dalai Lama to his meeting with the Qing dynasty's Shunzhi emperor (1644–62). The Qing dynasty opened border markets for the Kökenuur Mongols in 1658. Relations with the Zunghars soured as GALDAN BOSHOGTU KHAN (1678–97) overthrew Güüshi Khan's brother Ochirtu Tsetsen Khan in Zungharia and the Kökenuur princes welcomed dissident ZÜNGHARS. With Galdan Khan's defeat by the Manchus in 1697, the Kökenuur nobility, led by Güüshi Khan's youngest son, the Dalai Khung-Taiji Dashi-Baatur (d. 1714), submitted to Kangxi in a personal audience at Xi'an, receiving rich titles and gifts.

Göngchug Dalai Khan's son and successor, Lhazang Khan (Lha-bzang, 1698–1717), remained independent, however, and the Panchen and Dalai Lamas remained extremely influential in the Kökenuur Mongols' religious and secular affairs. When the deceased Fifth Dalai Lama's regent (sde-srid) Sangs-rgyas rGya-mtsho (r. 1679–1703) tried to expel the Khoshud from Tibet, Lhazang Khan seized Lhasa and killed Sangs-rgyas mGya-mtsho in 1705 before deposing the Sixth Dalai Lama (1683–1706) and imposing a new candidate as the true Sixth Dalai Lama. The Dalai Lama's deposition eventually generated serious opposition, and in 1717 the Zünghar ruler TSEWANG-RAB-TAN killed Lhazang and deposed his Dalai Lama. In 1720 a Qing army with the princes and INCARNATE LAMAS of Kökenuur and Mongolia escorted the recognized Seventh Dalai Lama (1708–57) from sKu-'bum Monastery (Kumbum or Ta'ersi) in Kökenuur to Lhasa as the Zünghar garrison fled without a fight.

LUBSANG-DANZIN'S REBELLION AND AFTERMATH

Stung by the Qing's cancellation of the line of the khans of Tibet and interference with his authority as Dalai Khung-Taiji, Dashi-Baatur's son Lubsang-Danzin (d. 1755) rebelled in June 1723 with the support of Tsaghan Nom-un Khan (King of the White Dharma) who was the throne holder of sKu-'bum Monastery and a powerful temporal lord as well. By April 1724 the Qing army had crushed Lubsang-Danzin's last forces, and in June it cowed the lamas and Tibetan nomads. Lubsang-Danzin fled to the Zünghars, where the Qing captured and executed him in 1755.

Following the recommendations of the Qing general Nian Gengyao, the Kökenuur Mongols were divided into 29 BANNERS (appanages): 21 Khoshud, two Choros (i.e., Zünghar), four Torghud, one Khoid, and one Khalkha, each under direct supervision of the Manchu AMBAN (imperial controller general) in Xining. The Upper Mongols' Tibetan subjects were organized into independent tribes also directly subject to the Qing *amban*. The Mongols of 'Dam-gzhung were put under the Lhasa authorities.

The separation of the Tibetan tribes from the Mongolian banners greatly weakened the Upper Mongols, leading from 1775 on to increasingly bold Tibetan attacks on Mongol princes and their subjects. From 1766 on small groups of Upper Mongols moved north into Gansu to escape Tibetan attacks, establishing the population of modern Subei county. Finally, in 1821 the Tibetan tribes south of the Huang (Yellow) River, themselves attacked by the feared mGo-log nomads to the south, made a mass migration north, sweeping away the Mongol banners between the Huang (Yellow) River and Kökenuur (Qinghai) Lake. Not until 1859 were elementary law and order restored as the *amban* in Xining recognized the fait accompli. Mongol banner nobility in Tibetan areas were allotted payments from Tibetan tribes, but Mongol communities remained only in the far southeast in modern Henan county and in the northwest around modern Dulaan and Ulaan, with a scattering north of Kökenuur Lake. In 1897 Hui (Chinese-speaking Muslim) rebels fled west through Qinghai, plundering and killing Mongols.

Although mostly of Oirat origin, the Upper Mongols (Deedü Monggol), or Mongols of Kökenuur, used the UIGHUR-MONGOLIAN SCRIPT. Tibetan influence was heavy. The Upper Mongols adopted Tibetan dress and jewelry, although they kept Mongolian yurts. Both the scattered Mongols north of Kökenuur Lake and the concentrated Mongol population of the four banners in modern Henan county were entirely Tibetan speaking by the 20th century, using Mongolian only for official purposes. Only the eight banners in the northwest retained Mongolian as a spoken language. The Mongols there generally occupied the lower valleys and were less extensively nomadic than were their Tibetan neighbors.

MODERN HISTORY

With the late Qing's reformist NEW POLICIES (1901 on), the Xining *amban* founded a Chinese-language, modern-

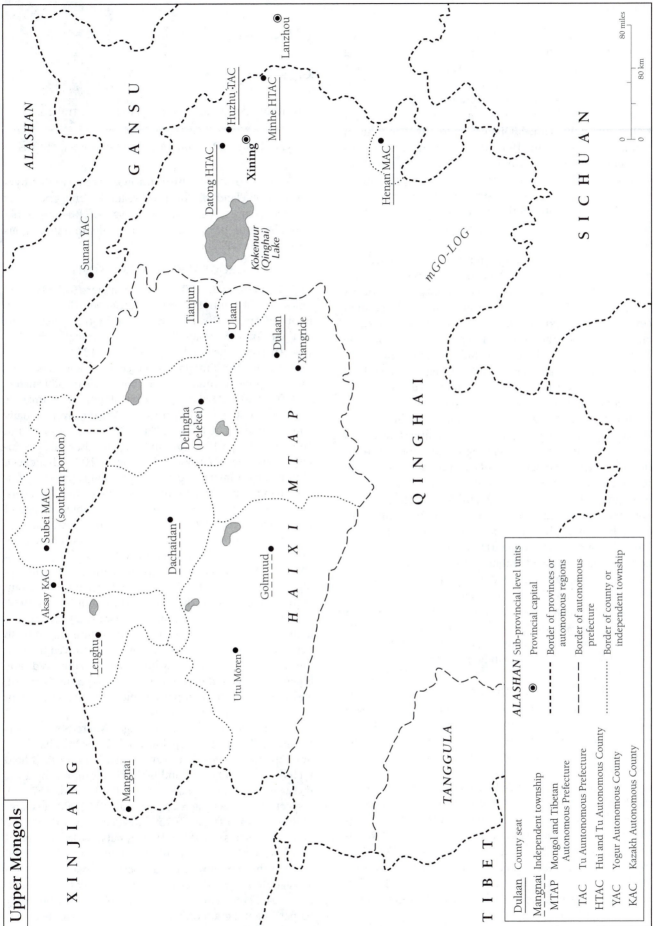

Upper Mongols

ALASHAN

GANSU

Lanzhou

Huzhu TAC

Minhe HTAC

Datong HTAC

Xining

Henan MAC

Suman YAC

Kökenuur
(Qinghai)
Lake

mGO-LOG

SICHUAN

Tianjun

Ulaan

Dulaan

Xiangride

H A I X I   M T A P

Delingha
(Delekei)

QINGHAI

Subei MAC
(southern portion)

Dachaidan

Golmuud

Aksay KAC

Lenghu

Utu Mören

X I N J I A N G

Mangnai

TANGGULA

T I B E T

80 miles

80 km

0

0

Dulaan County seat

Mangnai Independent township

MTAP Mongol and Tibetan
Autonomous Prefecture

TAC Tu Autonomous Prefecture

HTAC Hui and Tu Autonomous County

YAC Yogur Autonomous County

KAC Kazakh Autonomous County

ALASHAN Sub-provincial level units

⊙ Provincial capital

– – – – Border of provinces or
autonomous regions

– – – – Border of autonomous
prefecture

· · · · · · Border of county or
independent township

style Qinghai Mongolian Half-Day School in 1910 for the children of the nobility. In 1912 the 24 remaining Kökenuur banners declared their support for the 1911 RESTORATION of Mongolian independence in Outer Mongolia. Nevertheless, they soon were compelled to submit to the Hui warlords of the Ma family, who brought Kökenuur, now named Qinghai, into the Republic of China (1911–49). In 1930 the Guomingdang Party's national government funded a Qinghai Mongolian-Tibetan Cultural Advancement Society and established a Chinese-style county administration in Dulaan (northwest Qinghai). Colonization bureaus to settle impoverished peasants from eastern Qinghai in the northwest were set up in 1945.

The victorious Chinese Communists established two autonomous units for the Mongols in Haixi (northwest Qinghai) in 1951 and in Henan county in southeast Qinghai in 1954. The new government easily secured control over Haixi, working through Xining-educated elites and immigrant Inner Mongolian cadres, but the Tibetanized Henan Mongols, including many temple subjects (lha-sde) of Blabrang (Xiahe) Monastery, remained isolated, and resistance was not suppressed until 1953. Collectivization in 1956–58 sparked another serious insurrection in Henan. With liberalization after 1979 Haixi's Upper Mongols revived their cultural ties with Inner Mongolia, often seeking higher education in HÖH-HOT. The Henan Upper Mongols also began programs to revive the MONGOLIAN LANGUAGE. Several of China's most distinguished Tibetan-language authors are Henan Mongols: the fiction author Tsering-Dongrub (Tshe-ring Don-grub, b. 1961), the pioneer in avant-garde free verse Jangbu (lJang-bu; real name rDo-rje Tshe-ring, b. 1963), and the poetess Dejid-Dulma (bDe-skyid sGrol-ma, b, 1967). Of Qinghai's 50,400 Mongols in 1982, 37 percent lived in Haixi and 41 percent in Henan.

See also HAIXI MONGOL AND TIBETAN AUTONOMOUS PREFECTURE; HENAN MONGOL AUTONOMOUS COUNTY; KALMYK-OIRAT LANGUAGE AND SCRIPT; TIBETAN CULTURE IN MONGOLIA; TU LANGUAGE AND PEOPLE; YOGUR LANGUAGES AND PEOPLES.

Further reading: Uyunbilig Borjigidai, "The Hoshuud Polity in Khökhnuur (Kokonor)," *Inner Asia* 4 (2002): 181–196; Yangdon Dhondup, "Writers at the Cross-Roads: The Mongolian-Tibetan Authors Tsering Dondup and Jangbu," *Inner Asia* 4 (2002): 225–240; Naoto Kato, "The Accession to the Throne of Yung-cheng and the Lobdzang Danjin's Rebellion," in *Proceedings of the 35th Permanent International Altaistics Conference,* ed. Chieh-hsien Ch'en (Taipei: Center for Chinese Studies Materials, 1993), 189–192; Naoto Kato, "The 1723 Rebellion of Lobjang Danjin," in *Proceedings of the Fifth East Asian Altaistic Conference,* ed. Ch'en Chieh-hsien (Taipei: National Taiwan University, 1981), 182–191; Ho-chin Yang, trans., *Annals of Kokonur* (Bloomington: Indiana University, 1969).

Urdus   *See* ORDOS.

Urga   *See* ULAANBAATAR.

Urianhai   *See* ALTAI URIYANGKHAI; DUKHA; TUVANS.

Uriyangkhai   *See* ALTAI URIYANGKHAI; DUKHA; TUVANS.

Ust'-Orda Buriat Autonomous Area (Ust'-Ordyn-skiy) Homeland of the semipastoral, semiagricultural western BURIATS, Ust'-Orda was part of Russia's Buriat Republic until 1937, when it was made an autonomous area in Irkutsk Region.

GEOGRAPHY AND ECONOMY

Ust'-Orda covers 22,100 square kilometers (8,530 square miles) in the central Siberian plateau, north of Irkutsk. Both the Angara River (here flooded by the Bratsk Dam) and the Trans-Siberian Railway run through the area's western part. The total population of 135,870 in 1989 included 49,298 Buriats (36 percent). Ust'-Orda's territory is a mostly rolling plain about 450 to 800 meters (1,480–2,630 feet) above sea level, sloping from uplands in the north and east down to the Angara. Average daily temperatures range from –22° to –25°C (–8° to –13°F) in January to 14° to 18°C (57° to 64°F) in July, while precipitation averages 270–330 millimeters (10.6–13 inches), diminishing from west to east. Vegetation is primarily fescue steppe with thickets of sagebrush in the dry areas, couch grass steppe near the Angara, and forest steppe of larch, pine, and birch in the higher areas. Archaeology indicates, however, that this steppe was created by human activity in the last 300 to 400 years.

Ust'-Orda is one of Russia's most rural areas, supplying one-third of Irkutsk Region's total agricultural output. Only 18.1 percent of the population was urban in 1989, yet an unusually high number of persons, 29 percent, are employed in health, education, and culture. In 1998 46 percent of the working population was employed in farming, herding, and forestry, while industry employed only 8 percent. Coal and gypsum are the only products mined, and lumber the only important industry. Ust'-Ordynskiy, the capital, has 12,866 residents.

Compared to Buriatia and Aga, where Soviet plans emphasized raising sheep for wool, Ust'-Orda has been developed more as a dairy center. In 1975 the area's herd included 230,000 cattle and 302,000 sheep, but by 1991 these numbers had fallen to 170,600 and 157,300, respectively. Sown acreage reached 570,000 hectares (1,408,470 acres) in 1975 but declined to 483,100 (1,193,740 acres) in 1991. Wheat, oats, barley, and potatoes have replaced the traditional winter rye. From 1990 to 1998 the economy entered a serious crisis, with sown acreage dropping 10 percent, the cattle herd 43 percent, and pigs 27 percent, and milk production reached only 65 percent and grain only 81 percent of 1990 levels.

PREMODERN HISTORY

In 1628 Cossacks began raiding western Buriat territory, building forts and collecting *yasak* (fur tribute, from Mongolian *JASAQ*). The Buriat clans along the Angara and Lena sporadically resisted Cossack depredations until their final uprising was crushed in 1696. Once Russian conquest was secure, peasants slowly trickled into areas along the Angara and upper Lena. The western Buriats, now restricted to a territory around today's Ust'-Orda and extending north and east to Ol'khon and Verkholensk, were under Cossack *voevoda* (military governors) until the creation of the Irkutsk *guberniia* (province) in 1708.

From the late 18th century to about 1850 the western Buriat population grew rapidly, from about 50,000 in 1783 to 99,000 in 1839. Compared to the Transbaikal Buriats, they were more agricultural, less nomadic, less literate (and only in Russian), and generally shamanist or nominally Christian, as opposed to Buddhist. In 1822 the Buriats were divided into 14 autonomous "steppe dumas"; those of Balagan and Alair (Russian, Alar) west of the Angara and of Ida and Kuda east of the Angara covered modern Ust'-Orda. After 1840 a steady trickle of Buriats became Russified through intermarriage or Christian conversion. Called Karyms, they founded many villages, including Ust'-Ordynskiy.

BURIAT REVIVAL AND AUTONOMY

In the late 19th century Russian policy turned toward forced Russification, transferring 53 percent of communal Buriat land in Irkutsk province to Russian immigrants and abolishing the steppe dumas in 1901. Meanwhile, the completion of the Trans-Siberian Railway to Irkutsk in 1898 facilitated immigration. During the 1905 revolution western Buriat spokesmen protested forced Christianization and Russian colonization but did not support pan-Mongolist or pan-Buddhist programs.

The revolution against of the czar in March 1917 (February in the Old Style) allowed the spread of Buddhism. After 1917 six new *datsang*s (monasteries) were built in five years, and baptized Buriat Christians began turning to Buddhism or back to SHAMANISM in droves. Language policy was less clear. The all-Buriat National Committee advocated the UIGHUR-MONGOLIAN SCRIPT, but the western Buriats generally wrote Buriat, if at all, in the Cyrillic script.

In winter 1919–20, Bolsheviks regained firm control of Ust'-Orda. On January 9, 1922, a Mongol-Buriat Autonomous Region was created, led by the few Ust'-Orda Buriats in Bolshevik ranks. This new autonomous region contained five mostly noncontiguous AIMAGS (provinces): 1) Alair (including Balagan territory), 2) Bookhon (Russian, Bokhan, equivalent to the Ida steppe duma), 3) Ekhired-Bulagad (old Kuda and Ol'khon steppe dumas), 4) Tünkhen, and 5) Selenge south of Lake Baikal. Three of these—the Alair, Bookhon, and Ekhired-Bulagad areas—occupied present-day Ust'-Orda and together had 106,800

people, of whom 65,100, or 65 percent, were Buriat. When the Cisbaikal Buriat region was merged with the Transbaikal in May 1923, western Buriat officials such as MIKHEI NIKOLAEVICH ERBANOV dominated the party hierarchy of the new Buriat-Mongolian Autonomous Soviet Socialist Republic (ASSR).

From 1923 to 1937 the three Ust'-Orda *aimag*s were administratively unified with the rest of Buriatia. Theoretically, the UIGHUR-MONGOLIAN SCRIPT was the official language along with Russian, and a Bookhon high school was praised for its high level of Mongolian instruction. Nevertheless, Ust'-Orda offices were explicitly exempted from the 1924 exhortation to replace Russian with Buriat, and most Ust'-Orda Buriat schools still used Buriat teachers to teach from Russian-language textbooks with Buriat explanations.

After 1929 antireligious campaigns struck Buddhism, shamanism, and Russian Orthodoxy. Russian Orthodoxy disappeared among the Buriats, but while all the *datsang*s (monasteries) were closed, some identification of Buddhism with Buriat identity remained. Shamanism, however, remained the western Buriats' underground faith.

THE UST'-ORDA AUTONOMOUS AREA

On September 26, 1937, Moscow transferred Alair, Bookhon, and the Kuda area of the Ekhired-Bulagad *aimag*s from the Buriat-Mongolian Republic to the Irkutsk Region, creating the Ust'-Orda Buriat-Mongolian National Area (*okrug*). (The Ol'khon area of Ekhired-Bulagad was made a simple district of Irkutsk.) In 1977 the term *national area,* designating the lowest level of ethnic autonomy in the Soviet system, was changed to *autonomous area* without any real change of status.

The separation of Ust'-Orda from the BURIAT REPUBLIC ended any chance of developing Buriat there as a widely used written language. While a new Cyrillic script was officially introduced into all Buriat lands in 1939, Ust'-Orda had no Buriat periodical until 1954. By 1959 Russian immigration had reduced the Buriat percentage of Ust'-Orda's 113,200 people to only 37.4 percent. Official figures show 90 percent of the Buriats claiming Buriat as their native language, but surveys indicate those Buriats actually fluent in Buriat at hardly a third. Like other Russian rural areas, Ust'-Orda's population has been in decline; it peaked in 1970 at 146,412 people, of which 33.0 percent were Buriat. After 1960 many ambitious Ust'-Orda Buriats followed their landsman ANDREI URUPKHEEVICH MODOGOIEV, then head of the ASSR, in building careers in Buriatia. As a result, the Buriat population grew by only 2,000 persons between 1970 and 1989, while the non-Buriat population declined from 99,100 to 86,600.

During the pan-Buriat cultural revival since 1985, the Buriats of Ust'-Orda have revived shamanism, the GESER epic, and clan sacrifices. In 1993 Ust'-Orda was made an equal member within Russia's new federal system, but genuine autonomy has proven impossible with three-fourths of the budget dependent on federal subsidies. In the 1996 election a young ethnic Russian state farm director, Valerii Gennad'evich Maleev (b. 1964), defeated the area's incumbent Buriat chairman, Aleksei Nikolaevich Batagaev, by promising to negotiate closer relations with relatively wealthy Irkutsk. Ust'-Orda's financial difficulties resulted in Irkutsk taking over its pension fund in March 2003, a step believed to be the harbinger of eventual annexation.

Further reading: T. M. Mikhailov and V. P. Orsoev, *Land of Geser* (Irkutsk: Izdatelstvo Suiat, 1995).

Ust'-Ordynskiy *See* UST'-ORDA BURIAT AUTONOMOUS AREA.

Utrar Incident *See* OTRAR INCIDENT.

Uvs *See* UWS PROVINCE.

Uws, Lake (Uvs, Ubsa Nuur) Lake Uws is Mongolia's largest lake, with a surface area of 3,350 square kilometers (1,293 square miles). It lies in the northern part of the GREAT LAKES BASIN. Uws has no outlet and is weakly saline (approximately one-third as salty as the ocean). Roughly round in form (84 kilometers long and 79 kilometers wide, or 52 by 49 miles), the lake has a maximum depth of 20 meters (66 feet) and its total water volume is 40 cubic kilometers (9.6 cubic miles). Many waterfowl birds nest on Lake Uws, including rare and endangered species such as the Eurasian spoonbill, black stork, swan goose, barheaded goose, and white-tailed eagle. In 1994 the entire lake and its shore were made a strictly protected area.

See also ENVIRONMENTAL PROTECTION; FAUNA; MONGOLIAN PLATEAU; UWS PROVINCE.

Uws province (Uvs, Ubsa Nuur) Created in 1931, Uws province lies in northwestern Mongolia. Under the QING DYNASTY its territory was mostly occupied by the BANNERS (appanages) of the DÖRBÖD nobility, supervised by the Khowd AMBAN (imperial resident). These Dörböd banners also included as subjects the BAYAD and KHOTONG. In the THEOCRATIC PERIOD the Dörböd banners formed three provinces, but after 1923 all of western Mongolia was unified into Chandamani Uula province with its capital at Ulaangom in Dörböd territory. In 1931 the Dörböd territory was again separated and combined with neighboring KHALKHA Mongolian districts to make Uws province. The Kazakh-inhabited far western districts were given to the new Bayan-Ölgii province in 1940.

Uws province's 69,600 square kilometers (26,870 square miles) are almost wholly within the arid GREAT LAKES BASIN and contain two of Mongolia's largest lakes, Uws and Khyargas. Northern Uws has Mongolia's coldest average winters, and temperatures at Ulaangom have reached −50.0°C (−58.0°F). The province's population, 46,800 in 1956, was 86,800 in 2000; ethnically, it is 40.4 percent Dörböd, 34.5 percent Bayad, 16.3 percent Khalkha, and 6.0 percent Khotong. The Khalkhas of Uws are of the Eljigin and Sartuul subethnic groups. Uws province has 1,579,300 head of livestock, mostly SHEEP (858,600 head) and GOATS (521,900 head). The provincial capital of Ulaangom was settled as a Qing dynasty garrison and military farm in 1718 and then abandoned; a major monastery town was built there in 1870. Its present population is 26,300 (2000 figure), mostly Dörböds and Bayads.

See also BATMÖNKH, JAMBYN; THEOCRATIC PERIOD; TSEDENBAL, YUMJAAGIIN.

Üzemchin *See* ÜJÜMÜCHIN.

V

Vietnam   While Vietnam was a Mongol tributary from 1258, Qubilai Khan's effort to integrate Vietnam into the Yuan Empire resulted in a great defeat.

In 1225 Trân Thu Đô (d. 1264) placed his nephew Trân Nhât Quýnh (posthumous title, Trân Thai Tông, r. 1225–58, d. 1277) on the throne, ending the Lý dynasty (1009–1225) and beginning the Trân (1225–1400). The Trân strictly separated civil and military functions and furthered the bureaucratization of administration with an examination system based on Confucian, Buddhist, and Taoist (Daoist) classics.

When the Vietnamese imprisoned Mongol envoys sent from YUNNAN to find a route to attack the Song, the Mongol general Uriyangqadai (1199–1271) and his son AJU invaded in December 1257 with 3,000 Mongols and 10,000 Yunnanese Yi tribesmen. After the Mongols routed the Vietnamese and massacred the inhabitants of the capital, Thănh Long (modern Hanoi), Thai Tôong abdicated in March 1258 in favor of his son Quang Bính (posthumous title, Trân Thánh Tông, r. 1258–78, d. 1291). Thánh Tông paid tribute to Uriyangqadai, who had quickly evacuated Vietnam to escape malaria.

After QUBILAI KHAN's election as khan in 1260, Thánh Tông, enfeoffed as prince of Annam, sent tribute every three years and received a *DARUGHACHI* (overseer). By 1266, however, a standoff developed, as Thánh Tông sought to return to a loose tributary relationship while Qubilai demanded full submission to Mongol rule. The remoteness of communications through Yunnan, however, delayed armed conflict.

By winter 1278–79, with the conquest of South China, Qubilai ordered Mongol Yuan troops stationed along Vietnam's borders. Vietnam's new ruler, Trân Nhat Huyên (posthumous title, Trân Nhân Tông, r. 1278–93, d. 1308), resisted renewed Mongol demands for personal attendance at court but dispatched his uncle Trân Di Ái as hostage. In 1281 Qubilai tried to enthrone Di Ái as prince of Annam in place of Thánh Tông, but the plan failed miserably.

In summer 1284 Qubilai appointed his son Toghan to conquer Cham-pa, south of Vietnam. That December the Yuan general Sodu (d. 1284), defeated in Cham-pa, proposed the occupation of Vietnam as the key to pacifying all Southeast Asia, and Toghan was ordered to implement this plan. While Nhân Tông considered surrender, Prince Hu'ng Đao (1213–1300) rallied his troops, who all tattooed their arms with "Death to the Mongols." After defeating Prince Hu'ng Đao's army, Toghan, with Sodu and Li Heng and naval forces under 'Umar Ba'atur, reoccupied Thăng Long in June 1285, while the Vietnamese court fled. As the Yuan troops advanced down the Hong (Red) River, however, Prince Quang Khai counterattacked at Chu'o'ng Du'o'ng, forcing Toghan to evacuate Vietnam, while Prince Hu'ng Đao's armies annihilated the isolated vanguard at Tây Ket (near modern Hu'ng Yên), killing Sodu and Li Heng. The next March Qubilai enfeoffed Nhân Tông's younger brother Trân Ích Tăc, who had defected to the Yuan, as prince of Annam, but hardship in the Yuan's Hunan supply base aborted Qubilai's planned invasion. Finally, in 1287 Toghan invaded with 70,000 regular troops, 21,000 tribal auxiliaries from

Yunnan and Hainan, a 1,000-man vanguard under Abachi, and 500 ships under 'Umar and Fan Ji. Toghan reoccupied Thăng Long, but the Vietnamese captured the Mongol supply fleet and defeated the navy at Bach- Đằng River (near modern Haiphong), forcing Toghan to evacuate in March 1288. Abachi and Fan Ji died in the bloody retreat, and 'Umar was captured. Qubilai angrily banished Toghan to Yangzhou for life.

While Nhân Tông was willing to pay tribute to the Yuan, relations again foundered on the question of atten-dance at the Yuan court, and invasion plans continued. Qubilai's successor, Emperor Temür (1294–1307), finally recognized the futility of these plans and released all detained envoys, settling for Vietnam's traditional loose tributary relationship, which continued to the end of the Yuan. Prince Hu'ng Đao's command of the resistance became legendary in Vietnamese history.

See also EAST ASIAN SOURCES ON THE MONGOL EMPIRE; TRIBUTE SYSTEM.

W

weddings Traditional Mongolian weddings were extraordinarily rich in poetry and symbolism. Each Mongolian area had its own traditions, although the basic lines were similar. The complex Mongolian marriage described below was the ideal form, observed by the nobility and the middle and upper classes, but often not by the poor. In some cases sons-in-law moved in with the wife's parents, while many couples did not have a formal marriage at all. In Inner Mongolia hard-pressed families might marry their daughters to poor Chinese day-laborers working for them, while in respectable families a girl involved in a premarital liaison might be married to a Chinese peddler (*see* FAMILY; KINSHIP SYSTEM).

Little is known about weddings in medieval Mongolia, although the general similarity in wedding ceremonies among the Mongol groups suggests today's traditional ceremony is quite ancient.

ARRANGING A MARRIAGE

Traditional Mongol marriages were arranged by the parents, often as much as a few years before the children were actually old enough to marry. Sometimes two pregnant women agreed to marry their children before they were born, an engagement called an "egg betrothal" (*öndegen süi*).

Spouse selection was based primarily on the health and diligence of the bride, who as wife would carry the burden of physical labor in the household. Beauty was of importance for the wealthy. For the groom social status and dependability were the main attributes sought. Virginity of the bride was important among the Inner Mongolian CHAKHAR and KHORCHIN Mongols and was guarded by a severe stigma on girls with a "reputation," since brides did not marry before 18. Among the KALMYKS virginity of the bride was valued but guarded mainly by early marriage at age 14 or so, while in ORDOS where virginity was not important, brides married at age 16 or 17. Frequently, in pastoral families the groom was several years younger than the bride, although in noble families and in eastern Inner Mongolia the groom was usually older.

To the degree that genealogical information was maintained, marriage with patrilineal relations was forbidden. Marriage with close maternal relatives, however, was encouraged, as the families involved were already familiar. In the upper classes cross-banner (county) and even cross-AIMAG (province) marriage was preferred. If a first wife died leaving children, the husband often married her sister, since she would take care of the orphaned children better than a stranger. Once a marriage had been tentatively agreed on, a lama was sought to determine astrological compatibility (*see* ASTROLOGY). If the families were not set on the marriage, this could break the marriage, but if they were determined, this incompatibility could be rectified by reading the proper sutras.

THE ENGAGEMENT

The actual wedding was traditionally prepared in three visits, each accompanied by KHADAG scarves and other ceremonial gifts. First, after the groom's mother inquired about the prospective bride, a go-between (usually a mutual friend) was sent to propose marriage. If the go-between reported a favorable answer, astrological inquiries were made, and then the go-between, accompanied by the groom's father and a facile speaker, visited the bride's family, also represented by a speaker, where they negotiated the gifts to be given. The gifts having been settled, the groom's side placed an offering before the bride's

Wedding in Üjümüchin, Right Banner, Inner Mongolia, autumn 1987. The bride is having her hair done in the married woman's style before entering her in-laws' yurt with the groom. *(Courtesy Christopher Atwood)*

side, and the couple was then considered engaged. Later, the gifts were delivered at a third visit with the groom himself present.

Among the KHALKHA and the BURIATS the groom's family paid to the bride's family a bridewealth (*süi*) in livestock, while the bride's family provided the trousseau (*zasal*, or fixings, including jewelry, clothing, and household goods) and a dowry (*inj*; Buriat, *enzhe*, from Middle Mongolian INJE) of livestock or servants for the nobility. Among the Chakhar and Khorchin the groom's family provided the girl's jewelry (*jasal chimeg*), while the bride's side supplied the clothing and household goods and a dowry (*enj*), but there was no bridewealth. In Ordos the groom's side paid a bridewealth; the trousseau was divided as in Chakhar and Khorchin and a dowry given.

Once the engagement was made, the fiancée had to avoid her betrothed. Engagements usually lasted a year or more. In the weeks before the wedding, the bride paid farewell visits to her family and friends. Among the Buriats these visits were often raucous, with much drinking and dancing. In Chakhar and Khorchin, where standards for girls were much stricter, such visiting did not occur.

THE WEDDING

The wedding clothes of the bride and groom were new, bright, and festive versions of the Mongols' ordinary clothes. Red or green were favored colors for the bride, but there was no distinct color code. The only required element was the married woman's jewelry for the bride, which when put on marked her as a married woman.

On the wedding day the groom and his party rode to the bride's home. There the groom and his party were feasted, and the bride might perform prostrations before the household Buddhas. The groom's party then led off the bride and her party, followed by the trousseau and dowry. After arriving outside the groom's home, the bride's hair was redone in a married style, and the jewelry was put on. In Ordos, the bride passed between two purifying fires (see FIRE CULT). The bride then entered the house and performed prostrations with her new husband before the family fire, the Buddha of the groom's family, and the groom's parents, while a senior man of the groom's family delivered a *yörööl*, or benediction (see YÖRÖÖL and MAGTAAL). Then followed a vast wedding feast with abundant drunkenness.

Throughout the wedding the bride's and groom's sides were represented by fluent speakers who engaged in repeated verbal jousting. The language of the wedding poetry was largely traditional but often used skillfully by the bride's speaker at her home to challenge the groom, a challenge that the groom's side speaker had to meet. The bride was often miserable at leaving home, and in her songs before her departure she lamented (if bridewealth was paid) that she had been sold off by her father. By contrast, the wedding day poetry from the groom's side, contained frequent references to the customs of nature, the marriage of CHINGGIS KHAN and BÖRTE ÜJIN, and the necessity of reproduction as justification of the practice of weddings, exogamy, and daughters leaving home.

After the wedding night the bride was taken to visit the groom's relatives in her wedding dress. Sometimes the bride's parents visited the groom after a few days, but in all cases the bride and groom visited the bride's family. After the first child visits occurred regularly.

MODERN WEDDINGS

The main alternative to the traditional wedding today is one in a "cultural palace" or in the larger cities a specially built "wedding palace." In such weddings, the bride wears a white wedding dress and the groom a tuxedo, and the signing of the civil marriage registration replaces the prostrations that create the traditional wedding. However, many, if not most, Mongolian weddings today in Mongol lands follow roughly the traditional fashion. The main difference is in the engagement stage, with arranged marriages replaced by love matches, the abolition of contractual marriage payments (banned in Mongolia's 1940 CONSTITUTION), and the simplification and shortening of the engagement. However, wedding gifts (often lavish) from the bride's and groom's relatives fulfill the old role of the trousseau and dowry, and parents still exercise a strong role, sometimes amounting to a veto, on their children's marriage choices. Marriage within the patrilineage or outside the ethnic group (usually with Russians and Chinese) sometimes occurs in urban areas but is not common.

Further reading: Pao Kuo-yi [Ünensechen], "Marriage Customs of a Khorchin Village," *Central Asiatic Journal* 9 (1964): 29–59; Henry Serruys, "Four Manuals for Marriage Ceremonies among the Mongols, Parts I and II," *Zentralasiatische Studien* 8 (1974): 247–331, and 9 (1975): 275–360.

western Europe and the Mongol Empire Despite numerous envoys and the obvious logic of an alliance against mutual enemies, the papacy and the Crusaders never achieved the often-proposed Mongol alliance against Islam. western Europe first learned of the Mongols during the reign of ÖGEDEI KHAN (1229–41), when the Mongols pursued simultaneous western campaigns against eastern Europe in the north and against the Mid-

dle East in the south. Hungarian friars among the Bashkirs (Bashkort) in the Urals heard news of the Mongol invasion from 1237, but the scale of the subsequent Mongol campaign under BATU (d. 1255) against Central Europe from 1241 to 1242 exceeded all expectations. Meanwhile, the Mongol conquest of GEORGIA and the surrender of LESSER ARMENIA brought the Mongols to the attention of those Franks (the Middle Eastern term for all western Europeans) active in the eastern Mediterranean: Crusaders, papal representatives, and Italian merchants. Europeans showed their view of these invasions by changing *Tatar,* the common Middle Eastern name for the Mongols, to *Tartar,* that is, people from Tartarus, or Hell.

In 1245 Pope Innocent IV (1243–54) sent the Franciscan friar JOHN OF PLANO CARPINI as envoy to the Mongols. From Batu's camp on the Volga John traveled to the QURILTAI (assembly) that elected GÜYÜG Khan (1246–48). His mission was successful only in giving an alarming picture of the success and confidence of the Mongols. Dominican friars were sent to BAIJU in the Caucasus, but this mission was even less successful. In 1248 eastern Christians, posing as envoys from Eljigidei, Baiju's successor, to the French king St. Louis IX (r. 1226–70), first promoted the idea of a Christian alliance against the Muslims to recover Jerusalem. The Mongols later denied they had ever authorized those messengers. As this example shows, throughout the Mongol-Frankish relationship eastern Christian translators and envoys, particularly Armenians, were the most eager promoters of a Mongol-Frankish alliance against Islam. Nevertheless, Louis's purely evangelistic missions to the regent OGHUL-QAIMISH (d. 1251) and MÖNGKE KHAN (1251–59), the latter through the Franciscan friar WILLIAM OF RUBRUCK, both proved failures.

These early failures blocked cooperation for decades. As HÜLE'Ü (r. 1256–65), Möngke Khan's brother, invaded Syria, his tributary, King Het'um I (1230–69) of Lesser Armenia, persuaded the Crusader Bohemond of Antioch, his son-in-law, to participate, but the Crusaders at Acre (Akko) were hostile to the Mongols from the start. Even the reconquest of Syria by the great sultan Baybars (1260–77) of MAMLUK EGYPT and his destruction of Antioch (1268) did not change the Franks' anti-Mongol attitude. Hüle'ü's Mongol IL-KHANATE in the Middle East dropped the previous demand that the Franks submit, but his letter to France (1263) and Abagha Khan's (1265–81) repeated envoys to England and Rome a decade later received no reply.

Europe responded only as the Mamluk were preparing the final assault on the Crusaders' last outposts, Tripoli (taken 1289) and Acre (taken 1291). Arghun Khan (1284–91) in 1288 dispatched to Europe Rabban Sawma, an ÖNGGÜD Christian monk born in North China, with a proposal to join forces and take Jerusalem. From then until 1307 letters frequently passed back and forth but never resulted in any joint military action. The

Islamic conversion of the Il-Khans in 1295 did not influence Mongol eagerness for an alliance, but the 1323 peace treaty between the Il-Khans and Egypt ended all diplomatic interchange between the Il-Khanate and Western Europe.

Despite the failure of diplomatic relations, Italian trade with the western Mongol realms flourished, especially after 1300. The route from Ayas to Tabriz became the main path for exchange of Middle Eastern cotton, silk, and gold cloths for European silver and woolens. It also served as an emporium for Indian and Chinese goods, although routes through the Red Sea to Egypt offered stiff competition. Likewise, Italian colonies in CRIMEA exported East Asian goods and GOLDEN HORDE slaves, furs, and falcons all over the Mediterranean. "Tartar" slaves became a common sight in the town houses and country estates of Italy's noble families. The Venetian family of MARCO POLO was only one of many merchants who traveled these new trade routes. Catholic missionary activity proved more fruitful when yoked to trade than to diplomacy; Soltaniyeh (near Zanjan) in 1308, DAIDU (modern Beijing) in 1307, and Saray (on the lower Volga) in Toqto'a's reign (1291–1312) all received bishoprics. The BLACK DEATH and the continentwide crisis from 1345 on ended this flourishing European interaction with Asia.

See also CENTRAL EUROPE AND THE MONGOLS; CHRISTIAN SOURCES ON THE MONGOL EMPIRE; CHRISTIANITY IN THE MONGOL EMPIRE.

Further reading: Iris Origo, "The Domestic Enemy: The Eastern Slaves in Tuscany in the Fourteenth and Fifteenth Centuries," *Speculum* 30 (1955): 321–366. Igor de Rachewiltz, *Papal Envoys to the Great Khans* (London: Faber and Faber, 1971).

Western Mongols   *See* OIRATS.

White Horde   *See* BLUE HORDE.

White Month (Tsagaan Sar)   The White Month, or lunar new year, has been one of the two main Mongolian holidays since the time of the Mongol Empire. It is marked by religious rituals, new clothes, abundant food, and visiting of family and friends.

The White Month is determined by Mongolia's traditional lunar-solar calendar. This calendar has been used by the Mongols since at least the 12th century. Although the date varies according to the year, it generally falls around late January or early February. The name *White Month—chagha'an sara* in Middle Mongolian, *tsagaan sar* in modern Mongolian—derives from the auspicious character of the color white among the Mongols. The Buriat Mongolian name, *sagaalgan,* means "whitening."

During the world empire of the 13th and 14th centuries, the Mongols always nomadized on the eve of the White Month to the place where they would spend that month. On new year's day itself the Mongols visited one another wearing pure white clothes. On this day the khan held a QURILTAI (assembly). On the third day there was an assembly and a ceremony around the carts that held the ONGGHON and the standards. Despite scholarly speculation to the contrary, Chinese and Persian court annals of the MONGOL EMPIRE, both based directly on Mongolian sources, make it clear that the Mongols during the empire observed the late January–early February new year only.

In recent centuries people begin preparing for the White Month perhaps a month before, making new clothes, collecting foods and gifts, and cleaning the home and hearth. On the 23rd or 24th of the last month the offering to the fire is performed. On the *bitüün*, or last day of the last month, lamps are lit and prayers made to the household Buddhas. The *bitüün* meal consists of a whole sheep, of which part has first been offered to the Buddha, BUUZ (steamed dumplings), *bänsh* (dumplings in soup), fried bread, milks, and cheeses. On this day members of one camp visit one another and play games with astragali (sheep ankle bones, or *shagai*) until late at night. Visits outside the camp are not made, however. During the evening three grains of rice and a grain of millet are placed on the threshold as food for the mount of the fierce female protector-deity Lhamo, as she returns from suppressing hostile spirits.

The first day of the White Month begins early in the morning with the worship of heaven. Having built the previous day a temporary OBOO (heap) of dirt or snow southeast of the door, lamps are lit and incense sticks burned on the *oboo* as the men of the house bow down before heaven and perform aspersions (*satsal*) of TEA and DAIRY PRODUCTS. After eating breakfast the men of the family ride out in an auspicious direction and return by another auspicious direction; the direction is astrologically determined each year. (In the cities this often becomes a simple circumambulation of the residence.) With their return juniors begin presenting *khadags* (ceremonial scarves), bow down before the elders, and exchange sniffs from snuff bottles. Elders may speak a number of common blessings on the young.

Animals also participate in the White Month festivities. On the *bitüün* all animals are brought early into the camp and watered; only horse herds may be allowed to pasture overnight. On the first of the White Month rams and billygoats are brought to the *oboo,* censed with incense, anointed with milk, and fed soft cheeses.

Despite the seemingly festive nature of the day, it is traditionally one of considerable tension. Indeed, it is because this month and day are considered most inauspicious that so many "white" (auspicious) things need to be done. Omens for the coming year are sought in all actions, and rambunctiousness, arguments, drunkenness (despite the required presentations of liquor), working (particularly on anything left unfinished), and sleeping outside one's own home all presage a bad year.

Traditionally, Mongols did not celebrate individual birthdays. Instead, each White Month was taken to be the person's birthday. Those years with the animal under which one was born (*see* 12-ANIMAL CYCLE) were celebrated with gifts.

In the monasteries the White Month is marked with service to the fierce protectors of Buddhism beginning from the 28th of the last year's 12th moon. On the morning of the New Year a *lingka,* or figure of a naked man serving as the embodiment of all evil, is stabbed and cut up. A flamelike *sor,* or dough figure shaped as a flamelike pyramid to attack all enemies of the faith, is then burned in a bonfire outside the temple. On the 15th a TSAM dance or a procession for Maitreya (the future Buddha) was held.

Traditionally, the special observances of the White Month extended throughout the month. On the second day work was symbolically begun again, and families and friends paid visits. On the odd-numbered days leading up to the 13th, visiting was prohibited, however. The 10th day was for performing merit and avoiding sin, as all

karmic effects were magnified on this day. On the 19th to 21st days in prerevolutionary times, the banner offices, closed on *bitüün,* were reopened with a grand ceremony of worshiping the seal (*tamaga*), and a meeting of the high officials assigned tax quotas for the coming year. It was believed that Indra (Khormusta), king of the gods, assigned fates on the same day to influence which commoners made offerings.

The KALMYKS during the 18th century moved their new year from the White Month to the purely Buddhist Lamp Festival (*Zul*) celebrating the Nirvana (passing away) of Tsong-kha-pa (1372–1419), the great Tibetan lama. This took place on the 25th of the 10th lunar month, which was traditionally followed by the Jilin ezn (Lord of the Year, Mongolian, Jiliin ezen) celebration for the WHITE OLD MAN. Even so, the Kalmyks also still celebrated the White Month (Tsaghan Sar) with new clothes, housecleaning, family greetings, and visiting. While meat was eaten, the centerpiece of the holiday meal was plates of fried bread, or *boortsg* (Mongolian, *boortsog*), many

White Month spread at a pipe-fitter's house in Ulaanbaatar. In the center is a plate of fried dough and dairy products. To the left is a bowl of candy and to the right a partial *shüüs,* or boiled mutton. The food is being offered to the pipe-fitter's deceased parents, whose photograph is above the carpet on the wall. *(Courtesy Christopher Atwood)*

made in imitation meat form, which were presented to the household Buddhas on the eve. A large flat round *boortsg*, called either *tselwg* or *khawtkha* (flat, Mongolian, *khawtgai*), is a part of all such offerings. A sprinkling of tea outside the YURT was the main family religious ceremony on the first day of the White Month. The XINJIANG MONGOLS, largely descendants of the Kalmyks, have reverted to the general Mongolian calendar.

Since the White Month had obvious similarities to the Chinese lunar new year, China's ethnic Mongols, like all Chinese citizens, always received days off, even under the Communist government, although vacations were limited in the Maoist period. The holiday's religious elements were rigidly suppressed until 1979. In the Soviet bloc, however, the White Month was treated as an inherently Buddhist and antisocialist holiday, ironically following czarist scholarship, which exaggerated the Buddhist origins of the festival. These attacks began in the late 1920s among the Mongolian peoples in the Soviet Union, the BURIATS and Kalmyks. Despite a period of prohibition, by the 1960s observance of the holiday was still widespread among the Buddhist Buriats although officially ignored. In January 1990 Sagaalgan (the Buriat name) was officially declared a local holiday. Since then the Russian president regularly issues congratulations to the Buddhist clergy on that day. Perhaps due to the Soviet regime's aggressive identification of the holiday with Buddhism, the shamanist Buriats of Ust'-Orda, Ol'khon, and the SELENGE RIVER delta show little interest in the festival today.

In Mongolia attacks on the holiday were more circumspect. The attacks began in 1930 and the year 1932 saw an intense campaign against the holiday, but the campaign relented during the NEW TURN POLICY, from 1933 to 1936. During WORLD WAR II (1941–45) a decree of the legislature explicitly authorized the herders to celebrate the holiday again. In 1952, however, the ruler, MARSHAL CHOIBALSANG, died on *bitüün*, and the White Month that year and the next were replaced by official mourning. On January 26, 1954, the government officially decreed that the White Month would be a working day, beginning a new campaign against its observance. By 1960, however, the government again compromised and designated the first day of the lunar year the "Collective Herders' Day." Only in 1988 was the White Month again marked as a national holiday.

Observance of the day has changed significantly for urban Mongols, although the traditional foods, new clothes, and greetings continue, and many observe worship ceremonies. Since members of the extended family usually do not live together and the time for celebration has often been shortened, the first day of the White Month, traditionally an "at home" day, has become one of widespread visiting of family, friends, and respected acquaintances.

See also CALENDAR AND DATING SYSTEMS; FIRE CULT; FOOD AND DRINK; *TENGGERI*.

White Old Man   The White Old Man (Middle Mongolian, *chagha'an ebügen*, modern, *tsagaan öwgön*) is one of the most widespread and beloved Mongol deities and analogous to other aged gods of prosperity and blessing found throughout Tibet and East Asia. He is sometimes called Tserendug in Mongolia, from Tibetan Tshe-ring-drug.

The White Old Man is usually pictured as a bald and bearded white-haired old man leaning on a dragon-headed staff. He is dressed in white, the most auspicious color among the Mongols. Prayer texts speak of him as chief of the masters of the land and of the waters in the 24 directions. He resides on Fruitful (*jimislig*) Mountain and rides a deer. The White Old Man counts peoples' sins and governs the lengths of their lives, unleashing poxes, brigands, and slander against evildoers. Against these evils the White Old Man is to be worshiped twice a month on the second and 16th days of the month with aspersions (*satsal*) of liquor and offerings of butter and silk scraps to the household fire.

In Mongolian Buddhist apocrypha the White Old Man is described as a hermit who met Shakyamuni Buddha or the female bodhisattva Green Tara. He then received the prediction that he would be reborn as a Bud-

White Old Man. *Thangka* (mineral paints on cotton) from the Buriat Historical Museum *(From* Buddiiskaia zhivopis Buriatii *[1995])*

dha who would protect all living beings. The THIRD MERGEN GEGEEN (1717–66) composed an incense offering prayer text for the White Old Man.

See also TSAM.

White Tatars   *See* ÖNGGÜD.

William of Rubruck (fl. 1253–1256) *Missionary from France who visited the Mongols and wrote a valuable description of the Mongols' customs and religious life*

Born at Rubruck (French, Rubrouck, near Cassel) in French Flanders, William of Rubruck as a young Franciscan friar accompanied France's King Louis IX (St. Louis, r. 1226–70) on his 1248 crusade against Egypt. While staying in Acre (modern 'Akko), St. Louis was told that Sartaq, the Mongol prince ruling CRIMEA, was a Christian. Despite the failure of an earlier diplomatic mission to the Mongols, Louis sent William with elaborate vestments, vessels, and books, including a gold-illuminated Psalter from his wife Queen Marguerite, to instruct Sartaq and convert the Mongols. William reached the Black Sea in May 1253 and, landing at Sudak (Soldaia), proceeded to Sartaq's ORDO (palace-tent). Unfortunately, merchants had already spread the rumor that he came as an envoy of Louis offering submission. Constantly confused with an envoy, William was forwarded by Sartaq to his father, BATU, who in turn sent him to MÖNGKE KHAN (1251–59) in Mongolia, where he arrived on December 27. In July 1254 William was sent back with a letter from Möngke to St. Louis. William returned via Batu's court, the Caucasus, and TURKEY, reaching the Levantine Crusader fort of Tripoli on August 15, 1255. King Louis had already returned to France, and William wrote out a long account of his journey in Latin as a letter to Louis.

William of Rubruck's account of his journey is the best ethnographic description of medieval Mongol life, exceeding any other account in detail, accuracy, and range of interests. Unlike JOHN OF PLANO CARPINI, he discounted tales of monsters and other fantastic creatures often told of the East. While he eventually saw the Mongol khans as an alarming threat to Europe and regretted St. Louis's idea of evangelization, many aspects of Mongol life and craftsmanship impressed him. His account of Assyrian (Nestorian) and Armenian clergy at the courts of Sartaq and Möngke is the best description of Christian activities among the medieval Mongols. He resented how these clergymen spread misleading stories about the Mongols' eagerness to convert and believed that the Mongols had come to see Christianity as a kind of race or ethnic group. Thus, while the Mongol *khatuns* (ladies) often had a simple faith in the cross, the Mongol khans saw accepting Christianity as renouncing their Mongol ancestry.

After returning to Paris William of Rubruck met the philosopher Roger Bacon, who described William's experiences in his *Opus Majus*. No other medieval writer refers to his journey, however, and its importance was not recognized until the late 19th century.

See also CHRISTIAN SOURCES ON THE MONGOL EMPIRE; GOLDEN HORDE; WESTERN EUROPE AND THE MONGOLS.

Further reading: Peter Jackson, with David Morgan, *The Mission of Friar William of Rubruck: His Journey to the Court of Great Khan Möngke, 1253–1255* (London: Hakluyt Society, 1990).

Winter Palace   *See* PALACES OF THE BOGDA KHAN.

World War II Before World War II was officially declared Mongolia served as the theater for large Soviet-Japanese border clashes. When Nazi Germany invaded the Soviet Union in 1941, Mongolia made considerable sacrifices to deliver economic aid to the Soviet Red Army. Mongolia's later participation in the Soviet attack on Japan advanced its diplomatic recognition. Total Mongolian casualties in border clashes and battles against Japan from 1935 to 1945 were officially numbered at 2,039.

On June 22, 1941, Mongolia's ruler, MARSHAL CHOIBALSANG, responded to the German invasion by a declaration of full support for the Soviet Union, although Mongolia did not formally declare war. Aside from the largely symbolic mobilization of citizens' gifts, in February 1942 the Mongolian government gave 2.5 million tögrögs, 300 kilograms (661 pounds) of gold, and US $100,000 to the Soviet Union to equip a tank column, "Revolutionary Mongolia," and the next year gave another 2 million tögrögs to equip a fighter squadron, "Mongolian Arat" (i.e., commoners or herders).

The most costly forms of aid were the supply of livestock as food for the Soviet economy, mounts for the Red Army, and livestock to rebuild devastated areas. Mongolians donated 32,500 HORSES to the Soviet Union, and the state sold 722,000 CATTLE, 428,000 horses, and 4,931,000 SHEEP and GOATS. The low state-set procurement prices caused widespread popular discontent. Mongolia's total herd of 26.2 million in 1940 declined to about 24 million in 1944, before a massive winter ZUD (winter disaster) in 1944–45 killed 8 million head, leaving only 20.0 million head in summer 1945.

With Mongolia's dependent economy, the Soviet Union's war effort also led to shortages of consumer goods such as TEA, tobacco, flour, and grain; rationing was in effect until 1950. From 1942 to 1944 Mongolia's exports to the Soviet Union exceeded its imports by an average of 76 percent. To supply the lack of imported grain, cultivated acreage jumped from 27,000 hectares (66,720 acres) in 1941 to 74,000 hectares (182,854 acres) in 1943, and small factories were built to mill flour and manufacture scythes and plows. Again, droughts destroyed almost the whole harvest, however, in 1944–45.

During World War II Mongolia's armed forces expanded from about 18,000 in 1939 to 43,000 in 1945, not including 11,000 border guards, with many scarce professionals drafted into the army. With the conclusion of the European war, Mongolia joined the Soviet attack on Japanese forces in Manchuria and Inner Mongolia on August 9, 1945. Regular Mongolian troops participated in Colonel General I. A. Pliev's Mechanized Cavalry Group assaulting Japanese forces in central Inner Mongolia. This assault continued until August 23, reaching Zhangjiakou (Kalgan), Chengde, and Batu-Khaalga (Bailingmiao). A total of 2,000 Interior Ministry paramilitary units combed central Inner Mongolia and HULUN BUIR and assisted in arresting Japanese agents and KHALKHA refugees who had fled in the 1930s. Choibalsang also encouraged a grass-roots pan-Mongolist movement, particularly in Inner Mongolia's SHILIIN GOL, CHAKHAR, and Hulun Buir regions.

The war's main significance for Mongolia was diplomatic. According to the Anglo-American-Soviet accord at Yalta (February 1945), China would have to respect the "status quo" in Outer Mongolia. In negotiations leading up to the Sino-Soviet Friendship Treaty of August 14, Soviet ruler Joseph Stalin forced China's ruler, Chiang Kai-shek, to accept Mongolia's full independence within its current frontiers. As a result, pan-Mongolist agitation in Inner Mongolia was called off on August 30, and after a plebiscite China recognized Mongolian independence in February 1946. Mongolia had also formally declared war on Japan on August 10, a fact it believed entitled it to membership in the UNITED NATIONS. The first request, in June 1946, was, however, denied, and Mongolia would not be admitted until 1961.

See also ARMED FORCES OF MONGOLIA; DEMCHUNG-DONGRUB; PRINCE; KHALKHYN GOL, BATTLE OF; JAPAN AND THE MODERN MONGOLS; MONGOLIAN PEOPLE'S REPUBLIC; PLEBISCITE ON INDEPENDENCE.

wrestling The most popular sport in Mongolia since the 12th century, Mongolian wrestling is based on distinctive rules.

Stories of champion wrestlers (Middle Mongolian, *böke*, modern, *bökh*), including CHINGGIS KHAN's half-brother Belgütei, show that wrestling was popular throughout the empire period. Mongolian khans took pride in the strength of their wrestlers and set them fighting against those from subjugated countries. QAIDU KHAN's daughter Qutulun (d. 1306) became famous as a wrestler. Little, however, is known of the clothing or style of Mongolian wrestling then.

All rounds in modern Mongolian wrestling begin in a standing position. Whoever lets any part of his trunk, knees, or elbow touch the ground loses. The palms may touch the ground legally, allowing a wrestler on his hands and feet to stay in the match. Mongolian wrestling always takes place in the open on grassy ground, and the wrestlers do not need to stay within a defined ring. The feet can be used to trip the opponent, but kicking and punching are not allowed.

Champion wrestlers at the Great State Naadam *(Photo from Sotsialist Mongol [1988])*

Wrestlers' clothing varies but includes a tight-fitting *zodog* (Inner Mongolian, *jodog*), or cut-away shirt, which gives a standard grip for the wrestlers. Inner Mongolian wrestlers wear a short-sleeved *jodog* of brass-studded leather, belted over the lower belly but cut away to leave the upper belly, chest, and shoulders bare. Baggy pantaloons (*shuudag*), mostly white and covered with traditional appliqué patterns and designs, are tucked into traditional upturned leather Mongolian boots, also decorated with appliqué. Inner Mongolian wrestlers frequently wear ropes of twisted KHADAG scarves around their necks. Wrestlers in independent Mongolia wear an even shorter cloth *zodog* with sleeves, which is tied in front with a rope. Rather than pantaloons, they wear cloth briefs, also called *shuudag* and made of the same material as the *zodog*. Upturned Mongolian boots complete the costume. KHALKHA Mongolian wrestlers enter the field with a conical hat to which is tied a *khadag* (ceremonial scarf) that they give to the care of their coach during the actual bout. Buriat and Kalmyk wrestlers in Russia today compete in boxer shorts and athletic shoes.

Wrestling matches occur during NAADAM, or games held in conjunction with summertime religious ceremonies or national holidays. The wrestlers first perform a clockwise circumambulation of the field and traditionally make a libation of mare's milk to the gods. Before each match the wrestler's coach chants a *magtaal,* or praise for the wrestler (*see* YÖRÖÖL AND MAGTAAL). The wrestler then gives the coach his hat and performs a dance called "the flapping of the Garuda" (the mythic Indian king of birds) around the banner standard or national flag before touching the ground with his hands. During the bout the competitors' coaches stand next to them shouting advice in a ritualized language and sometimes slapping the wrestlers' buttocks or thighs if the contest seems slow. After one wins the loser passes under the winner's arm and is slapped on the buttocks, and the winner performs the Garuda dance again. The winner then takes from his coach a handful of crumbly Mongolian cheeses, which he tosses in offering to the local deities and/or the spectators. Young wrestlers eagerly vie to catch and eat these cheeses.

Mongolian wrestlers compete in single-elimination tournaments. Champions are matched with weak contenders in the early rounds so that the final rounds pit major champions against each other. Traditionally, there was no time limit on the rounds, but in the 1960s time limits were introduced, only to be eliminated again in 1996, when a final bout lasted four hours. During the National Holiday Naadam (Ulsynikh Bayar Naadam) in Mongolia's capital, 512 wrestlers compete. Winners receive prizes supplied by the organizer of the occasion. The titles of champions include, in ascending order, falcon (*nachin*), elephant (*zaan*), lion (*arslan*), and titan (*awarga*), which can be given at the provincial or national levels. The *ulsyn awarga* (titan of the state) is thus the current national champion in Mongolia. Wrestlers are Mongolia's most popular sports heroes, and their posters adorn shops, yurts, and rooms throughout Mongolia. In Inner Mongolia wrestling has less media presence, yet it is still the most popular and widely practiced sport.

Wrestling is the only one of the "three manly sports" from which women are, in fact, generally excluded. Indeed, legends in Khalkha speak of the current skimpy *zodog* and *shuudag* being adopted deliberately to exclude women. (This perhaps recalls the example of Qaidu's daughter Qutulun.) In Inner Mongolia women wrestlers, wearing T-shirts under their *jodog*s, have been included in recent years.

written Mongolian *See* UIGHUR-MONGOLIAN SCRIPT.

Wuhai Carved out of Ordos and Alashan territory, Wuhai city is the chief coal mining center of southwestern Inner Mongolia. Wuhai city was originally two towns, Wuda on the western side of the Huang (Yellow) River and Haibowan on the eastern side. In 1976 they were merged as Wuhai. With an area of 2,350 square kilometers (907 square miles), the total population is 314,148, of whom 8,554 are Mongol.

Coal mining began in Wuda in 1864, supplying Chinese settlers in the Hetao area with fuel. By 1949 annual output was around 30,000 metric tons (33,069 short tons). Haibowan was colonized by Chinese farmers around 1900. In 1958 large-scale prospecting and investment in the now-nationalized coal mining industry began. By 1990 proven reserves totaled 4.2 billion metric tons (4.6 billion short tons). In 1988 the city's total industrial output was 468,140,000 *yuan,* of which about 55 percent was coal.

See also INNER MONGOLIA AUTONOMOUS REGION.

Wulanchabu *See* ULAANCHAB.

Wulanfu *See* ULANFU.

Wuzhumuqin *See* ÜJÜMÜCHIN.

Xanadu *See* SHANGDU.

Xia dynasty (Tangut, Xixia, Hsi-Hsia) The Xia dynasty ruled Northwest China from 1038 to 1227, until its final destruction by CHINGGIS KHAN in five campaigns. It is often called the Western Xia or Xixia to distinguish it from the legendary Xia dynasty of China's remote past. The dynasty was founded by chiefs of the Mi-nyag people, who originated in the Chinese western borderlands between Sichuan, Gansu, and Tibet. Called Dangxiang by the Chinese and Tangut by the Turks and Mongols, the Mi-nyag spoke a language in the Tibeto-Burman family, most closely related to that of the Yi (Lolo) nationality in modern Sichuan and Yunnan and more distantly to Burmese and Tibetan.

RISE OF THE DYNASTY

Under the Tang dynasty (618–907) a body of Mi-nyag tribesmen settled the ORDOS plateau in southeastern Inner Mongolia. As a mark of honor their chieftains of the Weiming family bore the Tang imperial surname, Li. With the fall of the Tang dynasty the Weiming, or Li, family expanded its influence in Northwest China. Besides the local Chinese population, the Gansu corridor was occupied by nomadic Uighur and Shatuo (ÖNGGÜD) Turks. Tibetan occupied the mountainous southwest around modern Xining. While the SONG DYNASTY (960–1279) reunited most of North and South China, Li (Weiming) Yuanhao conquered the Ganzhou (modern Zhangye) UIGHURS in 1029, pushed the Tibetans south, and declared himself emperor of the Xia dynasty in 1038.

The Mi-nyag, or Tangut, people had long been in the Chinese orbit, and Li Yuanhao followed many institutions of Chinese administration. He also, however, commissioned a script for the Mi-nyag/Tangut language, which was still used into the 14th century. Buddhism was the state religion, and the Xia ruler had a religious and mystic reputation in Inner Asia exemplified by his Mongolian title of Burqan, or "Buddha," Khan. Earlier the Buddhism was primarily Chinese rite, but from the middle of the 12th century on Tibetan Buddhism became dominant as Xia rulers invited Tibetan clerics to hold the office of state preceptor (Chinese, *guoshi*).

The Xia dynasty's military success and a marriage alliance with the KITANS' Liao dynasty (907–1125), based in Inner Mongolia, eventually forced the Song dynasty to recognize Xia independence. After the Jurchen people destroyed the Kitan Liao and founded the JIN DYNASTY (1115–1234), driving the Song out of North China, the Xia recognized Jurchen suzerainty in return for de facto independence. The Gansu corridor had traditionally been an avenue of the famed "Silk Road," and the Xia tried to draw this trade, dominated by Uighurs and by Muslim Turkestanis, into its orbit, while the Kitans, Song, and Jin tried to bypass the empire. To the north the Xia rulers intermarried with the allied royal family of the KEREYID Khanate in central Mongolia.

MONGOL CONQUEST

When Chinggis Khan united the Mongolian plateau by defeating the Kereyid and NAIMAN khanates in 1203–04, Ilqa-Senggüm, son of the Kereyid ONG KHAN, sought refuge in the Xia. After his adherents took to plundering the locals, however, he was expelled. Perhaps in response to the initial offer of refuge, Chinggis Khan in 1205 launched the first of his five campaigns against the Xia, plundering border settlements. In 1207 he sacked

Wulahai, the main garrison along the Huang (Yellow) River in the northeast (near modern Wuyuan). In 1209 Chinggis undertook a larger campaign to secure the submission of the Xia. He again attacked Wulahai and followed the course of the Huang (Yellow) River up to the capital, Zhongxing (MARCO POLO's Egrigaia). He attempted to flood the capital by diverting the river, but instead only flooded his own camp, thus ending the siege. Even so, the new and insecure Xia emperor, Li (Weiming) Anquan (r. 1206–11), agreed to present a daughter to Chinggis Khan together with a large tribute in which countless herds of CAMELS held pride of place. Chinggis Khan always required tributary powers to send hostages and to contribute troops to his campaigns, but the Xia resisted these demands. The Mongols left a garrison, probably at Wulahai, and the Xia Empire entered the Mongol orbit.

Sending troops and hostages proved to be sticking points in Xia-Mongol relations. As the Mongols invaded the neighboring JIN DYNASTY in 1211, the Xia took advantage to pursue long-standing border claims against the Jin. In 1218 the Mongols in North China invaded the Xia a fourth time. The Mongols besieged the capital again, and the Xia emperor Li (Weiming) Zunxu (r. 1211–23) fled west, leaving his son and officials to make peace. How the conflict was resolved is uncertain, but the Tanguts did not contribute soldiers the next year, when Chinggis Khan demanded men for his great western campaign against KHORAZM. Xia territory gave easy access to Shaanxi province, a vital area of remaining Jin control, so in 1221 MUQALI, the Mongol commander in North China, crossed the Huang (Yellow) River into Xia territory. Xia envoys promised 50,000 soldiers, which in the end never arrived, and Muqali had to retreat without subduing Shaanxi. After Muqali's death in 1223 his Mongol and Chinese generals again raided the Xia.

When Chinggis Khan returned victorious from the conquest of Khorazm, he planned the final destruction of the recalcitrant Xia state. The campaign began in the northwest this time with the capture of Heishui (Khara-Khota, near modern Ejin Qi) in February–March 1226. The cities of the Gansu corridor were sacked one by one. Crossing the Huang (Yellow) River, the Mongols sacked Lingzhou near the capital in November, and on December 4 Chinggis Khan crossed back over the frozen Huang (Yellow) River to attack a relief column. The Mongols were victorious and besieged the capital. Confident the capital would fall, Chinggis Khan turned its capture over to his generals and left to attack the Jin cities along the Jin-Xia frontier in Gansu and Shaanxi. In July, when the last Xia ruler, Li Xian (r. 1226–27), finally surrendered, Chinggis Khan was on his deathbed to the south in Jin territory. After Chinggis's death the Xia royal family and the population of Zhongxing were massacred.

TANGUTS IN THE MONGOL EMPIRE

Even before the fall of the Xia, a number of Mi-nyag, or Tangut, men had come into Mongol service. These were not Xia subjects, but Tanguts from the Jiu or Jüyin tribal auxiliaries enrolled by the Jin in Inner Mongolia. The Tangut Jiu rebelled early against the Jin and formed an important part of the Mongol armies in North China. The Tangut ethnic group survived the Mongol conquest, and the Tangut language was one of those used in the famous inscription at Juyongguan Pass in the 1340s. At first few Tanguts from the Xia region achieved high position. Under the class system of the Mongol YUAN DYNASTY after 1260, however, ethnic Tanguts were classified as SEMUREN (various sorts) and not as North Chinese, giving them an advantage in the exams. Thus, after 1300 Tangut officials achieved higher positions. The most important legacy of the Xia state to the Mongols was its patronage of Tibetan Buddhism, revived in 1240 by KÖTEN, a son of ÖGEDEI KHAN, who had received his appanage in the former Xia area.

Tangut captives dwelling among the Mongols were eventually assimilated into the Mongolian people. In the 16th century the Tangut formed one of the 14 clans of the Khalkha and are still widespread in Mongolia.

Further reading: Ruth Dunnell, "The Fall of the Xia Empire: Sino-Steppe Relations in the Late 12th–Early 13th Centuries," in *Rulers from the Steppe: State Formation on the Eurasian Periphery*, ed. Gary Seaman and Daniel Marks (Los Angeles: Ethnographies Press, 1991), 158–185; Elliot Sperling, "Rtsa-mi Lo-ts-ba Sangs-rgyas Grags-pa and the Tangut Background to Early Mongol-Tibetan Relations," in *Tibetan Studies: Proceedings of the 6th Seminar of the International Association for Tibetan Studies*, ed. Per Kvaerne (Oslo: Institute for Comparative Research in Human Culture, 1994), 2: 801–824.

Xianbi (Xianbei, Hsien-pi) A branch of the Eastern Hu (Donghu, Tung-hu), the Xianbi (probably originally pronounced "Serbi") were the first Mongolic-speaking peoples to dominate the steppe and the first Inner Asian people to found a stable dynasty in China.

Around 209 B.C.E. the Eastern Hu peoples were defeated by the XIONGNU, to whom they paid skin and cloth taxes for the next two centuries. (In 443 a Xianbi delegation identified Gaxian Cave, now in Inner Mongolia's Oroqen Autonomous Banner, as its long-forgotten ancestral temple, to which it had fled from Xiongnu attacks.) The Eastern Hu were more sedentary than the Xiongnu, keeping pigs, for example. After 50 C.E. the Xianbi began moving into northern Mongolia, incorporating at one point 100,000 tents of the Xiongnu into their own people.

The Xianbi language contains a number of identifiable words preserved in Chinese transcription, particularly *qaghan*, "KHAN, emperor," and *qasun*, "queen" (cf.

592 Xiangyang, siege of

Mongolian KHATUN). Clearly, the Xianbi spoke a Turkic or Mongolic language, and historical considerations support a Mongolic ancestry. The relatively poor Xianbi remains resemble those of the Xiongnu but with differences: Graves frequently contain many bodies and have fewer animal remains, while animal figures are more static and have a distinct iconography, such as a little horse on top of a large one. Chinese histories treat the Xianbi as ancestors of the KITANS, Qai (Xi), and SHIWEI peoples.

Unlike the Xiongnu, the Xianbi did not form a centralized dynasty in Mongolia. Tanshihuai (r. 136?–81) unified the steppe but had no successor. Stable Xianbi dynasties emerged only as they settled on the Chinese frontiers in the late third century. After the Shanxi Xiongnu sacked the capital, Luoyang (316), these local dynasties began vying for power in North China. The Qifu clan, head of a four-clan Xianbi confederacy in eastern Gansu, founded the Later Qin dynasty (385–431) in Shaanxi. The more agricultural Murong family in Liaoning founded several dynasties named Yan around modern Beijing and Shandong from 337 to 410. Another branch of the Murong family migrated west and conquered the Qiang people in Qinghai (Kökenuur). There they founded the Achai (Tibetan, A-zha), or Tuyuhun, dynasty until their destruction by the new Tibetan empire around 638. Finally, the Tabghach (Chinese, Tuoba) occupied the Dai region in northern Shanxi and south-central Inner Mongolia and founded the Northern Wei dynasty (386–528) that reunited all North China.

The Wei created a script for Xianbi, which has not survived and in which were written a small number of books, including the Confucian *Classic of Filial Piety* and translated Chinese poetry. The Xianbi "Chele Song," celebrating the beauty of the steppe, has been preserved in Chinese translation.

Tabghach Hong (reign title Xiaowendi, 471–99) moved the capital from Datong south to Luoyang and ordered compulsory sinicization of Tabghach customs and surnames. Xiaowendi, however, extended the nomadic traditions of an armed populace to a depopulated North China, making each peasant a state militiaman farming state land. After a massive revolt of the tribal frontier armies in 523, Yuwen Tai, of an old Xianbi family, founded the Western Wei-Northern Zhou regime (535–81) in Shaanxi. The Yuwen regime reversed the sinicization policy yet relied on the peasant militia to conquer Sichuan and reunite the North (577). In 589, eight years after a Northern Zhou general, Yang Jian, had deposed the Yuwens and founded the Sui dynasty (581–617), the militia-based army he had inherited reunited China.

Culturally, the Tabghach regimes in North China showed an intense engagement with Chinese religions. Rulers built vast stone Buddhas near their capitals in Datong and Luoyang and received the title Tathagata (that is, Buddha), yet Tabghach Dao (reign title Taiwudi, 424–52) saw himself as a Taoist "Perfect Ruler of Great Peace" and persecuted Buddhism. Finally, both Taiwudi and Yuwen Tai dreamed of a Confucian primitivist return to the institutions of the Zhou dynasty (1122–256 B.C.E.), a viewpoint made official when the Yuwen rulers named their dynasty Zhou in 557.

The Tabghach dynasties neither conquered the Tarim Basin nor extended their rule to the Mongolian steppe, which by 400 was under the ROURAN dynasty. Even so, their prestige in North China resulted in the term *Tabghach* becoming the Old Turkish word both for China itself and for anything great and imposing.

See also ALTAIC LANGUAGE FAMILY; MONGOLIC LANGUAGE FAMILY.

Further reading: Emma Bunker, ed., *Ancient Bronzes of the Eastern Eurasian Steppe: From the Arthur W. Sackler Collections* (New York: Arthur M. Sackler Foundation, 1997); Adam Kessler, *Empires beyond the Great Wall: The Heritage of Genghis Khan* (Los Angeles: Natural History Museum of Los Angeles County, 1993).

Xiangyang, siege of (Hsiang-yang)

The twin cities of Xiangyang and Fancheng (modern Xiangfan in Hubei province) were a key SONG DYNASTY fortress straddling the south and north banks, respectively, of the Han River. The Mongol taking of the town in 1273 opened the way for an all-out assault on the Song.

Briefly held by the Mongols in 1236–38, the twin cities, with walls almost five kilometers (three miles) around and 200,000 people, withstood a Mongol assault in 1257. Lü Wende (d. 1270) commanded the Song dynasty's Middle Chang (Yangtze) sector, and his son-in-law Fan Wenhu and son Lü Wenhuan commanded Xiangyang. In 1268 QUBILAI KHAN assigned AJU and the Song defector Liu Zheng (1213–75) to take Xiangyang by siege. The two first blockaded the city with a ring of forts and in 1270 blocked the Han River with five stone platforms capped by arbalests. They also built 5,000 ships and trained 70,000 marines, yet Song food supplies still held out. In summer 1271 and April 1272 Song loyalist volunteers manned newly designed paddleboats to break the blockade, but the boats were eventually destroyed. Fan Wenhu was blamed for not offering land support and transferred. A breach of Fancheng's wall in April 1272 was repaired, but on January 25, 1273, the special mangonels of the deputy commander ARIQ-QAYA's Iraqi artillerymen, Isma'il and 'Ala'ud-Din, breached the walls again, while his marines cut the heavily defended pontoon bridge linking Fancheng to Xiangyang. The residents of Fancheng were butchered, but on March 14 Lü Wenhuan surrendered Xiangyang on more lenient terms. The Mongol victory opened the possibility of a full-scale assault on the Song.

See also MILITARY OF THE MONGOL EMPIRE.

Xilingol   *See* SHILIIN GOL.

Xilinguole *See* SHILIIN GOL.

Xing'an *See* KHINGGAN LEAGUE.

Xinjiang Mongols (Sinkiang)

The Mongols of Xinjiang form a small minority principally in the northern part of that land. They are primarily descendants of the TORGHUDS and KHOSHUDS who fled from Kalmykia and of the CHAKHAR stationed there as garrison soldiers.

SETTLEMENT

Xinjiang came under China's QING DYNASTY (1636–1912) in 1755–57. The destruction of the ZÜNGHARS opened the northern pastures for a large-scale immigration of KAZAKHS, whose loyalty the Qing suspected. At first the Qianlong emperor (1736–96) relied on small garrisons of Chakhar, Solon (i.e., Daur and Ewenki), and Manchu bannermen on regular three-year tours of duty to garrison the area. In 1762, however, those bannermen already on duty were assigned permanently to Xinjiang, and 5,000 new bannermen—Chakhars, Solons, Manchus, and Shibe—were selected for permanent assignment there. By 1767 1,837 Chakhar Mongol bannermen had been stationed in Rashiyan (modern Wenquan) and Borotala (modern Bole). Surviving Zünghars, except those of Tekes and Zhaosu in the Ili valley, were attached to Chakhar or Solon BANNERS (*see* EIGHT BANNERS).

In 1771 a tattered body of about 70,000 KALMYKS appeared on the frontier of Xinjiang (*see* FLIGHT OF THE KALMYKS). Originally hoping to conquer Züngharia for themselves, they had been too devastated by Kazakh and Kyrgyz attacks to do more than beg for admission. After an imperial audience in 1772, the Kalmyks were divided among 13 banners. The Torghud princes were organized in 1775 into four Ünen-Süzügtü LEAGUES distributed as follows: the South Route league, including the banner of the former Kalmyk viceroy Ubashi (1744–74), in the Zultus (modern Kaidu) River valley; the North Route league, including the banner of Tsebeg-Dorji (d. 1778), one of the chief instigators of the flight, around Khobogsair (Hoboksar); the East Route league around Kur-Kara-Usu (modern Usu); and the West Route league around Ebinur Lake. The Khoshud princes were organized into the Middle Route Batu-Sedkiltü league on the pastures around the lower Zultus River and Bosten Lake. Xinjiang's modern Mongolian population is about 50 percent Torghud, 20 percent Öölöd (Zünghars), 17 percent Chakhar, and almost 10 percent Khoshud.

UNDER THE QING AND EARLY REPUBLIC

The Mongols of Xinjiang, especially the strategically placed South Route Torghuds and the Khoshuds, formed an important reserve for the Qing Empire. In 1820 1,000 Torghud-Khoshud troops joined the Qing armies in defeating an invasion from the city of Kokand in the Ferghana valley. The great Turkestani rebellion in 1864 drove the Khoshuds into flight north of the Tianshan, with more than half the South Route Torghuds and Khoshuds being lost or scattered. In 1876 the Khoshuds joined the returning Qing armies, while the Chakhar and West Route Torghuds assisted cut-off Qing garrisons against the Russian occupation of Ili from 1871 to 1881. With the restoration of order Chakhar and Shibe bannermen were employed to open canals and begin military farms.

Culturally, the Torghud and Khoshud banners continued to use the Oirat CLEAR SCRIPT, which also became widely used by the Chakhar. The Borotala Chakhar dialect also acquired many Oirat features. Except among the Khoshuds and South Route Torghuds, the Mongols lived in close contact with the Kazakhs and developed a pidgin Mongol Kazakh developed to communicate with their neighbors. Compared to the Kazakhs, however, the Mongols practiced less extensive nomadization and had less contact with either the surrounding towns or Russian merchants.

During the Chinese Republican revolution Chakhar and Torghud troops fought for the Qing authorities in January–February 1912. The Chakhar commander Sumiya (Sumyaa, 1874–1935) defected to Mongolia with 116 households rather than join the Republicans, but more typical was the position of the Japanese-educated Torghud East Route prince Palta (1882–1920), who held the strategic Altai region first for the Qing and then for the republic. A small number of ALTAI URIYANGKHAI banner families were then caught on the Xinjiang side of the border when the Xinjiang-Mongolia border was demarcated. Until 1933 the new Chinese warlord regime made little change in Xinjiang Mongol life, although Chinese-style county administration was gradually extended. The South Route Torghuds, being the most numerous and strategic, had particularly strained relations with the Xinjiang governors.

REVOLUTION TO THE PRESENT

During the 1930s a Soviet-influenced educational movement spread through the Kazakhs and Mongols of northern Xinjiang. The lyrics to the widely sung *Altan surghuuli* (Golden school), by Torghud headmaster Tse. Ölzeibatu (1909–80) of Dörböljin (modern Emin), expressed the new schools' Mongol-nationalist, democratic, and antireactionary ideas. The Kazakh-led and Soviet-supported 1944 Three-Regions Revolution was the first Turkestani nationalist movement to gain Mongol support, establishing revolutionary regimes in every Mongol area except the Khoshud around Bosten Lake. In 1946 Ölzeibatu founded the first Xinjiang Mongolian newspaper *Aradiyin ayalgha* (People's voice) in the area controlled by the revolutionaries.

From 1949 to 1951 Chinese Communist troops occupied the various Mongol areas in Xinjiang, incorporating the Ili revolutionaries into the new regime. In 1954 the new government created two prefectural level

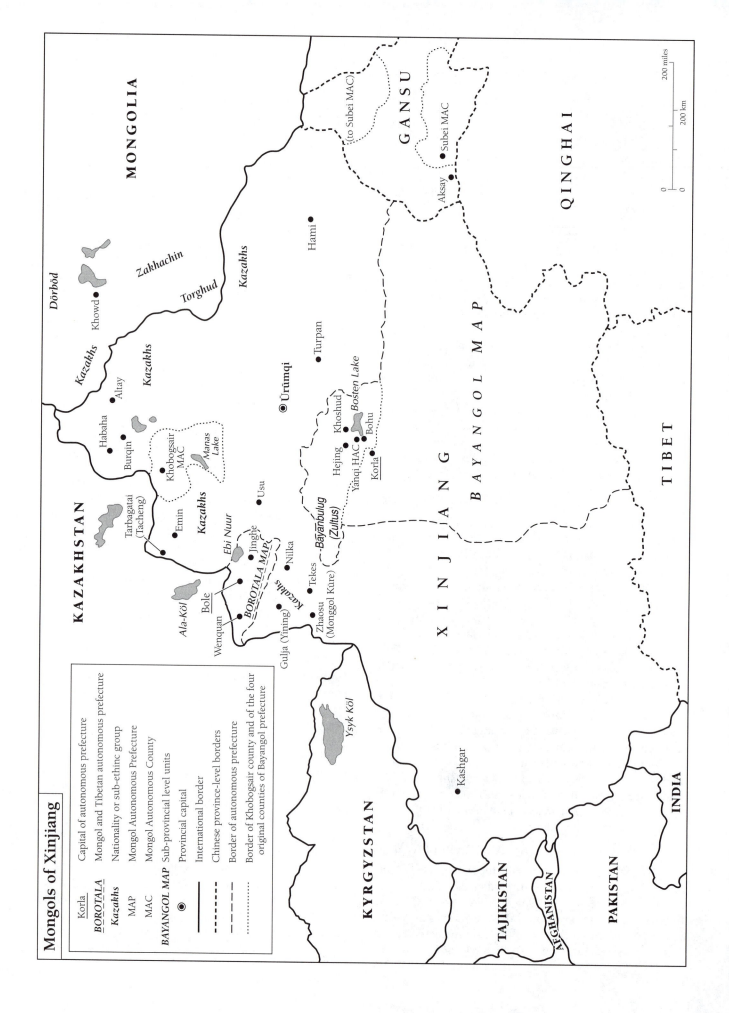

Mongols of Xinjiang

autonomous units, Bayangol (including the South Route Torghuds and the Khoshuds) and Borotala (including the Chakhar and the West Route Torghuds), and one county-level autonomous unit, Khobogsair (including the North Route Torghuds) territory.

The Mongol population of Xinjiang rapidly increased from 60,600 in 1954 to 138,000 in 1990. By 1982 the Mongols still formed the largest single nationality in Khobogsair, at 37 percent, but in Borotala and Bayangol the Mongols were only a small percentage outnumbered not only by recent Han Chinese immigrants but also by Kazakhs (Borotala), Hui, or Chinese-speaking Muslims (Bayangol), and UIGHURS (both). Virtually all Xinjiang Mongols still speak Mongolian.

See also BAYANGOL MONGOL AUTONOMOUS PREFECTURE; BOROTALA MONGOL AUTONOMOUS PREFECTURE; KALMYK-OIRAT LANGUAGE AND SCRIPT; KHOBOGSAIR MONGOL AUTONOMOUS COUNTY.

Further reading: C. R. Bawden, "A Mongol Document of 1764 concerning the Repopulation of Ili," *Zentralasiatische Studien* 5 (1971): 79–94; Baatar C. H. Hai, "The Family of Prince Palta," in *Meng-ku wen hua kuo chi hsueh shu yen tao hui lun wen chi,* ed. Chang Chün-i (Taipei: Mongolian and Tibetan Affairs Commission, 1993), 408–417; P. B. Tseren, "Traditional Pastoral Practice of the Oirat Mongols and Their Relationship with the Environment," in *Culture and Environment in Inner Asia,* vol. 2, *Society and Culture,* ed. Caroline Humphrey and David Sneath (Cambridge: White Horse Press, 1996), 147–159; Tsui Yenhu, "Development of Social Organization in the Pastoral Areas of North Xinjiang and Their Relationship with the Environment," in *Culture and Environment in Inner Asia,* vol. 2, *Society and Culture,* ed. Caroline Humphrey and David Sneath (Cambridge: White Horse Press, 1996), 205–230.

Xiongnu (Hsiung-nu, Khunnu, Huns) As the first great nomadic empire, the Xiongnu ruled Mongolia from 209 B.C.E. to 91 C.E. and established many of the classic steppe institutions. The first syllable of the Chinese transcription "Xiongnu" appears to be cognate to both "Khion" (in Central Asia and India) and "Hun" (in Europe). The second syllable means "slave." The idea of a link between the Xiongnu of Mongolia and the Huns of Europe, previously out of fashion, has now been strengthened by archaeological evidence.

ESTABLISHMENT OF THE XIONGNU EMPIRE

Xiongnu culture, as known archaeologically, is an outgrowth of that of the non-Chinese Rong in northern Hebei and the Di in western Shanxi, northern Shaanxi, and ORDOS (Inner Mongolia south of the Huang (Yellow) River) during the Spring and Autumn period (721–481 B.C.E.). The Rong and Di culture, as exemplified by the "Ordos bronzes," assimilated northern and western influences from the Scythian ANIMAL STYLE and Mongolian ELK

STONES. The Xiongnu name appears in Chinese histories in the late fourth century B.C.E. as the Chinese states began expanding north. Eventually, China's Qin dynasty (221–09) pushed the Xiongnu out of Ordos and into the Selenge-Orkhon River valley in northern Mongolia.

In 209 the Shanyu, or Xiongnu ruler, MODUN (209–174 B.C.E.) overthrew his father, unified the steppe, recovered Ordos, and conquered the farming peoples of the Tarim Basin. He forced China's new Han dynasty (206 B.C.E.–221 C.E.) to agree to a *heqin,* "peace and friendship" treaty, in which the Han gave the Shanyu tribute, an imperial princess, and recognition as an equal. In return Modun agreed to cease raids. Border markets were also opened, which allowed the ordinary Xiongnu access to Chinese goods. From 198 B.C.E to 134 C.E. the *heqin* system governed Han-Xiongnu relations, usually guaranteeing peace at the price of costly tribute and Chinese pride.

INSTITUTIONS

The position of Shanyu was basically hereditary, although minor sons could rarely enforce a claim to rule. Chinese historians do imply, however, the existence of some sort of confirmation assembly. As with the later Mongols, sons and younger brothers inherited their widowed stepmothers and sisters-in-law.

The highest posts under the Shanyu were those of Tuqi (Wise) Kings of the Left and the Right, who served as viceroys in the east and west, respectively. The Wise King of the Left was generally the heir apparent. A number of other offices existed, but their functions are not clear. The Xiongnu were the first to use the famed Inner Asian DECIMAL ORGANIZATION. Twenty-four myriarchs, each nominally ruling 10,000 households (although often as few as 4,000 in reality), appointed subordinate officers. Despite this bureaucratic-seeming structure, high offices were hereditary and filled by scions of the Huyan, the Lan, and later the Xubu clans.

The Shanyu bowed daily to the Sun in the morning and the Moon in the evening. Annual sacrifices at the assemblies of the first and fifth moon (approximately February and June) were made to the ancestors, heaven and earth, and other spirits. In 121 B.C.E. Han armies captured a "gold man which [a Xiongnu king] used in worshiping Heaven." Since Xiongnu art includes human images, this figure was most likely a native Xiongnu work. At the autumn assemblies (roughly August through October) men and animals were counted (*see* QURILTAI).

Militarily, the Xiongnu relied on mounted archery, using a compound bow lined with horn or bone and arrows with a range of tips, including "whistling arrows" used to guide volleys. Close combat was with short swords, halberds, and maces. They did not have stirrups.

LANGUAGE AND CULTURE

The only surviving materials of Xiongnu language are transcriptions in Chinese characters whose pronunciation at the time of the Xiongnu is very uncertain. (Note that the conventional transcriptions used in this article are of the Chinese characters' *modern* pronunciation and often far from the original one.) A few words are definitely Turco-Mongolian (*chengli* or *tengri*, heaven; *woluduo aotuo* or ORDO, palace-tent). Several scholars have claimed to analyze less obvious words, usually assuming an affiliation with either Oghur Turkic (related to ancient Bulghar/Bulgarian and modern Chuvash) or less probably Ket, a Siberian language isolate in the lower Yenisey valley. No attempt has yet won general credence, however.

Rich Xiongnu graves have been found in the ORDOS area and North China, the Selenge-Orkhon valley, and along the Yenisey River. The graves are characteristically single with double coffins oriented to the north, ceramic vessels near the head, extensive animal remains, especially of HORSES, and bronze cauldrons. Xiongnu bronzes and fabrics often were decorated in the ANIMAL STYLE, but other styles were also used. Goods from China and Central Asia were also welcomed. A number of Xiongnu forts and settlements have been excavated in northern Mongolia, Buriatia, and Khakassia. The architecture frequently shows Chinese features (*kangs*, or heated sleeping platforms, ceramic tiles, etc.).

WARS WITH THE HAN AND BREAKUP

The Chinese emperor Han Wudi (141–87 B.C.E.) turned against the *heqin* policy in 134 B.C.E., and from 129 to 119 massive Chinese expeditions seized Gansu and drove the Xiongnu north to their Selenge-Orkhon base. Trying to outflank the Xiongnu, the Han attempted from 108 on to control the Tarim Basin, only succeeding by 60. In 72–71 neighboring nomads attacked the weakened Xiongnu, which eventually split into five factions. Shanyu Huhanye (58–31 B.C.E.) eventually fled south to Inner Mongolia and agreed to submit personally to the Han court, receiving in return regular gifts of gold, fabrics, copper cash, and grain.

When civil war broke out in China, the Shanyu Hudu'ershi (19–46 C.E.) reunified the Xiongnu, conquered the Tarim Basin, and again demanded equal *heqin* relations with the Han. After his death, however, the southern Xiongnu elected a separate Shanyu and submitted to the Chinese court in 53 C.E., many being resettled within the Chinese frontiers, particularly in Shanxi. In 73 the Han responded to northern Xiongnu raids in Gansu by invading the Tarim Basin. After invasion by their nomadic neighbors in 85–87, the northern Xiongnu state collapsed; many fled to Inner Mongolia, and the Han armies drove the northern Shanyu's forces west to the Ili valley in 91. Again the reassertion of Chinese authority in the Tarim was lengthy and not completed until 127, when the Xiongnu in the Ili valley were definitively defeated.

By 90, with the resettlement of northern Xiongnu, the Xiongnu population in Shanxi reached 237,500 people. Although the Shanxi Xiongnu did not retain their nomadic material culture, they did retain a strong ethnic identity and repeatedly revolted against the unpopular Chinese-imposed Shanyus. In 216 the Shanyu office was abolished, but the Shanyu family, now taking the Han dynasty's imperial surname, Liu, still dominated the local administration. In 304, as the princes of the Jinn dynasty (265–420) waged civil war, Liu Yuan (d. 310), a descendant of the Shanyus, revolted in the name of the defunct Han dynasty. His son captured the western dynasty (265–316) Jinn capitals, Luoyang and Chang'an, and changed the dynasty name to Zhao. Unable to unify the north, his dynasty fell in 329. Anarchy ensued in which Xiongnu generals founded the northern Liang in Gansu (397–439) and the Xia in Shaanxi and Ordos (407–31). In 431 the XIANBI people's Wei dynasty (386–534) conquered the Xia, exterminating the Xiongnu ruling group and exiling the Xiongnu to the Inner Mongolian frontier as soldiers.

KHIONS AND HUNS IN THE WEST

By 350 the Khion people, probably a western branch of the Xiongnu, were invading Iran from Central Asia (modern Uzbekistan, Tajikistan, and Afghanistan). For the next two centuries the Khions were involved in Afghanistan-based dynasties such as the Kidarites (c. 360–400) and Heftalites (c. 460–550) and in tribal confederacies such as the "Red Khions" (Kermikhions) in Iran and the "White Huns" in India (c. 500–42). All these dynasties and confederacies were, however, more or less mixed with the native elements.

While no historical records trace their migration to Europe, characteristic Xiongnu remains can be followed from northern Mongolia, Zungharia, and the Yenisey valley through western Siberia and the upper Kama and Volga to the north Caucasus steppe, the lower Danube, and the Hungarian plain, the three known centers of Hun occupation after their invasion westward in 375. The western Huns lacked the institution of Shanyu; military needs raised charismatic chiefs such as Attila (444–53), based in Hungary. Attila's son, ruling in the lower Danube, appears on a list of the early kings of Bulgaria. The Huns of the north Caucasus remained a distinct people until at least 681, when they converted to Christianity.

See also BULGHARS; NOYON UUL; TRIBUTE SYSTEM.

Further reading: Emma Bunker, ed., *Ancient Bronzes of the Eastern Eurasian Steppe: From the Arthur W. Sackler Collections* (New York: Arthur M. Sackler Foundation, 1997); Nicola Di Cosmo, *Ancient China and Its Enemies: The Rise of Nomadic Power in East Asia History* (Cambridge: Cambridge University Press, 2002); Peter Golden, *An Introduction to the History of the Turkic Peoples: Ethno-*

genesis and State-Formation in Medieval and Early Modern Eurasia and the Middle East (Wiesbaden: Otto Harrassowitz, 1992); Adam Kessler, *Empires beyond the Great Wall: The Heritage of Genghis Khan* (Los Angeles: Natural History Museum of Los Angeles County, 1993); Sima Qian, "Account of the Xiongnu," trans. Burton Watson, in *Records of the Grand Historian: Han Dynasty II* (New York: Columbia University Press, 1993), 129–162; Ying-Shih Yü, "The Hsiung-nu," in *The Cambridge History of Early Inner Asia,* ed. Denis Sinor (Cambridge: Cambridge University Press, 1990), 118–149.

Xixia *See* XIA DYNASTY.

xöömii *See* THROAT SINGING.

Y

Yadamsüren, Ürjingiin (1905–1987) *One of the Mongolia's favored portrait artists who later helped create the neotraditional Mongol Zurag style*

Born in Erdene Zasag banner (modern Tümendelger Sum, Eastern) to an unwed mother, Yadamsüren learned wood carving from his maternal grandfather, Ürjin. In 1918 he began assisting Ürjin's monk brother, Choidashi, in block-printing scriptures. In 1930 Yadamsüren joined the MONGOLIAN REVOLUTIONARY YOUTH LEAGUE and migrated to ULAANBAATAR, where he become a typesetter. While attending Moscow's Communist University of the Toilers of the East in 1934 he began painting, and in 1939 he entered the Surikov Art Institute in Moscow. From his return to Mongolia in 1942 he became a professional painter. Until the late 1950s Yadamsüren painted revolutionary topics with oil paints in a European style. Well-known works included portraits of MARSHAL CHOIBALSANG (1941) and of GENERAL SÜKHEBAATUR (1942). He was a stage artist for the film *Tsogtu Taiji* (1945). In the 1950s Yadamsüren began collecting and drawing traditional artifacts, traveling throughout Mongolia to find good specimens. In 1958 Yadamsüren exhibited *Old Fiddler* (*Öwgön khuurch*) which became one of Mongolia's most frequently reproduced paintings. The work was a classic neotraditional work both in its then relatively new MONGOL ZURAG style and in its subject: an aged player of the traditional HORSE-HEAD FIDDLE. Yadamsüren also used the *Mongol Zurag* style for paintings on "modern" topics, such as *Friendship* (*Nökhörlöl*, 1967), showing Russian and Mongolian partisans exchanging smokes.

See also MONGOLIAN PEOPLE'S REPUBLIC; SOVIET UNION AND MONGOLIA.

Yahbh-Allaha, Mar (1245–1317) *Catholicos (patriarch) of the Assyrian Church of the East and confidante of the Mongol khans in the Middle East*

Born Marqos (Mark) in an ÖNGGÜD Christian family in North China, Yahbh-Allaha took monastic vows and set out on a pilgrimage to Jerusalem with Rabban Sawma (d. 1294). Once in the IL-KHANATE, the Assyrian catholicos (head of the Church of the East, or Nestorians), Mar Denkha (r. 1266–81), elevated Marqos in 1280 to be metropolitan of North China, but war in Turkestan prevented his return.

On Mar Denkha's death, Marqos was elected catholicos under the name Mar (Lord) Yahbh-Allaha (November 1281). Abagha's successor, Sultan Ahmad (1282–84), the first Muslim Il-Khan, briefly imprisoned Mar Yahbh-Allaha on charges of supporting his rival Arghun. After overthrowing Ahmad, Arghun Khan (1284–91) showed great favor to Mar Yahbh-Allaha and dispatched Rabban Sawma as an envoy to Europe in 1287–88.

In October 1295 GHAZAN KHAN (1295–1304) and NAWROZ (d. 1297) began a reign of terror against non-Islamic religions. Newly built churches were razed, and Mar Yahbh-Allaha was arrested and tortured until ransom was paid. From summer 1296 on Ghazan Khan moderated his policy toward non-Muslim religions and frequently visited the catholicos. Ghazan's brother Kharbanda (Sultan Öljeitü, 1304–16), despite having been baptized by the catholicos, treated him coldly, and after 1310 the catholicos retired in bitterness from the court until his death.

Further reading: E. A. Wallis Budge, *The Monks of Kublai Khan, Emperor of China* (1928; rpt., New York: AMS Press, 1973).

yaks See CATTLE.

Yalawachi See MAHMUD YALAVACH AND MAS'UD BEG.

yam See JAM.

Yan Shi (Yen Shih) (1182–1240) *North Chinese local strongman whose defection to the Mongols established Mongol power in Shandong province*
Born in a peasant household in Tai'an prefecture, Shandong, Yan Shi grew up as a gregarious and semiliterate tough, often on the wrong side of the law. In 1213, in response to the Mongol invasion, the JIN DYNASTY (1115–1234) authorities enrolled civilian volunteers, and Yan Shi became a company commander. In 1218 Yan Shi deserted to South China's SONG DYNASTY (960–1279), then active in Shandong. In 1220, as MUQALI, the supreme Mongol commander, moved south, Yan Shi deserted to him with eight prefectures and 300,000 households. In retaliation the Song generals slaughtered his clan. In 1221 Muqali and Yan Shi besieged Dongping, one of Shandong's major cities. After Muqali departed Yan Shi took the city and made it his base. In 1225 another Shandong strongman on the Song side, Peng Yibin, besieged Yan Shi in Dongping, and Yan Shi surrendered back to the Song. In July–August, however, he betrayed Peng Yibin in battle and rejoined the Mongols, decisively crushing the Song armies in North China and retaking Dongping. In 1230 he was granted an audience with ÖGEDEI KHAN and made a myriarch, or commander of 10,000. His subsequent performance in campaigns against the Jin and Song was mediocre. Despite his lack of learning, he generously patronized letters and education in Shandong. His sons served QUBILAI KHAN as military and civil officials.

Further reading: C. C. Hsiao, "Yen Shih," in *In the Service of the Khan: Eminent Personalities of the Early Mongol-Yuan Period (1200–1300)*, ed. Igor de Rachewiltz et al. (Wiesbaden: Harrassowitz, 1993), 60–74.

yarghuchi See JARGHUCHI.

yarligh See JARLIQ.

yarlyk See JARLIQ.

yasa See JASAQ.

yasaq See JASAQ.

yastuq (*ding, balish, iascot*) The MONGOL EMPIRE adopted as its money of account the *ding* silver ingot used by the Jin and Song dynasties in China for storing silver. Cast and certified by private moneychangers, ingots circulated in various weights. The *ding* contained 50 *taels* of silver (the Yuan used a large *tael* of more than 40 grams). Shaped with a narrow waist and wide end and looking like a double ax or a pillow, the ingots were called *süke*, "ax," in Mongolian and *yastuq/balish*, "pillow," in Uighur and Persian, respectively. (WILLIAM OF RUBRUCK mispronounced the Uighur name as *iascot*.) Ingots of one-tenth *yastuq*, called in Persian *sum* and by Italian traders *sommo*, also circulated and in the GOLDEN HORDE were used as the primary money of account. Balducci Pegolotti in 1340 gives the Golden Horde *sommo* as 206 grams (7.27 ounces) and .976 fine; the Yuan *sommo* was 224 grams (7.9 ounces). While the Persian historian, 'ALA'UD-DIN ATA-MALIK JUVAINI mentions both gold and silver *yastuq*s, silver was by far the predominant form. While the Mongols did not issue their own currency, local currencies were valued against the *yastuq* for official purposes. Thus, in the Middle East one *yastuq* equaled 75 gold dinars of standard purity. In the Mongol YUAN DYNASTY in China paper currency replaced silver as currency, but the unit for public accounting was still the *ding*, that is, paper bills worth one *ding* or *yastuq* of silver.

Yeh-lü Ch'u-ts'ai See YELÜ CHUCAI.

Yekhe Juu See ORDOS.

Yellow Uighurs See YOGUR LANGUAGES AND PEOPLE.

Yelü Ahai (1153–1225) **and Tuhua** (d. c. 1235) *Brothers who defected from the Jin dynasty and served as Chinggis's earliest civil administrators*
Yelü Ahai and Yelü Tuhua, members of the old Kitan imperial clan, served the JIN DYNASTY as officials in Huanzhou (near modern Zhenglan Qi, Inner Mongolia). Around 1200 Yelü Ahai went as the Jin's envoy to the KEREYID Khanate. There he met CHINGGIS KHAN, then a junior ally of the Kereyid, and offered to defect to Chinggis with his younger brother Tuhua as hostage. The brothers returned the next year, and Tuhua was enrolled in the KESHIG, or imperial guard. In 1203, when the Kereyid khan turned against Chinggis Khan, these two remained loyal and participated in the BALJUNA COVENANT. Both brothers served with JEBE in the vanguard against the Jin from 1211 to 1213. Yelü Ahai attempted, unsuccessfully, to moderate the violence of this first conquest of North China. When the Jin ruler fled south, Chinggis Khan allowed the brothers to set up a rudimentary civil administration. Ahai named himself grand preceptor (Taishi) and Tuhua grand mentor (Taifu); these were traditional Chinese titles for leading officials. After 1217 Yelü Ahai served in the Mongols'

western campaign and was great DARUGHACHI (overseer) in Samarqand, as was his son Miansige. Tuhua remained in Xuande city (modern Xuanhua) near Inner Mongolia, coordinating the Kitan and Han (ethnic Chinese) armies. Under ÖGEDEI KHAN (1229–41), YELÜ CHUCAI (no relation) reformed Mongol rule and eased Yelü Tuhua out of daily administration.

Further reading: Paul D. Buell, "Sino-Khitan Administration in Mongol Bukhara," *Journal of Asian History* 13 (1979): 121–151; ———, "Yeh-lü A-hai, Yeh-lü T'u-hua," in *In the Service of the Khan: Eminent Personalities of the Early Mongol-Yuan Period (1200–1300)*, ed. Igor de Rachewiltz et al. (Wiesbaden: Otto Harrassowitz, 1993), 112–121.

Yelü Chucai (Yeh-lü Ch'u-ts'ai, I-la Ch'u-ts'ai)

(1190–1244) *Chief minister of Ögedei Khan in North China and proponent of Confucian principles at the Mongol court*

Yelü Chucai was born in 1190 into a family of officials serving the Jurchen JIN DYNASTY (1115–1234), while deeply conscious of its past as the ruling family of the Kitan Liao dynasty (907–1123). Orphaned at age two, Yelü was raised and educated by his mother. By age 16 he had mastered the Chinese classical curriculum and entered an official career. When the Jin capital fell to the Mongols in 1215, he began to serve the conquerors as a scribe. From then on he never wavered in his conviction that for all the suffering of the conquests, CHINGGIS KHAN was the heavenly destined emperor and that he or his descendants would certainly unify "All under heaven."

Yelü Chucai from the beginning had a great interest in ASTROLOGY and calendrical sciences. His early influence on Chinggis Khan came from his skill at interpreting omens, taking auspices through SCAPULIMANCY, and predicting events as well as through his striking personal appearance. Extremely tall, his splendid whiskers made Chinggis nickname him Utu-Saqal, "Long Beard." Before 1223 he studied Dhyana (Zen or Meditation) Buddhism with the master Wansong Xingxiu (1166–1246). Yelü Chucai's mature belief, however, that CONFUCIANISM governed the state, Taoism (Daoism) cultivated one's nature, and Buddhism controlled the mind earned Wansong Xingxiu's criticism as denigrating Buddhism. Despite this ecumenism, Yelü Chucai strongly advocated state proscription of heretical subsects within these three main religions.

When Chinggis Khan died Yelü Chucai found a much greater scope for action with his son ÖGEDEI KHAN (1229–41). Ögedei appointed him governor (formally, director of the secretariat, Zhongshusheng ling) of North China. Modeling his career on those officials who slowly drew the emperors of the ancient Han dynasty (202 B.C.E.–220 C.E.) into Confucianism, Yelü Chucai patiently but tenaciously sought to reform traditional Mongol practices. His program of action included 1) reducing the power of the imperial clan; 2) separating civil and military authorities; 3) setting both tax payments and disbursements from the royal treasury according to fixed, low rates; 4) reduction and greater accuracy in the use of the death penalty; and 5) separation of mercantile and governmental activities by limiting ORTOQ partnerships. To further these plans he instructed Ögedei in the various classics of the Chinese tradition and built an observatory and a temple of Confucius in Ögedei's new capital at QARA-QORUM.

Yelü Chucai faced opposition from many other officials seeking the emperor's ear. Early on a Mongol official, Beter, proposed that the Han (ethnic Chinese) population of North China be exterminated and the land turned to pastures. Yelü Chucai used this proposal to set forth his plan for replacing unpredictable requisitions with regular tax payments. Ögedei allowed this plan on a trial basis and was astonished by the amount of goods collected. In reforming administration he had also to combat Mahmud Yalavach, governor of Turkestan, who wished to import Islamic methods of taxation into North China (see MAHMUD YALAVACH AND MAS'UD BEG). During the SIEGE OF KAIFENG he strenuously opposed SÜBE'ETEI BA'ATUR's proposal to slaughter the whole population, winning Ögedei's consent only after days of indecision. With the fall of Kaifeng Yelü Chucai protected Jin Confucian officials willing to serve the Mongols. In these debates his enemies charged Yelü Chucai with being more loyal to the fallen Jin dynasty than to the Mongol rulers, while he insisted that all his measures were for the long-term good of the dynasty.

Despite these victories, Yelü Chucai had to accept many compromises. Ögedei's assignment of new appanages to the aristocracy was not canceled, although their jurisdiction was limited. The *ortoq* partnerships were not curbed, and the continued demand for tax payments in silver, unprecedented in Chinese history, caused widespread hardship. In 1239 other officials, mostly Turkestani and Uighur, bid for the right to collect taxes in North China at levels double or more those Yelü Chucai had originally set. Hoping to continue his extravagant generosity, Ögedei consented and handed over tax policy to 'Abd-ur-Rahman, a protegé of Empress TÖREGENE. When Ögedei's drinking finally killed him in 1241, Empress Töregene tried to inveigle Yelü Chucai into supporting 'Abd-ur-Rahman's policies, but Yelü Chucai refused. He died in 1244, his life's work seemingly in ruins, yet in later decades his policies became precedents often appealed to by ministers of the Mongol YUAN DYNASTY. Yelü Chucai appears in later Mongolian legend as Chuu Mergen (Chu the Wise) of the Jurchen, one of Chinggis's "nine paladins."

See also BUDDHISM IN THE MONGOL EMPIRE; CALENDAR AND DATING SYSTEMS; CENSUS IN THE MONGOL EMPIRE;

PROVINCES IN THE MONGOL EMPIRE; RELIGIOUS POLICY IN THE MONGOL EMPIRE.

Further reading: Igor de Rachewiltz, "The *Hsi-yu Lu* by Yeh-lü Ch'u-ts'ai," *Monumenta Serica* 21 (1962): 1–128; Igor de Rachewiltz, "Yeh-lü Ch'u-ts'ai, Yeh-lü Chu, Yeh-lü Hsi-liang," in *In the Service of the Khan: Eminent Personalities of the Early Mongol-Yuan Period (1200–1300)*, ed. Igor de Rachewiltz et al. (Wiesbaden: Otto Harrassowitz, 1993), 136–175.

Yeme *See* JEBE.

Yen Shih *See* YAN SHI.

Yerbanov, Mikhey Nikolayevich *See* ERBANOV, MIKHEI NIKOLAEVICH.

Yesügei *See* YISÜGEI BA'ATUR.

Yike Zhao *See* ORDOS.

Yisügei Ba'atur (Yesügei) (d. 1171?) *Mongol chief and father of Chinggis Khan*

Yisügei Ba'atur was a member of the aristocratic BORJIGID lineage, the dominant lineage in the MONGOL TRIBE that occupied the northeast part of present-day Mongolia. (The title *ba'atur* means hero.) Yisügei was the grandson of the first Mongol chief to assume the title of KHAN, Qabul Khan, and the nephew of Qabul's second successor, Qutula Khan. Yisügei had two wives, one of obscure origin and another, Ö'ELÜN, whom he had captured from a MERKID tribesman who was leading her home after marrying her.

After Qutula Khan died in battle with the Tatar tribe, Yisügei Ba'atur became one of the main contenders for power among the Mongols. He strengthened his claim to leadership of the Mongols by becoming blood brother (ANDA) of Toghril Khan (later known as ONG KHAN), ruler of the powerful KEREYID Khanate to the west, and helping Toghril Khan secure his throne. On his way home from betrothing his nine-year-old son Temüjin (CHINGGIS KHAN's childhood name) to the daughter of a chieftain of the important QONGGIRAD clan, Yisügei stopped at a camp of the TATARS. Accepting their hospitality, he was poisoned, leaving his two wives widows and his sons orphans. The Kiyad-Borjigid clan he had built among his subjects and allies dispersed soon after his death. Chinggis Khan later said of his father that despite his battle prowess and hardiness, he ultimately failed because he did not know how to make allowance for his followers' weakness.

Yogur languages and people (Yugur, Yugu, Yellow Uighurs, Shera Yogur) The Yogurs are in part descendants of the Uighur Turks who fled south from Mongolia in the ninth century and in part descendants of Mongols settled along China's northwest frontier in the 13th and 14th centuries. Today they form a single small nationality in China's Gansu province, numbering 12,297 (1990), some speaking a Turkish language and some a Mongolic language.

ORIGINS

In 840, with the fall of the UIGHUR EMPIRE in Mongolia, a body of UIGHURS fled south to Ganzhou (modern Zhangye) in Gansu. The kingdom they established there was conquered in 1029 by the Tanguts (Mi-nyag) of the emerging XIA DYNASTY (1038–1227), although a body of "Yellow-Headed Uighurs," including members of the ruling Yaghlaqar lineage, remained in the Tsaidam area (modern Haixi). The designation "Yellow-Headed" may refer to fair-colored hair (found today in many Siberian peoples), yellow turbans, or possibly their imperial lineage. In 1226 the Mongol general SÜBE'ETEI BA'ATUR conquered these Sarigh Uighurs ("Yellow Uighurs") during his campaign against the Xia dynasty.

After 1374 the Yellow Uighurs, then nomadizing in yurts and raising CAMELS, HORSES, CATTLE, and SHEEP in the Subei-Aksay-Tsaidam areas, surrendered to the MING DYNASTY and were organized into the Anding, Aduan, Quxian, and Handong guards. The first ruler of the Yellow Uighurs in the Anding guard was a Chinggisid prince, Buyan-Temür. Meanwhile, the Chigil Mongol guard nomadized around modern Yumen. All these nomads were Buddhist, and the Chigil Mongols generously patronized Tibetan lamas (see NORTHERN YUAN DYNASTY). From 1472 to 1528 attacks from the Islamic Chinggisid state of MOGHULISTAN drove the Yellow Uighur and Chigil Mongol guards east to the mountains south of Suzhou (modern Jiuquan) and Ganzhou. From 1542 to 1596 ORDOS and TÜMED Mongols of Inner Mongolia subdued most of the Yellow Uighurs as part of their advance into Kökenuur (Qinghai; see UPPER MONGOLS).

By 1645 the remaining Yellow Uighurs had submitted as Huangfan, or "Yellow Barbarians," to the QING DYNASTY (1636–1912). Those in the west near Suzhou, who were Turkish speaking, were settled in seven OTOGS (camp-districts) totaling more than 7,000 around 1700, and those near Ganzhou, who were Mongolian speaking, were in five *otogs* totaling more than 6,000 in 1779. By this time the word *Uighur* had altered to *Yogur,* and the two groups called themselves Saregh (Turkish) or Shera (Mongolian) Yogur, both meaning "Yellow Yogur/Uighur." After a brief period subject to GALDAN BOSHOGTU KHAN (1678–97) of the ZÜNGHARS, the Yogurs returned to their obedience to the Qing in 1698. All the *otogs* had chiefs confirmed by the Qing and paid a fixed "tribute" of horses in return for "gifts" of TEA (see TRIBUTE SYSTEM). They also included a number of Heifan "Black Barbarians," or Tibetans, so-called from their black tents. By this time the Yogurs around Huangnibao were farmers.

LANGUAGES

The two languages of the Yogurs include Western Yogur, in the Turkic family, and Eastern Yogur, a language of the Mongolic family. It was estimated in the mid-1980s that about 3,000 spoke Eastern Yogur and about 4,600 spoke Western Yogur. Western Yogur is a relatively conservative Turkish language, showing many features of Old Turkish in pronunciation and the number system.

Eastern Yogur is a typical "peripheral" Mongolic language in preserving the Middle Mongolian initial h- (e.g., *heleghe*, liver, *hgu-*, to die). It also shares a number of features with the Gansu-Qinghai family of Tu, Dongxiang, and Bao'an, particularly the de-stressing of the first syllable, which leads to its frequent loss (e.g., *mudən* from Middle Mongolian *ömüdü(n)*, trousers) and the formation of consonant clusters in h- or r- (e.g., *hdoro* from Middle Mongolian *dotora*, inside, *hje-* from Middle Mongolian *hichi-*, to be ashamed, *rdə* from Middle Mongolian *urtu*). Other shared Gansu-Qinghai features include the fusion of the accusative and genitive forms, the ablative in -sa, and the terminal converb in -la (not -ra). They also share the transformation of b- to p- when followed by an aspirated stop (e.g., Middle Mongolian *bichig* becomes Eastern Yogur *puchig*). Unlike Tu, Dongxiang, and Bao'an, however, Eastern Yogur retains vowel harmony and separate front rounded vowels ö and ü, and its verbal forms and vocabulary are considerably closer to classical Mongolian. It is unclear whether Eastern Yogur thus represents a more conservative branch of the common Gansu-Qinghai subfamily or a branch that was secondarily "re-Mongolized" through contact with the Oirats, or West Mongols.

Both the Yellow Uighurs and the Mongols used the same Uighur script. As late as the early 18th century, Buddhist texts in both Uighur Turkish and in CLEAR SCRIPT Oirat Mongolian circulated among the Yogurs. By the 19th century, however, the Yogur languages were no longer written and only Chinese is now used for writing.

SOCIETY AND CONTEMPORARY SITUATION

The Hui (Chinese-speaking Muslim) rebellion of 1862–74 and Qing conscription into armies organized to suppress the rebellion caused great hardship among the Yogurs. By 1949 the Yogur population had declined to only about 3,000, who kept 43,030 sheep, 27,740 goats, 6,790 cattle (mostly yaks), and 1,740 horses. In the Kangle district, southeast of the Sunan county seat, the five Mongolian-speaking *otog*s still existed with their own chiefs. In Dahe district, northwest of the Sunan county seat, and at Huangnibao there were three Turkish-speaking *otog*s, including the Khurangat tribe and the Yaghlaqar tribe, and one Mongolian-speaking *otog*. The farming Yogurs around Huangnibao (modern Minghua district) spoke only Chinese, however. The Yogurs preserved scores of "bones," or clans, including the famous Mongol clans of Suldus, Arulad, QONGGIRAD, Tuman, and

Oirat, and the Turkish clans of Turgesh, Yaghlaqar, Kyrgyz, and Andijan, as well as many Tibetan clans. The pastoral Yogurs lived in Tibetan-style black tents. Married lamas gathered at Buddhist temples on holy days to perform services, and mostly male, but sometimes female, *yekheje* (shamans) sacrificed sheep to *Denggeri Khan*, "Khan Heaven."

In February 1954 the government of the new People's Republic of China proclaimed Sunan a Yogur Autonomous County. The county, which contains more than 75 percent of the Yogurs, consists of three discontinuous districts, two south and one (Minghua) north of the main railway. In 1982 the county's population was 33,816, of which the 8,088 Yogurs formed 23.92 percent, the Tibetans 22.03 percent, and the Han (ethnic Chinese) 50.86 percent. With illiteracy among those over six just more than 40 percent, primary school enrollment of school-age children at 40 percent and only 80 percent of the nationality employed in the herding and agriculture sector (1982 figures), the Yogur are relatively developed compared to other Gansu-Qinghai minorities.

See also ALTAIC LANGUAGE FAMILY; BAO'AN LANGUAGE AND PEOPLE; DONGXIANG LANGUAGE AND PEOPLE; MONGOLIC LANGUAGE FAMILY; TU LANGUAGE AND PEOPLE.

Further reading: Toru Saguchi, "Historical Development of the Sarïgh Uyghurs," *Memoirs of the Research Department of the Toyo Bunko* 44 (1986): 1–26; Henry Schwarz, *Minorities of Northern China: A Survey* (Bellingham: Western Washington University Press, 1984), 57–68.

yörööl** and **magtaal The *yörööl* (blessing or benediction) and *magtaal* (praise or panegyric) together form one of the major genres of Mongol folk poetry. The offering of a *yörööl* (Kalmyk-Oirat, *yörāl*, Buriat, *yerüül*) accompanies virtually all public ritual functions in traditional and in much modern Mongolian life. Occasions for a *yörööl* include dedication of newly made or acquired tools and implements (felt, YURT, saddles, rifles, etc.); the birth or acquisition of a valuable new animal; the making of a cradle for a newborn baby; the presentation of a whole sheep, liquor, or new KOUMISS; sacrifices to the household fire (see FIRE CULT), the OBOO, or war standard, aspersions (*tsatsal*) of mare's milk to heaven (see TENGGERI); and WEDDINGS. Such *yörööl*s often include descriptive *magtaal*s, which are also spoken separately for mountains and other features of the natural environment and especially during sporting events to announce the great qualities of the victorious horse and jockey, wrestler, or archer. Sometimes political addresses and wedding speeches are separated as *zorig*.

A typical *yörööl* begins with a syllable or line of invocation, such as *om sain amgalan boltugai* "Om (the sacred Tantric seed-syllable)! May there be a good peace!" or the exclamation *"Zee!"* The speaker then describes the occasion and the offerings made (where appropriate), praises the features of the object being blessed one by one, gives a predictive picture of its successful use, and concludes with the blessing proper. The poetic forms of *yörööls* and *magtaal*s are marked by groups of lines (couplets, tercets, or quatrains) alliterating on the first syllable. Parallelism between both lines and larger strophes is common, as are long cataloguelike lists. One of the most distinctive features of this genre and Mongolian ritual language generally is the combination of repeated restatement of obvious facts together with pervasive hyperbole. Thus, a YURT's latticework is jade and its door is garnet, an arrow is fledged with the "flight feathers of the King Garuda (the mythological Indian bird) who flies gracefully on high," and so on. This ritual hyperbole, found also in Mongolian EPICS, resembles a lay adaption of the language of Tantric visualizations, which re-creates this world in the form of a perfected world.

In Mongolian society men with a talent for speaking such praises and blessings, called *yöröölchi* (blessers) or *khonjin*, are widely sought for all sorts of ritual occasions. While the addresses are delivered orally and creative variations on existing patterns are valued, written exemplars have long circulated in booklets to help speakers develop their repertoire.

See also FOLK POETRY AND TALES.

Yuan dynasty (1206/1271–1368) Officially proclaimed in 1271, the Yuan dynasty represented both the continuation of the Mongol Empire and a new Mongol dynasty in China. The editors of the encyclopedic *YUAN SHI* (History of the Yuan), writing in the first years of the succeeding MING DYNASTY (1368–1644), treated the Yuan dynasty as synonymous with the MONGOL EMPIRE and naturally saw it beginning with the coronation in 1206 of CHINGGIS KHAN (Genghis) in Mongolia. Later Chinese historians, viewing the Yuan as a purely Chinese dynasty, put its beginning with the final fall of the Song in 1279. Officially, the name *Yuan* was not proclaimed until December 18, 1271, when it replaced *Great Mongol Empire* (Mongolian, Yeke Mongghol ulus; Chinese, Da Menggu guo) as the empire's formal title.

While the Mongol dynasty began in 1206, QUBILAI KHAN's (1260–94) rise created a new power center in North China that differed significantly from the earlier reigns of the Mongol khans. With Qubilai's 1260 coronation this new power center supplanted the old power center in Mongolia. In that sense the Yuan dynasty as the separate North China–based component of the divided Mongol Empire really began existence in 1260. It is in this sense that *Yuan* is used in this article.

FORMATION OF THE DYNASTY

The Yuan dynasty's origins lie in Qubilai's cultivation of a new ruling elite drawn from both the old officials of the JIN DYNASTY and the new SEMUREN (West and Central Asian) class of North China. Begun in the 1240s, Qubi-

lai's recruitment of Confucian-oriented officials created a network that would plan his coronation in 1260. As KHAN Qubilai's elder brother MÖNGKE KHAN (1251–59) appointed Qubilai supervisor of North China and Inner Mongolia, where he pursued experiments in Confucian governance and constructed a new seat at Kaiping (later SHANGDU).

Unlike earlier khans, Möngke had no powerful widow, so the empire was left without an obvious regent. Qubilai's brother ARIQ-BÖKE used his position in Mongolia proper to win the support of Möngke's old establishment and of the rulers in the GOLDEN HORDE and CHAGHATAY KHANATE. Qubilai, however, easily stripped Ariq-Böke of control in North China and, summoning a new general assembly (QURILTAI), had himself elected khan on April 15, 1260. His support came from Chinese and *semuren* Confucians and from Mongols living in or near China, descendants of the brothers of Chinggis Khan and the great noble families (JALAYIR, QONGGIRAD, Ikires, etc.) in North China and Inner Mongolia.

The succeeding conflict with Ariq-Böke largely turned on Qubilai's superior control of the civilian administration. Qubilai's new administration ordered widespread emergency mobilization of military equipment and manpower, both Mongol and Chinese, while blockading Ariq-Böke in QARA-QORUM. The resulting famine intensified when Alghu, the Chaghatayid ruler, betrayed Ariq-Böke and began supporting Qubilai. Eventually Ariq-Böke surrendered (August 21, 1264) and was pardoned.

With Ariq-Böke defeated, Berke, HÜLE'Ü, and Alghu, ruling the Golden Horde, the IL-KHANATE, and the Chaghatay Khanate, respectively, acknowledged Qubilai's victory and his precedence as ruler in the eastern homeland but declined to attend a new *quriltai*. The khanates were now all effectively separate, each choosing its own rulers with, at most, nominal recognition from the others.

GEOGRAPHY AND FOREIGN RELATIONS

Geographically, the core of the Yuan dynasty was North China, Manchuria, and its adjacent Inner Mongolian steppe. The Mongols had incorporated Inner Mongolia by 1211, while occupation of North China began in earnest in 1214. By the time of the death of Chinggis Khan in 1227, Hebei, Shanxi, Shandong, and Gansu provinces had been pacified, while Manchuria was partially settled by the Mongols. ÖGEDEI KHAN (1229–41) completed the conquest of Manchuria and of Shaanxi and Henan provinces in North China.

These provinces felt a very heavy Mongol influence. Chinese census figures indicate a catastrophic drop in North China's population during the first conquest. The Mongol rulers divided Inner Mongolia into grazing grounds for the nobility and for the allied tribes, such as the ÖNGGÜD and the Qonggirad. Manchuria was given over to the families of the descendants of Chinggis Khan's

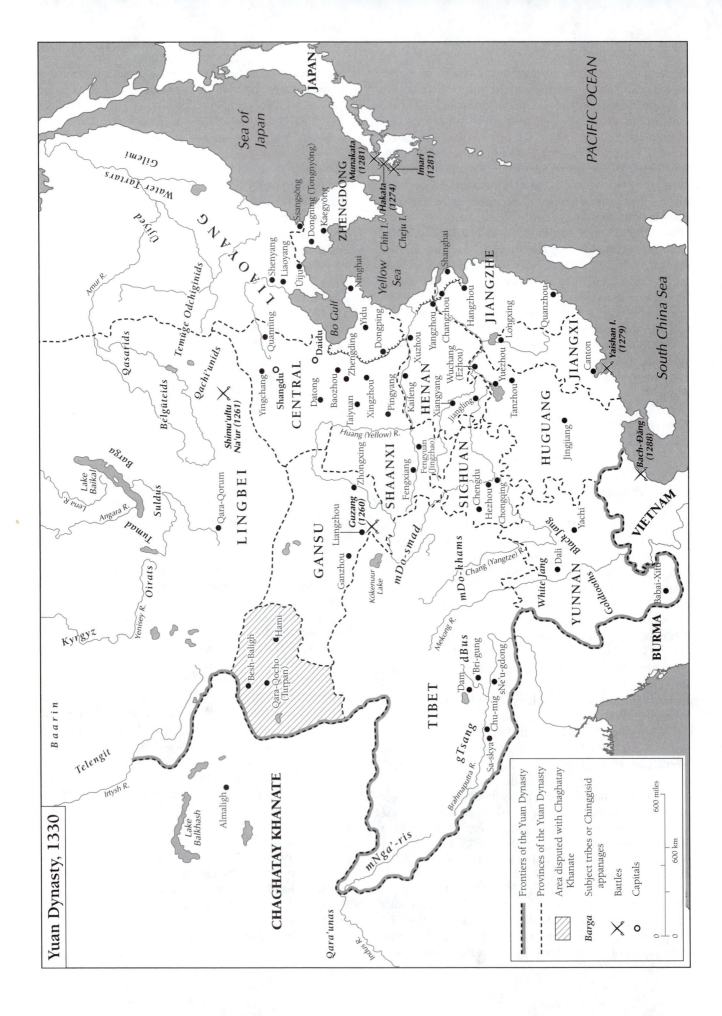

Yuan Dynasty, 1330

JAPAN

Sea of Japan

Water Tartars

Gilemi

Üjiyed

Amur R.

LIAOYANG

Ssangsŏng
Dongning (Tongnyŏng)
Kaegyŏng

Shenyang
Liaoyang
Üiju

ZHENGDONG

Munakata (1281)
Imari (1281)
Hakata (1274)
Chin I.
Cheju I.

PACIFIC OCEAN

Qasarids

Belgüteids

Temüge Odchiginids

Quanning

Bo Gulf

Ninghai
Yidu
Dongping
Zhengding

Yellow Sea

Shanghai

JIANGZHE

Hangzhou
Changzhou
Yangzhou

Longxing
Quanzhou

JIANGXI

South China Sea

Qachi'unids

○ Daidu

Shimu'ultu Na'ur (1261)

Yingchang
○ Shangdu

CENTRAL

Datong
Baozhou
Taiyuan
Xingzhou
Pingyang

HENAN

Kaifeng
Xuzhou
Wuchang (Ezhou)
Xiangyang

Lake Baikal

Barga

Lena R.

Suldus

Angara R.

Tumad

Qara-Qorum

LINGBEI

GANSU

Liangzhou
Guzang (1260)

Zhongxing

SHAANXI

Fengyuan (Jingzhao)
Fengxiang

Huang (Yellow) R.

Jiangling

SICHUAN

Chengdu
Hezhou
Chongqing

HUGUANG

Yuezhou
Tanzhou
Jingjiang

Canton
Yaishan I. (1279)

Bach-Đằng (1288)

VIETNAM

Yenisey R.
Oirats

Kyrgyz

Baarin

Almaligh

Lake Balkhash

Telengit

Irtysh R.

Qara-Qocho (Turpan)
Besh-Baligh
Hami

Ganzhou

Kökenuur Lake

mDo-smad

mDo-khams

Chang (Yangtze) R.

Mekong R.

YUNNAN

Dali
Yachi
Black Jiang
White Jiang
Golden Sands

BURMA

Babai-Xifu

CHAGHATAY KHANATE

TIBET

gTsang

Dam
dBus
Bri-gung
Chu-mig
sNe'u-gdong
Sa-skya

mNga'-ris

Brahmaputra R.

Qara'unas

Indus R.

Legend

— Frontiers of the Yuan Dynasty
‑ ‑ ‑ Provinces of the Yuan Dynasty
▨ Area disputed with Chaghatay Khanate

Barga Subject tribes or Chinggisid appanages
✕ Battles
○ Capitals

600 miles
600 km
0

brothers and the family of MUQALI of the Jalayir clan. About half of North China proper was divided into appanages granted to members of the nobility. Artisan colonies, both of conscripted Chinese and of deported Muslims from Central and West Asia, dotted the countryside. During the Mongol pacification campaigns the Mongols destroyed city walls, prohibited residence in remote mountain areas, and took over large areas as ranch lands for the herds of Mongol garrisons. Qubilai relocated his primary capital to Yanjing (modern Beijing), which was rebuilt and renamed DAIDU (Great Capital). Kaiping, now renamed Shangdu (Upper Capital), remained the summer capital.

Between Ögedei's death and Qubilai's accession, the Mongols took most of the major cities in Sichuan and Korea, raided Tibet, and subdued the Dali kingdom in modern YUNNAN. Qubilai peacefully induced Korea to submit, but only after further campaigns in 1269–73 was Korea fully integrated into the Yuan realm. The Korean kings received brides from the Mongol imperial family and served as senior grand councillors of the "Eastern Expeditionary Branch Secretariat" (Zhengdong xing zhongshu sheng), effectively a Yuan provincial administration. Yunnan was given a branch secretariat in 1273. Sichuan remained a military frontier zone until the fall of Chongqing in 1278 during the final conquest of the Song. Qubilai tried to rule central Tibet (dBus-gTsang) through the Sa-skya order, whose leader, 'PHAGS-PA LAMA, was Qubilai's private chaplain, but a rebellion in 1268 brought more direct Mongol rule through pacification commissions (xuanwei si) subject to the Commission for Buddhist and Tibetan Affairs (Xuanzhengyuan) based in Daidu.

The conquest of the SONG DYNASTY from 1274 to 1279 brought the Chang (Yangtze) valley and the South China coast under Yuan control. During the conquest Qubilai and his commander in chief, BAYAN CHINGSANG, diligently avoided the kind of massive destruction that had befallen North China. As a result, the population of South China remained much larger than that of North China—11.4 million households compared to 2.0 million households, according to the 1291 census. Grain from the Chang (Yangtze) valley breadbasket came north first through a reconstructed Grand Canal and later by sea.

Although Chinese writers hailed the unification of South and North China as one of the great achievements of the dynasty, the Mongols maintained a separation between the areas. Mongols always used two separate words (kitad and nanggiyad) to refer to South China and North China. The Mongol rulers distrusted Southern loyalties and discriminated against them in the selection of officials. When the exam system was restored in 1315, the quotas for North and South Chinese were equal despite the great difference in their populations. At the same time, the South was taxed much less heavily in pro-

portion to its wealth than was the North and the local soldiery in the south was mostly not Mongol but North Chinese and former Song soldiers.

Qubilai's conquest of the Southern Song did not end his territorial ambitions. Maritime invasions of Japan (1274 and 1280), Cham-pa (in modern central Vietnam, 1281), and Java (1292–93) all failed. More costly land invasions of BURMA (Myanmar, 1282–87) and VIETNAM (1285–88) secured only the payment of annual tribute. A final costly campaign against the Babai-Xifu of northern Thailand (1301) ended Yuan military ambitions in Southeast Asia.

With Ariq-Böke's surrender Qubilai recovered the Mongolian homeland and most of modern Xinjiang. From 1269 to 1285 the hostile Ögedeid prince QAIDU KHAN (1236–1301) raided the northwest frontier with increasing effect. A victory over the garrison in Besh-Baligh (ca. 1285) gave his coalition the entire Tarim Basin by 1288–89, and from then his raids went deep into Mongolia, even briefly occupying Qara-Qorum (1289). In 1293 the Yuan began a major counteroffensive in Mongolia, which concluded with Qaidu's death and the pacification of Mongolia as a branch secretariat in 1312. Xinjiang was not recovered, however, and a major westward expedition around 1314 had only ephemeral results. While no longer the capital, Mongolia retained its importance as a frontier post and the site of the imperial ancestors' burial grounds and palace-tents (ORDOS). Garrisoning Mongolia was a common route to power for princes until the 1329 death of Qoshila (titled Mingzong, 1328–29).

The Yuan dynasty, as the successor of the Mongol great khans, claimed authority over all the Mongol successor states. The Il-Khans in Iran, descended from Qubilai's brother Hüle'ü, and so likewise belonging to the Toluid branch of the Chinggisids, acknowledged this claim both in their coins and by accepting seals from the Yuan dynasty. After 1269 the other branches of the Chinggisid family resisted Qubilai and the Il-Khans, but in 1304 the various Mongol Khanates made peace. Yuan relations with the Il-Khans remained close until the latter's fall in 1335, while frequent diplomatic missions stimulated trade and intellectual exchange between China and Iran. The khans of the Golden Horde sent occasional embassies until at least 1341. Despite the peace of 1304, border clashes with the Changhatayids continued. The two regimes repeatedly interfered in each others' court politics, but neither ever successfully controlled the other.

ADMINISTRATION

The center of Yuan administration was, as in all Chinese dynasties, the emperor (qa'an in Mongolian, huangdi in Chinese). Unlike ethnically Chinese dynasties, however, the Mongols did not recognize primogeniture, leaving any descendant of Qubilai theoretically eligible. Up to 1311 the election quriltais (assemblies) saw genuine debate, but with the enthronement of Shidebala in 1320, they became a pure formality. For the next 20 years powerful empress-dowagers, rebellious guards units, or high officials dictated the successions.

The Yuan dynasty borrowed its formal administrative structure from that of the previous Jin dynasty in North China. The Secretariat (Zhongshusheng) served as the primary organ of civil governance. The Military Affairs Bureau (Shumiyuan, often translated Privy Council) commanded all military units in the North China–Inner Mongolia heartland except the KESHIG (imperial guard). The Censorate (Yushitai) supervised official conduct. The vast imperial household establishment, which included such Mongol institutions as the keshig (imperial guards of present and deceased emperors), the ordos (palacetents and staff of present and deceased emperors), the "houseboys" (ger-ün kö'üd), or enslaved artisans, and the ORTOQ, or government-affiliated merchants, was entirely independent of these organs, as were the large Commission for Buddhist and Tibetan Affairs and the smaller Commission for the Promotion of Religion (Chongfusi) directing Christian clergy (erke'ün). Other more traditional autonomous organizations included the various educational and literary organs, such as the Hanlin and Historiography Academy, which promoted Confucian studies and compiled historical records, the Academy of Scholarly Worthies, which supervised state schools and Taoist (Daoist) temples, and the Directorate of Astronomy (Sitianjian). Muslims dominated offices for "Turkestani" (Huihui) medicine, astronomy, and the ortoq administration.

All people in the empire were assigned to four different categories, in descending order of rank: Mongols, semuren ("various sorts," or western immigrants), the Han (North Chinese), and southerners. In local administration Qubilai decreed that the DARUGHACHIs (overseers) should be Mongol or semuren, while the administrators should be Han or Southerners. In the Central Secretariat the two grand councillors (chengxiang) after 1270 were always Mongols or semuren, while the four managers (pingzhang) who handled financial affairs included only an occasional Han and no Southerners. The privileged ortoq merchants were all semuren, while Han and Southern civilians could not bear arms.

Yuan administration was the forerunner of the modern Chinese province structure. The central Secretariat in Daidu directly administered only the dynasty's North Chinese–Inner Mongolian heartland. Elsewhere branch secretariats controlled administration. Overseers (darughachi), who by law were Mongols or semuren, served alongside all local officials. Tibet, Xinjiang, and Mongolia up to 1312 were not part of this secretariat system.

Qubilai resisted pressure to create an examination system, instead relying on recommendation and the yin privilege, by which officials could recommend a kinsman for office. Confucians despised most Yuan officials as mere

"clerks" (li), a partisan term that indicated any official without Confucian training. The Yuan also ignored the traditional Chinese law of avoidance, allowing officials to serve in their own districts. Prescribed terms of office were also widely ignored. Even so, the central government maintained its control over the provinces primarily by the selection and rotation of personnel.

FISCAL POLICY

One of Qubilai's earliest aims was to make the qubchiri, a direct silver tax, less onerous. The creation of a paper currency, which the government accepted for qubchiri payments, achieved this end. To make up lost revenue, Qubilai expanded the grain tax and enforced the tamgha, or commercial tax, on the ortoq merchants. The main source of revenue, however, was the salt monopoly, which by 1290 accounted for more than half the government's total revenue. As the court allowed the census and land registration to lapse, the role of commercial and monopoly taxes grew even more. By 1320 the salt monopoly reached 80 percent of government revenue.

The great achievement of Yuan finance was maintaining a reasonably stable paper currency for almost 100 years. Unlike the Jin dynasty, the Yuan issued paper currency only in proportion to actual silver reserves, which in turn depended on an international silver market linked to the Yuan by intercontinental trade. This policy of silver backing kept inflation more or less under control but made the Yuan vulnerable to periods of trade downturn. With the conquest of the Song, commerce on the South Sea proved another source of revenue and bullion.

Apart from the formal institutions of finance, the Chinggisid nobility, the great Mongol families, and later the Qipchaq and other imperial guards all disposed of vast private estates. Moreover, the Mongol tradition of entrusting favored persons—military commanders, messengers, ortoq merchants, court physicians, honored clerics, and so on—with PAIZA badges that allowed them to seize necessary goods was only partly curtailed. Thus, the decentralized Yuan upper class disposed of great resources, even as the formal government faced looming fiscal problems.

MILITARY POLICIES

By the time of the Yuan founding, the Mongolian military had already undergone major change. Chinggis Khan had put several tümens (10,000s) under Muqali as his TAMMACHI (permanent garrison) army. Under Ögedei Khan four Chinese generals, commanding armies personally loyal to themselves, were promoted to the rank of myriarch: YAN SHI, SHII TIANZE, ZHANG ROU, and Liu Heima. Qubilai inherited both of these armies in 1260 in addition to the Mongol armies subject to his princely supporters. In the early years of his reign, relentless conscription of Mongols and Chinese resident in North China and Inner Mongolia built a strong field army.

Qubilai also radically changed the guard's structure. Not until 1263 did he recruit the traditional *keshig*-type guard, which in any case during the Yuan was more political than military in function. Immediately upon his election as khan, he drafted a new guard army of Han Chinese, which by 1279 totaled 50,000. The conquest of the Song from 1274 to 1276 demonstrated the effectiveness of the new Mongol-Chinese army, as the Mongol aristocrats Bayan *Chingsang* and AJU, the low-born Uighur Ariq-Qaya, and Qubilai's Chinese guards commander, Dong Wenbing (1218–78), all worked together in a combined land-marine assault down the Han and Chang (Yangtze) Rivers. Much of the defeated Song army was then recruited into the Yuan military as "Newly Adhered Troops" (Xinfu Jun). The suppression of NAYAN'S REBELLION in 1287 also relied heavily on Chinese and Korean units.

The war against Qaidu and his partisans in Mongolia eventually brought new units to the fore. In 1278, gratified by the performance of a Qipchaq 1,000 under TUTUGH, Qubilai ordered that all Qipchaq Turks in his realm be mobilized under Tutugh. Similar guards were formed of displaced OSSETES (Alan or Asud), QARLUQS, Qangli, and Russians. These guards, composed of salaried professional fighters drawn from ethnic reserves, eventually became the dynasty's main fighting forces.

From the 1240s Chinese generals in Mongol service had been dealing with river-borne attacks from the Song dynasty. Mongol commanders such as Aju had begun experimenting with river warfare during campaigns against Dali and Vietnam in the 1250s. The defection of the Song general Liu Zheng (Liu Cheng, 1213–75) and the capture of 146 ships in Sichuan in 1265 stimulated the creation of an inland navy that eventually was organized in four wings. The conquest of Korea gave the Yuan dynasty its first ocean naval force, and the first invasion of Japan in 1274 involved 300 large ships. The conquest of the Song added tremendously to Yuan shipbuilding resources, and the second invasion in 1280 involved 900 vessels. The navy never became an independent branch of service, however, and was always deployed under the command of generals with primary experience in land fighting.

All military forces stationed in the area under the central Secretariat (North China and Inner Mongolia) came under the command of the Bureau of Military Affairs. These were primarily Mongol, *tammachi*, Han, and ethnic guards units. Areas of active military operations received Branch Bureaus of Military Affairs, but provincial garrisons were put under the Branch Secretariats in peacetime. Garrisons in South China were primarily Han and Newly-Adhered Troops, with only a scattering of Mongol units.

Both Mongol and Chinese units were organized according to the same DECIMAL ORGANIZATION, and both were expected to be self-supporting. Commanders of the decimal units served as civil administrators for the soldiers' home camps (*a'uruq*) in time of peace. Ordinary soldiers served tours of duty ranging from one to six years. Many Mongol soldiers benefited from the possession of slaves originally taken as prisoners of war—in Zhenjiang figures show the average Mongol held 15 slaves, while the Chinese rarely held any. Each regular Chinese military household supplying a soldier received financial assistance from one or two auxiliary military households. Soldiers were exempt from *qubchiri* taxes and partially exempt from the grain tax. Despite these benefits, shortages of male labor frequently drove soldier households into poverty. With the conclusion of the great campaigns against the Song, the effectiveness of the garrison armies, both Mongol and Chinese, began to decline. Only frequent reregistration to equalize burdens could prevent the paper strength from diverging from the real strength. After 1290 this reregistration lapsed, and the garrison forces gradually became ineffective.

POLITICAL HISTORY

After the defeat of Ariq-Böke in 1264, Qubilai's advisers began a period of institution building, proclaiming a dynastic title, a censorate, a regular civilian administration, and other classic institutions of Chinese rule. At the same time, 'Phags-pa Lama made Tibetan Buddhism the court religion. Qubilai eventually tired of what he saw as the doctrinaire attitude of the Confucian officials, dismissing the leading Confucians LIAN XIXIAN and Yelü Zhu from office in 1270 and elevating the Central Asian financier AHMAD FANAKATI. The fall of the great Song fortress Xiangyang in 1273 opened the possibility of the destruction of the Song. In 1274 Qubilai levied a force of 100,000 men to conquer the Song, whose capital fell in 1276. Military adventures in Japan and Southeast Asia occupied Qubilai until the end of his reign. Throughout Ahmad's dominance Qubilai's heir apparent, JINGIM (1243–85) and the *chingsangs* (grand councillors) Bayan and Hantum, both Mongols of distinguished families, covertly patronized Confucian officials. An abortive insurrection that killed Ahmad in 1282 strengthened the hands of the Confucians and their aristocratic Mongol supporters. SANGHA, a Tibetan financier, rose to high position by successfully addressing a revenue crisis. His fall in 1291 left the Mongol Confucian aristocrats in almost complete control of the government, although Sangha's policies were continued.

Jingim died in 1285, but the coronation of his youngest son, Temür (titled Chengzong, 1294–1307), after Qubilai's death in 1294 established the patterns of power for the next few decades. Temür's administration liquidated the adventure in Vietnam and, apart from the Pyrrhic victory against Babai-Xifu in northern Thailand, accepted the status quo on the frontiers. Mongols of aristocratic families dominated the higher levels of Temür's administration, which domestically abandoned Qubilai's activist remolding of society and adopted a nonconfrontational approach to social interests. Temür and his successors repudiated the anti-Taoist persecutions of Qubilai's late years and his hostility to Muslims and *ortoq* merchants.

From Qubilai's time the princes of the imperial family had married women of the Qonggirad clan. In 1284 Jingim's *ordo* (palace-tent) had received control of the *tammachi*, or garrison armies, in North China and Inner Mongolia, a position inherited by Jingim's Qonggirad widow, Bairam Egechi (Kökejin). Bairam Egechi played a key role in Temür's succession, but after his death without an heir, a rival QUDA (in-law) lineage tried to break Qonggirad influence. Empress Bulughan of the Baya'ud clan tried to secure the throne for Ananda, a son of Jingim's brother Manggala and a Muslim, but the Mongol Confucian HARGHASUN DARQAN of the Oronar clan, the senior grand councillor, arranged for the sons of Temür's brother Dharmabala and Dharmabala's Qonggirad widow Targi to converge on Daidu and kill Ananda. This action protected the throne for Jingim's descendants and the Qonggirad. After negotiations Targi's eldest son, Haishan (titled Wuzong, 1307–11), who had been garrisoning Mongolia, received the throne, with her younger son Ayurbarwada (titled Renzong, 1311–20) as heir apparent.

During the reigns of Haishan and Ayurbarwada the financial cost of the court's unwillingness to antagonize major interest groups became evident. By Mongol custom

Temür Öljeitü Khan, an emperor (1294–1307) of the Yuan dynasty. Anonymous court portrait (*Courtesy National Palace Museum, Taipei*)

every accession was followed by massive donatives to the aristocracy and the recruitment of a new *keshig*, so the repeated short reigns exacerbated the budget crisis. From 1309 to 1311 Haishan's administration attempted to push through a new nonconvertible silver currency but was defeated by public resistance. Ayurbarwada's administration, led by TEMÜDER, unsuccessfully attempted a new cadastral survey in 1314. Temüder also chipped away at the autonomy of the princely appanages. Opponents of fiscal centralization charged Temüder with corruption, and his execution of Confucian opponents stimulated such broad opposition that Ayurbarwada dismissed him in 1318. Despite these nagging problems, growth continued. By 1330 the Yuan's directly administered population had risen to 13.4 million households from 11.84 million in 1290.

Ayurbarwada also returned to Qubilai's early encouragement of CONFUCIANISM. In 1315 he restored the Confucian examination system for choosing officials, although with a quota system of 25 percent for each of the empire's four ethnolegal classes. From this time on lowborn Mongol and *semuren* Confucians used the exams for upward mobility.

When Ayurbarwada died in 1320 the fiscal, power-political, and ideological issues combined to create two decades of political turmoil. Temüder joined the Qonggirad empress Targi to put Ayurbarwada's son Shidebala (titled Yingzong, 1320–23) on the throne. When Targi and Temüder died in 1322, their opponents seemed to have triumphed, but in 1323 Temüder's faction linked up with the Ossetian (Alan) guard and assassinated both the emperor and his Mongol Confucian grand councillor, Baiju of the Jalayir. The conspirators invited Yisün-Temür (titled Taidingdi, 1323–28), the eldest son of Gammala, Jingim's eldest son, then stationed in Mongolia, to take the throne. Yisün-Temür's legitimacy was always in doubt, and his Muslim advisers Dawla-Shah and 'Ubaidullah increased opposition by their favoritism toward Muslims and Christians and lavish payments to *ortoq* merchants.

When Yisün-Temür died at Shangdu, the Qipchaq EL-TEMÜR and the Merkid BAYAN (1281?–1340) activated a conspiracy in Daidu to restore Haishan's exiled sons to the throne. The resulting two-month civil war split the ethnic guards' regiments, the great non-Chinggisid families, and the imperial family down the middle. The Confucian officials in the capital and the major provinces, however, strongly supported the conspirators. Victorious, El-Temür and Bayan executed Dawla-Shah and 'Ubaidullah, purged Temüder's old clique, curtailed Muslim privileges, and strengthened Confucian influence. At first, the military strength of Haishan's elder son, Qoshila (titled Mingzong, 1328–29), who had the support of the Chaghatayid Khanate, intimidated his brother Tuq-Temür (titled Wenzong, 1329–32), who had been exiled in South China. Tuq-Temür's entourage assassinated Qoshila in 1329.

When Tuq-Temür died of disease three years later, however, his Qonggirad empress Budashiri leagued with Bayan to put Qoshila's sons on the throne and to dominate the administration. Bayan, a lowborn loner in Yuan politics, canceled the exam system and tried to reverse the Confucianization of the Yuan administration. Executions and disappearances of prominent Mongol and *semuren* opponents increased opposition. Eventually the power of the Confucian officials became clear when Bayan's own nephew TOQTO'A (1314–55) secured an edict of dismissal from the emperor Toghan-Temür (title Shundi, 1333–70) in 1340.

COURT CULTURE AND MONGOL LIFE UNDER THE YUAN

The Yuan imperial court preserved its Mongol character until the end of the dynasty. The Mongol practice of long-standing *quda* (in-law) alliance with Mongol clans, particularly the Qonggirad and the Ikires, kept the imperial blood purely Mongol until Haishan's son Tuq-Temür, whose mother was a Tangut concubine. After 1340 Qonggirad influence declined. None of the emperors mastered written Chinese, although they could generally converse well in the language.

Perhaps Qubilai's most lasting legacy to Mongolian culture was his promotion of Tibetan Buddhism. From 1260, when 'Phags-pa Lama was made state preceptor (*guoshi*), all the Yuan emperors kept a Tibetan lama of the Sa-skya order at court to perform Tantric empowerments for the emperor and the numerous branches of the imperial family. Judging from personal names, the Qonggirad clan was perhaps even more actively involved in Buddhism than was the imperial family. Few members of the great *keshig* and DARQAN clans, such as the Jalayir, the Arulad, the Üüshin, and the Oronar, however, show Buddhist names, even in the 14th century.

Mongol patronage of Buddhism resulted in a number of monuments of Buddhist art. 'Phags-pa Lama invited Nepalese artists, including the famous ANIGA, although few of his Buddhist artworks survive. Monuments of a Sino-Tibetan style include the Tantric statues at Feilaifeng built under the direction of the Tibetan monk in Mongol service Yang Rin-chen-skyabs (fl. 1277–88), and the reliefs at the great gate of Juyongguan of 1345. Mongolian Buddhist translations, almost all from Tibetan originals, began on a large scale after 1300.

The other powerful influence on Mongol upper-class culture was Chinese, particularly Confucianism. Many members of Mongol aristocratic lineages, particularly the Jalayir and the Oronar, delighted in patronizing Confucian scholars and institutions, although their personal level of familiarity with Confucian texts in the original was rather slight. A considerable number of Confucian and Chinese historical works were translated into Mongolian. By the mid-14th century a significant number of Mongols were composing examination essays in classical

Mongol literati in the Yuan dynasty *(From the Yuan-era [i.e., 14th-century] printing of the* Shilin guangji)

Chinese and participating in the exchange of poetry with Chinese friends and colleagues. *Semuren* officials, particularly UIGHURS, Tanguts, and Önggüd, also joined in this appreciation of Chinese cultural traditions. At the same time, as late as 1345 Aruqtu of the Arulad clan had to admit to the emperor that he could not read the newly edited Chinese dynastic histories he was presenting to the throne.

The average Mongol garrison family seems to have lived a life of decaying rural leisure, with income from the harvests of their Chinese tenants eaten up by costs of equipping and dispatching men for their tours of duty. Social interaction with local Chinese was routine, and intermarriage was common. Membership in the *keshig*, open to handsome, able-bodied Mongols, offered one avenue of promotion for such Mongols, and after 1315 the exams offered another. The life of a late Yuan Mongol commander, Chagha'an-Temür, illustrates this milieu. His great-grandfather Kökedei, a NAIMAN from Uighuristan, had settled in Henan as a *tammachi* soldier in Ögedei's time. Chagha'an-Temür passed the local examinations, but his friends included Kuankuan, a non-Chinese village tough fond of hunting and horse riding, and Li Siqi, a Chinese police chief and tax clerk. Chagha'an-Temür's sister married another Chinese buddy, Wang Baobao, and when Chagha'an-Temür rose to fame he adopted their son, named Köke-Temür, as his own. When rebels began attacking officials and plundering landholding families in 1352, Chagha'an-Temür and his friends raised a multiethnic volunteer corps to defend their district.

FALL OF THE DYNASTY

Toqto'a's exile of Bayan and Empress Budashiri in 1340 ended the 20-year conflict over administration with victory for policy-oriented Confucians. El-Temür had sponsored the compilation of a Chinese-language administrative compendium, the *Jingshi dadian* (1330), and now Toqto'a restored the examinations, revived seminars in the classics for the young emperor, and promoted frustrated South Chinese scholars. Toqto'a also completed the long-delayed compilation of the dynastic histories of the Yuan's predecessors in 1344–45.

Unfortunately, the restoration of stable government coincided with a gathering socioeconomic crisis. In 1331 an epidemic in Henan had reportedly killed nine-tenths of the population, an outbreak that seems to mark the beginning of the medieval BLACK DEATH. In 1337–38 scattered uprisings broke out in South China, which Toqto'a blamed on the oppressive grand councillor Bayan. His own term in office saw turmoil among the tribal border populations and banditry in North China in 1341–43. In 1344 massive flooding foretold a change in the Huang (Yellow) River's course, while growing piracy menaced the seaborne transportation of southern grain north to Daidu. Meanwhile, plague, famine, and droughts struck Henan; plague ominously spread to the coastal provinces. Toqto'a proposed a program of restoring the Huang (Yellow) River to its old channel and rebuilding the Grand Canal, thus avoiding seaborne piracy. Given the chronic deficit, Toqto'a advocated paying for the massive works projects by issuing unbacked paper money.

Within a few weeks of the inauguration of Toqto'a's great project in May 1351, Buddhist millenarian sectarians among the canal workers revolted. These "Red Turbans" seized control of virtually the whole Huai River area. The garrisons proved useless, and several widely publicized defeats of poorly lead, disease-ridden imperial guards bolstered Red Turban morale and sparked more uprisings throughout the south. By 1354, however, Toqto'a and the Yuan establishment had broken the back of the uprising. Major victories showed the Ossetian and Qipchaq imperial guards units still had plenty of fight in them, but the bulk of the loyalist armies were volunteer forces, raised among Chinese officials and salt workers, Mongol *tammachi* households (such as that of Chagha'an-Temür), and Miao tribesmen. Toqto'a's dismissal in 1354, however, shattered the Yuan's military unity. Rebel leaders used the reprieve to retake the Chang (Yangtze) valley as pirates seized the coastline and remnants of the Red Turbans reoccupied Henan from 1355 to 1360, setting up a revived "Song dynasty."

In central Tibet Byang-chub rGyal-mtshan (1302–64), a cleric of the Phag-mo-gru-pa order and myriarch of sNe'u-gdong (modern Nêdong), gradually overthrew the Sa-skya order from 1351 to 1358. The Yuan court had no alternative but to recognize Byang-chub rGyal-mtshan as ruler of Tibet. Meanwhile, the Korean king Kongmin (1351–74) abolished the Branch Secretariat and exterminated the family of Toghan-Temür's wife, Empress Ki.

By 1355 virtually every aspect of the Yuan order was in shambles. Toqto'a's unbacked currency had entered a hyperinflationary spiral, forcing a return to silver ingots and copper cash as the main currency. By 1360 the value of silver in gold, stable from 1285 to 1350 at 1 to 10, had suddenly doubled to 1 to 5. Constant military operations and repeated outbreaks of plague from 1353 to 1362 in virtually every province led the population, which had been stable or increasing up to 1330, into another sharp decline. After 1351 the prohibition on weapons ownership by Chinese civilians became a dead letter, as rebels and loyalists alike armed volunteers.

After Toqto'a's fall the court lost control of the remaining loyalist armies, and most taxes were spent locally on warlord forces. Under Chagha'an-Temür and other volunteer commanders, nominally loyal Yuan armies defeated the Song regime, while along the Chang (Yangtze) the former monk Zhu Yuanzhang defeated his rivals and unified the south. The court managed to survive among the North Chinese warlords until Zhu Yuanzhang's great commander Xu Da drove north to Daidu, forcing the Mongolian court to flee to Inner Mongolia. Toghan-Temür died in 1370 in Yingchang, and his son Ayushiridara ascended the throne in the old Mongolian capital of Qara-Qorum. Zhu Yuanzhang declared the new Ming dynasty (1368–1644), but Ayushiridara and his descendants continued to claim the Yuan title in Mongolia until 1634. Within China hundreds of thousands of Mongol households joined the new dynasty as military households.

Why did the Yuan dynasty fall? Charges from the *Yuan shi* and Quan Heng's *Geng/shen waishi* (The unofficial history of 1380) of Toghan-Temür's outrageous immorality rely on selective use of the evidence. Modern historians often see the fall of the Yuan as a judgment on the decline of the Mongols, who became soft and lazy. Certainly, the Mongol military had radically changed, not so much in its fighting spirit or courage but its relation to the surrounding society. From the end of Qubilai's reign on the dynasty had renounced the systematic mobilization of men and materiel that marked the Mongol conquest. After several generations of living with the Chinese, it was simply impossible for the Mongol troops to fight them as alien conquerors. Nevertheless, men like Chagha'an-Temür proved successful enough fighting as defenders of the hierarchical, multiethnic Chinese rural society against sectarian religious violence.

The fall of the Yuan cannot be divorced from the pan-Eurasian crisis of the 14th century. The plagues, famine, hyperinflation, depopulation, and misery of China in the 1340s and 1350s resemble the contemporary situation in Europe and stand in sharp contrast to the increasing population, stable currency, and general prosperity evident in China up to 1330. The ultimate explanation of the socioeconomic crisis of the 1340s is thus best sought not in faults of Mongol administration but rather in the Black Death. Yet the chronic deficits of the Yuan government, which left the Yuan few options in dealing with the

Huang (Yellow) River flooding, and the political conflicts that diverted attention undoubtedly compounded the crisis. Even so, until the fall of Toqto'a, the Yuan administration showed remarkable resilience in dealing with the rebellions. Had the counterattack succeeded as it almost did until Toqto'a's dismissal in 1354, the Yuan might have ruled China, albeit in a less traditionally Mongol form, for many decades more.

THE IMPACT OF THE MONGOLS ON EAST ASIA

The influence of the Mongols on subsequent East Asian history was tremendous. Ironically, the Mongol military conquests were largely responsible for re-creating a unified, militarily powerful China. Since the decline of the Tang, independent, ethnically based Confucian regimes—Korea, Dali (Yunnan), Vietnam, the Kitan Liao, the Tangut XIA DYNASTY, and the Jurchen Jin—had boxed in the ethnic Chinese Song state. Outside traders began to treat North and South China as two separate countries. The Mongol conquest prevented a permanent division of North and South China and blocked the emergence of a permanent constellation of Confucian states, except for Vietnam and Korea. The Mongol rule of Tibet, Xinjiang, and Mongolia proper from a capital at modern Beijing also supplied the precedent for the QING DYNASTY's (1636–1912) Inner Asian empire, as well as that of the People's Republic today.

Culturally, the reunification of China had important consequences. From the Jurchen conquest of North China in 1127, innovative South Chinese cultural trends had diverged from the more conservative north. Confucianism, Buddhism, and Taoism all developed differing schools—the more literary Dongping Confucian school, the scholastic Caodong Dhyana (Sôtô Zen) school, and the ascetic Complete Realization (Quanzhen) Taoism in the north compared to the more philosophical Zhu Xi Confucianism, the more anti-intellectual Linji Dhyana (Rinzai Zen) school, and the less sectarian Celestial Master (Tianshi) Taoism in the south. By reunifying China the Mongols broke down sectarian boundaries both within and between the "Three Religions." At the same time, the choice of Zhu Xi Confucianism as the standard for the examinations marked its first adoption as the official state doctrine of late imperial China. The colloquial Chinese culture, encouraged by the Mongols' employment of non-Confucian clerks, also stimulated the further development of Chinese drama.

The other cultures and peoples in the Mongols' world empire permanently influenced China. The most obvious influence was the large Hui, or Chinese-speaking Muslim, community in North China, today numbering almost 9 million and stemming from the Muslim elements of the *semuren* community of the Yuan. Tibetan-rite Tantric Buddhism also took permanent root in Chinese Buddhism. The *semuren*, with the active sponsorship of the Yuan government, also introduced Middle Eastern cartography, astronomy, medicine, clothing, and foodways into China. Middle Eastern crops such as carrots, turnips, new varieties of lemons, eggplants, and melons, high-quality granulated sugar, and, most important, cotton were all either introduced or successfully popularized by the Yuan court.

Finally, the Yuan exercised a profound influence on the succeeding Ming dynasty. While its founder, Zhu Yuanzhang (titled Ming Taizu, 1368–97) admired the Yuan's unification of China and adopted its garrison system, he was disgusted by the broad role accorded the imperial family and the in-law families, the crude language and ideological laxity of the clerks, the predominant influence of military men, the monetized economy, the official patronage of *ortoq* merchants, and the persistent tradition of ad hoc requisitions by *paiza* holders. In organizing his new dynasty he sought to restrict policy making to the emperor and his classically trained Confucian civil officials alone. The ironic result was the rise of eunuchs as the emperor's only way around the Confucian elite. The strict enforcement of orthodox culture under Zhu himself led to massive purges and in the long run to widespread cynicism toward a regime of stifling hypocrisy. Creating an administration that tried as much as possible to dispense as far as possible with mercantile activity, large estates, and even the use of money, the Ming emperors proved incapable of emulating the Mongols' success in managing paper money, inadvertently returning China to a silver bullion currency. Zhu Yuanzhang's preferred policy of direct taxes, collected as much as possible in kind according to fixed schedules, limited the arbitrary requisitions of the autonomous Yuan upper class but eventually resulted in an almost complete budgetary paralysis that stymied any attempt to resolve pressing problems. Thus, much of China's subsequent imperial history can be understood as a reaction against the distinctive Mongolian administrative style.

See also APPANAGE SYSTEM; BUDDHISM IN THE MONGOL EMPIRE; CENSUS IN THE MONGOL EMPIRE; CHRISTIANITY IN THE MONGOL EMPIRE; EAST ASIAN SOURCES ON THE MONGOL EMPIRE; EIGHT WHITE YURTS; ISLAM IN THE MONGOL EMPIRE; JAPAN AND THE MONGOL EMPIRE; KOREA AND THE MONGOL EMPIRE; MANCHURIA AND THE MONGOL EMPIRE; MONGOLIAN SOURCES ON THE MONGOL EMPIRE; PAPER CURRENCY IN THE MONGOL EMPIRE; PROVINCES IN THE MONGOL EMPIRE; SIBERIA AND THE MONGOL EMPIRE; SOCIAL CLASSES IN THE MONGOL EMPIRE; SOUTH SEAS; RELIGIOUS POLICY IN THE MONGOL EMPIRE; TAOISM IN THE MONGOL EMPIRE; TIBET AND THE MONGOL EMPIRE.

Further reading: Thomas T. Allsen, *Culture and Conquest in Mongol Eurasia* (Cambridge: Cambridge University Press, 2001); Paul Heng-chao Ch'en, *Chinese Legal Tradition under the Mongols: The Code of 1291 as Reconstructed* (Princeton, N.J.: Princeton University Press, 1979). John W. Dardess, *Confucians and Conquerors: Aspects of Political*

Changes in Late Yüan China (New York: Columbia University Press, 1973); Elizabeth Endicott-West, *Mongolian Rule in China: Local Administration in the Yuan Dynasty* (Cambridge, Mass.: Harvard University Press, 1989); Herbert Franke and Denis Twitchett, eds., *Cambridge History of China*, vol. 6, *Alien Regimes and Border States, 907–1368* (Cambridge: Cambridge University Press, 1994); Ch'ich'ing Hsiao, *Military Establishment of the Yüan Dynasty* (Cambridge, Mass.: Harvard University Press, 1978); John D. Langlois, ed., *China under Mongol Rule* (Princeton, N.J.: Princeton University Press, 1981); Igor de Rachewiltz et al., eds., *In the Service of the Khan: Eminent Personalities of the Early Mongol-Yuan Period (1200–1300)* (Wiesbaden: Otto Harrassowitz 1993); Herbert Franz Schurmann, *Economic Structure of the Yüan Dynasty: Translation of Chapters 93 and 94 of the* Yüan Shih (Cambridge, Mass.: Harvard University Press, 1967).

Yuan shi (History of the Yuan)   The *Yuan shi* was a massive encyclopedia of the Mongol YUAN DYNASTY (1206/71–1368) compiled by the succeeding MING DYNASTY according to the standard format of Chinese dynastic histories. In January 1369, less than five months after the fall of the Yuan, the first emperor of the new Ming dynasty, Zhu Yuanzhang (titled Ming Taizu, 1368–98), assigned the task of compiling a history of the defunct dynasty to the Hanlin academician Song Lian (1310–81), seconded by edict attendant Wang Yi (1323–74). Song and Wang and their staff finished their first draft on September 12 the same year. The draft, however, lacked material on the long reign of the last Yuan emperor, Toghan-Temür (titled Shundi, 1333–70), and the emperor rejected the text. After a call for the officials of the empire to forward documentary material on the last reign, Song Lian, again assisted by Wang Yi, completed a version acceptable to the emperor on July 23, 1370.

The *Yuan shi* followed a format pioneered by Sima Qian's *Shi ji* (Historical records), which facilitated reference in the absence of an index. The standard format involved four sections: 1) strictly chronological annals of each emperor; 2) topical treatises on calendars, geography, rituals, personnel, finance, military, criminal punishments, and so on; 3) tables of the imperial family and high officials; and 4) biographies (including "biographies" of foreign countries). The editors dispensed with the usual assessment that often followed chapters in earlier histories, probably due to lack of time.

The compilation of a work of more than 4,000 pages in less than two years was possible only by wholesale borrowing from existing sources, and each of the three main sections—basic annals, treatises, and biographies—drew heavily on sources already compiled under the Yuan. The basic annals were based on the translated Veritable Records (*shilu*), which QUBILAI KHAN and his successors compiled about their predecessors in Mongolian.

Comparison of the *Yuan shi*'s relatively sparse annals of the early reigns with the extant veritable records of CHINGGIS KHAN and ÖGEDEI KHAN (known as the SHENGWU QINZHENG LU, or Record of the campaigns led by the lawgiving warrior) shows that the editors added many entries from other sources. The mode of compilation for the much denser annals of Qubilai and his successors, which contain hundreds of entries per year, is, however, not documented. Most of the treatises were compressed summaries of the corresponding chapters in the now mostly lost administrative encyclopedia *Jingshi dadian* (Compendium on administration of the world, 1330), compiled by the ÖNGGÜD high official Zhao Shiyan (1260–1336) and the South Chinese scholar Yu Ji (1272–1348). As a result, the treatises contain virtually no information on changes after 1330. Many of the biographies were copied almost verbatim from the extant *Guochao mingchen shilue* (Sketches of eminent ministers of the dynasty, 1328) and *Guochao wenlei* (Anthology of the dynasty) by Su Tianjue (1292–1354). Although these collections focused on Confucians, whether Mongol, SEMUREN, or Chinese, the *Yuan shi* biographies also incorporated biographical data from many now lost sources, Mongolian and Chinese, thus achieving an admirable ethnic and ideological catholicity.

Despite being a "standard history," the *Yuan shi* drew criticism from the start. Inconsistencies of fact appear repeatedly between the biographies and the annals. Characters for writing non-Chinese names were not standardized, which resulted in one father-son pair accidentally receiving two separate biographies each! Studies of these problems include the *Yuan shi ben zheng* (Textual corrections to the *History of the Yuan,* 1802) by Wang Huizu (1731–1807), while attempts to reorganize part or all of the *Yuan shi* materials include the *Yuan shi jishi benmo* (Topical Yuan history, 1616) by Chen Bangzhan (d. 1623), *Mengwu'r shiji* (Historical records of the Mongols) by Tu Ji (1856–1921), and Ke Shaomin's *Xin Yuan shi* (New history of the Yuan, 1919). Even so, the *Yuan shi*'s almost verbatim reproduction of numerous sources increases its value for the serious historian, making it an absolutely indispensable resource on all aspects of the MONGOL EMPIRE.

See also EAST ASIAN SOURCES ON THE MONGOL EMPIRE.

Further reading: Ch'i-ch'ing Hsiao, *Military Establishment of the Yüan Dynasty* (Cambridge, Mass.: Harvard University Press, 1978); Herbert Franz Schurmann, *Economic Structure of the Yüan Dynasty: Translation of Chapters 93 and 94 of the* Yüan Shih (Cambridge, Mass.: Harvard University Press, 1967).

Yugu   *See* YOGUR LANGUAGES AND PEOPLE.

Yugur   *See* YOGUR LANGUAGES AND PEOPLE.

Yunnan The Mongol conquest of the Dali kingdom began the integration of Yunnan into China proper. The Dali (Ta-li) kingdom (937–1253), successor to the Nanzhao (Nan-chao) dynasty (c. 653–902), centered on Dali, the capital, and Yachi (modern Kunming). The administration combined a Chinese system of prefectures and commanderies with the "White Jang" (Mongolian, Chagha'anjang, the modern Naxi) and "Black Jang" (Mongolian, Qarajang, the modern Yi) tribes. The ruling Duan dynasty was of the Chinese-influenced Bai people of Dali, but the "Black Jang" were numerous and powerful. (The idea that the Nanzhao and Dali kingdoms were formed by ethnically Thai peoples is no longer accepted.) Chinese-rite Buddhism was the city dwellers' dominant religion. Along the modern Chinese-Burmese border were the "Gold Tooths" (Persian, *Zardandan*, named from their gold-plated teeth), ancestors of the modern Dai (Tai) people but not yet Theravadin (Southeast Asian) Buddhist.

MÖNGKE KHAN (1251–59) dispatched Prince Qubilai to Dali in 1253 hoping to outflank the Song. The Gao family, probably Black Jang in origin, dominated the court and resisted. Qubilai took Dali on January 3, 1254, and spared the city, despite the slaying of the Mongol ambassadors. King Duan Xingzhi was confirmed as local ruler, with a Chinese pacification commissioner. After Qubilai's departure back for North China, unrest broke out among the Black Jang, which Uriyangqadai (1199–1271), son of SÜBE'ETEI BA'ATUR, ruthlessly suppressed, butchering Yachi and emptying recalcitrant mountain valleys. By 1256 the pacification was complete, yet difficult frontier conditions made Dali impossible to use for invading the Song.

The mountainous northern parts of the region proved excellent for horses, and Möngke Khan placed the region under 19 Mongol myriarchies. The small Mongol garrisons recruited Black Jang auxiliaries, and in their isolation from the Mongol world the two began to fuse. In 1267 QUBILAI KHAN (1260–94) made his younger son Hügechi prince of Yunnan, and in 1273 he dispatched SAYYID AJALL to implement civilian administration in the new Yunnan Branch Secretariat. Mongol Yuan rule in Yunnan was henceforth divided among the imperial princes, the Branch Secretariat under Sayyid Ajall and his family, the Mongol commanders, the Black Jang tribal leaders, and the Duan family in Dali. Yunnan used its distinctive cowrie money throughout the dynasty.

Under Emperor Temür (1294–1307) a disastrous expedition against the Babai-Xifu in northern Thailand spurred first a local official, Song Longji, and then the Gold-Tooths to revolt in 1301–03. The revolts were eventually suppressed.

After the expulsion of the Mongols from China in 1368, the Yuan prince Vajravarmi continued to rule Yunnan, refusing relations with the new MING DYNASTY. In 1382 the Ming defeated the Vajravarmi's armies and conquered Yunnan. A small population of Mongols (13,148 in 1990), with a heavily Yi (Black Jang)-influenced culture, are a legacy of Mongol rule in Yunnan.

Yün Tse *See* ULANFU.

Yun Ze *See* ULANFU.

yurt (*ger*) The Inner Asian yurt of recent centuries is the latest form of mobile Inner Asian residence, built with a collapsible wooden frame covered by felt. Once widespread over the Eurasian steppe, the yurt is still used by most of Mongolia's rural dwellers and among the Mongols of Inner Mongolia's high steppe, Xinjiang, and Kökenuur (*see* UPPER MONGOLS) in China. The KAZAKHS of Mongolia and Xinjiang and the Kyrgyz of Kyrgyzstan also dwell in yurts today. Mongolia's cities are all surrounded by districts of fixed yurt-courtyards.

The term *yurt* is Turkish in origin and actually means "homeland"; its use for the felt tent is something of a misnomer. In Mongolian the felt tent is called *ger* (home) or *isgii ger* (felt home), and in Kazakh *üy* (home) or *kigiz üy* (felt home).

STRUCTURE AND ASSEMBLY

The walls of a yurt in recent centuries are formed by latticework sections, or *khana* (term in Kalmyk-Oirat), which can be expanded or contracted. The *khana* are placed within a circle, completed by the door or door frame, and attached to one another with thongs. The roof is formed by a smoke-hole circle, or *toono* (*kharach* in Kalmyk-Oirat), which is attached to the walls by about 80 *uni*, or poles, radiating out from the *toono* to the *khana* like the spokes of a wheel. The *uni* and the *khana* are attached by leather thongs. Once built, the yurt framework is covered by wall and roof felts. The walls are cinched with rope sashes (*khoshlon*). An *örkh*, or felt smoke-hole cover, is attached on one corner to the rear of the yurt and can be opened to let sunlight in and smoke out or closed to keep in warmth.

The *khana* are roughly 1½ meters (5½ feet) high and 2⅓ meters (seven to eight feet) long. Yurt sizes are generally measured by how many *khana* they have; six to eight are normal. The average yurt thus has a diameter of about 5 to 6 meters (15 to 18 feet) and a living space of about 16 to 23 square meters (175 to 250 square feet).

The yurt and its furniture can be disassembled and reassembled in about one hour each and transported on two or three oxcarts or camels or on a single truck. Traditionally, yurts are assembled first by fixing the hearth site and placing the main chests and the door. Then the *khana* are set up. The *toono* (with either the attached *uni* or lashed-on pillars, depending on the type) is lifted in over the *khana* and set up, and the *uni* is fitted into position and lashed to the *khana*. Then the felt and smoke-hole flap are placed over the frame. Yurts are always assembled with the door to the south or southeast; in Mongolian "back"

Mongolian yurt and camp, Khöwsgöl 1992 *(Courtesy Christopher Atwood)*

(*khoino*), "front" (*ömnö*), "left" (*züün*), and "right" (*baruun*) also mean "north," "south," "east," and "west," respectively.

REGIONAL VARIATIONS

There are a number of regional variations in yurt construction. In Inner Mongolia and some eastern KHALKHA yurts the *uni* are permanently lashed to pegs wired to the *toono,* so that when the *uni* are lashed to the *khana,* the *toono* needs no support. Among the central and western Khalkha Mongols and the BURIATS and OIRATS the *uni* are not permanently attached but fitted separately into slots on the *toono.* As a result, two pillars (*bagana*) are needed to hold up the *toono.* Among the KALMYKS, although the *uni* are not attached to the *toono,* they are pushed up at a much higher angle, so that the *toono* does not need pillars.

Among the Mongols of Mongolia and Inner Mongolia the *toono* is constructed in two concentric circles, held together by crossbars. Among the Kazakhs, Kyrgyz, and Xinjiang's Oirat Mongols, however, the *toono* (called *shang'ïraq* in Kazakh and Kyrgyz and *kharach* by the Xinjiang Mongols) is formed of an outer circle and three pairs of perpendicularly intersecting crossbars. Among the Kalmyks the *kharach* is formed by an outer circle and a single cross.

In the MONGOL EMPIRE period felt flaps were used for doors, something still found among the Kalmyks of the 19th century. These were sewn with stitched patterns or colored patterns. In Mongolia and Inner Mongolia, however, the yurts of all but the poorest nomads have wooden doors. These doors also vary, with a more complicated double door being found in north-central Khalkha.

FURNISHING, USE, AND SYMBOLISM

In the 19th century traditional furnishings of the yurts consisted primarily of hides, felts, and sometimes imported pile rugs to cover the ground; at least two large chests for holding religious articles, clothes, and other valuables; a large wok (*togoo*) placed on a four-legged iron trivet (*tulga*) over an open fire; and low stools and tables for sitting and serving. Wealthier Mongols covered the inside *khana* with embroidered cloths or rugs and the outside roof with decorated felt covers. A single narrow bed was usually kept but used mostly to hold bedding; family members usually slept between quilts placed on the ground. The floor by the door was usually covered by boards. Today yurt dwellers all use an enclosed stove with a stovepipe. The stove may be a small manufactured one or assembled of bricks mortared with mud and dried grass and covered with a sheet of iron with a round hole for the wok. Large cots are now generally used, and sometimes the whole yurt is floored with wooden boards, especially if it is not frequently moved.

Yurt frameworks are made of willow wood and are often painted: Orange, bright red, and turquoise blue predominate. Wooden chests, stools, and tables are mostly orange with stereotyped decorations, including cloud patterns, auspicious Buddhist symbols (the unending knot, the wishing jewel, etc.), and the four friendly animals (elephant, rabbit, monkey, and bird).

The yurt's felt covering and its relatively small size make it relatively easy to heat even in extremely cold weather, so that it is the preferred winter dwelling even for semisedentarized Mongols with built houses (baishing). Yurts are generally heated with dried animal dung or else with wood in the northern forest-steppe. The lower flaps, or khayaa (kalmyk-Oirat, irg), of the yurt's felt walls are important for weather conditioning: In winter their outsides are buried in dirt, stones, and snow to block drafts, while in summer they are tied up, leaving about a 30-centimeter (one-foot) gap between the felt and the ground and allowing cross breezes into the yurt. Traditionally, poor people used reed or rawhide mats to help waterproof their patched and ragged felts.

The use of the yurt is bound with a strong symbolic structure based on the two polarities of honored and ordinary and male and female. The khoimor, or honored part of the yurt, is in the back, opposite the door. There is the Buddhist altar, if present, a display of family photographs and awards, and the master and mistress's bed. Honored guests are seated in that section. Near the door is the ordinary section, where horse tackle and cooking gear are kept and baby animals are nursed. The right side (looking from the khoimor to the door) is for men and their things, and the left for women and their things. Movement through the yurt should be clockwise, following the daily movement of the sunlight through the toono. The toono itself is seen in many myths and stories as the gateway between the human and the divine realm; from it hung the family ONGGHON (cloth or felt spirit figurine) in shamanist households or smoke offerings of grass and herbs in Buddhist ones. Saws are placed between the felt and the uni near the door and the rope hanging from the toono tucked in above the uni in a swivel pattern seen as a wolf's snout: These protect the yurt from harm. The making of a new yurt is accompanied by an anointing of the yurt with butter and a poetic benediction (see YÖRÖÖL AND MAGTAAL).

In the past, stepping on the threshold of the yurt is seen as stepping on the master's neck. In the Mongol Empire those who did so knowingly at the khan's court were executed; foreigners who did so ignorantly were excused but never again allowed into his presence.

HISTORY OF THE YURT

Despite its status as the exemplar of Mongolian tradition, nomadic housing has undergone many changes. From the first millennium B.C.E. through the XIONGNU (Hun) and TÜRK EMPIRES, Central Eurasian nomads dwelled in two-wheeled high carts with a pyramidal superstructure covered by black felt and pulled by draft animals: HORSES, oxen, or CAMELS. Camels were used to pull these carts through deep rivers. These tents were not collapsible and were moved with people inside them. The felt was coated with ewe's milk or tallow to make it waterproof. The earliest known collapsible yurts are pictured in Chinese art of the sixth century C.E. High carts were used by the western Turks until the 11th century, but among the KITANS of the 10th to 12th centuries such high cart tents were used only as shrines for the ancestors. The living all stayed in collapsible yurts.

During the Mongol Empire the collapsible yurt was used alongside the cart yurt. Some noncollapsible yurts kept permanently on carts had the form of a rounded-off square, while the smoke-hole area was like the top of a bell. These chomchog yurts are still found in the EIGHT WHITE YURTS of the CHINGGIS KHAN cult in ORDOS. WILLIAM OF RUBRUCK also describes round, presumably collapsible, yurts being moved fully assembled on carts. Some were almost 10 meters (30 feet) across and pulled by 22 oxen. The small pyramidal yurts on high carts, earlier used for residences, were used to keep goods and possessions and apparently as servants' dwellings. They were pulled by a single draft animal. During nomadization

The yurt-courtyards outside Mörön, Khöwsgöl province
(From N. Tsultem, Mongolian Architecture [1988])

each main yurt would go in front, and the cart yurts would be tied behind in single file and move at a very slow pace. When camped, the main yurt would be flanked by two lines of high carts behind and beside the main one.

High carts disappeared in the postimperial period; by the 16th century only the collapsible yurt remained. Large palatial yurts were now called *örgöö*, and Mongolian princes dwelt regularly in vast 12-*khana* yurts until the 20th century. By the 19th century yurt frameworks were built mostly in the monasteries by lama craftsmen. Much of the felt was made either in the monasteries or by Chinese seasonal laborers. The seminomadic western Buriats built not yurts but hexagonal or octagonal log cabins of the size and structure of yurts. In eastern Inner Mongolia mud-brick houses in the form of yurts also appeared in the 19th and early 20th centuries. In Khüriye (modern ULAANBAATAR) during the 19th century, lamas and layfolk alike lived in fixed yurts, establishing the pattern for the yurt-courtyard (*ger khashaa*) quarters that still exist today. Such fixed yurts are always surrounded by a wooden fence and often include a utility shed. In recent years providing clean water, sanitation, and electricity for these districts has taxed the abilities of urban planners.

The 20th century introduced technical improvements to the yurt even as social changes eliminated it among the Mongols of Russia and in the more densely inhabited regions of Inner Mongolia. Enclosed stoves and stovepipes, first introduced among the Transbaikal Buriats and spread by them into Mongolia and Inner Mongolia from the 1920s on, dramatically improved the air quality, while in the postwar period canvas covers over the felt greatly improved waterproofing. Yurt frameworks and felt in Mongolia became mostly the work of small urban factories, although with the economic crisis of the 1990s homemade felt became more common.

Further reading: Peter Alford Andrews, *Felt Tents and Pavilions: The Nomadic Tradition and Its Interaction with Princely Tentage,* 2 vols. (London: Melisende, 1999); Micheal V. Kriukov and Vadym P. Kurylev, "The Origins of the Yurt: Evidence from Chinese Sources of the Third Century B.C. to the Thirteenth Century A.D.," in Gary Seaman, *Foundations of Empire: Archeology and Art of the Eurasian Steppe* (Los Angeles: Ethnographics Press, 1992), 157–183; Jerzy Wasilewski, "Space in Nomadic Cultures—A Spatial Analysis of the Mongol Yurt," in *Altaica Collecta,* ed. Walther Heissig (Wiesbaden: Otto Harrassowitz, 1976), 345–360.

Zakchin *See* ZAKHACHIN.

Zakhachin (Zakhchin, Dzakhachin, Zakchin) The Zakhachin Mongols are a subethnic group, or *yastan,* in southern Khowd province. Originally in the Zünghar principality, certain subjects formed into a special OTOG (camp district) of *zakhachin*s (border wardens) directly subject to the Zünghar ruler. CLAN NAMES suggest many were actually of non-Zünghar origin, probably captured in Oirat wars with the Mongols. In 1754 a large body under the *zaisang* (local official) Maamud was captured southwest of the Altai and surrendered to the Qing armies. They were stationed as a directly administered Zakhachin banner along the Üyench and Bodonch Rivers, and two new monasteries were endowed.

In 1777 they were assigned to the Manchu AMBAN (assistant military governor) of KHOWD CITY fortress. Shortly thereafter, Maamud's nephew Jaltsan was granted hereditary jurisdiction over 30 households. From 1800 on the Zakhachin banner thus consisted of a banner with four *sumu*s and one independent hereditary *sumu* (SUM, or unit supplying 50 soldiers). The Zakhachins supplied horses to the Manchu garrison in ULIASTAI, farm labor for the fields at Khowd, and, after 1801, manning and provisioning of the five postroad stations between Khowd and Dihua (Ürümqi). The Zakhachins kept relatively few horses or camels but many sheep and goats. In 1878 a new monastery, Ölzöi Tsaghaan Padma, was established, and in 1906, on the occasion of the Dalai Lama's arrival in Mongolia, a *tsanid* (Tibetan, *mtshan-nyid,* or higher Buddhist studies) faculty was added. In 1929 the Zakhachin popula-tion was almost 8,000 and reached 10,800 in 1956 and 22,500 in 1989.

See also KHOWD PROVINCE.

Zakhchin *See* ZAKHACHIN.

Žamcarano *See* ZHAMTSARANO, TSYBEN ZHAMTSARA-NOVICH.

Zanabazar *See* JIBZUNDAMBA KHUTUGTU, FIRST.

zasag (Inner Mongolian, *jasag;* Chinese, *zhasake*) The *zasag,* or ruler, was the head of an autonomous banner or local district under the Mongolian administration of the QING DYNASTY (1636–1912).

The position of *zasag* was first created in the Qing dynasty's reorganization of Inner Mongolia in 1636. All of the Qing *zasag*s were TAIJI (noblemen), and virtually all were descendants of CHINGGIS KHAN or his brothers. Thus, the *zasag* was simultaneously a hereditary Qing official and a representative of Chinggis Khan. Qing dynasty regulations limited the BORJIGID (Chinggisid) ruler's classically patrimonial powers, reserving the right to depose serving *zasag*s, divide their banners, or alter the succession. Primogeniture was normal, however, and after 1670 in Inner Mongolia and 1765 in KHALKHA banner boundaries were not altered.

The *zasag* was the banner's supreme judge, but plaintiffs could appeal to the league and the LIFAN YUAN (Court of Dependencies) in Beijing. All capital cases were subject to mandatory review. The Qing regulations also enforced a rudimentary distinction between the banner finances and the *zasag*'s personal funds, although the precise boundaries were subject to constant lawsuits. Each banner office had a specified complement of officials. While they served theoretically at the pleasure of the *zasag*, the *zasag*s frequently lost power to their *tusalagchi*s (administrators), who were *taiji*s and often members of the *zasag*'s family.

While every *zasag* had the same powers within his banner, they and all the nobility were ranked according to their traditional prominence, seniority, and service to the dynasty. These ranks, from first-rank prince to mere *taiji* first degree, carried with them both symbolic distinctions and different salaries. The Qing used the possibilities of promotion or demotion to control the *zasag*s. The *zasag*s, along with the other titled *taiji*s, had the right and duty of audience at court every three (Inner Mongolia) or six (Khalkha) years, as well as participation in the imperial hunt.

After 1911 Mongolia's theocratic government preserved the *zasag* system and even extended it to HULUN BUIR and certain western Mongolian banners, where it had not previously existed. By contrast, Mongolia's revolutionary government after 1921 made the banner chiefs elective officials from 1922 to 1924. In Inner Mongolia under the Republic of China and Japan, the *zasag*s (*jasag*s) were partially transformed into appointive officials from 1929 to 1945, after which the old system collapsed.

See also DUGUILANG; THEOCRATIC PERIOD.

Zavchan   *See* ZAWKHAN PROVINCE.

Zavhan   *See* ZAWKHAN PROVINCE.

Zawkhan province (Dzavhan, Zavhan, Zavchan, Dzabkhan)   Created in the 1931 administrative reorganization, Zawkhan province lies in northwest Mongolia. Its territory includes parts of KHALKHA Mongolia's prerevolutionary Zasagtu Khan and Sain Noyan provinces. The western, Zasagtu Khan, sections are inhabited by the KHOTOGHOID and Eljigin Khalkhas. Part of the province borders the Tuvan Republic in Russia.

The province's territory of 82,500 square kilometers (31,850 square miles) covers the northwestern half of the wooded KHANGAI RANGE and the eastern part of the arid GREAT LAKES BASIN. Several landlocked rivers, including the Zawkhan River, from which the province is named, flow from the Khangai Range through the province to lakes in UWS PROVINCE and KHOWD PROVINCE.

The province's resident population grew from 55,100 in 1956 to 87,200 in 2000. In the 1980s and the early and mid-1990s Zawkhan had the largest livestock herd in Mongolia, at 2.1–2.4 million head, and the largest sheep herd, at 1.4–1.3 million. The livestock herd was hit heavily by the spring 2000 ZUD and declined to 1,941,300 head; sheep survived relatively well and now number 1,050,500 head. In the socialist era Zawkhan developed significant arable agriculture that proved unsustainable after 1990. The capital, ULIASTAI, founded as a QING DYNASTY garrison in the 18th century, had a population of 24,300 in 2000. The town of Tosontsengel, created in Mongolia's socialist industrialization after 1966, became Mongolia's largest lumber-processing center by 1980. Its current population is 12,700. Tosontsengel has posted one of Mongolia's coldest recorded temperatures at −52.9°C (−63.2°F).

See also JALKHANZA KHUTUGTU DAMDINBAZAR.

Zaya Pandita Namkhai-Jamtsu (Dzaya Pandita, Jaya Pandita) (1599–1662) *Oirat scholar and lama who designed the clear script used among the Oirats and Kalmyks*

Namkhai-Jamtsu was born in Gürööchin (Hunters) OTOG (camp-district) of the Khoshud tribe, the fifth son of Baabakhan. When he was 16 years old the Oirat nobles agreed to dispatch one child each to Tibet as a lama. Baibaghas Baatur Noyan (d. 1630), head of the Khoshud tribe, chose Namkhai-Jamtsu as a replacement for his own son. In 1617 he arrived in Tibet and after taking his *gelüng* vows from the Dalai Lama studied *tsanid* (Tibetan, *mtshan-nyid*, academic study of Buddhist philosophy). His examination for the Lharamba degree was flawless. In 1639 he returned to his homeland.

For the rest of his life he traveled constantly among the palace-yurts (*örgöö*) of the Oirat lords in Zungharia (Junggar basin) and the Ili valley, with occasional trips to the Volga KALMYKS and Khalkha, holding Buddhist services, particularly funerary and new year services, and consecrations for the nobles and their families. While offered lavish donations, he preferred to have donors send their gifts to the monasteries of Tibet, to which he felt an abiding gratitude for his education. In winter 1648–49 he created the CLEAR SCRIPT as an improvement on the UIGHUR-MONGOLIAN SCRIPT. From 1650 to 1662 he transcribed from the Uighur-Mongolian or translated freshly from the Tibetan 177 works. The colophons appended to his translations often feature accomplished devotional poetry. From 1657 to 1661 he and other clerics worked diligently, and more or less successfully, to negotiate a bloodless end to the bitter feud between Baibaghas's son Ablai (fl. 1638–72) and the Khoshud ruler Ochirtu Tsetsen Khan. He died in 1662 while on a journey to Tibet, and his disciples continued with his ashes to Lhasa. Zaya Pandita's biography, *Saran-u Gerel* (Light of the moon, 1690), written by a pupil, Ratnabhadra, is the first original prose work of Oirat clear script literature.

Namkhai-Jamtsu should not be confused with the founder of the incarnation lineage of Khalkha Zaya Panditas, Lubsang-Perenlai (1642–1715).

See also OIRATS; *SUTRA OF THE WISE AND FOOLISH; TREASURY OF APHORISTIC JEWELS;* ZÜNGHARS.

Zhamtsarano, Tsyben Zhamtsaranovich (Žamcarano, Tsewang, Jamsrangiin Tseween) (1881–1942) *Buriat folklorist, nationalist, and mentor in modern life for a generation of Mongolian revolutionaries* Born on April 26, 1881, in Khoito-Aga village in the Aga steppe, Tsyben was the son of the *zaisang* (petty headman) Zhamtsarano of the Sharaid clan. Growing up, Tsyben received both a formal education at the Chita primary school and an informal education from the tales and EPICS told by his great-grandmother, grandmother, and grandfather and the Indian stories and Buriat laws read to him by his father. In 1895 he attended the private gymnasium (academic high school) founded by the Buriat court physician Pëtr A. Badmaev (1856–1920) in St. Petersburg. After a period at the Irkutsk Pedagogical Academy he and his Aga landsman Bazar B. Baradiin (1878–1937) began auditing classes at the Imperial University of St. Petersburg.

Supplementing professorial instruction with private reading, the two became noted specialists in Buriat and Mongol culture, with Zhamtsarano specializing in folklore and SHAMANISM and Baradiin in Buddhism. Zhamtsarano received funding to collect folklore in the Buriat countryside in 1903–07 and in Inner Mongolia in 1909–10 between lecturing, editing folklore texts, and doing research in St. Petersburg.

After the 1911 RESTORATION of Mongol independence Zhamtsarano worked simultaneously in the Russian consulate in Khüriye (modern ULAANBAATAR) and in Mongolia's Foreign Ministry. There he instigated the founding of a modern-style school for Mongolian youth, a UIGHUR-MONGOLIAN SCRIPT movable-type press, and a monthly journal, *Shine toli khemekhü bichig* (New mirror). In the journal he published documents and treaties, discussions of general human development, and translations from works such as Leon Cahun's historical novel of the MONGOL EMPIRE, *La Bannière bleue* (Blue banner). Controversy over these works forced the journal to close down, but in 1915 Zhamtsarano began publishing *Neislel khüriyen-ü sonin bichig* (Capital Khüriye news).

In spring 1917, with the overthrow of czarism, Zhamtsarano returned to Buriatia. In December 1917 he was elected chairman of the Buriat National Committee (Russian abbreviation, Burnatskom). During the period of the Bolshevik seizure of power and White Russian rule, he was a member of the Chita Soviet and taught at Irkutsk University.

In summer 1920, after the Bolsheviks recovered Buriatia, Zhamtsarano linked up with Mongolian revolutionaries, several of whom he knew from the Foreign Ministry school, seeking Soviet aid against China. Zham-

tsarano joined the new Mongolian People's Party and at the March 1–3, 1921, conference drafted the new party's manifesto. After the success of the 1921 REVOLUTION Zhamtsarano remained a party and government leader in Mongolia until 1928. While in Mongolia in 1926, Zhamtsarano married Badamzhap Tsedenovna; they had no children. His primary sphere of activity was in promoting cultural activities, particularly in the "Philology Institute" (*Sudur bichig-ün khüriyeleng*), and Mongolian leaders sought his advice as a sort of elder statesman cum human encyclopedia. While Zhamtsarano did not spare obscurantist lamas, he believed the Buddha's views were fully compatible with communism and reprinted many Buddhist works. He hoped for a neutral Mongolia uniting all the Mongol peoples. Economically, he was an early and consistent advocate of using cooperatives to drive out Chinese merchants out of Mongolia.

In fall 1928, at the SEVENTH CONGRESS OF THE MONGOLIAN PEOPLE'S REVOLUTIONARY PARTY, Zhamtsarano was shouted down by leftists who were egged on by the Communist International. He remained in Mongolia until 1932 but was restricted to academic work. In 1932 he was finally expelled as a rightist and returned to the Oriental Institute of Leningrad. There he continued his academic work, writing a comprehensive ethnographic survey of Mongolia in Mongolian (1934) and defending his doctorate with the dissertation *Mongolian Chronicles of the Seventeenth Century* (1936, in Russian; English translation, 1955).

On August 10, 1937, Zhamtsarano was arrested in the first wave of the GREAT PURGE. Charged with being a pan-Mongolist Japanese agent, he denied the charges and did not implicate any others despite extreme torture. He died on April 14, 1942, in the labor camp of Sol'-Iletsk, near Orenburg.

See also ACADEMY OF SCIENCES; AGA BURIAT AUTONOMOUS AREA; BURIATS; MONGOLIAN PEOPLE'S REVOLUTIONARY PARTY; NEW SCHOOLS MOVEMENTS; REVOLUTIONARY PERIOD; THEOCRATIC PERIOD.

Further reading: Robert A. Rupen, "Cyben Žamcaranovič Žamcarano (1880–?1940)," *Harvard Journal of Asiatic Studies* 19 (1956): 126–145.

Zhangar *See* JANGGHAR.

Zhangjia *See* JANGJIYA KHUTUGTU.

Zhang Rou (Chang Jou) (1190–1268) *Chinese warlord who supported the Mongols in campaigns from Hebei to the Yangtze*
A prosperous landlord's son, Zhang Rou gathered a self-defense force when the Mongols invaded his native Hebei in 1213. The murder of his patron at the Jin court shook his loyalty, and in summer 1218 MUQALI, CHINGGIS KHAN'S viceroy in China, captured him. Muqali admired Zhang's

courage and after taking two sons of Zhang as hostages appointed him the local Mongol commander. Zhang made his base at Mancheng and by 1220 had carved out a semi-independent fiefdom in the central Hebei plain. In 1226 the Mongols made him chiliarch (commander of 1,000). After joining ÖGEDEI KHAN's final campaign against the Jin, he received an imperial audience and was promoted to myriarch (commander of 10,000) in 1234. From 1236 to 1255 Zhang Rou served three khans on the SONG DYNASTY frontier, gradually acquiring experience at checking the Song generals' river-borne incursions. In 1259 he joined QUBILAI KHAN's inconclusive invasion of the Song. Barely literate himself, Zhang Rou rescued many scholars and documents during the sack of Kaifeng in 1233 (see KAIFENG, SIEGE OF). In rebuilding Baozhou (modern Baoding) in Hebei and Bozhou (modern Boxian) in Anhui, he funded schools and Confucian temples. Qubilai Khan enfeoffed Zhang as duke, and his ninth song, Zhang Hongfan (1237–79), commanded the hunt for the last fugitive Song emperor.

Further reading: C. C. Hsiao, "Chang Jou," in *In the Service of the Khan: Eminent Personalities of the Early Mongol-Yuan Period (1200–1300)*, ed. Igor de Rachewiltz et al. (Wiesbaden: Otto Harrassowitz, 1993), 46–59.

Zhao Wuda   *See* JUU UDA.

Zhenhai   *See* CHINQAI.

Zhenjin   *See* JINGIM.

Zhongdu, sieges of (Chung-tu, Jungdu)   The Mongols' two sieges of the North Chinese capital city, Zhongdu, ended very differently: The first in spring 1214 with a negotiated settlement and the second from summer 1214 to May 1215 with the sack of the city and the establishment of Mongol control. Zhongdu (Central Capital) was the capital of North China's JIN DYNASTY, situated on the site of modern Beijing. On the North China plain, it was defended to the north and west by low but rugged ranges, through which the Juyongguan Pass to the northwest was the major pathway.

Mongol cavalry first appeared at Zhongdu in October 1211, but they soon withdrew. In 1213 the Mongols seized Juyongguan Pass again (see JUYONGGUAN PASS, BATTLES OF). The Mongols approached Zhongdu and defeated Marshal Shuhu Gaoqi in November 1213. Jin morale was weakened by the violent conflicts. Just at that time, Heshilie Hushahu had overthrown the previous emperor and enthroned his nephew, Wanyan Xun (titled Xuanzong, r. 1213–24). After Shuhu Gaoqi's defeat he killed Hushahu in his palace.

The Mongols left to reduce the rest of North China, but CHINGGIS KHAN and his men rendezvoused at Zhongdu on March 31, 1214. The Jin had lost hundreds of towns, but the Mongol army was being ravaged by famine and epidemics. Chinggis sent JABAR KHOJA to deliver his terms: The Jin would have to pay an immense ransom and surrender a princess of the imperial family. Negotiations continued through April, and grain supplies in the city grew increasingly tight. Finally, on April 30 the Jin councillors decided to secure a respite whatever the cost and agreed to Chinggis's terms. On May 11 Grand Councillor Wanyan Fuxing escorted the daughter of the emperor's murdered predecessor to Chinggis Khan's camp, and the siege was lifted. The Mongols withdrew from the North China plain, and the Jin emperor set about reestablishing control in North China.

After this respite the Jin court migrated to Kaifeng in Henan, south of the Huang (Yellow) River, as a better base for continued resistance. The crown prince, Shouzhong, was left as regent in Zhongdu, with Wanyan Fuxing to assist him. On their way south Kitan and Tatar tribal auxiliaries in the imperial entourage revolted, deserting to the Mongol banner. In September Shouzhong himself fled Zhongdu for Nanjing, leaving Wanyan Fuxing to guard the city.

Chinggis Khan, furious at the Jin's betrayal of the treaty, decided to take Zhongdu and conquer all North China. The KITANS and Tatar deserters began the siege of Zhongdu in July under the direction of Shimo Ming'an (see SHIMO MING'AN AND XIANDEBU). In March 1215 the Jin court dispatched Li Ying and Wugulun Qingshou to deliver supplies to the besieged defenders. The besiegers intercepted them in Bazhou (modern Baxian), about 60 miles south of Zhongdu, and seized their supplies for their own use. Famine and cannibalism raged in Zhongdu. On May 31, 1215, Wanyan Fuxing took poison, and the Mongols entered the city. The city was given over to pillage, and the gardens and estates were divided among the victorious commanders. Chinggis Khan, summering in Huanzhou in Inner Mongolia, sent SHIGI QUTUQU and others to confiscate the royal treasury. When order was reestablished the Kitan Shimo Ming'an and Jabar Khoja were put in charge of the city for the Mongols. Renamed DAIDU in 1272, Zhongdu remained the center of Mongol rule in China until 1368.

See also MASSACRES AND THE MONGOL CONQUEST; MILITARY OF THE MONGOL EMPIRE.

Zorig, Sanjaasürengiin (1962–1998) *One of the most charismatic leaders of the 1990 Democratic Revolution who was murdered on the eve of being nominated Mongolia's prime minister*
Zorig was the second son of Sanjaasüreng, rector of the Mongolian State University. His mother, the physician Dorjpalam, was actually the daughter of the Russian Andrei Dmitrievich Simukov (1902–42), a distinguished adviser to the Mongolian government in the 1930s.

When Simukov and his wife were arrested in the GREAT PURGE in 1939, Dorjpalam was adopted by Mongolians and raised as a Mongolian child.

In 1970 Zorig entered School No. 23, a Russian-language school for Mongolia's social elite, and from 1980 to 1985 studied philosophy (that is, Marxism-Leninism) at Moscow State University. Zorig was already dissatisfied with Mongolia's economic and intellectual development and desired to emulate Japan's successful modernization. From 1985 he worked for the MONGOLIAN REVOLUTIONARY YOUTH LEAGUE before teaching and researching on reforms at Mongolian State University. Zorig spoke softly and had a modest demeanor but was sometimes very stubborn.

On December 2–3, 1989, while writing a dissertation on political reform, Zorig was invited to attend sessions of the "Conference of Young Creative Artists" and was elected head of the Mongolian Democratic Association, which grew out of this meeting. During the ensuing demonstrations that toppled the one-party system, Zorig's public leadership and familiarity with Japanese reporters gave him a high international profile.

While denied leadership in the Mongolian Democratic Party, Zorig won a seat in the Great People's Khural and was one of the drafters of the 1992 CONSTITUTION. His visible role and reputation made him the object among opponents of scurrilous rumors and insinuations about his part-Russian descent. While originally a democratic socialist, by 1991 he was sponsoring discussions on the ideas of "neoconservatism," and in 1992 Zorig formed a new Republican Party with a classic liberal program. His name recognition made him one of only six democratic movement politicians to win a seat in the Great State Khural (from an ULAANBAATAR district) in July 1992. That October several democratic parties, including his Republican Party, merged, and he became a leader in the new Mongolian National Democratic Party.

After this party joined the winning Democratic Coalition in parliamentary elections in 1996, Zorig served on the Parliament's Committee on Security and Foreign Policy, emphasizing relations with Japan. In 1998, when Parliament members began serving in government, Zorig became minister of infrastructure, all the while steering clear of the allegations of corruption that dogged other Democratic politicians. After repeated attempts to nominate a Democratic Coalition acceptable to Mongolia's president, N. Bagabandi, Zorig was being considered as a new nominee when he was murdered by two assailants in his apartment on October 2, 1998. Neither the murderer nor the motive has yet been identified, but the murder was widely blamed on hostile political forces. In December Zorig's younger sister, the geologist S. Oyuun (b. 1964), won the by-election to his district and has gone on to a career as a good-government reformer. Zorig was survived by his wife, but they had no children.

See also 1990 DEMOCRATIC REVOLUTION; MONGOLIA, STATE OF; MONGOLIAN PEOPLE'S REPUBLIC.

zud Zud (or *jud* in Inner Mongolian) refers to any pastoral disaster that causes a massive die-off in the herds and widespread hunger. *Zud*s include "drought *zud*," or die-off caused by lack of rain in the summer, "white *zud*," or die-off caused by heavy snows in the winter, and "black *zud*," usually in the spring, caused by a prolonged cold snap that freezes the moisture from the previously melted snow cover and encloses the grass in a sheath of ice the animals cannot break.

Historically, *zud*s have sometimes had serious consequence for the nomads. In 839 a massive "white *zud*" caused the fall of the UIGHUR EMPIRE. In the 20th century serious winter *zud*s that killed millions of animals occurred in 1923–24, 1944–45, and 1968–69. That of 1944–45 killed 8 million animals. That and the 1968–69 *zud* occurred in years of the monkey, traditionally seen as a dangerous year (*see* 12-ANIMAL CYCLE). In recent years *zud*s struck twice in early spring 2000 and 2001. The massive die-off cut Mongolia's total herd from 33.5 million in December 1999 to 26.1 million in December 2001. Many herders lost their entire herds. Despite serious hardship, government intervention and international assistance prevented the crisis from reaching the point of starvation.

Further reading: Guy Templer, Jeremy Swift, and Polly Payne, "Changing Significance of Risk in the Mongolian Pastoral Economy," *Nomadic Peoples* 33 (1993): 105–122.

Zünghars The Zünghar tribe fashioned a powerful principality under GALDAN BOSHOGTU KHAN (r. 1678–97) and his successors that became the last great independent nomadic power on the steppe.

ORIGINS AND RISE OF THE ZÜNGHARS

The Zünghars as a tribal name first appear early in the 17th century as one part of the Oirat confederation (*see* OIRATS). The chiefs of the Zünghars were of the Choros lineage and reckoned their descent from the famous *taishi*s Toghoon (r. c.1417–38) and ESEN (r. 1438–54). The Choros, who also ruled the DÖRBÖD tribe, had an ancestral myth of descent from a boy nourished by a sacred tree, a legend shared with the Uighur royal family. The term *Zünghar* (the Left, i.e., Eastern, Hand, *Zöün Ghar* in CLEAR SCRIPT Oirat, *Zünghar* in modern Kalmyk, *Züüngar* in modern Mongolian) appears to have arisen as a way to distinguish them from the Dörböds, so that the Zünghars were the Dörböds to the east.

The Zünghars' rise to leadership among the Oirats began with Khara-Khula (d. 1634), who first appears in Russian diplomatic records in 1619. In the 1620s wars against the KHALKHA, Khara-Khula had hardly a third of the men of Khoshud khan Baibaghas (d. 1630), while Baatur Dalai Taishi of the Dörböds was considered the most powerful Oirat chief. Even so, Khara-Khula's son Baatur Khung-Taiji (d. 1653) joined the 1636–42 expedition to Tibet led by Baibaghas's brother TÖRÖ-BAIKHU GÜÜSHI KHAN (1582–1655). Baatur Khung-Taiji returned with the title Erdeni Baatur Khung-Taiji given him by the Dalai Lama, much booty, and Güüshi Khan's daughter Amin-Dara as wife. From around 1630 to 1677, TORGHUDS, KHOSHUDS, and Dörböds migrated west to the Volga or south to Kökenuur, increasing the Zünghars' relative power in Züngharia.

Baatur Khung-Taiji had given half his people to Sengge, his son by Amin-Dara. From 1657 on Amin-Dara's sons Sengge (d. 1670) and Galdan (1644–97) faced disaffection from their half brothers. This opposition they overcame with the backing of the Khoshud Ochirtu Tsetsen Khan (fl. 1639–76), son of Baibaghas. First Sengge and then Galdan married Ochirtu's granddaughter Anu-Dara. In 1676, however, the finally victorious Galdan overthrew his grandfather-in-law, and in 1678 he received from the Dalai Lama the title Boshogtu Khan. This confirmed the Zünghars as the confederation's new leading tribe.

While often called the "Zunghar Khanate," the Zünghar ruler bore the title of khan only rarely. Instead, the Zünghar ruler bore the title of Khung-Taiji, a title derived from Chinese *huang-taizi,* "crown prince" and originally meaning viceroy or regent for the khan. The title of khan was taken later, if at all, and only by special grant from an outside power, such as the Dalai Lama. While Galdan held the title of khan, his nephew and successor Tsewang-Rabtan was merely Khung-Taiji. GALDAN-TSEREN (r. 1727–45) is usually called khan, but it is unclear from whom he received the title.

ZÜNGHAR ORGANIZATION

Galdan made the Zünghars a major force in Inner Asian politics, establishing the basic lines of Zünghar foreign policy until its disintegration. From his time on the term *Zünghar* meant not just the Zünghar tribe but all the Oirats remaining in their homeland between the Altai and the Tianshan ranges. The Oirats nomadized along the Ili, Emil (modern Emin), and upper Irtysh Rivers and in the mountain pastures of Ürümqi, Zultus (along the Kaidu River), and Borotala (modern Bole). Baatur Khung-Taiji made the monastery at Khobogsair (Hoboksar) his center, and Galdan did so at Borotala. (*On political, military, and cultural life in this period, see* OIRATS.)

The total Zünghar population and military manpower underwent rapid expansion, largely through the incorporation of prisoners and subjugated tribes. In the late 16th century Mongolian chronicles speak of 8,000 Khoid and four *otogs* (camp districts) of Dörböd. In the 1620s the total manpower, excluding the Dörböd, was 36,000, yet during the civil strife of 1661 the Khoshud tribes alone fielded six *tümens* (nominally 10,000 each).

Galdan-Tseren reorganized the Zünghar principality, nominally numbering 200,000 households, into directly ruled *otogs* and appanages, or *anggis*. His directly subject

households, nomadizing in the Ili valley, numbered 24 *otogs* administered by 54 *albachi zaisang* (tax officials), with a nominal strength of 87,300 households. These were his personal Choros subjects, captured Siberian and Mongolian peoples, and functional units such as the 4,000 Kötöchi-Nar (equerries), 1,000 Buuchin (musketeers), 5,000 Uruud (craftsmen), and 2,000 ZAKHACHINS (borderers). The appanages of the great nobles, which surrounded the Ili center, were arranged into 21 *anggis*, specified as six Choros, one Khoshud, two Torghud, eight Khoid, and (presumably) four Dörböd. The *anggis* did not pay regular taxes to the ruler.

Given its general situation of two-front hostilities, the Zünghars never threw their full force against any external enemy. The 1688 and 1732 invasions of Khalkha both involved three *tümens*, or nominally 30,000 men.

ZÜNGHAR CONQUESTS

From the beginning of their conversion in 1615, the Oirats maintained unusually close relations with the Dalai and Panchen Lamas in central Tibet. After Güüshi Khan's and Baatur Khung-Taiji's pacification of Tibet, the Zünghars' slogan was "We are the main almsgivers [i.e., lay patrons] of the Holy Tsong-kha-pa [founder of the Yellow Hats]." The Fifth Dalai Lama, Ngag-dbang Blobzang rGya-mtsho (1617–82), encouraged this often bigoted devotion, advising Mongolian lamas to prevent any non-dGe-lugs-pa teaching there. This devotion often bore fruit in the plundering and desecration of competing Buddhist centers, whether monasteries of the JIBZUNDAMBA KHUTUGTU during Galdan's occupation in 1688–97 or rNying-ma-pa (a very traditional, non-dGe-lugs-pa order) monasteries during Tseren-Dondug's 1717–19 occupation of Lhasa.

To the east and southeast the Zünghars faced the Khalkha Mongols and the QING DYNASTY (1636–1912) in China. At first the Khalkhas and Oirats were in league, bound by the provisions of the MONGOL-OIRAT CODE (*Mongghol-Oirat tsaaji*) to common action against rebels and invaders. Eventually, the refusal of the Khalkhas' Tüshiyetü Khan Chakhundorji (r. 1655–99) to abide by arbitration broke the league and provoked Galdan's 1688 invasion of Khalkha. His invasion proved to be a disaster, however, driving the Khalkhas into the arms of the Qing.

Initially, relations with the Qing had been friendly. The Zünghars' main interest was in trade with China, which was, as under the MING DYNASTY, carried out through the TRIBUTE SYSTEM, really a form of state-subsidized monopoly trade. Until 1683 the Zünghar rulers allowed Turkestani merchants to freely join their "tribute" missions, which often reached 3,000 men in size. Galdan's invasion eventually provoked the Kangxi emperor (1662–1722) into a campaign of annihilation. Nevertheless, Kangxi was friendly to Galdan's nephew and successor, Tsewang-Rabtan (r. 1694–1727), until border conflicts with the Khalkhas and Hami, both under

Chinese protection, provoked war from the Altai to Lhasa that lasted off and on until 1732. A peace treaty of 1739 restored formal relations and "tribute" missions, although on a reduced scale.

More lasting conquests of Galdan's were the Tarim Basin cities in which Naqshbandi Sufi (Islamic mystic) masters had replaced the last Chaghatayid khans (*see* MOGHULISTAN). Galdan overthrew the Naqshbandi "Black Mountain" subsect and installed as his client rulers the exiled leader Afaq of the "White Mountain." The Zünghars kept control over the Tarim Basin until 1757. In 1678 Galdan decreed that the "Khotongs" (Turkestanis) would be judged by their own law except in cases affecting the state.

Farther to the west the Zünghars fought repeated wars against the KAZAKHS. Under Baatur Khung-Taiji the Zünghars raided the Zheti-Su (Seven Rivers, or Semirech'ie) between Lake Balkhash and the Tianshan, while Galdan's armies under his nephew Tsewang-Rabtan (1663–1727) reached Tashkent and the Syr-Dar'ya. After 1698 Tsewang-Rabdan's raids reached Tengiz Lake and Turkestan, and the Zünghars controlled Zheti-Su Tashkent until 1745.

Before the Russian conquest of Siberia, the Kyrgyz of Khakassia, the Telengits of the Altai, and the Baraba TATARS had paid the Oirats a fur tribute (*see* SIBERIA AND THE MONGOL EMPIRE). From 1607 the Russians, too, demanded *yasak* (fur-tribute) from the Siberians. Under Baatur Khung-Taiji it was agreed that the Siberian peoples would pay *yasak* to both Russia and the Zünghars. By 1707, however, new Russian forts blocked off Khakassia, and in 1720 they began blocking off the Baraba steppe between Omsk and Barnaul. Many Kyrgyz of Khakassia were moved south and incorporated into the Zünghars. Despite protests and raids, however, the Zünghar rulers never engaged in all-out war with Russia.

DOWNFALL OF THE ZÜNGHARS

At Galdan-Tseren's death in 1745 the Zünghar principality appeared still strong. Territory had been lost to both Russia and the Qing, but the core was still untouched. Less than 20 years later the Zünghars had not only disintegrated as a political structure, but the people had virtually disappeared. Politically, this sudden collapse stemmed from the strife between Galdan-Tseren's sons. In 1749 Lamdarja, Galdan-Tseren's son by a commoner wife,

Prince Dawachi of the Choros (left), last khan of the independent Zünghars, who surrendered to the Qing armies in 1755. Prince Tseren of the Dörböd (right), one of the "three Tserens" who led their tribe to surrender to the Qing in 1753. Qing court portraits, with subjects posed in summer and winter court robes, respectively *(Courtesy Staatliche Museen zu Berlin, Ethnologisches Museum)*

seized the throne from his younger brother. The next year the Zünghars began to desert to the Qing, which increased pressure by cutting off trade missions. In 1752 Lamdarja was overthrown by his second cousin Dawaachi and the Khoid AMURSANAA (1722?–57). In 1753 the "three Tserens" led the entire Dörböd tribe to surrender to the Qing dynasty, and in 1754 Amursanaa followed. Another wave of refugees flowed toward Siberia from 1753. In spring 1755 the Qing emperor, Qianlong (1736–1796), dispatched a massive army that found itself the master of Zungharia after a virtually bloodless campaign. Qianlong ordered the defeated confederation divided into four tribes—Dörböd, Khoshud, Choros, Khoid—each ruled by a subordinate khan. In autumn 1755 Amursanaa revolted against Qing rule. Zünghar refugees streamed north to the Cossack forts until Amursanaa's own flight and death.

What led to this sudden collapse? A few factors can be discounted. Neither the possession of firearms by the Qing nor some inherent weakness of nomadic polities seems plausible as an explanation, since the Zünghars had been overcoming these obstacles for many decades past. Certainly the irresponsibility of Lamdarja, Dawaachi, and Amursanaa contributed to the disaster. In particular, Dawaachi's and Amursanaa's alliances with the Kazakhs in 1752 and 1756–57 opened the Zünghar frontier to both plunder and immigration from their long-standing nomadic rivals. The impoverished condition of the Dörböd refugees who arrived in 1753 with little fight-ing indicates some natural disaster had already taken place. In Khalkha in 1754–55 a serious ZUD occurred, and in 1756–57 a smallpox epidemic broke out, and these disasters may have also affected the Zünghars.

With the suppression of Amursanaa's rebellion, Qian-long ordered that the remaining Zünghars be annihilated. When the killing stopped in 1759, the Qing authorities estimated that of all the Zünghars in 1755, 30 percent had been slain, 40 percent had died of disease, 20 percent had fled to Russia, and 10 percent remained. The Dör-böds, who had surrendered in 1753, together with two small bodies of Khoids who surrendered to the Qing in 1755, were resettled in modern UWS PROVINCE. Amursanaa's Khoids, who had surrendered in 1754, together with their subject Kyrgyz, were resettled as the Yekhe-Minggadai banner (modern Fuyu county, Heilongjiang). Zungharia was resettled by Kazakhs and bannermen from Manchuria and Inner Mongolia. The surviving Zünghars were officially renamed ÖÖLÖD and today constitute about 20 percent of Xinjiang's approximately 140,000 Mongols.

Further reading: Fred W. Bergholz, *The Partition of the Steppe: The Struggle of the Russians, Manchus, and the Zunghar Mongols for Empire in Central Asia, 1619–1758* (New York: Peter Lang, 1993); Junko Miyawaki, "Did a Dzungar Khanate Really Exist?" *Journal of the Anglo-Mongolian Society* 10 (1987): 1–5.

Zuu Ud   *See* JUU UDA.

RULERS AND LEADERS OF MONGOLIA AND THE MONGOL EMPIRE

GREAT KHANS AND REGENTS OF THE MONGOL EMPIRE

Name	Reign Years	Status
Temüjin Chinggis Khan	1206–1227	
Tolui	1227–1229	Regent
Ögedei Khan	1229–1241	
Töregene	1242–1246	Regent
Güyüg Khan	1246–1248	
Oghul-Qaimish	1248–1251	Regent
Möngke Khan	1251–1259	

EMPERORS (GREAT KHANS) OF THE YUAN DYNASTY

Name	Mongolian Title	Reign Years	Chinese Title
Qubilai	Sechen Khan	1260–1294	Shizu (Shih-tsu)
Temür	Öljeitü Khan	1294–1307	Chengzong (Ch'eng-tsung)
Haishan	Külüg Khan	1307–1311	Wuzong (Wu-tsung)
Ayurbarwada	Buyantu Khan	1311–1320	Renzong (Jen-tsung)
Shidebala	Gegeen Khan	1320–1323	Yingzong (Ying-tsung)
Yisün-Temür		1323–1328	Taidingdi (T'ai-ting-ti)
Qoshila		1328–1329	Mingzong (Ming-tsung)
Tuq-Temür	Jiya'atu Khan	1328, 1329–1332	Wenzong (Wen-tsung)
Irinchinbal		1332	Ningzong (Ning-tsung)
Toghan-Temür	Uqa'atu Khan	1332–1370	Shundi (Shun-ti)

THE IL-KHANS

Name	Reign Years	Other Names
Hüle'ü Khan	1256–1265	
Abagha Khan	1265–1282	
Sultan Ahmad	1282–1284	Born Tegüder
Arghun Khan	1284–1291	
Geikhatu Khan	1291–1295	Buddhist name Irinchin-Dorji
Baidu Khan	1295	
Ghazan Khan	1295–1304	Islamic name Mahmud
Sultan Öljeitü	1304–1316	Raised as Kharbanda; Islamic name, Muhammad Khudabanda
Sultan Abu Sa'id	1316–1335	Ba'atur Khan

KHANS OF THE GOLDEN HORDE

Name	Reign Years
Jochi	d. 1225?
Batu	d. 1255
Sartaq	1256–1257
Ula'achi	1257
Berke	1257–1266
Mengü-Temür	1267–1280
Töde-Mengü	1280–1287
Töle-Bugha	1287–1291
Toqto'a Khan	1291–1312
Özbeg	1313–1341
Tïnïbeg	1341–1342
Janibeg	1342–1357
Berdibeg	1357–1359
Qulpa	1359–1360
Nawroz	1360

(After the murder of Nawroz, rival dynasties seized power in the Golden Horde.)

KHANS OF THE CHAGHATAY KHANATE

Name	Reign Years
Cha'adai	d. 1242
Qara-Hüle'ü	1242–1246
Yisü-Möngke	1246–1251
[Orghina, regent for Mubarak-Shah, 1251–1260]	
Alghu	1260–1265/6
Mubarak-Shah	1265/6–1266
Baraq	1266–1271
Negübei	1271
Toqa-Temür	1272
interregnum	
Du'a	1282–1307
Könchek	1307–1308
Nalighu	1308–1309
Esen-Buqa	1309–1318?
Kebeg	1318?–1327
Eljigidei	1327–1330
Töre-Temür	1330–1331
Tarmashirin	1331–1334
Buzan	1334–1335
Changshi	1335–1338
Yisün-Temür	1338–1341/43
'Ali Khalil	1341–1343 (Ögedeid prince)
Muhammad	1342–1343
Qazan	1343–1346/47

(After the murder of Qazan, the Chaghatay split into Qara'una, Moghulistan, and Mawarannahr [Transoxiana] areas.)

EMPERORS (GREAT KHANS) OF THE NORTHERN YUAN DYNASTY

Name	Reign Title	Reign Years	Dynasty
Ayushiridara	Biligtü Khan	1370–1378	Qubilaid
Toghus-Temüs	Uskhal Khan	1378–1388	Qubilaid
Engke	Jorigtu Khan	1389?–1392?	
Elbeg	Nigülesegchi Khan	1393?–1399?	Qubilaid
Gün-Temür		1400?–1402?	
Guilichi		1403?–1408	Ögedeid?
Bunyashiri	Öljeitü Khan	1408–1411	Qubilaid?
Dalbag		1412–1414	Ariq-Bökid
Oiradai		1415?–1425?	Ariq-Bökid?
Adai		1426–1438	Ögedeid
Togtoo-Bukha	Taisung Khan	1433–1452	Qubilaid
Esen		1452–1454	Oirat (Choros)
Mar-Körgis		1455?–1466/7	Qubilaid
Molon Taiji		1467–1471?	Qubilaid
Manduul		1473–1479	Qubilaid
Batu-Möngke	Dayan Khan	1480?–1517?	Qubilaid/Dayan Khanid
Barsu Bolod	Sain-Alag Khan	1518?–1519?	Dayan Khanid
Bodi	Alag Khan	1519?–1547	Dayan Khanid
Daraisun	Küdeng Khan	1548–1557	Dayan Khanid
Tümen	Jasagtu Khan	1558–1592	Dayan Khanid
Buyan	Sechen Khan	1593–1603	Dayan Khanid
Ligdan	Khutugtu Khan	1604–1634	Dayan Khanid

KHOSHUD OR UPPER MONGOL KHANS OF TIBET

Name	Title	Years
Törö-Baikhu	Güüshi Khan	1642–1655
Dayan	Ochir Khan	1655–1669
Gönchug	Dalai Khan	1669–1698
Lhazang	Chinggis Khan	1698–1717

TORGHUD RULERS AND KHANS OF THE KALMYKS

Name	Title	Years
Khoo-Örlög		d. 1644
Shikür-Daiching		1644–1661
Puntsog		1661–1669
Ayuuki	Khan	1669–1724
Tseren-Dondug	Khan	1724–1735
Dondug-Ombo	Khan	1735–1741
Dondug-Dashi	Khan	1741–1761
Ubashi	Viceroy	1762–1771

RULERS OF THE ZÜNGHAR TRIBE

Name	Title	Years
Khara-Khula		d. 1634
Baatur	Khung-Taiji	1634–1653
Sengge		1653–1670
Galdan		1670–1697
	Khung-Taiji	1676–1678
	Boshogtu Khan	1678–1697
Tsewang-Rabtan	Khung-Taiji	1694–1727
Galdan-Tseren	Khan	1727–1745
Tsewang-Dorji-Namjil	Khung-Taiji	1746–1749
Lamdarja	Khung-Taiji	1749–1752
Dawaachi	Khung-Taiji	1752–1755

EMPERORS OF THE QING DYNASTY

Chinese Reign Title (and Personal Name)	Mongolian Reign Name	Years
Tianming (Nurhachi)	Tngri-yin Boshugtu	1616–1626
Tianchong, Congde (Hong Taiji)	Tngri-yin Sechen, Degedü Erdemtü	1627–1643
Shunzhi (Fulin)	Eye-ber Jasagchi	1644–1661
Kangxi (Xuanye)	Engkhe Amugulang	1662–1722
Yongzheng (Yinchen)	Nairaltu Töb	1723–1735
Qianlong (Hongli)	Tngri-yin Tedkhügsen	1736–1795
Jiaqing (Yunyan)	Saishiyaltu Irögeltü	1796–1820
Daoguang (Minning)	Törö Gereltü	1821–1850
Xianfeng (Yichu)	Tügemel Elbegtü	1851–1861
Tongzhi (Zaichun)	Bürintü Jasagchi	1862–1874
Guangxu (Zaitian)	Badaragultu Törö	1875–1908
Xuantong (Puyi)	Khebtü Yosu	1909–1912

THE JIBZUNDAMBA KHUTUGTUS

Number and Name	Dates	Ethnic Origin
I. Lubsang-Dambi-Jaltsan-Balsangbu (Zanabazar)	1635–1723	Mongol
II. Lubsang-Dambi-Döngmi	1724–1758	Mongol
III. Ishi-Dambi-Nima	1758–1773	Tibetan
IV. Lubsang-Tubdan-Wangchug	1775–1813	Tibetan
V. Lubsang-Tsültem-Jigmed	1815–1842	Tibetan
VI. Lubsang-Baldan-Damba	1842–1848	Tibetan
VII. Agwang-Choijin-Wangchug-Perenlai-Jamtsu	1850–1868	Tibetan
VIII. Agwanglubsang-Choijin-Nima-Danzin-Wangchug-Balsangbu	1870–1924	Tibetan

THEOCRATIC GOVERNMENT, 1911–1919

Emperor (Khaan)	Prime Ministers
Eighth Jibzundamba Khutugtu (1911–1924)	Sain Noyan Khan Namnangsüren (1912–1919)
	Badmadorji (1919)

PEOPLE'S GOVERNMENT AND PEOPLE'S REPUBLIC, 1921–1990

Name	Office	Years in Office
Bodô	Prime Minister	1921–1922
General Sükhebaatur	Commander in Chief	1921–1923
General Danzin	Commander in Chief	1923–1924
Elbek-Dorzhi Rinchino	Chairman of the Military Council	1922–1925
Dambadorji	Party Chairman	1924–1928
Badarakhu	Party Secretary (one of three)	1928–1932
Gendün	Party Secretary (one of three)	1928–1932
	Prime Minister	1932–1936
Choibalsang, Marshal	Commander in Chief	1924–1928, 1937–1950
	Prime Minister	1939–1952
Yu. Tsedenbal	Party First Secretary	1940–1954, 1958–1984
	Prime Minister	1952–1974
	Head of State	1974–1984
Ja. Batmönkh	Party First Secretary, Head of State	1984–1990

Note: The table above includes all who in practice were top leaders, regardless of their formal position. From 1928 to 1932 supreme authority was actually in the hands of the Comintern delegates, the Czech Bohumír Šmeral, and the Buriat M. I. Amagaev.

DEMOCRATIC MONGOLIA FROM 1990

President		Prime Minister
P. Ochirbat, 1990–1997	(MPRP, 1990–1993)	Sh. Gungaadorj, 1990 (MPRP)
		D. Byambasüren, 1990–1992 (MPRP)
	(Democrat, 1993–1997)	P. Jasrai, 1992–1996 (MPRP)
N. Bagabandi, 1997–	(MPRP)	M. Enkhsaikhan, 1996–1998 (Democrat)
		Ts. Elbegdorj, 1998 (Democrat)
		J. Narantsatsralt, 1998–1999 (Democrat)
		R. Amarjargal, 1999–2000 (Democrat)
		N. Enkhbayar, 2000– (MPRP)

CHRONOLOGY

209 B.C.E.	Modun kills his father and seizes the throne of the Xiongnu, who become the dominant nomadic people of the Mongolian plateau.		**924**	Yel Aboaji leads an expedition through Inner Mongolia into the former Uighur heartland.
198	Modun and the emperor Gaozu of China's Han dynasty sign a peace treaty, recognizing equality of the Xiongnu.		**925**	Kitan small script created.
			937	The Kitan emperor Deguang seizes 16 prefectures in northern China, around modern Beijing.
134	Han Wudi attacks the Xiongnu, beginning a decades-long Chinese offensive against the nomads.		**1114**	Wanyan (Onging) Aguda of the Jurchen defeats a Kitan army and declares himself emperor of the Jin dynasty in Manchuria.
53	After splitting into northern and southern dynasties, the southern Xiongnu *shanyu* (ruler) Huhanye surrenders and becomes tributary to the Han.		**1120**	Wanyan Aguda armies sack the Kitan capital Shangjing in Inner Mongolia.
85–87 C.E.	Attacked repeatedly by other nomadic peoples, the Xiongnu flee west to modern Kazakhstan and beyond and south to China. The Xianbi replace them as the dominant people in the steppe.		**1129**	Yelü Dashi, member of the Liao imperial family, rallies men of various nomadic tribes at Besh-Baligh in Turkestan, founding the Qara-Khitai dynasty of Central Asia.
502–510	Under Khan Shilun, the Rouran dynasty unifies the Mongolian plateau.		**1147**	After Mongol attacks, probably under Qabul Khan, the Jin dynasty of China pacifies the Mongols with lavish gifts.
552	Bumin of the Ashina family defeats the Rouran ruler and establishes the first Türk empire in Mongolia.		**1162**	Temüjin (later Chinggis/Genghis Khan) born as the eldest son of the Mongol chief Yisügei Ba'atur in northeastern Mongolia.
630	Xieli Qaghan of the eastern Türks is captured by the Chinese. Eastern Turks submit to China's Tang dynasty.		**1164**	Qutula Khan of the Mongols killed by the Tatars, in alliance with the Jin of north China.
c. 650	Earliest Old Turkish inscription at Ereen Kharganat (Bayan-Ölgii province).		**1171**	Yisügei Ba'atur poisoned by the Tatars.
659	Western Türks submit to China.		**1201**	The Mongol chief Jamugha elected as khan rival to Temüjin (Chinggis Khan).
682	Ilterish establishes second Türk empire.		**1202**	Mongols under Temüjin (Chinggis Khan) conquer and annihilate Tatars.
715	Runic Turkish inscription of Toñuquq.			
742	Second Türk empire overthrown by Uighur, Basmil, and Qarluq tribes.		**1203**	Ong Qa'an of the Kereyid Khanate and Temüjin (Chinggis Khan) come into conflict, and Temüjin emerges victorious, conquering the Kereyid.
744	Qulligh Boyla founds the Uighur empire.			
763	Under Bögü Qaghan, the Uighur empire adopts Manicheism as its state religion.		**1204**	At the battle of Keltegei Cliffs, Chinggis Khan defeats the Naiman Khanate; adopts Uighur-Mongolian Script
839	A catastrophic *zud* (winter disaster) devastates the Uighur herds.		**1206**	At a great *quriltai* or assembly, Chinggis Khan elected as khan of the Mongols.
840	The Kyrgyz sack Ordu-Baligh, Uighur capital in central Mongolia, the Uighurs flee to the Kitans in Inner Mongolia, to Gansu in northeast China, and to Turpan in Xinjiang.		**1209**	The Uighurs submit, and Chinggis Khan campaigns against the Xia, who agree to pay tribute.
907	Yelü Abaoji is elected Qaghan of the Kitans.			
920	Kitan large script created.			

1211	The Mongols attack the Jin dynasty in North China.
1215	Second siege of the Jin capital, Zhongdu, ends with the sack of the city by the Mongols.
1217	The Mongol general Muqali appointed as prince of state and given command of the *tammachi* (permanent garrison) army in north China.
1218–1219	Winter: The governor of Otrar in Central Asia massacres merchants in a trade delegation sent by Chinggis Khan.
1220	Chinggis Khan conquers Bukhara and Samarqand in Central Asia.
1221	Mongol armies destroy Balkh, Merv, Urganch, Nishapur, and Herat cities in Central Asia, Iran, and Afghanistan.
1222–1223	Taoist Master Changchun instructs Chinggis Khan in Taoism, receives edict setting him over all monks and priests.
1223	The Mongol generals Sübe'etei and Jebe defeat Russian-Qipchaq force at the battle of Kalka River.
1226	"Stone of Chinggis Khan," the earliest surviving monument in the Mongolian language, carved.
1227	Chinggis Khan destroys the Xia (Tangut) dynasty of northwest China, before his death.
1229	Ögedei elected khan, takes title of Great Khan (Qa'an).
1230	Regular tax system set up in Mongol-ruled North China under the Kitan official Yelü Chucai.
1233	Under Sübe'etei's command Mongol siege of the last Jin capital of Kaifeng ends with Mongol victory.
1235	Ögedei Khan builds the capital city of Qara-Qorum in central Mongolia.
1240	Mongol armies under the Mongol prince Batu sack Kiev and complete conquest of Russia.
1241	Mongol armies ravage Poland and Hungary; Ögedei Khan dies.
1243	Mongol armies under the Mongol general Baiju defeat the Seljük Turks at the Battle of Köse Dağı.
1246	Güyüg elected khan at a great *quriltai* in central Mongolia and receives the papal envoy John of Plano Carpini.
1248	Güyüg Khan dies at Qum-Senggir in East Turkestan.
1251	Möngke elected khan, and after discovering plot against him, purges his opponents.
1252	Possible date of authorship of the *Secret History of the Mongols*.
1252–1259	Persian official and historian 'Ala'ud-Din Ata-Malik Juvaini writes *History of the World Conqueror*.
1254	Mongol siege, led by Qubilai Khan, of Dali in Yunnan ends with the city's surrender.
1258	Last 'Abbasid caliph in Baghdad surrenders to the Mongols under the Mongol prince Hüle'ü; the caliph is executed with his family and the city sacked.
1259	Möngke Khan dies while campaigning in Sichuan against the Chinese Song dynasty.
1260	Qubilai and his brother Ariq-Böke elected khans at rival *quriltai*s; Mamluk Egyptian army defeats Mongol army of the Middle Eastern Il-Khanate in the Middle East at 'Ain Jalut (in modern Israel); Qubilai's officials introduce unified paper currency.
1262	Berke of the Golden Horde in the East European steppe invades Hüle'ü's Il-Khanate in the Middle East.
1264	Ariq-Böke surrenders to Qubilai Khan.
1269	Mengü-Temür of the Golden Horde, Baraq of the Chaghatay Khanate, and the Ögedeid Qaidu ally against the Il-Khanate in the Middle East and Qubilai Khan in the east; 'Phags-pa Lama creates the square script for Mongolian, based on Tibetan.
1271	Qubilai Khan renames the Mongol regime in China the Yuan dynasty.
1273	Song China's powerful Xiangyang fortress surrenders to Yuan armies under the Mongol general Aju and the Chinese general Liu Zheng.
1274	Qubilai Khan moves his court to his new capital, Daidu (modern Beijing).
1276	The Song court surrenders, and Grand Councillor Bayan Chingsang's troops peacefully enter the Song capital of Lin'an (Hangzhou).
1279	Mongols assault camp of the last Song emperor in Canton harbor; the Song emperor is drowned.
1281	Typhoons destroy Mongol fleet in invasion of Japan.
1282	Qubilai Khan's financial expert, Ahmad, murdered in unsuccessful palace coup.
1286	The Chaghatayid khan Du'a, of the Mongols' Chaghatay Khanate in Central Asia, captures Besh-Baligh city in East Turkestan, from Qubilai's forces.

1287	New nonconvertible Zhiyuan paper currency introduced in China under Mongols; Qubilai Khan defeats armies of the rebellious Mongol prince Nayan in Manchuria.
1288	Vietnamese crush the Mongol navy at Bach-Đăng River (near modern Haiphong).
1290	Mongol troops under Prince Buqa-Temür sack the 'Bri-gung-pa Monastery, crushing the last resistance to Mongol rule in Tibet.
1294	Qubilai Khan dies; unbacked paper currency introduced into the Il-Khanate but withdrawn after massive popular resistance.
1295	Ghazan Khan, new Muslim ruler of the Middle Eastern Il-Khanate, destroys churches, synagogues, and Buddhist temples.
1299	Toqto'a, khan of the Golden Horde, defeats the rival Prince Noqai.
1301	Qubilai's dogged opponent Qaidu Khan wins a battle against Yuan dynasty forces at Qaraqata in northwestern Mongolia, but is wounded and dies soon after.
1304	General peace declared between the five Mongol houses of the Yuan, the Chaghatay Khanate, the Ögedeids, the Il-Khanate, and the Golden Horde.
1305–1306	Persian official and historian Rashid-ud-Din completes the Mongol chapters of his *Compendium of Chronicles*.
1308–1309	The Il-Khan Öljeitü adopts Twelver (Ja'fari) Shi'ite Islam, but his attempts to impose this on the realm cause civil unrest.
1312	Buddhist monk and scholar Chosgi-Odsir's Mongolian translation of the Buddhist classic *Bodhicaryavatara* printed by imperial mandate.
1313	Özbeg Khan seizes power in the Golden Horde and executes emirs and Buddhist *baqshis* (teachers) who oppose his Islamization policy.
1315	Confucian examination system reestablished in Mongol (Yuan) China.
1323	Coup d'état by the Ossetian Guard, imperial bodyguard formed by Ossetes (Alans), kills the Yuan (Mongol) emperor Shidebala, and his distant cousin Yisün-Temür is made emperor; the Il-Khan commander in chief Chuban makes peace between the Il-Khanate and Mamluk Egypt.
1327	Fall of the Il-Khan's powerful commander in chief Chuban.
1328	After Yisün-Temür's death, the officials El-Temür and Bayan stage a coup d'état and reestablish the line of the late Mongol emperor Haishan.
1331	Massive plague in Henan, north China said to have killed nine-tenths of the population; Tarmashirin elected khan of the Chaghatay Khanate and begins Islamization.
1335	Grand Councillor Bayan abolishes Confucian examination system in Mongol China; the Il-Khan Abu-Sa'id dies without an heir, and Il-Khanate disintegrates.
1338	Chuban's grandson "Little" Hasan, founds the non-Chinggisid Suldus (Chubanid) dynasty in Azerbaijan, Iraq, and western Iran.
1338–1339	Outbreaks of the Black Death around Lake Ysyk Köl in the eastern Chaghatay Khanate.
1340	The Yuan official Toqto'a overthrows his uncle Bayan and restores examinations.
1346	Black Death reaches Saray on the Volga and then Crimea.
1346–1347	The Qara'una emir Qazaghan in Afghanistan and the Dughlat emir Dulaji in East Turkestan enthrone rival khans, splitting the Chaghatay Khanate.
1351	Grand Councillor Toqto'a begins vast project to reroute the Huang (Yellow) River, and rebellions breaks out against Yuan (Mongol) rule.
1355	After almost defeating the anti-Yuan rebels, Grand Councillor Toqto'a is dismissed due to court intrigues, and rebellions in south China revive.
1357	Janibeg Khan of the Golden Horde invades Azerbaijan, occupies Tabriz, and overthrows the Suldus dynasty.
1359	Sheikh Uwais enters Tabriz and revives the non-Chinggisid Jalayir dynasty.
1360	Shibanid Khizr Khan overthrows Nawroz, the last Batuid khan of the Golden Horde.
1368	Armies of the new Chinese Ming dynasty occupy the Yuan (Mongol) capital of Daidu (modern Beijing), and the Mongol (Yuan) emperors flee back to Mongolia.
1370	The non-Chinggisid Timur is elevated at a *quriltai* as de facto ruler of the Chaghatay Khanate in Central Asia.

1380	Grand Prince Dmitrii of Moscow defeats the Golden Horde army at the Battle of Kulikovo Pole (Snipe's Field).
1382	The Chinggisid prince Toqtamish, after reuniting the Golden Horde, sacks Moscow.
1388	Yisüder, a descendant of Ariq-Böke, allies with Oirats (West Mongols) and murders the emperor of the Yuan dynasty in Mongolia, beginning the Oirat-Mongol wars.
1389	Mongol tribes in eastern Inner Mongolia surrender to the Ming dynasty and are organized as "Three Guards."
1395	Timur invades the Golden Horde and sacks Saray and Astrakhan.
1405	Timur dies while organizing an invasion of China.
1412	Grand Prince Vasilii I is the last Moscow prince to "go to the Horde" to receive investiture from the Golden Horde.
1434	Toghoon Taishi of the Oirats kills Arugtai, the kingmaker of the surviving Yuan court in Mongolia.
1449	Esen Taishi of the Oirats captures the Ming dynasty's Zhengtong emperor, and the Ming frontier lines collapse.
1473–1474	To stave off Mongol attacks, the Ming border official Yu Zijun begins building the first strip of what becomes the Great Wall.
1480	Khan Ahmad of the Great Horde backs down after Czar Ivan III defies Tatar control at the stand on the Ugra River; Madukhai Sechen Khatun, widow of the previous Chinggisid khan, marries Batu-Möngke Dayan Khan and drives off the Oirats, beginning a Chinggisid revival in Mongolia.
1510	Dayan Khan defeats the Ordos and Tümed Mongols at the Battle of Dalan Terigün (Inner Mongolia), reunifying the Six Tümens of the Mongols.
1571	The Mongol princes Altan Khan and the Ming dynasty make peace and open horse fairs for trading.
1576	The Mongol prince Altan Khan and Khutugtai Sechen Khung-Taiji meet bSod-nam rGya-mtsho, the Third Dalai Lama, in northeast Tibet, beginning the Mongols' "Second Conversion" to Buddhism.
1585	Abatai Khan begins building Erdeni Zuu, the first monastery in Khalkha Mongolia.
1607	The *Jewel Translucent Sutra*, a versified history of Altan Khan and the Buddhist conversion, is written in the Inner Mongolian town Guihua (modern Höhhot).
1612–1615	Khorchins and southern Khalkha (later Juu Uda) ally with the rising Manchus.
1627	Most Mongols join a revolt against the supremacy of Ligdan Khan, the last Yuan emperor of the Mongols.
1628	Cossacks demanding *yasak* (fur tribute) first clash with Buriats along the Angara and Uda Rivers, in Siberia.
1628–1629	Ligdan Khan sponsors a complete translation of the bKa'-'gyur (Buddhist scriptures).
1630–1635	The Oirat (West Mongol) chief Khoo-Örlög leads most of the Torghuds west to the Volga, founding the Kalmyk people.
1632	The Manchu emperor Hong Taiji dispatches a large Manchu army with Mongol allies to destroy Ligdan Khan, who flees west to Ordos and then to northeast Tibet.
1634	Ligdan Khan dies of smallpox at Shara Tala (modern Tianzhu) in northwest China.
1636	Inner Mongolian princes acknowledge Hong Taiji as the first emperor of the Qing dynasty.
1639	Zanabazar, son of the Tüshiyetü khan, recognized as the First Jibzundamba Khutugtu, the supreme Buddhist lama of Mongolia.
1640	An assembly of Khalkha and Oirat princes issues the Mongol-Oirat Code.
1642	After the Khoshud ruler Törö-Baikhu Güüshi Khan defeats the enemies of the "Yellow Hat" Buddhist order, the Fifth Dalai Lama proclaims him Khan of Tibet.
1647	Khori Buriats surrender to the Cossacks and agree to pay *yasak* (fur tribute).
1648–1649	Buddhist cleric and scholar Zaya Pandita Namkhai-Jamtsu designs the clear script used by the Oirats.
1662	Saghang Sechen of Ordos (Inner Mongolia) writes the *Erdeni-yin Tobchi* (Precious summary), a famous chronicle of Mongolian history.
1667	The Qing authorities complete the deportation of all Solons (Daurs, Solon Ewenkis, and Old Barga) south from Siberia to Manchuria.
1676	Galdan of the Zünghar tribe overthrows Ochirtu Tsetsen Khan of the Khoshud,

establishing Zünghar supremacy among the Oirats.

1688 Galdan Boshogtu Khan of the Zünghars invades Khalkha.

1690 Ayuuki is recognized by the Dalai Lama as khan of the Kalmyks; Ratnabhadra in Zungharia writes *Sarayin gerel* (Light of the moon), a hagiography of the Buddhist cleric and scholar Zaya Pandita Namkhai-Jamtsu.

1691 At the Dolonnuur Assembly, the Khalkha princes and the Jibzundamba Khutugtu officially submit to the Qing dynasty's Kangxi emperor.

1693 The Tu (Monguor) lama, Agwang-Lubsang-Choidan from northwest China, appointed by the Kangxi emperor the first Jangjiya Khutugtu and supervisor of Inner Mongolian Buddhism.

1694 Tsewang-Rabtan revolts against his uncle Galdan Boshogtu Khan and takes control of the Zünghar homeland.

1705 The Khoshud Lhazang Khan deposes the Sixth Dalai Lama and kills the regent Sangs-rgyas rGya-mtsho.

1709 *Khalkha jirum* (Khalkha regulations) replaces the Mongol-Oirat Code among the Khalkha Mongols.

1717 Acting on an appeal by the Tibetan monasteries, the Zünghar army occupies Lhasa and kills Lhazang Khan.

1718 The Qing armies establish a garrison and military farm near modern Khowd city in western Mongolia.

1721 Arana, an ethnic Mongol official in the Eight Banners system, translates the Chinese religious novel *Journey to the West*.

1723 Lubsang-Danzin leads the Upper Mongols of Tibet into rebellion against the Qing dynasty.

1724–1735 After the death of Kalmyk ruler Ayuuki Khan, the Russian authorities attempt to interfere in the succession before accepting the more independent Kalmyk khan Dondug-Ombo.

1727 Kyakhta Treaty defines Russo-Qing frontier and divides the Buriats under Russia from the Khalkha Mongols under the Qing.

1732–1734 Qing authorities resettle the Solons (Daurs, Solon Ewenkis, and Old Barga) and the New Barga in Hulun Buir (northeast Inner Mongolia).

1741 Decree of Empress Elizabeth of Russia accords recognition and privileges to the Buddhist clergy among the Transbaikal Buriats.

1749 Mongolian translation of the bsTan-'gyur (canonical commentaries on the Buddhist scriptures) completed under the patronage of Qing emperor Qianlong.

1752 Dawaachi and Amursanaa overthrow the Zünghar ruler in Xinjiang; Dawaachi becomes new *khung-taiji* (ruler).

1755 The Qing armies occupy Zungharia in Xinjiang.

1756 Amursanaa and the Khotoghoid Khalkha prince Chinggünjab lead rebellions against Qing rule.

1758 Third Jibzundamba Khutugtu indentified in Eastern Tibet, not in Mongolia.

1771 Ubashi, viceroy of the Kalmyks, leads a great emigration from the Volga back to Xinjiang in northwest China.

1775 Inner Mongolian scholar and nobleman Rashipungsug's *Bolor Erikhe* is the first Mongolian chronicle to make extensive use of Chinese sources.

1779 Nom-un Yekhe Khüriye, the great monastery of the Jibzundamba Khutugtus, finally fixed at the present spot of Ulaanbaatar in Mongolia.

1789 Qing law replaces the native code, *Khalkha jirum*.

1811 *Tsam* dance, an exorcistic religious ceremony, introduced into Khüriye (modern Ulaanbaatar).

1822 Russian statesman Speransky reforms administration of the Buriats and other Siberian peoples.

1828 Earliest known *duguilang* (protest circle) formed in Ordos, Inner Mongolia; the Zinzili Decrees, a revision of the Mongol-Oirat Code for use among the Kalmyks, promulgated by decree of the czar.

1833 Danzin-Rabjai directs the opera *Saran Khökhögen-ü Namtar* (Tale of the moon cuckoo) in the Gobi Desert.

1836–1855 The Jibzundamba Khutugtu relocates from east Khüriye (now central Ulaanbaatar) to Gandan-Tegchinling Monastery to avoid Chinese merchants.

1838 Two-year Buddhist parochial school opened among Buzava Kalymks.

1840 The Christian western Buriat Iakov V. Boldonov designs Cyrillic script for

Buriat and begins printing catechetical literature.

1844 Sakhar Khamnaev founds first secular school for non-Cossack Buriats.

1846 The Buriat Cossack Dorzhi Banzarov becomes first person of Mongol ancestry to earn a European Ph.D. at University of Kazan' in Russia.

1863 Tugultur Toboev writes first Buriat chronicle.

1871 Inner Mongolia nobleman and scholar Injannashi's *Khökhe Sudur* (Blue chronicle) gives a highly romanticized picture of Chinggis Khan.

1891 Chinese rebels of the Jindandao (Way of the Golden Pill) sect launch massive pogroms against Mongols in southeastern Inner Mongolia.

1892 Legal privileges of the Kalmyk nobility are abolished, and Kalmyks are legally integrated into the Russian population.

1898 The Buriat monk Agwang Dorzhiev returns from Tibet to Russia as envoy of the Thirteenth Dalai Lama and begins founding new *tsanid* (higher Buddhist faculties) in Buriatia and Kalmykia.

1898–1900 Trans-Siberian Railway and Chinese Eastern Railway cut through Buriat territory in Siberia and Hulun Buir in Manchuria.

1900 Officials in Ordos, Inner Mongolia, organize large scale *duguilangs* to assist the Boxer movement in anti-Christian attacks.

1901 New Policies encouraging Chinese colonization and modernization in Mongolia announced by the Qing court; in Russia, the Speransky system abolished, and Buriats put under direct Russian administration.

1902 Mongol reformer and educator Prince Güngsangnorbu founds academy in Kharachin (Inner Mongolia) offering modern education in Mongolian, Chinese, and Japanese.

1906 Togtakhu Taiji launches insurrection against colonization and the New Policies in eastern Inner Mongolia.

1911 Khalkha Mongolia declares its independence with Eighth Jibzundamba Khutugtu as theocratic emperor.

1912 Hulun Buir, Dariganga, and the Oirats of western Mongolia join independent Khalkha Mongolia.

1915 Kyakhta Trilateral Treaty demotes Outer Mongolia to autonomous status under Russo-Chinese supervision; Hulun Buir separated from Outer Mongolia.

1919 Part-Buriat Cossack general Grigorii Semënov sponsors Buriat-Inner Mongolian pan-Mongolian movement; autonomy of Outer Mongolia revoked by Chinese authorities.

1920 Red Army advance in Russia gives Bolsheviks control of Buriat and Kalmyk territory; Kalmyk Autonomous Region organized.

1921 Russian Red Army and Mongolian partisans of the Mongolian People's Party drive Chinese and White Russians out of Outer Mongolia and found new revolutionary regime.

1922 Mongolian revolutionary Bodô and 14 others executed in Khüriye (modern Ulaanbaatar) by their former comrades.

1923 Buriat-Mongolian Autonomous Soviet Socialist Republic (BMASSR) created.

1924 Eighth Jibzundamba Khutugtu dies; Mongolian revolutionary General Danzin shot at the Third Congress of the Mongolian People's Party, and Mongolia declared a People's Republic.

1925 First Congress of the Inner Mongolian People's Revolutionary Party; Kalmyk-Oirat language switched from clear script to Cyrillic script.

1928 The Communist International engineers dismissal of Dambadorji and other Mongolian leaders and installs new far-left leadership that attacks Buddhism and the old aristocracy and pushes collectivization.

1929 Ts. Damdinsüren publishes Mongolia's first realist short story, "The Rejected Girl."

1931 Mongolian provinces reorganized; Uighur-Mongolian script replaced among the Buriats by the Latin script.

1932 Massive insurrection in northwest Mongolia against collectivization and persecution of religion; Joseph Stalin orders an end to the far-left policies; Natsugdorji writes the poem *Minii nutag* (My homeland); Japanese create autonomous Khinggan provinces for the Mongols in eastern Inner Mongolia.

1933 Hundreds executed or imprisoned in the manufactured "Lhümbe Case" in Mongolia.

1935 Kalmyk Autonomous Region made an Autonomous Soviet Socialist Republic (ASSR).

1936	Marshal Choibalsang appointed interior minister of the Mongolian People's Republic.
1937	Prince Demchugdongrub establishes autonomous government in central Inner Mongolia under Japanese patronage; the Buriat-Mongolian ASSR dismembered.
1937–1940	Great Purge and the campaign against Buddhism kills scores of thousands in Mongolia, Buriatia, and Kalmykia; all monasteries in those areas closed down.
1939	Soviet forces defeat the Japanese at the Battle of Khalkhyn Gol; Buriat language switched to Cyrillic script.
1940	New constitution in the Mongolian People's Republic; Rinchinkhorlo publishes first realist novella in Inner Mongolia; 500th anniversary of the Jangghar epic celebrated in Kalmykia.
1942	German armies occupy Kalmykia; Mongolia's first original European-style opera, *Uchirtai Gurwan Tolgoi* (Three fateful hills) performed.
1943	Kalmyks accused of collaboration with the Germans and deported as a people from their homeland on the Volga to Central Asia and Siberia.
1944	Gandan-Tegchinling Monastery reopened in Mongolia.
1945	Soviet and Mongolian troops invade Inner Mongolia, driving out the Japanese; Inner Mongolians form nationalist governments with pan-Mongolian aims; plebiscite on independence in Mongolia; *Tsogtu Taiji* is Mongolia's first successful feature film.
1947	Ts. Damdinsüren's modern adaption of the *Secret History of the Mongols* published in Mongolia; Chinese Communists organize Inner Mongolian Autonomous Government under Ulanfu, with its capital at Wang-un Süme (Ulanhot).
1949	Railway reaches Ulaanbaatar; Inner Mongolian Autonomous Government made an Autonomous Region in the new People's Republic of China and its capital moved to Zhangjiakou.
1950	Cyrillic-script Mongolian replaces the Uighur-Mongolian script in Mongolia.
1951–1955	The historical novel *Üriin Tuyaa* (Rays of the dawn) published by B. Rinchen in Mongolia.
1952	Marshal Choibalsang dies, and Yu. Tsedenbal, his successor as prime minister of the Mongolian People's Republic, is the first Mongolian leader to visit Beijing.
1952–1956	Daurs separated from the Mongols as a new nationality.
1954	Suiyuan province assigned to the Inner Mongolia Autonomous Region whose capital is moved to Höhhot; Mongol autonomous areas created in Xinjiang and Qinghai in northwest China.
1956	Trans-Mongolian Railway completed; de-Stalinization commission formed in Mongolia under B. Shirendew.
1957	Decrees exiling the Kalmyks revoked, and they begin to return to their homeland.
1958	Collectivization of pastoral regions in China completed with Great Leap Forward in China; Buriat-Mongolian ASSR renamed Buriat ASSR.
1959	Collectivization in the Mongolian People's Republic completed.
1960	New constitution in the Mongolian People's Republic.
1961	Mongolian People's Republic admitted to the United Nations; construction begins on the new Darkhan city in northern Mongolia.
1962	Yu. Tsedenbal denounces advocates of celebrating the 800th anniversary of Chinggis Khan's birth; Mongolia signs border treaty with China.
1963	Major historical and literary figures of Mongolia who had been killed in the Great Purge exonerated of criminal charges.
1966	Soviet leader Leonid Brezhnev visits Mongolia and signs alliance directed against China; Cultural Revolution begins in China, and Inner Mongolian chairman Ulanfu is deposed.
1968–1969	The manufactured "New Inner Mongolian People's Revolutionary Party" Case kills tens of thousands in Inner Mongolia.
1969	Inner Mongolia Autonomous Region dismembered.
1974	Construction begun on Erdenet city, built around the massive copper-molybdenum mine, which becomes Mongolia's major export enterprise.
1979	Inner Mongolia Autonomous Region restored to its former boundaries and given a Mongol chairman.
1981–1982	Student demonstrations in Inner Mongolia against Chinese policies.

1983–1985   Decollectivization of herds and pasture land in Inner Mongolia.

1984   Yu. Tsedenbal deposed while visiting Moscow; further agricultural colonization prohibited in Inner Mongolia.

1987   Mongolia and the United States establish diplomatic relations.

1990   J. Batmönkh resigns in response to popular demonstrations, and the Mongolian People's Revolutionary Party wins Mongolia's first free elections; Buriat legislature protests the illegality of the republic's dismemberment and renaming.

1991   Kalmyk language classes revived in Kalmykia.

1991–1993   Privatization of most of the Mongolian industrial and service economy.

1992   Mongolia renamed the State of Mongolia in the new democratic constitution; inflation peaks in Mongolia at 325.5 percent.

1992–1995   Mongolian pastoral economy decollectivized.

1993   Kirsan N. Ilümzhinov elected president of Kalmykia.

1996   The Democratic Coalition defeats the Mongolian People's Revolutionary Party in parliamentary elections.

1997   Apartments privatized in Mongolia.

2000   Massive *zud* in Mongolia, drought in Inner Mongolia; the Mongolian People's Revolutionary Party wins parliamentary elections.

2002   Locust plague in central Inner Mongolia.

2003   Farming and residential land privatization implemented in Mongolia; 180 Mongolian soldiers join U.S.-led forces in Iraq.

BIBLIOGRAPHY

Academy of Sciences, MPR. *Information Mongolia: The Comprehensive Reference Source of the People's Republic of Mongolia (MPR)*. Oxford: Pergamon Press, 1990.

Amitai-Preiss, Reuven, and David O. Morgan, eds. *The Mongol Empire and Its Legacy*. Leiden: E. J. Brill, 1999.

Badarch, Dendeviin, Raymond A. Zilinskas, and Peter J. Balint. *Mongolia Today: Science, Culture, Environment and Development*. London: Routledge Curzon, 2003.

Batbayar, Tsedendambyn. *Modern Mongolia: A Concise History*. Ulaanbaatar: Offset Printing, Mongolian Center for Scientific and Technological Information, 1996.

Bawden, Charles R. *An Anthology of Mongolian Traditional Literature*. London: Keegan Paul International, 2002.

———. *The Modern History of Mongolia*. 1969. Reprint, London: Keegan Paul International, 1989.

———. *Mongolian-English Dictionary*. London: Keegan Paul International, 1997.

Basilov, Vladimir N., ed. *Nomads of Eurasia*. Trans. Mary Fleming Zirin. Los Angeles: Natural History Museum Foundation, 1989.

Berger, Patricia, and Theresa Tse Bartholomew. *Mongolia: The Legacy of Chinggis Khan*. San Francisco: Asian Art Museum of San Francisco, 1995.

Bira, Sh. *Studies in the Mongolian History, Culture, and Historiography*. Tokyo: Institute for Languages and Cultures of Asia and Africa, 1994.

BNMAU-yn Shinjlekh Ukhaany Akademi. *Bügd Nairamdakh Mongol Ard Uls: ündesnii atlas*. Ulaanbaatar: State Geodesic and Cartographic Office of the State Construction Committee of the MPR, 1990.

Boyle, John Andrew, ed. *Cambridge History of Iran*. Vol. 5, *The Seljuk and Mongol Periods*. Cambridge: Cambridge University Press, 1968.

Brown, William A., and Urgunge Onon, trans. *History of the Mongolian People's Republic*. Cambridge, Mass.: East Asian Research Center, Harvard University, 1976.

Buell, Paul D. *Historical Dictionary of the Mongol World Empire*. Lanham, Md.: Scarecrow Press, 2003.

China's Inner Mongolia. Höhhot: Inner Mongolia People's Publishing House, 1987.

Dani, A. H., and V. M. Masson. *History of Civilizations of Central Asia*. 6 vols. Paris: UNESCO, 1992– .

Dorj, T., and S. Baatar, eds. *Mongolia in Brief*. Ulaanbaatar: n. p., 2000.

Forsyth, James. *A History of the Peoples of Siberia: Russia's North Asian Colony, 1581–1990*. Cambridge: Cambridge University Press, 1992.

Franke, Herbert, and Denis Twitchett, eds. *Cambridge History of China*. Vol. 6, *Alien Regimes and Border States, 907–1368*. Cambridge: Cambridge University Press, 1994.

Friters, Gerald H. *Mongolia and Its International Position*. Baltimore: Johns Hopkins University Press, 1949.

Ganbold, Da. *Facts about Mongolia*. Ulaanbaatar: n. p., 2000.

Grousset, Rene. *Empire of the Steppes: A History of Central Asia*. Trans. Naomi Wallford. New Brunswick, N.J.: Rutgers University Press, 1970.

Heissig, Walther, and Claudius Müller. *Die Mongolen*. Innsbruck: Pinguin-Verlag, 1989.

History of the Mongolian People's Republic. Moscow: Progress Publishers, 1973.

Humphrey, Caroline, and David Sneath. *Culture and Environment in Inner Asia*. 2 vols. Cambridge: White Horse Press, 1996.

Jagchid, Sechin. *Essays in Mongolian Studies*. Provo, Utah: David M. Kennedy Center for International Studies, Brigham Young University, 1998.

Jagchid, Sechin, and Paul Hyer. *Mongolia's Culture and Society*. Boulder, Colo.: Westview Press, 1979.

Kotkin, Stephen, and Bruce A. Elleman, eds. *Mongolia in the Twentieth Century: Landlocked Cosmopolitan*. Armonk, N.Y.: M. E. Sharpe, 1999.

Krouchkin, Yuri N. *Mongolia Encyclopedia*. Ulaanbaatar, 2000.

Morgan, David. *The Mongols*. London: Basil Blackwell, 1986.

Moses, Larry, and Stephen A. Halkovic, Jr. *Introduction to Mongolian History and Culture*. Bloomington: Indiana University, Research Institute for Inner Asian Studies, 1985.

National Statistical Office of Mongolia. *Mongolian Statistical Yearbook 2000*. Ulaanbaatar: National Statistical Office of Mongolia, 2001.

Nei Menggu da cidian. Höhhot: Inner Mongolia People's Publishing House, 1991.

Nordby, Judith, comp. *Mongolia*. Oxford: Clio Press, 1993.

Onon, Urgunge, ed. *Mongolian Heroes of the Twentieth Century*. New York: AMS Press, 1976.

Peng, Jianqun and Jia Laikuan, eds. *Prosperous Inner Mongolia*. Beijing: China Today Press, 1992.

Phillips, E. D. *The Mongols*. New York: Frederick A. Praeger, 1969.

Rachewiltz, Igor de, et. al., eds. *In the Service of the Khan: Eminent Personalities of the Early Mongol-Yuan Period (1200–1300)*. Wiesbaden: Otto Harrassowitz, 1993.

Rinchen, B. *Mongol ard ulsyn ugsaatny sudlal khelnii shinjleli-in atlas/Etnolingvisticheskii atlas MNR/Atlas éthnologique et linguistique de la République populaire de Mongolie*. 2 vols. Ulaanbaatar: Academy of Sciences, 1979.

Rupen, Robert A. *Mongols of the Twentieth Century*. 2 vols. Bloomington: Indiana University, Research Institute for Inner Asian Studies, 1964.

Sabloff, Paula L. W., ed. *Modern Mongolia: Reclaiming Genghis Khan*. Philadelphia: University of Pennsylvania Museum of Archaeology and Anthropology, 2001.

Sanders, Alan J. K. *Historical Dictionary of Mongolia*. 2d edition. Lanham, Md.: Scarecrow Press, 2003.

———. *Mongolia: Politics, Economics and Society*. Boulder, Colo.: Lynne Rienner Publishers, 1987.

Saunders, J. J. *History of the Mongol Conquests*. New York: Barnes and Nobles, 1971.

Schwarz, Henry G. *Bibliotheca Mongolica*. Bellingham, Wash.: Center for East Asian Studies, Western Washington University, 1978.

———. *Minorities of Northern China: A Survey*. Bellingham, Wash.: Center for East Asian Studies, Western Washington University, 1984.

Sinor, Denis. *The Cambridge History of Early Inner Asia*. Cambridge: Cambridge University Press, 1990.

Spuler, Berthold. *History of the Mongols: Based on Eastern and Western Accounts of the Thirteenth and Fourteenth Centuries*. Trans. Helga and Stuart Drummond. Berkeley: University of California Press, 1972.

State Statistical Office of the MPR. *National Economy of the MPR for 70 Years*. Ulaanbaatar: State Statistical Office of the MPR, 1991.

Storey, Robert, and Bradley Mayhew. *Lonely Planet Mongolia*. Hawthorne: Lonely Planet, 2001.

Tserenchunt, Legdengiin, and Sharon Luethy with B. Bold-Erdene. *Sain Baina uu? Mongolian Language Textbook*. 3 vols., with cassettes. Ulaanbaatar: T and U Printing, 2002–03.

Worden, Robert L., and Andree Matles Savada, eds. *Mongolia: A Country Study*. Washington, D.C.: Library of Congress Federal Research Division, 1991.

Zhukovskaia, N. L. *Istoriko-kul'turnyi atlas Buriatii*. Moscow: Design, Information, Cartography, 2001.

INDEX